S0-ARN-150

peng

GLOBAL BUSINESS

Second Edition

Mike W. Peng

*Provost's Distinguished Professor
of Global Business Strategy*

Executive Director, Center for Global Business

University of Texas at Dallas

SOUTH-WESTERN
CENGAGE Learning

Australia • Brazil • Japan • Korea • Mexico • Singapore • Spain • United Kingdom • United States

Global Business, Second Edition
Dr. Mike W. Peng

Vice President of Editorial, Business:
Jack W. Calhoun

Vice President/Editor-in-Chief: Melissa Acuña

Sr. Acquisitions Editor: Michele Rhoades

Developmental Editor: Jennifer King

Sr. Editorial Assistant: Ruth Belanger

Marketing Manager: Clint Kernan

Content Project Manager: Kelly Hillerich

Media Editor: Rob Ellington

Frontlist Buyer, Manufacturing:
Miranda Klapper

Sr. Marketing Communications Manager:
Jim Overly

Production Service: Christian Holdener,
S4Carlisle Publishing Services

Sr. Art Director: Tippy McIntosh

Internal Designer: Mike Stratton,
Stratton Design

Cover Designer: Mike Stratton,
Stratton Design

Cover Image: Ian McKinnell, Photographers
Choice/Getty Images

Sr. Rights Acquisitions Specialist:
Deanna Ettinger

© 2011, 2009 South-Western, Cengage Learning

ALL RIGHTS RESERVED. No part of this work covered by the copyright herein may be reproduced, transmitted, stored, or used in any form or by any means graphic, electronic, or mechanical, including but not limited to photocopying, recording, scanning, digitizing, taping, web distribution, information networks, or information storage and retrieval systems, except as permitted under Section 107 or 108 of the 1976 United States Copyright Act, without the prior written permission of the publisher.

For product information and technology assistance, contact us at
Cengage Learning Customer & Sales Support, 1-800-354-9706

For permission to use material from this text or product, submit all requests online at **www.cengage.com/permissions**
Further permissions questions can be emailed to
permissionrequest@cengage.com

Exam*View*® is a registered trademark of eInstruction Corp. Windows is a registered trademark of the Microsoft Corporation used herein under license. Macintosh and Power Macintosh are registered trademarks of Apple Computer, Inc. used herein under license. © 2008 Cengage Learning. All Rights Reserved.

Cengage Learning WebTutor™ is a trademark of Cengage Learning.

Library of Congress Control Number: 2010925628
ISBN-13: 978-1-4390-4224-3
ISBN-10: 1-4390-4224-1

South-Western Cengage Learning
5191 Natorp Boulevard
Mason, OH 45040
USA

Cengage Learning products are represented in Canada by Nelson Education, Ltd.

For your course and learning solutions, visit www.cengage.com
Purchase any of our products at your local college store or at our preferred online store **www.CengageBrain.com**

Printed in the United States of America
1 2 3 4 5 6 7 14 13 12 11 10

To Agnes, Grace, and James

BRIEF CONTENTS

CONTENTS

PREFACE

The first edition of *Global Business* aspired to set a new standard for international business (IB) textbooks. Based on enthusiastic support from students, professors, and instructors in Australia, Britain, Canada, China, Egypt, France, Hong Kong, Indonesia, Ireland, Israel, Lithuania, Malaysia, Puerto Rico, Russia, Slovenia, South Africa, South Korea, Taiwan, Thailand, and the United States, the first edition achieved unprecedented success. A Chinese translation is now available, an India edition specifically tailored for South Asia has been launched, and a European version with enhanced European flavor is being developed. In short, *Global Business* is global.

The second edition aspires to do even better. It continues the market-winning framework centered on one big question and two core perspectives pioneered in the first edition, and has been thoroughly updated to capture the rapidly moving research and events of the past few years. Written for undergraduate and MBA students around the world, the second edition will continue to make IB teaching and learning (1) more engaging, (2) more comprehensive, (3) more fun, and (4) more relevant.

More Engaging

As an innovation in IB textbooks, a unified framework integrates all chapters. Given the wide range of topics in IB, most textbooks present the discipline in a fashion that "Today is Tuesday, it must be Luxembourg." Very rarely do authors address: "*Why* Luxembourg today?" More important, why IB? What is the big question in IB? Our unified framework suggests that the discipline can be united by one big question and two core perspectives. The big question is: What determines the success and failure of firms around the globe? To address this question, we introduce two core perspectives, (1) institution-based view and (2) resource-based view, in *all* chapters. It is this relentless focus on our big question and core perspectives that enables this book to engage a variety of IB topics in an integrated fashion. This provides unparalleled continuity in the learning process.

Global Business further engages readers through an *evidence-based* approach. I have endeavored to draw on the latest research, as opposed to the latest fads. As an active researcher myself, I have developed the unified framework not because it just popped up in my head when I wrote the book, but as an extension of my own research that consistently takes on the big question and leverages the two core perspectives. This work has been published in the *Journal of International Business Studies* and other leading IB journals.[1]

Another vehicle to engage students is debates. Most textbooks present knowledge "as is" and ignore debates. However, it is debates that drive the field of practice and research forward. Obviously, our field has no shortage of debates. It is the responsibility of textbook authors to engage students by introducing cutting-edge

---

[1] M. W. Peng, 2004, Identifying the big question in international business research, *Journal of International Business Studies*, 35: 99–108; M. W. Peng, D. Wang, & Y. Jiang, 2008, An institution-based view of international business strategy: A focus on emerging economies, *Journal of International Business Studies*, 39: 920–936; M. W. Peng, 2001, The resource-based view and international business, *Journal of Management*, 27: 803–829.

debates. Thus, I have written a beefy "Debates and Extensions" section for *every* chapter (except Chapter 1, which is a big debate in itself).

Finally, this book engages students by packing rigor with accessibility. There is no "dumbing down." No other competing IB textbook exposes students to an article authored by a Nobel laureate (Douglass North—Integrative Case 1.1), a commentary by Jack Welch (former GE chairman—In Focus 15.2), and a *Harvard Business Review* article (authored by me—In Focus 12.2). These are not excerpts but full-blown, original articles—the first in an IB (and in fact in any management) textbook. These highly readable short pieces directly give students a flavor of the original insights.

More Comprehensive

Global Business offers the most comprehensive and innovative coverage of IB topics available on the market. Unique chapters not found in other IB textbooks are:

- Chapter 9 on entrepreneurship and small firms' internationalization.
- Chapter 11 on global competitive dynamics.
- Chapter 16 on corporate finance and governance.
- Chapter 17 on corporate social responsibility (in addition to one full-blown chapter on ethics, cultures, and norms, Chapter 3).
- Half of Chapter 12 (alliances and acquisitions) deals with the undercovered topic of acquisitions. Approximately 70% of market entries based on foreign direct investment (FDI) around the world use acquisitions. Yet, none of the other IB textbooks has a chapter on acquisitions—clearly, a missing gap that my Chapter 12 will fill.

The most comprehensive topical coverage is made possible by drawing on the latest and most comprehensive range of the research literature. Specifically, I have accelerated my own research, publishing a total of 30 articles between the time I finished the first edition (late 2007) and now (mid 2010).[2] Some of these recent articles appear in top-tier outlets in IB, such as the *Academy of Management Journal, Journal of International Business Studies, Journal of World Business,* and *Strategic Management Journal.* Thanks to writing the first edition that forced me to look into areas where I had not done research before, I have now broadened the scope of my research, publishing recently in top-tier journals in operations (*Journal of Operations Management*), entrepreneurship (*Entrepreneurship Theory and Practice*), and human resources (*International Journal of Human Resource Management*). I have drawn on this latest research to inject cutting-edge thinking into the second edition. In addition, I have also endeavored to consult numerous specialty journals. For example:

- The trade and finance chapters (Chapters 5–7) draw on the *American Economic Review* and *Quarterly Journal of Economics.*
- The entrepreneurship chapter (Chapter 9) consults with the *Journal of Business Venturing* and *Entrepreneurship Theory and Practice.*
- The marketing and supply chain chapter (Chapter 14) draws heavily from the *Journal of Marketing, Journal of International Marketing,* and *Journal of Operations Management.*
- The human resource chapter (Chapter 15) heavily cites from *Human Resource Management, International Journal of Human Resource Management, Journal of Applied Psychology,* and *Personnel Psychology.*

[2] All my articles are listed at www.mikepeng.com and www.utdallas.edu/~mikepeng. Go to "journal articles."

- The corporate finance and governance chapter (Chapter 16) is visibly guided by research published in the *Journal of Finance* and *Journal of Financial Economics*.
- The corporate social responsibility chapter (Chapter 17) borrows from work that appears in the *Journal of Business Ethics* and *Business Ethics Quarterly*.

The end result is the unparalleled, most comprehensive set of evidence-based insights on the IB market. While citing every article is not possible, I am confident that I have left no major streams of research untouched. Feel free to check the Name Index to verify this claim.

Finally, the second edition of *Global Business* continues to have the most comprehensive set of cases contributed by scholars around the world—an innovation on the IB market. Virtually all other IB textbooks have cases written by book authors. In comparison, this book has been blessed by a global community of case contributors who are based in Britain, Canada, China, Germany, Hong Kong, and the United States. Many are experts who are located in or are from the countries in which the cases take place—for example, among all IB textbooks, *Global Business* has the very first China case written by China-based case authors (see Integrative Case 2.2 Soybeans in China). Additionally, the new set of Video Cases brings you the insights and expertise of noted business leaders from Britain, Canada, France, and the United States.

More Fun

In case you think that this book must be very boring because it draws so heavily on the latest research, you are wrong. I have used a clear, engaging, conversational style to tell the "story." Relative to chapters in rival books, my chapters are generally more lively and shorter. For example, most books use two chapters to go over topics such as trade, FDI, and foreign exchange. I cut out a lot of "fat" and use one chapter to cover each of these topics, thus enhancing the "weight-to-contribution" ratio.

Throughout the text, I have woven a large number of interesting, non-traditional anecdotes, ranging from ancient Chinese military writings (Sun Tzu) to Roman empire's import quotas, from quotes in *Anna Karenina* to mutually assured destruction (MAD) strategy in the Cold War. Popular movies, such as *A Few Good Men*, *Devil's Advocate*, *GI Jane*, *High School Musical*, *Star Wars*, *Terminator*, *The Hunt for Red October*, and *The Informant* are also discussed.

In addition, numerous Opening Cases, Closing Cases, and In Focus boxes spice up the book. Check out the following fun-filled features:

- The McDonald's and Dell theory of world peace (Chapter 2 In Focus 2.2).
- Comparative advantage and *you* (Chapter 5 In Focus 5.1).
- Canada and the United States fight over pigs (Chapter 5 Closing Case).
- We unwind dreams (Chapter 9 In Focus 9.2).
- A fox in the hen house (Chapter 11 In Focus 11.2).
- Blunders in international marketing (Chapter 14 Table 14.2) and in international HRM (Chapter 15 Table 15.6).
- Dallas versus Delhi (Chapter 15 In Focus 15.3).

There is one Video Case to support every chapter. While virtually all competing books have some videos, none has a video package that is so integrated with the learning objectives of *every* chapter.

Finally, as a new feature for the second edition, the PengAtlas sections allow you to conduct IB research using informative maps and other geographic tools to enhance your learning.

More Relevant

So what? Chapters in most textbooks leave students to figure out the crucial "so what?" question for themselves. In contrast, I conclude every chapter with an action-packed section titled "Management Savvy." Each section has at least one table (or one teachable slide) that clearly summarizes the key learning points from a *practical* standpoint. No other competing IB book is so savvy and so relevant.

Further, ethics is a theme that cuts through the book, with at least one "Ethical Dilemma" feature and a series of Critical Discussion Questions on ethics in each chapter. Finally, many chapters offer *career* advice for students. For example:

- Chapter 4 develops a resource-based view of the individual—that is, about you, the student. The upshot? You want to make yourself into an "untouchable," who adds valuable, rare, and hard-to-imitate capabilities indispensable to an organization. In other words, you want to make sure your job cannot be outsourced.
- Chapter 15 offers tips on how to strategically and proactively invest in your career now—as a student—for future international career opportunities.

What's New in the Second Edition?

Pedagogically, two new tools have been introduced. The all-new PengAtlas at the end of each part reinforces the geographic dimension of IB teaching and learning. PengAtlas Map 1.1 provides a comprehensive and informative map of the world, while subsequent maps feature detailed information on such relevant topics as political freedom, religious heritage, imports and exports, FDI inflows and outflows, regional agreements, labor, unemployment, and more. A new feature, "Global Action," at the end of each chapter utilizes globalEDGE, the most current global business information portal available sponsored by Michigan State University.

Between the first and second editions, there was actually a 1.5 edition labeled "2009 Update." That was forced by the sudden and ferocious financial meltdown during 2008 and 2009. The second edition has leveraged the 1.5 edition and deepened the more timely coverage of the global economic crisis. Highlights include:

- Chapter 1 Opening Case: Avon fights recession—one lipstick at a time.
- Chapter 1 Closing Case: GE innovates from the base of the pyramid.
- Chapter 2 Opening Case: Adam Smith versus Deng Xiaoping.
- Chapter 2 debate on private ownership versus state ownership.
- Chapter 4 Closing Case: Why Amazon's Kindle cannot be made in the United States.
- Chapter 6 Closing Case: The fate of Opel.
- Chapter 9 Closing Case: Boom in busts: Good or bad?
- Chapter 11 In Focus 11.3: From trade wars to antitrust wars.
- Chapter 12 In Focus 12.3: Tata: Clawed by Jaguar and Land Rover.
- Chapter 12 Closing Case: Nomura integrates Lehman Brothers in Asia and Europe.
- Chapter 13 Closing Case: Moving headquarters overseas.
- Chapter 15 Closing Case: Cut salaries or cut jobs?
- Chapter 16 In Focus 16.3: Michael Jensen as an outside director.
- Chapter 17 Closing Case: From Kyoto to Copenhagen: Cut emissions or cut jobs?

Again, these are merely highlights of the changes throughout the chapters. A new set of Video Cases, which are interviews of global business and academic leaders conducted by a dedicated video provider (50 Lessons), has been assembled. Leading organizations featured include:

- The Coca-Cola Company
- McKinsey & Company
- Accenture
- Shell Canada
- 3M

In terms of Integrative Cases, half of them are new. They are:

- Fighting counterfeit motion pictures.
- Brazil's Embraer: From state-owned enterprise to global leader.
- Iceland's financial crisis.
- Huawei's internationalization.
- Mary Kay in China.
- Baosteel Europe.
- Socially responsible to whom? The case of the US ethanol industry.

Support Materials

A full set of supplements is available for students and adopting instructors, all designed to facilitate ease of learning, teaching, and testing.

Global Business CourseMate   Cengage Learning's Global Business Course-Mate brings course concepts to life with interactive learning, study, and exam preparation tools that support the printed textbook. Through this website, available for an additional fee, students will have access to their own set of Powerpoint® slides, flashcards, and games, as well as the Learning Objectives and Glossary for quick reviews. A set of auto-gradable, interactive quizzes (prepared by Timothy R. Muth of Florida Institute of Technology) will allow students to instantly gauge their comprehension of the material. The quizzes are all tagged to the book's Learning Objectives. Finally, Global Business CourseMate includes a set of four engaging, interactive maps that delve more deeply into key concepts presented in the book.

Product Support Website   The flashcards, Learning Objectives, and Glossary are available for quick reference on our complimentary student product support website.

Webtutor on BlackBoard® and Webtutor on WebCT™   Available on two different platforms, *Global Business* Webtutor enhances students' understanding of the material by featuring the Opening Cases and Video Cases, as well as e-lectures, the Glossary, study flashcards, and a set of four engaging, interactive maps that delve more deeply into key concepts presented in the book.

CengageNOW™ Course Management System   Designed by instructors for instructors, CengageNOW™ mirrors the natural teaching workflow with an easy-to-use online suite of services and resources, all in one program. With this system, instructors can easily plan their courses, manage student assignments, automatically grade, teach with dynamic technology, and assess student progress with pre- and post-tests tagged to AACSB standards. For students, study tools including e-lectures, flashcards, Powerpoint® slides, and a set of four interactive maps enhance comprehension of the material, while diagnostic tools create a personalized study plan for each student that focuses their study efforts. CengageNOW™ operates seamlessly with WebCT™, Blackboard® and other course management tools.

Global Economic Watch   Cengage Learning's Global Economic Watch helps instructors bring these pivotal current events into the classroom through a powerful, continuously updated online suite of content, discussion forums, testing tools, and more. The Watch, a first-of-its-kind resource, stimulates discussion and understanding of the global downturn with easily integrated teaching solutions:

- **A thorough overview and timeline of events** leading up to the global economic crisis are included in the ebook module, *Impact of the Global Economic Crisis on Small Business*
- **A content-rich blog** of breaking news, expert analysis and commentary—updated multiple times daily—plus links to many other blogs
- **A powerful real-time database** of hundreds of relevant and vetted journal, newspaper, and periodical articles, videos, and podcasts—updated four times every day
- **Discussion and testing content,** PowerPoint® slides on key topics, sample syllabi, and other teaching resources

History is happening now, so bring it into the classroom with The Watch at **www. cengage.com/thewatch.**

Instructor's Resource DVD-ROM   Instructors will find all of the teaching resources they need to plan, teach, grade, and assess student understanding and progress at their fingertips with this all-in-one resource for *Global Business*. The IR-DVD-ROM contains:

- Instructor's Manual—Written by John Bowen (Ohio State University, Newark and Columbus State Community College), this valuable, time-saving Instructor's Manual includes comprehensive resources to streamline course preparation, including teaching suggestions, lecture notes, and answers to all chapter questions. Also included are discussion guidelines and answers for the Integrative Cases found at the end of each part, as well as the 50 Lessons Video Cases.
- Test Bank—Prepared by Yi Jiang (California State University East Bay), the *Global Business* Test Bank in ExamView® software allows instructors to create customized tests by choosing from 35 True/False, 35 Multiple Choice, and at least 8 short answer/essay questions for each of the 17 chapters. Ranging in difficulty, all questions have been tagged to the text's Learning Objectives and AASCB standards to ensure students are meeting the course criteria.
- Powerpoint® Slides—Mike Giambattista (University of Washington) has created a comprehensive set of more than 250 Powerpoint® slides that will assist instructors in the presentation of the chapter material, enabling students to synthesize key concepts.
- Video Cases—Perhaps one of the most exciting and compelling bonus features of this program, these 17 short and powerful video clips, produced by 50 Lessons, provide additional guidance on international business strategies. A new set of video clips chosen expressly for this edition offers real-world business acumen and valuable learning experiences from an array of internationally known business and academic leaders.

Instructor Product Support Website   For those instructors who prefer to access supplements online, the Instructor's Manual, Powerpoint® slides, and Test Bank are also available through the instructor's product support website.

Acknowledgments

As *Global Business* launches its second edition, I first thank all our customers—students, professors, and instructors—around the world who have made the book's success possible. Most new products flop. Starting to use a new textbook entails substantial start-up cost on the part of instructors. Even worse, the first edition appeared in the worst economic times in recent memory. Given these tremendous entry barriers, the first edition's successful penetration into some 20 countries speaks volumes about our customers' vote of confidence.

A special thank you goes to my friend and colleague, Klaus Meyer (University of Bath), who is spearheading the development of *Global Business: A European View*, which is tailored for European students. When working on the second edition, I sent Klaus all my "global" chapters and he sent me all his "European" chapters. We commented on each other's work and literally practiced what we teach: "Think global, act local."

At UT Dallas, I thank my colleagues Tev Dalgic, Dave Ford, Marilyn Kaplan, Seung-Hyun Lee, Elizabeth Lim, John Lin, Livia Markoczy, Roberto Ragozzino, Orlando Richard, Jane Salk, Eric Tsang, Habte Woldu, and the leadership team—Hasan Pirkul (Dean), Varghese Jacob (Associate Dean), and Greg Dess (Area Coordinator)—for creating and nurturing a supportive intellectual environment.

At South-Western Cengage Learning, I thank the "Peng team" that not only publishes *Global Business*, but also *Global Strategy* and *GLOBAL*: Melissa Acuña (Editor-in-Chief); Michele Rhoades (Senior Acquisitions Editor); Jennifer King (Developmental Editor); Kelly Hillerich (Content Production Manager); Clinton Kernen (Marketing Manager); Tippy McIntosh (Senior Art Director); and Terri Coats (Executive Director, International).

In the academic community, I thank Ben Kedia (University of Memphis) for inviting me to conduct faculty training workshops in Memphis *every* year since 1999 on how to most effectively teach IB, and Michael Pustay (Texas A&M University) for co-teaching these workshops with me—known as the "M&M Show" in the IB field. Discussions with close to 150 colleagues who came to these faculty workshops over the last decade have helped shape this book into a better product.

I also appreciate the meticulous and excellent commentaries prepared by reviewers for the second edition:

Syed Ahmed (Cameron University)
Verl Anderson (Dixie State College of Utah)
George DeFeis (Monroe College, Bronx)
Lianlian Lin (California State Polytechnic University, Pomona)
Timothy R. Muth (Florida Institute of Technology)
Attila Yaprak (Wayne State University)

Continued thanks to the reviewers of the first edition:

Richard Ajayi (University of Central Florida, Orlando)
Basil Al-Hashimi (Mesa Community College)
Peter L. Banfe (Ohio Northern University)
Lawrence A. Beer (Arizona State University)
Tefvik Dalgic (University of Texas at Dallas)
Tim R. Davis (Cleveland State University)

Ping Deng (Maryville University)
Norb Elbert (Eastern Kentucky University)
Joe Horton (University of Central Arkansas)
Samira Hussein (Johnson County Community College)
Ann L. Langlois (Palm Beach Atlantic University)
Ted London (University of Michigan)
Martin Meznar (Arizona State University, West)
Dilip Mirchandani (Rowan University)
Don A. Okhomina (Fayetteville State University)
William Piper (Alcorn State University)
Charles A. Rarick (Barry University)
Tom Roehl (Western Washington University)
Bala Subramanian (Morgan State University)
Gladys Torres-Baumgarten (Kean University)
Susan Trussler (University of Scranton)
William R. Wilkerson (University of Virginia)

In addition, I thank a number of colleagues, who informally commented on the first edition:

Charles Byles (Virginia Commonwealth University)
Breena Coates (California State University, San Bernardino)
Ping Deng (Maryville University)
Juan España (National University)
Sungjin Hong (University of Texas at Dallas)
Ferry Jie (University of Technology, Australia)
Charles Mambula (Langston University)
John McIntyre (Georgia Institute of Technology)
Mike Poulton (Dickinson College)
Gongming Qian (Chinese University of Hong Kong, China)
Pradeep Kanta Ray (University of New South Wales, Australia)
Jordan Siegel (Harvard Business School)
Josè G. Vargas-Hernàndez (Universidad de Guadalajara, México)
George White III (University of Michigan, Flint)
Habte Woldu (University of Texas at Dallas)
Alan Zimmerman (City University of New York, College of Staten Island)

I also appreciate the contributions made by my PhD students. PhD students Erin Pleggenkuhle-Miles, Sunny Li Sun, and Weichieh Su have worked on the second edition as my assistants and made the book significantly better. I also thank Rachel Pinkham for her extraordinary assistance. A total of 27 colleagues from Britain, Canada, China, Germany, Hong Kong, and the United States contributed cases that have significantly enhanced the global flavor of this book. They are:

Masud Chand (Simon Fraser University, Canada)
Peggy Chaudhry (Villanova University)
Hao Chen (University of Texas at Dallas)
Yuan Yi Chen (Hong Kong Baptist University, China)
Juan España (National University)
Steven Globerman (Western Washington University)
C. Gopinath (Suffolk University)
Yi Jiang (California State University, East Bay)
Andreas Klossek (Technical University of Freiberg, Germany)
Lianlian Lin (California State Polytechnic University, Pomona)
Bernd Michael Linke (Friedrich Schiller University of Jena, Germany)

Yi Liu (Xi'an Jiaotong University, China)
Ted London (University of Michigan)
Hemant Merchant (Florida Atlantic University)
Klaus Meyer (University of Bath, UK)—two cases
Douglass North (Washington University at St. Louis)—Nobel laureate
Kenny Oh (University of Missouri at St. Louis)
Eydis Olsen (Drexel University)
Brian Pinkham (University of Texas at Dallas)
Erin Pleggenkuhle-Miles (University of Texas at Dallas)
Sunny Li Sun (University of Texas at Dallas)—two cases
Qingjiu (Tom) Tao (James Madison University)
Maulin Vakil (University of North Carolina at Chapel Hill)
Habte Woldu (University of Texas at Dallas)
Wei Yang (Xi'an Jiaotong University, China)
Michael N. Young (Hong Kong Baptist University, China)
Alan Zimmerman (City University of New York, College of Staten Island)

Last, but by no means least, I thank my wife Agnes, my daughter Grace, and my son James—to whom this book is dedicated. My eight-year old Grace is now a young writer who has recently completed her first chapter book: *High School Musical 4*. My six-year-old James can not only read, but also *laugh* at my Chapter 5 Closing Case (of course, just the title only): "Canada and the United States fight over pigs." For now, Grace wants to be a rock star and James a race car driver. As a third-generation professor in my family, I can't help but wonder whether one (or both) of them will become a fourth-generation professor. To all of you, my thanks and my love.

July 1, 2010

ABOUT THE AUTHOR

Mike W. Peng is the Provost's Distinguished Professor of Global Business Strategy at the University of Texas at Dallas and Executive Director of its Center for Global Business, which he founded. At UT Dallas, he has been the number one contributor to the list of 40 top academic journals tracked by *Financial Times*, which ranked UT Dallas as a top 20 school in research worldwide and ranked its EMBA program as 16th in the United States (2009).

Professor Peng holds a bachelor's degree from Winona State University, Minnesota, and a PhD degree from the University of Washington, Seattle, where he was advised by Professor Charles Hill. Professor Peng had previously served on the faculty at the Ohio State University, Chinese University of Hong Kong, and University of Hawaii. In addition, he has held visiting or courtesy appointments in Australia (University of Sydney and Queensland University of Technology), Britain (University of Nottingham), China (Xi'an Jiaotong University, Sun Yat-sen University, Renmin University, China-Europe International Business School, and Cheung Kong Graduate School of Business), Denmark (Copenhagen Business School), Hong Kong (Chinese University of Hong Kong, Hong Kong Polytechnic University, and University of Hong Kong), the United States (University of Memphis, University of Michigan, Seattle Pacific University, and Western Washington University), and Vietnam (Foreign Trade University).

Professor Peng is one of the most prolific and most influential scholars in international business (IB). During the decade 1996–2006, he was the top seven contributor to IB's number one journal, *Journal of International Business Studies*. His research is also among some of the most widely cited—both the United Nations and the World Bank have cited his work in major publications. Truly global in scope, his research has covered firm strategies in countries such as China, Egypt, Hong Kong, India, Indonesia, Japan, Malaysia, Russia, Singapore, South Africa, South Korea, Taiwan, Thailand, the United States, and Vietnam. He has authored approximately 80 articles in leading journals. Between the publication of *Global Business*'s first and second editions, Professor Peng has not only published his latest research in top journals in IB, such as the *Academy of Management Journal, Journal of International Business Studies*, and *Strategic Management Journal*, but also in leading outlets in operations (*Journal of Operations Management*), entrepreneurship (*Entrepreneurship Theory and Practice*), and human resources (*International Journal of Human Resource Management*).

Professor Peng has previously authored *Behind the Success and Failure of US Export Intermediaries* (Quorum, 1998) and *Business Strategies in Transition Economies* (Sage, 2000). His *Global Strategy* text has become the world's best-selling global strategy book and has been translated into Chinese and Portuguese. *Global Business* builds on and leverages the success of *Global Strategy*. In addition, he has also published *GLOBAL*, an innovative, colorful, and compact IB textbook.

Professor Peng is active in leadership positions in his field. At the Academy of International Business (AIB), he co-chaired the Research Frontiers Conference in San Diego (2006) and guest edited a *Journal of International Business Studies* special issue on "Asia and Global Business" (2010). At the Strategic Management Society (SMS), he was the first elected Chair of the Global Strategy Interest Group (2005–2008). He also co-chaired the first SMS conference on China in Shanghai (2007). Professor Peng has served on the editorial boards of the

Academy of Management Journal, Academy of Management Review, Journal of International Business Studies, Journal of Management Studies, Journal of World Business, and *Strategic Management Journal.* He recently completed a term as Editor-in-Chief of the *Asia Pacific Journal of Management,* during which he managed the doubling of submission numbers and the successful bid to gain entry into the Social Sciences Citation Index (SSCI).

Professor Peng has taught students at all levels—undergraduate, MBA, PhD, EMBA, executive, and faculty training programs. Some of his former PhD students are now professors at Babson College, California State University, Georgia State University, Hong Kong University of Science and Technology, Northeastern University, Oregon State University, Southern Methodist University, St. John's University, University of Colorado, University of Missouri, and University of Texas at Dallas.

Professor Peng is also an active consultant, trainer, and keynote speaker. He has provided on-the-job training to over 200 professors around the world. Every year since 1999, he has conducted faculty training workshops on how to teach IB at the University of Memphis with faculty participants from around the country. He has consulted for organizations such as BankOne, Berlitz International, Chinese Chamber of Commerce, Greater Dallas Asian American Chamber of Commerce, Hong Kong Research Grants Council, Manufacturers Alliance/MAPI, National Science Foundation, Nationwide Insurance, Ohio Polymer Association, SAFRAN, US-China Business Council, and The World Bank. His speaking engagements as a keynote speaker include the "China Goes Global" Conference at Harvard University Kennedy School of Government in Cambridge, Massachusetts, the Pacific Region Forum in Vancouver, Canada, and the Navy Reserve Officers Training Conference in Fort Worth, Texas.

Professor Peng has received numerous awards and recognitions. His world-class research has attracted close to $1 million in external research grants. His honors include a National Science Foundation CAREER Award, a Small Business Administration (SBA) Best Paper Award, and a Scholarly Contribution Award from the International Association for Chinese Management Research (IACMR). One of his *Academy of Management Review* papers has been found to be a "new hot paper" (based on citations) representing the *entire* field of Business and Economics by the Institute for Scientific Information (ISI). He has also been quoted in *Newsweek, Smart Business Dallas, The Exporter Magazine, Business Times* (Singapore), *Sing Tao Daily* (Vancouver), and Voice of America.

Part 1

Laying Foundations

©Image Source

Chapter

1

© AP Photo/Christopher Berkey

LEARNING OBJECTIVES

After studying this chapter, you should be able to:

1. explain the concepts of international business and global business.

2. give three reasons why it is important to study global business.

3. articulate one fundamental question and two core perspectives in the study of global business.

4. identify three ways of understanding globalization.

5. state the size of the global economy and its broad trends and understand your likely bias in the globalization debate.

Globalizing Business

Avon Fights Recession—One Lipstick at a Time

When numerous mighty, masculine companies in the banking and automobile industries were falling left and right during the recent recession, Avon Products, Inc. (NYSE: AVP), a self-styled "company for women," rose to new heights around the world. Avon is a leading global beauty products company with 42,000 employees and $10 billion in annual revenue. As the world's largest direct seller, Avon markets "smart value" products to women in more than 100 countries through 5.8 million independent sales representatives, often affectionately known as "Avon Ladies." Today, not all Avon representatives are women, and Avon has officially dropped the "Lady" title. Instead, they are now simply called "representatives," because Avon has been increasingly recruiting men to hawk its products. Although numerous companies in most industries lost money in 2008, Avon's revenue *grew* 5% (in local currency), to a record $10.7 billion. The growth continued in 2009: Its revenue *increased* 3%, 5%, and 7% (in local currency) in the first, second, and third quarters, respectively. The active number of representatives jumped 11% worldwide. In the United States alone, Avon recruited 200,000 more representatives in 2009 since its launch of an aggressive recruitment drive in March. At a time when most companies struggled for survival and forgot about dividends, Avon proudly declared regular quarterly dividends—$0.21 per share for each of the first three quarters in 2009. In an otherwise bleak environment, investors noticed Avon's enviable performance, pushing its share price from $14.40 on March 9, 2009, to $34.52 on October 16, 2009—a 140% increase (!).

Founded in 1886, Avon pioneered direct selling. In its long history, Avon has had its fair share of ups and downs. So why has its performance been so outstanding lately? Obviously, the severity of the 2008–2009 recession has rewritten a number of taken-for-granted rules of the game concerning job security, employment, and careers. Direct selling has always been a way (mostly for women) to earn supplemental income. It has now become all the more important for an increasingly large number of both women and men who have lost their jobs. Even currently employed individuals often join direct selling in case their jobs disappear. Burned by the recession, individuals who feel the need to "recession-proof" their income find direct selling to be a great new line of work. According to Richard Berry, director of the UK Direct Selling Association:

> Direct selling is almost uniquely immune to economic trends. When you have a recession and people want a low-cost way of making an extra income, direct selling is a great option. The reason our members tend not to suffer from a drop in consumer demand is that the products they sell are low-cost household and personal products, all of which are the last thing to suffer a downturn in demand.

Although direct selling is attractive, competition is tough. With essentially no entry barrier, laid-off bankers and stay-at-home moms are all rushing in. Why has Avon been doing so well? Avon's iconic brand certainly helps. Its massive army of Avon Ladies and Avon Dudes ensures unrivaled reach around the globe. Another reason is that a new generation of representatives find they do not have to go door-to-door if they do not want to. Instead, they take catalogs to church events, school functions, and sorority sister gatherings. They often operate on the "party-plan" model, pitching their wares at neighborhood potlucks and dessert parties. They are typically networked, using eBay and Twitter to creatively expand their business. Direct selling is not a get-rich-quick scheme. Representatives have to work hard. In the

United States, the average revenue for a party is $400, of which the representative makes 25%. So to be successful, a lot of parties will be needed.

Throughout its history, Avon has emphasized social responsibility. More than 120 years ago, the very idea that women could run their own entrepreneurial businesses selling products in their communities and recruiting others to do the same was revolutionary. Today, this idea of empowering women continues to be revolutionary in some parts of the world where women are discriminated against. Avon is the world's largest microfinance lender for women, extending some $1 billion in credit to help women (and some men) start their new ventures. Every time a representative joins Avon, a small loan is provided to cover the initial products up front. This is especially valuable and rare in a world where credit is drying up.

In addition, direct selling can be a low-risk way of experimenting with entrepreneurial ideas. Direct selling gives individuals an idea of how they like selling, how good they are at it, and how they manage their time, inventory, and finances to maximize profit—without necessarily having to quit current jobs, if they have jobs. For unemployed individuals, another benefit of direct selling is that it gets them out in the community, whereas the unemployed typically have a tendency to shy away from social engagements. One expert noted:

> If you are out of work, you can become out of touch. Direct selling gives you another point of contact with people. You never know what's going to land in your lap if you're out there meeting people.

Avon's chairman and CEO, Andrea Jung, proudly noted in her message to Avon's website visitors that Avon is "a true force for good, improving and changing the lives of others as we continue to fulfill our vision as the company for women." As governments, companies, and individuals around the world struggle to find ways to tame recession, Avon may indeed provide a glimmer of hope—one lipstick at a time.

Sources: Based on (1) *BusinessWeek*, 2009, Door-to-door sales revive in Britain, July 8 (www.businessweek.com); (2) *BusinessWeek*, 2009, The entrepreneurs born of recession, March 13 (www.businessweek.com); (3) *Shanghai Daily*, 2009, Avon Lady ranks boom in downturn, June 28 (www.shanghaidaily.com); (4) *Telegraph*, 2009, Avon Lady reborn in the USA, July 5 (www.telegraph.co.uk); (5) www.avoncompany.com (Avon reports fourth-quarter and 2008 results; Avon reports second-quarter results; CEO's message; all accessed on October 17, 2009).

How do firms such as Avon compete around the globe? How can Avon's direct-selling competitors such as Mary Kay and Tupperware keep up? How can beauty products competitors that market through traditional channels, such as Procter & Gamble (P&G), Unilever, and Kao, fight back? What determines the success and failure of these firms—and numerous others—around the world during a tumultuous recession? This book will address these and other important questions on global business.

LEARNING OBJECTIVE 1

Explain the concepts of international business and global business.

WHAT IS GLOBAL BUSINESS?

Traditionally, international business (IB) is defined as a business (or firm) that engages in international (cross-border) economic activities. It can also refer to the action of doing business abroad. A previous generation of IB textbooks almost always takes the foreign entrant's perspective. Consequently, these books deal with issues such as how to enter foreign markets and how to select alliance partners. The most frequently discussed foreign entrant is the multinational enterprise (MNE), defined as a firm that engages in foreign direct investment (FDI) by directly investing in, controlling, and managing value-added activities in other countries.[1] MNEs and their cross-border activities are important, but they only cover one side of IB: the foreign side. Students educated by these books often come away with the impression that the other side of IB—namely, domestic firms—does not exist. But domestic firms do not just sit around in the face of foreign entrants such as MNEs. Domestic firms actively compete and/or collaborate with foreign entrants. In Focus 1.1 shows how domestic Chinese firms in the video game industry compete head-to-head with global giants such as Microsoft, Nintendo, and Sony. In other words, focusing on the foreign entrant side captures only one side of the coin at best.[2]

It seems uncontroversial to suggest that there are *two* key words in IB: international (I) and business (B).[3] IB is most fundamentally about "B" before being "I." To put it differently, the IB course in the undergraduate and MBA curricula at numerous business schools is probably the *only* course with the word "business" in the course title. All other courses you take are labeled management, marketing, finance, and so on, representing one functional area but not the overall picture of business. Does it matter? Of course! It means that your IB course is an

International business (IB)
(1) A business (firm) that engages in international (cross-border) economic activities and/or (2) the action of doing business abroad.

Multinational enterprise (MNE)
A firm that engages in foreign direct investment (FDI).

Foreign direct investment (FDI)
Investment in, controlling, and managing value-added activities in other countries.

IN Focus 1.1

ETHICAL DILEMMA

Fighting the Online Video Game Wars in China

© Mario Tama/Getty Images

The $50-billion video game industry has two main segments. The first is personal computer (PC)- and console-based games, such as Nintendo's Wii, Sony's Playstation and PSP handhelds, and Microsoft's Xbox. The second is the relatively new online video games. Players (known as "gamers") compete in virtual worlds populated with thousands of players in large games known as massively multiplayer online games (MMOGs). With an army of close to 40 million gamers, China is emerging as a major battleground for video game wars. In the 2010s, China is likely to be the world's largest online video game market.

In the 1990s, the Chinese video game industry was growing slowly and not profitably. Rampant piracy and low income levels made it unattractive to Nintendo, Sony, and Microsoft. Further, the business model adopted in developed economies, based on sales of consoles and game cartridges to make a profit, made very slow progress in China. This was because the average Chinese found it prohibitively expensive to buy consoles or PCs. High-speed Internet connection, although rising fast, was expensive and thus rare in Chinese households.

In 2001, an innovative new business model pioneered by domestic firms significantly lowered the cost of playing games. This model centered on pre-paid cards for a small fee to use a PC at an Internet café. Games were hosted on secure company servers and accessed from Internet cafés. "Killing two birds with one stone," this new model solved two major problems: high cost to play and piracy. Since gamers only paid a few cents per hour, games now became affordable to numerous groups, ranging from school kids to retirees living on fixed incomes. Piracy was also largely eliminated because game content was maintained on secure company servers.

The impact of this innovation was immediate and profound. Instead of saving a lot of money to buy expensive equipment, anyone could go to an Internet café to have a good time now. This has steered the market toward MMOGs and away from consoles. China's explosive growth has not

In Focus 1.1 (continued)

escaped the attention of major international game companies. However, the China market does not play to these firms' traditional strengths in console games, thus forcing them to adapt and acquire new capabilities in MMOGs.

Foreign firms eyeing China will find the market dominated by four strong domestic players: (1) Shanda, (2) NetEase, (3) The9, and (4) Changyou. Shanda was a leader in the pre-paid card movement and, as a result, was successfully listed on NASDAQ (as SNDA) in 2004. NetEase is the current market leader strong on content built on Chinese mythology. Its top-selling game *Westward Journey* enjoyed 1.3 million *concurrent* users during its peak play time. The company generating a lot of buzz is The9 Ltd., which obtained a license for *World of Warcraft (WoW)* from the Irvine, California–based Blizzard Entertainment. *WoW* is the most successful online video game in history, generating closing to $1 billion a year in worldwide income. In China, *WoW* smashed opening-day sale records for the industry. The fastest-growing one is Changyou, whose net income increased 20 times between 2007 and 2009. On its opening day on NASDAQ (as CYOU) in April 2009, its stock soared 25%.

For foreign firms salivating for the spoils of China's video game wars, the fundamental question is: how to play the game when industry rules are fast changing and unpredictable? Sony and Microsoft are cultivating the console market. Microsoft operates an incubation center in Chengdu to help third-party developers create Xbox-compatible content. Sony is also working with local game developers. The Walt Disney Internet Group is partnering with Shanda to develop new games that include Disney characters. Blizzard has acquired a game development studio in Shanghai to incorporate China flavor into its next-generation games.

Not to be left alone, the Chinese government has intervened on two dimensions. First, upset with game addiction and other health concerns (one gamer died in 2007 after playing three consecutive days in an Internet café), the government has now demanded that game companies include "fatigue controls" that will automatically halt the game after several hours. Second, the Ministry of Culture announced that it would ban games "threatening state security, damaging the nation's glory, disturbing social order, and infringing on other's legitimate rights." Starting in 2004, the Ministry every year publishes a list of recommended games that were deemed "healthy" and "intelligent." Not surprisingly, all the 35 games on these lists were domestic games.

Finally, Chinese firms are not likely to sit around to see their home market invaded. Building on domestic success, they may become major game exporters to Asia and the rest of the world. Chinese firm Kingsoft's *Perfect World* has already entered Japan and South Korea. In 2008, China's CDC Games launched in North America a *manga-style* MMOG *Lunia* that is very popular in China and Japan.

Sources: Based on (1) *BusinessWeek*, 2009, Seeking the "next billion" gamers, July 6: 54; (2) *Economist*, 2009, Online gaming in China, April 4: 67; (3) R. Ewing, 2007, China's online video game wars, *China Business Review*, July–August: 45–49; (4) *Wall Street Journal*, 2009, Changyou.com IPO jumps 25% on NASDAQ, April 3, online.wsj.com.

integrative course that has the potential to provide you with an overall business perspective (as opposed to a functional view) grounded in a global environment. Consequently, it makes sense that your textbook should give you both the I and the B parts, not just the I part.

This is exactly why this book, which covers both the I and the B parts, is titled *Global Business*—not merely "international" business. **Global business**, consequently, is defined in this book as business around the globe. In other words, global business includes both (1) international (cross-border) business activities covered by traditional IB books *and* (2) domestic business activities. Such deliberate blurring of the traditional boundaries separating international and domestic business is increasingly important today, because many previously national (domestic) markets are now globalized. Consider the competition in college textbooks, such as this *Global Business* book you are studying now. Not long

Global business

Business around the globe.

ago, competition among college textbook publishers was primarily domestic. Before South-Western (our publisher) was acquired by Canada's Thomson and more recently by Britain's Apax partners and Canada's OMERS Partners (which created a new corporate parent company named Cengage Learning), and before Prentice-Hall was acquired by Britain's Pearson, South-Western, Prentice-Hall, and McGraw-Hill fought each other largely in the United States. A different set of publishers competed in other countries. UK publishers marketed textbooks authored by UK professors to UK students, Russian publishers marketed textbooks authored by Russian professors to Russian students, and so forth. Now South-Western Cengage Learning, Prentice-Hall Pearson, and McGraw-Hill have significantly globalized their competition. Thanks to rising demand for high-quality business textbooks in English, these top three publishers are now competing against each other in many markets around the globe. The first edition of *Global Business* not only won many customers in the United States, but also penetrated some 20 countries (noted in the Preface). It becomes difficult to tell in this competition what is "international" and what is "domestic." Thus, "global" is a better word to capture the essence of this competition.

This book also differs from other books on IB because most focus on competition in developed economies. Here, by contrast, we devote extensive space to competitive battles waged throughout **emerging economies**, a term that has gradually replaced the term "developing countries" since the 1990s. Another commonly used term is **emerging markets**. How important are emerging economies? Collectively, they now contribute approximately 45% of the global **gross domestic product (GDP)**, as shown in Figure 1.1.[4] Note that this percentage is

---

FIGURE 1.1   THE CONTRIBUTIONS OF EMERGING ECONOMIES RELATIVE TO DEVELOPED ECONOMIES (WORLD %)

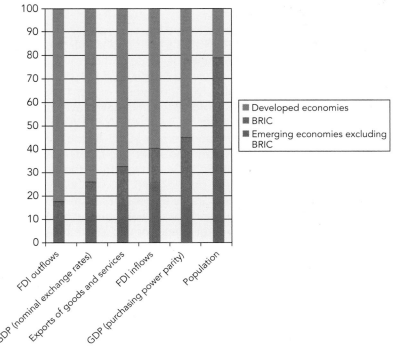

Emerging economies
A term that has gradually replaced the term "developing countries" since the 1990s.

Emerging markets
A term that is often used interchangeably with "emerging economies."

Gross domestic product (GDP)
The sum of value added by resident firms, households, and government operating in an economy.

Sources: Data extracted from (1) International Monetary Fund, 2009, *World Economic Outlook: Sustaining the Recovery* (p. 162), Washington: IMF; (2) United Nations, 2009, *World Investment Report 2009* (p. 247), New York and Geneva: UN; (3) World Bank, 2009, World Development Indicators database, Washington: World Bank. All data refer to 2008.

Purchasing power parity (PPP)
A conversion that determines the equivalent amount of goods and services different currencies can purchase.

BRIC
Brazil, Russia, India, and China.

Gross national product (GNP)
Gross domestic product (GDP) plus income from nonresident sources abroad.

Gross national income (GNI)
Gross domestic product (GDP) plus income from income from nonresident sources abroad. GNI is the term used by the World Bank and other international organizations to supersede the term GNP.

adjusted for **purchasing power parity (PPP)**, which is an adjustment to reflect the differences in cost of living (see In Focus 1.2). Using official (nominal) exchange rates without adjusting for PPP, emerging economies contribute about 26% of the global GDP. Why is there such a huge difference between the two measures? Because the cost of living (such as housing and haircuts) in emerging economies tends to be lower than that in developed economies. For example, one dollar spent in Mexico can buy a lot more than one dollar spent in the United States. Some emerging economies are growing rapidly.[5] During the 2008–2009 global recession, it was the strong recovery of China and India that spearheaded the global recovery.[6]

Table 1.1 (and PengAtlas Map 1.1) lists the 33 countries that are classified as "developed economies." The rest of the world (more than 150 countries) can be broadly labeled as "emerging economies." Of these emerging economies, Brazil, Russia, India, and China—commonly referred to as **BRIC**—command more attention. As a group, they generate 17% of world exports, absorb 16% of FDI inflows, and contribute 28% of world GDP (on a PPP basis). Commanding a lion's share, BRIC contribute 62% of the GDP of all emerging economies (on

IN Focus 1.2

Setting the Terms Straight

GDP, GNP, GNI, PPP—there is a bewildering variety of acronyms that are used to measure economic development. It is useful to set these terms straight before proceeding. Gross domestic product (GDP) is measured as the sum of value added by *resident* firms, households, and government operating in an economy. For example, the value added by foreign-owned firms operating in Mexico would be counted as part of Mexico's GDP. However, the earnings of *nonresident* sources that are sent back to Mexico (such as earnings of Mexicans who do not live and work in Mexico and dividends received by Mexicans who own non-Mexican stocks) are not included in Mexico's GDP. One measure that captures this is **gross national product (GNP)**. More recently, the World Bank and other international organizations have used a new term, **gross national income (GNI)**, to supersede GNP. Conceptually, there is no difference between GNI and GNP. What exactly is GNI/GNP? It comprises GDP plus income from nonresident sources abroad.

Although GDP, GNP, and now GNI are often used as yardsticks of economic development, differences in cost of living make such a direct comparison less meaningful. A dollar of spending in, say, Thailand can buy a lot more than in Japan. Therefore, conversion based on purchasing power

parity (PPP) is often necessary. The PPP between two countries is the rate at which the currency of one country needs to be converted into that of a second country to ensure that a given amount of the first country's currency will purchase the same volume of goods and services in the second country (Chapter 7 has more details). The Swiss per capita GNI is $64,011 based on official (nominal) exchange rates—*higher* than the US per capita GNI of $46,716. However, everything is more expensive in Switzerland. A Big Mac costs $5.98 in Switzerland versus $3.57 in the United States. Thus, Switzerland's per capita GNI based on PPP becomes $42,534—*lower* than the US per capita GNI based on PPP, $46,716 (the World Bank uses the United States as benchmark in PPP calculation). On a worldwide basis, measured at official exchange rates, emerging economies' share of global GDP is approximately 26%. However, measured at PPP, it is about 43% of the global GDP. Overall, when we read statistics about GDP, GNP, and GNI, always pay attention to whether these numbers are based on official exchange rates or PPP, which can make a huge difference.

Sources: Based on (1) *Economist*, 2009, The Big Mac index: Cheesed off, July 18; (2) *Economist*, 2006, Grossly distorted picture, February 11: 72; (3) World Bank, 2009, World Development Indicators database.

TABLE 1.1   CLASSIFYING DEVELOPED ECONOMIES VERSUS EMERGING ECONOMIES

33 developed economies as classified by the International Monetary Fund (IMF)		
Australia	Hong Kong	Portugal
Austria	Iceland	Singapore
Belgium	Ireland	Slovak Republic
Canada	Israel	Slovenia
Cyprus	Italy	South Korea
Czech Republic	Japan	Spain
Denmark	Luxembourg	Sweden
Finland	Malta	Switzerland
France	Netherlands	Taiwan
Germany	New Zealand	United Kingdom
Greece	Norway	United States
All the other 149 countries are classified by the IMF as emerging economies (see PengAtlas Map 1.1)		

Source: IMF, www.imf.org (accessed October 16, 2009). The IMF recognizes 182 countries and economies. It labels developed economies "advanced economies," and labels emerging economies "emerging and developing economies."

a PPP basis). BRIC also generate 8% of world FDI outflows, and MNEs from BRIC are increasingly visible in making investments and acquiring firms around the world.[7] Clearly, major emerging economies (especially BRIC) and their firms have become a force to be reckoned with in global business.[8]

The global economy can be viewed as a pyramid (Figure 1.2). The top consists of about one billion people with per capita annual income of $20,000

FIGURE 1.2   THE GLOBAL ECONOMIC PYRAMID

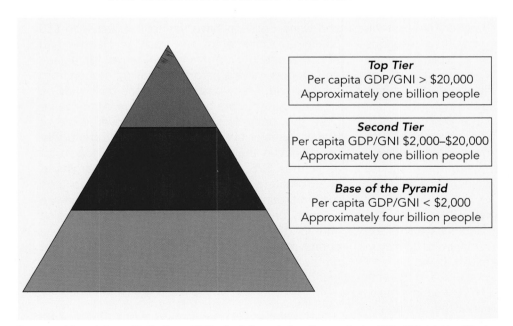

Top Tier
Per capita GDP/GNI > $20,000
Approximately one billion people

Second Tier
Per capita GDP/GNI $2,000–$20,000
Approximately one billion people

Base of the Pyramid
Per capita GDP/GNI < $2,000
Approximately four billion people

Sources: Adapted from (1) S. Hart, 2005, *Capitalism at the Crossroads* (p. 111), Philadelphia: Wharton School Publishing; (2) C. K. Prahalad & S. Hart, 2002, The fortune at the bottom of the pyramid, *Strategy+ Business*, 26: 54–67.

or higher. These are mostly people who live in the developed economies in the Triad, which consists of North America, Western Europe, and Japan. Another billion people earning $2,000 to $20,000 a year make up the second tier. The vast majority of humanity—about four billion people—earn less than $2,000 a year and comprise the base of the pyramid. Most MNEs focus on the top and second tiers and end up ignoring the base of the pyramid.[9] An increasing number of such low-income countries have shown a great deal of economic opportunities as income levels have risen (In Focus 1.3). More Western MNEs, such as GE, are investing aggressively in the base of the pyramid and leveraging their investment to tackle markets in both emerging economies and developed economies (see the Closing Case). Today's students—and tomorrow's business leaders—will ignore these opportunities at the base of the pyramid at their own peril. This book will help ensure that *you* will not ignore these opportunities.

Triad

North America, Western Europe, and Japan.

Base of the pyramid

Economies where people make less than $2,000 a year.

IN Focus 1.3

It's the Base of the Pyramid Calling

What magical device can boost entrepreneurship, provide an alternative to bad roads, widen farmers' and fishermen's access to markets, and allow swift and safe transfers of money? It is . . . a mobile (cell) phone! At the base of the global economic pyramid where fixed-line phones are rare or nonexistent, mobile phones are often the very first telephone networks widely deployed. In a typical country at the base of the pyramid, an increase of ten mobile phones per 100 people reportedly boosts GDP growth by 0.6%. Not surprisingly, the most explosive growth is found in the poorest region of the world: sub-Saharan Africa. Of course, such growth was based on a very low penetration level: In sub-Saharan Africa, there were three mobile phones per 100 people in 2001. Now there are eight mobile phones per 100.

The world's largest market, China now has 700 million users. In 2009, an additional 89 million signed up in China, 128 million in India, and 96 million across Africa. As demand takes off at the base of the pyramid, mobile phone makers and service providers cannot be happier. The reason is simple: At the top of the pyramid, market penetration is reaching saturation. The "race to the bottom" is challenging, since many customers demand rock

bottom prices of $50 or less per handset. For now, the only serious contenders for this segment are Nokia and Motorola, the world's No. 1 and No. 2 makers, respectively. Their tremendous volume gives them hard-to-beat economies of scale. Samsung, LG, and Sony Ericsson have yet to sell less-than-$50 handsets. Chinese makers such as Huawei and ZTE, despite their growing reputation for higher-end models, have a hard time making money from the low end. Many customers at the base may be illiterate, but they are brand conscious. At the same price, they prefer Nokia and Motorola over unknown brands. Already, both Nokia and Motorola are further consolidating their position by making models for as little as $25, while still maintaining margins at approximately 30%, which is comparable to their margin around the world. Overall, this is a win-win solution for numerous economies eager to develop and for the few far-sighted and capable mobile phone makers to do what C. K. Prahalad, a guru on the base of the pyramid, preaches—serving the world's poor, *profitably*.

Sources: Based on (1) *Economist*, 2009, Mobile marvels, September 26: 1–19; (2) *Economist*, 2006, Mobile phones in Africa, February 4: 94; (3) C. K. Prahalad & A. Hammond, 2002, Serving the world's poor, profitably, *Harvard Business Review*, September: 48–57.

WHY STUDY GLOBAL BUSINESS?

Global business (or IB) is one of the most exciting, challenging, and relevant subjects offered by business schools. Why study it? There are at least three compelling reasons why you should study global business—and study hard (Table 1.2).

First, mastering global business knowledge helps advance your employability and career in an increasingly competitive global economy. Take a look at the Opening Day Quiz in Table 1.3. Can you answer all the questions correctly? If not, you will definitely benefit from studying global business.

The answer to Question 1 is empirical—that is, based on data. You should guess first and then look at the label of your shirt yourself or ask a friend to help you. The key here is international trade. Do you wear a shirt made in your own country or another country? Why?

Students typically ask if the computer in Question 2 means the mother board or the keyboard. My answer is: "I mean the computer, all the production that went into making the machine." Then some students would respond: "But they could be made in different countries!" My point exactly. However, desktops or laptops have labels that specify in which country the final product was made or assembled. The point here is to appreciate the complexity of a global value chain, with different countries making different components and handling different tasks. Such a value chain is typically managed by an MNE, such as Dell, HP, or Lenovo. The capabilities necessary to organize a global supply chain hints at the importance of resources and capabilities—one of the two key themes of this book.

LEARNING OBJECTIVE 2

Give three reasons why it is important to study global business.

TABLE 1.2 WHY STUDY GLOBAL BUSINESS?

- Enhance your employability and advance your career in the global economy
- Better preparation for possible expatriate assignments abroad
- Stronger competence in interacting with foreign suppliers, partners, and competitors and in working for foreign-owned employers in your own country

---

TABLE 1.3 OPENING DAY QUIZ

1. Which country made the shirt you are wearing?

(A) China
(B) Malaysia
(C) Mexico
(D) Romania
(E) USA

2. Which country made your computer?

(A) China
(B) Germany
(C) Singapore
(D) Taiwan
(E) USA

3. How many countries does the G-20 have?

(A) 20
(B) 21
(C) 22
(D) 19
(E) 18

4. A 2,000-employee manufacturing plant is closing in a developed economy and production is moving to an emerging economy. How many jobs of the 2,000 will be kept by the company?

(A) 0
(B) 5–10
(C) 10–20
(D) 20–30
(E) 30–50

Question 3 is deceptively simple. Unfortunately, 100% of my own students—ranging from undergraduates to PhDs—*miss* it. Surprise! The Group of 20 (G-20) only has 19 member countries. The 20th member is the European Union (EU)—a regional bloc, not a single country (see PengAtlas Map 1.2). Why the G-20 is formed in such an interesting way will hopefully make you more curious about how the rules of the game are made around the world. In this case, why are 19 countries in, but numerous others are out? What is special about the EU? Why are other regional blocs not included? A focus on the rules of the game—more technically, institutions—is another key theme of this book.

Question 4 will really frighten you. Some students would typically clarify: "Do you mean the few security guards looking after the closed plant?" "Not necessarily," I would point out. "The question is: How many jobs will be kept by the *company*?" Students would eventually get it: even adding a few jobs as security guards at the closed plant, the most optimistic estimates are that only 30–50 jobs may be kept. Yes, you guessed it, these jobs typically are high-level positions such as the CEO, CFO, CIO, factory director, and chief engineer. These managers will be sent by the MNE to start-up operations in an emerging economy. You need to realize that in a 2,000-employee plant, even if you may be the 51st highest-ranked employee, your fate may be the same as the 2,000th employee. You really need to work hard and work smart to position yourself as one of the top 50 (preferably one of the top 30). Doing well in this class and mastering global business knowledge may help make it happen.

In addition to the first reason—to equip you with relevant knowledge—the second compelling reason why you should study global business is related to Question 4. Because many ambitious students aspire to join the top ranks of large firms, expertise in global business is often a prerequisite. Today, it is increasingly difficult, if not impossible, to find top managers at large firms without significant global competence. Of course, eventually hands-on global experience, not merely knowledge acquired from this course, will be required.[10] However, mastery of the knowledge of, and demonstration of interest in, global business during your education will set you apart as a more ideal candidate to be selected as an expatriate

What are some of the benefits you might enjoy as an expatriate manager?

Group of 20 (G-20)
The group of 19 major countries plus the European Union (EU) whose leaders meet on a biannual basis to solve global economic problems.

Expatriate manager (expat)
A manager who works abroad.

International premium
A significant pay raise when working overseas.

manager (or "expat" in short)—a manager who works abroad—to gain such an experience (see Chapter 15 for details).

Thanks to globalization, low-level jobs not only command lower salaries, but are also more vulnerable. However, high-level jobs, especially those held by expats, are both financially rewarding and relatively secure. Expats often command a significant international premium in compensation—a significant pay raise when working overseas. In US firms, an expat's total compensation package is approximately $250,000 to $300,000 (including perks and benefits). When they return to the United States after a tour of duty (usually 2 to 3 years), a firm that does not provide attractive career opportunities to experienced expats often find they are lured away by competitor firms. Competitor firms also want to globalize their business, and tapping into the expertise and experience of these former expats makes such expansion more likely to succeed. And yes, to hire away these internationally experienced managers, competitor firms have to pay an even larger premium. This indeed is a virtuous cycle.

Lastly, even if you do not aspire to compete for the top job at a large company and instead work at a small firm or are self-employed, you may find yourself dealing with foreign-owned suppliers and buyers, competing with foreign-invested firms in your home market, or perhaps even selling and investing overseas. Or alternatively, you may find yourself working for a foreign-owned firm your domestic employer acquired by a foreign player, or your unit ordered to shut down for global consolidation. Any of these are likely scenarios, because approximately 80 million people worldwide, including 18 million Chinese, six million Americans, and one million British, are employed by foreign-owned firms. Understanding how global business decisions are made may facilitate your own career in such firms.[11] If there is a strategic rationale to downsize your unit, you want to be prepared and start polishing your resume right away. In other words, it is your career that is at stake. Don't be the last in the know!

In short, in this age of global competition, "how do you keep from being Bangalored or Shanghaied" (that is, having your job being outsourced to India or China)?[12] A good place to start is to study hard and do well in your IB course. Also, don't forget to put this course on your resume!

A UNIFIED FRAMEWORK

Global business is a vast subject area. It is one of the few courses that will make you appreciate why your university requires you to take a number of seemingly unrelated courses in general education. We will draw on major social sciences such as economics, geography, history, political science, psychology, and sociology. We will also draw on a number of business disciplines such as strategy, finance, and marketing. The study of global business is thus very interdisciplinary. It is quite easy to lose sight of the forest while scrutinizing various trees or even branches. The subject is not difficult, and most students find it to be fun. The number one student complaint (based on previous student feedback) is that there is an overwhelming amount of information. Honestly, as your author this is also *my* number one complaint.

To proactively address your possible complaint and to make your learning more manageable (and hopefully more fun), we will develop a unified framework (shown in Figure 1.3). This will provide great continuity to facilitate your learning.

Articulate one fundamental question and two core perspectives in the study of global business.

FIGURE 1.3 A UNIFIED FRAMEWORK FOR GLOBAL BUSINESS

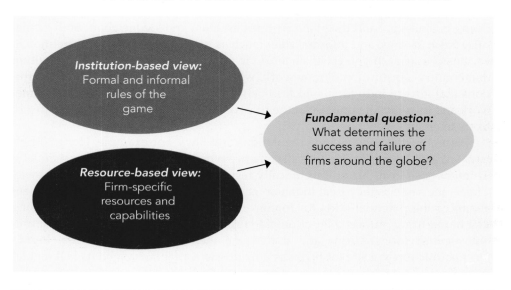

Specifically, we will discipline ourselves by focusing on only one most fundamental question. A fundamental question acts to define a field and to orient the attention of students, practitioners, and scholars in a certain direction. Our "big question" is: *What determines the success and failure of firms around the globe?*[13] To answer this question, we will introduce only two core perspectives throughout this book: (1) an institution-based view and (2) a resource-based view.[14] The remainder of this section outlines this framework.

One Fundamental Question

What is it that we do in global business? Why is it so important that practically all students in business schools around the world are either required or recommended to take this course? Although there are certainly a lot of questions to raise, a relentless interest in what determines the success and failure of firms around the globe serves to focus the energy of our field. Global business is fundamentally about not limiting yourself to your home country. It is about treating the entire global economy as your potential playground (or battlefield). Some firms may be successful domestically but fail miserably when they venture abroad. Other firms successfully translate their strengths from their home market to other countries. If you were expected to lead your firm's efforts to enter a particular foreign market, wouldn't you want to find out what drives the success and failure of other firms in that market?

Overall, the focus on firm performance around the globe defines the field of global business more than anything else. Numerous other questions and topics all relate in one way or another to this most fundamental question. Therefore, all chapters in this book will be centered on this consistent theme: What determines the success and failure of firms around the globe?

First Core Perspective: An Institution-Based View[15]

An institution-based view suggests that the success and failure of firms are enabled and constrained by institutions. By institutions, we mean the rules of the game. Doing business around the globe requires intimate knowledge about both formal rules (such as laws) and informal rules (such as values) that govern competition in various countries. If you establish a firm in a given country, you will work within that country's institutional framework, which is the formal and informal institutions that govern individual and firm behavior. Firms that do not do their homework and thus remain ignorant of the rules of the game in a certain country are not likely to emerge as winners.

Formal institutions include regulations and laws. For example, Hong Kong's laws are well-known for treating all comers—whether from neighboring mainland China (whose firms are still technically regarded as "nondomestic") or far-away Chile—the same as they treat indigenous Hong Kong firms. Such equal treatment enhances the potential odds for foreign firms' success. It is thus not surprising that Hong Kong attracts a lot of outside firms. Other rules of the game discriminate against foreign firms and undermine their chances for success. India's recent attraction as a site for FDI was only possible after it changed its FDI regulations from confrontational to accommodating. Prior to 1991, India's rules severely discriminated against foreign firms. As a result, few foreign firms bothered to show up, and the few that did had a hard time. For example, in the 1970s, the Indian government demanded that Coca-Cola either hand over the recipe for its secret syrup, which it does not even share with the US government, or get out of India. Painfully, Coca-Cola chose to leave India. Its return to India since the 1990s speaks volumes about how much the rules of the game have changed in India.

Informal institutions include cultures, ethics, and norms. They also play an important part in shaping the success and failure of firms around the globe. For example, individualistic societies, particularly the English-speaking countries such as Australia, Britain, and the United States, tend to have a relatively higher level of entrepreneurship as reflected in the number of business start-ups. Why? Because the act of founding a new firm is a widely accepted practice in individualistic societies. Conversely, collectivistic societies such as Japan often have a hard time fostering entrepreneurship. Most people there refuse to stick their necks out to found new businesses because it is contrary to the norm.[16] This explains why direct-selling companies such as Avon (see the Opening Case) have a hard time recruiting representatives in Japan.

Overall, an institution-based view suggests that institutions shed a great deal of light on what drives firm performance around the globe.[17] Next, we turn to our second core perspective.

Second Core Perspective: A Resource-Based View[18]

The institution-based view suggests that the success and failure of firms around the globe are largely determined by their environments. This is certainly correct. Indeed, India failed to attract much FDI prior to 1991 and Japan does not nurture a lot of internationally competitive start-ups because of their institutions. However, insightful as this perspective is, there is a major drawback. If we push this view to its logical extreme, then firm performance around the globe would be *entirely* determined by environments. The validity of this extreme version is certainly questionable.

The resource-based view has emerged to overcome this drawback. Although the institution-based view primarily deals with the *external* environment, the resource-based view focuses on a firm's *internal* resources and capabilities. It starts with a simple observation: In harsh, unattractive environments, most firms either suffer or exit. However, against all odds, a few superstars thrive in these environments. For example, despite the former Soviet Union's obvious hostility toward the United States during the Cold War, PepsiCo began successfully operating in the former Soviet Union in the 1970s (!). Most of the major airlines have been losing money since September 11, 2001. But a small number of players, such as Southwest in the United States and Ryanair in Ireland, have been raking in profits year after year (although, thanks to the recession, their profits are smaller than before). Most unusually, in the fiercely competitive beauty products industry, Avon has been able to grow its revenue during the devastating 2008–2009 recession (see the Opening Case). How can these firms succeed in such challenging environments? A short answer is that PepsiCo, Southwest, Ryanair, and Avon must have certain valuable and unique *firm-specific* resources and capabilities that are not shared by competitors in the same environments.

Doing business outside one's home country is challenging. Foreign firms have to overcome a **liability of foreignness**, which is the *inherent* disadvantage that foreign firms experience in host countries because of their non-native status.[19] Just

Liability of foreignness
The *inherent* disadvantage that foreign firms experience in host countries because of their nonnative status.

think about all the differences in regulations, languages, cultures, and norms. Against such significant odds, the primary weapon foreign firms employ is over-whelming resources and capabilities that not only offset the liability of foreignness, but also pose a significant competitive advantage. Today, many of us take it for granted that the Honda Civic is the best-selling car in the United States, Coca-Cola is the best-selling soft drink in Mexico, and Microsoft Word is the world's number one word-processing software. We really shouldn't. Why? Because it is *not* natural for these foreign firms to dominate non-native markets. These firms must possess some very rare and powerful firm-specific resources and capabilities that drive these remarkable success stories and are the envy of their rivals around the globe. This is a key theme of the resource-based view, which focuses on how winning firms acquire and develop such unique and enviable resources and capabilities and how competitor firms imitate and then innovate in an effort to outcompete the winning firms.

A Consistent Theme

Given our focus on the fundamental question of what determines the success and failure of firms around the globe, we will develop a unified framework by organizing the material in *every* chapter according to the two core perspectives, namely, the institution-based and resource-based views. With our unified framework—an innovation in IB books—we will not only explore the global business "trees," but also see the global business "forest."

Identify three ways of understanding globalization.

WHAT IS GLOBALIZATION?

Globalization, generally speaking, is the close integration of countries and peoples of the world. This abstract five-syllable word is now frequently heard and debated. Those who approve of globalization count its contributions to include greater economic growth and standards of living, increased technology sharing, and more extensive cultural integration. Critics argue that globalization undermines wages in rich countries, exploits workers in poor countries, grants MNEs too much power, and triggered the devastating economic recession that has engulfed the world since 2008. So what exactly is globalization? This section outlines three views on globalization, recommends the pendulum view, and introduces the idea of semiglobalization.

Three Views on Globalization

Depending on what sources you read, globalization could be

- a new force sweeping through the world in recent times
- a long-run historical evolution since the dawn of human history
- a pendulum that swings from one extreme to another from time to time

An understanding of these views helps put the debate about globalization in perspective. First, opponents of globalization suggest that it is a new phenomenon beginning in the late 20th century, driven by recent technological

Globalization
The close integration of countries and peoples of the world.

innovations and a Western ideology focused on exploiting and dominating the world through MNEs. The arguments against globalization focus on environmental stress, social injustice, and sweatshop labor, but present few clearly worked-out alternatives to the present economic order. Nevertheless, antiglobalization advocates and protesters often argue that globalization needs to be slowed down, if not stopped.[20]

A second view contends that globalization has always been part and parcel of human history. Historians are debating whether globalization started 2,000 or 8,000 years ago. The earliest traces of MNEs have been discovered in Assyrian, Phoenician, and Roman times.[21] International competition from low-cost countries is nothing new. In the first century A.D., the Roman emperor Tiberius was so concerned about the massive quantity of low-cost Chinese silk imports that he imposed the world's first known import quota of textiles.[22] Today's most successful MNEs do not come close to wielding the historical clout of some MNEs, such as Britain's East India Company during colonial times. In a nutshell, globalization is nothing new and will probably always exist.

A third view suggests that globalization is the "closer integration of the countries and peoples of the world which has been brought about by the enormous reduction of the costs of transportation and communication, and the breaking down of artificial barriers to the flows of goods, services, capital, knowledge, and (to a lesser extent) people across borders."[23] Globalization is neither recent nor one-directional. It is, more accurately, a process similar to the swing of a pendulum.

The Pendulum View on Globalization

The pendulum view probably makes the most sense because it can help us understand the ups and downs of globalization. The current era of globalization originated in the aftermath of World War II, when major Western countries committed to global trade and investment. However, between the 1950s and the 1970s, this view was not widely shared. Communist countries, such as China and the former Soviet Union, sought to develop self-sufficiency. Many noncommunist developing countries, such as Brazil, India, and Mexico, focused on fostering and protecting domestic industries. But refusing to participate in global trade and investment ended up breeding uncompetitive industries. In contrast, four developing economies in Asia—namely, Hong Kong, Singapore, South Korea, and Taiwan—earned their stripes as the "Four Tigers" by participating in the global economy. They became the *only* economies once recognized as less developed (low-income) by the World Bank to have subsequently achieved developed (high-income) status (see Table 1.1).

Inspired by the Four Tigers, more and more countries and regions—such as China in the late 1970s, Latin America in the mid-1980s, Central and Eastern Europe in the late 1980s, and India in the 1990s—realized that joining the world economy was a must. As these countries started to emerge as new players in the world economy, they became collectively known as "emerging economies." As a result, globalization rapidly accelerated. For example, between 1990 and 2000, while world output grew by 23%, global trade expanded by 80%, and the total flow of FDI increased fivefold.[24]

The pendulum view suggests, however, that globalization is unable to keep going in one direction. Rapid globalization in the 1990s and the 2000s saw some significant backlash. First, the rapid growth of globalization led to the historically inaccurate view that globalization is new. Second, it created fear among many people in developed economies that they would lose jobs. Emerging economies not only seem to attract many low-end manufacturing jobs away from developed economies, but they also increasingly appear to threaten some high-end jobs. Finally, some factions in emerging economies complained against the onslaught of MNEs, alleging that they destroy local companies as well as local cultures, values, and environments. During the 2008–2009 crisis, many citizens in emerging European countries, such as Hungary, Latvia, and Romania, were bitter.[25] Prior to 2008, these countries were infected with an irrational exuberance brought about by their integration with the EU. Many consumers in these countries thought they could afford to duplicate the rich living standards of the rest of Europe by excessive borrowing, which was often denominated in the euro even though the euro was not (and still is not) the legal currency in those countries. When emerging Europe collapsed in 2008, the International Monetary Fund (IMF) came to the rescue, but not without belt tightening, credit squeezing, and spending cuts. Not surprisingly, many citizens in emerging Europe further resented the IMF's "rescue" policies that some have accused of exacerbating the downturn (see Chapter 7).

Although small-scale acts of vandalizing McDonald's restaurants are reported in a variety of countries, the December 1999 antiglobalization protests in Seattle and the September 2001 terrorist attacks in New York and Washington are undoubtedly the most visible and most extreme acts of antiglobalization forces at work. As a result, international travel was curtailed, and global trade and investment flows slowed in the early 2000s.

In the middle of the 2000s, however, worldwide economic growth was again humming along. World GDP, cross-border trade, and per capita GDP all soared to historically high levels. Unfortunately, the party suddenly ended in 2008. Outlined in Table 1.4, the 2008–2009 global economic crisis was unlike anything the world had seen since the Great Depression (1929–1933). The year 2008 showed, for better or worse, how interconnected the global economy has become. Deteriorating housing markets in the United States, fueled by unsustainable subprime lending practices, led to massive government bailouts of financial services firms starting in September 2008. Initially most of the world probably shared the sentiment expressed by Brazilian President Luiz Inacio Lula da Silva that the crisis would be "Bush's crisis" (referring to President George W. Bush) and would have nothing to do with "us." Unfortunately, the crisis quickly spread around the world, forcing numerous governments to bail out their own troubled banks. Global output, trade, and investment plummeted, while unemployment skyrocketed.

TABLE 1.4   SYMPTOMS OF THE GLOBAL ECONOMIC CRISIS, 2008–2009

- The bursting of a real estate bubble
- The liquidity and solvency problems for major banks
- The refusal by consumers and companies to spend on consumption or investment
- Plummeting global output, trade, and investment
- Skyrocketing unemployment
- Rapid contagion around the world due to the closely interconnected nature of the global economy

After unprecedented intervention in developed economies where governments ended up being many banks' largest shareholders, confidence is growing that the global economy has turned the corner and that the recession is ending. However, economic recovery is likely to be slow in developed economies, whereas emerging economies are likely to rebound faster. The recession reminds all firms and managers of the importance of **risk management**—the identification and assessment of risks and the preparation to minimize the impact of high-risk, unfortunate events.[26] As a technique to prepare and plan for multiple scenarios (either high risk or low risk), **scenario planning** is now extensively used by firms around the world.[27] As far as the direction of economic globalization is concerned, the recovery may see more protectionist measures, since the stimulus packages and job creation schemes of various governments emphasize "buy national" (such as "buy American") and "hire locals." In short, the pendulum is swinging back.

Like the proverbial elephant, globalization is seen by everyone yet rarely comprehended. The sudden ferocity of the recent economic crisis surprised everybody—ranging from central bankers to academic experts. Remember all of us felt sorry when we read the story of a bunch of blind men trying to figure out the shape and form of the elephant. We really shouldn't. Although we are not blind, our task is more challenging than the blind men who study a standing animal. Our beast—globalization—does not stand still and often rapidly moves, back and forth (!). Yet, we try to live with it, avoid being crushed by it, and even attempt to profit from it. Overall, seeing globalization as a pendulum provides perhaps the most balanced and realistic perspective.

Semiglobalization

Despite the debate over the far-reaching impact of globalization, globalization is not complete. Most measures of market integration (such as trade and FDI) have recently scaled new heights but still fall far short of a single, globally integrated market. In other words, what we have may be labeled **semiglobalization**, which is more complex than extremes of total isolation and total globalization. Semiglobalization suggests that barriers to market integration at borders are high, but not high enough to completely insulate countries from each other.[28] Semiglobalization calls for more than one way for doing business around the globe. Total isolation on a nation-state basis would suggest localization—a strategy of treating each country as a unique market. Total globalization, on the other hand, would lead to standardization—a strategy of treating the entire world as one market. But semiglobalization has no single right strategy, resulting in a wide variety of experimentations. Overall, (semi)globalization is neither to be opposed as a menace nor to be celebrated as a panacea; it is to be *engaged*.[29]

Risk management
The identification and assessment of risks and the preparation to minimize the impact of high-risk, unfortunate events.

Scenario planning
A technique to prepare and plan for multiple scenarios (either high or low risk).

Semiglobalization
A perspective that suggests that barriers to market integration at borders are high, but not high enough to completely insulate countries from each other.

GLOBAL BUSINESS AND GLOBALIZATION AT A CROSSROADS

Twenty-first-century business leaders are facing an enormous challenge. This book provides a basic guide to meeting that challenge. As a backdrop for the remainder of this book, this section makes two points. First, a basic understanding of the global economy is necessary. Second, it is important to critically examine your own personal views and biases regarding globalization.

LEARNING OBJECTIVE

5

State the size of the global economy and its broad trends and understand your likely bias in the globalization debate.

A Glance at the Global Economy

At present, the global economy is approximately $60 trillion (total global GDP calculated at official, nominal exchange rates). Although there is no need to memorize a lot of statistics, it is useful to remember this $60-trillion figure to keep things in perspective.

A frequent observation in the globalization debate is the enormous size of MNEs.[30] This can be illustrated by comparing the sales of some of the largest MNEs with the GDP of countries. The world's largest MNE, ranked by sales, is Royal Dutch Shell headquartered in the Netherlands. If it were an independent country, it would be the 24th largest economy—its sales are smaller than Saudi Arabia's GDP but larger than Norway's. Exxon Mobil and Wal-Mart are the top two US firms, and also the top two and three global firms, respectively. Their respective sales equal the GDP of Austria and Iran, the 25th and 26th largest economies in the world measured by GDP. The sales of the largest Asia Pacific-based MNE, Sinopec of China, globally ranked number nine, are larger than the combined GDP of Malaysia, Singapore, Philippines, and New Zealand, all of which are sizeable Asia Pacific economies.

Today, approximately 82,000 MNEs control an estimated 810,000 subsidiaries overseas.[31] Figure 1.4 and Table 1.5 track the changes in the makeup of the 500 largest MNEs between 1990 and 2008. Broadly speaking, a country's economic strength is reflected by its number of firms on the *Fortune* Global 500 list. In general,

FIGURE 1.4 *FORTUNE* GLOBAL 500 (1990–2008)

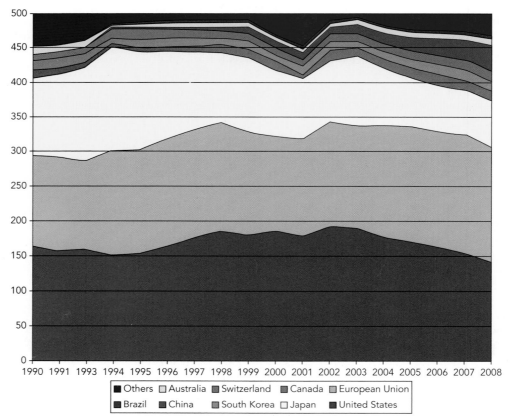

Sources: Based on data from various issues of *Fortune* Global 500.

TABLE 1.5   CHANGES IN THE *FORTUNE* GLOBAL 500 (1990–2008)

Country/bloc	1990	1995	2000	2001	2002	2003	2004	2005	2006	2007	2008
United States	164	153	185	178	192	189	176	170	162	153	140
European Union	129	148	136	139	150	147	161	165	165	170	163
Japan	111	141	95	88	88	100	81	70	67	64	68
Canada	12	6	13	5	14	12	13	14	16	14	14
South Korea	11	12	8	12	13	9	11	12	14	15	14
Switzerland	11	16	10	9	11	12	11	12	13	14	15
China	0	2	10	10	11	14	16	20	24	29	37
Australia	9	4	7	6	6	7	9	8	8	8	9
Brazil	3	4	3	4	4	3	3	4	5	5	6
Others	50	14	33	49	11	7	19	25	26	28	34
Total	500	500	500	500	500	500	500	500	500	500	500

Sources: Based on data from various issues of *Fortune* Global 500.

approximately 80% of the 500 largest MNEs come from the Triad. However, in 2008, thanks to the recession that originated from the Triad (in particular, from the United States), Triad-based MNEs only represented 74% of *Fortune* Global 500. Since 1990, the United States has contributed about one-third of these firms. In 2008, only 140 US MNEs made the *Fortune* Global 500, the lowest number for the United States since 1990. The EU has maintained a reasonably steady increase. With only 68 firms showing up on the *Fortune* Global 500 list in 2008, Japan has experienced the most dramatic variation (roughly corresponding to its economic boom and bust with several years of delay).

Among MNEs from emerging economies, those from South Korea and Brazil have largely maintained their presence in the *Fortune* Global 500. MNEs from China have come on strong—from zero in 1990 to 37 in 2008. Beijing is now headquarters to 26 *Fortune* Global 500 firms, eight *more* than New York. In some industries, these MNEs, often regarded as "Third World multinationals" or "dragon multinationals," have joined the top ranks.[32] Clearly, Western rivals cannot afford to ignore them, and students reading this book need to pay attention to these emerging multinationals.

The Globalization Debate and You

At the dawn of the 21st century, the seemingly one-directional march of globalization started to show its true color as a pendulum, which has direct ramifications for you as a future business leader, a consumer, and a citizen. Because the globalization debate directly affects *your* future, it is imperative that you participate in the debate instead of letting other people make decisions on globalization that will significantly affect your career, your consumption, and your country.[33]

It is important to know your own biases when joining the debate. By the very act of taking an IB course and reading this book, you probably already have some pro-globalization biases compared to nonbusiness majors elsewhere on campus and the general public in your country. You are not alone. In the last several decades, most executives, policymakers, and scholars in both developed and emerging economies, who are generally held to be the elite in these societies, are biased toward acknowledging the benefits of globalization.[34] Although it is

© AP Photo/Matt Rourke

Why do protestors object to globalization?

long known that globalization carries both benefits and costs, many of the elite have failed to take into sufficient account the social, political, and environmental costs associated with globalization. However, that these elites share certain perspectives on globalization does *not* mean that most other members of the society share the same views. Unfortunately, many of the elite fail to understand the limits of their beliefs and mistakenly assume that the rest of the world thinks like them. To the extent that powerful economic and political institutions are largely controlled by the elite in almost every country, it is not surprising that some antiglobalization groups, feeling powerless, end up resorting to unconventional tactics (such as mass protests) to make their point.

Many opponents of globalization are nongovernmental organizations (NGOs) such as environmentalists, human rights activists, and consumer groups. Ignoring them will be a grave failure when doing business around the globe.[35] Instead of viewing NGOs as opponents, many firms view them as partners. NGOs do raise a valid point when they insist that firms, especially MNEs, should have a broader concern for the various stakeholders affected by the MNEs' actions around the world.[36] At present, this view is increasingly moving from the peripheral to the mainstream.

It is certainly interesting and perhaps alarming to note that current business school students already exhibit values and beliefs in favor of globalization, which are similar to those held by executives, policymakers, and scholars, and are different from those held by the general public. Shown in Table 1.6, relative to the general public, US business students have significantly more positive (almost one-sided) views toward globalization than the general public. Although these data are based on US business students, my teaching and lectures around the world suggest that most business students—regardless of their nationality—seem to share such positive views on globalization. This is not surprising. Both self-selection to study business and socialization within the curriculum, in which free trade is widely regarded as positive, may lead to certain attitudes in favor of globalization. Consequently, business students may focus more on the economic gains of globalization and be less concerned with its darker sides.

Current and would-be business leaders need to be aware of their own bias embodied in such one-sided views toward globalization. Since business schools aspire to train future business leaders by indoctrinating students with the dominant values managers should hold, these results suggest that business schools may have largely succeeded in this mission. However, to the extent that current

Nongovernmental organizations (NGOs)

Organizations that are not affiliated with governments.

TABLE 1.6   VIEWS ON GLOBALIZATION: AMERICAN GENERAL PUBLIC VERSUS BUSINESS STUDENTS

Percentage answering "good" for the question: Overall, do you think globalization is *good* or *bad* for	General public[1] (N = 1,024)	Business students[2] (N = 494)
• US consumers like you	68%	96%
• US companies	63%	77%
• The US economy	64%	88%
• Strengthening poor countries' economies	75%	82%

Sources: Based on (1) A. Bernstein, 2000, Backlash against globalization, *BusinessWeek*, April 24: 43; (2) M. W. Peng & H. Shin, 2008, How do future business leaders view globalization? (p. 179), *Thunderbird International Business Review*, 50(3): 175–182. All differences are statistically significant.

managers (and professors) have strategic blind spots, these findings are potentially alarming. They reveal that business students already share these blind spots. Despite possible self-selection in choosing to major in business, there is no denying that student values are shaped, at least in part, by the educational experience business schools provide. Knowing such limitations, business school professors and students need to work especially hard to break out of this mental straitjacket.

In order to combat the widespread tendency to have one-sided, rosy views, a significant portion of this book is devoted to the numerous debates that surround globalization. Beyond this chapter, which illustrates a big debate in itself, debates are systematically introduced in *every* chapter to provoke more critical thinking and discussion. Our field has no shortage of debates. No doubt, debates drive practice and research forward. Therefore, it is imperative that students be exposed to cutting-edge debates and encouraged to form their own views when engaging in these debates.[37] In addition, ethics is emphasized throughout the book. A featured Ethical Dilemma and a series of Critical Discussion Questions on ethics can be found in every chapter. In addition, two whole chapters are devoted to ethics, norms, and cultures (Chapter 3) and corporate social responsibility (Chapter 17).

ORGANIZATION OF THE BOOK

This book has four parts. Part 1 is *foundations.* Following this chapter, Chapters 2, 3, and 4 deal with the two leading perspectives—institution-based and resource-based views. Part 2 covers *tools,* focusing on trade (Chapter 5), foreign investment (Chapter 6), foreign exchange (Chapter 7), and global and regional integration (Chapter 8). Part 3 sheds light on *strategy.* We start with the internationalization of small, entrepreneurial firms (Chapter 9), followed by ways to enter foreign markets (Chapter 10), to manage competitive dynamics (Chapter 11), to make alliances and acquisitions work (Chapter 12), and to strategize, structure, and learn (Chapter 13). Finally, Part 4 builds *excellence in different functional areas*: marketing and supply chain (Chapter 14), human resource management (Chapter 15), finance and corporate governance (Chapter 16), and corporate social responsibility (Chapter 17).

CHAPTER SUMMARY

1. Explain the concepts of international business and global business.
   - IB is typically defined as (1) a business (firm) that engages in international (cross-border) economic activities and (2) the action of doing business abroad.
   - Global business is defined in this book as business around the globe.
   - This book has gone beyond competition in developed economies by devoting extensive space to competitive battles waged in emerging economies and the base of the global economic pyramid.

2. Give three reasons why it is important to study global business.
   - Enhance your employability and advance your career in the global economy by equipping yourself with global business knowledge.
   - Better preparation for possible expatriate assignments abroad.
   - Stronger competence in interacting with foreign suppliers, partners, and competitors and in working for foreign-owned employers in your own country.

3. Articulate one fundamental question and two core perspectives in the study of global business.
   - Our most fundamental question is: What determines the success and failure of firms around the globe?
   - The two core perspectives are (1) the institution-based view and (2) the resource-based view.
   - We develop a unified framework by organizing materials in *every* chapter according to the two perspectives guided by the fundamental question.

4. Identify three ways of understanding globalization.
   - Some view globalization as a recent phenomenon, and others believe that it is a one-directional evolution since the dawn of human history.
   - We suggest that globalization is best viewed as a process similar to the swing of a pendulum.

5. State the size of the global economy and its broad trends and understand your likely bias in the globalization debate.
   - MNEs, especially large ones from developed economies, are sizeable economic entities in a global economy of $60 trillion (global GDP).
   - Current and would-be business leaders need to be aware of their own hidden pro-globalization bias.

KEY TERMS

Base of the pyramid   10
BRIC   8
Emerging economies   7
Emerging markets   7
Expatriate manager (expat)   12
Foreign direct investment (FDI)   5
Global business   6
Globalization   16
Gross domestic product (GDP)   7

Gross national income (GNI)   8
Gross national product (GNP)   8
Group of 20 (G-20)   12
International business (IB)   5
International premium   12
Liability of foreignness   15
Multinational enterprise (MNE)   5

Nongovernmental organizations (NGOs)   22
Purchasing power parity (PPP)   8
Risk management   19
Scenario planning   19
Semiglobalization   19
Triad   10

REVIEW QUESTIONS

1. What is the traditional definition of IB? How is global business defined in this book?

2. Discuss the importance of emerging economies in the global economy. Use current news.

3. What is your interest in studying global business? How do you think it may apply to your future?

4. If you were to work as an expatriate manager, where would you like to go and what would you like to do? Why?

5. How would you describe an institution-based view of global business?

6. How would you describe a resource-based view of global business?

7. After comparing the three views of globalization, which seems the most sensible to you and why?

8. What is semiglobalization and what factors contribute to it?

9. Why do some people protest against globalization? Do they make any point(s) that all people, whether for or against globalization, should consider?

10. You may view yourself as objective and neutral regarding globalization, but do you sense any bias that you may have one way or the other? What bias most likely exists on the part of other students taking this course?

11. Look at PengAtlas Maps 2.1 and 2.2. Compare the global position of the United States in merchandise trade versus service trade. Imagine that you were asked to give reasons why you think it is good from the US perspective that it is the world's largest importer in both merchandise and services. What reasons would you mention?

12. Some readers may be studying this book in one or more of the emerging economies shown on PengAtlas Map 1.2. Others may be descended from immigrants from these countries. If this is the case with you, pick one of the countries and do some research into current changes in that country. Indicate the reasons why you think that over the long run there may be a shift from an emerging status to a developed status.

CRITICAL DISCUSSION QUESTIONS

1. A classmate says: "Global business is relevant for top executives such as CEOs in large companies. I am just a lowly student who will struggle to gain an entry-level job, probably in a small domestic company. Why should I care about it?" How do you convince your classmate that global business is something to care about?

2. Thomas Friedman in his book *The World is Flat* (2005) suggests that the world is flattening—meaning it is increasingly interconnected by new technology such as the Internet. This can raise the poor from poverty, nurture a worldwide middle class, and even spread democracy. On the other hand, this presents significant challenges for developed economies, whose employees may feel threatened by competition from low-cost countries. How does this flattening world affect you?

3. *ON ETHICS:* What are some of the darker sides (in other words, costs) associated with globalization? How can business leaders make sure that the benefits of their various actions (such as outsourcing) outweigh their drawbacks (such as job losses in developed economies)?

4. **ON ETHICS:** Some argue that aggressively investing in emerging economies is not only economically beneficial but also highly ethical, because it may potentially lift many people out of poverty (see the Closing Case). However, others caution that in the absence of reasonable hopes of decent profits, rushing to emerging economies is reckless. How would you participate in this debate?

global**EDGE**

YOUR SOURCE FOR
**global business
knowledge**

http://globalEDGE.msu.edu

GLOBAL ACTION

1. Chemical companies are among the largest firms worldwide. Two approaches to evaluating operations of chemical companies are by capital spending and research and development (R&D) spending. Through the globalEDGE website, access a resource that provides this information about top global chemical producers. Then compare the top five capital-spending and R&D-spending chemical companies. Are any companies found on both lists? What insights does this information provide?

2. An important aspect of globalization is the fundamental stability of the global economic order currently in place. Thus, FDI intentions can be influenced by the perceived sustainability of the global economic order. Using the globalEDGE website, identify the three most important issues related to global economic stability over the next 20 years. Be sure to discuss the sample surveyed to provide the appropriate frame of reference for discussion.

VIDEO CASES

Watch "Integrating Global Business at a Local Level" by E. Neville Isdell of the Coca-Cola Company.

1. What is meant by the title of the video "Integrating Global Business at a Local Level"? What is being "integrated"?

2. In referring to past practices of global firms, Isdell referred to simply "parachuting in." What did he mean by that and how does it relate to his concern about economic nationalism?

3. How must global firms in the future be different regarding identifying with society as a whole?

4. How does a franchise system with its use of local entrepreneurs contribute to the integration desired by Isdell?

5. Isdell warned against simply extracting and not putting something back. What challenge did Coca-Cola have in that regard? Think of an example of another firm or industry that may heed Isdell's warning and explain the reason for your selection.

Closing Case

GE Innovates from the Base of the Pyramid

Although the 130-year-old General Electric (GE) is usually regarded as a model of management excellence, the recent recession has been brutal. An *Economist* article in March 2009 on GE used the following unflattering title: "Losing Its Magic Touch"—for a good reason. Since 2008, GE has slashed its dividends by two-thirds, lost a prized AAA credit rating, and seen $269 billion wiped off its stock market value due to concerns about the quality of some loans made by its financial services unit, GE Capital.

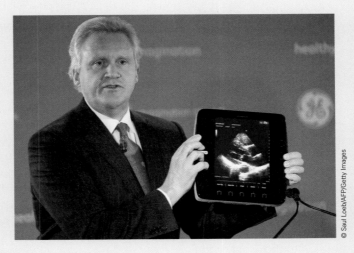

© Saul Loeb/AFP/Getty Images

One glimmer of hope out of GE's recent mess is a new initiative called "reverse innovation," which has attracted GE chairman and CEO Jeff Immelt's personal attention. MNEs such as GE historically innovate new products in developed economies, and then localize these products by tweaking them for customers in emerging economies. Unfortunately, a lot of these expensive products, with well-off customers in developed economies in mind, flop in emerging economies not only because of their price tag, but also because of their lack of consideration for the specific needs and wants of local customers. Being the exact opposite, reverse innovation turns innovative products created for emerging economies into low-cost offerings for developed economies.

Take a look at GE's conventional ultrasound machines, originally developed in the United States and Japan and sold for $100,000 and up (up to $350,000). In China, these expensive, bulky devices sold poorly because not every sophisticated, urban hospital-based imaging center could afford to have them. GE's team in China realized that more than 80% of China's population relies on rural hospitals or clinics that are poorly funded. Conventional ultrasound machines are simply out of reach for these

facilities. Patients thus have to travel to urban hospitals to access ultrasound. However, transportation to urban hospitals, especially for the sick, is challenging. Since most Chinese patients could not come to the ultrasound machines, the machines need to go to the patients. Scaling down its existing bulky, expensive, and complex ultrasound machines was not going to serve that demand. GE realized that it needed a revolutionary product—a compact, portable ultrasound machine. In 2002, GE in China launched its first compact ultrasound, which combined a regular laptop computer with sophisticated software. The machine sold for only $30,000. In 2008, GE introduced a new model that sold for $15,000, less than 15% of the price tag of its high-end conventional ultrasound models. While portable ultrasounds have naturally become a hit in China, especially in rural clinics, they have also generated dramatic growth throughout the world, including *developed* economies. These machines combine a new dimension previously unavailable to ultrasound machines—portability—with an unbeatable price in developed economies where containing health care cost is increasingly paramount. Before the global recession, portable ultrasounds by 2008 were a $278 million global product line for GE, growing at 50% to 60% annually. Even in the midst of a severe global recession, this product line is expected to grow 25% annually in China.

GE's experience in developing portable ultrasound machines in China is not alone. For rural India, it has pioneered a $1,000 handheld electrocardiogram (ECG) device that brings down the cost by a margin of 60% to 80%. In the Czech Republic, GE developed an aircraft engine for small planes that slashes its cost by half. This allows GE to challenge

---

TABLE 1.7   GE'S MENTAL MAP OF THE WORLD

2000	2010
• United States	• People-rich regions, such as China and India
• Europe	• Resource-rich regions, such as the Middle East, Australia, Brazil, Canada, and Russia
• Japan	
• Rest of the world	• Rest of the world, such as the United States, Europe, and Japan

Source: Extracted from text in J. Immelt, V. Govindarajan, & C. Trimble, 2009, How GE is disrupting itself (p. 59), *Harvard Business Review,* October: 56–65. Jeff Immelt is chairman and CEO of GE.

Pratt & Whitney's dominance of the small turboprop market in developed economies.

Such outstanding performance in and out of emerging economies, in combination with GE's dismal recent experience in developed economies, has rapidly transformed GE's mental map of the world (see Table 1.7). Ten years ago, it focused on the Triad and paid relatively minor attention to the "rest of the world." Now strategic attention is on emerging economies and other resource-rich regions, and the Triad becomes the "rest of the world." In an October 2009 *Harvard Business Review* article, Immelt wrote:

To be honest, the company is also embracing reverse innovation for defensive reasons. If GE doesn't come up with innovations in poor countries and take them global, new competitors from the developing world—like Mindray, Suzlon, Goldwind, and Haier—will…GE has tremendous respect for traditional rivals like Siemens, Philips, and Rolls-Royce. But it knows how to compete with them; they will never destroy GE. By introducing products that create a new price-performance paradigm, however, the emerging giants very well could. Reverse innovation isn't optional; it is oxygen.

Case Discussion Questions:

1. What are the similarities and differences between GE's traditional innovation and reverse innovation?
2. Why is GE so interested in reverse innovation?
3. What are the main concerns that prevent Western MNEs from aggressively investing in emerging economies? What are the costs if they choose not to focus on emerging economies?
4. Why is a leading US MNE such as GE afraid of emerging multinationals from emerging economies?

Sources: Based on (1) *BusinessWeek,* 2009, The joys and perils of "reverse innovation," October 5: 12; (2) *Economist,* 2009, GE: Losing its magic touch, March 21: 73–75; (3) GE Report, 2009, www.gereports.com; (4) J. Immelt, V. Govindarajan, & C. Trimble, 2009, How GE is disrupting itself, *Harvard Business Review,* October: 56–65.

NOTES

[Journal acronyms] **AMP**—*Academy of Management Perspectives;* **AMR**—*Academy of Management Review;* **APJM**—*Asia Pacific Journal of Management;* **BW**—*BusinessWeek;* **HBR**—*Harvard Business Review;* **JIBS**—*Journal of International Business Studies;* **JIM**—*Journal of International Management;* **JM**—*Journal of Management;* **JMS**—*Journal of Management Studies;* **JWB**—*Journal of World Business;* **MIR**—*Management International Review;* **SMJ**—*Strategic Management Journal*

[1] This definition of the MNE can be found in R. Caves, 1996, *Multinational Enterprise and Economic Analysis,* 2nd ed. (p. 1), New York: Cambridge University Press; J. Dunning, 1993, *Multinational Enterprises and the Global Economy* (p. 30), Reading, MA: Addison-Wesley. Other terms are multinational corporation (MNC) and transnational corporation (TNC), which are often used interchangeably with MNE. To avoid confusion, in this book, we will use MNE.

[2] O. Shenkar, 2004, One more time: International business in a global economy (p. 165), *JIBS,* 35: 161–171.

[3] C. Pitellis, 2009, IB at 50, *AIB Insights,* 9 (1): 2–8.

[4] *Economist,* 2006, Climbing back, January 21: 69–70.

[5] T. Hasfi & M. Farashahi, 2005, Applicability of management theories to developing countries, *MIR*, 45: 483–513; R. Ramamurti, 2004, Developing countries and MNEs, *JIBS*, 35: 277–283; M. Wright, I. Filatotchev, R. Hoskisson, & M. W. Peng, 2005, Strategy research in emerging economies, *JMS*, 42: 1–33.

[6] M. W. Peng, R. Bhagat, & S. Chang, 2010, Asia and global business, *JIBS* (in press).

[7] A. Bhattacharya & D. Michael, 2008, How local companies keep multinationals at bay, *HBR*, March: 85–95; A. Cuervo-Cazurra, 2007, Sequence of value-added activities in the multinationalization of developing country firms, *JIM*, 13: 258–277; I. Filatotchev, R. Strange, J. Piesse, & Y. Lien, 2007, FDI by firms from newly industrialized economies in emerging markets, *JIBS*, 38: 556–572; M. Garg & A. Delios, 2007, Survival of the foreign subsidiaries of TMNCs, *JIM*, 13: 278–295; S. Klein & A. Worcke, 2007, Emerging global contenders, *JIM*, 13: 319–337; N. Kumar, 2009, How emerging giants are rewriting the rules of M&A, *HBR*, May: 115–121; J. Lee & J. Slater, 2007, Dynamic capabilities, entrepreneurial rent-seeking, and the investment development path, *JIM*, 13: 241–257; P. Li, 2007, Toward an integrated theory of multinational evolution, *JIM*, 13: 296–318; Y. Luo & R. Tung, 2007, International expansion of emerging market enterprises, *JIBS*, 38: 481–498; D. Yiu, C. Lau, & G. Bruton, 2007, International venturing by emerging economy firms, *JIBS*, 38: 519–540.

[8] G. Gao, J. Murray, M. Kotabe, & J. Lu, 2010, A "strategy tripod" perspective on export behaviors, *JIBS* (in press); S. Gubbi, P. Aulakh, S. Ray, M. Sarkar, & R. Chittoor, 2010, Do international acquisitions by emerging-economy firms create shareholder value? *JIBS* (in press).

[9] T. London, 2009, Making better investments at the base of the pyramid, *HBR*, May: 106–113; T. London & S. Hart, 2004, Reinventing strategies for emerging markets, *JIBS*, 35: 350–370; C. K. Prahalad, 2005, *The Fortune at the Bottom of the Pyramid*, Philadelphia: Wharton School Publishing.

[10] A. Yan, G. Zhu, & D. Hall, 2002, International assignments for career building, *AMR*, 27: 373–391.

[11] W. Newburry, 2001, MNC interdependence and local embeddedness influences on perceptions of career benefits from global integration, *JIBS*, 32: 497–508.

[12] *BW*, 2007, The changing talent game (p. 68), August 20: 68–71.

[13] M. W. Peng, 2004, Identifying the big question in international business research, *JIBS*, 35: 99–108.

[14] K. Meyer, S. Estrin, S. Bhaumik, & M. W. Peng, 2009, Institutions, resources, and entry strategies in emerging economies, *SMJ*, 30: 61–80.

[15] M. W. Peng, S. L. Sun, B. Pinkham, & H. Chen, 2009, The institution-based view as a third leg for a strategy tripod, *AMP*, 23: 63–81; M. W. Peng, D. Wang, & Y. Jiang, 2008, An institution-based view of international business strategy: A focus on emerging economies, *JIBS*, 39: 920–936.

[16] S. Lee, M. W. Peng, & J. Barney, 2007, Bankruptcy laws and entrepreneurship development, *AMR*, 32: 257–272.

[17] B. Kim & J. Prescott, 2005, Deregulatory forms, variations in the speed of governance adaptation, and firm performance, *AMR*, 30: 414–425; I. Mahmood & C. Rufin, 2005, Government's dilemma, *AMR*, 30: 338–360; P. Ring, G. Bigley, T. D'Aunno, & T. Khanna, 2005, Perspectives on how governments matter, *AMR*, 30: 308–320.

[18] M. W. Peng, 2001, The resource-based view and international business, *JM*, 27: 803–829.

[19] B. Elango, 2009, Minimizing effects of liability of foreignness, *JWB*, 44: 51–62.

[20] A. Giddens, 1999, *Runaway World*, London: Profile; S. Strange, 1996, *The Retreat of the State*, Cambridge: Cambridge University Press.

[21] K. Moore & D. Lewis, 1999, *Birth of the Multinational*, Copenhagen: Copenhagen Business School Press.

[22] D. Yergin & J. Stanislaw, 2002, *The Commanding Heights* (p. 385), New York: Simon & Schuster.

[23] J. Stiglitz, 2002, *Globalization and Its Discontents* (p. 9), New York: Norton.

[24] United Nations, 2000, *World Investment Report 2000*, New York and Geneva: United Nations.

[25] S. Leong et al., 2008, Understanding consumer animosity in an international crisis, *JIBS*, 39: 996–1009.

[26] L. Purda, 2008, Risk perception and the financial system, *JIBS*, 39: 1178–1196; N. Taleb, D. Goldstein, & M. Spitznagel, 2009, The six mistakes executives make in risk management, *HBR*, October: 78–81.

[27] S. Lee & M. Makhija, 2009, Flexibility in internationalization, *SMJ*, 30: 537–555.

[28] P. Ghemawat, 2003, Semiglobalization and international business strategy, *JIBS*, 34: 138–152.

[29] M. Guillen, 2001, *The Limits of Convergence* (p. 232), Princeton, NJ: Princeton University Press.

[30] All data described in this section refer to 2008. GDP data are from the World Bank, and Global 500 data are from *Fortune*.

[31] United Nations, 2009, *World Investment Report 2009* (p. xxi), New York and Geneva: UN.

[32] J. Mathews, 2006, Dragon multinationals as new features of globalization in the 21st century, *APJM*, 23: 5–27; R. Ramamurti & J. Singh (eds.), 2009, *Emerging Multinationals from Emerging Markets*, New York: Cambridge University Press. See also P. Aulakh, 2007, Emerging multinationals from developing economies, *JIM*, 13: 235–240.

[33] T. Friedman, 2005, *The World is Flat*, New York: Farrar, Straus, & Giroux.

[34] A. Bird & M. Stevens, 2003, Toward an emergent global culture and the effects of globalization on obsolescing national cultures, *JIM*, 9: 395–407.

[35] H. Teegen, J. Doh, & S. Vachani, 2004, The importance of non-governmental organizations (NGOs) in global governance and value creation, *JIBS*, 35: 463–483.

[36] A. Peredo & J. Chrisman, 2006, Toward a theory of community-based enterprise, *AMR*, 31: 309–328; C. Robertson & W. Crittenden, 2003, Mapping moral philosophies, *SMJ*, 24: 385–392.

[37] B. Kedia & A. Mukherji, 1999, Global managers, *JWB*, 34: 230–251; D. Ricks, 2003, Globalization and the role of the global corporation, *JIM*, 9: 355–359.

LEARNING OBJECTIVES

After studying this chapter, you should be able to:

1. identify two types of institutions—formal and informal.

2. explain how institutions reduce uncertainty.

3. identify the two core propositions underpinning an institution-based view of global business.

4. understand the differences between democracy and totalitarianism.

5. list the differences among civil law, common law, and theocratic law.

6. articulate the importance of property rights and intellectual property rights.

7. outline the differences among market economy, command economy, and mixed economy.

8. participate in two leading debates on politics, laws, and economics.

9. draw implications for action.

© UPI Photo/Landov

Understanding Formal Institutions: Politics, Laws, and Economics

 ETHICAL DILEMMA

O P E N I N G   C A S E

Adam Smith versus Deng Xiaoping

Adam Smith would probably turn in his grave if he heard that in 2008, the fundamental principle of his theory first published in *The Wealth of Nations* in 1776, *laissez faire* (the idea that governments should be hands-off when managing the economy), would be severely challenged. The challenge came neither from the remaining practitioners of socialism such as Cuba, nor from countries traditionally strong on government intervention such as Russia. Instead, these challenges came from the United States and United Kingdom—the two countries so deeply in love with Adam Smith that they had often preached "free market principles" around the world until recently.

To be sure, the times were tough: Financial markets were melting down, banks were failing left and right, and consumer and investor confidence were reaching all-time lows since the Great Depression. However, the solutions turned the unthinkable into a new orthodoxy. Labeled "radical intervention" or even "financial socialism," the solutions centered on nationalization of failing banks and financial

services firms. Yet, for over three decades (since the 1980s), privatization—the complete opposite of nationalization—was largely in the air.

On October 3, 2008, the Emergency Economic Stabilization Act, commonly known as the $700-billion bank bailout plan or the Paulson plan (named after then US Treasury Secretary Henry Paulson in the George W. Bush administration), was passed and signed into law. The congressional debate prior to its passage was ferocious because critics argued that this would clearly violate the enshrined free market principle of nonintervention. On October 15, Paulson announced the first step of implementation, by injecting $125 billion into nine banks: Bank of America, JP Morgan Chase, Citigroup, and Wells Fargo each obtained $25 billion; Goldman Sachs and Morgan Stanley $10 billion each; and Bank of New York and State Street between $2 billion and $3 billion each. In return, the US government, having turned these banks into (partially) state-owned enterprises (SOEs), would take nonvoting preference shares paying 5% interest. This action was so at odds with the free market tradition in the United States that its principal architect Paulson admitted that it was "objectionable." In Paulson's own words at a press conference:

> Government owning a stake in any private US company is objectionable to most Americans, me included. Yet the alternative of leaving businesses and consumers without access to financing is totally unacceptable.

Similarly, on October 8, 2008, the UK government announced a £400 billion ($692 billion) rescue package to inject cash into UK banks. The justification was that if the government had not acted, UK banks faced the real risk of collapse. So used to being lectured by the British about "free markets," other EU governments were reluctant to believe this initially. But they quickly followed UK actions by bailing out their own troubled banks. By the end of 2008, governments in most developed economies became the largest shareholders in their financial industries, reversing three decades of deregulation and privatization.

Although these are certainly extreme measures for extreme times, their long-term significance in terms of changing economic ideology has been noted by numerous experts. No doubt, these actions will be recorded as an important turning point in economic history, triggering a fundamental rethink regarding the merits of private ownership and state ownership. The once-cherished assumptions about the superiority of the US economic model, centered on more market forces and less government intervention, are now in doubt. Recently, French President Nicolas Sarkozy announced that such "*laissez faire* capitalism is over." The irony was that he had been elected in 2007 on a campaign platform promising to practice more "Anglo-Saxon capitalism" in France.

"Forget Adam Smith. Whatever Works." This is the title of a *BusinessWeek* article in October 2008. On October 11, Federal Reserve Bank of Dallas President Richard Fisher gave a speech at the Group of Seven (G-7) finance ministers meeting in Washington, and borrowed a line from the late Chinese leader Deng Xiaoping: "Regardless of whether it is a white cat or a black cat, as long as it can catch mice, it is a good cat."

Of course, Deng in the early 1980s popularized his pragmatic "cat theory" in an effort to transform China from a command economy to a market economy. Interestingly, nearly three decades later, the "cat theory" was being invoked in a totally *opposite* direction. The upshot is that to the same extent that a pure command economy does not exist, a pure free market economy does not exist either. No doubt the post-bailout United States and United Kingdom can still be labeled "market economies," but it is prudent to drop the "F" word. In other words, let us drop the "free" from the term "free market economies."

Sources: Based on (1) *BusinessWeek*, 2008, Forget Adam Smith. Whatever works. October 27: 22–24; (2) *Economist*, 2009, Business in America, May 30-June 5: special report; (3) *Economist*, 2008, Is Sarkozy a closet socialist? November 15: 61–62; (4) *Financial Times*, 2008, US injection lifts confidence, October 15: 1; (5) *Financial Times*, 2008, Whatever it took, October 15: 11; (6) R. Reich, 2009, Government in your business, *Harvard Business Review*, July–August: 94–99.

Institutions
Formal and informal rules of the game.

Institutional transitions
Fundamental and comprehensive changes introduced to the formal and informal rules of the game that affect firms as players.

Institution-based view
A leading perspective in global business that suggests that the success and failure of firms are enabled and constrained by institutions.

What are the benefits and costs of free markets and private ownership? What are the pros and cons of government intervention and state ownership? What are the political ideologies behind such ownership arrangements? Why are the stakes so high behind these decisions? As the Opening Case illustrates, these decisions are affected by **institutions**, commonly known as the "rules of the game." As economic players, firms play by these rules. However, institutions are not static and they may change, resulting in **institutional transitions**—"fundamental and comprehensive changes introduced to the formal and informal rules of the game that affect firms as players."[1]

Overall, the success and failure of firms around the globe are to a large extent determined by firms' ability to understand and take advantage of the different rules of the game. In other words, how firms play the game and win (or lose), at least in part, depends on how the rules are made, enforced, and changed. This calls for firms to constantly monitor, decode, and adapt to the changing rules of the game in order to survive and prosper. As a result, such an **institution-based view** has emerged as a leading perspective in global business.[2] This chapter first introduces the institution-based view. Then, we focus on *formal* institutions (such as political systems, legal systems, and economic systems). *Informal* institutions (such as cultures, ethics, and norms) will be discussed in Chapter 3.

UNDERSTANDING INSTITUTIONS

Building on the "rules of the game" metaphor, Douglass North, a Nobel laureate in economics, more formally defines institutions as "the humanly devised constraints that structure human interaction."[3] An **institutional framework** is made up of both the formal and informal institutions governing individual and firm behavior. Richard Scott, a leading sociologist, identifies three pillars that support these institutions: regulatory, normative, and cognitive pillars.[4]

LEARNING OBJECTIVE 1

Identify two types of institutions—formal and informal.

Formal institutions include laws, regulations, and rules, as shown in Table 2.1. In global business, formal institutions may be imposed by home countries and host countries. Their primary supportive pillar, the **regulatory pillar**, is the coercive power of governments. For example, although many individuals may pay taxes out of a sense of patriotic duty, many others pay taxes out of fear—if they did not pay and got caught, they would go to jail. In other words, it is the coercive power of governments' tax laws that forms the regulatory pillar to compel many individuals to pay taxes.

On the other hand, informal institutions include norms, cultures, and ethics. Informal institutions are supported by two pillars: normative and cognitive. The **normative pillar** refers to how the values, beliefs, and actions of the relevant players—collectively known as norms—influence the behavior of focal individuals and firms. For example, a recent norm is the rush to invest in China and India. This norm prompted many Western firms to imitate each other without a clear understanding of how to make such moves work.[5] Cautious managers who resist such herding are often confronted by board members, investors, and reporters with the question: "Why don't you invest in China and India?" In other words, "Why don't you follow the norm?"

The **cognitive pillar** is the second support for informal institutions. It refers to the internalized (or taken-for-granted) values and beliefs that guide individual and firm behavior. For example, a few whistleblowers reported Enron's wrongdoing out of a belief in what was right and wrong. Although many Enron employees might not feel comfortable with organizational wrongdoing that they were aware of, the social norm in the firm was to not rock the boat. Essentially, whistleblowers chose to follow their internalized personal beliefs on what was right by overcoming the social norms that encouraged silence.

How do these three forms of supportive pillars *combine* to shape individual and firm behavior? Let us use two examples—one at the individual level and another at

Institutional framework
Formal and informal institutions governing individual and firm behavior.

Formal institutions
Institutions represented by laws, regulations, and rules.

Regulatory pillar
The coercive power of governments.

Normative pillar
The mechanism through which norms influence individual and firm behavior.

Cognitive pillar
The internalized (or taken-for-granted) values and beliefs that guide individual and firm behavior.

TABLE 2.1   DIMENSIONS OF INSTITUTIONS

Degree of formality	Examples	Supportive pillars
Formal institutions	• Laws • Regulations • Rules	• Regulatory (coercive)
Informal institutions	• Norms • Cultures • Ethics	• Normative • Cognitive

the firm level. First, speed limits formally define how fast drivers can go. However, many drivers adjust their speed in relation to the speed of *other* vehicles—a form of the normative pillar. When police ticket some motorists for driving at speeds above the legal limit, they protest: "We are barely keeping up with traffic!" This statement indicates that the drivers do not have a clear cognitive pillar regarding what is the right speed. Never mind the posted speed limit signs, they have followed the norm and let other drivers define what is the right speed. Second, in 2008, while Wall Street had to be bailed out by trillions of taxpayer dollars, Wall Street executives paid themselves $18 billion in bonuses. The resulting public outcry was understandable. However, by paying themselves so handsomely, these executives did not commit any crime or engage in any wrongdoing. Therefore, the regulatory pillar had little teeth. Rather, this is a case of major clashes between the normative pillar and cognitive pillar held by these executives. In the minds of these executives, supported by their own cognitive pillar, they deserved such bonuses. What they failed to read was the normative pressure coming from an angry public.

WHAT DO INSTITUTIONS DO?

Explain how institutions reduce uncertainty.

Although institutions do many things, their key role is to *reduce uncertainty*. Specifically, institutions influence the decision-making process of both individuals and firms by signaling what conduct is legitimate and acceptable and what is not. Basically, institutions constrain the range of acceptable actions. Why is it so important to reduce uncertainty? Because uncertainty can be potentially devastating.[6] Political uncertainty such as a coup may render long-range planning obsolete. Economic uncertainty such as failure to carry out transactions as spelled out in contracts may result in economic losses. An extreme case of economic uncertainty is the 2008–2009 recession, during which consumption by individuals and investment by firms around the world plummeted. Uncertain about how long the recession would last, even consumers with jobs and firms with profits felt compelled to preserve cash, collectively driving global economic growth to a new record low.

Uncertainty surrounding economic transactions can lead to **transaction costs**, which are the costs associated with economic transactions or, more broadly, the costs of doing business. A leading theorist and winner of the 2009 Nobel Prize in economics, Oliver Williamson, makes the comparison to frictions in mechanical systems: "Do the gears mesh, are the parts lubricated, is there needless slippage or other loss of energy?" He goes on to suggest that transaction costs can be viewed as "the economic counterpart of frictions: Do the parties to exchange operate harmoniously, or are there frequent misunderstandings and conflicts?"[7]

An important source of transaction costs is **opportunism**, defined as self-interest seeking with guile. Examples include misleading, cheating, and confusing other parties in transactions that will increase transaction costs. Attempting to reduce such transaction costs, institutional frameworks increase certainty by spelling out the rules of the game so that violations (such as failure to fulfill a contract) can be mitigated with relative ease (such as through formal arbitration and courts).

Without stable institutional frameworks, transaction costs may become prohibitively high, to the extent that certain transactions simply would not take place. For example, in the absence of credible institutional frameworks that protect investors, domestic investors may choose to put their money abroad. Although Africa is starving for capital, rich people in Africa put a striking 39% of their assets outside of Africa.[8] Similarly, rich Russians often prefer to purchase a soccer club in London or a seaside villa in Cyprus, rather than investing in Russia.

Transaction costs
The costs associated with economic transactions or, more broadly, the costs of doing business.

Opportunism
The act of seeking self-interest with guile.

Institutions are not static. Institutional transitions are widespread in the world (see the Opening Case). Institutional transitions in some emerging economies, particularly those moving from central planning to market competition (such as China, Poland, Russia, and Vietnam), are so pervasive that these countries are simply called "transition economies" (a *subset* of "emerging economies"). Institutional transitions in these countries as well as in India and South Africa (see the Closing Case) create both huge challenges and tremendous opportunities for domestic and international firms. For example, IKEA, a leading Swedish furniture retailer, aggressively entered Russia beginning in 2000. Over the next decade, IKEA invested $4 billion, and Russian yuppies became known as the "IKEA Generation." However, even as one of the largest foreign investors in Russia, IKEA has been frustrated by the difficulties, especially those associated with corruption at the local level. In 2009, it put on hold all new investment in Russia (see In Focus 2.1).

Having outlined the definitions of various institutions and their supportive pillars as well as the key role of institutions in uncertainty reduction, next we will introduce the first core perspective on global business: an institution-based view.

IN Focus 2.1

The Russia Puzzle

Russia is not the Soviet Union. But what is it? Since the collapse of the former Soviet Union in 1991, Russia has undergone a series of extraordinary institutional transitions. Russia changed from a communist totalitarian state into a democracy with regular elections. Its centrally planned economy was transformed into a capitalist economy of mostly private firms. Yet, Russia has remained a huge puzzle to policy makers, scholars, and business practitioners both in Russia and abroad, thus provoking a constant debate.

The debate centers on political, economic, and legal dimensions. Politically, does Russia really have a democracy? Some critics labeled Russia's democracy to be "phony." In 2004, Russia was *downgraded* from "Partly Free" to "Not Free"—on a 1 to 3 scale of "Free," "Partly Free," and "Not Free"—by Freedom House, a leading nongovernmental organization (NGO) promoting political freedom (see PengAtlas Map 1.3). This was driven by Russia's recent steady drift toward more authoritarian rule under then-president Vladmir Putin. Yet, Russia under Putin between 2000 and 2008 grew 7% annually, whereas Russia under Boris Yeltsin during the 1990s, when it was "Partly Free," experienced a catastrophic economic decline. Most Russians, who were economically better off in the 2000s, do not

seem to mind living in a "less democratic" country (relative to what Russia was in the 1990s).

Economically, just how bad was the decline? Official statistics indicated that GDP fell approximately 40% in the 1990s. One side of the debate argues that the actual decline might have been far worse. However, the other side suggests that Russia's economic performance was actually far *better*, because some decline in output, by reducing military goods and shoddy consumer products for which there was no demand, was actually good for the economy. For example, there was no reason why the former Soviet Union should produce 80% more steel than the United States. Also, the level of output at the outset of reforms was exaggerated because the central planning system rewarded managers who *overreported* their output. However, managers now *underreport* output in order to reduce their tax bill. Thus, the real decline was probably smaller than officially reported. In addition, Russia's unofficial economy blossomed since the early 1990s, significantly compensating for the decline of the official sector. Thus, Russia's decline might not have been as bad as commonly thought.

Legally, establishing the rule of law that respects private property is one of the main goals of Russia's institutional transitions. In a society where nobody

In Focus 2.1 (continued)

had any significant private property until recently, how a small number of individuals became super-rich oligarchs (tycoons) almost overnight is intriguing. By 2003, the top 10 families or groups owned 60% of Russia's total market capitalization. Should the government protect private property if it is acquired through illegitimate or "gray" means? Most oligarchs obtained their wealth during the chaotic 1990s. Once these oligarchs have acquired assets, they demand that the government respect and protect these private assets. The government thus faces a dilemma: Redistributing wealth by confiscating assets from the oligarchs creates more uncertainty, whereas respecting and protecting the property rights of the oligarchs results in more resentment among the population. Thus far, except when a few oligarchs, notably Mikhail Khodorkovsky, threatened to politically challenge the government, the Russian government sided with the oligarchs. Not surprisingly, oligarchs have emerged as a strong force in favor of property rights protection. In Russia, oligarchs run their firms more efficiently than other types of business owners (except foreign owners). Although the emergence of oligarchs no doubt has increased income inequality and caused mass resentment, on balance, oligarchs are often argued to have contributed to Russia's more recent boom.

Where exactly is Russia heading? Key to solving this puzzle is to understand Putin (who has been the prime minister since 2008) and his chosen successor, President Dmitry Medvedev. While Russia becomes economically richer and stronger (thanks to high oil prices), the government is bolder and more assertive in foreign affairs by being willing to challenge the United States and to dominate neighbors. In August 2008, Russia invaded Georgia. At home, the government is also sliding back to more authoritarian ways. But, one argument goes, if the government delivers economic growth or at least survives the recent downturn, so what?

Finally, another group of writers point out that despite its former superpower status, Russia has become a "normal," middle-income country. With GDP per capita around $8,000, Russia in 2010 is at a level similar to that of Argentina in 1991 and Mexico in 1999. Democracies in this income range are rough around the edges. They tend to have corrupt governments, high income equality, concentrated corporate ownership, and turbulent economic performance. In all these aspects, Russia may be quite "normal." However, these flaws are not necessarily incompatible with further political, economic, and legal progress down the road. For example, consumers in normal, middle-income countries naturally demand bank loans, credit cards, and mortgages, which have only appeared in Russia for the first time and created lucrative opportunities for Russian and foreign firms.

Because Russia is so large and complex, news from Russia is often simultaneously good and bad. For example, IKEA, a leading Swedish furniture retailer, aggressively entered Russia in 2000, investing $4 billion over a decade during which Russia's yuppies became known as the "IKEA Generation." However, even as one of the largest foreign investors in Russia, IKEA has been frustrated by the difficulties, especially those associated with corruption at the local level. In 2009, IKEA put on hold all new investment in Russia. At the same time, despite such bad news, big political risks overall, which might deter foreign investors, seem reasonably remote. More foreign firms are now rushing into Russia, which is the R in BRIC. Russia is simply too big and too rich to ignore. Disposable household income in Russia is one-third higher than Brazil's, four times China's, and 10 times India's. However, the Russian economy seems overly dependent on raw materials exports (such as oil and minerals). The global collapse of demand, due to reduced production, is hurting Russia. Among BRIC, Russia's economy is likely to shrink 8.5% in 2009, whereas Brazil's would shrink slightly (by 1%), and China's and India's would grow by 7% and 5%, respectively. Overall, solving the Russia puzzle has more than academic importance; it has a direct bearing on firms' assessment of the risks of operating in Russia relative to the risks of operating in other countries such as Brazil, India, and China.

Sources: Based on (1) *BusinessWeek*, 2009, IKEA in Russia: Enough is enough, July 13 & 20: 33; (2) *BusinessWeek*, 2009, The peril and promise of investing in Russia, October 5: 48–51; (3) *Economist*, 2007, Dancing with the bear, February 3: 63–64; (4) *Economist*, 2007, Russia and America, February 17: 60–61; (5) *Economist*, 2008, Enigma variations, November 29: 3–18; (6) S. Guriev & A. Rachinsky, 2005, The role of oligarchs in Russian capitalism, *Journal of Economic Perspectives*, 19: 131–150; (7) S. Puffer & D. McCarthy, 2007, Can Russia's state-managed, network capitalism be competitive? *Journal of World Business*, 42: 1–13; (8) A. Shleifer & D. Treisman, 2005, A normal country: Russia after communism, *Journal of Economic Perspectives*, 19: 151–174; (9) www.freedomhouse.org.

AN INSTITUTION-BASED VIEW OF GLOBAL BUSINESS

Identify the two core propositions underpinning an institution-based view of global business.

An institution-based view of global business, as shown in Figure 2.1, focuses on the dynamic interaction between institutions and firms and considers firm behavior as the outcome of such an interaction.[9] Specifically, firm behavior is often a reflection of the formal and informal constraints of a particular institutional framework.[10] In short, institutions matter.

How do institutions matter? The institution-based view suggests two core propositions, shown in Table 2.2. First, managers and firms *rationally* pursue their interests and make choices within institutional constraints. In Brazil, government tax revenues at all levels reach 35% of GDP, much higher than the average for emerging economies (for example, Mexico's is 18% and China's is 16%). Not surprisingly, the World Bank estimates the gray market in Brazil to be a much higher percentage of the economy than in Mexico or China.[11] Likewise, in the United States, the Obama Administration's 2009 proposal to tax the overseas earnings of US-based multinationals, which are currently exempt from US taxes, has met

FIGURE 2.1   INSTITUTIONS, FIRMS, AND FIRM BEHAVIOR

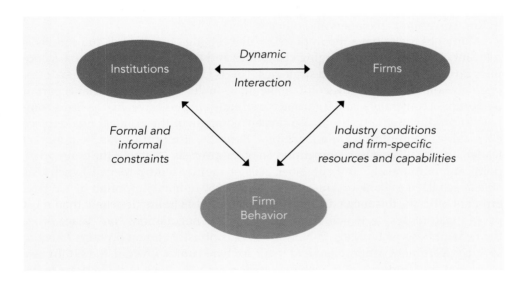

TABLE 2.2   TWO CORE PROPOSITIONS OF THE INSTITUTION-BASED VIEW

Proposition 1	Managers and firms pursue their interests and make choices *rationally* within the formal and informal constraints in a given institutional framework.
Proposition 2	Although formal and informal institutions combine to govern firm behavior, in situations where formal constraints are unclear or fail, informal constraints will play a *larger* role in reducing uncertainty and providing constancy to managers and firms.

fierce resistance from the business community. Having already paid overseas taxes, US-based multinationals naturally resent having to pay $190 billion extra in US taxes, when their global competitors pay lower taxes. "Doesn't the Obama Administration recognize that most big US companies are multinationals that happen to be headquartered in the United States?" asked Duncan Niederauer, CEO of NYSE Euronext in a *BusinessWeek* interview.[12] A case in point is Seagate Technology. Formerly based in Silicon Valley, the disk-drive maker incorporated in the Cayman Islands a few years ago.[13] One of the reasons behind Seagate's move was to avoid such a financial hit, and more US-based multinationals are likely to follow if the Obama tax proposal goes through. The upshot? Fewer good jobs in the United States because high-end executive, R&D, and finance jobs are likely to be located wherever the headquarters are.[14] Further, high-quality service providers, such as lawyers, bankers, and accountants, are likely to follow their clients. Both Brazilian firms' migration to the gray market and US firms' interest in migrating overseas are rational responses to formal institutional constraints within their respective countries.

Second, while formal and informal institutions combine to govern firm behavior, informal constraints play a *larger* role in reducing uncertainty and providing constancy for managers and firms in situations where formal constraints are unclear or fail. For example, when the former Soviet Union collapsed and with it the formal regime, the growth of many entrepreneurial firms was facilitated by informal constraints based on personal relationships and connections (called *blat* in Russian) among managers and officials.[15]

Many observers have the impression that relying on informal connections is relevant only to firms in emerging economies and that firms in developed economies pursue only market-based strategies. This is far from the truth. Even in developed economies, formal rules only make up a small (although important) part of institutional constraints, and informal constraints are pervasive. Just as firms compete in product markets, firms also fiercely compete in the political marketplace characterized by informal relationships.[16] Basically, if a firm cannot be a market leader, it may still beat the competition on other grounds—namely, the nonmarket, political environment.[17] In September 2008, a rapidly failing Merrill Lynch was able to sell itself to Bank of America for a hefty $50 billion. Supported by US government officials, this mega deal was arranged over 48 hours (less time than most people take to decide which car to buy) and the negotiations took place *inside* the Federal Reserve building in New York. In contrast, Lehman Brothers failed to secure government support and had to file for bankruptcy. Overall, the skillful use of a country's institutional frameworks to acquire advantage is at the heart of the institution-based view.

Although there are numerous formal and informal institutions, in this chapter we focus on *formal* institutions. (Informal institutions will be covered in Chapter 3.) Chief among formal institutions are political systems, legal systems, and economic systems. We will now briefly introduce each in turn.

Political system

The rules of the game on how a country is governed politically.

Understand the differences between democracy and totalitarianism.

POLITICAL SYSTEMS

A political system refers to the rules of the game on how a country is governed politically. At the broadest level, there are two primary political systems: democracy and totalitarianism. This section first outlines these two systems and then discusses their ramifications for political risk.

Democracy

Democracy is a political system in which citizens elect representatives to govern the country on their behalf. Usually the political party with the majority of votes, such as the ANC in the post-apartheid South Africa (see the Closing Case), wins and forms a government. Democracy was pioneered by Athens in ancient Greece. In today's world, Great Britain has the longest experience of running a democracy (its Parliament was founded in the 1200s), and India has the largest democracy (by population).

A fundamental aspect of democracy that is relevant to global business is an individual's right to freedom of expression and organization. For example, starting up a firm is an act of economic expression, essentially telling the rest of the world: "I want to be my own boss! And I want to make some money!" In most modern democracies, the right to organize economically has been extended not only to domestic individuals and firms, but also to *foreign* individuals and firms that come to do business. While those of us fortunate enough to have been brought up in a democracy take the right to establish a firm for granted, we should be reminded that this may not necessarily be the case under other political systems. Before the 1980s, if someone dared to formally establish a private firm in the former Soviet Union, he or she would be arrested and *shot* by the authorities.

What fundamental aspect of democracy is relevant to the conduct of global business?

Totalitarianism

On the opposite end of the political spectrum from democracy is **totalitarianism** (also known as **dictatorship**), which is defined as a political system in which one person or party exercises absolute political control over the population. There are four major types of totalitarianism:

- Communist totalitarianism centers on a communist party. This system had been embraced throughout Central and Eastern Europe and the former Soviet Union until the late 1980s. It is still practiced in China, Cuba, Laos, North Korea, and Vietnam.
- Right-wing totalitarianism is characterized by its intense hatred of communism. One party, typically backed by the military, restricts political freedom because its members believe that such freedom would lead to communism. In the decades following World War II, the Philippines, South Africa (see the Closing Case), South Korea, Taiwan, and most Latin American countries practiced right-wing totalitarianism. Most of these countries have recently become democracies.
- Theocratic totalitarianism refers to the monopolization of political power in the hands of one religious party or group. Iran and Saudi Arabia are leading examples. Another example is Afghanistan, which had been ruled by the Taliban until 2001 when US forces removed that group from formal power.
- Tribal totalitarianism refers to one tribe or ethnic group (which may or may not be the majority of the population) monopolizing political power and oppressing other tribes or ethnic groups. Rwanda's bloodbath in the 1990s was due to some of the most brutal practices of tribal totalitarianism.

Democracy

A political system in which citizens elect representatives to govern the country on their behalf.

Totalitarianism (dictatorship)

A political system in which one person or party exercises absolute political control over the population.

Political Risk

Although the degree of hostility toward business varies among different types of totalitarianism (some can be more pro-business than others), totalitarianism in general is not as good for business as democracy. Totalitarian countries often experience wars, riots, protests, chaos, and breakdowns, which result in higher **political risk**—risk associated with political changes that may negatively impact domestic and foreign firms. The most extreme political risk may lead to the nationalization (expropriation) of foreign assets.[18] This happened in many totalitarian countries from the 1950s until the 1970s. Consider the oil industry in Argentina. In 1955, the government canceled international contracts signed by a previous president, Peron, in 1952. The next president signed new contracts in 1958, which were nullified in 1963 by a different president. Foreign oil companies were invited to return in 1966, expelled in 1973, and again encouraged to enter after 1976.[19] It is hardly surprising that foreign oil companies are reluctant to repeat the cycle yet again, and would rather go to "greener pastures" elsewhere.

Firms operating in democracies also confront political risk. However, such risk is qualitatively lower than that in totalitarian states. For example, Quebec's possible independence from the rest of Canada creates some political risk. Although firms highly exposed to Quebec experience some drop in their stock price, there is no general collapse of stock price in Canada or flight of capital out of Canada.[20] Investors are confident that, should Quebec become independent, the Canadian democracy is mature enough to manage the break-up process in a relatively non-disruptive way.

No two democracies have reportedly gone to war with each other (see In Focus 2.2 for an interesting extension of this point). Obviously, when two countries are at each other's throats, we can forget about doing business between them (perhaps other than smuggling). In this regard, the recent advance of democracy and retreat of totalitarianism is highly beneficial for global business. It is not a coincidence that globalization took off in the 1990s, a period during which both communist and right-wing totalitarianism significantly lost its power and democracy expanded around the world (see Chapter 1).

List the differences among civil law, common law, and theocratic law.

Political risk

Risk associated with political changes that may negatively impact domestic and foreign firms.

Legal system

The rules of the game on how a country's laws are enacted and enforced.

Civil law

A legal tradition that uses comprehensive statutes and codes as a primary means to form legal judgments.

LEGAL SYSTEMS

A **legal system** refers to the rules of the game on how a country's laws are enacted and enforced. By specifying the do's and don'ts, a legal system reduces transaction costs by minimizing uncertainty and combating opportunism. This section first introduces three different legal traditions and then discusses crucial issues associated with property rights and intellectual property.

Civil Law, Common Law, and Theocratic Law

Laws in different countries typically are not enacted from scratch but are often transplanted—voluntarily or otherwise—from three legal traditions (or legal families): civil law, common law, and theocratic law (Table 2.3). Each is briefly introduced here.

Civil law was derived from Roman law and strengthened by Napoleon's France. It is "the oldest, the most influential, and the most widely distributed around the world."[21] It uses comprehensive statutes and codes as a primary means to form legal judgments. Over 80 countries practice civil law.

IN Focus 2.2

The McDonald's and Dell Theory of World Peace

Thomas Friedman, a *New York Times* columnist and author of the 1999 book *The Lexus and the Olive Tree*, reported that no two countries that both had McDonald's had ever fought a war against each other since they got their McDonald's. He theorized that the country does not necessarily have to operate a democracy, but if its political system can foster a middle class whose population is large enough to support a chain of McDonald's, people don't like to fight wars anymore. They prefer to wait in line for burgers. Although this "theory" was offered slightly tongue in cheek, the serious point was that as countries are woven into the fabric of global trade and rising standards of living, which are symbolized by McDonald's, the cost of war becomes too prohibitive.

More recently, in a 2005 bestseller, *The World is Flat*, Friedman upgraded his McDonald's theory and suggested a new Dell theory: No two countries that are both part of a major global supply chain, like Dell's, will ever fight a war against each other as long as they are both part of the same global supply chain. Countries involved in major global supply chains focus on just-in-time deliveries of goods and services, which raise standards of living. In the case of Dell, the following countries are involved: China, Costa Rica, Germany, Israel, Malaysia, Philippines, South Korea, Taiwan, Thailand, and the United States.

The biggest test of the Dell theory is whether China will go to war with Taiwan, which is regarded as a renegade province by Beijing. With the recent détente between China and Taiwan (including the inauguration of direct flights), the Dell theory has been supported 100% so far. However, the McDonalds' theory has been violated by Russia's invasion of Georgia in August 2008. Both countries have a chain of McDonalds' and the joke is that Russian and Georgian soldiers went to war with each other while wolfing down their Big Macs.

Sources: Based on (1) T. Friedman, 1999, *The Lexus and the Olive Tree*, New York: Farrar, Straus, and Giroux; (2) T. Friedman, 2005, *The World is Flat*, New York: Farrar, Straus, and Giroux.

TABLE 2.3   THREE LEGAL TRADITIONS[1]

Civil law countries	Common law countries	Theocratic law countries
Argentina, Austria, Belgium, Brazil, Chile, China, Egypt, France, Germany, Greece, Indonesia, Italy, Japan, Mexico, Netherlands, Russia, South Korea, Sweden, Switzerland, Taiwan	Australia, Canada, Hong Kong, India, Ireland, Israel, Kenya, Malaysia, New Zealand, Nigeria, Singapore, South Africa, Sri Lanka, United Kingdom, United States, Zimbabwe	Iran, Saudi Arabia, United Arab Emirates (UAE)[2]

[1] The countries are examples, and do not exhaustively represent all countries practicing a particular legal system.
[2] Certain parts of Dubai (an emirate within the UAE) practice common law (see In Focus 2.3).

Common law, which is English in origin, is shaped by precedents and traditions from previous judicial decisions. Common law has spread to all English-speaking countries, most of which were at one time colonies of the British empire.

Relative to civil law, common law has more flexibility because judges have to resolve specific disputes based on their *interpretation* of the law, and such

Common law

A legal tradition that is shaped by precedents and traditions from previous judicial decisions.

interpretation may give new meaning to the law, which will in turn shape future cases. Civil law has less flexibility because judges only have the power to *apply* the law. Thus, civil law is less confrontational because comprehensive statutes and codes serve to guide judges. Common law, on the other hand, is more confrontational because plaintiffs and defendants, through their lawyers, must argue and help judges to favorably interpret the law largely based on precedents. This confrontation is great material for movies. Hollywood movies such as *A Few Good Men* and *Devil's Advocate* dramatically illustrate common law in action. In contrast, movies rarely show a civil law court in action because civil law lacks the drama and its proceedings tend to be boring.[22] In addition, contracts in common law countries tend to be long and detailed to cover all possible contingencies, because common law tends to be relatively under-defined. In contrast, contracts in civil law countries are usually shorter and less specific, because many issues typically articulated in common law contracts are already covered in comprehensive civil law codes.

The third legal family is **theocratic law**, a legal system based on religious teachings. Examples include Jewish and Islamic laws. Although Jewish law is followed by some elements of the Israeli population, it is *not* formally embraced by the Israeli government. Islamic law is the only surviving example of a theocratic legal system that is formally practiced by some governments, including those in Iran and Saudi Arabia. Despite the popular characterization of Islam as anti-business, it is important to note that Mohammed was a merchant trader and the tenets of Islam are pro-business in general. The holy book of Islam, the Koran, does, however, advise against *certain* business practices. In Saudi Arabia, McDonald's operates "ladies only" restaurants in order to comply with the Koran's ban on direct, face-to-face contact between unrelated men and women (who often wear a veil) in public. Moreover, banks in Saudi Arabia have to maintain two retail branches: One for male customers staffed by men and another for female customers staffed by women. This requirement obviously increases property, overhead, and personnel costs. To reduce costs, some foreign banks such as HSBC staff their back-office operations with both male and female employees who work side by side.[23]

Overall, legal systems are a crucial component of the institutional framework because they form the first, regulatory pillar that supports institutions. They directly impose the do's and don'ts on businesses around the globe. Legal reforms (such as importing common law–based frameworks into civil law or theocratic law countries) are difficult, but not impossible. In Focus 2.3 introduces how Dubai in the United Arab Emirates (UAE), which uses theocratic law as the country's legal system, is able to create a common law oasis within Dubai. A legal system is complex, and there are numerous components under its broad umbrella. Two of these, property rights and intellectual property, are discussed next.

Theocratic law
A legal system based on religious teachings.

Property rights
The legal rights to use an economic property (resource) and to derive income and benefits from it.

Articulate the importance of property rights and intellectual property rights.

Property Rights

One fundamental economic function that a legal system serves is to protect **property rights**—the legal rights to use an economic property (resource) and to derive income and benefits from it. Examples of property include homes, offices, and factories. Intellectual property will be discussed in the next section.

What difference do property rights supported by a functioning legal system make? A lot. Why did developed economies become developed (remember, for example, the United States was a "developing" or "emerging" economy 100 years ago)?

IN Focus 2.3

Dubai International Finance Centre: A Common Law Oasis

As one of the seven emirates that consist of the United Arab Emirates (UAE), Dubai is known for its aggressive drive for modernization in the Arab world. Both UAE federal laws and Dubai laws are based on the Islamic legal framework known as *sharia*. This framework imposes a number of Islamic finance principles on the do's and don'ts of business, such as banning interest payment. Within Dubai, 15 free zones enjoy a relatively autonomous legal status with more business-friendly regulations. The most extreme example is the Dubai International Finance Centre (DIFC), a 110-acre free zone that has a most unusual legal

© Mosab Omar/Reuters/Landov

framework. In its ambitious bid to become a world-class financial center, DIFC has totally embraced *English common law* and operates an independent, common law–based, parallel legal framework, which is backed by a judicial system that is independent from UAE and Dubai laws. Since DIFC's opening in September 2004, it has attracted high-caliber financial services firms from around the globe. NASDAQ Dubai opened in DIFC in September 2005.

Sources: Based on (1) A. Carballo, 2007, The law of the Dubai International Financial Centre, *Arab Law Quarterly*, 21: 91–104; (2) Dubai International Finance Centre, 2009, www. difc.ae; (3) R. Nasra & M. T. Dacin, 2010, Institutional arrangements and international entrepreneurship, *Entrepreneurship Theory and Practice* (in press).

Although there are many answers, Hernando de Soto, a Peruvian economist, forcefully put forward an answer centered on the role played by formal institutions, in particular the protection of property rights afforded by a functioning legal system.[24] In Africa, only approximately 1% of land is formally registered.[25] In developed economies, every parcel of land, every building, and every trademark is represented in a property document that entitles the owner to derive income and benefits from it. That property document is also important when violators are prosecuted through legal means.

When a legal system is stable and predictable, tangible property also makes other, less tangible economic activities possible. For example, property can be used as collateral for credit. The single most important source of funds for new start-ups in the United States is the mortgage of entrepreneurs' houses. But this cannot be done without documented right to the property. If you live in a house but cannot produce a title document specifying that you are the legal owner of the house (which is a very common situation throughout the developing world, especially in "shanty towns"), no bank in the world will allow you to use your house as collateral for credit. To start up a new firm, you end up borrowing funds from family members, friends, and other acquaintances through *informal* means. But funds through informal means are almost certainly more limited than funds that could have been provided formally by banks. Because of such under-funding, in the aggregate, the average firm size in the developing world is smaller than that in the developed world. Insecure property rights also result in using technologies that employ little fixed capital and do not entail long-term investment (such as R&D). These characteristics of developing countries do not bode well in global competition where leading firms reap benefits from economies of scale, capital-intensive technologies, and sustained investment in R&D. What the developing world lacks and desperately needs is formal protection of property rights in order to facilitate economic growth.

Intellectual Property Rights

Although the term "property" traditionally refers to *tangible* pieces of property, such as land, **intellectual property** specifically refers to *intangible* property that is the result of intellectual activity (such as books, videos, and websites). **Intellectual property rights (IPR)** are rights associated with the ownership of intellectual property, such as patents, copyrights, and trademarks.

- **Patents** are legal rights awarded by government authorities to inventors of new products or processes. The inventors are given exclusive (monopoly) rights to derive income from such inventions through activities such as manufacturing, licensing, or selling.
- **Copyrights** are the exclusive legal rights of authors and publishers to publish and disseminate their work. This book, for example, is protected by copyright laws.
- **Trademarks** are the exclusive legal rights of firms to use specific names, brands, and designs to differentiate their products from others.

Because IPR are usually protected on a country-by-country basis, a pressing issue arises internationally: how to protect IPR, when countries have uneven levels of IPR enforcement? The Paris Convention for the Protection of Industrial Property is the "gold standard" for a higher level of IPR protection. Adopting the Paris Convention is required in order to become a signatory country to the WTO's Agreement on Trade-Related Aspects of Intellectual Property Rights (TRIPS). Given the global differences in the formal rules, much stricter IPR protection is provided by TRIPS. Once countries join TRIPS, firms are often forced to pay more attention to innovation.

IPR need to be asserted and enforced through a *formal* system, which is designed to punish violators and to provide an incentive for people and firms to innovate. However, the intangible nature of IPR makes their protection difficult.[26] Around the world, piracy—unauthorized use of IPR—is widespread, ranging from unauthorized sharing of music files to deliberate counterfeiting of branded products. Different countries have developed "distinctive competencies." For example, China is known for fake DVDs and Rolexes. Russia is emerging as a powerhouse for counterfeit software. Ukraine is famous for bootlegged optical discs. Paraguay is well known for imitation cigarettes. Italy is a leading producer of counterfeit luxury goods. Florida has developed a strong reputation for fake aircraft parts.[27]

Overall, an institution-based view suggests that the key to understanding IPR violation is realizing that IPR violators are not amoral monsters, but ordinary people and firms. Given an institutional environment of weak IPR protection, IPR violators make a rational decision by investing in skills and knowledge in this business (Proposition 1 in Table 2.2). When filling out a survey on "What is your dream career?" no high school graduate anywhere in the world will answer,

---

Intellectual property

Intangible property that is the result of intellectual activity.

Intellectual property rights (IPR)

Rights associated with the ownership of intellectual property.

Patents

Exclusive legal rights of inventors of new products or processes to derive income from such inventions.

Copyrights

Exclusive legal rights of authors and publishers to publish and disseminate their work.

Trademarks

Exclusive legal rights of firms to use specific names, brands, and designs to differentiate their products from others.

"Counterfeiting." Nevertheless, thousands of individuals and firms *voluntarily* choose to be involved in this business worldwide. Stronger IPR protection may reduce their incentive to do so. For example, counterfeiters in China will be criminally prosecuted only if their profits exceed approximately $10,000. No counterfeiters are dumb enough to keep records to show that they make that much money. If they are caught and are found to make less than $10,000, they are usually fined $1,000, which is widely regarded as a (small) cost of doing business. However, IPR reforms to criminalize *all* counterfeiting activities regardless of the amount of profits, currently being discussed in China, may significantly reduce counterfeiters' incentive.[28]

ECONOMIC SYSTEMS

An **economic system** refers to the rules of the game on how a country is governed economically. At the two ends of a spectrum, we can find a market economy and a command economy. In between, there is a mixed economy.

A pure **market economy** is characterized by the "invisible hand" of market forces first noted in 1776 by Adam Smith in *The Wealth of Nations*. The government takes a hands-off approach known as *laissez faire*. All factors of production should thus be privately owned. The government performs only those functions the private sector cannot perform, such as providing roads and defense.

A pure **command economy** is defined by a government taking, in the words of Lenin, the "commanding height" in the economy. All factors of production should be owned and controlled by the government. During the heydays of communism, the former Soviet Union and China approached such an ideal.

A **mixed economy**, by definition, has elements of both a market economy and a command economy. It boils down to the relative distribution of market forces versus command forces. In practice, no country has ever completely embraced Adam Smith's ideal *laissez faire* approach. Question: Which economy has the highest degree of economic freedom (the lowest degree of government intervention)? Hint: Given extensive government intervention since 2008, it is obviously not the United States (see the Opening Case). Answer: A series of surveys report that it is Hong Kong (the post-1997 handover to Chinese sovereignty does not make a difference).[29] The crucial point here is that there is still some noticeable government intervention in the economy, even in Hong Kong. During the aftermath of the 1997 economic crisis when the share price of all Hong Kong–listed firms took a nose dive, the Hong Kong government took a highly controversial action. It used government funds to purchase 10% of the shares of all the blue chip firms listed in the Hang Seng index. This action slowed down the sliding of share prices and stabilized the economy, but it turned all the blue chip firms into state-owned enterprises (SOEs)—at least 10% owned by the state. At present, most governments in developed economies have bailed out their banks, which have become SOEs.

Likewise, no country has ever had a complete command economy, despite the efforts of communist zealots throughout the Eastern Bloc during the Cold War. Poland never nationalized its agriculture. Hungarians were known to have second (and private!) jobs while all of them theoretically worked only for the state. Black markets hawking agricultural produce and small merchandise existed in practically all former communist countries. Although the former Soviet Union and Central and Eastern European countries have recently thrown away communism, even ongoing practitioners of communism such as China and Vietnam have

LEARNING OBJECTIVE 7

Outline the differences among market economy, command economy, and mixed economy.

Economic system
Rules of the game on how a country is governed economically.

Market economy
An economy that is characterized by the "invisible hand" of market forces.

Command economy
An economy that is characterized by government ownership and control of factors of production.

Mixed economy
An economy that has elements of both a market economy and a command economy.

embraced market reforms. Cuba has a lot of foreign-invested hotels. Even North Korea is now interested in attracting foreign investment.

Overall, the economic system of most countries is a mixed economy. In practice, when we say a country has a market economy, it is really a short-hand version for a country that organizes its economy *mostly* (but not completely) by market forces and that still has certain elements of a command economy. China, France, Russia, Sweden, and the United States all claim to have a market economy now, but the meaning is different in each country. In other words, free markets are not totally "free." It boils down to a matter of degree. The point is that we probably need to consider dropping the "F" word ("free") when discussing "free market economy."

LEARNING OBJECTIVE

8

Participate in two leading debates on politics, laws, and economics.

DEBATES AND EXTENSIONS

Formal institutions such as political, legal, and economic systems represent some of the broadest and most comprehensive forces affecting global business. They provoke some significant debates. In this section, we focus on two major debates: (1) drivers of economic development and (2) private ownership versus state ownership.

Drivers of Economic Development: Culture, Geography, or Institutions?

The differences in economic development around the globe are striking (see PengAtlas Map 3.4). Table 2.4 shows the highest and lowest per capita income countries to be Norway ($76,450) and Burundi ($110), respectively. Why are countries such as Norway so developed (rich), and countries such as Burundi so underdeveloped (poor)? More generally, what drives economic development in different countries?

Scholars and policymakers have debated this very important question since Adam Smith's time. Various debate points boil down to three explanations: culture,

TABLE 2.4   TOP TEN AND BOTTOM TEN COUNTRIES BY PER CAPITA GROSS NATIONAL INCOME (GNI)

Richest ten	US$	Poorest ten	US$
Norway	$76,450	Mozambique	$320
Switzerland	$59,880	Rwanda	$320
Denmark	$54,910	Niger	$280
Ireland	$48,140	Sierra Leone	$260
Sweden	$46,060	Malawi	$250
United States	$46,040	Eritrea	$230
Netherlands	$45,820	Ethiopia	$220
Finland	$44,400	Liberia	$150
United Kingdom	$42,740	Democratic Republic of Congo (Zaire)	$140
Austria	$42,700	Burundi	$110

Source: Adapted from The World Bank, 2009, *World Development Report 2009: Reshaping Economic Geography*, Washington: The World Bank. GNI is gross domestic product (GDP) plus net receipts of primary income (compensation of employees and property income) from nonresident sources.

geography, and institutions. The culture side argues that rich countries tend to have a smarter and harder working population driven by a stronger motivation for economic success (such as the Protestant work ethic identified by Max Weber—see Chapter 3). However, it is difficult to imagine that an average Norwegian is nearly *700 times* smarter and harder at work than an average Burundian. This line of thinking, bordering on racism, is no longer acceptable in the 21st century.

The geography school of thought in this debate suggests that rich countries (such as the United States) tend to be well endowed with natural resources. However, one can easily point out that some poor countries (such as the Democratic Republic of Congo [Zaire]) also possess rich natural resources, and that some rich countries (such as Denmark and Japan) are very poor in natural resources. In addition, some countries are believed to be cursed by their poor geographic locations, which may be land-locked (such as Malawi) and/or located near the hot equator zone infested with tropical diseases (such as Burundi). This argument is not convincing either, because some land-locked countries are phenomenally well developed (such as Switzerland) and some countries near the equator have accomplished enviable growth (such as Singapore). Geography is important, but not destiny.

Finally, institutional scholars argue that institutions are "the basic determinants of the performance of an economy."[30] Because institutions provide the incentive structure of a society, formal political, legal, and economic systems have a significant impact on economic development by affecting the incentives and the costs of doing business. In short, rich countries are rich because they have developed better market-supporting institutional frameworks. Specifically, several points can be made:

- It is economically advantageous for individuals and firms to grow and specialize in order to capture the gains from trade. This is the "division of labor" thesis first advanced by Adam Smith (see Chapter 5).
- A lack of strong, formal, market-supporting institutions forces individuals to trade on an informal basis with a small neighboring group and forces firms to remain small, thus foregoing the gains from a sharper division of labor by trading on a large scale with distant partners. For example, most of the transactions in Africa are local in nature and most firms are small. Over 40% of Africa's economy is reportedly informal, the highest proportion in the world.[31]
- Emergence of formal, market-supporting institutions encourages individuals to specialize and firms to grow in size to capture the gains from complicated long-distance trade (such as transactions with distant, foreign countries). As China's market institutions progress, many Chinese firms have grown in size.
- When formal, market-supporting institutions protect property rights, they fuel more innovation, entrepreneurship, and thus economic growth. Even though spontaneous innovation existed throughout history, why has its pace accelerated significantly since the Industrial Revolution, which started in the 1700s? In no small measure, this was because of the Statute of Monopolies enacted in Great Britain in 1624, which was the world's first patent law to formally protect the IPR of inventors and make innovation financially lucrative.[32] This law has been imitated around the world. Its impact is still felt today, as we now expect *continuous* innovation to be the norm. This would not have happened had there not been a system of IPR protection. Why do we now routinely expect IT products to double their computing power roughly every ten years? The answer is certainly not because humans (or even IT geniuses) are two times smarter every decade—the key is institutions affording better and stronger IPR protection that fuels such relentless (and effectively routine!) innovation.[33]

These arguments, of course, are the backbone of the institution-based view of global business. Championed by Douglass North, the Nobel laureate quoted earlier, this side has clearly won the debate on the drivers of economic development.[34] However, the debate does not end, because it is still unclear *exactly* what kind of political system facilitates economic development.

Is a democracy conducive for economic growth? Although champions of democracy shout "Yes," the fastest-growing major economy in the last three decades, China, remains totalitarian. The growth rate of India, the world's largest democracy, in the same period is only about half of China's. On the other hand, no one in his or her right mind can seriously argue for a case for totalitarianism in order to facilitate economic development. The few examples of "benign" totalitarian regimes that protected property rights and delivered strong growth, such as South Korea and Taiwan, have become democracies in the last two decades. Overall, there is no doubt that democracy has spread around the world (from 69 countries in the 1980s to 117 in the 2000s). However, whether democracy necessarily leads to strong economic development is still subject to debate (see In Focus 2.1 and Integrative Case 1.1).

Private Ownership versus State Ownership[35]

Private ownership is good. State ownership is bad. Although crude, these two statements fairly accurately summarize the intellectual and political reasoning behind three decades of privatization around the world since the Thatcher Revolution in Britain in the early 1980s. Table 2.5 summarizes the key differences between private ownership and state ownership. As providers of capital, private owners

TABLE 2.5   PRIVATE OWNERSHIP VERSUS STATE OWNERSHIP

	Private ownership	State ownership
Objective of the firm	Maximize profits for private owners who are capitalists (and maximize shareholder value for shareholders if the firm is publicly listed).	Optimal balance for a "fair" deal for all stakeholders. Maximizing profits is not the sole objective of the firm. Protecting jobs and minimizing social unrest are legitimate goals.
Establishment of the firm	Entry is determined by entrepreneurs, owners, and investors.	Entry is determined by government officials and bureaucrats.
Financing of the firm	Financing is from private sources (and public shareholders if the firm is publicly traded).	Financing is from state sources (such as direct subsidiaries or banks owned or controlled by governments).
Liquidation of the firm	Exit is forced by competition. A firm has to declare bankruptcy or be acquired if it becomes financially insolvent.	Exit is determined by government officials and bureaucrats. Firms deemed "too big to fail" may be supported by taxpayer dollars indefinitely.
Appointment and dismissal of management	Management appointments are made by owners and investors largely based on merit.	Management appointments are made by government officials and bureaucrats who may also use noneconomic criteria.
Compensation of management	Managers' compensation is determined by competitive market forces. Managers tend to be paid more under private ownership.	Managers' compensation is determined politically with some consideration given to a sense of fairness and legitimacy in the eyes of the public. Managers tend to be paid less under state ownership.

Source: Extracted from text in M. W. Peng, 2000, *Business Strategies in Transition Economies* (p. 19), Thousand Oaks, CA: Sage.

are known as "capitalists," and their central role in the economic system gave birth to the term "capitalism." State ownership emphasizes the social and public nature of economic ownership, and leads to the coinage of the term "socialism." Both forms of ownership have their own pros and cons. The debate is which form of ownership is better—whether the pros outweigh the cons.

The debate on private versus state ownership underpins much of the global economic evolution since the early 20th century. The Great Depression (1929–1933) was seen as a failure of capitalism, and led numerous elites in developing countries and a nontrivial number of scholars in developed economies to favor the Soviet-style socialism centered on state ownership. As a result, the postwar decades saw an increase in state ownership and a decline in private ownership. State ownership was not only extensive throughout the former Eastern Bloc (the former Soviet Union, Central and Eastern Europe, China, and Vietnam), but was also widely embraced throughout developed economies in Western Europe. By the early 1980s, close to half of the GDP in major Western European countries such as Britain, France, and Italy was contributed by SOEs.

Experience throughout the former Eastern Bloc and Western Europe indicated that SOEs typically suffer from a lack of accountability and a lack of concern for economic efficiency. SOEs were known to feature relatively equal pay between the executives and the rank and file. Since extra work did not translate into extra pay, employees had little incentive to improve the quality and efficiency of their work. Given the generally low pay and the nondemanding work environment, former Soviet SOE employees summed it up well: "They pretend to pay us, and we pretend to work."[36]

As Britain's prime minister, Margaret Thatcher privatized a majority of British SOEs in the 1980s. Very soon, SOEs throughout Central and Eastern Europe followed suit. After the former Soviet Union collapsed, the new Russian government unleashed some most aggressive privatization schemes in the 1990s. Eventually, the privatization movement became global, reaching Brazil, India, China, Vietnam, and most countries in Africa. In no small part, such a global movement was championed by the Washington Consensus, spearheaded by two Washington-based international organizations: the International Monetary Fund (IMF) and the World Bank. A core value of the Washington Consensus is the unquestioned belief in the superiority of private ownership over state ownership. The widespread privatization movement suggested that the Washington Consensus had clearly won the day—or so it seemed.

But in 2008, the pendulum suddenly swung back (see the Opening Case). During the unprecedented recession, major governments in developed economies, led by the US government, bailed out numerous failing private firms using public funds, effectively turning them into SOEs. As a result, all the arguments in favor of private ownership and "free market" capitalism collapsed. Since SOEs had such a dreadful reputation (essentially a "dirty word"), the US government has refused to acknowledge that it has SOEs. Instead, the US government refers to them as "government-sponsored enterprises" (GSEs). GSEs include the bankrupt General Motors (GM), whose equity is held by the US government (61%) and the Canadian government (8%). GM is now popularly known as Government Motors, and Citigroup, which is 30% owned by the US government, is now nicknamed Citigovernment.

Conceptually, what are the differences between SOEs and GSEs? Hardly any! The right column in Table 2.5 is based on my own research on the "classical" SOEs

Are the income and jobs of these automobile manufacturing workers in China affected by the move toward privatization in that country?

Washington Consensus
A view centered on the unquestioned belief in the superiority of private ownership over state ownership in economic policy making, which is often spearheaded by two Washington-based international organizations: the International Monetary Fund and the World Bank.

in pre-reform China and Russia published more than a decade ago. This column also accurately summarizes what is happening in developed economies featuring GSEs now. For example, protecting jobs is one of the stated goals behind bailouts. Entry and exit are determined by government officials, and some firms that have been clearly run to the ground, such as AIG and GM, are deemed "too big to fail" and are bailed out with taxpayer dollars. The US government forced the exit of GM's former chairman and CEO and is now directly involved in the appointment of executives at GM and other GSEs. Not surprisingly, the US government is now drafting rules to regulate executive compensation.

Scholars who have studied "classical" SOEs in emerging economies and gurus who are worried about the pendulum swinging toward more state ownership in developed economies agree on one thing: Despite noble goals to rescue the economy, protect jobs, and fight recession, government bailouts serve to heighten **moral hazard**—recklessness when people and organizations (including firms and governments) do not have to face the full consequences of their actions.[37] In other words, capitalism without the risk of failure becomes socialism. It is long known that executives in SOEs face a "soft budget constraint" in that they can always dip into state coffers to cover their losses.[38] When executives in private firms make risky decisions that turn sour, but their firms do not go under—thanks to generous bailouts—they are likely to embrace *more* risk in the future. In other words, bailouts foster a "heads I win, tails you lose" kind of thinking among executives regarding state coffers and taxpayer dollars. Per Proposition 1 (Table 2.2), these executives are being perfectly rational: Taking on risks, if successful, will enrich their private firms, their owners (shareholders), and themselves; if unsuccessful, Uncle Sam will come to the rescue. Having bailed out failing private firms once, governments that not long ago were the strongest champions of "free markets" now increasingly find it hard to draw the line.

Although the worst fear about the recession is now over, debate continues to rage. Although the Obama administration is clearly interested in having the government play a larger and more active role in the economy, it is also becoming a stronger and more powerful regulator as well as a shareholder and manager in banks and automobile companies. As a core institution behind the Washington Consensus, the IMF still believes that state ownership is not healthy and needs to be eventually withdrawn. But it is pragmatic enough to acknowledge the realities of bailouts and stimulus packages. In October 2009, the IMF advised great care in disengaging from state ownership. Specifically, the IMF opined in its *World Economic Outlook*:

> The key policy priorities remain to restore the health of the financial sector and to maintain supportive macroeconomic policies until the recovery is on a firm footing, even though policymakers must also begin preparing for an eventual unwinding of extraordinary levels of public intervention. . . . The challenge is to map a middle course between unwinding public interventions too early, which would jeopardize the progress made in securing financial stability and recovery, and leaving these measures in place too long, which carries the risk of distorting incentives and damaging public balance sheet.[39]

Moral hazard
Recklessness when people and organizations (including firms and governments) do not have to face the full consequences of their actions.

LEARNING OBJECTIVE

9

Draw implications for action.

MANAGEMENT SAVVY

Focusing on *formal* institutions, this chapter has sketched the contours of an institution-based view of global business, which is one of the two core perspectives we introduce throughout this book. (Chapter 3 will flesh out the institution-based view with a focus on *informal* institutions.) How does the institution-based view help us answer our fundamental question of utmost concern to managers around the globe: What determines the success and failure of firms around the globe? In a nutshell, this chapter suggests that firm performance is determined, at least in part, by the institutional frameworks governing firm behavior. It is the growth of the firm that, in the aggregate, leads to the growth of the economy. Not surprisingly, most developed economies are supported by strong, effective, and market-supporting formal institutions, and most underdeveloped economies are pulled back by weak, ineffective, and market-depressing formal institutions. In other words, when markets work smoothly in developed economies, formal market-supporting institutions are almost invisible and taken for granted. However, when markets work poorly, the absence of strong formal institutions may be conspicuous.

For managers doing business around the globe, this chapter suggests two broad implications for action, shown in Table 2.6. First, managerial choices are made rationally within the constraints of a given institutional framework. Therefore, managers aiming to enter a new country need to do their homework by having a thorough understanding of the formal institutions affecting their business. The rules for doing business in a democratic market economy are certainly different from the rules in a totalitarian command economy. In short, "when in Rome, do as the Romans do." Although this is a good start, managers also need to understand *why* "Romans" do things in a certain way by studying the formal institutions governing "Roman" behavior. Of course, merely mastering the rules of the game will not be enough. The firm will also need to develop firm-specific resources and capabilities to take advantage of the rules of the game. In the midst of a horrific recession, Merrill Lynch's skillful maneuvers to save itself and Lehman Brothers' failed attempt to garner political support serve as two contrasting cases in point.

Second, although this chapter has focused on the role of formal institutions, managers should follow the advice of the second proposition of the institution-based view: In situations where formal constraints are unclear or fail, informal constraints such as relationship norms will play a *larger* role in reducing uncertainty. If, for example, you are doing business in a country with a strong propensity for informal, relational exchanges, it may not be a good idea to insist on formalizing the contract right away. Such a plan could backfire.[40] In a country with relatively weak legal systems, personal relationship building is often used to substitute for the lack of strong legal protection.[41] Attitudes such as "business first, relationship afterwards" (have a drink *after* the negotiation) may clash with the norm that puts things the other way around (lavish entertainment first, talk about business later). We often hear that, because of their culture, the Chinese prefer to cultivate personal relationships (*guanxi*) first. This is *not* entirely true. Investing in personal relationships up front may simply be the initial cost one has to pay if interested in eventually doing business together, given the absence of a strong and credible legal and regulatory regime in China. In other words, the value on personal relationships has as much to do with the absence of institutional constraints as it does with cultural norms. In fact, personal relationships are key to business in a

TABLE 2.6   IMPLICATIONS FOR ACTION

- When entering a new country, do your homework by having a thorough understanding of the formal institutions governing firm behavior.
- When doing business in countries with a strong propensity for informal relational exchanges, insisting on formalizing the contract right away may backfire.

broad range of countries from Argentina to Zimbabwe, each with *different* cultural traditions. So the interest in cultivating what the Chinese call *guanxi*, the Russians call *blat*, or the Vietnamese call *guan he* is not likely to be driven by culture alone, but also by the fact that these countries have in common a lack of formal market-supporting institutions.

CHAPTER SUMMARY

1. Identify two types of institutions—formal and informal.
   - Institutions are commonly defined as the rules of the game.
   - Formal institutions include laws, regulations, and rules, which are underpinned by the regulatory pillar.
   - Informal institutions include norms, cultures, and ethics, which are supported by the normative and cognitive pillars.

2. Explain how institutions reduce uncertainty.
   - The key function of institutions is to reduce uncertainty, curtail transaction costs, and combat opportunism.

3. Identify the two core propositions underpinning an institution-based view of global business.
   - Proposition 1: Managers and firms *rationally* pursue their interests and make choices within formal and informal institutional constraints in a given institutional framework.
   - Proposition 2: When formal constraints are unclear or fail, informal constraints will play a *larger* role.

4. Understand the differences between democracy and totalitarianism.
   - Democracy is a political system in which citizens elect representatives to govern the country.
   - Totalitarianism is a political system in which one person or party exercises absolute political control.

5. List the differences among civil law, common law, and theocratic law.
   - Civil law uses comprehensive statutes and codes as a primary means to form legal judgments.
   - Common law is shaped by precedents and traditions from previous judicial decisions.
   - Theocratic law is a legal system based on religious teachings.

6. Articulate the importance of property rights and intellectual property rights.
   - Property rights are legal rights to use an economic resource and to derive income and benefits from it.
   - Intellectual property refers to intangible property that is the result from intellectual activity.

7. Outline the differences among market economy, command economy, and mixed economy.
   - A pure market economy is characterized by *laissez faire* and total control by market forces.

- A pure command economy is defined by government ownership and control of all means of production.
- Most countries operate mixed economies, with a different emphasis on market versus command forces.

8. Participate in two leading debates on politics, laws, and economics.
   - What drives economic development: culture, geography, or institutions?
   - Private ownership versus state ownership.

9. Draw implications for action.
   - Have a thorough understanding of the formal institutions before entering a country.
   - Insisting on formalizing the contract in initial negotiations may backfire in some countries.

KEY TERMS

Civil law 40	Institution-based view 32	Political risk 40
Cognitive pillar 33	Institutions 32	Political system 38
Command economy 45	Intellectual property 44	Property rights 42
Common law 41	Intellectual property rights	Regulatory pillar 33
Copyrights 44	(IPR) 44	Theocratic law 42
Democracy 39	Legal system 40	Totalitarianism
Economic system 45	Market economy 45	(dictatorship) 39
Formal institutions 33	Mixed economy 45	Trademarks 44
Institutional	Moral hazard 50	Transaction costs 34
framework 33	Normative pillar 33	Washington
Institutional	Opportunism 34	Consensus 49
transitions 32	Patents 44	

REVIEW QUESTIONS

1. In what ways do institutions influence individual and firm behaviors? Explain your answer.

2. Define institutional transitions and give three examples of where they can be found.

3. Explain the two core propositions behind the institution-based view of global business.

4. Which are generally more significant: formal or informal constraints? Explain your answer.

5. Suppose your firm has an opportunity to expand into a totalitarian state. What are some of the issues that you may consider (other than profitability) before taking advantage of the opportunity?

6. To what extent should your firm become involved in politics within another country?

7. Compare PengAtlas Maps 1.1 and 1.2 with PengAtlas Maps 1.3. To what extent does there appear to be a relationship between political freedom and a country's economic development and power as reflected in its G-20 status? Are there any exceptions to the rule? What is your explanation?

8. Describe the differences among the three types of legal systems.

9. Give an example of how theocratic law may affect daily business operations.

10. Describe intellectual property and explain its importance.

11. Is intellectual property easier or more difficult to protect than other types of property? Why?

12. Name and describe the three economic systems.

13. Which economic system is the most common and why?

14. Generally speaking, what is the result of strong, effective, market-supporting formal institutions?

15. Why should managers guard against a herd mentality?

16. If formal constraints are unclear or ineffective, what else can managers use to reduce uncertainty?

CRITICAL DISCUSSION QUESTIONS

1. How do you explain your country's economic success (or failure)?

2. What is your view on the debate between private ownership and state ownership?

3. *ON ETHICS:* As manager, you discover that your firm's products are counterfeited by small family firms that employ child labor in rural Bangladesh. You are aware of the corporate plan to phase out the products soon. You also realize that once you report the counterfeiting to the authorities, these firms will be shut down, employees will be out of work, and families and children will starve. How do you proceed?

4. *ON ETHICS:* Your multinational is the largest foreign investor and enjoys good profits in Sudan, where government forces are reportedly cracking down on rebels and killing civilians, and also in Vietnam, where religious leaders are reportedly being persecuted. As country manager, you understand that your firm is pressured by activists to exit these countries. The alleged government actions, which you personally find distasteful, are not directly related to your operations. How would you proceed?

GLOBAL ACTION

1. Evaluating political risk is an important element of country risk analysis. In fact, your personal interest relates to countries in the Middle East and North Africa region that have a high political risk. After searching the globalEDGE website, provide a brief overview of the region and the reasoning behind assessing these countries that have been assessed with high political risk. From this list, which country has the highest overall country risk?

2. Since you work for a diversified multinational corporation, economic risk across different sectors of the world economy is an integral part of analysis as it indicates the future business prospects for specific industries. Using the globalEDGE website, evaluate the risk assessment of three industry sectors that are available to analyze. Prepare a report and provide a recommendation concerning which industry and region would be most beneficial to your company.

VIDEO CASES

Watch "Entering the Chinese Market" by Eric Tarchoune of Dragonfly Group, Ltd.

1. In what ways did Tarchoune's knowledge of the Chinese language contribute to his success? Why was it particularly important given the areas of China he visited?

2. Western businesses depend on documents and written contracts. What challenge did Tarchoune encounter and how did he cope?

3. What did Tarchoune mean when he said that the rules were "not written on the wall"? What does that suggest when doing business in other countries and cultures?

4. In many parts of Asia, respect is gained with age but Tarchoune was quite young when he went to China. If a young foreign manager were to be sent to China, what could he or she do to improve his or her managerial effectiveness in that country?

5. Tarchoune indicated that there would be some differences in doing business in the larger modern cities of China as compared to where he went. To what extent do you think that such might be the case in other parts of the world? Do you think that Western businesspeople may have a preference for cities that may cause them to ignore opportunities in rural areas? Why?

Closing Case

Managing Risks in the New South Africa

With a population of 49 million, South Africa represents 10% of Africa's population and 45% of the continent's gross domestic product (GDP). Its GDP is almost as big as the rest of sub-Saharan Africa's 47 countries *combined*. As the engine of growth for Africa, South Africa had been growing at 5% annually until 2008. As Africa's sole member of the G-20 group, South Africa has the 20th-largest GDP in the world and is among the top ten emerging economies.

Before 1994, South Africa had been ruled by a white minority government that earned notoriety for its apartheid (racial segregation) policy. In 1994, South Africa accomplished a peaceful transition of power, with the black majority party, African National Congress (ANC), taking over power. ANC's leader, Nelson Mandela, a Nobel Peace Prize laureate, served as its first post-apartheid president. Since then, South Africa has embarked on a new journey toward political reconciliation and economic liberalization.

Yet, doing business in South Africa has always been risky. Although the risks associated with apartheid are well known, managing risks in the post-apartheid era is no less challenging. Since 1994, South Africa has introduced fundamental and comprehensive changes to its rules of the game, unleashing both uncertainties and opportunities. The democratically elected ANC government has adopted a Black Economic Empowerment (BEE) policy aiming to increase blacks' share in the economy. While the neighboring Zimbabwe has violently expropriated land from white farmers and redistributed it to blacks, the South African government is committed to protecting property rights. BEE aims to accomplish its goals through peaceful means.

In principle, few South Africans disagree with BEE. In practice, there has been much grumbling over the way BEE has been implemented. This is because BEE is clearly intrusive, setting quotas and timetables in terms of black ownership, executive position, employment, and affirmative action procurement. South African firms, which are predominantly owned and managed by whites, are compelled to sell a substantial percentage (25% to 50%) of their equity to black-owned businesses and investors often at discounted prices. A number of leading South African firms listed on the New York Stock Exchange, such as AngloGold, SAPPI, SASOL, and Telkom, have disclosed BEE as a risk to shareholders, because these firms cannot guarantee that BEE transactions would take place at fair market price. BEE also affects foreign firms. Foreign firms interested in securing government contracts in excess of $10 million are required to invest at least 30% of the sales in local black-owned firms. In the case of defense contracts, the percentage increases to 50%. Firms such as SASOL complain that in a country whose official unemployment rate is stubbornly high at 25% (which may really be as high as 40%), BEE scares away investment and deters foreign firms. Further, although BEE has rapidly created a new black business elite (who often have connections with the ANC), it has not created jobs for the millions of poor and unemployed blacks. In other words, BEE has sliced up the economic cake differently, but has done little to expand it. Then-president Thabo Mbeki labeled firms such as SASOL "bigoted," and accused them of bad-mouthing South Africa's attempt to address the legacy of racism.

© Mike Hutchings/Reuters/Landov

In addition to BEE, heavy-handed labor regulations are another area attracting business complaint. Unions are given broad power to block layoffs and limit the outsourcing of contracts, making a lot of firms reluctant to hire in the first place. The HIV/AIDS epidemic has reached epic proportions, affecting 5.5 million individuals, one-ninth of the population. Since laid-off HIV-positive employees will be on government support, the government has more incentive to make it harder to fire employees. The upshot? Skyrocketing absenteeism and heath care costs. Crime is another problem. Security expenditures and crime-related losses cost South African firms approximately 1% of sales, higher than in Russia or Brazil.

Despite the risks, many firms—both domestic and foreign—are charging ahead. For large domestic firms, noncompliance with BEE may not be an option in the long run. Thus, they adopt two strategies. The first is "fronting": relying on businesses controlled by blacks to acquire procurement contracts. Second, lobbying to renegotiate the BEE terms becomes a frequent coping strategy. The Chamber of Mines, an industry association for the important mining sector, successfully reduced the targeted ten-year equity quota for black ownership from 51% to 26%. Many foreign firms find it attractive to form joint ventures (JVs) or merge with black-owned firms. For instance, Tsavliris Salvage Group of Greece formed a JV with Cape Diving & Salvage of South Africa that has a 66% black equity stake. This JV thus is well positioned to go after government contracts in the offshore oil industry. PricewaterhouseCoopers's South African subsidiary merged with MSGM Masuku Jeena, the largest black-owned accounting firm in the country. The merger opened doors for more lucrative contracts.

In May 2009, Jacob Zuma became the third post-apartheid president of South Africa. After the heroic, aristocratic Mandela and the aloof, technocratic Mbeki, the charismatic and relaxed Zuma is a highly popular president among the public. However, his lack of formal education and his promise to trade unions have made the business community nervous. There are concerns that Zuma may reduce judicial independence, foster corruption and patronage, and undermine democracy. None of these concerns is substantiated as of this writing. In the meantime, the global crisis has hit South Africa, which is experiencing its first recession since 1994. Business confidence is at a ten-year low, and the economy is shrinking. To numerous South African businesses and foreign firms interested in the country, how to survive the economic downturn and the new presidential regime is a multimillion dollar (or rand) question.

Case Discussion Questions:

1. How do firms in South Africa play the game when the rules are uncertain?
2. There is a proposition that democracy usually goes hand in hand with a functioning market economy. Does the government's insistence on BEE, often involving nonmarket-based quotas and below-market prices for equity sales to black firms and investors, support or refute this proposition?
3. Should foreign firms be interested in entering South Africa? Why or why not?

Sources: I thank Professor Steve Burgess (University of Cape Town) for his assistance. This case is based on (1) S. Burgess, 2003, Within-country diversity: Is it key to South Africa's prosperity in a changing world? *International Journal of Advertising*, 22: 157–182; (2) *Economist*, 2006, Chasing the rainbow, April 8: 1–12; (3) *Economist*, 2006, The way to BEE, December 23: 99; (4) *Economist*, 2007, The long journey of a young democracy, March 3: 32–34; (5) *Economist*, 2009, Africa's new Big Man, April 18: 11; (6) *Economist*, 2009, Still on a roll, September 26: 60–61; (7) *Economist*, 2009, Voting for the people's man, April 18: 23–25; (8) J. van Wyk, W. Dahmer, & M. Custy, 2004, Risk management and the business environment in South Africa, *Long Range Planning*, 37: 259–276.

NOTES

[Journal acronyms] AER—*American Economic Review;* AME—*Academy of Management Executive;* AMJ—*Academy of Management Journal;* AMP—*Academy of Management Perspectives;* AMR—*Academy of Management Review;* APJM—*Asia Pacific Journal of Management;* B&P—*Business & Politics;* BW—*BusinessWeek;* CBR—*China Business Review;* HBR—*Harvard Business Review;* JEL—*Journal of Economic Literature;* JIBS—*Journal of International Business Studies;* JIM—*Journal of International Management;* JMS—*Journal of Management Studies;* JPE—*Journal of Political Economy;* JWB—*Journal of World Business;* SMJ—*Strategic Management Journal;* WSJ—*Wall Street Journal*

1 M. W. Peng, 2003, Institutional transitions and strategic choices (p. 275), *AMR*, 28: 275–296.

2 M. W. Peng, S. Sun, B. Pinkham, & H. Chen, 2009, The institution-based view as a third leg for a strategy tripod, *AMP*, 23: 63–81; M. W. Peng, D. Wang, & Y. Jiang, 2008, An institution-based view of international business strategy, *JIBS*, 39: 920–936.

3 D. North, 1990, *Institutions, Institutional Change, and Economic Performance* (p. 3), New York: Norton.

4 W. R. Scott, 1995, *Institutions and Organizations*, Thousand Oaks, CA: Sage.

5 M. Guillen, 2003, Experience, imitation, and the sequence of foreign entry, *JIBS*, 34: 185–198; J. Lu, 2002, Intra- and inter-organizational imitative behavior, *JIBS*, 33: 19–37.

6 S. Elbanna & J. Child, 2007, Influences on strategic decision making, *SMJ*, 28: 431–453; V. Hoffmann, T. Trautmann, & J. Hemprecht, 2009, Regulatory uncertainty, *JMS*, 46: 1227–1253.

7 O. Williamson, 1985, *The Economic Institutions of Capitalism* (pp. 1–2), New York: Free Press.

8 P. Collier & J. Gunning, 1999, Explaining African economic performance, *JEL*, 37: 64–111.

9 M. W. Peng, 2002, Towards an institution-based view of business strategy, *APJM*, 19: 251–267; C. Stevens & J. Cooper, 2010, A behavioral theory of governments' ability to make credible commitments to firms, *APJM* (in press).

10 N. Biggart & R. Delbridge, 2004, Systems of exchange, *AMR*, 29: 28–49; R. Greenwood & R. Suddaby, 2006, Institutional entrepreneurship in mature fields, *AMR*, 49: 27–46; R. Mudambi & C. Paul, 2003, Domestic drug prohibition as a source of foreign institutional instability, *JIM*, 9: 335–349; A. Parkhe, 2003, Institutional environments, institutional change, and international alliances, *JIM*, 9: 305–216.

11 *Economist*, 2007, Heavy going (p. 5), April 14: 5–7.

12 *BW*, 2009, NYSE chief Duncan Niederauer on Obama and business (p. 15), June 8: 15–16.

13 *BW*, 2009, The overseas tax squeeze, May 18: 18–20.

14 *BW*, 2010, Taxes: Ready to rumble, February 1: 38–41.

15 M. W. Peng, 2001, How entrepreneurs create wealth in transition economies, *AME,* 15: 95–108; S. Puffer & D. McCarthy, 2007, Can Russia's state-managed, network capitalism be competitive? *JWB*, 42: 1–13.

16 A. Hillman & W. Wan, 2005, The determinants of MNE subsidiaries' political strategies, *JIBS*, 36: 322–340; A. McWilliams, D. van Fleet, & K. Cory, 2002, Raising rivals' costs through political strategy, *JMS*, 39: 707–723; M. Ozer & S. Lee, 2009, When do firms prefer individual action to collective action in the pursuit of corporate political strategy? *B&P*, 11: 1–21; D. Schuler, K. Rehbein, & R. Cramer, 2002, Pursuing strategic advantage through political means, *AMJ*, 45: 659–672.

17 J. Bonardi, G. Holburn, & R. Bergh, 2006, Nonmarket strategy performance, *AMJ*, 49: 1209–1228.

18 R. Click, 2005, Financial and political risks in US direct foreign investment, *JIBS*, 36: 559–575.

19 M. Guillen, 2001, *The Limits of Convergence* (p. 135), Princeton, NJ: Princeton University Press.

20 M. Beaulieu, J. Cosset, & N. Essaddam, 2005, The impact of political risk on the volatility of stock returns, *JIBS*, 36: 701–718.

21 R. La Porta, F. Lopez-de-Silanes, A. Shleifer, & R. Vishny, 1998, Law and finance (p. 1118), *JPE*, 106: 1113–1155.

22 M. W. Peng & K. Meyer, 2011, *Global Business: A European View*, London: Cengage Learning (in press).

23 The author's interview, Middle East Women's Delegation visiting the University of Texas at Dallas, January 23, 2006.

24 H. de Soto, 2000, *The Mystery of Capital*, New York: Basic Books.

25 W. Easterly, 2008, Institutions: Top down or bottom up? *AER*, 98: 95–99.

26 P. Chaudhry & A. Zimmerman, 2009, *The Economics of Counterfeit Trade*, Berlin: Springer; C. Hill, 2007, Digital piracy, *APJM*, 24: 9–25.

27 M. W. Peng, 2006, Dealing with counterfeiting, in M. W. Peng, *Global Strategy* (pp. 137–138), Cincinnati: South-Western Cengage Learning.

28 J. Simone, 2006, Silk market fakes, *CBR*, January–February: 16–17.

29 Heritage Foundation, www.heritage.org.

30 D. North, 2005, *Understanding the Process of Economic Change* (p. 48), Princeton, NJ: Princeton University Press.

31 *Economist*, 2005, Doing business in Africa, July 2: 61.

32 D. North, 1981, *Structure and Change in Economic History* (p. 164), New York: Norton.

33 Y. Lu, E. Tsang, & M. W. Peng, 2008, Knowledge management and innovation in the Asia Pacific (p. 359), *APJM*, 25: 361–374.

34 D. Acemoglu, S. Johnson, & J. Robinson, 2001, The colonial origins of comparative development, *AER*, 91: 1369–1401; R. Barro & X. Sala-i-Martin, 2003, *Economic Growth*, Cambridge, MA: MIT Press; G. Roland, 2000, *Transition and Economics*, Cambridge, MA: MIT Press.

35 State ownership is also often referred to as "public ownership." However, since a lot of privately owned firms are publicly listed and traded, this can cause confusion. I have decided to use "state ownership" here to minimize confusion.

36 M. W. Peng, 2000, *Business Strategies in Transition Economies* (p. 24), Thousand Oaks, CA: Sage.

37 P. Bernstein, 2009, The moral hazard economy, *HBR*, July–August: 101–102; S. Harrington, 2009, Moral hazard and the meltdown, *WSJ*, May 23, online.wsj.com.

38 J. Kornai, 1992, *The Socialist System*, Princeton, NJ: Princeton University Press.

39 International Monetary Fund, 2009, *World Economic Outlook: Sustaining the Recovery* (p. xvi), Washington: IMF.

40 D. Malhotra, 2009, When contracts destroy trust, *HBR*, May: 25.

41 C. Su, Z. Yang, G. Zhuang, N. Zhou, & W. Dou, 2009, Interpersonal influence as an alternative channel behavior in emerging markets, *JIBS*, 40: 668–689.

Chapter
3

© AP Photo/Nasser Shiyoukhi

LEARNING OBJECTIVES

After studying this chapter,
you should be able to:

1. explain where informal
   institutions come from.

2. define culture and
   articulate its four
   main manifestations:
   language, religion,
   social structure, and
   education.

3. discuss how cultures
   systematically differ
   from each other.

4. explain why ethics
   is important and
   identify ways to combat
   corruption.

5. identify norms
   associated with
   strategic responses
   when firms deal with
   ethical challenges.

6. participate in three
   leading debates on
   cultures, ethics, and
   norms.

7. draw implications for
   action.

Emphasizing Informal Institutions: Cultures, Ethics, and Norms

ETHICAL DILEMMA

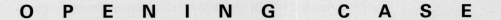

O P E N I N G   C A S E

Cartoons that Exploded

In September 2005, Danish newspaper *Jyllands-Posten* (*Jutland Post*) published a dozen cartoons of the Muslim prophet Muhammad. These cartoons not only violated the Muslim norm against picturing prophets, but also portrayed Muhammad in a highly negative, insulting light, especially those that pictured him as a terrorist. *Jyllands-Posten* knew that it was testing the limits of free speech and good taste. But it had no idea about the ferociousness of the explosion its cartoons would ignite. For Denmark itself, this incident became the biggest political crisis since the Nazi occupation during World War II. Beyond Denmark, publishers in a total of 22 countries, such as Belgium, France, Germany, the Netherlands, and Norway, reprinted these cartoons to make a point about their right to do so in the name of freedom of expression. Muslims around the world were outraged, protests were organized, Danish flags were burned, and Western embassies in Indonesia, Iran, Lebanon, and Syria were attacked. In Khartoum, Sudan, a crowd of 50,000 chanted "Strike, strike, bin Laden!" At least ten people were killed in protests against the cartoons, as police in Afghanistan shot into crowds besieging Western installations.

In addition to mob reactions in the street, Muslim governments also took action. In protest of the cartoons, Iran, Libya, Saudi Arabia, and Syria withdrew their ambassadors from Denmark. The Justice Minister of the United Arab Emirates argued: "This is cultural terrorism, not freedom of expression." However, Anders Rasmussen, the Danish Prime Minister, when meeting ambassadors from ten Muslim countries, indicated that however distasteful the cartoons were, the government could not apologize on behalf of the newspaper. This was because in principle freedom of speech was enshrined in Denmark (and the West), and in practice even if the Danish government preferred to take action against the newspaper, there were no laws empowering it to do so.

While acknowledging the importance of freedom of speech, Western governments expressed sympathy to Muslims. French President Jacques Chirac issued a plea for "respect and moderation" in exercising freedom of expression. British Foreign Minister Jack Straw called the cartoons "insensitive." US President George W. Bush called on world governments to stop the violence and be "respectful." Carsten Juste, editor of *Jyllands-Posten*, who received death threats, said that the drawings "were not in violation of Danish law but offended many Muslims, for which we would like to apologize."

Although Muslim feelings were hurt, Danish firms active in Muslim countries were devastated. Arla Foods, one of Denmark's (and Europe's) largest dairy firms, had been selling to the Middle East for 40 years, had had production in Saudi Arabia for 20 years, and normally had sold approximately $465 million a year to the region, including the best-selling butter in the Middle East. Arla's sales to the region plummeted to zero in a matter of days after the protests began. Arla lost $1.8 million every *day*, and was forced to lay off 170 employees. Other affected firms included Carlsberg (a brewer), Lego (a toy maker), and Novo Nordisk (an insulin maker). In addition, Carrefour, a French supermarket chain active in the region, voluntarily pulled Danish products from shelves in the Middle East, and boasted about it to customers.

In response, Arla took out full-page advertisements in Saudi newspapers, reprinting the news release from the Danish Embassy in Riyadh saying that Denmark respected all religions. That failed to stop the boycott. Other Danish firms kept a low profile. Some switched "Made in Denmark" labels to "Made in European Union." Others used foreign subsidiaries to camouflage their origin. Danish shipping companies, such as Maersk, took down the Danish flag when docking in ports in Muslim countries. Overall, although Muslim countries represented only approximately 3% of all Danish exports, a worst-case scenario would lead to 10,000 job losses, which would be a significant blow to a small country with a population of only 5.4 million.

Sources: Based on (1) A. Browne, 2006, Denmark faces international boycott over Muslim cartoons, *Times Online*, January 31 (www.timesonline.co.uk); (2) *Economist*, 2006, Mutual incomprehension, mutual outrage, February 11: 29–31; (3) *Economist*, 2006, When markets melted away, February 11: 56; (4) J. Lausen, 2009, *The Cartoons that Shook the World*, New Haven, CT: Yale University Press; (5) E. Pfanner, 2006, Danish companies endure snub by Muslim consumers, *New York Times*, February 27: 2; (6) P. Reynolds, 2006, A clash of rights and responsibilities, *BBC News* Website, February 6 (news.bbc.co.uk).

Although publishing the offending cartoons is legal in Denmark, is it ethical? Should the editor of *Jyllands-Posten*, the Danish prime minister, and managers at Arla have reacted differently? Why should many Danish firms, which have nothing to do with the cartoons, suffer major economic losses in Muslim countries? Why do non-Danish and non-Muslim firms such as Carrefour withdraw Danish products from their shelves in the Middle East? More fundamentally, what informal institutions govern individual and firm behavior in different countries?

This chapter continues our coverage on the institution-based view, which began with formal institutions in Chapter 2. Now we will focus on informal institutions represented by cultures, ethics, and norms. Remember that the institution-based view involves two propositions. First, managers and firms rationally pursue their interests within a given institutional framework. Second, in situations where formal institutions are unclear or fail, informal institutions play a larger role in reducing uncertainty. The first proposition deals with both formal and informal institutions. The second proposition hinges on the informal institutions we are about to discuss. As the Opening Case shows, informal institutions are about more than just basic customs such as how to present business cards correctly and how to wine and dine properly. Informal institutions can make or break firms, which is why they deserve a great deal of our attention.[1]

WHERE DO INFORMAL INSTITUTIONS COME FROM?

Explain where informal institutions come from.

Recall that any institutional framework consists of formal and informal institutions. Although formal institutions such as politics, laws, and economics (see Chapter 2) are important, they make up a small (although important) part of the rules of the game that govern individual and firm behavior. As pervasive features of every economy, informal institutions can be found almost *everywhere*.[2]

Where do informal institutions come from? They come from socially transmitted information and are a part of the heritage that we call cultures, ethics, and norms. Those within a society tend to perceive their own culture, ethics, and norms as "natural, rational, and morally right."[3] This self-centered mentality is known as **ethnocentrism**. For example, many Americans believe in "American exceptionalism," a view that holds that the United States is exceptionally well endowed to lead the world. The Chinese call China *zhong guo*, which literally means "the country in the middle" or "middle kingdom." Ancient Scandinavians called their country by a similar name (*midgaard*). Some modern Scandinavians, such as some Danes, believe in their freedom to publish whatever they please. Unfortunately, as shown in the Opening Case, those from other societies may beg to differ. In other words, common sense in one society may be uncommon elsewhere.[4]

Recall from Chapter 2 that informal institutions are underpinned by the normative and cognitive pillars, whereas formal institutions are supported by the regulatory pillar. Although the regulatory pillar clearly specifies the do's and don'ts, informal institutions, by definition, are more elusive. Yet they are no less important.[5] Thus, it is imperative that we pay attention to three different informal institutions: culture, ethics, and norms.

CULTURE

Define culture and articulate its four main manifestations: language, religion, social structure, and education.

Out of many informal institutions, culture is probably the most frequently discussed. This section first defines culture, and then highlights its four major components.

Definition of Culture

Although hundreds of definitions of culture have appeared, we will use the definition proposed by the world's foremost cross-cultural expert, Geert Hofstede, a Dutch professor. He defines **culture** as "the collective programming of the mind which distinguishes the members of one group or category of people from another."[6] Before proceeding, it is important to make two points to minimize confusion. First, although it is customary to talk about American culture or Brazilian culture, no strict one-to-one correspondence between cultures and nation-states exists. Many subnational cultures exist within multiethnic countries such as Belgium, China, India, Indonesia, Russia, South Africa, Switzerland, and the United States.[7] In Focus 3.1 shows the importance of the Hispanic culture within the United States. Second, culture has many layers, such as regional, ethnic, and religious. Even firms may have a specific organizational culture. Companies such as IKEA are well-known for their distinctive corporate cultures. Acknowledging the validity of these two points, we will, however, follow Hofstede by using the term "culture" to

Ethnocentrism

A self-centered mentality held by a group of people who perceive their own culture, ethics, and norms as natural, rational, and morally right.

Culture

The collective programming of the mind that distinguishes the members of one group or category of people from another.

discuss *national* culture unless otherwise noted. Although this is a matter of expediency, it is also a reflection of the institutional realities of the world with about 200 nation-states.

Each one of us is a walking encyclopedia of our own culture. Although culture is too complex to dissect in the space we have here, we will highlight four major components of culture that impact global business: language, religion, social structure, and education.

IN Focus 3.1

Marketing to Hispanics in the United States

According to the US Census Bureau definition, "Hispanic" refers to individuals of Latin American descent living in the United States who may be of any race or ethnic group (such as white or black). With approximately 45 million people (15% of the US population), Hispanics represent the largest minority group in the United States. To put things in perspective, the US Hispanic population is larger than the population of Australia, Denmark, Finland, Norway, and Sweden *combined*. The print media advertising revenues for the US Hispanic market, $1.5 billion, have now surpassed the advertising revenues for the total UK magazine market.

How to effectively market products and services to this sizable group of customers is a leading challenge among many marketers. Although most US Hispanics speak some English, Spanish is likely to remain their language of preference. Approximately 38% of Hispanics surveyed report English-language ads to be less effective than Spanish-language ads in terms of recall. Half of US Hispanics who watch TV during prime time watch Spanish language programming. The Spanish-language TV network, Univision, is now the fifth-largest TV network in the United States, behind ABC, CBS, Fox, and NBC.

The typical debate in *international* marketing, standardization versus localization, is relevant here in the context of adapting marketing messages and media *within* a country. Direct translation of English-language campaigns is often ineffective, because it often misses the emotional and culturally relevant elements. Savvy marketers thus call for "transcreation." For instance, Taco Bell's tagline

"Think outside the bun" evolved into a Hispanic adaptation: "*No solo de pan vive el hombre*" ("A man does not live by bread alone"). Volkswagen completely changed its "Drivers Wanted" English slogan, and marketed to US Hispanics with a new slogan, "*Agarra Calle*" ("Hit the Road"), with a specific, Spanish-language website, agarracalle. com. When marketing its minivans on TV, Chrysler showed a grandfather figure engaged in a puppet show at a child's birthday party—a traditional way for Hispanics to entertain children.

Interestingly, although about 60% of the US Hispanic population can trace their roots to Mexican heritage, direct importation of ads used in Mexico may not necessarily be successful either. The reasons are twofold. First, the US Hispanic culture, with influences from numerous other Latin American countries, is much more diverse than the Mexican culture. Second, mainstream (Anglo) media in the United States has asserted substantial influence on US Hispanics. A case in point is that 40% of Spanish-dominant Hispanics regularly watch English-language TV programming.

Overall, US Hispanics possess a distinctive cultural identity that is neither mainstream (Anglo) American nor pure Mexican. One size does not fit all. Any firm interested in marketing products and services to the "US market" needs to use both caution and creativity when marketing to Hispanics.

Sources: Based on (1) the author's interviews; (2) *Advertising and Marketing Review*, 2009, Hispanic marketing, www.admarketreview.com; (3) N. Singh & B. Bartikowski, 2009, A cross-cultural analysis of print advertising targeted to Hispanic and non-Hispanic American consumers, *Thunderbird International Business Review*, 51: 151–164; (4) US Census Bureau, 2009, Hispanics in the United States, www.census.gov.

Language

Approximately 6,000 languages are spoken in the world. In terms of the number of native speakers, Chinese is the world's largest language (20% of the world population).[8] English is a distant second, followed closely by Hindi and Spanish (Figure 3.1). Yet, the dominance of English as a global business language, or *lingua franca*, is unmistakable. This is driven by two factors. First, English-speaking countries contribute the largest share (approximately 40%) of global output (Figure 3.2). Such economic dominance not only drives trade and investment ties between English-speaking countries and the rest of the world, but also generates a constant stream of products and services marketed in English. Think about the ubiquitous Hollywood movies, *Economist* magazine, and Google's search engine.

Second, recent globalization has called for the use of one common language. Countries sharing a common official language obviously find it easier and cheaper to trade with each other. Interestingly, countries that do not share a common official language but share a common *foreign* language may still benefit from increased trade and investment. In European countries where English is not an official language, the ability to speak English fluently helps bilateral trade significantly. Hypothetically, if English proficiency in all European countries increased 10% (while keeping UK and Irish proficiency levels constant), intra-Europe trade

FIGURE 3.1   NATIVE SPEAKERS OF TOP SIX LANGUAGES AS PERCENTAGE OF WORLD POPULATION

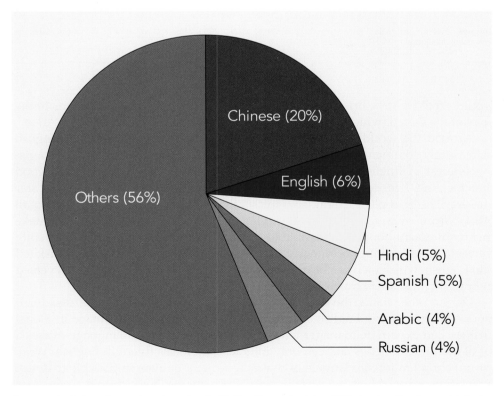

Sources: Author's estimates based on data in (1) *The Economist Atlas*, 2005, London: The Economist Books; (2) D. Graddol, 2004, The future of language, *Science*, 303: 1329–1331; (3) S. Huntington, 1996, *The Clash of Civilizations and the Remaking of World Order*, New York: Simon & Schuster. Only native speakers (people who speak a language as a *first* language/mother tongue) are included in our calculations.

Lingua franca
A global business language.

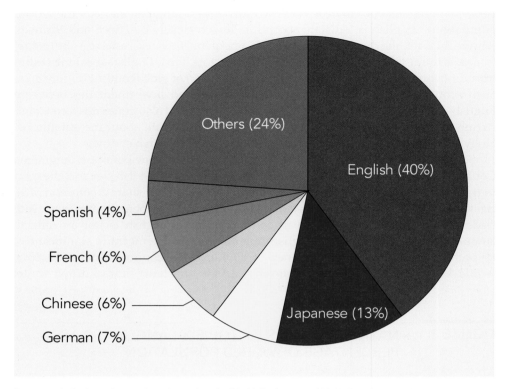

FIGURE 3.2   NATIVE SPEAKERS OF TOP SIX LANGUAGES AS PERCENTAGE OF CONTRIBUTION TO WORLD OUTPUT

Sources: Author's estimates based on data in World Bank, 2009, World Development Indicators database (www.worldbank.org).

would grow by 15%. Bringing up the English proficiency of all Europeans to the level of the Dutch (which is very high) would boost intra-Europe trade by 70%.[9]

Around the world, non-native speakers of English who can master English increasingly command a premium in jobs and compensation, and this fuels a rising interest in English. Think, for example, of the Taiwanese-born Hollywood director Ang Lee, Icelandic-born singer Björk, and Colombian-born pop star Shakira. The European Union (EU) insists that documents be translated into all other official languages. The 23 official languages for 27 member countries make this requirement almost impossible to satisfy. For example, nobody can fluently translate Estonian into Portuguese. An Estonian document needs to be translated into English, which then can be translated into Portuguese. Translators well versed in English, thus, are in much greater demand.

On the other hand, the dominance of English may also lead to a disadvantage. Although native English speakers have a great deal of advantage in global business, an expatriate manager who does not know the local language misses a lot of cultural subtleties and can only interact with locals fluent in English. Weak (or no) ability in foreign languages makes it difficult or even impossible to detect translation errors, which may result in embarrassments. For example, Coors Beer translated its slogan, "Turn it loose!" into Spanish as "Drink Coors and get diarrhea!" Ford marketed its Nova car in Latin America with disastrous results—"No va" means "no go" in Spanish.[10] To avoid such embarrassments, you will be better off if you can pick up at least one foreign language during your university studies.

Religion

Religion is another major manifestation of culture. Approximately 85% of the world's population reportedly have some religious belief (see PengAtlas Map 1.4). The four leading religions are Christianity (approximately 1.7 billion adherents), Islam (1 billion), Hinduism (750 million), and Buddhism (350 million). Of course, not everybody claiming to be an adherent actively practices a religion. For instance, some Christians may go to church only *once* every year—at Christmas.

Because religious differences have led to numerous challenges, knowledge about religions is crucial even for nonreligious managers. For example, in Christian countries, the Christmas season represents the peak in shopping and consumption. In the United States, half of toy sales for a given year occur during the month before Christmas. Since kids in America consume half of the world's toys and virtually all toys are made outside the United States (mostly in Asia), this means 25% of the world toy output is sold in one country in a month, thus creating severe production, distribution, and coordination challenges. For toy makers and stores, "missing the boat" from Asia, whose transit time is at least two weeks, can literally devastate an entire holiday season and probably the entire year. Overall, managers and firms ignorant of religious traditions and differences may end up with embarrassments and, worse, disasters. A US firm blundered in Saudi Arabia by sending a meticulously prepared proposal bound with an expensive pigskin leather cover, hoping to impress the clients. The proposal was rejected out of hand because Muslims avoid pig products. Although this is a relatively minor embarrassment, Danish insensitivity to Muslim religious traditions sparked riots, as the Opening Case illustrates. The hope is that historically and religiously sensitive managers and firms will avoid such blunders in the future.

Social Structure

Social structure refers to how a society broadly organizes its members—with rigidity or flexibility. Two terms are key to this discussion. Social stratification is the hierarchical arrangement of individuals into social categories (strata) such as classes, castes, or divisions within a society. Social mobility refers to the degree to which members from a lower social category can rise to a higher status. In general, highly stratified societies have a low degree of social mobility. For example, India is well known for its caste system: traditionally, individuals born into the lowest caste would have little chance of breaking into the social circles and jobs occupied by members of the highest caste. Britain historically had a rigid class system with low social mobility. Only in newer environments, such as Australia, Canada, and the United States, could upwardly mobile but lower-class British individuals have greater chances of advancing socially and economically. The relatively loose social structure combined with high social mobility attracted waves of British immigrants from the lower social strata to the newly founded English-speaking colonies and countries.

Social structure is the outcome of a society's formal and informal rules of the game that, in turn, give birth to its norms and values. In China, pronounced social stratification can be found along the urban-rural divide. Although urban dwellers around the world often look down on rural residents (by calling them "rednecks" or "country bumpkins"), in China such discrimination is enhanced by formal laws known as the official residence (*hukou*) system. Approximately 80% of Chinese citizens whose identification (ID) cards specify their official residence to be in rural areas have no health insurance, cannot compete for high-class urban jobs at state-owned firms, and cannot send their children to urban schools—all of which are privileges enjoyed by urban dwellers. As migrant workers, many rural residents travel

Social stratification
The hierarchical arrangement of individuals into social categories (strata) such as classes, castes, or divisions within a society.

Social mobility
The degree to which members from a lower social category can rise to a higher status.

to urban areas to find low-end jobs and live in shanty towns. Although they may be unofficially living in urban areas, they have little hope of achieving social mobility.

Multinational enterprises (MNEs) operating in highly socially stratified countries need to be sensitive to local hiring and staffing norms. The most suitable person for a job may not necessarily be the most technically qualified individual. Hiring managers from traditionally lower socioeconomic strata to supervise employees from more prestigious socioeconomic backgrounds may torpedo workplace morale and create ill feeling.

At the same time, it is important to note that all societies evolve. Even socially rigid societies such as India, Britain, and China have experienced institutional transitions that have facilitated social mobility in recent decades. For example, in India, the caste system has been legally banned (although it is still widely practiced informally). In the last two decades, Britain may be moving toward a relatively "classless" society similar to the United States.[11] Likewise, the last three decades of economic reforms in China have made a large number of entrepreneurs with rural backgrounds very affluent. Owning companies and properties and creating jobs in urban areas, they can hardly care less about their lack of urban ID cards. Although these entrepreneurs are clearly exceptions rather than the rule, they do help break down barriers for social mobility during China's institutional transitions.

Education

Education is an important component of any culture. From an early age, schools teach children the mainstream values and norms and foster a sense of cultural identity. In collectivistic societies, schools often foster collectivistic values and emphasize the "right" answers in learning. In individualistic societies, schools emphasize individual initiatives and encourage more independent thinking, emphasizing questions with "no right or wrong answers."

In socially rigid societies, education—especially access to a small number of elite schools and universities—is one of the primary means to maintain social stratification. In an effort to limit access, until recently Cambridge and Oxford Universities guaranteed a certain percentage of entry positions for graduates from prestigious private schools (such as Eton). Here is a quiz: Which is the most selective university in the world? The answer is the Indian Institute of Management (IIM). Every year, its seven campuses accept only 1,500 students out of approximately 300,000 applicants—a 0.5% acceptance ratio (!). Such limited access to higher education fosters social stratification.

On the other hand, in socially mobile societies, education is typically one of the leading forces in breaking down social barriers. In Britain, the number of universities expanded from 46 to 84 in the 1990s and then to 115 in the 2000s, resulting in significantly broader access to higher education by more members of the society. Britain is not alone in this regard. Overall, the dramatic expansion of higher education around the world in the postwar decades has increased social mobility.

© Chris Schmidt/iStockPhoto

How is education related to social stratification?

In addition to language, religion, social structure, and education, culture is manifested in numerous other ways. However, if we kept going with these differences, this chapter—in fact, this book—may never end, given the tremendous differences around the world. Students will be frustrated with a seemingly random collection of the facts and rules of the game: do this in Muslims countries, don't do that in Catholic countries, and so on. Although all these are interesting "trees," let us not forget that we are more interested in the "forest." Next, we will study the "forest" to understand how cultures are *systematically* different.

CULTURAL DIFFERENCES

This section outlines three different ways to systematically understand cultural differences: context, cluster, and dimension approaches. Then, culture is linked with different firm behavior.

Discuss how cultures systematically differ from each other.

The Context Approach

Of the three main approaches probing into cultural differences, the context approach is the most straightforward because it relies on a single dimension: context.[12] **Context** is the underlying background upon which social interaction takes place. Figure 3.3 outlines the spectrum of countries along the dimension of low-context versus high-context. In **low-context cultures** (such as North American and Western European countries), communication is usually taken at face value without much reliance on unspoken context. In other words, "no" means "no." In contrast, in **high-context cultures** (such as Arab and Asian countries), communication relies a lot on the underlying unspoken context, which is as important as the words used. In such cultures, "no" does not necessarily mean "no."

Context is important because failure to understand the differences in interaction styles may lead to misunderstanding. For example, in Japan, a high-context culture, negotiators prefer not to give a flat "no" to a request. They will say "We will study it" or "We will get back to you later." Their negotiation partners are supposed to understand from context that these responses lack enthusiasm, and so essentially mean "no" (although "no" is never mentioned). In the United States, a low-context culture, lawyers are often involved in negotiations to remove the "context"—a contract should be as straightforward as possible and parties are not supposed to "read between the lines." For the same reason, negotiators from high-context countries (such as China) often prefer *not* to involve lawyers until the very last phase of contract drafting. In high-context countries, initial rounds

Context
The underlying background upon which social interaction takes place.

Low-context culture
A culture in which communication is usually taken at face value without much reliance on unspoken context.

High-context culture
A culture in which communication relies a lot on the underlying unspoken context, which is as important as the words used.

FIGURE 3.3   HIGH-CONTEXT VERSUS LOW-CONTEXT CULTURES

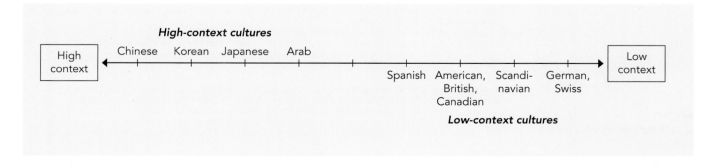

of negotiations are supposed to create the "context" for mutual trust and friendship. For individuals brought up in high-context cultures, decoding the context and acting accordingly is second nature, but the straightforward communication and confrontation typical in low-context cultures is often baffling to them.

The Cluster Approach

The cluster approach groups countries that share similar cultures together as one **cluster**. There are three influential sets of clusters (Table 3.1). The first is the Ronen and Shenkar clusters, proposed by management professors Simcha Ronen and Oded Shenkar.[13] In alphabetical order, these clusters are: (1) Anglo, (2) Arabic, (3) Far Eastern, (4) Germanic, (5) Latin American, (6) Latin European, (7) Near Eastern, and (8) Nordic.

The second set of clusters is called the GLOBE clusters, named after the Global Leadership and Organizational Behavior Effectiveness project led by management

TABLE 3.1   CULTURAL CLUSTERS[1]

Ronen and Shenkar Clusters[2]	GLOBE Clusters[3]	Huntington Civilizations
Anglo	Anglo	Western (1)[4]
Arabic	Middle East	Islamic
Far East	Confucian Asia	Confucian (Sinic)
Germanic	Germanic Europe	Western (2)
Latin America	Latin America	Latin American
Latin Europe	Latin Europe	Western (3)
Near Eastern	Southern Asia	Hindu
Nordic	Nordic Europe	Western (4)
Central and Eastern Europe	Eastern Europe	Slavic-Orthodox
Sub-Saharan Africa	Sub-Saharan Africa	African
Independents: Brazil, India, Israel, Japan		Japanese

[1] This table is the *first* time these three major systems of cultural clusters are compiled side by side. Viewing them together can allow us to see their similarities. However, there are also differences. Across the three systems (columns), even though sometimes clusters share the same labels, there are still differences. For example, Ronen and Shenkar's Latin America cluster does not include Brazil (which is regarded as an "independent"), whereas GLOBE and Huntington's Latin America includes Brazil.

[2] Ronen and Shenkar originally classified eight clusters (in alphabetical order, from Anglo to Nordic), covering 44 countries. They placed Brazil, India, Israel, and Japan as "independents." Upon consultation with Oded Shenkar, my colleagues and I more recently added Central and Eastern Europe and Sub-Saharan Africa as two new clusters—see Peng, Hill, and Wang (2000) cited as (3) below.

[3] GLOBE includes ten clusters, covering 62 countries.

[4] Huntington includes eight civilizations, in theory covering *every* country. For the Western civilization, he does not use such labels as Western 1, 2, 3, and 4 as in the table. They are added by the present author to establish some rough correspondence with the respective Ronen and Shenkar and GLOBE clusters.

Sources: Based on (1) R. House, P. Hanges, M. Javidan, P. Dorfman, & V. Gupta (eds.), 2004, *Culture, Leadership, and Organizations: The GLOBE Study of 62 Societies*, Thousand Oaks, CA: Sage; (2) S. Huntington, 1996, *The Clash of Civilizations and the Remaking of World Order*, New York: Simon & Schuster; (3) M. W. Peng, C. Hill, & D. Wang, 2000, Schumpeterian dynamics versus Williamsonian considerations, *Journal of Management Studies*, 37: 167–184; (4) S. Ronen & O. Shenkar, 1985, Clustering countries on attitudinal dimension, *Academy of Management Review*, 10: 435–454.

Cluster

Countries that share similar cultures.

professor Robert House.[14] The GLOBE project identifies ten clusters, five of which use nearly identical labels as the Ronen and Shenkar clusters: (1) Anglo, (2) Germanic Europe, (3) Latin American, (4) Latin Europe, and (5) Nordic Europe. In addition, GLOBE has (6) Confucian Asia, (7) Eastern Europe, (8) Middle East, (9) Southern Asia, and (10) Sub-Saharan Africa, which roughly (but not completely) correspond with the respective Ronen and Shenkar clusters.

The third set of clusters is the Huntington civilizations, popularized by political scientist Samuel Huntington. A civilization is "the highest cultural grouping of people and the broadest level of cultural identity people have."[15] Shown in Table 3.1, Huntington divides the world into eight civilizations: (1) African, (2) Confucian (Sinic), (3) Hindu, (4) Islamic, (5) Japanese, (6) Latin American, (7) Slavic-Orthodox, and (8) Western. Although this classification shares a number of similarities with the Ronen and Shenkar and GLOBE clusters, Huntington's Western civilization is a very broad cluster that is subdivided into Anglo, Germanic, Latin Europe, and Nordic clusters by Ronen and Shenkar and GLOBE. Although the classification scheme is not controversial, Huntington has advanced a highly controversial idea that the Western civilization will clash with the Islamic and Confucian civilizations in the years to come. Incidents such as "9/11," Iraq, and more recently the Danish cartoons (see the Opening Case) have often been cited as evidence of such clash.

For our purposes, we do not need to debate the validity of Huntington's idea of the "clash of civilizations"—we will leave that debate to your political science or international relations classes. However, we do need to appreciate the underlying idea that people and firms are more comfortable doing business with other countries within the same cluster/civilization. This is because common language, history, religion, and customs within the same cluster/civilization reduce the liability of foreignness when operating abroad (see Chapter 1). For example, Hollywood movies are more likely to succeed in English-speaking countries, and most foreign investors in China are from Hong Kong and Taiwan—in other words, they are not very "foreign."

The Dimension Approach

Although both the context and cluster approaches are interesting, the dimension approach is more influential. The reasons for such influence are probably twofold. First, insightful as the context approach is, context only represents one dimension. What about other dimensions? Second, the cluster approach has relatively little to offer regarding differences between countries *within* one cluster. For example, what are the differences between Italy and Spain, both of which belong to the same Latin Europe cluster according to Ronen and Shenkar and GLOBE? By focusing on multiple dimensions of cultural differences both within and across clusters, the dimension approach has endeavored to overcome these limitations. Although there are several competing frameworks,[16] the work of Hofstede and his colleagues is by far the most influential, and thus is our focus here.

Hofstede and his colleagues have proposed five dimensions (Table 3.2). First, power distance is the extent to which less powerful members within a country expect and accept that power is distributed unequally. For example, in high power distance Brazil, the richest 10% of the population receives approximately 50% of the national income, and everybody accepts this as "the way it is." In low power distance Sweden, the richest 10% only get 22% of the national income.[17] Major differences occur even within the same cluster. For example, in the United States, subordinates often address their bosses on a first name basis, a reflection of a relatively low power distance. Although your boss, Mary or Joe, still has the power to

Civilization

The highest cultural grouping of people and the broadest level of cultural identity people have.

Power distance

The extent to which less powerful members within a country expect and accept that power is distributed unequally.

TABLE 3.2 HOFSTEDE DIMENSIONS OF CULTURE[1]

1. Power Distance	2. Individualism	3. Masculinity	4. Uncertainty avoidance	5. Long-term orientation
Malaysia (104)[2]	USA (91)	Japan (95)	Greece (112)	China (118)
Guatemala (95)	Australia (90)	Austria (79)	Portugal (104)	Hong Kong (96)
Panama (95)	UK (89)	Venezuela (73)	Guatemala (101)	Taiwan (87)
Philippines (94)	Canada (80)	Italy (70)	Uruguay (100)	Japan (80)
Mexico (81)	Netherlands (80)	Switzerland (70)	Belgium (94)	South Korea (75)
Venezuela (81)	New Zealand (79)	Mexico (69)	El Salvador (94)	Brazil (65)
Arab countries (80)	Italy (76)	Ireland (68)	Japan (92)	India (61)
Ecuador (78)	Belgium (75)	Jamaica (68)	Yugoslavia (88)	Thailand (56)
Indonesia (78)	Denmark (74)	Germany (66)	Peru (87)	Singapore (48)
India (77)	France (71)	UK (66)	Argentina (86)	Netherlands (44)
West Africa (77)	Sweden (71)	Colombia (64)	Chile (86)	Bangladesh (40)
Yugoslavia (76)	Ireland (70)	Philippines (64)	Costa Rica (86)	Sweden (33)
Singapore (74)	Norway (69)	Ecuador (63)	France (86)	Poland (32)
Brazil (69)	Switzerland (68)	South Africa (63)	Panama (86)	Australia (31)
France (68)	Germany (67)	USA (62)	Spain (86)	Germany (31)
Hong Kong (68)	South Africa (65)	Australia (61)	South Korea (85)	New Zealand (30)
Colombia (67)	Finland (63)	New Zealand (58)	Turkey (85)	USA (29)
El Salvador (66)	Austria (55)	Greece (57)	Mexico (82)	UK (25)
Turkey (66)	Israel (54)	Hong Kong (57)	Israel (81)	Zimbabwe (25)
Belgium (65)	Spain (51)	Argentina (56)	Colombia (80)	Canada (23)
East Africa (64)	India (48)	India (56)	Brazil (76)	Philippines (19)
Peru (64)	Argentina (46)	Belgium (54)	Venezuela (76)	Nigeria (16)
Thailand (64)	Japan (46)	Arab countries (53)	Italy (75)	Pakistan (0)
Chile (63)	Iran (41)	Canada (52)	Austria (70)	
Portugal (63)	Jamaica (39)	Malaysia (50)	Pakistan (70)	
Uruguay (61)	Arab countries (38)	Pakistan (50)	Taiwan (69)	
Greece (60)	Brazil (38)	Brazil (49)	Arab countries (68)	
South Korea (60)	Turkey (37)	Singapore (48)	Ecuador (67)	
Iran (58)	Uruguay (36)	Israel (47)	Germany (65)	
Taiwan (58)	Greece (35)	Indonesia (46)	Thailand (64)	
Spain (57)	Philippines (32)	West Africa (46)	Finland (59)	
Pakistan (55)	Mexico (30)	Taiwan (45)	Iran (59)	
Japan (54)	East Africa (27)	Turkey (45)	Switzerland (58)	
Italy (50)	Puerto Rico (27)	Panama (44)	West Africa (54)	
Argentina (49)	Yugoslavia (27)	Iran (43)	Netherlands (53)	
South Africa (49)	Malaysia (26)	France (43)	East Africa (52)	
Jamaica (45)	Hong Kong (25)	Peru (42)	Australia (51)	
USA (40)	Chile (23)	Spain (42)	Norway (50)	
Canada (39)	Singapore (20)	East Africa (41)	New Zealand (49)	
Netherlands (38)	Thailand (20)	El Salvador (40)	South Africa (49)	
Australia (36)	West Africa (20)	South Korea (39)	Canada (48)	
Cost Rica (35)	El Salvador (19)	Uruguay (38)	Indonesia (48)	
Germany (35)	South Korea (18)	Guatemala (37)	USA (46)	
UK (35)	Taiwan (17)	Thailand (34)	Philippines (44)	
Switzerland (34)	Peru (16)	Portugal (31)	India (40)	
Finland (33)	Costa Rica (15)	Chile (28)	Malaysia (36)	

1. Power Distance	2. Individualism	3. Masculinity	4. Uncertainty avoidance	5. Long-term orientation
Norway (31)	Indonesia (14)	Finland (26)	Ireland (35)	
Sweden (31)	Pakistan (14)	Costa Rica (21)	UK (35)	
Ireland (28)	Colombia (13)	Yugoslavia (21)	Hong Kong (29)	
New Zealand (22)	Venezuela (12)	Denmark (16)	Sweden (29)	
Denmark (18)	Panama (11)	Netherlands (14)	Denmark (23)	
Israel (13)	Ecuador (8)	Norway (8)	Jamaica (13)	
Austria (11)	Guatemala (6)	Sweden (8)	Singapore (8)	

[1] Differences in score do not imply whether a high (or low) score is good (or bad). When scores are the same, countries are tied according to their alphabetical order. Arab, East Africa, and West Africa are clusters of multiple countries. Germany and Yugoslavia refer to the former West Germany and the former Yugoslavia, respectively.
[2] Scores reflect relative standing among countries, not absolute positions. They are measures of differences only.

Sources: Adapted from G. Hosftede, 1997, *Cultures and Organizations: Software of the Mind* (pp. 25, 26, 53, 84, 113, 166), New York: McGraw-Hill.

fire you, the distance appears to be shorter than if you had to address your boss as Mrs. Y or Dr. Z. In low power distance American universities, all faculty members, including the lowest ranked assistant professors, are commonly addressed as "Professor A." In high power distance British universities, however, only full professors are called "Professor B"; everybody else is called "Dr. C" or "Ms. D" if D does not have a PhD. German universities are perhaps most extreme: Full professors with PhDs must be addressed as "Prof. Dr. X."

Second, **individualism** refers to the idea that an individual's identity is fundamentally his or her own, whereas **collectivism** refers to the idea that an individual's identity is fundamentally tied to the identity of his or her collective group, be it a family, village, or company. In individualistic societies, led by the United States, ties between individuals are relatively loose and individual achievement and freedom are highly valued. American elementary schools disband classes at the end of every school year, and kids join new classes each fall. After several years, kids realize that the particular class that they are in is not that important. In collectivist societies, such as many countries in Africa, Asia, and Latin America, ties between individuals are relatively close and collective accomplishments are often sought after. Kids in Chinese elementary schools stay in the same class until they graduate. Collective identity associated with a particular class thus is stronger in Chinese than in American elementary schools.

Third, the **masculinity** versus **femininity** dimension refers to sex role differentiation. In every traditional society, men tend to have occupations such as politician, soldier, or executive that reward assertiveness. Women, on the other hand, usually work in caring professions such as teacher and nurse in addition to being homemakers. High masculinity societies (led by Japan) continue to maintain a sharp role differentiation along gender lines. In low masculinity societies (led by Sweden), women are increasingly likely to become politicians, scientists, and soldiers (think about the movie *GI Jane*), and men frequently assume the role of nurses, teachers, and househusbands.

Fourth, **uncertainty avoidance** refers to the extent to which members in a culture accept or avoid ambiguous situations and uncertainty. Members of high uncertainty avoidance cultures (led by Greece) place a premium on job security and retirement benefits. They also tend to resist change, which often creates uncertainty. Low uncertainty avoidance cultures (led by Singapore) are characterized by a greater willingness to take risk and less resistance to change.

Finally, **long-term orientation** emphasizes perseverance and saving for future betterment. China, which has the world's longest continuous written history

Individualism
The idea that an individual's identity is fundamentally his or her own.

Collectivism
The idea that an individual's identity is fundamentally tied to the identity of his or her collective group.

Masculinity
A relatively strong form of societal-level sex role differentiation whereby men tend to have occupations that reward assertiveness and women tend to work in caring professions.

Femininity
A relatively weak form of societal-level sex role differentiation whereby more women occupy positions that reward assertiveness and more men work in caring professions.

Uncertainty avoidance
The extent to which members in a culture accept or avoid ambiguous situations and uncertainty.

Long-term orientation
Dimension of how much emphasis is placed on perseverance and savings for future betterment.

of approximately 4,000 years and the highest contemporary savings rate, leads the pack. On the other hand, members of short-term orientation societies (led by Pakistan) prefer quick results and instant gratification.

Overall, Hofstede's dimensions are interesting and informative. They are also largely supported by subsequent work. It is important to note that Hofstede's dimensions are not perfect and have attracted some criticisms (see In Focus 3.2). However, it is fair to suggest that these dimensions represent a *starting point* for us to figure out the role of culture in global business.

IN Focus 3.2

Criticizing Hofstede's Framework

Despite the influence of Hofstede's framework, it has attracted a number of criticisms.

- Cultural boundaries are not the same as national boundaries.
- Although Hofstede was careful to remove some of his own cultural biases, "the Dutch software" of his mind, as he acknowledged, "will remain evident to the careful reader." Being more familiar with Western cultures, Hofstede might inevitably be more familiar with dimensions relevant to Westerners. Thus, crucial dimensions relevant to Easterners (Asians) could be missed.
- Hofstede's research was based on surveys of more than 116,000 IBM employees working at 72 national subsidiaries during 1967–1973. This had both pros and cons. On the positive side, it not only took place in the same industry, but also in the same company. Otherwise, it would have been difficult to attribute whether findings were due to differences in national cultures or industry/organizational cultures. However, because of such a single firm/single industry design, it was possible that Hofstede's findings captured what was unique to that industry or to IBM. Given anti-American sentiments in some countries, some individuals might refuse to work for an American employer. Thus, it was difficult to ascertain whether employees working for IBM were true representatives of their respective national cultures.
- Because the original data are now 40 years old, critics contend that Hofstede's framework would simply fail to capture aspects of recent cultural change.

Hofstede responded to all four criticisms. First, he acknowledged that his focus on national culture was a matter of expediency with all its trappings. Second, since the 1980s, Hofstede and colleagues relied on a questionnaire derived from cultural dimensions most relevant to the Chinese, and then translated it from Chinese to multiple languages. That was how he uncovered the fifth dimension, long-term orientation (originally labeled "Confucian dynamism"). In response to the third and fourth criticisms, Hofstede pointed out a large number of more recent studies conducted by other scholars, using a variety of countries, industries, and firms. Most results were supportive of his original findings. Overall, although Hofstede's work is not perfect, on balance, its values seem to outweigh its drawbacks.

Sources: I thank Professor **Geert Hosftede** for working with me on an article for the *Asia Pacific Journal of Management* where I served as Editor-in-Chief—see (5) cited below—and Professor **Tony Fang** (Stockholm University) for their assistance. Based on (1) T. Fang, 2010, Asian management research needs more self-confidence: Reflection on Hofstede (2007) and beyond, *Asia Pacific Journal of Management*, 27: 155–170; (2) S. Gould & A. Grein, 2005, Think glocally, act glocally, *Journal of International Business Studies*, 40: 237–254; (3) G. Hofstede, 1997, *Cultures and Organizations*, New York: McGraw-Hill; (4) G. Hosftede, 2006, What did GLOBE really measure? *Journal of International Business Studies*, 37: 882–896; (5) G. Hosftede, 2007, Asian management in the 21st century, *Asia Pacific Journal of Management*, 24: 411–420; (6) M. Javidan, R. House, P. Dorfman, P. Hanges, & M. Luque, 2006, Conceptualizing and measuring cultures and their consequences, *Journal of International Business Studies*, 37: 897–914; (7) B. Kirkman, K. Lowe, & C. Gibson, 2006, A quarter century of *Culture's Consequences*, *Journal of International Business Studies*, 37: 285–320; (8) K. Leung, R. Bhagat, N. Buchan, M. Erez, & C. Gibson, 2005, Culture and international business, *Journal of International Business Studies*, 36: 357–378; (9) R. Maseland & A. van Hoorn, 2009, Explaining the negative correlation between values and practices: A note on the Hofstede–GLOBE debate, *Journal of International Business Studies*, 40: 527–532; (10) B. McSweeney, 2002, Hofstede's model of national cultural differences and their consequences, *Human Relations*, 55: 89–118; (11) P. Smith, 2006, When elephants fight, the grass gets trampled, *Journal of International Business Studies*, 37: 915–921; (12) L. Tang & P. Keveos, 2008, A framework to update Hofstede's cultural value indices, *Journal of International Business Studies*, 39: 1045–1063.

Culture and Global Business

A great deal of global business activity is consistent with the context, cluster, and dimension approaches to cultural differences.[18] For instance, the average length of contracts is longer in low-context countries such as Germany than in high-context countries such as Vietnam where a lot of agreements are unspoken and not necessarily put in a legal contract.

Also, as pointed out by the cluster approach, firms are a lot more serious in preparation when doing business with countries in other clusters compared to how they deal with fellow countries within the same cluster. Countless new books have recently been published on how to do business in China. Two decades ago, gurus wrote about how to do business in Japan. Evidently, there is a huge demand for English-speaking business people to read such books before heading to China and Japan. But has anyone ever seen a book in English on how to do business in Canada?

Hofstede's dimension approach can be illustrated by numerous examples. For instance, managers in high power distance countries such as France and Italy have a greater penchant for centralized authority. Although widely practiced in low power distance Western countries, asking for feedback and participation from subordinates—known as empowerment—is often regarded as a sign of weak leadership and low integrity in high power distance countries such as Egypt, Russia, and Turkey.[19]

Individualism and collectivism also affect business activities. Individualist US firms may often try to differentiate themselves, whereas collectivist Japanese firms tend to follow each other. Because entrepreneurs stick their necks out by founding new firms, individualistic societies tend to foster a relatively higher level of entrepreneurship.

Likewise, masculinity and femininity affect managerial behavior. The stereotypical manager in high masculinity societies is "assertive, decisive, and 'aggressive,'" and the word "aggressive" carries positive connotations. In contrast, high femininity societies generally consider "aggressive" a negative term, and managers are "less visible, intuitive rather than decisive, and accustomed to seeking consensus."[20]

Managers in low uncertainty avoidance countries such as Britain rely more on experience and training, whereas managers in high uncertainty avoidance countries such as China rely more on rules. In addition, cultures with a long-term orientation are likely to nurture firms with long horizons. For example, Japan's Matsushita has a 250-year plan, which was put together in the 1930s.[21] Although this is certainly an extreme case, Japanese and Korean firms tend to focus more on the long term. In comparison, Western firms often focus on relatively short-term profits (often on a *quarterly* basis).

Overall, there is strong evidence pointing out the importance of culture.[22] Sensitivity to cultural differences does not guarantee success but can at least help to avoid blunders. For instance, if one Chinese manufacturer had had more cultural sensitivity, it would not have exported to the West a premium brand of battery under the brand name White Elephant given the meaning of this phrase in Western culture. In another example, when a French manager was transferred to a US subsidiary and met his American secretary (a woman) the first time, he greeted her with an effusive cheek-to-cheek kiss, a harmless "Hello" in France. However, the secretary later filed a complaint for sexual harassment. More seriously, Mitsubishi Motors encountered major problems when operating in the United States. Although Japan leads the world in masculinity, the company's US facilities had more female participation in the labor force, as would be expected in a country with a relatively higher level of femininity. Yet, its North American division reportedly tolerated sexual discrimination and sexual harassment behaviors. In 1998, Mitsubishi paid $34 million to settle these charges in the United States.

Explain why ethics is important and identify ways to combat corruption.

ETHICS

Cross-cultural differences can be interesting. But they can also be unethical, all depending on the institutional frameworks in which firms are embedded. This is dealt with next.

Definition and Impact of Ethics

Ethics refers to the principles, standards, and norms of conduct that govern individual and firm behavior.[23] Ethics is not only an important part of informal institutions, but is also deeply reflected in formal laws and regulations. To the extent that laws reflect a society's minimum standards of conduct, there is a substantial overlap between what is ethical and legal as well as between what is unethical and illegal. However, in some cases, there is a gray area because what is legal may be unethical (see the Opening Case).

Recent scandals (such as those at Siemens discussed in the Closing Case) have pushed ethics to the forefront of global business discussions. Numerous firms have introduced a code of conduct—a set of guidelines for making ethical decisions—but firms' ethical motivations are still subject to debate.[24] Three views have emerged:

Ethics
The principles, standards, and norms of conduct that govern individual and firm behavior.

Code of conduct
A set of guidelines for making ethical decisions.

Ethical relativism
A perspective that suggests that all ethical standards are relative.

- A *negative view* suggests that firms may simply jump onto the ethics bandwagon under social pressure to *appear* more legitimate without necessarily becoming better.
- A *positive view* maintains that some (although not all) firms may be self-motivated to do things right regardless of social pressure.
- An *instrumental view* believes that good ethics may simply be a useful instrument to help make money.[25]

Perhaps the best way to appreciate the value of ethics is to examine what happens after some crisis. As a reservoir of goodwill, the value of an ethical reputation is *magnified* during a time of crisis. One study found that any US firm engulfed in crisis (such as the *Exxon Valdez* oil spill) takes an average hit of 8% of their stock market value in the first week. After ten weeks, however, firms with positive ethical reputations actually saw their stock value *rise* 5%, whereas those without such reputations dropped 15%.[26] Ironically, catastrophes may allow more ethical firms to shine. The upshot seems to be that ethics pays.[27]

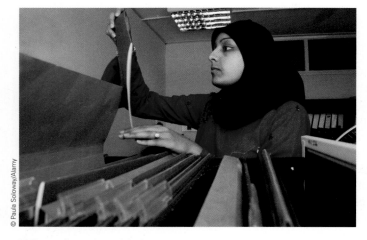

What do you think a company's code of conduct should say about respect for people's religious beliefs and practices?

Managing Ethics Overseas

Managing ethics overseas is challenging because what is ethical in one country may be unethical elsewhere.[28] There are two schools of thought.[29] First, **ethical relativism** follows the cliché, "When in Rome, do as the Romans do." For example,

TABLE 3.3 MANAGING ETHICS OVERSEAS: THREE "MIDDLE-OF-THE-ROAD" APPROACHES

- Respect for human dignity and basic rights
- Respect for local traditions
- Respect for institutional context

Sources: Based on text in (1) T. Donaldson, 1996, Values in tension: Ethics away from home, *Harvard Business Review*, September–October: 4–11; (2) J. Weiss, 2006, *Business Ethics*, 4th ed., Cincinnati: South-Western Cengage Learning.

if Muslim countries di _____ ? Likewise, if industry rivals in China fix pri _____ mans" do in "Rome"? Second, **ethical imperi** _____ t "There is only one set of Ethics (with a capit _____ e especially renowned for believing that thei _____ universally.[30] For example, since sexual discr _____ g in the United States, they must be wrong e _____ ther of these schools of thought is realistic. A _____ uld have to accept any local practice, where _____ sentiment and backlash among locals.

Three middle-of-t _____ n proposed by Thomas Donaldson, a busine _____ le 3.3. First, respect for human dignity and b _____ lth, safety, and the need for young children to _____ uld determine the absolute, minimal ethical _____ the world.

Second, firms sho _____ bans giving gifts, it can forget about doing b _____ gift giving is part of the business norm. Whi _____ relatives instead of more qualified applicants _____ equal opportunity laws, it is routine practice _____ d to strengthen employee loyalty. What should _____ es in India do? Donaldson advises that such ne _____ ast not in India.

Finally, respect _____ careful understanding of local institutions. C _____ re not very useful unless accompanied by g _____ appropriate gift giving/receiving. Citigrou _____ ash gifts whose nominal value is less than $ _____ ists to accept any gift that can be consumed i _____ eptable, but a case of wine is not.[31] Overall, th _____ n perfect, can help managers make decisions _____ y comfortable.

Ethics and _____

Ethics helps to co _____ e abuse of public power for private benefits u _____ h or in kind.[32] Competition should be based o _____ on distorts that basis, causing misallocation _____ velopment.[33] Transparency International, hea _____ obably the most influential anti-corruption n _____ . It reports a strong correlation between a high level of corruption and a low level of economic development

Ethical imperialism
A perspective that suggests that "there is one set of Ethics (with a capital E) and we have it."

Corruption
The abuse of public power for private benefits, usually in the form of bribery.

(Table 3.4). In other words, corruption and poverty go together. Some evidence indicates that corruption discourages foreign direct investment (FDI).[34] If the level of corruption in Singapore, which is very low, were to increase to the mid-range level in Mexico, it reportedly would have the same negative effect on FDI inflows as raising the tax rate by 50%.[35]

However, there are exceptions. Russia, whose corruption level ranks 147th out of a total of 180 countries (tied with Bangladesh, Kenya, and Syria), is an obvious case. Some high-profile foreign firms in Russia, such as IKEA, have scaled back FDI citing the level of corruption (see In Focus 2.1). Although better than Russia, China (ranked 72nd), Brazil (80th), and India (85th) also have corruption problems. So why are these countries popular FDI destinations? This is likely due to the vast potential of these economies, which may outweigh the drawbacks of corruption.

Given the widespread corruption and the frequent use of bribes by competitors such as Siemens around the world (see the Closing Case), many US firms complain that they are unfairly restricted by the **Foreign Corrupt Practices Act (FCPA)**, a law enacted in 1977 that bans bribery of foreign officials. Even with the FCPA, however, there is no evidence that US firms are inherently more ethical than others. The FCPA itself was triggered in the 1970s by investigations of many corrupt US firms. Even the FCPA makes exceptions for small grease payments to get through customs abroad. Most alarmingly, the World Bank reported that despite over two decades of FCPA enforcement, US firms "exhibit systematically *higher* levels of corruption" than other firms in the Organization for Economic Co-operation and Development (OECD).[36]

Foreign Corrupt Practices Act (FCPA)

A US law enacted in 1977 that bans bribery of foreign officials.

TABLE 3.4   TOP 20 LEAST CORRUPT AND BOTTOM 20 MOST CORRUPT COUNTRIES

Rank	Top 20 least corrupt countries out of 180	Index: 10 (highly clean) – 0 (highly corrupt)	Rank	Bottom 20 most corrupt countries out of 180	Index: 10 (highly clean) – 0 (highly corrupt)
1	Denmark	9.3	158	Angola	1.9
	New Zealand	9.3		Azerbaijan	1.9
	Sweden	9.3		Burundi	1.9
4	Singapore	9.2		Sierra Leone	1.9
5	Finland	9.0		Venezuela	1.9
	Switzerland	9.0	166	Cambodia	1.8
7	Iceland	8.9		Kyrgyzstan	1.8
	Netherlands	8.9		Turkmenistan	1.8
9	Australia	8.7		Uzbekistan	1.8
	Canada	8.7		Zimbabwe	1.8
11	Luxembourg	8.3	171	Democratic Republic of Congo	1.7
12	Austria	8.1		Equatorial Guinea	1.7
	Hong Kong	8.1	173	Chad	1.6
14	Germany	7.9		Guinea	1.6
	Norway	7.9		Sudan	1.6
16	Ireland	7.7	176	Afghanistan	1.5
	United Kingdom	7.7	177	Haiti	1.4
18	Belgium	7.3	178	Iraq	1.3
	Japan	7.3		Myanmar	1.3
	United States	7.3	180	Somalia	1.0

Source: Adapted from Transparency International, 2009, *Global Corruption Report 2009* (pp. 397–402), Berlin: Transparency International (www.transparency.org).

Overall, the FCPA can be regarded as an institutional weapon in the global fight against corruption. Despite the FCPA's formal *regulatory* teeth, for a long time, it had neither a *normative* pillar nor a *cognitive* pillar. Until recently, the norm among other OECD firms was to pay bribes first and get tax deductions later, a clear sign of ethical relativism (see the Closing Case). Only in 1997 did the OECD Convention on Combating Bribery of Foreign Public Officials commit all 30 member countries (essentially all developed economies) to criminalize bribery. The regulation went into force in 1999. A more ambitious campaign is the UN Convention against Corruption, signed by 106 countries in 2003 and activated in 2005. If every country criminalizes bribery and every firm resists corruption, their combined power will eradicate it.[37] But this will not happen unless FCPA-type legislation is institutionalized and *enforced* in every country.

NORMS AND ETHICAL CHALLENGES

As an important informal institution, norms are the prevailing practices of relevant players—the proverbial "everybody else"—that affect the focal individuals and firms. How firms strategically respond to ethical challenges is often driven, at least in part, by norms. Four broad strategic responses are (1) reactive, (2) defensive, (3) accommodative, and (4) proactive strategies. These are illustrated in Table 3.5.

Identify norms associated with strategic responses when firms deal with ethical challenges.

A reactive strategy is passive. Firms do not feel compelled to act when problems arise, and denial is usually the first line of defense. In the absence of formal regulation, the need to take action is neither internalized through cognitive beliefs nor embodied in any norm in practice. For example, in the early 1970s, Ford marketed the Pinto car even though the company knew the gas tank had a fatal design flaw that made the car susceptible to exploding in rear-end collisions. Citing high costs, Ford decided against adding an $11-per-car improvement. Sure enough, accidents happened and people were burned and killed in Pintos. Ford refused to recall the Pinto until 1978. Then, under intense formal pressures from the government and informal pressures from the media and consumer groups, Ford belatedly recalled all 1.5 million Pintos.[38]

A defensive strategy focuses on regulatory compliance. In the absence of regulatory pressures, firms often fight informal pressures coming from the media and activists. In the early 1990s, media and activist groups charged Nike with running sweatshops. Nike's initial response was "We don't make shoes" because Nike did not directly own and manage the factories. Its contractors in Indonesia and Vietnam were in charge. This response, however, failed to convey any ethical responsibility. Only when several senators began to suggest legislative solutions did Nike become more serious.

TABLE 3.5   STRATEGIC RESPONSES TO ETHICAL CHALLENGES

Strategic responses	Strategic behaviors	Examples in the text
Reactive	Deny responsibility; do less than required.	*Ford Pinto fire (the 1970s)*
Defensive	Admit responsibility but fight it; do the least that is required.	*Nike (the early 1990s)*
Accommodative	Accept responsibility; do all that is required.	*Ford Explorer rollovers (the 2000s)*
Proactive	Anticipate responsibility; do more than is required.	*BMW (the 1990s)*

In an accommodative strategy, accepting responsibility becomes an organizational norm, and cognitive beliefs and values are increasingly internalized. These normative and cognitive values may be shared by a number of firms, leading to new industry norms. In other words, higher levels of ethical and moral responsibility, beyond simply the minimum of what is legally required, are accepted standards. In this fashion, Nike and the entire sportswear industry became more accommodative about the issue of sweatshops in the late 1990s.

Companies can change their strategic response. Ford evidently learned the painful lesson from its Pinto fire fiasco in the 1970s. When Ford Explorer vehicles equipped with Firestone tires had a large number of fatal rollover accidents in 2000, Ford aggressively initiated a speedy recall, launched a media campaign featuring its CEO, and discontinued the 100-year-old relationship with Firestone. Although critics argue that Ford's accommodative strategy was to place the blame squarely on Firestone, the institution-based view (especially Proposition 1 in Chapter 2) suggests that such highly rational actions are to be expected. Even if Ford's public relations campaign was only window dressing designed to make the company look good to the public, it publicized a set of ethical criteria against which the company can be judged and opened doors for more scrutiny by concerned stakeholders. It is probably fair to say that Ford was a better corporate citizen in 2000 than it was in 1975.

Finally, firms that take a proactive strategy anticipate institutional changes and do more than is required. In 1990, the German government proposed a "take-back" policy, requiring automakers to design cars whose components can be taken back by the same manufacturers for recycling. With this policy in mind, BMW anticipated its emerging responsibility. It not only designed easier-to-disassemble cars, but also enlisted the few high-quality dismantler firms as part of an exclusive recycling infrastructure. Further, BMW actively participated in public discussions and succeeded in establishing its approach as the German national standard for automobile disassembly. Other automakers were thus required to follow BMW's lead. However, other automakers had to fight over smaller, lower-quality dismantlers or develop in-house dismantling infrastructures from scratch.[39] Through such a proactive strategy, BMW set a new industry standard for environmentally friendly norms in both car design and recycling.

Overall, although there is probably a certain element of window dressing in proactive strategies, the fact that proactive firms go beyond the current regulatory requirements is indicative of the normative and cognitive beliefs held by many managers at these firms on the importance of doing the right thing.[40]

LEARNING OBJECTIVE 6

Participate in three leading debates on cultures, ethics, and norms.

DEBATES AND EXTENSIONS

Informal institutions such as cultures, ethics, and norms provoke a series of significant debates. In this section, we focus on three of them: (1) Western values versus Eastern values, (2) cultural convergence versus divergence, and (3) opportunism versus individualism/collectivism.

Economic Development: Western Values versus Eastern Values

This is another component of the debate on the drivers of economic development first discussed in Chapter 2. Here our focus is on the role of informal cultural values. About 100 years ago, at the apex of Western power (which ruled most of Africa and Asia as colonies), German sociologist Max Weber argued that it was the Protestant work ethic that led to the "spirit of capitalism" and strong economic development. As a branch of Christianity (the other two branches are Roman Catholic and Orthodox), Protestantism is widely practiced in English-speaking countries, Germany, the Netherlands, and Scandinavia. This is where the Industrial Revolution (and modern capitalism) took off. Weber suggested that the Protestant emphasis on hard work and frugality is necessary for capital accumulation—hence the term "capitalism." Adherents of other religious beliefs are believed to lack such traits. At that time, Weber's view was widely accepted.

Such belief in the superiority of Western values has recently been challenged by two sets of Eastern values: (1) Islam and (2) Asian (Confucian). The first is the challenge from Islamic fundamentalism, which, rightly or wrongly, argues that it is Western dominance that *causes* the lackluster economic performance of Muslim countries. Aggressive marketing of Western products in these countries is seen as a cultural invasion. Islamic fundamentalists prefer to go "back to the roots," by moving away from Western influence. Although the majority of Islamic fundamentalists are peaceful, a small number of radical fundamentalists have become terrorists (such as those involved in "9/11").

A second challenge comes from East Asia, whose values center on Confucianism, based on the teachings of Confucius, an ancient Chinese scholar who lived more than 2,000 years ago. Confucianism is not a religion, but a set of moral codes guiding interpersonal relationships that emphasize respect, loyalty, and reciprocity. A hundred years ago, Confucianism was criticized by Weber as a leading cause of Asian backwardness. However, times change. In the postwar decades, although Western economic growth has been stagnant, it is Confucian Asia—first led by Japan in the 1960s, then the four Tigers in the 1970s, and China since the 1980s—that generated the fastest economic growth in the world and for the longest time. Interestingly, the same Confucianism, trashed by Weber, has been widely viewed as the engine behind such an "Asian economic miracle." Not only do Asians proudly proclaim the validity of such "Asian values," but Western scholars also increasingly endorse such a view.[41] For example, Hofstede's fifth dimension, long-term orientation, was originally labeled simply as "Confucian dynamism."[42]

Although Islamic fundamentalists prefer to drop out of the game of economic development, Asian value proponents claim to have beaten the West in its own game. However, any declaration of winning the game needs to be viewed with caution. By 1997, much of Asia was suddenly engulfed in a financial crisis. Then—guess what?—Confucianism was blamed, by both Asians and non-Asians, for having *caused* such hardship (!). Respect, loyalty, and reciprocity become inertia, nepotism, and cronyism. Fast forward to 2010: Asia has not only recovered from the 1997 crisis, but also quickly rebounded from the 2008–2009 recession.[43] With the emergence of both China and India (although India has very little Confucian influence) as global economic powerhouses, the Asian value gurus again are practicing their craft—although with a lower voice this time.

As we can see from this wide-ranging debate, our understanding of the connection between cultural values and economic development is very superficial. To advocate certain cultural values as key to economic development may not be justified. A new generation of students and managers needs to be more sophisticated and guard against such ethnocentric thinking. One speculation is that if there will ever be an African economic take-off, there will be no shortage of gurus pontificating on how the African cultural values provide such a booster behind Africa's yet-to-happen economic take-off.

Cultural Change: Convergence versus Divergence

Every culture evolves. A great debate thus erupts on the *direction* of cultural change. In this age of globalization, one side of the debate argues that there is a great deal of convergence, especially toward more "modern" Western values such as individualism and consumerism. As evidence, convergence gurus point out the worldwide interest in Western products, such as Blackberries, Levi jeans, iPods, and MTV, especially among the youth.[44]

However, another side suggests that Westernization in consumption does not necessarily mean Westernization in values. In a most extreme example, on the night of September 10, 2001, "9/11" terrorists enjoyed some American soft drinks, pizzas, and movies, and then went on to kill thousands of Americans the next day.[45] More broadly, the popularity of Western brands in the Middle East does not change Muslim values (see the Opening Case). In another example, the increasing popularity of Asian foods and games in the West does not necessarily mean that Westerners are converging toward "Asian values" (see In Focus 3.3). In short, the world continues to be characterized by cultural divergence.

A "middle-of-the-road" group makes two points. First, the end of the Cold War, the rise of the Internet, and the ascendance of English as the language of business all offer evidence of some cultural convergence—at least on the surface and among the youth. For example, relative to the average citizens, younger Chinese, Georgian, Japanese, and Russian managers are becoming more individualistic and less collectivistic.[46] Second, deep down, cultural divergence may continue to be the norm. Therefore, perhaps a better term is "crossvergence" that acknowledges the validity of both sides of the debate.[47] This idea suggests that when marketing products and services to younger customers around the world, a more "global" approach (featuring uniform content and image) may work, whereas when dealing with older, more tradition-bound consumers, local adaptation may be a must.

Opportunism versus Individualism/ Collectivism[48]

As noted in Chapter 2, opportunism is a major source of uncertainty that adds to transaction costs, and institutions emerge to combat opportunism.[49] However, critics argue that emphasizing opportunism as "human nature" may backfire.[50] If firm A insists on specifying minute details in a contract in order to prevent firm B from behaving opportunistically *in the future*, A is likely to be regarded by B as being not trustworthy and being opportunistic *now*. This is especially likely to be the case if B is from a high-context (or collectivist) society. Thus, A's attempts to combat opportunism may beget opportunism.

Transaction cost theorists acknowledge that opportunists are a minority in any population. However, theorists contend that because of the difficulty in identifying such a minority of opportunists *before* they cause any damage, it is imperative to place safeguards that, unfortunately, treat everybody as a potential opportunist. For example, thanks to the work of only 19 terrorists on September 11, 2001, millions of air travelers around the world now have to put up with heightened security. Everybody hates it, but nobody argues that it is unnecessary. This debate, therefore, seems deadlocked.

One cultural dimension—individualism/collectivism—may hold the key to an improved understanding of opportunism. A common stereotype is that players

Are We All "Asians" Now?

Around the world, there is now a rising popularity of Asian foods (such as tofu and sushi), martial arts (such as kung fu, taekwondo, and judo), toys (such as Pokemon), cartoons (such as *Astro Boy*), and practices (such as feng shui). Asian business words, such as *guanxi*, *keiretsu*, and *chaebol*, now routinely appear in English publications without any explanation provided in brackets. In the main pedestrian shopping street in Copenhagen, Denmark, there are two competing Chinese restaurants: one called "Beijing" and another "Shanghai." When watching a sport as quintessentially American as baseball, you

© Yoshikazu Tsuno/AFP/Getty Images

can buy a box of sushi to wash down with your beer in the ball park. School kids in the West can't get enough of toys, cartoons, comics, and video games originating from Japan—ranging from Hello Kitty for girls and Godzilla and Bokugan for boys. To combat declining reader interest in newspapers especially among young readers, a number of US newspapers, including the *Los Angeles Times*, have introduced *manga*-style comics (Japanese comics with wide-eyed characters) to their Sunday funny pages. The lead theme is *Peach Fuzz*, a playful chronicle of a nine-year-old girl and her pet ferret. The sight of a ferret where Snoopy once reigned may lead some old-timers to exclaim: "Good grief!"

Until recently, the United States had been the only place that had muscle to generate "cultural exports," such as movies, music, and food. But winds are changing. Japan now sells approximately $15 billion cultural exports, three times the value of its exports of TV sets. Publishers, toy makers, and game developers increasingly look east to spot new trends. Hasbro, a leading US toymaker, teamed with Shogakukan, a major *manga* publisher, to create *Duel Masters*, a new TV show and trading card game. Sony synched *Astro Boy* characters' lips with both Japanese and English to maximize their appeal.

Some have long argued that consumption of Western products, ranging from Coca-Cola to credit cards, would "Westernize" the world. Obviously, not everyone agrees. Now, if you are not an Asian, ask yourself: if you carried a Samsung mobile (cell) phone, had fried rice and egg rolls for lunch, enjoyed *Peach Fuzz* comics, and practiced taekwondo for your exercise, are you really becoming more "Asian" in values and outlook?

Sources: Based on (1) T. Bestor, 2000, How sushi went global, *Foreign Policy*, December: 54–63; (2) *BusinessWeek*, 2005, Can *manga* ferret out young readers, November 28: 16; (3) *BusinessWeek*, 2004, Is Japanese style taking over the world, July 26: 56–58; (4) C. Robertson, 2000, The global dispersion of Chinese values, *Management International Review*, 40: 253–268; (5) E. Tsang, 2004, Superstition and decision-making, *Academy of Management Executive*, 18 (4): 92–104.

from collectivist societies (such as China) are more collaborative and trustworthy, and that those from individualist societies (such as America) are more competitive and opportunistic.[51] However, this is not necessarily the case. Collectivists are more collaborative *only* when dealing with **in-group** members—individuals and firms regarded as a part of their own collective. The flip side is that collectivists discriminate more harshly against **out-group** members—individuals and firms not regarded as a part of "us." On the other hand, individualists, who believe

In-group

Individuals and firms regarded as a part of "us."

Out-group

Individuals and firms not regarded as a part of "us."

that every person (firm) is on his or her (its) own, make less distinction between in-group and out-group. Therefore, although individualists may indeed be more opportunistic than collectivists when dealing with in-group members (this fits the stereotype), collectivists may be *more* opportunistic when dealing with out-group members. Thus, on balance, the average Chinese is not inherently more trustworthy than the average American.

This helps explain why the United States, the leading individualist country, is among societies with a higher level of spontaneous trust, whereas there is greater interpersonal and interfirm *distrust* in the large society in China.[52] This also explains why it is so important to establish *guanxi* (relationship) for individuals and firms in China; otherwise, life can be very challenging in a sea of strangers.

Although this insight is not likely to help improve airport security screening, it can help managers and firms better deal with one another. Only through repeated social interactions can collectivists assess whether to accept newcomers as in-group members. If foreigners who, by definition, are from an out-group refuse to show any interest in joining the in-group, then it is fair to take advantage of them. For example, refusing a friendly cup of coffee from a Saudi businessman is considered an affront. Most of us do not realize that feeling free to say "no" when offered food or drink reflects a cultural underpinning of individualism. This misunderstanding, in part, explains why many cross-culturally naïve Western managers and firms often cry out loud for being taken advantage of in collectivist societies. They are simply being treated as "deserving" out-group members.[53]

LEARNING OBJECTIVE

7

Draw implications for action.

MANAGEMENT SAVVY

The institution-based view emphasizes the importance of informal institutions—cultures, ethics, and norms—in propelling or constraining business around the globe. How does this perspective answer our fundamental question: What determines the success and failure of firms around the globe? The institution-based view argues that firm performance is, at least in part, determined by the informal cultures, ethics, and norms governing firm behavior.

For savvy managers around the globe, this emphasis on informal institutions suggests two broad implications. First, it is necessary to enhance **cultural intelligence**, defined as an individual's ability to understand and adjust to new cultures.[54] Nobody can become an expert, the chameleon in Table 3.6, in all cultures. However, a genuine interest in foreign cultures will open your eyes. Acquisition of cultural intelligence passes through three phases: (1) awareness, (2) knowledge, and (3) skills.[55] *Awareness* refers to the recognition of both the pros and cons of your "mental software" and the appreciation of people from other cultures. *Knowledge* refers to the ability to identify the symbols, rituals, and taboos in other cultures, also known as cross-cultural literacy. Although you may not share (or may disagree with) their values, you will at least understand the informal institutions governing their behavior. Finally, *skills* are based on awareness and knowledge, plus good practice (Table 3.7). Of course, culture is not everything. It is advisable not to read too much into culture, which is one of many variables affecting global business.[56] However, it is imprudent to ignore culture.

Although skills can be taught, the most effective way to gain cultural intelligence is total immersion within a foreign culture. Even for gifted individuals, learning a new language and culture well enough to function at a managerial level will take at least several months of full-time studies. Most employers do not give their

Cultural intelligence
An individual's ability to understand and adjust to new cultures.

TABLE 3.6   FIVE PROFILES OF CULTURAL INTELLIGENCE

Profiles	Characteristics
The Local	A person who works well with people from similar backgrounds but does not work effectively with people from different cultural backgrounds.
The Analyst	A person who observes and learns from others and plans a strategy for interacting with people from different cultural backgrounds.
The Natural	A person who relies on intuition rather than on a systematic learning style when interacting with people from different cultural backgrounds.
The Mimic	A person who creates a comfort zone for people from different cultural backgrounds by adopting their general posture and communication style. This is not pure imitation, which may be regarded as mocking.
The Chameleon	A person who may be mistaken for a native of the foreign country. He/she may achieve results that natives cannot, due to his/her insider's skills and outsider's perspective. This is very rare.

Sources: Based on (1) P. C. Earley & S. Ang, 2003, *Cultural Intelligence: Individual Interactions Across Cultures*, Palo Alto, CA: Stanford University Press; (2) P. C. Earley & E. Mosakowski, 2004, Cultural intelligence, *Harvard Business Review*, October: 139–146.

TABLE 3.7   IMPLICATIONS FOR ACTION: SIX RULES OF THUMB WHEN VENTURING OVERSEAS

- Be prepared
- Slow down
- Establish trust
- Understand the importance of language
- Respect cultural differences
- Understand that no culture is inherently superior in all aspects

expatriates that much time to learn before sending them abroad. Thus, most expatriates are inadequately prepared, and the costs for firms, individuals, and families are tremendous (see Chapter 15). This means that you, a student studying this book, are advised to invest in your own career by picking up at least one foreign language, spending one semester (or year) abroad, and reaching out to make some international friends who are taking classes with you (perhaps sitting next to you). Such an investment during university studies will make you stand out among the crowd and propel your future career to great heights.

Second, managers need to be aware of the prevailing norms and their transitions globally. The norms around the globe in the 21st century are more culturally sensitive and ethically demanding than they were in, say, the 1970s. This is not to suggest that every local norm needs to be followed. However, failing to understand and adapt to the changing norms by behaving in an insensitive and unethical way may lead to unsatisfactory or disastrous results (see the Opening and Closing Cases). The best managers expect norms to shift over time and constantly decipher the changes in the informal rules of the game and take advantage of new opportunities. How BMW managers proactively shaped the automobile recycling norms serves as a case in point. Firms that fail to realize the passing of old norms and adapt accordingly are likely to fall behind or even go out of business.

CHAPTER SUMMARY

1. Explain where informal institutions come from.
   - Informal institutions primarily come from socially transmitted information and are a part of the heritage that we call cultures, ethics, and norms.

2. Define culture and articulate its four major manifestations: language, religion, social structure, and education.
   - Culture is the collective programming of the mind which distinguishes one group from another.
   - Managers and firms ignorant of foreign languages and religious traditions may end up with embarrassments and, worse, disasters when doing business around the globe.
   - Highly stratified societies have a low degree of social mobility, and vice versa.
   - Education fosters a sense of cultural identity by teaching mainstream values and norms.

3. Discuss how cultures systematically differ from each other.
   - The context approach differentiates cultures based on the high- versus low-context dimension.
   - The cluster approach groups similar cultures together as clusters and civilizations.
   - Hofstede and colleagues have identified five cultural dimensions: (1) power distance, (2) individualism/collectivism, (3) masculinity/femininity, (4) uncertainty avoidance, and (5) long-term orientation.

4. Explain why ethics is important and identify ways to combat corruption.
   - When managing ethics overseas, two schools of thought are ethical relativism and ethical imperialism.
   - Three "middle-of-the-road" principles help guide managers make ethical decisions.
   - The fight against corruption around the world is a long-term, global battle.

5. Identify norms associated with strategic responses when firms deal with ethical challenges.
   - When confronting ethical challenges, individual firms have four strategic choices: (1) reactive, (2) defensive, (3) accommodative, and (4) proactive strategies.

6. Participate in three leading debates on cultures, ethics, and norms.
   - These are (1) Western values versus Eastern values, (2) cultural convergence versus divergence, and (3) opportunism versus individualism/collectivism.

7. Draw implications for action.
   - It is important to enhance cultural intelligence, leading to cross-cultural literacy.
   - It is crucial to understand and adapt to the changing norms globally.

KEY TERMS

Civilization 71	Ethical relativism 76	*Lingua franca* 65
Cluster 70	Ethics 76	Long-term orientation 73
Code of conduct 76	Ethnocentrism 63	Low-context culture 69
Collectivism 73	Femininity 73	Masculinity 73
Context 69	Foreign Corrupt Practices	Out-group 83
Corruption 77	Act (FCPA) 78	Power distance 71
Cultural intelligence 84	High-context culture 69	Social mobility 67
Culture 63	Individualism 73	Social stratification 67
Ethical imperialism 77	In-group 83	Uncertainty avoidance 73

REVIEW QUESTIONS

1. What is ethnocentrism and what is its cause?

2. What are the four major components of a country's culture?

3. What is the difference between a low-context culture and a high-context culture? How would you classify your home country's culture?

4. Describe the three systems for classifying cultures by clusters.

5. Indicate where you feel your country generally fits in each of Hofstede's five dimensions.

6. What is the difference between ethical relativism and ethical imperialism?

7. How would you define corruption in a business setting?

8. Explain the difference between a reactive strategy and a defensive strategy when dealing with an ethical challenge.

9. What is the FCPA and why has it not ended corruption in global business?

10. What might be the outcome if several firms within an industry decide to adopt the same accommodative strategy to a shared ethical challenge?

11. Give an example of a proactive strategy to an ethical challenge.

12. How is Western capitalism viewed by the two major sets of Eastern values, Islam and Confucianism?

13. In general, how do collectivists typically behave toward in-group members compared to out-group members?

14. What is cross-cultural literacy and why is it important?

15. Describe cultural intelligence and its development.

16. Look at the developed countries shown on PengAtlas Map 1.1 and review what you learned in this chapter regarding culture. Based on what you know concerning these countries, what generalizations can you make regarding cultural commonalities that tend to exist among the majority of the developed countries?

17. As you look at PengAtlas Maps 1.1 and 1.3, which countries do you think will most likely undergo changes in political freedom and economic development in the years ahead as a result of cultural change? Why?

CRITICAL DISCUSSION QUESTIONS

1. You are on a flight and the passenger sitting next to you is trying to have a conversation with you. He asks: "What do you do?" You would like to be nice, but you don't want to give too much information about yourself (such as your name). How would you answer this question? A typical US manager may say: "I am a marketing manager" without mentioning the employer. A typical Japanese manager may say: "I work for Honda." What explains such differences?

2. *ON ETHICS*: Assume you work for a New Zealand company exporting a container of kiwis to Haiti or Iraq. The customs official informs you that there is a delay in clearing your container through customs and it may last a month. However, if you are willing to pay an "expediting fee" of US$200, he will try to make it happen in one day. What are you going to do?

3. *ON ETHICS*: Most developed economies have some illegal immigrants. The United States has the largest number: approximately 10 to 11 million. Without legal US identification (ID) documents, they cannot open bank accounts or buy houses. Many US firms have targeted this population and accept the ID issued by their native countries when selling them products and services. Some Americans are furious with these business practices. Other Americans suggest that illegal immigrants represent a growth engine in an economy with relatively little growth elsewhere. How would you participate in this debate?

YOUR SOURCE FOR
global business knowledge

http://globalEDGE.msu.edu

GLOBAL ACTION

1. Religion is an integral component of your company's operations because it manufactures food products according to Islam's Halal requirements. Top management wants information concerning the largest populations of Islam worldwide to develop your company's distribution capabilities. Provide a report with any information found on the globalEDGE website relevant to this company-wide initiative. What recommendations can you provide to the company?

2. One approach to understanding corruption perceptions is to compare information across a variety of countries. As such, your company has had operations in South America for some time. However, there has not been an internal evaluation of perceived regional corruption to date. Therefore, you have been asked to provide insight on this topic for each country in South America. Based on an annual corruption perceptions index found on globalEDGE, develop a brief report and recommendations for the entire company.

VIDEO CASES

Watch "Communicating Across Cultures" by Sir David Bell of Pearson.

1. Bell gave an example in which a group of people were offended when they were told that what they did was "quite good." Why were they offended and what was his point?

2. What did Bell's example of the pantomime illustrate? Can you think of forms of verbal or nonverbal communication in your country that could be misunderstood by people from other parts of the world?

3. One of his objectives is to have people from various countries feel that they are all part of the same company and to value the same things. To what extent would that help overcome communication barriers among different cultures?

4. Bell indicated that one approach to improving cross-cultural communication is to periodically shift people around so that they are exposed to different parts of an organization and the world. What are the limitations and opportunities? Do you think technology could help in shifting people as he suggests?

Closing Case

ETHICAL DILEMMA

Siemens Needs to Clean Up around the Globe

© Imagine China via AP Images

Founded in 1847, Siemens, headquartered in Munich and Berlin, is an engineering conglomerate whose revenues in 2008 reached €77 billion ($108 billion) from 190 countries. As a global firm, Siemens is not only subject to German regulations, but also subject to regulations in many countries, especially in the United States since its shares have been publicly listed on the New York Stock Exchange since 2001.

Recently, Siemens found itself engulfed in a sea of scandals around the globe. In November 2007, Siemens disclosed in its Form 6-K to the US Securities and Exchange Commission (SEC): Authorities around the world were conducting investigations of Siemens "regarding allegations of public corruption, including criminal breaches of fiduciary duty including embezzlement, as well as bribery, money laundering, and tax evasion, among others." According to the report, authorities from the following countries/regions were involved:

- Brazil
- China
- Czech Republic
- European Union/European Commission
- Germany
- Greece
- Hungary
- Indonesia
- Italy
- Japan
- Mexico
- New Zealand
- Norway
- Poland
- South Africa
- Switzerland
- Turkey
- United States

In the same report, Siemens disclosed that its internal investigation uncovered $1.9 billion in questionable payments made to outsiders by the company from 2000 to 2006. In its own words:

These payments raise concerns in particular under the Foreign Corrupt Practices Act (FCPA) of the United States, anti-corruption legislation in Germany, and similar legislation in other countries. The payments identified were recorded as deductible business expenses in prior periods [2000–2006] in determining income tax provisions . . . the Company's investigation determined that certain of these payments were nondeductible under tax regulations of Germany and other jurisdictions.

In December 2008, Siemens pleaded guilty to corruption charges and settled with the US and German governments for a combined total of $1.6 billion in fines, including $800 million to US authorities. This represented the largest fine ever imposed in an FCPA case since the act was passed by Congress in 1977. Siemens was alleged to have bribed officials in Africa, Asia, Europe, the Middle East, and the Americas approximately 4,200 times to the tune of $1.4 billion between 2000 and 2006 with the goal of winning contracts abroad. Linda Thomsen of the SEC noted in a press release:

The scope of the bribery scheme is astonishing, and the tone set at the top at Siemens was a corporate culture in which bribery was tolerated and even rewarded at the highest levels of the company. The SEC portion of the Siemens settlement, $350 million in disgorgement, is by far the largest settlement amount ever obtained by the SEC under the FCPA. To put this in context, the largest prior SEC FCPA settlement was reached in 2007 and was for $33 million. The SEC settlement with Siemens is more than 10 times that amount.

Joseph Persichini, Assistant Director of the Federal Bureau of Investigation (FBI), noted:

a massive, willful, and carefully orchestrated criminal corruption scheme. Their actions were not an anomaly. They were standard operating procedures for corporate executives who viewed bribery as a business strategy.

However, the settlement stopped the case from going to trial in both the United States and Germany—although authorities in other countries may still pursue a court trial. When asked why, despite such strong words, the US government had not pressed criminal charges against the company or its executives, Persichini said that Siemens had cooperated fully in the investigation, engaged in significant reforms, and hired a former German finance minister as an independent compliance monitor for the next four years. "In this case, one weighed all the factors," he said, "This was the right disposition. And the court agreed with our proposal."

During 2006–2008, in response to the scandals, Siemens undertook a number of measures: Its Supervisory Board established a Compliance Committee, its Managing Board engaged an external attorney to provide a protected communication channel for employees and third parties, the company appointed a Chief Compliance Officer, marketed a Compliance hotline to employees, and adopted a Global Amnesty Program for employees who voluntarily provided useful information regarding their wrongdoing. In an effort to distance itself from the scandals, Siemens in July 2007 broke convention from internal promotion and hired an outside candidate, Peter Löscher from pharmaceutical giant Merck, as CEO. In December 2008, after its guilty plea, Siemens released a statement, in which it noted that the US authorities recognized its "extraordinary cooperation" with the investigation as well as its recent compliance efforts. Siemens also noted that the US Defense Logistics Agency confirmed that "Siemens remains a responsible contractor for US government business." Gerhard Cromme, chairman of Siemens' Supervisory Board, noted in the statement:

Siemens is closing a painful chapter in its history . . . For Siemens, the corruption cases in Germany and the United States are now over. Today marks the end of an unprecedented two-year effort to resolve extremely serious matters for the company. Based on robust leadership processes, Siemens has established a sustainable culture of compliance . . . We regret what happened in the past. But we have learned from it and taken appropriate measures. Siemens is now a stronger company.

Talk is cheap, according to critics. Many critics wonder whether the new measures would transform a "bad barrel." Within one week of the settlement, Siemens announced in late December 2008 that it won a $2.1 billion contract in Iraq for high-efficiency gas turbines. This would be one of the biggest orders

Siemens ever booked in the Middle East. Critics are naturally suspicious of deals like this.

Case Discussion Questions:

1. What are the costs and benefits of bribery?
2. Is the FCPA unnecessarily harsh or do its provisions dispense the appropriate level of punishment?
3. In your view, how heavy should Siemens be fined? In addition to fines, what else can be done?
4. Are some of Siemens employees "bad apples" or is Siemens a "bad barrel"?

Sources: Based on (1) *BusinessWeek*, 2007, Siemens braces for a slap from Uncle Sam, November 6: 78–79; (2) *Deutsche Welle*, 2008, Siemens wins big Iraq contract after global corruption scandal, December 22 (www.dw-word.de); (3) *Los Angeles Times*, 2008, Siemens makes $1.3 billion in plea deals, December 16 (articles.latimes.com); (4) *Managing Automation*, 2008, Siemens guilty of US corruption, December 16 (www.managingautomation.com); (5) Siemens AG, 2007, Form 6-K Report of Foreign Private Issuer, November 8, New York: SEC; (6) www.siemens.com.

NOTES

[Journal acronyms] **AMJ**—*Academy of Management Journal;* **AMR**—*Academy of Management Review;* **APJM**—*Asia Pacific Journal of Management;* **CMR**—*California Management Review;* **HBR**—*Harvard Business Review;* **IJHRM**—*International Journal of Human Resource Management;* **JBE**—*Journal of Business Ethics;* **JIBS**—*Journal of International Business Studies;* **JM**—*Journal of Management;* **JMS**—*Journal of Management Studies;* **JWB**—*Journal of World Business;* **MIR**—*Management International Review;* **OD**—*Organizational Dynamics;* **OSt**—*Organization Studies;* **RES**—*Review of Economics and Statistics;* **SMJ**—*Strategic Management Journal.*

1 J. Salk & M. Brannen, 2000, National culture, networks, and individual influence in a multinational management team, *AMJ*, 43: 191–202; M. Witt & G. Redding, 2009, Culture, meaning, and institutions, *JIBS*, 40: 859–885; H. Woldu, P. Budhwar, & C. Parkes, 2006, A cross-national comparison of cultural value orientations of India, Polish, Russian, and American employees, *IJHRM*, 17: 1076–1094.

2 S. Nadkarni & P. Barr, 2008, Environmental context, managerial cognition, and strategic action, *SMJ*, 29: 1395–1427; B. Olson, Y. Bao, & S. Parayitam, 2007, Strategic decision making within Chinese firms, *JWB*, 42: 35–46; B. Tyler & D. Gnyawali, 2009, Managerial collective cognitions, *JMS*, 46: 93–126.

3 G. Hofstede, 1997, *Cultures and Organizations* (p. xii), New York: McGraw-Hill.

4 S. Michailova, 2002, When common sense becomes uncommon, *JWB*, 37: 180–187.

5 L. Busenitz, C. Gomez, & J. Spencer, 2000, Country institutional profiles, *AMJ*, 43: 994–1003; M. Lounsbury, 2007, A tale of two cities, *AMJ*, 50: 289–307; S. Rangan & A. Drummond, 2002,

Explaining outcomes in competition among foreign multinationals in a focal host market, *SMJ*, 25: 285–293.

6 Hofstede, 1997, *Cultures and Organizations* (p. 5).

7 C. Chan, S. Makino, & T. Isobe, 2010, Does sub-national region matter? *SMJ* (in press).

8 D. Graddol, 2004, The future of language, *Science*, 303: 1329–1331.

9 J. Fidrmuc & J. Fidrmuc, 2009, Foreign languages and trade, working paper, Uxbridge, UK: Brunel University.

10 D. Ricks, 1999, *Blunders in International Business*, 3rd ed., Oxford, UK: Blackwell.

11 C. Hill, 2007, *International Business*, 6th ed. (p. 98), New York: McGraw–Hill/Irwin.

12 E. Hall & M. Hall, 1987, *Hidden Differences*, Garden City, NY: Doubleday.

13 S. Ronen & O. Shenkar, 1985, Clustering countries on attitudinal dimension, *AMR*, 10: 435–454.

14 R. House, P. Hanges, M. Javidan, P. Dorfman, & V. Gupta (eds.), 2004, *Culture, Leadership, and Organizations: The GLOBE Study of 62 Societies*, Thousand Oaks, CA: Sage.

15 S. Huntington, 1996, *The Clash of Civilizations and the Remaking of World Order* (p. 43), New York: Simon & Schuster.

16 S. Schwartz, 1994, Cultural dimensions of values, in U. Kim et al. (eds.), *Individualism and Collectivism* (pp. 85–119), Thousand Oaks, CA: Sage; V. Taras, J. Rowney, & P. Steel, 2009, Half a century of measuring culture, *JIM*, 15: 357–373; F. Trompenaars, 1993, *Riding the Waves of Culture*, Chicago: Irwin.

17 World Bank, 2004, World Development Indicators (www.worldbank.org).

18 J. Evans & F. Mavondo, 2002, Psychic distance and organizational performance, *JIBS*, 33: 515–532; J. Lee, T. Roehl, & S. Choe, 2000, What makes management style similar or distinct across border? *JIBS*, 31: 631–652; J. Li, K. Lam, & G. Qian, 2001, Does culture affect behavior and performance of firms? *JIBS*, 32: 115–131; J. West & J. Graham, 2004, A linguistic–based measure of cultural distance and its relationship to managerial values, *MIR*, 44: 239–260.

19 C. Fey & I. Bjorkman, 2001, The effect of HRM practices on MNC subsidiary performance in Russia, *JIBS*, 32: 59–75; J. Parnell & T. Hatem, 1999, Behavioral differences between American and Egyptian managers, *JMS*, 36: 399–418; E. Pellegrini & T. Scandura, 2006, Leader-member exchange (LMX), paternalism, and delegation in the Turkish business context, *JIBS*, 37: 264–279.

20 Hofstede, 1997, *Cultures and Organizations* (p. 94).

21 C. Bartlett & S. Ghoshal, 1989, *Managing Across Borders* (p. 41), Boston: Harvard Business School Press.

22 X. Chen & S. Li, 2005, Cross-national differences in cooperative decision-making in mixed-motive business contexts, *JIBS*, 36: 622–636; R. Friedman, S. Chi, & L. Liu, 2006, An expectancy model of Chinese-American differences in conflict-avoiding, *JIBS*, 37: 76–91; K. Lee, G. Yang, & J. Graham, 2006, Tension and trust in international business negotiations, *JIBS*, 37: 623–641; S. Lee, O. Shenkar, & J. Li, 2008, Cultural distance, investment flow, and control in cross-border cooperation, *SMJ*, 29: 1117–1125; L. Metcalf, A. Bird, M. Shankarmahesh, Z. Aycan, J. Larimo, & D. Valdelamar, 2006, Cultural tendencies in negotiation, *JWB*, 41: 382–394; W. Newburry & N. Yakova, 2006, Standardization preferences, *JIBS*, 37: 44–60; G. Van der Vegt, E. Van de Vliert, & X. Huang, 2005, Location-level links between diversity and innovative climate depend on national power distance, *AMJ*, 48: 1171–1182.

23 L. Treviño & K. Nelson, 2004, *Managing Business Ethics*, 3rd ed. (p. 13), New York: Wiley; L. Treviño, G. Weaver, & S. Reynolds, 2006, Behavioral ethics in organizations, *JM*, 32: 951–990.

24 R. Durand, H. Rao, & P. Monin, 2007, Code of conduct in French cuisine, *SMJ*, 28: 455–472; I. Maignan & D. Ralston, 2002, Corporate social responsibility in Europe and the US, *JIBS*, 33: 497–514; J. Stevens, H. K. Steensma, D. Harrison, & P. Cochran, 2005, Symbolic or substantive document? *SMJ*, 26: 181–195.

25 T. Jones, 1995, Instrumental stakeholder theory, *AMR*, 20: 404–437.

26 C. Fombrun, 2001, Corporate reputations as economic assets, in M. Hitt, R. E. Freeman, & J. Harrison (eds.), *The Blackwell Handbook of Strategic Management* (pp. 289–312), Cambridge, UK: Blackwell.

27 E. G. Love & M. Kraatz, 2009, Character, conformity, or the bottom line? *AMJ*, 52: 314–335.

28 J. B. Hamilton, S. Knouse, & V. Hill, 2009, Google in China, *JBE*, 86: 143–157; K. Parboteeah, J. Cullen, B. Victor, & T. Sakano, 2005, National culture and ethical climates, *MIR*, 45: 459–519; D. Ralston et al., 2009, Ethical preferences for influencing superiors, *JIBS*, 40: 1027–1045; A. Spicer, T. Dunfee, & W. Bailey, 2004, Does national context matter in ethical decision making? *AMJ*, 47: 610–620.

29 This section draws heavily from T. Donaldson, 1996, Values in tension, *HBR*, September–October: 4–11.

30 D. Vogel, 1992, The globalization of business ethics, *CMR*, Fall: 30–49.

31 *Economist*, 2006, How to grease a palm (p. 116), December 23: 115–116.

32 A. Cuervo-Cazurra, 2006, Who cares about corruption? *JIBS*, 37: 807–822; N. Khatri, E. Tsang, & T. Begley, 2006, Cronyism, *JIBS*, 37: 61–75; S. Lee & K. Oh, 2007, Corruption in Asia, *APJM*, 24: 97–114.

33 C. Dirienzo, J. Das, K. Cort, & J. Burbridge, 2006, Corruption and the role of information, *JIBS*, 38: 320–332; C. Robertson & A. Watson, 2004, Corruption and change, *SMJ*, 25: 385–396; U. Weitzel & S. Berns, 2006, Cross-border takeovers, corruption, and related aspects of governance, *JIBS*, 37: 786–806; J. H. Zhao, S. Kim, & J. Du, 2003, The impact of corruption and transparency on foreign direct investment, *MIR*, 43: 41–62.

34 S. Globerman & D. Shapiro, 2003, Governance infrastructure and US foreign direct investment, *JIBS*, 34: 19–39.

35 S. Wei, 2000, How taxing is corruption on international investors? *RES*, 82: 1–11.

36 J. Hellman, G. Jones, & D. Kaufmann, 2002, Far from home: Do foreign investors import higher standards of governance in transition economies (p. 20), Working paper, Washington: World Bank (www.worldbank.org).

37 C. Kwok & S. Tadesse, 2006, The MNC as an agent of change for host-country institutions, *JIBS*, 37: 767–785.

38 D. Gioia, 2004, Pinto fires, in Treviño & Nelson, 2004, *Managing Business Ethics* (pp. 105–108).

39 S. Hart, 2005, *Capitalism at the Crossroads*, Philadelphia: Wharton School Publishing.

40 M. Barnett & A. King, 2008, Good fences make good neighbors, *AMJ*, 51: 1150–1170; A. King, M. Lenox, & A. Terlaak, 2005, The strategic use of decentralized institutions, *AMJ*, 48: 1091–1106.

41 World Bank, 1993, *The East Asian Miracle*, Washington: World Bank.

42 R. Franke, G. Hofstede, & M. Bond, 1991, Cultural roots of economic performance, *SMJ*, 12: 165–173; G. Hofstede & M. Bond, 1988, The Confucian connection, *OD*, 16: 4–21.

43 M. W. Peng, R. Bhagat, & S. Chang, 2010, Asia and global business, *JIBS* (in press).

44 T. Levitt, 1983, The globalization of markets, *HBR*, May–June: 92–102.

45 National Commission on Terrorist Attacks on the United States, 2004, *The 9/11 Report* (p. 364), New York: St Martin's.

46 A. Ardichvili & A. Gasparishvili, 2003, Russian and Georgian entrepreneurs and nonentrepreneurs, *OSt*, 24: 29–46; D. Ralston, C. Egri, S. Stewart, R. Terpstra, & K. Yu, 1999, Doing business in the 21st century with the new generation of Chinese managers, *JIBS*, 30: 415–428.

47 C. Carr, 2005, Are German, Japanese, and Anglo-Saxon strategic decision styles still divergent in the context of globalization? *JMS*, 42: 1155–1188; G. Hirst, P. Budhwar, B. Cooper, M. West, C. Long, C. Xu, & H. Shipton, 2008, Cross-cultural

variations in climate for autonomy, stress, and organizational productivity relationships, *JIBS*, 39: 1343–1358; D. Ralston, D. Holt, R. Terpstra, & K. Yu, 1997, The impact of national culture and economic ideology on managerial work values, *JIBS*, 28: 177–207; S. Speck & A. Roy, 2008, The interrelationships between television viewing, values, and perceived well-being, *JIBS*, 39: 1197–1219.

[48] This section draws heavily from C. Chen, M. W. Peng, & P. Saparito, 2002, Individualism, collectivism, and opportunism: A cultural perspective on transaction cost economics, *JM*, 28: 567–583.

[49] O. Williamson, 1985, *The Economic Institutions of Capitalism*, New York: Free Press.

[50] S. Ghoshal & P. Moran, 1996, Bad for practice, *AMR*, 21: 13–47.

[51] J. Cullen, K. P. Parboteeah, & M. Hoegl, 2004, Cross-national differences in managers' willingness to justify ethically suspect behaviors, *AMJ*, 47: 411–421.

[52] F. Fukuyama, 1995, *Trust*, New York: Free Press.

[53] S. Goodman, 2009, *Where East Eats West*, Charleston, SC: BookSurge/Amazon.

[54] P. C. Earley & E. Mosakowski, 2004, Cultural intelligence, *HBR*, October: 139–146; J. Johnson, T. Lenartowicz, & S. Apud, 2006, Cross-cultural competence in international business, *JIBS*, 37: 525–543.

[55] Hofstede, 1997, *Cultures and Organizations* (p. 230).

[56] O. Shenkar, 2001, Cultural distance revisited, *JIBS*, 32: 519–535; K. Singh, 2007, The limited relevance of culture to strategy, *APJM*, 24: 421–428; L. Tihanyi, D. Griffith, & C. Russell, 2005, The effect of cultural distance on entry mode choice, international diversification, and MNE performance, *JIBS*, 36: 270–283.

Chapter 4

© John Keatley

LEARNING OBJECTIVES

After studying this chapter, you should be able to:

1. define resources and capabilities.

2. explain how value is created from a firm's resources and capabilities.

3. articulate the difference between keeping an activity in-house and outsourcing it.

4. explain what a VRIO framework is.

5. participate in two leading debates on leveraging resources and capabilities.

6. draw implications for action.

Leveraging Resources and Capabilities

Saturna Capital: A Leading Company in Islamic Finance

Saturna Capital Corporation, adviser to both the Saturna Investment Trust and the Amana Mutual Funds Trust, is one of the world's most successful companies in the rapidly growing and specialized activity of Islamic investing. As of the fall of 2009, Saturna managed approximately $2.6 billion in assets, representing a tenfold increase since the beginning of 2005. The vast majority of these assets are invested in equities according to Islamic finance principles, which prohibit the use of interest and forbid investments in firms involved in alcohol, tobacco, and gambling activities. Indeed, the Amana Mutual Funds Trust's two largest equity mutual funds, the Amana Income Fund (AMANX) and the Amana Growth Fund (AMAGX), are recognized as the largest in the world that invest according to *sharia* (Islamic law).

Considering its unlikely location, Saturna's success within the global market of Islamic finance products is even more remarkable. Its headquarters is located in the small city of Bellingham, Washington (population: 67,200), located about midway between the much larger cities of Seattle, Washington, and Vancouver, British Columbia. Saturna is named for one of the larger islands in northern Puget Sound's beautiful San Juan archipelago, easily visible from Bellingham. Furthermore, it is a relatively small company—operating with only about 40 employees. Therefore, Saturna provides an apt example of a firm's ability to transcend geographical barriers and compete on a global scale through persistent leverage of core competence.

In the mid-1980s, when Saturna's founder Nicholas Kaiser was initially approached by a group of Islamic investors with the idea for an Islamic mutual fund, Islamic investing was certainly off the radar of major financial players in the United States. In fact, the group's idea had already been rejected by at least one well-established firm. It was Mr. Kaiser's openness to learning about *sharia* compliant investment principles and his willingness to enter uncharted territory that allowed him, as a non-Muslim, native-born American, to acquire a skill set that would prove to complement his portfolio management expertise. Today, Saturna is the beneficiary of the corporate-wide transfer of his highly developed knowledge of Islamic investing, which allows the company to compete successfully in an important global market.

To some extent, Saturna's rapid growth mirrors the rapid growth of the Islamic financial industry. By some estimates, the industry more than doubled in size between 1998 and 2008 with the growth driven by, among other things, a surge in oil-related wealth. Nevertheless, Saturna's growth has markedly exceeded that of the industry as a whole that includes hundreds of financial institutions located in major financial capitals that also compete for clients who want to invest in accordance with Islamic law. Saturna's competitors include such corporate behemoths as HSBC, Citicorp, Deutsche Bank, and UBS, as well as large banks headquartered in the Persian Gulf region and Southeast Asia where the majority of the world's Muslims live.

In light of what many might see as formidable competitive disadvantages related to its location and relatively small size, how does one explain Saturna's remarkable success? One of the most compelling explanations is Mr. Kaiser's exceptional talent as an investment manager. The Amana Income and Amana Growth mutual funds are consistently ranked in the top of their peer categories for long-term performance, despite being measured against funds with no restrictions on where they can invest. The Amana funds for example, are prohibited from investing in companies that earn a significant amount of revenue from alcohol, tobacco, or gambling as well as investments based on interest (such as bonds or financial derivatives). While avoiding investments in banks and other financial companies proved fortuitous in the aftermath of the collapse of financial stocks in 2008, such limitations can handicap overall financial performance.

Saturna's outstanding corporate governance also undoubtedly contributes to its success. In particular, it has a sterling reputation for financial integrity, including vigilance in complying with financial regulations governing the mutual fund industry. Its commitment to upholding the ethical principles of its investors is supported by its board of directors mostly consisting of prominent Muslim community leaders, as well as its use of *sharia* scholars as advisors regarding its compliance with Islamic laws of investing. Saturna's director of Islamic investing, Monem Salam, serves as a vital interface between the company and the population of potential Islamic investors. Both a devout Muslim and an MBA graduate, Salam is very effective in ensuring that

Saturna's investments meet the needs of its Muslim clientele as well as communicating Saturna's remarkable performance to potential Muslim investors.

The investment management business is ultimately about serving the needs of customers. Besides providing industry-leading financial returns, Saturna dedicates considerable resources to providing value-added services for its current customers and to the broader American Muslim community. For example, Saturna will estimate *zakah* (the percentage of investment earnings to set aside for charitable giving according to *sharia*) on behalf of investors in affiliated accounts. It also creates a worksheet to help investors save for *Hajj* (a Muslim's obligatory pilgrimage to Mecca).

Perhaps the most impressive evidence of Saturna's success is the fact that many Amana Fund shareowners are not Muslim. They are quite happy to abide by the Islamic law and appreciate Saturna's uncompromising standards of customer service. Saturna and the dedicated efforts of its employees clearly demonstrate how a small firm in an unlikely location can cultivate a culture of principled financial operations and leverage a niche market strategy to earn respect and recognition in a global industry.

Sources: This case was written by Professor **Steven Globerman** (Kaiser Professor of International Business, Western Washington University). It is based on (1) the author's interviews with Nick Kaiser; (2) D. Kathman, 2009, Nick Kaiser, Saturna Capital, *Morningstar Advisor*, January 30.

Resource-based view
A leading perspective in global business that posits that firm performance is fundamentally driven by differences in firm-specific resources and capabilities.

SWOT analysis
An analytical tool for determining a firm's strengths (S), weaknesses (W), opportunities (O), and threats (T).

Why is Saturna able to outcompete its much larger and more visible rivals in a global industry? What is so special about this company? The answer must be that certain resources and capabilities specific to Saturna are not shared by competitors. This insight has been developed into a **resource-based view**, which has emerged as one of the two core perspectives on global business.[1]

One leading tool in global business is **SWOT analysis**. A SWOT analysis determines a firm's strengths (S), weaknesses (W), opportunities (O), and threats (T). In global business, the institution-based view deals with the *external* O and T, enabled and constrained by formal and informal rules of the game (see Chapters 2 and 3). The resource-based view builds on the SWOT analysis,[2] and concentrates on the *internal* S and W to identify and leverage sustainable competitive advantage.[3] In this chapter, we first define resources and capabilities, and then discuss the value chain analysis concentrating on the decision to keep an activity in-house or outsource it. We then focus on value (V), rarity (R), imitability (I), and organization (O) through a VRIO framework. Debates and extensions follow.

UNDERSTANDING RESOURCES AND CAPABILITIES

Define resources and capabilities.

A basic proposition of the resource-based view is that a firm consists of a bundle of productive resources and capabilities.[4] **Resources** are defined as "the tangible and intangible assets a firm uses to choose and implement its strategies."[5] There is some debate regarding the definition of capabilities. Some scholars define them as "a firm's capacity to dynamically deploy resources," suggesting a "dynamic capabilities" view that emphasizes a crucial distinction between resources and capabilities.[6]

Although scholars may debate the fine distinctions between resources and capabilities, these distinctions are likely to "become badly blurred" in practice.[7] Is Saturna's ability to pick winning stocks in which to invest a resource or capability? How about its ability to achieve enviable financial returns while following Islamic finance principles? What about its ability to offer superb customer service? For current and would-be managers, the key is to understand how these attributes help improve firm performance, not to figure out whether they should be defined as resources or capabilities. Therefore, in this book, we will use the terms "resources" and "capabilities" *interchangeably* and often in *parallel*. In other words, **capabilities** are defined here the same as resources.

All firms, even the smallest ones, possess a variety of resources and capabilities. How do we meaningfully classify such diversity? A useful way is to separate the resources and capabilities into two categories: tangible and intangible (Table 4.1). **Tangible resources and capabilities** are assets that are observable and easily quantified. They can be broadly organized in four categories: financial, physical, technological, and organizational resources and capabilities.

TABLE 4.1   EXAMPLES OF RESOURCES AND CAPABILITIES

Tangible resources and capabilities	Examples
Financial	• Ability to generate internal funds • Ability to raise external capital
Physical	• Location of plants, offices, and equipment • Access to raw materials and distribution channels
Technological	• Possession of patents, trademarks, copyrights, and trade secrets
Organizational	• Formal planning, command, and control systems • Integrated management information systems
Intangible resources and capabilities	**Examples**
Human	• Managerial talents • Organizational culture
Innovation	• Research and development capabilities • Capacities for organizational innovation and change
Reputational	• Perceptions of product quality, durability, and reliability • Reputation as a good employer • Reputation as a socially responsible corporate citizen

Resource
The tangible and intangible assets a firm uses to choose and implement its strategies.

Capability
The tangible and intangible assets a firm uses to choose and implement its strategies.

Tangible resources and capabilities
Assets that are observable and easily quantified.

Sources: Adapted from (1) J. Barney, 1991, Firm resources and sustained competitive advantage, *Journal of Management*, 17: 101; (2) R. Hall, 1992, The strategic analysis of intangible resources, *Strategic Management Journal*, 13: 135–144.

By definition, **intangible resources and capabilities** are harder to observe and more difficult (or even impossible) to quantify (Table 4.1). Yet, it is widely acknowledged that they must be there, because no firm is likely to generate competitive advantage by only relying on tangible resources and capabilities alone.[8] Examples of intangible assets include human, innovation, and reputational resources and capabilities.

It is important to note that all resources and capabilities discussed here are merely *examples*, and that they do not represent an exhaustive list. As firms forge ahead, discovery and leveraging of new resources and capabilities are likely.

RESOURCES, CAPABILITIES, AND THE VALUE CHAIN: IN-HOUSE VERSUS OUTSOURCING

If a firm is a bundle of resources and capabilities, how do they come together to add value? A value chain analysis allows us to answer this question. Shown in Figure 4.1 Panel A, most goods and services are produced through a chain of vertical activities (from upstream to downstream) that add value—in short, a value chain. The **value chain** consists of two areas: primary and support activities.[9]

Each activity requires a number of resources and capabilities. Value chain analysis forces managers to think about resources and capabilities at a very micro, activity-based level.[10] Given that no firm is likely to have enough resources and capabilities to be good at all primary and support activities, the key is to examine whether the firm has resources and capabilities to perform a *particular* activity in a manner superior to competitors—a process known as **benchmarking** in SWOT analysis. If managers find that their firm's particular activity is unsatisfactory, a two-stage decision model can remedy the situation, as shown in Figure 4.2. In the first stage, managers ask: "Do we really need to perform this activity in-house?" Figure 4.3 introduces a framework to take a hard look at this question. The answer boils down to two factors: whether an activity is industry-specific or common across industries and whether this activity is proprietary (firm-specific) or not. So an activity that falls in Cell 2 of Figure 4.3 would be answered "No, we don't need to perform this activity in-house" because the activity has a great deal of commonality across industries and little need for keeping it proprietary. As a product loses its ability to command high prices and high margins through market competition, it undergoes a process known in the recent jargon as **commoditization** (in short, it becomes a low-price "commodity"). The answer may also be "No" if the activity is in Cell 1, which is industry-specific but also with a high level of commoditization. In this case, the firm may want to outsource the activity, sell the unit involved, or lease the unit's services to other firms (see Figure 4.2). This is because operating multiple stages of activities in the value chain may be cumbersome.

Think about steel, definitely a crucial component for automobiles. The question for automakers is: "Do we need to make steel ourselves?" The requirements for steel are common across end user industries—that is, the steel for automakers is essentially the same for construction, defense, and other steel-consuming end users (ignoring minor technical differences for the sake of our discussion). Although it is imperative for automakers to keep the automaking activity (especially engine and final assembly) proprietary (Cell 3 in Figure 4.3), there is no need to make steel in-house. Therefore, although many automakers such as Ford and GM were historically involved in steel making, none of them does it now. In other words, steel making is outsourced and steel commoditized.

LEARNING OBJECTIVE 2

Explain how value is created from a firm's resources and capabilities.

Intangible resources and capabilities

Assets that are hard to observe and difficult (if not impossible) to quantify.

Value chain

A chain of vertical activities used in the production of goods and services that add value.

Benchmarking

An examination on whether a firm has resources and capabilities to perform a particular activity in a manner superior to competitors.

Commoditization

A process of market competition through which unique products that command high prices and high margins gradually lose their ability to do so, thus becoming commodities.

FIGURE 4.1   THE VALUE CHAIN

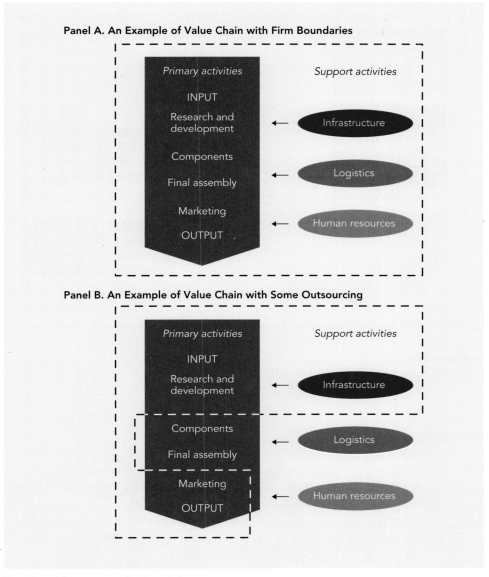

Panel A. An Example of Value Chain with Firm Boundaries

Primary activities

INPUT

Research and development

Components

Final assembly

Marketing

OUTPUT

Support activities

Infrastructure

Logistics

Human resources

Panel B. An Example of Value Chain with Some Outsourcing

Primary activities

INPUT

Research and development

Components

Final assembly

Marketing

OUTPUT

Support activities

Infrastructure

Logistics

Human resources

Note: Dotted lines represent firm boundaries.

Outsourcing is defined as turning over an organizational activity to an outside supplier that will perform the activity on behalf of the focal firm.[11] Many consumer products companies such as Nike that possess strong capabilities in upstream activities (such as design) and downstream activities (such as marketing) have outsourced manufacturing to suppliers in low-cost countries. A total of 80% of the value of Boeing's new 787 Dreamliner is provided by outside suppliers. This compares with 51% for Boeing's previous aircraft.[12] Not only is manufacturing often outsourced, there is a recent trend toward outsourcing a number of service activities such as information technology (IT), human resources (HR), and logistics. The driving force is that many firms, which previously considered certain activities such as airline reservations and bank call centers a special part of their industries, now believe that these activities have relatively generic attributes that can be

LEARNING OBJECTIVE

3

Articulate the difference between keeping an activity in-house and outsourcing it.

Outsourcing

Turning over an organizational activity to an outside supplier that will perform it on behalf of the focal firm.

FIGURE 4.2   A TWO-STAGE DECISION MODEL IN VALUE CHAIN ANALYSIS

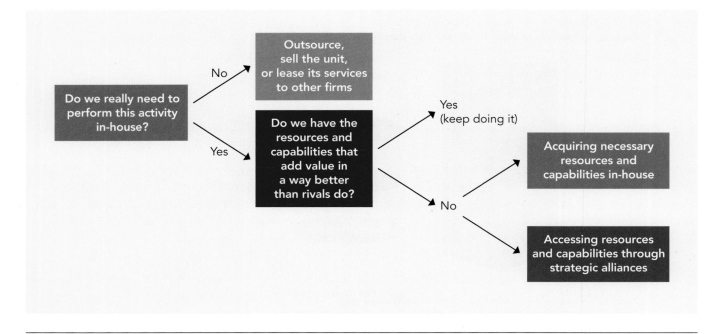

FIGURE 4.3   IN-HOUSE VERSUS OUTSOURCE

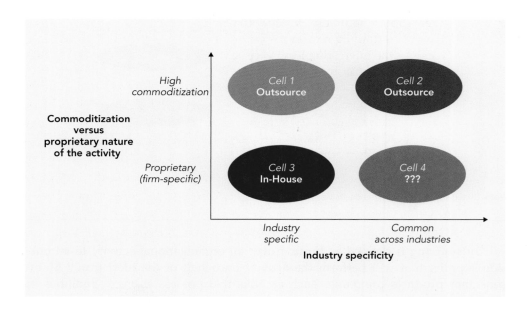

Note: At present, no clear guidelines exist for Cell 4, where firms either choose to perform activities in-house or outsource.

shared across firms or industries. Of course, this changing viewpoint is fueled by the rise of service providers such as EDS (now known as HP Enterprise Services) and Infosys in IT, Manpower in HR, Flextronics in contract manufacturing, and DHL and UPS in logistics. These specialist firms argue that such activities can be broken off from the various client firms (just as steel making was broken off from automakers decades ago) and leveraged to serve multiple clients with greater economies of scale.[13] For client firms, such outsourcing results in "leaner and meaner" organizations that can focus on core activities better (see Figure 4.1 Panel B).

If the answer to the question "Do we really need to perform this activity in-house?" is "Yes" (Cell 3 in Figure 4.3) but the firm's current resources and capabilities are not up to the task, then there are two second-stage choices (Figure 4.2). First, the firm may want to acquire and develop capabilities in-house so that it can perform this particular activity better. Or it may go with the second option if it does not have enough skills to develop these capabilities in-house and access them through strategic alliances. For example, neither Sony nor Ericsson was strong enough on their own to elbow into the competitive mobile handset market. So they formed a joint venture named Sony Ericsson to penetrate it.

Conspicuously absent in both Figures 4.2 and 4.3 is the *geographic* dimension—domestic versus foreign locations.[14] Because the two terms "outsourcing" and "offshoring" have emerged rather recently, there is a great deal of confusion, especially among some journalists who often casually (and erroneously) equate the two. So to minimize confusion, we identify four terms in Figure 4.4 based on locations and modes (in-house versus outsource):

- **captive sourcing**—setting up subsidiaries abroad (the work done is in-house but the location is foreign)
- **offshoring**—international/foreign outsourcing
- domestic in-house activity
- **inshoring**—domestic outsourcing[15]

Despite this set of new labels, we need to be aware that "offshoring" and "inshoring" are simply international and domestic variants of outsourcing, respectively, and that "captive sourcing" is conceptually identical to foreign direct investment (FDI), which is nothing new in the world of global business (see Chapters 1 and 6 for details). One interesting lesson we can take away from Figure 4.4 is that value-adding activities may be geographically dispersed around the world, even

FIGURE 4.4   LOCATION, LOCATION, LOCATION

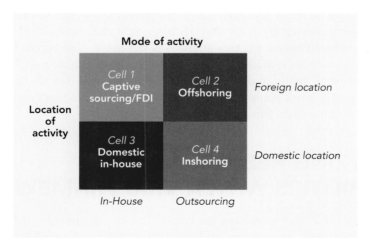

Note: "Captive sourcing" is a new term, which is conceptually identical to "foreign direct investment" (FDI), a term widely used in global business. See Chapter 6 for details.

Captive sourcing

Setting up subsidiaries abroad so that the work done is in-house but the location is foreign. Also known as foreign direct investment (FDI).

Offshoring

Outsourcing to an international or foreign firm.

Inshoring

Outsourcing to a domestic firm.

IN Focus 4.1

NCR: More Careful about Outsourcing

NCR is a leading US-based manufacturer of bank automated teller machines (ATMs) and supermarket self-checkout kiosks. In 2007, NCR shut down its own ATM factories in Canada and Scotland, and split ATM production between its own remaining factories and an outside supplier, Flextronics. Although Flextronics is a leader in contract manufacturing, NCR found that outsourcing to Flextronics was not worth it. A major headache was that because ATMs were so complex, NCR engineers often had to jet around the world to sort out design changes and production glitches, causing costly delays and customer frustration. These delays took place during a time NCR's customers—banks and supermarkets—were cutting back on spending but demanding more.

In response, in 2009, NCR changed course again, this time bringing back more outsourced production in-house and back home—to Columbus, Georgia. This doesn't mean NCR was ditching

outsourcing. It was just being more careful. Flextronics was still retained as an outsourced producer, whose scope of work was now limited to ATMs produced in larger quantities with less complexity. In Figure 4.4, Flextronics' work can be positioned in Cell 2 (offshoring). NCR used its own factories in Asia, Europe, and Latin America to serve these regions' high-end, more demanding customers (Cell 1 in Figure 4.4: FDI). It would supply North America entirely from its Columbus, Georgia, factory, employing 800 highly skilled workers. This can be positioned in Cell 3 in Figure 4.4: Domestic in-house manufacturing. NCR's saga suggests that value chain decisions regarding outsourcing versus in-house production needs to be examined and re-examined rigorously and continuously, and that outsourcing is not necessarily the panacea for competitiveness problems.

Sources: Based on (1) *BusinessWeek*, 2009, Why NCR said, "Let's go back home," August 24: 19; (2) www.ncr.com.

for a single firm, to take advantage of the best locations and modes to perform certain activities. For example, a Dell laptop may be designed in the United States (domestic in-house activity), its components may be produced by suppliers in Taiwan (offshoring) as well as the United States (inshoring), and its final assembly may be done in China (captive sourcing/FDI). When customers call for help, the call center may be with an outside service provider—Dell may have outsourced the service activities through offshoring.

Overall, a value chain analysis enables managers to ascertain a firm's strengths and weaknesses on an activity-by-activity basis, *relative to rivals*, in a SWOT analysis. As shown in In Focus 4.1, this analysis is not static. The recent proliferation of new labels is intimidating, causing some gurus to claim that "twenty-first century offshoring really is different."[16] In reality, we still see the time-honored SWOT analysis at work behind the new vocabulary. The next section introduces a framework on how to do this.

VRIO framework

The resource-based framework that focuses on the value (V), rarity (R), imitability (I), and organizational (O) aspects of resources and capabilities.

LEARNING OBJECTIVE 4

Explain what a VRIO framework is.

ANALYZING RESOURCES AND CAPABILITIES WITH A VRIO FRAMEWORK[17]

The resource-based view focuses on the value (V), rarity (R), imitability (I), and organizational (O) aspects of resources and capabilities, leading to a **VRIO framework**. Looking at a firm from the perspective of these four important aspects has a number of ramifications for competitive advantage (see Table 4.2). This framework can be illustrated by the example of Saturna in our Opening Case. Nicholas Kaiser's exceptional talent as an investment manager is certainly *valuable*. What is *rare* is Kaiser's ability,

TABLE 4.2   THE VRIO FRAMEWORK: IS A RESOURCE OR CAPABILITY . . .

Valuable?	Rare?	Costly to imitate?	Exploited by organization?	Competitive implications	Firm performance
No	—	—	No	Competitive disadvantage	Below average
Yes	No	—	Yes	Competitive parity	Average
Yes	Yes	No	Yes	Temporary competitive advantage	Above average
Yes	Yes	Yes	Yes	Sustained competitive advantage	Persistently above average

Sources: Adapted from (1) J. Barney, 2002, *Gaining and Sustaining Competitive Advantage*, 2nd ed. (p. 173), Upper Saddle River, NJ: Prentice Hall; (2) R. Hoskisson, M. Hitt, & R. D. Ireland, 2004, *Competing for Advantage* (p. 118), Cincinnati: South-Western Cengage Learning.

as a non-Muslim, native-born American, to make Islamic finance principles work for Saturna's clients. Bundling exceptional American investment talent with Islamic finance principles makes it challenging for rivals to *imitate* this unbeatable combination. Given the uneasy relationship between the United States and the Muslim world since "9/11," Saturna's non-Muslim American clients may be reluctant to let an investment company led by a Muslim run their investments. The fact that Kaiser is a native-born American who is not a Muslim himself serves to reassure Saturna's non-Muslim clients that their investments are "safe." Although relatively small, Saturna is a 40-person company that has a lot more *organizational* resources and capabilities than a lot of smaller investment firms that are essentially one-man (or one-woman) shows. In short, Saturna's success can be explained by its ability to overcome the VRIO hurdles—a point that we develop more systematically in the next four sections.

Value

Do firm resources and capabilities add value? Value chain analysis suggests that this is the most fundamental question.[18] Only value-adding resources can possibly lead to competitive advantage, whereas non-value-adding capabilities may lead to competitive *disadvantage*. As the competitive landscape changes, what was previously value-adding may become obsolete. The evolution of IBM is a case in point. IBM historically has excelled in making hardware, including tabulating machines in the 1930s, mainframes in the 1960s, and personal computers (PCs) in the 1980s. However, as competition for hardware heats up, IBM's core capabilities in hardware not only add little value but increase core rigidities, which hinder its efforts to move into new areas.[19] Since the 1990s, IBM has focused on more lucrative software and services and has developed new value-adding capabilities. Now it is an on-demand computing *service* provider for corporations. As part of this new strategy, IBM sold its PC division to China's Lenovo in 2004.

The relationship between valuable resources and capabilities and a firm's performance is straightforward. Non-value-adding resources and capabilities, such as IBM's historical expertise in hardware, may become weaknesses instead of strengths. If firms are unable to get rid of non-value-adding resources and capabilities, they are likely to suffer below-average performance.[20] In the ongoing recession, consumers no longer purchase luxury goods when the goods are no longer viewed as valuable. In 2009, fashion design houses such as France's Christian Lacroix and Germany's Escada went bankrupt.[21] On the other hand, the 50-year-old Barbie provides some inspiration on how to *continuously* add value in the eyes of some of the most fickle consumers (In Focus 4.2).

Barbie at 50

© Scott Houston/Sygma/Corbis

Frowned upon by feminists but fought over by five-year-olds, Barbie has been a victim of controversy as much as fashion ever since her birth 50 years ago in March 1959. The charge sheet against the pint-sized piece of plastic is long. She teaches the supremacy of looks over substance; she stereotypes outdated gender roles; she celebrates an impossible body ideal; and she spreads platinum hair, plastic limbs, and a nauseating shade of pink into households from Honolulu to Hamburg.

Yet, could it be that Barbie, far from being a relic from another era, is in fact a woman for our troubled economic times? For a start, she may benefit from having a strong, reassuring brand in a downturn. Although global Barbie sales fell by 9% in 2008, battering profits at Mattel, her maker, Barbie topped the 2008 survey by America's National Retail Federation of the most popular girls' toys, relegating even the Nintendo Wii to fifth place. And she has just seen off her hipper rival, Bratz. After a long legal battle, a federal judge recently ordered Bratz's maker, MGA, to transfer the trademark rights to Mattel.* Barbie is once again the queen of the toyshop. In previous recessions toy sales held up reasonably well, as parents cut back elsewhere.

As the recession deepens, Barbie's conservative values are also back in vogue. Amid concern about rampant individualism and excess, she evokes a simpler, gentler era. And since staying in is the new going out, little girls will have more time for old-fashioned play.

Barbie also embodies career flexibility, a valuable attribute in difficult times. Having starting out as a fashion model in a black-and-white striped bathing suit, she tiptoed into other professions as fast as they were invented. She was a flight attendant in the 1960s as mass aviation took off, an aerobics instructor with leg-warmers in the 1980s, and even a black presidential candidate four years before Barack Obama. Time for a new Barbie, dressed as a distressed-debt investor?

Source: *Economist*, 2009, Barbie at 50: In the pink, March 7: 72. © Economist Group. Reprinted by permission.

*[Editor's Note] In 2001, MGA launched the Bratz dolls. In 2004, Mattel sued. In 2008, a jury ruled that Mattel, not MGA, owns the Bratz line because Bratz's designer worked for Mattel when he created Bratz. Retailers quickly stopped ordering Bratz, whose sales collapsed. As of late 2009, MGA is still appealing the verdict.

Rarity

Simply possessing valuable resources and capabilities may not be enough. The next question is: How rare are the valuable resources and capabilities? At best, valuable but common resources and capabilities will lead to competitive parity but no advantage. Consider the identical aircraft made by Boeing and Airbus and used by Southwest, Ryanair, and most other airlines. The aircraft are certainly valuable, but it is difficult to derive competitive advantage from the aircraft alone. Airlines have to compete on how to use the same aircraft differently. The same is true for

bar codes, enterprise resource planning (ERP) software, and radio frequency identification (RFID) tags. Their developers are too willing to sell them everywhere,
thus undermining their novelty (or rarity).

Resources and capabilities must, therefore, be both valuable and *rare* to have
the potential to provide some temporary competitive advantage. However cliché,
rarity boils down to a simple point: If everyone has it, you can't make money from
it. For example, the quality of the American Big Three automakers is now comparable with the best Asian and European rivals. But high quality is now expected by
car buyers and is no longer rare, so it provides no advantage. Case in point: Even
in their home country, the Big Three's quality improvements have not translated
into stronger sales. The point is simple: Flawless high quality is now expected
among car buyers, is no longer rare, and thus provides no advantage.

Imitability

Valuable and rare resources and capabilities can be a source of competitive advantage only if they are also difficult to imitate by competitors. Although it is relatively
easier to imitate a firm's *tangible* resources such as plants, it is a lot more challenging
and often impossible to imitate *intangible* capabilities such as tacit knowledge, superior motivation, and managerial talents.[22] In an effort to maintain a high-quality
manufacturing edge, many Japanese firms intentionally employ "super technicians" (or *supaa ginosha*)—an honor designated by the Japanese government—to
handle mission-critical work, such as mounting tiny chips onto circuit boards for
laptops at Sharp. The quality of the work performance of these super technicians is
better than robots.[23] Although robots can be purchased by rivals, no robots, and few
humans elsewhere, can imitate the skills and dedication of these super technicians.

Imitation is difficult. Why? In two words: **causal ambiguity**, which means the
difficulty of identifying the actual cause of a firm's successful performance.[24] For
three decades, Toyota has been meticulously studied by automakers and even
nonautomakers around the world. Yet no one has figured out what exactly gives
Toyota its edge, so no one has been able to challenge it. In the past 25 years during
which every firm has allegedly been "learning from Toyota," Toyota's productivity has grown sevenfold, twice as much as Detroit's finest despite their serious
efforts to keep up.

A natural question is: How can Toyota do it? Usually a number of resources and
capabilities will be nominated, including its legendary "Toyota production system," its aggressive ambition, and its mystical organizational culture. Even though
all of these resources and capabilities are plausible, what *exactly* is it? Knowing
the answer to this question is not only intriguing to scholars and students, it can
also be hugely profitable for Toyota's rivals. Unfortunately, outsiders usually have
a hard time understanding what a firm does inside its boundaries. We can try, as
many rivals have, to identify Toyota's recipe for success by drawing up a long list
of possible reasons labeled as resources and capabilities in our classroom discussion. But in the final analysis, as outsiders we are not sure.[25]

What is even more fascinating for scholars and students, and frustrating for
rivals, is that managers of a focal firm such as Toyota often do not know exactly
what contributes to their success. When interviewed, they can usually generate
a long list of what they do well, such as a strong organizational culture, a relentless drive, and many other attributes. To make matters worse, different managers
of the same firm may suggest different lists. When probed as to which resource
or capability is "it," they usually suggest that it is all of the above in *combination*. This is probably one of the most interesting (and frustrating) aspects of the

Causal ambiguity
The difficulty of identifying
the causal determinants of
successful firm performance.

resource-based view: If insiders have a hard time figuring out what unambiguously contributes to their firm's performance, it is not surprising that outsiders' efforts in understanding and imitating these capabilities are usually flawed and often fail.[26]

Overall, valuable and rare but imitable resources and capabilities may give firms some temporary competitive advantage, leading to above-average performance for some time. But such an advantage is not likely to be sustainable. As the Toyota example shows, only valuable, rare, and *hard-to-imitate* resources and capabilities may potentially lead to sustained competitive advantage. But even sustained competitive advantage does not mean it will last forever. In 2010, Toyota painfully recalled millions of vehicles due to accelerator irregularities, severely eroding its competitive advantage.

Organization

Even valuable, rare, and hard-to-imitate resources and capabilities may not give a firm sustained competitive advantage if the firm is not properly organized. Although movie stars represent some of the most valuable, rare, hard-to-imitate, and certainly highest-paid resources, *most* movies flop. More generally, the question of organization asks: How should a firm such as a movie studio be organized to develop and leverage the full potential of its resources and capabilities?

Numerous components within a firm are relevant to the question of organization.[27] In a movie studio, these components include talents in "smelling" good ideas, photographers, musicians, singers, makeup specialists, animation artists, and managers on the business side who deal with sponsors, distributors, and local sites. These components are often called **complementary assets**,[28] because they cannot generate box office hits by themselves. For the last movie you saw, did you remember the name of the makeup artist? Of course not—you probably only remember the stars. However, stars alone cannot generate hit movies either. It is the *combination* of star resources and complementary assets that create hit movies. "It may be that not just a few resources and capabilities enable a firm to gain a competitive advantage but that literally thousands of these organizational attributes, bundled together, generate such advantage."[29]

Another idea is **social complexity**, which refers to the socially intricate and interdependent ways firms are typically organized. Many multinationals consist of thousands of people scattered throughout many different countries. How they overcome cultural differences and achieve common organizational goals is profoundly complex. Oftentimes it is their invisible relationships that add value.[30] Such organizationally embedded capabilities are thus very difficult for rivals to imitate. This emphasis on social complexity refutes what is half-jokingly called the "Lego" view of the firm, in which a firm can be assembled and disassembled from modules of technology and people, like Lego toy blocks. By treating employees as identical and replaceable blocks, the Lego view fails to realize that the social capital associated with complex relationships and knowledge permeating many firms can be a source of competitive advantage.

Overall, only valuable, rare, and hard-to-imitate resources and capabilities that are organizationally embedded and exploited can possibly lead to persistently above-average performance. Because resources and capabilities cannot be evaluated in isolation, the VRIO framework presents four interconnected and increasingly difficult hurdles for them to become a source of sustainable competitive advantage (Table 4.2). In other words, V, R, I, and O come together as one package.

Complementary assets

The combination of numerous resources and assets that enable a firm to gain a competitive advantage.

Social complexity

The socially intricate and interdependent ways firms are typically organized.

DEBATES AND EXTENSIONS

Like the institution-based viewed outlined in Chapters 2 and 3, the resource-based view has its fair share of controversies and debates. Here, we introduce two leading debates: (1) domestic resources versus international (cross-border) capabilities and (2) offshoring versus not offshoring.

LEARNING OBJECTIVE 5

Participate in two leading debates on leveraging resources and capabilities.

Domestic Resources versus International (Cross-Border) Capabilities

Do firms that are successful domestically have what it takes to win internationally? If you ask managers at The Limited Brands, their answer would be "No." The Limited Brands is the number one US fashion retailer. It has a successful retail empire of 4,000 stores throughout the country and leading brands such as The Limited, Victoria's Secret, and Bath & Body Works. Yet, it has refused to go abroad—not even Canada. On the other hand, the ubiquitous retail outlets of LVMH, Zara, and United Colors of Benetton in major cities around the world suggest that their answer would be "Yes!"

Some domestically successful firms continue to succeed overseas. For example, Swedish furniture retailer IKEA has found that its Scandinavian-style furniture combined with do-it-yourself, flat packaging is popular around the globe. IKEA thus has become a global cult brand. The young generation in Russia is now known as the "IKEA Generation." However, many other firms that are formidable domestically are burned badly overseas. Wal-Mart withdrew from Germany and South Korea. Similarly, Wal-Mart's leading global rival, France's Carrefour, had to exit the Czech Republic, Japan, Mexico, and South Korea recently. Starbucks has failed to turn its bitter brew into sweet profits overseas.

Are domestic resources and cross-border capabilities essentially the same? The answer can be either "Yes" or "No." This debate is an extension of the larger debate on whether international business (IB) is different from domestic business. The argument that IB is different from domestic business is precisely the argument for having stand-alone IB courses in business schools. If the two are essentially the same, then it is possible to argue that IB fundamentally is about "business," which is well covered by strategy, finance, and other courses (most textbooks in these areas have at least one chapter on "international topics"). This question is obviously very important for companies and business schools. However, there is no right or wrong answer.

Offshoring versus Not Offshoring

As noted earlier, offshoring—or, more specifically, international (offshore) outsourcing—has emerged as a leading corporate movement in the 21st century. Outsourcing low-end manufacturing to countries such as China and Mexico is now widely practiced. But increased outsourcing of more high-end services, particularly IT and other business process outsourcing (BPO) services, to countries such as India is controversial. Because digitization and commoditization of service work is enabled only by the very recent rise of the Internet and the reduction of international communication costs, it is debatable whether such offshoring proves to be a long-term benefit or hindrance to Western firms and economies.[31]

In recent years, some firms have offshored their customer service operations. What are the advantages and disadvantages of this practice?

Proponents argue that offshoring creates enormous value for firms and economies. Western firms are able to tap into low-cost yet high-quality labor, translating into significant cost savings. Firms can also focus on their core capabilities, which may add more value than dealing with noncore (and often uncompetitive) activities. In turn, offshoring service providers, such as Infosys and Wipro, develop *their* core competencies in IT/BPO. A McKinsey study reported that for every dollar spent by US firms' offshoring in India, the US firms save 58 cents (see Table 4.3). Overall, $1.46 of new wealth is created, of which the US economy captures $1.13, through cost savings and increased exports to India, which buys made-in-USA equipment, software, and services. India captures the other 33 cents through profits, wages, and taxes.[32] Although acknowledging that some US employees may regrettably lose their jobs, offshoring proponents suggest that on balance, offshoring is a win-win solution for both US and Indian firms and economies. In other words, offshoring can be conceptualized as the latest incarnation of international trade (in tradable services), which theoretically will bring mutual gains to all involved countries (see Chapter 5).

Critics of offshoring make three points on strategic, economic, and political grounds. Strategically, according to some outsourcing gurus, if "even core functions like engineering, R&D, manufacturing, and marketing can—and often should—be moved outside,"[33] what is left of the firm? In manufacturing, US firms have gone down this path before with disastrous results. In the 1960s, Radio Corporation of America (RCA) invented the color TV and then outsourced its production to Japan, a *low-cost* country at that time. Fast forward to 2010: the United States no longer has any US-owned color TV producers left. The nationality of RCA itself, after being bought and sold several times, is now *Chinese* (France's Thomson sold RCA to China's TCL in 2003). Critics argue that offshoring nurtures rivals.[34] Why are Indian IT/BPO firms now emerging as strong rivals to EDS and IBM? It is in part because they built up their capabilities doing work for EDS and IBM in the 1990s, particularly by working to help the IT industry prevent the "millennium bug" (Y2K) problem.

TABLE 4.3   BENEFIT OF $1 US SPENDING ON OFFSHORING TO INDIA

Benefit to the United States	$	Benefit to India	$
Savings accruing to US investors/customers	0.58	Labor	0.10
Exports of US goods/services to providers in India	0.05	Profits retained in India	0.10
Profit transfer by US-owned operations in India back to the United States	0.04	Suppliers	0.09
Net direct benefit retained in the United States	*0.67*	Central government taxes	0.03
Value from US labor reemployed	0.46	State government taxes	0.01
Net benefit to the United States	*1.13*	*Net benefit to India*	*0.33*

Source: Based on text in D. Farrell, 2005, Offshoring: Value creation through economic change, *Journal of Management Studies*, 42: 675–683. Farrell is director of the McKinsey Global Institute, and she refers to a McKinsey study.

In manufacturing, many Asian firms, which used to be **original equipment manufacturers (OEMs)** executing design blueprints provided by Western firms, now want to have a piece of the action in design by becoming **original design manufacturers (ODMs)** (see Figure 4.5). Having mastered low-cost and high-quality manufacturing, Asian firms such as BenQ, Compal, Flextronics, Hon Hai, HTC, and Huawei are indeed capable of capturing some design function from Western firms such as Dell, HP, Kodak, and Nokia. Therefore, increasing outsourcing of design work by Western firms may accelerate their own long-run demise. A number of Asian OEMs, now quickly becoming ODMs, have openly announced that their real ambition is to become **original brand manufacturers (OBMs)**. Thus, according to critics of offshoring, isn't the writing already on the wall? A new case in point is the inability of US firms to manufacture the Amazon Kindle (see the Closing Case).

Economically, critics contend that they are not sure whether developed economies, on the whole, actually gain more. Although shareholders and corporate high-flyers embrace offshoring (see Chapter 1), offshoring increasingly results in job losses in high-end areas such as design, R&D, and IT/BPO. Even though white-collar individuals who lose jobs will naturally hate it, the net impact (consolidating all economic gains and losses including job losses) on developed economies may still be negative (see the Closing Case).

Finally, critics make the political argument that many large US firms claim that they are global companies and, consequently, that they should neither represent nor be bound by American values any more. According to this view, all these firms are interested in is the cheapest and most exploitable labor. Not only is work commoditized, people (such as IT programmers) are degraded as tradable commodities that can be jettisoned. As a result, large firms that outsource work to emerging economies are often accused of being unethical, destroying jobs at home, ignoring corporate social responsibility, violating customer privacy (for example, by sending medical records, tax returns, and credit card numbers to be processed

FIGURE 4.5   FROM ORIGINAL *EQUIPMENT* MANUFACTURER (OEM) TO ORIGINAL *DESIGN* MANUFACTURER (ODM)

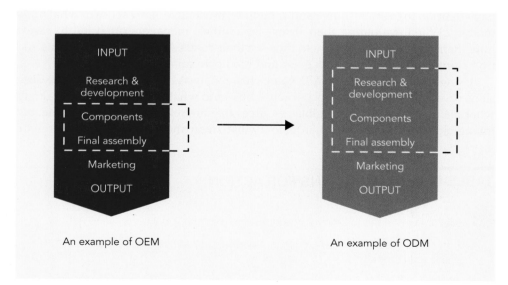

An example of OEM   An example of ODM

Note: Dotted lines represent organizational boundaries. A further extension is to become an original *brand* manufacturer (OBM), which would incorporate brand ownership and management in the marketing area. For graphic simplicity, it is not shown here.

Original equipment manufacturer (OEM)

A firm that executes design blueprints provided by other firms and manufactures such products.

Original design manufacturer (ODM)

A firm that both designs and manufactures products.

Original brand manufacturer (OBM)

A firm that designs, manufactures, and markets branded products.

overseas), and in some cases undermining national security. Not surprisingly, the debate often becomes political, emotional, and explosive when such accusations are made.

For firms in developed economies, the choice is not really offshoring versus not offshoring, but *where* to draw the line on offshoring. It is important to note that this debate primarily takes place in developed economies. There is relatively little debate in emerging economies because they clearly stand to gain from such offshoring to them. Taking a page from the Indian playbook, the Philippines, with numerous English-speaking professionals, is trying to eat some of India's lunch. Northeast China, where Japanese is widely taught, is positioning itself as an ideal location for call centers for Japan.[35] Central and Eastern Europe gravitates towards serving Western Europe. Central and South American countries want to grab call center contracts for the large Hispanic market in the United States.

LEARNING OBJECTIVE

6

Draw implications for action.

MANAGEMENT SAVVY

How does the resource-based view answer the big question in global business: What determines the success and failure of firms around the globe? The answer is straightforward. Fundamentally, some firms outperform others because they possess some valuable, rare, hard-to-imitate, and organizationally embedded resources and capabilities that competitors do not have.[36] This view is especially insightful when we see firms such as Mattel (the maker of Barbie in In Focus 4.2) persistently succeed in difficult industries while their competitors struggle.

The resource-based view thus suggests four implications for action (see Table 4.4). First, the proposition that firms "compete on resources and capabilities" is not novel. The subtlety comes when managers attempt, via the VRIO framework, to distinguish resources and capabilities that are valuable, rare, hard-to-imitate, and organizationally embedded from those that do not share these attributes. In other words, the VRIO framework can greatly aid the time-honored SWOT analysis, especially the S (strengths) and W (weaknesses) parts. Managers, who cannot pay attention to every resource and capability, must have some sense of what *really* matters. When evaluating their firms' capabilities, managers often fail to assess how their capabilities compare to those of their rivals. As a result, most firms end up having a mixed bag of both good and mediocre capabilities.

Using the VRIO framework, a value chain analysis helps managers make decisions on what capabilities to focus on in-house and what to outsource. Increasingly, what really matters is not tangible resources that are relatively easy to imitate, but intangible capabilities that are harder for rivals to wrap their arms around. At present,

---

TABLE 4.4   IMPLICATIONS FOR ACTION

- Managers need to build firm strengths based on the VRIO framework.
- Relentless imitation or benchmarking, while important, is not likely to be a successful strategy.
- Managers need to build up resources and capabilities for future competition.
- Students need to make yourself into an "untouchable" whose job cannot be easily outsourced.

as much as 75% of the value of publicly traded corporations in the United States comes from intangible, knowledge-based assets, up from approximately 40% in the early 1980s.[37] This is a crucial reason that we often label the new global economy as a "knowledge-based economy." Therefore, managers need to identify, develop, and leverage valuable, rare, hard-to-imitate, and organizationally embedded resources and capabilities, which are often intangible. It is thus not surprising that capabilities that don't meet these criteria are increasingly outsourced.

Second, relentless imitation or benchmarking, although important, is not likely to be enough. Follower firms have a tendency to mimic the most visible and, consequently, the *least* important practices of winning firms. At best, follower firms that meticulously replicate every resource possessed by winning firms can hope to attain competitive parity. Firms endowed with enough resources to imitate others may be better off by developing their own unique capabilities. This is a challenge confronting ambitious firms such as Hyundai that want to join the top league in the world (In Focus 4.3).

Third, even a sustainable competitive advantage will not last forever, particularly in today's global competition. All a firm can hope for is to sustain a competitive advantage for as long as possible. However, over time, all advantages may erode. As noted earlier, each of IBM's product-related advantages associated with tabulating machines, mainframes, and PCs were sustained for a period of time. But eventually, these advantages disappeared. In another example, Toyota's legendary advantages have been severely eroded when some of its vehicles allegedly experienced uncontrollable acceleration, which forced Toyota to recall millions of vehicles in 2010. Therefore, the lesson for all firms, including current market leaders, is to develop strategic *foresight*—"over-the-horizon radar" is a good metaphor. Such strategic foresight enables them to anticipate future needs and move early to identify, develop, and leverage resources and capabilities for future competition.[38]

IN Focus 4.3

Hyundai's Uphill Battle

Would you be surprised that Hyundai's Genesis was named the North American Car of the Year for 2009 by its auto industry peers, beating all the usual suspects? Would you believe an authoritative J.D. Power survey reported that Hyundai has better quality than Toyota and Honda? Trouble is, just like you, most American car buyers don't buy it. Only 23% of all new-car buyers in the United States bother to consider buying a Hyundai. This compares with 65% and 50% for Toyota and Honda, respectively (before Toyota's mass recalls in 2010).

Make no mistake: Hyundai is very capable. It is the fastest-growing automaker in the US market in the 2000s. Between 2008 and 2009, it *doubled* its market share from 2% to 4%, whereas most rivals lost market share. Hyundai benefitted from

consumers' desire to "trade down" in hard times. Elbowing its way into the entry-level market, Hyundai captured many value-conscious buyers, who appreciated the more *tangible* equipment and performance at lower prices. For high-end buyers, it is the *intangible* reputation and mystique that count. Hyundai audaciously compared its Genesis luxury sedan with both the BMW 5 series and the Lexus ES350, but does Hyundai have what it takes to win the hearts, minds, and wallets of high-end car buyers?

Sources: Based on (1) *BusinessWeek*, 2007, Hyundai still gets no respect, May 21: 68–70; (2) *Economist*, 2009, Sui Genesis, March 7: 71; (3) PR Newswire, 2009, Hyundai leads all automotive brands in market share growth this year, November 3, www.prnewswire.com; (4) www.jdpower.com.

Finally, here is a very personal and relevant implication for action. As a student who is probably studying this book in a developed (read: high-wage and thus high-cost!) country such as the United States, you may be wondering: What do I get out of this? How do I cope with the frightening future of global competition? There are two lessons you can draw. First, the whole debate on offshoring, a part of the larger debate on globalization, is very relevant and directly affects your future as a manager, a consumer, and a citizen (see Chapter 1). So don't be a couch potato! You should be active, get involved, and be prepared because it is not only "their" debate, it is *yours* as well. Second, be very serious about the VRIO framework of the resource-based view. Although the resource-based view has been developed to advise firms, there is no reason you cannot develop that into a resource-based view of the *individual*. In other words, you can use the VRIO framework to make yourself into an "untouchable"—a person whose job cannot be outsourced, as Thomas Friedman defines it in *The World is Flat* (2005). An untouchable individual's job cannot be outsourced because he or she possesses valuable, rare, and hard-to-imitate capabilities indispensable to an organization. This won't be easy. But you really don't want to be mediocre. A generation ago, parents told their kids: "Eat your food—kids in China and India are starving." Now, Friedman would advise you: "Study this book and leverage your education—students in China and India are starving for your job."[39]

CHAPTER SUMMARY

1. Define resources and capabilities.
   - "Resources" and "capabilities" are tangible and intangible assets a firm uses to choose and implement its strategies.

2. Explain how value is created from a firm's resources and capabilities.
   - A value chain consists of a stream of activities from upstream to downstream that add value.
   - A SWOT analysis engages managers to ascertain a firm's strengths and weaknesses on an activity-by-activity basis relative to rivals.

3. Articulate the difference between keeping an activity in-house and outsourcing it.
   - Outsourcing is defined as turning over all or part of an organizational activity to an outside supplier.
   - An activity with a high degree of industry commonality and a high degree of commoditization can be outsourced, and an industry-specific and firm-specific (proprietary) activity is better performed in-house.
   - On any given activity, the four choices for managers in terms of modes and locations are (1) offshoring, (2) inshoring, (3) captive sourcing/FDI, and (4) domestic in-house activity.

4. Explain what a VRIO framework is.
   - A VRIO framework centers on value (V), rarity (R), imitability (I), and organizational (O) attributes of resources and capabilities.
   - A VRIO framework suggests that only resources and capabilities that are valuable, rare, inimitable, and organizationally embedded will generate sustainable competitive advantage.

5. Participate in two leading debates on leveraging resources and capabilities.
   • Are domestic capabilities the same as international (cross-border) capabilities?
   • For Western firms and economies, is offshoring beneficial or detrimental in the long run?

6. Draw implications for action.
   • Managers need to build firm strengths based on the VRIO framework.
   • Relentless imitation or benchmarking, although important, is not likely to be a successful strategy.
   • Managers need to build up resources and capabilities for future competition.
   • Students are advised to make yourself into an "untouchable" whose job cannot be outsourced.

KEY TERMS

Benchmarking   98
Capability   97
Captive sourcing   101
Causal ambiguity   105
Commoditization   98
Complementary assets   106
Inshoring   101
Intangible resources and capabilities   98

Offshoring   101
Original brand manufacturer (OBM)   109
Original design manufacturer (ODM)   109
Original equipment manufacturer (OEM)   109
Outsourcing   99
Resource   97

Resource-based view   96
Social complexity   106
SWOT analysis   96
Tangible resources and capabilities   97
Value chain   98
VRIO framework   102

REVIEW QUESTIONS

1. Describe at least three types of tangible and intangible resources and capabilities.

2. Explain the differences between primary activities and support activities in a value chain.

3. What is meant by "commoditization?"

4. When analyzing a value chain with a VRIO framework, what is the most important question to begin with and why?

5. How does the rarity of a firm's resources and capabilities affect its competitive advantage?

6. Which is more difficult: imitating a firm's tangible resources or its intangible resources?

7. How do complementary assets and social complexity influence a firm's organization?

8. If a firm is successful domestically, is it likely to be successful internationally? Why or why not?

9. After reviewing the arguments for and against offshoring, state your opinion on this issue.

10. Identify a developed economy on PengAtlas Map 1.1 and explain why it might be the location of offshoring from a firm in an emerging economy.

11. What is one common mistake that managers often make when evaluating their firm's capabilities?

12. What is the likely result of relentless imitation or benchmarking?

13. How would you characterize strategic foresight?

14. Check PengAtlas Map 1.1 and imagine that your firm is headquartered in a developed economy. Pick an emerging economy in which your firm may enter. Explain your firm's resources and capabilities that may enable it to succeed in this new market.

CRITICAL DISCUSSION QUESTIONS

1. Pick any pair of rivals (such as Samsung/Sony, Nokia/Motorola, Boeing/Airbus, and Cisco/Huawei) and explain why one outperforms another.

2. Rank your business school relative to the top three rival schools in terms of the following six dimensions. If you were the dean with a limited budget, from a VRIO standpoint, where would you invest precious financial resources to make your school number one among rivals? Why?

	Your school	Competitor 1	Competitor 2	Competitor 3
Perceived reputation				
Faculty strength				
Student quality				
Administrative efficiency				
Information systems				
Building maintenance				

3. *ON ETHICS*: Since managers read information posted on competitors' websites, is it ethical to provide false information on resources and capabilities on corporate websites? Do the benefits outweigh the costs?

GLOBAL ACTION

1. Currently, your firm has manufacturing and logistics units in the Russian cities of Moscow and Saint Petersburg, which provide access to Russia's vast country-wide market. However, recent business regulations have discouraged growth in specific portions of the country. As such, you have been asked to reconfigure your firm's strategy in Russia. Using the globalEDGE website, identify the location(s) where you should move operations. Provide detailed and compelling rationale to support your decision.

2. The technology company that you work for wants to enter a foreign market for the first time. The objective is for the firm to make a sustainable international investment that can create long-term competitive advantages and allow it to be recognized as important in the industry. Evaluate the opportunities available to your company by assessing the national conditions among leading emerging economies, data available on the globalEDGE website.

VIDEO CASES

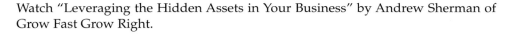

Watch "Leveraging the Hidden Assets in Your Business" by Andrew Sherman of Grow Fast Grow Right.

1. Although Sherman did not specifically refer to "SWOT," how did he illustrate one element of SWOT analysis?

2. Sherman referred to a professor who claims that the balance sheets of S&P 500 companies reflect only 15% of their value. What point was this professor trying to make?

3. Sherman urged small business people to find "Rembrandts in the attic." What did he mean by that? How does one do that?

4. Do you agree with Sherman's comments about intellectual capital? For a small business firm seeking to expand globally, how does leveraging intellectual capital compare with leveraging financial capital?

5. Imagine that you own a small firm that has a limited amount of expertise in technology but you are concerned about your lack of expertise in many other areas of business. How could leveraging your expertise provide a means of obtaining the capabilities that you lack?

Closing Case

ETHICAL DILEMMA

Why Amazon's Kindle Cannot Be Made in the United States

© Marcus Brandt/dpa/Landov

The Amazon Kindle is a revolutionary e-reader device developed by Amazon's Lab126 unit based in California. Kindle 1, which retailed for $399 and could hold approximately 200 e-books, sold out in its first six *hours* when it debuted in November 2007. In October 2009, Amazon unleashed Kindle 2, which was lighter, could hold 1,500 e-books, and had a more attractive price tag: $259. For such a cutting-edge, high-tech product, unfortunately, no US-based manufacturer is able to make it in the United States. Its components are made in China, Taiwan, and South Korea, and its final assembly is in China.

Why Kindle cannot be made in its home country has become "Exhibit A" in the debate about the future of the US economy. Since no US-based manufacturer has the capabilities to produce Kindle at home, Amazon has no choice but to outsource Kindle's production to Asia. Critics argue that after decades of outsourcing production to low-cost countries, US firms have not only lost millions of low-skill jobs, but also the ability to make the next generation of high-tech, high-value goods. In addition to Kindle, the not-made-in-USA list includes electric-car batteries, light-emitting diodes, and carbon-fiber components of Boeing's 787 Dreamliner.

The common belief is that as long as US firms control upstream R&D and design activities and downstream branding, marketing, and distribution services in a value chain, their competitiveness will remain unchallenged in global competition. Outsourcing basic manufacturing will not be a grave problem. However, critics argue that when a large chunk of value-adding activities, such as manufacturing, is taken out of a country, employment opportunities for these activities shrink, experienced people change careers, and smart students avoid these "dead-end" fields. Eventually, a critical mass of capabilities is lost, and will no longer be able to support upstream and downstream activities, which will be forced to migrate too.

Consider the migration of PC production. Original equipment manufacturers (OEMs) in Asia, for sure, offered compelling low-cost solutions to US firms. US firms initially did not feel threatened. However, product innovation for new gadgets and process innovation in manufacturing are intertwined. PC designers need to frequently interact with manufacturing specialists in order to optimize the design. When the loss of US-based manufacturing makes US design engineers less able to handle complex new designs, plenty of such opportunities to work with manufacturing specialists in Asia makes Asian design engineers more capable. Thus, the erosion of PC manufacturing capabilities leads to the erosion of PC design skills. Ferocious product market competition often forces US firms then to relinquish the design function to their Asian suppliers, which then become original design manufacturers (ODMs) (see Figure 4.5). Of course, one solution is to jettison a US PC brand all together, as evidenced by IBM's sale of its PC division to China's Lenovo. Lenovo thus becomes an original brand manufacturer (OBM). Today for all the remaining US-owned PC brands, with the exception of Apple, every laptop is not only manufactured but also designed in Asia. Competing with them are a bunch of PC brands from Taiwan, such as Acer, BenQ, ASUS, Advantech, HTC, and MSI—in addition to Lenovo from China and Samsung and LG from South Korea.

Nevertheless, the migration of PC production still fits the theory of product life cycle (that is, US-based firms manufactured and designed PCs first, and then gradually the production and design functions migrated to Asia). However, the theory of product life cycle no longer seems valid in the case of Amazon Kindle. US-based firms simply do not have a chance to manufacture it, which does not generate a single US manufacturing job at a time when the US unemployment rate is sky-high. In another high-tech industry, the $30 billion global solar industry, the United States has a chance to be a contender in manufacturing. But odds are not great. This is because the United States produces just 5% of the world's solar panel cells, whereas China is already the number-one player making 35%.

General Electric (GE) CEO Jeff Immelt has recently admitted that GE has probably gone too far in outsourcing. He has labeled the notion that the United States could remain an economic superpower by relying solely on services and consumption "flat wrong." Recently, Ford chairman Bill Ford and Dow Chemical CEO Andrew Liveris have openly called for "industrial policy," an unpopular term (in the United States at least) that is otherwise known

as government intervention by picking winners. However, by bailing out Detroit and rescuing Wall Street, the Obama administration is being dragged into "industrial policy" without much of a clear long-term policy. At a time when global competition is heating up, how to beef up the manufacturing (and other) capabilities of US firms in order to enhance US competitiveness undoubtedly remains job number one for numerous executives and policymakers. But what does the future hold for Amazon Kindle 3?

Case Discussion Questions:

1. From a resource-based view, what resources and capabilities do Asian firms involved in the production of Amazon Kindle have that US firms do not have?
2. What are the differences between the production of PCs and the production of Amazon Kindle?
3. From an institution-based view, what should the US government do to foster US competitiveness?

Sources: Based on (1) *BusinessWeek*, 2009, Can the future be built in America? September 21: 46–51; (2) *BusinessWeek*, 2009, Top 20 Taiwan global brands 2009, November 23: 43; (3) C. Weigelt, 2009, The impact of outsourcing new technologies on integrative capabilities and performance, *Strategic Management Journal*, 30: 595–616; (4) L. Pierce, 2009, Big losses in ecosystem niches: How core firm decisions drive complementary product shakeouts, *Strategic Management Journal*, 30: 323–347; (5) G. Pisano & W. Shih, 2009, Restoring American competitiveness, *Harvard Business Review*, July–August: 114–125; (6) Y. Su, E. Tsang, & M. W. Peng, 2009, How do internal capabilities and external partnerships affect innovativeness? *Asia Pacific Journal of Management*, 26: 309–331.

NOTES

[Journal acronyms] **AME**—*Academy of Management Executive;* **AMJ**—*Academy of Management Journal;* **AMR**—*Academy of Management Review;* **BW**—*BusinessWeek;* **CBR**—*China Business Review;* **HBR**—*Harvard Business Review;* **JIBS**—*Journal of International Business Studies;* **JIM**—*Journal of International Management;* **JM**—*Journal of Management;* **JMS**—*Journal of Management Studies;* **JWB**—*Journal of World Business;* **MIR**—*Management International Review;* **SMJ**—*Strategic Management Journal.*

[1] M. W. Peng, 2001, The resource-based view and international business, *JM*, 27: 803–829. For historical development of this view, see J. Barney, 1991, Firm resources and sustained competitive advantage, *JM*, 17: 99–120.

[2] G. Dess, T. Lumpkin, & M. Eisner, 2007, *Strategic Management*, 3rd ed. (p. 78), Chicago: McGraw-Hill; G. Gao, J. Murray, M. Kotabe, & J. Lu, 2010, A "strategy tripod" perspective on export behaviors, *JIBS* (in press); K. Meyer, S. Estrin, S. Bhaumik, & M. W. Peng, 2009, Institutions, resources, and entry strategies in emerging economies, *SMJ*, 30: 61–80.

[3] F. Acedo, C. Barroso, & J. Galan, 2006, The resource-based theory, *SMJ*, 27: 621–636; J. A. Adegbesan, 2009, On the origins

of competitive advantage, *AMR*, 34: 463–475; S. Newbert, 2007, Empirical research on the resource-based view of the firm, *SMJ*, 28: 121–146; D. Sirmon, M. Hitt, & R. D. Ireland, 2007, Managing firm resources in dynamic environments to create value, *AMR*, 32: 273–292; M. Sun & E. Tse, 2009, The resource-based view of competitive advantage in two-sided markets, *JMS*, 46: 45–64.

[4] M. W. Peng & P. Heath, 1996, The growth of the firm in planned economies in transition, *AMR*, 21: 492–528. See also W. Egelhoff & E. Frese, 2009, Understanding managers' preferences for internal markets versus business planning, *JIM*, 15: 77–91; H. Greve, 2008, A behavioral theory of firm growth, *AMJ*, 51: 476–494; J. Steen & P. Liesch, 2007, A note on Penrosian growth, resource bundles, and the Upssala model of internationalization, *MIR*, 47: 193–206; T. Reus, A. Ranft, B. Lamont, & G. Adams, 2009, An interpretive systems view of knowledge investments, *AMR*, 34: 382–400.

[5] J. Barney, 2001, Is the resource-based view a useful perspective for strategic management research? (p. 54) *AMR* 26: 41–56.

[6] C. Helfat & M. Peteraf, 2003, The dynamic resource-based view, *SMJ*, 24: 997–1010; G. Lee, 2008, Relevance of organizational

capabilities and its dynamics, *SMJ*, 29: 1257–1280; D. Teece, G. Pisano, & A. Shuen, 1997, Dynamic capabilities and strategic management, *SMJ*, 18: 509–533.

[7] J. Barney, 2002, *Gaining and Sustaining Competitive Advantage*, 2nd ed. (p. 157), Upper Saddle River, NJ: Prentice Hall; R. Makadok, 2001, Toward a synthesis of the resource-based and dynamic capability views of rent creation, *SMJ*, 22: 387–401.

[8] A. Carmeli & A. Tishler, 2004, The relationships between intangible organizational elements and organizational performance, *SMJ*, 25: 1257–1278; S. Dutta, O. Narasimhan, & S. Rajiv, 2005, Conceptualizing and measuring capabilities, *SMJ*, 26: 277–285.

[9] M. Porter, 1985, *Competitive Advantage*, New York: Free Press.

[10] T. Hutzschenreuter & F. Grone, 2009, Changing vertical integration strategies under pressure from foreign competition, *JMS*, 46: 269–307; A. Parmigiani, 2007, Why do firms both make and buy? *SMJ*, 28: 285–311.

[11] J. Hatonen & T. Eriksson, 2009, 30+ years of research and practice of outsourcing, *JIM*, 15: 142–155; F. Rothaermel, M. Hitt, & L. Jobe, 2006, Balancing vertical integration and strategic outsourcing, *SMJ*, 27: 1033–1056.

[12] *BW*, 2006, The 787 encounters turbulence, June 19: 38–40.

[13] M. Jacobides & S. Winter, 2005, The co-evolution of capabilities and transaction costs (p. 404), *SMJ*, 26: 395–413; M. Kang, J. Mahoney, & D. Tan, 2009, Why firms make unilateral investments specific to other firms, *SMJ*, 30: 117–135.

[14] S. Beugelsdijk, T. Pedersen, & B. Petersen, 2009, Is there a trend towards global value chain specialization? *JIM*, 15: 126–141; S. Chen, 2009, A transaction cost rationale for private branding and its implications for the choice of domestic versus offshore outsourcing, *JIBS*, 40: 156–175; J. Doh, K. Bunyaratavej, & E. Hahn, 2009, Separable but not equal, *JIBS*, 40: 926–943; M. Kotabe & R. Mudambi, 2009, Global sourcing and value creation, *JIM*, 15: 121–125.

[15] K. Coucke & L. Sleuwaegen, 2008, Offshoring as a survival strategy, *JIBS*, 39: 1261–1277; D. Gregorio, M. Musteen, & D. Thomas, 2009, Offshore outsourcing as a source of international competitiveness of SMEs, *JIBS*, 40: 969–988; D. Griffith, N. Harmancioglu, & C. Droge, 2009, Governance decisions for the offshore outsourcing of new product development in technology intensive markets, *JWB*, 44: 217–224; R. Javalgi, A. Dixit, & R. Scherer, 2009, Outsourcing to emerging markets, *JIM*, 15: 156–168; P. Jensen, 2009, A learning perspective on the offshoring of advanced services, *JIM*, 15: 181–193; M. Kenney, S. Massini, & T. Murtha, 2009, Offshoring administrative and technical work, *JIBS*, 40: 887–900; B. Kedia & D. Mukherjee, 2009, Understanding offshoring, *JWB*, 44: 250–261; K. Kumar, P. van Fenema, & M. von Glinow, 2009, Offshoring and the global distribution of work, *JIBS*, 40: 642–667; S. Lahiri & B. Kedia, 2009, The effects of internal resources and partnership quality on firm performance, *JIM*, 15: 209–224; A. Lewin, S. Massini, & C. Peeters, 2009, Why are companies offshoring innovation? *JIBS*, 40: 901–925; K. S. Swan & B. Allred, 2009, Does the "China option" influence subsidiary technology sourcing strategy? *JIM*, 15: 169–180; S. Zaheer, A. Lamin, & M. Subramani, 2009, Cluster capabilities or ethnic ties? *JIBS*, 40: 944–968.

[16] D. Levy, 2005, Offshoring in the new global political economy (p. 687), *JMS*, 42: 685–693.

[17] This section draws heavily from Barney, 2002, *Gaining and Sustaining* (pp. 159–174).

[18] R. Adner & P. Zemsky, 2006, A demand-based perspective on sustainable competitive advantage, *SMJ*, 27: 215–239; J. Anderson, J. Narus, & W. Van Rossum, 2006, Customer value propositions in business markets, *HBR*, March: 91–99; V. La, P. Patterson, & C. Styles, 2009, Client-perceived performance and value in professional B2B services, *JIBS*, 40: 274–300; J. Morrow, D. Sirmon, M. Hitt, & T. Holcomb, 2007, Creating value in the face of declining performance, *SMJ*, 28: 271–283.

[19] B. Vissa & A. Chacar, 2009, Leveraging ties, *SMJ*, 30: 1179–1191.

[20] D. Lavie, 2006, Capability reconfiguration, *AMR*, 31: 153–174.

[21] *Economist*, 2009, The substance of style, September 19: 79–81.

[22] J. Grahovac & D. Miller, 2009, Competitive advantage and performance, *SMJ*, 30: 1192–1212; G. Ray, J. Barney, & W. Muhanna, 2004, Capabilities, business processes, and competitive advantage, *SMJ*, 25: 23–37; B. Skaggs & M. Youndt, 2004, Strategic positioning, human capital, and performance in service organizations, *SMJ*, 25: 85–99.

[23] *BW*, 2005, Better than robots, December 26: 46–47.

[24] S. Jonsson & P. Renger, 2009, Normative barriers to imitation, *SMJ*, 30: 517–536; A. King, 2007, Disentangling interfirm and intrafirm casual ambiguity, *AMR*, 32: 156–178; T. Powell, D. Lovallo, & C. Caringal, 2006, Causal ambiguity, management perception, and firm performance, *AMR*, 31: 175–196.

[25] M. Lieberman & S. Asaba, 2006, Why do firms imitate each other? *AMR*, 31: 366–385.

[26] A. Lado, N. Boyd, P. Wright, & M. Kroll, 2006, Paradox and theorizing within the resource-based view, *AMR*, 31: 115–131.

[27] G. Hoetker, 2006, Do mudular products lead to modular organizations? *SMJ*, 27: 501–518; M. Kotabe, R. Parente, & J. Murray, 2007, Antecedents and outcomes of modular production in the Brazilian automobile industry, *JIBS*, 38: 84–106.

[28] T. Chi & A. Seth, 2009, A dynamic model of the choice of mode for exploiting complementary capabilities, *JIBS*, 40: 365–387; N. Stieglitz & K. Heine, 2007, Innovations and the role of complementarities in a strategic theory of the firm, *SMJ*, 28: 1–15; A. Tiwana, 2008, Does interfirm modularity complement ignorance? *SMJ*, 29: 1241–1252.

[29] J. Barney, 1997, *Gaining and Sustaining Competitive Advantage* (p. 155), Reading, MA: Addison-Wesley. See also J. Jansen, F. Van den Bosch, & H. Volberda, 2005, Managerial potential and related absorptive capacity, *AMJ*, 48: 999–1015; Y. Kor & J. Mahoney, 2005, How dynamics, management, and governance of resource deployments influence firm-level performance, *SMJ*, 26: 489–496.

[30] T. Kostova & K. Roth, 2003, Social capital in multinational corporations and a micro-macro model of its formation, *AMR*, 28: 297–317; P. Moran, 2005, Structural vs. relational embeddedness, *SMJ*, 26: 1129–1151.

[31] J. Doh, 2005, Offshore outsourcing, *JMS*, 42: 695–704.

[32] D. Farrell, 2005, Offshoring, *JMS*, 42: 675–683.

[33] M. Gottfredson, R. Puryear, & S. Phillips, 2005, Strategic sourcing (p. 132), *HBR*, February: 132–139.

[34] C. Rossetti & T. Choi, 2005, On the dark side of strategic sourcing, *AME*, 19 (1): 46–60.

[35] N. Wright, 2009, China's emerging role in global outsourcing, *CBR*, November–December: 44–48.

[36] W. DeSarbo, C. Nenedetto, M. Song, & I. Sinha, 2005, Revisiting the Miles and Snow strategic framework, *SMJ*, 26: 47–74; G. T. Hult, D. Ketchen, & S. Slater, 2005, Market orientation and performance, *SMJ*, 26: 1173–1181.

[37] *Economist*, 2005, A market for ideas, October 22: 3.

[38] G. Hamel & C. K. Prahalad, 1994, *Competing for t* Boston: Harvard Business School Press.

[39] The author's paraphrase based on T. Friedman, 2005, *The World is Flat* (p. 237), New York: Farrar, Straus, & Giroux.

pengatlas Part 1

MAP 1.1   DEVELOPED ECONOMIES AND EMERGING ECONOMIES

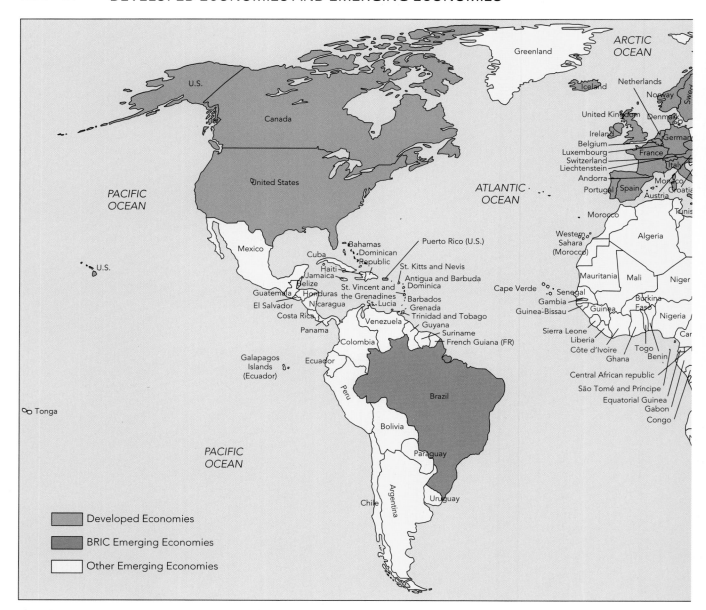

Source: International Monetary Fund (IMF), www.imf.org (accessed October 16, 2009). The IMF recognizes 182 countries and economies. It labels developed economies "advanced economies," and labels emerging economies "emerging and developing economies." See Table 1.1 on page 9 for the list of developed economies.

Finland
Lithuania
Czech Republic
Slovak Republic
Belarus
Hungary
Slovenia
San Marino
Moldova
Georgia
Armenia
Estonia
Latvia
Poland
Romania
Ukraine
Serbia
Bulgaria
Bosnia and
Macedonia Herzegovina
Turkey
Albania
Montenegro
Malta
Greece
Cyprus Lebanon Syria
Israel
Libya
Egypt
Jordan
Bahrain
Chad
Sudan
Eritrea
Yemen
Cameroon
Uganda
Rwanda
Burundi
Kenya
Democratic
Republic of
Congo
Tanzania
Angola
Zambia
Malawi
Namibia
Botswana
South
Africa
Lesotho
Zimbabwe
Swaziland
Mozambique
Madagascar
Comoros
Mauritius
Seychelles
Maldives
Djibouti
Ethiopia
Somalia
Saudi
Arabia
Oman
United
Arab
Emirates
Iraq
Kuwait
Qatar
Azerbaijan
Iran
Afghanistan
Pakistan
Turkmenistan
Tajikistan
Kyrgyzstan
Uzbekistan
Kazakhstan
Russia
Mongolia
China
Nepal
Bhutan
India
Bangladesh
Myanmar (Burma)
Sri Lanka
Thailand
Laos
Vietnam
Cambodia
Malaysia
Singapore
East Timor
Indonesia
Brunei
Philippines
Hong Kong
Taiwan
North
Korea
South
Korea
Japan
PACIFIC
OCEAN
Micronesia
Palau
Micronesia
Marshall Islands
Nauru
Tuvalu
Papua
New guinea
Solomon
Islands
Vanuatu
Samoa
Fiji
Australia
New Zealand
INDIAN
OCEAN

MAP 1.2   THE GROUP OF 20 (G-20)

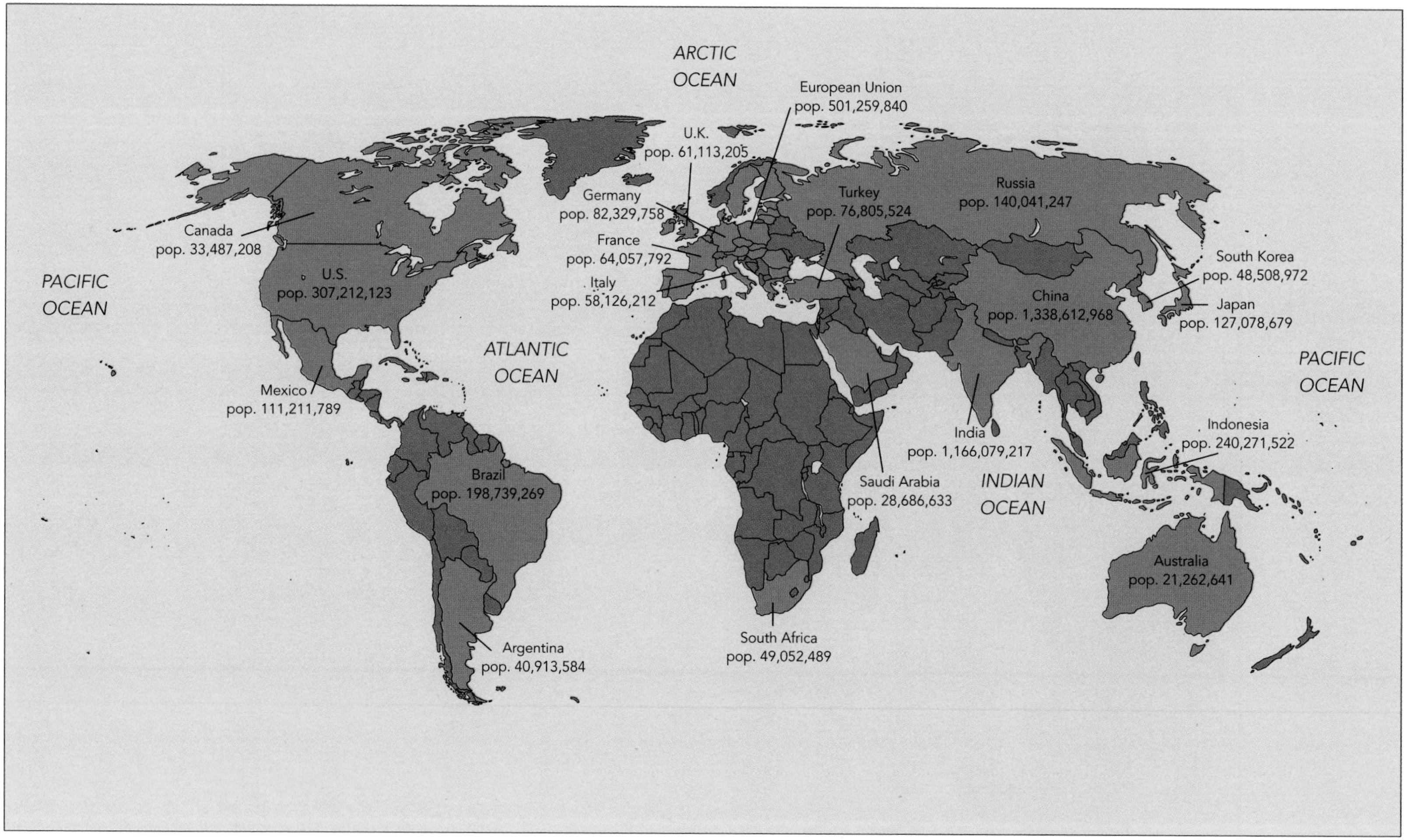

THE GROUP OF 20 (G-20)

ARCTIC OCEAN

PACIFIC OCEAN

European Union
pop. 501,259,840

Russia
pop. 140,041,247

China
pop. 1,338,612,968

South Korea
pop. 48,508,972

Japan
pop. 127,078,679

Indonesia
pop. 240,271,522

Australia
pop. 21,262,641

INDIAN OCEAN

India
pop. 1,166,079,217

Saudi Arabia
pop. 28,686,633

South Africa
pop. 49,052,489

Turkey
pop. 76,805,524

U.K.
pop. 61,113,205

Germany
pop. 82,329,758

France
pop. 64,057,792

Italy
pop. 58,126,212

ATLANTIC OCEAN

Argentina
pop. 40,913,584

Brazil
pop. 198,739,269

Mexico
pop. 111,211,789

U.S.
pop. 307,212,123

Canada
pop. 33,487,208

PACIFIC OCEAN

Source: U.S. Census Bureau, International Database, and The World Factbook, 2009. Factbook, 2009. The EU's population is 501,259,840. See PengAtlas Map 2.4 for a map of EU member countries.

MAP 1.3   POLITICAL FREEDOM AROUND THE WORLD

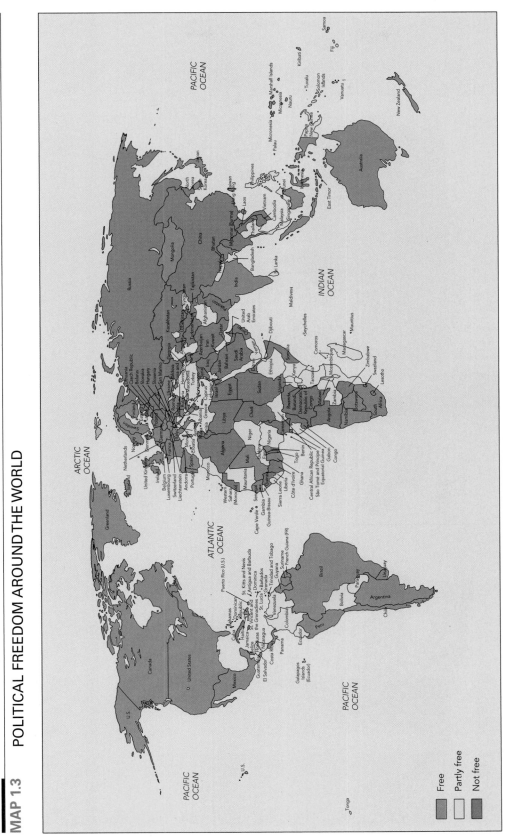

Source: Countries are ranked according to political rights and civil liberties on a scale from 1.0 (most free) to 7.0 (least free). Freedom in the World, 2007, published by Freedom House.

MAP 1.4   RELIGIOUS HERITAGES OF THE WORLD

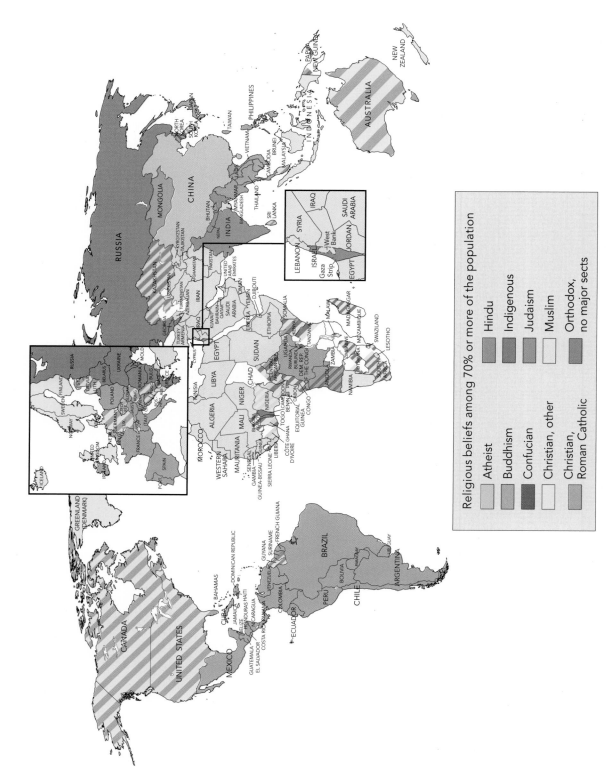

Religious beliefs among 70% or more of the population

Atheist
Buddhism
Confucian
Christian, other
Christian, Roman Catholic
Hindu
Indigenous
Judaism
Muslim
Orthodox, no major sects

Source: CIA—The World Factbook 2000. Note that Confucianism, strictly speaking, is not a religion but a set of moral codes guiding interpersonal relationships.

INTEGRATIVE CASE 1.1

THE CHINESE MENU (FOR DEVELOPMENT)

Douglass C. North, *Washington University*

How does China's recent economic success inform the debate on the best political and economic models for economic development?

In the years since the end of World War II, we, and other developed nations, have devoted immense amounts of resources to the development of poor countries. The result has not been a success story. This is puzzling, since during that time we have learned a great deal about the process of economic and political change: not only the underlying source of economic growth—productivity increase—but also the factors that make for such increase. And in the past several decades, as economists have become aware of the role of institutions in providing the correct incentives for economic growth, we have incorporated an understanding of the significance of well-specified and -enforced property rights as key structural requirements in that process.

Despite our increased understanding, the record at promoting development is not impressive, largely because we fail to see the importance of open-access political systems as well as open-access competitive markets. Yes, the world has gotten richer, the percentage of the world's population subsisting on less than a dollar a day has fallen, and there have been a few spectacular success stories, most particularly China. But sub-Saharan Africa remains a part of the world where per capita income has absolutely fallen, Latin America continues to have stop-and-go development, and the efforts at promoting development by the World Bank have been, to put it politely, nothing to brag about.

Yet, none of the standard models of economic and political theory can explain China. After a disastrous era of promoting collective organization, in which approximately 30 million people died of starvation, China gradually fumbled its way out of the economic disaster it had created by instituting the Household Responsibility System which provided peasants with incentives to produce more. This system in turn led to the town-village enterprises (TVEs) and sequential development built on their cultural background. But China still does not have well-specified property rights, TVEs hardly

resembled the standard firm of economics, and it remains to this day a communist dictatorship.

What kind of a model is that for the developing world? It is not a good model and it is still not clear what the outcome will be, but the Chinese experience should force economists to rethink some of the fundamental tenets of economics as they apply to development. Two features stand out: (1) While the institutions China employed are different from developed nations, the incentive implications were similar; and (2) China has been confronting new problems and pragmatically attempting new solutions.

Two implications are clear. First, there are many paths to development. The key is creating an institutional structure derived from your particular cultural institutions that provide the proper incentives—not slavishly imitating Western institutions. Second, the world is constantly changing in fundamental ways. The basics of economic theory are essential elements of every economy, but the problems countries face today are set in new and novel frameworks of beliefs, institutions, technologies, and radically lower information costs than ever before. The secret of success is the creation of adaptively efficient institutions—institutions that readily adapt to changing circumstances. Just how do we create such an institutional framework?

Institutions are the way we structure human interaction—political, social, and economic—and are the incentive framework of a society. They are made up of formal rules (constitutions, laws, and rules), informal constraints (norms, conventions, and codes of conduct), and their enforcement characteristics. Together they define the way the game is played, whether as a society or an athletic game. Let me illustrate from professional football. There are formal rules defining the way the game is supposed to be played; informal norms—such as not deliberately injuring the quarterback of the opposing team; and enforcement characteristic—umpires, referees—designed to see that the game is played according to the intentions underlying the rules. But enforcement is always imperfect and it frequently pays for a team to violate rules. Therefore,

This case was written by Douglass C. North (Washington University) and first published as "The Chinese Menu (for Development)" in the *Wall Street Journal*, April 7, 2005, A14. © Dow Jones & Company, Inc. Reprinted with permission. North received the Nobel Prize in Economics in 1993. Case discussion questions were added by Mike Peng.

the way a game is actually played is a function of the underlying intentions embodied in the rules, the strength of informal codes of conduct, the perception of the umpires, and the severity of punishment for violating rules.

It is the same way with societies. Poorly performing societies have rules that do not provide the proper incentives, lack effective informal norms that would encourage productivity, and/or have poor enforcement. Underlying institutions are belief **systems** that provide our understanding of the world around us and, therefore, the incentives that we face. Creating institutions that will perform effectively is, thus, a difficult task. Effective performance entails the creation of open-access societies—the essential requirement for the dynamic market that Adam Smith envisioned. Let me illustrate from the contrasting histories of North and South America.

North America was settled by British colonists bringing with them the property-rights structure that had evolved by that time in the home country. Because the British did not regard the colonies as critical to their own development, they were allowed a large measure of self-government. In the context of relative political and economic freedom with a setting of endless resource opportunities, the result was the gradual evolution of an open-access society in the decades following independence.

Latin America, in contrast, was settled by the Spanish (and Portuguese) to exploit the discovery and extraction of treasure. The resultant institutional structure was one of monopoly and political control from Madrid and Lisbon. Independence in the 19th century led to efforts to follow the lead of the United States and constitutions were written with that objective. The results, however, were radically different. With no heritage of self-government (political and economic), the result was a half-century of civil wars to attempt to fill the vacuum left by Iberian rule. It also was the creation of political and economic institutions dominated by personal exchange that led to political instability and economic monopolies that persist in much of that continent to this day, with adverse consequences for dynamic economic growth.

The perpetuation of open-access societies like the United States in a world of continuous novel change raises a fundamental institutional dilemma at the heart of the issue of economic development and of successful dynamic change. By uncertainty, we mean that we do not know what is going to happen in the future, and that condition characterizes the world we have been creating. How can our minds make sense of new and novel conditions that are continually occurring? The answer that in fact has proven successful in the case of the United States and other open-access societies is the creation of an institutional structure that maximizes trials and eliminates errors and, therefore, maximizes the potential for achieving a successful outcome—a condition first prescribed by Friedrich Hayek many years ago and still the prescription for an adaptively efficient society. Such an institutional structure is derived from an underlying belief system that recognizes the tentative nature of our understanding of the world around us.

What about China? China partially opened competitive access to its economic markets. But China is barely halfway there. The society is still dominated by a political dictatorship and, as a result, personal exchange rather than impersonal rules dominate the economy. How will China evolve? It could continue to evolve open-access economic markets built on impersonal rules and gradually dissolve the barriers to open political markets. . . . Or the political dictatorship could perceive the evolving open-access society as a threat to the existing vested interests, and halt the course of the past decades.

Case Discussion Questions:

1. What role do institutions play in economic development?
2. What is behind the differences in economic development between North and South America?
3. Some argue that a democratic political system is conducive for economic growth. How does the experience of recent Chinese economic development support or refute this statement?
4. If you were a policymaker in a poor country or a World Bank official, what would be your advice, based on North's article and China's experience, for most effective economic development?

INTEGRATIVE CASE 1.2

FIGHTING COUNTERFEIT MOTION PICTURES

Alan Zimmerman, *City University of New York, College of Staten Island*

Peggy Chaudhry, *Villanova University*

The scale and scope of counterfeiting, especially in motion pictures, make it very challenging to combat counterfeiting. Are current anticounterfeiting measures effective?

Counterfeiting is big business. It is a problem that has been haunting businesspeople for millennia. The first producer's marks appeared on pottery in China about 4,000 years ago. And it was not too soon after that counterfeiters saw the advantage of copying successful products. In the Roman Empire, a well-known brand name for oil lamps was FORTIS. So many artifacts with this name have been found that it is evident that widespread product copying took place at the time.

What exactly is a counterfeit product? A common definition is that "any unauthorized manufacturing of goods whose special characteristics are protected as intellectual property rights (IPR) constitutes product counterfeiting." IPR include copyrights, patents, and trademarks. The scope of counterfeiting is widespread with traditional products ranging from footwear to computer software to watches to cigarettes. The pirates have also diversified their product offerings to non-traditional goods in health and safety areas, such as pharmaceuticals and aircraft parts. The total size of the counterfeit market is nearly impossible to accurately determine, but it appears to be growing rapidly. In 1985, the annual worldwide product counterfeit market was estimated at about $25 billion. Today, a number of organizations claim that more than 5% of world trade consists of counterfeit goods and estimate the total at about $500 billion annually.

A number of reasons have been given for the growth of counterfeits. An in-depth analysis shows many driving forces, including the low investment required to get into a market combined with easily available cheap technology, globalization and lower trade barriers, powerful worldwide brands, ongoing consumer willingness to buy counterfeit product, and especially weak national and international enforcement of IPR. Each of these forces relates to the basic issues discussed in this text. Industry structures such as

entry barriers that can be overcome by technology and the continuing importance of worldwide brands are important. Firm-specific resources such as the ability to copy product, find distribution outlets, and secure financing make certain pirate firms successful.

But it is clear that the overriding driver of the growth of counterfeit products lies within institutional frameworks. A number of multilateral organizations exist to protect IPR, including the World Trade Organization's Trade-Related Aspects of Intellectual Property Rights (TRIPS) and the World Intellectual Property Organization (WIPO), that are charged with implementing the provisions of the Paris Convention dealing with patents and trademarks, and the Berne Convention that focuses on copyrights. In addition there are nongovernmental organizations (NGOs) such as the International Anticounterfeiting Coalition (IACC), the Business Software Alliance (BSA), and the Software Information Industry Association that deal with chronic piracy. A critical problem lies in enforcement. While in the United States, convicted counterfeiters may be fined millions of dollars and spend years in prison even for a first offense, in many countries counterfeiters can get away with small fines and virtually no danger of a prison sentence. The US Trade Representative (USTR) reports each year on the intellectual property environment within each US trading partner. Countries that fail to enforce their IPR laws are subject to penalties from the US government. Despite the plethora of governmental and nongovernmental agencies attempting to control counterfeit product, the failure of enforcement at national and international levels has allowed pirates to operate with impunity in many countries. For example, the infamous Ciudad del Este in Paraguay has been described as the Wild West for its illicit trade. Other problem countries for IPR protection described in our 2009 book, *The Economics of Counterfeit Trade: Governments, Consumers, Pirates, and Intellectual Property Rights,* are Argentina, Brazil, Chile, China, Egypt, India, Israel, Lebanon, Mexico, Russia,

This case was written by Alan Zimmerman (City University of New York, College of Staten Island) and Peggy Chaudhry (Villanova University). © Alan Zimmerman and Peggy Chaudhry. Reprinted with permission.

Thailand, Turkey, Ukraine, and Venezuela. They host some notorious counterfeit shopping districts, such as Xiushui Market (formerly known as Silk Alley) in Beijing.

One critical worldwide problem is the illegal copying of motion pictures. The box office for films in the United States was estimated at $9.79 billion in 2008 (a 1.8% increase over 2007) and globally at $28.1 billion (a 5.2% increase over 2007). For example, Disney's *Ratatouille* was launched simultaneously in 33 countries in multiple languages and earned more than $300 million in international sales on the third weekend of its debut in 2007. With this type of revenue, the Motion Picture Association of America (MPAA) tries to improve the image of "Hollywood" and reports several reasons why the industry should be nurtured since it employs over 2.5 million professionals (ranging from costume designers to set builders), contributes almost $80 billion per year to the US economy, and is the only US industry that has a positive balance of trade in all of its foreign markets.

The Motion Picture Association (MPA), the international branch of the MPAA, has focused heavily on fighting pirated product. An MPA study on piracy reported the following:

- The major US motion picture studios lost $6.1 billion in 2005 to piracy worldwide.
- Approximately 80% of those losses resulted from piracy overseas, and 20% from piracy in the United States.
- 62% of the $6.1 billion loss results from piracy of hard goods such as DVDs and 38% from Internet piracy.
- Piracy rates are highest in China (90%), Russia (79%), and Thailand (79%).
- The worldwide motion picture industry, including foreign and domestic producers, distributors, theaters, video stores, and pay-per-view operators, lost $18.2 billion in 2005 as a result of piracy.
- The typical pirate is aged between 16 and 24 and male. Approximately 44% of MPA company losses in the United States are attributable to college students.

Exhibit 1 lists the top piracy rates from the MPA study, yielding an overall estimate of the percentage of the potential market that is lost to counterfeits. The estimate for the US market is 7%. A 2009 article in *The Wall Street Journal* authored by one of us (Chaudhry), "Getting Real About Fakes," reported that over 50% of 2,000 consumers surveyed in Brazil, Russia, India, China, and the United States had obtained a fake movie in either a physical or virtual market and that the average frequency of acquisition was three times during the past year. Despite the well-publicized efforts

EXHIBIT 1   PERCENTAGE OF TOTAL MARKET LOST TO PIRACY

Country	Percent	Country	Percent
China	90%	Mexico	61%
Russia	79%	Taiwan	54%
Thailand	79%	Spain	32%
Hungary	76%	India	29%
Poland	65%	Italy	25%

Source: Motion Picture Association of America, 2005, *The Cost of Movie Piracy.*

of many national governments and international as well as nongovernmental institutions, the counterfeit product market appears to be growing at a rapid pace. The world of counterfeiting seems subject mainly to informal norms and beliefs. The advent of easy and inexpensive communications allows all the players in this business to rely on relationship-based informal networks while easily avoiding detection.

Many actions aimed at slowing down product counterfeiting have been offered by a number of researchers. Studies of these recommended actions show that some are particularly ineffective. In particular, actions directed at consumers, whose willingness to buy counterfeit products including pirated movies is undaunted, seem fruitless. The MPA is targeting young consumers on its website and even has prepared material for the *Weekly Reader* that educates fifth-grade students through a story of "Lucky and Flo," two dogs who sniff out fake DVDs by sensing the chemicals used to manufacture this product. Obviously, the goal is to create better cybercitizens by educating youth to reinforce the concept that watching fake movies is stealing and analogous to shoplifting. Nevertheless, most studies report that consumers generally see purchasing a counterfeit good as a victimless crime. In addition, the industry has followed in the footsteps of Apple iTunes and there are now several ways to obtain movies *legally* through the web at places like MovieFlex and Netflix. Today, consumers can obtain *Ice Age: Dawn of the Dinosaurs* at Amazon Video on Demand for $6.99 that gives them the flexibility to watch this film through their television, a computer, a portable video device, or "save it later" in a video library.

The most effective anticounterfeiting action is straightforward—registering trademarks/patents/copyrights in the relevant jurisdictions. In addition, other effective actions focus on distributors and employees and local law enforcement. The MPA has developed a multipronged action plan ranging from publication of the "Top 25 University Piracy Schools" to commercials featuring Jackie Chan and Arnold Schwarzenegger riding motorcycles in their "Mission to Stop Piracy" advertisement. A few years ago, the MPA used the "You Can Click But Can't Hide" campaign to educate consumers about the ease of finding someone who has illegally downloaded a movie from the web. This prompted bloggers to create their own *anti*-antipiracy campaign, "You Can Sue, But You Can't Catch Everyone." Current ads at the MPA website focus on illegally filming movies in the theater with the slogans, "Lights. Camera. Busted." and "Leave Your Camera at Home. Do Not Record in This Theater."

It may be that over time the growth and sophistication of particular markets will reduce counterfeiting. Pressures from legitimate suppliers have certainly made product counterfeiting less widespread in the United States, Japan, Hong Kong, Taiwan, and South Korea as these markets mature. In the meantime, to limit the harm counterfeiters can do to their brands, owners of IPR must have effective ongoing antipiracy programs that has the attention of top management.

Case Discussion Questions:

1. Why do some entrepreneurs choose a strategy of product counterfeiting?
2. What are the main drivers in the growth of product counterfeiting?
3. Review the antipiracy advertisements of the MPAA on the web at http://www.mpaa.org/piracy.asp. Do you think these types of ads will effectively deter illegally filming movies in the theater and posting on the web? In your opinion, what anti-counterfeiting actions would the MPAA have to develop to realistically get consumers to stop using illegal movies?
4. What roles do the institution-based and resource-based views play in curbing the growth of the counterfeit product market?
5. What are the most effective actions firms can take to protect their products from being counterfeited?

Sources: Based on (1) K. Barry, 2007, *Counterfeits and Counterfeiters: The Ancient World*; (2) C. Bialik, 2006, Efforts to quantify sales of pirated goods lead to fuzzy figures, *Wall Street Journal*, October 19: B1; (3) P. Chaudhry & S. Stumpf, 2009, Getting real about fakes, *Wall Street Journal*, August 19, http://online.wsj.com; (4) P. Chaudhry & A. Zimmerman, 2009, *The Economics of Counterfeit Trade: Governments, Consumers, Pirates and Intellectual Property Rights*, Heidelberg, Germany: Springer-Verlag; (5) V. Cordell, N. Wongtada, & R. Kieschnick, 1996, Counterfeit purchase intentions: Role of lawfulness attitudes and product traits as determinants, *Journal of Business Research*, 35: 41–53; (6) International Anti-Counterfeiting Coalition, 2007, *Get Real—The Truth about Counterfeiting*; (7) J. Kay, 2007, *Ratatouille becomes 10th Disney film to gross $300m overseas*, http://www.screendaily.com; (8) Motion Picture Association of America, 2005, *The Cost of Movie Piracy*; (9) Motion Picture Association of America, http://www.mpaa.org; (10) S. Ono, 1999, *Overview of Japanese Trademark Law*, Chapter 2; (11) T. Stern, 1985, Foreign product counterfeiting, *Vital Speeches of the Day*, Volume LI, No. 22; (12) G. Tom, B. Garibaldi, Y. Zeng, & J. Pilcher, 1998, Consumer demand for counterfeit goods, *Psychology and Marketing*, 15: 405–421; (13) D. J. Weinterfeldt, L. Dow, & P. Albertson, 2002, *Historical Trademarks: In Use since 4000 BC*, International Trademark Association; (14) United States Trade Representative, 2007, *Special 301 Report*.

INTEGRATIVE CASE 1.3

BRAZIL'S EMBRAER: FROM STATE-OWNED ENTERPRISE TO GLOBAL LEADER

Juan España, *National University*

How does Embraer grow to become a global leader in the highly competitive aircraft manufacturing industry?

In 1994, when Fernando Henrique Cardoso was elected as Brazil's new president, the economy was unstable and experiencing hyperinflation of about 2,000% per year. As a finance minister in the previous administration, Cardoso and his team had

Embraer jet in flight

introduced economic measures centered on the *Real Plan*. This plan was very successful and by 1997 inflation had been brought down to international levels. Macroeconomic reforms and price stability revived the economy. Brazil had been the world's economic miracle of the 1970s and most of the 1980s, and with a steady course, it could now look forward to a new era of growth. An important part of the reforms was the privatization of key state-owned enterprises (SOEs). One of them was Embraer, the short form for Empresa Brasileira de Aeronautica, S.A. (Brazilian Aeronautics Company). Embraer's stock is traded on the Sao Paulo Bovespa and has been listed on the New York Stock Exchange (NYSE: ERJ) since 2000.

Origins

Embraer was created in 1969 by a military government determined to provide Brazil with the capacity to produce military aircraft. The company was set up as a mixed enterprise, with the Brazilian state retaining a 51% majority of the voting shares and the rest held by private investors. Production started in 1970 and the company became profitable the next year and remained so until 1981. Propelled by government procurement and fiscal support, Embraer soon produced internationally successful models, such as the turboprop models EMB 110 Bandeirante transport aircraft

and its larger, 30-seat successor, the EMB 120 Brasilia, as well as the Tucano military trainer.

The company is located in San Jose dos Campos, in the state of Sao Paulo, in the corridor between the cities of Sao Paulo and Rio de Janeiro. This part of Brazil is called "Technology Valley," with industrial clusters in the aerospace, telecommunications, automobile, and petroleum sectors. Educational centers have been created in the area offering aerospace-related programs. Embraer's distinctive competencies are the areas of R&D, design, product development, system integration, assembly, and technical assistance in aircraft manufacturing.

Product Range

Embraer's product range includes commercial, military, and corporate aircraft, with commercial sales in 2009 accounting for 66% and the fast-growing corporate segment (also known as executive aviation) representing 14% (see Exhibits 1, 2, and 3 on the next page). By comparison, commercial and corporate sales represented about 80% and 6% of total sales in 2002.

In 1989, Embraer introduced the 35-seat ERJ 135 and the 50-seat ERJ 145 regional jets to meet increasing demand for jets to replace turboprop models. Regional jets are smaller and less costly to acquire and operate than larger jets such as the Boeing 737. They are a cost-effective alternative to serve mid-range routes and to feed passengers from smaller airports to major hubs replacing larger planes that were underutilized in short(er) flights. Sales of Embraer's new family of regional jets took off rapidly.

By 1994, Embraer had reached world market shares of 31% and 42% in the regional jet and the military

This case was written by Juan España (National University). © Juan España. Reprinted with permission.

EXHIBIT 1   REVENUE BY SEGMENT

Source: http://www.embraer.com.

EXHIBIT 2   REVENUE BY REGION

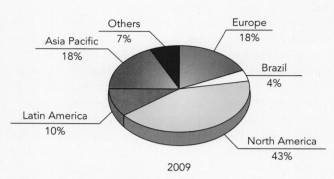

2009

Source: http://www.embraer.com.

EXHIBIT 3   PRODUCT RANGE

Commercial Aircraft	
Turboprop	EMB 110 Bandeirante (produced until 1990)
	EMB 120 Brasilia
Regional Jets	ERJ 145 family (37 to 50 passengers)
	ERJ 170, 175, 190, 195 (80 to 122 passengers)
Military Aircraft	
	Tucano: Military trainer, produced since 1980, used by air forces around the world
	EMB 314 Super Tucano
	AMX International Fighter, in service at the Brazilian and Italian Air Forces
	ERJ 145 military variants: EMB 145 AEW&C, EMB 145 RS/AGS
	KC 390 Military tanker/transport being developed for the Brazilian military
Corporate Aircraft	
	Phenom 100, 300
	EMB Legacy 450, 500, 600
	EMB Lineage 1000
Agriculture Aircraft	
	Ipanema: The world's first alcohol-powered airplane, more than 4,000 units sold

trainer markets, respectively. However, it was facing severe challenges. A downturn in demand in the airline industry had led to a serious decline in commercial aircraft sales, while export financing was drying up due to the expiration of the Brazilian government Finex program. These and other factors contributed to a sense of disarray at Embraer at a time when major reforms such as privatization were transforming the Brazilian economy. In December 1994, Embraer was privatized, and acquired by a consortium of Brazilian institutions headed by a local investment bank. The Brazilian government retained a golden share that allowed it to veto certain strategic actions such as a takeover by a foreign company.

By 1998, buoyed by the success of its ERJ family of jets introduced in 1989, Embraer had become the world's leader in the regional jet market, surpassing its main rival, Bombardier of Canada. In 1999, Embraer became Brazil's leading exporter and accounted for about 7% of all of Brazil's exports of manufactured goods.

In 1999, after a $1 billion investment in development, Embraer introduced the E-Jet family, consisting of the

80-seat ERJ 170, the 110-seat ERJ 190, and the 122-seat ERJ 195 airliners. They are comparable to Boeing 737 and DC-9 airliners. These jets proved to be very successful and the first one was delivered in 2002. Bombardier had no comparable models to compete against this new line of Embrarer planes. Currently, Bombardier offers the original jet series, the 50-seat CRJ 100 and CRJ 200, which are identical except that CRJ 200 has more powerful engines. Bombardier also developed the CRJ 700, CRJ 900, and CRJ 1000, which are simply stretched versions of the CRJ 200 and have a capacity of 70, 90, and 100 passengers, respectively. However, in July 2004, Bombardier announced the development of the C Series consisting of the CS 100 (100–125 seats) and the CS 300 (120–150 passengers). The launch year has been set to be 2013. The C Series jets are comparable to the Boeing 787 and the Airbus 350.

Supply Chain

Embraer's production structure gives the company a competitive edge. Its supply network consists of three layers. At the first level, risk (or strategic) partners carry most of the risk of innovation and operate on the basis of long-term contracts. At the second level, international suppliers provide equipment, systems, and components. At the third level are the national subcontractors that supply services and products following Embraer's specifications. They are retained on the basis of purchase orders and can be easily replaced. Embraer trains employees of these suppliers. They represent a diversified local network of about 30 small and medium-sized firms mostly located in close proximity of Embraer and are typically founded by previous employees of the company. The number of these suppliers has gradually been reduced. For instance, while the ERJ 145 program had about 400 suppliers, the newer ERJ 170/190 program had around 20. Suppliers must be ISO9000 certified.

Embraer develops new products using a "co-design" approach that involves risk partners that carry most of the risk of innovation. Risk partners are also responsible for aggregating subsystems and components into "modules" (complete, recognizable subunits of the airplane). This modular assembly system reduces the number of suppliers and shifts risk and costs from the company to suppliers. These supply chain innovations provide Embraer with a competitive edge resulting from reduced levels of risk, reduced R&D costs, reduced complexity of the production process, increased quality, increased innovation, and—in the case of ERJ 170/190—a 33% shorter product development process (from 54 to 36 months).

The new family of regional jets, the ERJ 170/190, was designed through a cooperative system. Embraer's design process consists of three phases: (1) the initial definition phase that is performed before the risk partners are selected; (2) the joint definition phase that is carried out by all risk partners and involves assigning the design of different parts of the aircraft to different partners; and (3) the detailed design and certification phase during which the risk partners finish all details and the aircraft seeks certification in different national markets.

Over the years, Embraer has attempted to address issues of strategic importance such as dependency on international suppliers, low local content of its products, a lack of government support for R&D, and a lack of an internal market intelligence unit. To alleviate these obstacles, Embraer has engaged in corporate capacity building at various levels.

The level of dependency on international contractors is illustrated by the fact that about 95% (by volume) of the equipment, materials, and components are purchased on international markets. The total national (Brazilian) content in each airplane is only about 40%, with risk partners accounting for an additional 38% of the total cost of an airplane. Embraer is attempting to increase local sourcing, mainly by attracting international suppliers to set up operations in Brazil. Some progress has been made in this area. For example, in 2003, Japan's Kawasaki opened a wing-production plant within Embraer's Gaviao Peixoto facility, joining other international companies that have set up plants in Brazil such as C&D Aerospace, Sonaca, Goodyear, and ELEB. In 2008, Embraer took full ownership of ELEB, a former joint venture (JV) of Embraer with Liebherr of Germany, and this subsidiary now exports landing gear and hydraulic equipment to aerospace firms in the United States, Asia, and Europe.

Embraer faces hurdles in the creation of knowledge and specialized suppliers. It lacks a targeted government program focusing on R&D and the creation of small high-tech suppliers to the aerospace industry. In addition, the company's relationships with universities are rather informal and not comparable to the structured ties found between companies and university-based R&D centers in the United States and Europe. In order to expedite the process of innovation and knowledge creation, Embraer is considering creating its own corporate university.

For many years, Embraer had relied on external consultants to produce market studies of the commercial aircraft industry. In 1998, it established its own market intelligence unit, with the ultimate goal of producing good estimates while at the same time internalizing market analysis into the company's competitive strategy.

International Operations

Embraer sells civil and military aircraft around the world, and has established plants, sales, and maintenance centers in China, France, Portugal, Singapore, and the Unites States. A new dimension in Embraer's relations with the outside world was initiated in 1999 when the company established a strategic alliance with a French consortium formed by Dassault, Aerospatiale Matra, Thompson-CSF, SNECMA, and EADS (the parent company of Airbus). These companies acquired about 8% of Embraer's equity. The pact would have allowed Embraer access to new military and civil aviation technology. Among other projects, the agreement envisaged the assembly of France's Mirage fighter jets in Brazil. However, EADS sold its equity in 2007 and the Mirage project was never carried out. In 2005, a consortium consisting of Embraer and EADS acquired control of OGMA, Portugal's formerly state-owned aerospace firm. OGMA will provide service and perform certification procedures for Embraer aircraft in Europe.

In 2002, Embraer established a JV with Aviation Industry of China II (AVIC II), opening a plant in Harbin, China, to produce ERJ 145 regional jets. The first jet was produced in 2003, and a total of 25 will be delivered to Hainan Airlines by 2011.

Challenges for the Future

As the year 2010 begins, Embraer can look back to major achievements that have turned it into the world's third largest commercial aircraft manufacturer in terms of sales, surpassed only by Boeing and Airbus. However, many significant challenges lie ahead.

Embraer is preparing to face another difficult year as the world economy and commercial carriers experience the worst crisis since World War II. Many orders have been downsized or cancelled, and Embraer is expecting a 10% sales decline for 2010. The company is reacting to the crisis by cutting staff and adopting other cost-reduction measures, but there is no end in sight for the downturn in the world economy. To make things worse, Bombardier has received several orders for its new C Series jets due for delivery starting in 2013, and Embraer, whose models go up to 122 seats, has nothing to offer in the 149-seat range. In addition, the Brazilian real appreciated by 35% against the US dollar in 2009, and this will ultimately show as increased costs at Embraer, where about 40% of expenditures are denominated in the real.

There are a few bright spots in this otherwise bleak landscape: Sales of the expanded line of corporate jets are growing fast and making up for lost revenue in other areas, and domestic sales are expected to reach $500 million in 2010 driven by purchases by the new Brazilian discount airline Azul (founded by Brazilian-born David Neeleman, the previous CEO of a US discount airline JetBlue). Azul ordered 76 of the 118-seat ERJ 190. In addition, new lines of financing have been offered: China's CDB Leasing Co., a unit of China's Development Bank, awarded Embraer a $2.2 billion loan for the sale of Embraer planes, and the Brazilian state bank BNDES plans to step up financing of Embraer sales from the previous level of 30% to as much as 60% in 2010. With an order backlog of about $18 billion at the beginning of 2010 and new sources of financing lined up, Embraer is confident that it can weather the current crisis and grow again.

Case Discussion Questions:

1. Perform a brief SWOT analysis of Embraer.
2. From a resource-based view, what are the key factors behind Embraer's success in the market for regional jets?
3. What changes do you foresee in the market for regional jets over the next five years?
4. Since September 11, 2001, demand in the airline industry has been unstable or deteriorating. How can Embraer grow and remain profitable in such an environment?
5. How can Embraer's international operations be upgraded to increase its competitiveness?

Sources: Based on (1) R. Bernardes, 2003, *Passive Innovation System and Local Learning: A Case Study of Embraer in Brazil*, Fundação SEADE, November; (2) Bloomberg, 2009, Embraer bets on Brazil market as global sales decline, December 23; (3) Bombardier's website, www.bombardier.com; (4) Embraer's website, www.embraer.com; (4) J. España, 2004, Explaining Embraer's hi-tech success: Porter's diamond, new trade theory, or the market at work, *Journal of the American Academy of Business*, 4(1), March; (5) P. Figueiredo, S. Gutenberg, & R. Sbragia, 2008, Risk sharing partnerships with suppliers: The case of Embraer, *Journal of Technology Management and Innovation*, 3(1); (6) V. Frigant & Y. Lung, 2003, Geographical proximity and supplying relationship in modular production, *Actes du GERPISA*, No. 34; (7) E. Leslie, 2002, *How Brazil Beat Hyperinflation*, UCLA Latin American Center; (8) *Newsweek*, 2006, Embraer: An ugly duckling finds its wings, July 31.

INTEGRATIVE CASE 1.4

SHAKTI: UNILEVER COLLABORATES WITH WOMEN ENTREPRENEURS IN RURAL INDIA

Ted London, *University of Michigan*

Maulin Vakil, *University of North Carolina at Chapel Hill*

By collaborating with women entrepreneurs in rural India, Unilever's India subsidiary, Hindustan Lever Limited, reaches the base of the economic pyramid.

Unilever in India

From ice cream to washing powder, the Anglo-Dutch group Unilever is one of the world's biggest makers of fast-moving consumer goods (FMCGs). The company grew out of a merger in 1930 between Dutch company Margarine Unie and British company Lever Brothers. Today, Unilever markets renowned household names such as Pond's, Dove, Hellman's, Surf, Lipton, Axe, Bertolli, and numerous others, and operates in over 100 countries. The company is a leader in several product categories in North America and Europe, such as frozen foods, margarines, olive oil, detergents, and tea.

Unilever products made their first appearance in India in 1888, when India was still a British colony. In 1956, the company merged its Indian operations to form Hindustan Lever Limited (HLL). HLL offered 10% of its equity to the Indian public, being the first among international companies in India to do so. Unilever, which has gradually divested its stake in HLL (also known as Unilever India), now holds 52% equity in HLL. The rest of the shares is distributed among about 380,000 individual shareholders and financial institutions.[1]

Today, India contributes approximately $2.5 billion of Unilever's nearly $40 billion sales revenues. HLL is comprised of two operating divisions: Home and Personal Products (HPC), consisting of its detergents, soaps, personal care lines of products; and Foods, consisting of staple foods, bakery, confectionary, beverages, and frozen foods. In past years, leading national and international publications like *The Economic Times, Business World, Far Eastern Economic Review,* and *Business Today* have frequently rated HLL as one of India's best managed and most admired companies, and commended its achievements at enhancing value for its shareholders.

Selling to the Wealthy: A Strategy Rooted in Consumer Marketing and Distribution

HLL brought a scientific, consumer-oriented approach and competitive acumen to its business in India. Early on, the company became known and recognized for its various products that had slowly but steadily appeared on virtually every shop shelf across urban and semi-urban India.

The company's philosophy as a maker of high quality, mostly premium-priced products strongly influenced its marketing strategy. In the 1970s, HLL emerged as a prominent advertiser on the radio, magazines and daily press, as well as billboards across the country, and spent as much as 10% of its annual turnover on advertising and media. Its brands quickly captured the imagination of the wealthy and middle class with the clever use of characters such as the Liril waterfall girl, and leading Indian cinema celebrities that endorsed Lux bath soap.

At the same time, HLL invested in an extensive distribution system in India that eventually became a source of its competitive advantage. By focusing on efficiencies, reach, and visibility, it was able to stitch together a vast network of retail outlets that were connected seamlessly by the country's most sophisticated distribution chain. These retailers were loyal because a large portion of revenues typically comprised of Unilever products. Using this distribution chain, HLL could efficiently provide its products to consumers in a convenient fashion, offering the company with an advantage that was the envy of its competitors.

Yet, even HLL's large network was insufficient to cater to a majority of Indian people who lived in remote villages where supplying and selling every-day products was not amenable to the company's existing distribution methods. Indeed, its vaunted distribution network failed to serve more than 500,000 rural villages, meaning that the company was ignoring over 500 million potential customers (nearly half of the

Research Assistant Maulin Vakil and Professor Ted London at the William Davidson Institute and the Ross School of Business at the University of Michigan prepared this case as a basis for class discussion. It is not intended to serve as an endorsement, sources of primary data, or illustration of effective or ineffective management. © Ted London and the William Davidson Institute. Reprinted with permission.

country's population) located at the base of the economic pyramid.[2] With this gap in distribution, HLL had little access to market knowledge about how the less-affluent purchased and used personal care and food products that were the staple of the company's product line.

A New Challenge: Slowdown in Growth

The 1980s and 1990s proved to be outstanding years for HLL's businesses. It systematically outcompeted global giants such as Procter & Gamble and Colgate Palmolive, as well as local rivals such as Tata and Godrej. It took up leadership positions in several categories within the consumer packaged goods space. But after nearly two decades of heady expansion, HLL seemingly stopped growing in 1999. During 1993–1999, sales surged five-fold to $2.3 billion. But since 1999, growth had stagnated and the company closed calendar year 2004 at $2.33 billion.[3] HLL's series of mergers had added market clout and created opportunities for efficiencies, but had also made it difficult to maintain growth momentum.

Analysts highlighted some obvious areas of concern: a high margin structure, large overheads relative to those of its local competitors, and a lack of genuine product and business model innovation.[4] With a lack of growth, increasing attention was placed on HLL's Millennium Plan—an ambitious blueprint outlining the company's growth strategies for the 21st century.

HLL's Millennium Plan

Rural demand and consumption of consumer products is set to explode. The challenge for most companies is to be able to offer appropriate products in an affordable way in relatively remote locations. It is our view that India will soon see an Inflexion Point in rural consumption.[5]

On April 25, 2000, at the annual shareholder's meeting, then Chairman K. B. Dadiseth (who was quoted above) unveiled the much-talked Millennium Plan—a strategic blueprint for the company that had been prepared in consultation with external consultants. Ideas for growth were extensively debated and the team of consultants and company managers identified nine ventures to further explore. These ventures were selected based on an assessment of the changing business environment in India, HLL's existing resources, and the company's ability to build new capabilities over time. A New Ventures Group was formed within the company to implement these new growth opportunities.

Among those that were selected was an idea that would later be dubbed Shakti, an initiative to increase HLL's penetration into rural India, a market that the company had only scratched the surface with to date. The centerpiece of this initiative was a fundamentally different rural distribution system based on Self-Help Groups (SHG), such as those used by Grameen Bank in Bangladesh.[6]

Rural India: Challenges and Opportunities

Approximately one-tenth of the world's population (and approximately three-quarters of India's) live in rural Indian villages. India's nearly 639,000 villages are spread over 128 million households and have a rural population of 742 million.[7] The Indian rural population is substantially poorer, with a per capita annual income below Rs. 10,000 ($227),[8] compared to the national average of approximately Rs. 21,000 ($477).[9] Exhibit 1 shows the dispersion of rural income by household.

Due to the sheer size of the population, HLL saw this is as a potentially lucrative market for its consumer products. Indeed, rural India's consumption has also been growing steadily since the 1980s and is now bigger than the urban market for both FMCGs (53% share of the total market) and consumer durables (59%). More than half of HLL's products were bought by rural consumers. Yet when HLL considered that its products were currently available in less than 15% of the villages, the company recognized the vast untapped potential that is rural India.

For HLL and other consumer companies, several infrastructural and economic challenges make the task of reaching these small, dispersed markets extremely daunting. First, villages do not have the same infrastructure connectivity as large towns, making flow of goods difficult. For example, in the last 50 years only 40% of villages have been connected by paved, "permanent" roads.[10]

Second, the majority of the 638,691 villages are highly scattered with relatively small populations (see Exhibit 2). HLL, with the most extensive distribution network in the country, was able to reach only 100,000 of these directly. This geographic dispersion, coupled with low per capita volume demand, means that these markets are less cost effective to distribute into using traditional approaches due to the distribution challenges and high capital and operating expenditures.

Third, these villages have poor literacy levels and limited availability of electricity, resulting in low reach of traditional media such as print and television. And finally, there was the question of the need for consumer awareness to influence rural consumers into trying non-local alternatives for hygiene, personal care, and diet.

EXHIBIT 1   DISTRIBUTION OF RURAL INCOME BY HOUSEHOLD

Consumer class	Annual income	Distribution by percentage of total population 1995–1996	Distribution by percentage of total population 2006–2007 (estimates)
Very Rich	Above Indian Rupees 215,000	0.3	0.9
Consuming Class	Indian Rupees 45,001–215,000	13.5	25.0
Climber	Indian Rupees 22,001–45,000	31.6	49.0
Aspirant	Indian Rupees 16,001–22,000	31.2	14.0
Destitute	Indian Rupees 16,000 & Below	23.4	11.1
Total		100.0	100.0

Notes: In December 1995, the exchange rate was US$1 = 35.2 Indian Rupees; in May 2005, it was US$1 = 44 Indian Rupees.

Source: National Council for Applied Economic Research. The NCAER study is based on the population data provided by the Census of India, which is conducted every 10 years. In 2001 (most recent data), the ratio of rural to urban population in India was 742 million to 285 million. The same ratio was 628 million to 217 million in 1991.

EXHIBIT 2   DISTRIBUTION OF RURAL POPULATION

Size of population	Number of villages	% of total villages
Less than 200	92,541	15.6
200–500	127,054	21.4
501–1000	144,817	24.4
1001–2000	129,662	21.9
2001–5000	80,313	13.5
5001–10000	18,758	3.2
Total number of villages	593,154*	100.0

* Total inhabited villages is 638,691.

Source: Census of India, 2001.

A Need for a New System

In the past, HLL had tried traditional approaches to expand reach such as appointing new distributors and wholesalers. However, these projects were limited in their ability to solve the entire problem. To begin with, these projects required setting up an expensive distribution system in small markets. In addition, these efforts were unable to stimulate demand in villages where there was low awareness of Unilever products. They also failed to overcome logistical challenges such as getting products into markets without good roads or telephone networks. In the end, these efforts yielded only limited results, and what the company was looking for was a fundamentally different approach that overcame these distribution and marketing challenges.

Indeed, Shakti (which means "strength" or "empowerment" in many of the local Indian languages) was different from other rural expansion efforts by HLL, as well as by other consumer products companies in India, for two key reasons. First, it was designed to overcome most, if not all, of the hurdles encountered in prior rural forays while still maintaining channel control and cost efficiency. Second, the Shakti mindset provided the company an opportunity to participate in social and economic development of rural areas, a significant shift in the selling-only model that previously dictated multinational activities in rural markets.

How Shakti Works

The team at HLL manages three separate initiatives under the Shakti umbrella: (1) the Shakti Entrepreneur Program, (2) the Shakti Vani Program, and (3) the I-Shakti community portal. Shakti leverages the network of self-help groups that had been created by the federal and state governments across villages in India. These self-help groups were development initiatives targeted at enhancing local savings and industry (such as handicrafts and other hand-made products) and creating a stronger social system within rural villages.

A typical self-help group consisted of 8–20 members and activities included learning new vocational skills, airing grievances, and resolving local disputes. Moreover, these groups also acted as savings cooperatives. Daily contributions by the members are invested in a joint account and then loaned internally to members as per their needs. Based on savings, these groups also gained access to institutions engaged in micro-credit lending activities, many of them supported by the government or local or international non-profits.

However, a continuing gap in the rural economy and the development of self-help groups was the limited number of opportunities to use micro-credit in developing new ventures. Most micro-enterprises usually consisted of small ventures such as basket-weaving, local handicraft, and agriculture projects that produced outputs that were sold within the same community. The managers at HLL recognized the opportunity to create a new type of profitable venture by applying micro-finance to building a local business that had long-term profit and growth potential for the entrepreneur.

Shakti Entrepreneur Program

The longest running and most successful Shakti initiative is the entrepreneurship program. The Shakti Entrepreneur program seeks to expand HLL's reach by involving the village communities, specifically rural women, into its business venture. Leveraging the participants of existing self-help groups, HLL invites one woman (or sometimes more, depending on the size of the area to be served) from a target village to become a Shakti entrepreneur or Shakti-amma[11] to promote and distribute Unilever products within a group of 4–6 neighboring communities. Often in collaboration with local partners, the Shakti team holds a local Concept Selling Meeting in which prospective entrepreneurs are screened on a range of criterion. These include support extended to the entrepreneur from her family and community, access to funds and current sources of income, ability to devote time and energy to Shakti, and ability to manage the business without on-going active supervision.

Initially, Shakti entrepreneurs are expected to invest around Rs.10,000 ($227, which is approximately equal to the annual per capita income in rural India) to buy the necessary inventory of Unilever products. These funds are usually made available via micro-credit loans through self-help groups, since perspective rural entrepreneurs may not have access to traditional means of credit. Sometimes though, bank loans may be obtained

against collateral such as cattle and livestock. Unilever products such as soaps, laundry detergent, oral and skin care products, hair oil and shampoos, flour, tea, and salt are provided in affordable, small, "daily-use" sizes (e.g., sachets), each costing between Rs.2 to Rs.18 ($0.04 to $0.38). The entrepreneur is supported by a HLL team member, the Rural Sales Promoter (RSP), who is responsible for training each Shakti entrepreneur in the skills required to be a distributor.

Shakti entrepreneurs are encouraged to sell to the village community as well as to small local retailers. They sell to consumers at the retail prices and to retailers at the trade price, earning 11%–13% on consumer sales and 3% on trade sales. Monthly turnover is expected to be approximately equivalent to the initial inventory of Rs.10,000 ($227), although in the case of mature entrepreneurs it is known to exceed Rs.25,000 ($568). For the typical entrepreneur, this leaves her with a net monthly profit of Rs.700–1200 ($16–27), which is equal to or exceeds the average monthly income in rural India. Moreover, for most Shakti entrepreneurs these business activities are designed to be supplemental in nature, leaving sufficient time for existing local livelihoods activities.

Entrepreneurs are known to apply ingenuity in overcoming the infrastructural challenges faced in rural India. For example, an entrepreneur in Nalgonda district was able to expand her market reach by contracting the back-hauling services of an auto-rickshaw that plied between neighboring villages. Others are known to hire relatives and friends in surrounding villages to act as salespersons. HLL's RSPs also assist the entrepreneur in creating sales promotions and special events, such as a health day,[12] which brings a doctor to the village to disseminate information about health and hygiene, and Shakti day, which creates a village fair atmosphere with games, songs, and product giveaways.

Shakti Vani Program

The second initiative in Shakti is a communication-led program, called Shakti "Vani" (Sanskrit for "speech"). Vani is a socially led communication effort which involves a "Vani" (speaker), appointed from the community, to spread information and awareness on important issues such as health, hygiene, sanitation, and personal care. The objective for this program is to be an advertising medium within the rural markets for both health challenges and company solutions. Hence, Vani helps create awareness of not only the problems but also how HLL's products offer ways to overcome them.

The Vani is appointed from the self-help group, and after a training program, travels from village to village spreading information about Unilever products at gatherings such as village events, local schools, and self-help group meetings. The Vani earns a fixed salary per day based on the route and villages covered. The program does not generate any direct revenues for HLL. Rather, it is designed to be a cost effective approach to promoting company brands. The program had covered 10,000 villages in 2004 and targets 50,000 more in 2005 and was expected to cost around Rs. 9,000–11,000 per village per year.

Shakti Community Portal

A recent addition to Shakti is the "I-Shakti" community-based portal. I-Shakti makes available Internet connectivity, relevant information, and education services to rural areas. Currently, the project has been rolled out in Andhra Pradesh in South-Central India in cooperation with the local government, which has set up computer kiosks in local villages. The portal has modules covering important information such as health, sanitation, agriculture, and animal husbandry and has also linked to the Internet via a once-daily dial-up connection. For villages poorly connected with road transport, this results in a significant advantage when compared with the need to travel to towns for basic information about prices of agricultural outputs, local weather forecasts, and medical queries.

While the I-Shakti program was designed primarily as a resource for the local community, the company can also use this as a medium to convey its brand messages. In an area which was not conducive to traditional advertising methods, these community-based portals provided a useful marketing tool. By building brand messages into the software package, HLL's I-Shakti portal can help the company market to areas with limited media coverage and low literacy. To scale up the program to other regions, the cost was estimated to be approximately Rs.29,000 (US$648) per portal.

Shakti Today

Since inception in 2001, Shakti has expanded its network to cover 80,000 villages through 25,000 Shakti entrepreneurs in 12 out of 28 states of India. What makes the project especially intriguing is that it offers a model for generating economic benefits for the company while also producing social benefits for rural communities.

Economically, HLL sees considerable advantages from the Shakti model as an entrepreneurial approach to entering new markets in rural India. First, it leads to greater reach without having to augment an expensive distribution chain built around large volumes. Second, it creates goodwill and awareness for the company and its products, by using local talent to act as spokespersons in areas where traditional advertising media cannot reach. In this environment, word-of-mouth is an effective source of influence and persuasion. Third and finally, it creates a stake in the communities within which Shakti operates, creating first-mover advantage over rival FMCG companies as well as countering the future growth of possible imitation products.

EXHIBIT 3   SCENES FROM SHALIGOVARAM VILLAGE IN RURAL ANDHRA PRADESH

Photos by Maulin Vakila

A Shakti entrepreneur

Photos by Maulin Vakila

An I-Shakti kiosk

An important component of the local social impact of Shakti comes from its focus on women entrepreneurs. As other micro-credit initiatives serving the rural poor have shown, women are better borrowers than men. Women have better repayment rates and are more likely to invest profits in opportunities to improve their families' condition.

Furthermore, HLL also believed that improving the condition of women could positively impact their status in the family and in the community. Gaining control over some portion of household income can empower women and help alleviate some of the gender inequality that exists in families in rural India. Additionally, being a Shakti entrepreneur can generate new found respect for these women by others in the community. To quote a Shakti entrepreneur, "Now, when I go out of the house, everyone immediately recognizes me and calls out 'Shakti-amma'. . . . I want my children to have even greater opportunities and I think that this can only happen with education."

Shakti: The Challenges Ahead

The Shakti model took some time to develop before it was ready for large-scale implementation. The project was approved within HLL in 2000, and by the end of 2003, there were less than 3000 entrepreneurs. By mid-2005 scale-up was beginning to occur, and the Shakti team was looking to extend its reach to 100,000 villages and 30,000 entrepreneurs by the end of 2006. HLL, however, is still looking to refine its model. The Shakti management team is exploring ways to increase the income of the individual Shakti entrepreneurs, which they feel will help manage the drop-out rates. They also recognize that additional training is crucial for the entrepreneur to improve her earning capabilities. Although drop-out rates are declining, they are still around 5%–7% per quarter.

The sheer size of operations as the initiative scales up has also brought challenges. Shakti began as a two-member team at HLL with ambitious goals. Today, the project has relationships with over 350 non-profit organizations and other non-traditional partners. For Shakti, local and international non-profits play a vital role in providing an understanding of local communities. Moreover, they act as aggregators of the local communities through the self-help groups that they run and offer Shakti local credibility due to the goodwill established in rural villages. To help manage these new partnerships, the Shakti team has grown to 45 at HLL. Collaborating with such a diverse and growing group of partners, however, brings out a set of challenges around relationship management and social performance expectations that are new for HLL.

Is Shakti a Solution to the Growth Crisis at HLL?

Since 2000, Shakti has taken off. By the end of 2006, it is poised to reach 100,000 villages and 30,000 entrepreneurs. As a result, the Shakti model has been extensively studied by other Unilever subsidiaries, journalists, and students as well as competitors. Currently, Shakti-inspired models are being implemented in Unilever Bangladesh and Unilever Sri Lanka. Yet crucial questions remain: Will Shakti and the base-of-the-pyramid markets it targets deliver to HLL much-needed long term growth and become a key source of future profitability? If other competitors introduce similar distribution approaches, will Shakti need to modify its business model? And can HLL convert this ambitious new rural thrust into a source of sustainable competitive advantage?

Case Discussion Questions:

1. From a resource-based view, what were HLL's competitive advantages prior to launching Shakti?
2. From an institution-based view, what are the barriers against ventures such as Shakti?
3. Why is HLL pursuing Shakti? Is Shakti successful?
4. From the perspective of those at the base of the pyramid, what is the impact of Shakti's activities on poverty alleviation?
5. What metrics can Shakti use to measure its impact on poverty?
6. What should Shakti do to increase its effectiveness in relieving poverty?

NOTES

[1] Hindustan Lever Limited Corporate Profile (www.hll.com).

[2] C. K. Prahalad & S. Hart, 2002, The fortune at the bottom of the pyramid, *Strategy + Business*, 26 (First Quarter): 2–14.

[3] A new improved HLL, Rediff.com.

[4] *Economic Times*, 2004, A premium future for HLL, September 4.

[5] Excerpt from Hindustan Lever Limited Chairman Mr. K. B. Dadiseth's address at the Annual Shareholders Meeting held on April 25, 2000.

[6] Grameen Bank was a pioneering micro-credit organization started in 1976 in Bangladesh by economics professor Mohammad Yunus. The Bank defied conventional banking rules by lending to the poor with no collateral and relied on self-help groups as a means to ensure accountability of borrowers. As of 2005, Grameen Bank had made cumulative loans of over US$5 billion and maintained a repayment rate of 96%, higher than that of traditional commercial banks. Widely admired by the development community, Grameen's model has been replicated in a number of other emerging economies.

[7] Census of India, 2001.

[8] Census of India, 2001; US$1 = Indian Rs.44, as per foreign exchange rate in May 2005.

[9] National Council for Applied Economic Research.

[10] Issues in Rural Markets, Pradeep Kashyap.

[11] -amma: literally, mother, but also a general term for elder women in India.

[12] C. K. Prahalad, 2004, *The Fortune at the Bottom of the Pyramid: Eradicating Poverty Through Profits*, Upper Saddle River, NJ: Wharton School Publishing.

Acquiring Tools

©David Young-Wolff Photography

Chapter 5

LEARNING OBJECTIVES

After studying this chapter, you should be able to:

1. use the resource-based and institution-based views to explain why nations trade.

2. understand the classical and modern theories of international trade.

3. explain the importance of political realities governing international trade.

4. participate in two leading debates on international trade.

5. draw implications for action.

© Taylor Peden/Transtock/Corbis

Trading Internationally

Why Are German Exports So Competitive?

Until 2009, Germany had been the world's export champion for a long time. Although China snatched the world's export champion title in 2009, Germany's export volume (approximately $1.4 trillion a year) routinely outperforms other powerhouses such as the United States and Japan. On the road, BMW and Mercedes cars visibly set global standards. In information technology (IT), SAP is king of the hill for enterprise resource planning (ERP). In sportswear, many of us wear Adidas shoes. Nivea touches the skins of many female (and some male) readers of this book around the world. In addition to these high-profile firms, Germany also has a lot of less visible but equally successful firms in their respective domains. These typically small- and medium-sized *Mittelstand* firms account for 40% of German exports. Krones (beverage bottling and packaging systems), Heidenhain (encoders for manufacturing equipment), and Dorma (moveable walls) may not be household names, but they hold up to 90% worldwide market share in their niches. Also, consider Neumann microphones, which have captured songs from singers ranging from Elvis Presley to Céline Dion. These tiny microphones can last 22 years before they need repair. But they don't come cheap: A single top-of-the line, made-in-Germany Neumann microphone costs $6,450 (!).

In a world dominated by price-chopping Wal-Mart stores and their suppliers that often produce in China, why do German exports that typically compete in the high end win the hearts, minds, and wallets of so many customers around the world? What is unique about German exports? German products and firms are world renowned for their excellent engineering, superb craftsmanship, and obsession for perfection. Although manufacturing only contributes 30% of Germany's GDP, manufacturing products enjoy a lion's share of Germany's exports.* Not surprisingly, these exports center on engineering driven products, such as automobiles, machinery, and chemical goods. Overall, German exports are not cheap, but they are often "worth it."

Although these positive country-of-origin images associated with German exports are well known to practically every reader of this book, what is typically not appreciated is the formal and informal rules in Germany that are behind its export prowess. Formally, the German government has sought to avoid large-scale deindustrialization (otherwise known as loss of manufacturing jobs) and encouraged firms to produce at home. In an effort to push more unemployed to seek jobs, the German government has trimmed unemployment benefits. The unique "co-determination" scheme implemented since the postwar decades has allowed labor union representatives to occupy half of the seats on firms' supervisory boards, and they naturally are not interested in voting for outsourcing jobs to lower-cost countries. In the face of relentless global cost competition and relatively inflexible labor markets, German managers have been holding down wage increases. German wages have been more or less frozen since the mid-1990s.

Hovering between 1% and 2% in much of the 2000s (before 2008), German economic growth was slow. In part this was due to relatively modest consumer spending. Informally, Germans often tell visitors that saving is a national obsession that goes far back into their history. The post-WWI Great Depression and post-WWII devastation are often pointed out as sources for such understandably thrifty habits. Between 2000 and 2008, consumer spending remained flat in Germany, and it has declined since the 2008–2009 crisis.

* The typical impression that services are underdeveloped in Germany is wrong: 69% of its GDP is contributed by services (and agriculture has another 1%) and Germany is the world's third-largest *exporter* of commercial services (behind the United States and Britain. To avoid confusion, we use the term "German exports" to refer to "manufacturing exports" here.

Powerful industrial infrastructure and modest domestic consumption combine to suggest that exports are often the only source of German economic growth. And what a growth engine German exports are. Between 2000 and 2008, exports grew by 80%, resulting in a hefty trade *surplus* of 8% of GDP in 2008—in contrast, the US trade *deficit* was 6% of GDP and Spain's was 10%. Such an outstanding export performance is also helped by Germany's trading partners. Nine out of the top ten importers of German products are within the European Union (EU), with France in the lead. Of the top ten, the United States is the second-largest importer. Prior to the 2008–2009 crisis, most of these countries experienced a consumption binge and import boom fueled by cheap credit. So in a way, rather like China and Japan, Germany has earned its surplus by living off the consumption overindulgence of its export customers. Unfortunately, Germany's export success has irritated some of its EU trading partners within the euro area, which have failed to hold down wages but cannot resort to currency devaluation.

However, when the 2008–2009 crisis hit, virtually all the top ten countries that bought German exports cut back on their spending. The collapse of demand has caused a collapse of German exports, forcing the entire German economy to shrink—estimated to be a 6% drop of GDP for 2009. There is some soul searching both inside and outside of Germany on whether the country has relied too much on exports. In October 2009, German chancellor Angela Merkel, after her re-election for the second term, responded to such critics in a major speech:

> Germany's strength lies largely in the fact that the Federal Republic is a center of industry and that it is an export nation. . . . All those who now say we have depended too much on exports are undermining our biggest source of prosperity and must be rebuffed.

Sources: I thank Professor Klaus Meyer (University of Bath) for his assistance. This case is based on (1) Bloomberg, 2009, German exports remain key, October 15, www.bloomberg.com; (2) *Economist*, 2009, The export model sputters, May 9: 53–54; (3) *Economist*, 2009, The lives of others, August 8: 65–66; (4) *Economist*, 2009, Unbalanced Germany, August 8: 10; (5) B. Venohr & K. Meyer, 2009, Uncommon common sense, *Business Strategy Review*, Spring: 39–43.

Why are German exports so competitive in the world? How does international trade contribute to Germany's economic growth and prosperity? Why has its export success irritated some of its trading partners? International trade is the oldest and still the most important building block of international business. It has never failed to generate debate. Debates on international trade tend to be fierce because, as illustrated so powerfully by our Opening Case, so much is at stake. Thanks to the recession, the World Trade Organization (WTO) estimated a 9% decline of world trade in 2009, the biggest such contraction since World War II.[1]

We begin by addressing a crucial question: Why do nations trade? Then we outline how the two core perspectives introduced in earlier chapters, namely, resource-based and institution-based views, can help answer this question. The remainder of the chapter deals with the theories and realities of international trade. As before, debates and implications for action follow.

Exporting
Selling abroad.

Importing
Buying from abroad.

Merchandise
Tangible products being traded.

Services
Intangible services being traded.

Use the resource-based and institution-based views to explain why nations trade

WHY DO NATIONS TRADE?

International trade consists of **exporting** (selling abroad) and **importing** (buying from abroad). Table 5.1 provides a snapshot of the top ten exporting and importing nations in the two main sectors: **merchandise** and **services**. In merchandise exports, although Germany was the world champion, China was not far behind in 2008. In 2009, China dethroned Germany. In merchandise imports, Germany was the second-largest importer behind the United States. In services, the United States was both the largest exporter and the largest importer in 2008.

TABLE 5.1   LEADING TRADING NATIONS

	Top 10 merchandise exporters	Value ($ billion)	World share (%)	Annual change (%)		Top 10 merchandise importers	Value ($ billion)	World share (%)	Annual change (%)
1	Germany	1,465	9.1%	11%	1	United States	2,166	13.2%	7%
2	China	1,428	8.9%	17%	2	Germany	1,206	7.3%	14%
3	United States	1,301	8.1%	12%	3	China	1,133	6.9%	19%
4	Japan	782	4.9%	10%	4	Japan	762	4.6%	22%
5	Netherlands	634	3.9%	15%	5	France	708	4.3%	14%
6	France	609	3.8%	10%	6	United Kingdom	632	3.8%	1%
7	Italy	540	3.3%	10%	7	Netherlands	574	3.5%	16%
8	Belgium	477	3.0%	10%	8	Italy	556	3.4%	10%
9	Russia	472	2.9%	33%	9	Belgium	470	2.9%	14%
10	United Kingdom	458	2.8%	4%	10	South Korea	435	2.7%	22%
	World total	16,127	100%	15%		World total	16,415	100%	15%

	Top 10 service exporters	Value ($ billion)	World share (%)	Annual change (%)		Top 10 service importers	Value ($ billion)	World share (%)	Annual change (%)
1	United States	522	14.0%	10%	1	United States	364	10.5%	7%
2	United Kingdom	283	7.6%	2%	2	Germany	285	8.2%	11%
3	Germany	235	6.3%	11%	3	United Kingdom	199	5.7%	1%
4	France	153	4.1%	6%	4	Japan	166	4.8%	11%
5	Japan	144	3.9%	13%	5	China	152	4.4%	10%
6	Spain	143	3.8%	11%	6	France	137	3.9%	6%
7	China	137	3.7%	8%	7	Italy	132	3.8%	12%
8	Italy	123	3.3%	12%	8	Spain	108	3.1%	10%
9	India	106	2.8%	4%	9	Ireland	103	3.0%	9%
10	Netherlands	102	2.7%	8%	10	South Korea	93	2.7%	12%
	World total	3,730	100%	11%		World total	3,470	100%	11%

Source: Adapted from World Trade Organization, 2009, *Word Trade Report 2009* (Appendix Table 5 and Table 3). All data are for 2008.

Relative to domestic trade, international trade entails much greater complexities (see PengAtlas Map 2.1 and 2.2). So why do nations go through the trouble of trading internationally? More importantly, such gains must be shared by *both* sides. Otherwise, there would be no willing exporters and importers. In other words, international trade is a *win-win* deal. Figure 5.1 shows that world trade growth (averaging about 6% during 1998–2008) routinely outpaces GDP growth (averaging 3% during the same period). Even in 2008, a very difficult year, trade growth (2.2%) still exceeded GDP growth (1.8%).

Why are there gains from trade? How do nations benefit from such gains? The remainder of this chapter will answer these questions. But before proceeding, we need to clarify that it is misleading to say that *nations* trade. A more accurate expression would be: "*Firms* from different nations trade."[2] Unless different governments

FIGURE 5.1   GROWTH IN WORLD TRADE OUTPACES GROWTH IN WORLD GDP (ANNUAL % CHANGE)

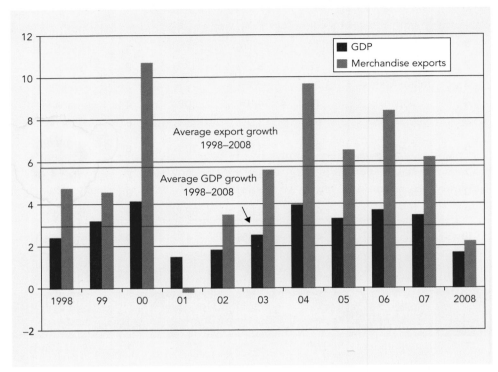

Source: World Trade Organization, 2009, *World Trade 2008, Prospects for 2009*, press release, March 23 (www.wto.org).

Trade deficit

An economic condition in which a nation imports more than it exports.

Trade surplus

An economic condition in which a nation exports more than it imports.

Balance of trade

The aggregation of importing and exporting that leads to the country-level trade surplus or deficit.

directly buy and sell from each other (such as arms sales), the majority of trade is conducted by firms that pay little attention to country-level ramifications. For example, Wal-Mart imports large quantities of goods into the United States and does not export much. Wal-Mart thus directly contributes to the US trade deficit. A **trade deficit** occurs when a nation imports more than it exports. The US government is alarmed by the trade deficit, which is contributed to, in part, by Wal-Mart's massive imports and insignificant exports. But in most countries, governments cannot tell firms such as Wal-Mart what to do (and not to do) unless those firms engage in illegal activities. Likewise, when we discuss US-China trade, we are really referring to thousands of US firms buying from and selling to China, which also has thousands of firms buying from and selling to the United States. Unlike the United States, China has a **trade surplus**, which occurs when a nation exports more than it imports. The aggregation of such buying (importing) and selling (exporting) by both sides leads to the country-level **balance of trade**—namely, whether a country has a trade surplus or deficit. Overall, we need to be aware that when we ask "Why do nations trade?" we are really asking "Why do *firms* from different nations trade?"

Having acknowledged the limitations of the expression that *nations* trade, we will still use it. Why? Because it has been commonly used and also serves as a shorthand version of the more accurate but more cumbersome "firms from different nations trade." This clarification also enables us to use the two *firm-level* perspectives introduced earlier, namely, the resource-based and institution-based views, to shed light on why nations trade.

Recall from Chapter 4 that valuable, rare, inimitable, and organizationally derived (VRIO) products determine a firm's competitive advantage. Applying this insight, we can suggest that valuable, rare, and inimitable products generated by organizationally strong firms in one nation (such as Germany in the Opening Case) can lead to the competitive advantage of a nation's exports.[3] Further, recall from Chapters 2 and 3 that numerous politically and culturally derived rules of the game, known as institutions, constrain individual and firm behavior. Institutions can either limit or facilitate trade. For example, although American movies dominate the world market, Canada, France, and South Korea limit the market share of American movies in order to protect their domestic movie industries. On the other hand, we also see the rise of rules that facilitate trade, such as those promoted by the WTO (see Chapter 8).

Overall, why are there economic gains from international trade? According to the resource-based view, it is because some firms in one nation generate exports that are valuable, unique, and hard to imitate that firms from other nations find it beneficial to import. How do nations benefit from such gains? According to the institution-based view, different rules governing trade are designed to determine how such gains are shared. The remainder of this chapter expands on these two perspectives.

THEORIES OF INTERNATIONAL TRADE

Theories of international trade provide one of the oldest, richest, and most influential bodies of economic literature. Although the publication of Adam Smith's *The Wealth of Nations* in 1776 is usually considered the founding of modern economics, theories of international trade predate Adam Smith. In fact, Adam Smith wrote *The Wealth of Nations* to challenge an earlier theory: mercantilism. In this section, we outline six major theories of international trade: (1) mercantilism, (2) absolute advantage, (3) comparative advantage, (4) product life cycle, (5) strategic trade, and (6) national competitive advantage of industries. The first three are often regarded as **classical trade theories**, and the last three are viewed as **modern trade theories**.

Understand the classical and modern theories of international trade.

Classical trade theories
The major theories of international trade that were advanced before the 20th century, which consist of (1) mercantilism, (2) absolute advantage, and (3) comparative advantage.

Modern trade theories
The major theories of international trade that were advanced in the 20th century, which consist of (1) product life cycle, (2) strategic trade, and (3) national competitive advantage of industries.

Theory of Mercantilism
A theory that suggests that the wealth of the world is fixed and that a nation that exports more and imports less will be richer.

Mercantilism

Widely practiced during the 17th and 18th centuries, the **theory of mercantilism** viewed international trade as a zero-sum game. Its theorists, led by French statesman Jean-Baptiste Colbert, suggested that the wealth of the world (measured in gold and silver at that time) was fixed, and so a nation that exported more and imported less would enjoy the net inflows of gold and silver and become richer. On the other hand, a nation experiencing a trade deficit would see its gold and silver flowing out and, consequently, would become poorer. The upshot? Self-sufficiency would be best.

Although mercantilism is the oldest theory in international trade, it is not an extinct dinosaur. Very much alive, mercantilism is the direct intellectual ancestor of modern-day **protectionism**, which is the idea that governments should actively protect domestic industries from imports and vigorously promote exports. Even today, many modern governments may still be mercantilist at heart.

Protectionism
The idea that governments should actively protect domestic industries from imports and vigorously promote exports.

Absolute Advantage

The theory of absolute advantage, advocated by British economist Adam Smith in 1776, opened the floodgates for the free trade movement that is still going on today. Smith argued that, in the aggregate, the "invisible hand" of the free market, not government, should determine the scale and scope of economic activities. This is known as *laissez faire* (see Chapter 2). Thus, the principles of a market economy should apply for international trade as they apply for domestic trade. By trying to be self-sufficient and to (inefficiently) produce a wide range of goods, mercantilist policies *reduce* the overall wealth of a nation in the long run. Smith thus argued for **free trade**, which is the idea that free market forces should determine how much to trade with little or no government intervention.

Specifically, Smith proposed a **theory of absolute advantage**: With free trade, a nation gains by specializing in economic activities in which that nation has an absolute advantage. What is absolute advantage? A nation that is more efficient than anyone else in the production of any good or service is said to have an **absolute advantage** in the production of that good or service. For example, Smith argued that Portugal enjoyed an absolute advantage over England in producing grapes and wines because Portugal had better soil, water, and weather. Likewise, England had an absolute advantage in raising sheep and producing wool compared to Portugal. It cost England more to grow grapes: an acre of land that could raise sheep and produce fine wool would only produce an inferior grape and a lower-quality wine. Has anyone heard of any world famous English wines? Smith recommended that England specialize in sheep and wool, that Portugal specialize in grapes and wines, and that they trade with each other. Smith's two greatest insights are: (1) By specializing in the production of goods for which each has an absolute advantage, both can produce more. (2) Both can benefit more by trading. By specializing, England produces more wool than it can use and Portugal produces more wine than it can drink. When both countries trade, England gets more

Free trade
The idea that free market forces should determine how much to trade with little or no government intervention.

Theory of absolute advantage
A theory that suggests that under free trade, a nation gains by specializing in economic activities in which it has an absolute advantage.

Absolute advantage
The economic advantage one nation enjoys that is absolutely superior to other nations.

© Radius Images

Is it necessary for a country to have an absolute advantage in some activity, such as the production of a particular crop, in order to participate in international trade?

(and better) wine and Portugal more (and better) wool than either country could produce on its own. In other words, international trade is not a zero-sum game as mercantilism suggests. It is a *win-win* game.

How can this be? Smith's England-Portugal example offered a general example, but let us use a specific example with hypothetical numbers (Figure 5.2 and Table 5.2). For the sake of simplicity, assume there are only two nations in the world: China and the United States. They perform only two economic activities: grow wheat and make aircraft. Production of wheat or aircraft, naturally, requires resources such as labor, land, and technology. Assume that both countries are equally endowed

FIGURE 5.2   ABSOLUTE ADVANTAGE

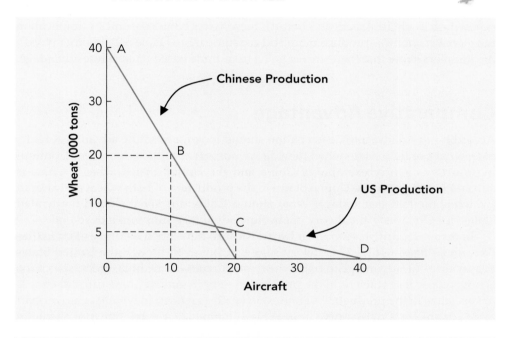

TABLE 5.2   ABSOLUTE ADVANTAGE

Total units of resources = 800 for each country		Wheat	Aircraft
(1) Resources required to produce 1,000 tons of wheat and 1 aircraft	China US	20 resources 80 resources	40 resources 20 resources
(2) Production and consumption with no specialization and without trade (each country devotes *half* of its resources to each activity)	China (point B) US (point C) *Total production*	20,000 tons 5,000 tons *25,000 tons*	10 aircraft 20 aircraft *30 aircraft*
(3) Production with specialization (China specializes in wheat and produces no aircraft, and the United States specializes in aircraft and produces no wheat)	China (point A) US (point D) *Total production*	40,000 tons 0 *40,000 tons*	0 40 aircraft *40 aircraft*
(4) Consumption after each country trades 1/4 of its output while producing at points A and D, respectively (as in Scenario #3)	China US *Total consumption*	30,000 tons 10,000 tons *40,000 tons*	10 aircraft 30 aircraft *40 aircraft*
(5) *Gains* from trade: Increase in consumption as a result of specialization and trade (Scenario #4 versus #2)	China US	+10,000 tons +5,000 tons	0 +10 aircraft

with 800 units of resources. Between the two activities, the United States has an absolute advantage in the production of aircraft. It takes 20 resources to produce an aircraft (for which China needs 40 resources) and the total US capacity is 40 aircraft if it does not produce wheat (point D in Figure 5.2). China has an absolute advantage in the production of wheat. It takes 20 resources to produce 1,000 tons of wheat (for which the United States needs 80 resources) and the total Chinese capacity is 40,000 tons of wheat if it does not make aircraft (point A). It is important to note that the United States can grow wheat and China can make aircraft, albeit inefficiently. Both nations need wheat and aircraft. Without trade, each nation would have to produce *both* by spending half of their resources on each—China at point B (20,000 tons of wheat and 10 aircraft) and the United States at point C (5,000 tons of wheat and 20 aircraft). Interestingly, if they stay at points A and D, respectively, and trade one-quarter of their output with each other (that is, 10,000 tons of Chinese wheat with 10 American aircraft), these two countries—and by implication the global economy—produce more and consume more (Table 5.2). In other words, the numbers show that there are *net* gains from trade based on absolute advantage.

Comparative Advantage

According to Adam Smith, each nation should look for absolute advantage. However, what can nations do when they do *not* possess absolute advantage? Continuing our two-country example of China and the United States, what if China is absolutely inferior to the United States in the production of both wheat and aircraft (which is the real case today)? What should China do? What should the United States do? Obviously, the theory of absolute advantage runs into a dead end.

In response, British economist David Ricardo developed a **theory of comparative advantage** in 1817. This theory suggests that even though the United States has an absolute advantage in both wheat and aircraft over China, as long as China is not equally less efficient in the production of both goods, China can still choose to specialize in the production of one good (such as wheat) in which it has comparative advantage. **Comparative advantage** is defined as the relative (not absolute) advantage in one economic activity that one nation enjoys in comparison with other nations. Figure 5.3 and Table 5.3 show that China's comparative advantage lies in its *relatively less inefficient* production of wheat. If China devotes all resources to wheat, it can produce 10,000 tons, which is 4/5 of the 12,500 tons the United States can produce. However, at a maximum, China can produce only 20 aircraft, which is merely half of the 40 aircraft the United States can make. By letting China specialize in the production of wheat and importing some wheat from China, the United States is able to leverage its strengths by devoting its resources to aircraft. For example, if the United States devotes four-fifths of its resources to aircraft and one-fifth to wheat (point C in Figure 5.3), if China concentrates 100% of its resources on wheat (point E), and if the two trade with each other, then both countries produce and consume more than what they would produce and consume if they inefficiently devoted half of their resources to each activity (see Table 5.3). Again, the numbers show that there are *net* gains from trade, this time from comparative advantage.

One crucial concept here is **opportunity cost**, which refers to the cost of pursuing one activity at the expense of another activity, given the alternatives. For the United States, the opportunity cost of concentrating on wheat at point A in Figure 5.3 is tremendous relative to producing aircraft at point D, because it is only 25% more productive in wheat than China but is 100% more productive in aircraft.

Theory of comparative advantage

A theory that focuses on the relative (not absolute) advantage in one economic activity that one nation enjoys in comparison with other nations.

Comparative advantage

Relative (not absolute) advantage in one economic activity that one nation enjoys in comparison with other nations.

Opportunity cost

Cost of pursuing one activity at the expense of another activity, given the alternatives (other opportunities).

FIGURE 5.3 COMPARATIVE ADVANTAGE

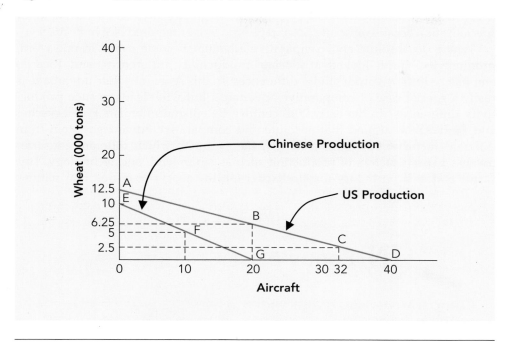

TABLE 5.3 COMPARATIVE ADVANTAGE

Total units of resources = 800 for each country		Wheat	Aircraft
(1) Resources required to produce 1,000 tons of wheat and 1 aircraft	China US	80 resources 64 resources	40 resources 20 resources
(2) Production and consumption with no specialization and without trade (each country devotes *half* of its resources to each activity)	China (point F) US (point B) *Total production*	5,000 tons 6,250 tons *11,250 tons*	10 aircraft 20 aircraft *30 aircraft*
(3) Production with specialization (China devotes all resources to wheat, and the United States devotes 1/5 of its resources to wheat and 4/5 of its resources to aircraft)	China (point E) US (point C) *Total production*	10,000 tons 2,500 tons *12,500 tons*	0 32 aircraft *32 aircraft*
(4) Consumption after China trades 4,000 tons of wheat for 11 US aircraft while producing at points E and C, respectively (as in Scenario #3)	China US *Total consumption*	6,000 tons 6,500 tons *12,500 tons*	11 aircraft 21 aircraft *32 aircraft*
(5) *Gains* from trade: Increase in consumption as a result of specialization and trade (Scenario #4 versus #2)	China US	+1,000 tons +250 tons	+1 aircraft +1 aircraft

Relative to absolute advantage, the theory of comparative advantage seems counterintuitive. But comparative advantage is actually far more realistic and useful when applied in the real world than absolute advantage. It is easy to identify an absolute advantage in a highly simplified, two-country world like the one we posited in Figure 5.2, but how can each nation decide what to specialize in when there are over 200 nations in the world? It is simply too challenging to ascertain that one nation is absolutely better than all others in one activity. Is the United States *absolutely* better than not only China, but also all other 200 nations in aircraft production? European nations that produce Airbus planes obviously beg to differ. The theory of comparative advantage suggests that, even without an absolute advantage, the United States can still specialize profitably in aircraft as long as it is relatively more efficient than others. This insight has greatly lowered the threshold for specialization because absolute advantage is no longer required (see In Focus 5.1).

Where do absolute and comparative advantages come from? In one word: productivity. Smith looked at *absolute* productivity differences, and Ricardo emphasized *relative* productivity differences. In this sense, absolute advantage is really a special case of comparative advantage. But what leads to such productivity differences? In the early 20th century, Swedish economists Eli Heckscher and Bertil Ohlin argued that absolute and comparative advantages stem from different **factor endowments**, namely, the extent to which different countries possess various factors of production such as labor, land, and technology. This **factor endowment theory (or Heckscher-Ohlin theory)** proposed that nations

Factor endowment
The extent to which different countries possess various factors of production such as labor, land, and technology.

Factor endowment theory (Heckscher-Ohlin theory)
A theory that suggests that nations will develop comparative advantages based on their locally abundant factors.

IN Focus 5.1

Comparative Advantage and *You*

Despite the seemingly abstract reasoning, the theory of comparative advantage is very practical. Although you may not be aware of it, you have been a practitioner of this theory almost *every day*. How many of you grow your own food, knit your own sweaters, and write your own software? Hardly any! You probably buy everything you consume. By doing this, you are actually practicing this theory. This is because buying your food, sweaters, and software from producers frees up the time it would have taken you to grow your own food, knit sweaters, and write software—even assuming you are multitalented and capable of doing all of the above. As a student, you are probably using this time wisely to pursue a major (ranging from accounting to zoology) in which you may have some comparative advantage. After graduation, you will trade your skills (via your employer) with others who need these skills from you. By specializing and trading, rather than producing everything yourself, you help channel the production of food, sweaters, and software to more efficient producers. Some of them may be foreign firms. You and these producers mutually benefit, because they can produce more for everyone to consume, and you can concentrate on your studies and build your tradable skills.

Let's assume that in your school, you are the best student receiving all As. At the same time, you also drive a cab at night to earn enough money to put you through school. In fact, you become the best cab driver in town, knowing all the side streets, never getting lost, and making more money than other cab drivers. Needless to say, by studying hard during the day and driving a cab at night, you don't have a life. However, your efforts are handsomely rewarded when the best company in town hires you after graduation and very soon, as a fast tracker, you become the best manager in town. Of course, you quit driving a cab. The best cab driver (who doesn't sleep) can earn about $50,000 a year, whereas the best manager (who does sleep) can make $500,000—your choice is obvious. One day, you jump into a cab from your office to rush to the airport. The cab driver who is a recent immigrant and who doesn't speak your language well misunderstands your instruction, gets lost, and is unnecessarily stuck in a bad traffic jam. As soon as you become irritated because you may miss your flight, you start to smile because you remember today's lecture. "Yes, I have an absolute advantage both in driving a cab and being a good manager compared with this poor cab driver. But by focusing on my comparative advantage in being a good manager," you remember what your professor said, "this cab driver, whose abilities are nowhere near my cab driving skills, can tap into his comparative advantage (funny, he has one!), trade his skills with me, and can still support his family." With this pleasant thought, you end up giving the driver a big tip when arriving at the airport.

will develop comparative advantages based on their *locally abundant* factors.[4] Numerous examples support the theories of comparative advantage and factor endowments (see In Focus 5.2 on Brazil). For example, labor shortages in the West led to the development of telephone automation technology. However, Indian call centers that service Western clients (a form of service export) use human labor, an abundant factor in India, to replace some automation functions when answering the phone. This makes Western clients happier, because they can actually talk to a live person instead of talking to a machine or pushing buttons (push 1 for this, push 2 for that), which they hate.

In summary, the *classical* theories of mercantilism, absolute advantage, and comparative advantage have laid the foundation. More recently (since the mid-20th century), three *modern* theories, outlined next, have emerged.

Product Life Cycle

The three classical theories all paint a *static* picture: If England has an absolute or comparative advantage in textiles, which it does mostly because of its factor endowments such as favorable weather and soil, it should keep making textiles.

IN Focus 5.2

Brazil's Comparative Advantage in Agriculture

A pine tree in a forest in Finland needs 50 years before it can be felled to make paper. A eucalyptus tree in coastal Brazil is ready in seven. Grapes in France can only be harvested once a year. Grapes in northeastern Brazil can bear fruit twice a year. Chicken and hog farmers in Canada have to consume energy to heat the barns. Their competitors in Brazil need no energy to heat their animals' dwellings. Blessed by an abundant supply of sun, soil, and water, Brazil is a preeminent player in agricultural products such as beef, coffee, rubber, soya, and sugar. Although Brazil's agricultural prowess may be the envy of many less endowed countries, in Brazil it has become a source of frustration. For much of the 20th century, the Brazilian government sought to deviate from Brazil's dependence on agriculture-based commodities and to industrialize, often with little regard to comparative or competitive advantage. Their favorite policy was protectionism, which often did not succeed.

Brazil's market opening since the 1990s has led more Brazilians to realize that the country's comparative advantage indeed lies in agriculture. One commodity that can potentially transform the low prestige associated with agricultural products is sugar cane–based ethanol. Brazil is a world leader in the production of ethanol, which has been mandated as an additive to gasoline used in cars since the 1970s. A system to distribute ethanol to gas stations, an oddity in the eyes of the rest of the world until recently, now looks like a national treasure that is the envy of the world. At present, no light vehicle in Brazil is allowed to run on pure gasoline. Since 2007, the mandatory blend for car fuels is at least 25% ethanol. Brazil currently produces 18 billion liters of ethanol, of which it exports 4 billion—more than half of worldwide exports. Ethanol now accounts for 40% for the fuel used by cars in Brazil. As the global ethanol trade is estimated to rise 25-fold by 2020, Brazil's comparative advantage in agricultural products is destined to shine more brightly.

Sources: Based on (1) *Economist*, 2007, The economy of heat, April 14: 8–9; (2) World Bank, 2008, Biofuels: The promise and the risks, in *World Development Report 2008* (pp. 70–71), Washington: World Bank.

But factor endowments and trade patterns change over time, so the assumption that trade is static does not always hold in the real world. Although England in Adam Smith's time, over 200 years ago, was a major exporter of textiles, today England's textile industry is rather insignificant. So what happened? Although one may argue that the weather in England has changed and the soil has become less fertile for sheep (and wool), it is difficult to believe that weather and soil have changed so much in 200 years, which is a relatively short period for long-run climatic changes. Now consider another example that has nothing to do with weather or soil change. Since the 1980s, the United States changed from a net exporter to a net importer of personal computers (PCs), whereas Malaysia went from being a net importer to a net exporter. Why did patterns of trade in PCs change over time? Classic theories would have a hard time answering this intriguing question.

In 1966, American economist Raymond Vernon developed the **product life cycle theory**, which is the first *dynamic* theory to account for changes in the patterns of trade over time.[5] Vernon divided the world into three categories: the lead innovation nation (which, according to him, is typically the United States), other developed nations, and developing nations. Further, every product has three life cycle stages: new, maturing, and standardized. Shown in Figure 5.4, the first stage involves production of a new product (such as a VCR) that commands a price premium. Such production will concentrate in the United States, which exports to other developed nations. In the second, maturing stage, demand and ability to produce grow in other developed nations such as Australia and Italy, so it becomes worthwhile to produce there. In the third stage, the previously new product is standardized (or commoditized). Therefore, much production will now move to low-cost developing nations that export to developed nations. In other words, comparative advantage may change over time.

Although this theory was first proposed in the 1960s, some later events such as the migration of the PC production have supported its prediction. However, this theory has been criticized on two accounts. First, it assumes that the United States will always be the lead innovation nation for new products. This may be increasingly invalid. For example, the fanciest cell phones are now routinely pioneered in Asia and Europe. Second, this theory assumes a stage-by-stage migration of production, taking at least several years, if not decades. In reality, however, an increasing number of firms now launch new products such as iPods *simultaneously* around the globe.

Strategic Trade

Except mercantilism, none of the theories above say anything about the role of governments. Since the days of Adam Smith, government intervention is usually regarded by economists as destroying value because, they contend, it distorts free trade. But government intervention is extensive and is not going away. In fact, thanks to the global recession, government intervention has been increasing around the world since 2008. Can government intervention actually add value? Since the 1970s, a new theory, strategic trade theory, has been developed to address this question.[6]

Strategic trade theory suggests that strategic intervention by governments in certain industries can enhance their odds for international success. What are these industries? They tend to be highly capital-intensive industries with high barriers to entry where domestic firms may have little chance of entering and succeeding without government assistance. These industries also feature substantial first-mover advantages, namely, advantages that first entrants enjoy and do not share with late entrants. A leading example is the commercial aircraft industry. Founded in 1915 and strengthened by large military orders during World War II,

Product life cycle theory
A theory that accounts for changes in the patterns of trade over time by focusing on product life cycles.

Strategic trade theory
A theory that suggests that strategic intervention by governments in certain industries can enhance their odds for international success.

FIGURE 5.4   THEORY OF PRODUCT LIFE CYCLES

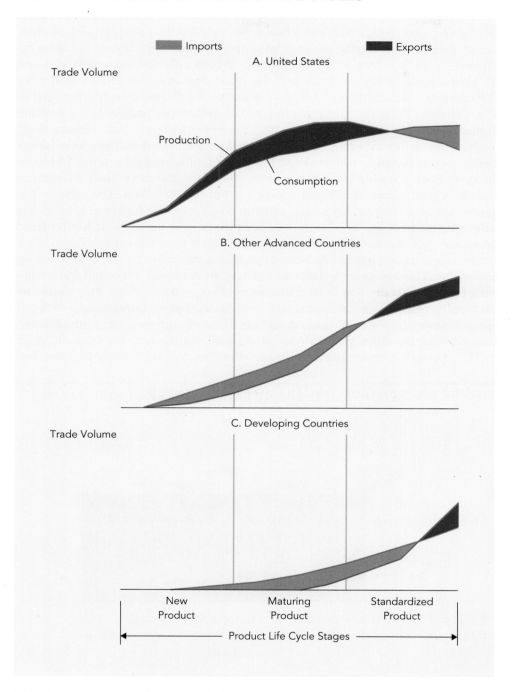

Boeing has long dominated this industry. In the jumbo jet segment, Boeing's first-mover advantages associated with its 400-seat 747, first launched in the late 1960s, are still significant today. Alarmed by such US dominance, British, French, German, and Spanish governments realized then that individual European aerospace firms might be driven out of business by US rivals if these governments did not intervene. So these European governments agreed to launch and subsidize Airbus. Over the past four decades, Airbus has risen from having zero market share to splitting the global market 50-50 with Boeing.

How do European governments help Airbus? Let us use the super-jumbo aircraft, which is larger than the Boeing 747, as an example. Both Airbus and Boeing are interested in entering this market. However, the demand in the next 20 years is only about 400 to 500 aircraft and a firm needs to sell at least 300 just to break even, which means that only one firm can be supported profitably. Shown in Figure 5.5 (Panel A), the outcome will be disastrous if both enter because each will lose $5 billion (Cell 1). If one enters and the other does not, the entrant will make $20 billion (Cells 2 and 3). It is also possible that both will choose not to enter (Cell 4). If a number of European governments promise Airbus a **subsidy** of, say, $10 billion if it enters, then the picture changes to Panel B. Regardless of what Boeing does, Airbus finds it lucrative to enter. In Cell 1, if Boeing enters, it will lose $5 billion as before, whereas Airbus will make $5 billion ($10 billion subsidy minus $5 billion loss). So Boeing has no incentive to enter. Therefore, the more likely outcome is Cell 2, where Airbus enters and enjoys a profit of $30 billion. The subsidy has given Airbus a *strategic* advantage and the policy to assist Airbus is known as a **strategic trade policy**.[7] This has indeed been the case, as the 550-seat A380 entered service in 2007 and became a formidable competitor for the Boeing 747.

Strategic trade theorists do not advocate a mercantilist policy to promote all industries. They propose to help only a few strategically important industries. However, this theory has been criticized on two accounts. First, many scholars and policymakers are uncomfortable with government intervention. What if governments are not sophisticated and objective enough to do this job? Second, many industries claim that they are strategically important. For example, after 9/11, American farmers extracted more subsidies by successfully arguing that

FIGURE 5.5   ENTERING THE VERY LARGE, SUPER-JUMBO MARKET

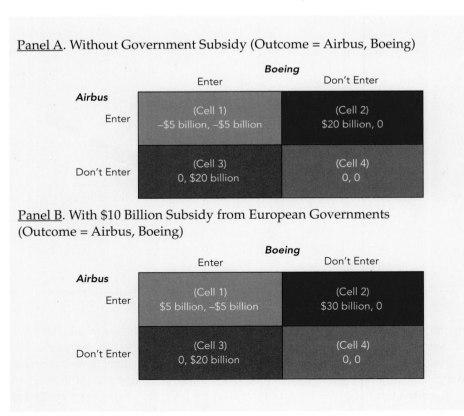

Panel A. Without Government Subsidy (Outcome = Airbus, Boeing)

Panel B. With $10 Billion Subsidy from European Governments (Outcome = Airbus, Boeing)

Subsidy

Government payment to domestic firms.

Strategic trade policy

Government policy that provides companies a strategic advantage in international trade through subsidies and other supports.

agriculture is a strategic industry because the food supply needs to be guarded against terrorists. Since the 2008–2009 crisis, practically every self-respecting industry in every country that has dished out a stimulus package can expect some handouts from its government. Overall, where to draw the line between strategic and nonstrategic industries is tricky.

National Competitive Advantage of Industries

The most recent theory is known as the **theory of national competitive advantage of industries**. This is popularly known as the **diamond theory** because its principal architect, Harvard strategy professor Michael Porter, presents it in a diamond-shaped diagram, as shown in Figure 5.6.[8] This theory focuses on why certain *industries* (but not others) within a nation are competitive internationally. For example, whereas Japanese electronics and automobile industries are global winners, Japanese service industries are notoriously inefficient. Porter is interested in finding out why.

Porter argues that the competitive advantage of certain industries in different nations depends on four aspects, which form a "diamond." First, he starts with factor endowments, which refer to the natural and human resources as noted by the

How did strategic trade policy contribute to the creation of the Airbus A380?

FIGURE 5.6   NATIONAL COMPETITIVE ADVANTAGE OF INDUSTRIES: THE PORTER DIAMOND

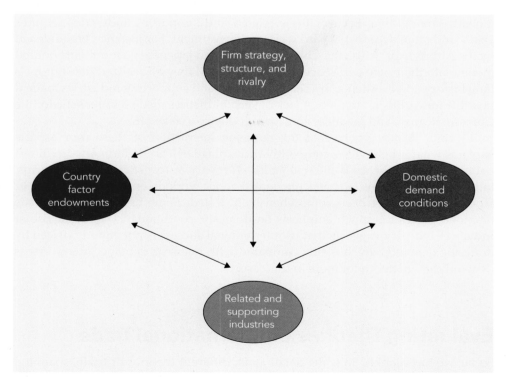

Source: M. Porter, 1990, The competitive advantage of nations (p. 77), *Harvard Business Review*, March–April: 73–93. Reprinted with permission.

Theory of national competitive advantage of industries (diamond theory)

A theory that suggests that the competitive advantage of certain industries in different nations depends on four aspects that form a "diamond."

Heckscher-Ohlin theory. Some countries (such as Saudi Arabia) are rich in natural resources but short on population, whereas others (such as Singapore) have a well-educated population but few natural resources. Not surprisingly, Saudi Arabia exports oil, and Singapore exports semiconductors (which need abundant skilled labor). While building on these insights from previous theories, Porter argues that factor endowments are not enough.

Second, tough domestic demand propels firms to scale new heights. Why are American movies so competitive worldwide? One reason might be the level of extraordinary demand in the US market for exciting movies. Endeavoring to satisfy domestic demand, US movie studios unleash *High School Musical* first and then *High School Musical 2* and *3,* or *Spider-Man* first and then *Spider-Man 2* and *3,* each time packing in more excitement. Most movies—in fact, most products—are created to satisfy domestic demand first. Thus, the ability to satisfy a tough domestic crowd may make it possible to successfully deal with less demanding overseas customers.

Third, domestic firm strategy, structure, and rivalry in one industry play a huge role in its international success or failure. Both sports giants Adidas and Puma hail from Herzogenaurach, a small town in Germany that few have heard of. Yet, they manage to turn the cross-town rivalry into global battles. One reason the Japanese electronics industry is so competitive globally is because its *domestic* rivalry is probably the most intense in the world. When shopping for a digital camera or camcorder in a typical Japanese electronics store, you will find about 200 models (!) to choose from. Most firms producing such a bewildering range of models do not make money. However, the few top firms such as Canon that win the tough competition domestically may have a relatively easier time when venturing abroad because overseas competition is less demanding.

Finally, related and supporting industries provide the foundation upon which key industries can excel. In the absence of strong related and supporting industries, such as engines, avionics, and materials, an aerospace industry cannot become globally competitive. Each of these related and supporting industries requires years (and often decades) of hard work and investment. For instance, emboldened by the Airbus experience, the Chinese, Korean, and Japanese governments poured money into their own aerospace firms. Eventually, they all realized that Europe's long history and excellence in a series of related and supporting industries made it possible for Airbus to succeed. A lack of such industries made it unrealistic for the Chinese, Korean, and Japanese aerospace industry to take off.

Overall, Porter argues that the dynamic interaction of these four aspects explains what is behind the competitive advantage of leading industries in different nations. This theory is the first *multilevel* theory to realistically connect firms, industries, and nations, whereas previous theories work on only one or two levels. However, it has not been comprehensively tested. Some critics argue that the diamond places too much emphasis on domestic conditions.[9] The recent rise of India's IT industry suggests that its international success is not entirely driven by domestic demand, which is tiny compared with overseas demand; it is overseas demand that matters a lot more in this case.

Evaluating Theories of International Trade

So far we have looked in some detail at six different theories of trade, spanning some 300 years of research, debates, and policy changes around the world. Let us now step back and look at the big picture in Table 5.4.

TABLE 5.4 THEORIES OF INTERNATIONAL TRADE: A SUMMARY

Classical theories	Main points	Strengths and influences	Weaknesses and debates
Mercantilism (Colbert, 1600s–1700s)	• International trade is a zero-sum game—trade deficit is dangerous • Governments should protect domestic industries and promote exports	• Forerunner of modern-day protectionism	• Inefficient allocation of resources • Reduces the wealth of the nation in the long run
Absolute advantage (Smith, 1776)	• Nations should specialize in economic activities in which they have an absolute advantage and trade with others • By specializing and trading, each nation produces more and consumes more • The wealth of all trading nations, and the world, increases	• Birth of modern economics • Forerunner of the free trade movement • Defeats mercantilism, at least intellectually	• When one nation is absolutely inferior than another, the theory is unable to provide any advice • When there are many nations, it may be difficult to find an absolute advantage
Comparative advantage (Ricardo, 1817; Heckscher, 1919; Ohlin, 1933)	• Nations should specialize in economic activities in which they have a comparative advantage and trade with others • Even if one nation is absolutely inferior than another, the two nations can still gainfully trade • Factor endowments underpin comparative advantage	• More realistic guidance to nations (and their firms) interested in trade but having no absolute advantage • Explains patterns of trade based on factor endowments	• Relatively static, assuming that comparative advantage and factor endowments do not change over time
Modern theories			
Product life cycle (Vernon, 1966)	• Comparative advantage first resides in the lead innovation nation, which exports to other nations • Production migrates to other advanced nations and then developing nations in different product life cycle stages	• First theory to incorporate dynamic changes in patterns of trade • More realistic with trade in industrial products in the 20th century	• The United States may not always be the lead innovation nation • Many new products are now launched simultaneously around the world
Strategic trade[1] (Brander, Spencer, Krugman, 1980s)	• Strategic intervention by governments may help domestic firms reap first-mover advantages in certain industries • First-mover firms, aided by governments, may have better odds at winning internationally	• More realistic and positively incorporates the role of governments in trade • Provides direct policy advice	• Ideological resistance from many "free trade" scholars and policymakers • Invites all kinds of industries to claim they are strategic
National competitive advantage of industries (Porter, 1990)	• Competitive advantage of different industries in different nations depends on the four interacting aspects of a "diamond" • The four aspects are (1) factor endowments; (2) domestic demand; (3) firm strategy, structure, and rivalry; and (4) related and supporting industries	• Most recent, most complex, and most realistic among various theories • As a multilevel theory, it directly connects research on firms, industries, and nations	• Has not been comprehensively tested • Overseas (not only domestic) demand may stimulate the competitiveness of certain industries

[1] This theory is sometimes referred to as "new trade theory." However, it is now more than 25 years old and no longer that new. In some ways, all the modern trade theories can be regarded as "new" trade theories relative to classical theories. Therefore, to avoid confusion, we label this "strategic trade theory."

Focus 5.3

North Korea versus South Korea

How much difference does international trade make? A lot. The comparison between North Korea and South Korea provides an interesting clue. In 1945, at the time of Korea's liberation from Japanese colonial occupation, the North was slightly more advantageous economically because the North had more industry, whereas the South only had agriculture. However, this mattered very little because the Korean War (1950–1953) devastated the economic fundamentals of both. After the war, both essentially started from scratch and were roughly equal in terms of backwardness. Fast forward to 2009: the differences were striking, as evidenced by this nighttime satellite image of the two countries. North Korea's per capita GDP was $1,800 (based on purchasing power parity, PPP), 155th in the world. In contrast, South Korea had a per capita GDP of $27,939 (based on PPP), 23rd in the world. So what happened to these two equally devastated countries populated by the same people sharing the same cultural heritage?

After the Korean War, North Korea adopted an isolationist policy of self-sufficiency. Although North Korea received aid from the Soviet Union and China, it refused to join the communist "common market"—the Council for Mutual Economic Assistance (CMEA), which was hardly a practitioner of "free trade." The collapse of the Soviet Union has exacerbated North Korea's economy, which has suffered from chronic food shortages. At present, North Korea's only reliable exports are illegal drugs, weapons, and counterfeits. North Korea's nuclear weapons are viewed by experts as an *economic*, not a military, weapon. Sadly, with nothing else to trade with the rest of the world, North Korea's only bargaining chip to extract more donations of rice, oil, and technology from its reluctant donor countries (led by the United States) is to wave its nukes.

© Jason Reed/Reuters/Landov

In contrast, South Korea undertook a strong export strategy. Since the early 1960s, the government provided extensive export subsidies, adopted policies to encourage inflows of foreign capital, and reduced import barriers. As a result, South Korea became one of the "four tigers" in East Asia known for its economic prowess—the other three are Hong Kong, Singapore, and Taiwan. This is not to say that the South Korean economy is perfect. It is not, as illustrated by the devastation of the 1997–1998 financial crisis that showed its structural problems. Nevertheless, economically, a weakened South Korea is still much stronger than North Korea. In the last decade, South Korea has bounced back from the crisis and embraced the Internet era. Since 1996, South Korea has been a proud member of the Organization for Economic Cooperation and Development (OECD)—known as "the rich countries' club," whose only other Asian members are Japan and Singapore. At present, South Korea is one of the world's leaders in per capita broadband usage.

Overall, between 1968 and 2008, the average annual GDP growth rate in South Korea was approximately 8%, whereas North Korea trailed increasingly behind, averaging about 3%. Although there are many reasons behind the radically different economic performance between the two Koreas, international trade is a crucial component of any answer offered. In 1968, North Korea's international trade volume was about two-thirds of South Korea's. By 2008, South Korea's trade volume beat North Korea's by 180 *times*.

Sources: This case was prepared by Professor **Kenny K. Oh** (University of Missouri at St. Louis). It was based on (1) *Business Week*, 2003, The other Korean crisis, January 20: 44–52; (2) *CIA World Factbook*, 2009, www.cia.gov; (3) S. Kim, B. Kim, & K. Lee. 2006, Assessing the economic performance of North Korea, 1954–1989, *Proceedings of Annual Meetings of Allied Social Sciences Association*; (4) World Bank, 2009, World Development Indicators database.

The classical pro-free trade theories seem like common sense today, but they were *revolutionary* in the late 1700s and early 1800s in a world dominated by mercantilistic thinking. These theories attracted numerous attacks. But eventually, they defeated mercantilism, at least intellectually.

All theories simplify to make their point. Classical theories rely on highly simplistic assumptions of a model consisting of only two nations and two goods. The theories also assume perfect **resource mobility**—the assumption that a resource used in producing a product for one industry can be shifted and put to use in another industry. One resource removed from wheat production, for example, can be moved to make aircraft. In reality, though, not all resources can be moved. Farm hands, for example, will probably have a hard time assembling modern aircraft. Further, classical theories assume no foreign exchange complications and zero transportation costs. So is free trade still as beneficial as Smith and Ricardo suggested in the real word of many countries, numerous goods, imperfect resource mobility, fluctuating exchange rates, high transportation costs, and product life cycle changes? The answer is still *"Yes!"* Worldwide data support the *basic* arguments of free traders such as Smith and Ricardo.[10] In Focus 5.3 compares the economic performance of North Korea versus South Korea to drive home this point. (See "Debates and Extensions" for disagreements.)

Instead of relying on simple factor analysis, modern theories rely on more realistic product life cycles, first-mover advantages, and Porter's diamond to explain and predict patterns of trade. Overall, classical and modern theories have significantly contributed to today's ever-deepening trade links around the world. Yet, the victory of pro-free trade theories is not complete. The political realities governing international trade, outlined next, indicate that mercantilism is still alive and well.

REALITIES OF INTERNATIONAL TRADE

International trade has substantial mismatches between theories and realities. The political realities are that plenty of trade barriers exist. Although some trade barriers are being dismantled, many will remain. Let us examine why this is the case. To do so, we will first discuss the two broad types of trade barriers: tariff barriers and nontariff barriers.

Explain the importance of political realities governing international trade.

Tariff Barriers

A **tariff barrier** is a means of discouraging imports by placing a tariff (tax) on imported goods. As a major tariff barrier, an **import tariff** is a tax imposed on a good brought in from another country. Figure 5.7 uses rice tariffs in Japan to show *unambiguously* that net losses, known as **deadweight costs**, occur when import tariffs are imposed.

- Panel A: In the absence of international trade, the domestic price is P_1 and domestic rice farmers produce Q_1, determined by the intersection of domestic supply and demand curves.

- Panel B: Because Japanese rice price P_1 is higher than world price P_2, foreign farmers export to Japan. Japanese farmers reduce output to Q_2. Japanese consumers enjoy more rice at Q_3 at a much lower price P_2.

Resource mobility
Assumption that a resource used in producing a product for one industry can be shifted and put to use in another industry.

Tariff barrier
Trade barrier that relies on tariffs to discourage imports.

Import tariff
A tax imposed on imports.

Deadweight cost
Net losses that occur in an economy as a result of tariffs.

FIGURE 5.7   TARIFF ON RICE IMPORTS IN JAPAN

<u>Panel A.</u> No international trade

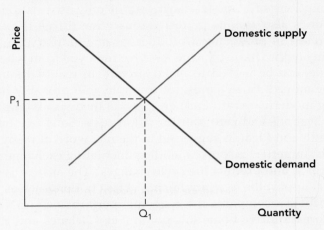

<u>Panel B.</u> Imports with no Tariff

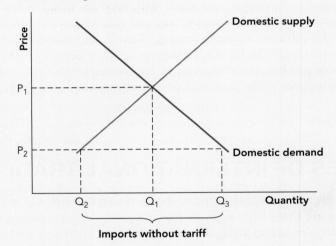

<u>Panel C.</u> Imports with Tariff

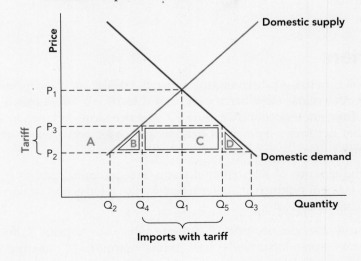

- Panel C: The government imposes an import tariff, effectively raising price from P_2 to P_3. Japanese farmers increase production from Q_2 to Q_4, and consumers pay more at P_3 and consume less by reducing consumption from Q_3 to Q_5. Imports fall from Q_2Q_3 in Panel B to Q_4Q_5 in Panel C.

Classical theorists such as Smith and Ricardo would have advised Japan to enjoy the gains from trade in Panel B. But political realities land Japan in Panel C, which, by limiting trade, introduces total inefficiency represented by the area consisting of A, B, C, and D. However, Japanese rice farmers gain the area of A and the government pockets tariff revenues in the area of C. Therefore:

Net losses (deadweight) = Total inefficiency − Net gain

$$= \text{Area } (A + B + C + D) - \text{Area } (A + C)$$

$$= \text{Area } (B + D)$$

The net losses (areas B and D) represent unambiguous economic inefficiency to the nation as a whole. Japan is not alone in this regard. A Microsoft Xbox 360 console that retails for $360 in the United States costs $1,000 (!) in Brazil, after adding import tariffs.[11] In 2009, the United States slapped a 35% import tariff on tires made in China. Brazilian Xbox gamers and American tire buyers have to pay more, and some may be unable to afford the products. Although not being able to lay your hands on an Xbox will have no tangible damage, some economically struggling US drivers who should have replaced their worn-out tires may be forced to delay replacing their tires—and some may be *killed* should they be involved in accidents before they are able to afford the now more expensive tires.[12]

Given the well-known net losses, why are tariffs imposed? The answer boils down to the political realities. Although (almost) everybody in a country suffers because of higher prices, it is very costly to politically organize individuals and firms that are geographically scattered in order to advance the case for free trade.[13] On the other hand, certain special interest groups tend to be geographically concentrated and skillfully organized to advance their interest. Although farmers represent less than 5% of the Japanese population, they represent disproportionate votes in the Diet (Japanese congress). Why? Diet districts were drawn up in the aftermath of World War II when most Japanese lived in rural areas. Although the majority of the population now lives in urban areas, such districts were never re-zoned. Thus, when the powerful farm lobby speaks, the Japanese government listens. Likewise, in the United States, the United Steelworkers union pushed for tariffs to be imposed on Chinese tires, and President Obama thought the tariffs would generate support among the union members for his controversial health care reforms.[14]

Nontariff Barriers (NTBs)

Today, tariff barriers are often criticized around the world, and nontariff barriers are now increasingly the weapon of choice in trade wars. A **nontariff barrier (NTB)** discourages imports using means other than taxes on imported goods. NTBs include subsidies, import quotas, export restraints, local content requirements, administrative policies, and antidumping duties.

Subsidies, as noted earlier, are government payments to domestic firms. Much like their Japanese counterparts, European farmers are masters of extracting subsidies even though they constitute only 2% of the EU population. The EU's Common

Nontariff barrier (NTB)
Trade barrier that relies on nontariff means to discourage imports.

Agricultural Policy (CAP) costs European taxpayers $47 billion a year, eating up 40% of the EU budget.[15] European consumers do not like CAP, and governments and farmers in developing countries eager to export their foodstuffs to the EU hate it.

Import quotas are restrictions on the quantity of goods that can be brought into a country. Import quotas are worse than tariffs because foreign goods can still be imported if tariffs are paid. Quotas are thus the most straightforward denial of absolute or comparative advantage. For example, the textile industry in developed economies had been "temporarily" protected by quotas for about 30 years—until 2005.[16] As soon as the protectionist Multifiber Agreement (MFA) was phased out and textile quotas were lifted on January 1, 2005, China's comparative (and probably absolute) advantage in textiles *immediately* became apparent. In the first quarter of 2005, the number of Chinese pants exported to the United States rose 1,573%, T-shirts 1,277%, and underwear 318%.[17] In the second quarter of 2005, both the United States and EU said "Enough!" and slapped quotas on Chinese textiles again.

Because import quotas are protectionist pure and simple, they force countries to shoulder certain political costs in today's largely pro-free trade environment. In response, **voluntary export restraints (VERs)** have been developed to show that, on the surface, exporting countries *voluntarily* agree to restrict their exports. In essence, VERs are export quotas. One of the most (in)famous examples is the VERs that the Japanese government agreed to in the early 1980s to restrict US-bound automobile exports. The voluntary export restraints, of course, were a euphemism because the Japanese did not really volunteer to restrict their exports. Only when faced with concrete threats did the Japanese reluctantly agree.

Another NTB is **local content requirements**, which are rules stipulating that a certain proportion of the value of the goods made in one country must originate from that country. The Japanese automobile VERs are again a case in point. Starting in the mid-1980s, because of VERs, Japanese automakers switched to producing cars in the United States through foreign direct investment (FDI; see Chapter 6). Initially such factories were "screwdriver plants," because a majority of components were imported from Japan and only the screwdrivers were needed to tighten the bolts. To deal with this issue, many countries impose local content requirements, mandating that a domestically produced product will still be treated as an "import" subject to tariffs and NTBs unless a certain fraction of its value (such as the 51% specified by the Buy America Act) is produced locally.

Administrative policies are bureaucratic rules that make it harder to import foreign goods. Since 2008, Indonesia and Malaysia have limited imports to certain ports. India has banned Chinese toys, citing safety concerns. Argentina has revived the import licensing regime.[18] The United States has recently tightened requirements to label the origin of pigs and pork products imported from Canada, and caused Canada to appeal to the WTO (see the Closing Case).

Finally, the arsenal of trade weapons also includes **antidumping duties**. Chapter 11 will expand the discussion on dumping (selling below cost) and antidumping duties in much greater detail.

Economic Arguments against Free Trade

Taken together, trade barriers undermine international trade. Although certain domestic industries and firms benefit from them, the entire country—or at least a majority of its consumers—tends to suffer. Given these well-known negative aspects, why do people make arguments against free trade? This section outlines

Import quota
Restriction on the quantity of imports.

Voluntary export restraint (VER)
An international agreement that shows that exporting countries voluntarily agree to restrict their exports.

Local content requirement
A requirement stipulating that a certain proportion of the value of the goods made in one country must originate from that country.

Administrative policy
Bureaucratic rules that make it harder to import foreign goods.

Antidumping duty
Tariffs levied on imports that have been "dumped" (selling below costs to "unfairly" drive domestic firms out of business).

economic arguments against free trade; we will deal with political arguments in the next section. There are two prominent economic arguments against free trade: (1) the need to protect domestic industries and (2) the need to shield infant industries.

The oldest and most frequently used economic argument against free trade is the urge to protect domestic industries, firms, and jobs from allegedly "unfair" foreign competition—in short, protectionism. The following excerpt is from an 1845 petition of the French candle makers to the French government:

> We are subject to the intolerable competition of a foreign rival, who enjoys such superior capabilities for the production of light, that he is flooding the domestic market at an incredibly low price. From the moment he appears, our sales cease, all consumers turn to him, and a branch of French industry whose ramifications are innumerable is at once reduced to complete stagnation. This rival is nothing other than the sun. We ask you to be so kind as to pass a law requiring the closing of all windows, skylights, shutters, curtains, and blinds—in short, all openings, holes, chinks, and fissures through which sunlight penetrates.[19]

Although this was a hypothetical satire written by a French free trade advocate Fredric Bastiat 160 years ago, these points are often heard today. Such calls for protection are not limited to commodity producers like candle makers. Highly talented individuals, such as American mathematicians and Japanese sumo wrestlers, have also called for protection. Foreign math PhDs grab 40% of US math jobs, and recent US math PhDs face a jobless rate of 11%. Many American math PhDs have thus called for protection of their jobs. Similarly, Japanese sumo wrestlers insist that foreign sumo wrestlers should not be allowed to throw their weight around in Japan.[20]

The second argument is the **infant industry argument**. Young domestic firms need government protection. Otherwise, they stand no chance of surviving and will be crushed by mature foreign rivals. It is thus imperative that governments level the playing field by assisting infant industries. Although this argument is sometimes legitimate, governments and firms have a tendency to abuse it. Some protected infant industries may never grow up and continue to request subsidies. When Airbus was a true infant in the 1960s, it no doubt deserved some subsidies. However, by the 2000s, Airbus has become a giant that can take on Boeing. In some years, Airbus *outsells* Boeing. Nevertheless, Airbus continues to ask for subsidies, which European governments continue to provide.

Political Arguments against Free Trade

Political arguments against free trade are based on advancing a nation's political, social, and environmental agenda regardless of possible economic gains from trade. These arguments include (1) national security, (2) consumer protection, (3) foreign policy, and (4) environmental and social responsibility.

First, national security concerns are often invoked to protect defense-related industries. France has always insisted on maintaining an independent defense industry to produce nuclear weapons, aircraft carriers, and combat jets. Although the French can purchase such weapons at much lower costs from the United States, which is eager to sell them, the French answer has usually been: "No, thanks!"

Second, consumer protection has frequently been used as an argument for nations to erect trade barriers. American hormone-treated beef was banned by the European Union (EU) between 1989 and 1995 because of the alleged health risks.

Infant industry argument
The argument that if domestic firms are as young as "infants," in the absence of government intervention, they stand no chances of surviving and will be crushed by mature foreign rivals.

© Justin Guariglia

Which political arguments against free trade did environmental activists use to try to stop the importation of Asian shrimp into the United States?

Even though the United States won a WTO battle on this, the EU still has refused to remove the ban.

Third, trade intervention is often used to meet foreign policy objectives. **Trade embargoes** are politically motivated trade sanctions against foreign countries to signal displeasure. Many Arab countries maintain embargoes against Israel. The United States has enforced embargoes against Cuba, Iran, North Korea, Sudan, and Syria. In 2009, DHL paid a record fine of $9.4 million because it violated US embargoes and sent shipments to Iran, Sudan, and Syria. Specifically, DHL, according to a US Treasury Department statement, "may have conferred a significant economic benefit to these sanctioned countries that potentially created extraordinarily adverse harm." What are such dangerous shipments? Condoms, Tiffany jewelry, and radar detectors for cars, according to the same Treasury Department statement.[21]

Finally, environmental and social responsibility can be used as political arguments to initiate trade intervention against certain countries. In a "shrimp-turtle" case, the United States banned shrimp imports from India, Malaysia, Pakistan, and Thailand. Although the shrimp were not harvested from US waters, they were caught using a technique that also accidentally trapped sea turtles, an endangered species protected by the United States. India, Malaysia, Pakistan, and Thailand were upset and brought the case to the WTO, alleging that the United States invoked an environmental law as a trade barrier. The WTO sided with these nations and demanded that the US ban be lifted, with which the United States later complied (see In Focus 8.1).

DEBATES AND EXTENSIONS

LEARNING OBJECTIVE

4

Participate in two leading debates on international trade.

International trade has no shortage of debates. This section highlights two leading debates: (1) trade deficit versus surplus and (2) classic theories versus new realities.

Trade Deficit versus Trade Surplus

A leading debate in international trade deals with trade deficit. Smith and Ricardo would probably turn in their graves if they heard that one of today's hottest trade debates still echoes the old debate between mercantilists and free traders 200 years ago. Nowhere is the debate more ferocious than in the United States, which runs the world's largest trade deficit (combining the US deficit in merchandise trade with its surplus in service trade). In 2006, it reached a record-breaking $760 billion (6% of GDP). Then it dropped to $731 billion in 2007 and $681 billion in 2008. Thanks to the recent recession, US trade deficit shrank to about 3% of GDP in 2009.[22] Should this level of trade deficit be of concern? Armed with classic theories, free traders argue that the deficit is not a grave concern. They argue that the United States and its trading partners mutually benefit by developing a deeper division of labor based on comparative advantage. Former Treasury Secretary Paul O'Neill went so far as to say that trade deficit was "an antiquated theoretical construct."[23] The 2008 Nobel laureate in economics Paul Krugman argued in an earlier article in 1993:

International trade is not about competition, it is about mutually beneficial exchange.... Imports, not exports, are the purpose of trade. That is, what

Trade embargo
Politically motivated trade sanctions against foreign countries to signal displeasure.

a country gains from trade is the ability to import things it wants. Exports are not an objective in and of themselves: the need to export is a burden that a country must bear because its import suppliers are crass enough to demand payment.[24]

Critics strongly disagree. They argue that international trade *is* about competition—about markets, jobs, and incomes. Trade deficit has always been blamed on a particular country with which the United States runs the largest deficit: Japan in the 1980s and 1990s and China in the 2000s. Therefore, the recent trade deficit debate is otherwise known as the China trade debate. Unlike Japan that is a democratic, military ally of the United States, China's status as the last surviving communist power makes matters a lot worse when the US trade deficit with it reached $266 billion in 2008—more than one-third of the total deficit. "China bashing" thus is in vogue among some US politicians, journalists, and executives. The United States runs trade deficits with all of its major trading partners—Canada, the EU, Japan, and Mexico—and is in trade disputes with them most of the time (see the Closing Case). Nevertheless, the China trade debate is by far the most emotionally charged and politically explosive.

Major arguments and counterarguments in the China debate are in Table 5.5. It is obvious that in this seemingly intractable debate, emotions are high, and clear answers are few.[25] Two things are certain. Given Americans' appetite for imports, the US trade deficit is difficult to disappear. Drastic measures proposed by some protectionist members of US Congress (such as slapping all Chinese imports with 20% to 30% tariffs if the yuan does not appreciate "satisfactorily") are unrealistic—these would violate the US commitments to the WTO. As China's export drive continues, according to the *Economist*, China will be the "scapegoat of choice" for America's economic problems for a long time.[26] (We will discuss the currency issue in Chapter 7.)

Classical Theories versus New Realities

Although the China trade debate is primarily about *merchandise* trade and unskilled manufacturing jobs that classical theories talk about, another debate (mostly on India) is about *service* trade and high-skill jobs in high technology such as IT. Typically dealing with wheat from Australia to Britain on a slow boat, classical theorists certainly could not have dreamed about using the Internet to send *this* manuscript to India to be typeset and counted as part of India's service exports.

We already discussed a part of this debate in Chapter 4 when focusing on outsourcing. That debate deals with *firm*-level capabilities; here let us examine *country*-level and *individual*-level ramifications. Classical theorists and their modern-day disciples argue that the United States and India trade by tapping into each other's comparative advantage: India leverages its abundant, high-skill, and low-wage labor and Americans will channel their energy and resources to higher-skill, higher-paying jobs. Although regrettably certain Americans will lose jobs, the nation as a whole benefits—so the theory goes.

But, not so fast, argued retired MIT economics professor Paul Samuelson. In an influential 2004 paper, Samuelson suggested that, in a more realistic world, India can innovate in an area, such as IT, where the United States traditionally enjoys comparative advantage.[27] Indian innovation can reduce the price of US software exports and curtail the wage of US IT workers. Despite the availability of cheaper goods (which is a plus), the net effect may be that the United States is *worse* off as a whole. Samuelson is not an anti-globalization ideologue. Instead, he won a

TABLE 5.5 DEBATE ON THE US TRADE DEFICIT WITH CHINA[1]

US trade deficit with China is a huge problem	US trade deficit with China is not a huge problem
Naïve trader versus unfair protectionist (in China)	**Market reformer versus unfair protectionist (in America)**
• The United States is a "naïve" trader with open markets. China has "unfairly" protected its markets.	• China's markets are already unusually open. Its trade volume (merchandise and services) is 75% of GDP, whereas the US volume is only 25%—so is Japan's.
Greedy exporters	**Eager foreign investors**
• Unscrupulous Chinese exporters are eager to gut US manufacturing jobs and drive US rivals out of business.	• Two-thirds of Chinese exports are generated by foreign-invested firms in China, and numerous US firms have invested in and benefited from such operations in China.
The demon who has caused deflation	**Thank China (and Wal-Mart) for low prices**
• Cheap imports sold at "the China price" push down prices and cause deflation.	• Every consumer benefits from cheap prices brought from China by US firms such as Wal-Mart.
Intellectual property (IP) violator	**Inevitable step in development**
• China is a blatant violator of IP rights, and US firms lose $2 billion a year.	• True, but (1) the United States did that in the 19th century (to the British), and (2) IP protection will improve in China.
Currency manipulator[2]	**Currency issue is not relevant**
• The yuan is severely undervalued (maybe up to 40%), giving Chinese exports an "unfair" advantage in being priced at an artificially low level.	• The yuan is somewhat undervalued, but (1) US and other foreign firms producing in China benefit, and (2) yuan appreciation will not eradicate US trade deficit.
Trade deficit will make the United States poorer	**Trade deficit does not cause a fall in the US standard of living**
• Since imports have to be paid, the United States borrows against its future with disastrous outcomes.	• As long as the Chinese are willing to invest in the US economy (such as Treasury bills), what's the worry?
Something has to be done	**Remember the gains from trade argued by classic theories?**
• If the Chinese don't do it "our way," the United States should introduce drastic measures (such as slapping 20%–30% tariffs on all Chinese imports).	• Tariffs will not bring back US jobs, which will simply go to Mexico or Malaysia, and will lead to retaliation from China, a major importer of US goods and services.

[1] This table is a representative sample—but not an exhaustive list—of major arguments and counterarguments in this debate. Other issues include (1) statistical reporting differences, (2) environmental damage, and (3) national security, which are not discussed in order to make this table manageable.
[2] The currency issue will be discussed at length in Chapter 7 (see especially the Closing Case).

Sources: Based on (1) *BusinessWeek*, 2004, The China price, December 6: 102–112; (2) *BusinessWeek*, 2009, Free trade in the slow lane, September 21: 50; (3) *China Business Review*, 2008, US exports to China hit new high, September–October: 36–39; (4) *Economist*, 2005, From T-shirts to T-bonds, July 30: 61–63; (5) *Economist*, 2005, The dragon comes calling, September 3: 24–25; (6) O. Shenkar, 2005, *The Chinese Century*, Philadelphia: Wharton School Publishing; (7) L. Tyson, 2003, The folly of slapping quotas on China, *BusinessWeek*, December 8: 30; (8) *Wall Street Journal*, 2009, Geithner is exactly wrong on China trade, January 26.

Nobel Prize for his penetrating research on the gains from international trade and he wrote one of the most influential mainstream economics textbooks. Now even Samuelson is not so sure about comparative advantage, one of the founding pillars of modern economics.

The reaction has been swift. Within the same year (2004), Jagdish Bhagwati, an Indian-born, Columbia University trade expert, and his colleagues countered Samuelson by arguing that classical pro-free trade theories still hold.[28] Bhagwati and colleagues wrote:

Imagine that you are exporting aircraft, and new producers of aircraft emerge abroad. That will lower the price of your aircraft, and your gains from trade will diminish. You have to be naïve to believe that this can never happen.

But you have to be even more naïve to think that the policy response to the reduced gains from trade is to give up the remaining gains as well. The critical policy question we must address is: When external developments, such as the growth of skills in China and India, for instance, do diminish the gains from trade to the US, is the harm to the US going to be reduced or increased if the US turns into Fortress America? The answer is: The US will only increase its anguish if it closes its markets.[29]

In any case, according to Bhagwati and colleagues, the "threat" posed by Indian innovation is vastly exaggerated and offshoring is too small to matter much. Although approximately 3.4 million US jobs may be outsourced by 2015, we have to realize that in any given year, the US economy destroys 30 million jobs and creates nearly the same, thus dwarfing the effect of offshoring. Further, Bhagwati argues that newer and higher-level jobs will replace those lost to offshoring.

But here is a huge problem: Where are such newer and higher-level jobs? Will there be enough of such jobs in the United States? Bhagwati has no concrete answer. As discussed in Chapter 4's Closing Case, when Amazon launched the Amazon Kindle e-reader, no US-based producer was able to make it, and the manufacturing jobs went to China, South Korea, and Taiwan.[30] In the rapidly expanding $30 billion global solar industry, China is already the number one player making 35% of the world's cells. The United States produces just 5%. In a best case scenario, it will account for less than 15% in 2011, compared with 60% or more from Asia. The Tempe, Arizona-based First Solar is the world's leader in thin film, a crucial component for making solar cells. In 2009, it invested $1 billion to double its capacity and created 4,000 jobs. However, 86% of its output is from Germany and Malaysia and a major new plant is being built in France.[31] If the United States not only loses jobs in traditional manufacturing but also in these new, cutting-edge industries one after another, what does the future hold?

MANAGEMENT SAVVY

Draw implications for action.

How does this chapter answer the big question in global business, adapted for the context of international trade: What determines the success and failure of firms' exports around the globe? The two core perspectives lead to two answers. Fundamentally, the various economic theories underpin the resource-based view, suggesting that successful exports are valuable, unique, and hard-to-imitate products generated by certain firms from a nation. However, the political realities stress the explanatory and predictive power of the institution-based view: As rules of the game, laws and regulations promoted by various special interest groups can protect certain domestic industries, firms, and individuals. These rules can erect trade barriers and make the nation as a whole worse off.

Listed in Table 5.6, three implications for action emerge. First: Location, location, location! In international trade, a savvy manager's first job is to leverage the comparative advantage of world-class locations. For instance, as managers aggressively tapped into Argentina's comparative advantage in wine production, its wine exports grew from $6 million in 1987 to $500 million in 2008.

Second, comparative advantage is not fixed. Managers need to constantly monitor and nurture the current comparative advantage of a location and take advantage of new promising locations. Managers who fail to realize when a location no longer has a comparative advantage are likely to fall behind. For example, numerous German managers have moved production out of Germany, citing the

---

TABLE 5.6   IMPLICATIONS FOR ACTION

- Discover and leverage comparative advantage of world-class locations.

- Monitor and nurture the current comparative advantage of certain locations and take advantage of new locations.

- Be politically active to demonstrate, safeguard, and advance the gains from international trade.

country's reduced comparative advantage in basic manufacturing. However, they still concentrate top-notch, high-end manufacturing in Germany, leveraging its excellence in engineering.

Third, managers need to be politically savvy if they appreciate the gains from trade. In times of economic difficulties, governments are often under pressure to adopt protectionist policies. Although managers at many uncompetitive firms have long mastered the game of using politicians to gain protection, managers at competitive firms tend to shy away from politics. But they often fail to realize that free trade is *not* free—it requires constant efforts to demonstrate and advance the gains from such trade. For example, the US-China Business Council, a pro-free trade (in particular, pro-China trade) group consisting of 250 large US corporations, has spoken out in defense of trade with China.

CHAPTER SUMMARY

1. Use the resource-based and institution-based views to explain why nations trade.
   - The resource-based view suggests that nations trade because some firms in one nation generate valuable, unique, and hard-to-imitate exports that firms in other nations find it beneficial to import.
   - The institution-based view argues that as rules of the game, different laws and regulations governing international trade aim to share gains from trade.

2. Understand the classical and modern theories of international trade.
   - Classical theories include (1) mercantilism, (2) absolute advantage, and (3) comparative advantage.
   - Modern theories include (1) product life cycles, (2) strategic trade, and (3) "diamond."

3. Explain the importance of political realities governing international trade.
   - The net impact of various tariffs and NTBs is that the whole nation is worse off while certain special interest groups (such as certain industries, firms, and regions) benefit.
   - Economic arguments against free trade center on (1) protectionism and (2) infant industries.
   - Political arguments against free trade focus on (1) national security, (2) consumer protection, (3) foreign policy, and (4) environmental and social responsibility.

4. Participate in two leading debates on international trade.
   - (1) Trade deficit versus trade surplus and (2) classical theories versus new realities.

5. Draw implications for action.
   - Discover and leverage comparative advantage of world-class locations.
   - Monitor and nurture the current comparative advantage and take advantage of new locations.
   - Be politically active to demonstrate, safeguard, and advance the gains from international trade.

KEY TERMS

Absolute advantage   150
Administrative policy   166
Antidumping duty   166
Balance of trade   148
Classical trade
   theories   149
Comparative
   advantage   152
Deadweight cost   163
Exporting   146
Factor endowment   154
Factor endowment theory
   (Heckscher-Ohlin
   theory)   154
Free trade   150
Import quota   166
Import tariff   163

Importing   146
Infant industry
   argument   167
Local content
   requirement   166
Merchandise   146
Modern trade theories   149
Nontariff barrier
   (NTB)   165
Opportunity cost   152
Product life cycle
   theory   156
Protectionism   149
Resource mobility   163
Services   146
Strategic trade policy   158
Strategic trade theory   156

Subsidy   158
Tariff barrier   163
Theory of absolute
   advantage   150
Theory of comparative
   advantage   152
Theory of
   mercantilism   149
Theory of national
   competitive advantage
   of industries (diamond
   theory)   159
Trade deficit   148
Trade embargo   168
Trade surplus   148
Voluntary export restraint
   (VER)   166

REVIEW QUESTIONS

1. Look at PengAtlas Maps 2.1 and 2.2. Compare the global position of the United States in merchandise versus service exports.
   a. Does the United States have an advantage globally in either merchandise or services? Does it have an advantage in both? If it has any type of advantage, is it absolute or comparative? Or does it have a disadvantage in both? Explain your answers.
   b. Imagine that you were asked to give reasons why you think that it is good from the US perspective that it is the world's biggest importer in both merchandise and services. What reasons would you mention?

2. International trading is quite complex, so why do nations routinely engage in this activity?

3. Name and describe the two key components of a balance of trade.

4. Briefly summarize the three classical theories of international trade.

5. Compare and contrast the three modern theories of international trade.

6. What are two primary economic arguments that critics use against free trade?

7. Summarize four political arguments against free trade.

8. Is a persistent trade deficit a matter of grave concern? Why or why not?

9. Will the service trade benefit or hurt rich countries?

10. What are some of the factors managers might need to consider when assessing the comparative advantage of various locations around the world?

11. Why is it necessary for business people to monitor political activity concerning international trade?

CRITICAL DISCUSSION QUESTIONS

1. Is the trade policy of your country's government protectionist? Why?

2. What is the ratio of international trade (exports + imports) to GDP in your country? How about the ratio for the United States, the EU, Japan, Russia, China, and Singapore? Why are there such differences?

3. *ON ETHICS:* As a foreign policy tool, trade embargoes, such as US embargoes against Cuba, Iraq (until 2003), and North Korea, are meant to discourage foreign governments. But they also cause a great deal of misery among the population (such as shortage of medicine and food). Are embargoes ethical?

4. *ON ETHICS:* Although the nation as a whole may gain from free trade, certain regions, industries, and individuals may lose livelihood due to foreign competition. How can the rest of the nation help those less fortunate to cope with the impact of international trade?

globalEDGE

YOUR SOURCE FOR
**global business
knowledge**

http://globalEDGE.msu.edu

GLOBAL ACTION

1. Cities worldwide differ considerably along many dimensions. However, one facet of trading internationally is to identify global cities to base a network of operations. Choose one dimension on which to measure different cities. Then, using resources found on the globalEDGE website, develop a report that discusses your findings in detail.

2. At times, corporate tax rates in specific locations can be considered a trade barrier to business development. As a result, locations that have lower tax rates may be trying to encourage corporations to conduct operations or relocate headquarters there. On the globalEDGE website, find a list of tax rates for a variety of locations. If you were part of a company seeking to relocate its operations, which location(s) would you recommend, and why?

VIDEO CASES

Watch "New Ventures" by John Stewart of McKinsey & Company.

1. Stewart discussed how difficult it may be to successfully get into a new venture or industry. Why are there such difficulties?

2. Explain the connection between shifting into a new venture and the considerations of cost, time, quality, and function.

3. Stewart discussed a friend who worked for an oil company. The friend began in oil exploration, then moved into petrochemicals, and finally into plastics. Each type of business had different demands upon that friend and required major adjustments. Do you think that entire countries have a similar problem in terms of having an absolute or comparative advantage in various industries? Why or why not? To what extent could that be used to support the concept of comparative advantage?

4. Stewart pointed out that there are many instances of firms that have failed in new ventures. Why? Governments often seek to develop new industries to compete in global trade. Do his comments suggest anything they may keep in mind?

Closing Case

ETHICAL DILEMMA

Canada and the United States Fight over Pigs

Sharing the world's longest undefended border, Canada and the United States are the best of friends. Their bilateral trading relationship is the world's largest, with $560 billion in volume. The two-way traffic that crosses the Ambassador Bridge between Windsor, Ontario, and Detroit, Michigan, equals all US exports to Japan. Approximately 76% of Canada's exports (about a quarter of its GDP) go to its southern neighbor, making it the largest exporter to the United States. Canadian products command approximately 20% of the US import market share. In comparison, China, the second-largest exporter to the United States, commands slightly over 10%. Canada is also the largest importer of US products, absorbing about a quarter of US exports. The United States runs a sizeable trade deficit with Canada, at $78 billion in 2008. Despite such a close relationship, they fight like "cats and dogs" in trade disputes. Most recently, they have traded blows over pigs.

In an effort to tighten food labeling, the Obama administration in 2009 implemented the Mandatory Country of Origin Labeling (COOL) legislation, requiring US firms to track and notify customers of the country of origin of meat and other agricultural products at each major stage of production, including at the retail level. Unfortunately, such a seemingly innocent move in the name of protecting consumers provoked fierce protests from the Canadian government, hog farmers, and other agricultural producers. In a normal year, Canada would export approximately $3 billion hogs (live pigs) to the United States. In the first three quarters of 2009, such exports suffered from a disastrous 60% drop.

The reason is that many young Canadian pigs are exported to the United States, and they are mixed and raised together with indigenous US pigs for fattening and slaughter. After several months, separating the (immigrant) Canadian pigs from the (native-born) US pigs is challenging and costly. The US Department of Agriculture (USDA) estimates that it will cost the food industry $2.5 billion to comply with the new rules. When facing such hassles, several major US pork producers, including the top five that account for more than half of all pork sold in the United States (Cargill, Hormel, JBS SA, Seaboard, and Smithfield), simply stopped buying hogs from Canada or gradually phased out such purchases. In addition to damaging livestock exports, processed meat products from Canada, including the legendary Canadian bacon, were also broadly affected.

Starting in May 2009, the Canadian and US governments negotiated. While the United States modified some rules to alleviate Canadian concerns, the negotiations eventually broke down. Canada's frustrated Trade Minister Stockwell Day said in October 2009:

© AP Photo/The Waterloo Courier, Greg Brown

> The US requirements are so onerous that they affect the ability of our hog and cattle exporters to compete fairly in the US market. The US law leaves the Canadian government with no choice but to escalate its first formal trade dispute with the Obama Administration by pressing charges at the WTO.

In response, US Trade Representative Ron Dirk and Agriculture Secretary Tom Vilsack in a joint statement in October 2009 argued:

> We believe that our implementation of COOL provides information to consumers in a manner consistent with our WTO commitments. Countries have agreed since long before the existence of the WTO that country-of-origin labeling is a legitimate policy. It is common for other countries to require that goods be labeled as to their origin.

The COOL pig fight is not the only dispute between Canada and the United States. The first edition of *Global Business* reported disputes over

salmon and softwood lumber. The list of Canada's trade grievances has since grown to include "Buy American" purchasing rules and generous US biofuel tax breaks for paper mills.

While Canada and the United States fight over item by item on their long list of trade grievances, a useful mental exercise is to ask: What if these two friendly countries stopped trading all together? Normally, scholars studying this intriguing question would have to use simulation methods based on hypothetical data to entertain what would happen if they stopped trading. Thanks to 9/11, such an unthinkable scenario did take place. Immediately after the terrorist attacks on September 11, 2001, the United States closed all airports, seaports, and land crossings with Canada (and Mexico). The world's largest bilateral trading relationship literally shut down. When the borders reopened days later, US officials undertook intensive inspections of commercial traffic that, among other things, delayed truck carriers for up to 18 hours. An exhaustive study found that Canadian exports to the United States in the fourth quarter of 2001 were 20% lower than they would have been in the absence of the border security consequences of 9/11. Even by 2005, exports from Canada were $12 billion less than they would otherwise have been, had 9/11 and the US security responses not occurred. By the same time (2005), US exports to Canada resumed their "normal" level. In other words, Canadian exporters will suffer disproportionate damage due to any unilateral tightening of the border by the United States—whether for security reasons in the post-9/11 period or for food safety reasons at present. As Canadian hog producers struggle with the recession, the high Canadian dollar, a spike in feed costs, and widespread swine flu fears, it remains to be seen whether cool heads will prevail when fighting over COOL.

Case Discussion Questions:

1. Why do Canada and the United States have the largest bilateral trading relationship in the world?

2. Why do Canadian products have such a large market share in the United States?

3. While 98% of Canada-US trade flows smoothly, trade disputes only affect the remaining 2%. Some argue that the Canadians have overreacted in this case. What do you think?

Sources: I thank Professor Steven Globerman (Western Washington University) for his assistance. It is based on (1) I. Fergusen, 2006, *United States-Canada Trade and Economic Relationship*, Washington: Congressional Research Service; (2) *Globe and Mail*, 2009, Canada turns to WTO over US label law, October 8: B7; (3) S. Globerman & P. Storer, 2008, *The Impacts of 9/11 on Canada-US Trade*, Toronto: University of Toronto Press; (4) *Pig Progress*, 2009, US-COOL dispute proceeds by WTO, October 8, www.pigprogress.net.

NOTES

[Journal acronyms] AER—*American Economic Review;* **BW**—*BusinessWeek;* **HBR**—*Harvard Business Review;* **JEP**—*Journal of Economic Perspectives;* **JIE**—*Journal of International Economics;* **JIBS**—*Journal of International Business Studies;* **JM**—*Journal of Management;* **JMS**—*Journal of Management Studies;* **QJE**—*Quarterly Journal of Economics*

[1] World Trade Organization, 2009, WTO sees 9% global trade decline in 2009, press release, March 23, www.wto.org.

[2] J. Baggs & J. Brander, 2006, Trade liberalization, profitability, and financial leverage, *JIBS*, 37: 196–211.

[3] M. W. Peng, 2001, The resource-based view and international business, *JM*, 27: 803–829.

[4] B. Ohlin, 1933, *Interregional and International Trade*, Cambridge, MA: Harvard University Press. In this work, Ohlin summarized and extended E. Heckscher's research first published in 1919.

[5] R. Vernon, 1966, International investments and international trade in product life cycle, *QJE*, May: 190–207.

[6] J. Brander & B. Spencer, 1985, Export subsidies and international market share rivalry, *JIE*, 18: 83-100; P. Krugman (ed.), 1986, *Strategic Trade Policy and the New International Economics*, Cambridge, MA: MIT Press.

[7] P. Krugman, 1994, *Peddling Prosperity* (p. 238), New York: Norton.

[8] M. Porter, 1990, *Competitive Advantage of Nations*, New York: Free Press.

[9] H. Davies & P. Ellis, 2001, Porter's *Competitive Advantage of Nations*: Time for the final judgment? *JMS*, 37: 1189–1215.

[10] D. Bernhofen & J. Brown, 2005, An empirical assessment of the comparative advantage gains from trade, *AER*, 95: 208–225.

[11] *BW*, 2009, Seeking the next billion gamers, July 6: 54.

[12] Tire Industry Association (TIA), 2009, Tire Industry Association expresses disappointment with President's decision concerning Chinese tire tariff, September 14, Bowie, MD: TIA, www.tireindustry.org.

[13] J. Bhagwati, 2004, *In Defense of Globalization*, New York: Oxford University Press.

[14] *Economist*, 2009, Vandalism: America's mad trade war with China, September 17: Lead story.

[15] *Economist*, 2009, Agricultural subsidies, July 25: 93.

[16] H. Nordas, 2004, The global textile and clothing industry beyond the Agreement on Textiles and Clothing (p. 34), Discussion paper No. 5, Geneva: WTO Secretariat.

[17] *Economist*, 2005, The great stitch-up, May 28: 61–62.

[18] *Economist*, 2009, The nuts and bolts come apart, March 28: 79–81.

[19] F. Bastiat, 1964, *Economic Sophisms*, edited and translated by A. Goddard, New York: Van Norstrand.

[20] M. Kreinin, 2006, *International Economics*, 10th ed. (p. 82), Cincinnati: South-Western Cengage Learning.

[21] *USA Today*, 2009, DHL will pay $9.4M fine to settle shipping dispute, August 7: 2A.

[22] World Trade Organization, 2009, *World Trade Report* (Overview) (p. 4), Geneva: WTO.

[23] *BW*, 2005, America's trade deficit: Expect some storm damage, October 3: 31.

[24] P. Krugman, 1993, What do undergrads need to know about trade? (p. 24), *AER*, 83: 23–26.

[25] L. Dobbs, 2004, *Exporting America: Why Corporate Greed is Shipping American Jobs Overseas*, New York: Warner; O. Shenkar, 2005, *The Chinese Century*, Philadelphia: Wharton School Publishing.

[26] *Economist*, 2003, Tilting at dragons (p. 65), October 25: 65–66.

[27] P. Samuelson, 2004, Where Ricardo and Mill rebut and confirm arguments of mainstream economists supporting globalization, *JEP*, 18 (3): 135–146.

[28] J. Bhagwati, A. Panagariya, & T. Sribivasan, 2004, The muddles over outsourcing, *JEP*, 18 (4): 93–114.

[29] J. Bhagwati & A. Panagariya, 2004, Trading opinions about free trade (p. 20), *BW*, December 27: 20.

[30] G. Pisano & W. Shih, 2009, Restoring American competitiveness, *HBR*, July–August: 114–125.

[31] *BW*, 2009, Can the future be built in America? September 21: 46–51.

Chapter 6

© Siphiwe Sibeko/Reuters/Landov

LEARNING OBJECTIVES

After studying this chapter, you should be able to:

1. define the key terms associated with foreign direct investment (FDI).

2. explain how FDI results in ownership, location, and internalization (OLI) advantages.

3. identify ownership advantages associated with FDI.

4. list ways firms can acquire and neutralize location advantages.

5. appreciate the benefits of internalization advantages.

6. articulate the different political views on FDI and FDI's benefits and costs.

7. understand how multinational enterprises (MNEs) and host country governments bargain.

8. participate in three leading debates on FDI.

9. draw implications for action.

Investing Abroad Directly

South African Firms Invest Abroad

Since apartheid was removed in 1994, South Africa has brewed a series of multinationals that are increasingly active abroad. Although most readers of this book probably have heard about SABMiller (beers) and De Beers (diamonds), how many of you have heard of Didata, MTN, Old Mutual, SASOL, and Standard Bank? If you have not heard of them, watch out as they may soon come to a city near you (if they have not already arrived).

Naturally, South African firms started by entering sub-Saharan African countries. In fact, South Africa is the number one foreign investor in sub-Saharan Africa with more than $8.5 billion plowed into the region. South African Breweries (SAB) first pioneered the concept of the pan-African beer market, and then went on to become the global titan known as SABMiller after acquiring Miller Beer of the United States in 2002. As an early mover in cellular (mobile) phones, telecom provider MTN was one of a handful companies to defy conventional wisdom and prove that Africa could be a huge market for mobile services. Retailers such as Massmart, Shoprite, and Game are bringing Western-style shopping to Malawi, Mozambique, Nigeria, Uganda, and others. Standard Bank has charged into 16 African countries that previously often lacked even basic financial services. "Africa is the next China," one South African businessman noted. South African firms have every intention of enjoying first-mover advantages there.

After a short time cutting their teeth in Africa, many South African firms spread their wings beyond the shores of Africa. In the early 1990s, SAB moved into China and Central and Eastern Europe, establishing strong positions in major emerging economies ahead of global rivals. Since becoming SABMiller, it has further globalized. It is now the second-largest brewer in South America. Old Mutual, South Africa's biggest financial services firm, bought Sweden's oldest insurance house in 2005. Dimension Data (Didata), an IT firm, competes in over 30 countries. SASOL, a chemicals and energy firm, operates in more than 20 countries.

What explains such a surge of internationalization from South Africa? From an institution-based view, the lifting of anti-apartheid sanctions by other countries and the generally open trade and investment environment worldwide have made such global expansion possible. From a resource-based standpoint, since South Africa represents 10% of Africa's population but 45% of its GDP, winning firms in South Africa not surprisingly have a competitive edge in other less competitive African countries. Capabilities that serve African customers well can then be leveraged to more effectively compete in more distant emerging economies such as China, Central and Eastern Europe, and South America. "South Africans do well when they go elsewhere," noted another expert, "because they're not afraid, having done well in the most difficult continent on earth."

Sources: Based on (1) S. Burgess, 2003, Within-country diversity: Is it key to South Africa's prosperity in a changing world? *International Journal of Advertising*, 22: 157–182; (2) *BusinessWeek*, 2008, Africa's dynamo, December 15: 51–56; (3) *Economist*, 2006, Going global, July 15: 59–60; (4) *Economist*, 2009, Africa's new Big Man, April 18: 11.

Why are South African firms increasingly interested in foreign direct investment (FDI)?[1] Is it because of the push from intense competition at home or the pull of lucrative markets abroad? Perhaps both? Recall from Chapter 1 that FDI is defined as investing in activities that control and manage value creation in other countries. Also recall from Chapter 1 that firms that engage in FDI are known as multinational enterprises (MNEs). Because international trade and FDI are closely related, this chapter continues our coverage of international trade in Chapter 5. About 40% of US merchandise trade is either between overseas subsidiaries of US MNEs and US-based units or between US subsidiaries of non-US MNEs and their non-US-based units.[2] Two-thirds of Chinese exports are generated by MNE affiliates producing in that country.

This chapter starts by first defining key terms related to FDI. Then we address a crucial question: Why do firms engage in FDI? We outline how the two core perspectives—namely, resource-based and institution-based views—can help answer this question. Debates and implications for action follow.

Define the key terms associated with FDI.

UNDERSTANDING THE FDI VOCABULARY

Part of FDI's complexity is associated with its vocabulary. This section will try to reduce the complexity by setting the terms straight.

The Key Word Is *Direct*

International investment takes place in two basic ways: FDI and foreign portfolio investment (FPI). FPI refers to holding securities, such as stocks and bonds, of companies in countries outside one's own but does not entail the active management of foreign assets. Essentially, FPI is foreign *indirect* investment. In contrast, the key word in FDI is *direct*—namely, the direct, hands-on management of foreign operations.

For statistical purposes, the United Nations defines FDI as an equity stake of 10% or more in a foreign-based enterprise.[3] A lower percentage invested in a foreign firm is, by definition, FPI. Without a sufficiently large equity, it is difficult to exercise management control rights, namely, the authority to appoint key managers and establish control mechanisms. Many firms invest abroad for the explicit purpose of managing foreign operations, and they need a large equity, sometimes up to 100%, to be able to do that.

Horizontal and Vertical FDI

FDI can be horizontal or vertical. Recall the value chain from Chapter 4, whereby firms perform value-adding activities stage-by-stage in a vertical fashion, from upstream to downstream. When a firm takes the same activity at the same value-chain stage from its home country and *duplicates* it in a host country through FDI, we call this *horizontal FDI* (see Figure 6.1). For example, SABMiller brews beer

Foreign portfolio investment (FPI)
Investment in a portfolio of foreign securities such as stocks and bonds.

Management control rights
The rights to appoint key managers and establish control mechanisms.

in South Africa. Through horizontal FDI, it does the same thing in host countries such as Russia, Thailand, and the United States (see the Opening Case). Overall, horizontal FDI refers to producing the same products or offering the same services in a host country as firms do at home.

If a firm moves upstream or downstream in different value-chain stages in a host country through FDI, we label this vertical FDI (Figure 6.2). For example, if BMW (hypothetically) only assembled cars and did not manufacture components in Germany but entered into components manufacturing through FDI in the

FIGURE 6.1   HORIZONTAL FDI

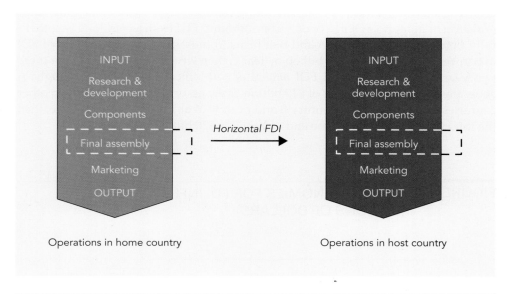

FIGURE 6.2   VERTICAL FDI

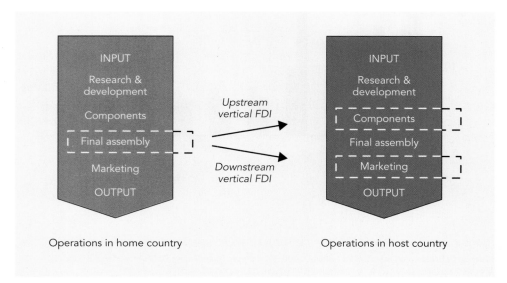

Horizontal FDI

A type of FDI in which a firm duplicates its home country-based activities at the same value chain stage in a host country.

Vertical FDI

A type of FDI in which a firm moves upstream or downstream at different value chain stages in a host country.

United States (an upstream activity in the value chain), this would be **upstream vertical FDI**. Likewise, if BMW did not engage in car distribution in Germany but invested in car dealerships in Egypt (a downstream activity in the value chain), it would be **downstream vertical FDI**.

FDI Flow and Stock

"Flow" and "stock" are often used to describe FDI. **FDI flow** is the amount of FDI moving in a given period (usually a year) in a certain direction. **FDI inflow** usually refers to FDI moving into a country in a year, and **FDI outflow** typically refers to FDI moving out of a country in a year. Figures 6.3 and 6.4 illustrate the top 10 economies receiving inflows and generating outflows. **FDI stock** is the total accumulation of inbound FDI in a country or outbound FDI from a country. Hypothetically, between two countries A and B, if firms from A undertake $10 billion of FDI in B in Year 1 and another $10 billion in Year 2, then we can say that in each of these two years, B receives annual FDI *inflows* of $10 billion and, correspondingly, A generates annual FDI *outflows* of $10 billion. If we assume that firms from no other countries undertake FDI in country B and prior to Year 1 no FDI was possible, then the total *stock* of FDI in B by the end of Year 2 is $20 billion.

Upstream vertical FDI

A type of vertical FDI in which a firm engages in an upstream stage of the value chain in a host country.

Downstream vertical FDI

A type of vertical FDI in which a firm engages in a downstream stage of the value chain in a host country.

FDI flow

The amount of FDI moving in a given period (usually a year) in a certain direction.

FDI inflow

Inbound FDI moving into a country in a year.

FDI outflow

Outbound FDI moving out of a country in a year.

FDI stock

Total accumulation of inbound FDI in a country or outbound FDI from a country across a given period (usually several years).

FIGURE 6.3   TOP 10 ECONOMIES FOR FDI INFLOWS (BILLIONS OF DOLLARS)

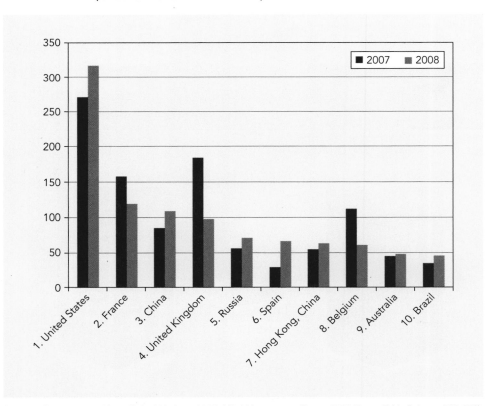

Sources: Data extracted from United Nations, 2009, *World Investment Report 2009* (Annex Table B.1, pp. 247–250), New York and Geneva: UN. Top 10 rankings are based on the magnitude of 2008 FDI inflows.

The differences between flow and stock are important. Figure 6.5 shows the fluctuation of annual FDI inflows, which have dropped since 2008. Since most developed economies are now in recession, they do not appear to be attractive FDI destinations. In contrast, emerging economies as a group attracted 43% of the FDI inflows in 2008 and their share may grow further. Brazil, Russia, India, and China (BRIC) as a group attracted 16% of the global FDI inflows. Firms from emerging economies, such as those from South Africa (see the Opening Case), generated 20% of FDI outflows worldwide. Figure 6.6 shows that the inward FDI stock had been rising until 2007. Essentially, flow is a snapshot of a given point in time, and stock represents the cumulative volume. (See also PengAtlas Map 2.3.)

MNE versus non-MNE

An MNE, by definition, is a firm that engages in FDI when doing business abroad. Note that non-MNE firms can also do business abroad by exporting and importing, licensing and franchising, outsourcing, or engaging in FPI. What sets MNEs apart from non-MNEs is FDI. An exporter has to undertake FDI in order to become

FIGURE 6.4   TOP 10 ECONOMIES FOR FDI OUTFLOWS (BILLIONS OF DOLLARS)

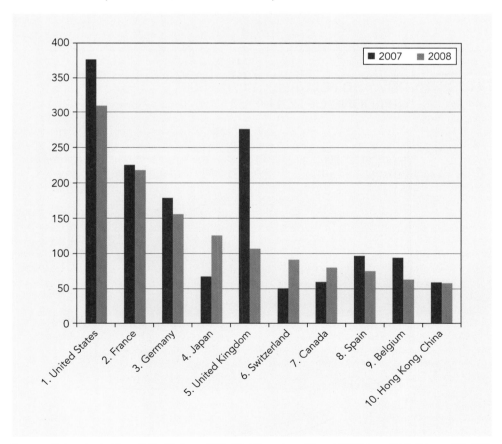

Sources: Data extracted from United Nations, 2009, *World Investment Report 2009* (Annex Table B.1, pp. 247–250), New York and Geneva: UN. Top 10 rankings are based on the magnitude of 2008 FDI outflows.

FIGURE 6.5   ANNUAL FDI INFLOWS, 1990–2008
(BILLIONS OF DOLLARS)

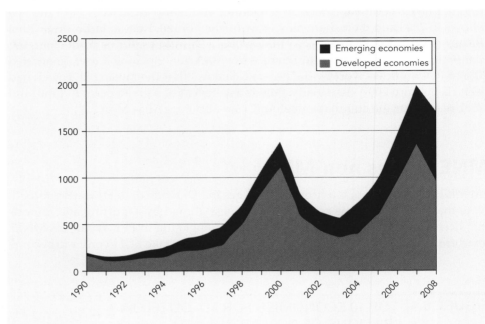

Source: Based on data from United Nations, 2009, *World Investment Report 2009*, New York and Geneva: UN (with additional data from stats.unctad.org). Data on "emerging economies" combine data on "developing economies" and "transition economies" in the source.

FIGURE 6.6   INWARD FDI STOCK, 1990–2008
(BILLIONS OF DOLLARS)

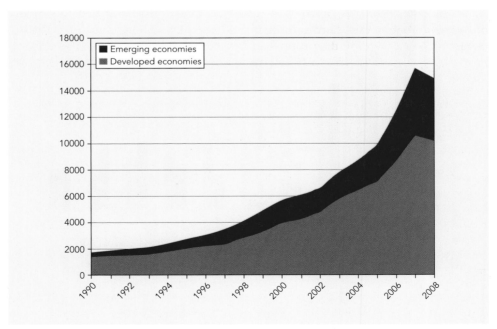

Source: Based on data from United Nations, 2009, *World Investment Report 2009*, New York and Geneva: UN (with additional data from stats.unctad.org). Data on "emerging economies" combine data on "developing economies" and "transition economies" in the source.

an MNE. In other words, SABMiller would not be an MNE if it brewed all its beers in South Africa and exported them around the world. SABMiller became an MNE only when it started to directly invest abroad, as the Opening Case illustrates.

Although some people argue that MNEs are a new organizational form that emerged after World War II, that is simply not the case. MNEs have existed for at least 2,000 years, with some of the earliest examples found in the Phoenician, Assyrian, and Roman times.[4] In 1903 when Ford Motor Company was founded, it exported its sixth car. Ford almost immediately engaged in FDI by having a factory in Canada that started producing cars in 1904.[5] MNEs have experienced significant growth since World War II. In 1990, there were 37,000 MNEs with 170,000 foreign affiliates. At present, over 82,000 MNEs (more than *double* the number in 1990) control approximately 810,000 foreign affiliates (close to *five times* the number in 1990).[6] Clearly, there is a proliferation of MNEs lately.

WHY DO FIRMS BECOME MNEs BY ENGAGING IN FDI?

Explain how FDI results in ownership, location, and internalization (OLI) advantages.

Having set the terms straight, we need to address a fundamental question: Why do so many firms—ranging from those in the ancient world to today's BMW, Wal-Mart, and SABMiller—become MNEs by engaging in FDI? Without getting into details, we can safely say that there must be economic gains from FDI. More importantly, given the tremendous complexities associated with FDI, such gains must significantly outweigh the costs.[7] What are the sources of such gains? The answer, as suggested by British scholar John Dunning and illustrated in Figure 6.7, boils down to firms' quest for ownership (O) advantages, location (L) advantages, and internalization (I) advantages—collectively known as **OLI advantages**.[8] The two core perspectives introduced earlier, resource-based and institution-based views, enable us to probe into the heart of this question.

In the context of FDI, **ownership** refers to MNEs' possession and leveraging of certain valuable, rare, hard-to-imitate, and organizationally embedded (VRIO) assets overseas. Owning the proprietary technology and the management know-how that goes into making a BMW helps ensure that the MNE can beat rivals abroad.

FIGURE 6.7   WHY DO FIRMS BECOME MNEs BY ENGAGING IN FDI? AN OLI FRAMEWORK

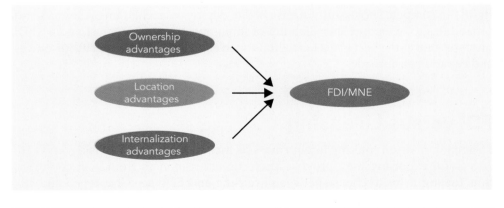

OLI advantages

A firm's quest for ownership (O) advantages, location (L) advantages, and internalization (I) advantages via FDI.

Ownership

An MNE's possession and leveraging of certain valuable, rare, hard-to-imitate, and organizationally embedded (VRIO) assets overseas in the context of FDI.

Location advantages are those enjoyed by firms because they do business in a certain place. Features unique to a place, such as its natural or labor resources or its location near particular markets, provide certain advantages to firms doing business there. For example, South Africa provides a convenient platform for BMW's operations to cover sub-Saharan Africa. From a resource-based view, an MNE's pursuit of ownership and location advantages can be regarded as flexing its muscles—its resources and capabilities—in global competition.

Internalization refers to the replacement of cross-border markets (such as exporting and importing) with one firm (the MNE) locating and operating in two or more countries. For example, BMW could sell its technology to a Chinese firm for a fee. This would be a non-FDI-based market entry mode technically called licensing. BMW chooses to have some FDI in China by assembling cars. In other words, external market transactions (in this case, the market for buying and selling of technology through licensing) are replaced by internalization. From an institution-based view, internalization is a response to the imperfect rules governing international transactions, known as **market imperfections** (or **market failure**). Evidently, Chinese regulations governing the protection of intellectual property such as BMW's proprietary technology do not give BMW sufficient confidence that those rights will be protected. Therefore, internalization is a must.

Overall, firms become MNEs because FDI provides ownership, location, and internalization advantages that they otherwise would not obtain. The next three sections explain why this is the case.

LEARNING OBJECTIVE

3

Identify ownership advantages associated with FDI.

OWNERSHIP ADVANTAGES

All investments, including both FDI and FPI, entail ownership of assets. So what is unique about FDI? This section highlights the benefits of direct ownership, and compares and contrasts FDI with licensing when considering market entries abroad.

The Benefits of Ownership

Remember that "direct" (D) is the key word in FDI. FDI requires a significant equity ownership position. The benefits of direct ownership lie in the *combination* of equity ownership rights and management control rights. Specifically, the ownership rights provide the much-needed management control rights. In contrast, FPI represents essentially insignificant ownership rights and no management control rights. To compete successfully, firms need to deploy overwhelming resources and capabilities to overcome their liability of foreignness (see Chapters 1 and 4). FDI provides one of the best ways to facilitate such extension of firm-specific resources and capabilities abroad.

Location

Advantages enjoyed by firms operating in a certain location.

Internalization

The replacement of cross-border markets (such as exporting and importing) with one firm (the MNE) locating and operating in two or more countries.

Market imperfection (market failure)

The imperfect rules governing international transactions.

FDI versus Licensing

Basic choices when entering foreign markets include exporting, licensing, and FDI. Successful exporting may provoke protectionist responses from host countries, thus forcing firms to choose between licensing and FDI (see Chapters 5 and 10). Between licensing and FDI, which is better? Table 6.1 shows three reasons that may compel firms to prefer FDI to licensing.

TABLE 6.1   WHY FIRMS PREFER FDI TO LICENSING

- FDI reduces dissemination risks.

- FDI provides tight control over foreign operations.

- FDI facilitates the transfer of tacit knowledge through "learning by doing."

First, FDI affords a high degree of direct management control that reduces the risk of firm-specific resources and capabilities being taken advantage of. One of the leading risks abroad is **dissemination risk,** defined as the possibility of unauthorized diffusion of firm-specific know-how. If a foreign company grants a license to a local firm to manufacture or market a product, "it runs the risk of the licensee, or an employee of the licensee, disseminating the know-how or using it for purposes other than those originally intended."[9] For example, Pizza Hut found out that its long-time licensee in Thailand disseminated its know-how and established a direct competitor, simply called The Pizza Company, which recently controlled 70% of the market in Thailand.[10] Although owning and managing proprietary assets through FDI does not completely shield firms from dissemination risks (after all, their employees can quit and join competitors), FDI is better than licensing because licensing does not provide such management control. Understandably, FDI is extensively used in knowledge-intensive, high-tech industries such as automobiles, electronics, chemicals, and IT.[11]

Second, FDI provides more direct and tighter control over foreign operations. Even when licensees (and their employees) harbor no opportunistic intention to take away secrets, they may not always follow the wishes of the foreign firm that provides the know-how. Without FDI, the foreign firm cannot control its licensee. For example, Starbucks entered South Korea by licensing its format to ESCO. Although ESCO soon opened ten stores, Starbucks felt that ESCO was not aggressive enough in growing the chain. But there was little Starbucks could do. Eventually, Starbucks switched from licensing to FDI, which allowed it to directly promote the aggressive growth of the chain in South Korea.

Finally, certain knowledge (or know-how) calls for FDI as opposed to licensing. Even if there is no opportunism on the part of licensees and if they follow the wishes of the foreign firm, certain know-how may be simply too difficult to transfer to licensees without FDI. There are two basic categories of knowledge: explicit and implicit. Explicit knowledge is codifiable and can be written down and transferred without losing much of its richness. Tacit knowledge, on the other hand, is noncodifiable and its acquisition and transfer requires hands-on practice. For example, a driving manual represents a body of explicit knowledge. However, mastering the manual without any road practice does not make you a good driver. Tacit knowledge is clearly more important and harder to transfer and learn—it can only be acquired through learning by doing (in this case, practice driving under the supervision of an experienced driver). Likewise, operating a Wal-Mart store involves a great deal of knowledge, some explicit (often captured in an operational manual) and some tacit. As such, simply giving foreign licensees a copy of the Wal-Mart operational manual will not be enough. Foreign employees will need to learn directly from Wal-Mart personnel by actually doing the job.

From a resource-based standpoint, it is Wal-Mart's tacit knowledge that gives it competitive advantage (see Chapter 4). Wal-Mart owns such crucial tacit knowledge, and it has no incentive to give that knowledge away to licensees without

Dissemination risk
The risk associated with unauthorized diffusion of firm-specific know-how.

having some management control over how that knowledge is used. Therefore, properly transferring and controlling tacit knowledge calls for FDI. Overall, ownership advantages enable the firm, now becoming an MNE, to more effectively extend, transfer, and leverage firm-specific capabilities abroad.[12]

LEARNING OBJECTIVE

4

List ways firms can acquire and neutralize location advantages.

LOCATION ADVANTAGES

The second key word in FDI is F, referring to a *foreign* location. Given the well-known liability of foreignness, foreign locations must offer compelling advantages to make it worthwhile to undertake FDI.[13] We may regard the continuous expansion of international business, such as FDI, as an unending saga in search of location-specific advantages. This section (1) highlights the sources of location advantages and (2) outlines ways to acquire and neutralize location advantages.

Location, Location, Location

Certain locations possess geographical features that are difficult to match by others. For example, although Austria politically and culturally belongs to the West, the country is geographically located in the heart of Central and Eastern Europe (CEE) and its capital Vienna is actually *east* of Prague, the Czech Republic, and Ljubljana, Slovenia. Not surprisingly, Vienna is an attractive site as MNE regional headquarters for CEE. Similarly, Miami is blessed by its location that is close to Latin America and the Caribbean. It also has excellent air links with all major cities in North America. Miami thus advertises itself as the "Gateway of the Americas." South Africa is a great launch pad for business in sub-Saharan Africa. These locations naturally attract a lot of FDI.

Beyond natural geographical advantages, location advantages also arise from the clustering of economic activities in certain locations, referred to as **agglomeration**.[14] For instance, the Netherlands grows and exports two-thirds of the world's exported cut flowers. Slovakia produces more cars per capita than any other country in the world, thanks to the quest for agglomeration benefits by global automakers. Dallas attracts all the world's major telecom equipment makers and many telecom service providers, making it the Telecom Corridor. In Focus 6.1 highlights how agglomeration has made Wichita, Kansas, the "Air Capital of the World." Overall, agglomeration advantages stem from:

- **knowledge spillover**—the diffusion of knowledge from one firm to others among closely located firms that attempt to hire individuals from competitors.
- industry demand that creates a skilled labor force whose members may work for different firms without moving out of the region.
- industry demand that facilitates a pool of specialized suppliers and buyers also located in the region.[15]

Beyond the quest for geographical and agglomeration advantages, sometimes firms undertake FDI in search of markets. Airbus is building an assembly plant in China, *not* because it is cheap to make planes in China; the country's inefficiencies in advanced aerospace manufacturing more than offset the savings brought by cheap labor (see Chapter 5). Instead, Airbus has one clear goal: greater access to the Chinese aviation market.[16]

Agglomeration
Clustering of economic activities in certain locations.

Knowledge spillover
Knowledge diffused from one firm to others among closely located firms.

IN Focus 6.1

Air Capital of the World—Wichita, Kansas

Although the Wichita, Kansas, metro area only has a population of about 600,000 people, the *entire* population of major aerospace companies in the West is represented here: Airbus (North American Wing Design), Boeing (Integrated Defense Systems), Bombardier Aerospace/Learjet, Textron/Cessna Aircraft, Raytheon/Beech Aircraft, and Spirit AeroSystems. Although Boeing, Cessna, and Raytheon are US-owned, Airbus, Bombardier, and Spirit have come to Wichita via FDI—the latter two companies are Canadian-owned. The city proudly claims itself to be the "Air Capital of the World." Why is Wichita so attractive? In one word, agglomeration (clustering of economic activities). In Wichita, the aerospace industry employs 35,000 workers, and makes up 60% of manufacturing earnings. In Kansas, $22 out of every $100 in earnings comes from this industry.

Wichita's aerospace industry started in the 1920s. Flat land, good winds, and excellent year-round flying weather were initially important. In 1929, Boeing came by acquiring a local start-up. During World War II, Boeing produced numerous military aircraft including the B-29 bomber in Wichita. In postwar decades, Wichita has become one of Boeing's prime engineering, fabrication, assembly, and modification centers. The two US presidential Boeing 747s, known as Air Force One when the president is on board, were made in Everett, Washington, but modified, equipped, and serviced

in Wichita. In addition to large aircraft made by Boeing, Wichita is also the undisputed leader in small aircraft for general aviation (often known as business jets). All three top players—Learjet, Cessna, and Beech—are here. Although Cessna and Beech were acquired by US-owned Textron and Raytheon, respectively, Learjet was bought by Canada's Bombardier. Airbus does not manufacture in Wichita. Instead, it set up an R&D center, employing 200 engineers. In 2005, Boeing spun off its commercial aircraft division in Wichita and sold it for $1.5 billion to a Canadian company that nobody had heard of in the aerospace industry, Onex Corporation. Although Onex (TSX: OCX) is one of Canada's largest diversified companies with $16 billion annual sales, it had never operated in the aerospace industry before. Onex named its new Wichita-based subsidiary Spirit AeroSpace. Spirit has continued to be a major supplier to Boeing. In addition, exercising the spirit of an independent company, Spirit has also secured new contracts to supply Airbus in Europe. Since then, Boeing's work in Wichita has been entirely focused on the military side.

Sources: I thank Professor Dharma DeSilva (Wichita State University) for his assistance. Based on (1) R. Whyte, 2006, Competitiveness in the global aircraft industry, Presentation at Wichita State University, May 20; (2) Wichita Metro Chamber of Commerce, 2009, www.wichitakansas. org; (3) www.boeing.com; (3) www.learjet.com; (4) www.cessna. textron.com; (5) www.onex.com; (6) www.raytheon.com; (7) www. wingsoverkansas.com.

Acquiring and Neutralizing Location Advantages

Note that from a resource-based view, location advantages do *not* entirely overlap with country-level advantages such as the factor endowments discussed in Chapter 5. Location advantages refer to the advantages one firm obtains when operating in a location due to its *firm-specific* capabilities. In 1982, General Motors (GM) ran its Fremont, California, plant to the ground and had to close it. Reopening the same plant in 1984, Toyota initiated its first FDI project in the United States in a joint venture (JV) with GM. Since then, Toyota (together with GM) has leveraged this plant's location advantages by producing award-winning cars that American customers particularly like, the Toyota Corolla and Tacoma. The point here is that it is Toyota's unique capabilities, applied to the California location, that literally saved the plant from its demise. The California location in itself does not provide location advantages per se, as shown by GM's inability to make it work prior to 1982.

Firms do not operate in a vacuum. When one firm enters a foreign country through FDI, its rivals are likely to increase FDI in that host country either to acquire location advantages themselves or to at least neutralize the first mover's location advantages. These actions to imitate and follow competitors are especially likely in **oligopolies**—industries (such as aerospace and semiconductors) dominated by a small number of players.[17] The automobile industry is a typical oligopolistic industry. Volkswagen was the first foreign entrant in China, starting production in 1985 and enjoying a market share of 60% in the 1990s. Now, every self-respecting global automaker has entered China trying to eat some of Volkswagen's lunch. Overall, competitive rivalry and imitation, especially in oligopolistic industries, underscores the importance of acquiring and neutralizing location advantages around the world.

LEARNING OBJECTIVE 5

Appreciate the benefits of internalization advantages.

INTERNALIZATION ADVANTAGES

Known as internalization, another great advantage associated with FDI is the ability to replace the external market relationship with one firm (the MNE) owning, controlling, and managing activities in two or more countries.[18] Internalization is important because of significant imperfections in international market transactions. The institution-based view suggests that markets are governed by rules, regulations, and norms that are designed to reduce uncertainties. Uncertainties introduce transaction costs—costs associated with doing business (see Chapter 2). This section outlines the necessity of combating market failure and describes the benefits brought by internalization.

Market Failure

International transaction costs tend to be higher than domestic transaction costs. Because laws and regulations are typically enforced on a nation-state basis, enforcement can be problematic at the international level. Suppose two parties from different countries are doing business. If the party from country A behaves opportunistically, the other party from country B will have a hard time enforcing the contract. Suing the other party in a foreign country is not only costly but also uncertain. In the worst case, such imperfections are so grave that markets fail to function, and many firms simply choose not to do business abroad to avoid being burned. High transaction costs can therefore result in market failure. The imperfections of the market mechanisms make transactions prohibitively costly and sometimes make transactions unable to take place. However, recall from Chapter 5 that there are gains from trade. Not doing business together prevents firms from reaping such gains. In response, MNEs emerge to overcome and combat such market failure through FDI.

Oligopoly
Industry dominated by a small number of players.

Overcoming Market Failure through FDI

How do MNEs combat market failure through internalization? Let us use a simple example involving an oil importer, BP in Britain, and an oil exporter, Nigerian National Petroleum Corporation (NNPC), in Nigeria. For the sake of our discussion, assume that BP does all its business in Britain and NNPC does all its business in Nigeria—in other words, neither of them is an MNE. BP and NNPC negotiate a contract which specifies that NNPC will export a certain amount of crude oil from Nigeria to BP's oil refinery facilities in Britain for a certain amount of money. Shown in Figure 6.8, this is both an export contract (from NNPC's perspective) and an import contract (from BP's standpoint) between two firms. In other words, it is a market transaction.

A market transaction between an importer and an exporter like BP and NNPC may suffer from high transaction costs. What is especially costly is the potential opportunism on both sides. For example, NNPC may demand a higher-than-agreed-upon price, citing a variety of reasons such as inflation, natural disasters, or simply rising oil prices after the deal is signed. BP then has to either pay more than the agreed-upon price or refuse to pay and suffer from the huge costs of keeping expensive refinery facilities idle. In other words, NNPC's opportunistic behavior can cause a lot of losses for BP.

Opportunistic behavior can go both ways in a market transaction. In this particular example, BP can also be opportunistic. It may refuse to accept a shipment after its arrival from Nigeria citing unsatisfactory quality, but the real reason could be BP's inability to sell refined oil downstream because gasoline demand is going down. Perhaps people are driving less due to skyrocketing oil prices and the recession—the jobless do not need to commute to work that much. NNPC is thus forced to find a new buyer for a huge tanker load of crude oil on a last-minute, "fire sale" basis with a deep discount, losing a lot of money.

Overall, once one side in a market (export/import) transaction behaves opportunistically, the other side will not be happy and will threaten or initiate law suits. But the legal and regulatory frameworks governing such international transactions

---

FIGURE 6.8 AN INTERNATIONAL MARKET TRANSACTION BETWEEN TWO COMPANIES IN TWO COUNTRIES

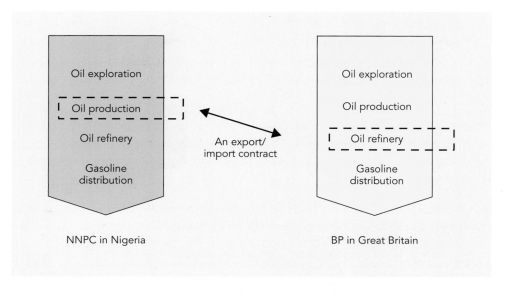

How does Russian MNE LukOil benefit from internalization by owning and operating gas stations in the United States?

are generally not as effective as those governing domestic transactions. Therefore, the injured party will generally be frustrated; whereas the opportunistic party can often get away with it. All of these are examples of transaction costs that increase international market inefficiencies and imperfections, ultimately resulting in market failure.

In response, FDI combats such market failure through internalization, which involves replacing the external market with in-house links. The MNE reduces cross-border transaction costs and increases efficiencies by replacing an external market relationship with a single organization spanning both countries.[19] In our example, there are two possibilities for internalization: BP could undertake *upstream* vertical FDI by owning oil production assets in Nigeria, or NNPC could undertake *downstream* vertical FDI by owning oil refinery assets in Great Britain (see Figure 6.9). As a real-life example, Russian firm LukOil has undertaken FDI in the United States by owning and operating US gas stations. FDI essentially transforms the international trade between two independent firms in two countries to **intrafirm trade** between two subsidiaries in two countries controlled by the same MNE.[20] The MNE is thus able to coordinate cross-border activities better and achieve an internalization advantage.

Overall, the motivations for FDI are complex. The quest for OLI advantages, although analytically distinct as discussed above, may overlap in practice.[21] Based on resource-based and institution-based views, we can see FDI as a reflection of both a firm's motivation to extend its firm-specific capabilities abroad and its responses to overcome market imperfections and failures.

FIGURE 6.9   COMBATING MARKET FAILURE THROUGH FDI: ONE COMPANY (MNE) IN TWO COUNTRIES[1]

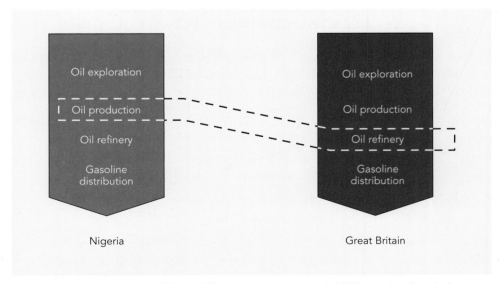

Intrafirm trade

International transactions between two subsidiaries in two countries controlled by the same MNE.

[1] In theory, there can be two possibilities: (1) BP undertakes *upstream* vertical FDI by owning oil production assets in Nigeria, or (2) NNPC undertakes *downstream* vertical FDI by owning oil refinery assets in Great Britain. In reality, the first scenario is more likely.

REALITIES OF FDI

The realities of FDI are intertwined with politics. This section starts with three political views on FDI and follows with a discussion of pros and cons of FDI for home and host countries.

Articulate the different political views on FDI and FDI's benefits and costs.

Political Views on FDI

There are three primary political views on FDI. First, the radical view is hostile to FDI. Tracing its roots to Marxism, the **radical view on FDI** treats FDI as an instrument of imperialism and a vehicle for exploiting domestic resources and people by foreign capitalists and firms. Governments embracing the radical view often nationalize MNE assets or simply ban (or discourage) inbound FDI. Between the 1950s and the early 1980s, the radical view was influential throughout Africa, Asia, Eastern Europe, and Latin America.[22] However, the popularity of this view is in decline worldwide, because (1) economic development in these countries was poor in the absence of FDI, and (2) the few developing countries (such as Singapore) that embraced FDI attained enviable growth (see Chapter 1).

On the other hand, the **free market view on FDI** suggests that FDI, unrestricted by government intervention, will enable countries to tap into their absolute or comparative advantages by specializing in the production of certain goods and services. Similar to the win-win logic for international trade as articulated by Adam Smith and David Ricardo (see Chapter 5), free market-based FDI should lead to a win-win situation for both home and host countries. Since the 1980s, a series of countries such as Brazil, China, Hungary, India, Ireland, and Russia have adopted more FDI-friendly policies.

However, a totally free market view on FDI does not really exist in practice. Most countries practice **pragmatic nationalism on FDI**, considering both the pros and cons of FDI and approving FDI only when its benefits outweigh its costs. The French government, invoking "economic patriotism," has torpedoed several foreign takeover attempts of French firms. The German government insists that German jobs be protected at General Motor's (GM) Opel subsidiary when providing state aid loans (see the Closing Case).

Overall, more and more countries in recent years have changed their policies to be more favorable to FDI. Restrictive policies towards FDI succeed only in driving out MNEs to countries with more favorable policies. Even hard core countries such as Cuba and North Korea that had a radical view on FDI are now experimenting with opening up to some FDI. This openness is indicative of the emerging pragmatic nationalism in their thinking.

Benefits and Costs of FDI to Host Countries

Underpinning pragmatic nationalism is the need to assess the various benefits and costs of FDI to host (recipient) countries and home (source) countries. In a nutshell, Figure 6.10 outlines these considerations. In Focus 6.2 raises a provocative question: Is FDI in agriculture in some of poorest countries detrimental in the form of land grabs or beneficial in the form of outsourced agricultural production? This section focuses on *host* countries, and the next section deals with *home* countries.

Radical view on FDI
A political view that is hostile to FDI.

Free market view on FDI
A political view that suggests that FDI unrestricted by government intervention is the best.

Pragmatic nationalism on FDI
A political view that only approves FDI when its benefits outweigh its costs.

FIGURE 6.10   EFFECTS OF FDI ON HOME AND HOST COUNTRIES

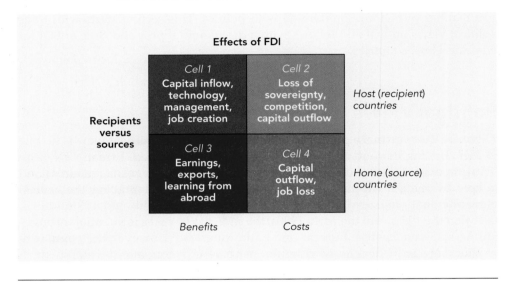

Effects of FDI

	Benefits	Costs	
	Cell 1 Capital inflow, technology, management, job creation	**Cell 2** Loss of sovereignty, competition, capital outflow	Host (recipient) countries
	Cell 3 Earnings, exports, learning from abroad	**Cell 4** Capital outflow, job loss	Home (source) countries

Recipients versus sources

IN Focus 6.2

ETHICAL DILEMMA

Land Grabs or Outsourcing 3.0?

If you believe FDI only involves manufacturing and services, welcome to FDI in agriculture. Recently, many countries that export capital but import food are outsourcing production to countries that need capital but have land to spare. FDI in foreign farms is nothing new. The term "banana republic" refers to exactly this phenomenon in an earlier era: US firms invested in banana plantations in Central America. What is unusual is the scale of recent land deals. Since 2005, 20 million hectares (48 million acres)—an area as big as France's sprawling farmland or 20% of Europe's farmland—has been acquired by capital exporting countries such as Saudi Arabia, Kuwait, United Arab Emirates, South Korea, and China. They buy or lease millions of acres, grow staple crops or biofuels, and ship output back home. The countries doing the selling are some of the world's least developed ones, such as Congo, Ethiopia, Madagascar, Malawi, Mali, Pakistan, and Sudan.

A triggering event seems to be the skyrocketing oil prices several years ago, which resulted in spikes of food prices around the world. In an effort to combat food price hikes, governments in major food exporting countries such as Argentina, India, and Ukraine imposed food export bans. Although more recently oil and food prices came down and food export bans were removed, food importing countries were alarmed, reaching the conclusion that the OLI advantages associated with FDI outweigh the beauty of relying on international food trade. Critics argue that these land deals are neocolonialist "land grabs" that are detrimental to host countries. Defenders claim these deals represent outsourcing 3.0 (1.0 being in manufacturing in the 1980s and 2.0 being in services in the 1990s), which would tap into the comparative advantages of both home and host countries.

Sources: Based on (1) *Economist*, 2009, Outsourcing's third wave, May 23: 61–63; (2) United Nations, 2009, *World Investment Report 2009: Transnational Corporations, Agricultural Production, and Development*, New York: UN.

Cell 1 in Figure 6.10 shows four primary benefits to host countries:

- Capital inflow can help improve a host country's balance of payments. (See Chapter 7 for more details.)
- Technology, especially more advanced technology from abroad, can create **technology spillovers** that benefit domestic firms and industries. Technology spillover is the domestic diffusion of foreign technical knowledge and processes. Local rivals, after observing such technology, may recognize its feasibility and strive to imitate it. This is known as the **demonstration effect**, sometimes also called the **contagion** (or **imitation**) **effect**.[23] It underscores the important role that MNEs play in stimulating competition in host countries.[24]
- Advanced management know-how may be highly valued. In many developing countries, it is often difficult for the development of management know-how to reach a world-class level if it is only domestic and not influenced by FDI.
- FDI creates jobs. For example, more than 50% of manufacturing employees in Ireland work for MNEs.[25] Indirect benefits include jobs created when local suppliers increase hiring and when MNE employees spend money locally, which also results in more jobs.

Cell 2 in Figure 6.10 outlines three primary costs of FDI to host countries: (1) loss of sovereignty, (2) adverse effects on competition, and (3) capital outflow. The first concern is the loss of some (but not all) economic sovereignty associated with FDI. Because of FDI, decisions to invest, produce, and market products and services in a host country are being made by foreigners. Even if locals serve as heads of MNE subsidiaries, they represent the interest of foreign firms. Will foreigners and foreign firms make decisions that are in the best interest of host countries? This is truly a million dollar question, which has frustrated the German government in its dealings with GM on the fate of its Opel subsidiary (see the Closing Case). According to the radical view, the answer is "No!" because foreigners and foreign firms are likely to maximize their own profits by exploiting people and resources in host countries. Such deep suspicion of MNEs leads to policies that discourage or even ban FDI. On the other hand, countries embracing free market and pragmatic nationalism views agree that, despite some acknowledged differences between foreign and host country interests, the interests of MNEs and host countries overlap sufficiently. Host countries are therefore willing to live with some loss of sovereignty.

A second concern is associated with the negative effects on local competition. Although we have just discussed the positive effects of MNEs on local competition, it is possible that MNEs may drive some domestic firms out of business. Having driven domestic firms out of business, in theory, MNEs may be able to monopolize local markets. Although this is a relatively minor concern in developed economies, it is a legitimate concern for less developed economies where MNEs are generally so much larger and financially stronger compared to local firms. For example, as Coca-Cola and PepsiCo have extended their "cola wars" from the United States to countries around the world, they have almost "accidentally" wiped out much of the world's indigenous beverages companies, which are—or were—much smaller.

A third concern is associated with capital outflow. When MNEs make profits in host countries and repatriate (send back) such earnings to headquarters in home countries, host countries experience a net outflow in the capital account in

Technology spillover
Technology diffused from foreign firms to domestic firms.

Demonstration (contagion or imitation) effect
The reaction of local firms to rise to the challenge demonstrated by MNEs through learning and imitation.

their balance of payments. As a result, some countries have restricted the ability of MNEs to repatriate funds. Another issue arises when MNE subsidiaries spend a lot of money to import components and services from abroad, which also results in capital outflow.

Benefits and Costs of FDI to Home Countries

As exporters of capital, technology, management, and, in some cases, jobs, home (source) countries often reap benefits and endure costs associated with FDI that are *opposite* to those experienced by host countries. Cell 3 of Figure 6.10 shows three benefits to home countries:

- Repatriated earnings from profits from FDI
- Increased exports of components and services to host countries
- Learning via FDI from operations abroad

Cell 4 in Figure 6.10 shows that the costs of FDI to home countries primarily center on capital outflow and job loss. First, since host countries enjoy capital inflow because of FDI, home countries naturally suffer from some capital outflow. Less confident home country governments often impose capital controls to prevent or reduce FDI from flowing abroad.

The second concern is now more prominent: job loss. Many MNEs invest abroad and increase employment overseas but lay off domestic employees. So it is not surprising that politicians, union members, journalists, and social activists in developed economies have increasingly called for restrictions on FDI outflows.

Understand how MNEs and host country governments bargain.

HOW MNEs AND HOST GOVERNMENTS BARGAIN

MNEs react to various policies by bargaining with host governments. The outcome of the MNE–host government relationship, namely, the scale and scope of FDI in a host country, is a function of the relative **bargaining power** of each side—the ability to extract favorable outcome from negotiations due to one party's strengths. MNEs typically prefer to minimize host government intervention while maximizing the incentives provided by the host government. Not surprisingly, host governments usually want to ensure a certain degree of control while minimizing the incentives provided to MNEs. As shown in the Closing Case, sometimes host governments "must coerce or cajole the multinationals into undertaking roles that they would otherwise abdicate."[26] However, host governments have to "induce, rather than command," because MNEs have options elsewhere.[27] Different countries, in effect, are competing with each other for precious FDI dollars.

FDI is not a zero-sum game. The negotiations are characterized by the "three Cs": common interests, conflicting interests, and compromises[28] (see Figure 6.11). The upshot is that despite a variety of conflicts, conditions exist where the interests of both sides may converge on an outcome that benefits both sides.[29]

Typically, FDI bargaining is not a one-round affair. After the initial FDI entry, both sides may continue to exercise bargaining power. A well-known phenomenon

Bargaining power
Ability to extract favorable outcome from negotiations due to one party's strengths.

FIGURE 6.11   HOW MNEs NEGOTIATE WITH HOST GOVERNMENTS: THE THREE Cs

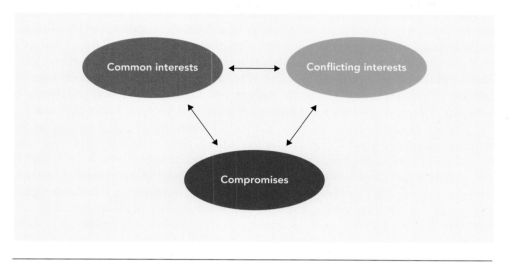

is the **obsolescing bargain**, in which the requirements of the deal previously struck between MNEs and host governments is changed *after* the initial FDI entry. It typically unfolds in three rounds:

- In Round One, the MNE and the government negotiate a deal. The MNE usually is not willing to enter in the absence of some government assurance of property rights and incentives (such as tax holidays).
- In Round Two, the MNE enters and, if all goes well, earns profits that may become visible.
- In Round Three, the government, often pressured by domestic political groups, may demand renegotiations of the deal because it seems to yield "excessive" profits to the foreign firm (which, of course, regards these as "fair" and "normal" profits). The previous deal, thus, becomes obsolete. The government's tactics include removing incentives, demanding a higher share of profits and taxes, and even **expropriation** (confiscating foreign assets).

At this time, the MNE has already invested substantial sums of resources (called **sunk costs**) and often has to accommodate some new demands. Otherwise, it may face expropriation or exit at a huge loss. Not surprisingly, MNEs do not appreciate the risk associated with such obsolescing bargains. Unfortunately, recent actions in Venezuela, Bolivia, and Ecuador suggest that obsolescing bargains are not necessarily becoming obsolete (see the next section for details).

Obsolescing bargain
The deal struck by MNEs and host governments, which change their requirements after the initial FDI entry.

Expropriation
Government's confiscation of foreign assets.

Sunk cost
Cost that a firm has to endure even when its investment turns out to be unsatisfactory.

DEBATES AND EXTENSIONS

As an embodiment of globalization, FDI has stimulated numerous debates. This section highlights three: (1) FDI versus outsourcing, (2) facilitating versus confronting inbound FDI, and (3) welcoming versus restricting sovereign wealth fund investment.

Participate in three leading debates on FDI.

FDI versus Outsourcing

Although this chapter has focused on FDI, we need to be aware that FDI is *not* the only mode of foreign market entry. Especially when undertaking a value chain analysis regarding specific activities (see Chapter 4), a decision to undertake FDI will have to be assessed relative to the benefits and costs of outsourcing. Recall from Chapter 4 that in a foreign location, overseas outsourcing becomes "offshoring," whereas FDI—that is, performing an activity in-house at an overseas location—has been recently labeled "captive sourcing" by some authors (see Figure 4.4). A strategic debate is whether FDI (captive sourcing) or outsourcing will better serve a firm's purpose.

The answer boils down to three factors: (1) How critical is the activity to the core mission of the firm? (2) How common is the activity within multiple end-user industries? (3) How readily available is overseas talent to perform this activity? If the activity is marginal, is common (or similar) across multiple end-user industries, and can be provided by proven talents overseas, then outsourcing is called for. Otherwise, FDI is often necessary. For example, when Travelocity outsourced its call center operations to India, its rival Sabre carefully considered its options. It eventually decided to avoid outsourcing and to initiate FDI in Uruguay (see In Focus 6.3).

Facilitating versus Confronting Inbound FDI

Despite the general trend toward more FDI-friendly policies around the world, debates continue to rage. At the heart of these debates is the age-old question discussed earlier and illustrated in the Closing Case: Can we trust foreign firms in making decisions important to our economy?

IN Focus 6.3

Sabre Travel Network: FDI versus Outsourcing

Sabre Travel Network, headquartered in Southlake, Texas (a suburb of Dallas), is the world's largest marketer and distributor of travel-related products and services. It has 9,000 employees in 59 countries. More than 55,000 travel agencies subscribe to Sabre's services, which provide access to over 400 airlines, 88,000 hotels, 24 car rental companies, 13 cruise lines, 35 railroads, and 220 tour operators worldwide. One out of every two travelers with trips originating in the United States uses Sabre in some fashion.

Because "9/11" attacks devastated the travel industry, Sabre was forced to have its first layoffs and pay careful attention to its cost structure. In 2003, Travelocity, a leading rival, outsourced its call center operations to India, forcing Sabre to weigh its options between outsourcing and FDI.

Sabre viewed its proprietary systems and its relationships with travel agencies to be its key assets. Therefore, it ruled out outsourcing and focused on FDI. Then it searched Canada, India, and Poland, and eventually decided to move its customer service center and software and hardware help desks to Uruguay. Unlike its bigger neighbor Argentina, Uruguay is politically stable. It offered significant incentives. Uruguay's well-educated labor force, thanks to universal free college tuition, is 40% cheaper than the United States. Better yet, the country is in the same time zone with most of the United States.

Sources: Based on (1) *Economist*, 2006, Uruguay: Paper dreams, October 8: 47; (2) Sabre Travel Network, 2009, www.sabretravelnetwork.com; (3) M. Tapp, 2006, Sabre Travel Network, MBA case study, University of Texas at Dallas.

In developed economies, backlash against inbound FDI from certain countries is not unusual. In the 1960s, Europeans were concerned about the massive US FDI in Europe. In the 1980s, Americans were alarmed by the significant Japanese inroads into the United States. Over time, such concerns have subsided. More recently, in 2006, a controversy erupted when Dubai Ports World (DP World), a Dubai government-owned company, purchased US ports from another *foreign* firm, Britain's P&O. This entry gave DP World control over terminal operations at the ports of New York/New Jersey, Philadelphia, Baltimore, Miami, and New Orleans. Although Dubai, as an emirate within the United Arab Emirates (UAE), has been a US ally for three decades, many politicians, journalists, and activists opposed such FDI. In this "largest political storm over US ports since the Boston Tea Party,"[30] DP World eventually withdrew. Similarly, Chinese firm CNOOC's bid for the US firm Unocal and another Chinese firm Chinalco's bid for Australia's Rio Tinto were torpedoed by a politicized process. Cases such as these make many wonder whether a wave of protectionism is emerging in developed economies.

In some parts of the developing world, foreign ownership can be a touchy issue. Between the 1950s and the 1970s, numerous cases of nationalization and expropriation of MNE assets occurred throughout the developing world. Given the recent worldwide trend toward more FDI-friendly policies, many people thought that such actions were a thing of the past. However, in March 2006, Venezuelan President Hugo Chavez ordered Chevron, Royal Dutch, Total, ENI, and other oil and gas MNEs to convert their Venezuelan operations into forced JVs with state-owned Venezuelan firm PDVSA in which PDVSA would be granted at

© AP Photo/Roberto Candia

How should MNE managers in the oil and gas industry (and other industries) approach countries such as Venezuela, whose President Hugo Chavez is openly hostile to oil and gas MNEs?

least 60% of the equity. When France's Total and Italy's ENI rejected such terms, their fields were promptly seized by the government.[31] On May 1, 2006, the Bolivian military stormed MNEs' oil fields and proclaimed control.[32] President Evo Morales declared, "The plunder [by MNEs] has ended."[33] Soon after, in late May 2006, Ecuador expropriated the oil fields run by America's Occidental Petroleum.

Although the rapidity of the anti-MNE events in Latin America was surprising, it is important to note that these actions were not sudden, impulsive policy changes. The politicians initiating these actions were all democratically elected. These actions were the result of lengthy political debates concerning FDI in the region, and the takeovers were popular among the public. Bolivian President Morales' action, in fact, fulfilled his campaign promise. Until the 1970s, Latin American governments had often dealt harshly with MNEs. It was only in the 1990s that these countries became democratic and opened their oil fields to inbound FDI. Therefore, the policy reversal is both surprising (considering how these governments recently welcomed MNEs) and yet not surprising (considering the history of how MNEs were dealt with in the region). Although some argue that the recent actions were driven by industry-specific dynamics (sky-high oil prices that tempted cash-hungry governments), others suggest that these actions represent the swing of a "pendulum" toward more confrontation (see Chapter 1).

Welcoming versus Restricting Sovereign Wealth Fund Investments

A **sovereign wealth fund (SWF)** is "a state-owned investment fund composed of financial assets such as stocks, bonds, real estate, or other financial instruments funded by foreign exchange assets."[34] Investment funds that we now call SWFs were first created in 1953 by Kuwait. In 1976, the Alaska Permanent Fund and the Alberta Heritage Fund were founded in the United States and Canada, respectively. Table 6.2 lists the major SWFs in the world.

In the recent financial crisis, SWFs came to the rescue.[35] For example, in November 2007, the Abu Dhabi Investment Authority injected $7.5 billion (4.9% of equity) into Citigroup. In early 2008, China Investment Corporation (CIC) invested $5 billion for a 10% equity stake in Morgan Stanley. As discussed earlier, the threshold between FDI and FPI is 10%. Although most SWFs make relatively passive FPI, some have become more active, direct investors as they hold larger stakes in recipients.

It is such large-scale investments that have ignited the debate on SWFs. On the one hand, SWFs have brought much needed cash to rescue desperate Western firms. On the other hand, concerns are raised by host countries, which are typically developed economies. A primary concern is national security in that SWFs may be politically (as opposed to commercially) motivated. Another concern is SWFs' inadequate transparency. Currently, governments in several developed economies, in fear of the "threats" from SWFs, are erecting measures to defend their companies from SWF takeovers.

As discussed earlier, foreign investment certainly has both benefits and costs to host countries.[36] However, in the absence of any evidence that the costs outweigh benefits, the rush to erect anti-SWF barriers is indicative of protectionist (or, some may argue, even racist) sentiments. For executives at hard-pressed Western firms, it would not seem sensible to ask for government bailouts on the one hand, and to reject cash from SWFs on the other. Most SWF investment is essentially free cash with few strings attached. For example, CIC, which now holds 10% of Morgan Stanley equity, did not demand a board seat or a management role. For policymakers, it makes little sense to spend taxpayers' dollars to bail out failed firms, run huge budget deficits, and then turn away SWFs. Commenting on inbound Chinese investment in the United States (including SWF investment), two experts note:

Sovereign wealth fund (SWF)

A state-owned investment fund composed of financial assets such as stocks, bonds, real estate, or other financial instruments funded by foreign exchange assets.

TABLE 6.2   THE SIX LARGEST SOVEREIGN WEALTH FUNDS

Country	Sovereign wealth fund	Assets ($ billion)	Inception	Approximate wealth per citizen ($)
United Arab Emirates	Abu Dhabi Investment Authority	$875 billion	1976	$100,000
Norway	Government Pension Fund of Norway	$391 billion	1990	$81,500
Singapore	Government of Singapore Investment Corporation	$330 billion	1981	$100,000
Kuwait	Kuwait Investment Authority	$264 billion	1953	$80,000
China	China Investment Corporation	$200 billion	2007	$151
Russia	Stabilization Fund of the Russian Federation	$158 billion	2008	$1130

Source: Data extracted from various items posted at Sovereign Wealth Fund Institute, 2009, Current news, www.swfinstitute.org.

It seems feckless on the part of US policymakers to stigmatize Chinese invest-ment in the United States based upon imprecise and likely exaggerated esti-mates of the relevant costs and risks of that investment.[37]

At least some US policymakers agree. In the September/October 2008 issue of *Foreign Affairs*, then-Secretary of the Treasury Henry Paulson (when he still held the position) commented:

> These concerns [on Chinese investment] are misplaced . . . the United States would do well to encourage such investment from anywhere in the world—including China—because it represents a vote of confidence in the US econ-omy and it promotes growth, jobs, and productivity in the United States.[38]

Lastly, thanks to the deteriorating financial crisis in 2008–2009, recent SWF investment in developed economies suffered major losses for SWFs. Such a "double whammy"—both the political backlash and the economic losses—has severely discouraged government officials and SWFs. As a result, the current FDI recession "puts a premium on maintaining a welcoming investment climate."[39] As part of the effort to foster such a welcoming investment climate in times of great political and economic anxiety, both US and Chinese governments con-firmed the following in the US-China Strategic and Economic Dialogue (S&ED) on July 28, 2009:

> The United States confirms that the Committee on Foreign Investment in the United States (CFIUS) process ensures the consistent and fair treatment of all foreign investment without prejudice to the place of origin. The United States welcomes sovereign wealth fund investment, including that from China. China stresses that investment decisions by its state-owned invest-ment firms will be based solely on commercial grounds.[40]

Beyond bilateral negotiations such as the US-China S&ED, in September 2008, major SWFs of the world at a summit in Santiago, Chile, agreed to a voluntary code of conduct known as the Santiago Principles. These principles are designed to alle-viate some of the concerns for host countries of SWF investment and to enhance the transparency of such investment. These principles represent an important milestone of SWFs' evolution.

MANAGEMENT SAVVY

The big question in global business, adapted to the context of FDI, is: What deter-mines the success and failure of FDI around the globe? The answer boils down to two components. First, from a resource-based view, some firms are good at FDI because they leverage ownership, location, and internalization advantages in a way that is valuable, unique, and hard to imitate by rival firms. Second, from an institution-based view, the political realities either facilitate or constrain FDI. Therefore, the success and failure of FDI also significantly depends on how institutions as rules of the game govern FDI.

Shown in Table 6.3, three implications for action emerge. First, you should carefully assess whether FDI is justified in light of other possibilities such as outsourcing and licensing. This exercise needs to be conducted on an activity-by-activity basis as part of the value-chain analysis (see Chapter 4). If owner-ship and internalization advantages are not deemed critical, then FDI is not recommended.

LEARNING OBJECTIVE 9

Draw implications for action.

TABLE 6.3   IMPLICATIONS FOR ACTION

- Carefully assess whether FDI is justified, in light of other foreign entry modes such as outsourcing and licensing.
- Pay careful attention to the location advantages in combination with the firm's strategic goals.
- Be aware of the institutional constraints and enablers governing FDI and enhance FDI's legitimacy in host countries.

Second, once a decision to undertake FDI is made, you should pay attention to the old adage, "Location, location, location!" The quest for location advantages has to fit with the firm's strategic goals. For example, if a firm is searching for the innovation hot spots, then low-cost locations that do not generate sufficient innovations will not be attractive (see Chapters 10 and 13).

Finally, given the political realities around the world, you should be aware of the institutional constraints. Recent events suggest that savvy MNE managers should not take FDI-friendly policies for granted. Setbacks are likely. In the short run, an FDI recession has happened. The global economic slowdown makes key markets less attractive to invest, and the credit crunch means that firms are less able to invest abroad. Attitudes toward certain forms of FDI are changing, which may cause FDI policies to become more protectionist. In the long run, the interests of MNEs in host countries can be best safeguarded if MNEs accommodate, rather than neglect or dominate, the interests of host countries. In practical terms, contributions to local employment, job training, education, and pollution control will tangibly demonstrate an MNE's commitment to the host country.

CHAPTER SUMMARY

1. Define the key terms associated with FDI.
   - The key word for FDI is *direct (D)*.
   - FDI can be horizontal or vertical, and FDI measures are typically expressed in flow and stock.

2. Explain how FDI results in ownership, location, and internalization (OLI) advantages.
   - Ownership refers to MNEs' possession and leveraging of certain valuable, rare, hard-to-imitate, and organizationally embedded (VRIO) assets overseas.
   - Location refers to certain locations' advantages that can help MNEs attain strategic goals.
   - Internalization refers to the replacement of cross-border market relationship with one firm (the MNE) locating in two or more countries.

3. Identify ownership advantages associated with FDI.
   - Ownership advantages center on direct management control, which reduces the risk of firm-specific resources and capabilities being taken advantage of.

4. List ways firms can acquire and neutralize location advantages.
   - Firms can acquire and neutralize location advantages by entering locations with great geographical features or with great agglomeration benefits.

5. Appreciate the benefits of internalization advantages.
   - Internalization combats market failure by replacing the external market with in-house links within the MNE.

6. Articulate the different political views on FDI and FDI's benefits and costs.
   - The radical view is hostile to FDI, and the free market view calls for minimum intervention in FDI. Most countries practice pragmatic nationalism.
   - FDI brings a different (and often opposing) set of benefits and costs to host and home countries.

7. Understand how MNEs and host country governments bargain.
   - MNE-host country negotiations center on common interests, conflicting interests, and compromises.

8. Participate in three leading debates on FDI.
   - They are (1) FDI versus outsourcing, (2) facilitating versus confronting inbound FDI, and (3) welcoming versus restricting SWFs.

9. Draw implications for action.
   - Carefully assess whether FDI is justified, in light of other options such as outsourcing and licensing.
   - Pay careful attention to the location advantages in combination with the firm's strategic goals.
   - Be aware of the institutional constraints governing FDI and enhance FDI's legitimacy in host countries.

KEY TERMS

Agglomeration   188
Bargaining power   196
Contagion (imitation) effect   195
Demonstration effect   195
Dissemination risk   187
Downstream vertical FDI   182
Expropriation   197
FDI flow   182
FDI inflow   182
FDI outflow   182
FDI stock   182

Foreign portfolio investment (FPI)   180
Free market view on FDI   193
Horizontal FDI   181
Internalization   186
Intrafirm trade   192
Knowledge spillover   188
Location   186
Management control rights   180
Market imperfection (market failure)   186

Obsolescing bargain   197
OLI advantages   185
Oligopoly   190
Ownership   185
Pragmatic nationalism on FDI   193
Radical view on FDI   193
Sovereign wealth fund (SWF)   200
Sunk cost   197
Technology spillover   195
Upstream vertical FDI   182
Vertical FDI   181

REVIEW QUESTIONS

1. What is the primary difference between FDI and FPI?

2. How does horizontal FDI compare to vertical FDI?

3. Briefly summarize each of the three OLI advantages.

4. Discuss the pros and cons of ownership versus a contractual relationship that provides control.

5. Devise your own example of agglomeration that demonstrates your understanding of the concept.

6. Compare and contrast the three political views of FDI.

7. Describe two benefits and two costs to a host country of FDI and to a home country of FDI.

8. Given that outsourcing is a viable alternative to FDI, what issues should be considered before a firm decides between the two?

9. Why do some countries object to inbound FDI?

10. What issues should a savvy manager consider when evaluating a particular location for FDI?

11. Some Americans feel that US-based firms should not undertake FDI in other countries because it results in expanding business opportunities in those countries and does not benefit the United States. How might 2008 data on PengAtlas Map 2.3 be used to refute that view?

12. Consider PengAtlas Map 2.3 showing US FDI in other countries and then look at PengAtlas Maps 2.1 and 2.2. Which countries receiving US FDI are also countries that export merchandise and services to the United States? Given the possibility that some US imports are from operations in which US firms have made FDI, how does that affect your view of the trade deficit? Does it make the deficit seem like less of a problem or greater? Explain your answer.

CRITICAL DISCUSSION QUESTIONS

1. Identify the top five (or 10) *source* countries of FDI into your country. Then identify the top five (or 10) foreign MNEs that have undertaken inbound FDI in your country. Why do these countries and companies provide the bulk of FDI into your country?

2. Identify the top five (or 10) *recipient* countries of FDI from your country. Then identify the top five (or 10) MNEs headquartered in your country that have made outbound FDI elsewhere. Why do these countries attract FDI from the top MNEs from your country?

3. **ON ETHICS**: Undertaking FDI, by definition, means not investing in the MNE's home country. What are the ethical dilemmas here? What are your recommendations, as (1) an MNE executive, (2) a labor union leader in your domestic (home country) labor force, (3) a host country official?

GLOBAL ACTION

1. Your MNE is looking to evaluate the industrial capability of various locations worldwide. Based on readily available data concerning the potential and performance of different countries, the information you provide will drive future investment by your company. Choose a country each from Asia, Europe, North America, and South America, and summarize your globalEDGE findings about each. Of the four countries from four continents, how would you rank them? Why?

2. The main premise for development at your company in the coming years is to shift its offshore services to Africa. As such, you have been asked to develop a report using resources from the globalEDGE website that evaluates which African countries have increased the possibility of creating a long-term advantage for your company. Also, be sure to include the African countries that have *decreased* their capacity to create a long-term advantage. Can you generate a top five list and a bottom five list from Africa for this purpose?

VIDEO CASES

Watch "Maximizing Investors: Contributions" by Candice Brown Elliott at Clairvoyante.

1. What did Elliott mean when she compared "dumb money" to "smart money"?

2. What did Elliott mean by a "double bottom line" and how could the concept be applied to FDI?

3. How could her reference to the "Rolodex" be applied to a firm entering a new market in a new overseas location?

4. Elliott had different objectives for the first level of investors as opposed to the second level. What were those objectives and how might they be applied when developing a venture in another country?

5. Elliott talked about turning away those who were interested in investing in her company. Why would anyone do that regardless of whether the venture is domestic or international?

Closing Case

ETHICAL DILEMMA

The Fate of Opel

Opel is a German automaker. It began making cars in 1899, and was acquired by General Motors (GM) in 1929. The GM-Opel relationship survived World War II, during which Opel factories were seized by the Nazis and then bombed by the Allies. Only in 1948 did GM regain control of Opel. In 2008, Opel generated €18 billion in sales and a 7% market share in Western Europe. It had 50,000 employees and eight factories in Europe. About half of the jobs and four factories were in Germany. In addition, Opel ran one factory each in Belgium, Poland, Spain, and the UK—the latter is a Vauxhall plant that produced cars with its own Vauxhall brand. Opel formed the backbone of GM Europe.

© Ronald Wittek/dpa/Landov

Unfortunately, the 80-year-old relationship between GM and Opel experienced some unprecedented turbulence in 2009, during which GM itself declared bankruptcy on June 1. Before June 1, the German (federal) government, in an effort to protect Opel assets and jobs in the event of a GM bankruptcy, took unprecedented action by offering a €1.5 billion bridge loan to Opel and pushing GM to form an Opel Trust. The Opel Trust controlled and protected Opel assets during GM's bankruptcy. The board of the trust consisted of representatives from GM, German employees, the German federal government, and the governments of the four German states in which Opel operated. Losing money for a decade, Opel was indeed struggling desperately despite repeated restructuring efforts. In 2008, GM Europe lost $2.8 billion. In the first quarter of 2009, it burned an additional $2 billion with a 25% drop in sales.

After June 1, 2009, although the US and Canadian governments bailed out GM by injecting billions of dollars and taking over 61% and 8% of its equity, respectively, there were specific requirements preventing GM from using American and Canadian taxpayer dollars to fund overseas operations such as Opel's. In desperation, GM felt it had to sell Opel to prevent the financial hemorrhage.

Although initially reluctant, GM in early September 2009 agreed to support a proposal favored by the German government to sell 55% of Opel's equity to a consortium led by Magna, a Canadian auto parts maker that would take 20% of equity. Magna has two Russian partners—Sherbank and GAZ, Russia's second-largest automaker—that would take 35% of equity. German employees would get 10% and GM the remaining 35%. Magna agreed to invest €500 million while the German government pledged an additional €4.5 billion in state aid loans, in addition to the €1.5 billion bridge loan already provided. German Chancellor Angela Merkel invested significant political capital in brokering the deal, which extracted a promise from Magna to keep job cuts to a minimum (not exceeding 2,500 jobs) in Germany—a significantly better outcome than a more ruthless restructuring process during which 20% of Opel's jobs (10,000) might disappear in Germany. In part due to her extraordinary efforts, Merkel was reelected for the second term in late September.

GM was never enthusiastic about the sale to the Magna consortium. Of the four bids GM received, it quickly dropped one from Italy's Fiat and another from China's Beijing Automotive, but strongly favored one from RHJ International, a Belgian private equity firm, which would eventually consider selling Opel back to GM in the future. The Germans saw RHJ as a pawn for GM. From a fair bidding standpoint, the fact that RHJ offered only €275 million (substantially lower than the €400 million offered by the Magna consortium) made it impossible for GM to offer Opel to RHJ and bypass the Magna consortium. To lock in the sale to Magna, the German government also announced that its financing would only support Magna and its partners, but not RHJ.

GM had legitimate concerns for the sale to the Magna consortium. It would be hit by a "double whammy." First, GM would lose important passenger car expertise that has fueled a lot of GM's models beyond those carrying the Opel and Vauxhall plates, including many models that are branded as Cadillac, Buick, and Chevrolet. Second, the sale would turn Magna into a major competitor overnight, although the deal forbade Opel from selling in China until 2015 and forbade any entry into the United States. Further, GAZ will take advantage of Opel technology and boost its position in Russia, soon to overtake Germany as Europe's largest car market. RHJ would present none of these strategic headaches.

In October 2009, a significant player previously not involved entered the fray. The European Commissioner for Competition, Neelie Kroes, was pressured by the Belgian, Polish, Spanish, and UK governments that complained that Opel's sale to Magna would result in disproportionate and thus "unfair" job losses in these countries. Kroes wrote to the German government, expressing her concerns that state aid promised by the German government to the "new Opel" was tied to one bidder and discriminated against other bidders such as RHJ. The letter demanded that GM and the Opel Trust "be given the opportunity to reconsider the outcome of the bidding process," because state aid "cannot be used to impose political constraints concerning the location of production activities within the EU." After talks between Berlin and the EU, Germany clarified that its state aid would be available to any investor with a decent plan. Unfortunately, RHJ had already walked away, so this assurance was entirely theoretical. Satisfied by the assurance, the Eurocrats eventually backed off. They argued that the assurance set a good precedent in the future, and that dragging Germany's previously unacceptable behavior into a full-scale EU probe would push Opel into legal limbo, possibly causing the firm to collapse.

However, in the middle of such intense politicking and strategizing, in November 2009, GM's board announced a startling shift in direction by cancelling the sale to the Magna consortium and keeping Opel. Outraged, Opel workers took to the streets. German media pointed out that GM might close two factories and lay off 10,000 workers in Germany. The German Minister for Economy and Technology said that "the behavior of GM against the Opel workers as well as against Germany is completely unacceptable." The German government demanded that its €1.5 billion bridge loan be repaid. Once GM has repaid the loan, GM can dissolve Opel Trust and can do whatever it pleases with Opel. The fate of Opel, thus, hangs in the balance.

Case Discussion Questions:

1. What are the costs and benefits of FDI inflows for a host country such as Germany?
2. Will foreign firms such as GM always make decisions in the best interest of the host country?
3. In an effort to preserve German jobs, the Magna plan would close a more efficient plant in Spain. What would you do if you were a Spanish government official? What if you were a German official?
4. How would you vote if you were a member of the GM board regarding the fate of Opel?

Sources: Based on (1) *BusinessWeek*, 2009, Green light for Opel? November 2; (2) *Economist*, 2009, Looking for reverse, August 29: 55; (3) *Just Auto*, 2009, Government denies GM-Opel-Magna scrutiny needed, October 19, www.just-auto.com; (4) *New York Times*, 2009, GM opts to keep Opel, scraps sale to Magna, November 3, www.nytimes.com; (5) *Wall Street Journal*, 2009, At last, GM sets deal to cede control of Opel, September 11, online.wsj.com; (6) *Wall Street Journal*, 2009, GM advances Opel restructuring, November 7, online.wsj.com.

NOTES

[Journal acronyms] **AER**—*American Economic Review*; **AMJ**—*Academy of Management Journal*; **AMR**—*Academy of Management Review*; **APJM**—*Asia Pacific Journal of Management*; **BW**—*Business Week*; **CFDIP**—*Columbia Foreign Direct Investment Perspectives*; **FA**—*Foreign Affairs*; **FEER**—*Far Eastern Economic Review*; **JIBS**—*Journal of International Business Studies*; **JMS**—*Journal of Management Studies*; **JWB**—*Journal of World Business*; **MIR**—*Management International Review*; **SMJ**—*Strategic Management Journal*; **TIBR**—*Thunderbird International Business Review*

1 R. Caves, 1996, *Multinational Enterprise and Economic Analysis*, 2nd ed. (p. 1), New York: Cambridge University Press.

2 US Census Bureau, 2006, US goods trade: Imports and exports by related parties, 2005, News release, May 12.

3 United Nations, 2005, *World Investment Report 2005* (p. 4), New York and Geneva: United Nations.

4 K. Moore & D. Lewis, 1999, *Birth of the Multinational*, Copenhagen: Copenhagen Business School Press.

5 M. Wilkins, 2001, The history of multinational enterprise (p. 13), in A. Rugman & T. Brewer (eds.), *The Oxford Handbook of International Business*, 3–35, New York: Oxford University Press.

6 United Nations, 2009, *World Investment Report 2009* (p. xxi), New York and Geneva: United Nations.

7 A. Madhok, 1997, Cost, value, and foreign market entry mode, *SMJ*, 18: 39–61.

8 J. Dunning, 1993, *Multinational Enterprises and the Global Economy*, Reading, MA: Addison-Wesley.

9 C. Hill, P. Hwang, & C. Kim, 1990, An eclectic theory of the choice of international entry mode (p. 124), *SMJ*, 11: 117–128.

10 R. Tasker, 2002, Pepperoni power, *FEER*, November 14: 59–60.

11 M. Cannice, R. Chen, & J. Daniels, 2004, Managing international technology transfer risk, *MIR*, 44: 129–139.

12 B. Elango & C. Pattnaik, 2007, Building capabilities for international operations through networks, *JIBS*, 38: 541–555; D. Yiu, C. M. Lau, & G. Bruton, 2007, International venturing by emerging economy firms, *JIBS*, 38: 519–540.

13 J. Dunning, 1998, Location and the multinational enterprise, *JIBS*, 29: 45–66; R. Grosse & L. Treviño, 2005, New institutional economics and FDI location in Central and Eastern Europe, *MIR*, 45: 123–135.

14 E. Maitland, S. Nicholas, W. Purcell, & T. Smith, 2004, Regional learning networks, *MIR*, 44: 87–100.

15 A. Kalnins & W. Chung, 2004, Resource-seeking agglomeration, *SMJ*, 25: 689–699; B. McCann & T. Folta, 2009, Demand- and supply-side agglomerations, *JMS*, 46: 362–392; S. Tallman, M. Jenkins, N. Henry, & S. Pinch, 2004, Knowledge, clusters, and competitive advantage, *AMR*, 29: 258–271.

16 *BW*, 2006. Airbus may hit an air pocket over China, April 24: 44.

17 F. Knickerbocker, 1973, *Oligopolistic Reaction and Multinational Enterprise*, Boston: Harvard Business School Press.

18 S. Feinberg & A. Gupta, 2009, MNC subsidiaries and country risk, *AMJ*, 52: 381–399.

19 P. Buckley & M. Casson, 1976, *The Future of the Multinational Enterprise*, London: Macmillan.

20 I. Filatotchev, R. Strange, J. Piesse, & Y. Lien, 2007, FDI by firms from new industrialized economies in emerging markets, *JIBS*, 38: 556–572.

21 J. Galan & J. Gonzalez-Benito, 2006, Distinctive determinant factors of Spanish foreign direct investment in Latin America, *JWB*, 41: 171–189.

22 R. Vernon, 1977, *Storm over the Multinationals*, Cambridge, MA: Harvard University Press.

23 C. Altomonte & E. Pennings, 2009, Domestic plant productivity and incremental spillovers from FDI, *JIBS*, 40: 1131–1148; B. Javorcik, 2004, Does foreign direct investment increase the productivity of domestic firms? *AER*, 94: 605–627.

24 G. Blalock & D. Simon, 2009, Do all firms benefit equally from downstream FDI? *JIBS*, 40: 1095–1112; K. Meyer, 2004, Perspectives on multinational enterprises in emerging economies, *JIBS*, 35: 259–276.

25 F. Barry & K. Kearney, 2006, MNE and industrial structure in host countries, JIBS, 37: 392–406.

26 P. Evans, 1979, *Dependent Development* (p. 44), Princeton, NJ: Princeton University Press.

27 C. Lindblom, 1977, *Politics and Markets* (p. 173), New York: Basic Books.

28 T. Agmon, 2003, Who gets what, *JIBS*, 34: 416–427.

29 M. W. Peng, 2000, Controlling the foreign agent, *MIR*, 40: 141–165.

30 *Economist*, 2006, Trouble on the waterfront, February 25: 33–34.

31 *BW*, 2006, Venezuela: You are working for Chavez now, May 15: 76–78.

32 Throughout the socialist world, May 1 (May Day) is celebrated as the International Workers' Day against capitalism. President Morales deliberately chose this day to seize MNE oil fields in Bolivia.

33 *Economist*, 2006, Bolivia: Now it's the people's gas, May 6: 37–38.

34 Sovereign Wealth Fund Institute, 2009, About sovereign wealth fund, www.swfinstitute.org.

35 V. Fotak & W. Megginson, 2009, Are SWFs welcome now? *CFDIP*, No. 9, July 21, www.vcc.columbia.edu.

36 T. Hemphill, 2009, Sovereign wealth funds, *TIBR*, 51: 551–566.

37 S. Globerman & D. Shapiro, 2009, Economic and strategic considerations surrounding Chinese FDI in the United States (p. 180), *APJM*, 26: 163–183.

38 H. Paulson, 2008, The right way to engage China, FA, September/October, www.foreignaffairs.org.

39 K. Sauvant, 2008, The FDI recession has begun, *CFDIP*, No. 1, November 22, www.vcc.columbia.edu.

40 US Department of the Treasury, 2009, *The First US-China Strategic and Economic Dialogue Economic Track Joint Fact Sheet*, July 28, Washington.

Chapter

7

© Super Stock Rf/Super Stock

LEARNING OBJECTIVES

After studying this chapter, you should be able to:

1. list the factors that determine foreign exchange rates.

2. articulate the steps in the evolution of the international monetary system.

3. identify strategic responses firms can take to deal with foreign exchange movements.

4. participate in two leading debates on foreign exchange movements.

5. draw implications for action.

Dealing with Foreign Exchange

O P E N I N G   C A S E

A Strong Dollar versus a Weak Dollar

The value of the US dollar is a trillion dollar question. At present, 65% of the world's foreign exchange holdings are in dollars. The recent economic turmoil has intensified the global debate on the proper value of the dollar (see Table 7.1). In terms of international trade competitiveness, a strong dollar may make it harder for US firms to export and to compete on price when combating imports. Conversely, a weak dollar may facilitate more US exports and stem import growth. Since the Plaza Accord of 1985, after which the dollar declined sharply against the Japanese yen, the United States has been pursuing a "cheap dollar" policy in order to facilitate more exports and reduce trade deficits. Unfortunately, the policy has backfired. Although US exports did rise, US trade deficits grew even more. In part this was due to China's policy to peg its yuan to the dollar, which made the yuan also cheap. In addition to spending on a shopping binge on made-in-China goods, all these "more competitive" dollars had to go somewhere. The *Wall Street Journal* noted that "with amazing efficiency they found their way into subprime mortgages."

That was before the subprime bubble collapsed in 2008. Now after being burned by one of the most horrific economic recessions that the world had seen since the Great Depression, a number of governments, firms, and experts around the world are arguing for the proper valuation of the dollar. In addition to debating what the "fair" value of the dollar is, a new voice is now calling for *abandoning* the dollar as a reserve currency.* Leading this new global movement is China. China is America's number one creditor country that holds about $2.2 trillion in foreign exchange reserves, two-thirds of which are denominated in dollars. Since the yuan is not internationally accepted (technically nonconvertible), China does not suggest that the yuan be used to replace the dollar. Instead, China has proposed to use Special Drawing Rights (SDRs), already created by the International Monetary Fund (IMF), to replace the dollar as a global reserve currency. Although this proposal is made in the name of promoting global stability, China is not totally altruistic. Since the US budget deficit has exploded and the US Federal Reserve is printing a ton of new money to fund stimulus packages, China is deeply worried that a cheapening dollar will be a nasty hit to Chinese holdings of US Treasury bonds. There is some fundamental soul-searching among Beijing's economic mandarins. Their policy of keeping the yuan low versus the dollar to promote exports and then to recycle export earnings to buy US Treasury bonds has backfired. Even the typically timid, state-controlled media in China is now full of criticisms of the Chinese government's "irresponsible" investment policy, which ends up investing hard-earned dollars from a developing economy to subsidize a very rich economy. China's proposal to dethrone the dollar as a dominant currency, although clearly a long shot, quickly garnered support from Russia and Brazil. In September 2009, the United Nations Conference on Trade and Development issued a supportive opinion:

> An economy whose currency is used as a reserve currency is not under the same obligation as others to make the necessary macroeconomic or exchange-rate adjustments for avoiding continuing current account

* Technically, since the demise of the Bretton Woods system in the early 1970s, the US dollar is no longer the official reserve currency of the world. However, the dollar, due to its "soft power," has been treated as the de facto reserve currency by most countries in the world. Read this chapter for more details.

deficits. Thus, the dominance of the dollar as the main means of international payments also played an important role in the build-up of the global imbalances in the run up to the financial crisis.

The United States, on the other hand, has every interest to keep the dollar's status quo as a (de facto) reserve currency around the world so that China and other surplus countries will keep buying Treasury bonds for lack of a better alternative. In June 2009, when the US Treasury Secretary, Tim Geithner, in a public speech at Peking University assured students that China's holdings of Treasury bonds were safe, the audience laughed. In 2009, while China continued to buy new Treasury bonds, it took two concrete steps. First, China arranged more than $120 billion in currency swaps with its trading partners such as Argentina, Belarus, Indonesia, Malaysia, and South Korea. The People's Bank of China, the central bank, will make yuan available to pay for imports from these countries if they are short on dollars. Second, China in July 2009 started to use yuan to settle certain transactions with Hong Kong—the first step for the yuan's eventual international convertibility.

TABLE 7.1   A STRONG DOLLAR VERSUS A WEAK DOLLAR

Panel A. A Strong (Appreciating) Dollar	
Advantages	**Disadvantages**
• US consumers benefit from low prices on imports	• US exporters have a hard time to compete on price abroad
• Lower prices on foreign goods help keep US price level and inflation level low	• US firms in import-competing industries have a hard time competing with low-cost imports
• US tourists enjoy lower prices abroad	• Foreign tourists find it more expensive when visiting the US
• US firms find it easier to acquire foreign targets	
Panel B. A Weak (Depreciating) Dollar	
Advantages	**Disadvantages**
• US exporters find it easier to compete on price abroad	• US consumers face higher prices on imports
• US firms face less competitive pressure to keep prices low	• Higher prices on imports contribute to higher price level and inflation level in the US.
• Foreign tourists enjoy lower prices in the US.	• US tourists find it more expensive when traveling abroad
• Foreign firms find it easier to acquire US targets	• Governments, firms, and individuals outside the US holding dollar-denominated assets suffer from value loss of their assets
• The US can print more dollars to export its problems to the rest of the world	

Sources: Based on (1) *BusinessWeek*, 2009, China's doubts about the dollar, June 8: 20; (2) *BusinessWeek*, 2009, What happens if the dollar crashes, October 26: 18–20; (3) *Economist*, 2009, Time for a Beijing bargain, May 30: 15–16; (4) *Economist*, 2009, Yuan small step, July 11: 71–72; (5) *Wall Street Journal*, 2009, Geithner is exactly wrong on China trade, January 26; (6) *Wall Street Journal*, 2009, UN panel calls for dollar reserve role to be eliminated, September 8.

International Monetary Fund (IMF)

An international organization that was established to promote international monetary cooperation, exchange stability, and orderly exchange arrangements.

Why is the value of the dollar so important? What determines foreign exchange rates? How do foreign exchange rates affect trade and investment? What is the role of global institutions such as the **International Monetary Fund (IMF)**? Finally, how can firms respond strategically? Continuing from our two previous chapters on trade (Chapter 5) and foreign direct investment (FDI) (Chapter 6), this chapter addresses these crucial questions. At the heart of our discussion lie the two core perspectives introduced earlier: the institution-based and resource-based views. Essentially, the institution-based view suggests that, as the rules of the game, domestic and international institutions (such as the IMF) influence foreign exchange rates and affect capital movements. In turn, the resource-based view sheds light on how firms such as

Wal-Mart and its suppliers (see the Closing Case) can profit from favorable foreign exchange movements by developing their own firm-specific resources and capabilities.

We start with a basic question: What determines foreign exchange rates? Then, we track the evolution of the international monetary system culminating in the IMF. How firms strategically respond is outlined next. We conclude with some discussion of debates and extensions.

WHAT DETERMINES FOREIGN EXCHANGE RATES?

A **foreign exchange rate** is the price of one currency, such as the dollar ($), in terms of another, such as the euro (€). Table 7.2 provides some examples. This section addresses a key question: What determines foreign exchange rates?

LEARNING OBJECTIVE 1

List the factors that determine foreign exchange rates.

Basic Supply and Demand

The concept of an exchange rate as the price of a commodity—in this case, a country's currency—helps us understand its determinants. Basic economic theory suggests that a commodity's price is fundamentally determined by its supply and demand. Strong demand will lead to price hikes, and oversupply will result in price drops. Of course, we are dealing with a most unusual commodity here—money—but the basic underlying principles still apply. When the United States sells products to China, US exporters often demand that they be paid in US dollars because the Chinese yuan is useless (technically, nonconvertible) in the United States. Chinese importers of US products must somehow generate US dollars in order to pay for US imports. The easiest way to generate US dollars is to *export* to the United States, whose buyers will pay in US dollars. In this example, the dollar is the common transaction currency involving both US imports and US exports. As a result, the demand for dollars is much stronger than the demand for yuans (while holding the supply constant). A wide variety of users outside the United States, such as Chinese exporters, Russian mafia members, and Swiss bankers, prefer to hold and transact in US dollars, thus fueling the demand

Foreign exchange rate
The price of one currency in terms of another.

TABLE 7.2   EXAMPLES OF KEY CURRENCY EXCHANGE RATES

	US Dollar (US$)	Euro (€)	UK Pound (£)	Swiss Franc (SFr)	Mexican Peso	Japanese Yen (¥)	Canadian Dollar (C$)
Canadian Dollar (C$)	1.08	1.58	1.79	1.05	0.08	0.012	—
Japanese Yen (¥)	90.92	132.94	150.64	87.93	6.80	—	83.98
Mexican Peso	13.36	19.54	22.14	12.92	—	0.147	12.34
Swiss Franc (SFr)	1.03	1.51	1.713	—	0.08	0.011	0.96
UK Pound (£)	0.60	0.88	—	0.58	0.04	0.007	0.56
Euro (€)	0.68	—	1.13	0.66	0.05	0.008	0.63
US Dollar (US$)	—	1.46	1.66	0.97	0.07	0.011	0.92

Source: These examples are from September 14, 2009. The rates may change. Adapted from *Wall Street Journal,* 2009, Key currency cross rates, September 14 (www.wsj.com). Reading *vertically,* the first column means US$1 = C$1.08 = ¥91 = Mexican Peso 13.36 = SFr 1.03 = £0.60 = €0.68. Reading *horizontally,* the last row means €1 = US$1.46; £1 = US$1.66; SFr 1 = US$0.97; Mexican Peso 1 = US$0.07; ¥1 = US$0.011; C$1 = US$0.92.

TABLE 7.3   THE ROLE OF THE US DOLLAR OUTSIDE THE UNITED STATES

Common reference	Most international statistics (such as exports, imports, and GDP) reported by national governments and international organizations (such as the UN, IMF, and WTO) are expressed in US dollars.
Intervention currency	Most central banks buy and sell US dollars in their respective foreign exchange markets to influence their exchange rates. Many countries peg their currencies to the dollar.
Reserve currency	Most central banks hold US dollars as official reserves to intervene in their respective markets. (The US Federal Reserve System maintains its foreign currency reserves in euros and yens.)
Vehicle currency	Transaction between two less commonly used ("exotic") currencies, such as between the Brazilian real and the Czech koruna, is often through dollars. There is always an active market for dollars in every country.

FIGURE 7.1   WHAT DETERMINES FOREIGN EXCHANGE RATES?

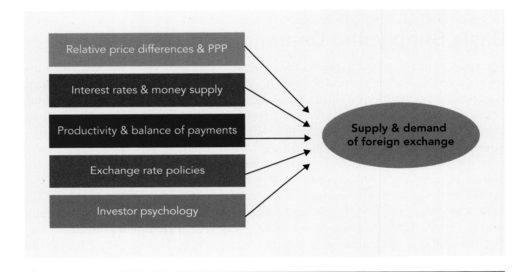

for dollars. Such a strong demand explains why the US dollar is the most sought after currency in postwar decades (see Table 7.3). At present, approximately 65% of the world's foreign exchange holdings are in US dollars, followed by 26% in euros, 4% in pounds, and 3% in yen.[1]

Because foreign exchange involves such a unique commodity, its markets are influenced not only by economic factors, but also by a lot of political and psychological factors. The next question is: What determines the supply and demand of foreign exchange? Figure 7.1 sketches the five underlying building blocks: (1) relative price differences, (2) interest rates and money supply, (3) productivity and balance of payments, (4) exchange rate policies, and (5) investor psychology.

Relative Price Differences and Purchasing Power Parity

Some countries (such as Switzerland) have famously expensive prices, and others (such as the Philippines) are known to have cheap prices. How do these price differences affect exchange rate? An answer is provided by the theory of purchasing power parity (PPP), which is essentially the "law of one price."

Purchasing power parity (PPP) is a conversion that determines the equivalent amount of goods and services different currencies can purchase. This conversion is usually used to capture the differences in cost of living between countries. The theory suggests that, in the absence of trade barriers (such as tariffs), the price for identical products sold in different countries must be the same. Otherwise, traders (or arbitragers) may "buy low" and "sell high," eventually driving prices for identical products to the same level around the world. The PPP theory argues that in the long run, exchange rates should move towards levels that would equalize the prices of an identical basket of goods in any two countries.[2]

One of the most influential (and perhaps the most fun-filled) applications of the PPP theory is the Big Mac index, popularized by the *Economist* magazine. The *Economist*'s "basket" is McDonald's Big Mac hamburger produced in about 120 countries. According to the PPP theory, a Big Mac should cost the same anywhere around the world. In reality, it does not. In July 2009, a Big Mac cost $3.57 in the United States and 12.5 yuan in China. If the Big Mac did indeed cost the same, the de facto exchange rate based on the Big Mac would be 3.50 yuan to the dollar (that is, 12.5 yuan/$3.57), whereas the nominal (official) rate at that time was 6.83 yuan to the dollar. According to this calculation, the yuan was 49% undervalued against the dollar—the second most extreme in the Big Mac universe behind the Hong Kong dollar, which was 52% undervalued (Table 7.4). In other words, Big Macs in Hong Kong and China have the best "value" in the world, costing only $1.72 in Hong Kong and $1.83 in China, respectively.[3]

Although the Big Mac index is never a serious exercise, it has been cited by some US politicians as "evidence" that the yuan is artificially undervalued. This

TABLE 7.4   THE BIG MAC INDEX

	Big Mac price in local currency	Big Mac price in US dollars	Implied PPP of the US dollar	Official exchange rate of the US dollar at present	Under (−) / over (+) valuation of the US dollar
United States	$3.57	$3.57	—	—	—
Brazil	Real 8.03	$4.02	2.25	2.00	+13%
Britain	£2.29	$3.69	1.09	1.16	+3%
Canada	C$3.89	$3.35	1.14	1.05	−6%
China	Yuan 12.5	$1.83	3.50	6.83	−49%
Denmark	DK 29.5	$5.53	8.26	5.34	+55%
Egypt	Pound 13	$2.33	3.64	5.58	−35%
Euro area	€3.31	$4.62	1.08	1.39	+29%
Hong Kong	HK$13.3	$1.72	3.73	7.75	−52%
Iceland	Krona 640	$4.99	179	128	+40%
Japan	¥320	$3.46	89.6	92.6	−3%
Mexico	Peso 33	$2.39	9.24	13.8	−33%
Norway	Kroner 40	$6.15	11.2	6.51	+72%
Philippines	Peso 99.39	$2.04	18.8	32.8	−43%
Russia	Ruble 67	$2.03	15.2	25.6	−41%
Singapore	S$4.22	$2.88	1.18	1.46	−19%
Sweden	SKr 39	$4.93	10.9	7.90	+38%
Switzerland	SFr 6.5	$5.98	1.82	1.09	+68%

Source: Adapted from *Economist*, 2009, The Big Mac Index: Cheesed off, July 18. PPP = Price in local currency divided by price in the United States ($3.57).

claim has been disavowed by the *Economist* itself. More seriously, we can make three observations:

- The Big Max index confirms that prices in some European countries are very expensive. Big Macs in Norway and Switzerland were the most expensive in the world, costing $6.15 and $5.98, respectively.
- Prices in developing countries are cheaper. Big Macs in Russia and the Philippines cost only $2.03 and $2.04, respectively. This makes sense because a Big Mac is a product with both traded and nontraded inputs. To simplify our discussion, let us assume that the costs for traded inputs (such as flour for the bun) are the same. It is obvious that nontraded inputs (such as labor and real estate) are cheaper in developing countries.
- The Big Mac is not a traded product. No large number of American hamburger lovers would travel to Hong Kong and China simply to get the best deal on the Big Mac, and then somehow (perhaps in portable freezers) return with large quantities of made-in-Hong-Kong and made-in-China Big Macs. If they did, the Big Mac price in Hong Kong and China would be driven up and the price in the United States would be pushed down. Remember supply and demand?

After having a laugh, we shouldn't read too much into this index. PPP signals where exchange rates may move in the *long run*. But it does not suggest that the yuan should appreciate by 49% or the Swiss franc should depreciate by 68% next year. According to the *Economist*, anyone interested in the PPP theory "would be unwise to exclude the Big Mac index from their diet, but Super Size servings (of this index) would equally be a mistake."[4]

Interest Rates and Money Supply

Although the PPP theory suggests the long-run direction of exchange rate movement, what about the short run? In the short run, variations in interest rates have a powerful effect. If one country's interest rate is high relative to other countries, the country will attract foreign funds. Because inflows of foreign funds usually need to be converted to the home currency, a high interest rate will increase the demand for the home currency, thus enhancing its exchange value.

In addition, a country's rate of inflation, relative to that prevailing abroad, affects its ability to attract foreign funds and hence its exchange rate. A high level of inflation is essentially too much money chasing too few goods in an economy. Technically, it is an an expansion of a country's money supply. When a government faces budgetary shortfalls, it may choose to print more currency, which tends to stimulate inflation. In turn, this would cause its currency to depreciate. This makes sense because, as the supply of a given currency (such as the Mexican peso) increases while the demand stays the same, the per unit value of that currency (such as one peso) goes down. Therefore, the exchange rate is highly sensitive to changes in monetary policy. It responds swiftly to changes in money supply. To avoid losses, investors often sell assets denominated in a depreciating currency for assets denominated in other currencies. Such massive sell-offs may worsen the depreciation.

Productivity and Balance of Payments

In international trade, the rise of a country's productivity relative to other countries will improve its competitive position. This is the basic proposition of the theories of absolute and comparative advantage discussed in Chapter 5. In turn, more FDI will be attracted to the country, fueling demand for its home currency.

One recent example is China. All the China-bound FDI inflows in dollars, euros, and pounds have to be converted to local currency, boosting the demand for the yuan and hence its value. Other examples are not hard to find. The rise in relative Japanese productivity over the past three decades led to a long-run appreciation of the yen, which rose from about ¥300 = $1 in 1975 to ¥90 = $1 in 2009.

Recall from Chapter 5 that changes in productivity will change a country's balance of trade. A country highly productive in manufacturing may generate a merchandise trade surplus, whereas a country less productive in manufacturing may end up with a merchandise trade deficit. These have ramifications for the balance of payments—officially known as a country's international transaction statement, including merchandise trade, service trade, and capital movement. Table 7.5 shows that the United States had a merchandise trade deficit of $821 billion and a service trade surplus of $140 billion in 2008. In addition to merchandise and service trade, we add receipts on US assets abroad (such as repatriated earning from US multinational enterprises (MNEs) in Brazil and dividends paid by Japanese firms to American shareholders), subtract payments on US-based foreign assets (such as repatriated earnings from Canadian MNEs in the United States to Canada and dividends paid by US firms to Dutch shareholders), and government grants and private remittances (such as US foreign aid sent to Iraq and the money that Mexican farm hands in America sent home). After doing all of the math, we can see that the United States ran a $667 billion current account deficit.[5] Technically, the current account balance consists of exports minus imports of merchandise and services, plus income on US assets abroad, minus payments on foreign assets in the United States, plus unilateral government transfers and private remittances.

Balance of payments
A country's international transaction statement, which includes merchandise trade, service trade, and capital movement.

TABLE 7.5   THE SIMPLIFIED US BALANCE OF PAYMENTS (BILLION DOLLARS)

I. Current Account		
1. Exports of goods (merchandise)	1,291	
2. Imports of goods (merchandise)	−2,112	
3. Balance on goods (merchandise trade—lines 1 + 2)		**−821**
4. Exports of services	544	
5. Imports of services	−404	
6. Balance on services (service trade—lines 4 + 5)		**140**
7. Balance on goods and services (trade deficit/surplus—lines 3 + 6)		**−681**
8. Income receipts on US-owned assets abroad	752	
9. Income payments on foreign-owned assets in the US	−618	
10. Government grants and private remittances	−120	
11. Balance on current account (current account deficit/surplus—lines 7 + 8 + 9 + 10)		**−667**
II. Financial Account		
12. US-owned private assets abroad (increase/financial outflow = − [negative sign])	−52	
13. Foreign-owned private assets in the US.	599	
14. Balance on financial account (lines 12 + 13)		**547**
15. Overall balance of payments (Official reserve transactions balance—lines 11 + 14)		**−120**

Sources: This is a simplified table adapted from US Department of Commerce, Bureau of Economic Analysis, 2009, *US International Transactions: Fourth Quarter and Year 2008*, Table 1, March 18, Washington: BEA (www.bea.gov [accessed July 13, 2009]). This table refers to 2008. Numbers may not add due to rounding.

A current account deficit has to be financed by financial account consisting of purchases and sales of assets. This is because a country needs to balance its accounts in much the same way as a family deals with its finances. Any deficit in a family budget has to be financed by spending from savings or by borrowing.[6] In a similar fashion, the overall US deficit of $120 billion was financed by spending from savings and borrowing (selling US government securities such as Treasury bonds to foreign central banks—see the Opening Case).

To make a long story short, a country experiencing a current account surplus will see its currency appreciate. Conversely, a country experiencing a current account deficit will see its currency depreciate. This may not happen overnight but may materialize over a span of years and decades. The current movement between the yuan (appreciating) and the dollar (depreciating) is but one example (see the Opening and Closing Cases). Going back to the 1950s and 1960s, the rise of the dollar was accompanied by a sizable US surplus on merchandise trade. By the 1970s and 1980s, the surplus gradually turned into a deficit. By the 1990s and 2000s, the US current account deficit increased, forcing the dollar to depreciate relative to other currencies such as the yuan, the euro, and the Canadian dollar. Broadly speaking, the value of a country's currency is an embodiment of its economic strengths as reflected in its productivity and balance of payments positions. Overall, the recent pressure for the US dollar to depreciate is indicative of the relative (not absolute) decline of the US economic strengths, compared with its major trading partners.

Exchange Rate Policies

There are two major exchange rate policies: (1) floating rate and (2) fixed rate. Governments adopting the **floating** (or **flexible**) **exchange rate policy** tend to be free market believers, willing to let the supply-and-demand conditions determine exchange rates, usually on a daily basis via the foreign exchange market. However, few countries adopt a **clean** (or **free**) **float**, which would be a pure market solution. Most countries practice a **dirty** (or **managed**) **float**, with selective government interventions. Of the major currencies, the US, Canadian, and Australian dollars, the yen, and the pound have been under managed float since the 1970s (after the collapse of the Bretton Woods system—see next section). Since the late 1990s, several emerging economies, such as Brazil, Mexico, and South Korea, have also joined the managed float regime.

The severity of intervention is a matter of degree. Heavier intervention moves the country closer to a fixed exchange rate policy, and less intervention enables a country to approach the free float ideal. A main objective for intervention is to prevent the emergence of erratic fluctuations that may trigger macroeconomic turbulence. Some countries do not adhere to any particular rates. Others choose **target exchange rates**, also known as **crawling bands**, which are specified upper and lower bounds within which the exchange rate is allowed to fluctuate. A country that uses target exchange rates—an approach colorfully termed "snake in a tube"—will intervene only when the snake (the exchange rate) crawls out of the tube (the upper or lower bounds).

Another major exchange rate policy is the fixed rate policy. A country adopting a **fixed exchange rate policy** fixes the exchange rate of its currency relative to other currencies. Both political and economic rationales may influence this choice. During the German reunification in 1990, the West German government, for political considerations, fixed the exchange rate between the West and East German mark as 1:1. In economic terms, the East German mark was not worth that much. Politically, this exchange

---

Floating (flexible) exchange rate policy

A government policy to let supply-and-demand conditions determine exchange rates.

Clean (free) float

A pure market solution to determine exchange rates.

Dirty (managed) float

Using selective government intervention to determine exchange rates.

Target exchange rates (crawling bands)

Specified upper or lower bounds within which an exchange rate is allowed to fluctuate.

Fixed exchange rate policy

A government policy to set the exchange rate of a currency relative to other currencies.

rate reduced the feeling of alienation and resentment among East Germans, thus facilitating a smoother unification process. Of course, West Germans ended up paying more for the costs of unification.

Economically, many developing countries peg their currencies to a key currency (often the US dollar). There are two benefits for a peg policy. First, a peg stabilizes the import and export prices for developing countries. Second, many countries with high inflation have pegged their currencies to the dollar in order to restrain domestic inflation because the United States has relatively low inflation. (See Debates and Extensions for more discussion.)

During reunification with East Germany, what were some of the economic consequences of West Germany's decision to fix the exchange rate between the West and East German marks at parity (a 1:1 rate)?

Investor Psychology

Although theories on price differences (PPP), interest rates and money supply, balance of payments, and exchange rate policies predict long-run movements of exchange rates, they often fall short of predicting short-run movements. What then determines short-run movements? They are largely driven by investor psychology, some of which is fickle and thus very hard to predict. Professor Richards Lyons at the University of California, Berkeley, is an expert on exchange rate theories. However, he was baffled when he was invited by a friend—a currency trader—to observe currency trading firsthand:

> As I sat there, my friend traded furiously all day long, racking up over $1 billion in trades each day. This was a world where the standard trade was $10 million, and a $1 million trade was a "skinny one." Despite my belief that exchange rates depend on macroeconomics, only rarely was news of this type his primary concern. Most of the time he was reading tea leaves that were, at least to me, not so clear . . . It was clear my understanding was incomplete when he looked over, in the midst of his fury, and asked me: "What should I do?" I laughed. Nervously.[7]

Investors—currency traders such as the one Lyons observed, foreign portfolio investors, and average citizens—may move like a "herd" at the same time in the same direction, resulting in a bandwagon effect. The bandwagon effect seemed to be at play in the second half of 2008, when the Icelandic krona, which showed signs of being overvalued by the Big Mac index (see Table 7.4), lost more than half of its value against key currencies such as the US dollar, the euro, and the pound sterling. Essentially, a large number of individuals and firms exchanged the krona for the key foreign currencies in order to minimize their exposure to Iceland's financial crisis—a phenomenon known as capital flight. This pushed down the demand for, and thus the value of, domestic currencies. Then, more individuals and companies jumped on the bandwagon, further depressing the exchange rate and worsening a major economic crisis.

Overall, economics, politics, and psychology are all at play. The stakes are high, yet consensus is rare regarding the determinants of foreign exchange rates. As a result, predicting the direction of currency movements remains an art or, at best, a highly imprecise science.

Peg

A stabilizing policy of linking a developing country's currency to a key currency.

Bandwagon effect

The effect of investors moving in the same direction at the same time, like a herd.

Capital flight

A phenomenon in which a large number of individuals and companies exchange domestic currency for a foreign currency.

LEARNING OBJECTIVE

2

Articulate the steps in the evolution of the international monetary system.

EVOLUTION OF THE INTERNATIONAL MONETARY SYSTEM

Having outlined the basic determinants of exchange rates, let us trace the history of the three eras of the evolution of the international monetary system: (1) the gold standard, (2) the Bretton Woods system, and (3) the post–Bretton Woods system.

The Gold Standard (1870–1914)

The **gold standard** was a system in place between 1870 and 1914, when the value of most major currencies was maintained by fixing their prices in terms of gold. Gold was used as the **common denominator** for all currencies. This was essentially a global peg system with little volatility and every bit of predictability and stability. To be able to redeem its currency in gold at a fixed price, every central bank needed to maintain gold reserves. The system provided powerful incentives for countries to run current account surpluses, resulting in net inflows of gold.

The Bretton Woods System (1944–1973)

The gold standard was abandoned in 1914 when World War I broke out and several combatant countries printed excessive amounts of currency to finance their war efforts. After World War I, especially during the Great Depression (1929–1933), countries engaged in competitive devaluations in an effort to boost exports at the expense of trading partners. But no country could win such a "race to the bottom," and the gold standard had to be jettisoned.

Towards the end of World War II, at an allied conference in Bretton Woods, New Hampshire, a new system—known simply as the **Bretton Woods system**—was agreed upon by 44 countries. The Bretton Woods system was centered on the US dollar as the new common denominator. All currencies were pegged at a fixed rate to the dollar. Only the dollar—the official reserve currency—was convertible into gold at $35 per ounce. Other currencies were not required to be gold convertible.

The Bretton Woods system propelled the dollar to the commanding heights of the global economy (see Table 7.3). This system reflected the higher US productivity level and the large trade surplus the United States had with the rest of the world in the first two postwar decades. This was not surprising, because the US economy contributed approximately 70% of the global GDP at the end of World War II and was the export engine of the world.

The Post–Bretton Woods System (1973–Present)

By the late 1960s and early 1970s, a combination of rising productivity elsewhere and US inflationary policies led to the demise of Bretton Woods. First, in the 1960s, President Lyndon Johnson increased government spending in order to finance both the Vietnam War and Great Society welfare programs. He did this not by additional taxation but by increasing the money supply. These actions led to rising inflation levels and strong pressures for the dollar to depreciate. Second, the United States ran its first post-1945 trade deficit in 1971 as (West) Germany and other countries caught up to the United States in productivity and increased their exports. This pushed the (West) German mark to appreciate and the dollar to depreciate—a situation very similar to the yen-dollar relationship in the 1980s and the current yuan-dollar relationship in the 2000s.

Gold standard

A system in which the value of most major currencies was maintained by fixing their prices in terms of gold.

Common denominator

A currency or commodity to which the value of all currencies are pegged.

Bretton Woods system

A system in which all currencies were pegged at a fixed rate to the US dollar.

As currency traders bought more German marks, Germany's central bank, the Bundesbank, had to buy billions of dollars in order to maintain the dollar/mark exchange rate fixed by Bretton Woods. Being stuck with massive amounts of the dollar that was worth less now, Germany unilaterally allowed its currency to float in May 1971.

The Bretton Woods system also became a pain in the neck for the United States because the exchange rate of the dollar was not allowed to unilaterally change. Per Bretton Woods agreements, the US Treasury was obligated to dispense one ounce of gold for every $35 brought to it by a foreign central bank such as the Bundesbank. Consequently, the United States was hemorrhaging gold into the coffers of foreign central banks. In order to stop the flow of gold out of the US Treasury, President Richard Nixon unilaterally announced in 1971 that the dollar was no longer convertible into gold. After tense negotiations, major countries collectively agreed in 1973 to allow their currencies to float, thus hammering the nails into the coffin of the Bretton Woods system. In retrospect, the Bretton Woods system had been built on two conditions: (1) the US inflation rate had to be low, and (2) the US could not run a trade deficit. When both of these conditions were violated, the demise of the system became inevitable.

As a result, today we live in the **post–Bretton Woods system**. Its strengths lie in its flexibility and diversity of exchange rate regimes (including various floating systems and fixed rates). Its drawbacks are turbulence and uncertainty. Since the early 1970s, the US dollar has not been the official reserve currency (or common denominator). However, it has retained a significant amount of "soft power" as a key currency (see Table 7.3).

The International Monetary Fund (IMF)

Although the Bretton Woods system is no longer with us, one of its most enduring legacies is the IMF, founded in 1944 as a Bretton Woods institution. (The World Bank is the other Bretton Woods institution.) With 186 member countries, the IMF is very much alive today. Its mandate is to promote international monetary cooperation and provide temporary financial assistance to member countries in order to help overcome balance of payments problems.

Lending is a core responsibility of the IMF. The IMF can be viewed as a lender of last resort to help member countries should they get into financial difficulty. Where does the IMF get its funds? The answer boils down to the same principle as where insurance companies get their funds to pay out insurance claims. Similar to insurance companies collecting premiums from subscribers to accumulate the funds necessary to cover claims, the IMF collects funds from member countries. Each member country is assigned a **quota** that determines its financial contribution to the IMF (technically known as its "subscription"), its capacity to borrow from the IMF, and its voting power. The quota is broadly based on a country's relative size in the global economy.

By definition, the IMF makes loans, not free grants. IMF loans usually have to be repaid in 1–5 years. Although payment schedules have been extended in some cases, no member country has defaulted. An ideal IMF scenario would be a country that has found itself in a balance of payments crisis that threatens to severely disrupt its financial stability, such as when a country imports more than it exports and cannot pay for the imports. The IMF could step in and inject funds in the short term to help stabilize the financial system.

Although an IMF loan provides short-term financial resources, it also comes with strings attached: long-term policy reforms that recipient countries must undertake as conditions of receiving the loan. These conditions usually entail belt-tightening,

Post–Bretton Woods system

A system of flexible exchange rate regimes with no official common denominator.

Quota

The weight a member country carries within the IMF, which determines the amount of its financial contribution (technically known as its "subscription"), its capacity to borrow from the IMF, and its voting power.

pushing governments to embark on painful reforms that they otherwise probably would not have undertaken (Table 7.6). For instance, when the IMF provided a $30 billion loan to Brazil in 2002, the Brazilian government agreed to maintain a budget surplus of 3.75% of GDP or higher in order to pay for government debt. Between the mid-1990s and the early 2000s, the IMF frequently went into action in emerging economies, such as Mexico (1994), Russia (1996 and 1998), Asia (Indonesia, South Korea, and Thailand, 1997), and Brazil (2002). Between 2002 and 2008, thanks to the generally stable global economy, there was a relative lack of crises that called for the IMF. However, as a "global economic fireman," IMF provided rapid-fire bailouts to 10 countries (mostly in emerging Europe) in five *months* (!) starting in November 2008 (see Figure 7.2). Although the IMF has noble goals, its actions are not without criticisms (see In Focus 7.1). Critics call for reforms, some of which represent a total change from the IMF's previous directions.[8]

TABLE 7.6   TYPICAL IMF CONDITIONS ON LOAN RECIPIENT COUNTRIES: FROM IMF 1.0 TO IMF 2.0

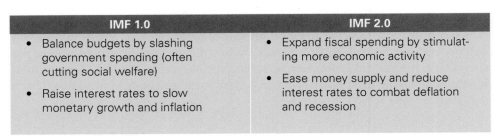

IMF 1.0	IMF 2.0
• Balance budgets by slashing government spending (often cutting social welfare)	• Expand fiscal spending by stimulating more economic activity
• Raise interest rates to slow monetary growth and inflation	• Ease money supply and reduce interest rates to combat deflation and recession

FIGURE 7.2   THE IMF'S RAPID-FIRE BAILOUTS ($ BILLION AND PERCENTAGE OF GDP)

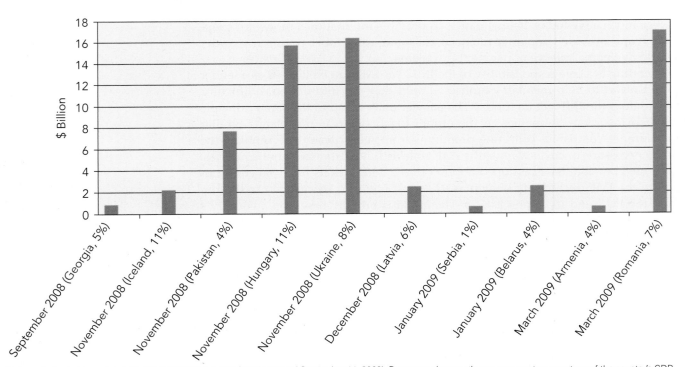

Source: Extracted from data from the IMF, 2009, www.imf.org (accessed September 14, 2009). Percentage in parentheses represents percentage of the country's GDP.

 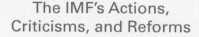 

IN Focus 7.1

The IMF's Actions, Criticisms, and Reforms

The complexity of the IMF's actions means that it cannot please everyone. First, the IMF's critics argue that the IMF's lending may *facilitate* more problems because of moral hazard. Moral hazard refers to recklessness when people and organizations (including governments) do not have to face the full consequences of their actions. Moral hazard is inherent in all insurance arrangements, including the IMF. Basically, knowing that the IMF would come to the rescue, certain governments may behave more recklessly. For example, between 1958 and 2001, Turkey was rescued by 18 (!) IMF loans.

A second criticism centers on the IMF's lack of accountability. Although the IMF can dictate terms over a host country that is being rescued and receiving loans, none of the IMF officials is democratically elected, and most of them do not have any deep knowledge of the host country. Consequently, they sometimes make disastrous decisions. For example, in 1997–1998, the IMF forced the Indonesian government to drastically cut back on food subsidies for the poor. Riots exploded the next day. Hundreds of people were killed and property damaged. Then, the IMF reversed its position by restoring food subsidies. However, in some quarters, the bitterness was all the greater. A lot of protesters argued: If food subsidies could have been continued, why were they taken away in the first place?

A third and perhaps most challenging criticism is that the IMF's "one-size-fits-all" strategy may be inappropriate. Since the 1930s, in order to maintain more employment, most Western governments have abandoned the idea to balance the budget. Deficit spending has been used as a major policy weapon to pull a country out of an economic crisis. Yet, the IMF often demands governments in more vulnerable developing countries, in the midst of a major crisis, to balance their budgets by slashing spending (such as cutting food subsidies). These actions often make the crisis far worse than it needs to be. After the IMF "rescued" countries affected by the 1997 Asian financial crisis, the unemployment rate went up threefold in Thailand, fourfold in South Korea, and tenfold in Indonesia. Many scholars are surprised that the IMF would pursue its agenda in

the absence of conclusive research and with the knowledge of repeated failures.

After a period of relative inactivity in the early 2000s, the IMF went back into action again starting in late 2008, rescuing 10 countries, mostly in emerging Europe (Georgia, Hungary, Ukraine, Latvia, Serbia, Belarus, Armenia, and Romania), in five *months* (see Figure 7.2). Shown in Table 7.6, balancing budgets and raising interest rates are the IMF's standard weapons of choice that it imposes on loan recipient countries. In most emerging European countries, the IMF has still prescribed such bitter "medicines."

However, the momentum of the criticisms, the severity of the global crisis, and the desire to better serve the international community have facilitated a series of IMF reforms since 2009. Some of these reforms represent a total (180 degrees) change from its previous directions, resulting in what *Time* dubbed "IMF 2.0." For example, the IMF is now starting to promote more fiscal spending in order to stimulate the economy and to ease the money supply and reduce interest rates, given the primary concern for the global economy now is deflation and recession, but not inflation. Obviously, the IMF's change of heart is affected by the tremendous stimulus packages unleashed by developed economies since 2008, which have resulted in skyrocketing budget deficits. If the developed economies can (hopefully) use greater fiscal spending and budget deficits to pull themselves out of the crisis, the IMF simply cannot lecture developing economies that receive its loans to balance their budgets in the middle of a crisis. Further, given the stigma of receiving IMF loans and listening to and then implementing IMF lectures, many countries avoid the IMF until they run out of options. In response, in April 2009, the IMF unleashed a new Flexible Credit Line (FCL), which would be particularly useful for crisis prevention by providing the flexibility to draw on it at any time, with no strings attached—a radical contrast to the requirement to be in compliance with IMF-imposed targets as in traditional IMF loans. Mexico is the first country that has requested and been approved

In Focus 7.1 (continued)

to tap the FCL for up to $47 billion, which is the largest financial arrangement in IMF's history.

Further, the IMF 2.0 is likely to become three times bigger—leaders in the G-20 Summit in London in April 2009 agreed to enhance the IMF's funding from $250 billion to $750 billion. Of the $500 billion new funding (technically Special Drawing Rights [SDRs]), the United States, the EU, and Japan are each expected to contribute $100 billion. China has signed up for $40 billion. However, this is still not a done deal, because it is possible that the US Congress may veto the $100 billion spending on "other countries' problems" at a time when the American economy is hurting. Further, injection of substantial funding from emerging economies has led the finance ministers of Brazil, Russia, India, and China (BRIC) who met in March 2009 to call for

greater representation of these countries. However, enhancing voting rights for emerging economies would result in reduced shares for developed economies. Even with the IMF's new proposed change to vote shares, Brazil, with 1.72% of the votes (up from the current 1.38%), will still carry less weight than Belgium (with 1.86%, down from the current 2.09%). Such points of contention continue to rage throughout IMF discussions. Therefore, IMF reforms will be a long-term undertaking that will not stop anytime soon.

Sources: Based on (1) *Economist*, 2009, Mission possible, April 11: 69–71; (2) *Economist*, 2009, New fund, old fundamentals, May 2: 78; (3) A. Ghosh, M. Chamon, C. Crowe, J. Kim, & J. Ostry, 2009, Coping with the crisis: Policy options for emerging market countries, IMF staff position paper, Washington: IMF; (4) J. Stiglitz, 2002, *Globalization and Its Discontents*, New York: Norton; (5) *Time*, 2009, International Monetary Fund 2.0, April 20.

LEARNING OBJECTIVE 3

Identify strategic responses firms can take to deal with foreign exchange movements.

STRATEGIC RESPONSES TO FOREIGN EXCHANGE MOVEMENTS

From an institution-based view, knowledge about foreign exchange rates and international monetary system (including the role of the IMF) helps paint a broad picture of the rules of the game that govern financial transactions around the world. Armed with this knowledge, savvy managers need to develop firm-specific resources and capabilities so they can rise to the challenge or at least prevent their firms from being crushed by unfavorable currency movements. This section outlines the strategic responses of two types of firms: financial and nonfinancial companies.

Strategies for Financial Companies

One of the leading strategic goals for financial companies is to profit from the foreign exchange market. The **foreign exchange market** is a market where individuals, firms, governments, and banks buy and sell currencies. Unlike a stock exchange, the foreign exchange market has no central, physical location. This market is truly global and transparent. Buyers and sellers are geographically dispersed but constantly linked, and quoted prices change as often as 20 times a minute.[9] Every Monday morning, the market opens first in Tokyo, then Hong Kong and Singapore (when it is still Sunday evening in New York). Gradually, Frankfurt, Zurich, Paris, London, New York, Chicago, and San Francisco "wake up" and come online.

Operating on a 24/7 basis, the foreign exchange market is the largest and most active market in the world. On average, the worldwide volume exceeds $2 trillion per day. To put this mind-boggling number in perspective, the amount of one single *day* of foreign exchange transactions roughly doubles the amount of entire worldwide FDI outflows in one *year*, and roughly equals close to one-quarter of

Foreign exchange market

The market where individuals, firms, governments, and banks buy and sell foreign currencies.

worldwide merchandise exports in one *year*. Of course, trade and FDI are directly related to foreign exchange transactions because traders and investors need to convert home currencies into foreign currencies. But the strikingly large scale of the foreign exchange market, compared to the more modest levels of trade and FDI, suggests that something else must be going on beyond the need to service trade and FDI. Specifically, the foreign exchange market has two functions: (1) to service the needs of trade and FDI and (2) to trade in its own commodity—namely, foreign exchange.

There are three primary types of foreign exchange transactions: (1) spot transactions, (2) forward transactions, and (3) swaps. **Spot transactions** are the classic single-shot exchange of one currency for another. Although Australian tourists vacationing in Italy can buy several thousand euros with Australian dollars

What type of foreign exchange transaction might an individual like yourself engage in?

from a bank right away, companies exchanging large amounts such as several million Australian dollars for several million euros cannot settle their transaction right away. However, as long as settlement is done within two business days—a period conceptually known as *immediate delivery*—the transaction is still considered a "spot transaction."

Forward transactions allow participants to buy and sell currencies now for future delivery, typically in 30, 90, or 180 days, after the date of the transaction. The primary benefit of forward transactions is to protect traders and investors from being exposed to the fluctuations of the spot rate, an act known as **currency hedging**. Currency hedging is essentially a way to minimize the foreign exchange risk inherent in all nonspot transactions, which include most trade and FDI deals. Traders and investors expecting to make or receive payments in a foreign currency in the future are concerned that they could be forced to make either a greater payment or receive less in terms of the domestic currency should the spot rate change. For example, if the forward rate of the euro (€/US$) is exactly the same as the spot rate, the euro is "flat." If the forward rate of the euro per dollar is *higher* than the spot rate, the euro has a **forward discount**. If the forward rate of the euro per dollar is *lower* than the spot rate, the euro then has a **forward premium**.

Hypothetically, assume that (1) today's exchange rate of €/US$ is 1, (2) a US firm expects to be paid €1 million six months later, and (3) the euro is at a 180-day forward discount of 1.1 (or €1/US$1.1). The US firm could take out a forward contract now and convert euro earnings into a dollar revenue of $909,091 (€1 million/1.1) after six months. Does such a move make sense? Maybe. The move makes sense if the firm believes that the future spot rate will be higher. So in six months if the spot rate is 1.25, then the forward contract provides the US firm with $909,091 instead of $800,000 (€1 million/1.25)—the difference is $109,091 (or 14% of $800,000). However, the move would not make sense if after six months the spot rate were actually below 1.1. If the spot rate remained at 1, the firm could have earned $1 million *without* the forward contract, instead of only $909,091 with the contract. This simple example suggests a powerful observation: Currency hedging *requires* firms to have expectations or forecasts of future spot rates relative to forward rates.

A third major type of foreign exchange transactions is swap. A **currency swap** is the conversion of one currency into another in Time 1, with an agreement to revert it back to the original currency at a specific Time 2 in the future. Let's say that Deutsche Bank has an excess balance of pounds but needs dollars now. At the same time, Union Bank of Switzerland (UBS) has more dollars than it needs at the

Spot transaction

The classic single-shot exchange of one currency for another.

Forward transaction

A foreign exchange transaction in which participants buy and sell currencies now for future delivery.

Currency hedging

A transaction that protects traders and investors from exposure to the fluctuations of the spot rate.

Forward discount

A condition under which the forward rate of one currency relative to another currency is higher than the spot rate.

Forward premium

A condition under which the forward rate of one currency relative to another currency is lower than the spot rate.

Currency swap

A foreign exchange transaction between two firms in which one currency is converted into another at Time 1, with an agreement to revert it back to the original currency at a specified Time 2 in the future.

moment but is looking for more pounds. They can negotiate a swap agreement in which Deutsche Bank agrees to exchange pounds for dollars with UBS today and dollars for pounds at a specific point in the future.

The primary participants of the foreign exchange market are large international banks such as Citigroup, Deutsche Bank, and UBS that trade among themselves. How do these banks make money by trading money? They make money by capturing the difference between their **offer rate** (the price to sell) and **bid rate** (the price to buy). The bid rate is *always* lower than the offer rate. In other words, banks buy low and sell high. The difference between the offer rate and the bid rate is technically called the **spread**. For example, Citigroup may quote offer and bid rates for the Swiss franc at $0.5854 and $0.5851, respectively, and the spread is $0.0003. That is, Citigroup is willing to sell 1 million francs for $585,400 and buy 1 million francs for $585,100. If Citigroup can simultaneously buy and sell 1 million francs, it can make $300 (the spread of $0.0003 × 1 million francs). Given the instantaneous and transparent nature of the electronically linked foreign exchange market around the globe (one new quote in London can reach New York before you finish reading this *sentence*), the opportunities for trading, or arbitrage, can come and go very quickly. The globally integrated nature of this market leads to three outcomes:

- a razor-thin spread
- quick (often literally split-second) decisions on buying and selling (remember Professor Lyon's observation earlier)
- ever-increasing volume in order to make more profits (recall the daily volume of $2 trillion).

In the example above, $300 is obviously just a few "peanuts" for Citigroup. Do a little math: How much trading in Swiss francs does Citigroup have to do in order to make $1 million in profits for itself?

Strategies for Nonfinancial Companies

How do nonfinancial companies cope with the potential losses they could incur due to fluctuations in the foreign exchange market, broadly known as **currency risks**? There are two primary strategies: (1) currency hedging (as discussed earlier) and (2) strategic hedging.[10] Currency hedging is risky because in trying to predict currency movements your bets could be all wrong. For example, most airlines in the world engage in currency hedging to manage fuel cost fluctuations, and most suffered losses in 2008. In July 2008, oil price was at a record high, $147 per barrel. Some airlines entered 180-day forward transactions with foreign exchange traders at, say, $100 per barrel. This looked like a fantastic deal, representing 32% savings. However, by early January 2009, oil was only trading at $41 per barrel. These airlines were bound by the contract to purchase the oil at $100 per barrel, thus paying 144% (!) more than they needed to for their fuel.

Strategic hedging means spreading out activities in a number of countries in different currency zones in order to offset any currency losses in one region with gains in other regions.[11] Therefore, strategic hedging can be considered as currency diversification. It reduces exposure to unfavorable foreign exchange movements. Strategic hedging is conceptually different from currency hedging. Currency hedging focuses on using forward contracts and swaps to contain currency risks, a financial management activity that can be performed by in-house financial specialists or outside experts (such as currency traders). Strategic hedging refers to geographically dispersing operations—through sourcing or FDI—in multiple currency zones.[12] By definition, this is more strategic because it involves managers from many functional

---

Offer rate
The price to sell a currency.

Bid rate
The price to buy a currency.

Spread
The difference between the offer price and the bid price.

Currency risk
The potential for loss associated with fluctuations in the foreign exchange market.

Strategic hedging
Spreading out activities in a number of countries in different currency zones to offset any currency losses in one region through gains in other regions.

areas such as production, marketing, and sourcing in addition to those from finance. Strategic hedging was one of the key motivations behind Toyota's 1998 decision to set up a new factory in France instead of expanding its existing British operations. Although expanding the British site would have cost less in the short run, France is in the euro area, which the British have refused to join.

Overall, the importance of foreign exchange management for firms of all stripes interested in doing business abroad cannot be over-stressed. Firms whose performance is otherwise stellar can be devastated by unfavorable currency movements. For example, Honda is hurt by the strong yen, which has appreciated against the dollar since 2000. Since Honda makes 80% of its profits in the United States, their value becomes much lower when translated into the Japanese yen.

From a resource-based view, it seems imperative that firms develop resources and capabilities that can combat currency risks in addition to striving for excellence in areas such as operations and marketing.[13] Although MNE subsidiary managers in certain countries may believe that there are lucrative opportunities to expand production, if these countries suffer from high currency risks, it may be better for the multinational as a whole to curtail such expansion and channel resources to other countries whose currency risks are more manageable. Developing such expertise is no small accomplishment because, as noted earlier, prediction of currency movements remains an art or a highly imprecise science. These challenges mean that firms able to profit from (or at least avoid being crushed by) unfavorable currency movements will possess some valuable, rare, and hard-to-imitate capabilities that are the envy of rivals.

DEBATES AND EXTENSIONS

In the highly uncertain world of foreign exchange movements, stakes are high, yet consensus is rare and debates are numerous. We review two major debates here: (1) fixed versus floating exchange rates and (2) hedging versus not hedging.

Participate in two leading debates on foreign exchange movements.

Fixed versus Floating Exchange Rates[14]

Since the collapse of the Bretton Woods system in the early 1970s, debate has never ended on whether fixed or floating exchange rates are better. Proponents of fixed exchange rates argue that fixed exchange rates impose monetary discipline by preventing governments from engaging in inflationary monetary policies (essentially, printing more money). Proponents also suggest that fixed exchange rates reduce uncertainty and thus encourage trade and FDI, not only benefiting the particular economy but also helping the global economy.

Proponents of floating exchange rates believe that market forces should take care of supply, demand, and thus price of any currency. Floating exchange rates may avoid large balance-of-payments deficits, surprises, and even crises. In other words, flexible exchange rates may help avoid the crises that occur under fixed exchange rates when expectations of an impending devaluation arise. For example, Thailand probably would not have been devastated so suddenly in July 1997 (generally regarded as the triggering event for the 1997 Asian financial crisis) had it operated a floating exchange rate system. In addition, floating exchange rates allow each country to make its own monetary policy. A major problem associated with the Bretton Woods system was that other countries were not happy about fixing their currencies to the currency of a country with inflationary monetary policies, as practiced by the United States in the late 1960s.

There is no doubt that floating exchange rates are more volatile than fixed rates. Many countries have no stomach for such volatility. The most extreme fixed rate policy is through a **currency board**, which is a monetary authority that issues notes and coins convertible into a key foreign currency at a *fixed* exchange rate. Usually, the fixed exchange rate is set by law, making changes to the exchange rate politically very costly for governments. To honor its commitment, a currency board must back the domestic currency with 100% of equivalent foreign exchange. In the case of Hong Kong's currency board, every HK$7.8 in circulation is backed by US$1. By design, a currency board is passive. When more US dollars flow in, the board issues more Hong Kong dollars and interest rates fall. When more US dollars flow out, the board reduces money supply and interest rates rise. The Hong Kong currency board has been jokingly described as an Asian outpost of the US Federal Reserve. This is technically accurate, because interest rates in Hong Kong are essentially determined by the US Federal Reserve. Although the Hong Kong currency board has been a successful bulwark against speculative attacks on the Hong Kong dollar, a currency board is not necessarily a panacea, as evidenced by Argentina's experience (In Focus 7.2).

Currency board

A monetary authority that issues notes and coins convertible into a key foreign currency at a fixed exchange rate.

IN Focus 7.2

Hong Kong and Argentina: A Tale of Two Currency Boards

Hong Kong is usually cited as an example that has benefited from a currency board. In the early 1980s, Hong Kong had a floating exchange rate. As Britain and China intensified their negotiations over the colony's future, the fear that the "Hong Kong way of life" might be abandoned after 1997 shook business confidence, pushed down real estate values, and caused panic buying of vegetable oil and rice. The result was a 16% depreciation in the Hong Kong dollar against the US dollar. In 1983, the Hong Kong government ended the crisis by adopting a currency board that pegged the exchange rate at HK$7.8 = US$1. The currency board almost immediately restored confidence. The second major test of the currency board came in 1997, in the first autumn after Hong Kong was returned to Chinese sovereignty. During the Asian financial crisis of 1997–1998, Hong Kong's currency board stood like a rock and successfully repelled speculative attacks and maintained its peg to the US dollar. At present, the peg is still in effect.

In Argentina, hyperinflation was rampant in the 1980s. Prices increased by more than 1,000% (!) in both 1989 and 1990. In 1991, to tame its tendency to finance public spending by printing pesos, Argentina's government adopted a currency board and pegged the peso at parity to the US dollar (1 peso = US$1). At first, the system worked, as inflation was brought down to 2% by 1995. However, by the late 1990s, Argentina was hit by multiple problems. First, appreciation of the dollar made its exports less competitive. Second, rising US interest rates spilled over to Argentina. Third, depreciation of Brazil's real (R$) resulted in more imports from Brazil and fewer exports from Argentina to Brazil. To finance budget deficits, Argentina borrowed dollars on the international market, as printing more pesos was not possible under the currency board. When further borrowing became impossible in 2001, the government defaulted on its $155 billion public debt (a world record), ended the peso's convertibility, and froze most dollar-denominated deposits in banks. In 2002, Argentina was forced to give up its currency board. After the de-link, the peso plunged, hitting a low of 3.5 to the dollar. Riots broke out as people voiced their displeasure with politicians.

Sources: Based on (1) R. Carbaugh, 2007, *International Economics*, 11th ed. (pp. 492–495), Cincinnati: South-Western Cengage Learning; (2) F. Gunter, 2004, Why did Argentina's currency board collapse? *The World Economy*, May: 697–704; (3) M. W. Peng, 2006, Coping with institutional uncertainty in Argentina, in M. W. Peng, *Global Strategy* (p. 111), Cincinnati: South-Western Cengage Learning.

Currency Hedging versus Not Hedging

Given the unpredictable nature of foreign exchange rates, it seems natural that firms that deal with foreign transactions—both financial and nonfinancial types, both large and small firms—may want to engage in currency hedging. For instance, many Irish exporters use forward contracts to hedge (In Focus 7.3). Firms that fail to hedge are at the mercy of the spot market.

Yet, surprisingly, many firms do not bother to engage in currency hedging. Some Irish exporters simply insist on payment in euros (see In Focus 7.3). Among the largest US firms, only approximately one-third hedge. The standard argument for currency hedging is increased stability of cash flows and earnings. In essence, currency hedging may be regarded as a form of insurance, the cost of which may be outweighed by the protection it provides. However, many large firms, such as 3M, Deere, Eastman Kodak, ExxonMobil, and IBM, do not care about such insurance. Managers argue that currency hedging eats into profits. A simple forward contract may cost up to half a percentage point per year of the revenue being hedged. More complicated transactions may cost more. As a result, many firms believe that the ups and downs of various currencies even out in the long run. Some firms, such as IBM, focus on strategic hedging (geographically dispersing activities) while refraining from currency hedging. Whether such a "no currency hedging" strategy outperforms a currency hedging strategy remains to be seen.

IN Focus 7.3

Irish Exporters Cope with Currency Fluctuation

A member of the euro area, Ireland has strong exporters that sell not only throughout Europe, but also in many other parts of the world. The downside of selling around the world is the complication of having to deal with currency fluctuation. Approximately 50% of the Irish export invoicing is done in either British pounds or US dollars, which have fluctuated substantially during the 2008–2009 crisis. Although hedging using forward contracts is an obvious coping strategy, many smaller exporters cannot afford the expenses. In addition, hedging is not risk-free. Wrong bets may end up burning firms big time.

To better cope with currency fluctuation, a straightforward mechanism is to insist on payment in euros. As a growing number of buyers of Irish exports have agreed, this strategy seems to have worked. A survey in late 2008 conducted by the Irish Exporters Association found that 38% of buyers in the UK, 18% in North America, 48% in the Middle East, 45% in Asia, 67% in Latin America, and 83% in noneuro area European countries were willing to pay Irish exporters in euros, thus eliminating the problem of currency fluctuation for Irish exporters. Although this is a small piece of evidence, it does help paint a picture of the euro's rising popularity as a major currency for international trade around the world.

Sources: Based on (1) The Euro Information Website, 2009, ww.ibiblio. org/theeuro/InformationWebsite.htm; (2) *The Independent*, 2009, Exporters get resourceful to fight currency fluctuation, November 21, www. independent.ie; (3) Irish Exporters Association, 2009, http://www. irishexporters.ie.

Draw implications for action.

MANAGEMENT SAVVY

The big question in global business, adapted to the context of foreign exchange movements, is: What determines the success and failure of currency management around the globe? The answer boils down to two components. First, from an institution-based standpoint, the changing rules of the game—economic, political, and psychological—enable or constrain firms. Shown in the Closing Case, Wal-Mart's low-cost advantage from made-in-China products stems at least in part from the Chinese government's policy of pegging its yuan at a favorable level against the dollar. Consequently, Wal-Mart's low-cost advantage may be eroded as the yuan appreciates. Second, from a resource-based perspective, how firms develop valuable, unique, and hard-to-imitate capabilities in currency management may make or break them.

As a result, three implications for action emerge (Table 7.7). First, foreign exchange literacy must be fostered. Savvy managers need to not only pay attention to the broad long-run movements informed by PPP, productivity changes, and balance of payments, but also to the fickle short-run fluctuations triggered by interest rate changes and investor mood swings.

Second, risk analysis of any country must include its currency risks. Previous chapters have advised managers to pay attention to political, regulatory, and cultural risks of various countries. Here, a crucial currency risk dimension is added. An otherwise attractive country may suffer from high inflation, resulting in devaluation of its currency on the horizon. Countries in Southeast Asia prior to 1997 and in Central and Eastern Europe (CEE) prior to 2008 represented such a scenario. Numerous firms ignoring such a currency risk dimension were burned badly in the Asian financial crisis of 1997–1998 and in the CEE financial crisis of 2008–2009 (see Figure 7.2).

Finally, a country's high currency risks do not necessarily suggest that this country needs to be totally avoided. Instead, it calls for a prudent currency risk management strategy via currency hedging, strategic hedging, or both. Not every firm has the stomach or capabilities to do both. Smaller, internationally inexperienced firms may outsource currency hedging to specialists, such as currency traders, and may find strategic hedging unrealistic. On the other hand, many larger, internationally experienced firms (such as 3M) choose not to touch currency hedging, citing its unpredictability. Instead, they focus on strategic hedging. Although no one has found a fixed formula, firms without a well-thought-out currency management strategy will be caught off guard when currency movements take a nasty turn.

TABLE 7.7   IMPLICATIONS FOR ACTION

- Fostering foreign exchange literacy is a must.
- Risk analysis of any country must include an analysis of its currency risks.
- A currency risk management strategy is necessary—via currency hedging, strategic hedging, or both.

CHAPTER SUMMARY

1. List the factors that determine foreign exchange rates.
   - A foreign exchange rate is the price of one currency expressed in another.
   - Basic determinants of foreign exchange rates include (1) relative price differences and PPP, (2) interest rates, (3) productivity and balance of payments, (4) exchange rate policies, and (5) investor psychology.

2. Articulate the steps in the evolution of the international monetary system.
   - The international monetary system evolved from the gold standard (1870–1914), to the Bretton Woods system (1944–1973), and eventually to the current post–Bretton Woods system (1973–present).
   - The IMF serves as a lender of last resort to help member countries fight balance of payments problems.
   - In response to the criticisms, the IMF has initiated major reforms recently.

3. Identify strategic responses firms can take to deal with foreign exchange movements.
   - Three foreign exchange transactions are: (1) spot transactions, (2) forward transactions, and (3) swaps.
   - Firms' strategic responses include: (1) currency hedging, (2) strategic hedging, or (3) both.

4. Participate in two leading debates on foreign exchange movements.
   - (1) Fixed versus floating exchange rates and (2) currency hedging versus not hedging.

5. Draw implications for action.
   - Fostering foreign exchange literacy is a must.
   - Risk analysis of any country must include an analysis of its currency risks.
   - A currency risk management strategy is necessary—via currency hedging, strategic hedging, or both.

KEY TERMS

REVIEW QUESTIONS

1. Briefly summarize the six major factors that influence foreign exchange rates.

2. What is the difference between a floating exchange rate policy and a fixed exchange rate policy?

3. Why did the gold standard evolve to the Bretton Woods system? Why then did the Bretton Woods system evolve to the present post–Bretton Woods system?

4. Describe the IMF's roles and responsibilities.

5. Name and describe the three primary types of foreign exchange transactions made by financial companies.

6. Name and describe two ways nonfinancial companies can cope with currency risks.

7. Is the strength of the American dollar important to the rest of the world? Why?

8. In recent years, the value of the US dollar has decreased compared to other major currencies. In view of the impact that tends to have on trade, does PengAtlas Map 2.1 reflect that impact relative to the United States? What is a potential explanation?

9. In view of the impact that the decrease in the value of the dollar tends to have on trade, does PengAtlas Map 2.2 reflect that impact relative to the United States? Why does the United States seem to be doing better in this aspect of trade than in that covered in PengAtlas Map 2.1? What else might explain US trade as seen in this map besides a change in the value of the dollar?

10. Why might it be easier for a large firm to engage in currency hedging? Why then do some of the largest global corporations fail to do so?

11. What concepts must a savvy manager understand to be considered literate about foreign exchange?

12. If a firm lacks the skills to hedge currencies, what are its choices?

CRITICAL DISCUSSION QUESTIONS

1. Suppose US$1 = €0.63 in New York and US$1 = €0.65 in Paris, how can foreign exchange traders profit from these exchange rates? What actions can they take to make the dollar/euro exchange rate the same in both New York and Paris?

2. Identify the currencies of the top three trading partners of your country in the last 10 years. Find the exchange rates of these currencies, relative to your country's currency, 10 years ago and now. Explain the changes. Then predict the movement of these exchange rates 10 years from now.

3. As a manager, you are choosing to do business in two countries: one has a fixed exchange rate and another a floating rate. Which country would you prefer? Why?

4. *ON ETHICS:* You are an IMF official going to a country whose export earnings are not able to pay for imports. The government has requested a loan from the IMF. Which areas would you recommend the government to cut: (1) education, (2) salaries for officials, (3) food subsidies, and/or (4) tax rebates for exporters?

GLOBAL ACTION

1. Based in the United States, your firm trades extensively in European countries that have adopted the euro. You have been asked to evaluate the impact of currency fluctuations on sales in this region over the past month. The first step in this process is to develop an exchange rate table for daily exchange rates over the past month between the US dollar and the euro, using resources from the globalEDGE website. Once this has been accomplished, what general trends do you notice? How could these trends impact your firm's sales in countries that use the euro?

2. Your company is examining possible market opportunities in the Asia Pacific region. As a part of this possible strategic shift, the benchmark currencies of the region must be identified to diversify currency risk for future operations. Using a globalEDGE resource that examines foreign exchange, determine which predominant currencies are likely candidates for your analysis.

VIDEO CASES

Watch "Interpret Numbers With Care" by Sir Peter Middleton of Camelot.

1. Sir Peter Middleton quoted an instructor who wanted everyone to be above average. What is the problem with everyone being above average? Middleton then indicated that actually everyone was above average except for one person. How was that possible?

2. Middleton argued that almost everything you do is affected by numbers. Show how numbers are related to each major heading of this chapter.

3. According to Middleton, one could produce six versions of a balance sheet or a profit-and-loss statement. If you have had accounting, show how one could produce two versions of either of those financial statements. If you have never had an accounting class, use what you learned about currency exchange rates to show how those changes could affect what is reported as profit.

4. Middleton recommended that one ask how a number would look if things were different. One way to do that is to not simply compare performance in Period B to Period A but to compare actual performance in Period B to what was forecast for Period B. For example, suppose your firm's exports drop by 10%, which would appear to be bad. How might that be good?

5. Numbers can be misleading according to Middleton. That could be true in the currency market. For example, when the value of the dollar increases many people would feel that is a good thing. How might it be bad?

Closing Case

Wal-Mart and the Yuan Debate

© Rob Crandall

According to US critics (including plenty of politicians in US Congress), the Chinese government has kept the value of the yuan artificially low (maybe up to 40%), making China's exports cheaper and thus representing an "unfair" advantage. Therefore, it is argued, the yuan needs to appreciate, and the dollar will consequently depreciate. As a result, Americans will benefit because with a cheap dollar, US exports would be more price competitive when sold in China and elsewhere (see the Opening Case). This us-versus-them story seems straightforward, and US firms should applaud the efforts to push China to raise the value of its yuan. Well, not so fast! Plenty of US firms may not like this idea. Wal-Mart is one such US company standing in the middle of the debate. Wal-Mart is not an average American company. It is the largest company in America and in the world (by sales).

Estimating the impact of Wal-Mart on the US and global economy has become a cottage industry in itself. Wal-Mart is unrivaled; it is as big as Costco, Home Depot, Kmart, Kroger, Sears, and Target *combined*. In 2010, it operated 4,200 stores in the United States and 3,600 stores in 15 other countries. Beyond sales, Wal-Mart is the largest private employer in the US and in the world. It employs an army of 2.1 million employees worldwide, including 1.4 million in the United States. It is now the largest corporate employer in both Mexico and Canada, and the second-largest grocer in Britain. Worldwide, more than 176 million people, including 127 million Americans, shop at Wal-Mart every week. Why is Wal-Mart so attractive? Its tag line (used during 1980–2007) said it all: "Always low prices. *Always.*" The second *always* was italicized and underlined to avoid any confusion. Wal-Mart claims that it saves the average American household more than $2,500 every year.

How can Wal-Mart deliver consistently attractive and low prices? In one word: China. Wal-Mart's suppliers and competitors widely acknowledge that there exists a wholesale price, a retail price, and a Wal-Mart price, but what they really mean is an unbeatable *China price*. Although Wal-Mart sources from suppliers in more than 70 countries, China is no doubt at the center of Wal-Mart's supplier base. Of Wal-Mart's 6,000 suppliers, at least 80% produce in China, often at Wal-Mart's urging in an effort to cut costs. China is the largest exporter to the US economy in consumer goods, and Wal-Mart is the leading retailer in consumer goods. Therefore, China and Wal-Mart, according to an influential PBS documentary, *Is Wal-Mart Good for America?* are a "joint venture made in heaven." It is not a coincidence that the rise of Wal-Mart and the rise of China have taken place during roughly the same period.

At present, the United States runs the largest trade deficit with China, totaling $266 billion in 2008 (about 40% of the $681 billion US trade deficit). A debate is thus raging in the United States on how to deal with the deficit (see Chapter 5, especially Table 5.5). The debate is complicated because it is much more than just us versus them. It is us versus them + our Wal-Mart + Wal-Mart's suppliers producing in China (!). Over 60% of "Chinese" exports are not produced by Chinese-owned companies but by foreign-invested enterprises producing in China. If Wal-Mart were an independent country, it would rank as China's eighth-largest trading partner, ahead of Russia, Australia, and Canada. Regardless of whether the yuan is unfairly low, all foreign-invested enterprises in China benefit from the yuan's low valuation, including about 5,000 of Wal-Mart's non-Chinese-owned suppliers producing in China. Standing in the middle, Wal-Mart has definitely made this debate more complicated.

In July 2005, China abandoned the yuan's peg to the dollar at 8.3 yuan per dollar. Since then, the pace of yuan appreciation has gathered steam, reaching 6.8 yuan per dollar in July 2009, an 18% increase in four years. However, if the yuan appreciates sharply, it could put Wal-Mart's entire business model in jeopardy. Consider this: Approximately 70% of Wal-Mart's products are made in China. If the yuan (hypothetically) appreciates by 30%, 70% of its products may experience a 30% price *jump* (holding everything else constant). A strong yuan could potentially wipe out Wal-Mart's entire profit margin almost overnight. The leading practitioner of "always low prices" will naturally do everything possible to prevent this from happening. Although Wal-Mart closely guards its corporate plans, it makes sense to imagine that Wal-Mart may have a two-pronged strategy. First, Wal-Mart will likely work with its suppliers to lobby extensively against efforts to push the yuan to appreciate sharply. Second, the Chinese government, while denying the influence of US political pressure, admits that some appreciation of the yuan seems inevitable for China's own good (such as cooling off the overheated economy in the long term). As a result, Wal-Mart may seek to minimize the damage caused by a stronger yuan by currency hedging, strategic hedging (diversifying its supplier base), or both.

Case Discussion Questions:

1. Why is the value of the yuan so important?
2. If you were the CEO of Wal-Mart and were preparing for a meeting with the most vocal members of the US Congress on China's currency "manipulation," what would you say to them?
3. Should Wal-Mart do something about the US trade deficit with China?
4. Assuming that the yuan will appreciate further against the dollar, what should Wal-Mart do?

Sources: Based on (1) C. Fishman, 2006, *The Wal-Mart Effect*, New York: Penguin; (2) R. E. Freeman, 2006, The Wal-Mart effect and business, ethics, and society, *Academy of Management Perspectives*, 20: 38–40; (3) PBS/Frontline, 2004, Is Wal-Mart good for America? www.pbs.org; (4) *South China Morning Post*, 2007, Yuan soars to highest level since 2005, July 20: 1; (5) Wal-Mart, 2010, Corporate facts: Wal-Mart by the numbers, www.walmartstores.com; (6) *Wall Street Journal*, 2009, Geithner is exactly wrong on China trade, January 26.

NOTES

[Journal acronyms] JEP—*Journal of Economic Perspectives*; JIBS—*Journal of International Business Studies*

[1] *Economist*, 2009, Yuan small step, July 11: 71–72.

[2] A. Taylor & M. Taylor, 2004, The purchasing power parity debate, *JEP*, 18: 135–158.

[3] *Economist*, 2009, The Big Mac Index: Cheesed off, July 18: 74.

[4] *Economist*, 2006, McCurrencies, May 27: 74.

[5] US Department of Commerce, Bureau of Economic Analysis, 2009, *US International Transactions: Fourth Quarter and Year 2008*, Table 1, March 18, Washington: BEA, www.bea.gov (accessed July 13, 2009).

[6] M. Kreinin, 2006, *International Economics* (p. 183), Cincinnati: South-Western Cengage Learning.

[7] R. Lyons, 2001, *The Microstructure Approach to Exchange Rates* (p. 1), Cambridge, MA: MIT Press.

[8] *Economist*, 2009, Mission possible, April 11: 69–71; *Economist*, 2009, New fund, old fundamentals, May 2: 78; A. Ghosh, M. Chamon, C. Crowe, J. Kim, & J. Ostry, 2009, Coping with the crisis: Policy options for emerging market countries, IMF staff position paper, Washington: IMF; *Time*, 2009, International Monetary Fund 2.0, April 20.

[9] R. Carbaugh, 2007, *International Economics*, 11th ed. (p. 360), Cincinnati: South-Western Cengage Learning.

[10] F. Carrieri & B. Majerbi, 2006, The pricing of exchange risk in emerging stock markets, *JIBS*, 37: 372–391; L. Jacque & P. Vaaler, 2001, The international control conundrum with exchange risk, *JIBS*, 32: 813–832.

[11] C. Pantzalis, B. Simkins, & P. Laux, 2001, Operational hedges and the foreign exchange exposure of US multinational corporations, *JIBS*, 32: 793–812.

[12] S. Lee & M. Makhija, 2009, The effect of domestic uncertainty on the real option value of international investments, *JIBS*, 40: 405–420.

[13] R. Faff & A. Marshall, 2005, International evidence on the determinants of foreign exchange rate exposure of multinational corporations, *JIBS*, 36: 539–558; R. Weiner, 2005, Speculation in international crises, *JIBS*, 36: 576–587.

[14] This section draws heavily from B. Yarbrough & R. Yarbrough, 2006, *The World Economy*, 7th ed. (p. 683), Cincinnati: South-Western Cengage Learning.

Chapter
8

© Avatra Images/Alamy

LEARNING OBJECTIVES

After studying this chapter, you should be able to:

1. make the case for global economic integration.

2. explain the evolution of the GATT and the WTO, including current challenges.

3. make the case for regional economic integration.

4. list the accomplishments, benefits, and costs of the EU.

5. identify the five organizations that facilitate regional trade in the Americas and describe their benefits and costs.

6. identify the three organizations that promote regional trade in the Asia Pacific and describe their benefits and costs.

7. understand why regional trade deals are not effective in Africa.

8. participate in two leading debates on global and regional economic integration.

9. draw implications for action.

Capitalizing on Global and Regional Integration

A Closer Continent

When Kurt Wilson's pals told him they were throwing him a bachelor party in Vilnius, Lithuania, back in 2002, the British entrepreneur was less than thrilled. Aside from cheap beer, what could this grim former Soviet bloc city offer? Plenty, as it turned out. Wilson, now 32, fell so in love with Vilnius, with its friendly people and beautiful medieval old town, that he has since made it his second home.

A Brit commuting to Lithuania? A few years ago, such an idea would have been unthinkable. Now, thanks to airfare as low as $100 round-trip on Ryanair or its local competitor, Air Baltic, Wilson and his wife travel between London and Vilnius at least once a month. The couple owns two apartments in Vilnius. And Wilson, impressed with the skilled and inexpensive local workforce, opened a local office of Advansys, his Reading, UK–based software development company. "When I first came here, my friends thought I was mad," he says. "Low-cost airlines are opening up places that used to be beyond most people's comfort zones."

Ryanair, easyJet, and nearly 40 other low-cost airlines across Europe are accomplishing what the politicians in the expanding European Union couldn't.

When the discount airlines came on strong, millions of Europeans started to cross borders en masse for business and pleasure. Airlines last year [2005] logged more than 420 million passengers on intra-European flights, an increase of some 40% from five years ago. In the process, they've played a major role in breaking down cultural barriers, revitalizing local economies, and opening up new business opportunities. "Bureaucrats in Brussels have been blathering on about European unity for ages," says Michael O'Leary, CEO of Dublin-based Ryanair. "But low-cost airlines are at the forefront of delivering it."

Jetting around Europe used to be a luxury. Now it is possible to crisscross the region for as little as $30 round-trip—less than the fare on a taxi ride to the local airport. The British pop over to Budapest for budget root canals and cut-price nip-and-tucks. Irish property speculators fly to Estonia to bag a bargain. Latvian construction workers head to Dublin to cash in on that city's construction boom, while Polish doctors and nurses jet over to Britain to fill hospital staffing shortages. "I've been to places I've never even heard of just because it's so cheap," says Dave Marsden, a 38-year-old dispatch manager at a Manchester printing company who recently spent a weekend in Santiago de Compostela in Spain.

The explosion in low-cost flights has given rise to a new group of Euro-commuters. For six years, Herman Bynke, a 34-year-old Swede who runs London-based Hela Ltd., a maker of ergonomic computer accessories, endured the stress and high cost of living in London. But when Ryanair began offering direct flights from London to Gothenburg, Bynke decided it was time to move back home. Now for $85 or less round-trip, he makes the three-hour door-to-door trip from his home in Sweden to his office in London biweekly. "I can spend more time with my family, save more money, and have a better quality of life," he says.

The trend originated in 1997 when Brussels deregulated the aviation industry, enabling discounters to get airborne. Ryanair was one of the first. The Irish carrier launched service from Britain to the Continent in 1997, keeping fares low by flying to smaller, out-of-the-way airports, a model pioneered by Southwest Airlines in the United States. Today, Ryanair is Europe's leading discounter, flying 334 routes to 23 countries. The company is on course to log a 6% increase in pretax profit in 2006, to $409 million, on revenues of $2.1 billion. O'Leary's fleet of 105 Boeing 737s will ferry some 42 million passengers this year, more than British Airways (BA). To fight back, BA, Air France, Lufthansa, and the other flag carriers have been slashing their own fares. The fare wars could set the stage for an industry-wide European shakeout, but for now consumers are the big winners. In Sweden, for instance, the average international airfare fell from $160 in 2001 to $110 last year.

The resulting surge in European travel is turning once-sleepy backwaters into boomtowns. Bratislava's airport used to be a grim, deserted place. But that was before Slovakian upstart SkyEurope turned it into its hub four years ago. Traffic has more than quadrupled since 2002, from 300,000 passengers a year to more than 1.3 million, as easyJet PLC and Ryanair have followed SkyEurope's lead and added Bratislava to their routes.

To cater to Europe's new commuters, savvy entrepreneurs are setting up businesses that offer every service imaginable. Frances Sargent, a 56-year-old Briton, discovered Slovenia after vacationing there a decade ago. Now she and her family spend weekends at their second home, in the Julian Alps, and she runs Slovenian Properties, a company that helps Slovenian real estate agents market their properties to English-speaking buyers. Since low-cost flights to Slovenia started two years ago, values in areas such as the tiny lakeside town of Bled have risen 30%. Sargent's own property has doubled in value since she bought it 18 months ago. "I realized that Slovenes hadn't anticipated the interest from British buyers," she says.

Thanks to low fares, Britons are even flocking to dentists in Budapest. Hungarian Dental Travel Ltd., a one-year-old London-based outfit, has built a brisk business referring travelers to English-speaking dentists in Hungary. "In Britain the average cost of an implant is $3,500, but in Hungary you can get it done for $1,000," says Managing Director Christopher Hall. British consumers aren't just stopping in Hungary for their teeth—they're also headed to the Czech Republic for the rest of their bodies. Tamara Zdinakova, 28, runs Beauty in Prague, a Web site that refers English-speaking patients to plastic surgeons in the Czech Republic, where prices are a fraction of those in the West. British builder Tony Barham and his wife, Maureen, both 55, flew easyJet to Prague for a 17-day holiday—and Maureen's face-lift. "It should be called Plastic Surgery Airline," Tony says. At $3,700, they'll pay one-quarter what they would for the same procedure back in Britain. Zdinakova says the business wouldn't exist without discount airlines. "It just wipes out the barriers," she says of the cheap airlines. "Prague has not been this close ever before."

By all accounts, low-cost carriers will only keep shrinking Europe. Cheap air travel has "changed my life for the better," says Peter Allegretti, a 44-year-old Italian hypnotherapist who regularly commutes from his home in Barcelona to work in London. "National boundaries are disappearing." Now, that sounds like a true European Union.

Source: Reprinted from the May 8, 2006 issue of Bloomberg *BusinessWeek* by special permission. Copyright © 2006 by Bloomberg L.P.

Regional economic integration

Efforts to reduce trade and investment barriers within one region.

Why are Ryanair, easyJet, Air Baltic, SkyEurope, and 40 other low-cost airlines able to shrink Europe? Why are firms such as Advansys, Beauty in Prague, Hungarian Dental Travel, and Slovenian Properties thriving? In two words: economic integration. Economic integration is taking place both regionally and globally. **Regional economic integration** refers to efforts to reduce trade and investment barriers within one region, such as the **European Union (EU)**. **Global economic integration**, in turn, refers to efforts to reduce trade and investment barriers around the globe.

This chapter is fundamentally about how the two core perspectives in global business interact. Specifically, how do changes in the rules of the game for global and regional economic integration, as emphasized by the institution-based view, lead firms to better develop and leverage their capabilities, as highlighted by the resource-based view? In other words, how do firms around the world capitalize on global and regional economic integration? We start with a description of global economic integration. Next we introduce regional economic integration. Debates and extensions follow.

GLOBAL ECONOMIC INTEGRATION

Current frameworks of regional and global economic integration date back to the end of World War II. The world community was mindful of the mercantilist trade wars in the 1930s, which worsened the Great Depression and eventually led to World War II. Two new developments after the war were initiated to prevent a repeat of these circumstances. Globally, the **General Agreement on Tariffs and Trade (GATT)** was created in 1948 as a multilateral agreement governing the international trade of goods (merchandise). In Europe, regional integration started in 1951. The agreement and ensuing integration proved so successful that they are now considerably expanded. The GATT became the **World Trade Organization (WTO)**, and economic integration in Europe led to the EU.

Political Benefits for Global Economic Integration

Recall from Chapters 5 and 6 that, theoretically, economic gains occur when firms from different countries can freely trade and engage in foreign direct investment (FDI). However, these insights had not been accepted by most governments until the end of World War II. In the late 1920s and early 1930s, virtually all governments tried to protect domestic industries by imposing protectionist policies through tariffs and quotas. Collectively, these beggar-thy-neighbor policies triggered retaliation that further restricted trade (Figure 8.1). Eventually, trade wars turned into World War II.

The postwar urge for global economic integration grew out of the painful lessons of the 1920s and 1930s. While emphasizing economic benefits, global economic integration is *political* in nature. Its fundamental goal is to promote peace (Table 8.1). Simply put, people who buy and sell from each other are usually reluctant to fight or kill each other. Japan only decided to attack Pearl Harbor in 1941 *after* the United States cut off oil sales to Japan in protest of Japanese aggression in China. Global economic integration also seeks to build confidence. The mercantilist trade policies in the 1930s were triggered by a lack of confidence. Confidence building is key to avoiding the tragedies of the 1930s. Governments, if they are confident that other countries will not raise trade barriers, will not be tempted to do the same.

At this moment when the world economy is engulfed in one of the worst economic crises since the Great Depression, there is a grave danger of rising protectionism around the globe. During the G-20 summits in Washington in

LEARNING OBJECTIVE

1

Make the case for global economic integration.

European Union (EU)

The official title of European economic integration since 1993.

Global economic integration

Efforts to reduce trade and investment barriers around the globe.

General Agreement on Tariffs and Trade (GATT)

A multilateral agreement governing the international trade of goods (merchandise).

World Trade Organization (WTO)

The official title of the multilateral trading system and the organization underpinning this system since 2005.

FIGURE 8.1　DOWN THE TUBE: CONTRACTION OF WORLD TRADE DURING THE GREAT DEPRESSION (1929–33, MILLIONS $)

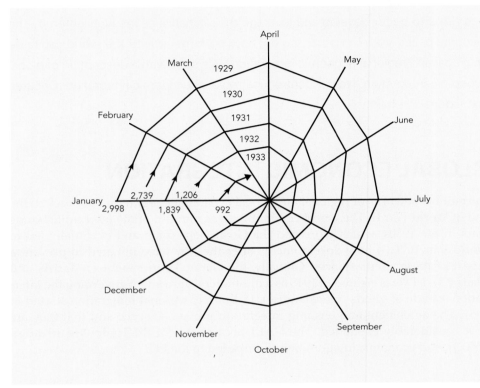

Source: Charles Kindleberger, The World in Depression, p. 170 (Berkeley: University of California Press, 1975). Reprinted by permission in print and electronic format via Copyright Clearence Center.

TABLE 8.1　BENEFITS OF GLOBAL ECONOMIC INTEGRATION

Political benefits

- Promote peace by promoting trade and investment
- Build confidence in a multilateral trading system

Economic benefits

- Disputes are handled constructively
- Rules make life easier and discrimination impossible for all participating countries
- Free trade and investment raise incomes and stimulate economic growth

November 2008, in London in April 2009, and in Pittsburgh in September 2009, world leaders affirmed their commitment to promote world trade, investment, and ultimately peace. Hopefully, leaders of the 21st century will be smarter and wiser than the leaders of the 1920s and the 1930s. Although protectionism may lead to short-term gains at the expense of trading partners, the world as a whole has "been there, done that" with disastrous outcomes and tremendous wartime losses.

Economic Benefits for Global Economic Integration

In addition to political benefits, there are at least three compelling economic reasons for global economic integration. The first is to handle disputes constructively. This is especially evident in the WTO's dispute resolution mechanisms (discussed later in this chapter). Although there is an escalation in the number of disputes brought to the WTO, such an increase, according to the WTO, "does not reflect increasing tension in the world. Rather, it reflects the closer economic ties throughout the world, the WTO's expanding membership, and the fact that countries have faith in the system to solve their differences."[1] In other words, it is so much better to bring disputes to the WTO for resolution than to declare war on each other.

A second benefit is that global economic integration makes life easier for all participants. Officially, the GATT/WTO system is called the **multilateral trading system** because it involves all participating countries (the key word being *multilateral*) and not just two countries (*bilateral*). A crucial principle in the multilateral trading system is **nondiscrimination**. Specifically, a country cannot discriminate against any of its trading partners. Every time a country lowers a trade barrier, it has to do the same for *all* WTO member countries, except when giving preference to regional partners (an exception we will discuss later). Such nondiscrimination makes life easier for all. The alternative would be continuous bilateral negotiations with numerous countries. Each pair may end up with a different deal, significantly complicating trade and investment (see the Closing Case) and probably substantially reducing the bargaining power of most small countries.

Finally, global economic integration raises incomes, generates jobs, and stimulates economic growth. The WTO estimates that cutting global trade barriers by a third may raise worldwide income by approximately $600 billion. That is equivalent to contributing an economy the size of Canada to the world.[2] Although countries as a whole benefit, individuals also benefit because more and better jobs are created. In the United States, 12 million people owe their jobs to exports. In China, 18 million people work for foreign-invested firms, which have the highest level of profits and pay among all China-based firms.[3]

Of course, global economic integration has its share of problems. Critics may not be happy with the environmental impact and distribution of the benefits from more trade and investment among the haves and have-nots in the world. However, when weighing all the pros and cons, most governments and people agree that global economic integration generates enormous benefits, ranging from preserving peace to generating jobs.

Multilateral trading system
The global system that governs international trade among countries—otherwise known as the GATT/WTO system.

Nondiscrimination
A principle that a country cannot discriminate among its trading partners.

ORGANIZING WORLD TRADE

In this section, we will examine the two principal mechanisms of global economic integration: the GATT and WTO. First, we outline the WTO's evolution from the GATT. Then, we consider in more detail what the WTO does.

LEARNING OBJECTIVE 2

Explain the evolution of the GATT and the WTO, including current challenges.

General Agreement on Tariffs and Trade: 1948–1994

The GATT was created in 1948. Unlike the WTO, the GATT was technically an agreement but *not* an organization. Its major contribution was to reduce the level of tariffs by sponsoring "rounds" of multilateral negotiations. As a result, the average tariff in developed economies dropped from 40% in 1948 to 3% in 2005. In other words, the GATT facilitated some of the highest growth rates in international trade recorded in history. Between 1950 and 1995, when the GATT was phased out to become the WTO, world GDP grew about fivefold, but world merchandise exports grew about 100 times (!). During the GATT era, trade growth consistently outpaced GDP growth.

Despite the GATT's phenomenal success in bringing down tariff barriers, by the mid-1980s three concerns had surfaced that made it clear that reforms would be necessary. First, because of the GATT's declared focus on merchandise trade, neither trade in services nor intellectual property protection was covered. Both of these areas were becoming increasingly important. Second, the many loopholes in merchandise trade needed reforming. The most (in)famous loophole was the Multifibre Arrangement (MFA) designed to limit free trade in textiles, a direct violation of the letter and spirit of the GATT. Finally, although the GATT had been successful in reducing tariffs, the global recessions in the 1970s and 1980s led many governments to invoke nontariff barriers (NTBs) such as subsidies and local content requirements (see Chapter 5). Unlike tariff barriers, which were relatively easy to verify and challenge, NTBs were more subtle but more pervasive, thus triggering a growing number of trade disputes. The GATT, however, lacked effective dispute resolution mechanisms. Thus, at the end of the Uruguay Round in 1994, participating countries agreed to upgrade the GATT and launch the WTO.

World Trade Organization: 1995–Present

Established on January 1, 1995, the WTO is the GATT's successor. This transformation turned the GATT from a provisional treaty serviced by an ad hoc secretariat to a full-fledged international organization, headquartered in Geneva, Switzerland. Although the WTO seems to be one of the youngest major international organizations, it actually is not. Because the GATT still exists as part of the WTO, we can date the organization's history back to 1948.

Significantly broader than the GATT, the WTO has six main areas (Figure 8.2):

General Agreement on Trade in Services (GATS)

A WTO agreement governing the international trade of services.

Trade-Related Aspects of Intellectual Property Rights (TRIPS)

A WTO agreement governing intellectual property rights.

- An umbrella agreement, simply called the Agreement Establishing the WTO.
- An agreement governing the international trade of goods, still using the old title as the General Agreement on Tariffs and Trade (GATT), technically called "GATT 1994."
- An agreement governing the international trade of services, the General Agreement on Trade in Services (GATS).
- An agreement governing intellectual property rights, the Trade-Related Aspects of Intellectual Property Rights (TRIPS)—see Chapter 2.
- Trade dispute settlement mechanisms, which allow for the WTO to adjudicate trade disputes among countries in a more effective and less time-consuming way (discussed next).
- Trade policy reviews, which enable other members to "peer review" a country's trade policy.

FIGURE 8.2   SIX MAIN AREAS OF THE WTO

Umbrella	Agreement Establishing the WTO		
Three main areas	Goods (GATT)	Services (GATS)	Intellectual Property (TRIPS)
Dispute settlement	Dispute Settlement Mechanisms		
Transparency	Trade Policy Reviews		

Source: Adapted from World Trade Organization, 2003, *Understanding the WTO* (p. 22), Geneva: WTO.

Overall, the WTO has a far wider scope, bringing into the multilateral trading system—for the first time—trade in services, intellectual property, dispute settlement, and peer review of policy. The next two sections outline two of its major initiatives: dispute settlement and the Doha Round.

Trade Dispute Settlement

One of the main objectives for establishing the WTO was to strengthen the trade dispute settlement mechanisms. The old GATT mechanisms experienced (1) long delays, (2) blocking by accused countries, and (3) inadequate enforcement. The WTO addresses all three of these problems. First, it sets time limits for a panel, consisting of three neutral countries, to reach a judgment. Second, it removes the power of the accused countries to block any unfavorable decision. WTO decisions will be final. Third, in terms of enforcement, although the WTO has earned the nickname of "the world's supreme court in trade," it does *not* have real enforcement capability. The WTO simply recommends the losing countries to change its laws or practices and authorizes the winning countries to use tariff retaliation to compel the offending countries to comply with the WTO rulings.

Fundamentally, a WTO ruling is a *recommendation* but not an order, which means the rulings have relatively little "teeth." After all, no higher-level entity can order a sovereign government to do something against its wishes, thus the offending country decides whether to implement a WTO recommendation. Because the WTO has no real power to enforce its rulings, a country that has lost a dispute case can choose one of two options: change its laws or practices to be in compliance or defy the ruling by doing nothing and suffer trade retaliation by the winning country known as "punitive duties." Most of the WTO's trade dispute rulings, however, are resolved without resorting to trade retaliation.

As shown in the "shrimp-turtle" case (In Focus 8.1), even some of the most powerful countries, such as the United States, have lost cases and have painfully adjusted their own laws and practices to comply with the WTO rulings. This supports the first proposition in the institution-based view (see Chapter 2): most offending countries have made a *rational* decision to respect the rules of the game, believing that the benefits of compliance with the rulings, however unfavorable to them, outweigh the costs of "rocking the boat."

IN Focus 8.1

The WTO's "Shrimp-Turtle" Case

ETHICAL DILEMMA

In 1997, India, Malaysia, Pakistan, and Thailand brought a joint complaint to the WTO against a US ban on shrimp imports from these countries. The protection of sea turtles was at the heart of the ban. Shrimp trawlers from these countries often caught shrimp with nets that trapped and killed an estimated 150,000 sea turtles each year. The US Endangered Species Act, enacted in 1989, listed as endangered or threatened five species of sea turtles, and required US shrimp trawlers to use turtle excluder devices (TEDs) in their nets when fishing in areas where sea turtles may be found. It also placed embargoes on shrimp imports from countries that do not protect sea turtles from deadly entrapment in nets. The complaining countries, unwilling to equip their fleets with TEDs, argued that the US Endangered Species Act was an illegal trade barrier. The WTO panel ruled in favor of the four Asian countries, and provoked a firestorm of criticisms from environmentalists, culminating in some violence in the Seattle protests against the WTO in 1999. The United States appealed but lost again. In its final ruling, the WTO Appellate Body argued that the United States lost the case, *not* because it sought to protect the environment but because it violated the principle of nondiscrimination. It provided countries in the Western Hemisphere, mainly in the Caribbean, technical and financial assistance to equip their fishermen with TEDs. However, it did not give the same assistance to the four complaining

© Rontography/Stock Photo

countries. The WTO opined:

We have not decided that the protection and preservation of the environment is of no significance to members of the WTO. Clearly, it is. We have not decided that the sovereign nations that are members of the WTO cannot adopt effective measures to protect endangered species, such as sea turtles. Clearly, they can and should....What we decided in this appeal is simply this: although the measure of the United States in dispute in this appeal serves an environmental objective that is recognized as legitimate...this measure has been applied by the United States in a manner which constitutes arbitrary and unjustifiable discrimination between members of the WTO....WTO members are free to adopt their own policies aimed at protecting the environment as long as, in so doing, they fulfill their obligations and respect the rights of other members under the WTO Agreement.

After its appeal failed, the United States reached agreements with the four complaining countries to provide technical and financial assistance on TEDs to be implemented on their shrimp boats.

Sources: Based on (1) R. Carbaugh, 2005, *International Economics*, 10th ed. (pp. 186–187), Cincinnati: South-Western Cengage Learning; (2) WTO, 2003, *Understanding the WTO* (pp. 68–69), Geneva: WTO.

The Doha Round—"The Doha Development Agenda"

The **Doha Round** (since 2001) was the only round of trade negotiations sponsored by the WTO. In 1999, the WTO intended to start a new round of trade talks in Seattle, but the meeting was not only devastated by the appearance of 30,000 protesters, it was also derailed by significant differences between developed and developing countries. The meeting thus became known as the "Battle of Seattle" (see Chapter 1).

Undeterred by the backlash, WTO member countries went ahead to launch a new round of negotiations in Doha, Qatar, in November 2001. The Doha Round was significant for two reasons. First, it was launched in the aftermath of the 9/11 attacks. Members had a strong resolve to make global free trade work in order to defeat the terrorist agenda to divide and terrorize the world. Second, this was the first round in the history of the GATT/WTO to aim specifically at promoting economic development in developing countries in order to make globalization more inclusive and help the world's poor. Consequently, the official title of the Doha Round was the "Doha Development Agenda." The agenda was ambitious: Doha would (1) reduce agricultural subsidies in developed countries to facilitate exports from developing countries; (2) slash tariffs, especially in industries like textiles that might benefit developing countries; (3) free up trade in services; and (4) strengthen intellectual property protection. Note that in the Doha Round, *not* all meetings were held in Doha. Subsequent meetings took place in Cancun, Mexico (2003); Hong Kong (2005); and Geneva (2006 and 2008).

Unfortunately, in the Cancun meeting in September 2003, numerous countries failed to deliver on promises made two years before in Doha. The hot potato turned out to be agriculture. Australia, Argentina, and most developing countries demanded that Japan, the EU, and the United States reduce farm subsidies. Japan rejected any proposal to cut rice tariffs. The EU refused to significantly reduce farm subsidies, which consumed 40% of its budget. The United States actually *increased* farm subsidies. On the other hand, many developing countries, led by India, refused to tighten protection for intellectual property, particularly for pharmaceuticals, citing their need for cheap generic drugs to combat diseases such as HIV/AIDS. Overall, developing countries refused to offer concessions in intellectual property and service trade in part because of the failure of Japan, the EU, and the United States to reduce farm subsidies.

Doha Round

A round of WTO negotiations to reduce agricultural subsidies, slash tariffs, and strengthen intellectual property protection that started in Doha, Qatar, in 2001. Officially known as the "Doha Development Agenda," it was suspended in 2006 due to disagreements.

© Yuri cortez/AFP/Getty images

What were some factors that led to the collapse of the Doha Round?

IN Focus 8.2

Why a Global Fix Is So Far Off

Can a global financial system be made safe without creating a global regulator? Hoping to avoid future crises, the Obama administration released its plan for financial regulation reform on June 17, 2009. The proposal, loaded with good ideas, would help US regulators monitor financial stress during good times and give them new powers to deal with troubled US financial institutions.

But the reform proposal is unsatisfying, precisely because in an increasingly global economy it focuses mainly on beefing up US regulation. Until now that was a workable strategy. Even globe-spanning giants like Citigroup and Goldman Sachs got the bulk of their income and revenue at home, enabling them plausibly to be regulated by the US government. For example, in 2006, Citigroup received 56% of its income from the United States, roughly matching the location of the company's loans. In the future, however, the successful big financial players will expand beyond the reach of a single national government. Rather than being concentrated in New York or even London, they will go where the growth is. As a result, they will have revenues and assets spread more or less equally across the United States, Europe, and Asia.

The current crisis already has given us a glimpse of the damage that can be done by financial institutions operating beyond the reach of US regulators. A recent *BusinessWeek* story, "The Perils of Global Banking," described in detail how Lehman Brothers was able to issue $35 billion in complex bonds from a small office in Amsterdam—bonds which might have raised a lot more questions if they had been issued in the United States.

Globalization also makes it more difficult to figure out which government will lay out the big bucks to support a mammoth financial institution in the event of a crisis. Until now the United States had enough economic heft to serve as the global lender of last resort. For example, when the US government threw enormous sums at AIG to keep the embattled insurer afloat, at least $58 billion went to banks and other creditors based outside the United States—an altruistic move that helped contain the global crisis. In the future the United States may no longer be able to afford to spend in this way.

The Obama officials who wrote the financial regulation proposal are aware of the problem. In a section on international cooperation, the report calls for "further work on the feasibility and desirability of moving towards the development of methods of allocating the financial burden associated with the failure of large, multinational financial firms."

But that's just talk. In theory, what's needed is a global board with the power in a crisis to decide how much each country will contribute to the financial bailouts and guarantees. But be serious—can you imagine Barack Obama, President Hu Jintao of China, Chancellor Angela Merkel of Germany, and other G-20 leaders allowing a global authority to control trillion dollar spending decisions during a crisis? In early June 2009, Merkel publicly criticized US policies, saying: "I view with great skepticism the powers of the Fed."

True, Europe is also moving towards imposing stricter regulations and creating new European financial supervisors. But the new agencies won't have the power to force European countries to pony up money to bail out foreign banks.

As strange as this may sound, it may be that this crisis was not bad enough to force nations into the difficult step of giving up some sovereignty. Remember that in the United States, the Federal Reserve was created only after the Panic of 1907 frightened Wall Street bankers. With the global economy seemingly on the mend, we will have to live with reform proposals that only go partway.

Source: Reprinted from the July 6, 2009, issue of Bloomberg *BusinessWeek* by special permission. Copyright © 2009 by Bloomberg L.P. The author is Michael Mandel, chief economist of *BusinessWeek*.

After the failed Cancun meeting, member countries tried again in Hong Kong in December 2005. Finally, in Geneva in July 2006, it became evident that they could not talk any more because they were still miles apart. The Doha Round was thus officially suspended, dampening the hope of lifting millions out of poverty through free trade. Labeled "the biggest threat to the postwar [multilateral] trading system" by the *Economist*,[4] the Geneva fiasco of the Doha Round disappointed almost every country involved. Naturally, finger-pointing started immediately. To be fair, no country was totally responsible for Doha's collapse, and all members collectively were culpable. The sheer complexity of reaching an agreement on *everything* among 153 member countries in the Doha Round was simply mind boggling.

What happens next? Officially Doha was suspended but not terminated or dead. In 1990, the Uruguay Round was similarly suspended, only to rise again in 1994 with a far-reaching agreement that launched the WTO. Whether history will repeat itself remains to be seen. During the 2008–2009 global economic crisis and its aftermath, the pressures for protectionism mounted, thus preventing politicians around the world from arguing too forcefully in favor of free trade as promoted by Doha.

Efforts to solve a global problem with a global fix must address additional challenges as well. In Focus 8.2 suggests that as bad as the 2008–2009 crisis was, it may not have been bad enough to force countries to globally coordinate bailouts in a severe crisis. On the other hand, regional deals have been moving "at twice the speed and with half the fuss."[5] The upshot is stagnation of multilateralism and acceleration of regionalism—a topic we turn to next.

REGIONAL ECONOMIC INTEGRATION

Make the case for regional economic integration.

There is now a proliferation of regional trade deals. All WTO members but one—Mongolia—are now involved in some regional trade arrangement. This section first introduces the benefits of regional economic integration, followed by a discussion of its major types.

The Pros and Cons of Regional Economic Integration

Similar to global economic integration, the benefits of regional economic integration center on both political and economic dimensions (see Table 8.1). Politically, regional economic integration promotes peace by fostering closer economic ties and building confidence. Only in the last six decades have the Europeans broken away from their centuries-old habit of war and violence among themselves. A leading cause of this dramatic behavioral change is economic integration. In addition, regional integration enhances the collective political weight of a region, which has also helped fuel postwar European integration, particularly when dealing with superpowers such as the United States.

Economically, the three benefits associated with regional economic integration are similar to those associated with global economic integration: (1) Disputes are handled constructively. (2) Consistent rules make life easier and discrimination impossible for participating countries within one region. (3) Free trade and investment raise incomes and stimulate economic growth (see Table 8.1). Regional economic integration may bring additional benefits such as a larger market, simpler standards, reduced distribution costs, and economies of scale for firms based in that region.

However, not everything is rosy in regional integration. A case can be made *against* it. Politically, regional integration, centered on preferential treatments for firms within a region, may lead to discrimination against firms outside a region and thus undermine global integration. Of course, in practice, global deals such as the Doha Round are so challenging to accomplish that regional deals emerge as realistic alternatives. Economically, regional integration may result in some loss of sovereignty. For example, the 16 EU members adopting the euro can no longer implement independent monetary policies.

The simultaneous existence of both pros and cons means that countries are often cautious in joining regional economic integration. Norway and Switzerland chose not to join the EU. Even when countries are part of a regional deal, they sometimes choose to stay out of certain areas. For example, Britain, Denmark, and Sweden refused to adopt the euro. Overall, different levels of enthusiasm call for different types of regional economic integration, which are outlined next.

Types of Regional Economic Integration

Free trade area (FTA)
A group of countries that remove trade barriers among themselves.

Customs union
One step beyond a free trade area (FTA), a customs union imposes common external policies on nonparticipating countries.

Common market
Combining everything a customs union has, a common market, in addition, permits the free movement of goods and people.

Figure 8.3 shows five main types of regional economic integration.

- A **free trade area (FTA)** is a group of countries that remove trade barriers among themselves. Each still maintains different external policies regarding nonmembers, and there is no free movement of people among member countries. An example is NAFTA.
- A **customs union** is one step beyond an FTA. In addition to all the arrangements of an FTA, a customs union imposes common external policies on nonparticipants in order to combat trade diversion. One example is the Andean Community in South America (see the "Regional Economic Integration in the Americas" section later in this chapter).
- A **common market** carries everything a customs union has. In addition, it permits the free movement of goods and people. Today's EU used to be a common market.

FIGURE 8.3   TYPES OF REGIONAL ECONOMIC INTEGRATION

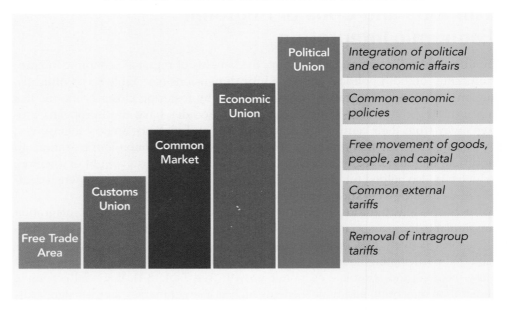

- An **economic union** combines all the features of a common market. In addition, members also coordinate and harmonize economic policies (monetary, fiscal, and taxation) in order to blend their economies into a single economic entity. Today's EU is an economic union. One possible dimension of an economic union is to establish a **monetary union**, which has been accomplished by 16 EU members through the adoption of the euro (see next section).
- A **political union** is the integration of political and economic affairs of a region. The United States and the former Soviet Union are two examples. Whether the EU will eventually turn into a political union is subject to debate. At present, the EU is not a political union.

Overall, these five major types feature an intensification of the level of regional economic integration. Next, we tour the world to visit concrete examples of these arrangements.

REGIONAL ECONOMIC INTEGRATION IN EUROPE

List the accomplishments, benefits, and costs of the EU.

At present, the most ambitious economic integration takes place in Europe. The current system of economic integration in Europe is called the EU. This section (1) outlines its origin and evolution, (2) introduces its current structure, and (3) discusses its challenges.

Origin and Evolution

Although European economic integration is now often noted for its economic benefits, its origin was political in nature. More specifically, it was an effort by European statesmen to stop the vicious cycle of hatred and violence. In 1951, Belgium, France, Germany (technically the western part of today's Germany), Italy, Luxembourg, and the Netherlands signed the European Coal and Steel Community (ECSC) Treaty, which was the first step toward what is now the EU. The six founding members and the two industries involved were highly motivated. France and Germany each lost millions of soldiers and civilians in World Wars I and II, not to mention losses in previous major European wars. Reflecting the public mood, statesmen in both countries realized that such killing needed to stop. Italy had the misfortune of being dragged along and devastated whenever France and Germany went to war. Belgium, the Netherlands, and Luxembourg (known collectively as Benelux) are small countries geographically sandwiched between France and Germany and were usually wiped out when their two larger neighbors went to war. Naturally Italy and Benelux would be happy to do anything to stop France and Germany from fighting again. Also, the industry focus on coal and steel was not an accident. These two industries traditionally supplied the raw materials for war. Integrating these two industries among the six members might help prevent future hostilities.

In 1957, six member countries of ECSC signed the Treaty of Rome, which launched the European Economic Community (EEC), later known as the European Community (EC). Starting as an FTA, the EEC/EC progressed to become a customs union and eventually a common market. Over time, more countries joined. In 1991, 12 member countries signed the Treaty on European Union in Maastricht,

Economic union

Having all the features of a common market, members also coordinate and harmonize economic policies (in areas such as monetary, fiscal, and taxation) to blend their economies into a single economic entity.

Monetary union

A group of countries that use a common currency.

Political union

The integration of political and economic affairs of a region.

the Netherlands (in short, the "Maastricht Treaty"), to complete the single market and establish an economic union. The title "European Union" (EU) was officially adopted in 1993 when the Treaty went into effect.

The EU Today

Headquartered in Brussels, Belgium, today's EU has experienced four waves of expansion (PengAtlas Map 2.4 and Table 8.2) and now encompasses 27 member countries, 500 million citizens, and $15 trillion GDP—approximately 25% of the world's GDP. Here is how the EU describes itself in an official publication:

> The European Union is not a federation like the United States. Nor is it simply an organization for cooperation between governments, like the United Nations. Neither is it a state intended to replace existing states, but it is much more than any other organization. The EU is, in fact, unique. Never before have countries voluntarily agreed to set up common institutions to which they delegate some of their sovereignty so that decisions on specific matters of joint interest can be made democratically at a higher, in this case European, level. This pooling of sovereignty is called "European integration."[6]

The EU today is an economic union. Internal trade barriers have been mostly removed. In aviation, the EU now has a single market, which means all European carriers compete on equal terms across the EU, including routes within other European countries. US airlines are not allowed to fly between pairs of cities within Germany, but non-German, EU airlines can fly between any pair of German cities. Such deregulation has allowed discount airlines such as Ryanair and easyJet to thrive (see the Opening Case). On the ground, it used to cost French truck drivers 24 hours to cross the border into Spain due to numerous paperwork requirements and checks. Since 1992, passport and customs control among 12 of the member countries of the EU has been disbanded, and checkpoints at border crossings are no longer manned. This area became known as the **Schengen** passport-free travel zone. Now French trucks can move from France to Spain nonstop, similar to how American trucks go from Texas to Oklahoma. Citizens of the EU 15 (the 15 "core" countries that joined between 1957 and 1995), but not those of the newer members, are free to live and work throughout the EU. Thus, when Germany did not generate enough jobs, a lot of Germans went to Ireland to seek employment.

As an economic union, the EU's proudest accomplishment is the introduction of a common currency, the **euro**, in 12 of the EU 15 countries—known as the **euro area**—between 1999 and 2002. Since then four more countries have joined the euro area, resulting in a total of 16 countries currently using the euro. Today's euro area accounts for approximately 330 million population and 21% of world GDP (relative to 30% for the United States).

The euro was introduced in two phases. First, it became available in 1999 as "virtual money" only used for financial transactions but not in circulation. Exchange rates with various national currencies were also fixed at that point. Second, in 2002, the euro was introduced as banknotes and coins. To meet the cash needs of over 300 million people, the EU printed 14.25 billion banknotes and minted 56 billion coins with a total value of 660 billion euros ($558 billion). The new banknotes would cover the distance between the earth and the moon *five* times (!).[7] Overall, the introduction of the euro was a great success.[8]

Schengen

A passport-free travel zone within the EU.

Euro

The currency currently used in 16 EU countries.

Euro area

The 16 EU countries that currently use the euro as the official currency.

TABLE 8.2   THE EUROPEAN UNION AT A GLANCE (see also PengAtlas Map 2.4)

Member countries	Year of entry	Population (millions)	GDP (PPP in billion €)	GDP (PPP in €) per capita	Percentage of EU 27 per capita GDP	Current currency
Six founding members						
Belgium	1957	10.7	314	28,800	115%	Euro
France	1957	63.7	1,727	26,900	107%	Euro
Germany	1957	82.5	2,390	29,100	116%	Euro
Italy	1957	58.5	1,489	25,200	101%	Euro
Luxembourg	1957	0.5	32	63,500	253%	Euro
Netherlands	1957	16.4	553	33,800	135%	Euro
Expansion in the 1970s						
Denmark	1973	5.4	163	29,700	118%	Danish crown
Ireland	1973	4.1	160	35,000	140%	Euro
United Kingdom	1973	60.4	1,802	29,500	118%	Pound sterling
Expansion in the 1980s						
Greece	1981	11.2	272	23,900	95%	Euro
Portugal	1986	10.5	201	18,900	75%	Euro
Spain	1986	45.3	1,193	26,100	104%	Euro
Expansion in the 1990s						
Austria	1995	8.3	261	30,900	123%	Euro
Finland	1995	5.3	153	28,900	115%	Euro
Sweden	1995	9.2	285	30,500	121%	Swedish crown
Expansion in the 2000s						
Cyprus	2004	0.7	19	23,800	95%	Euro
Czech Republic	2004	10.7	210	20,200	80%	Czech koruna
Estonia	2004	1.3	22	16,900	67%	Estonian kroon
Hungary	2004	10.1	155	15,800	63%	Forint
Latvia	2004	2.3	31	14,000	56%	Lats
Lithuania	2004	3.4	51	15,400	61%	Litas
Malta	2004	0.4	8	19,200	76%	Euro
Poland	2004	38.2	528	14,400	58%	Zloty
Slovakia	2004	5.4	95	18,000	72%	Euro
Slovenia	2004	2.0	46	22,500	90%	Euro
Bulgaria	2007	7.3	77	10,100	40%	Lev
Romania	2007	22.3	242	11,500	46%	Leu

Source: Population data are from Europe, http://europa.eu; GDP data are from Eurostat (the Statistics Office of the EU), various documents, http://epp.eurostat.ec.europa.eu/portal/page/portal/eurostat/home/ (accessed September 1, 2009). All data refer to 2008.

TABLE 8.3   BENEFITS AND COSTS OF ADOPTING THE EURO

Benefits	Costs
• Reduce currency conversion costs	• Unable to implement independent monetary policy
• Facilitate direct price comparison	• Limit the flexibility in fiscal policy (in areas such as deficit spending)
• Impose monetary disciplines on governments	

Adopting the euro has three great benefits (Table 8.3). First, it reduces currency conversion costs. Travelers and businesses no longer need to pay numerous processing fees to convert currencies for tourist activities or hedging purposes (see Chapter 7). Second, direct and transparent price comparison is now possible, thus channeling more resources toward more competitive firms. Third, adopting the euro imposes strong macroeconomic disciplines on participating governments. Prior to adopting the euro, different governments determined exchange rates independently. Italy, for example, sharply devalued its lire in 1992 and 1995. While Italian exports became cheaper and more competitive overseas, other EU members, especially France, were furious. Also, when confronting recessions, governments often printed more currency and increased government spending. Such actions cause inflation, which may spill over to neighboring countries. By adopting the euro, euro area countries agreed to abolish monetary policy—which involves activities such as manipulating exchange rates and printing more currency—as a tool to solve macroeconomic problems. These efforts provide much-needed macroeconomic stability. Overall, the euro has boosted intra-EU trade by approximately 10%. Commanding one-fourth of global foreign currency reserves, the euro has quickly established itself as the only plausible rival to the dollar.[9]

However, there are also significant costs involved. The first, noted above, is that countries lose the ability to implement independent monetary policy. Especially in the 2008–2009 crisis, economic life for many EU countries without devaluation is tough (see In Focus 8.3). The possibility of leaving the euro area has surfaced in public discussion in some countries.[10] The second cost is the lack of flexibility in implementing fiscal policy in areas such as deficit spending. When a country runs into fiscal difficulties, it may be faced with inflation, high interest rates, and a run on its currency. When a number of countries share a common currency, the risks are spread. But some countries can become "free riders"; they may not feel the need to fix their own fiscal problems because other, more responsible members will shoulder the burden.

To prevent such free riding, euro area governments signed the Stability and Growth Pact (SGP) in 1997, in which they committed to limiting their budget deficits to no more than 3% of GDP. Otherwise, countries could be fined. Essentially, the tools for fighting a recession—namely tax reductions and deficit spending—are severely constrained by the SGP. Yet the SGP did not prevent free riding. Even before the 2008–2009 crisis, France and Germany had failed to curtail their deficit to less than 3%. In other words, they were in open defiance of the SGP, essentially free riding. When the recent recession hit, virtually all EU members adopted fiscal stimulus measures to cope. In 2009, the EU fingered France, Greece, Ireland, Latvia, Malta, and Spain as violators of the SGP because they ran a budget deficit of more than 3% in 2008. It is hard to imagine how the EU can fine these countries, whose governments are already short on cash and have to run a deficit in order to prevent economic collapse. Overall, the SGP has been severely undermined by the recent crisis.

IN Focus 8.3

Boom and Bust in Spain

Spain embraced the euro from the outset, and enjoyed a decade of successful economic growth. GDP grew by an annual average of 3.7% over the decade to 2006, compared to 2.1% in the remainder of the euro area. Spain created over five million new jobs, and attracted waves of immigration. The euro contributed to this success story: The euro lowered Spain's costs of servicing government debt, and confidence in the stability of the currency attracted foreign investment—not to mention heightened self-esteem of Spaniards feeling that they now had taken their rightful place in the European family. This prosperity was strengthened by prudent fiscal policy running budget surpluses when times were good and a comparatively robust banking sector.

However, the prosperity had side effects. Private consumers and businesses took advantage of the combination of a solid currency and low interest rates, and went on a spending spree. This led to a current account deficit of 10% in 2007 and rapidly rising property prices, resulting in a real estate bubble. When the 2008–2009 economic crisis hit, credit flows dried up and the housing bubble burst. Construction projects were stopped, and unemployment surged.

What options did the Spanish government have to tackle the crisis? Monetary policy was transferred to the European Central Bank, and thus devaluation of the currency was not an option. The Spanish economy needed other sources of flexibility to get back on its feet. Prudent fiscal policy gave the government some leverage to increase government spending that softened the impact. One might also expect pressure on wages to keep costs down and thus maintain international competitiveness of Spanish exports, yet this did not happen. The Spanish labor market had a two-tier structure. Two-thirds of workers enjoyed safe long-term employment, whereas the rest was on short-term contracts. The recession hit the two parts of the labor market unequally. Those on long-term contracts were even able to negotiate pay raises of 3% in real terms, whereas those in short-term employment bore the brunt of rising unemployment. Spain's increase in unemployment from 11% in 2007 to 18% in 2009 was among the sharpest. In July 2009, its unemployment rate, at 18%, was the highest in the EU, doubling the EU average of 9%. Under flexible exchange rates, wage increase above the rate of productivity increase is normally compensated by currency devaluation. But thanks to the euro, this tool is not feasible now.

Although the euro undoubtedly helps Spain in the long run, it is hard to say whether a flexible exchange rate might have eased the impact of the crisis in the short run. Assuming Spain may entertain the notion of abandoning the euro, two scenarios can be considered: (1) A devaluation of the revived Spanish peseta, similar to that of the British pound in 2008, might have stimulated exports, thus allowing the Spanish economy to recover more quickly albeit from a lower level of real income. (2) Wild speculation and high volatility of the exchange rates within Europe, which might have further accelerated the disruptive effects of the economic crisis, possibly even leading to an Iceland-style collapse.

Sources: This case was written by Professor **Klaus Meyer** (University of Bath). It was based on (1) *Economist*, 2009, Unemployment in Spain: Two-tier flexibility, July 11; (2) C. Giles & V. Mallet, 2009, Britain and Spain: A tale of two housing bubbles, *Financial Times*, January 11; (3) V. Mallet, 2009, Spain's recession: After the fiesta, *Financial Times*, February 17; (4) J. Pérez-Campanero, 2009, Diez años del euro: Evaluación y perspectivas tras las crisis financiera, *Claves de la Economía Mundial 2009*.

The EU's Challenges

In 2007, the EU celebrated its 50th anniversary of the signing of the Treaty of Rome. Politically, the EU, together with its predecessors (ECSC, EEC, and EC), has delivered more than half a century of peace and prosperity, and turned some Cold War opponents into fellow members. Although some people complain of the EU's expenses and bureaucratic meetings, they need to be reminded that one

© Sean Gallup/Stringer/Getty images

What are some advantages to the adoption of the euro as the EU's common currency?

day spent talking in meetings is one day member countries are not shooting at one another. Considering that most European countries, until the mid-20th century, were involved in wars as their primary mechanism to resolve differences, negotiating to resolve differences via EU platforms is not only cheaper, but also far better in the long run. Economically, the EU has launched a single currency, and built a single market in which people, goods, services, and capital—known as the "four freedoms of movement"—can move freely within the core Schengen area (not completely within the EU, however). Although the accomplishments are enviable in the eyes of other regional organizations, the EU seems to be engulfed in a midlife crisis.[11] Significant challenges lie ahead, especially in terms of internal divisions and enlargement concerns.

Internally, there is a significant debate on whether the EU should be an economic and political union or just an economic union. One school of thought, led by France, argues that an economic union should inevitably evolve toward a political union through which Europe speaks as one voice. Proponents of this view frequently invoke the famous term enshrined in the 1957 Treaty of Rome, *"ever closer union."* In this spirit, a Constitution for Europe was drafted in 2004, urging for more centralization of power at the EU level. Another school of thought, led by the United Kingdom, views the EU as primarily an economic union, which should focus on free trade, pure and simple. For the Constitution to enter into force, it would have to be ratified by every member country. In 2005, popular referendums in France and the Netherlands saw "no" votes prevail by wide margins, torpedoing further progress toward a political union.[12]

Interestingly, in December 2007, EU members signed the Lisbon Treaty in an effort to rework the EU Constitution rejected by French and Dutch voters. In December 2009, with some complicated political maneuvers, the Lisbon Treaty entered into force. As another landmark treaty, the Lisbon Treaty amended both the 1992 Maastricht Treaty that established the EU and the 1957 Rome Treaty that launched the EEC. Major changes included more qualified majority voting in EU-wide decision making and the creation of a long-term President of the European Council (a position first occupied by a Belgian official) and a High Representative of the Union for Foreign Affairs and Security Policy (a position first occupied by a UK official) to present a united position on EU policies.

There are also significant concerns associated with enlargement. The EU's largest expansion took place in 2004 with the addition of 10 new members. Eight of these were former eastern bloc Central and Eastern Europe (CEE) countries, including three Baltic states that were part of the former Soviet Union (Table 8.2). While taking on 10 new members was a political triumph, it was also an economic burden. The 10 new members added 20% to the total population but contributed only 9% to GDP and had an average GDP per capita that was 46% of the average for the EU 15. Until the 2008–2009 crisis, CEE had displayed the strongest economic growth rates within the EU and provided low-cost production sites for EU 15 firms that engaged in a lot of "nearshoring."[13] However, the rich EU 15 countries had to provide billions of euros in aid to bring CEE up to speed. The cost for such support has skyrocketed during the 2008–2009 crisis when CEE countries have collapsed one after another (more details later in this section). Many EU citizens, especially those in the rich EU 15 countries, are increasingly sick and tired of taking on additional burdens to absorb new and usually poor member countries, which will then have to be bailed out.

In the same spirit, only three of the EU 15 countries—Britain, Ireland, and Sweden—opened their labor markets to citizens from the 10 new member countries in 2004. The rest of the EU 15, which typically had unemployment rates of 9% (before the 2008 recession), were fearful of an onslaught of job seekers from CEE. They had good reason to worry. Between 2004 and 2006, approximately 200,000 CEE citizens came to Ireland and about 600,000 (including half a million Poles) came to Britain in search of jobs—the biggest single wave of immigration inflows in British history.[14] However vibrant the British and Irish economies, there was a limit to the absorptive capacity of their labor markets, resulting in second thoughts on the wisdom of such an open door policy. When Bulgaria and Romania joined the EU in 2007, they brought down the EU average GDP per capita further and would likely send another wave of job seekers if they were allowed. Even Britain restricted immigration from Bulgaria and Romania.

Another major debate regarding enlargement is Turkey, whose average income is even lower. In addition, its large Muslim population is also a concern for a predominantly Christian EU. If Turkey were to join, its population of 73 million would make it the second most populous EU country behind only Germany, whose population is 83 million now. Given the current demographic trends such as high birth rates in Turkey and low birth rates in Germany and other EU countries, if Turkey were to join the EU, it would become the most populous and thus the most powerful member by 2020, by commanding the most significant voting power. Turkey's combination of low incomes, high birth rates relative to current EU members, and Muslim majority visibly concern current member countries, especially given the history of Christian-Muslim tension in Europe.

During the 2008–2009 crisis, the EU's challenges have magnified. Although the EU's banks avoided dealing in subprime mortgages as those in the United States, they had something worse: subprime *countries*.[15] Consumers in many new EU member countries in CEE felt they could afford to enjoy rich Europe's living standards by borrowing excessively. Even for countries that had not yet adopted the euro, such loans were often denominated in the euro and financed by banks headquartered in the EU 15, resulting in a housing bubble and a consumption binge. When the bubble collapsed, the subprime countries did not suffer from financial meltdown because, according to the *Economist*, "they lack much to melt."[16] Instead, they required massive bailouts from the International Monetary Fund (IMF, see Chapter 7, especially Figure 7.2) and from the EU 15 governments, which felt compelled to support their own banks that were dangerously exposed to CEE. At the same time, thanks to the global recession, EU 15 economies have also suffered a tremendous recession. For example, Spain's unemployment rose from 11% in 2007 to 18% in 2009. Europe's (and the world's) export champion, Germany, endured a 20% export *decline* in 2009. Not surprisingly, Germany, France, and other relatively well-off EU countries in the middle of their own crisis are reluctant to foot the bill for bailing out other countries.

Overall, we can view the EU enlargement as a miniature version of globalization and the "enlargement fatigue" as part of the recent backlash against globalization.[17] Given the accomplishments and challenges, how does the future of the EU look? One possible scenario is that there will be an "EU à la carte," where different members pick and choose certain mechanisms to join and opt out of other mechanisms.[18] Seeking consensus among 27 members during negotiations may be impractical. If every country's representative spends 10 minutes on opening remarks, 4.5 *hours* would be gone before discussions even begin. The translation and interpretation among the 23 official languages now costs the EU €1.1 billion ($1.4 billion) a year.[19] Since not every country needs to take part in everything, ad hoc groupings of member countries with similar interests are increasingly common and discussions are more efficient. To some extent, "EU à la carte" has already taken place, as evidenced by the three countries that refused to adopt the euro and 12 countries that blocked job seekers from CEE. Although "EU à la carte" is at odds with the ideal of an "ever closer union," it seems a more realistic outcome given the recent backlash and economic crisis.

LEARNING OBJECTIVE

5

Identify the five organizations that facilitate regional trade in the Americas and describe their benefits and costs.

REGIONAL ECONOMIC INTEGRATION IN THE AMERICAS

Two sets of regional economic integration efforts in the Americas have taken place along geographic lines, one in North America and the other in South America.

North America: North American Free Trade Agreement (NAFTA)

Because of the very different levels of economic development, when NAFTA was launched in 1994 it was labeled "one of the most radical free trade experiments in history."[20] NAFTA is a free trade agreement among Canada, Mexico, and the United States. Politically, the Mexican government was interested in cementing market liberalization reforms by demonstrating its commitment to free trade. Economically, Mexico was interested in securing preferential treatment for 80% of its exports that went to the United States and Canada. Consequently, by the stroke of a pen, Mexico declared itself as a *North* American country. However, many Americans thought it was not the best time to open the borders because the US unemployment rate was 7% at the time and they feared that American jobs would be further jeopardized by free trade. H. Ross Perot, a presidential candidate in 1992, described NAFTA's potential destruction of thousands of US jobs as a "giant sucking sound."

As NAFTA went into effect in 1994, tariffs on half of exports and imports among members were removed immediately. Remaining tariffs would be phased out by 2010. These changes in the rules of the game significantly shaped the strategies of both NAFTA and non-NAFTA firms.[21]

NAFTA celebrated its 10th anniversary in 2004. By most statistical measures, NAFTA was a great success. In its first decade, trade between Canada and the United States grew twice as fast as it did before NAFTA. Expanding even faster, US exports to Mexico grew threefold, from $52 billion to $161 billion. US FDI in Mexico averaged $12 billion a year, three times what India took in. Mexico's US-bound exports grew threefold, and its GDP rose to become the 9th in the world, up from 15th in 1992. In ten years Mexico's GDP per capita rose 24% to over $4,000 (by 2004), several times that of China.[22]

What about jobs? *Maquiladora* (export assembly) factories blossomed under NAFTA, with jobs peaking at 1.3 million in 2000. Beyond *maquiladora*, the export boom NAFTA caused reportedly has accounted for more than half of the 3.5 million

North American Free Trade Agreement (NAFTA)

A free trade agreement among Canada, Mexico, and the United States.

jobs created in Mexico since 1994. Yet no "giant sucking sound" has been heard in the United States. Approximately 300,000 US jobs were lost due to NAFTA, but about 100,000 jobs have been created. The net loss was small, since the US economy generated 20 million new jobs during the first decade of NAFTA. NAFTA's impact on job destruction versus creation in the United States was essentially a "wash."[23] However, a hard count on jobs misses a pervasive but subtle benefit. NAFTA has allowed US firms to *preserve* more US jobs, because 82% of the components used in Mexican assembly plants are US-made, whereas factories in Asia use far fewer US parts. Without NAFTA, entire industries might be lost, rather than just the labor-intensive portions.

What are some of the advantages and disadvantages Mexico has experienced as part of NAFTA?

Although economic theory suggests that trade benefits all partners (see Chapter 5), the impact of trade is different among members. Over 85% of Canadian and Mexican exports go to the United States, but only 40% of US exports go to NAFTA partners (about 22% to Canada and 18% to Mexico). Because US imports from Mexico amounted to less than 1.5% of US GDP, their impact was relatively small. Low-priced Mexican imports helped hold down inflation but only modestly, shaving about 0.1% off the annual inflation in the United States.[24]

As NAFTA celebrated its 15th anniversary in 2009, not all was rosy. Opponents of globalization in both Canada and the United States no longer focus on the negative impact of competition from Mexico but rather on China and India. Despite the impressive gains in their country, many Mexicans feel betrayed by NAFTA. Thanks to Chinese competition, Mexican real wages in manufacturing have stagnated. Many US, Canadian, European, and Japanese multinationals are shifting some of their factory work to China, which has now replaced Mexico as the second-largest exporter to the United States (after Canada).[25] About 1,000 *maquiladora* factories have closed down since 2000. NAFTA might have been oversold by its sponsors as a cure-all for Mexico to become the next South Korea, but it can be argued that the Mexican government has not capitalized on the tremendous opportunities it has been offered. There is only so much free trade can do; other reforms in infrastructure and education need to keep up.

South America: Andean Community, Mercosur, FTAA, USAN/UNASUR, and CAFTA

Whatever NAFTA's imperfections, it is much more effective than the two customs unions in South America: **Andean Community** and **Mercosur**. Members of the Andean Community (launched in 1969) and Mercosur (launched in 1991)

Andean Community
A customs union in South America that was launched in 1969.

Mercosur
A customs union in South America that was launched in 1991.

are mostly countries on the *western* and *eastern* sides of the Andean mountains, respectively (see PengAtlas Map 2.5). There is much mutual suspicion and rivalry between both organizations as well as within each of them. Mercosur is relatively more protectionist and suspicious of the United States, whereas the Andean Community is more pro–free trade. When Colombia and Peru, both Andean Community members, signed trade deals with the United States, Venezuela, led by the anti-American President Hugo Chavez, pulled out of the Andean Community in protest and joined Mercosur in 2006. At the same time, Uruguay, a Mercosur member, demanded permission from the group to sign a separate trade deal with the United States—otherwise, it would quit Mercosur.[26]

Both regional initiatives have not been effective, in part because only 5% of member countries' trade is within the Andean Community and 20% within Mercosur. Their largest trading partner, the United States, lies outside the region. A free trade deal with the United States, not among themselves, would generate the most significant benefits. Emboldened by NAFTA, in 1998, all Latin American countries (except Cuba) launched negotiations with Canada and the United States for a possible **Free Trade Area of the Americas (FTAA)**. However, by November 2005, Argentina, Brazil, Paraguay, Uruguay, and Venezuela changed their minds and announced that they opposed FTAA, thus undermining the chances that FTAA would ever be set up.

Instead of pursuing FTAA, Andean Community and Mercosur countries in May 2008 agreed to form the **Union of South American Nations (USAN**, more commonly known by its Spanish acronym, **UNASUR**, which refers to *Unión de Naciones Suramericanas*). Inspired by the EU, USAN/UNASUR announced its intention to eventually adopt a common currency, parliament, and passport. A functioning union similar to that of the EU may be possible in 2019. This is the newest development of large-scale regional integration mechanisms to watch.

In the absence of the FTAA, one recent accomplishment is the **United States-Dominican Republic-Central America Free Trade Agreement (CAFTA)**, which took effect in 2005. Modeled after NAFTA, CAFTA is an agreement "between a whale and six minnows" (five Central American countries—Costa Rica, El Salvador, Guatemala, Honduras, and Nicaragua—plus the Dominican Republic).[27] Although small, the six CAFTA countries collectively represent the second-largest US export market in Latin America (behind only Mexico). Globally, CAFTA is the tenth-largest US export market, importing more than Russia, India, and Indonesia *combined*.[28]

Free Trade Area of the Americas (FTAA)

A proposed free trade area for the entire Western Hemisphere.

Union of South American Nations (USAN/UNASUR)

A regional integration mechanism integrating two existing customs unions (Andean Community and Mercosur) in South America.

United States-Dominican Republic-Central America Free Trade Agreement (CAFTA)

A free trade agreement between the United States and five Central American countries and the Dominican Republic.

LEARNING OBJECTIVE

6

Identify the three organizations that promote regional trade in the Asia Pacific and describe their benefits and costs.

REGIONAL ECONOMIC INTEGRATION IN THE ASIA PACIFIC

This section introduces regional integration efforts between Australia and New Zealand, in Southeast Asia, and throughout the Asia Pacific. Their scale and scope differ.

Australia-New Zealand Closer Economic Relations Trade Agreement (ANZCERTA or CER)

Australia-New Zealand Closer Economic Relations Trade Agreement (ANZCERTA or CER)

A free trade agreement between Australia and New Zealand that was launched in 1983.

The CER, launched in 1983, turned the historical rivalry between Australia and New Zealand into a partnership. As an FTA, the CER removed tariffs and NTBs over time. For example, both countries agreed not to charge exporters from another country for dumping. Citizens from both countries can also freely work and reside in the other country. Mostly due to the relatively high level of geographic proximity and cultural homogeneity, CER has been regarded as a very successful FTA.

Association of Southeast Asian Nations (ASEAN)

Founded in 1967, ASEAN (PengAtlas Map 2.6) was inspired by the EU's success and set up the ASEAN Free Trade Area (AFTA) in 1992. ASEAN suffers from a similar problem that Latin American countries face: ASEAN's main trading partners—the United States, the EU, Japan, and China—are outside the region. Intra-ASEAN trade usually accounts for less than a quarter of total trade. The benefits of AFTA thus may be limited. In response, in 2002, ASEAN signed an ASEAN-China Free Trade Agreement (ACFTA) to be launched by the early 2010s. Given the increasingly strong competition in terms of Chinese exports and China-bound FDI that could have come to ASEAN, ACFTA hopes to turn such rivalry into a partnership. ACFTA is estimated to boost ASEAN's exports to China by 48% and China's exports to ASEAN by 55%, thus raising ASEAN's GDP by 0.9% and China's by 0.3%.[29] Similar FTAs are being negotiated with Japan and South Korea.

Asia-Pacific Economic Cooperation (APEC)

Although ASEAN was deepening its integration, Australia was afraid that it might be left out and suggested in 1989 that ASEAN and CER countries form APEC. Given the lack of a global heavyweight in both ASEAN and CER, Japan was invited. Although the Japanese happily agreed to join, ASEAN and CER countries also feared that Japan might dominate the group and create a de facto "yen bloc." Many people remembered how a desire for economic leadership before and during World War II led Japan to invade many countries in the region, and bitter memories of Japanese wartime atrocities in the region seemed to die hard. At that time, China was far less significant economically than it is now, and thus could hardly counterbalance Japan. Then the United States requested to join APEC, citing its long West Coast that would qualify it as a Pacific country. Economically, the United States did not want to be left out of the most dynamically growing region in the world. Politically, the United States was interested in containing Japanese influence in any Asian regional deals. Although the United States could certainly serve as a counterweight for Japan, the US membership would also change the character of APEC, which had been centered on ASEAN and CER. To make its APEC membership less odd, the United States brought on board two of its NAFTA partners, Canada and Mexico. Canada and Mexico were equally interested in the economic benefits but probably cared less about the US political motives to contain Japanese influence. Once the floodgates for membership were open, Chile, Peru, and Russia all eventually got in, each citing their long Pacific coast lines (!).

Shown in PengAtlas Map 2.6, APEC's 21 member economies span four continents, are home to 2.6 billion people, contribute 46% of world trade ($7 trillion), and command 57% of world GDP ($21 trillion), making it the largest regional integration grouping by geographic area and by GDP.[30] Although it is nice to include so many members, APEC may be too big. The goal of free trade by industrialized members no later than 2010 and by developing members no later than 2020 is *not* binding. Essentially as a talking shop, APEC—nicknamed "a perfect excuse to chat"—provides a forum for members to make commitments that are largely rhetorical.

Association of Southeast Asian Nations (ASEAN)

The organization underpinning regional economic integration in Southeast Asia.

Asia-Pacific Economic Cooperation (APEC)

The official title for regional economic integration involving 21 member economies around the Pacific.

Understand why regional trade deals are not effective in Africa.

REGIONAL ECONOMIC INTEGRATION IN AFRICA

Regional integration initiatives in Africa are both numerous and ineffective. Each country often has memberships in multiple regional deals, making it difficult to map out any one country's membership in any one regional deal. In fact, any attempt to diagram African regional deals, like the one shown in Figure 8.4, creates a "spaghetti bowl." This hopelessly complicated diagram also suggests that no sane professor will want to quiz students on the membership of these different deals on your exam (!). Although various African countries are interested in reaping the benefits from regional economic integration, there is relatively little trade within Africa (amounting to less than 10% of the continent's total trade) and protectionism often prevails. Frustration with a current regional deal often leads to a new deal, typically with a different set of countries, which has resulted in the messy spaghetti bowl.

Participate in two leading debates on global and regional economic integration.

DEBATES AND EXTENSIONS

As discussed earlier, global and regional economic integration is characterized by numerous debates (What caused Doha to collapse? How to enlarge the EU?). This section outlines two additional major debates: (1) building blocks versus stumbling blocks and (2) impact of the WTO.

FIGURE 8.4   REGIONAL ECONOMIC INTEGRATION IN AFRICA

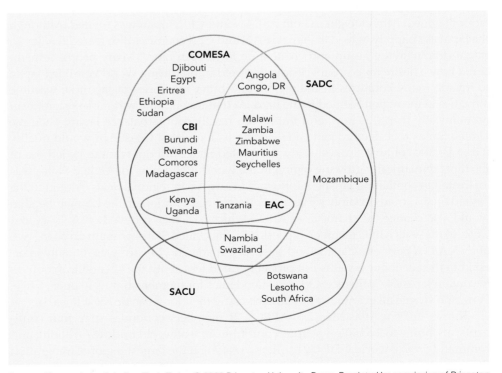

Source: Bhagwati, Jagdish, Free Trade Today. © 2002 Princeton University Press. Reprinted by permission of Princeton University Press. CBI—Cross Border Initiative; COMESA—Common Market for Eastern and Southern Africa; EAC—Commission for East Africa Co-operation; SADC—Southern Africa Development Community; SACU—Southern Africa Customs Union.

Building Blocks or Stumbling Blocks

In the absence of global economic integration, regional economic integration is often regarded as the next best thing to facilitate free trade, at least within a region. Some may even argue that regional integration represents building blocks for eventual global integration. For example, the EU now participates in WTO negotiations as one entity, which seems like a building block. Individual EU member countries no longer enter such talks.

However, another school of thought argues that regional integration has become a stumbling block for global integration. By design, regional integration provides preferential treatment to members and, at the same time, *discriminates* against nonmembers. Although it is allowed by WTO rules, it is still a form of protectionism centered on us versus them, except "us" is now an expanded group of countries. The proliferation of regional trade deals thus may be alarming. For example, in the first few decades after World War II, the United States avoided regional deals. Partly due to concerns about the power of the EU, the United States launched NAFTA with Canada and Mexico. Likewise, China signed its first FTA agreement (ACFTA) in 2002 with ASEAN. Then in 2005, China signed FTA deals with Chile and Pakistan. Clearly, the trend is accelerating.

Of course, all countries party to some regional deals participate in WTO talks, arguing that they are walking on two legs: regional and global. Yet, instead of walking on two legs, critics such as Columbia professor Jagdish Bhagwati argued that "we have wound up on all fours"—in other words, crawling with slow progress.[31] This sorry state is triggered by individual countries pursuing their interest in a globally uncoordinated fashion. As regional deals proliferate, nonmembers feel that they are squeezed out and begin plotting their own regional deals. Very soon, we end up having a global spaghetti bowl.

Does the WTO Really Matter?

Frustration over the collapse of the Doha Round and other WTO initiatives hinges on a crucial assumption that the WTO actually matters. However, this assumption itself is now subject to debate. Academic research has failed to find any compelling evidence that the WTO (and the GATT) has a significantly positive effect on trade. True, trade has blossomed since the GATT was established in 1948. But Andrew Rose, a professor at the University of California, Berkeley, reports that trade has blossomed for the GATT/WTO members and nonmembers alike. Therefore, it is difficult to find that the GATT/WTO membership *caused* more trade.[32] The *Economist* thus commented that "the 'hoopla' and 'hype' that surrounds the WTO's successes, failures, and admissions of new members are just that: hoopla and hype."[33]

Defenders of the WTO point out Rose's methodological imperfections.[34] Beyond such methodological hair-splitting, in the real world the collapse of Doha has not caused any noticeable collapse of global trade and investment—certainly not as much damage as the 2008–2009 recession. So, perhaps the WTO does not matter much. This debate is much more than just academic. It directly speaks to the possibility that perhaps we may not need to place so much hope on the WTO, which means we do not need to be so depressed over Doha's collapse.

Draw implications for action.

MANAGEMENT SAVVY

Of the two major perspectives on global business (institution-based and resource-based views), this chapter has focused on the institution-based view. In order to address the question, "What determines the success and failure around the globe?" the entire chapter has been devoted to an introduction of the rules of the game as institutions governing global and regional economic integration. How does this knowledge help managers? Managers need to combine the insights from the institution-based view with those from the resource-based view to come up with strategies and solutions on how their firms can capitalize on opportunities presented by global and regional economic integration. Two broad implications for action emerge (Table 8.4).

First, given the slowdown of multilateralism and the acceleration of regionalism, managers are advised to focus their attention more on regional than global levels.[35] To a large extent, they are already doing that. The majority of the multinational enterprises (MNEs) generate most of their revenues in their home region (such as within the EU or NAFTA).[36] The largest MNEs may have a presence all over the world, but their center of gravity (measured by revenues) is often still their home region. Thus, they are not really global. Regional strategies make sense because most countries within a region share some cultural, economic, and geographic similarities that can lower the liability of foreignness when moving within one region, as opposed to moving from one region to another. From a resource-based standpoint, most firms are better prepared to compete at a regional as opposed to global level. Despite the hoopla associated with global strategies, managers, in short, need to think local and downplay—while not necessarily abandoning—global.

Second, managers also need to understand the rules of the game and their transitions at both global and regional levels. Although trade negotiations involve a lot of politics that many managers think they could hardly care less about, managers ignore these rules and their transitions at their own peril. Although the MFA was phased out in 2005, numerous managers at textile firms, who had become comfortable under the MFA's protection, decried the new level of competition and complained about their lack of preparation. In fact, they had 30 *years* to prepare for such an eventuality. When the MFA was signed in 1974, it was agreed that it would be phased out by 2005. The typical attitude that "We don't care about (trade) politics" can lead to a failure in due diligence. The best managers expect their firm strategies to shift over time, constantly decipher the changes in the big picture, and are willing to take advantage of new opportunities brought by global and regional trade deals. Ryanair and Hungarian Dental Travel (see the Opening Case) represent some interesting examples of such firms.

TABLE 8.4   IMPLICATIONS FOR ACTION

- Think regional, downplay global
- Understand the rules of the game and their transitions, at both global and regional levels

CHAPTER SUMMARY

1. Make the case for global economic integration.
   - There are both political and economic benefits for global economic integration.

2. Understand the evolution of the GATT and the WTO, including current challenges.
   - The GATT (1948–94) significantly reduced tariff rates on merchandise trade.
   - The WTO (1995–present) was set up to not only incorporate the GATT, but also cover trade in services, intellectual property, trade dispute settlement, and peer review of trade policy.
   - The Doha Round to promote more trade and development thus far failed to accomplish its goals.

3. Make the case for regional economic integration.
   - Political and economic benefits for regional integration are similar to those for global integration.
   - Regional integration may undermine global integration and lead to some loss of countries´ sovereignty.

4. List the accomplishments, benefits, and costs of the EU.
   - The EU has delivered more than half a century of peace and prosperity, launched a single currency, and constructed a single market.
   - Its challenges include internal divisions and enlargement concerns.

5. Identify the five organizations that facilitate regional trade in the Americas and describe their benefits and costs.
   - Despite problems, NAFTA has significantly boosted trade and investment among members.
   - South American countries have merged two customs unions, Andean Community and Mercosur, to form the new USAN/UNASUR.
   - In effect since 2005, CAFTA facilitates trade between the United States and five Central American countries and the Dominican Republic.

6. Identify the three organizations that promote regional trade in the Asia Pacific and describe their benefits and costs.
   - Regional integration in the Asia Pacific centers on CER, ASEAN, and APEC.

7. Understand why regional trade deals are not effective in Africa.
   - Regional integration deals in Africa are both numerous and ineffective, because countries often have memberships in different regional deals.

8. Participate in two leading debates on global and regional economic integration.
   - Are regional integration building blocks or stumbling blocks for global integration?
   - Does the WTO really matter?

9. Draw implications for action.
   - Think regional, downplay global.
   - Understand the rules of the game and their transitions, at both global and regional levels.

KEY TERMS

Andean Community   257
Asia-Pacific Economic Cooperation (APEC)   259
Association of Southeast Asian Nations (ASEAN)   259
Australia-New Zealand Closer Economic Relations Trade Agreement (ANZCERTA or CER)   258
Common market   248
Customs union   248
Doha Round   245
Economic union   249
Euro   250

Euro area   250
European Union (EU)   239
Free trade area (FTA)   248
Free Trade Area of the Americas (FTAA)   258
General Agreement on Tariffs and Trade (GATT)   239
General Agreement on Trade in Services (GATS)   242
Global economic integration   239
Mercosur   257
Monetary union   249
Multilateral trading system   241
Nondiscrimination   241

North American Free Trade Agreement (NAFTA)   256
Political union   249
Regional economic integration   238
Schengen   250
Trade-Related Aspects of Intellectual Property Rights (TRIPS)   242
Union of South American Nations (USAN/UNASUR)   258
United States-Dominican Republic-Central America Free Trade Agreement (CAFTA)   258
World Trade Organization (WTO)   239

REVIEW QUESTIONS

1. Name and describe three compelling economic benefits of global economic integration.

2. Why do some critics question the benefits of global economic integration?

3. Briefly summarize the history of the WTO.

4. What are the six main areas of concern for the WTO?

5. In what ways are the benefits of regional economic integration similar to global economic integration?

6. What is one possible negative outcome of regional integration?

7. What are the advantages of the EU's adoption of the euro?

8. After reviewing the two sides of the debate over whether the EU should be just an economic union or also a political union, state your opinion on the issue and explain your reasons.

9. In PengAtlas Map 2.4, consider the EU countries that do not use the euro. Why might current and historic leadership in international trade and finance be a factor in one of those countries? Do you think that a country would be better off if it shifted from its current currency to the euro? Why?

10. What achievements do NAFTA supporters point to as evidence of NAFTA's success?

P9. 257

11. Why have the Andean Community and Mercosur not been more effective?

12. Name and describe three examples of regional integration in the Asia Pacific.

13. Note the countries shown in PengAtlas Map 2.6 that are involved in some aspect of regional integration in the Asia Pacific. What do you think is the potential for economic growth of those countries compared to the EU? Explain.

14. What is the largest regional integration by geographic area? To what extent might its size be a problem?

15. How can regional economic integration be a barrier to global economic integration?

16. What evidence suggests that the WTO may not be as significant as its supporters claim it is?

17. What two trends indicate that managers should focus more on regional as opposed to global issues?

18. How important is it for a manager to understand the political ramifications of global and regional trade negotiations?

CRITICAL DISCUSSION QUESTIONS

1. The Doha Round collapsed because many countries believed that no deal was better than a bad deal. Do you agree or disagree with this approach? Why?

2. Will Turkey become a full-fledged member of the EU? Why or why not?

3. The German chancellor wanted to consult with you, a leading expert on the EU. For years, Germany advocated both the single currency and the EU's enlargement to include more CEE countries. At the same time, Germany insisted, via the SGP, that countries in the euro area must tame their public finances and could not be bailed out. Now CEE countries and Greece are in desperate need of bailouts. But the German economy has also suffered a major recession itself and has already been running a budget deficit. How would you advise the chancellor: to bail out or not to bail out EU members such as CEE countries and Greece?

4. *ON ETHICS*: Critics argue that the WTO single-mindedly promotes trade at the expense of the environment (see In Focus 8.1). Therefore, trade, or more broadly, globalization, needs to slow down. What is your view on the relationship between trade and the environment?

YOUR SOURCE FOR
**global business
knowledge**

http://globalEDGE.msu.edu

GLOBAL ACTION

1. The WTO membership is viewed by some as a signal of a country's ability to guarantee and protect trade among companies in stable macroeconomic conditions. Since your company is looking to expand internationally for the first time since 1999, a list of countries that have been admitted to the WTO since 2000 is required, and can be found on globalEDGE. This will update your company's market entry initiative so that it can review the international opportunities in a more thorough manner.

2. Your firm is considering developing business in the Middle East. Many in your company are aware that there is considerable economic cooperation currently underway in the region. However, there is very little information in current internal entry evaluation documents concerning the possible regional trade agreements that may already exist. Using resources available on globalEDGE, identify at least one regional trade agreement and its member countries in the Middle East.

VIDEO CASE

Watch "Delivering High Performance Research Through Cross-Sector Collaboration" by Peter Lacy of Accenture.

1. Lacy covered collaboration in projects involving different "cultures" in academic, business, and government areas. How would you apply his discussion to the challenge of bringing together leaders from various national cultures in regional economic integration?

2. Lacy stated that business people solve problems in months with real-world applications, as opposed to academics who may take many years and attempt to build on previous studies. Show how globalization and the expanded use of technology could create a need for businesspeople to actually spend *more* time and academics to spend *less* time in problem solving.

3. Suppose you are the CEO of a global corporation and you wish to achieve boundary spanning through experience. What would be the benefit of using that approach as opposed to developing empathy? How would you go about doing that?

4. Lacy applied the stakeholder concept to projects. What stakeholders exist when attempting to create or expand regional economic integration?

Closing Case

Whose Law Is Bigger: Arbitrating Government—Firm Investment Disputes in the EU

One of the key concerns as a multinational enterprise (MNE) making foreign direct investment (FDI) is how to take advantage of incentives in different host countries while safeguarding investor interests if something goes wrong. This issue may arise when countries change regimes like when the Central and Eastern European (CEE) countries joined the EU in 2004–2007. Similarly, when a country nationalizes an industry like Argentina did with utilities (such as water and gas) in 2001, it would leave many foreign investors without recourse for recouping their investments. Courts in Argentina were unable to enforce investor contracts and the government refused to repay foreign investors. However, since these contracts fall under the protection of a series of bilateral investment treaties (BITs) between Argentina and other countries (typically one BIT covers one pair of countries), aggrieved firms can file for binding arbitration proceedings through the International Center for Settlement of Investment Disputes (ICSID), which is based in Washington, DC.

© Pixtal Images

Binding arbitration is a private forum for contract dispute resolution. Its functions are similar to those of an international court, but it uses experts, rather than judges, to resolve complex disputes. Although arbitration awards do not change laws (they merely interpret laws), binding arbitration has the benefit of enforcement in multiple jurisdictions under the New York Convention of 1958 and the ICSID Convention. A total of 144 countries are signatories. Therefore, binding arbitration awards made in one country are enforceable in 143 other countries. This includes awards made against other signatory countries, such as Argentina. Generally, countries that have lost cases pay voluntarily. However, even as recently as 2008 Argentina continues to be reluctant to pay. Many of these firms, such as Vivendi and Siemens, are seeking Argentine assets in other signatory countries.

The EU law is starting to feel the pressure of these government–firm investment disputes. To attract FDI before joining the EU, Hungary and Romania in the 1990s and early 2000s offered large and lucrative incentives in long-term contracts. However, because Hungary and Romania joined the EU in 2004 and 2007, respectively, the incentives became illegal under the EU law. This is because the EU law forbids any discrimination against any EU member countries and firms. Any BIT between, for example, Hungary (a nonmember until 2004) and Austria (an EU member) that gives Austrian firms preferential treatments and investment incentives, by definition, discriminates against firms from other EU countries. Therefore, such BITs were declared illegal by the EU and contracts signed under the BITs were forcibly withdrawn by Hungary and Romania in 2008.

MNEs from the EU (Sweden and Belgium) and the United States responded to the 2008 abrogation of their contracts in Hungary and Romania by seeking remedies in arbitration instead of national courts. For example, Micula, a firm from Sweden, is suing Romania for unilaterally removing tax and custom duties from the contacts. In Hungary (shown in the photo above), several foreign electricity producers are suing for breach of long-term power supply contracts based on unilateral change of electricity pricing. These contracts fall under the BITs between the contracting countries. Because the contracts are unenforceable under EU law, but enforceable under the BITs in place at the time of contracting, these cases present a larger question: *Which law takes precedence?*

Recent arbitration suggests that the EU law is *secondary* to original commitments—that is, local laws and BITs at the time of original contracting are to be respected if they clash with the EU law.

For example, in 2008, a Dutch sugar company received an award of €25 million against the Czech Republic based on a contract under a Dutch-Czech BIT from the 1990s. The arbitration tribunal sent a clear message by excluding the argument that the BIT ceased to have force upon the Czech Republic's entry into the EU in 2004. Likely responding to this message, the EU Commission is taking an active role in the current proceedings involving Hungary and Romania, seeking to intervene in the arbitration decisions.

Case Discussion Questions:

1. If the EU law is bigger, the MNEs lose billions of euros. If the EU law is secondary, the governments (and ultimately the taxpayers) in the host countries must pay. Which law should come first?
2. From an institution-based view, explain why the MNEs in this case filed through arbitration and not courts in the host countries.
3. As a foreign investor, do you want to support BITs and arbitration or rely on local court systems?

Sources: This case was written by **Brian Pinkham** (University of Texas at Dallas) under the supervision of Professor Mike W. Peng. It was based on (1) International Center for Settlement of Investment Disputes, 2009, http://icsid.worldbank.org/ICSID/Index.jsp; (2) L. E. Peterson, 2009, *Investment Arbitration Reporter*, 2(8); (3) S. Pignal & N. Tait, 2009, EU leaves sour aftertaste, *Financial Times*, June 22; (4) United Nations Commission on International Trade Law, 2009, http://www.uncitral.org.

NOTES

[Journal acronyms] AER—*American Economic Review*; BW—*Business Week*; JIBS—*Journal of International Business Studies*; JWB—*Journal of World Business*; SMJ—*Strategic Management Journal*.

1 World Trade Organization, 2005, *10 Benefits of the WTO Trading System* (p. 3), Geneva: WTO.

2 *10 Benefits of the WTO Trading System* (p. 8).

3 D. Xu, Y. Pan, C. Wu, & B. Yim, 2006, Performance of domestic and foreign-invested enterprises in China (p. 268), *JWB*, 41: 261–274.

4 *Economist*, 2006, The future of globalization (p. 11), July 29: 11.

5 *Economist*, 2006, In the twilight of Doha (p. 63), July 29: 63–64.

6 Delegation of the European Commission to the USA, 2005, *The European Union: A Guide for Americans* (p. 2), Washington: Delegation of the European Commission to the USA.

7 G. Zestos, 2006, *European Monetary Integration: The Euro* (p. 64), Cincinnati: South-Western Cengage Learning.

8 P. Whyman, 2002, Living with the euro, *JWB*, 37: 208–215.

9 *Economist*, 2007, The quest for prosperity, March 17: 6–9.

10 *Economist*, 2009, No exit, June 13: 7–8.

11 *Economist*, 2007, Europe's mid-life crisis, March 17: 13.

12 *Economist*, 2005, The Europe that died, June 4: 13–14.

13 K. Meyer & M. W. Peng, 2005, Probing theoretically in Central and Eastern Europe, *JIBS*, 36: 600–621.

14 *Economist*, 2006, A survey of Poland (p. 3), May 13: 3–12.

15 *BW*, 2009, What's dragging Europe down? March 9: 36–41.

16 *Economist*, 2009, The whiff of contagion (p. 28), February 28: 27–29.

17 *Economist*, 2006, A case of enlargement fatigue, May 13: 64.

18 *Economist*, 2004, Europe à la carte, September 25: 14–16.

19 *Economist*, 2006, Babelling on, December 16: 50.

20 *BW*, 2003, Mexico: Was NAFTA worth it? December 22.

21 A. Rugman & J. Kirton, 1998, Multinational enterprise strategy and the NAFTA trade and environment regime, *JWB*, 33: 438–454.

22 *BW*, 2003, Happy birthday, NAFTA, December 22; *BW*, 2003, Mexico: Was NAFTA worth it? December 22.

23 J. Garten, 2003, At 10, NAFTA is ready for an overhaul, *BW*, December 22.

24 *BW*, 2001, NAFTA's scorecard, July 9.

25 J. Sargent & L. Matthews, 2006, The drivers of evolution/upgrading in Mexico's maquiladoras, *JWB*, 41: 233–246.

26 *Economist*, 2006, Mercosur's summit: Downhill from here, July 29: 36.

27 *Economist*, 2005, Another such victory, July 30: 66.

28 US Trade Representative, 2005, *The Case for CAFTA*, February, Washington: USTR (www.ustr.gov).

29 ASEAN Secretariat, 2002, *Southeast Asia: A Free Trade Area*, Jakarta: ASEAN Secretariat (www.asean.org).

30 APEC Secretariat, 2005, *APEC at a Glance*, Singapore: APEC Secretariat (www.apec.org).

31 J. Bhagwati, 2002, *Free Trade Today* (p. 119), Princeton, NJ: Princeton University Press.

32 A. Rose, 2004, Do we really know that the WTO increases trade? *AER*, 94: 98–114.

33 *Economist*, 2005, Is there any point to the WTO? August 6: 62.

[34] A. Subramanian & S. Wei, 2005, The WTO promotes trade strongly but unevenly, Working paper, IMF.

[35] M. Fratianni & C. Oh, 2009, Expanding RTAs, trade flows, and the multinational enterprise, *JIBS*, 40: 1206–1277; A. Rugman, 2005, *The Regional Multinationals*, Cambridge, UK: Cambridge University Press.

[36] G. Qian, T. Khoury, M. W. Peng, & Z. Qian, 2010, The performance implications of intra- and inter-regional geographic diversification, *SMJ* (in press).

pengatlas Part 2

MAP 2.1   TOP TEN MERCHANDISE IMPORTERS AND EXPORTERS

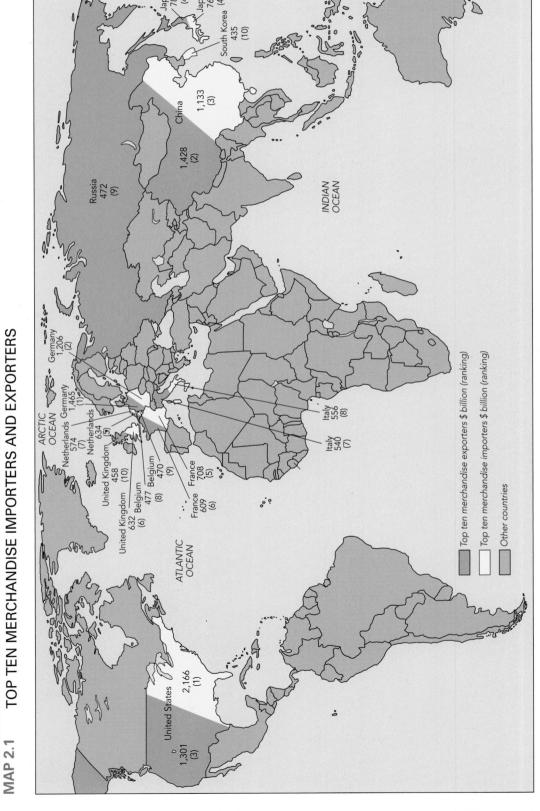

Germany
1,206
(2)

Germany
1,465
(1)

Netherlands
574
(7)

Netherlands
634
(5)

United Kingdom
458
(10)

United Kingdom
632
(6)

Belgium
477
(8)

Belgium
470
(9)

France
708
(5)

France
609
(6)

Russia
472
(9)

China
1,428
(2)

China
1,133
(3)

Japan
782
(4)

Japan
762
(4)

South Korea
435
(10)

Italy
556
(8)

Italy
540
(7)

United States
2,166
(1)

United States
1,301
(3)

ARCTIC
OCEAN

ATLANTIC
OCEAN

INDIAN
OCEAN

☐ Top ten merchandise exporters $ billion (ranking)

☐ Top ten merchandise importers $ billion (ranking)

☐ Other countries

Source: Adapted from World Trade Organization, 2009, *World Trade Report 2009* (Appendix Table 5 and Table 3). All data are for 2008. See Table 5.1 on page 147.

MAP 2.2   TOP TEN SERVICE IMPORTERS AND EXPORTERS

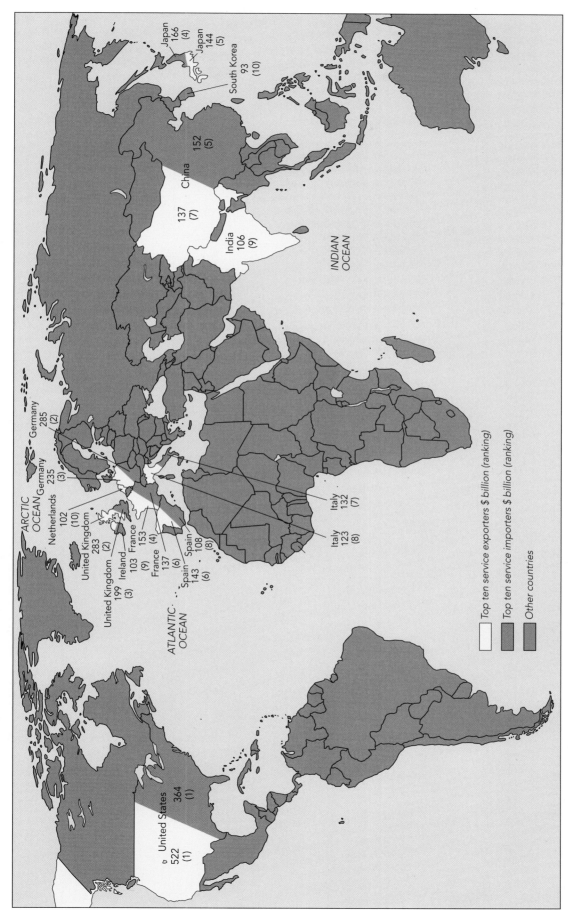

Japan 166 (4)
Japan 144 (5)
South Korea 93 (10)

China 152 (5)
137 (7)

India 106 (9)

INDIAN OCEAN

ARCTIC OCEAN

Germany 285 (2)
Germany 235 (3)

Netherlands 102 (10)

United Kingdom 283 (2)
United Kingdom 199 (3)

Ireland 103 (9)
France 153 (4)
France 137 (6)

Spain 143 (6)
Spain 108 (8)

Italy 132 (7)
Italy 123 (8)

ATLANTIC OCEAN

United States 364 (1)
United States 522 (1)

Top ten service exporters $ billion (ranking)
Top ten service importers $ billion (ranking)
Other countries

Source: Adapted from World Trade Organization, 2009, *World Trade Report 2009* (Appendix Table 5 and Table 3). All data are for 2008. See Table 5.1 on page 147.

MAP 2.3   TOP TEN ECONOMIES FOR FDI INFLOWS AND OUTFLOWS

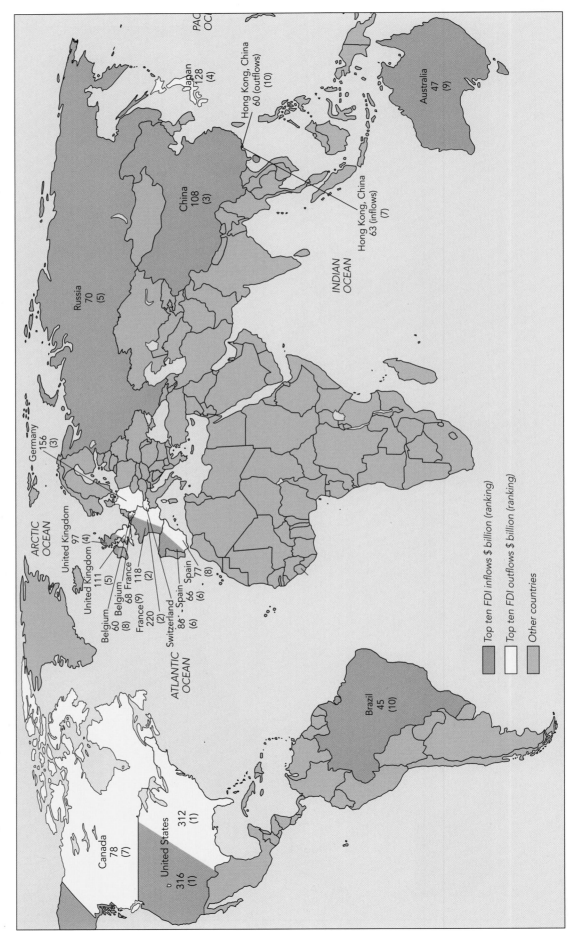

Canada
78
(7)

United States
312
(1)

United States
316
(1)

ARCTIC
OCEAN

United Kingdom
97
(4)

United Kingdom
111
(5)

Belgium
60
(8)

Belgium
68
(9)

France
220
(2)

France
118
(2)

Switzerland
86
(6)

Spain
66
(6)

Spain
77
(8)

Germany
156
(3)

ATLANTIC
OCEAN

Russia
70
(5)

China
108
(3)

Japan
128
(4)

Hong Kong, China
60 (outflows)
(10)

Hong Kong, China
63 (inflows)
(7)

INDIAN
OCEAN

Australia
47
(9)

Brazil
45
(10)

PAC
OC

Top ten FDI inflows $ billion (ranking)

Top ten FDI outflows $ billion (ranking)

Other countries

Source: Adapted from United Nations, 2009, *World Investment Report 2009* (Annex Table B.1, pp. 247–250), New York and Geneva: UN. All data are for 2008. See Figure 6.3 on page 182 and Figure 6.4 on page 183.

MAP 2.4   THE EUROPEAN UNION

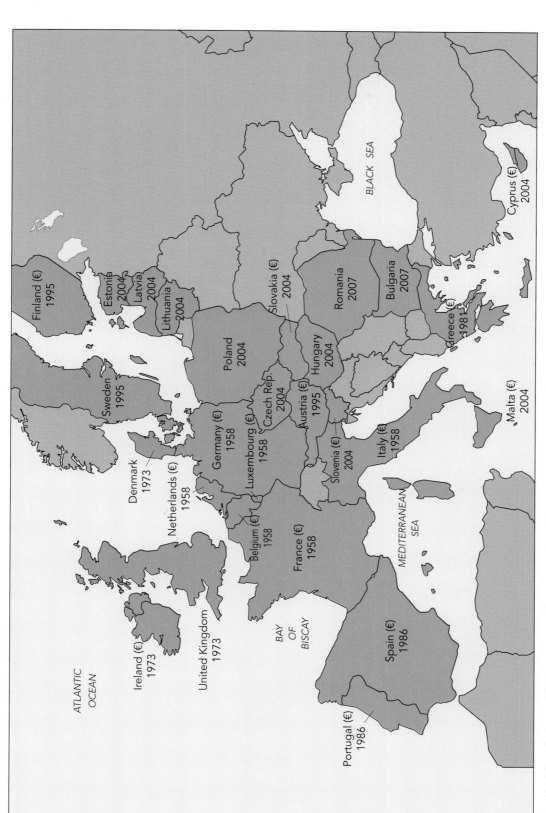

Croatia, Macedonia, and Turkey are candidate countries. All the other Western Balkan countries (Albania, Bosnia and Herzegovina, Montenegro, Serbia, and Kosovo) are potential candidate countries. Iceland submitted an application for membership in July 2009.

Note: Countries showing the € symbol have adopted the euro. See Table 8.2 on page 251.

MAP 2.5   REGIONAL INTEGRATION IN SOUTH AMERICA

In May 2008, Andean Community and Mercosur agreed to merge to form the Union of South American Nations (USAN, more commonly known by its Spanish acronym, UNASUR, which refers to *Unión de Naciones Suramericanas*).

MAP 2.6 REGIONAL INTEGRATION IN THE ASIA PACIFIC

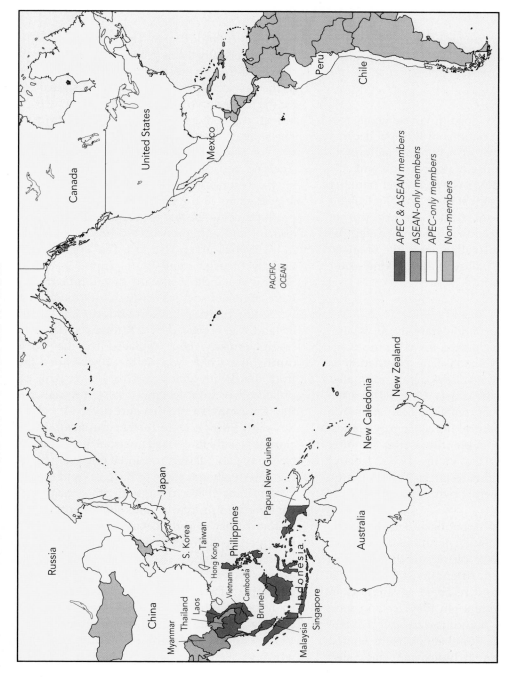

Legend:
- APEC & ASEAN members
- ASEAN-only members
- APEC-only members
- Non-members

PACIFIC OCEAN

Russia, China, Myanmar, Thailand, Laos, Vietnam, Cambodia, Brunei, Malaysia, Singapore, Indonesia, Hong Kong, Taiwan, S. Korea, Japan, Philippines, Papua New Guinea, New Caledonia, Australia, New Zealand, Canada, United States, Mexico, Peru, Chile

INTEGRATIVE CASE 2.1

ICELAND'S FINANCIAL CRISIS

Eydis Olsen, *Drexel University*

How did one of the wealthiest nations in Europe become the most dramatic example of the financial meltdown in 2008? What are some of the root causes? How effective are the countermeasures?

In the midst of the 2008 global financial crisis, Iceland, one of the wealthiest nations of Europe, became the most dramatic example of economic meltdown. Iceland experienced a collapse of its economy and currency as a result of a fatally over-leveraged banking sector. With a population of just over 300,000, Iceland became an active participant in globalization during the first decade of the 21st century, following deregulation, tax reforms, and the privatization of the financial sector. In October 2008, the failure of the banking sector led to a severe financial crisis.

Background

Iceland is an independent nation-state on an island, about the size of Kentucky, located between the Scandinavian Peninsula and Canada. The population is concentrated around the capital, Reykjavik, and smaller towns and farms around the coasts. Over 90% of the land is uninhabited but features an exotic landscape ranging from glaciers to natural hot springs. Geothermal and hydraulic energy is plentiful. After winning a political battle with the UK in the 1970s, Iceland has exclusive territorial rights to large portions of the North Atlantic Ocean, which is rich in fisheries but is yet to be explored for oil.

The history of the Icelandic nation and the Icelandic language goes back to Viking explorations 1,000 years ago. However, the economic history of the Republic of Iceland is relatively short. After almost 500 years of Danish colonial rule, Iceland received sovereignty in 1918 and declared independence in 1944. Iceland soon emerged as a prosperous Scandinavian-style welfare state. In 2007, Iceland ranked number one on the United Nations Human Development Index and was listed as the fifth richest nation in the world as measured by GDP per capita (on purchasing power parity basis).

The source of prosperity was primarily a highly literate population and rich maritime resources from the North Atlantic Ocean. The key industries in Iceland have historically been fishing and renewable energy resources, though most of the growth as of the 1990s was in the service sector. The traditional source of growth for the Icelandic economy was the export driven fishing industry and the geothermal-based hydro fuel sector. The energy sector attracted foreign investment centered on energy intensive operations, such as aluminum smelting. Agriculture and manufacturing is limited and most consumer goods are imported. Trade accounts for largest share of the GDP, with fish and other marine products being the key export products. Product development and entrepreneurship related to the maritime industry has given rise to a few successful internationally focused small- to medium-sized companies. Several Icelandic software development companies have achieved success through international sales.

As for political background, during World War II Iceland was occupied by UK forces in defense against Nazi Germany, later replaced by the US military during the Cold War. In the 1990s, after the threat from the Soviet Union was no longer real, US forces pulled away from Iceland. Strong ties remained with the Scandinavian nations and political and economic ties with Europe were further pursued. The political climate was characterized by social democracy, personal freedom, general welfare, and a relatively high level of regulation when it came to business and finance.

Until the 1980s, along with other major industries, banking was primarily state owned and directed. The history of banking in Iceland goes back to the beginning of the 20th century, when the state controlled Landsbanki Islands (the National Bank of Iceland) was established and the currency (Icelandic Krona) was developed. Landsbanki issued all bank notes until a traditional central bank was established in 1961. The roots of a private banking system go back to the early 1980s with the establishment of a free capital market, which gave rise to private banks and brokerage firms. In 1990, Glitnir Bank was established through a merger of smaller privately held banks, and in 2002 the largest brokerage firm in the nation, Kaupthing, was granted a commercial banking license. Deregulation and

This case was written by Eydis Olsen (Drexel University). © Eydis Olsen. Reprinted with permission.

privatization in the banking industry took place gradually throughout the 1990s and was completed in 2003. During the transition period, the relatively newly established banks competed with the dominant Landsbanki, using aggressive international expansion.

Once fully privatized, the former state owned bank followed suit. The relatively unregulated Icelandic financial sector and a global environment of easily available credit instruments provided a fertile ground for creative investment bankers and ambitious business people. The banking sector grew faster than any other sector of the economy. By 2008 banking assets were almost ten times the size of GDP. All three of Iceland's major banks had overseas branches and subsidiaries. Most notably, Landsbanki had marketed its Icesave deposit accounts to British, Dutch, and German customers. Because Landsbanki used its own branches, rather than locally established subsidiaries, they were able to offer its foreign customers Icelandic interest rates on the accounts. This also meant that Icelandic deposit insurance was expected to cover the foreign depositors. The Icesave accounts alone had accumulated foreign deposits worth roughly 70% of Iceland's GDP.

The idea of privatization was generally accepted by the population in the late 1980s and the early 1990s, particularly in light of the fact that Iceland had been one of the most regulated (although democratic) economies of Europe. The global trend was towards deregulation, increased openness to trade and investment, and the principles of a market economy. Prior to the move towards privatization, prices on consumer goods and services, from basic food items to telecommunication and transportation, were extremely high. Increased openness and competition delivered a clear benefit to the average consumer. When it came to wealth accumulation resulting from privatization, the first beneficiaries included only a few families. First to mention are individuals who were associated with the members of the political party that stood in the forefront of privatization, including the owners and directors of major industries. Second, the individual beneficiaries of the privatization in the maritime industry were given private rights to fishing quotas, which could be bought, sold, and used as collateral on loans. Third, a new generation of entrepreneurial "Vikings" embraced the ease of obtaining credit in international financial markets. At the same time, the currency was strong and this enabled Icelandic firms to expand internationally through acquisitions in various business sectors, including retail and real estate. Icelandic companies grew extensively in Denmark and the UK through mergers and acquisitions of major

retail chains including House of Fraiser, Karen Millen, and Hainleys Toys. Even one of Britain's soccer teams, West Ham United of London, was acquired by an Icelandic banking tycoon. There seemed to be plenty of wealth to go around.

Iceland's Economic Meltdown

In the years prior to the crisis, although the banking sector was extremely large compared to the size of the economy, the banks appeared to be well funded. What became apparent was that the banks were dependent on borrowing aggressively in international capital markets. At the same time, Iceland's high interest rates and strong sovereign rating had attracted foreign investments funds. The balance of payments was positive and the government was debt free.

The prelude to the crisis included a downgrade in sovereign debt rating in the spring of 2008. Major credit rating agencies and investor services, including Moody's and Fitch, lowered the credit rating. The reasons for the downgrade included the concern over the government having to cover the bank debts, reduced ability of the government to obtain funding under plausible stress conditions, and concerns over economic stability. The downgrade led to capital flight due to the loss of confidence in the economy and the currency. The Icelandic Krona (a free floating currency as of 2001) weakened by 35% against the US dollar and 20% against the euro in the six months prior to October 2008. To counter the capital flight, Iceland raised the interest rates. By the time of the collapse, interest rates were at 15%. With the departure of foreign deposits and diminished ability to obtain foreign currency loans, the private banks looked to the Icelandic Central Bank as a lender of last resort.

In October 2008, a series of events led to the official burst of the Icelandic economic bubble. The banks had serious liquidity problems that resulted in the Icelandic government essentially nationalizing the three major banks under emergency law. The first takeover was in response to Glitnir's plea for help from the Central Bank. In the days to follow, the remaining internationally active banks were taken over by the Iceland's Financial Supervisory Authority (FSA), which is an independent state authority responsible for regulating and supervising the financial sector. The operations were transferred to new bank entities, fully owned by the Icelandic government.

When it became evident that there was severe trouble in the banking sector, the negative reaction by markets quickly made the situation worse. There was a run on the currency and the Krona weakened by 70% against major currencies in a matter of days.

As the Icelandic government struggled with its newly acquired liability, which was many times the size of the Central Bank's reserves, Icesave deposit account holders panicked as it was not clear whether the Icelandic government was able to guarantee its deposits. The British government reacted by offering Icesave account holders its own government protection. But it froze the assets of Icelandic banks and companies in the UK under a law which had been enacted post-9/11 for the purpose of combating terrorism. The Icelandic banks were cut off from international credit card and ATM systems, leaving Icelandic citizens abroad unable to access their accounts for several days. Krona-based currency trading was suspended temporarily but later resumed with strict limits.

Seeking Solutions

Essentially, Iceland was bankrupt. Since national bankruptcy is not a real option, a contingency plan was in dire need. The first step in seeking solutions was to find a way for Iceland's citizens and businesses to import necessities and the best prospect for immediate help was the International Monetary Fund (IMF). The IMF approved a $2.1 billion loan, which went directly into foreign exchange reserves in an attempt to strengthen the currency. Northern European neighbors, Norway and Sweden, also provided assistance. Therefore, a month after the collapse, Iceland became the first developed nation in over 30 years to accept an emergency loan from the IMF.

The IMF, which has received strong criticism for its track record with many developing nations, went through a reform in 2006. The strings attached to the IMF loan to Iceland included fiscal tightening and some systematic cut-backs in welfare spending. Negotiating a payback to the British and Dutch governments for the guarantee on the Iceesave accounts was another contingency. However, since the debt burden and the financial crisis was originally private sector driven, the primary focus on was on stabilizing the currency and getting the economy back on track. By the recommendation of the IMF, interest rates were increased to 18% to prevent capital flight. Currency restrictions remained in place but the IMF issued recommendations to gradually ease controls.

The economic crisis soon became a political issue. Iceland has a parliamentary political system, where the political party with the majority vote is in power, led by the Prime Minister, though with a President as a ceremonial head of state and last resort veto power. The economic crisis was soon met by political turmoil and persistent (non-violent though) citizen protests. In February 2009, an interim government was appointed

by the President, following the resignation of the previous government. Protests that mainly consisted of concerned citizens banging pots and pans in a steady rhythm outside the parliament house might not have been the cause, but contributed to the resignation of the right wing, economically liberal government of the late 1990s through 2008.

A national election in April 2009 resulted in a coalition government of Social Democrats and the Left Green Party, with the conservative Independence Party in government opposition. Notably, the new government included representatives from the newly formed Citizens Party led by leaders of the "pot and pan revolution." The new coalition government faced the task of negotiating the repayment of the Iceasave account government guarantee to the British and Dutch governments, both of which had made good on deposits for their citizens. This was not only a condition of getting further IMF assistance, but also crucial to maintain integrity as a nation. Moreover, the new government faced the task of seeking a viable long-term solution for the citizens of Iceland who had been left with an unimaginable debt burden.

In October 2009, Iceland passed the first review by the IMF as the economy showed more resilience than expected and as a deal had been reached for the repayment of the Icesave loans. An IMF press release following the review stated that "creditors must be treated fairly and equably, in line with applicable law, but it also remains imperative for the government not to further absorb losses from the private sector." At the time of this writing (January 2010), there is an end in sight to the short-term solution of preventing shortages. However, a long-term solution is not clear.

In an attempt to replace the failed currency, Icelandic officials approached the European Union (EU) with the idea of taking up the euro as the official currency. Iceland is already a member of the European Free Trade Area (EFTA) consisting of the EU on the one hand and Switzerland, Norway, Liechtenstein, and Iceland on the other hand. Iceland is also a member of the European Economic Area (EEA), which is a common market between the EU, Norway, Liechtenstein, and Iceland. Prior to the crisis, Iceland had never applied for EU membership due to popular opposition rooted in the fear of lost sovereignty and the potential economic consequences of giving up exclusive fishing rights in the North Atlantic Ocean. After learning that there is "no back door" for taking up the euro and the only way to replace the Krona with the euro would be to become a full member of the EU, Iceland submitted an application for membership in July 2009. In order to become an EU member, a prospect nation must meet a set of criteria for democracy, human rights, and economic conditions as well as the willingness to take on the EU's treaties and shared policies. Prospects for acceptance are relatively positive, as Iceland is a long-standing democracy with respect for human rights. The economic conditions, though severe for Iceland, are not likely to have an impact on the EU as a whole. As a member of the EEA, Iceland has already adopted the majority of EU legislation and the "four freedoms" of the EU—free movement of people, goods, services, and capital. However, the common fisheries policy of the EU, Icelandic fishing territory, and fishing quotas as well as the right to exploration for oil in the Atlantic Ocean will be difficult issues to resolve.

More than a year after the crisis, Iceland's credit rating has been further downgraded. Interest rates have been lowered to 12%, currency restrictions are still in place though they have been eased from the beginning of the crisis. The Icelandic nation struggles to adjust to the reality of an overleveraged future while seeking viable solutions.

Case Discussion Questions:

1. Is there a link between the US sub-prime crisis and the Icelandic financial crisis?
2. How could the Icelandic financial crisis have been avoided?
3. Why is political and economic sovereignty so important to Iceland?
4. If you were the head of state, what steps would you take to get the Icelandic economy back on track?
5. What are some of the business opportunities created by the crisis?
6. On Ethics: How did the financial crisis and the IMF bailout affect an ordinary Icelandic citizen, such as a teacher, nurse, or police officer? Was the increase in interest rates and the transfer of private debt to the taxpayer "fair"?

Sources: Based on (1) Central Bank of Iceland, www.sedlabanki.is (2) J. Jackson, 2008, Iceland's Financial Crisis, CRC Report to Congress, November 20; (3) Á. Jónsson, 2009, *Why Iceland? How One of the World's Smallest Countries became the Meltdown's Biggest Casualty*, New York: McGraw-Hill; (4) G. Magnússon, Professor of Economics at the University of Iceland, currently Iceland's Minister of Industry, interviewed by the author, November 20, 2008; (5) www.ruv.is; (6) www.mbl.is.

INTEGRATIVE CASE 2.2

SOYBEANS IN CHINA

Liu Yi and Yang Wei, *Xi'an Jiaotong University, China*

Although soybeans were first grown in China, China's comparative advantage eroded recently. What does the future hold for this industry?

Soybeans were first grown in China over 5,000 years ago and today China is the world's largest producer of non-genetically modified (GM) soybeans. China's Northeast region (Manchuria), the Inner Mongolian Autonomous Region, and the Yellow River and Huaihai River valleys are some of the most advantageous locations in the world to grow soybeans.

In 1938, the soybean growing area in China reached 9.07 million hectares and the total output was 12.1 million tons, accounting for 93% of the world output. Since then, other countries have caught up, with the United States, Brazil, and Argentina all progressing greatly. Soybean production is concentrated in Asia and the Americas, accounting for 96% of total area and 90% of total output. At present, the United States, Brazil, China, and Argentina are the world's top four soybean producing countries (in that order), with North America accounting for 45% total area and 49% output, followed by Latin America and Asia.

Soybeans in China: From Exporter to Importer

As economic growth increases, so does the demand of soybean production. Before 1995, China was a net exporting country of soybeans. However, since 1996, it has become a net import country. From 2003 to 2005, the annual import amount was more than 20 million tons. In 2005, while China produced 17.8 million tons, it imported 26.6 million tons, which accounted for one-third of global trade. China thus became the largest soybean importing country. Experts estimate that by 2020, China will need to import 36 million tons of soybeans—in other words, about 80% of China's soybeans will be imported.

Unfortunately, this strong increase in demand brings no benefits to the soybean farmers in China. In 2005, the acreage of soybean planting in the Heilongjiang province decreased from 108 million mu[1] to 82 million mu, a 24% decrease from the previous year.

During the same period, the soybean acreage in the Inner Mongolian Autonomous Region also decreased by 17%, from 28 million mu in 2004 to 23 million mu in 2005. At the same time, soybean supplies stockpiled due to low prices. Many farmers who had planted and harvested soybeans with the expectation of increased income instead lost profits. For example, in the Heilongjiang province, which had the largest acreage and highest output of soybeans, the average sales price was only $0.271 per kilogram, which was lower than the farmers' cost. Consequently, farmers in Heilongjiang collectively lost $419 million, had incentive to reduce output, and the number of unemployed soybean farmers soared to approximately 1.2 million.

Subsidies and Imports

While soybean farmers suffer, farmers who grow wheat and corn are "luckier." To encourage farmers' enthusiasm toward these commodities, the government offers subsidies every year. For example, in 2005, the Henan provincial government gave $1.23 for every mu of wheat grown, resulting in $3.6 million of total subsidies to wheat farmers in the province. In 2006, the Beijing municipality government adjusted its subsidies for corn growers upward to $1.88 per mu. One county government in the Chongqing municipality announced that it would subsidize $0.64 per mu to wheat growers in 2007. At the national level, the central government uses strategic storage of wheat and corn to ensure that sales prices farmers command are not lower than minimum prices. In contrast, subsidies for soybeans are negligible.

Falling soybean prices and the rise of imports also affect downstream soybean oil processing firms. No. 93 Seed-Oil Corporation was set up by one of the state-owned farms in Heilongjiang in China's Northeast (Manchuria) with the specific purpose of absorbing and processing soybeans produced by farms in the province. The annual soybean output of Heilongjiang province is about six million tons, and the company purchases two million tons (1/3 of the

This case was written by Professor Liu Yi and Yang Wei (both at Xi'an Jiaotong University, Xi'an, China) for teaching purposes. The authors thank Professor Mike Peng and Erin Pleggenkuhle-Miles for editorial assistance on the English version. © Liu Yi and Yang Wei. Reprinted with permission. A Chinese version is available upon request from the authors. Please email Professor Liu at liuyi@mail.xjtu.edu.cn.

EXHIBIT 1   SOYBEAN PRODUCTION, CONSUMPTION, AND IMPORTS IN CHINA

Year	Planting area (million hectare)	Output (million tons)	Consumption (million tons)	Import (million tons)	Domestic purchase price($/kg)	Import price ($/kg)
1998	8.500	15.152	22.020	3.196	0.273	0.181
1999	7.962	14.245	26.290	4.317	0.297	0.183
2000	9.299	15.300	31.810	10.420	0.261	0.193
2001	8.700	15.000	30.700	13.940	0.266	0.242
2002	8.720	16.507	32.690	11.320	0.267	0.220
2003	9.133	16.400	37.900	20.740	0.346	0.312
2004	9.600	18.000	38.150	20.229	0.326	0.338
2005	9.103	17.800	40.000	26.590	0.331	0.278

Source: http://www.93.com.cn.

total output from that province). Yet, even such a firm crucial to soybean production and processing in the Northeast had to yield to the pressures from the rise of imports. In 2004, five of its soybean oil processing subsidiaries in the Northeast went bankrupt. As a result, two new subsidiaries were built in 2005: one in Tianjin and another in Dalian. However, both of these new soybean oil processing subsidiaries exclusively used *imported* soybeans, which commanded more than half of all the soybeans processed by No. 93 Seed-Oil Corporation.

Aside from the lack of subsidies, one crucial reason that domestic soybeans are not as competitive as imports is because soybeans are primarily grown in China's Northeast, whereas soybean oil processing companies concentrate along the coast. If No. 93 Seed-Oil Corporation used locally grown soybeans, taking into account transportation, storage, and capital requirements, the cost of domestic soybeans is $20.54 more than imported soybeans per ton. Because of economies of scale, industrialized production, foreign government subsidies, and topographical and climatic conditions, the cost of imported soybeans is far lower than that of domestic soybeans. In 2003, the production cost of soybeans per ton in the United States was $168, in Brazil $119, and in China $192. Exhibit 1 has more detailed comparison of prices between domestic and imported soybeans in recent years.

More than half of this huge difference in price can be attributed to agriculture subsidies. Among the 30 OECD members, the ratio of agriculture subsidies (percentage of subsidies over total agricultural income) varies tremendously (see Exhibit 2). While in many competing countries agricultural subsidy ratios

EXHIBIT 2   AGRICULTURAL SUBSIDIES

Country	Subsidy ratio[a]
Switzerland	71%
Iceland	69%
Norway	68%
South Korea	63%
Japan	56%
European Union	33%
Canada	21%
United States	18%
China	8.5%

[a] Subsidy ratio = percentage of subsidies over total agricultural income.

are over 20%, in China the overall agricultural subsidy ratio is only 8.5%, as pledged by the government's commitment to the WTO in 2001.

The quality of soybeans depends on the quantity of oil that can be extracted from the bean. A 1% variance can lead to a profit difference of $1.9 million for every 100,000 tons of soybeans produced. At present, the ratio of oil extraction from domestic soybeans is only 16%–17%, which is 2%–3% lower than imported soybeans. Not surprisingly, when confronting higher prices and lower quality domestic soybeans, oil processing firms in China, such as No. 93 Seed-Oil Corporation, choose to import soybeans.

International Competition

In the international agricultural market for basic foodstuffs such as soybeans, about 80% of the market share is dominated by four *Fortune* Global

500 companies: Archer Daniels Midland (ADM), Bunge, and Cargill of the United States and Louis Dreyfus of France—collectively known as "ABCD." Since 2005, these multinational firms have intensified their acquisitions in the Chinese soybean oil processing industry. In 2000, the number of Chinese soybean oil processing firms exceeded 1,000. In 2006, there were only 90—64 of which were wholly or partially controlled by foreign investors. These 64 foreign-invested firms command 85% of the production capability.

In 2005, Baogang Seed-Oil Corporation, once a leading seed oil manufacturing company in Jiangsu province, declared bankruptcy as a result of capital shortage. The company could not pay its debt, so the Nantong municipality government authorized it to be leased by Cargill. However, employees clearly knew that the "lease" was just a transition form, and that the company's eventual fate would be an acquisition by Cargill. In addition to acquisitions, foreign firms are also shifting some attention to soybean research. For example, Kwok Brothers Corporation of Singapore held talks with the Academy of Agricultural Sciences in Heilongjiang province, hoping that the Academy would license the output of its research to the Singapore company. By popularizing the new breed of soybeans pioneered by the Academy, the Singapore company hoped to be able to purchase such soybeans directly from farmers when harvested, and then to gradually monopolize the soybean industry of Heilongjiang province (and perhaps even the whole country).

The Soybean Value Chain

An extensive industry value chain can be derived from soybeans. First, soybeans can be made into a variety of food products, including tofu and other bean curd–based products, soy milk, and soy-protein drinks. Second, oil can be pressed from soybeans. Finally, the soybean oil extraction process generates a by-product, soybean residue, which contains abundant proteins. Soybean residue is a main ingredient in animal feed for livestock and poultry. Animal feed, in turn, connects soybeans with livestock and poultry production, another crucial component of the agricultural industry.

Nowadays, foreign direct investment (FDI) has mainly penetrated the soybean oil production process (other than some attempts to be involved in upstream production as noted above). What is the attitude of other players in the soybean value chains toward FDI? Consider Qinghe Technology, Ltd., a large animal-feed producer. Because soybean residue represents 60% of the raw materials used in production, the market price of soybeans directly affects the company's production cost. Obviously, the low price of imported soybeans makes Qinghe happy. Therefore, managers in the animal feed industry are interested in more imported soybeans.

The Future of Soybeans in China

As the country that proudly pioneered soybean production, China has been producing non-GM soybeans for more than 5000 years. Except for Qinghai province, soybeans are grown everywhere in China, and the variety of soybean categories in China is the most complete in the world. We can say, without exaggeration, that China cultivates soybeans, and in turn, soybeans nurture our country. At present, soybeans are at a crucial historical crossroads between progress and decline. Fortunately, on October 1, 2006, the central government passed new regulations on the labeling standards of edible oil, requiring that "GM-based" or "non-GM-based" soybeans be clearly labeled for consumers. Can this "institutional change" in the rules of the game governing soybean oil labeling and consumption bring new hope to domestic soybeans?

Case Discussion Questions:

1. Does China have an absolute or comparative advantage in soybean production?
2. In China, what is the current crisis of the soybean industry? Do you think the government should or should not intervene? If intervention is called for, what measures should be taken?
3. What difficulties do Chinese soybean farmers face? How can they compete with international producers?
4. Will the new labeling standards for non-GM-based soybeans used for edible oil production have any impact on domestic Chinese soybeans?
5. Facing the imminent wave of consolidations led by FDI, what can the soybean oil processing companies do to promote locally grown soybeans? Is this their responsibility?

NOTE

[1] Mu is the standard Chinese unit for acreage. The conversion is: 1 mu = 1/15 hectare = 1/6 acre.

INTEGRATIVE CASE 2.3

DP WORLD

C. Gopinath, *Suffolk University*

Why was DP World's foreign direct investment in US ports unable to sail through?

On February 13, 2006, the shareholders of Peninsular & Oriental Steam Navigation Co., of London (P&O) confirmed the sale of their company to DP World (Dubai Ports World). Through this act, the management of port operations in five US ports also came under DP World's purview. On March 9, DP World announced that it would divest the US port operations.

The intervening 25 days saw a flurry of activity in the US with politicians of all shades of opinion, news programs, administration officials, and assorted experts debating the pros and cons of the deal. The outcome of the deal was seen to have much larger implications than mere port management. It raised issues of national security, the investments of petrodollars around the world, US policy towards foreign investment, political risk, and the attitudes of Americans towards the Arabs.

A Dubai Company

Since 1999, DP World, a Dubai-government owned company, had begun a strategy of aggressive growth. With the acquisition of P&O, it became the world's third largest port operator, with operations in 13 countries, including China, India, Germany, Australia, UK, and the Dominican Republic. The acquisition of P&O was the successful outcome of a bidding war against Singapore's Temasek Holdings for $6.8 billion. (Being privately owned, DP World's revenues and profit figures are not publicly accessible.)

Dubai is the second largest of a federation of seven semi-autonomous city states, which became the United Arab Emirates in 1971. It has a population of about 4 million, of whom only about 20% are citizens. Like most of the other countries in the region, Dubai depends on a large number of expatriate workers from South Asia (India, Pakistan, and Bangladesh) to run the country. It has also attracted a number of British, Australian, and Americans who have come to work or retire.

Dubai attempts to balance the demands on its being a Middle Eastern state with its desire to play a larger role in the world. The UAE is a part of the boycott of Israel called by the Arab League since the early 1990s, although it ignores the boycott in practice. It also does not recognize US sanctions against Iran. As the UAE does not have any direct links with Israel, products are not shipped directly from Israel, but are allowed to enter from third countries.

Unlike some of its neighboring states, Dubai gets only a small share of its income from oil, and has worked hard over the years to build the country as a business hub and tourism destination. It does not have income taxes. Dubai is a popular shopping center in the region with glitzy malls, extravagant hotels, and amusement parks. All major luxury brands of the world have outlets there. Apart from tourism, Dubai is also the regional headquarters of many of the world's large financial institutions. Dubai has built its port to world class levels, and it also operates the biggest airline of the area, Emirates Air. More than 500 US companies operate in the UAE.

The Dubai government has been using its oil revenues to make major investments around the world. It has purchased hotels and property in the US and UK. It recently purchased a $1 billion stake in DaimlerChrysler AG, and became the third largest shareholder.[1]

Given its strategic geographic location and small size, the country has tried to maintain good relations with countries in the region and outside. It stayed neutral during the Iran-Iraq war in the 1980s. The UAE is considered a key ally by the US administration. It cooperates militarily, hosting US naval vessels since its ports are capable of receiving large aircraft carriers and nuclear submarines. It also has an airbase for refueling US military planes. On the other hand, two of the hijackers who participated in the September 11, 2001, terrorist attacks in the US were from the UAE. Even before that, it was one of three countries (apart from Pakistan and Saudi Arabia) that officially recognized the Taliban regime in Afghanistan. The UAE was also seen as a transit point for Iran and Pakistan to move contraband

This case was written by C. Gopinath (Suffolk University, Boston, MA). © C. Gopinath. Reprinted with permission of the author.

nuclear materials and its banking facilities are believed to be used by terrorist groups. After the terrorist attacks, the country had worked hard to strengthen controls on its financial system.

Investment in US Ports

Through this purchase, the operations by P&O in five ports in the US passed on to DP World's hands. These included: New York/New Jersey, Philadelphia, Baltimore, Miami, and New Orleans. Of these, the New York/New Jersey and Miami terminals are considered the more attractive ones, and in these two, P&O shared ownership with other operators. Apart from the five marine terminal operations, P&Os operations in the US include cargo handling and cruise ship services in 22 ports in the US.[2]

The management of the five ports was not the first venture of DP World in the US. In a previous deal, DP World had purchased the international terminal business of CSX Corp. of Jacksonville, Florida, for $1.15 billion, in December 2004.

All foreign investment in the US needs to be approved by the Committee on Foreign Investment in the US (CFIUS). The late 1980s saw a lot of debate in the US about increasing Japanese investments. In response, US Congress passed the Omnibus Trade and Competitiveness Act of 1988 (Exon-Florio Amendment) to amend the Defense Production Act of 1950 which empowered the President to block foreign acquisition proposals on grounds of national security. This role was assigned to CFIUS.

CFIUS comes under the Department of Treasury and is an interagency committee chaired by the Treasury Secretary. There are 12 members including the Secretaries of State, Defense, Commerce, and Homeland Security, Attorney General, Director of the Office of Management and Budget, US Trade Representative, Chairman of the Council of Economic Advisers, Assistant to the President for Economic Policy, Assistant to the President for National Security, and Director of the Office of Science and Technology. On receipt of notification, it undertakes a 30-day review, and in some cases, an additional 45-day period for investigation is allowed, after which it makes a recommendation to the President. The committee since 1988 had reviewed about 1,600 transactions. Of these, only about 25 were investigated further.

In mid-October 2005, even before formally approaching P&O about the acquisition, DP World retained the services of two lawyers in Washington, DC, to informally negotiate with CFIUS and seek their approval. This is normal practice, and often a lot of the work involved in such reviews are undertaken even before a formal application. After completing the deal with P&O and the deal was formally announced, DP World, in mid-November 2005, made its formal application to CFIUS and was approved on January 16, 2006. The company, at that time, also put forward a package of commitments on security, such as allowing US officials to examine company records and check the background of its employees, and to separate the port terminal operations from the rest of the company.

When information about the deal appeared in the press, Eller & Co., a stevedoring company in Miami that had a joint venture with P&O, decided it did not want to be an "involuntary partner" of DP World pursuant to the acquisition.[3] Therefore, Eller retained the services of a lobbyist in Washington, Mr. Joe Muldoon, who began researching the issues involved in the P&O acquisition and contacted several legislators in February, when they returned from their January recess. One of those senators was Mr. Charles Schumer, a Democrat from New York (where one of the ports is situated) and a member on the Banking Committee in the Senate. Meanwhile, the Associated Press also contacted Mr. Schumer, and issued a report making a connection between the acquisition, the country of Dubai, terrorists, and the vulnerability of the ports to terrorism.[4]

Politicians of different hues were quick to react to the deal. Mr. Schumer addressed a press conference along with the families of those who suffered from the terrorist attack on September 11, 2001, calling the President to step in and prevent the deal. On February 17, Senator Hillary Clinton, the other senator from New York and also a Democrat, said, "Our port security is too important to place in the hands of foreign governments." Even Republicans (the same party as the President) were opposed to the deal, saying "Dubai can't be trusted with our critical infrastructure" and another saying "It is my intention to lay the foundation to block the deal."[5] Senator Lindsey Graham (Republican) said, "It's unbelievably tone-deaf politically . . . four years after 9/11, to entertain the idea of turning port security over to a company based in the UAE, [a country that] vows to destroy Israel."[6]

Some political observers felt that the President's low standing in public opinion polls due to dissatisfaction on the progress in the war in Iraq was making some Republican lawmakers challenge, and distance themselves from, him in preparation for their own re-election battles in November 2006.

News commentators began to raise alarms about the deal. On the same day that P&O announced its purchase, Lou Dobbs, a business anchor on CNN News Channel said, "a country with ties to the Sept. 11

terrorists could soon be running significant operations at some of our most important and largest seaports with full blessing of the Bush White House."[7] Mr. Dobbs was known for taking a nationalist position on issues like immigration, outsourcing, and the effects on jobs in the US. Several radio talk shows picked up the story filling the airwaves with different interpretations. Moreover, many among the public and security professionals who had been concerned that the government had not been doing enough for port safety and scanning of containers found the ports takeover as another example of a government that was slackening on security.

In an effort to manage the debate around the deal, the administration clarified that it had asked and received additional security commitments from DP World before giving its clearance. An Israeli shipping company, ZIM Integrated Shipping Services Ltd., even sent a letter to US senators stating that they have used the services of DP World at Dubai and have had no concern about their level of security.[8]

Officials also clarified that security screening was not the responsibility of the commercial port operators but that of US law enforcement agents. However, the misperception that the Middle East company would be responsible for port security persisted in the public impression and was repeated in talk shows.

Ports and Container Operations

Container shipping was pioneered by a US company, Sea Land, in the 1950s. However, during the 1980s, US companies found it difficult to face the competition from companies that were operating under flags of convenience, were thus subject to less stringent tax and regulatory policies, and also used cheaper cost labor. The shipping industry has been globalized for some time now. None of the major global container shipping company is US owned. Shipping companies often have subsidiaries to manage terminals, in order to facilitate the cargo they carry.

Most ports are owned by port authorities that are set up by local governments. The authorities lease a terminal to an individual company, which is responsible for port management and operations such as moving the containers from the ships to the warehouses.

Large ports have multiple terminals and these are operated by different companies. US companies have exited from this business over time as it requires heavy investment and returns are seen only over the long term. At the Los Angeles port, the terminals are managed by companies from China, Denmark, Japan, Singapore, and Taiwan. The big ports of the US, namely, Los Angeles, Long Beach, and Oakland in California

and New York/New Jersey handle about half of all containers that pass through the US. At these ports, about 80% of the container terminals are handled by foreign companies, some of whom are owned by foreign governments.

The purchase of P&O by DP World would give it control over terminal operations at New York/New Jersey, Philadelphia, Baltimore, Miami, and New Orleans. Other terminals in these ports are run by other companies, some of whom are foreign.

Companies that manage terminals were often subsidiaries of shipping companies. About 80% of global cargo was handled by five companies around the world, headquartered in Hong Kong (Hutchison Whampoa), Singapore (PSA), Dubai (DP World), Denmark (APMoler Maersk Terminals), and Germany (Eurogate).

Security[9]

Regardless of who operates the terminal, whether a US or a foreign company, security at the ports including inspection of containers is the responsibility of federal agencies such as the US Coast Guard and the US Customs and Border Protection. The Coast Guard is also authorized to inspect a vessel at sea or at the harbor entrance. About 26,000 containers arrive at US ports every day and customs agents inspect about 5% of them. About 37% of containers that leave the ports for the highways are screened. Security in the area surrounding the ports are part of the responsibility of the local police.

There are several areas that can do with strengthening to improve security and they have very little to do with who manages port operations. There is a voluntary program operated by the US government to protect incoming shipments. Many companies have signed up for this, under which the companies develop voluntary security procedures to protect the shipment from the factory to the port. In return, their cargo is processed at a faster pace at the port. Shipments from companies that don't take part in the program may not always be inspected. Even those who do participate, security is not perfect as the cargo may be open to tampering in transit.

About 40 ports around the world ship about 80% of the cargo entering the US. At the port of shipment, the carrier is required to electronically provide the manifest (list of items being shipped) at least 24 hours before loading. This list is analyzed in a screening center in the US and Customs Agents who identify any suspicious items can ask their counterparts at the port of dispatch to screen the containers. However, US Government Accountability Office reports that as of

2005 about one third of the containers were not being analyzed, and about 25% of those identified as high-risk were not being inspected. Scanners and radiation detectors to screen every single container are available and their use was estimated to add about $20 to the container.

Opposition Gathers Momentum

Faced with rising criticism, DP World also had a crew of lobbyists and attorneys working on its behalf in Washington. Officials of the UAE embassy were also working closely with people like Senator John Warner (Republican) who was in favor of the deal. Legislation was also being planned to allow the deal subject to conditions such as the terminals being operated by US citizens.

When some members of Congress threatened to pass legislation blocking the sale, President Bush responded on February 21 by saying that he would veto it. He also said that he learned about the deal only after it was approved by his administration. Expressing concern about the implications of the deal, he was quoted as saying, "I want those who are questioning to step up and explain why all of a sudden a Middle Eastern company is held to a different standard that a [British] company. I am trying to [say] to the people of the world, 'We'll treat you fairly.'"[10]

By end of February, a CBS News Poll revealed that 70% of participants said that a UAE company should not be permitted to operate US shipping ports. With political objections mounting, DP World, on February 26, requested a fresh 45-day review of the deal and offered to hold the American operations separate until the review was completed. The administration agreed to undertake the review.

Although the Administration had taken a hard stand initially in supporting the deal, the opposition from within the President's party was strong. Both the leader of the party in the Senate (upper house) and the Speaker (in the lower house) were opposed to the President on the issue.

Although the US operations only accounted for about 10% of P&O's profits, DP World was keen on making the deal work. The US operations of the company was the destination of cargo from its more significant holdings in Asia and the company wanted this as a foothold to expand its US operations in the future. Its CEO, Mr. Ted Bilkey, told a US news channel, "We'll do anything possible to make sure this deal goes through."[11]

In keeping with this, the company, on March 7, offered three Republican senators a package of security measures titled "Proposed solution to the DP World Issue."[12] These proposals, which were in addition to the commitments the company made earlier in January, included:

- Paying for screening devices at all current and future ports the company operates around the world.
- Giving the Department of Homeland Security the right to disapprove the choice of Chief Executive, board members, security officials, and all senior officers.
- A "supermajority" of the board would be US citizens.
- All records pertaining to its security operations would be maintained on US soil and these records would be turned over at the request of the US government.
- Its US subsidiary, now managed by a UK citizen, would in the future also only be headed by a US or UK citizen.
- A Security and Financial Oversight Board would be established headed by a prominent American which would report annually to the Department of Homeland Security.

Some observers felt that this was truly extraordinary for a foreign company to offer. Although such an offer, if made earlier, may have swayed the debate, by the time it came, positions had already hardened. On March 8, the House Appropriations Committee voted 62 to 2 to block the DP World deal. To make the President's threat of a veto more difficult, the Committee attached this as an amendment to a spending bill for the wars in Iraq and Afghanistan. The next day, the Republican congressional leaders conveyed to the President that Congress would kill the deal.

The Bush administration then conveyed a request to Dubai's ruler to sever the US operations in order to allay fears in the US about security. Officials in the UAE saw this as a situation where President Bush was incurring a loss of face in his dealings with the Congress. Consequently, DP World on March 9, 2006 offered to divest the US port operations.

Case Discussion Questions:

1. From a resource-based view, why was DP World interested in acquiring US ports? What advantages did it have or was it interested in acquiring?
2. From an institution-based view, did this acquisition violate any *formal* laws, rules, or regulations?
3. Also from an institution-based view, what *informal* rules and norms did this acquisition "violate" that triggered such a strong negative reaction in the United States?

4. Did DP World and its American lawyers and other advisors do their homework properly beforehand?

5. Combining the institution- and resource-based views, what advantages did Eller have that DP World did not have? Did Eller's political strategy make sense?

6. If you were CEO of Hong Kong's Hutchison Whampoa, Singapore's PSA, Denmark's Maersk, or Germany's Eurogate, what lessons would you draw from this case when entertaining the idea of acquiring US port operations?

NOTES

[1] *Wall Street Journal*, 2006, Dubai: Business partner of terrorist hotbed, February 25–26, p. A9.

[2] D. Machalaba, 2006, DP World's ports sale may not pinch, *Wall Street Journal*, March 11–12, p. A6.

[3] P. Overby, 2006, Lobbyist's last-minute bid set off ports controversy, *National Public Radio*, March 8, http://www.npr.org/templates/story/story.php?storyId=5252263.

[4] T. Bridis, 2006, United Arab Emirates firm may oversee 6 US ports, *Washington Post*, February 12, p. A17.

[5] D. E. Sanger, 2006, Under pressure, Dubai company drops port deal, *New York Times*, March 10, p. 1.

[6] Dubai: Business partner of terrorist hotbed.

[7] G. Hitt & S. Ellison, 2006, Dubai firm bows to public outcry, *Wall Street Journal*, March 26, p. A1.

[8] T. Al-Issawi, 2006, Port company ignores boycott, *Boston Globe*, March 3.

[9] Much of the data in this section is from *New York Times*, 2006, Our porous port protections, March 10, p. A18.

[10] Dubai: Business partner of terrorist hotbed.

[11] *Wall Street Journal*, 2006, In ports furor, a clash over Dubai, February 23, p. A1.

[12] N. King, Jr., 2006, DP World tried to soothe US waters, *Wall Street Journal*, March 14, p. A4.

INTEGRATIVE CASE 2.4

COMPETING IN CHINA'S AUTOMOBILE INDUSTRY

Qingjiu (Tom) Tao, *James Madison University*

How do various foreign and domestic automakers compete in the fastest-growing automobile market in the world, which has also recently become the largest market in the world?

For automakers seeking relief from the most severe global recession in decades, China is the only game in town. With just ten vehicles per 1,000 residents in China as of 2006 (as opposed to 940 in the United States and 584 in Western Europe), there seems to be plenty of growth opportunities. Not surprisingly, nearly every major auto company has jumped into China, quickly turning the country into a new battleground for dominance in this global industry. In addition, China has become a major auto parts supplier. Of the world's top 100 auto parts suppliers, 70% have a presence in China.

China vaulted past the United States to become the world's number-one vehicle market in the first 10 months of 2009. Reports of record sales, new production, and new venture formations were plenty. After China's accession to the World Trade Organization (WTO) in 2001, the industry has been advancing by leaps and bounds (see Exhibit 1). Between 2002 and

2007, China's automobile market grew by an average 21%, or one million vehicles year-on-year. At the global level, China has also moved to the first position in production passing the United States and Japan, and is slated to produce 13 million vehicles in 2009. Around 50% of the world's activity in terms of capacity expansion has been seen in China for the last few years.

Because the Chinese government does not approve wholly owned subsidiaries for foreign carmakers (even after the WTO accession), foreign firms interested in final-assembly operations have to set up joint ventures (JVs) or licensing deals with domestic players. By the mid-1990s, most major global auto firms had managed to enter the country through these means (Exhibit 2). Among the European companies, Volkswagen (VW), one of the first entrants (see below), has dominated the passenger car market. In addition, Fiat-Iveco and Citroen are expanding.

Japanese and Korean automakers are relatively late entrants. In 2003, Toyota finally committed $1.3 billion to a 50/50 JV. Guangzhou Honda, Honda's JV, quadrupled its capacity by 2004. Formed in 2003, Nissan's new JV with Dongfeng, which is the same partner for

---

EXHIBIT 1   AUTOMOBILE PRODUCTION VOLUME AND GROWTH RATE IN CHINA (1996–2009)

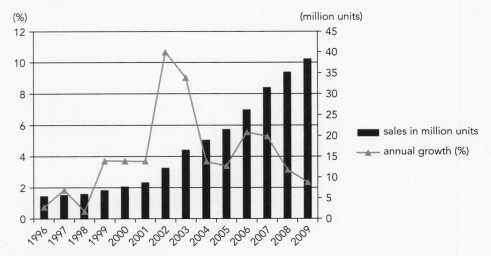

Source: Yearbook of China's Automobile Industry (1996–2009).

This case was written by Qingjiu (Tom) Tao (James Madison University). © Qingjiu (Tom) Tao. Reprinted with permission.

EXHIBIT 2 TIMING AND INITIAL INVESTMENT OF MAJOR CAR PRODUCERS

	Formation	Initial investment ($ million)	Foreign equity	Chinese partner	Foreign partner
Beijing Jeep*	1983	223.93	42.4%	Beijing Auto Works	Daimler, Chrysler
Shanghai Volkswagen	1985	263.41	50%	SAIC	Volkswagen
Guangzhou Peugeot	1985	131.40	22%	Guangzhou Auto Group	Peugeot
FAW VW	1990	901.84	40%	First Auto Works	Volkswagen
Wuhan Shenlong Citroen	1992	505.22	30%	Second Auto Works	Citroen
Shanghai GM	1997	604.94	50%	SAIC	GM
Guangzhou Honda	1998	887.22	50%	Guangzhou Auto Group	Honda
Changan Ford	2001	100.00	50%	Changan Auto Motors	Ford
Beijing Hyundai	2002	338.55	50%	Beijing Auto Group	Hyundai
Tianjin Toyota	2003	1300.00	50%	First Auto Works	Toyota

* Since 2005, the JV formerly called Beijing Jeep has taken the name "Beijing-Benz DaimlerChrysler Automotive Co., Ltd." After DamilerChrysler's divestiture of Chrysler in 2007, the name has remained the same but ownership has been restructured, currently with 25% owned by Daimler, 25% by Chrysler, and 50% by Beijing Auto Works.

the Citroen JV, is positioned to allow Nissan to make a full fledged entry. Meanwhile, Korean auto players are also keen to participate in the China race, with Hyundai and Kia having commenced JV production recently.

American auto companies have also made significant inroads into China. General Motors (GM) has an important JV in Shanghai, whose cumulative investment by 2006 would be $5 billion. Although Ford does not have a high-profile JV as GM, it nevertheless established crucial strategic linkages with several of China's second-tier automakers, such as Changan Auto Group. Chrysler's Beijing Jeep venture, established since the early 1980s, has continued to maintain its presence.

The Evolution of Foreign Direct Investment (FDI) in the Automobile Industry

In the late 1970s, when Chinese leaders started to transform the planned economy to a market economy, they realized that China's roads were largely populated by inefficient, unattractive, and often unreliable vehicles that needed to be replaced. However, importing large quantities of vehicles would be a major drain on the limited hard currency reserves. China thus saw the need to modernize its automobile industry. Attracting FDI through JVs with foreign companies seemed ideal. However, unlike the new China at the dawn of the 21st century that attracted automakers of every stripe, China in the late 1970s and early 1980s was not regarded as attractive by many global automakers.

In the early1980s, Toyota, for example, refused to establish JVs with Chinese firms even when invited by the Chinese authorities (Toyota chose to invest in a more promising market, the United States, in the 1980s). In the first wave, three JVs were established during 1983–84 by VW, American Motors,[1] and Peoguet, in Shanghai, Beijing, and Guangzhou, respectively. These three JVs thus started the three decades of FDI in China's automobile industry.

There are two distinctive phases of FDI activities in China's automobile industry. The first phase is from the early 1980s to the early 1990s, as exemplified by the three early JVs mentioned above. The second phase is from the mid-1990s to present. Because of the reluctance of foreign automakers, only approximately 20 JVs were established by the end of 1989. FDI flows into this industry started to accelerate sharply from 1992. The accumulated number of foreign invested enterprises was 120 in 1993 and skyrocketed to 604 in 1998 with the cumulated investment reaching $20.9 billion.

The boom of the auto market, especially during the early 1990s, brought significant profits to early entrants such as Shanghai VW and Beijing Jeep. The bright prospect attracted more multinationals to invest. This new wave of investment had resulted in an overcapacity. Combined with the changing customer base from primarily selling to fleets (government agencies, state-owned enterprises, and taxi companies) to private buyers, the auto market has turned into a truly competitive arena. The WTO entry in 2001 has further intensified the competition as government regulations weaken. Given the government mandate for JV entries and the limited number of worthy local firms as partners, multinationals have to fight their way in to secure the last few available local partners. By the end of 2002, almost all major Chinese motor vehicle assemblers set up JVs with foreign firms. For numerous foreign automakers which entered China, the road to the Great Wall has been a bumpy and crowded one. Some firms lead, some struggle, and some had to drop out (see Exhibit 3). The leading players are profiled below.

Volkswagen

After long and difficult negotiations that began in 1978, VW in 1984 entered a 50/50 JV with the Shanghai Automotive Industrial Corporation (SAIC) to produce the Santana model using completely knocked down (CKD) kits. The Santana went on to distinguish itself as China's first mass produced modern passenger car. As a result, VW managed to establish a solid market position. Four years later, VW built on its first-mover

advantage and secured a second opening in the China market when the central authorities decided to establish two additional passenger car JVs. After competing successfully against GM, Ford, Nissan, Renault, Peugeot, and Citroen, VW was selected to set up a second JV with the First Auto Works (FAW) in Changchun in northeast China in 1988 for CKD assembly of the Audi 100 and the construction of a state-of-the-art auto plant to produce the VW Jetta in 1990.

Entering the China market in the early 1980s, VW took a proactive approach in spite of great potential risks. The German multinational not only committed enormous financial resources but also practiced a rather bold approach in its dealings in China. This involved a great deal of high-level political interaction with China's central and local government authorities for which the German government frequently lent its official support. Moreover, VW was willing to avail the Chinese partners a broad array of technical and financial resources from its worldwide operations. For example, in 1990 VW allowed FAW a 60% in its JV while furnishing most

EXHIBIT 3   EVOLUTION OF RELATIVE MARKET SHARE AMONG MAJOR AUTO MANUFACTURERS IN CHINA

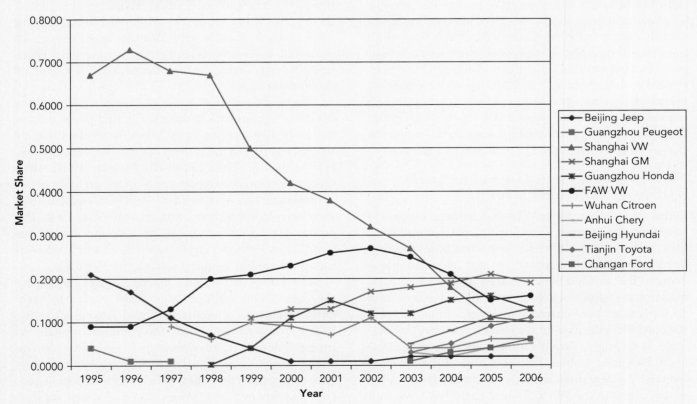

of the manufacturing technology and equipment for its new FAW-Volkswagen Jetta plant in Changchun. Moreover, VW has endeavored to raise the quality of local produced automotive components and parts. For the remainder of the 1980s and most of the 1990s, VW enjoyed significant first mover advantages. With a market share (Shanghai VW and FAW VW combined) of more than 70% for passenger cars over a decade, VW, together with its Chinese partners, benefited considerably from the scarcity of high-quality passenger cars and the persistence of a seller's market.

However, by the late 1990s, the market became a more competitive buyer's market. As the leading incumbent, VW has been facing vigorous challenges brought by its global rivals which by the late 1990s made serious commitments to compete in China. Consequently, VW's passenger car market share in China dropped from over 70% in 1999 to 39% in 2004. In 2005, GM took the number one position in China from VW. How to defend VW's market position thus is of paramount importance.

General Motors

In 1995, GM and SAIC, which was also VW's partner, signed a 50/50, $1.57 billion JV agreement—GM's first JV in China—to construct a greenfield plant in Shanghai. The new plant was designed to produce 100,000 sedans per year, and it was decided to produce two Buick models modified for China. The plant was equipped with the latest automotive machinery and robotics and was furnished with process technology transferred from GM's worldwide operations. Initially, Shanghai GM attracted a barrage of criticisms about the huge size of its investment and the significant commitments to transfer technology and design capabilities to China. These criticisms notwithstanding, GM management reiterated at numerous occasions that China was expected to become the biggest automotive market in the world within two decades and that China represented the single most important emerging market for GM.

Since launching Buick in China in 1998, GM literally started from scratch. Unlike its burdens at home, GM is not saddled with billions in pensions and health-care costs. Its costs are competitive with rivals, its reputation does not suffer, and it does not need to shell out $4,000 per vehicle in incentives to lure new buyers—even moribund brands such as Buick are held in high esteem in China. Consequently, profits are attractive: The $437 million profits GM made in 2003 in China, selling just 386,000 cars, compares favorably with $811 million profits it made in North America

on sales of 5.6 million autos. In 2004, GM had about 10,000 employees in China and operated six JVs and two wholly owned foreign enterprises (which were allowed to be set up more recently in non-final assembly operations). Boasting a combined manufacturing capacity of 530,000 vehicles sold under the Buick, Chevrolet, and Wuling nameplates, GM offers the widest portfolio of products among JV manufacturers in China. In 2009, the bankruptcy filing of GM in the United States had a minimal impact on its China operations. GM vehicle sales in China, its largest overseas market, surged 50% to a monthly record of 151,084 units in April 2009, in contrast with a sharp decline in the United States.

Peugeot

Together with VW and American Motors (the original partner for the Beijing Jeep JV), Peugeot was one of the first three entrants in the Chinese automobile industry. In 1980, it started to search for JV partners. In 1985, it set up a JV, Guangzhou Peugeot, in south China. The JV mainly produced the Peugeot 504 and 505, both out-of-date models of the 1970s. While many domestic users complained about the high fuel consumption, difficult maintenance, and expensive parts, the French car manufacturer netted huge short-term profits at approximately $480 million by selling a large amount of CKD kits and parts. Among its numerous problems, the JV also reportedly repatriated most of its profits and made relatively few changes to its 1970s era products, whereas VW in Shanghai reinvested profits and refined its production, introducing a new "Santana 2000" model in the mid-1990s. Around 1991, Guangzhou Peugeot accounted for nearly 16% share of China's passenger car market. But it began to go into the red in 1994 with its losses amounting to $349 million by 1997, forcing Peugeot to retreat from China. It sold its interest in the JV to Honda in 1998 (see the following page).

While the sour memories of the disappointing performance of its previous JV were still there, Peugeot (now part of PSA Peugeot Citroen) decided to return to the battlefield in 2003. This time, the Paris-based carmaker seemed loaded with ambitious expectations to grab a slice of the country's increasingly appealing auto market sparked by the post-WTO boom. One of its latest moves in China is an agreement in 2003 under which PSA Peugeot Citroen would further its partnership with Hubei-based Dongfeng Motor, one of China's top three automakers which originally signed up as a JV partner with Citroen, to produce Peugeot vehicles in China. According to the new deal, a Peugeot production platform will be installed at the Wuhan plant of the JV, Dongfeng Citroen. Starting from 2004, the new facility has turned out car models tailored for domestic consumers, including the Peugeot 307, one of the most popular models in Europe since 2003.

Honda

Peugeot's 1998 pullout created a vacuum for foreign manufacturers that missed the first wave of FDI into this industry. These late entrants included Daimler-Benz, GM, Opel (a German subsidiary of GM), and Hyundai. Against these rivals, Honda won the fierce bidding war for the takeover of an existing auto plant in Guangzhou of the now defunct Guangzhou Peugeot JV. The partner selection process had followed a familiar pattern: Beijing was pitting several bidders against each other to extract a maximum of capital, technology, and manufacturing capabilities, as well as the motor vehicle types deemed appropriate for China. Honda pledged to invest $887 million and committed the American version of the Honda Accord, whose production started in 1999. Two years later, Guangzhou Honda added the popular Odyssey minivan to its product mix. In less than two years, Honda had turned around the loss-making Peugeot facility into one of China's most profitable passenger car JVs.

It is important to note that well before its JV with the Guangzhou Auto Group, Honda had captured a significant market share with exports of the popular Honda Accord and a most effective network of dealerships and service and repair facilities all over China. These measures helped Honda not only to attain an excellent reputation and brand recognition, but also strengthened Honda's bargaining power with the Chinese negotiators.

Emerging Domestic Players

The original thinking behind the Open Door policy in China's auto market by forming JVs with multinationals was to access capital and technology and to develop Chinese domestic partners into self-sustaining independent players. However, this market-for-technology strategy failed to achieve its original goal. Cooperation with foreign car companies did bring in capital and technology, but also led to over-dependence on foreign technology and inadequate capacity (or even incentive) for independent innovations. By forming JVs with all the major domestic manufacturers and controlling brands, designs, and key technologies, multinationals effectively eliminated the domestic competition for the most part of the last two decades. Only in the last few years did Chinese manufacturers start to design, produce, and market independent brands.

In 2006, domestic companies controlled some 27% of the domestic market (mostly in entry- to mid-level segments). They have become masters at controlling costs and holding prices down, with a typical Chinese auto worker earning $1.95 an hour against a German counterpart making $49.50 an hour.

Ironically, the breakthrough came from newly established manufacturers without foreign partners. Government-owned Chery (Qirui) Automobile, which started with $25 million using second-hand Ford production equipment, produced only 2,000 vehicles six years ago.[2] In 2006, it sold 305,236 cars, a surge of 118% over 2005, with plans to double that again by 2008. Privately owned Geely Group obtained its license only six year ago and began with crudely built copycat hatchbacks powered by Toyota-designed engines. With an initial output of 5,000 cars in 2001, Geely today produces 180,000 a year, with various models of sedans and sports cars, including those equipped with self-engineered six-cylinder engines.

Beyond the domestic market, Chery now exports cars to 29 countries. In 2006, the company produced 305,000 cars and exported 50,000. Chery cars are expected to hit Europe soon. Geely Group plans to buy a stake in the UK taxi maker Manganese Bronze Holdings and start producing London's black taxis in Shanghai. It also aims to sell its affordable small vehicles in the US within several years.

In an effort to get closer to overseas markets, the Chinese players are starting to open overseas factories too. Chery has assembly operations in Egypt, Indonesia, Iran, and Russia. The company now is planning to extend its reach in South America by opening an assembly plant to produce its Tigo-brand sport-utility vehicle in Uruguay. Brilliance produces vehicles in three overseas factories in North Korea, Egypt, and Vietnam, and Geely has a factory in Russia.

One notable trend is the use of acquisition as a key mode for Chinese players to gain ownership of technologies, brands, and access to markets in developed countries with the profit from the domestic market. As the domestic competition and the pressure to consolidate from the central government intensifies, firms have participated in many high-profile bidding wars to acquire international brands/firms, such as BAIC's bid for Opel and Saab, Geely's bid for Volvo, and the acquisition of Hummer from GM by Tengzhong Heavy Industrial Corporation in 2009.

Another significant development is the effort on "green vehicles." At present, energy conservation and environmental protection have represented a new wave of innovations. The development of new energy technologies becomes an opportunity for China's auto industry to shorten the gap and enhance its international competitiveness. Total investment into this area in China has exceeded $850 million for the last decade and automakers have made certain noticeable achievements. Of all the Chinese automakers that pursue new energy cars, perhaps the most significant is BYD, which has a promising breakthrough electric vehicle technology through its self-developed ferrous batteries. BYD Auto is a subsidiary of BYD Group, the leading provider of lithium-ion cell phone batteries (with a 30% global market share).

BYD has only been an automaker since 2003, when it acquired a small car company called Qinchuan Motor. The company's core business is producing batteries for mobile phones made by the likes of Nokia and Motorola. Since then BYD has developed its auto business, selling more than 100,000 cars in China in 2007. BYD sees major synergy between its batteries and its cars.

At the moment, there is a worldwide race in producing the first commercially viable "plug-in hybrid" car. Among about a dozen competitors, GM is planning to offer Chevy Volt and Toyota is working on a plug-in model of Prius—both have a target launching time of 2010. The key to the race is the battery technology, which BYD claims to have mastered through its own R&D efforts. The lithium-iron phosphate batteries are much safer than the common lithium-ion batteries seen in early development efforts.

Chinese automakers, especially the independent brand holders, have made significant progress toward producing competitive vehicles for domestic market as well as external markets through licensing, self-development, outsourcing, and acquisition of technologies. However, the real breakthrough may not come from the traditional vehicles powered by internal combustion engines where Chinese firms are perceived to be still 10–20 years behind multinationals. With a coordinated effort from government, research centers, universities, as well as R&D centers established by auto firms, China is not far behind in the area of new energy vehicle technologies. Some firms such as BYD may even be among the leaders in offering a commercially viable "plug-in hybrid" and a pure electric car in the near future. Such kind of new technology-based vehicles will overcome many entry barriers to the mature markets like the United States.

The Road Ahead

China's automobile industry, which has almost exclusively focused on the domestic market, still has much room for future development and may maintain an annual growth rate of 10%–15% for the next few years. In the long run, as domestic growth inevitably slows down, there will be fiercer market competition and industry consolidation. The entry barriers will be higher and resource development will be more crucial to the sustainability of the competitive advantage. In order to survive and maintain healthy and stable growth, China's JVs and indigenous automobile companies, having established a solid presence domestically, must be able to offer their own products that are competitive in the global market.

No doubt, the road to success in China's automobile industry is fraught with plenty of potholes. As latecomers, Hyundai, Toyota, Honda, and Nissan had fewer options in the hunt for appropriate JV partners and market positioning than did the first mover VW during the 1980s. All the way through the early 1990s, foreign auto companies were solicited to enter China and encountered very little domestic competition or challenge. This situation has changed significantly. Today the industry is crowded with the world's top players vying for a share of this dynamic market. Success in China may also significantly help contribute to the corporate bottom line for multinationals that often struggle elsewhere. For example, China, having surpassed the United States, is now Volkswagen's largest market outside of Germany.

There are two competing scenarios confronting executives contemplating a move into China or expand in China: (1) At the current rate of rapid foreign and domestic investment, the Chinese industry will rapidly develop overcapacity. Given the inevitable cooling down of the overall growth of the economy, a blood-bath propelled by self-inflicted wounds such as massive incentives looms on the horizon. (2) Given the low penetration of cars among the vast Chinese population whose income is steadily on the rise, such a rising tide will be able to list all boats—or wheels—for a long while at least.

Case Discussion Questions:

1. Why do all multinational automakers choose to use FDI to enter this market? What are the drawbacks of using other entry modes such as exporting and licensing?
2. Some early entrants (such as VW) succeeded and some early entrants (such as Peugeot) failed. Similarly, some late entrants (such as Honda) did well and some late entrants (such as Ford) are struggling. From a resource-based standpoint, what role does entry timing play in determining performance?

3. From an institution-based view, explain the initial reluctance of most multinational automakers to enter China in the 1980s. Why happened recently that made them to change their minds?

4. You are a board member at one of the major multinational companies. At a board meeting you have just heard two presentations outlining the two contrasting scenarios for the outlook of the Chinese automobile industry (as described in the last paragraph of the case). Would you vote "Yes" or "No" for a $2 billion proposal to fund a major FDI project in China?

Sources: Based on (1) W. Arnold, 2003, The Japanese automobile industry in China, JPRI Working Paper No. 95; (2) *Economist*, 2003, Cars in China: The great leap forward, February 1: 53–54; (3) G. Edmondson, 2004, Volkswagen slips into reverse, *BusinessWeek*, August 9: 40; (4) H. Huang, 1999, Policy reforms and foreign direct investment: The case of the Chinese automotive industry, *Fourin*, 9 (1): 3–66; (5) M. W. Peng, 2000, Controlling the foreign agent: How governments deal with multinationals in a transition economy, *Management International Review*, 40: 141–166; (6) Q. Tao, 2004, The Road to Success: A Resource-Base View of Joint Venture Evolution in China's Auto Industry, PhD dissertation, University of Pittsburgh; (7) D. Welch, 2004, GM: Gunning it in China, *BusinessWeek*, June 21: 112–115; (8) G. Zeng & W. Peng, 2003, China's automobile industry boom, *Business Briefing: Global Automobile Manufacturing & Technology 2003*, 20–22; (9) E. Thun, 2006, *Changing lanes in China*, China Business Review (online); (10) Xinhua News Agency, 2009, GM bankruptcy to have minimal impact on China business.

NOTES

[1] American Motors was later acquired by Chrysler, which, in turn, was acquired by Daimler to form DaimlerChrysler in 1998. Between 1983 and 2005, the JV in China maintained its name as "Beijing Jeep Corporation" while experiencing ownership changes. In 2005, its name was changed to "Beijing-Benz DaimlerChrysler Automotive Co., Ltd." In 2007, DaimlerChrysler divested the Chrysler part. Interestingly, despite the divestiture, the JV's name has not been changed. But its ownership has been restructured, currently with 25% owned by Daimler, 25% by Chrysler, and 50% by Beijing Auto Works.

[2] In May 2005, GM sued Chery in a Chinese court for counterfeiting the design of a vehicle developed by GM's South Korean subsidiary Daewoo. While this case created some media sensation, in November 2005, the parties, encouraged by the Chinese government, reached "an undisclosed settlement." The settlement terms were not revealed. It was not known whether Chery had to pay for its alleged infringement or whether it was barred from using the purportedly infringing design (http://iplaw.blogs.com/content/2005/11/gm_piracy_case_.html).

Strategizing around the Globe

LEARNING OBJECTIVES

After studying this chapter, you should be able to:

1. define entrepreneurship, entrepreneurs, and entrepreneurial firms.

2. understand the institutions and resources that affect entrepreneurship.

3. identify three characteristics of a growing entrepreneurial firm.

4. differentiate international strategies that enter foreign markets and that stay in domestic markets.

5. participate in two leading debates on growing and internationalizing the entrepreneurial firm.

6. draw implications for action.

© Paulo Whitaker/Reuters/Landov

Growing and Internationalizing the Entrepreneurial Firm

Azul Takes Off from Brazil

David Neeleman was born in São Paolo to parents who were Mormon missionaries. He spent several years living the life of a well-to-do Brazilian child in the country's southeast, which typically revolves around beaches, barbecues, and private sports clubs. Many Brazilians lament the contrast between the rich and the poor. But it is less marked now than it was in Neeleman's childhood thanks to a recent spell of growth that has favored the poor in particular. In that he sees an opportunity. Brazil's middle class is swelling: at the last count there were 97 million people in marketing bracket "C," which means they are rich enough to contemplate getting on an airplane. Neeleman, in turn, has some experience getting people onto planes, having founded JetBlue, an American airline that aims to combine low cost with relatively lavish service.

Neeleman insists that he was "pretty much done with the airline business" last year [2008], when he resigned as chairman of JetBlue, which he had taken from an idea to an initial public offering (IPO) and is now valued at $1.6 billion. The previous year [2007] he had ceased to be chief executive after blunders had left passengers stranded during a spell of bad weather.

When he tried to put all this behind him by returning to Brazil, he found airfares that were 70% higher than America in a country that is considerably poorer, in a market in which the two biggest carriers, TAM and Gol, had a combined share of 85%, and large areas of the country that were scantily served by airlines. All this tempted him back into a business that in the words of Sir Richard Branson, British founder of the Virgin family of carriers, excels at turning billionaires into millionaires.

Making air travel more accessible in a country the size of the continental United States, where infrastructure is weak and many families have been scattered by internal migration, is a noble aim—and potentially a lucrative one. "It sometimes feels like this country is built for 20 million people," says Neeleman, when in fact it has close to 190 million souls. His Brazilian airline Azul (which means blue) was born in December 2008. On some routes, its tickets are cheaper than a bus for the same journey.

In nine months, the company has gone from having no employees to a staff of 1,300. It has 12 planes made by Embraer, a local firm, which pleases the Brazilian government; it will have 14 by the end of 2009. Azul is already the country's third biggest carrier, although it is still a long way behind the big two.

The speed with which Neeleman has got his new company airborne is perhaps surprising given Brazil's reputation as a bureaucratic place where life is hard for entrepreneurs. In its *Doing Business* survey, the World Bank ranks Brazil 121 places lower than America on ease of starting a business. According to Neeleman, lots of things that companies need, from capital to telephone lines and computing expertise, are indeed more expensive in Brazil than in America. Labor is not much cheaper when taxes are taken into account. The corporate tax rate is lower than in America but Azul needs an army of accountants to pay it correctly. Customers have less access to credit than American ones do, so Azul has had to perform some of the services of a bank, offering interest-free credit for ten months, and so on.

But the feebler competition and growing market compensate for this. "America has an excess of everything: cars, credit," says Neeleman. "Down here people are getting their first car, first credit card, owning their first home. It feels like the beginning of the cycle."

Source: Excerpted from "Missionary Man", *The Economist*, August 29, 2009, p. 58. Copyright © 2009 The Economist Newspaper Limited. Reprinted with permission. All rights reserved.

How do entrepreneurial firms such as Azul and JetBlue grow? How do they enter international markets? What are the challenges and constraints they face? This chapter deals with these important questions. This is different from many international business (IB) textbooks that typically focus on large firms. To the extent that *every* large firm today started small and that some (although not all) of today's **small- and medium-sized enterprises (SMEs)** may become tomorrow's multinational enterprises (MNEs), current and would-be managers will not gain a complete picture of the global business landscape if they only focus on large firms. In addition, since SMEs (in contrast to most large firms, which often have to downsize) generate most jobs now, most students will join SMEs. Some readers of this book may also start up SMEs, thus further necessitating our attention on these numerous starts-ups (such as Azul) instead of on the smaller number of giants (such as the two big airlines, TAM and Gol, in Brazil).

Small- and medium-sized enterprises (SMEs)

Firms with fewer than 500 employees in the United States and with fewer than 250 employees in the European Union.

This chapter first defines entrepreneurship. Next, we outline how our two leading perspectives, institution-based and resource-based views, shed light on entrepreneurship. Then we introduce characteristics of a growing entrepreneurial firm and multiple ways to internationalize.

LEARNING OBJECTIVE

1

Define entrepreneurship, entrepreneurs, and entrepreneurial firms.

Entrepreneurship

The identification and exploitation of previously unexplored opportunities.

ENTREPRENEURSHIP AND ENTREPRENEURIAL FIRMS

Although entrepreneurship is often associated with smaller and younger firms, no rule bans larger and older firms from being entrepreneurial. In fact, many large firms, which tend to be more established and bureaucratic, are often urged to become more entrepreneurial. So, what exactly is entrepreneurship? Recent research suggests that firm size and age are *not* defining characteristics of entrepreneurship. Instead, **entrepreneurship** is defined as "the identification and exploitation of previously unexplored opportunities."[1] Specifically, it is concerned with "the sources of opportunities; the processes of discovery, evaluation, and exploitation of opportunities; and the set of individuals who discover, evaluate, and exploit them."[2] **Entrepreneurs** are founders and owners of new businesses or managers of existing firms. **International entrepreneurship** is defined as "a combination of innovative, proactive, and risk-seeking behavior that crosses national borders and is intended to create wealth in organizations."[3]

Although SMEs are not the exclusive domain of entrepreneurship, many people often associate entrepreneurship with SMEs because, on average, SMEs tend to be more entrepreneurial than large firms. To minimize confusion, the remainder of this chapter will follow that convention, although it is not totally accurate. That is, although we acknowledge that managers at large firms can be entrepreneurial, we will limit the use of the term "entrepreneur" to owners, founders, and managers of SMEs. Further, we will use the term "entrepreneurial firms" when referring to SMEs. We will refer to firms with more than 500 employees in the United States and more than 250 employees in the European Union as "large firms."

SMEs are important. Worldwide, they account for over 95% of the number of firms, create approximately 50% of total value added, and generate 60% to 90% of employment, depending on the country.[4] Obviously, entrepreneurship has both rewarding and punishing aspects.[5] Many entrepreneurs will try and many SMEs will fail—in fact, approximately 60% of start-ups in the United States will fail within 6 years.[6] Only a small number of entrepreneurs and SMEs will succeed.

INSTITUTIONS, RESOURCES, AND ENTREPRENEURSHIP

LEARNING OBJECTIVE 2

Understand the institutions and resources that affect entrepreneurship.

Both institution-based and resource-based views shed light on entrepreneurship, as shown in Figure 9.1. In this section, we will look at how institutions constrain or facilitate entrepreneurs and how firm-specific (and in many cases entrepreneur-specific) resources and capabilities determine entrepreneurial success and failure.

FIGURE 9.1   INSTITUTIONS, RESOURCES, AND ENTREPRENEURSHIP

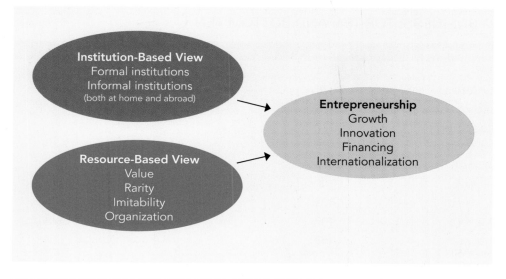

Entrepreneurs

Founders and/or owners of new businesses or managers of existing firms who identify and exploit new opportunities.

International entrepreneurship

A combination of innovative, proactive, and risk-seeking behavior that crosses national borders and is intended to create wealth in organizations.

Institutions and Entrepreneurship

First introduced in Chapters 2 and 3, both formal and informal institutional constraints, as rules of the game, affect entrepreneurship (see Figure 9.1). Although entrepreneurship is thriving around the globe in general, its development is uneven. Formal institutions that govern how entrepreneurs start up new firms either help or hinder the growth of new SMEs.[7] A World Bank survey, *Doing Business*, reports some striking differences in government regulations concerning start-ups, such as registration, licensing, incorporation, taxation, and inspection (Table 9.1 and PengAtlas Map 3.1).[8] In Focus 9.1 tracks the procedures, time, and direct costs to obtain electricity for a newly constructed commercial building. In developed economies, governments impose fewer procedures (an average of 4.6 procedures for OECD high-income countries) and a lower total cost (free in Japan and 5.1% of per capita GDP in Germany). In poor countries, entrepreneurs frequently face higher hurdles. As a class of its own, Burundi imposes a total cost of 430 times of its per capita GDP for entrepreneurs to obtain electricity. Sierra Leone leads the world in time needed for entrepreneurs to obtain electricity for their businesses: an astounding 441 days.

Overall, it is not surprising that when formal institutional requirements are more entrepreneur-friendly, entrepreneurship flourishes, and in turn the economy develops—and vice versa (Figure 9.2). As a result, more and more developing economies are reforming their formal institutions to become more entrepreneur-friendly. The World Bank's *Doing Business 2010* report noted that the top ten countries making significant entrepreneur-friendly reforms were all developing economies—for the first time led by a Sub-Saharan Africa country, Rwanda.[9]

In addition to formal institutions, informal institutions such as cultural values and norms also affect entrepreneurship. For example, because entrepreneurs necessarily take more risk, individualistic and low uncertainty-avoidance societies tend to foster relatively more entrepreneurs, whereas collectivistic and high uncertainty-avoidance societies may result in relatively fewer entrepreneurs. Since Chapter 3 discussed this issue at length, we will not repeat it here other than to stress its importance. Overall, the institution-based view suggests that institutions matter. Later sections in this chapter will discuss how they matter.

TABLE 9.1   EASE OF DOING BUSINESS: TOP TEN AND BOTTOM TEN

Rank	Top ten countries	Rank	Bottom ten countries
1	Singapore	174	Niger
2	New Zealand	175	Eritrea
3	Hong Kong, China	176	Burundi
4	United States	177	Venezuela
5	United Kingdom	178	Chad
6	Denmark	179	Republic of Congo
7	Ireland	180	Sao Tome and Principe
8	Canada	181	Guinea-Bissau
9	Australia	182	Democratic Republic of Congo (Zaire)
10	Norway	183	Central African Republic

Source: Data extracted from World Bank, 2010, *Doing Business 2010* (database at www.doingbusiness.org).

Getting Electricity

The World Bank's *Doing Business 2010* report tracks all procedures, time, and direct costs required for a new business to obtain electricity for a newly constructed commercial building. To ensure that the data are comparable across economies, the respondents were presented with a standard case study:

An entrepreneur would like to connect his newly built warehouse for cold meat storage to electricity. The internal wiring up to the metering point has already been completed by the electrician employed by the construction firm, and the entrepreneur would now like to obtain the final electricity connection from the local distribution utility. The electrician working for the entrepreneur estimates that the warehouse will need a 140 kilo Volt Ampere (kVA) connection.

Electricity distribution utilities in the largest business city of each of the 140 economies were surveyed. The results are very informative.

Selected countries	Direct cost (% of per capita GDP)	Time (days)	Procedures (number)
Japan	0*	105	3*
Hong Kong, China	1.8%	101	4
Germany	5.1%	17*	3*
Australia	15.4%	46	5
United States	16.8%	48	5
Singapore	34.2%	76	5
United Kingdom	42.2%	111	5
Brazil	163.2%	36	6
Canada	164.4%	133	8**
India	504.9%	67	6
China	835.7%	118	4
Sierra Leone	1,279.1%	441**	8**
Russia	4,521.6%	272	8**
Burundi	43,020.5%**	158	4
Regional averages			
OECD (high income)	58.3%	87.6	4.6
Latin America & Caribbean	526.3%	65.4	5.3
Eastern Europe & Central Asia	804.0%	156.4	5.8
East Asia & Pacific	1,108.9%	91.1	4.8
Middle East & North Africa	1,355.0%	78.9	4.8
South Asia	1,695.8%	172.5	5.5
Sub-Saharan Africa	6,409.0%	162.4	5.2

Source: Data extracted from World Bank, 2010, *Doing Business 2010* (database at www.doingbusiness.org).
*Lowest in the world.
**Highest in the world.

FIGURE 9.2   AVERAGE RANKING ON THE EASE OF DOING BUSINESS

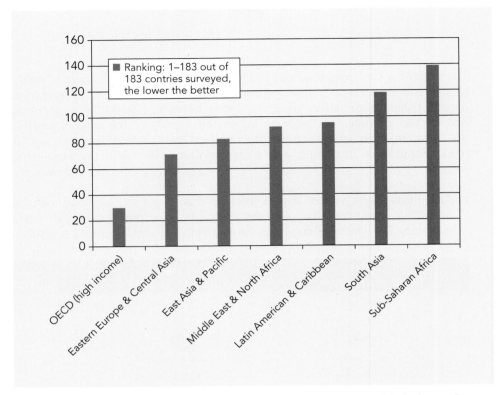

Source: Data extracted from World Bank, 2010, *Doing Business 2010* (database at www.doingbusiness.org).

Resources and Entrepreneurship

The resource-based view, first introduced in Chapter 4, sheds considerable light on entrepreneurship, with a focus on its value (V), rarity (R), imitability (I), and organizational (O) aspects (see Figure 9.1). An entrepreneurial firm must take the VRIO framework into account as it considers how to develop and leverage its resources.

First, entrepreneurial resources must create *value*.[10] For example, networks and contacts are great potential resources for would-be entrepreneurs. However, unless networks and contacts are channeled to create economic value, they remain only *potential* resources.

Second, resources must be *rare*. As the cliché goes, "If everybody has it, you can't make money from it." The best-performing entrepreneurs tend to have the rarest knowledge and insights about business opportunities.[11] Although the global recession means many entrepreneurs and their firms are struggling, the recession turns out to be a wonderful opportunity for a rare breed of entrepreneurs known as liquidators (see In Focus 9.2).

Third, resources must be *inimitable*. For example, Amazon's success prompted a number of online bookstores to directly imitate it. Amazon rapidly built the world's largest book warehouses, which, ironically for an online company, are brick-and-mortar. It is Amazon's "best-in-the-breed" physical inventories—not its online presence—that are more challenging to imitate.

Fourth, entrepreneurial resources must be *organizationally* embedded. For example, as long as there are wars, there have been mercenaries, soldiers who fight on a country's or group's behalf in exchange for wages. But only in

We Unwind Dreams

Dreadful economic times turn out to be a wonderful time for some entrepreneurs. Skyrocketing corporate bankruptcies prove to be great business for a network of dismantler firms, such as online auction companies, intellectual-property brokers, used-equipment liquidation outfits, and law firms specializing in bankruptcies. Silicon Valley is famed for its start-up–generating ecosystem, but brutal efficiency in winding down failed start-ups is part of that ecosystem too. "We unwind dreams," blatantly stated Martin Pichinson, in a *Business Week* interview. Pichinson is managing director of Sherwood Partners, a liquidation firm that specializes in selling the remains of failing start-ups. Known as Marty the Liquidator, Pichinson is the go-to guy for shutdowns. From 2002 until 2008, he managed to get two or three deals a month. Starting in 2008, he has been working two or three deals a *week*.

Pichinson and Sherwood Partners, of course, are not the only ones profiting from the recession. Lehman Brothers may be dead, but insolvency lawyers, restructuring experts, and other businesses may eventually bag $1 billion in court-awarded fees from its demise. This will be substantially above the $757 million such experts made from Enron's demise, the record for a bankruptcy case until now. Another case in point: Jones Day, a law firm working on Chrysler's bankruptcy case, claimed fees of more than $12 million for the first month of work. No wonder the *Economist* used the following title to describe such highly valuable, rare, and hard-to-imitate work: "Boom, bust, *bonanza*."

Sources: Based on (1) *BusinessWeek*, 2008, Enter the Liquidators, December 15: 66–67; (2) *Economist*, 2009, Boom, bust, bonanza, September 12: 82; (3) *Economist*, 2009, The boom in busts, July 2: 30.

modern times have private military companies (PMCs) become a global industry (see Integrative Case 3.1). Entrepreneurial PMCs thrive on their organizational capabilities to provide military and security services in dangerous conflict and post-conflict environments, particularly in situations like Iraq where individuals shy away and even national militaries withdraw.

In sum, the resource-based view suggests that firm-specific (and in many cases entrepreneur-specific) resources largely determine entrepreneurial success and failure. Overall, institution-based and resource-based views combine to shed light on entrepreneurial strategies.

GROWING THE ENTREPRENEURIAL FIRM

This section discusses three major characteristics associated with a growing entrepreneurial firm: (1) growth, (2) innovation, and (3) financing. A fourth one, internationalization, will be highlighted in the next section. Before proceeding, it is important to note that these strategies are not mutually exclusive and that they are often pursued in combination by entrepreneurial firms.[12]

Identify three characteristics of a growing entrepreneurial firm.

Growth

For many entrepreneurs, like David Neeleman in the Opening Case, the excitement associated with growing a new company is the very thing that attracts them in the first place.[13] Recall from the resource-based view that a firm can be conceptualized as a bundle of resources and capabilities. The growth of an entrepreneurial firm can thus be viewed as an attempt to more fully utilize currently under-utilized resources and capabilities.[14] What are these resources and capabilities? An entrepreneurial firm can leverage its vision, drive, and leadership in order to grow, even though it may be short on resources such as financial capital.[15]

A hallmark of entrepreneurial growth is a dynamic, flexible, guerrilla strategy. As underdogs, entrepreneurial SMEs cannot compete against their larger and more established rivals head-on. "Going for the crumbs" (at least initially), smaller firms often engage in indirect and subtle attacks that large rivals may not immediately recognize as competitive challenges.[16] In the lucrative market of US defense contracts, large firms such as Boeing and Raytheon like "doing the impossible." Meanwhile, smaller firms, such as Alliant Techsystems (known for its stock symbol ATK), focus on the possible and the cheap—upgrading missiles and making mortar munitions more accurate based on proven, off-the-shelf solutions. As a result, ATK is able to consistently beat a number of "top guns" and to supply the US military, which has become increasingly concerned about cost overruns.[17]

Innovation

Innovation is at the heart of entrepreneurship.[18] Evidence generally shows a positive relationship between a high degree of innovation and superior profitability.[19] Innovation allows for a more sustainable basis for competitive advantage. Google's ability to continuously unleash innovations—ranging from ever more powerful search engines to free gmail accounts and Google Scholar references—provides a good case in point. Entrepreneurial firms that come up with "disruptive technologies" may define the rules of competition.[20]

Entrepreneurial firms are uniquely ready for innovation. Owners, managers, and employees at entrepreneurial firms tend to be more innovative and risk-taking than those at large firms.[21] In fact, many SMEs are founded by former employees of large firms who were frustrated by their inability to translate innovative ideas into realities at the large firms.[22] Intel, for example, was founded by three former employees of Fairchild Semiconductor who quit in 1968. Innovators at large firms also have limited ability to personally profit from innovations because property rights usually belong to the corporation. In contrast, innovators at entrepreneurial firms are better able to reap the financial gains associated with innovations, thus fueling their motivation to charge ahead.

Financing

All start-ups need to raise capital. What are the sources? Here is a quiz (also a joke). Three of the "4F" sources of entrepreneurial financing are founders, family, and friends. What is the other "F" source? The answer is . . . *fools* (!). Although this is a joke, it strikes a chord in the entrepreneurial world. Given the well-known failure risks of start-ups (a *majority* of them will fail), why would anybody other than a fool be willing to invest in start-ups? In reality, most outside, strategic investors, who can be wealthy individual investors (often called angels), venture capitalists, banks, foreign entrants, and government agencies, are not fools. They often demand some assurance (such as collateral), examine business plans, and require a strong management team.[23]

Around the world, the extent to which entrepreneurs draw on resources from outside investors (such as venture capitalists) rather than family and friends varies. Figure 9.3 shows that Sweden, South Africa, Belgium, and the United States lead the world in venture capital (VC) investment as a percentage of GDP. In contrast, Greece and China have the lowest level of VC investment. Figure 9.4 illustrates a different picture: informal investment (mostly by family and friends) as a percentage of GDP. In this case, China leads the world with the highest level of informal investment as a percentage of GDP. In comparison, Brazil and Hungary have the lowest level of informal investment. Although there is a lot of "noise" in such worldwide data, the case of China (second lowest in VC investment and highest in informal investment) is easy to explain: China's lack of formal market-supporting institutions, such as venture capitalists and credit-reporting agencies, requires a high level of informal investment for Chinese entrepreneurs and new ventures, particularly during a time of entrepreneurial boom.[24]

A highly innovative solution, called microfinance, has emerged in response to the lack of financing for entrepreneurial opportunities in many developing countries. Microfinance involves lending small sums ($50–$300) to entrepreneurs with the intention of ultimately lifting them out of poverty. Although microfinance started in the 1970s in countries such as Bangladesh and India, the In Focus 9.3 feature shows that it has now become a global movement.

Microfinance

A practice to provide micro loans ($50–$300) used to start small businesses with the intention of ultimately lifting the entrepreneurs out of poverty.

FIGURE 9.3 VENTURE CAPITAL INVESTMENT AS A PERCENTAGE OF GDP

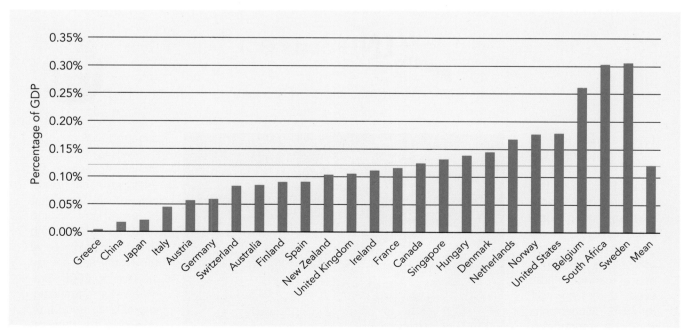

Source: Adapted from M. Minniti, W. Bygrave, & E. Autio, 2006, *Global Entrepreneurship Monitor 2006 Executive Report* (p. 49), Wellesley, MA: Babson College/GEM.

FIGURE 9.4   INFORMAL INVESTMENT AS A PERCENTAGE OF GDP

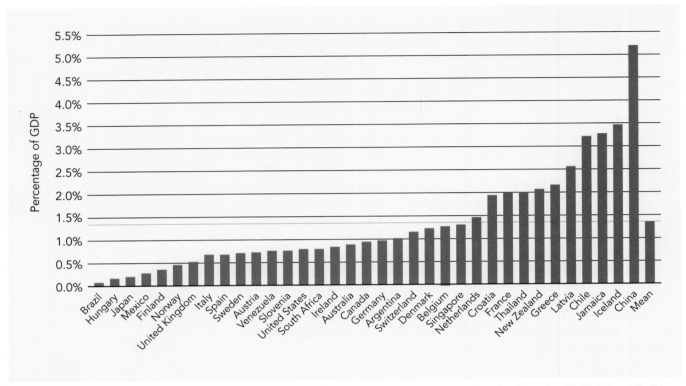

Source: Adapted from M. Minniti, W. Bygrave, & E. Autio, 2006, *Global Entrepreneurship Monitor 2006 Executive Report* (p. 53), Wellesley, MA: Babson College/GEM.

IN Focus 9.3

Microfinance, Macro Success

Teach a man to fish, and he'll eat for a lifetime. But here is a catch: He has to buy a fishing rod. Sadly, in many poor countries, numerous eager "fishermen"—also known as entrepreneurs—cannot afford even a fishing rod. In 1976, Muhammad Yunus, a young economics professor in Bangladesh, lent $27 out of his own pocket to a group of poor craftsmen and helped found a village-based enterprise called the Grameen Project. It never occurred to Yunus that he would inspire a global movement for entrepreneurial financing, much less that 30 years later he and the Grameen Bank he founded would receive the Nobel Peace Prize in 2006. In 2009, Grameenphone, a subsidiary of Grameen Bank, enjoyed the biggest initial public offering (IPO) in Bangladesh's history.

Also known as microloans, microfinance features tiny sums of $50 to $300. But in Bangladesh per capita GDP is about $440, so such loans are not small. Used to buy everything ranging from milk cows to mobile phones (to be used as pay phones by the entire village), these loans can make a huge difference. The poor tend to have neither assets (necessary for collateral) nor credit history, making traditional loans risky. The innovative, simple solution is to lend to women. Women, on average, are more likely to use their earnings to support family needs than men, who may be more likely to indulge in drinking, gambling, or drugs. A more sophisticated solution is to organize the women in a village into a collective and lend money to the collective but not to individuals. Overall, 84% of microloan recipients are women and repayment rates are between 95% and 98%. Although

interest rates average a hefty 35%, they are far below rates charged by local loan sharks. By 2009, more than 7,000 microfinance institutions had served 113 million borrowers around the world.

However, as microfinance grows from periphery to mainstream, it may have to change some of its practices. From an ethical standpoint, it is questionable whether clearly discriminatory lending practices against men can be sustained in the long run. In this age of gender equality, aspiring male entrepreneurs in the developing world probably do not appreciate being automatically discriminated against.

Sources: Based on (1) *BusinessWeek*, 2005, Microcredit missionary, December 26: 20; (2) *BusinessWeek*, 2006, Taking tiny loans to the next level, November 27: 76-80; (3) www.grameenfoundation.org, 2009.

INTERNATIONALIZING THE ENTREPRENEURIAL FIRM

LEARNING OBJECTIVE 4

Differentiate international strategies that enter foreign markets and that stay in domestic markets.

There is a myth that only large MNEs do business abroad and that SMEs mostly operate domestically. This myth, based on historical stereotypes, is being increasingly challenged, as more and more SMEs become internationalized. Further, some start-ups attempt to do business abroad from inception. These are often called **born global** firms (or international new ventures).[25] This section examines how entrepreneurial firms internationalize.

Transaction Costs and Entrepreneurial Opportunities

Compared with domestic transaction costs (the costs of doing business), international transaction costs are qualitatively higher. Some costs are due to numerous innocent differences in formal institutions and informal norms (see Chapters 2 and 3). Other costs, however, may be due to a high level of deliberate opportunism that is hard to detect and remedy. For example, suppose a small business in Texas with $5 million annual revenues received an unsolicited order of $1 million from an unknown buyer in Alaska. Most likely the Texas firm would fill the order and allow the Alaska buyer to pay within 30 or 60 days after receiving the goods—a typical practice among domestic transactions in the United States. But what if an order came from an unknown buyer in Algeria (an importer in this case)? If the Texas firm shipped the goods but foreign payment did not arrive on time (after 30 or 60 days), it is difficult to assess whether punctual payment is not a norm for Algerian firms or if that particular importer is being deliberately opportunistic. If the latter is indeed the case, suing the Algerian importer in an Algerian court where Arabic is the official language may be so costly that it is not an option for a small US exporter.

Born global

Start-up companies that attempt to do business abroad from inception.

TABLE 9.2   INTERNATIONALIZATION STRATEGIES FOR ENTREPRENEURIAL FIRMS

Entering foreign markets	Staying in domestic markets
• Direct exports	• Indirect exports (through export intermediaries)
• Franchising/licensing	• Supplier of foreign firms
• Foreign direct investment (through strategic alliances, green-field wholly owned subsidiaries, and/or foreign acquisitions)	• Franchisee/licensee of foreign brands
	• Alliance partner of foreign direct investors
	• Harvest and exit (through sell-off to and acquisition by foreign entrants)

Maybe the Algerian importer is an honest and capable firm with every intention and ability to pay, but because the Texas firm cannot determine *prior to the transaction* if the Algerian side will pay upon receiving the goods, the Texas firm may simply say "No, thanks!" Conceptually, this is an example of transaction costs being too high that many firms may choose not to pursue international opportunities. Therefore, entrepreneurial opportunities exist to lower transaction costs and bring distant groups of people, firms, and countries together. Shown in Table 9.2, although entrepreneurial firms can internationalize by entering foreign markets, they can also add an international dimension without having to go abroad. Next, we discuss how SMEs can undertake some of these strategies.

International Strategies for Entering Foreign Markets

SMEs have three broad modes for entering foreign markets: (1) direct exports, (2) licensing/franchising, and (3) foreign direct investment (FDI) (see Chapter 10 for more details). First, **direct exports** involve the sale of products made by entrepreneurial firms in their home country to customers in other countries. This strategy is attractive because entrepreneurial firms are able to reach foreign customers directly. When domestic markets experience some downturns, sales abroad may compensate for such drops.[26] However, a major drawback is that SMEs may not have enough resources to turn overseas opportunities into profits, and that some opportunities have to be given up due to potentially high transaction costs.

Export transactions are complicated. One particular concern is how to overcome the lack of trust between exporters and importers when receiving an export order from unknown importers abroad. For example, although the US exporter in Figure 9.5 does not trust the Chinese importer, banks on both sides can facilitate this transaction by a **letter of credit (L/C)**, which is a financial contract that states that the importer's bank (Bank of China in this case) will pay a specific sum of money to the exporter upon delivery of the merchandise. It has several steps:

• The US exporter may question the unknown Chinese importer's assurance that it will promptly pay for the merchandise. An L/C from the highly reputable Bank of China will assure the US exporter that the importer has good creditworthiness and sufficient funds for this transaction. If the US exporter is not sure whether Bank of China is a credible bank, it can consult its own bank, Bank of America, which will confirm that an L/C from Bank of China is as good as gold.

Direct exports
The sale of products made by firms in their home country to customers in other countries.

Letter of credit (L/C)
A financial contract that states that the importer's bank will pay a specific sum of money to the exporter upon delivery of the merchandise.

FIGURE 9.5 AN EXPORT/IMPORT TRANSACTION

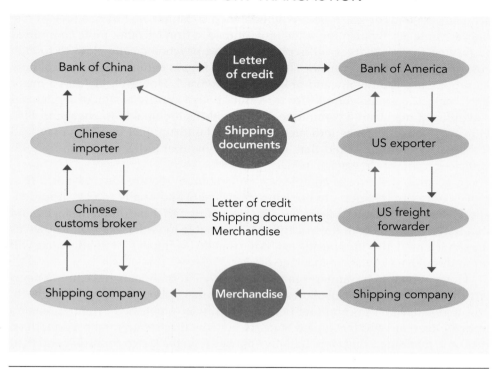

- With this assurance through the L/C, the US exporter can release the merchandise, which goes through a US freight forwarder, then a shipping company, and then a Chinese customs broker. Finally, the goods will reach the Chinese importer.
- Once the US exporter has shipped the goods, it will present to Bank of America the L/C from Bank of China and shipping documents. On behalf of the US exporter, Bank of America will then collect payment from Bank of China, which, in turn, will collect payment from the Chinese importer.

In short, instead of having unknown exporters and importers deal with each other, transactions are facilitated by banks on both sides that have known each other quite well because of numerous such dealings. In other words, the L/C reduces transaction costs.

A second way to enter international markets is through licensing and/or franchising. Usually used in *manufacturing* industries, **licensing** refers to Firm A's agreement to give Firm B the rights to use A's proprietary technology (such as a patent) or trademark (such as a corporate logo) for a royalty fee paid to A by B. **Franchising** is essentially the same idea, except it is typically used in *service* industries such as fast food. A great advantage is that SME licensors and franchisors can expand abroad while risking relatively little capital of their own.[27] Foreign firms interested in becoming licensees or franchisees have to put their own capital up front. For example, a franchise from McDonald's costs approximately one million dollars, whereas a franchise from Wendy's costs half-a-million dollars. But licensors and franchisors also take a risk because they may suffer a loss of control over how their technology and brand names are used. If foreign licensees produce substandard products that damage the brand and refuse to improve quality, licensors are left with the difficult choices. They can (1) sue licensees in an unfamiliar foreign court or (2) discontinue the relationship. Either choice is complicated and costly.

Licensing

Firm A's agreement to give Firm B the rights to use A's proprietary technology (such as a patent) or trademark (such as a corporate logo) for a royalty fee paid to A by B. This is typically done in manufacturing industries.

Franchising

Firm A's agreement to give Firm B the rights to use A's proprietary assets for a royalty fee paid to A by B. This is typically done in service industries.

A third entry mode is FDI, which is discussed in detail in Chapter 6. FDI may involve strategic alliances with foreign partners (such as joint ventures), foreign acquisitions, and/or green-field wholly owned subsidiaries. FDI has several distinct advantages. By planting some roots abroad, a firm becomes more committed to serving foreign markets. It is physically and psychologically close to foreign customers. Relative to licensing/franchising, a firm is better able to control how its proprietary technology and brand name are used. However, FDI has a major drawback: its cost and complexity. It requires both a nontrivial sum of capital and a significant managerial commitment. Many SMEs are unable to engage in FDI. However, some evidence indicates that in the long run, FDI by SMEs may lead to higher performance, and that some entrepreneurial SMEs can come up with sufficient resources to engage in FDI.[28]

In general, the level of complexity and resources required increase as a firm moves from direct exports to licensing/franchising and finally to FDI. Traditionally, it is thought that most firms will have to go through these different stages, and that SMEs (perhaps with few exceptions) are unable to undertake FDI. Known as the **stage model**, this idea posits that SMEs that do eventually internationalize will do so through a slow, stage-by-stage process.[29]

However, enough counterexamples of *rapidly* internationalizing entrepreneurial firms, known as born globals, exist to challenge stage models. Consider Logitech, now a global leader in computer peripherals. It was established by entrepreneurs from Switzerland and the United States, where the firm set up dual headquarters. R&D and manufacturing were initially split between these two countries, and then quickly spread to Ireland and Taiwan through FDI. Its first commercial contract was with a Japanese company. The information technology advancements of the past decade have given instant worldwide reach to most Internet firms, allowing them to internationalize rapidly.[30]

Given that most SMEs still fit the stereotype of slow (or no) internationalization but some entrepreneurial SMEs seem to be born global, a key question is: What leads to rapid internationalization? The key differentiator between rapidly and slowly (or no) internationalizing SMEs seems to be the international experience of entrepreneurs.[31] If entrepreneurs have solid previous experience abroad (such as David Neeleman's earlier experience in Brazil), then doing business internationally is not so intimidating. Otherwise, the apprehension associated with the unfamiliar foreign business world may take over and entrepreneurs will simply want to avoid troubles overseas.

Although many entrepreneurial firms have aggressively gone abroad, it is probably true that a majority of SMEs will be unable to do so—they already have enough headaches struggling domestically. However, as discussed next, some SMEs can still internationalize by staying at home.

Stage model

Model of internationalization that portrays the slow step-by-step (stage-by-stage) process an SME must go through to internationalize its business.

Indirect exports

A way to reach overseas customers by exporting through domestic-based export intermediaries.

International Strategies for Staying in Domestic Markets

Shown in Table 9.2, there are at least five strategies for entrepreneurial SMEs to internationalize without leaving their home country: (1) export indirectly, (2) become suppliers for foreign firms, (3) become licensees or franchisees of foreign brands, (4) become alliance partners of foreign direct investors, and (5) harvest and exit through sell-offs. First, whereas direct exports may be lucrative, many SMEs simply do not have the resources to handle such work. But they still can reach overseas customers through **indirect exports**, which involve exporting through domestic-based export intermediaries. **Export intermediaries** perform an important middleman function by linking domestic sellers and overseas buyers that otherwise would not have been connected.[32] Being entrepreneurs themselves, export intermediaries facilitate the internationalization of many SMEs.[33]

A second strategy is to become a supplier for a foreign entrant. Most foreign firms, in order to save costs, are interested in looking for local suppliers. For example, when Subway opened restaurants in Northern Ireland, it secured supply contracts for chilled part-bake bread with a domestic bakery. This relationship was so successful that the Northern Irish firm now supplies Subway franchisees throughout Europe.[34] SME suppliers thus may be able to internationalize by piggybacking on the larger foreign entrants.

Third, entrepreneurial firms may consider becoming licensees or franchisees of foreign brands. Foreign licensors and franchisors provide training and technology transfer—for a fee of course. Consequently, an SME can learn a great deal about how to operate at world-class standards. Furthermore, licensees and franchisees do not have to be permanently under the control of licensors and franchisors. If enough learning has been accomplished and enough capital has been accumulated, it is possible to discontinue the relationship and reap greater entrepreneurial profits. For example, in Thailand, Minor Group, which had held the Pizza Hut franchise for 20 years, broke away from the relationship. Its new venture, The Pizza Company, has now become the market leader in Thailand.[35]

A fourth strategy is to become alliance partners of a foreign direct investor.[36] Facing an onslaught of aggressive MNEs, many entrepreneurial firms may be unable to successfully defend their market positions. Then it makes great sense to follow the old adage, "If you can't beat them, join them!" Although dancing with the giants is tricky, it seems to be a much better outcome than being crushed by the giants. (See Chapters 10, 11, and 12 for examples on how smaller, domestic firms become alliance partners with MNEs.)

Finally, as a harvest and exit strategy, entrepreneurs may sell an equity stake or the entire firm to foreign entrants.[37] An American couple, originally from Seattle, built a Starbucks-like coffee chain in Britain called Seattle Coffee. When Starbucks entered Britain, the couple sold the chain of 60 stores to Starbucks for a hefty $84 million. In light of the high failure rates of start-ups, being acquired by foreign entrants may help preserve the business in the long run.

DEBATES AND EXTENSIONS

Entrepreneurship throughout the world has attracted significant controversies and debates (see the Closing Case). This section discusses two leading debates: (1) traits versus institutions and (2) slow versus rapid internationalization.

Traits versus Institutions

Probably the oldest debate on entrepreneurship focuses on the question: What motivates entrepreneurs to establish new firms, whereas most others are simply content to work for bosses? The "traits" school of thought argues that it is personal traits that matter. Compared with nonentrepreneurs, entrepreneurs seem more likely to possess a stronger desire for achievement and are more willing to take risks and tolerate ambiguities. Overall, entrepreneurship inevitably deviates from the norm to work for others, and this may be in the blood of entrepreneurs.[38]

Participate in two debates on growing and internationalizing the entrepreneurial firm.

Export intermediary
A firm that performs an important middleman function by linking domestic sellers and foreign buyers that otherwise would not have been connected.

Critics, however, argue that some of these traits, such as a strong achievement orientation, are not necessarily limited to entrepreneurs but are characteristic of many successful individuals. Moreover, the diversity among entrepreneurs makes any attempt to develop a standard psychological or personality profile futile. Critics suggest that what matters are the institutions, particularly the formal and informal rules of the game (see PengAtlas Map 3.2).[39] Consider the ethnic Chinese for example. As a group, they have exhibited a high degree of entrepreneurship throughout Southeast Asia. In countries such as Indonesia and Thailand where they are a minority group (usually less than 10% of the population), they control 70% to 80% of the national wealth. Yet from the 1950s until the end of the 1970s mainland China saw virtually no entrepreneurship, thanks to harsh communist policies. In the last three decades, as government policies become more entrepreneur-friendly, the institutional transitions have opened the floodgates of entrepreneurship in China.

A high-profile case documents how institutions can either constrain or enable entrepreneurship. In 2005, on the first day a Chinese Internet start-up Baidu listed on the NASDAQ, its shares surged 354% (from $27 to $154), marking the biggest one-day stock surge in US capital markets since 2000. Although some "irrational exuberance" among US investors chasing "China's Google" might account for some of the gain, it is evident that they did not discriminate against Baidu. The sad reality is that the Chinese securities authorities blatantly discriminated against Baidu right on its home turf. Because Baidu is a private start-up, Chinese securities authorities did not allow it to be listed on China's stock exchanges—only state-owned firms were allowed. Essentially, Baidu was pushed out of China and forced to list in the United States, where entrepreneur-friendly institutional frameworks, such as NASDAQ regulations, are able to facilitate more entrepreneurial success.[40] In a nutshell, it is not what is in people's blood that makes or breaks entrepreneurship; it is institutions that encourage or constrain entrepreneurship.

Beyond the macro societal-level institutions, micro institutions also matter. Family background and educational attainment have been found to correlate with entrepreneurship. Children of wealthy parents, especially parents who own businesses, are more likely to start their own firms, as are better educated people. Taken together, informal norms governing one's socioeconomic group, in terms of whether starting a new firm is legitimate or not, assert a powerful impact on the propensity to create new ventures. Overall, this debate is an extension of the broader debate on "nature versus nurture." Most scholars now agree that entrepreneurship is the result of both nature *and* nurture.

Slow Internationalizers versus Born Global Start-ups

This debate has two questions: (1) *Can* SMEs internationalize faster than what has been suggested by traditional stage models? (2) *Should* they rapidly internationalize? The dust has largely settled on the first question: it is possible for some (but not all) SMEs to make very rapid progress in internationalization. What is currently being debated is the second question.[41]

Advocates argue that every industry has become "global" and that entrepreneurial firms need to go after these opportunities rapidly.[42] Opponents argue that the stage models suggest that firms need to enter culturally and institutionally close markets first, spend enough time there to accumulate overseas experience, and then gradually move from more primitive modes such as exports to more sophisticated strategies such as FDI in distant markets. Consistent with stage models, Sweden's IKEA waited 20 years (1943–1963) before entering neighboring Norway. Only more recently has IKEA accelerated its internationalization.[43] According to stage models, caution should be used because inexperienced companies may sink in unfamiliar and turbulent foreign waters.

A key issue, therefore, is whether it is better for entrepreneurs to start the internationalization process soon after founding (as born global firms do) or to postpone until the firm has accumulated significant resources (as IKEA did). One study in Finland supports rapid internationalization.[44] Specifically, firms following the prescription of stage models, when eventually internationalizing, must

Although Sweden's IKEA is now active in distant markets such as China, it waited 20 years (1943–1963) before first entering a neighboring country, Norway. Did IKEA's slow, cautious approach in initial internationalization—suggested by stage models—make sense?

overcome substantial inertia because of their domestic orientation. In contrast, firms that internationalize earlier had fewer of these barriers to overcome. Therefore, SMEs without an established domestic orientation (such as Logitech) may outperform their rivals that wait longer to internationalize.[45] In other words, contrary to the inherent disadvantages for SMEs in internationalization as suggested by the stage model, being smaller while venturing abroad may have inherent advantages.[46]

On the other hand, opponents of rapid globalization point to a study in Hungary that shows foreign sales during the first few years of the new venture may *reduce* its chances for survival.[47] Consequently, indiscriminate advice for new ventures to go global may not be warranted.[48] Some scholars argue that "the born-global view, although appealing, is a dangerous half-truth." They maintain that "You must first be successful at home, then move outward in a manner that anticipates and genuinely accommodates local differences."[49] In other words, the teachings of stage models are still relevant.

Given the split findings, there are no hard and fast rules on whether entrepreneurial firms should rapidly internationalize or not. Although the entrepreneurial urge to "be bold" should be encouraged, the virtues of "not being too bold" should also be recognized.

MANAGEMENT SAVVY

Entrepreneurs and their firms are quintessential engines of the "creative destruction" process underpinning global capitalism first described by Joseph Schumpeter. What determines the success and failure of entrepreneurial firms around the globe? The answers boil down to two components. First, the institution-based view

LEARNING OBJECTIVE

6

Draw implications for action.

argues that the larger institutional frameworks explain a great deal about what is behind the differences in entrepreneurial and economic development around the world. Second, the resource-based view posits that it is largely intangible resources such as vision, drive, and willingness to take risk that fuels entrepreneurship around the globe. Overall, the performance of entrepreneurial firms depends on how they take advantage of formal and informal institutional resources and leverage their capabilities at home, abroad, or both.

Two clear implications for action emerge (Table 9.3). First, institutions that facilitate entrepreneurship development—both formal and informal—are important. As a result, savvy entrepreneurs have a vested interest in pushing for more entrepreneur-friendly formal institutions in various countries, such as rules governing how to set up new firms (see Table 9.1, Figure 9.2, and In Focus 9.1). Entrepreneurs also need to cultivate strong informal norms granting legitimacy to entrepreneurs. Talking to high school and college students, taking on internships, and providing seed money as angels for new ventures are some of the actions that entrepreneurs can undertake.

Second, when internationalizing, entrepreneurs are advised to get their feet "wet" abroad. Thanks to globalization, the costs of doing business abroad have fallen recently. But being bold does not mean being reckless. One specific managerial insight from this chapter is that it is possible to internationalize without venturing abroad. A variety of international strategies enable entrepreneurial firms to stay in domestic markets. When the entrepreneurial firm is not ready to take on higher risk abroad, this more limited involvement may be appropriate. In other words, be bold, but not too bold.[50]

TABLE 9.3   IMPLICATIONS FOR ACTION

- Push for institutions that facilitate entrepreneurship development—both formal and informal

- When internationalizing, be bold, but not too bold

CHAPTER SUMMARY

1. Define entrepreneurship, entrepreneurs, and entrepreneurial firms.
   - Entrepreneurship is the identification and exploitation of previously unexplored opportunities.
   - Entrepreneurs may be founders and owners of new businesses or managers of existing firms.
   - Entrepreneurial firms in this chapter are defined as SMEs.

2. Understand how institutions and resources affect entrepreneurship.
   - Institutions—both formal and informal—enable and constrain entrepreneurship around the world.
   - Resources and capabilities largely determine entrepreneurial success and failure.

3. Identify the three characteristics associated with a growing entrepreneurial firm.
   • (1) Growth, (2) innovation, and (3) financing.

4. Differentiate international strategies that enter foreign markets and that stay in domestic markets.
   • Entrepreneurial firms can internationalize by entering foreign markets, through entry modes such as (1) direct exports, (2) licensing/franchising, and (3) foreign direct investment.
   • Entrepreneurial firms can also internationalize without venturing abroad, by (1) exporting indirectly, (2) supplying foreign firms, (3) becoming licensees/franchisees of foreign firms, (4) joining foreign entrants as alliance partners, and (5) harvesting and exiting through sell-offs to foreign entrants.

5. Participate in two leading debates on growing and internationalizing the entrepreneurial firm.
   • (1) Traits versus institutions and (2) slow versus rapid internationalization.

6. Draw implications for action.
   • Push for both formal and informal institutions that facilitate entrepreneurship development.
   • When internationalizing, be bold, but not too bold.

KEY TERMS

Born global 309	Franchising 311	Licensing 311
Direct exports 310	Indirect exports 312	Microfinance 307
Entrepreneur 301	International	Small- and medium-sized
Entrepreneurship 300	entrepreneurship 301	enterprises (SMEs) 300
Export intermediary 313	Letter of credit (L/C) 310	Stage model 312

REVIEW QUESTIONS

1. How do you define entrepreneurship?

2. How prevalent and important are small entrepreneurial firms in economies around the globe?

3. Which societal norms tend to encourage entrepreneurship and which discourage it?

4. How important are an entrepreneur's resources and capabilities in determining his or her success? Why?

5. Name and describe three major characteristics associated with an entrepreneurial firm's growth.

6. What qualities typically compensate for an entrepreneurial firm's lack of tangible resources?

7. Briefly summarize three modes an SME can use to enter foreign markets.

8. Name and describe at least three of the five ways entrepreneurial SMEs can internationalize without leaving their home countries.

9. Compare PengAtlas Maps 3.1 and 3.4. Based on that information, which country would be most attractive to you as a place to expand your business? The global economy is subject to constant change. In your opinion, what potential changes in one of the countries shown may make that country less attractive as a place to expand?

10. In the entrepreneurial nature versus nurture debate, which do you think carries more power: traits (nature) or institutions (nurture)? Why?

11. We know that it is possible for an SME to be born global by jumping immediately to the highest stage, FDI, but do you think it is wise? Why?

12. Describe two or three examples of institutions that could be made friendlier and more supportive of entrepreneurs.

13. In comparing PengAtlas Maps 3.1 and 3.4, note that some of the countries that are at the bottom of the list regarding ease of doing business are also among the poorest. Note also that the two groups are not identical. However, to what extent could ease of doing business impact the wealth of a country?

CRITICAL DISCUSSION QUESTIONS

1. Given that most entrepreneurial start-ups fail, why do entrepreneurs start so many new firms? Why are (most) governments interested in promoting more start-ups?

2. Some suggest that foreign markets are graveyards where entrepreneurial firms overextend themselves. Others argue that foreign markets represent the future for SMEs. If you were the owner of a small, reasonably profitable domestic firm, would you consider expanding overseas? Why or why not?

3. Devise your own example of an entrepreneurial action that demonstrates your understanding of the difference between being bold and being reckless.

4. *ON ETHICS*: Your former high school buddy invites you to join an entrepreneurial start-up that specializes in cracking the software that protects CDs and DVDs from being copied. He has developed the pioneering technology and lined up financing. The worldwide demand for this technology appears to be enormous. He offers you the job of CEO and 10% of the equity of the firm. You are currently unemployed. How would you respond to his proposition?

GLOBAL ACTION

1. You work for a small foreign language services company. You have been asked to present a market assessment of the largest translation companies for competitor evaluation. Your report must include the following attributes for the global industry: company, size, locations, and ownership status. What do your findings gathered from the globalEDGE website suggest about possible worldwide opportunities?

2. An entrepreneurship research firm has asked you to identify the most entrepreneurial countries in the world. Based on your knowledge of the entrepreneurship field, find a database on globalEDGE that may assist in your research. Once the information has been secured, compare the top five countries across the multiple years included in the database. Are there any countries that appear in all years included in the database? What is the general percentage of new start-ups in the overall economy for each of the top countries? Is the size of each country similar? Explain these dynamics in your report.

VIDEO CASES

Watch "The Essence of the Entrepreneur" by Lord Kalms of Dixons Group.

1. To most people, it seems that a successful entrepreneur would be satisfied. However, Lord Kalms claimed that the successful entrepreneur needs to be continually dissatisfied. Explain how his claim makes sense.

2. In global markets, why is it especially important to follow Lord Kalm's advice to always seek new things?

3. Lord Kalms mentioned three characteristics of a growing firm. Which is most important? Which is most under an entrepreneur's control? Why?

4. Do you think it is possible to develop the entrepreneurial traits described by Lord Kalms? Why or why not? If you were to try to do so, how would you go about it?

Closing Case

Boom in Busts: Good or Bad?

Corporate bankruptcies* have climbed new heights in the recession, as firms ranging from huge General Motors to tiny entrepreneurial outfits are crushed left and right around the world. Since bankruptcies sound neither good nor inspiring, is there anything that we—governments, financial institutions, consumers, taxpayers, or the society at large—can do to prevent widespread bankruptcies?

Efforts to rescue failing firms from bankruptcies stem from an "anti-failure" bias widely shared among entrepreneurs, scholars, journalists, and government officials. Although a majority of entrepreneurial firms fail, this "anti-failure" bias leads to widespread interest in entrepreneurial success. (Remember how many times Google and eBay were written up by the press?) Scant attention is devoted to the vast majority of entrepreneurial firms that end up in failure and bankruptcy. However, one perspective suggests that bankruptcies, which are undoubtedly painful to individual entrepreneurs and employees, may be *good* for society overall. Consequently, bankruptcy laws need to be reformed to become more entrepreneur-friendly by making it easier for entrepreneurs to declare bankruptcies and to move on. Consequently, financial, human, and physical resources stuck with failed firms can be redeployed in a socially optimal way.

A leading debate is how to treat failed entrepreneurs who file for bankruptcy. Do we let them walk away from debt or punish them? Historically, entrepreneur-friendliness and bankruptcy laws are like an "oxymoron," because bankruptcy laws are usually harsh and even cruel. The very term "bankruptcy" is derived from a harsh practice: In me-

dieval Italy, if bankrupt entrepreneurs did not pay their debt, debtors would destroy the trading bench of the bankrupt traders—the Italian word for broken bench, "banca rotta," has evolved into the English word "bankruptcy." The pound of flesh demanded by the creditor in Shakespeare's *The Merchant of Venice* is only a slight exaggeration. The world's first bankruptcy law, passed in England in 1542, considered a bankrupt individual a criminal and penalties ranged from incarceration to death.

Recently, however, many governments have realized that entrepreneur-friendly bankruptcy laws can not only lower exit barriers, but also lower *entry* barriers for entrepreneurs. Even though many start-ups will end up in bankruptcy, at present it is impossible to predict up front which ones will go under. From an institution-based standpoint, entrepreneurship would be encouraged, if the pain associated with bankruptcy is reduced by allowing entrepreneurs to walk away from debt. This is the case for bankrupt entrepreneurs in the United States. In contrast, bankrupt German entrepreneurs may remain liable for unpaid debt for up to 30 years. Further, German and Japanese managers of bankrupt firms can also be liable for criminal penalties, and numerous bankrupt Japanese entrepreneurs have committed suicide. Not surprisingly, many failed entrepreneurs in Germany and Japan try to avoid business exit despite escalating losses, so societal and individual resources cannot be channeled to more productive uses. Therefore, as rules of the "end game," harsh bankruptcy laws become grave exit barriers. They can also create significant entry barriers, as fewer would-be entrepreneurs decide to risk launching their ventures.

* The term "bankruptcies" in this case refers to *corporate* bankruptcies and does not deal with *personal* bankruptcies.

At a societal level, if many would-be entrepreneurs abandon their ideas for fear of failure, the entrepreneurial sector will not thrive. Given the risks and uncertainties, it is not surprising that many entrepreneurs do not make it the first time. However, if they are given second, third, or more chances, some of them will succeed. For example, approximately 50% of US entrepreneurs who filed bankruptcy resumed a new venture in four years. This high level of entrepreneurialism is, in part, driven by the relatively entrepreneur-friendly bankruptcy laws in the United States (such as the provision of Chapter 11 bankruptcy, which is reorganization instead of straight liquidation). On the other hand, a society that severely punishes failed entrepreneurs (such as forcing financially insolvent firms to liquidate instead of offering a US Chapter 11-style reorganization option) is not likely to foster widespread entrepreneurship. Failed entrepreneurs have nevertheless accumulated a great deal of experience and lessons on how to avoid their mistakes. If they drop out of the entrepreneurial game (or, in the worst case, kill themselves), their wisdom will be permanently lost.

Institutionally, some of the anti-failure bias urgently needs to be removed, and entrepreneur-friendly bankruptcy policies designed so that failed entrepreneurs can be given more chances. At a societal level, entrepreneurial failures may be beneficial, since it is through a large number of entrepreneurial experimentations—although many will fail—that winning solutions will emerge and that economies will develop. In short, the boom in busts is not necessarily bad.

Case Discussion Questions:

1. What are the pros and cons for entrepreneur-friendly bankruptcy laws?
2. Why can bankruptcy laws become an exit barrier for an entrepreneurial firm? An entry barrier?
3. Having studied this case, how would you respond to a friend's comment: "Recent news about the boom in bankruptcies is so depressing"?

Sources: I thank Seung-Hyun Lee (University of Texas at Dallas), Yasuhiro Yamakawa (Babson College), and Jay Barney (Ohio State University) for collaboration on related research. Based on (1) S. Lee, M. W. Peng, & J. Barney, 2007, Bankruptcy law and entrepreneurship development, *Academy of Management Review*, 32: 257–272; (2) S. Lee, Y. Yamakawa, & M. W. Peng, 2007, How does bankruptcy law affect entrepreneurship development? Washington: US Small Business Administration (SBA Best Research Papers Collection, www.sba.gov/advo/research/rs326tot.pdf); (3) M. W. Peng, Y. Yamakawa, & S. Lee, 2010, Bankruptcy laws and entrepreneur-friendliness, *Entrepreneur Theory and Practice* (in press).

NOTES

[Journal acronyms] **AME**—*Academy of Management Executive;* **AMJ**—*Academy of Management Journal;* **AMR**—*Academy of Management Review;* **APJM**—*Asia Pacific Journal of Management;* **BW**—*BusinessWeek;* **ETP**—*Entrepreneurship Theory and Practice;* **FEER**—*Far Eastern Economic Review;* **JBV**—*Journal of Business Venturing;* **JIBS**—*Journal of International Business Studies;* **JIM**—*Journal of International Management;* **JM**—*Journal of Management;* **JMS**—*Journal of Management Studies;* **JWB**—*Journal of World Business;* **MIR**—*Management International Review;* **QJE**—*Quarterly Journal of Economics;* **SEJ**—Strategic Entrepreneurship Journal; **SMJ**—*Strategic Management Journal;* **SMR**—*MIT Sloan Management Review*

[1] M. Hitt, R. D. Ireland, S. M. Camp, & D. Sexton, 2001, Strategic entrepreneurship (p. 480), *SMJ*, 22: 479–491.

[2] S. Shane & S. Venkataraman, 2000, The promise of entrepreneurship as a field of research (p. 218), *AMR*, 25: 217–226.

[3] P. McDougall & B. Oviatt, 2000, International entrepreneurship (p. 903), *AMJ*, 43: 902–906.

[4] Z. Acs & C. Armington, 2006, *Entrepreneurship, Geography, and American Economic Growth*, New York: Cambridge University Press.

[5] V. Lau, M. Shaffer, & K. Au, 2007, Entrepreneurial career success from a Chinese perspective, *JIBS*, 38: 126–146.

[6] J. Timmons, 1999, *New Venture Creation* (pp. 32–34), Boston: Irwin McGraw-Hill. See also R. Mudambi & S. Zahra, 2007, The survival of international new ventures, *JIBS*, 38: 333–352.

[7] A. Fadahunsi & P. Rosa, 2002, Entrepreneurship and illegality, *JBV*, 17: 397–429; F. Luthans & E. Ibrayeva, 2006, Entrepreneurial self-efficacy in Central Asian transition economies, *JIBS*, 37: 92–110.

[8] S. Djankov, R. La Porta, F. Lopez-de-Silanes, & A. Shleifer, 2002, The regulation of entry, *QJE*, 67: 1–37.

[9] World Bank, 2010, *Doing Business 2010: Overview* (p. 2), Washington: World Bank (www.doingbusiness.org).

[10] A. Chatterji, 2009, Spawned with a silver spoon? *SMJ*, 30: 185–206; R. Doern & C. Fey, 2006, E-commerce developments and

strategies for value-creation, *JWB*, 41: 315–327; G. Knight & D. Kim, 2009, International business competence and the contemporary firm, *JIBS*, 40: 255–273; D. Lepak, K. Smith, & M. S. Taylor, 2007, Value creation and value capture, *AMR*, 32: 180–194.

[11] L. Busenitz & J. Barney, 1997, Differences between entrepreneurs and managers in large organizations, *JBV*, 12: 9–30.

[12] J. Baum, E. Locke, & K. Smith, 2001, A multidimensional model of venture growth, *AMJ*, 44: 292–303; B. Gilbert, P. McDougall, & D. Audretsch, 2006, New venture growth, *JM*, 32: 926–950.

[13] M. Cardon, J. Wincent, J. Singh, & M. Drnovsek, 2009, The nature and experience of entrepreneurial passion, *AMR*, 34: 511–532; V. Rindova, D. Barry, & D. Ketchen, 2009, Entrepreneuring as emancipation, *AMR*, 34: 477–491.

[14] G. Bruton & Y. Rubanik, 2002, Resources of the firm, Russian high-technology start-ups, and firm growth, *JBV*, 17: 553–576.

[15] C. Nicholls-Nixon, 2005, Rapid growth and high performance, *AME*, 19: 77–88; W. Sine, H. Mitsuhashi, & D. Kirsch, 2006, Revisiting Burns and Stalker, *AMJ*, 49: 121–132.

[16] J. Ebben & A. Johnson, 2005, Efficiency, flexibility, or both? *SMJ*, 26: 1249–1259; G. George, 2005, Slack resources and the performance of privately held firms, *AMJ*, 48: 661–676.

[17] *BW*, 2005, The little contractor that could, July 4: 78–79.

[18] R. Katila & S. Shane, 2005, When does lack of resources make new firms innovative? *AMJ*, 48: 814–829; G. Lumpkin & G. Dess, 1996, Clarifying the entrepreneurial orientation construct and linking it to performance, *AMR*, 21: 135–172; F. Santos & K. Eisenhardt, 2009, Constructing markets and shaping boundaries, *AMJ*, 52: 643–671.

[19] A. Phene, K. Fladmoe-Lindquist, & L. Marsh, 2006, Breakthough innovations in the US biotechnology industry, *SMJ*, 27: 369–388; N. Stieglitz & K. Heine, 2007, Innovations and the role of complementarities in a strategic theory of the firm, *SMJ*, 28: 1–15.

[20] C. Christensen, 1997, *The Innovator's Dilemma*, Boston: Harvard Business School Press.

[21] G. Qian & L. Li, 2003, Profitability of small and medium-sized enterprises in high-technology industries, *SMJ*, 24: 881–887.

[22] S. Dobrev & W. Barnett, 2005, Organizational roles and transition to entrepreneurship, *AMJ*, 48: 433–449.

[23] D. Kirsch, B. Goldfarb, & A. Gera, 2009, Form or substance, *SMJ*, 30: 487–515.

[24] K. Au & H. Kwan, 2009, Start-up capital and Chinese entrepreneurs, *ETP*, 33: 889–908; D. Ahlstrom, G. Bruton, & K. Yeh, 2007, Venture capital in China: Past, present, future, *APJM*, 24: 247–268; M. Wright, 2007, Venture capital in China: A view from Europe, *APJM*, 24: 269–282.

[25] G. Knight & S. T. Cavusgil, 2004, Innovation, organizational capabilities, and the born-global firm, *JIBS*, 35: 124–141; B. Oviatt & P. McDougall, 1994, Toward a theory of international new ventures, *JIBS*, 25: 45–64.

[26] R. Chen & M. Martin, 2001, Foreign expansion of small firms, *JBV*, 16: 557–574.

[27] J. Combs & D. Ketchen, 1999, Can capital scarcity help agency theory explain franchising? *AMJ*, 42: 196–207; A. Fosfuri, 2006, The licensing dilemma, *SMJ*, 27: 1141–1158.

[28] J. Lu & P. Beamish, 2001, The internationalization and performance of SMEs, *SMJ*, 22: 565–586; S. Zahra, R. D. Ireland, & M. Hitt, 2000, International expansion by new venture firms, *AMJ*, 43: 925–950.

[29] J. Johanson & J. Vahlne, 1977, The internationalization process of the firm, *JIBS*, 4: 20–29; L. Li, D. Li, & T. Dalgic, 2004, Internationalization process of small and medium-sized enterprises, *MIR*, 44: 93–116.

[30] S. Kotha, V. Rindova, & F. Rothaermel, 2001, Assets and actions, *JIBS*, 32: 769–791.

[31] S. Chetty, K. Eriksson, & J. Lindbergh, 2006, The effect of specificity of experience on a firm's perceived importance of institutional knowledge in an ongoing business, *JIBS*, 37: 699–712; N. Coviello, 2006, The network dynamics of international new ventures, *JIBS*, 37: 713–731; Z. Fernandez & M. Nieto, 2006, Impact of ownership on the international involvement of SMEs, *JIBS*, 37: 340–351.

[32] M. W. Peng & A. Y. Ilinitch, 1998, Export intermediary firms, *JIBS*, 29: 609–620; H. Trabold, 2002, Export intermediation: An empirical test of Peng and Ilinitch, *JIBS*, 33: 327–344.

[33] M. W. Peng & A. York, 2001, Behind intermediary performance in export trade, *JIBS*, 32: 327–346; M. W. Peng, Y. Zhou, & A. York, 2006, Behind make or buy decisions in export strategy, *JWB*, 41: 289–300.

[34] J. Bell, R. McNaughton, & S. Young, 2001, "Born-again global" firms (p. 184), *JIM*, 7: 173–189.

[35] R. Tesker, 2002, Pepperoni power, *FEER*, November 14: 59–60.

[36] V. Aggarwal & D. Hsu, 2009, Modes of cooperative R&D commercialization by start-ups, *SMJ*, 30: 835–864; P. Ozcan & K. Eisenhardt, 2009, Origin of alliance portfolios, *AMJ*, 52: 246–279.

[37] M. Graebner, 2009, Caveat venditor, *AMJ*, 52: 435–472.

[38] B. Barringer, F. Jones, & D. Neubaum, 2005, A quantitative content analysis of the characteristics of rapid-growth firms and their founders, *JBV*, 20: 663–687; J. Dyer, H. Gregerson, & C. Christensen, 2008, Entrepreneur behaviors, opportunity recognition, and the origin of innovative ventures, *SEJ*, 2: 317–338.

[39] L. Busenitz, C. Gomez, & J. Spencer, 2000, Country institutional profiles, *AMJ*, 43: 994–1003; J. Oxley & B. Yeung, 2001, E-commerce readiness, *JIBS*, 32: 705–724; H. K. Steensma, L. Marino, M. Weaver, & P. Hickson, 2000, The influence of national culture on the formation of technology alliances by entrepreneurial firms, *AMJ*, 43: 951–973.

[40] Y. Yamakawa, M. W. Peng, & D. Deeds, 2008, What drives new ventures to internationalize from emerging to developed economies? *ETP*, 32: 59–82.

[41] H. Sapienza, E. Autio, G. George, & S. Zahra, 2006, A capabilities perspective on the effects of early internationalization on firm survival and growth, *AMR*, 31: 914–933.

[42] V. Govindarajan & A. Gupta, 2001, *The Quest for Global Dominance*, San Francisco: Jossey-Bass.

[43] K. Kling & I. Goteman, 2003, IKEA CEO Anders Dahlvig on international growth, *AME*, 17: 31–45.

[44] E. Autio, H. Sapienza, & J. Almeida, 2000, Effects of age at entry, knowledge intensity, and imitability in international growth, *AMJ*, 43: 909–924.

[45] J. Mathews & I. Zander, 2007, The international entrepreneurial dynamics of accelerated internationalization, *JIBS*, 38: 387–403; S. Nadkarni & P. Perez, 2007, Prior conditions and early international commitment, *JIBS*, 38: 160–176.

[46] P. Liesch & G. Knight, 1999, Information internationalization and hurdle rates in small and medium enterprise internationalization, *JIBS*, 30: 383–394.

[47] M. Lyles, T. Saxton, & K. Watson, 2004, Venture survival in a transition economy, *JM*, 30: 351–373.

[48] L. Lopez, S. Kundu, & L. Ciravegna, 2009, Born global or born regional? *JIBS*, 40: 1228–1238.

[49] S. Rangan & R. Adner, 2001, Profits and the Internet (pp. 49–50), *SMR*, summer: 44–53.

[50] M. W. Peng, C. Hill, & D. Wang, 2000, Schumpeterian dynamics versus Williamsonian considerations, *JMS*, 37: 167–184.

Chapter 10

© Peter Harmsen/AFP/Getty Images

LEARNING OBJECTIVES

After studying this chapter, you should be able to:

1. identify ways in which institutions and resources affect the liability of foreignness.

2. match the quest for location-specific advantages with strategic goals.

3. compare and contrast first-mover and late-mover advantages.

4. list the steps in the comprehensive model of foreign market entries.

5. participate in three leading debates on foreign market entries.

6. draw implications for action.

Entering Foreign Markets

Pearl River Goes Abroad: Exports, Green-fields, Acquisitions

Pearl River is likely to be the world's largest piano maker that you have never heard of. It is also the fastest growing piano maker in North America, with the largest dealer network (over 300 dealers) in Canada and the United States. Pearl River US subsidiary's website proudly announces that Pearl River is "the world's best selling piano." Some of you may say: "Sorry, I don't play piano, so I don't know anything about leading piano brands." However, you most likely have heard about Yamaha and Steinway. Therefore, your defense for not knowing Pearl River would collapse.

The problem is with both you (consumers) and Pearl River itself. Given the relatively low prestige associated with made-in-China goods, a fine musical instrument such as a piano is not typically associated with a Chinese firm. Pearl River Piano Group (PRPG) is China's largest piano maker and has recently dethroned Japan's Yamaha to become the world champion by volume. Despite PRPG's outstanding capabilities, it is difficult for one firm to change the negative country-of-origin image associated with made-in-China goods.

PRPG was founded in 1956 in Guangzhou, China, where the Pearl River flows by. Pearl River in fact exported its very first piano to Hong Kong. Yet, its center of gravity has remained in China. Pianos have become more affordable with rising income. The one-child policy has made families willing to invest in their only child's education. As a result, the Chinese now buy half of the pianos produced in the world.

If you think life will be easy for the leading firm in the largest market in the world, sorry, you are wrong. In fact, life is increasingly hard for PRPG. This is because rising demand has attracted numerous new entrants, many of which compete at the low end in China. More than 140 competitors have pushed PRPG's domestic market share from 70% at its peak a decade ago to about 25% now, although it is still the market leader.

Savage domestic competition has pushed PRPG to look increasingly for overseas opportunities. It now exports to over 80 countries. In North America, PRPG started in the late 1980s by relying on US-based importers. Making its first ever foreign direct investment (FDI) in 1999, it set up a US-based sales subsidiary, PRPG America, Ltd. (more commonly known as Pearl River USA), in Ontario, California. This subsidiary is a green-field—namely, a new entity built from scratch. Acknowledging the importance of the US market and the limited international caliber of his own managerial rank, PRPG's CEO, Tong Zhi Cheng, attracted Al Rich, an American with long experience in the piano industry, to head the subsidiary. In two years, the green-field subsidiary succeeded in getting Pearl River pianos into about one-third of the specialized US retail dealers. In ten years, the Pearl River brand became the undisputed leader in the low end of the upright piano market in North America. Efforts to penetrate the high end market, however, were still frustrated.

Despite the enviable progress made by PRPG itself in general and by its US subsidiary in particular, the Pearl River brand suffers from all the usual trappings associated with Chinese brands. "We are very cognizant that our pricing provides a strong incentive to buy," Rich noted in a media interview, "but $6,000 is still a lot of money." In an audacious move to overcome buyers' reservation about purchasing a high-end Chinese product, PRPG made its second major FDI move in 2000, by acquiring Ritmüller of Germany.

Ritmüller was founded in 1795 by Wilhelm Ritmüller, during the lifetimes of composers Beethoven and Haydn. It was one of the first piano makers in Germany (and in the world). It soon became one of Europe's most innovative manufacturers. Ritmüller conceived of the double soundboard that resulted in the characteristic warm, rich tone now called the "Euro Sound." Unfortunately, Ritmüller's style of small-scale, handicraft-based piano making had a hard time surviving the disruptive, mass-production technologies unleashed by Yamaha and more recently by Pearl River. Prior to being acquired by Pearl River, Ritmüller ended up being inactive for a long time. Today, Ritmüller has entered a new era in its proud history and operates a factory in Germany with full capacity. The entire product line has been re-engineered to reflect a new commitment to a classic heritage and standard of excellence. PRPG has commissioned international master piano designer Lothar Thomma to marry German precision craftsmanship with the latest piano making technology.

PRPG executives as well as branding experts and media gurus have constantly debated whether PRPG should invest solely in building up the Pearl River brand or to inject major resources into reviving the Ritmüller brand. Pointing out the success of Japanese brands such as Yamaha, critics both inside and outside PRPG argue that acquiring Ritmüller reflects a lack of confidence in the Pearl River brand. Defenders of this practice argue that this is a realistic step given PRPG's lack of international branding prowess and China's lack of positive country-of-origin image. If you compare

PRPG's corporate home page with its US subsidiary's home page, both brag about Pearl River (not Ritmüller), but you can see how modest the Chinese are in pushing their brand:

- Line 1 from PRPG's home page (www.pearlriver piano.com): "If you have not heard of us, it may surprise you to know that we are a formidable competitor in the world piano market, and we're growing fast."
- Line 1 from the US subsidiary's home page (www. pearlriverusa.com): "Why is Pearl River the fastest growing piano company in North America? Pearl River delivers the best quality for the price you pay. In fact, when it comes to value, Pearl River has no competition."

Sources: I thank Professors Klaus Meyer (University of Bath) and Yuan Lu (Chinese University of Hong Kong) for their assistance. Based on (1) *Beijing Review*, 2009, The return of the king, May 21, www.bjreview.com; (2) Funding Universe, 2009, Guangzhou Pearl River Piano Group Ltd., www.fundinguniverse.com; (3) Y. Lu, 2009, Pearl River Piano Group's international strategy, in M. W. Peng, *Global Strategy*, 2nd ed. (pp. 437–440), Cincinnati: South-Western Cengage Learning; (4) Pearl River Piano Group, 2009, www.pearlriverpiano.com; (5) Pearl River USA, 2009, www.pearlriverusa.com.

How do companies such as Pearl River enter foreign markets? Why do they enter certain countries but not others? Why do they sometimes export, sometimes set up green-field subsidiaries, and sometimes use acquisitions when entering foreign markets? These are some of the key questions we will address in this chapter. Entering foreign markets is one of the most important topics in international business (IB). First, we will draw on the institution-based and resource-based views to discuss ways to overcome the liability of foreignness.[1] Then we will focus on three crucial dimensions: where (W), when (W), and how (H)—known as the 2W1H dimensions. Our discussion continues with a comprehensive model, followed by three leadings debates. We conclude with practical tips for entering foreign markets.

LEARNING OBJECTIVE

1

Identify ways in which institutions and resources affect the liability of foreignness.

OVERCOMING THE LIABILITY OF FOREIGNNESS

It is not easy to succeed in an unfamiliar environment. Recall from Chapter 1 that foreign firms such as Pearl River have to overcome a liability of foreignness, which is the *inherent* disadvantage foreign firms experience in host countries because of their non-native status.[2] Such a liability is manifested in at least two ways. First, numerous differences in formal and informal institutions govern the rules of the game in different countries. Although local firms are already well versed in these rules, foreign firms have to learn the rules. For example, European firms that have subsidiaries operating in the United States are busy learning the new "Buy American" rules in US stimulus packages that may qualify them as "US firms."[3] Many governments ban foreigners from owning assets in certain strategic sectors. Rupert Murdoch (owner of News Corporation) had to become a US citizen in order to acquire US broadcast properties.

Second, although customers in this age of globalization *supposedly* no longer discriminate against foreign firms, the reality is that foreign firms are often still discriminated against, sometimes formally and other times informally. In government procurement, "buy national" (such as "buy American") is often required. In consumer products, the discrimination against foreign firms is less, but still far from disappearing. For years, American rice and beef, suspected (although never proven) to contain long-term health hazards because of genetic modification, are informally resisted by individual consumers in Japan and Europe, *after* formal discriminatory policies imposed by their governments were removed. Activists in India accused both Coca-Cola and Pepsi products of containing higher than permitted levels of pesticides but did not test any Indian soft drinks, even though pesticide residues are present in virtually all groundwater in India. Although both Coca-Cola and Pepsi denied these charges, their sales suffered.

Against such significant odds, how do foreign firms crack new markets? The answer boils down to our two core perspectives introduced earlier (see Figure 10.1). The institution-based view suggests that firms need to undertake actions deemed legitimate and appropriate by the various formal and informal institutions governing market entries.[4] Differences in formal institutions may lead to regulatory risks due to differences in political, economic, and legal systems (see Chapter 2). There may be numerous trade and investment barriers on a national or regional basis (see Chapters 5, 6, and 8). In addition, the existence of multiple currencies—and currency risks as a result—may be another formal barrier (see Chapter 7). The experience of the euro shows how much more trade and investment can take place when multiple countries remove barriers by adopting the same currency (see Chapter 8). Informally, numerous differences in cultures, norms, and values create another major source of liability of foreignness (see Chapter 3).[5]

FIGURE 10.1   INSTITUTIONS, RESOURCES, AND FOREIGN MARKET ENTRIES

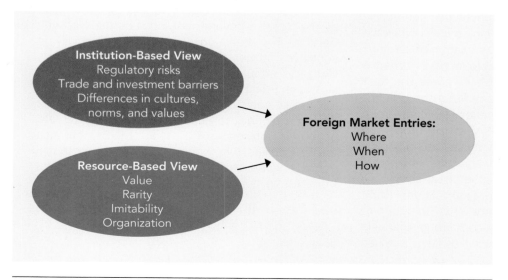

The resource-based view argues that foreign firms need to deploy *overwhelming* resources and capabilities to offset the liability of foreignness.[6] Applying the VRIO framework introduced in Chapter 4 to our Opening Case, we can suggest that Pearl River has some overwhelmingly valuable and rare capabilities in successfully becoming the king of the low-end pianos in North America. Yet, no US rivals are able to imitate Pearl River's combination of excellent quality with attractive pricing. However, thanks to the liability of foreignness (in this case, "Chineseness"), it has a hard time breaking into the high-end market. In response, it has acquired a classic but inactive German brand Ritmüller to reduce such liability of foreignness. Acquiring and integrating a foreign firm requires an enormous amount of organizational capabilities, and many acquisitions fail. Pearl River's organizational capabilities have proven to be a tremendous asset.

Overall, our two core perspectives shed a lot of light on firms' internationalization.[7] For example, In Focus 10.1 illustrates why there is a recent surge of multinational enterprises (MNEs) from Russia. Next, we investigate the 2W1H dimensions associated with foreign market entries.

IN Focus 10.1

Russian Firms Spread Their Wings Abroad

Although outward FDI from companies based in China and India often grabs media headlines, Russia has the largest stock of outward FDI among all emerging economies. At the end of 2008, at $203 billion, Russia held more outward FDI stock than Brazil ($162 billion), China ($148 billion), and India ($62 billion).

After the fall of the Berlin Wall in 1989, Russia suffered a decade of turmoil. Since 1999, the Russian economy staged a spectacular comeback, largely thanks to consistently high prices of its main export items, oil and gas. Accumulation of earnings and lucrative opportunities abroad have turned a series of Russian firms into MNEs spreading their wings around the globe. Russian firms active in FDI can be found in three categories: (1) One group targets acquisition targets in Western Europe and North America in an effort to access technological innovations and advanced management know-how. (2) Another group focuses on the "near abroad"— the Commonwealth of Independent States (CIS), whose member countries were all formerly a part of the Soviet Union. (3) The last group channels funds through offshore financial centers such as

Cyprus and British Virgin Islands and reinvests back in Russia—a process known as capital round-tripping. Experts estimate that about 10% of the Russian outward FDI is involved in round-tripping, leaving the other 90% to be "real" FDI.

Russian FDI abroad is not without controversies. Host country governments and the media often voice concern that Russian MNEs, especially large energy companies, may represent the "long arm of the Kremlin." The political hard line recently taken by the Russian government (such as the war with Georgia) heightens such concerns, especially in sensitive, former Soviet bloc countries such as Hungary, Lithuania, and Poland. Russian MNEs claim that their FDI is solely driven by profit motives. However, host country governments face the dilemma of how to accommodate the legitimate economic interests of Russian MNEs, harness the FDI dollars they bring, and limit the potential damage when dealing with the bears (or eagles) from Russia.

Sources: Based on (1) A. Panibratov & K. Kalotay, 2009, Russia outward FDI and its policy context, *Columbia FDI Profiles*, No. 1, www.vcc.columbia.edu; (2) United Nations, 2009, *World Investment Report 2009*, New York: UN.

WHERE TO ENTER?

Similar to real estate, the motto for IB is "Location, location, location." In fact, such a *spatial* perspective (that is, doing business outside of one's home country) is a defining feature of IB.[8] Two sets of considerations drive the location of foreign entries: (1) strategic goals and (2) cultural and institutional distances.

LEARNING OBJECTIVE

2

Match the quest for location-specific advantages with strategic goals.

Location-Specific Advantages and Strategic Goals

Favorable locations in certain countries may give firms operating there what are called location-specific advantages. Location-specific advantages are the benefits a firm reaps from features specific to a particular place. Certain locations simply possess geographical features that are difficult for others to match. Miami, the self-styled "Gateway of the Americas," is an ideal location both for North American firms looking south and Latin American companies coming north. Vienna is an attractive site as MNE regional headquarters for Central and Eastern Europe. Rotterdam is at the center of a vast transportation network spanning Europe (In Focus 10.2 and PengAtlas Map 3.3). We may regard the continuous expansion of IB as an unending saga in search of location-specific advantages.

We also learned in Chapter 6 about agglomeration, or location-specific advantages that arise from the clustering of economic activities in certain locations. The basic idea dates back at least to Alfred Marshall, a British economist who first published it in 1890. Recall that location-specific advantages stem from (1) knowledge spillovers among closely located firms that attempt to hire individuals from competitors, (2) industry demand that creates a skilled labor force whose members may work for different firms without having to move out of the region, and (3) industry demand that facilitates a pool of specialized suppliers and buyers to also locate in the region.[9] Agglomeration explains why certain cities and regions can attract businesses even in the absence of obvious geographic advantages. For example, due to agglomeration, aerospace firms cluster around Wichita, Kansas (see In Focus 6.1), and financial services firms flock to Ireland.

Given that different locations offer different benefits, it is imperative that a firm match its strategic goals with potential locations as shown in Table 10.1. First, firms seeking *natural resources* have to go to particular foreign locations where those resources are found. For example, the Middle East, Russia, and Venezuela

Location-specific advantages
The benefits a firm reaps from the features specific to a place.

TABLE 10.1 MATCHING STRATEGIC GOALS WITH LOCATIONS

Strategic goals	Location-specific advantages	Examples in the text
Natural resource seeking	Possession of natural resources and related transport and communication infrastructure	*Oil in the Middle East, Russia, and Venezuela*
Market seeking	Abundance of strong market demand and customers willing to pay	*Seafood in Japan*
Efficiency seeking	Economies of scale and abundance of low-cost factors	*Manufacturing in China*
Innovation seeking	Abundance of innovative individuals, firms, and universities	*IT in Silicon Valley and Bangalore; financial services in New York and London; aerospace in Russia*

Focus 10.2

Rotterdam: Gateway to the World

Photo Credit

The Netherlands has long been a nation of traders. The hub of trade is the Port of Rotterdam, Europe's largest. It stretches over 40 kilometers (25 miles) and covers over 10,000 hectares (24,000 acres) of land. Over one million tons of goods are loaded, unloaded, and distributed in Rotterdam *every day*—more than twice the turnover of the next largest European ports, which are Antwerp, Belgium, and Hamburg, Germany. Worldwide, Rotterdam ranks fourth behind the East Asian hubs of Shanghai, Ningbo, and Singapore. Shipments involve all types of cargo, including chemicals, ores, liquid bulk, dry bulk, vehicles, and refrigerated cargo such as fruit. Every year, 33,000 ocean going ships call in the port, 6.5 million containers pass through, and 120 million m³ crude oil arrive to be refined and distributed throughout Europe. The transportation businesses in the port add €6.6 billion to Dutch GDP, while other industries located in the vicinity add another €5 billion.

The Port of Rotterdam serves as the main hub for sea-bound transportation into and out of Europe, a market of over 500 million consumers (see PengAtlas Map 3.3). Containers arrive from Asia on mega ships that are too large even for other large ports such as Hamburg or Copenhagen. Thus, containers are transferred in Rotterdam to smaller ships sailing to ports along the Atlantic coast, into the North and Baltic Seas, up the river Rhine, and across to the UK. More than 500 liner services connect Rotterdam with over 1,000 ports worldwide.

Huge investments have gone into the port. Essential is the *Nieuwe Waterweg* (New Channel), which opened in 1870 and connects the city of Rotterdam directly to the North Sea. It has been continuously widened and deepened, while far out in the North Sea, a man-made channel

allows easy access even for the largest ships of the world, including mammoth tankers, ore carriers, and container vessels. With a depth of 20 meters the port is accessible for container ships that are unable to berth in other European ports. *Maasvlakte 1*, which contains the largest container terminals, was reclaimed from the estuary 30 years ago. A new expansion of the port, called *Maasvlakte 2*, is to extend the port further into the North Sea, creating 1,000 hectares of industrial land.

Rotterdam is connected to its hinterland by an integrated transportation infrastructure, including regional shipping lines, inland waterways (especially the Rhine connecting to Germany, France, and Switzerland), oil pipelines, roads, and railways—along with suitably located trans-shipment points between different transport modes. Many goods from the German industrial heartlands of the Ruhr region are loaded on riverboats or direct trains in Duisburg, Germany, then shipped downstream to Rotterdam, and from there out to the world. Yet, traffic jams hold up trucks, and the regional and national authorities are under pressure to invest in upgrading the infrastructure connecting Rotterdam with Duisburg and other secondary hubs.

Rotterdam has attracted many businesses relying on imported goods, especially petroleum refinery and chemicals processing plants. Many Japanese and American MNEs set up their European distribution centers in the Rotterdam area, using the South-West of the Netherlands as a hub.

Sources: This case was written by Professor **Klaus Meyer** (University of Bath). It is based on (1) A. Granzow & R. Reichstein, 2008, Alle Wege führen über Duisburg, *Handelsblatt*, April 11; (2) Port of Rotterdam, 2009, *Port Statistics*, mimeo, www.portofrotterdam.com (accessed October 2009); (3) R. Wrights, 2007, Rotterdam struggles to contain its enthusiasm as demand surges ahead, *Financial Times*, December 5.

are all rich in oil. Even when the Venezuelan government became more hostile, Western oil firms had to put up with it.

Second, *market-seeking* firms go to countries that have a strong demand for their products and services. For example, the Japanese appetite and willingness to pay for seafood has motivated seafood exporters around the world—ranging from nearby China and Korea to distant Norway and Chile—to ship their catch to Japan in order to fetch top dollars (or yen).

Third, *efficiency-seeking* firms often single out the most efficient locations featuring a combination of scale economies and low cost factors.[10] It is the search for efficiency that induced numerous MNEs to enter China. China now manufactures two-thirds of the world's photocopiers, shoes, toys, and microwave ovens; half of the DVD players, digital cameras, and textiles; one-third of the desktop computers; and a quarter of the mobile phones, TV sets, and steel.[11] Reportedly Shanghai alone has a cluster of over 300 of the *Fortune* Global 500 firms. It is important to note that China does not present the absolutely lowest labor costs in the world, and Shanghai is the *highest* cost city in China. China's attractiveness lies in its ability to enhance efficiency for foreign entrants by lowering *total* costs. However, the rising labor costs and the appreciating yuan have eroded some of China's cost advantage recently, making Mexico a relatively more attractive production location, especially for US MNEs (see Table 10.2).

Finally, *innovation-seeking* firms target countries and regions renowned for generating world-class innovations, such as Silicon Valley and Bangalore (in information technology), New York and London (in financial services), and Russia (in aerospace). Such entries can be viewed as "an option to maintain access to innovations resident in the host country, thus generating information spillovers that may lead to opportunities for future organizational learning and growth."[12] (See Chapter 13 for details.)

It is important to note that these four strategic goals, although analytically distinct, are not mutually exclusive. A firm may have to weigh more than one concern as it decides where to locate. Also, location-specific advantages may grow, change, and/or decline, prompting a firm to relocate. If policymakers fail to maintain the institutional attractiveness (for example, by raising taxes) and if companies overcrowd and bid up factor costs such as land and talents, some firms may move out of certain locations previously considered advantageous.[13] For example, Mercedes and BMW had proudly projected a 100% "Made in Germany" image until the early 1990s. Now both companies produce in a variety of countries such as Brazil, China, Mexico, South Africa, the United States, and Vietnam, and instead boast "Made by Mercedes" and "Made by BMW." Both the relative decline of Germany's location-specific advantages and the rise of other countries' advantages prompted Mercedes and BMW to shift their emphasis from location-specific advantages to firm-specific advantages.

TABLE 10.2   CHINA'S RISING MANUFACTURING COST IN PRODUCING AN ALUMINUM AUTO PART

	2005	2008
China	$17	$25
Mexico	$18	$20
United States	$24	$29

Source: Adapted from *BusinessWeek*, 2009, China's eroding advantage, June 15: 54–55.

Cultural/Institutional Distances and Foreign Entry Locations

In addition to strategic goals, another set of considerations centers on cultural/institutional distances (see also Chapters 2 and 3). **Cultural distance** is the difference between two cultures along identifiable dimensions such as individualism. Considering culture as an informal part of institutional frameworks governing a particular country, **institutional distance** is "the extent of similarity or dissimilarity between the regulatory, normative, and cognitive institutions of two countries."[14] Broadly speaking, cultural distance is a subset of institutional distance. For example, many Western cosmetics firms, such as L'Oreal, have shied away from Saudi Arabia, citing its stricter rules of personal behavior. In essence, Saudi Arabia's cultural and institutional distance from Western cultures is too large.

Two schools of thought have emerged in terms of where to enter. The first is associated with the stage model. According to the stage model, firms will enter culturally similar countries during their first stage of internationalization and will then gain more confidence to enter culturally distant countries in later stages.[15] This idea is intuitively appealing: It makes sense for Belgian firms to enter France first and Russian firms to enter Ukraine first to take advantage of common cultural and language traditions. On average, business between countries that share a language is three times greater than between countries without a common language. Firms from common-law countries (English-speaking countries and Britain's former colonies) are more likely to be interested in other common-law countries. Colony-colonizer links boost trade significantly. In general, MNEs from emerging economies perform better in other developing countries, presumably because of their closer institutional distance and similar stages of economic development.[16] Overall, some evidence documents certain performance benefits of competing in culturally and institutionally adjacent countries.[17]

Citing numerous counterexamples, a second school of thought argues that it is more important to consider strategic goals such as market and efficiency rather than culture and institutions.[18] For example, natural-resource-seeking firms have some compelling reasons to enter culturally and institutionally distant countries (such as Papua New Guinea for bauxite, Zambia for copper, and Nigeria for oil). Major Western oil producers on Sakhalin Island, a remote part of the Russian Far East, have no choice but to accept Russia's unfriendly, strong-arm tactics to grab more shares and profits—tactics described as "thuggish ways" by the *Economist*.[19] Because major Western oil producers have few alternatives elsewhere, cultural, institutional, and geographic distance in this case does not seem relevant. These Western oil producers simply have to be there and let the Russians dictate the terms. Some counterintuitive (although inconclusive) evidence suggests that for any particular host country, firms from distant countries do not necessarily underperform those from neighboring countries.[20] Overall, in the complex calculus underpinning entry decisions, location represents only one of several important considerations. As shown next, entry timing and modes are also crucial.

Cultural distance
The difference between two cultures along identifiable dimensions such as individualism.

Institutional distance
The extent of similarity or dissimilarity between the regulatory, normative, and cognitive institutions of two countries.

First-mover advantages
Benefits that accrue to firms that enter the market first and that late entrants do not enjoy.

Compare and contrast first-mover and late-mover advantages.

WHEN TO ENTER?

Entry timing refers to whether there are compelling reasons to be an early or late entrant in a particular country. Some firms look for **first-mover advantages**, defined as the benefits that accrue to firms that enter the market first and that late entrants do not enjoy.[21] Speaking of the power of first-mover advantages, "Xerox,"

"FedEx," and "Google" have now become verbs describing the actions or services they perform (such as "Google it"). In many African countries, "Colgate" is the generic term for toothpaste. Unilever, a late mover, is disappointed to find out that its African customers call its own toothpaste "the red Colgate" (!). However, first movers may also encounter significant disadvantages which, in turn, become **late-mover advantages**. Table 10.3 shows a number of first-mover advantages.

First movers may gain advantage through proprietary technology. They also ride the learning curve in pursuit of scale and scope economies in new countries. For example, Yahoo! has become a search engine leader in Japan, thanks to its pioneering efforts in that country (see the Closing Case). First movers may also make preemptive investments. A number of Japanese multinational enterprises (MNEs) have cherry picked leading local suppliers and distributors in Southeast Asia as new members of the expanded *keiretsu* networks (or alliances of Japanese businesses with interlocking business relationships and shareholdings), and blocked access to these suppliers and distributors by late entrants from the West.[22] In addition, first movers may erect significant entry barriers for late entrants, such as high switching costs due to brand loyalty. Parents who used a particular brand of disposable diapers (such as Huggies or Pampers) for their first baby often use the same brand for any subsequent babies. Buyers of expensive equipment are likely to stick with the same producers for components, training, and other services for a long time. That is why American, British, French, German, and Russian aerospace firms competed intensely for Poland's first post–Cold War order of fighters—America's F-16 eventually won.

Intense domestic competition may drive some nondominant firms abroad to avoid clashing with dominant firms head-on in their home market. Matsushita, Toyota, and NEC were the market leaders in Japan, but Sony, Honda, and Epson all entered the United States in their respective markets ahead of the leading firms. Finally, first movers may build precious relationships with key stakeholders such as customers and governments. Motorola, for example, entered China in the early 1980s and has benefited from its lengthy presence in the country. Later, China

Late-mover advantages
Benefits that accrue to firms that enter the market later and that early entrants do not enjoy.

TABLE 10.3 FIRST-MOVER VERSUS LATE-MOVER ADVANTAGES

First-mover advantages	Examples in the text	Late-mover advantages	Examples in the text
Proprietary, technological leadership	*Yahoo! in Japan*	Opportunity to free ride on first-mover investments	*Ericsson won big contracts in Saudi Arabia, free riding on Cisco's efforts*
Preemption of scarce resources	*Japanese MNEs in Southeast Asia*	Resolution of technological and market uncertainty	*IBM and Matsushita have patience to wait*
Establishing entry barriers for late entrants	*Huggies and Pampers diapers for the first born; Poland's F-16 fighter jet contract*	First mover's difficulty to adapt to market changes	*Kodak and Fujifilm are pushed aside by Canon, Samsung, and Sony*
Avoidance of clash with dominant firms at home	*Sony, Honda, and Epson went to the US market ahead of their Japanese rivals*		
Relationships with key stakeholders such as customers and governments	*Motorola's technology became China's national paging standard*		

adopted Motorola's technology as its national paging standard, locking out other rivals (at least for the initial period).

The potential advantages of first movers may be counterbalanced by various disadvantages, listed in the second column of Table 10.3. Numerous first-mover firms have lost market dominance in the long run, such as EMI in CT scanners, de Haviland in jet airliners, and Netscape in Internet browsers. It is such late-mover firms as GE, Boeing, and Microsoft (Explorer), respectively, that win. Specifically, late-mover advantages are manifested in three ways. First, late movers may be able to free ride on the huge pioneering investments. For example, Cisco invested millions of dollars to rub shoulders with dignitaries in Saudi Arabia, including the king, in order to help officials grasp the promise of the Internet in fueling economic development, only to lose out to late movers such as Ericsson and Huawei that offered lower cost solutions. In one case, the new King Abdullah Economic City awarded an $84 million citywide telecom project to Ericsson whose bid was more than 20% lower than Cisco's, in part because Ericsson did not have to offer a lot of basic education and did not have to entertain that much. "We're very proud to have won against a company that did as much advance work as Cisco did," an elated Ericsson executive noted.[23]

Second, first movers face greater technological and market uncertainties. After some of these uncertainties are removed, late movers may join the game with massive firepower. Some MNEs such as IBM and Matsushita are known to be hard-hitting late movers. Finally, as incumbents, first movers may be locked into a given set of fixed assets or reluctant to cannibalize existing product lines in favor of new ones. Late movers may be able to take advantage of the inflexibility of first movers by leapfrogging them. For example, first movers in traditional photo technology, such as Kodak and Fujifilm, have recently been pushed aside by late movers, led by Canon, Samsung, and Sony, which excel in digital technology.

Overall, some evidence points out first-mover advantages,[24] and other evidence points out late-mover advantages.[25] Unfortunately, a mountain of research is still unable to conclusively recommend a particular entry timing strategy. Although first movers may have an *opportunity* to win, their pioneering status is not a guarantee of success.[26] For example, among the three first movers into the Chinese automobile industry in the early 1980s, Volkswagen captured significant advantages, Chrysler had very moderate success, and Peugeot failed and had to exit. Although many of the late movers that entered in the late 1990s are struggling, GM, Honda, and Hyundai gained significant market shares. It is obvious that entry timing cannot be viewed in isolation, and entry timing per se is not the sole determinant of success and failure of foreign entries. It is through *interaction* with other strategic variables that entry timing has an impact on performance.[27]

HOW TO ENTER?

List the steps in the comprehensive model of foreign market entries.

In this section, we will first consider on what scale—large or small—a firm should enter foreign markets. Then we will look at a comprehensive model for entering foreign markets. The first step is to determine whether to pursue an equity or nonequity mode of entry. As we will see, this crucial decision differentiates MNEs (involving equity modes) from non-MNEs (relying on nonequity modes). Finally, we outline the pros and cons of various equity and nonequity modes.

Scale of Entry: Commitment and Experience

One key dimension in foreign entry decisions is the scale of entry, which refers to the amount of resources committed to entering a foreign market. A number of European financial services firms, such as ABN Amro and HSBC, have recently spent several billion dollars to enter the United States through a series of acquisitions. Such large-scale entries demonstrate a strategic commitment to certain markets. This helps assure local customers and suppliers ("We are here for the long haul!") as well as deterring potential entrants. The drawbacks of such a hard-to-reverse strategic commitment are (1) limited strategic flexibility elsewhere and (2) huge losses if these large-scale bets turn out to be wrong. (See In Focus 10.3 for DHL's big-time failure.)

Small-scale entries are less costly. They focus on organizational learning by getting a firm's feet wet—learning by doing—while limiting the downside risk.[28] For example, to enter the market of Islamic finance whereby no interest can be charged (according to the Koran), Citibank set up a subsidiary Citibank Islamic Bank, HSBC established Amanah, and UBS launched Noriba. They were all designed to experiment with different interpretations of the Koran on how to make money while not committing religious sins. It is simply not possible to acquire such an ability outside the Islamic world. Overall, there is evidence that the longer foreign firms stay in host countries, the less liability of foreignness they experience.[29] The drawback of small-scale entries is a lack of strong commitment, which may lead to difficulties in building market share and capturing first-mover advantages.

Modes of Entry: The First Step on Equity versus Nonequity Modes

Managers are unlikely to consider the numerous modes of entry (methods used to enter a foreign market) all at the same time. Given the complexity of entry decisions, it is imperative that managers *prioritize* and consider only a few key

Scale of entry
The amount of resources committed to entering a foreign market.

Mode of entry
Method used to enter a foreign market.

IN Focus 10.3

DHL Fails to Deliver

Conquering the world is one thing, conquering the United States is another. That is the lesson from DHL's November 10, 2008, announcement that it would abandon the US express delivery market after losses of nearly $10 billion over five years. Although DHL is No. 1 around the globe, DHL could not dislodge FedEx and UPS in their home market. Faced with steep sales declines because of the economic downturn, it decided to lay off some 10,000 US workers and close all 18 of its land hubs. DHL will still make international deliveries to and from the United States. Its rivals immediately hustled to grab its customers.

Source: Reprinted from the November 24, 2008 issue of *Bloomberg Business-Week* by special permission. Copyright © 2008 by Bloomberg L.P.

variables first and then consider other variables later.[30] The comprehensive model shown in Figure 10.2 and explained in Table 10.4 is helpful.

In the first step, considerations for small-scale versus large-scale entries usually boil down to the equity (ownership) issue. **Nonequity modes** include exports and contractual agreements and tend to reflect relatively smaller commitments to overseas markets. **Equity modes**, on the other hand, include JVs and wholly owned subsidiaries and are indicative of relatively larger, harder-to-reverse commitments. Equity modes call for the establishment of independent organizations overseas (partially or wholly controlled). Nonequity modes do not require such independent establishments. Overall, these modes differ significantly in terms of cost, commitment, risk, return, and control.

The distinction between equity and nonequity modes is not trivial. In fact, it is what defines an MNE: An MNE enters foreign markets via equity modes through foreign direct investment (FDI). A firm that merely exports/imports with no FDI is usually not regarded as an MNE. As discussed at length in Chapter 6, an MNE, relative to a non-MNE, enjoys the three pronged advantages of ownership, location, and internalization, collectively known as the OLI advantages.[31] Overall, the first step in entry mode considerations is crucial. A strategic decision has to be made in terms of whether or not to undertake FDI and to become an MNE.

Nonequity mode

A mode of entry (exports and contractual agreements) that tends to reflect relatively smaller commitments to overseas markets.

Equity mode

A mode of entry (JV and WOS) that indicates a relatively larger, harder-to-reverse commitment.

FIGURE 10.2   THE CHOICE OF ENTRY MODES: A COMPREHENSIVE MODEL

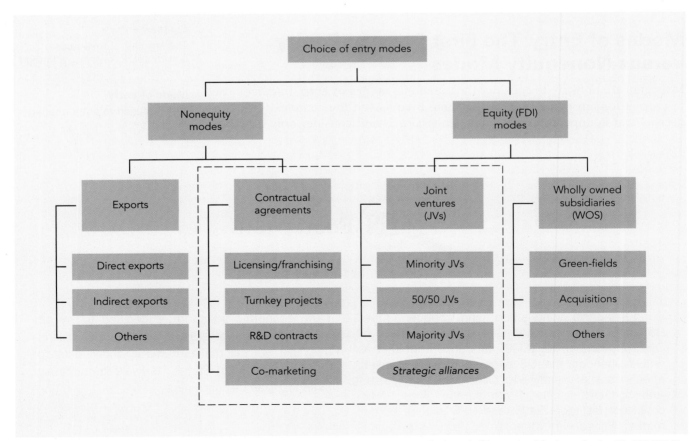

Source: Adapted from Y. Pan & D. Tse, 2000, The hierarchical model of market entry modes (p. 538), *Journal of International Business Studies*, 31: 535–554. The dashed area labeled "strategic alliances" is added by the present author.

TABLE 10.4 MODES OF ENTRY: ADVANTAGES AND DISADVANTAGES

Entry modes (examples in the text)	Advantages	Disadvantages
1. Nonequity modes: Exports		
Direct exports (*Pearl River piano exports to over 80 countries*)	• Economies of scale in production concentrated in home country • Better control over distribution	• High transportation costs for bulky products • Marketing distance from customers • Trade barriers and protectionism
Indirect exports (*Commodities trade in textiles, wood products, and meats*)	• Focus on production • Avoid export processes	• Less control over distribution • Inability to learn how to compete overseas
2. Nonequity modes: Contractual agreements		
Licensing/Franchising (*Pizza Hut in Thailand*)	• Low development costs • Low risk in overseas expansion	• Little control over technology and marketing • May create competitors • Inability to engage in global coordination ·
Turnkey projects (*A German, Italian, and Iranian consortium on a BOT project in Iran*)	• Ability to earn returns from process technology in countries where FDI is restricted	• May create efficient competitors • Lack of long-term presence
R&D contracts (*IT work in India and aerospace research in Russia*)	• Ability to tap into the best locations for certain innovations at low costs	• Difficult to negotiate and enforce contracts • May nurture innovative competitors • May lose core innovation capabilities
Co-marketing (*McDonald's campaigns with movie studios and toy makers; airline alliances such as OneWorld and Star Alliance*)	• Ability to reach more customers	• Limited coordination
3. Equity modes: Partially owned subsidiaries		
Joint ventures (*Sony Ericsson and Shanghai Volkswagen*)	• Sharing costs, risks, and profits • Access to partners' assets • Politically acceptable	• Divergent goals and interests of partners • Limited equity and operational control • Difficult to coordinate globally
4. Equity modes: Wholly owned subsidiaries		
Green-field operations (*Pearl River USA; Japanese auto transplants in the United States*)	• Complete equity and operational control • Protection of know-how • Ability to coordinate globally	• Potential political problems and risks • High development costs • Add new capacity to industry • Slow entry speed (relative to acquisitions)
Acquisitions (*Pearl River's acquisition of Ritmüller; Santander and Bilbao Vizcaya's acquisitions in Latin America*)	• Same as green-field (above) • Do not add new capacity • Fast entry speed	• Same as green-field (above), except adding new capacity and slow speed • Post-acquisition integration problems

Modes of Entry: The Second Step on Making Actual Selections

During the second step, managers consider variables within *each* group of nonequity and equity modes.[32] If the decision is to export, then the next consideration is direct exports or indirect exports. Direct exports are the most basic mode of entry, capitalizing on economies of scale in production concentrated in the home country and providing better control over distribution.[33] This strategy essentially treats foreign demand as an extension of domestic demand, and the firm is geared toward designing and producing first and foremost for the domestic market. Pearl River, for example, exports its pianos from China to over 80 countries. Although direct exports may work if the export volume is small, it is not optimal when the firm has a large number of foreign buyers. "Marketing 101" suggests that the firm needs to be closer, both physically and psychologically, to its customers, prompting the firm to consider more intimate overseas involvement such as FDI. In addition, direct exports may provoke protectionism. In 1981, the success of direct automobile exports from Japan led the US government to impose a voluntary export restraint (VER) agreement on Japanese exports—never mind that in the absence of protectionist threats, the Japanese would not have voluntarily agreed to do so.

As you will recall from Chapter 9, another export strategy is indirect exports, namely, exporting through domestically based export intermediaries.[34] This strategy not only enjoys the economies of scale in domestic production (similar to direct exports) but is also relatively worry-free. A significant amount of export trade in commodities such as textiles, woods, and meats that compete primarily on price is indirect through intermediaries.[35] Indirect exports have some drawbacks. For example, third parties such as export trading companies do not share the same agendas and objectives as exporters.[36] Exporters choose intermediaries primarily because of information asymmetries concerning risks and uncertainties associated with foreign markets. Intermediaries with international contacts and knowledge essentially make a living by taking advantage of such information asymmetries. They may have a vested interest in making sure that such asymmetries are not reduced. Intermediaries, for example, may repackage the products under their own brand and insist on monopolizing the communication with overseas customers. If the exporter is interested in knowing more about how its products perform overseas, indirect exports would not provide such knowledge.[37]

The next group of nonequity entry modes involves the following types of contractual agreement: (1) licensing or franchising, (2) turnkey projects, (3) R&D contracts, and (4) co-marketing. Recall from Chapter 9 that, in licensing/franchising agreements, the licensor/franchisor sells the rights to intellectual property such as patents and know-how to the licensee/franchisee for a royalty fee. The licensor/franchisor thus does not have to bear the full costs and risks associated with foreign expansion. On the other hand, the licensor/franchisor does not have tight control over production and marketing.[38] Its worst fear is to find that it nurtured a competitor, as Pizza Hut found out in Thailand. Pizza Hut's long-term licensee in Thailand, once it learned Pizza Hut's tricks, terminated the licensing agreement and set up its own pizza restaurant chain to eat Pizza Hut's lunch.

In **turnkey projects**, clients pay contractors to design and construct new facilities and train personnel. At project completion, contractors hand clients the proverbial "key" to facilities ready for operations—hence the term "turnkey." This mode allows firms to earn returns from process technology (such as power generation) in countries where FDI is restricted. The drawbacks, however, are twofold. First, if foreign clients are competitors, selling them state-of-the-art technology through turnkey projects may boost their competitiveness. Second, turnkey projects do

Turnkey project
A project in which clients pay contractors to design and construct new facilities and train personnel.

not allow for a long-term presence after the key is handed to clients. To obtain a longer-term presence, build-operate-transfer agreements are now often used, instead of the traditional build-transfer type of turnkey projects. A **build-operate-transfer (BOT) agreement** is a nonequity mode of entry used to build a longer-term presence by building and then operating a facility for a period of time before transferring operations to a domestic agency or firm. For example, a consortium of German, Italian, and Iranian firms obtained a large-scale BOT power-generation project in Iran. After completion of the construction, the consortium will operate the project for 20 years before transferring it to the Iranian government.

R&D contracts refer to outsourcing agreements in R&D between firms. Firm A agrees to perform certain R&D work for firm B. Firms thereby tap into the best locations for certain innovations at relatively low costs, such as IT work in India and aerospace research in Russia. However, three drawbacks may emerge. First, given the uncertain and multidimensional nature of R&D, these contracts are often difficult to negotiate and enforce. Although delivery time and costs are relatively easy to negotiate, quality is often difficult to assess. Second, such contracts may cultivate competitors. A number of Indian IT firms, nurtured by such work, are now on a global offensive to take on their Western rivals. Finally, firms that rely on outsiders to perform a lot of R&D may lose some of their core R&D capabilities in the long run.

Co-marketing refers to efforts among a number of firms to jointly market their products and services. Toy makers and movie studios often collaborate in co-marketing campaigns with fast-food chains such as McDonald's to package toys based on movie characters in kids' meals. Airline alliances such as One-World and Star Alliance engage in extensive co-marketing through code sharing. The advantages are the ability to reach more customers. The drawbacks center on limited control and coordination.

Next are equity modes, all of which entail some FDI and transform the firm to an MNE. A **joint venture (JV)** is a "corporate child," a new entity created and jointly owned by two or more parent companies. It has three principal forms: Minority JV (less than 50% equity), 50/50 JV, and majority JV (more than 50% equity). JVs, such as Sony Ericsson and Shanghai Volkswagen, have three advantages. First, an MNE shares costs, risks, and profits with a local partner, so the firm possesses a certain degree of control but limits risk exposure. Second, the MNE gains access to knowledge about the host country; the local firm, in turn, benefits from the MNE's technology, capital, and management. Third, JVs may be politically more acceptable in host countries.

In terms of disadvantages, JVs often involve partners from different backgrounds with different goals, so conflicts are natural. Effective equity and operational control may be difficult to achieve since everything has to be negotiated—in some cases, fought over. Finally, the nature of the JV does not give an MNE the tight control over a foreign subsidiary that it may need for global coordination (such as simultaneously launching new products around the world). Overall, all sorts of nonequity-based contractual agreements and equity-based JVs can be broadly considered as strategic alliances (within the *dashed area* in Figure 10.2). Chapter 12 will discuss them in detail.

The last entry mode is to establish a **wholly owned subsidiary (WOS)**, defined as a subsidiary located in a foreign country that is entirely owned by the parent multinational. There are two primary means to set up a WOS.[39] One is to establish **green-field operations**, building new factories and offices from scratch (on a proverbial piece of "green field" formerly used for agricultural purposes). Pearl River's first subsidiary, PRPG America Ltd. (more commonly known as "Pearl River USA"), is such a green-field WOS (see the Opening Case). There are three advantages.

Build-operate-transfer (BOT) agreement
A nonequity mode of entry used to build a longer-term presence by building and then operating a facility for a period of time before transferring operations to a domestic agency or firm.

R&D contract
Outsourcing agreement in R&D between firms.

Co-marketing
Efforts among a number of firms to jointly market their products and services.

Joint venture (JV)
A new corporate entity created and jointly owned by two or more parent companies.

Wholly owned subsidiary (WOS)
A subsidiary located in a foreign country that is entirely owned by the parent multinational.

Green-field operations
Building factories and offices from scratch (on a proverbial piece of "green field" formerly used for agricultural purposes).

First, a green-field WOS gives an MNE complete equity and management control, thus eliminating the headaches associated with JVs. Second, this undivided control leads to better protection of proprietary technology. Third, a WOS allows for centrally coordinated global actions. Sometimes, a subsidiary will be ordered to launch actions that by design will *lose* money. In the semiconductor market, Texas Instruments (TI) faced competition from Japanese rivals such as NEC and Toshiba that maintained low prices outside of Japan by charging high prices in Japan and using domestic profits to cross-subsidize overseas expansion. By entering Japan via a WOS and slashing prices there, TI incurred a loss but forced the Japanese firms to defend their profit sanctuary at home, where they had more to lose. Japanese rivals had a much larger market share in Japan, so when the price level in Japan collapsed thanks to the aggressive price cutting unleashed by TI's WOS in the country, NEC and Toshiba had to drop prices, thus suffering much more significant losses. Consequently, Japanese rivals had to reduce the ferocity of their price wars outside of Japan. Local licensees/franchisees or JV partners are unlikely to accept such a subservient role as being ordered to lose money (!).

In terms of drawbacks, a green-field WOS tends to be expensive and risky, not only financially but also politically. The conspicuous foreignness embodied in such a WOS may become a target for nationalistic sentiments. Another drawback is that green-field operations add new capacity to an industry, which will make a competitive industry more crowded. For example, think of all the Japanese automobile plants built in the United States, which have severely squeezed the market share of US automakers and forced General Motors (GM) and Chrysler into bankruptcy. Finally, green-field operations suffer from a slow entry speed of at least one to two years (relative to acquisitions).

The other way to establish a WOS is through an acquisition. Pearl River's acquisition of Ritmüller is such an example. Although this is the last mode we discuss here, it represents approximately 70% of worldwide FDI. Acquisition shares all the benefits of green-field WOS but enjoys two additional advantages, namely: (1) adding no new capacity and (2) faster entry speed. For example, just since the 1990s, two leading banks in Spain with little prior international experience, Santander and Bilbao Vizcaya, became the largest foreign banks in Latin America through some 20 acquisitions. In terms of drawbacks, acquisition shares all the disadvantages of green-field WOS except adding new capacity and slow entry speed. But acquisition has a unique and potentially devastating disadvantage: post-acquisition integration problems. (See Chapter 12 for more details.)

Overall, although we have focused on one entry mode at a time, in practice firms are not limited by any single entry choice.[40] For example, IKEA stores in China are JVs and its stores in Hong Kong and Taiwan are separate franchises. In addition, entry modes may change over time.[41] Starbucks, for example, first used franchising. It then switched to JVs and more recently to acquisitions. As shown in the Opening Case, Pearl River has used exports, green-fields, and acquisitions to tackle various markets.

LEARNING OBJECTIVE 5

Participate in three leading debates on foreign market entries.

DEBATES AND EXTENSIONS

This chapter has already covered some crucial debates, such as first-mover versus late-mover advantages. Here we discuss three heated *recent* debates: (1) liability versus asset of foreignness, (2) global versus regional geographic diversification, and (3) old-line versus emerging multinationals.

Liability versus Asset of Foreignness

Although we do not need to spend much more time discussing the "liability of foreignness," one contrasting view argues that under certain circumstances, being foreign can be an *asset* (that is, a competitive advantage).[42] Americans often consider Japanese and German cars to be of superior quality. American cigarettes are "cool" among smokers in Eastern Europe. Anything Korean—ranging from handsets and TV shows to *kimchi* (pickled cabbage) flavored instant noodles—are considered hip in Southeast Asia. Conceptually, this is known as the **country-of-origin effect**, which refers to the positive or negative perception of firms and products from a certain country.[43] Pearl River's promotion of the Ritmüller brand, which highlights the product's German origin, suggests that the negative country-of-origin effect can be (at least partially) overcome (see the Opening Case). Pearl River is not alone in this regard. Here is a quiz: What is the country of origin of Häagen-Dazs ice cream? Students typically answer Germany, Belgium, Switzerland, or some other European country. Sorry, all wrong. Häagen-Dazs is American and always has been (!).

Whether foreignness is indeed an asset or a liability remains tricky. Disneyland Tokyo became wildly popular in Japan because it played up its American image. But Disneyland Paris received relentless negative press coverage in France because it insisted on its "wholesome American look." Thus Disneyland Hong Kong and (soon) Disneyland Shanghai must carefully consider how much foreignness (i.e., "Americanness") to emphasize.

Over time, the country-of-origin effect may shift. A number of UK firms used to proudly sport names such as British Telecom and British Petroleum. Recently, they have shied away from being "British" and rebranded themselves simply as BT and BP. In Britain, these changes are collectively known as the "B phenomenon." These costly rebranding campaigns are not casual changes. They reflect less confidence in the positive country-of-origin effect. Recently, BAE Systems, formerly British Aerospace, has complained that its British origin is causing problems in its largest

In Hong Kong Disneyland, is foreignness an asset or a liability?

market, the US defense market. Only US citizens are allowed to know the details of its most sensitive US contracts, and even its British CEO cannot know such details. This is untenable now that two-fifths of the company's sales are in the United States. Thus, BAE Systems is seriously considering becoming "American." However, in an interesting twist, an "Americanized" BAE Systems may encounter liability of foreignness in Britain.[44] Not surprisingly, the "B phenomenon" is controversial in Britain. One lesson we can draw is that foreignness can either be a liability or an asset, and that changes are possible.

Global versus Regional Geographic Diversification

This age of globalization brews an ongoing debate on the optimal geographic scope for MNEs. Despite the widely held belief (and frequently voiced criticism from antiglobalization activists) that MNEs are expanding globally, Alan Rugman and Alain Verbeke report that, surprisingly, few of even the largest *Fortune* Global 500

Country-of-origin effect
The positive or negative perception of firms and products from a certain country.

TABLE 10.5 THERE ARE ONLY NINE "GLOBAL" MULTINATIONAL ENTERPRISES (MNEs) MEASURED BY SALES

1	IBM
2	Sony
3	Philips
4	Nokia
5	Intel
6	Canon
7	Coca-Cola
8	Flextronics
9	LVMH

Source: Adapted from A. Rugman & A. Verbeke, 2004, A perspective on regional and global strategies of multinational enterprises (pp. 8–10), *Journal of International Business Studies*, 35: 3–18. "Global" MNEs have at least 20% of sales in each of the three regions of the Triad (Asia, Europe, and North America) but less than 50% in any one region.

MNEs are truly "global."[45] They develop a criteria based on sales. Looking at firms that had at least 20% of sales in *each* of the three regions of the Triad, which consists of Asia, Europe, and North America, but had less than 50% in any one region, they find a total of only *nine* MNEs to be "global" (see Table 10.5). The majority of the remaining *Fortune* Global 500 (over 450 companies) are "home-region-oriented" MNEs. In other words, they may be labeled regional, but *not* global, firms.

Should most MNEs further globalize? There are two answers. First, most MNEs know what they are doing and their current geographic scope is the maximum they can manage.[46] Others may have already over-diversified and will need to narrow their geographic scope. Second, these data only capture a snapshot (in the early 2000s), and some MNEs may become more globalized over time. While the debate goes on, it has at least taught us one important lesson: Be careful when using the word "global."[47] The *majority* of the largest MNEs are not necessarily global in their geographic scope.

Old-line versus Emerging Multinationals: OLI versus LLL

As discussed extensively in Chapter 6, MNEs presumably possess ownership, location, and internalization (OLI) advantages. The OLI framework is based on the experience of MNEs headquartered in developed economies that typically possess high-caliber technology and management know-how. However, emerging multinationals from emerging economies, such as those from China (Opening Case) and Russia (In Focus 10.1), are challenging some of this conventional wisdom.[48] Although these emerging multinationals, like their old-line counterparts, hunt for lucrative locations and internalize transactions—conforming to the L and I parts of the OLI framework—they typically do not own better proprietary technology, and their management capabilities are usually not world class. In other words, the O part is largely missing. How can we make sense of these emerging multinationals?

One interesting new framework is the "linkage, leverage, and learning" (LLL) framework advocated by John Mathews.[49] Linkage refers to emerging MNEs' ability to identify and bridge gaps. Pearl River has identified the gap between what its pianos can actually offer and what price it can command given the negative country-of-origin effect associated with Chinese products. Pearl River's answer has been two-pronged: (1) develop the economies of scale to bring down the unit cost of pianos while maintaining a high standard for quality, and (2) acquire and revive the Ritmüller brand to reduce some of the negative country-of-origin effect. Thus, Pearl River links China and Germany to propel its global push (see the Opening Case).

Leverage refers to emerging multinationals' ability to take advantage of their unique resources and capabilities, which are typically based on a deep understanding of customer needs and wants. For example, Naver enjoys a 76% market share for Internet searches in South Korea. It intends to leverage its deep understanding of Asian languages and cultures by moving into Japan, a foreign market it has studied for eight years. In the long run, it also has ambitions to launch other culturally specific search engines, such as "Naver Korean-American" and "Naver Chinese-American." On a global scale, Naver's skills clearly pale in comparison with Google's capabilities, but Naver and other emerging multinationals have been beating Google in certain markets, such as South Korea (see the Closing Case).

Learning probably is the most unusual aspect among the motives behind the internationalization push of many emerging multinationals.[50] Instead of the "I-will-tell-you-what-to-do" mentality typical of old-line MNEs from developed economies, many MNEs from emerging economies openly profess that they go abroad to learn. Skills they need to absorb range from basic English skills to high-level executive skills in transparent governance, market planning, and management of diverse multicultural workforces.

Of course, OLI and LLL frameworks overlap a great deal. So the debate boils down to whether the differences are fundamental, which would justify a new theory such as LLL, or just a matter of degree, in which case OLI would be just fine to accommodate the new MNEs. In addition to LLL, there may be new theories to be developed from the arrival of MNEs from emerging economies. Given the rapidly moving progress of these emerging multinationals, one thing for certain is that our learning and debate about them will not stop anytime soon.[51]

MANAGEMENT SAVVY

Draw implications for action.

Entry into a foreign market represents a *foundation* for IB. Without these crucial first steps, firms will remain domestic players. The challenges associated with internationalization are daunting, the complexities enormous, and the stakes high. Returning to our fundamental question, we ask: What determines the success and failure in foreign market entries? The answers boil down to the two core perspectives: institution-based and resource-based views. Shown in Table 10.6, three implications for action emerge. First, from an institution-based view, managers need to understand the rules of the game, both formal and informal, governing competition in foreign markets. Failure to understand these rules can be costly. Why did Chinese MNEs' high-profile acquisition attempts to take over US and Australian firms (such as CNOOC's bid for Unocal and Chinalco's for Rio Tinto, respectively) often fail? Arabic MNEs' similar attempts (such as DP World's bid for US ports) often fail too, as do Russian MNEs' high-profile acquisitive forays (such as Sherbank's bid—in alliance with Canada's Magna—for Opel). Although the reasons are numerous, one key reason is that these foreign entrants often fail to understand the informal, unwritten rules of the game that often have protectionist (or even racist) undertones in developed economies. Knowing these rules of the game does not mean these emerging MNEs need to be discouraged. They just need to do their homework better, keep their heads low, and work on *low*-profile acquisitions, which are routinely approved in developed economies.

TABLE 10.6   IMPLICATIONS FOR ACTION

- Understand the rules of the game—both formal and informal—governing competition in foreign markets
- Develop overwhelming resources and capabilities to offset the liability of foreignness
- Match efforts in market entry with strategic goals

Second, from a resource-based view, managers need to develop overwhelming capabilities to offset the liability of foreignness. Merely outstanding, but not overwhelming, capabilities cannot ensure success in the face of strong incumbents—a painful lesson DHL has learned at the cost of $10 billion (!) (see In Focus 10.3).

Finally, managers need to match entries with strategic goals. If the goal is to deter rivals in their home markets through price slashing as TI did in Japan, then be prepared to fight a nasty price war and lose money. If the goal is to generate decent returns, then it may be necessary to withdraw from some tough markets to crack, as when Wal-Mart withdrew from Germany and South Korea.

CHAPTER SUMMARY

1. Identify ways in which institutions and resources affect the liability of foreignness.
   - When entering foreign markets, firms confront a liability of foreignness.
   - Both institution-based and resource-based views advise managers on how to overcome such liability.

2. Match the quest for location-specific advantages with strategic goals.
   - Where to enter depends on certain foreign countries' location-specific advantages and firms' strategic goals, such as seeking (1) natural resources, (2) market, (3) efficiency, and (4) innovation.

3. Compare and contrast first-mover and late-mover advantages.
   - Each has pros and cons, and there is no conclusive evidence pointing to one direction.

4. List the steps in the comprehensive model of foreign market entries.
   - How to enter depends on the scale of entry: Large-scale versus small-scale entries.
   - A comprehensive model of foreign market entries first focuses on the equity (ownership) issue.
   - The second step focuses on making the actual selection, such as exports, contractual agreements, JVs, and WOS.

5. Participate in three leading debates on foreign market entries.
   - They are (1) liability versus asset of foreignness, (2) global versus regional geographic diversification, and (3) old-line versus emerging multinationals.

6. Draw implications for action.
   - Understand the rules of game—both formal and informal—governing competition in foreign markets.
   - Develop overwhelming resources and capabilities to offset the liability of foreignness.
   - Match efforts in market entry with strategic goals.

KEY TERMS

Build-operate-transfer
  (BOT) agreement   339
Co-marketing   339
Country-of-origin effect   341
Cultural distance   332
Equity mode   336
First-mover advantage   332

Green-field operations   339
Institutional distance   332
Joint venture (JV)   339
Late-mover advantage   333
Location-specific
  advantage   329
Mode of entry   335

Nonequity mode   336
R&D contract   339
Scale of entry   335
Turnkey project   338
Wholly owned subsidiary
  (WOS)   339

REVIEW QUESTIONS

1. How do foreign firms suffer from their liability of foreignness?

2. What does the institution-based view suggest how a firm should deal with the liability of foreignness? What does the resource-based view advise?

3. What are some of the location-specific advantages found in agglomeration?

4. Describe how four strategic goals may affect the decision of where to enter.

5. Summarize the advantages of being a first mover.

6. What are the possible benefits of being a late mover?

7. How does a large-scale entry differ from a small-scale entry?

8. What are some of the hallmarks of each type of equity mode?

9. How does the country-of-origin effect change for a firm over time?

10. Devise your own example of how a firm may use its capabilities to overwhelmingly offset the liability of foreignness as it moves into a new foreign market.

11. If you were a manager charged with choosing a new location for your firm's business, how would you go about matching the location options with your firm's strategic goals?

12. Compare PengAtlas Maps 3.1 and 3.4.
    a. To what extent are the richest countries also among the easiest in which to do business? Are any of the richest countries among the most difficult in which to do business? Indicate whether you think the relationship is coincidental or causal and why you think that way.

b. If you were thinking of expanding your firm's operations, you would probably wish to go where it is easier to do business and where income is higher. Furthermore, at least some of the poorest countries may like to have your firm expand into them to help lift income. If such is the case, why don't they simply make it easier to do business? What do you think?

CRITICAL DISCUSSION QUESTIONS

1. Pick an internationally active industry in your country. What are the top five most favorite foreign markets for firms in this industry? Why?

2. From institution-based and resource-based views, identify the obstacles confronting MNEs from emerging economies interested in expanding overseas. How can such firms overcome them?

3. *ON ETHICS:* Entering foreign markets, by definition, means not investing in a firm's home country. For example, Nissan closed factories in Japan and added a new factory in the United States. GM shut down factories in the United States but kept them open in Europe. What are the ethical dilemmas here?

GLOBAL ACTION

1. The most important element of your company's success in its domestic market thus far has been its electronic readiness and competitiveness. This has allowed the organization to develop very stringent internal processes and controls that are the envy of the industry. As such, entering a foreign market requires a sufficient level of technological prowess among possible target locations. An evaluation of the "e-readiness" of specific locations can provide considerable insight for your company's anticipated internationalization in Asia. Using globalEDGE, gather information and provide an overview of the five most technologically ready Asian locations.

2. Global competition is determined in part by both efficiency and innovation. To develop a foreign market entry strategy for your company, a colleague informed you of a competitiveness report that is published periodically to evaluate the standing of each specific economy worldwide. Locate this report on globalEDGE for assessment. Which countries rank highest on both measures of efficiency and innovation? Which regions of the world appear to rank well for each category? What conclusions may be drawn from this information?

VIDEO CASES

Watch "Researching and Understanding Markets" by Luke Johnson of Channel 4 Television. In the following questions, imagine that your company is seeking to expand into another country through the use of an acquisition or at least a major equity position in a local firm.

1. Which would be better, to gain control of a small firm that you then seek to expand, or to acquire a company that is among the top five in its industry? Why?

2. What would be the benefit of expanding in an industry that is fragmented?

3. Johnson indicated that sometimes instead of investing in a given industry, it may be best to expand into one that can benefit from that industry. How did he use FedEx and UPS as an example of that concept? Evaluate the pros and cons of that approach.

4. Johnson pointed out the benefit of looking for a niche. Do you think there is more or less risk in entering a niche overseas market through acquisitions?

5. Pick a specific firm or industry and show how you would use Johnson's advice in entering a foreign market.

Closing Case

Google in Asia

© Jung Yeon-Je/AFP/Getty Images

In South Korea, people who want to look something up on the Internet do not "Google it." Instead they "ask Naver." Among the 35 million South Koreans who use the Internet every day, the nine-year-old search engine is wildly popular, accounting for 76% of Internet searches, compared with less than 3% each for Google and Yahoo!. Naver owes its popularity, in part, to the fact that it is not just a search engine. Like Yahoo!, it is also a portal, drawing together news, e-mail, discussion groups, stock market information, videos, restaurant reviews, and so on. Some 17 million people visit its home page every day, and since January 2009 they have been able to customize it according to their own taste.

But Naver is also dominant—too dominant, say some—because it caters to the interests of South Koreans. "Google and Yahoo! have a very American, English-based search engine," says Chae Hwi-Young, the chief executive of NHN, Naver's parent company. If you go to Google and type in "rain," for example, the result is lots of pages of water falling from the sky. In South Korea, however, it makes more sense to return pages, as Naver does, about a popular singer and actor called Rain.

Naver pioneered the idea of presenting search results from several categories—web pages, images, videos, books—on the same page, something that Google later adopted. Another

FIGURE 10.3   SEARCH ENGINE MARKET SHARE AS A PERCENTAGE: GOOGLE VERSUS MARKET LEADER

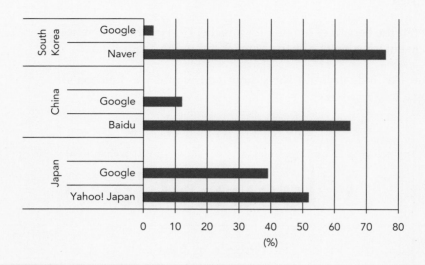

popular feature is Naver's "Knowledge Search" service, launched in 2002. It enables people to ask questions, the answers to which are served up from a database provided by other users. If an answer is incomplete or inaccurate, it can be easily changed, Wikipedia-style, for the benefit of others who ask the same question in the future. A points system rewards users who submit questions, provide answers, or rate the answers provided by other people.

On February 4, 2009, NHN announced record sales and profits for 2008, becoming the first South Korean Internet company to record sales of more than 1 million won ($660 million). Such is Naver's grip on the market that Google and Yahoo! have just agreed to combine some of their services in South Korea, in order to give them greater clout against the local giant.

Although Google is having trouble making any headway in South Korea, it may have more of a chance in China, where the market leader, Baidu, has been hit by a series of scandals. In September 2008, at the height of the scandal over melamine-tainted milk, rumors began to spread that Baidu had accepted payment to suppress stories on the subject from its search results. Baidu denied any wrongdoing. A few weeks later the firm was accused of giving prominence in its

search results to unlicensed drug firms in return for payment.

This led to speculation in the local media that web users might be turning against Baidu. Whether or not this is true, it does not help that unlike Google and other rivals, Baidu does not distinguish in search results between paid links (i.e., advertisements) and unpaid ones—a practice that was criticized in a report by CCTV, a state-run broadcaster, in November 2008.

As Chinese web users become more sophisticated, they may be gaining a preference for search results that are separate from advertising, which could benefit Google. Advertisers, at least, seem to be switching: The most recent figures suggest that Google increased its market share of Internet advertising by 4.4% during 2008, compared to Baidu's 2.9%. Baidu has announced plans to delineate more clearly between paid and unpaid links, and has removed links to unlicensed providers of drugs and medical care from its index.

In the Japanese market, meanwhile, Google plays second fiddle to Yahoo! Japan, despite frantic efforts to catch up by launching more Japan-specific services. It will soon face a new rival, Naver, which has decided to enter the Japanese market on the basis that Japan, like South Korea, has a unique and distinctive culture and language. After eight years studying and collecting data on Japanese tastes,

Mr Chae is confident that Naver can become the leading search engine in Japan—despite the failure of his firm's previous foray into the country.

After that, Mr Chae says he plans to launch several more culturally specific search engines, such as "Naver California," "Naver Korean-American," or "Naver Chinese-American." That would be attacking Google on its home turf. Is this too ambitious? Naver say never.

Editor's Note: In early 2010, Google threatened to withdraw from China, due to disputes with the Chinese government over censorship.

Case Discussion Questions:

1. What resources and capabilities does Naver have that Google does not?
2. Why are the top two search engine providers in Japan foreign entrants, whereas in South Korea and China, it is a domestic incumbent that dominates the industry?
3. Does Naver have what it takes to succeed in overseas markets, such as Japan and the United States?

Source: *Economist*, 2009, Google in Asia: Seeking success, February 28: 71. © The Economist Newspaper Limited. Reprinted with permission. All rights reserved.

NOTES

[Journal acronyms]: AMJ—*Academy of Management Journal*; **AMR**—*Academy of Management Review*; **APJM**—*Asia Pacific Journal of Management*; **BW**—*BusinessWeek*; **JIBS**—*Journal of International Business Studies*; **JIM**—*Journal of International Management*; **JM**—*Journal of Management*; **JMS**—*Journal of Management Studies*; **JWB**—*Journal of World Business*; **MIR**—*Management International Review*; **SMJ**—*Strategic Management Journal*

[1] K. Meyer, S. Estrin, S. Bhaumik, & M. W. Peng, 2009, Institutions, resources, and entry strategies in emerging economies, *SMJ*, 30: 61–80.

[2] S. Hymer, 1976, *The International Operations of National Firms*, Cambridge, MA: MIT Press; J. Mezias, 2002, Identifying liabilities of foreignness and strategies to minimize their effects, *SMJ*, 23: 229–244; S. Miller & A. Parkhe, 2002, Is there a liability of foreignness in global banking? *SMJ*, 23: 55–75.

[3] *BW*, 2009, Europe's rush to grab US stimulus cash, May 4: 52.

[4] C. Asmussen, T. Pedersen, & C. Dhanaraj, 2009, Host-country environment and subsidiary performance, *JIBS*, 40: 42–57.

[5] C. Chan, S. Makino, & T. Isobe, 2006, Interdependent behavior in FDI, *JIBS*, 37: 642–665; J. Gimeno, R. Hoskisson, B. Beal, & W. Wan, 2005, Explaining the clustering of international expansion modes, *AMJ*, 48: 297–319.

[6] M. W. Peng, 2001, The resource-based view and international business, *JM*, 27: 803–829. See also M. Augier & D. Teece, 2007, Dynamic capabilities and MNEs, *MIR*, 47: 175–192; D. Brock, T. Yaffe, & M. Dembovsky, 2006, International diversification and performance, *JIM*, 12: 473–489; M. Chari, S. Devaraj, & P. David, 2007, International diversification and firm performance, *JWB*, 42: 184–197.

[7] H. Berry, 2006, Shareholder valuation of foreign investment expansion, *SMJ*, 27: 1123–1140; D. Tan & J. Mahoney, 2007, The dynamics of Japanese firm growth in US industries, *MIR*, 47: 259–279.

[8] J. Dunning, 2009, Location and the MNE: A neglected factor? *JIBS*, 40: 5–19. See also R. Belderbos & L. Sleuwaegen, 2005, Competitive drivers and international plant configuration strategies, *SMJ*, 26: 577–593; J. Cantwell, 2009, Location and the MNE, *JIBS*, 40: 35–41; M. Enright, 2009, The location of activities of manufacturing multinationals in the Asia-Pacific, *JIBS*, 40: 818–839.

[9] L. Canina, C. Enz, & J. Harrison, 2005, Agglomeration effects and strategic orientations, *AMJ*, 48: 565–581; J. Kuilman & J. Li, 2009, Grades of membership and legitimacy spillovers, *AMJ*, 52: 229–245; E. Maitland, E. Rose, & S. Nicholas, 2005, How firms grow, *JIBS*, 36: 435–451; L. Nachum & C. Wymbs, 2005, Product differentiation, external economies, and MNE location choices, *JIBS*, 36: 415–434.

[10] D. Sethi, S. Guisinger, S. Phelan, & D. Berg, 2003, Trends in FDI flows, *JIBS*, 34: 315–326.

[11] Economist Intelligence Unit, 2006, *CEO Briefing* (p. 9), London: EIU.

[12] M. W. Peng & D. Wang, 2000, Innovation capability and foreign direct investment (p. 80), *MIR*, 40: 79–93. See also W. Chung & S. Yeaple, 2008, International knowledge sourcing, *SMJ*, 29: 1207–1224; B. Petersen, T. Pedersen, & M. Lyles, 2008, Closing knowledge gaps in foreign markets, *JIBS*, 39: 1097–1113.

[13] F. Molina-Morales & M. Martinez-Fernandez, 2009, Too much love in the neighborhood can hurt, *SMJ*, 30: 1013–1023.

[14] D. Xu & O. Shenkar, 2002, Institutional distance and the MNE (p. 608), *AMR*, 27: 608–618. See also S. Estrin, D. Baghdasaryan, & K. Meyer, 2009, The impact of institutional and human resource distance on international entry strategies, *JMS*, 46: 1172–1196.

[15] K. Meyer & M. Gelbuda, 2006, Process perspectives in international business research in CEE, *MIR*, 46: 143–164.

[16] E. Tsang & P. Yip, 2008, Economic distance and survival of FDI, *AMJ*, 50: 1156–1168.

[17] M. Myers, C. Droge, & M. Cheung, 2007, The fit of home to foreign market environment, *JWB*, 42: 170–183.

[18] J. Johanson & J. Vahlne, 2006, Commitment and opportunity development in the internationalization process, *MIR*, 46: 165–178; J. Steen & P. Liesch, 2007, A note on Penrosian growth,

resource bundles, and the Uppsala model of internationalization, *MIR*, 47: 193–206.

[19] *Economist*, 2006, Don't mess with Russia, December 16: 11.

[20] J. Evans & F. Mavondo, 2002, Psychic distance and organizational performance, *JIBS*, 33: 515–532.

[21] G. Dowell & A. Swaminathan, 2006, Entry timing, exploration, and firm survival, *SMJ*, 27: 1159–1182; J. G. Frynas, K. Mellahi, & G. Pigman, 2006, First mover advantages in IB and firm-specific political resources, *SMJ*, 27: 321–345.

[22] M. W. Peng, S. Lee, & J. Tan, 2001, The *keiretsu* in Asia, *JIM*, 7: 253–276.

[23] *BW*, 2008, Cisco's brave new world (p. 68), November 24: 56–68.

[24] T. Isobe, S. Makino, & D. Montgomery, 2000, Resource commitment, entry timing, and market performance of FDI in emerging economies, *AMJ*, 43: 468–484.

[25] J. Boyd & R. Bresser, 2008, Performance implications of delayed competitive responses, *SMJ*, 29: 1017–1096; J. Yoo, R. Reed, S. Shin, & D. Lemak, 2009, Strategic choice and performance in late movers, *JMS*, 46: 308–335.

[26] V. Gaba, Y. Pan, & G. Ungson, 2002, Timing of entry in international market, *JIBS*, 33: 39–55.

[27] M. W. Peng, 2000, Controlling the foreign agent, *MIR*, 40: 141–165; F. Suarez & G. Lanzolla, 2007, The role of environmental dynamics in building a first mover advantage theory, *AMR*, 32: 377–392.

[28] Y. Luo & M. W. Peng, 1999, Learning to compete in a transition economy, *JIBS*, 30: 269–296.

[29] A. Delios & W. Henisz, 2003, Political hazards, experience, and sequential entry strategies, *SMJ*, 24: 1153–1164.

[30] C. Bouquet, A. Morrison, & J. Birkinshaw, 2009, International attention and MNE performance, *JIBS*, 40: 108–131; L. Brouthers, S. Mukhopadhyay, T. Wilkinson, & K. Brouthers, 2009, International market selection and subsidiary performance, *JWB*, 44: 262–273.

[31] S. Chen, 2005, Extending internalization theory, *JIBS*, 36: 231–245; J. Galan & J. Gonzalez-Benito, 2006, Distinctive determinant factors of Spanish foreign direct investment in Latin America, *JWB*, 41: 171–189; H. Zou & M. Adams, 2008, Corporate ownership, equity risk, and returns in the People's Republic of China, *JIBS*, 39: 1149–1168.

[32] D. Dow, 2006, Adaptation and performance in foreign markets, *JIBS*, 37: 212–226; H. Zhao, Y. Luo, & T. Suh, 2004, Transaction cost determinants and ownership-based entry mode choice, *JIBS*, 35: 524–544.

[33] R. Salomon & J. M. Shaver, 2005, Export and domestic sales, *SMJ*, 26: 855–871.

[34] M. W. Peng & A. York, 2001, Behind intermediary performance in export trade, *JIBS*, 32: 327–346.

[35] M. W. Peng, Y. Zhou, & A. York, 2006, Behind make or buy decisions in export strategy, *JWB*, 41: 289–300; H. Trabold, 2002, Export intermediation: An empirical test of Peng and Ilinitch, *JIBS*, 33: 327–344.

[36] H. Lau, 2008, Export channel structure in a newly industrialized economy, *APJM*, 25: 317–333.

[37] M. W. Peng, 1998, *Behind the Success and Failure of US Export Intermediaries*, Westport, CT: Quorum; F. Wu, R. Sinkovics, S. T. Cavusgil, & A. Roath, 2007, Overcoming export manufacturers' dilemma in international expansion, *JIBS*, 38: 283–302.

[38] J. Barthelemy, 2008, Opportunism, knowledge, and the performance of franchise chains, *SMJ*, 29: 1451–1463; M. Jiang, P. Aulakh, & Y. Pan, 2009, Licensing duration in foreign markets, *JIBS*, 40: 559–577; H. Mitsuhashi, S. Shane, & W. Sine, 2008, Organization governance form in franchising, *SMJ*, 29: 1127–1136.

[39] A. Harzing, 2002, Acquisitions versus greenfield investments, *SMJ*, 23: 211–227.

[40] T. Jandik & R. Kali, 2009, Legal systems, information asymmetry, and firm boundaries, *JIBS*, 40: 578–599.

[41] J. Puck, D. Holtbrugge, & A. Mohr, 2009, Beyond entry mode choice, *JIBS*, 40: 388–404; D. Tan, 2009, Foreign market entry strategies and post-entry growth, *JIBS*, 40: 1046–1063.

[42] D. Kronborg & S. Thomsen, 2009, Foreign ownership and long-term survival, *SMJ*, 30: 207–219.

[43] L. Brouthers, E. O'Connell, & J. Hadjimarcou, 2005, Generic product strategies for emerging market exports into Triad nation markets, *JMS*, 42: 225–245; J. Knight, D. Holdsworth, & D. Mather, 2007, Country-of-origin and choice of food imports, *JIBS*, 38: 107–125; P. Verlegh, 2007, Home country bias in product evaluation, *JIBS*, 38: 361–373.

[44] *Economist*, 2006, BAE Systems: Changing places, October 28: 66–67.

[45] A. Rugman & A. Verbeke, 2004, A perspective on regional and global strategies of MNEs, *JIBS*, 35: 3–18

[46] G. Qian, T. Khoury, M. W. Peng, & Z. Qian, 2010, The performance implications of intra- and inter-regional geographic diversification, *SMJ* (in press).

[47] J. Arregle, P. Beamish, & L. Hebert, 2009, The regional dimension of MNEs' foreign subsidiary localization, *JIBS*, 40: 86–107; C. Asmussen, 2009, Local, regional, or global? *JIBS*, 40: 1192–1205; P. Dastidar, 2009, International corporate diversification and performance, *JIBS*, 40: 71–85; L. Li, 2005, Is regional strategy more effective than global strategy in the US service industries? *MIR*, 45: 37–57; E. Yin & C. Choi, 2005, The globalization myth, *MIR*, 45: 103–120.

[48] P. Aulakh, 2007, Emerging multinationals from developing countries, *JIM*, 13: 235–240; R. Ramamurti & J. Singh (eds.), 2009, *Emerging Multinationals in Emerging Markets*, New York: Cambridge University Press.

[49] J. Mathews, 2006, Dragon multinationals: Emerging players in 21st century globalization, *APJM*, 23: 5–27.

[50] Y. Luo & R. Tung, 2007, International expansion of emerging market enterprises, *JIBS*, 38: 481–498.

[51] M. W. Peng, R. Bhagat, & S. Chang, 2010, Asia and global business, *JIBS* (in press).

Chapter 11

© Imaginechina via AP Images

LEARNING OBJECTIVES

After studying this chapter, you should be able to:

1. understand the industry conditions conducive for cooperation and collusion.

2. outline how formal instutitions affect domestic and international competition.

3. articulate how resources and capabilities influence competitive dynamics.

4. identify the drivers for attacks, counterattacks, and signaling.

5. discuss how local firms fight multinational enterprises (MNEs).

6. participate in two leading debates on global competitive dynamics.

7. draw implications for action.

Managing Global Competitive Dynamics

Cisco versus Huawei: War and Peace

Founded in 1986, Cisco is a worldwide leader in networking for the Internet. Numerous rivals challenged Cisco but none were viable threats—until the rise of Huawei. Founded in 1987, Huawei distinguished itself as an aggressive company that led the telecommunications equipment market in China. Remarkably, despite not being a state-owned company, Huawei not only beat all state-owned rivals but also a series of multinationals in China. In 1999, Huawei launched an overseas drive. Starting with $50 million sales (4% of overall sales) in international markets in 1999, Huawei's sales outside of China reached $18 billion (75% of overall sales) in 2008. What is Huawei's secret weapon? Relative to offerings from competitors such as Cisco, Lucent, Nokia, and Siemens, Huawei's products offer comparable performance at a 30% lower price. This is music to the ears of telecom operators. As a result, Huawei not only penetrated many emerging economies, but also achieved significant breakthroughs in developed markets such as Japan and Western Europe. As of 2009, Huawei served 31 of the world's top 50 telecom operators, including Vodafone, Telefonica, KPN, FT/Orange, and Italia Telecom. Yet North America remained the toughest nut to crack.

In 2002, Huawei turned its guns on North America—Cisco's stronghold. Huawei's debut in North America was at a trade show in Atlanta, Supercomm, in 2002. Two people visited the Huawei booth and asked detailed questions for 20 minutes. Only after they had left did one of Huawei's executives at the booth realize that one of the visitors was John Chambers, Cisco's CEO. Chambers thus personally experienced the aggressive arrival of his archrival from China. Thanks to Huawei,

Cisco's sales in China peaked in 2001 at $1 billion and then never reached anything above $600 million. Correspondingly Cisco's share in the Chinese router market went from 80% to 50%. In North America, facing suspicious buyers, Huawei offered "blind" performance tests on Huawei and Cisco machines whose logos were removed. Buyers often found that the only difference was price.

Cisco's response was both audacious and unexpected. On January 22, 2003, Cisco filed a lawsuit in Texas alleging that Huawei unlawfully copied and misappropriated Cisco's software and documentation. Cisco's actions totally caught Huawei off guard—it was the first time Huawei had been sued by a foreign rival. Even the day of the attack was deliberately chosen: the start of the Spring Festival, the main annual holiday in China. Instead of spending time with their families, Huawei top executives had to forego the holiday and keep working. The media noted that this lawsuit squarely put Huawei "on the map" as Cisco's acknowledged enemy number one.

Huawei's response was also interesting. Huawei noted that as a firm that consistently invested at least 10% of its sales on R&D, it had always respected intellectual property rights (IPR).* Several days before the court hearing in March 2003, Huawei announced a joint venture with Cisco's rival 3Com. Consequently, 3Com's CEO, Bruce Claflin, provided testimony supporting Huawei. By using an American CEO to fight off another American firm, Huawei thus skillfully eroded the "us versus them" feeling permeating this case at a time when "China bashing" was popular.

---

* In 2008, Huawei filed the largest number of patent applications in the *world* (see Table 11.3).

While both Cisco and Huawei fought in court, negotiations between them, which often involved both American and Chinese officials, also intensified. In July 2004, Cisco dropped the case. Although the settlement details were confidential, *both* Cisco and Huawei declared victory. Huawei agreed to change the software and documentation in question, thus partially meeting Cisco's goals. More importantly, Cisco delayed Huawai's North America offensive by one and a half years. However, Huawei not only refuted most of Cisco's accusations, but also received media attention for its products, which amounted to free advertising. In part thanks to this high-profile case, Huawei's international sales *doubled*—from approximately $1 billion in 2003 to $2 billion in 2004. Clearly, Huawei had become a force to be reckoned with. In December 2005, Chambers visited Huawei and for the first time met its CEO Ren Zhengfei. The former plaintiff and the former defendant shook hands and had friendly discussions like pals, as if nothing had happened between them.

Sources: I thank Sunny Li Sun (University of Texas at Dallas) for his assistance. Based on (1) www.cisco.com; (2) *Cisco Systems et al. v. Huawei Technologies, Co. et al.*, Civil Action No. 2:03-CV-027, Marshall, TX: US District Court for the Eastern District of Texas; (3) www.huawei.com; (4) J. Wu & Y. Ji, 2006, *Huawei's World*, Beijing: China CITIC Press.

In the rivalry between Cisco and Huawei, why were certain actions taken but not others? Once one side initiates an action, how does the other side respond? These are some of the key questions in this chapter, which focuses on such **competitive dynamics**—actions and responses undertaken by competing firms. Since one firm's actions rarely go unnoticed by rivals, the initiating firm would naturally like to predict its rivals' responses *before* making its move.[1] In anticipating rivals' actions, the initiating firm may revise its original plan and/or prepare to deal with rivals' responses. This process is called **competitor analysis**, advocated by the ancient Chinese strategist Sun Tzu who taught that you must not only know "yourself" but also "your opponents."

As military officers have long known, a good plan never lasts longer than the first contact with the enemy because the enemy does not act according to our plan. The key word is *interaction*—how firms interact with rivals. This chapter first deals with competition, cooperation, and collusion. Then, we draw on institution-based and resource-based views to shed light on competitive dynamics. Attack, counterattack, and signaling are then outlined, with one interesting extension on how local firms fight multinational enterprises (MNEs) in emerging economies. Debates and extensions follow.

Competitive dynamics
Actions and responses undertaken by competing firms.

Competitor analysis
The process of anticipating rivals' actions in order to both revise a firm's plan and prepare to deal with rivals' response.

LEARNING OBJECTIVE 1

Understand the industry conditions conducive for cooperation and collusion.

COMPETITION, COOPERATION, AND COLLUSION

War and Peace

While militaries fight over territories, waters, and air spaces, firms compete over markets. Note the military tone of such terms as "attack" and "price wars."[2] Although it often seems that "business is war," it is obvious that military principles cannot be completely applied in business. The marketplace, after all, is not a battlefield where participants must either "kill or be killed." In business, it is possible to compete and win without destroying the opposition. In a nutshell, business is simultaneously war *and* peace.

Alternatively, most competitive dynamics terms and concepts can also be explained in terms of sports analogies. Terms such as "offense" and "defense" should be very familiar to sports enthusiasts.

Cooperation and Collusion

In *The Wealth of Nations* (1776), Adam Smith wrote, "People of the same trade seldom meet together, even for merriment and diversion, but their conversation often ends in a conspiracy against the public." In modern jargon, this means that competing firms in an industry may have an incentive to engage in collusion, defined as collective attempts to reduce competition.

Collusion can be either tacit or explicit. Firms engage in tacit collusion when they indirectly coordinate actions by signaling their intentions, often in an attempt to reduce output and maintain pricing above competitive levels. Explicit collusion exists when firms *directly* negotiate output and pricing and divide markets. Explicit collusion leads to a cartel—an output- and price-fixing entity involving multiple competitors. A cartel is also known as a trust, because members have to trust each other to honor agreements. Since the Sherman Act of 1890, cartels have often been labeled "anticompetitive" and outlawed by antitrust laws in many countries. Recent globalization, by fostering competition in many formerly protected markets, may have *increased* some firms' incentive to collude.[3] The 2009 movie, *The Informant*, vividly documented the true story of an international price-fixing cartel led by a US firm, ADM. The ADM investigation, which took place during the 1990s, convinced antitrust prosecutors that international price-fixing was a more pervasive problem than they had suspected (see In Focus 11.1).

Beyond antitrust laws, collusion often collapses under the weight of its own incentive problems. Of the cartels prosecuted in the 1990s, the average duration was only six years. Chief among these problems is the prisoners' dilemma, which underpins game theory. The term "prisoners' dilemma" derives from a simple game in which two prisoners are suspected of a major joint crime (such as burglary), but police do not have strong evidence. The two prisoners are interrogated separately and told that if either one confesses, the confessor will get a one-year sentence while the other will go to jail for ten years. If neither confesses, both will be convicted of a lesser charge (such as trespassing) with each serving two years. If both confess, both will go to jail for ten years. At a first glance, the solution seems clear enough. The maximum *joint* payoff would be for neither of them to confess. However, both prisoners have tremendous incentives to confess or to "defect."

Translated to an airline setting, Figure 11.1 illustrates the payoff structure for two airlines, A and B, in a given market between Hong Kong and Singapore. Assuming a total of 200 passengers, Cell 1 represents the most ideal outcome. Maintaining a price of $500, each airline gets 100 passengers and makes $50,000; the "industry" revenue reaches $100,000. However, Cell 2 shows the results if B maintains its price at $500 while A drops its price to $300: B is likely to lose all its customers. Assuming perfectly transparent pricing information on the Internet, who would want to pay $500 when you can get a ticket for $300? Thus, A would make $60,000 on 200 passengers and B would get nothing. In Cell 3, the situation is reversed. In both Cells 2 and 3, although industry revenue *decreases* by 40%, the price dropper *increases* its revenue by 20%. Thus, both A and B have strong incentives to charge the lower price and hope the other side becomes a "sucker."

Collusion
Collective attempts between competing firms to reduce competition.

tacit collusion
Firms indirectly coordinate actions by signaling their intention to reduce output and maintain pricing above competitive levels.

Explicit collusion
Firms directly negotiate output and pricing and divide markets.

Cartel (trust)
An output- and price-fixing entity involving multiple competitors.

Antitrust laws
Laws in various countries that outlaw cartels (trusts).

Prisoners' dilemma
In game theory, a type of game in which the outcome depends on two parties deciding whether to cooperate or to defect.

Game theory
A theory that studies the interactions between two parties that compete and/or cooperate with each other.

The Global Vitamin Cartel

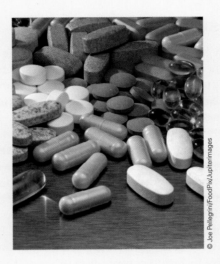

The largest and most wide-reaching cartel ever convicted is the global vitamin cartel in operation during 1990–1999. It involved mainly four firms that controlled more than 75% of worldwide production: (1) Hoffman-La Roche of Switzerland, (2) BASF of Germany, (3) Rhône-Poulenc of France (Now Aventis), and (4) Eisai of Japan. Four other Dutch, German, and Japanese firms were also involved. The ringleader was the industry leader, Hoffman-La Roche. This cartel was truly extraordinary: by 1999, prices were meticulously set in at least *nine* currencies. The discovery of the cartel led to numerous convictions and fines during 1999–2001 by US, EU, Canadian, Australian, and South Korean antitrust authorities. According to the US Assistant Attorney General:

> The criminal conduct of these companies hurt the pocketbook of virtually every American consumer—anyone who took a vitamin, drank a glass of milk, or had a bowl of cereal. . . These companies fixed the price; they allocated sales volumes; they allocated consumers; and in the United States they even rigged bids to make absolutely sure that their cartel would work. The conspirators actually held "annual meetings" to fix prices and to carve up world markets, as well as frequent follow-up meetings to ensure compliance with their illegal scheme.

Although this statement only referred to the damage to the US economy, it is plausible to argue that *every* vitamin consumer in the world was ripped off. Average buyers paid 30% to 40% more. The total illegal profits—known as "global injuries"—were estimated to be $9 billion to $12 billion, of which 15% occurred in the US and 26% in the EU. Firms and managers in this conspiracy paid a heavy price: Worldwide, firms paid record fines of about $5 billion, including $500 million from Hoffman-La Roche and $225 million from BASF to the United States alone. In addition, for the first time in US antitrust history, Swiss and German executives working for Hoffman-La Roche and BASF served prison terms of 3–4 months and paid personal fines of $75,000–$350,000.

This case has both triumphs and frustrations. A leading triumph stems from the US Corporate Leniency Program. Tapping into the powerful incentives to defect in this *real* "prisoner's dilemma," this Program offers the first company to voluntarily confess blanket amnesty from criminal prosecution while its fingered co-conspirators are hit with criminal fines and jail time. The amnesty prize goes only to the *first* company that comes forward. In this case, it was Rhône-Poulenc that provided antitrust authorities overwhelming evidence that made other defendants decide not to contest the charges and to plead guilty. In terms of frustrations, despite the record fines and penalties, the criminal and civil justice systems of the world have failed to recover more than half of the cartel's illegal profits. In other words, given the low probability of detection, as experts noted, it may still be "utterly rational for would-be cartelists to form or join an international price-fixing conspiracy." Overall, the deterrence, as powerful as this case indicates, may still not be enough.

Sources: Based on (1) D. Bush et al., 2004, *How to Block Cartel Formation and Price-Fixing*, Washington: AEI-Brookings Joint Center for Regulatory Studies; (2) *Guardian*, 2001, Vitamin cartel fined for price fixing, November 21; (3) C. Hobbs, 2004, The confession game, *Harvard Business Review*, September: 20–21; (4) US Department of Justice, 2000, Four foreign executives agree to plead guilty to participating in international vitamin cartel, April 6, Washington: DOJ.

FIGURE 11.1   A "PRISONER'S DILEMMA" FOR AIRLINES AND PAYOFF STRUCTURE (TOTAL NUMBER OF PASSENGERS = 200)

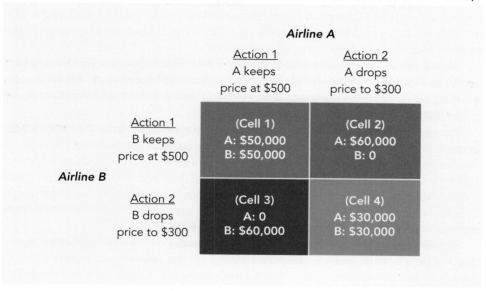

However, neither side likes to be a "sucker." Thus, the more likely outcome is Cell 4. Each airline still gets 100 passengers, but revenue for both firms and the industry is reduced 40%. A key insight of game theory is that even if A and B have a prior agreement to fix the price at $500, both still have strong incentives to cheat, thus pulling the industry to Cell 4 where both are clearly worse off.

Given the benefits of collusion and incentives to cheat, what industries are most susceptible to collusion? Five factors emerge (Table 11.1). The first is the number of firms or, more technically, the **concentration ratio**—the percentage of total industry sales accounted for by the top four, eight, or twenty firms. In general, the higher the concentration, the easier it is to organize collusion. In the vitamin cartel, the top four firms controlled 75% of the global supply of bulk vitamins (In Focus 11.1).

Second, the existence of a **price leader**—defined as a firm that has a dominant market share and sets "acceptable" prices and margins in the industry—helps tacit collusion. The price leader needs to possess the **capacity to punish** defectors, which requires sufficient resources to deter and combat defection. The most frequently used punishment is to undercut the defector by flooding the market, thus making defection fruitless. Such punishment is costly because it brings significant short-run financial losses to the price leader. The price leader needs to be both willing

Concentration ratio
The percentage of total industry sales accounted for by the top four, eight, or twenty firms.

Price leader
A firm that has a dominant market share and sets "acceptable" prices and margins in the industry.

Capacity to punish
Sufficient resources possessed by a price leader to deter and combat defection.

TABLE 11.1   INDUSTRY CHARACTERISTICS AND POSSIBILITY OF COLLUSION VIS-À-VIS COMPETITION

Collusion possible	Collusion difficult (competition likely)
• Few firms (high concentration)	• Many firms (low concentration)
• Existence of an industry price leader	• No industry price leader
• Homogeneous products	• Heterogeneous products
• High barriers to entry	• Low barriers to entry
• High market commonality (mutual forbearance)	• Lack of market commonality (no mutual forbearance)

and able to punish and bear the costs. Prior to the 1980s, General Motors (GM) served as the price leader in car manufacturing. GM would set price increases, and Ford and Chrysler would follow or GM would punish them. More recently, however, Asian and European automakers refused to follow GM's lead, and GM is no longer willing and able to play this role. Thus, the US automobile industry has become much more turbulent and competitive.

Third, collusion is likely in an industry with homogeneous products where rivals are forced to compete on price rather than differentiation. Because price competition is often "cut-throat," firms in commodity industries may have stronger incentives to collude (see In Focus 11.1).

Fourth, collusion is more likely in an industry with high barriers to entry (such as shipbuilding) rather than low barriers to entry (such as restaurants).[4] In order to overcome barriers, new entrants are likely to ignore the existing industry "order" and to introduce less homogeneous products with newer technologies (in other words, "disruptive technologies").[5] As "mavericks," new entrants "can be thought of as loose cannons in otherwise placid and calm industries."[6] Thus, existing firms may collude to keep new firms from disrupting the market.

Finally, **market commonality**, defined as the degree of overlap between two rivals' markets, also has a significant bearing on the intensity of rivalry.[7] A high degree of market commonality may restrain firms from aggressively going after each other. **Multimarket competition** occurs when firms engage the same rivals in multiple markets. Multimarket firms may respect their rivals' spheres of influence in certain markets, and their rivals may reciprocate, leading to tacit collusion—an outcome known as **mutual forbearance**.[8] Such mutual forbearance stems primarily from deterrence. A high degree of market commonality suggests that if a firm attacks in one market, its rivals have the ability to engage in **cross-market retaliation**, leading to a costly all-out war that nobody can afford.

Overall, the effectiveness of a firm's actions depends significantly on the domestic and international institutions governing competitive dynamics as well as firm-specific resources and capabilities. The next two sections expand on these points, which are summarized in Figure 11.2.

FIGURE 11.2   INSTITUTIONS, RESOURCES, AND COMPETITIVE DYNAMICS

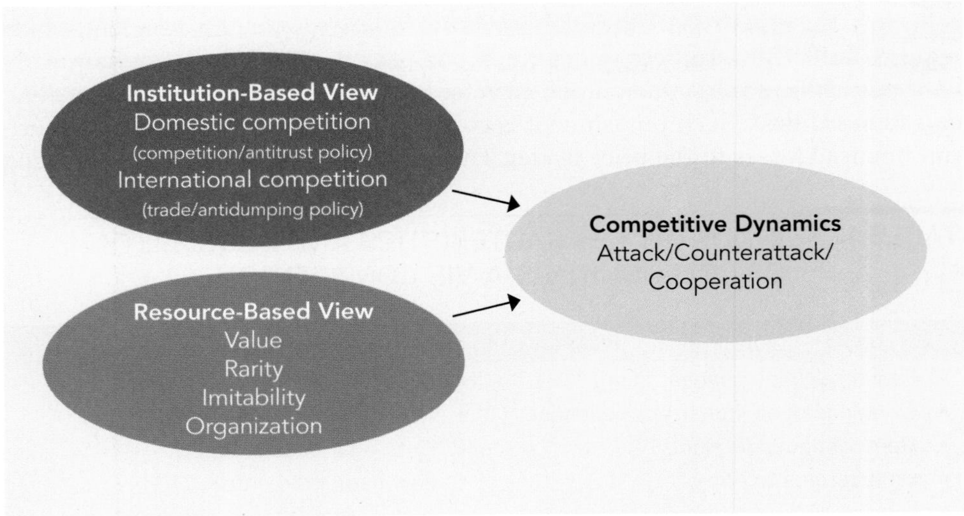

Market commonality
The overlap between two rivals' markets.

Multimarket competition
Firms engage the same rivals in multiple markets.

Mutual forbearance
Multimarket firms respect their rivals' spheres of influence in certain markets, and their rivals reciprocate, leading to tacit collusion.

Cross-market retaliation
Retaliatory attacks on a competitor's other markets if this competitor attacks a firm's original market.

INSTITUTIONS GOVERNING DOMESTIC AND INTERNATIONAL COMPETITION

Outline how formal institutions affect domestic and international competition.

The institution-based view advises managers to be well versed in the rules governing domestic and international competition. A lack of understanding of these institutions may land otherwise successful firms (such as Microsoft) in deep trouble.

Formal Institutions Governing Domestic Competition: A Focus on Antitrust

Formal institutions governing domestic competition are broadly guided by competition policy, which "determines the institutional mix of competition and cooperation that gives rise to the market system."[9] Of particular relevance to us is one branch called antitrust policy, which is designed to combat monopolies and cartels. Competition and antitrust policy seeks to balance efficiency and fairness. Although efficiency is relatively easy to understand, it is often hard to agree on what is fair. In the United States, fairness means equal opportunities for incumbents and new entrants. It is "unfair" for incumbents to fix prices and raise entry barriers to shut out new entrants (see *The Informant*). However, in Japan, fairness means the *opposite*—that is, incumbents that have invested in and nurtured an industry for a long time deserve to be protected from new entrants. What Americans approvingly describe as "market dynamism" is negatively labeled by Japanese as "market turbulence." The Japanese ideal is "orderly competition" (a euphemism for incumbent dominance).

Overall, the American antitrust policy is *pro-competition* and *pro-consumer*, whereas the Japanese approach is *pro-incumbent* and *pro-producer*. It is difficult to argue who is right or wrong here, but we need to be aware of such crucial differences. In general, because of stronger, pro-consumer antitrust laws, competitive forces have been stronger in the United States than in most other developed economies. As a result, American consumers enjoy the lowest prices on average (except for drugs) and Japanese consumers endure the highest prices (except for cars) (see Table 11.2).

Competition policy
Government policy governing the rules of the game in competition.

Antitrust policy
Government policy designed to combat monopolies and cartels.

TABLE 11.2   INTERNATIONAL PRICE COMPARISONS (RATIO OF DOMESTIC RETAIL PRICES TO WORLD PRICES)

	Australia	Canada	Germany	Japan	Netherlands	UK	US
Agriculture and fisheries	*1.067*	1.112	1.529	1.584	1.080	1.648	1.158
Processed food	*1.086*	1.192	1.447	2.099	1.299	1.202	1.090
Textiles	1.111	1.163	1.101	1.478	1.140	1.237	*1.051*
Printing and publishing	1.120	1.205	1.024	1.186	1.342	1.029	*1.005*
Drugs and medicines	*1.001*	2.680	2.643	1.217	3.349	1.845	3.105
Petroleum and coal	2.127	1.320	2.847	3.359	4.335	4.067	*1.007*
Motor vehicles	1.224	1.197	1.315	*1.000*	1.648	1.680	1.106
Professional goods	1.125	1.082	1.379	1.077	1.369	1.586	*1.074*
Weighted means	1.266	1.270	1.539	1.567	1.541	1.48	*1.118*

Source: Adapted from OECD, 2004, Product market competition and economic performance in the United States (p. 14), Economics Department Working Paper 398, Paris: OECD. **Bold** type face indicates the lowest price of this category.

Competition and antitrust policy focuses on (1) collusive price setting and (2) predatory pricing. Collusive price setting refers to price setting by monopolists or collusion parties at a level higher than the competitive level. This was exactly what cartel members in the movie *The Informant* were trying to do. In the largest collusive pricing case ever prosecuted, the global vitamin cartel of the 1990s artificially jacked up prices by 30% to 40% (see In Focus 11.1).

Another area of concern is predatory pricing, which is defined as (1) setting prices below cost *and* (2) intending to raise prices after eliminating rivals to cover losses in the long run ("an attempt to monopolize"). This is an area of significant contention. First, it is not clear what exactly constitutes "cost." Second, even when firms are found to be selling below cost, US courts have ruled that if rivals are too numerous to eliminate, one firm cannot recoup the losses incurred due to charging low prices by later jacking up prices, so its pricing cannot be labeled "predatory." This seems to be the case in most industries that are very competitive in nature. These two legal tests have made it extremely difficult to win a (domestic) predation case in the United States.

Formal Institutions Governing International Competition: A Focus on Antidumping

This section primarily deals with antidumping. In the same spirit of predatory pricing, dumping is defined as (1) an exporter selling below cost abroad and (2) planning to raise prices after eliminating local rivals. While domestic predation is usually labeled "anticompetitive," cross-border dumping is often emotionally accused of being "unfair" (see Chapter 5).

Consider the following two scenarios. First, a steel producer in *Indiana* enters a new market in Texas, where it offers prices lower than those in Indiana, resulting in a 10% market share in Texas. Texas firms have two choices. The first one is to initiate a lawsuit against the Indiana firm for "predatory pricing." However, it is difficult to prove (1) that the Indiana firm is selling below cost *and* (2) that its pricing is an "attempt to monopolize." Under US antitrust laws, a predation case like this will have no chance of succeeding. In other words, domestic competition/antitrust laws offer no hope for protection. Thus, Texas firms are most likely to opt for their second option—to retaliate in kind by offering lower prices to customers in Indiana, leading to lower prices in both Texas and Indiana.

Now in the second scenario, the "invading" firm is not from Indiana but *India*. Holding everything else constant, Texas steel firms can argue that the Indian firm is dumping. Under US antidumping laws, Texas steel producers "would almost certainly obtain legal relief on the very same facts that would not support an antitrust *claim*, let alone antitrust relief."[10] Note that imposing antidumping duties on Indian steel imports reduces the incentive for Texas firms to counterattack by entering India, resulting in *higher* prices in both Texas and India, where consumers are hurt. These two scenarios are not merely hypothetical; they are highly realistic. An OECD study in Australia, Canada, the EU, and the US reports that 90% of the practices found to be unfairly dumping in these countries would never have been questioned under their own antitrust laws if used by a domestic firm in making a domestic sale.[11] In a nutshell, foreign firms are discriminated against by the formal rules of the game.

Discrimination is also evident in the actual antidumping investigations. A case is usually filed by a domestic firm with the relevant government authorities. In the United States, the authorities are the International Trade Administration

Collusive price setting
Price setting by monopolists or collusion parties at a level higher than the competitive level.

Predatory pricing
An attempt to monopolize a market by setting prices below cost and intending to raise prices to cover losses in the long run after eliminating rivals.

Dumping
An exporter selling goods below cost.

Antidumping laws
Laws that make it illegal for an exporter to sell goods below cost abroad with the intent to raise prices after eliminating local rivals.

(a unit of the Department of Commerce) and International Trade Commission (an independent government agency). These government agencies then send lengthy questionnaires to the foreign firms accused of dumping and request comprehensive, proprietary data on their cost and pricing, in English, using US generally accepted accounting principles (GAAP), within 45 days. Many foreign defendants fail to provide such data on time because they are not familiar with US GAAP. The investigation can have one of the four following outcomes.

- If no data are forthcoming from abroad, the estimated data provided by the accusing firm become the evidence, and the accusing firm can easily win.
- If foreign firms do provide data, the accusing firm can still argue that these unfair foreigners have lied—"There is no way their costs can be so low!" In the case of Louisiana versus Chinese crawfish suppliers, the authenticity of the $9 per *week* salary made by Chinese workers was a major point of contention.
- Even if the low cost data are verified, US (and EU) antidumping laws allow the complainant to argue that these data are not "fair." In the case of China, the argument goes, its cost data reflect huge distortions due to government intervention because China is still a "nonmarket" economy. Wages may be low, but workers may also be provided with low-cost housing and government-subsidized benefits. Thus the crawfish case boiled down to how much it would cost hypothetically to raise crawfish in a market economy. In this particular case, Spain was mysteriously chosen. Because Spanish costs were about the same as Louisiana costs, the Chinese suppliers, despite their vehement objections, were found guilty of dumping in America by selling below *Spanish* costs. Thus, 110% to 123% import duties were levied on Chinese crawfish.
- The fourth possible outcome is that the defendant wins the case (see the Closing Case). But this is rare and happens to only 5% of the antidumping cases in the United States.[12]

One study reports that simply filing an antidumping petition (regardless of the outcome) may result in a nontrivial 1% increase in the stock price for US listed firms (an average of $46 million increase in market value).[13] Evidently, Wall Street knows that Uncle Sam favors US firms. Globally, this means that governments usually protect their domestic firms in antidumping investigations. So it is not surprising that antidumping cases have proliferated throughout the world. Although the EU and the United States have initiated the largest number of cases, Argentina and South Africa, on per dollar of imports, have 20 times more cases than the United States; India, seven times; and Brazil, five times.[14]

Overall, institutional conditions such as the availability of antidumping protection are not just the "background." They determine directly what weapons a firm has in its arsenal to wage competitive battles. In addition to formal institutions, informal norms and beliefs also play a significant role. Since many previous chapters have already dealt with these issues, we will not expand on this point here.

RESOURCES AND CAPABILITIES INFLUENCING COMPETITIVE DYNAMICS

A number of resource-based imperatives, informed by the VRIO framework first outlined in Chapter 4, drive decisions and actions associated with competitive dynamics (see Figure 11.2).

Articulate how resources and capabilities influence competitive dynamics.

TABLE 11.3   TOP TEN PATENT APPLICANT COMPANIES

	Patent applicant companies	Number of applications		Patent applicant companies	Number of applications
1	Huawei (China)	1,737	6	Siemens (Germany)	1,089
2	Panasonic (Japan)	1,729	7	Nokia (Finland)	1,005
3	Philips (Netherlands)	1,551	8	LG Electronics (South Korea)	992
4	Toyota (Japan)	1,364	9	Ericsson (Sweden)	984
5	Robert Bosch (Germany)	1,273	10	Fujitsu (Japan)	983

Source: Data extracted from World Intellectual Property Organization, 2009, Top 50 PCT applicants in 2008, Geneva: WIPO, www.wipo.int. The number of applications refers to international patent filings under WIPO's Patent Cooperation Treaty (PCT) during 2008.

Value

Firm resources must create value when engaging rivals. For example, the ability to attack in multiple markets—like Gillette did when it launched its Sensor razors in 23 countries *simultaneously*—throws rivals off balance, thus adding value. Likewise, the ability to respond rapidly to challenges also adds value.[15] Another example is holding a dominant position in key markets, such as flights in and out of London Heathrow airport for British Airways and Dallas-Fort Worth for American Airlines. Such a sphere of influence poses credible threats to rivals, which understand that the firm will defend its core markets vigorously.

Another way to add value is patenting. While patents are obviously valuable, firms are expanding the scale and scope of patenting, resulting in a "patent race."[16] Huawei now leads the world in terms of the number of patents filed, with more than 1,700 patents a year (see Table 11.3). On average, one patent will cost a firm half a million dollars in R&D, but only 5% of patents end up having any economic value. So why do firms spend so much money on the "patent race"? The answer is purely defensive. The proliferation of patents makes it easy for one firm to inadvertently infringe on rivals' patents. When being challenged, a firm without a defensive portfolio of patents is at a severe disadvantage: It has to pay its rivals to use their patents. On the other hand, a firm with strong patents can challenge rivals for infringement, thus making it easier to reach some understanding—or mutual forbearance. Patents thus become a valuable weapon in fighting off rivals. Huawei's aggressive patenting strategy is in part driven by Cisco's lawsuit against it in 2003 (see the Opening Case).

Rarity

Either by nature or nurture (or both), certain assets are rare, thus generating significant advantage. Saudi Arabia's vast oil reserves enable it to become the enforcer (price leader) of OPEC cartel agreements. Singapore Airlines, in addition to claiming as its home base one of the best locations connecting Europe and the Asia Pacific, has often been rated as the world's best airline. This rare combination of both geography and reputation allows Singapore Airlines to charge higher prices compared to rivals. In turn, this means Singapore Airlines can buy newer and better equipment than its rivals; it is the first airline in the world to fly the all new Airbus A380.

© Reuters/The Straits Times/Landov

Singapore Airlines was the first to fly the new Airbus A380. What type of advantage does this give the airline?

Imitability

Most rivals watch each other and probably have a fairly comprehensive (although not necessarily accurate) picture of how their rivals compete. However, the next hurdle is how to imitate successful rivals. It is well known that fast-moving rivals tend to perform better.[17] Competitively passive and slow-moving firms find it difficult to imitate rivals' actions. Many major airlines have repeatedly tried to imitate successful discount carriers such as Southwest and Ryanair but have failed.

Organization

Some firms are better organized for competitive actions, such as stealth attacks and a willingness to answer challenges "tit-for-tat."[18] The intense "warrior-like" culture not only requires top management commitment, but also employee involvement down to the "soldiers in the trenches." It is such a self-styled "wolf" culture that propelled Huawei to become Cisco's leading challenger (see the Opening Case). It is difficult, however, for slow-moving firms to suddenly become more aggressive.

More centrally coordinated firms may be better mutual forbearers than firms whose units are loosely controlled. An MNE competing with rivals across many countries may pursue a mutual forbearance strategy and require some units to hold back and sacrifice possible market gains out of respect for a rival's sphere of influence. Such coordination helps other units with dominant market positions to maximize performance, thus helping the MNE as a whole. Successfully carrying out such mutual forbearance calls for organizational reward systems and structures (such as those concerning bonuses and promotions) that encourage cooperation between units (see Chapter 13). Conversely, if a firm has competitive reward systems and structures (for example, bonuses linked to unit performance), unit managers may be unwilling to give up market gains for the greater benefits of other units and the whole firm, thus undermining mutual forbearance.[19]

Resource Similarity

Extended from the resource-based view, **resource similarity** is defined as "the extent to which a given competitor possesses strategic endowment comparable, in terms of both type and amount, to those of the focal firm."[20] Firms with a high degree of resource similarity are likely to have similar competitive actions. American Airlines and Japan Airlines may have a higher degree of resource similarity than that between American Airlines and Air Botswana.

If we put resource similarity and market commonality (discussed earlier) together, we can yield a framework of competitor analysis for any pair of rivals. In Figure 11.3, Cell 4 represents two firms with a high degree of resource similarity but a low degree of market commonality (little mutual forbearance), and the intensity of rivalry is likely to be the highest. Conversely, in Cell 1, since both firms have little resource similarity but a high degree of market commonality, the intensity of their rivalry may be the lowest. Cells 2 and 3 present an intermediate level of competition. Such conscientious mapping can help managers sharpen their analytical focus and allocate resources in proportion to the degree of threat each rival presents.

Resource similarity
The extent to which a given competitor possesses strategic endowment comparable, in terms of both type and amount, to those of the focal firm.

FIGURE 11.3   A FRAMEWORK FOR COMPETITOR ANALYSIS BETWEEN A PAIR OF RIVALS

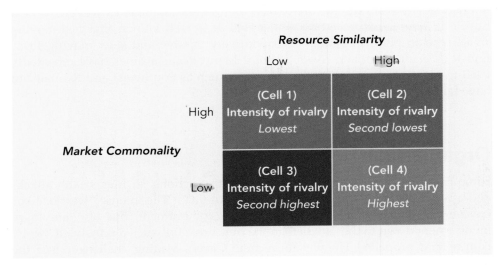

Sources: Adapted from (1) M. Chen, 1996, Competitor analysis and interfirm rivalry: Toward a theoretical integration, *Academy of Management Review*, 21: 108; (2) J. Gimeno & C. Y. Woo, 1996, Hypercompetition in a multimarket environment: The role of strategic similarity and multimarket contact in competitive de-escalation, *Organization Science*, 7: 338.

To illustrate, In Focus 11.2 describes why Fox's entry into the US broadcasting industry has intensified the rivalry. One lesson the Big Three TV networks learned too late was that they should have gone abroad earlier and established mutual forbearance with News Corporation when it was financially possible. By the time Fox entered the market, however, it was too late for the Big Three to start thinking about expanding overseas. As the saying goes, "The best defense is a good offense." The next section discusses how to launch successful offensive attacks.

Identify the drivers for attacks, counterattacks, and signaling.

Attack
An initial set of actions to gain competitive advantage.

Counterattack
A set of actions in response to attack.

Blue ocean strategy
Strategy that focuses on developing new markets ("blue ocean") and avoids attacking core markets defended by rivals, which is likely to result in a bloody price war or a "red ocean."

ATTACK, COUNTERATTACK, AND SIGNALING

Attack and Counterattack

In the form of price cuts, advertising campaigns, market entries, and new product introductions, attack can be defined as an initial set of actions to gain competitive advantage, and counterattack is consequently defined as a set of actions in response to attack. This section focuses on a key question: What kinds of attack are more likely to be successful?

Obviously, unopposed attacks are more likely to be successful. Thus, attackers need to be aware of the three drivers for counterattacks: (1) awareness, (2) motivation, and (3) capabilities.

- *Awareness* is a prerequisite for any counterattack. If an attack is so subtle that rivals are not aware of it, then the attacker's objectives are likely to be attained. One interesting idea is the blue ocean strategy, which avoids attacking core markets defended by rivals.[21] A thrust on rivals' core markets is likely to result in a bloody price war—in other words, a "red ocean." In the 1990s,

IN Focus 11.2

A Fox in the Hen House

Prior to 1996, the US TV broadcasting industry could be viewed as a relatively tranquil "hen house." The Big Three networks (ABC, NBC, and CBS) dominated mainstream programming and CNN ran its 24-hour news show. Like hens sharing a house, there was some rivalry. But there were well-understood rules of engagement, such as not raiding each other's affiliate stations. Overall, competition was gentlemanly.

However, the 1996 arrival of Fox News Channel, a subsidiary of Rupert Murdoch's News Corporation, has transformed the industry. First, Fox violated industry norms by raiding Big Three affiliate stations. Fox convinced some affiliates to switch and become Fox stations. In some markets, affiliate defections gave Fox overnight success at the expense of one of the Big Three. Second, Fox paid up to $11 per subscriber to cable operators. This violated another norm where cable operators only paid stations carriage fees for programming. Having outfoxed the Big Three, Fox turned its guns on CNN. When Time Warner bought CNN owned by Ted Turner, Time Warner was required by an antitrust consent to carry a second news channel in addition to CNN. Time Warner chose MSNBC instead of Fox, and then Fox sued Time Warner. The media war became dirty: Turner publicly compared Murdoch to Adolf Hitler, while Murdoch's *New York Post* questioned Turner's sanity. Perhaps controversy was exactly what Fox wanted. Critics have repeatedly accused Fox of promoting a conservative (allegedly Republican) point of view. Viewers did not care. By 2006, Fox was the most watched news channel in the United States, reaching 96% of US households.

Using Figure 11.3, we can suggest that the pre-1996 industry was in Cell 2. The intensity of rivalry was the second *lowest* because the Big Three and CNN had high market commonality (all focusing on the United States) and high resource similarity (TV programming). However, Fox's entry has transformed the game. News Corporation is a global player that was historically headquartered in Australia but is now headquartered and listed in New York. In addition to its Australian roots, News Corporation has a major presence in Asia, Canada, and Europe. Its first US acquisition took place in 1973, and Murdoch became an American citizen in 1985 to satisfy a requirement that only US citizens could own American TV stations. In other words, although Fox shares high resource similarity with the Big Three and CNN, it has low market similarity with the Big Three because they have little non-US presence. The upshot? The industry is now in Cell 4 with the *highest* intensity of rivalry. Fox can beat up the Big Three because it has little fear of retaliation against its non-US markets. The Big Three thus pay a heavy price for their US-centric mentality. Being more international, CNN is in a better position to fight Fox. In 1997, Turner and Murdoch settled, with Time Warner agreeing to carry Fox and News Corporation giving Time Warner access to News Corporation's satellites in Asia and Europe. In other words, they have established some mutual forbearance.

Sources: Based on (1) *BusinessWeek*, 2006, August 21/28: 82; (2) www.newscorp.com.

Netscape drew tremendous publicity by labeling Microsoft the "Death Star" (of *Star Wars* fame) and predicting that the Internet would make Windows obsolete. Such a public challenge helped make Netscape Microsoft's enemy number one, and eventually contributed to Netscape's demise (or its drowning in the "red ocean").

- *Motivation* is also crucial. If the attacked market is of marginal value, managers may decide not to counterattack. Consider Haier's entry into the US white goods market. Although Haier dominates in China, its home market, with a broad range of products, it chose to enter the US market in a most nonthreatening segment: compact refrigerators (also known as mini-bars) for hotels and dorms. Does anyone remember the brand of the compact refrigerator in the last hotel room where you stayed? Probably not. Evidently, not only you failed to pay attention to that brand, incumbents such as GE and Whirlpool also dismissed this segment as peripheral and of low marginal value. In other words, they were not motivated to counterattack. Thanks to incumbents' lack of motivation to counterattack, Haier now commands a 50% US market share in compact refrigerators, and has built a factory in South Carolina to go after more lucrative product lines.
- Finally, even if an attack is identified and a firm is motivated to respond, it requires strong *capabilities* to carry out counterattacks. In 2008, Microsoft identified that Apple's share of the PC market neared double-digit numbers, despite Mac's $2,700 price tag. Further pressure came from Linux, a free operating system that was coming already installed on a new generation of $500 "netbook" computers. Microsoft fought back by leveraging its deep pockets (a hard-to-imitate capability). Instead of charging PC makers the normal $70, Microsoft only charged $15 for Windows. As a result, Mac sales are no longer increasing, and Linux has disappeared from most netbooks. In 2009, approximately 95% of netbooks run Windows, up from 10% in 2008.[22]

Overall, minimizing opponents' awareness, motivation, and capabilities is more likely to result in successful attacks. Frontal, infrequent, and predictable attacks typically find rivals well prepared. Winning firms excel at making subtle, frequent, but unpredictable moves.

Cooperation and Signaling

Some firms choose to compete and attack, whereas others choose to cooperate. How do firms signal an intention to cooperate in order to *reduce* competitive intensity? Short of talking directly to rivals, which is illegal, firms have to resort to signaling: Although you can't talk to your competitors on pricing, you can always *wink* at them.

- Firms may enter new markets, not necessarily to challenge incumbents but to seek mutual forbearance by establishing multimarket contact. Thus, MNEs often chase each other, entering one country after another.[23] Airlines that meet in many routes are often less aggressive than airlines that meet in one or a few routes.[24]
- Firms can send an open signal for a truce. As GM faced grave financial difficulties in 2005, Toyota's chairman told the media *twice* that Toyota would "help GM" by raising Toyota prices in the United States. As far as signaling goes, Toyota's signal could not have been more unambiguous, short of talking directly to GM, which would have been illegal. US antitrust authorities reportedly took note of such remarks—essentially an open message to GM for price fixing.[25]
- Sometimes firms can send a signal to rivals by enlisting the help of governments. Although it is illegal to hold direct negotiations with rivals on what constitutes "fair" pricing, holding such discussions is legal under the auspices of government investigations. Thus, filing an antidumping petition or suing a rival does not necessarily indicate a totally hostile intent. Rather, it sends a

signal that it is ~~time to talk~~. When Cisco sued Huawei, Cisco was able to *legally* discuss a number of strategic issues during settlement negotiations, which were mediated by US and Chinese government officials. In the end, Cisco dropped its case against Huawei after both firms negotiated a solution (see the Opening Case).

• Finally, firms can organize strategic alliances with rivals for cost reduction. Although price fixing is illegal, reducing cost by 10% through an alliance, which is legal, has the same impact on the financial bottom line as collusively raising prices by 10%. See Chapter 12 for details.

LOCAL FIRMS VERSUS MULTINATIONAL ENTERPRISES

Although managers, students, and journalists are often fascinated by MNE rivals such as Coca-Cola and Pepsi, Intel and AMD, and Sony and Samsung, much less is known about how local firms cope with attacks from MNEs. Given the broad choices of competing and/or cooperating, local firms can adopt one of four strategic postures, depending on (1) the industry conditions and (2) the nature of competitive assets. Shown in Figure 11.4, these factors suggest four strategic actions.[26]

Discuss how local firms fight multinational enterprises (MNEs).

Cell 3 shows how in some industries, the pressures to globalize are relatively low and local firms' strengths lie in a deep understanding of local markets. In this case, local assets where MNEs are weak are leveraged in a **defender** strategy. For example, facing an onslaught from MNE cosmetics firms, a number of local Israeli firms turned to focus on products suited to the Middle Eastern climate and managed to defend their turf. Ahava has been particularly successful, partly because of its highly unique components, which are extracted from the Dead Sea and unavailable elsewhere. In other words, although local firms such as Ahava cede

FIGURE 11.4 HOW LOCAL FIRMS IN EMERGING ECONOMIES RESPOND TO MULTINATIONAL ACTIONS

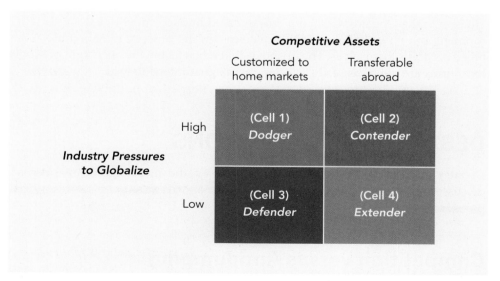

Source: Adapted from N. Dawar & T. Frost, "Competing with giants: Survival strategies for local companies in emerging markets," *Harvard Business Review* (March–April 1999): 122. Reprinted by permission of Harvard Business Publishing.

Defender
Strategy that centers on local assets in areas in which MNEs are weak.

some markets (such as mainstream cosmetics) to MNEs, they build strongholds in narrower but deeper product markets (such as the Dead Sea mud). Ahava's Dead Sea mud is now likely to be available in a cosmetics store near you.

Cell 4 shows industries where pressures for globalization are relatively low and local firms may possess some skills and assets that are transferable overseas, thus leading to an extender strategy. This strategy centers on leveraging home-grown competencies abroad. For example, Asian Paints controls 40% of the house paint market in India. Asian Paints developed strong capabilities tailored to the unique environment in India, which is characterized by thousands of small retailers serving numerous poor consumers who can only afford small quantities of paint that can be diluted to save money. Such capabilities are not only a winning formula in India but also in much of the developing world. In contrast, MNEs, whose business model typically centers on affluent customers in developed economies, have had a hard time coming up with profitable low-end products.

Cell 1 depicts local firms that compete in industries with high pressures for globalization. Thus, a dodger strategy is necessary. This is largely centered on cooperating through joint ventures (JVs) with MNEs and sell-offs to MNEs. In the Chinese automobile industry, *all* major domestic automakers have entered JVs with MNEs. In the Czech Republic, the government sold Skoda to Volkswagen. In essence, to the extent that local firms are unable to successfully compete head-on against MNEs, cooperation becomes necessary. In other words, if you can't beat them, join them!

Finally, in Cell 2, some local firms, through a contender strategy, engage in rapid learning and then expand overseas. A number of Chinese mobile phone makers such as TCL and Bird have rapidly caught up with global heavyweights such as Motorola and Nokia. Domestic firms in China went from a 5% market share in the early 2000s to more than 50% market share by the end of the decade. Following their success at home, TCL and Bird have now entered foreign markets.

Particularly in emerging economies, how domestic firms respond is crucial for managers. Despite initial dominance, MNEs in China do not always stay on top. In numerous industries (such as sportswear, cellular phones, personal computers, and home appliances), many MNEs have been "dethroned." Although weak domestic players are washed out, some of the stronger domestic firms (such as Huawei in the Opening Case) not only succeed in the competitive domestic environment, but now challenge MNEs overseas. In the process, they become a new breed of MNEs themselves. The upshot is that when facing the onslaught of MNEs, local firms are not necessarily "sitting ducks" guaranteed to lose.

Extender
Strategy that centers on leveraging homegrown competencies abroad.

Dodger
Strategy that centers on cooperating through joint ventures with MNEs and sell-offs to MNEs.

Contender
Strategy that centers on a firm engaging in rapid learning and then expand overseas.

Participate in two leading debates on global competitive dynamics.

DEBATES AND EXTENSIONS

Debates abound in this sensitive area. Two of the most significant ones are discussed: (1) competition versus antidumping and (2) managers versus antitrust policy makers.

Competition versus Antidumping

There are two arguments against the practice of imposing antidumping restrictions on foreign firms. First, because dumping requires selling "below cost," it is often difficult (if not impossible) to prove the case given the ambiguity concerning "cost."

Second, does it matter if foreign firms are indeed selling below cost? This is simply a commonly used competitive action. When entering a new market, virtually all firms lose money on Day 1 (and often in Year 1). Until some point when the firm (finally) breaks even, it loses money because it is selling below cost. Domestically, cases of such "dumping" are both numerous and perfectly legal. For example, coupon items are frequently sold (or given away) below cost. Do consumers complain about such good deals? Generally not. "If the foreigners are kind enough (or dumb enough) to sell their goods to our country below cost, why should we complain?"[27]

The classic counterargument is: What if, through "unfair" dumping, foreign rivals drive out domestic firms and then jack up prices? Given the competitive nature of most industries, it is often difficult (if not impossible) to eliminate all rivals and then recoup losses by charging higher monopoly prices. The fear of foreign monopoly is often exaggerated by special interest groups who benefit at the expense of consumers in the domestic economy (see Chapter 5). Joseph Stiglitz, a Nobel laureate in economics and then chief economist of the World Bank, wrote that antidumping duties "are simply naked protectionism" and one country's "fair trade laws" are often known elsewhere as "unfair trade laws."[28] Our Closing Case has a vivid discussion of some of these "fair trade laws" in action.

One solution is to phase out antidumping laws and use the same standards as applied to domestic predatory pricing. Such a waiver of antidumping charges has been in place between Australia and New Zealand, between Canada and the United States, and within the EU. Thus, a Canadian firm, essentially treated as a US firm, can be accused of predatory pricing but cannot be accused of dumping in the United States. Since antidumping is about "us versus them," such harmonization represents essentially an expanded notion of "us." However, as noted earlier, a domestic predation case is very difficult to make. In such a way, competition can be fostered, aggressiveness rewarded, and "dumping" legalized.

Competitive Strategy versus Antitrust Policy

Managers strive to lead their firms to compete. But antitrust policy makers sometimes get in the way by accusing firms (such as Microsoft) of being "anticompetitive." This debate, therefore, is crucial. Unfortunately, *none* of the other international business (IB) textbooks covers this debate. As a result, most business school students do not know antitrust policy, and when they graduate and become managers, they do not care either. Antitrust officials, on the other hand, tend to be trained in economics and law but not business. A background in economics and law, however, does not give antitrust officials an intimate understanding of how firm-level competition and/or cooperation unfolds, which is something that a business school education provides. As a result, policy makers trained in economics and law but with little sense of how real companies make decisions end up deciding and enforcing the rules governing competition. Such a disconnect naturally breeds mutual suspicion and frustration on both sides. Business school students and managers will be better off if they are familiar with antitrust concerns.

Because the United States has the world's oldest antitrust frameworks (dating back to the 1890 Sherman Act), the US debate is the most watched in the world and so is the focus here. Rather than adopting a US-centric approach, here we treat the US debate as a *case study* that may have global ramifications. In fact, antitrust issues, which originated from a domestic orientation, have been globalized recently (see In Focus 11.3).

On behalf of managers, concerned management scholars have made four arguments.[29] First, antitrust laws were often created in response to the old realities of

Focus 11.3

From Trade Wars to Antitrust Wars

In the 21st century, trade wars are often threatened but seldom fought. However, a new style of trade wars centered on protectionism is on the rise. These new trade wars are increasingly known as antitrust wars, because antitrust policy, which historically focuses on domestic competition, has been used to score international points.

In the name of promoting competition in Europe, the EU antitrust authorities in 2001 torpedoed the proposed merger of two US-headquartered firms, GE and Honeywell. In 2009, the EU fined Intel $1.45 billion for alleged anticompetitive conduct against its smaller US-based rival, AMD. While Intel was also being investigated by US antitrust authorities, the EU ruling appeared ahead of the US decision (still pending as of this writing). In 2004, the EU fined Microsoft $660 million for bundling its own Media Player with Windows and thus excluding market access for RealNetworks, a Seattle-based US rival. In 2009, the EU prosecuted Microsoft for tying Windows with its own web browser, Internet Explorer, and stifling competition from other browsers—exactly the same alleged crime as pursued by US authorities a decade ago. The only viable US competitor from the earlier US case against Microsoft, Netscape had essentially vanished by 2009, accounting for less than 1% of browsers usage. This time, the EU case against Microsoft was triggered by a complaint from Opera Software, an Oslo, Norway–based browser maker. In comparison with Explorer's 86% global browser market share in 1999, the 2009 case came at a time when Microsoft's dominance in browsers was weakened. In 2009, Explorer only had 68% of the global market, and its nearest competitor, Firefox (developed by California-based Mozilla) enjoyed 20%. In Europe, Microsoft was even weaker, with Explorer accounting for only 60% of the

market, followed by Opera's 5% and Firefox's 3%. Overall, the EU antitrust authorities, rather than the US authorities, appear to more vigorously pursue leading US firms, suggesting a potential protectionist undertone.

Not to be outdone, the fledgling Chinese antitrust authorities entered the fray by enforcing China's new Antimonopoly Law in 2008. Mergers of firms not headquartered in China, as long as their combined China turnover reached $120 million in the previous year, had to notify Chinese authorities for clearance. For example, the merger between the Belgium-based InBev and the US-based Anheuser-Busch had to be approved by the Chinese authorities, subject to some conditions. What is the most controversial is the very first decision to stop an acquisition announced in March 2009: the proposed acquisition of China's leading fruit juice maker Huiyuan by Coca-Cola. At $2.4 billion, the price was 50 times Huiyuan's expected earnings in 2008 and a 200% premium to Huiyuan's share price. Huiyuan's delighted owners agreed to sell. The only party blocking the transaction was the Chinese Ministry of Commerce. The Ministry cited the adverse impact on small and medium-sized domestic juice makers as a major reason—in other words, protectionism. Beyond the antitrust merit of this individual case, there is a possibility that the Chinese authorities used this case to signal displeasure to the United States and Australia, which recently disallowed high-profile Chinese acquisitions in these countries.

Sources: Based on (1) M. Bachrack, 2009, Merger control under China's Antimonopoly Law, *China Business Review*, July–August: 18–21; (2) J. Clougherty, 2005, Antitrust holdup source, cross-national institutional variation, and corporate political strategy implications for domestic mergers in a global context, *Strategic Management Journal*, 26: 769–790; (3) *Wall Street Journal*, 2009, EU hits Microsoft with new antitrust charges, January 17–18; (4) www.intel.com.

mostly domestic competition—the year 1890 for the Sherman Act is *not* a typo for 1990. However, the largely global competition today means that a large, dominant firm in one country (think of Boeing) does not automatically translate into a dangerous monopoly. The existence of foreign rivals (such as Airbus) forces the large domestic incumbent to be more competitive.

Second, the very actions accused of being "anticompetitive" may actually be highly "competitive" or "hypercompetitive." In the 1990s, the hypercompetitive

Microsoft was charged with "anticompetitive" behavior. Its alleged crime? *Not* voluntarily helping its competitors. Just imagine: if your manager asked you to voluntarily help your firm's competitors, would you just do it or think that your manager was out of his or her mind?

Third, US antitrust laws create strategic confusion. Because the intention to destroy your firm's rivals is the smoking gun of antitrust cases, managers are forced to use milder language. Don't say or write a memo that says, "We want to beat our competitors!" Forget freedom of speech: US managers could end up in court if they wrote such a memo. In contrast, non-US firms often use war-like language: Komatsu is famous for "Encircling Caterpillar!" and Honda for "Annihilate, crush, and destroy Yamaha!" The inability to talk straight creates confusion among lower-level managers and employees in US firms. A confused firm is not likely to be aggressive.

Finally, US antitrust laws may be unfair because these laws discriminate *against* US firms. In 1983, if GM and Ford were to propose to jointly manufacture cars, antitrust officials would have turned them down, citing an (obvious!) intent to collude. Ironically, starting in 1983, GM was allowed to make cars with Toyota. Now 27 years later, Toyota is the number one automaker in the United States. The upshot? American antitrust laws have helped Toyota but not Ford or GM. Although the protectionist undertones of one country's (or region's) antitrust laws against other countries' firms may be disgraceful, they are understandable (see In Focus 11.3). But it is puzzling why US antitrust laws may unfairly discriminate against certain US firms. Overall, business students and future managers should be prepared to enter this debate head-on. Its outcome may shape future competition around the world to a large degree.

MANAGEMENT SAVVY

Let us revisit our fundamental question: What determines the success and failure in managing competitive dynamics around the world? Drawing on the two core perspectives (institution-based and resource-based views), we suggest that to successfully manage competitive dynamics, managers not only need to become masters of maneuvers (both confrontation and cooperation), but also experts in government regulations at home and abroad if they aspire to succeed globally.

Consequently, three implications emerge for savvy managers (Table 11.4). First, managers need to understand the rules of the game governing competition around the world. In countries such as the United States, aggressive language such as "Let's kill competitors" is not allowed. However, carefully crafted ambitions such as Wal-Mart's "We want to be number one in the grocery business"

LEARNING OBJECTIVE

7

Draw implications for action.

TABLE 11.4   IMPLICATIONS FOR ACTION

- Understand the rules of the game governing domestic and international competition around the world.

- Strengthen resources and capabilities that more effectively compete and/or cooperate.

- Develop skills in competitor analysis that guide decision making on attacks, counterattacks, and cooperation.

are legal, because such wording (at least on paper) shows no illegal intention to destroy rivals. Too bad, 31 US supermarket chains have declared bankruptcy since Wal-Mart entered the grocery market in the 1990s—just a tragic coincidence (!) according to Wal-Mart. Wal-Mart's "everyday low prices" cannot be charged as predatory pricing because after rivals drop out, Wal-Mart does *not* raise prices.

The necessity to understand the rules of the game is crucial when venturing abroad. What is legal domestically may be illegal elsewhere. Imagine Chinese managers' shock when expanding abroad to discover they cannot approach rivals in the United States to discuss pricing, a typical practice in China. They may go to jail in the United States (see *The Informant*). Indeed, several German and Swiss managers involved in the vitamin cartel served jail time in America (In Focus 11.1). Another crucial area is antidumping. Many Chinese managers are surprised that their low-cost strategy is labeled "illegal" dumping in the very countries that often brag about "free market" competition. In reality, "free markets" are not free. However, managers well versed in the rules of the game may launch subtle attacks without incurring the wrath of antidumping officials. Imports commanding less than 3% market share or below in a 12-month period are regarded by US antidumping laws as "negligible imports" not worthy of investigation.[30] Thus, foreign firms not crossing such a "red line" would be safe. As a manager exporting to the United States, would you like to maintain a steady 3% US market share every year over ten years or a dramatic 30% upsurge in Year 1, which would attract antidumping actions preventing further growth in Year 2 and beyond?

Second, managers need to strengthen capabilities that more effectively compete and/or cooperate. In attacks and counterattacks, subtlety, frequency, complexity, and unpredictability are helpful. In cooperation, market similarity and mutual forbearance may be better. As Sun Tzu advised a long time ago, managers need to "know yourself," including your unit, your firm, and your industry.

Finally, savvy managers also need to "know your opponents," by developing skills in competitor analysis (see Figure 11.3). Managers need to develop skills and instinct to think like their opponents who are eager to collect competitive intelligence (Table 11.5). Overall, since business is simultaneously war *and* peace, a winning formula, as in war and chess, is "Look ahead, reason back."

TABLE 11.5   TIPS ON COMPETITIVE INTELLIGENCE AND COUNTERINTELLIGENCE

- If you are bidding against a major local rival in a foreign country, expect aggressive efforts to gather your information. If you leave your laptop in a hotel room, expect the hard drive to be copied.

- Be careful about cell phones because signals can be intercepted. If you lose your cell phone for 30 seconds, your opponents may be able to put in a look-alike battery with a chip that will record and transmit your calls. This chip can also secretly turn your phone on and use it as a microphone.

- Be careful about the high-speed Internet service at your hotel. Go to the office of your local subsidiary. If there isn't such a safe, local office, a random WiFi spot may be safer than the hotel Internet service.

- If your negotiation counterparts offer to book you into a luxurious suite or hotel, turn it down. Book your own.

Source: Based on text in G. Morse, 2005, H. Keith Melton on corporate espionage, *Harvard Business Review*, November: 26. Note this is an interesting but extremely cautious view.

CHAPTER SUMMARY

1. Understand the industry conditions conducive for cooperation and collusion.
   - Such industries tend to have (1) a smaller number of rivals, (2) a price leader, (3) homogenous products, (4) high entry barriers, and (5) high market commonality (mutual forbearance).

2. Outline how formal institutions affect domestic competition and international competition.
   - Domestically, antitrust laws focus on collusion and predatory pricing.
   - Internationally, antidumping laws discriminate against foreign firms and protect domestic firms.

3. Articulate how resources and capabilities influence competitive dynamics.
   - Resource similarity and market commonality can yield a powerful framework for competitor analysis.

4. Identify the drivers for attacks, counterattacks, and signaling.
   - Attackers need to be aware of the three drivers for counterattacks: (1) awareness, (2) motivation, and (3) capabilities.
   - Without talking directly to competitors, firms can use various means to signal rivals.

5. Discuss how local firms fight MNEs.
   - When confronting MNEs, local firms can choose a variety of strategic choices: (1) defender, (2) extender, (3) dodger, or (4) contender. They may not be as weak as many people believe.

6. Participate in two leading debates on global competitive dynamics.
   - They are (1) competition versus antidumping and (2) competitive strategy versus antitrust policy.

7. Draw implications for action.
   - Understand the rules of the game governing domestic and international competition around the world.
   - Strengthen resources and capabilities for more effective competitor analysis.
   - Develop skills in competitor analysis that guide decision-making on attacks, counterattacks, and cooperation.

KEY TERMS

Antidumping laws 360	Competitor analysis 354	Game theory 355
Antitrust laws 355	Concentration ratio 357	Market commonality 358
Antitrust policy 359	Contender 368	Multimarket
Attack 364	Counterattack 364	competition 358
Blue ocean strategy 364	Cross-market	Mutual forbearance 358
Capacity to punish 357	retaliation 358	Predatory pricing 360
Cartel (trust) 355	Defender 367	Price leader 357
Collusion 355	Dodger 368	Prisoners' dilemma 355
Collusive price setting 360	Dumping 360	Resource similarity 363
Competition policy 359	Explicit collusion 355	Tacit collusion 355
Competitive dynamics 354	Extender 368	

REVIEW QUESTIONS

1. Explain the differences between tacit and explicit collusion.

2. Name and describe the five factors that make an industry particularly conducive to collusion.

3. Some countries' competition and antitrust policies are pro-competition and pro-consumer, whereas other countries' policies are pro-incumbent and pro-producer. How do they differ?

4. What is the difference between collusive price setting and predatory pricing?

5. Use your own examples to identify how resources and capabilities affect competitive dynamics.

6. How does a firm's corporate culture and organization affect its ability to engage in competitive actions?

7. Name and describe three drivers for counterattacks.

8. Describe at least three ways a firm may signal its intention to cooperate with a competitor.

9. Under what conditions might a firm assume a defender strategy?

10. Under what conditions might a firm adopt an extender strategy?

11. What criteria might induce a firm to choose a dodger strategy over a contender strategy, and vice versa?

12. Do you support or oppose antidumping restrictions? Explain your answer.

13. Using the United States as a case study, describe four arguments that managers may make regarding antitrust law.

14. What are some qualities you could develop in yourself to strengthen your capabilities for engaging in competitive dynamics?

15. As part of your firm's strategy to gain competitive advantage, it wants to cut prices by looking for alternate locations in which to manufacture its products. You are part of a committee attempting to select a new manufacturing location based on information in PengAtlas Map 3.4. What will your committee recommend and why?

CRITICAL DISCUSSION QUESTIONS

1. ***ON ETHICS***: As a CEO of a US firm, you feel the price war in your industry is killing profits for all firms. However, you have been warned by corporate lawyers not to openly discuss pricing with rivals, who you know personally because you went to school with them. How would you signal your intentions?

2. *ON ETHICS*: As a CEO, you are concerned that your firm and your industry in the United States are being devastated by foreign imports. Trade lawyers suggest filing an antidumping case against leading Chinese rivals and assure you a win. Would you file an antidumping case? Why or why not?

3. *ON ETHICS*: As part of a feint attack, your firm (firm A) announces that in the next year, it intends to enter country X where the competitor (firm B) is strong. Your firm's real intention is to march into country Y whereby B is weak. There is actually *no* plan to enter X. However, in the process of trying to "fool" B, customers, suppliers, investors, and the media are also being intentionally misled. What are the ethical dilemmas here? Do the pros of this action outweigh its cons?

GLOBAL ACTION

1. An element of understanding global competitive dynamics is to assess the industry concentration of different industries. To accomplish this, the percentage of overall industry sales coming from the largest manufacturing companies in an industry can be used as a proxy. Based on this approach, categorize the following four industries from most to least concentrated by using the sales of the top four companies in the report you locate on globalEDGE: aerospace and defense, beverages, chemicals, and food. Which countries are represented across these four industries? What insights concerning competitive dynamics in each industry can your evaluation provide?

2. The structure of international trade and tariff systems is highly complex. To maintain order, the United Nations Conference on Trade and Development (UNCTAD) has developed a coding system that categorizes the different trade control measures that may be required when conducting business internationally. Find this coding system on globalEDGE and then outline the nature of the main categories included.

VIDEO CASES

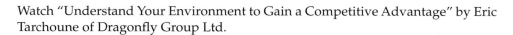

Watch "Understand Your Environment to Gain a Competitive Advantage" by Eric Tarchoune of Dragonfly Group Ltd.

1. How can one gain a competitive advantage in global markets by using the advice of the ancient Chinese military strategist, Sun Tzu?

2. Tarchoune discussed the Chinese contrasts of the big versus small fish and the quick versus slow fish. What is the application of that discussion to competition in global markets?

3. In many countries, the key to strategic business intelligence involves building relationships. Briefly explain.

4. Tarchoune suggested the Internet can be a means of gaining strategic intelligence. Do you agree? Why or why not?

5. Why do you think that many firms fail to understand the change in the business environment when entering new countries?

Closing Case

ETHICAL DILEMMA

The US Antidumping Case against Chinese Apple Juice Concentrate Producers

© Rigoulet Gilles

On September 11, 2009, President Obama decided to impose a 35% punitive tariff on Chinese-made car tires. This decision triggered an *immediate* reaction from China, which launched a pair of antidumping investigations against US autos and chicken products. Although in this case the Chinese tire makers were found not guilty of dumping (but still had to swallow the high tariffs), in the past, the US Commerce Department ("Commerce") has frequently initiated antidumping investigations of Chinese imports. In most cases, Chinese producers were found guilty of dumping in the United States and had to suffer high punitive tariffs. The nonfrozen apple juice concentrate (AJC) case in 2004 was the first time Chinese agricultural product firms ever won.

Commerce's probe into AJC production in China started in June 1999 in response to a petition filed by a couple of American apple juice producers. The US petitioners requested a 92% antidumping tariff rate and then dropped it to 52% after they heard that Chinese AJC producers actually responded. If the Chinese producers did not respond to the investigation, they would obviously lose. If they chose to respond, their chances of winning the case were estimated to be 25%.

China was the world's largest apple producer, AJC producer, and exporter. A total of 90% of China's AJC production was exported. In 2003, AJC exports reached 417,000 tons worth $254 million. The proposed antidumping rate of 52%, if imposed, would be devastating to Chinese AJC producers and apple growers. Among China's roughly 30 AJC producers involved in the US antidumping investigation, 15 companies agreed to respond. Subsequently 11 of them collectively hired experienced American lawyers, with one firm later dropping out. The case took four and a half years (1999–2004) and cost about $3.6 million in legal fees for the Chinese producers.

A key point of contention was how much it would cost to produce AJC in a market economy. Since China was not considered a "market economy," Commerce chose India and other surrogate factors of production for valuation purpose. Commerce concluded that Chinese AJC exports were sold at less than "fair market value" and the US International Trade Commission determined that the Chinese dumping materially injured US industry. As a result, an antidumping rate of 15% was imposed on the Chinese producers that had responded with one firm receiving zero tariff, and the Chinese firms that did not respond paying the original 52% rate. Nine Chinese respondents appealed the case to the US Court of International Trade and challenged Commerce's improper selection of India as a surrogate country and using Indian prices for juice apple and calculation of expenses.

Surprisingly, the US Court of International Trade did not support Commerce's decision, and the Chinese AJC producers won the case. When choosing India as a surrogate country for China, Commerce relied on the data in a private market study prepared for US petitioners by a paid consultant. There were no official country-wide data about AJC production in India and the Chinese companies had not provided information to reject this market study. According to the Court, secondary information might not be entirely reliable and could be used if it had probative value—serving as proving evidence. The burden of verifying secondary information such as the market study from independent sources fell squarely on Commerce. Commerce failed to adequately explain how the data in the market study could serve as substantial evidence of the Indian AJC industry as a whole and thereby led to its conclusion that India was a significant producer of comparable merchandise (AJC) to be a proper surrogate country.

Another source Commerce used to conclude that India was a significant producer of AJC was the data from an Indian company, Himachal Pradesh Horticultural Produce Marketing & Processing Corp. (HPMC). However, Commerce failed to show that HPMC produced most of the AJC in India and that such output was significant. It also failed to establish that significant production of AJC by other Indian producers could be extrapolated from the HPMC data. HPMC was a government-controlled company and historically had not made a profit, in part because its main activity was to administer an Indian government's Market Intervention Scheme (MIS) by purchasing apples to stabilize prices. Its losses were made up by loans from the state and other government sources. Therefore, HPMC activities did not appear to be market driven and the MIS tended to increase the price paid for juice apples.

Accordingly, Commerce observed the Court's decisions and used Turkey as the surrogate country. It then amended the weighted average dumping

margins to 1.5% (3.83% for four Chinese respondent firms and 0% for six firms), while the same rate (52%) was applied to other Chinese AJC exporters that had not responded. For the ten Chinese respondents, reducing the punitive tariff first from 92% to 52%, then to 15%, and finally to 1.5% on average was regarded as a major victory in the US antidumping game where the rules were typically stacked against them.

Case Discussion Questions:

1. What are the costs and benefits for the Chinese AJC producers to respond to the antidumping investigation by the US Commerce Department?
2. Why did the US Court of International Trade disapprove Commerce's selection of India and Indian apple juice prices as surrogate factors for China?
3. If you were CEO of a US petitioner, what lessons can be drawn from this antidumping case?
4. If you were CEO of a Chinese exporter not involved in this case, what lessons can you draw?

Sources: This case was written by Professor **Lianlian Lin** (California State Polytechnic University, Pomona). It was based on (1) Department of Commerce, International Trade Administration, 2004, Certain nonfrozen apple juice concentrate from the People's Republic of China: Notice of amended final determination and amended order pursuant to final court decision, *Federal Register*, 69 (30), February 13, A-570-855; (2) X. Wang, 2004, Taking 4.5 years, Chinese agricultural product firms won US Commerce Department for the first time, *Economic Information Newspaper*, February 12, http://news.xinhuanet.com.

NOTES

[Journal acronyms] **AMJ**—*Academy of Management Journal;* **AMR**—*Academy of Management Review;* **BW**—*BusinessWeek;* **CJE**—*Canadian Journal of Economics;* **HBR**—*Harvard Business Review;* **IE**—*International Economy;* **JIBS**—*Journal of International Business Studies;* **JM**—*Journal of Management;* **JWB**—*Journal of World Business;* **SMJ**—*Strategic Management Journal*

[1] K. Coyne & J. Horn, 2009, Predicting your competitors' reaction, HBR, April: 90–97; N. Kumar, 2006, Strategies to fight low-cost rivals, HBR, December: 104–112.

[2] G. Markman, P. Gianiodis, & A. Buchholtz, 2009, Factor-market rivalry, AMR, 34: 423–441; V. Rindova, M. Becerra, & I. Contardo, 2004, Enacting competitive wars, AMR, 29: 670–686.

[3] S. Evenett, M. Levenstein, & V. Suslow, 2001, International cartel enforcement, IE, 24: 1221–1245.

[4] A. Mainkar, M. Lubatkin, & W. Schulze, 2006, Toward a product-proliferation theory of entry barriers, AMR, 31: 1062–1075.

[5] C. Christensen, 1997, *The Innovator's Dilemma*, Boston: Harvard Business School Press.

[6] J. Barney, 2002, *Gaining and Sustaining Competitive Advantage* (p. 359), Upper Saddle River, NJ: Prentice Hall.

[7] M. Chen, 1996, Competitor analysis and interfirm rivalry, AMR, 21: 106.

[8] M. Semadeni, 2006, Minding your distance, SMJ, 27: 169–187.

[9] E. Graham & D. Richardson, 1997, Issue overview (p. 5), in E. Graham & D. Richardson (eds.), 1997, *Global Competition Policy* (pp. 3–46), Washington: Institute for International Economics.

[10] R. Lipstein, 1997, Using antitrust principles to reform antidumping law, in E. Graham & D. Richardson (eds.), 1997, *Global Competition Policy* (p. 408), Washington: Institute for International Economics, original italics.

[11] OECD, 1996, *Trade and Competition: Frictions After the Uruguay Round* (p. 18), Paris: OECD.

[12] T. Prusa, 2001, On the spread and impact of antidumping, CJE, 34: 598.

[13] S. Marsh, 1998, Creating barriers for foreign competitors, SMJ, 19: 25–37.

[14] M. Finger, F. Ng, & S. Wangchuk, 2001, Antidumping as safeguard policy (p. 6), Working paper, World Bank.

[15] J. R. Baum & S. Wally, 2003, Strategic decision speed and firm performance, *SMJ*, 24: 1107–1129.

[16] This paragraph draws heavily from *Economist*, 2005, A market for ideas, October 22: 1–18.

[17] W. Ferrier, K. Smith, & C. Grimm, 1999, The role of competitive action in market share erosion and industry dethronement, *AMJ*, 42: 372–388.

[18] D. Basdeo, K. Smith, C. Grimm, V. Rindova, & P. Derfus, 2006, The impact of market actions on firm reputation, *SMJ*, 27: 1205–1219.

[19] J. Anand, L. Mesquita, & R. Vassolo, 2009, The dynamics of multimarket competition in exploration and exploitation activities, *AMJ*, 52: 802–821; B. Golden & H. Ma, 2003, Mutual forbearance, *AMR*, 28: 479–493; A. Kalnins, 2004, Divisional multimarket contact within and between multiunit organizations, *AMJ*, 47: 117–128; T. Yu, M. Subramaniam, & A. Cannella, 2009, Rivalry deterrence in international markets, *AMJ*, 52: 127–147.

[20] M. Chen, 1996, Competitor analysis and interfirm rivalry, *AMR*, 21: 107. See also W. Desarbo, R. Grewal, & J. Wind, 2006, Who competes with whom? *SMJ*, 27: 101–129; L. Fuentelsaz & J. Gomez, 2006, Multipoint competition, strategic similarity, and entry into geographic markets, *SMJ*, 27: 477–499.

[21] W. C. Kim & R. Mauborgne, 2005, *Blue Ocean Strategy*, Boston: Harvard Business School Press.

[22] *BW*, 2009, How Microsoft is fighting back (finally), April 20: 63–64.

[23] G. McNamara & P. Vaaler, 2000, The influence of competitive positioning and rivalry in emerging market risk assessment, *JIBS*, 31: 337–347; K. Ito & E. Rose, 2002, Foreign direct investment location strategies in the tire industry, *JIBS*, 33: 593–602.

[24] J. Prince & D. Simon, 2009, Multimarket contact and service quality, *AMJ*, 52: 336–354.

[25] *USA Today*, 2005, Price remarks by Toyota chief could be illegal, June 10: 5B.

[26] This section draws heavily from N. Dawar & T. Frost, 1999, Competing with giants, *HBR*, March–April: 119–129.

[27] R. Griffin & M. Pustay, 2003, *International Business*, 3rd ed. (p. 241), Upper Saddle River, NJ: Prentice Hall.

[28] J. Stiglitz, 2002, *Globalization and Its Discontent*, (pp. 172–173), New York: Norton.

[29] R. D'Aveni, 1994, *Hypercompetition*, New York: Free Press.

[30] M. Czinkota & M. Kotabe, 1997, A marketing perspective of the US International Trade Commission's antidumping actions, *JWB*, 32: 183.

LEARNING OBJECTIVES

After studying this chapter, you should be able to:

1. define alliances and acquisitions.

2. articulate how institutions and resources influence alliances and acquisitions.

3. describe how alliances are formed.

4. outline how alliances are evolved and dissolved.

5. discuss how alliances perform.

6. explain why firms undertake acquisitions.

7. understand why acquisitions often fail.

8. participate in two leading debates on alliances and acquisitions.

9. draw implications for action.

© Daniel Acker/Bloomberg via Getty Images

Making Alliances and Acquisitions Work

ETHICAL DILEMMA

O P E N I N G   C A S E

Danone and Wahaha: From Alliance to Divorce

In 1996, France's Groupe Danone SA established five joint ventures (JVs) with China's Wahaha Group. Danone owned 51% of each of these JVs, and Wahaha and its employees owned the remainder. Founded in 1987, Wahaha has one of the best-known beverage brands in China. By 2006, the total number of JVs between Danone and Wahaha had grown from 5 to 39. A huge financial success for both Danone and Wahaha, their JVs' revenues increased from $100 million in 1996 to $2.25 billion in 2006. These JVs, which cost Danone $170 million, paid Danone a total of $307 million in dividends over the past decade. By 2006, Danone's 39 JVs (or more accurately, JV subsidiaries) in China, jointly owned and managed by Wahaha, contributed 6% of Danone's total global profits.

In addition to the JVs with Wahaha, Danone also bought stakes in more than seven Chinese food and dairy firms, spending another $170 million (besides what was spent on Wahaha) over the past decade in China. In 2006, Danone became the biggest beverage maker by volume in China, ahead of rivals such as Coca-Cola and PepsiCo. At the same time, Wahaha also pursued aggressive growth in China, some of which was beyond the scope of the JVs with Danone. By 2006, Wahaha Group managed 70 subsidiaries scattered throughout China. All these subsidiaries use the same brand "Wahaha," but only 39 of them had JV relationships with Danone.

A major dispute erupted concerning Wahaha's other 31 subsidiaries that had no JV relationships with Danone. In 2006, after profits from the 39 JVs jumped 48% to $386 million, Danone wanted to buy Wahaha's other subsidiaries. This would enable Danone to control the "Wahaha" brand once and for all. This proposal was rejected by Wahaha's founder Zong Qinghou, who served as chairman of the 39 JVs with Danone. Zong viewed this offer as unreasonable because the book value of the non-JV subsidiaries' assets was $700 million with total profits of $130 million, while the price/earnings ratio of Danone's $500 million offer was lower than 4. Zong also asserted that the buyout would jeopardize the existence of the "Wahaha" brand, because Danone would phase it out and promote global brands such as Danone and Evian.

The heart of the dispute stemmed from the master JV agreement between Danone and Wahaha, which granted the subsidiary JVs exclusive rights to produce, distribute, and sell food and beverage products under the "Wahaha" brand. This meant that every product using the "Wahaha" brand should be approved by the board of the master JV. Danone thus claimed that the non-JV subsidiaries set up by Zong and his managers were illegally selling products using the "Wahaha" brand and were making unlawful use of the JVs' distributors and suppliers. However, Zong claimed that the original JV agreement to grant exclusive rights to use the "Wahaha" brand was never approved by the Chinese trademark office and so was not in force or effect. He further stated that Danone had not made an issue when Wahaha embarked on its expansion and openly used the subsidiary JVs' assets—it seemed that Danone preferred Wahaha to shoulder the risk first. According to Zong, when Wahaha's expansion proved successful, Danone, driven by greed, wanted to reap the fruits. Finally, Zong argued that forcing Wahaha Group to grant the exclusive rights for the "Wahaha" brand to the JVs with Danone was unfair to Wahaha Group, because Danone was actively investing in other beverage companies around the country and competing with Wahaha. Wahaha pointed out that in human marriage terms, these would be extra-marital affairs.

The board room dispute spilled into the public domain when Zong publicly criticized Danone in April 2007. In response, Danone issued statements and initiated arbitrations against Wahaha in Stockholm, Sweden. Danone also launched a lawsuit against a company owned by Zong's daughter in the United States, alleging that it was using the Wahaha brand illegally. Outraged, Zong resigned from his board chairman position at all the JVs with Danone. Wahaha's trade union, representing about 10,000 workers of Wahaha Group, sued Danone in late 2007, demanding $1.36 million in damages. This made the dispute worse, and revenues of the JVs only increased 3% in 2007, 17% less than the industry's average growth.

Between 2007 and 2009, both sides spent most of their energy dealing with over 21 lawsuits and arbitrations in several countries, including British

Virgin Islands, China, France, Italy, Sweden, and the United States. Even the French president and Chinese minister of commerce called for the two parties to stop lawsuits and to settle. Danone spent $83 million in litigation fees in three years but won no victory. Finally, Danone gave up its 51% share in the JVs and sold it to Wahaha in September 2009. No financial terms were publicly disclosed. A person familiar with the matter said the settlement amount was "slightly below" the figure Danone cited in previously published financial accounts as the value of its Wahaha holdings: $555 million.

From an ethical standpoint, we can wonder whether the divorce was caused by opportunism from the start or by "changed circumstances" as the relationship evolved. Even with the painful divorce, Danone still earned enviable financial returns. A Danone spokesman defended the JV strategy: "If we now have 30% of our sales in emerging markets and we built this in only ten years, it's thanks to this specific [JV] strategy. We have problems with Wahaha. But we prefer to have problems with Wahaha now to not having had Wahaha at all for the last ten years." Wahaha's Zong said in the settlement announcement: "Chinese companies are willing to cooperate and grow with the world's leading peers on the basis of equality and reciprocal benefit."

Sources: This case was written by **Sunny Li Sun** and **Hao Chen** (both at the University of Texas at Dallas) under the supervision of Professor Mike W. Peng. It was based on (1) *China Daily*, 2007, Chinese drinks giant brands Danone "despicable" over lawsuit, June 8; (2) finance.sina.com.cn/focus/2007wahaha; (3) M. W. Peng, S. L. Sun, & H. Chen, 2008, Managing divorce: How to disengage from joint ventures and strategic alliances, *Peking University Business Review*, April; (4) *Wall Street Journal*, 2009, Danone pulls out of disputed China venture, October 1.

ninos!

Why did Danone and Wahaha form strategic alliances? Among many forms of alliances, why did they choose joint ventures (JVs)? Why did the JVs fail? Why did Wahaha agree to acquire Danone's equity in the failed JVs? These are some of the key questions we address in this chapter. Alliances and acquisitions are two major strategies for growth used by firms around the world, thus necessitating our attention.[1] This chapter first defines alliances and acquisitions and follows with a discussion of how institution-based and resource-based views shed light on these topics. We then discuss the formation, evolution, and performance of alliances and acquisitions. Finally, we introduce two leading debates and discuss some tips on managing alliances and acquisitions.

DEFINING ALLIANCES AND ACQUISITIONS

A **strategic alliance** is a voluntary agreement between firms involving exchange, sharing, or co-developing of products, technologies, or services.[2] Figure 12.1 illustrates this further, depicting alliances as degrees of *compromise* between pure market transactions and acquisitions. **Contractual (non-equity-based) alliances** are alliances between firms that are based on contracts and do not involve the sharing of ownership. They include co-marketing, research and development (R&D) contracts, turnkey projects, strategic suppliers, strategic distributors, and licensing/franchising. **Equity-based alliances**, on the other hand, are based on ownership or financial interest between the firms. They include **strategic investment** (one partner invests in another) and **cross-shareholding** (each partner invests in the other). Equity-based alliances also include JVs, which involve the establishment of a new legally independent entity (in other words, a new firm) whose equity is provided by two or more partners.

Although JVs are often used as examples of alliances (as in the Opening Case), *not* all alliances are JVs. A JV is a corporate child produced by two or more parent firms, as is the case with Sony Ericsson. A non-JV, equity-based alliance can be regarded as two firms getting married but not having children. For example, Renault is a strategic investor in Nissan, but both automakers still operate independently and they have *not* given birth to a new car company; if they did, the new company would be a JV.

An **acquisition** is a transfer of the control of operations and management from one firm (target) to another (acquirer), the former becoming a unit of the latter. For example, Merrill Lynch is now a unit of Bank of America. A **merger** is the combination of operations and management of two firms to establish a new legal entity. For instance, the merger between South African Brewery and Miller Beer resulted in SABMiller.

Although the phrase "mergers and acquisitions" (M&As) is often used, in reality, acquisitions dominate the scene. Only 3% of M&As are mergers. A *World Investment Report* opines that "The number of 'real' mergers is so low that, for practical purposes, 'M&As' basically mean 'acquisitions.'"[3] Consequently, we will use "M&As" and "acquisitions" interchangeably. Specifically, we focus on cross-border (international) M&As (Figure 12.2). This is not only because of our global interest, but also because of (1) the high percentage (about 30%) of international deals among all M&As and (2) the high percentage (about 70%) of M&As among foreign direct investment (FDI) flows.

LEARNING OBJECTIVE 1

Define alliances and acquisitions

Strategic alliance
A voluntary agreement between firms involving exchange, sharing, or co-developing of products, technologies, or services.

Contractual (non-equity-based) alliances
Alliances between firms that are based on contracts and do not involve the sharing of ownership.

Equity-based alliances
Alliances based on ownership or financial interest between firms.

Strategic investment
One firm invests in another as a strategic investor.

Cross-shareholding
Both firms invest in each other to become cross-shareholders.

Acquisition
Transfer of the control of operations and management from one firm (target) to another (acquirer), the former becoming a unit of the latter.

Merger
The combination of operations and management of two firms to establish a new legal entity.

FIGURE 12.1   THE VARIETY OF STRATEGIC ALLIANCES

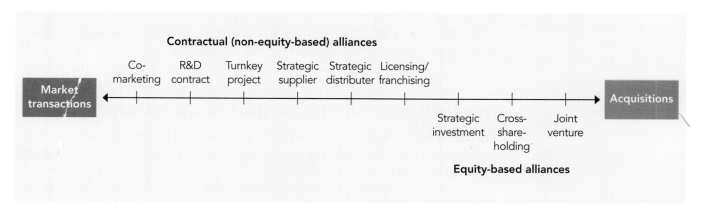

FIGURE 12.2   THE VARIETY OF CROSS-BORDER MERGERS AND ACQUISITIONS

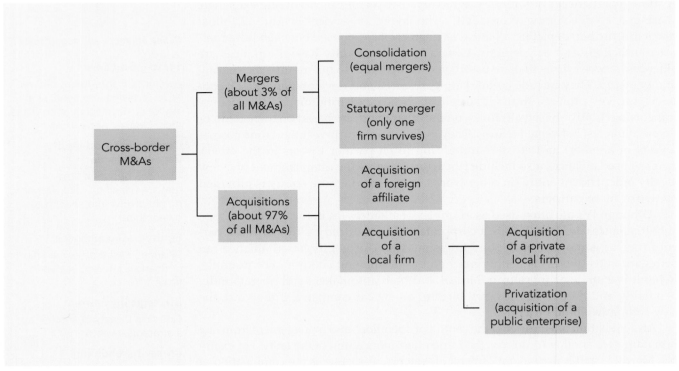

Source: Adapted from United Nations, 2000, *World Investment Report 2000* (p. 100), New York: UNCTAD.

Articulate how institutions and resources influence alliances and acquisitions.

INSTITUTIONS, RESOURCES, ALLIANCES, AND ACQUISITIONS

What drives alliances? What drives acquisitions? The institution-based and resource-based views shed light on these important questions. The institution-based view suggests that, as rules of the game, institutions affect how a firm chooses between alliances and acquisitions in terms of its strategy. However, rules are not made just for one firm. The resource-based view argues that, although a number of firms may be governed by the same set of rules, some excel more than others because of the differences in firm-specific capabilities that make alliances and acquisitions work (see Figure 12.3).

Institutions, Alliances, and Acquisitions

Formal Institutions   Alliances function within a set of formal legal and regulatory frameworks. The impact of these *formal institutions* on alliances and acquisitions can be found along two dimensions: (1) antitrust concerns and (2) entry mode requirements. First, many firms establish alliances with competitors. For example, Siemens and Bosch compete in automotive components and collaborate in household appliances. Antitrust authorities suspect at least some tacit collusion when competitors cooperate. However, because integration within alliances is usually

FIGURE 12.3   INSTITUTIONS, RESOURCES, ALLIANCES, AND ACQUISITIONS

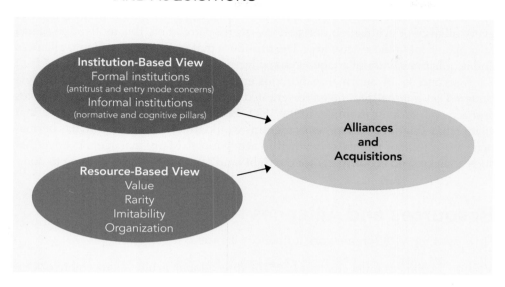

not as tight as acquisitions (which would eliminate one competitor), antitrust authorities are more likely to approve alliances as opposed to acquisitions.[4] A proposed merger of American Airlines and British Airways was blocked by both US and UK antitrust authorities. But the two airlines were allowed to form an alliance that has eventually grown to become the multipartner OneWorld.

Another way formal institutions affect alliances and acquisitions is through formal requirements on market entry modes. In many countries, governments discourage or simply ban acquisitions to establish wholly-owned subsidiaries (WOS), thereby leaving some sort of alliance with local firms as the only choice.[5] The Indian government dictates the maximum ceiling of foreign firms' equity position in the retail sector to be 51%, forcing foreign entrants to set up alliances such as JVs with local firms. For example, Wal-Mart formed a 50/50 JV with Bharti—Bharti Wal-Mart Private Limited—with the goal of setting up wholesale cash-and-carry stores, branded as Best Price Modern Wholesale, throughout India.

Recently, two trends have emerged in the entry mode requirements dictated by formal government policies. First, there is a general trend toward more liberal policies. Many governments that historically approved only JVs as an entry mode (such as those in Mexico and South Korea) now allow WOS. As a result, JVs have declined and acquisitions have increased in emerging economies.[6] Despite the general movement toward more liberal policies, a second noticeable trend is that many governments still impose considerable requirements, especially when foreign firms acquire domestic assets. The strategically important Chinese automobile assembly industry and the Russian oil industry permit only JVs, thus eliminating acquisitions as a choice. US regulations limit foreign carriers to a maximum 25% of the equity in any US airline, and EU regulations limit non-EU ownership of EU-based airlines to 49%.

Informal Institutions   The first set of informal institutions centers on collective norms, supported by a normative pillar. A core idea of the institution-based view is that, because firms want to enhance or protect their legitimacy, copying what other reputable organizations are doing—even without knowing the direct performance benefits of doing so—may be a low-cost way to gain legitimacy.

Therefore, when a firm sees competitors entering alliances, that firm may jump on the alliance bandwagon just to be "safe" rather than risk ignoring industry trends. When M&As are "in the air," even managers with doubts about the wisdom of M&As may nevertheless be tempted to hunt for acquisition targets. Although not every alliance or acquisition decision is driven by imitation, this motivation seems to explain a lot of these activities.[7] The flipside is that many firms rush into alliances and acquisitions without adequate due diligence and then get burned big time.[8]

A second set of informal institutions emphasizes the cognitive pillar, which is centered on internalized, taken-for-granted values and beliefs that guide alliances and acquisitions. For example, in the 1990s Britain's BAE Systems announced that *all* its future aircraft development programs would involve alliances. GE has permanent full-time staff members devoted to acquisitions. Many managers believe that such alliances and acquisitions are the right (and sometimes the only) thing to do.

Resources and Alliances

How does the VRIO framework influence alliances?

Value   Alliances must create *value*.[9] The three global airline alliance networks—OneWorld, Sky Team, and Star Alliance—create value by reducing ticket costs by 18% to 28% on two-stage flights compared with separate flights on the same route if the airlines were not allied.[10] Table 12.1 identifies three broad categories of value creation in terms of how advantages outweigh disadvantages. First, alliances may reduce costs, risks, and uncertainties.[11] As Google rises to preeminence, rivals such as eBay, Yahoo!, and Microsoft (MSN) are now exploring alliances to counter Google's influence while not taking on excessive risks. Microsoft is also exploring an alliance with News Corporation in which Microsoft's Bing would be the only search engine to deliver the content of the *Wall Street Journal*, which is owned by News Corporation.[12]

Second, alliances allow firms to tap into partners' complementary assets and facilitate learning.[13] In Focus 12.1 illustrates how MiG and Sukhoi, two of Russia's leading aerospace firms, collaborated.

Finally, an important advantage of alliances lies in their value as real options. Conceptually, an option is the right but not obligation to take some action in the future. Technically, a financial option is an investment instrument permitting its holder, having paid for a small fraction of an asset, the right to increase investment by eventually acquiring the asset if necessary. A **real option** is an investment in real operations as opposed to financial capital.[14] A real options view suggests two propositions:

- In the first phase, an investor makes a small, initial investment to buy an option, which leads to the right to future investment without being obligated to do so.
- The investor then holds the option until a decision point arrives in the second phase and then decides between exercising the option or abandoning it.

Real option
An investment in real operations as opposed to financial capital.

TABLE 12.1   STRATEGIC ALLIANCES: ADVANTAGES AND DISADVANTAGES

Advantages	Disadvantages
Reducing costs, risks, and uncertainties	Choosing wrong partners
Accessing complementary assets and learning opportunities	Potential partner opportunism
Possibilities to use alliances as real options	Risks of helping nurture competitors (learning race)

Russia's MiG and Sukhoi Join Hands

During the Cold War, thousands of MiG fighter jets made by the Mikoyan Moscow Production Organization (MAPO) were synonymous with "bogeys" widely recognized and respected by military pilots in the free world. In the post–Cold War era, MAPO ran into great difficulties because the Russian government cut back its orders (no orders for new aircraft during 1992–1998), and with the dissolution of the Warsaw Pact, Central and Eastern European air forces started to import fighters from the West. Poland, for example, ordered F-16s from the United States. MAPO thus was forced to look for new export markets. However, in new markets, MAPO found that its previously popular MiG aircraft were not as successful as those made by its traditional rival, Sukhoi Aircraft Military and Industrial Group. Although Sukhoi jets had not been as famous as MiGs during the Cold War, Sukhoi scored big hits in the 1990s by securing high-profile contracts from China, India, and Vietnam, including more than 150 Su-27s as direct exports and 300 under licensed production. What was more impressive was that the Indonesian and South Korean air forces, traditionally exclusive markets for US fighters, expressed an interest in Sukhoi (although eventually had to cancel because of the 1997 Asian financial crisis). In comparison, MAPO only sold 80 MiG-29s to India and Malaysia in the 1990s. As a result, MAPO found that it had little choice but to cooperate with Sukhoi. To be sure, initial cooperation was limited, involving only a joint marketing strategy and a sharing of some avionics. Such cooperation, however, intensified as competition in the global arms market heated up. In 2006, both MAPO and Sukhoi, together with several other aircraft producers, were merged by the Russian government to form the new United Aircraft Corporation (UAC).

Sources: Based on (1) M. W. Peng, 2000, *Business Strategies in Transition Economies* (p. 96), Thousand Oaks, CA: Sage; (2) www.migavia.ru; (3) www.sukhoi.org; (4) www.uacrussia.ru.

For firms interested in eventually acquiring other companies but uncertain about such moves, working together in alliances thus affords an insider view to the capabilities of these partners. This is similar to trying on new shoes to see if they fit before buying them. Since acquisitions are not only costly but also very likely to fail, alliances permit firms to *sequentially* increase their investment should they decide to pursue acquisitions. If, after working together as partners, a firm finds that an acquisition is not a good idea, there is no obligation to pursue it. Overall, alliances have emerged as great instruments of real options because of their flexibility to sequentially scale the investment *up* or *down*.[15]

On the other hand, alliances have a number of nontrivial drawbacks. First, there is always a possibility of being stuck with the wrong partner(s).[16] Firms are advised to choose a prospective partner with caution, preferably a known entity. Yet, the partner should also be sufficiently differentiated to provide some complementary (nonoverlapping) capabilities.[17] Many firms find it difficult to evaluate the true intentions and capabilities of their prospective partners until it is too late.

A second disadvantage is potential partner opportunism. Although opportunism is likely in any kind of economic relationship, the alliance setting may provide especially strong incentives for some (but not necessarily all) partners to be opportunistic. A cooperative relationship always entails some elements of trust that may be easily abused.[18] In an alliance with Britain's Rover, Honda shared a great deal of proprietary technology beyond what was contractually called for. Honda was stunned when Rover's parent firm announced that Rover would be sold to BMW and that Honda would be literally kicked out. Unfortunately, such an example is not an isolated incident.

Rarity   The ability to successfully manage interfirm relationships—often called **relational (or collaborative) capabilities**—may be rare. Managers involved in alliances require relationship skills rarely covered in the traditional business school curriculum, which typically emphasizes competition rather than collaboration.[19] To truly derive benefits from alliances, managers need to foster trust with partners yet be on guard against opportunism.[20]

As much as alliances represent a strategic and economic arrangement, they also constitute a social, psychological, and emotional phenomenon: words such as "courtship," "marriage," and "divorce" are often used when discussing alliances. Given that the interests of partner firms do not fully overlap and are often in conflict, managers involved in alliances live a precarious existence, trying to represent the interests of their respective firms while attempting to make the complex relationship work.[21] Given the general shortage of good relationship management skills in the population (remember, for example, 50% of the human marriages in the United States fail), it is not surprising that sound relational capabilities necessary to successfully manage alliances are in short supply.

Imitability   Imitability occurs at two levels in alliances: (1) firm level and (2) alliance level. Alliances between rivals can be dangerous because they may help competitors. By opening their doors to outsiders, alliances make it *easier* to observe and imitate firm-specific capabilities. A **learning race** can arise in which partners aim to learn the other firm's tricks—*imitate* its resources—as fast as possible.[22] For example, in the late 1980s, McDonald's set up a JV with the Moscow Municipality Government to help the fast-food chain enter Russia. During the 1990s, however, the Moscow mayor set up a rival fast-food chain, The Bistro. The Bistro replicated many of the fast-food giant's products and practices. McDonald's could do little about the situation because nobody sues the mayor in Moscow and hopes to win.

Another imitability issue is the trust and understanding among partners in successful alliances. Firms without genuine trust and understanding may have a hard time faking it. CFM International, a JV set up by GE and Snecma to produce jet engines in France, has successfully operated for over 30 years. Rivals would have a hard time imitating such a successful relationship.

Organization   Some successful alliance relationships are organized in a way that is difficult to replicate. Tolstoy makes the observation in the opening sentence of *Anna Karenina*: "All happy families are alike; each unhappy family is unhappy in its own way." Much the same can be said for business alliances. Each failed alliance has its own mistakes and problems, and firms in unsuccessful alliances (for whatever reason) often find it exceedingly challenging, if not impossible, to organize and manage their interfirm relationships better.

Relational (collaborative) capability
Capability to successfully manage interfirm relationships.

Learning race
A situation in which alliance partners aim to outrun each other by learning the "tricks" from the other side as fast as possible.

Resources and Acquisitions

Value   Do acquisitions create *value*?[23] Overall, their performance record is sobering. As many as 70% of acquisitions reportedly fail. On average, the performance of acquiring firms does not improve after acquisitions.[24] Target firms, after being acquired and becoming internal units, often perform worse than when they were independent, stand-alone firms. The only identifiable group of winners is the shareholders of target firms, who may experience on average a 24% increase in their stock value during the transaction. This increase is due to the **acquisition premium**, which is defined as the difference between the acquisition price and the market value of target firms.

Acquirers of US firms on average pay a 20% to 30% premium, and acquirers of EU firms pay a slightly lower premium (about 18%).[25] Shareholders of acquiring firms experience a 4% loss in their stock value during the same period. The combined wealth of shareholders of both acquiring and target firms is only marginally positive, less than 2%.[26] Unfortunately, many M&As destroyed value.[27] Consider DaimlerChrysler. In 1998, Daimler paid $35 billion for Chrysler. In 2007, Chrysler was sold to Cerberus Capital, a private equity firm, for $7.4 billion, one-fifth of what Daimler paid for.

Rarity For acquisitions to add value, one or all of the firms involved must have *rare* (unique) skills that enhance the overall strategy. In 2004, an executive team at Lenovo, China's leading PC maker, planned to acquire IBM's PC division. Lenovo's board, however, raised a crucial question: If a venerable American technology company had failed to profit from the PC business, did Lenovo have what it takes to do better when managing such a complex global business? The answer was actually "No." The board gave its blessing to the plan only when the acquisition team agreed to acquire the business *and* to recruit top American executives.

Imitability Although many firms undertake acquisitions, a much smaller number of them have mastered the art of post-acquisition integration.[28] Consequently, firms that excel in integration possess *hard-to-imitate* capabilities. For example, each of Northrop's acquisitions must conform to a carefully orchestrated plan of nearly 400 items, from how to issue press releases to which accounting software to use. Unlike its bigger defense rivals such as Boeing and Raytheon, Northrop thus far has not stumbled with any of its acquisitions.

Organization Fundamentally, whether acquisitions add value boils down to how merged firms are *organized* to take advantage of the benefits while minimizing the costs. Pre-acquisition analysis often focuses on **strategic fit**, which is the effective matching of complementary strategic capabilities.[29] Yet many firms do not pay adequate attention to **organizational fit**, which is the similarity in cultures, systems, and structures. On paper, Daimler and Chrysler in 1998 had great strategic fit in terms of complementary product lines and geographic scope, but there was little organizational fit. Despite the official proclamation of a merger of equals, the American unit in DaimlerChrysler saw itself as Occupied Chrysler. American managers resented answering to German managers, and Germans disliked being paid two-thirds less than their Chrysler colleagues. These clashes led to a mass exodus of American managers from Chrysler, a common phenomenon in acquired firms.

Overall, institutions and resources significantly affect alliances and acquisitions. In Focus 12.2 sheds light on how to enhance the odds for M&A success in China. The next few sections discuss in some detail the formation, evolution, and performance of alliances and acquisitions.

© Jason Lee/Reuters/Landov

What conditions must be present to make an acquisition, like Lenovo's acquisition of IBM's PC division, successful?

Acquisition premium
The difference between the acquisition price and the market value of target firms.

Strategic fit
The effective matching of complementary strategic capabilities between firms.

Organizational fit
The similarity in cultures, systems, and structures between firms.

Focus 12.2

Making M&As Fly in China

The first wave of foreign direct investment (FDI) in China in the 1980s mostly took the form of joint ventures (JVs). A second wave followed in the 1990s in the form of wholly foreign-owned enterprises (WFOEs). Now a third wave of FDI—cross-border mergers and acquisitions (M&As)—is gaining strength.

Consider the forces driving this third wave. China has a massive appetite for FDI; it is one of the world's largest FDI recipients. Yet, M&As account for only 10% to 15% of FDI flowing into China, compared with approximately 70% of FDI outside of China that takes the form of M&As. One reason for this disparity is that, until China joined the World Trade Organization in 2001, national regulations often encouraged (or required) foreign entrants to form JVs or set up WFOEs, while explicitly discouraging M&As. But China has since gradually loosened the regulations that govern foreign takeovers of Chinese assets, especially state-owned enterprises (SOEs), and has made explicit moves to attract foreign M&As. In many industries, including financial services and manufacturing, constraints on M&As are just now being lifted. At the same time, Chinese firms are increasingly engaging in cross-border M&As of their own, as evidenced by their bids for Unocal, Maytag, and IBM's personal computer division. To the extent that the Chinese government supports the outbound M&As, it must in most cases clear the path for inbound M&As, according to international norms of reciprocity.

Given the environment, how should foreign companies proceed? In many ways, strategies for M&As in China overlap with those for M&As elsewhere. But recent research has uncovered some idiosyncrasies that are specific to acquisitions in China. First, Chinese SOEs are rife with organizational slack. Government agencies have restructured some SOEs to reduce underutilized resources and to make the SOEs more attractive

M&A targets for foreign firms. Although slack usually indicates inefficiency, in certain firms, some slack—such as unabsorbed cash flow in the form of depreciation funds, reserve funds, and retained earnings—may indicate the potential for increased performance, actually enhancing targets' attractiveness.

Second, it is well known that many Chinese SOEs maintain three sets of books: one set that exaggerates performance, to brag to administrative superiors; one that underreports performance, for tax purposes; and one that is fairly accurate, for managers themselves. Acquisition targets are likely to show foreign negotiators the bragging books initially. As a result, foreign firms need to be aggressive in conducting due diligence to uncover an accurate picture of targets' assets and resources. This is particularly relevant when investigating slack.

Finally, most Western firms launching JVs and WFOEs in China have believed that ethnic Chinese managers—those from overseas Chinese economies, such as Hong Kong and Taiwan, who are well versed in the local language—were the best choice for running their operations in China. Meanwhile, they have presumed that Western managers would be less effective because of language and cultural barriers. But research evidence suggests the *opposite*: Using surveys, interviews, and other tools, researchers are finding that ethnic Chinese managers hired by Western companies to run these businesses are, on average, *less* effective than their non-Chinese counterparts, as measured by the length of their tenures and attainment of performance goals. How could this be?

One reason appears to be that ethnic Chinese managers often struggle with an ambiguous managerial identity: Western corporate headquarters views them as "us," whereas local Chinese employees also expect them to be "us." When these managers favor headquarters on issues where headquarters and locals conflict—such as whether Western employees and locals should receive equal compensation or whether chopsticks or forks should be used at company banquets—local employees may regard them as traitors of sorts. That corrodes employees' trust, ultimately undermining ethnic Chinese managers' performance. On the other hand, employees give Western managers the benefit of the doubt. They expect these managers to behave differently, to commit cultural errors, and to show allegiance to the parent firm. This tolerance by local employees of Western managers' differences can enhance these managers' confidence and performance.

Of course, not every non-Chinese manager outperforms every ethnic Chinese manager. It is clear, however, that managerial effectiveness in China does not depend on one's ability to use chopsticks. This point is crucial as more M&As flow into China and more acquiring companies staff their target firms' management.

Sources: Adapted from M. W. Peng, 2006, Making M&A fly in China, *Harvard Business Review*, March: 26–27. For underlying research, see (1) Z. Lin, M. W. Peng, H. Yang, & S. Sun, 2009, How do networks and learning drive M&As? An institutional comparison between China and the United States, *Strategic Management Journal*, 30: 1113–1132; (2) M. W. Peng, 2005, From China strategy to global strategy, *Asia Pacific Journal of Management*, 22: 123–141; (3) J. Tan & M. W. Peng, 2003, Organizational slack and firm performance during economic transitions, *Strategic Management Journal*, 24: 1249–1263.

FORMATION OF ALLIANCES

LEARNING OBJECTIVE

3

Describe how alliances are formed.

How are alliances formed? Figure 12.4 illustrates a three-stage model to address this question.[30] In Stage One, a firm must decide if growth can be achieved strictly through market transactions, through acquisitions, or through cooperative alliances.[31] To grow by pure market transactions, the firm has to confront competitive challenges independently. This is highly demanding, even for resource-rich multinationals.[32] Also, as noted earlier in the chapter, acquisitions have some unique drawbacks, leading many managers to conclude that alliances are the way to go.

In Stage Two, a firm must decide whether to take a contractual or an equity approach. As noted in Chapters 6 and 10, the choice between contract and equity is crucial. The first driving force is shared capabilities (see Table 12.2). The more tacit (that is, hard to describe and codify) the capabilities, the greater the preference for equity involvement. Although not the only way, the most effective way to learn *complex* processes is through learning by doing. A good example is learning to cook by actually cooking and not by simply reading cookbooks. Many business processes are the same way. A firm that wants to produce cars will find that the codified knowledge found in books, reports, and manuals is not enough. Much tacit knowledge can only be acquired via learning by doing, preferably with experts as alliance partners.

A lot of tacit knowledge dealing with complex skills and know-how is embedded in specific organizational settings and is "sticky" (that is, hard to be isolated out of the particular firm that possesses such knowledge).[33] Hypothetically, assuming Toyota is able to codify all the tacit knowledge associated with the legendary "Toyota production system" (TPS)—of course impossible to do in reality—and sell it, the buyer will probably find that no matter how hard it tries, it is simply unable to completely replicate TPS. This is because TPS is, by definition, firm-specific and has a high degree of "stickiness" associated with Toyota. Short of completely acquiring Toyota (an extremely costly proposition), no other firm can hope to totally master this system. Further, if many Toyota employees leave after the acquisition (a realistic scenario at most acquired firms), again the acquirer will

FIGURE 12.4   ALLIANCE FORMATION

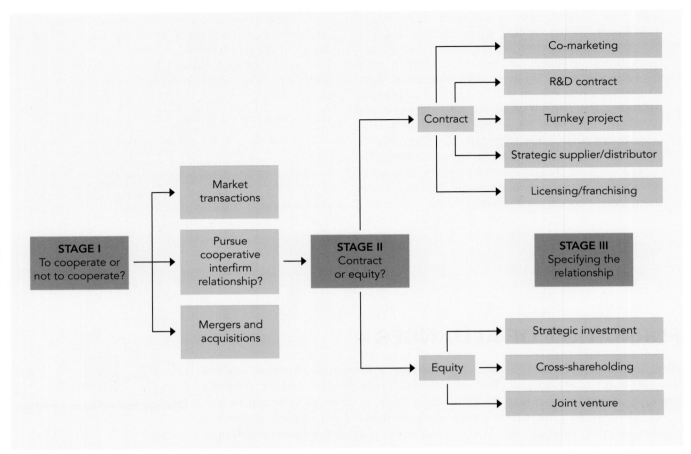

Source: Adapted from S. Tallman & O. Shenkar, 1994, A managerial decision model of international cooperative venture formation (p. 101), *Journal of International Business Studies*, 25 (1): 91–113.

TABLE 12.2   EQUITY-BASED VERSUS NON-EQUITY-BASED ALLIANCES

Driving forces	Equity-based alliances	Non-equity-based alliances
Nature of shared resources and capabilities (degree of tacitness)	High	Low
Importance of direct organizational monitoring and control	High	Low
Potential as real options	High (for possible upgrading to M&As)	High (for possible upgrading to equity-based relationships)
Influence of formal institutions	High (when required or encouraged by regulations)	High (when required or encouraged by regulations)

find that its mastery of the system is incomplete. Thus, the most realistic way to access TPS is to establish an equity-based alliance in order to learn how to "do it" side by side with Toyota, as GM did through its NUMMI JV with Toyota. In general, equity-based alliances are more likely to be formed when dealing with more complex technology and know-how (such as NUMMI) than with less complex skills that can be more efficiently transferred between two organizations (such as McDonald's franchising).

A second driving force is the importance of direct monitoring and control. Equity relationships allow firms to have some direct control over joint activities on a continuing basis, whereas contractual relationships usually do not.[34] In general, firms that fear their intellectual property may be expropriated prefer equity alliances (and a higher level of equity). This, for example, explains why China has so many JVs but so few licensing and franchising agreements.

A third driver is real options thinking. Some firms prefer to first establish contractual relationships, which can be viewed as real options (or stepping-stones) for possible upgrading into equity alliances should the interactions turn out to be mutually satisfactory. Finally, the choice between contract and equity also boils down to institutional constraints.[35] Some governments eager to help domestic firms climb the technology ladder either require or actively encourage the formation of JVs between foreign and domestic firms. The Chinese auto industry is a case in point.

Eventually, firms need to choose a specific format that is either equity-based or contractual (non-equity-based), depending on the choice made in Step Two. Figure 12.4 lists the different format options. Since Chapter 10 has already covered this topic as part of the discussion on entry modes, we will not repeat it here.

EVOLUTION AND DISSOLUTION OF ALLIANCES

4

Outline how alliances are evolved and dissolved.

All relationships evolve—some grow, others fail.[36] This section deals with two aspects of such evolution: (1) combating opportunism and (2) evolving from corporate marriage to divorce.

Combating Opportunism

The threat of opportunism looms large on the horizon. Most firms want to make their relationship work, but also want to protect themselves in case the other side is opportunistic.[37] Although it is difficult to completely eliminate opportunism, it is possible to minimize its threat by (1) walling off critical capabilities or (2) swapping critical capabilities through credible commitments.

First, both sides can contractually agree to wall off critical skills and technologies not meant to be shared. For example, GE and Snecma cooperated to build jet engines, yet GE was not willing to share its proprietary core technology fully with Snecma. GE thus presented several sealed "black box" components, the inside of which Snecma had no access to. At the same time, GE granted Snecma access to final assembly. This type of relationship, in human marriage terms, is like married couples whose premarital assets are protected by prenuptial agreements. As long as both sides are willing to live with these agreements designed to minimize the threat of opportunism, these relationships can prosper.

The second approach, swapping skills and technologies, is the exact *opposite* of the first approach. Both sides not only agree not to hold critical skills and technologies back, but also make credible commitments to hold each other as a "hostage." Motorola, for instance, licensed its microprocessor technology to Toshiba, which, in turn, licensed its memory chip technology to Motorola. In a nutshell, such mutual "hostage taking" reduces the threat of opportunism.

In human marriage terms, mutual "hostage taking" is similar to the following commitment: "Honey, I will love you forever. If I betray you, feel free to kill me. But likewise if you dare to betray me, I'll cut your head off!" To think slightly outside the box, the precarious peace during the Cold War can be regarded as a case of mutual "hostage taking" that worked. Because both the United States and Soviet Union held each other as a "hostage," nobody dared to launch a first nuclear strike. As long as the victim of the first strike had only *one* nuclear ballistic missile submarine (such as the American Ohio class or the Soviet Typhoon class) left, this single submarine would have enough retaliatory firepower to wipe the top 20 US or Soviet cities off the surface of earth, an outcome that neither of the two superpowers found acceptable (see the movie *The Hunt for Red October*). In other words, the Cold War did not turn hot in part because of such "mutually assured destruction" (MAD!)—a real jargon used in the military.

Both of these approaches help minimize the threat of opportunism in alliances. Unfortunately, sometimes none of these approaches works and the relationship deteriorates, as shown next.

From Corporate Marriage to Divorce[38]

Alliances are often described as corporate marriages and, when terminated, as corporate divorces. Figure 12.5 portrays an alliance dissolution model. To apply the metaphor of divorce, we focus on the two-partner alliance. Following the convention in research on human divorce, the party who begins the process of ending the alliance is labeled the **initiator**, whereas the other party is termed the "partner"—for lack of a better word. We will draw on our Opening Case to explain this process.

FIGURE 12.5   ALLIANCE DISSOLUTION

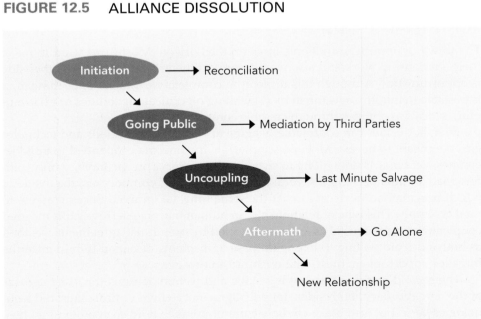

Initiator

The party who begins the process of ending the alliance.

Source: M. W. Peng & O. Shenkar, 2002, Joint venture dissolution as corporate divorce (p. 95), *Academy of Management Executive*, 16 (2): 92–105.

The first phase is initiation. The process begins when the initiator starts feeling uncomfortable with the alliance (for whatever reason). Dissatisfaction leads to quiet, unilateral pressure from the initiator, which was Danone in this case. After repeated demands to modify Wahaha's behavior failed, Danone began to sense that the alliance was probably unsalvageable. At this point, the display of discontent became bolder. Initially, Wahaha, the partner, might simply not "get it." The initiator's apparently sudden dissatisfaction might confuse the partner. As a result, initiation tends to escalate.

The second phase is going public. The party that breaks the news first has a first-mover advantage. By presenting a socially acceptable reason in favor of its cause, this party is able to win sympathy from key stakeholders such as parent company executives, investors, and journalists. Not surprisingly, the initiator is likely to go public first, blaming the failure on the partner. Alternatively, the partner may preempt the initiator, laying the blame on the initiator and establishing the righteousness of its own position. This was exactly what Wahaha did. Eventually, both Danone and Wahaha were eager to publicly air their grievances.

The third phase is uncoupling. Like divorce, alliance dissolution can be either friendly or hostile. In uncontested divorces, both sides attribute the separation to an outside cause such as a change in circumstances. For example, Eli Lilly and Ranbaxy phased out their JV in India and remained friendly with each other. In contrast, contested divorces involve accusations from one or both parties. The worst scenario is a "death by a thousand cuts" inflicted by either or both parties at every turn.

The last phase is aftermath. Like most divorced individuals, most (but not all) divorced firms are likely to search for new partners. Understandably, the new alliance is often negotiated more extensively.[39] One Italian executive reportedly signed *each* of the 2,000 pages (!) of an alliance contract.[40] However, excessive formalization may signal a lack of trust in the same way that prenuptials may scare away some prospective marriage partners.

PERFORMANCE OF ALLIANCES

Discuss how alliances perform.

Although managers naturally focus on alliance performance, opinions vary on how to measure it.[41] A combination of objective measures (such as profit and market share) and subjective measures (such as managerial satisfaction) can be used. Figure 12.6 shows that four factors may influence alliance performance: (1) equity, (2) learning and experience, (3) nationality, and (4) relational capabilities. However, none of them asserts an unambiguous, direct impact on performance.[42] What has been found is that they may have some *correlations* with performance.

The level of equity may be crucial in how an alliance performs. A greater equity stake may indicate a higher-level commitment, which is likely to result in higher performance.[43] Second, whether firms have successfully learned from partners is important when assessing alliance performance.[44] Since learning is abstract, experience is often used as a proxy because it is relatively easy to measure.[45] Although experience certainly helps, its impact on performance is not linear. There is a limit beyond which further increase in experience may not enhance performance.[46] Third, nationality may affect performance. For the same reason that marriages where both parties have similar backgrounds are more stable, dissimilarities in national culture may create strains in alliances.[47] Not

FIGURE 12.6   WHAT IS BEHIND ALLIANCE PERFORMANCE?

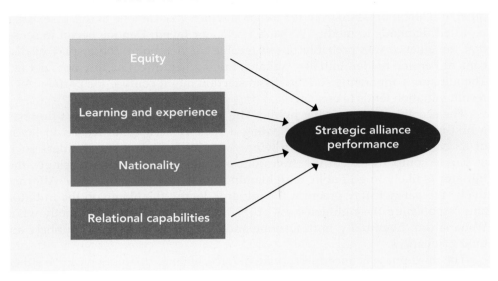

surprisingly, international alliances tend to have more problems than domestic ones.[48] When disputes and conflicts arise, it is often difficult to ascertain whether the other side is deliberately being opportunistic or is simply being (culturally) different. Finally, alliance performance may fundamentally boil down to soft, hard-to-measure relational capabilities. The art of relational capabilities, which are firm-specific and difficult to codify and transfer, may make or break alliances.[49]

Overall, it would be naïve to think that any of these four single factors would guarantee success. It is their *combination* that jointly increases the odds for the success of strategic alliances.

Explain why firms undertake acquisitions.

MOTIVES FOR ACQUISITIONS

What drives acquisitions? Table 12.3 shows three motives for acquisition: (1) synergistic, (2) hubristic, and (3) managerial motives. All three can be explained by the institution-based and resource-based views. From an institution-based view, synergistic motives for acquisitions are often a response to formal institutional constraints and transitions that affect a company's search for synergy. It is not a coincidence that the number of cross-border acquisitions has skyrocketed in the last two decades. This is the same period during which trade and investment barriers have gone down and FDI has risen (see In Focus 12.2).

From a resource-based standpoint, the most important synergistic rationale is to leverage superior resources.[50] Lufthansa recently acquired Air Dolomiti, an award-winning regional airline in northern Italy. At a time when many small airlines go out of business, Lufthansa's willingness to leverage its superior resources helps ensure Air Dolomiti's survival despite its loss of independence. Another synergistic rationale is to enhance market power. After the Belgian beer giant InBev (number one in the world) acquired the US-based Anheuser-Busch (number three in the world), the combined entity has significantly larger market power relative

TABLE 12.3   MOTIVES FOR ACQUISITIONS

	Institution-based issues	Resource-based issues
Synergistic motives	• Respond to formal institutional constraints and transitions	• Leverage superior managerial capabilities • Enhance market power and scale economies • Access to complementary resources
Hubristic motives	• Herd behavior—following norms and chasing fads of M&As	• Managers' over-confidence in their capabilities
Managerial motives	• Self-interested actions such as empire-building guided by informal norms and cognitions	

to the second-largest beer maker SABMiller. Such M&As not only eliminate rivals but also reduce redundant assets. Finally, another rationale is to gain access to complementary resources, as evidenced by Lenovo's interest in IBM's worldwide client base.

Although all the synergistic motives, in theory, add value, hubristic and managerial motives reduce value. Hubris refers to over-confidence in one's capabilities.[51] Managers of acquiring firms make two strong statements.[52] The first is "We can manage *your* assets better than you (target firm managers) can!" The second statement is even bolder. Given that purchasing a publicly listed firm requires paying an acquisition premium, managers of an acquiring firm essentially say: "We are smarter than the market!" To the extent that the capital market is efficient and that the market price of target firms reflects their intrinsic value, there is simply no hope to profit from such acquisitions. Even when we assume the capital market to be inefficient, it is still apparent that when the premium is too high, acquiring firms must have overpaid.[53] This attitude is especially dangerous when multiple firms are bidding for the same target. The winning acquirer may suffer from what is called the "winner's curse" in auctions—the winner has overpaid. From an institution-based view, hubristic motives are at play when managers join the acquisition bandwagon. The fact that M&As come in waves speaks volumes about such herd behavior. After a few first-mover firms start making some deals in an industry, waves of late movers, eager to catch up, may rush in, prompted by a "Wow! Get it!" mentality. Not surprisingly, many of those deals turn out to be bust.

Although the hubristic motives suggest that some managers may *unknowingly* overpay for targets, some managers may *knowingly* overpay for targets. Such self-interested actions are fueled by managerial motives, defined as managers' desire for power, prestige, and money, which may lead to decisions that do not benefit the firm overall in the long run. As a result, some managers may deliberately over-diversify their firms through M&As for such personal gains. These are known as agency problems (see Chapter 16 for details).

Hubris
Over-confidence in one's capabilities.

Managerial motives
Managers' desire for power, prestige, and money, which may lead to decisions that do not benefit the firm overall in the long run.

PERFORMANCE OF ACQUISITIONS

Why do as many as 70% of acquisitions reportedly fail? Problems can be identified in both pre- and post-acquisition phases (Table 12.4). During the pre-acquisition phase, executive hubris and/or managerial motives may cause acquiring firms

LEARNING OBJECTIVE

7

Understand why acquisitions often fail.

TABLE 12.4   SYMPTOMS OF ACQUISITION FAILURES

	Problems for all M&As	Particular problems for cross-border M&As
Pre-acquisition: Overpayment for targets	• Managers overestimate their ability to create value • Inadequate pre-acquisition screening • Poor strategic fit	• Lack of familiarity with foreign cultures, institutions, and business systems • Nationalistic concerns against foreign takeovers (political and media levels)
Post-acquisition: Failure in integration	• Poor organizational fit • Failure to address multiple stakeholder groups' concerns	• Clashes of organizational cultures compounded by clashes of national cultures • Nationalistic concerns against foreign takeovers (firm and employee levels)

to pay too much for targets and fall into a synergy trap.[54] In 1998, Daimler paid $35 billion, a 40% premium over market value, to acquire Chrysler. Such a high premium was indicative of a strong capability to derive synergy, a high level of hubris, a significant managerial self-interest—or *all of the above*. In another example, in 2006, Google paid $1.6 billion to acquire the 20-month-old YouTube, which had *zero* profits. Microsoft CEO Steven Ballmer commented that "there's no business model for YouTube that would justify $1.6 billion."[55]

Another primary pre-acquisition problem is inadequate screening and failure to achieve strategic fit. In September 2008, Bank of America spent $50 billion to acquire Merrill Lynch. How much time did Bank of America take to do due diligence? A total of *48 hours*—less than the time most people spend to buy a car. It is not surprising that inadequate homework led to numerous problems centered on the lack of strategic fit. Consequently, this acquisition was labeled by the *Wall Street Journal* as "a deal from hell" and Bank of America's CEO Ken Lewis had to announce his resignation within one year. A less well-known case that took place at roughly the same time (September 2008) was Nomura's decision to acquire the remnants of Lehman in Asia and Europe within *24 hours*. Nomura's stock suffered a 70% drop as a result (see the Closing Case).

Why do you think Google agreed to pay $1.6 billion to acquire YouTube in 2006? Was it worth it?

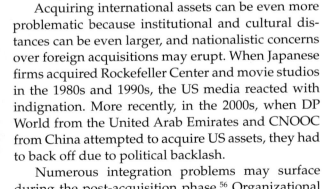

Acquiring international assets can be even more problematic because institutional and cultural distances can be even larger, and nationalistic concerns over foreign acquisitions may erupt. When Japanese firms acquired Rockefeller Center and movie studios in the 1980s and 1990s, the US media reacted with indignation. More recently, in the 2000s, when DP World from the United Arab Emirates and CNOOC from China attempted to acquire US assets, they had to back off due to political backlash.

Numerous integration problems may surface during the post-acquisition phase.[56] Organizational fit is just as important as strategic fit (see the Closing Case). One study reports that a surprising 80% of acquiring firms do *not* analyze organizational fit with targets.[57] Firms may also fail to address multiple stakeholders' concerns, including job losses and diminished power. Figure 12.7 illustrates the substantial concerns among a variety of stakeholders

© Jewel Samad/AFP/Getty Images

FIGURE 12.7   STAKEHOLDERS' CONCERNS DURING MERGERS AND ACQUISITIONS

Investors	Will synergy benefits be downscaled?	Optimistic view of return on investment?	Will efficiency & short-term revenues fall?
Top management	Synergies difficult to attain	Internal conflicts: fractious management groups, key staff leave	Unrealistic euphoria
Middle management	Concern over job security	Expect to do M&A + day jobs at the same time	Overwelmed by scale and scope
Front-line employees	What should I tell my customers?	When do lay-offs begin?	Who is setting my priorities and objectives?
Customers	So what?	Service quality dips, relationship suffers	No one is listening to me. Do I still matter?

at all levels, and Figure 12.8 humorously portrays one particular challenge. Most firms focus first on task issues such as standardizing reporting and pay inadequate attention to people issues, which typically results in low morale and high turnover.

In cross-border M&As, integration difficulties may be much worse because clashes of organizational cultures are compounded by clashes of national cultures (see the Closing Case).[58] When Four Seasons acquired a hotel in Paris, the simple American request that employees smile at customers was resisted by French employees and laughed at by the local media as *"la culture Mickey Mouse."*[59]

Although acquisitions are often the largest capital expenditures most firms ever make, they are frequently the worst planned and executed activities of all. Unfortunately, while merging firms are sorting out the mess, rivals are likely to launch aggressive attacks. In 1996, while Boeing struggled in near total chaos with its acquisition of McDonnell Douglas (including a complete production halt), Airbus quickly increased its share from one third to one half of the global market. When HP was distracted by its highly controversial acquisition of Compaq during 2002–2003, Dell invaded HP's printer market and unleashed a price war. Adding all of the above, it is hardly surprising that most M&As fail.

DEBATES AND EXTENSIONS

Although this chapter has introduced a number of debates (such as the merits of acquisitions), this section discusses two other leading debates: (1) M&As + alliances and (2) majority JVs versus minority JVs.

LEARNING OBJECTIVE **8**

Participate in two leading debates on alliances and acquisitions.

FIGURE 12.8   A CHALLENGE IN POST-ACQUISITION INTEGRATION

" As you know, some details of the new merger
have yet to be resolved. "

Source: *Harvard Business Review*, February 2005, p. 102. Reprinted with permission.

M&As + Alliances

Although alliances and acquisitions are alternatives, many firms seem to plunge straight into "merger mania." Between 2005 and 2009, Microsoft, IBM, and HP swallowed 79, 60, and 34 firms, respectively.[60] In many firms, an M&A group reports to CFO, while a separate unit, headed by the VP or director for business development, deals with alliances. M&As and alliances are thus often undertaken in isolation. A smaller number of firms, such as Eli Lilly, have a separate "office of alliance management." Few firms have established a combined "mergers, acquisitions, *and* alliance" function.[61] In practice, it may be advisable to explicitly compare acquisitions vis-à-vis alliances.[62]

Compared with acquisitions, alliances cost less and allow for opportunities to learn from working with each other before engaging in full-blown acquisitions.[63] Although alliances do not preclude acquisitions and may lead to acquisitions, acquisitions are often one-off deals swallowing both the excellent capabilities and mediocre units of target firms, leading to "indigestion" problems. Many acquisitions (such as DaimlerChrysler) probably would have been better off had firms pursued alliances first.

Majority JVs as Control Mechanisms versus Minority JVs as Real Options

A long-standing debate focuses on the appropriate level of equity in JVs. Although the logic of having a higher level of equity control in majority JVs is straightforward, its actual implementation is often problematic. Asserting one party's control rights, even when justified based on a majority equity position, may irritate the other party. Local partners in JVs in emerging economies in particular resent the dominance of Western multinationals (see the Opening Case). Despite the obvious needs for foreign capital, technology, and management, Russian managers often refuse to acknowledge that their country, which they still regard as a superpower, is an emerging or developing country.[64] Consequently, a 50/50 share of management control is often advised even when the MNE has majority equity.[65]

As alluded to earlier, a key benefit associated with minority JVs is their value as real options. In general, the more uncertain the conditions, the higher the value of real options. In highly uncertain but potentially promising industries and countries, M&As or majority JVs may be inadvisable because the cost of failure may be tremendous. Thus, minority JVs are recommended *toehold* investments; they provide possible stepping-stones for future scaling up, if necessary, while limiting the risks.

MANAGEMENT SAVVY

Draw implications for action.

What determines the success and failure in alliances and acquisitions? Our two core perspectives shed light on this big question. The institution-based view argues that alliances and acquisitions depend on a thorough understanding and skillful manipulation of the rules of the game governing alliances and acquisitions. The resource-based view calls for the development of firm-specific capabilities to make a difference in enhancing alliance and acquisition performance.

Consequently, three clear implications for action emerge (Tables 12.5, 12.6, and 12.7). First, managers need to understand and master the rules of the game—both formal and informal—governing alliances and acquisitions around the world. Lenovo clearly understood and tapped into the Chinese government's support for home-grown multinationals. IBM likewise understood the necessity for the new Lenovo to maintain an American image when it persuaded Lenovo to give up the idea of having dual headquarters in China and the United States and to set up its world headquarters in the United States. This highly symbolic action made it easier to win approval from the US government. In contrast, GE and Honeywell, two US-headquartered firms, proposed to merge and cleared US antitrust scrutiny

---

TABLE 12.5 IMPLICATIONS FOR ACTION

- Understand and master the rules of the game governing alliances and acquisitions around the world

- When managing alliances, pay attention to the "soft" relationship aspects

- When managing acquisitions, do not overpay, focus on both strategic and organizational fit, and thoroughly address integration concerns

TABLE 12.6   IMPROVING THE ODDS FOR ALLIANCE SUCCESS

Areas	Do's and don'ts
Contract versus "chemistry"	No contract can cover all elements of the relationship. Relying on a detailed contract does not guarantee a successful relationship. It may indicate a lack of trust.
Warning signs	Identify symptoms of frequent criticism, defensiveness (always blaming others for problems), and stonewalling (withdrawal during a fight).
Invest in the relationship	Like married individuals working hard to strengthen their ties, alliances require continuous nurturing. Once a party starts to waver, it is difficult to turn back the dissolution process.
Conflict resolution mechanisms	"Good" married couples also fight. Their secret weapon is to find mechanisms to avoid unwarranted escalation of conflicts. Managers need to handle conflicts—inevitable in any alliance—in a credible and controlled fashion.

Sources: Based on text in M. W. Peng & O. Shenkar, 2002, Joint venture dissolution as corporate divorce (pp. 101–102), *Academy of Management Executive*, 16 (2): 92–105.

TABLE 12.7   IMPROVING THE ODDS FOR ACQUISITION SUCCESS

Areas	Do's and don'ts
Pre-acquisition	• Do not overpay for targets and avoid a bidding war when premiums are too high. • Engage in thorough due diligence concerning both strategic and organizational fit.
Post-acquisition	• Address the concerns of multiple stakeholders and try to keep the best talents. • Be prepared to deal with roadblocks thrown up by people whose jobs and power may be jeopardized.

in 2001. But they failed to anticipate the power of the EU antitrust authorities and their incentive for killing the deal. In the end, the deal was torpedoed by the EU. The upshot is that, in addition to the economics of alliances and acquisitions, managers need to pay attention to the politics behind such high-stakes strategic moves.

Second, when managing alliances, managers need to pay attention to the soft relational capabilities that often make or break relationships (see Table 12.6). To the extent that business schools usually provide a good training on hard number-crunching skills, it is time for all of us to beef up soft but equally important (and perhaps more important) relational capabilities.

Finally, when managing acquisitions, managers are advised not to overpay for targets and to focus on both strategic and organizational fit (see Table 12.7). There is now systematic evidence that MNEs from emerging economies, such as Tata, are likely to overpay for targets in developed economies, relative to other bidders from developed economies for the same targets.[66] The upshot? More headaches down the road (see In Focus 12.3).

IN Focus 12.3

Tata: Clawed by Jaguar and Land Rover

To show off the new Jaguar XJ, Tata Motors in July 2009 rented a gallery in London's fashionable Chelsea district and flew in Jay Leno and other stars. With its muscular new design, the $73,000 car has won rave reviews. Tata, which a year ago paid Ford Motor $2.3 billion for Jaguar Cars and its cousin, Land Rover, seemed to have good reason to be upbeat.

Yet buying Jaguar and Land Rover has so far not worked out well for Ratan Tata, chairman of both the sprawling $64 billion Tata Group and Tata Motors. Unit sales of Jaguar and Land Rover are down 52% for the June 2009 quarter. The brands lost some $1.1 million a day in the same period, pushing the otherwise profitable Tata Motors to a $67 million loss. Tata still needs to spend $1 billion-plus a year in R&D on new models and making power-hungry Jaguars and Land Rovers meet new European emission standards. Among the options: replacing heavy steel with aluminum and more efficient engines such as hybrids. In Mumbai on August 26, 2009, Ratan Tata defended the acquisition as "very much worthwhile," whereas Tata Motors Vice-Chairman Ravi Kant said on August 31 that the R&D spending would likely continue for five more years.

Funding all this activity has been a headache. Tata this spring rustled up a $480 million loan from the European Investment Bank to help make its cars greener, and it wanted an extra $290 million to cover operating expenses for Jaguar and Land

Rover. But Tata needed loan guarantees from the British government. In exchange, Peter Mandelson, the Business Secretary, wanted a seat on the board and the right to fire David Smith, the chief of Jaguar and Land Rover, according to Tata executives. Tata balked, and in August the company gave up on the government and got guarantees from private banks. The British government maintained it could not go forward unless it was assured that UK taxpayers' money would be protected.

Tata was stung by the experience. It has lowered inventories, saving $250 million, cut three British factories to single shifts, and eliminated some 2,500 jobs. Unite, a union representing Jaguar and Land Rover workers, agreed to $110 million in cuts such as pay freezes and shorter work hours.

Jaguar and Land Rover won't likely break even before 2011. With less than $300 million in cash on hand, Tata Motors may need to sell equity to raise more funds. The biggest expense is apt to be Land Rover, which may require a major rethink as Americans and Europeans shun sport utility vehicles (SUVs). "Land Rover needs to tweak its entire image," says Paul Newton, a London analyst at research firms HIS Global Insight. "The complication is the huge amounts of money that will take."

Source: Excerpts reprinted from the September 3, 2009 issue of Bloomberg *BusinessWeek* by special permission. Copyright © 2009 by Bloomberg L.P.

CHAPTER SUMMARY

1. Define alliances and acquisitions.
   - A strategic alliance is a voluntary agreement between firms involving exchange; sharing; or co-developing of products, technologies, or services.
   - An acquisition is a transfer of the control of operations and management from one firm (target) to another (acquirer), the former becoming a unit of the latter.

2. Articulate how institutions and resources influence alliances and acquisitions.
   - Formal institutions influence alliances and acquisitions through antitrust and entry mode concerns.

- Informal institutions affect alliances and acquisitions through normative and cognitive pillars.
- The impact of resources on alliances and acquisitions is illustrated by the VRIO framework.

3. Describe how alliances are formed.
   - Alliances are typically formed when managers go through a three-stage decision process.

4. Outline how alliances are evolved and dissolved.
   - Managers need to combat opportunism and, if necessary, manage the dissolution process.

5. Discuss how alliances perform.
   - (1) Equity, (2) learning and experience, (3) nationality, and (4) relational capabilities may affect alliance performance.

6. Explain why firms undertake acquisitions.
   - Acquisitions are often driven by synergistic, hubristic, and managerial motives.

7. Understand why acquisitions often fail.
   - Many acquisitions fail because managers fail to address pre- and post-acquisition problems.

8. Participate in two leading debates on alliances and acquisitions.
   - They are (1) M&As + alliances and (2) majority versus minority JVs.

9. Draw implications for action.
   - Understand and master the rules of the game governing alliances and acquisitions around the world.
   - When managing alliances, pay attention to the soft relationship aspects.
   - When managing acquisitions, do not overpay and focus on both strategic and organizational fit.

KEY TERMS

Acquisition 383
Acquisition premium 389
Contractual (non-equity-based) alliances 383
Cross-shareholding 383
Equity-based alliances 383

Hubris 397
Initiator 394
Learning race 388
Managerial motives 397
Merger 383
Organizational fit 389

Real option 386
Relational (collaborative) capability 388
Strategic alliance 383
Strategic fit 389
Strategic investment 383

REVIEW QUESTIONS

1. List several examples of contractual and equity-based alliances.

2. Are mergers or acquisitions more common? Why?

3. In what two primary areas do formal institutions affect alliances?

4. Describe at least one norm (or collective assumption) and how it would affect a firm's perspective on creating an alliance.

5. Using the VRIO framework, describe the difference between an alliance and an acquisition.

6. Explain the three stages involved in the formation of an alliance.

7. Of the two methods allied firms can use to combat opportunism, which one do you think is better? Why?

8. What happens when an alliance fails and must be terminated? Summarize the process.

9. Of the four factors that may influence alliance performance shown in Figure 12.6, which do you think is the most important and which the least important? Why?

10. Describe the three most common motives for acquisition.

11. What are some criteria managers should consider to avoid pre- and post-acquisition problems?

12. If you were part of a firm's leadership, under what conditions would you choose an acquisition over an alliance and vice versa?

13. When does a majority JV seem more appropriate, and when is a minority JV more appealing?

14. Is it necessary for managers to pay attention to the politics behind alliances and acquisitions? Why?

15. Identify a country or region on PengAtlas Map 3.1 in which it is relatively difficult to do business. In spite of any difficulty, suppose you wish to expand into that country. Would you expand through an acquisition or an alliance? Why?

CRITICAL DISCUSSION QUESTIONS

1. M&As are a rare event for most companies. How can they enhance their capabilities for M&As?

2. *ON ETHICS:* During the courtship and negotiation stages, managers often emphasize "equal partnerships" and do not reveal (or try to hide) their true intentions. What are the ethical dilemmas here?

3. *ON ETHICS:* As a CEO, you are trying to acquire a foreign firm. The size of your firm will double and it will become the largest in your industry. On the one hand, you are excited about the opportunity to be a leading captain of industry and to attain the associated power, prestige, and income (you expect your salary, bonus, and stock option to double next year). On the other hand, you have just read this chapter and are troubled by the fact that 70% of M&As reportedly fail. How would you proceed?

globalEDGE
YOUR SOURCE FOR
global business
knowledge

http://globalEDGE.msu.edu

GLOBAL ACTION

1. You are an entrepreneur seeking to develop alliances in Ireland and generate new business ideas. Based on information found on globalEDGE, which region of Ireland may be most conducive to developing your global entrepreneurship network? What information and details support your thinking?

2. Identifying new sources of energy has been an important business opportunity for quite some time. Given recent growth in Asia, your company is seeking the acquisition of geothermal and solar energy firms in the region. Based on your firm's energy and resource development emphasis, use resources found on globalEDGE to identify three Asian countries in which this is most possible.

VIDEO CASES

Watch "Why a Deal is Done" by Stuart Grief of Textron.

1. Grief presented reasons for separating the analysis of potential M&As into the "why" and the "how" with emphasis on the "why." Develop a scenario in which the "how" may be the most important question and could influence the "why."

2. In Textron's M&As, the "why" is handled by the firm's strategic function and the "how" by the M&A function. Discuss both the pros and cons of that approach.

3. Grief said that when Textron is considering an acquisition, it asks if it is the best "parent" for the potential acquisition. What did he mean by that and does that make sense to you? Why or why not?

4. In global acquisitions, it is possible that a focus on the "why" may yield a decision to go ahead with an M&A that fails due to overlooking the cultural issues in the "how" question. Explain why that is possible.

Closing Case

Nomura Integrates Lehman Brothers in Asia and Europe

Everyone knows Lehman Brothers went bankrupt in September 2008. But what happened to its remains? Britain's Barclay Capital bought Lehman's North America operations as well as its securities and cash for $3.75 billion. Lehman's assets in Asia and Europe were purchased by Japan's Nomura for the bargain-basement price of $200 million. Founded in 1925, Nomura is the oldest and largest securities brokerage and investment banking firm in Japan. Although Nomura had operated in 30 countries prior to its acquisition of Lehman assets in 2008, it had al-

© Katsumi Kasahara

ways been known as a significant but still primarily regional (Asian) player in the big league of the financial services industry. In addition to Lehman, the list of elite investment banking firms in early 2008 would include Goldman Sachs, Morgan Stanley, Bear Stearns, JP Morgan, and Citigroup of the United States; Credit Suisse and UBS of Switzerland; Deutsche Bank of Germany; and ING Group of the Netherlands. No one would include Nomura in this group. Nomura viewed itself primarily as an Asian version of Merrill Lynch.

The tumultuous 2008 left Bear Stearns dead first, Lehman second, and all of the firms in the big league named above in deep financial trouble. To the conservatively managed Nomura, this became the opportunity of a lifetime. Within a lightning 24 hours, CEO Kenichi Watanabe decided to acquire Lehman's remnants in Asia and Europe. Some of the Lehman assets were dirt cheap. For example, its French investment banking operations was sold to Nomura

for only one euro (that is, €1!). Overall, by cherry-picking Lehman's Asia and Europe operations and adding 8,000 employees who tripled Nomura's size outside Japan, Nomura transformed itself into a global heavyweight overnight. The question is: Does Nomura have what it takes to make this acquisition a success?

The answer was a decisive "No!" from Nomura's investors, who drove its shares down by 70% in March 2009. Over the past five years, Nomura consistently underperformed the Nikkei 225 index, and this

acquisition broke a new low record for Nomura. Since the purchase price seemed reasonable and there was little evidence that Nomura overpaid, the biggest challenge is post-acquisition integration, merging a hard-charging New York investment bank with a hierarchical Japanese firm that still largely practices lifetime employment.

Clearly, Lehman's most valuable, rare, and hard-to-imitate assets are its talents. To ensure that Nomura retain most of the ex-Lehman talents, Nomura set aside a compensation pool of $1 billion (five times the $200 million it used to acquire Lehman assets) and guaranteed all ex-Lehman employees who chose to stay with Nomura not only their jobs, but also their 2007 pay level (including bonuses) for three years. About 95% of them accepted Nomura's offer. Given the ferociousness of the financial meltdown in 2008–2009 (which, if you remember, was triggered by Lehman's collapse), many employees at other firms that were not bankrupt lost their jobs.

The fact that Nomura guaranteed both jobs and pay levels was widely appreciated by ex-Lehman employees who otherwise would have been devastated.

Instead, acquiring Lehman introduced significant stress to Nomura's long-held traditions. A leading challenge is pay level. Most senior executives at Lehman made on average $1 million in 2007. Although concrete data were not available on how much money specific Nomura executives made, media reported that on average, Nomura employees only received *half* the pay of their Lehman counterparts. Not surprisingly, guaranteeing ex-Lehman employees at such an astronomical pay level (viewed from a Nomura perspective) created a major problem among Nomura's Japanese employees. In response, Nomura in 2009 offered its employees in Japan higher pay and bonuses that would start to approach the level ex-Lehman employees were commanding, in exchange for less job security—in other words, they could be fired more easily if they underperform. So far, about 2,000 Japanese employees accepted the offer, which would link pay to individual and departmental performance rather the firm as a whole.

Another challenge is the personnel rotation system. Like many leading Japanese firms, Nomura periodically rotates managers to different positions. For example, Yoshihiro Fukuta, who was appointed as head of Nomura International Hong Kong Ltd. in 2008, was rotated back to Tokyo as head of the Internal Audit Division in 2009. Although these practices produce well-rounded generalist managers, they generate a rigid hierarchy: a manager in a later cohort year, no matter how superb his (always a male) performance is, is unlikely to supervise a manager in an earlier cohort year. These Nomura practices directly clash with Western norms evidenced by two aspects

of Lehman practices: (1) work is increasingly done by specialists who develop deep expertise and (2) super stars are typically on a fast track rocketing ahead. Although the personnel rotation system largely did not apply to Nomura's overseas employees, it resulted in a top echelon that entirely consists of Japanese executives who have gone through the rotations. In an effort to globalize, Nomura's top echelon needs to attract diverse talents, especially those from Lehman. How the rotation system can accommodate the arrival of ex-Lehman employees who had neither experience nor stomach for it remains to be seen.

The performance of Nomura's acquisition of Lehman is mixed at this point. For the fiscal year ended in March 2009, Nomura lost $7.5 billion, calling into question the sustainability of paying ex-Lehman employees at such high levels. However, ex-Lehman employees indeed delivered some enviable performance. In Asia, Nomura advised 19 high-profile M&A deals in 2009; in 2008, it did two. In Europe, Nomura's equity-trading business jumped from eighty-second to the third biggest on the London Stock Exchange (Lehman used to be number one). Stay tuned for further transformation of Nomura.

Case Discussion Questions:

1. What is the strategic fit between Nomura and Lehman?
2. Is there any organizational fit? How do you bridge the gaps between the cultures of these two firms?
3. How does Nomura alleviate the concerns of multiple stakeholders?
4. How would you predict the effectiveness of Nomura's transformation after this acquisition?

Sources: Based on (1) *BusinessWeek*, 2009, Nomura is starting to flex its Lehman muscles, September 28; (2) E. Choi, H. Leung, J. Chan, S. Tse, & W. Chu, 2009, How can Nomura be a true global financial company? case study, University of Hong Kong; (3) *The Economist*, 2009, Numura's integration of Lehman, July 11; (4) A. Huo, E. Liu, R. Gampa, & R. Liew, 2009, Nomura's bet on Lehman, case study, University of Hong Kong.

NOTES

[Journal acronyms] AME—*Academy of Management Executive*; AMJ—*Academy of Management Journal*; AMP—*Academy of Management Perspectives*; AMR—*Academy of Management Review*; APJM—*Asia Pacific Journal of Management*; BW—*BusinessWeek*; CMR—*California Management Review*; HBR—*Harvard Business Review*; JB—*Journal of Business*; JEP—*Journal of Economic Perspectives*; JFE—*Journal of Financial Economics*; JIBS—*Journal of*

International Business Studies; JIM—*Journal of International Management*; JM—*Journal of Management*; JMS—*Journal of Management Studies*; JWB—*Journal of World Business*; OSc—*Organization Science*; SMJ—*Strategic Management Journal*; WSJ—*Wall Street Journal*

[1] X. Yin & M. Shanley, 2008, Industry determinants of the "merger versus alliance" decision, *AMR*, 33: 473–491.

2 R. Gulati, 1998, Alliances and networks (p. 293), *SMJ*, 19: 293–317. See also P. Beamish & N. Lupton, 2009, Managing JVs, *AMP*, May, 75–94; P. Kale & H. Singh, 2009, Managing strategic alliances, *AMP*, August: 45–62.

3 United Nations, 2000, *World Investment Report 2000* (p. 99), New York: United Nations.

4 Federal Trade Commission & US Department of Justice, 2000, *Antitrust Guidelines for Collaborations among Competitors*, Washington, DC: FTC & DOJ.

5 D. Chen, Y. Paik, & S. Park, 2010, Host-country policies and MNE management control in IJVs, *JIBS* (in press).

6 M. W. Peng, 2006, Making M&A fly in China, *HBR*, March: 26–27. See also P. Kale & J. Anand, 2006, The decline of emerging economy JVs, *CMR*, 48: 62–76; S. Rossi & P. Volpin, 2004, Cross-country determinants of M&As, *JFE*, 74: 277–304; H. K. Steensma, L. Tihanyi, M. Lyles, & C. Dhanaraj, 2005, The evolving value of foreign partnerships in transitioning economies, *AMJ*, 48: 213–235.

7 Z. Lin, M. W. Peng, H. Yang, & S. Sun, 2009, How do networks and learning drive M&As? An institutional comparison between China and the United States, *SMJ*, 30: 1113–1132.

8 M. Hayward & K. Shimizu, 2006, De-commitment to losing strategic action, *SMJ*, 27: 541–557; J. Reuer & R. Ragozzino, 2006, Agency hazards and alliance portfolios, *SMJ*, 27: 27–43.

9 R. Z. Ainuddin, P. Beamish, J. Hulland, & M. Rouse, 2007, Resource attributes and firm performance in IJVs, *JWB*, 42: 47–60; J. Dyer & N. Hatch, 2006, Relation-specific capabilities and barriers to knowledge transfers, *SMJ*, 27: 701–719; E. Fang & S. Zou, 2009, Antecedents and consequences of marketing dynamic capabilities in IJVs, *JIBS*, 40: 742–761; S. Lazzarini, 2007, The impact of membership in competing alliance constellations, *SMJ*, 28: 345–367.

10 *The Economist*, 2003, Open skies and flights of fancy (p. 67), October 4: 65–67.

11 S. Ang, 2008, Competitive intensity and collaboration, *SMJ*, 29: 1057–1075; R. Sampson, 2007, R&D alliances and firm performance, *AMJ*, 50: 364–386.

12 *BW*, 2009, Murdoch vs. Google, December 7: 26; *The Economist*, 2009, Web-wide war, November 28: 70.

13 B. Bourdeau, J. Cronin, & C. Voorhees, 2007, Modeling service alliances, *SMJ*, 28: 609–622; A. Tiwana & M. Keil, 2007, Does peripheral knowledge complement control? *SMJ*, 28: 623–634.

14 T. Tong, J. Reuer, & M. W. Peng, 2008, International joint ventures and the value of growth options, *AMJ*, 51: 1014–1029.

15 R. Belderbos & J. Zou, 2009, Real options and foreign affiliate divestments, *JIBS*, 40: 600–620; T. Chi, 2000, Option to acquire or divest a JV, *SMJ*, 21: 665–687; M. Santoro & J. McGill, 2005, The effect of uncertainty and asset co-specialization on governance in biotechnology alliances, *SMJ*, 26: 1261–1269.

16 G. Ahuja, F. Polidoro, & W. Mitchell, 2009, Structural homophily or social asymmetry? *SMJ*, 30: 941–958.

17 Z. Lin, H. Yang, & B. Arya, 2009, Alliance partners and firm performance, *SMJ*, 30: 921–940; X. Luo & L. Deng, 2009, Do birds of a feather flock higher? *JMS*, 46: 1005–1030.

18 S. Currall & A. Inkpen, 2002, A multilevel approach to trust in JVs, *JIBS*, 33: 479–495.

19 D. Zoogah & M. W. Peng, 2010, What determines the performance of strategic alliance managers? *APJM* (in press).

20 J. Li, C. Zhou, & E. Zajac, 2009, Control, collaboration, and productivity in IJVs, *SMJ*, 30: 865–884; L. Mesquita, 2007, Starting over when the bickering never ends, *AMR*, 32: 72–91; H. Ness, 2009, Governance, negotiations, and alliance dynamics, *JMS*, 46: 451–480.

21 D. Chen, S. Park, & W. Newburry, 2009, Parent contribution and organizational control in IJVs, *SMJ*, 30: 1133–1156.

22 J. Hennart, T. Roehl, & D. Zietlow, 1999, "Trojan horse" or "workhorse"? *SMJ*, 20: 15–29; J. Li & C. Zhou, 2008, Dual-edged tools of trade, *JWB*, 43: 463–474.

23 S. Gubbi, P. Aulakh, S. Ray, M. Sarkar, & R. Chittoor, 2010, Do international acquisitions by emerging-economy firms create shareholder value? *JIBS* (in press); K. Uhlenbruck, M. Hitt, & M. Semadeni, 2006, Market value effects of acquisitions involving Internet firms, *SMJ*, 27: 899–913; C. Zhou & J. Li, 2008, Product innovation in emerging market-based IJVs, *JIBS*, 39: 1114–1132.

24 D. King, D. Dalton, C. Daily, & J. Covin, 2004, Meta-analyses of post-acquisition performance, *SMJ*, 25: 187–200.

25 C. Moschieri & J. Campa, 2009, The European M&A industry (p. 82), *AMP*, November: 71–87.

26 G. Andrade, M. Mitchell, & E. Stafford, 2001, New evidence and perspectives on mergers, *JEP*, 15: 103–120.

27 J. Doukas & O. Kan, 2006, Does global diversification destroy firm value? *JIBS*, 37: 352–371.

28 J. Haleblian, J. Kim, & N. Rajagopalan, 2006, The influence of acquisition experience and performance on acquisition behavior, *AMJ*, 49: 357–370.

29 J. Kim & S. Finkelstein, 2009, The effects of strategic and market complementarity on acquisition performance, *SMJ*, 30: 617–646.

30 This section draws heavily from S. Tallman & O. Shenkar, 1994, A managerial decision model of international cooperative venture formation, *JIBS*, 25: 91–113.

31 B. Garrette, X. Castaner, & P. Dussauge, 2009, Horizontal alliances as an alternative to autonomous production, *SMJ*, 30: 885–894.

32 S. Park, R. Chen, & S. Gallagher, 2002, Firm resources as moderators of the relationship between market growth and strategic alliances in semiconductor start-ups, *AMJ*, 45: 527–545.

33 R. Jensen & G. Szulanski, 2004, Stickiness and the adaptation of organizational practices in cross-border knowledge transfers, *JIBS*, 35: 508–523; B. Simonin, 2004, An empirical investigation of the process of knowledge transfer in international strategic alliances, *JIBS*, 35: 407–427.

34 Y. Pan & X. Li, 2000, JV formation of very large multinational firms, *JIBS*, 31: 179–189.

35 J. Hagedoorn, D. Cloodt, & H. van Kranenburg, 2005, Intellectual property rights and the governance of international R&D partnerships, *JIBS*, 36: 175–186.

36 J. Reuer, M. Zollo, & H. Singh, 2002, Post-formation dynamics in strategic alliances, *SMJ*, 23: 135–152; J. Robins, S. Tallman, & K. Fladmoe-Lindquist, 2002, Autonomy and dependence of international cooperative ventures, *SMJ*, 23: 881–901.

[37] Y. Luo, 2007, Are JV partners more opportunistic in a more volatile environment? *SMJ*, 28: 39–60; S. White & S. Lui, 2005, Distinguishing costs of cooperation and control in alliances, *SMJ*, 26: 913–932.

[38] This section draws heavily from M. W. Peng & O. Shenkar, 2002, JV dissolution as corporate divorce, *AME*, 16: 92–105.

[39] D. Faems, M. Janssens, A. Madhok, & B. Looy, 2008, Toward an integrative perspective on alliance governance, *AMJ*, 51: 1053–1078; N. Pangarkar, 2009, Do firms learn from alliance terminations? *JMS*, 46: 982–1004; J. Reuer & A. Arino, 2007, Strategic alliance contracts, *SMJ*, 28: 313–330.

[40] A. Arino & J. Reuer, 2004, Designing and renegotiating strategic alliance contracts (p. 44), *AME*, 18: 37–48.

[41] A. Goerzen & P. Beamish, 2005, The effect of alliance network diversity on MNE performance, *SMJ*, 26: 333–354; J. Lu & D. Xu, 2006, Growth and survival of IJVs, *JM*, 32: 426–448; P. Meschi, 2005, Stock market valuation of JV sell-offs, *JIBS*, 36: 688–700; A. Mohr, 2006, A multiple constituency approach to IJV performance measurement, *JWB*, 41: 247–260; A. Shipilov, 2006, Network strategy and performance of Canadian investment banks, *AMJ*, 49: 590–604.

[42] A. Gaur & J. Lu, 2007, Ownership strategies and survival of foreign subsidiaries, *JM*, 33: 84–110; A. Madhok, 2006, How much does ownership really matter? *JIBS*, 37: 4–11.

[43] J. Barden, H. K. Steensma, & M. Lyles, 2005, The influence of parent control structure on parent conflict in Vietnamese IJVs, *JIBS*, 36: 156–174.

[44] R. Aguilera, 2007, Translating theoretical logics across borders, *JIBS*, 38: 38–46; P. Lane, J. Salk, & M. Lyles, 2001, Absorptive capacity, learning, and performance in IJVs, *SMJ*, 22: 1139–1161; K. Meyer, 2007, Contextualizing organizational learning, *JIBS*, 38: 27–37; E. Tsang, 2002, Acquiring knowledge by foreign partners from IJVs in a transition economy, *SMJ*, 23: 835–854.

[45] F. Evangelista & L. Hau, 2009, Organizational context and knowledge acquisition in IJVs, *JWB*, 44: 63–73; R. Gulati, D. Lavie, & H. Singh, 2009, The nature of partnering experience and the gains from alliances, *SMJ*, 30: 1213–1233; B. Nielsen & S. Nielsen, 2009, Learning and innovation in international strategic alliances, *JMS*, 46: 1031–1058.

[46] Y. Luo & M. W. Peng, 1999, Learning to compete in a transition economy, *JIBS*, 30: 269–296.

[47] D. Sirmon & P. Lane, 2004, A model of cultural differences and international alliance performance, *JIBS*, 35: 306–319.

[48] M. Acquaah, 2009, IJV partner origin, strategic choice, and performance, *JIM*, 15: 46–60; D. Hambrick, J. Li, K. Xin, & A. Tsui, 2001, Compositional gaps and downward spirals in IJV management groups, *SMJ*, 22: 1033–1053.

[49] K. Brouthers & G. Mamossy, 2006, Post-formation processes in Eastern and Western European JVs, *JMS*, 43: 203–229; R. Krishnan, X. Martin, & N. Noorderhaven, 2006, When does trust matter to alliance performance? *AMJ*, 49: 894–917.

[50] J. Anand & A. Delios, 2002, Absolute and relative resources as determinants of international acquisitions, *SMJ*, 23: 119–134; T. Saxton & M. Dollinger, 2004, Target reputation and appropriability, *JM*, 30: 123–147.

[51] R. Roll, 1986, The hubris hypothesis of corporate takeovers, *JB*, 59: 197–216.

[52] P. Buckley & P. Ghauri, 2002, *International Mergers and Acquisitions* (p. 2), London: Thomson.

[53] S. Moeller, F. Schlingemann, & R. Stulz, 2004, Firm size and the gains from acquisitions, *JFE*, 73: 201–228.

[54] J. M. Shaver, 2006, A paradox of synergy, *AMR*, 31: 962–976; M. Sirower, 1997, *The Synergy Trap*, New York: Free Press.

[55] *BW*, 2006, Ballmer: They paid how much for that? October 23: 37.

[56] M. Brannen & M. Peterson, 2009, Merging without alienating, *JIBS*, 40: 468–489; R. Chakrabarti, S. Gupta–Mukherjee, & N. Jayaraman, 2009, Mars–Venus marriages, *JIBS*, 40: 216–236; K. Ellis, T. Reus, & B. Lamont, 2009, The effects of procedural and informational justice in the integration of related acquisitions, *SMJ*, 30: 137–161; C. Homburg & M. Bucerius, 2006, Is speed of integration really a success factor of M&As? *SMJ*, 27: 347–367.

[57] T. Grubb & R. Lamb, 2000, *Capitalize on Merger Chaos* (p. 14), New York: Free Press.

[58] A. Slangen, 2006, National cultural distance and initial foreign acquisition performance, *JWB*, 41: 161–170; K. Uhlenbruck, 2004, Developing acquired foreign subsidiaries, *JIBS*, 35: 109–123.

[59] R. Hallowell, D. Bowen, & C. Knoop, 2002, Four Seasons goes to Paris (p. 19), *AME*, 16: 7–24.

[60] *BW*, 2009, Oracle has customers over a barrel, September 21: 52–55.

[61] J. Dyer, P. Kale, & H. Singh, 2004, When to ally and when to acquire, *HBR*, July–August: 109–115; A. Goerzen, 2007, Alliance networks and firm performance, *SMJ*, 28: 487–509.

[62] D. Yiu & S. Makino, 2002, The choice between JV and wholly owned subsidiary, *OSc*, 13: 667–683.

[63] H. Yang, S. Sun, Z. Lin, & M. W. Peng, 2010, Behind M&As in China and the United States, *APJM* (in press).

[64] N. Napier & D. Thomas, 2004, *Managing Relationships in Transition Economies*, New York: Prager; S. Puffer, D. McCarthy, & N. Alexander, 2000, *The Russian Capitalist Experiment*, Cheltenham, UK: Edward Elgar.

[65] C. Choi & P. Beamish, 2004, Split management control and IJV performance, *JIBS*, 35: 201–215; H. K. Steensma & M. Lyles, 2000, Explaining IJV survival in a transition economy, *SMJ*, 21: 831–851.

[66] O. Hope, W. Thomas, & D. Vyas, 2009, The cost of pride: Why do firms from developing countries bid higher? Working paper, University of Toronto.

LEARNING OBJECTIVES

After studying this chapter, you should be able to:

1. describe the relationship between multinational strategy and structure.

2. explain how institutions and resources affect strategy, structure, and learning.

3. outline the challenges associated with learning, innovation, and knowledge management.

4. participate in two leading debates on multinational strategy, structure, and learning.

5. draw implications for action.

KIKKOMAN

NATURALLY BREWED

Soy Sauce

150 ml e

© MediaBlitz Images (UK) Limited/Alamy

Strategizing, Structuring, and Learning around the World

Kikkoman's Sauce of Success

At the International Trade Fair in Chicago in 1959, visitors were delighted by the salty-savory taste of roast beef marinated in a novel condiment called soy sauce: slices were being given away by young Japanese men. What the nibblers did not know was that the foreigners were not merely demonstration staff but workers at the sauce maker's new American unit, who wanted to see firsthand how American consumers responded to their product. Among them was Yazaburo Mogi, a 24-year-old student at Columbia Business School and the scion of one of the founding families behind Kikkoman, a soy sauce maker that traces its origins to the 17th century.

By the time he reached the top of the firm in 1995, Mr. Mogi was well on his way to transforming it into an international food business and turning an obscure Asian seasoning into a mainstream global product. "We tried to appeal to the non-Japanese, general-market consumer," says Mr. Mogi, who speaks fluent English—a rarity among Japanese bosses. Kikkoman is now the world's largest maker of naturally brewed soy sauce. Foreign sales of its sauce have grown by nearly 10% a year for 25 years. Its distinctive curvy bottle has become commonplace in restaurants and kitchens the world over, alongside other condiments such as Italian olive oil or French mustard. Interbrand,

a brand consultancy, ranks Kikkoman among the most recognizable Japanese names in a list otherwise dominated by carmakers and electronics firms.

Indeed, this family-owned Japanese firm is unusual in several ways. In 1973, it became the first Japanese food company to open a factory in America; Mr. Mogi was running the American division by this time. Whereas many Japanese firms eschew mergers and acquisitions, Kikkoman has been active, buying American and Japanese companies in the course of its expansion. (In January 2009, Kikkoman adopted a holding-company structure that will make acquisitions easier, among other things.) Mr. Mogi speaks with pride about corporate governance reforms he has instituted, including succession planning. Since 2004, the firm's presidents have come from outside the founding families. And rather than being centrally run from Tokyo, Kikkoman is known for devolving power to the bosses of its foreign subsidiaries.

Under Mr. Mogi's leadership, Kikkoman's sales have grown to more than $4 billion a year, of which soy sauce accounts for 20%. Most of the firm's revenue now comes from selling other food products in Japan and abroad. Kikkoman is the biggest wholesaler of Asian foodstuffs in America, with similar operations in Europe, China, and Australia. It sells canned fruit and vegetables in Asia under the Del Monte brand, and one of its subsidiaries is Coca-Cola's bottling affiliates in Japan. Foreign sales account for 30% of revenue but 55% of operating profit, three-quarters of which comes from North America. By some measures Kikkoman is the Japanese firm most dependent on the American market. The recession has hit Kikkoman's profits, but it is relatively well protected. "In a recession, demand shifts from restaurants to household consumption," Mr. Mogi explains, so what his company loses in one market, it makes up in the other.

Kikkoman's move into America in the 1950s set the template for the company's foreign expansion. America was the perfect place to venture abroad, says Mr. Mogi. It is open to new things and is willing to incorporate novel ingredients into its cuisine. During his time at business school, Mr. Mogi travelled across America, visiting Asian restaurants. There were very few: in New York he found only eight Japanese eateries. Kikkoman, he realized, had to adapt its sauce to the local cuisine if it was going to succeed. Kikkoman promoted soy sauce in America by hiring chefs to concoct recipes that incorporated the sauce into classic American dishes. The firm then sent the recipes to local newspapers, prompting housewives to cut them out and shop for the ingredients. In the process, it started to position soy sauce not as a Japanese product, but as an "all-purpose

seasoning," as a housewife puts it in Kikkoman's 1950s television advertisements. The same words can still be seen emblazoned on its bottles.

In 1961, the company picked up many new customers by introducing teriyaki sauce—a mixture of soy sauce and other ingredients devised specifically for the American market as a barbecue glaze. Kikkoman is now devising products for South American and European tastes, such as a soy sauce that can be sprinkled on rice—something that is not done in Japan. In Europe and Australia, where consumers are suspicious of biotechnology, Kikkoman's sauce is made without genetically modified ingredients. Mr. Mogi is also taking Kikkoman into a foreign market rather close to home: China. It is a more difficult market to enter than America or Europe, because soy sauce is already part of Chinese cuisine and cheap products abound, often chemically synthesized rather than naturally brewed. Mr. Mogi hopes to establish Kikkoman's sauce as a premium product aimed at wealthier buyers. His early recognition of the importance of adapting his firm's product for foreign markets is Kikkoman's real special sauce.

Source: "Sauce of success", *The Economist*, April 11, 2009, p. 68. Copyright © 2009 The Economist Newspaper Limited. Reprinted with permission. All rights reserved.

How can multinational enterprises (MNEs) such as Kikkoman be appropriately structured so that they can be successful both locally and internationally? How can they learn national tastes, global trends, and market transitions that require structural changes? How can they improve the odds for better innovation? These are some of the key questions we address in this chapter. The focus here is on relatively large MNEs with significant internationalization. We start by discussing the crucial relationship between four strategies and four structures. Next, we consider how the institution-based and resource-based views shed light on these issues. Then, we discuss worldwide learning, innovation, and knowledge management and look at two leading debates. Finally, we go over some tips for making MNEs successful.

Describe the relationship between multinational strategy and structure.

MULTINATIONAL STRATEGIES AND STRUCTURES

This section first introduces an integration-responsiveness framework centered on the pressures for cost reductions and local responsiveness. We then outline the four strategic choices and the four corresponding organizational structures that MNEs typically adopt.

Pressures for Cost Reductions and Local Responsiveness

MNEs primarily confront two sets of pressures: cost reduction and local responsiveness. These two sets of pressures are dealt with in the **integration-responsiveness framework**, which allows managers to deal with the pressures for both global integration and local responsiveness. Cost pressures often call for global integration, whereas local responsiveness pushes MNEs to adapt locally.[1] In both domestic and international competition, pressures to reduce costs are almost universal. International competition is unique in the pressure for **local responsiveness**, which means reacting to different consumer preferences and host country demands. Consumer preferences vary tremendously around the world. For example, McDonald's beef-based hamburgers obviously would find few customers in India, where cows are held sacred by the Hindu majority. Host country demands and expectations add to the pressures for local responsiveness. Throughout Europe, Canadian firm Bombardier manufactures an Austrian version of railcars in Austria, a Belgian version in Belgium, and so on. Bomdardier believes that such local responsiveness, although not required, is essential for making sales to railway operators in Europe, which tend to be state-owned.

Taken together, being locally responsive certainly makes local customers and governments happy but unfortunately increases costs. Given the universal interest in lowering cost, a natural tendency is to downplay or ignore the different needs and wants of various local markets and instead market a global version of products and services like Ford's world car or MTV's global song. The intellectual underpinning of the movement to globalize offerings can be traced to a 1983 article by Theodore Levitt: "The Globalization of Markets."[2] Levitt argued that worldwide consumer tastes are converging. As evidence, Levitt pointed to sales of Coke Classic, Levi Strauss jeans, and Sony color TVs, all of which were successful worldwide. Levitt predicted that such convergence would characterize most product markets in the future.

Levitt's idea has often been the intellectual force propelling many MNEs to globally integrate their products while minimizing local adaptation. Ford experimented with world car designs. MTV pushed ahead with the belief that viewers would flock to global (essentially American) programming. Unfortunately, most of these experiments are not successful. Ford found that consumer tastes ranged widely around the globe. MTV eventually realized that there is no global song. In a nutshell, one size does not fit all. This leads us to look at how MNEs can pay attention to *both* dimensions: cost reductions and local responsiveness.

Four Strategic Choices

Based on the integration-responsiveness framework, Figure 13.1 plots the four strategic choices for MNEs: (1) home replication, (2) localization, (3) global standardization, and (4) transnational.[3] Each strategy has a set of pros and cons, as outlined in Table 13.1. (Their corresponding structures shown in Figure 13.1 are discussed in the next section.)

Home replication strategy, often known as international (or export) strategy, duplicates home country-based competencies in foreign countries. Such competencies include production scales, distribution efficiencies, and brand power. In manufacturing, this is usually manifested in an export strategy. In services, this is often done through licensing and franchising. This strategy is relatively easy to implement and usually the first one adopted when firms venture abroad.

Integration-responsiveness framework

A framework of MNE management on how to simultaneously deal with two sets of pressures for global integration and local responsiveness.

Local responsiveness

The necessity to be responsive to different customer preferences around the world.

Home replication strategy

A strategy that emphasizes the replication of home country-based competencies in foreign countries.

TABLE 13.1 FOUR STRATEGIC CHOICES FOR MULTINATIONAL ENTERPRISES

	Advantages	Disadvantages
Home replication	• Leverages home country-based advantages • Relatively easy to implement	• Lack of local responsiveness • May result in foreign customer alienation
Localization	• Maximizes local responsiveness	• High costs due to duplication of efforts in multiple countries • Too much local autonomy
Global standardization	• Leverages low-cost advantages	• Lack of local responsiveness • Too much centralized control
Transnational	• Cost efficient while being locally responsive • Engages in global learning and diffusion of innovations	• Organizationally complex • Difficult to implement

FIGURE 13.1 MULTINATIONAL STRATEGIES AND STRUCTURES: THE INTEGRATION-RESPONSIVE FRAMEWORK

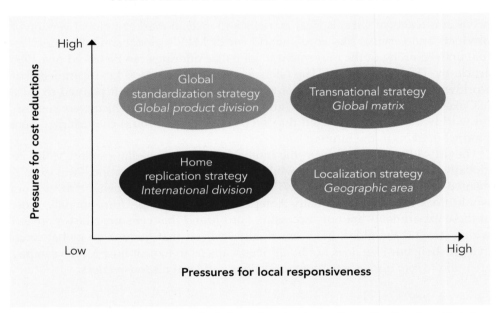

Note: In some other textbooks, "home replication" may be referred to as "international" or "export" strategy, "localization" as "multidomestic" strategy, and "global standardization" as "global" strategy. Some of these labels are confusing, because one can argue that all the four strategies here are "international" or "global," thus resulting in some confusion if we label one of these strategies as "international" and another as "global." The present set of labels is more descriptive and less confusing.

On the disadvantage side, home replication strategy often lacks local responsiveness because it focuses on the home country. This strategy makes sense when the majority of a firm's customers are domestic. However, when a firm aspires to broaden its international scope, failing to be mindful of foreign customers' needs and wants may alienate those potential customers. For example, when Wal-Mart entered Brazil, the stores initially were exactly the same copy as its US stores, including having a large number of *American* footballs. Considering that Brazil has won soccer's World Cup five times, more wins than any other country, nobody (except a few homesick American expatriates in their spare time) plays American football there.

Localization strategy is an extension of the home replication strategy. **Localization (multidomestic) strategy** focuses on a number of foreign countries/regions, each of which is regarded as a stand-alone local (domestic) market worthy of significant attention and adaptation. While sacrificing global efficiencies, this strategy is effective when differences among national and regional markets are clear and pressures for cost reductions are low. As noted earlier, MTV started with a home replication strategy when first venturing overseas; it simply broadcast American programming. It has now switched to a localization strategy by broadcasting in local languages.

In terms of disadvantages, localization strategy has high costs due to duplication of efforts in multiple countries. The costs of producing such a variety of programming for MTV are obviously greater than the costs of producing one set of programming. As a result, this strategy is only appropriate in industries where the pressures for cost reductions are not significant. Another potential drawback is too much local autonomy, which happens when each subsidiary regards its country as so unique that it is difficult to introduce corporate-wide changes. For example, Unilever had seventeen country subsidiaries in Europe in the 1980s and it took four *years* to persuade all seventeen subsidiaries to introduce a single new detergent across Europe.

As the opposite of localization strategy, **global standardization strategy** is sometimes simply referred to as global strategy. Its hallmark is the development and distribution of standardized products worldwide in order to reap the maximum benefits from low-cost advantages. Although home replication and global standardization strategies both minimize local responsiveness, a crucial difference is that an MNE pursuing a global standardization strategy is not limited to its major operations at home. In a number of countries, the MNE may designate **centers of excellence**, defined as subsidiaries explicitly recognized as a source of important capabilities, with the intention that these capabilities be leveraged by and/or disseminated to other subsidiaries.[4] For example, Merck Frosst Canada, the Canadian subsidiary of Merck, is a center of excellence in R&D. Centers of excellence are often given a **worldwide** (or **global**) **mandate**, namely, a charter to be responsible for one MNE function throughout the world. HP's Singapore subsidiary, for instance, has a worldwide mandate to develop, produce, and market all of HP's handheld products.

In terms of disadvantages, a global standardization strategy obviously sacrifices local responsiveness. This strategy makes great sense in industries where pressures for cost reductions are paramount and pressures for local responsiveness are relatively minor (particularly in commodity industries such as semiconductors and tires). However, as noted earlier, in industries ranging from automobiles to consumer products, a one-size-fits-all strategy may

Localization (multidomestic) strategy

A strategy that focuses on a number of foreign countries/regions, each of which is regarded as a stand-alone local (domestic) market worthy of significant attention and adaptation.

Global standardization strategy

A strategy that focuses on development and distribution of standardized products worldwide in order to reap the maximum benefits from low-cost advantages.

Center of excellence

An MNE subsidiary explicitly recognized as a source of important capabilities, with the intention that these capabilities be leveraged by and/or disseminated to other subsidiaries.

Worldwide (global) mandate

A charter to be responsible for one MNE function throughout the world.

© Jin Lee/Bloomberg News/Landov

Why do you think HP has issued a mandate to its Singapore subsidiary to develop, produce, and market all of HP's handheld products?

be inappropriate. Consequently, arguments such as "all industries are becoming global" and "all firms need to pursue a global (standardization) strategy" are potentially misleading.

Transnational strategy aims to capture the best of both worlds by endeavoring to be both cost efficient and locally responsive.[5] In addition to cost efficiency and local responsiveness, a third hallmark of this strategy is global learning and diffusion of innovations. Traditionally, the diffusion of innovations in MNEs is a one-way flow, from the home country to various host countries—the label "home replication" says it all (!). Underpinning such a one-way flow is the assumption that the home country is the best location for generating innovations. However, this assumption is increasingly challenged by critics who suggest that innovations are inherently risky and uncertain and that there is no guarantee that the home country will generate the highest-quality innovations.[6]

MNEs that engage in a transnational strategy promote global learning and diffusion of innovations in multiple ways. Innovations not only flow from the home country to host countries (which is the traditional flow), but also flow from host countries to the home country and among subsidiaries in multiple host countries.[7] Kia Motors, for example, not only operates a design center in Seoul, Korea, but also has two other design centers in Los Angeles and Frankfurt, tapping into automotive innovations generated in North America and Europe.[8]

On the disadvantage side, a transnational strategy is organizationally complex and difficult to implement. The large amount of knowledge sharing and coordination may slow down decision making. Trying to achieve cost efficiencies, local responsiveness, and global learning simultaneously places contradictory demands on the organizational capabilities of MNEs (to be discussed in the next section).

Transnational strategy

A strategy that endeavors to be cost efficient, locally responsive, and learning driven simultaneously around the world.

International division

An organizational structure that is typically set up when firms initially expand abroad, often engaging in a home replication strategy.

Four Organizational Structures

Figure 13.1 also shows four organizational structures that are appropriate for each of the strategic choices: (1) international division, (2) geographic area, (3) global product division, and (4) global matrix.

International division is typically used when firms initially expand abroad, often engaging in a home replication strategy. Figure 13.2 shows Starbucks'

FIGURE 13.2   INTERNATIONAL DIVISION STRUCTURE AT STARBUCKS

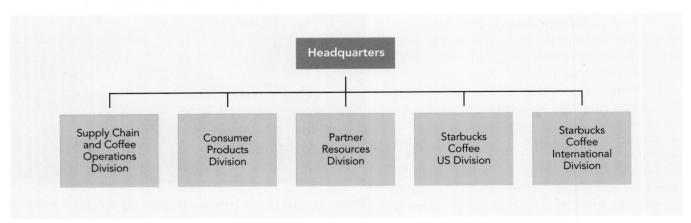

Sources: Adapted from (1) www.cogmap.com; (2) www.starbucks.com. Headquartered in Seattle, Starbucks is a leading international coffee and coffeehouse company.

International Division and its four other divisions that primarily focus on the United States. Although this structure is intuitively appealing, it often leads to two problems. First, foreign subsidiary managers, whose input is channeled through the international division, are not given sufficient voice relative to the heads of domestic divisions.[9] Second, by design, the international division serves as a silo whose activities are not coordinated with the rest of the firm, which is focusing on domestic activities. Consequently, many firms phase out this structure after their initial stage of overseas expansion.

Geographic area structure organizes the MNE according to different geographic areas (countries and regions). It is the most appropriate structure for a localization strategy. Figure 13.3 illustrates such a structure for Avon Products (see the Chapter 1 Opening Case). A geographic area can be a country or a region, led by a **country or regional manager**. Each area is largely stand-alone. In contrast to the limited voice of subsidiary managers in the international division structure, country and regional managers carry a great deal of weight in a geographic area structure. Interestingly and paradoxically, *both* the strengths and weaknesses of this structure lie in its local responsiveness. Although being locally responsive can be a virtue (see the Opening Case), it also encourages the fragmentation of the MNE into fiefdoms.[10]

Global product division structure, which is the opposite of the geographic area structure, supports the global standardization strategy by assigning global responsibilities to each product division. Figure 13.4 shows such an example from EADS, whose most famous unit is Airbus. This structure treats each product division as a stand-alone entity with full worldwide—as opposed to domestic—responsibilities. This structure is highly responsive to pressures for cost efficiencies, because it allows for consolidation on a worldwide (or at least regional) basis and reduces inefficient duplication in multiple countries. For example, Unilever reduced the number of soap-producing factories in Europe from ten to two after adopting this structure. Recently, because of the popularity of the global standardization strategy (noted earlier), the global product division structure is on the rise. The structure's main drawback is that local responsiveness suffers, as Ford discovered when it phased out the geographical area structure in favor of the global product division structure.

A **global matrix** alleviates the disadvantages associated with both geographic area and global product division structures, especially for MNEs adopting a transnational strategy. Shown in Figure 13.5, its hallmark is the sharing and coordination

Geographic area structure
An organizational structure that organizes the MNE according to different geographic areas (countries and regions).

Country (regional) manager
Manager of a geographic area, either a country or a region.

Global product division structure
An organizational structure that assigns global responsibilities to each product division.

Global matrix
An organizational structure often used to alleviate the disadvantages associated with both geographic area and global product division structures, especially for MNEs adopting a transnational strategy.

FIGURE 13.3 GEOGRAPHIC AREA STRUCTURE AT AVON PRODUCTS

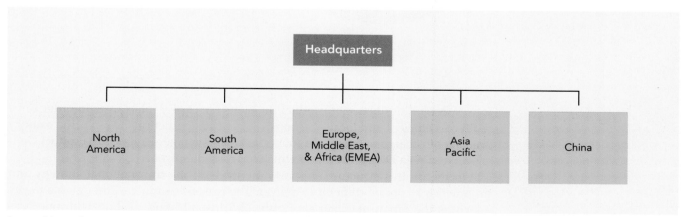

Source: Adapted from www.avoncompany.com. Headquartered in New York, Avon is a leading global beauty products company (see Chapter 1 Opening Case).

FIGURE 13.4   GLOBAL PRODUCT DIVISION STRUCTURE AT EUROPEAN AERONAUTIC
DEFENSE AND SPACE COMPANY (EADS)

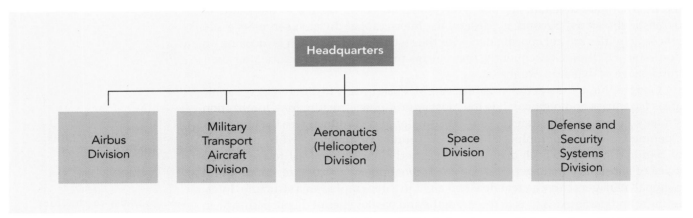

Source: Adapted from www.eads.com. Headquartered in Munich, Germany, and Paris, France, EADS is the largest commercial aircraft maker and the largest defense contractor in Europe.

FIGURE 13.5   A HYPOTHETICAL GLOBAL MATRIX STRUCTURE

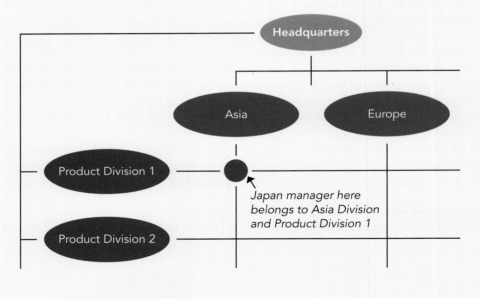

of responsibilities between product divisions and geographic areas in order to be both cost efficient and locally responsive. In this hypothetical example, the country manager in charge of Japan—in short, the Japan manager—reports to Product Division 1 and Asia Division, both of which have equal power.

In theory this structure supports the goals of the transnational strategy, but in practice it is often difficult to deliver. The reason is simple: Although managers (such as the Japan manager in Figure 13.5) usually find dealing with one boss headache enough, they find having two bosses who are often in conflict (!) even more difficult to deal with. For example, Product Division 1 may decide that Japan is too tough a nut to crack and that there are more promising markets elsewhere, thus ordering the Japan manager to *curtail* her investment and channel resources elsewhere. This makes sense because Product Division 1 cares about its global market position and is not wedded to any particular country. However, Asia Division, which is evaluated by how well it does in Asia, may beg to differ. Asia Division argues that it cannot afford to be a laggard in Japan if it expects to be a leading player in Asia. Therefore, Asia Division demands that the Japan manager *increase* her investment in the country. Facing these conflicting demands, the Japan manager, who prefers to be politically correct, does not want to make any move before consulting corporate headquarters. Eventually, headquarters may provide a resolution. But crucial time may be lost in the process and important opportunities for competitive actions may be missed.

Despite its merits on paper, the matrix structure may add layers of management, slow down decision speed, and increase costs while not showing significant performance improvement. There is no conclusive evidence for the superiority of the matrix structure.[11] Having experimented with the matrix structure, a number of MNEs have now moved back to the simpler and easier-to-manage global product structure. Even when the matrix structure is still in place, global product divisions are often given more power than geographic area divisions. The following quote from a CEO of Dow Chemical, an early adopter of the matrix structure, is sobering:

> We were an organization that was matrixed and depended on teamwork, but there was no one in charge. When things went well, we didn't know whom to reward; and when things went poorly, we didn't know whom to blame. So we created a global product division structure, and cut out layers of management. There used to be 11 layers of management between me and the lowest level employees, now there are five.[12]

Overall, the positioning of the four structures in Figure 13.1 is not random. They develop from the relatively simple international division through either geographic area or global product division structures and may finally reach the more complex global matrix stage. It is important to note that not every MNE experiences all these structural stages and the movement is not necessarily in one direction. For example, the matrix structure's "poster child," the Swiss-Swedish conglomerate ABB, recently withdrew from this structure.

The Reciprocal Relationship between Multinational Strategy and Structure

In one word, the relationship between strategy and structure is *reciprocal*. Three key ideas stand out. First, strategy usually drives structure. The fit between strategy and structure, as exemplified by the *pairs* in each of the four cells in Figure 13.1, is crucial.[13] A misfit, such as combining a global standardization strategy with a geographic area structure, may have grave performance consequences.

Second, the relationship is not a one-way street. As much as strategy drives structure, structure also drives strategy. The withdrawal from the unworkable matrix structure at MNEs such as ABB has called into question the wisdom of the transnational strategy.

Finally, neither strategies nor structures are static. It is often necessary to change strategy, structure, or both.[14] In an effort to move toward a global standardization strategy, many MNEs have adopted a global product division structure while de-emphasizing the role of country headquarters. However, unique challenges in certain countries, especially China, have now pushed some MNEs to revive the country headquarters, such as the China headquarters, so that it can coordinate numerous activities within a large, complex, and important host country.[15] A further experimentation is to have an emerging economies division, which is not dedicated to any single country but dedicated to pursuing opportunities in a series of emerging economies ranging from Brazil to Saudi Arabia. Cisco pioneered this structure, which has been followed by rivals such as IBM.[16]

Explain how institutions and resources affect strategy, structure, and learning.

HOW INSTITUTIONS AND RESOURCES AFFECT MULTINATIONAL STRATEGIES, STRUCTURES, AND LEARNING

Having outlined the basic strategy/structure configurations, let us introduce how the institution-based and resource-based views shed light on these issues (see Figure 13.6).

Institution-Based Considerations

MNEs face two sets of rules of the game: Formal and informal institutions governing (1) *external* relationships and (2) *internal* relationships. Each is discussed in turn.

Externally, MNEs are subject to the formal institutional frameworks erected by various home-country and host-country governments. For example, in order to protect domestic employment, the British government taxes the foreign earnings of British MNEs at a higher rate than their domestic earnings. The Obama administration is threatening similar moves.

Host-country governments, on the other hand, often attract, encourage, or coerce MNEs into undertaking activities that they otherwise would not. For

FIGURE 13.6   HOW INSTITUTIONS AND RESOURCES AFFECT MULTINATIONAL STRATEGY, STRUCTURE, AND LEARNING

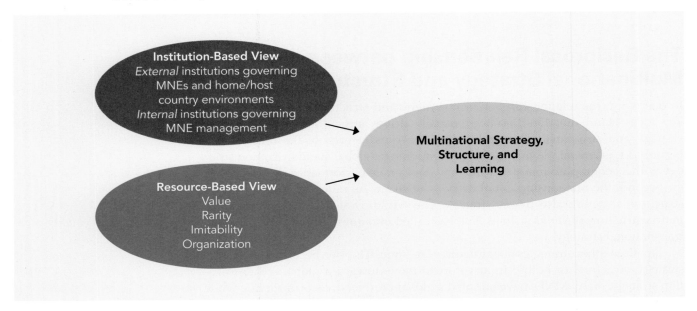

example, basic manufacturing generates low-paying jobs, does not provide sufficient technology spillovers, and carries little prestige. Advanced manufacturing, R&D, and regional headquarters (see the Closing Case), on the other hand, generate better and higher-paying jobs, provide more technology spillovers, and lead to better prestige. Therefore, host-country governments (such as those in China, Hungary, and Singapore) often use a combination of carrots (such as tax incentives and free infrastructure upgrades) and sticks (such as threats to block market access) to attract MNE investments in higher value-added areas. (See Chapter 6.)

In addition to formal institutions, MNEs also confront a series of informal institutions governing their relationships with *home* countries.[17] In the United States, few laws ban MNEs from aggressively setting up overseas subsidiaries, although the issue is a hot button in public debate and is always subject to changes in political policy. However, managers contemplating such moves must consider the informal but vocal backlash against such activities due to the associated losses in domestic jobs.

Dealing with *host* countries also involves numerous informal institutions. For example, Airbus devotes 40% of its procurement budget to US suppliers in more than 40 states. Although there is no formal requirement for Airbus to farm out supply contracts, its sourcing decisions are guided by the informal norm of reciprocity: If one country's suppliers are involved with Airbus, airlines based in that country are more likely to buy Airbus aircraft.

Institutional factors affecting MNEs are not only external. How MNEs are governed *internally* is also determined by various formal and informal rules of the game. Formally, the organizational charts, such as in Figures 13.2–13.5 specify the scope of various parties' responsibilities.[18] Most MNEs have systems of evaluation, reward, and punishment in place based on these formal rules.

What the formal organizational charts do not reveal are the informal rules of the game, such as organizational norms, values, and networks. The nationality of the head of foreign subsidiaries is such an example. Given the lack of formal regulations, MNEs essentially can have three choices:

- a home country national as the head of a subsidiary (such as an American for a subsidiary of a US-headquartered MNE in India)
- a host country national (such as an Indian for the same subsidiary above)
- a third country national (such as an Australian for the same subsidiary above)

MNEs from different countries have different norms when making these appointments. Most Japanese MNEs seem to follow an informal rule: Heads of foreign subsidiaries, at least initially, need to be Japanese nationals.[19] In comparison, European MNEs are more likely to appoint host and third country nationals to lead subsidiaries. As a group, US MNEs are somewhere between Japanese and European practices. These staffing approaches may reflect strategic differences.[20] Home country nationals, especially long-time employees of the same MNE at home, are more likely to have developed a better understanding of the informal workings of the firm and to be better socialized into its dominant norms and values. Consequently, the Japanese propensity to appoint home country nationals is conducive to their preferred global standardization strategy, which values globally coordinated and controlled actions. Conversely, the European comfort in appointing host and third country nationals is indicative of European MNEs' (traditional) preference for a localization strategy. Interestingly, some emerging MNEs from China have chosen to appoint host country nationals to head their first overseas subsidiaries. For example, Pearl River Piano appointed an American executive to be in charge of its first US-based subsidiary (see Chapter 10 Opening Case).

© Manish Swarup

What are some of the challenges faced by non-native top executives, such as Pepsi's CEO Indra K. Nooyi?

Beyond the nationality of subsidiary heads, the nationality of top executives at the highest level (such as chairman, CEO, and board members) seems to follow another informal rule: They are almost always home country nationals. To the extent that top executives are ambassadors of the firm and that the MNE headquarters' country of origin is a source of differentiation (for example, a German MNE is often perceived to be different from an Italian MNE), home country nationals would seem to be the most natural candidates for top positions.

In the eyes of stakeholders such as employees and governments around the world, however, a top echelon consisting of largely one nationality does not bode well for an MNE aspiring to globalize everything it does. Some critics even argue that this "glass ceiling" reflects "corporate imperialism."[21] Consequently, such leading MNEs as Coca-Cola, GSK, Nissan, PepsiCo, and Sony have appointed foreign-born executives to top posts. Such foreign-born bosses bring substantial diversity to the organization, which may be a plus. However, such diversity puts an enormous burden on these non-native top executives to clearly articulate the values and exhibit behaviors expected of senior managers of an MNE associated with a particular country.[22] For example, Procter & Gamble (P&G) appointed Durk Jager, a native of the Netherlands, to be its chairman and CEO in 1999. Unfortunately, Jager's numerous change initiatives almost brought the venerable company to a grinding halt and he was quickly forced to resign in 2000. Since then, the old rule is back: P&G has been led by an American executive (A. G. Lafley between 2000 and 2009 and Robert McDonald since 2009).

Overall, although formal internal rules on how the MNE is governed may reflect conscientious strategic choices, informal internal rules are often taken for granted and deeply embedded in administrative heritages, thus making them difficult to change.

Resource-Based Considerations

Shown in Figure 13.6, the resource-based view—exemplified by the VRIO framework—adds a number of insights. First, when looking at structural changes, it is critical to consider whether a new structure (such as a matrix) adds concrete *value*. The value of innovation must also be considered.[23] A vast majority of innovations simply fail to reach market, and most new products that do reach market end up being financial failures.[24] The difference between an innovator and a *profitable* innovator is that the latter has not only plenty of good ideas but also lots of complementary assets (such as appropriate organizational structures and marketing muscles) to add value to innovation. Philips, for example, is a great innovator. The company invented rotary shavers, video cassettes, and compact discs (CDs). Still, its abilities to profit from these innovations lag behind those of Sony and Matsushita, which have much stronger complementary assets.

A second question is *rarity*. Certain strategies or structures may be in vogue at a given point in time. So, for example, when a company's rivals all move toward a global standardization strategy, this strategy cannot be a source of differentiation. To improve global coordination, many MNEs spend millions of dollars to equip themselves with enterprise resource planning (ERP) packages provided by SAP and Oracle. However, such packages are designed to be implemented widely and appeal to a broad range of firms, thus providing no firm-specific advantage for the adopting firm.

Even when capabilities are valuable and rare, they have to pass a third hurdle, namely, *imitability*. Formal structures are easier to observe and imitate than informal structures. This is one of the reasons why the informal, flexible matrix is in vogue now. The informal, flexible matrix "is less a structural classification than a broad organizational concept or philosophy, manifested in organizational capability and management mentality."[25] Obviously imitating an intangible mentality is much harder (if it is even possible) than imitating a tangible structure.

The last hurdle is *organization*—namely, how MNEs are organized, both formally and informally, around the world. One elusive but important concept is organizational culture. Recall from Chapter 3 that culture is defined by Hofstede as "the collective programming of the mind which distinguishes the members of one group or category of people from another." We can extend this concept to define **organizational culture** as the collective programming of the mind that distinguishes the members of one organization from another. China's Huawei, for example, is known to have a distinctive "wolf" culture, whose core values center on "continuous hunting" and "relentless pursuit" with highly motivated employees who routinely work over time and sleep in their offices. Although rivals can endeavor to imitate everything Huawei does technologically, their biggest hurdle lies in their lack of ability to wrap their arms around Huawei's elusive but important "wolf" culture. As discussed above, if MNEs are able to derive the organizational benefits of the matrix without being burdened by a formal matrix structure (that is, building an informal, flexible, invisible matrix), they are likely to outperform rivals.

WORLDWIDE LEARNING, INNOVATION, AND KNOWLEDGE MANAGEMENT

LEARNING OBJECTIVE 3

Outline the challenges associated with learning, innovation, and knowledge management.

Having outlined how institutions and resources affect multinationals, next let us devote our attention to the crucial issue of learning, innovation, and knowledge management.

Knowledge Management

Underpinning the recent emphasis on worldwide learning and innovation is the emerging interest in knowledge management. **Knowledge management** can be defined as the structures, processes, and systems that actively develop, leverage, and transfer knowledge.[26]

Many managers regard knowledge management as simply information management. Taken to an extreme, "such a perspective can result in a profoundly mistaken belief that the installation of sophisticated information technology (IT) infrastructure is the be-all and end-all of knowledge management."[27] Knowledge management depends not only on IT but also on informal social relationships within the MNE. This is because there are two categories of knowledge: (1) explicit knowledge and (2) tacit knowledge. **Explicit knowledge** is codifiable—it can be written down and transferred with little loss of richness. Virtually all the knowledge captured, stored, and transmitted by IT is explicit. **Tacit knowledge** is non-codifiable, and its acquisition and transfer require hands-on practice.[28] For example, reading a driver's manual (which contains a ton of explicit knowledge) without any road practice does not make you a good driver. Tacit knowledge is evidently more important and harder to transfer and learn; it can only be acquired

Organizational culture
The collective programming of the mind that distinguishes the members of one organization from another.

Knowledge management
The structures, processes, and systems that actively develop, leverage, and transfer knowledge.

Explicit knowledge
Knowledge that is codifiable (can be written down and transferred with little loss of richness).

Tacit knowledge
Knowledge that is non-codifiable, and its acquisition and transfer require hands-on practice.

through learning by doing (driving, in this case). Consequently, from a resource-based view, explicit knowledge captured by IT may be strategically *less* important. What counts is the hard-to-codify and hard-to-transfer tacit knowledge.

Knowledge Management in Four Types of MNEs

Differences in knowledge management among four types of MNEs in Figure 13.1 fundamentally stem from the interdependence (1) between the headquarters and foreign subsidiaries and (2) among various subsidiaries, as illustrated in Table 13.2.[29] In MNEs pursuing a home replication strategy, such interdependence is moderate and the role of subsidiaries is largely to adapt and leverage parent company competencies. Thus, knowledge on new products and technologies is mostly developed at the center and flown to subsidiaries, representing the traditional one-way flow. Starbucks, for example, insists on replicating its US coffee shop concept around the world, down to the elusive "atmosphere."

When MNEs adopt a localization strategy, the interdependence is low. Knowledge management centers on developing insights that can best serve local markets. Ford of Europe used to develop cars for Europe, with a limited flow of knowledge to and from headquarters.

In MNEs pursuing a global standardization strategy, on the other hand, the interdependence is increased. Knowledge is developed and retained at the headquarters and a few centers of excellence. Consequently, knowledge and people flow between headquarters and these centers to other subsidiaries. For example, Yokogawa Hewlett-Packard, HP's subsidiary in Japan, won a coveted Japanese Deming Award for quality. The subsidiary was then charged with transferring such knowledge to the rest of HP, which resulted in a tenfold improvement in *corporate*-wide quality in ten years.[30]

A hallmark of transnational MNEs is a high degree of interdependence and extensive and bidirectional flows of knowledge.[31] For example, Häagen-Dazs developed a popular ice cream in Argentina that was based on a locally popular caramelized milk dessert. The company then took the new flavor and sold it

TABLE 13.2   KNOWLEDGE MANAGEMENT IN FOUR TYPES OF MULTINATIONAL ENTERPRISES

Strategy	Home replication	Localization	Global standardization	Transnational
Interdependence	Moderate	Low	Moderate	High
Role of foreign subsidiaries	Adapting and leveraging parent company competencies	Sensing and exploiting local opportunities	Implementing parent company initiatives	Differentiated contributions by subsidiaries to integrate worldwide operations
Development and diffusion of knowledge	Knowledge developed at the center and transferred to subsidiaries	Knowledge developed and retained within each subsidiary	Knowledge mostly developed and retained at the center and key locations	Knowledge developed jointly and shared worldwide
Flow of knowledge	Extensive flow of knowledge and people from headquarters to subsidiaries	Limited flow of knowledge and people in both directions (to and from the center)	Extensive flow of knowledge and people from center and key locations to subsidiaries	Extensive flow of knowledge and people in multiple directions

Sources: Adapted from (1) C. Bartlett & S. Ghoshal, 1989, *Managing Across Borders: The Transnational Solution* (p. 65), Boston: Harvard Business School Press; (2) T. Kostova & K. Roth, 2003, Social capital in multinational corporations and a micro-macro model of its formation (p. 299), *Academy of Management Review,* 28 (2): 297–317.

as Dulce De Leche throughout the United States and Europe. Within one year, it became the second most popular Häagen-Dazs ice cream, next only to vanilla.[32] Particularly fundamental to transnational MNEs is knowledge flows among dispersed subsidiaries. Instead of a top-down hierarchy, the MNE thus can be conceptualized as an integrated network of subsidiaries. Each subsidiary not only develops locally relevant knowledge but also aspires to contribute knowledge that will enhance *corporate*-wide competitiveness and thus benefit the MNE as a whole.

Globalizing Research and Development

R&D represents an especially crucial arena for knowledge management. Relative to production and marketing, only more recently has R&D emerged as an important function to be internationalized—often known as innovation-seeking investment (see Chapter 10). Intense competition for innovation drives the globalization of R&D.[33] Such R&D provides a way to gain access to a foreign country's local talents and expertise.[34] Recall earlier discussions in Chapters 6 and 10 on the importance of *agglomeration* of high caliber, innovative firms within a country or region. For foreign firms, an effective way to access such a cluster is through FDI—as Shiseido did in France (In Focus 13.1).

Shiseido Smells at Innovations in France

France is the undisputed global innovation leader in perfumes. Blending ancient art with modern R&D, the knowledge about how to make attractive perfumes is tacit and hard to codify. Non-French firms, such as Japan's Shiseido, face the significant challenge of how to access—or "plug into"—and manage such knowledge efficiently. In 1984, Shiseido established its Europe TechnoCentre in France, led by Japanese expatriates, to gather and transfer intelligence for the head office in Japan, which would then process and digest such knowledge. However, Shiseido perfumes developed in Japan initially failed in France.

In 1990, Shiseido realized that to plug into the fragrance knowledge in France, it had to have some of its people work side by side with the French masters of the trade. Consequently, it established a new subsidiary, Beauté Prestige International

© Yoshikazu Tsuno/AFP/Getty Images

(BPI), aiming at the top end of the French market. In a very unusual step for a Japanese MNE, Shiseido hired a reputable French female CEO, who leveraged her social capital to recruit a staff of top notch French perfume developers. Despite some cultural conflicts, the Japanese let the French "run the show" in R&D, whereas Japanese expatriates learned by close observation, interaction, and simply "smelling." Then, Shiseido opened its own plant in Gien in the heart of the French perfume "cluster." In 1992, Shiseido successfully launched two "designer brand" perfumes in France: Eau d'Issey and Jean Paul Gaultier. Since then, Shiseido has transferred such knowledge to Japan and elsewhere. At present, Shiseido is the world's fourth-largest cosmetics firm.

Sources: Based on (1) Y. Doz, J. Santos, & P. Williamson, 2001, *From Global to Metanational* (pp. 66–67), Boston: Harvard Business School Press; (2) www.shiseido-europe.com.

From a resource-based standpoint, a fundamental basis for competitive advantage is innovation-based firm heterogeneity (that is, being different).[35] Decentralized R&D work performed by different locations and teams around the world virtually guarantees that there will be persistent heterogeneity in the solutions generated.[36] Britain's GSK, for example, aggressively spun off R&D units as it became clear that simply adding more researchers in centralized R&D units did not necessarily enhance global learning and innovation. GE's China units have developed low-cost, portable ultrasound machines at a fraction of the cost of existing machines developed in the United States. GE has not only been selling the developed-in-China machines throughout emerging economies, but has also brought them back to the United States and other developed economies, which also benefit tremendously from such low-cost machines (see Chapter 1 Closing Case).

Problems and Solutions in Knowledge Management[37]

Institutionally, how MNEs employ formal and informal "rules of the game" has a significant bearing on the success or failure of knowledge management. Shown in Table 13.3, a number of informal "rules" can become problems in knowledge management. In knowledge acquisition, many MNEs prefer to invent everything internally. However, for large firms, R&D actually has *diminishing* returns.[38] Consequently, a new model, "open innovation," is emerging.[39] It relies on more collaborative research, among various internal units, external firms, and university labs. Evidence shows that firms that skillfully share research (including publishing results in the public domain) outperform those that fail to do so.[40]

In knowledge retention, the usual problem of employee turnover is compounded when exiting employees are key R&D personnel, whose departure will lead to knowledge leakage.[41] Knowledge outflow has a "How does it help me?" syndrome. Specifically, managers of the source subsidiary may view outbound sharing of knowledge as a diversion of scarce time and resources. Further, some managers may believe that "knowledge is power"—monopolizing certain knowledge may be viewed as the currency to acquire and retain power within the MNE.[42]

Even when certain subsidiaries are willing to share knowledge, inappropriate transmission channels may still limit effective knowledge sharing.[43] Given the advancement in IT, it is tempting to establish **global virtual teams**, which do not meet face to face, to transfer knowledge. Unfortunately, such teams often have to confront tremendous communication and relationship barriers.[44] For example, videoconferences can hardly show body language and Skype can be unreliable. As a result, face-to-face meetings are still often necessary.

Global virtual team
A team whose members are physically dispersed in multiple locations in the world and often operate on a virtual basis.

TABLE 13.3   PROBLEMS IN KNOWLEDGE MANAGEMENT

Elements of knowledge management	Common problems
Knowledge acquisition	Failure to share and integrate external knowledge
Knowledge retention	Employee turnover and knowledge leakage
Knowledge outflow	"How does it help me?" syndrome and "knowledge is power" mentality
Knowledge transmission	Inappropriate channels
Knowledge inflow	"Not invented here" syndrome and absorptive capacity

Source: Adapted from A. Gupta & V. Govindarajan, 2004, *Global Strategy and Organization* (p. 109), New York: Wiley.

Finally, recipient subsidiaries may present two problems that block successful knowledge inflows. First, the "not invented here" syndrome causes some managers to resist accepting ideas from other units. Second, recipient subsidiaries may have limited **absorptive capacity**—the "ability to recognize the value of new information, assimilate it, and apply it."[45]

To combat these problems, corporate headquarters can manipulate the formal "rules of the game." For example, headquarters can (1) tie bonuses with measurable knowledge outflows and inflows; (2) use high-powered, corporate-based or business-unit-based incentives (as opposed to individual-based and single-subsidiary-based incentives); and/or (3) invest in codifying tacit knowledge. Siemens has used some of these measures when promoting its knowledge portal, ShareNet. However, these formal policies fundamentally boil down to the very challenging (if not impossible) task of how to accurately measure

© Triangle Images

Describe the various ways global virtual team members can effectively communicate knowledge among themselves.

inflows and outflows of tacit knowledge. The nature of tacit knowledge simply resists such formal bureaucratic practices. Consequently, MNEs often have to rely on a great deal of informal integrating mechanisms, such as facilitating management and R&D personnel networks among various subsidiaries through joint teamwork, training, and conferences and promoting strong organizational (that is, MNE-specific) culture and shared values and norms for cooperation among subsidiaries.[46]

The key idea is that instead of using traditional, formal command-and-control structures that are often ineffective, knowledge management is best facilitated by informal **social capital**, which refers to the informal benefits individuals and organizations derive from their social structures and networks.[47] Social capital motivates colleagues to go out of their way to help friends. Managers of a Chinese subsidiary are more likely to help managers of a Canadian subsidiary with needed knowledge if they know each other and have some social relationship. In contrast, managers of a Chinese subsidiary may not be as eager to help managers at a Chilean subsidiary, with whom they have no social relationship. Overall, the micro, informal interpersonal relationships among managers of various units may greatly facilitate macro, inter-subsidiary cooperation—in short, a **micro-macro link**.[48]

Absorptive capacity

The ability to recognize the value of new information, assimilate it, and apply it.

Social capital

The informal benefits individuals and organizations derive from their social structures and networks.

Micro-macro link

The micro, informal interpersonal relationships among managers of various units that may greatly facilitate macro, inter-subsidiary cooperation among these units.

DEBATES AND EXTENSIONS

The question of how to manage complex MNEs has led to numerous debates, some of which have been discussed earlier (such as the debate on the matrix structure). Here we outline two of the leading debates not previously discussed: (1) corporate controls versus subsidiary initiatives and (2) customer-focused dimensions versus integration, responsiveness, and learning.

LEARNING OBJECTIVE

4

Participate in two leading debates on multinational strategy, structure, and learning.

Corporate Controls versus Subsidiary Initiatives

One of the leading debates on how to manage large firms is whether control should be centralized or decentralized. In an MNE setting, the debate boils down to central controls versus subsidiary initiatives. Subsidiaries are not necessarily receptive to headquarters' commands. When headquarters require that certain practices (such as quality circles) be adopted, some subsidiaries may be in full compliance, others may pay lip service, and still others may simply refuse to adopt the practice, citing local differences.[49]

In addition to reacting to headquarters' demands differently, some subsidiaries may actively pursue their own, *subsidiary*-level strategies and agendas.[50] These activities are known as **subsidiary initiatives**, defined as the proactive and deliberate pursuit of new opportunities by a subsidiary to expand its scope of responsibility.[51] For example, Honeywell Canada requested that it be designated as a global "center for excellence" for certain Honeywell product lines (see In Focus 13.2). Many authors argue that such initiatives may inject a much-needed spirit of entrepreneurship throughout the larger, more bureaucratic corporation.

From corporate headquarters' perspective, however, it is hard to distinguish between good-faith subsidiary initiative and opportunistic empire-building on the part of subsidiary managers. Much is at stake when determining whether subsidiaries should be named "centers of excellence" with worldwide mandates. Subsidiaries that fail to attain this status may see their roles marginalized or, worse, their facilities closed. Subsidiary managers are often host country nationals (such as the Canadian managers at Honeywell Canada) who would naturally prefer to strengthen their subsidiary, if only to protect local (and their own!) employment and not necessarily to be patriotic. However natural and legitimate these

Subsidiary initiative
The proactive and deliberate pursuit of new opportunities by a subsidiary to expand its scope of responsibility.

IN Focus 13.2

A Subsidiary Initiative at Honeywell Canada

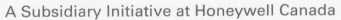

Honeywell Limited is a wholly owned Canadian subsidiary—hereafter "Honeywell Canada"—of the Minneapolis-based Honeywell, Inc. Until the mid-1980s, Honeywell Canada was a traditional branch plant that mainly produced for the Canadian market in volumes approximately one-tenth of those of the main manufacturing operations in Minneapolis. By the late 1980s, the winds of change unleashed by the US-Canadian Free Trade Agreement (later to become NAFTA in the 1990s) threatened the very survival of Honeywell Canada, whose relatively inefficient (sub-optimal scale) operations could face closure when the high tariffs came down and made-in-USA products could enter Canada duty-free. Canadian managers in the subsidiary entrepreneurially proposed to the headquarters that their plant be given the mandate to produce certain relatively more efficient product lines for all of North America. In exchange, they agreed to shut down some inefficient lines. Although some

US managers were understandably negative, the head of the homes division was open-minded. Negotiations followed and the Canadian proposal was eventually adopted. Consequently, Honeywell Canada was designated as a Honeywell "Center of Excellence" for valves and actuators. At present, Honeywell Canada is Canada's leading controls company.

Although this is a successful case of subsidiary initiative, a potential ethical problem is that from a corporate headquarters' standpoint, it is often difficult to ascertain whether the subsidiary is making good-faith efforts acting in the best interest of the MNE or the subsidiary managers are primarily promoting their self-interest such as power, prestige, and their own jobs. How corporate headquarters can differentiate good-faith efforts from more opportunistic maneuvers remains a challenge.

Sources: Based on (1) J. Birkinshaw, 2000, *Entrepreneurship in the Global Firm* (p. 26), London: Sage; (2) www.honeywell.ca; (3) www.honeywell.com.

tendencies are, they are not necessarily consistent with the MNE's *corporate*-wide goals. These tendencies, if not checked and controlled, can surely lead to chaos for the MNE as a whole.

Customer-Focused Dimensions versus Integration, Responsiveness, and Learning[52]

As discussed earlier, juggling integration, responsiveness, and learning has often made the global matrix structure so complex that it is unworkable. However, instead of simplifying, many MNEs have added new dimensions that make their structure even *more* complex. Often, new, customer-focused dimensions of structure are placed on top of an existing structure, resulting in a four- or five-dimension matrix.

There are two primary customer-focused dimensions. The first is a **global account structure** to supply customers (often other MNEs) in a coordinated and consistent way across various countries. The structure is used by most original equipment manufacturers (OEMs)—namely, contract manufacturers that produce goods *not* carrying their own brands, such as the makers of Nike shoes and Microsoft's Xbox. Singapore's Flextronics, the world's largest electronics OEM, has dedicated global accounts for Dell, Palm, and Sony Ericsson. Second, a **solutions-based structure** is often used. As a "customer solution" provider, IBM will sell whatever combination of hardware, software, and services that customers prefer, whether that means selling IBM's or rivals' products.

The typical starting point is to put informal or temporary solutions in place rather than create new layers or units. However, this ad hoc approach can quickly get out of control with subsidiary managers reporting to three or four "informal bosses" (global account managers) on top of doing their "day jobs." Eventually, new formal structures may be called for, resulting in inevitable bureaucracy. One solution is to *simplify*. For instance, ABB, when facing grave performance problems, transformed its sprawling "Byzantine" matrix structure to a mere two global product divisions—power technology and automation.

MANAGEMENT SAVVY

MNEs are the ultimate large, complex, and geographically dispersed business organizations. What determines the success or failure of multinational strategies, structures, and learning? The answer boils down to the institution-based and resource-based dimensions. The institution-based view calls for thorough understanding and skillful manipulation of the rules of the game, both at home and abroad. The resource-based view focuses on the development and deployment of firm-specific capabilities to enhance the odds for success.

Consequently, three clear implications emerge for savvy managers, listed in Table 13.4. First, understanding and mastering the external rules of the game governing MNEs and home/host country environments become a must. For example, some MNEs take advantage of the rules that subsidiaries in different countries need to be registered as independent legal entities in these countries, and claim that other subsidiaries do not have to be responsible for the wrongdoing of another subsidiary in another country (see In Focus 13.3). Other MNEs abandon their original countries of origin and move their headquarters to be governed by more market-friendly and politically stable laws and regulations in their new countries of domicile (see the Closing Case).

Draw implications for action.

Global account structure

A customer-focused dimension that supplies customers (often other MNEs) in a coordinated and consistent way across various countries.

Solutions-based structure

A customer-focused solution in which a provider sells whatever combination of goods and services the customers prefer, including rivals' offerings.

TABLE 13.4 IMPLICATIONS FOR ACTION

- Understand and master the external rules of the game governing MNEs and home/host country environments

- Understand and be prepared to change the internal rules of the game governing MNE management

- Develop learning and innovation capabilities to leverage multinational presence as an asset—"think global, act local"

IN Focus 13.3

ETHICAL DILEMMA

One Multinational versus Many National Companies

We often treat each MNE as one firm, regardless of how many countries it operates in. However, from an institution-based standpoint, one can argue that a *multinational* enterprise may be a total fiction that does not exist. This is because, legally, incorporation is only possible under national law, so every so-called MNE is essentially a bunch of *national* companies (subsidiaries) registered in various countries. Although some pundits argue that globalization is undermining the power of national governments, there is little evidence that the modern nation-state system, in existence since the 1648 Treaty of Westphalia, is retreating.

This debate is not just academic hair-splitting. It is very relevant and stakes are high. One case in point is the bankruptcy of General Motors (GM). Although the US and Canadian governments bailed out GM by taking over 61% and 8% of its equity, respectively, they technically only bailed out GM's North American operations. GM could not use US and Canadian taxpayer dollars to fund overseas operations. As a result, GM's Opel subsidiary based in Germany had to be rescued by the German government, creating a major political firestorm (see Chapter 6 Closing Case).

Another case in point is brought by Indian firm Satyam's recent scandal (see In Focus 16.2). PricewaterhouseCooper (PwC) endorsed Satyam's books even though $1 billion cash did not exist at all. Although such sloppy auditing was done by PwC India, some Satyam shareholders have filed suits against PwC International Limited headquartered in New York. But a PwC International spokesman argued in interviews that "there is no such a thing as a global firm because we are a membership organization." That is to say: PwC India, registered in India, is a legally independent firm whose conduct has nothing to do with other nationally registered firms such as PwC International or PwC Hong Kong. On PwC India's website, it is noted that PwC "refers to the network of member firms of PricewaterhouseCoopers International Limited, each of which is a separate and independent legal entity." Whether such a defense can repel legal challenges remains to be seen in court battles.

Sources: Based on (1) *BusinessWeek*, 2009, For accounting giants, nowhere to hide? February 16: 56–57; (2) S. Kobrin, 2009, Sovereignty@ bay, in A. Rugman (ed.), *The Oxford Handbook of International Business* (pp. 183–204), New York: Oxford University Press; (3) www.pwc.com/in/en/index.jhtml.

Second, managers need to understand and be prepared to change the internal rules of the game governing MNE management. Different strategies and structures call for different internal rules. Some facilitate and others constrain MNE actions. A firm using a home replication strategy should not look to hire a foreigner as its CEO. Yet, as an MNE becomes more global in its operations, its managerial outlook needs to be broadened as well.

Finally, managers need to actively develop learning and innovation capabilities to leverage multinational presence. A winning formula is: *Think global, act local.* Failing to do so may be costly. From 1999 until 2000, Ford Explorer SUVs were involved in numerous fatal rollover accidents in the United States. Most of these accidents were blamed on faulty tires made by Japan's Bridgestone and its US subsidiary Firestone. However, before the increase in US accidents, an alarming number of similar accidents had already taken place in warmer weather countries such as Brazil and Saudi Arabia—tires wear out faster in warmer weather. Local Firestone managers dutifully reported the accidents to headquarters in Japan and the United States. Unfortunately, these reports were dismissed by the higher-up as due to driver error or road conditions. Bridgestone/Firestone thus failed to leverage its multinational presence as an asset. It should have learned from these reports and proactively probed into the potential for similar accidents in cooler weather countries. In the end, lives were lost unnecessarily, and informed car buyers abandoned the Bridgestone/Firestone brand.

CHAPTER SUMMARY

1. Describe the relationship between multinational strategy and structure.
   - Governing multinational strategy and structure is an integration-responsiveness framework.
   - There are four strategy/structure pairs: (1) home replication strategy/international division structure, (2) localization strategy/geographic area structure, (3) global standardization strategy/global product division structure, and (4) transnational strategy/global matrix structure.

2. Explain how institutions and resources affect strategy, structure, and learning.
   - MNEs are governed by external and internal rules of the game around the world.
   - Management of MNE strategy, structure, and learning needs to take into account VRIO.

3. Outline the challenges associated with learning, innovation, and knowledge management.
   - Knowledge management primarily focuses on tacit knowledge.
   - Globalization of R&D calls for capabilities to combat a number of problems associated with knowledge creation, retention, outflow, transmission, and inflow.

4. Participate in two leading debates on multinational strategy, structure, and learning.
   - (1) Corporate controls versus subsidiary initiatives and (2) customer-focused dimensions versus integration, responsiveness, and learning.

5. Draw implications for action.
   - Understand and master the external rules of the game from home/host country environments.
   - Understand and be prepared to change the internal rules of the game governing MNEs.
   - Develop learning and innovation capabilities around the world—"think global, act local."

KEY TERMS

Absorptive capacity   429

Center of excellence   417

Country (regional)
   manager   419

Explicit knowledge   425

Geographic area
   structure   419

Global account
   structure   431

Global matrix   419

Global product division
   structure   419

Global standardization
   strategy   417

Global virtual team   428

Home replication
   strategy   415

Integration-responsiveness
   framework   415

International
   division   418

Knowledge
   management   425

Local responsiveness   415

Localization (multi-
   domestic) strategy   417

Micro-macro link   429

Organizational culture   425

Social capital   429

Solutions-based
   structure   431

Subsidiary initiative   430

Tacit knowledge   425

Transnational strategy   418

Worldwide (global)
   mandate   417

REVIEW QUESTIONS

1. The pressure to reduce costs is common to both domestic and international competition, but what additional kind of pressure is unique to international competition?

2. Referring to Figure 13.1, describe the four strategic choices and the four corresponding organizational structures in the integration-responsiveness framework.

3. What are three key lessons derived from understanding the reciprocal nature of the relationship between strategy and structure?

4. List three examples of how formal and informal external institutions affect MNEs.

5. Describe some of the informal rules of the game that govern what type of individual an MNE can appoint to be the head of a foreign subsidiary.

6. Summarize the insights revealed by using a VRIO framework to analyze a potential structural change.

7. How would you characterize the two types of knowledge found in an MNE?

8. How is knowledge developed and disseminated in each of the four types of MNEs?

9. What are some of the problems inherent in the functioning of a global virtual team?

10. What are some of the actions that MNEs can take to combat common problems in knowledge management?

11. Which do you think would be more integral to a firm's success: corporate controls or subsidiary-level strategies and agendas?

12. Describe the two primary customer-focused dimensions that many MNEs add to their global matrix structures.

13. From time to time, a manager may be faced with the need to change the internal rules of the game within his or her MNE. What skills and capabilities might be useful in achieving this?

14. What is your interpretation of the phrase "Think global, act local"?

15. Suppose a firm is primarily an importer. After reviewing PengAtlas Map 2.1, in your opinion, what form of organizational structure covered in this chapter would be most useful? Why?

16. Suppose a firm is primarily an exporter. After reviewing PengAtlas Map 2.1, in your opinion, what form of organizational structure covered in this chapter would be most useful? Why?

CRITICAL DISCUSSION QUESTIONS

1. In this age of globalization, some gurus argue that all industries are becoming global and that all firms need to adopt a global standardization strategy. Do you agree? Why or why not?

2. *ON ETHICS:* You are the manager of the best-performing subsidiary in an MNE. Because bonuses are tied to subsidiary performance, your bonus is the highest among managers of all subsidiaries. Now headquarters is organizing managers from other subsidiaries to visit and learn from your subsidiary. You are worried that if performance at other subsidiaries improves, then your subsidiary will no longer be a star unit and your bonus will go down. What are you going to do?

3. *ON ETHICS:* You are a corporate R&D manager at Boeing and are considering to transfer some R&D work to China, India, and Russia, where the work performed by a US engineer making $70,000 a year can be done by an equally capable engineer making less than $7,000 per year. However, US engineers at Boeing have staged protests against such moves. US politicians are similarly vocal concerning job losses and national security hazards. What are you going to do?

YOUR SOURCE FOR
**global business
knowledge**

http://globalEDGE.msu.edu

GLOBAL ACTION

1. Currently, considerable growth has been documented in Latin American and Caribbean economies. Based on the specific regulations in each country, part of your company's strategy in the Western Hemisphere is to ensure that contracts made by the firm are agreed to and abided by in all business dealings. Since your company has sales offices in every Latin American and Caribbean economy, where should your company focus first? Provide detailed justification for your choices using globalEDGE resources.

2. To remain competitive, a steel company needs to reconfigure its operations to align with worldwide production. As a consultant on world steel production, use globalEDGE to provide a report that indicates appropriate personnel and resource allocation to each region of the world. As a part of your analysis, be sure to include your analysis for specific countries in which your client should maintain regional headquarters.

VIDEO CASES

Watch "Freedom to Plan" by Phillip Kotler of Kellogg School of Management, Northwestern University.

1. Kotler discussed a plea by a district manager for IBM who was concerned about his Chicago market. On a global basis, which strategic response would best relate to his plea? Why might the ability to apply that response internationally be different than domestically?

2. Do you agree with Kotler's assertion that "all markets are local"? Why?

3. The district manager wanted to be able to run his part of the company as a business. Obviously he was already running part of a business, so what did he mean by that?

4. Do you agree with the assertion that corporate headquarters cannot have the same feel for opportunity as those at the local level? Given a firm's limited resources and given the possibility that all local managers may see an opportunity for the company (or an opportunity to build their own empires), how should headquarters determine which local manager has the best feel for opportunity?

5. Accountability was stressed as key in granting greater autonomy to local managers who are willing to go out on a limb. However, remember that such managers are not only going out on a limb with their careers, but also with the firm's resources. How would you implement such autonomy in a way that would limit the risks to the firm?

Closing Case

Moving Headquarters Overseas

Although many MNEs have been moving operations around the world, a small number of them have also moved headquarters (HQ) overseas. In general, there are two levels of HQ: *business unit* HQ and *corporate* HQ. At the business unit level, examples are numerous. In 2004, Nokia moved its corporate finance HQ from Helsinki, Finland, to New York. In 2006, IBM's global procurement office moved from New York to Shenzhen, China. Examples for corporate HQ relocations are fewer, but they tend to be of higher profile. In 1981, Tetra Pak, the pioneer of soft packaging for beverages, moved corporate HQ from Sweden to Switzerland. In 1992, HSBC moved corporate HQ from Hong Kong to London. Similarly, Anglo American, Old Mutual, and SAB (later to become SABMiller after acquiring Miller Beer) moved from South Africa to London. In 2004, News Corporation moved corporate HQ from Melbourne, Australia, to New York. In 2005, Lenovo set up corporate HQ in Raleigh, North Carolina, home of IBM's former PC division that Lenovo acquired. The question is: Why?

If you have moved from one house to another in the same city, you can easily appreciate the logistical challenges (and nightmares!) associated with relocating HQ overseas. A simple answer is that the benefits of such moves must significantly outweigh their drawbacks. At the business unit level, the answer is straightforward: the "center of gravity" of the activities of a business unit may pull its HQ toward a host country. See the following

© AP Photo/Sang Tan

letter to suppliers from IBM's chief procurement officer informing them of the move to China:

> IBM Global Procurement is taking a major step toward developing a more geographically distributed executive structure . . . By anchoring the organization in this location, we will be better positioned to continue developing the skills and talents of our internal organization in the region . . . Clearly, this places us closer to the core of the technology supply chain which is important, not only for IBM's own internal needs, but increasingly for the needs of external clients whose supply chains we are managing via our Procurement Services offering. As IBM's business offerings continue to grow, we must develop a deeper supply chain in the region to provide services and human resource skills to clients both within Asia and around the world.

At the corporate level, there are at least five strategic rationales. First, a leading symbolic value is an unambiguous statement to various stakeholders that the firm is a global—rather than domestic or local—player. News Corporation's corporate HQ relocation to New York is indicative of its global status, as opposed to being a relatively parochial firm from "down under." Lenovo's coming of age as a global player is no doubt underpinned by the establishment of its worldwide HQ in the United States.

Second, there may be significant efficiency gains. If the new corporate HQ is in a major financial center such as New York or London, the MNE can have more efficient, more direct, and more frequent communication with institutional shareholders, financial analysts, and investment banks. The MNE also increases its visibility in a financial market, resulting in a broader shareholder base and greater market capitalization. As a result, three leading (former) South African firms, Anglo American, Old Mutual, and SABMiller, have now joined FTSE 100—the top 100 UK-listed firms by capitalization.

Third, firms may benefit from their visible commitment to the laws of the new host country. By making such a commitment, firms benefit from the higher-quality legal and regulatory regime they now operate under. These benefits are especially crucial for firms from emerging economies where local rules are not world-class. A lack of confidence about South Africa's political stability drove Anglo American, Old Mutual, and SABMiller to London. By coming to London, HSBC likewise deviated from its Hong Kong roots at a time before the 1997 handover when the political future of Hong Kong was uncertain.

Fourth, moving corporate HQ to a new country clearly indicates a commitment to that country's market. In addition to political motivation, HSBC's move to London signaled its determination to become a more global player, instead of being a regional player centered on Asia. HSBC indeed carried out this more global strategy since the 1990s. However, in an interesting twist of events, HSBC's CEO and the principal office of the CEO will relocate back to Hong Kong in February 2010. Technically, HSBC's corporate headquarters is still in London, and it will remain domiciled in the UK for registration and tax purposes. Its chairman and two executive directors will remain in London. However, the symbolism of the CEO's return to Hong Kong is clear. As China and Asia become more economically powerful, HSBC is interested in demonstrating its commitment to that part of the world, which was where HSBC started (HSBC was set up in Hong Kong in 1865 as Hongkong and Shanghai Banking Corporation).

Finally, by moving (or threatening to move) HQ locations, firms enhance their bargaining power vis-à-vis that of their (original) home country governments. Tetra Pak's move of its corporate HQ to Switzerland was driven primarily by the owners' tax disputes with the Swedish government. A few years ago, Seagate Technology, formerly registered in Silicon Valley, changed its incorporation to Cayman Islands in search of lower taxes. More US firms may follow this move. Having already paid overseas taxes, US-based MNEs naturally resented the Obama administration's proposal to force them to pay $190 billion extra in US taxes. "Doesn't the Obama Administration recognize that most big US companies are multinationals that happen to be headquartered in the United States?" asked Duncan Niederauer, CEO of NYSE Euronext in a *BusinessWeek* interview. The message is clear: If the home country government treats us harshly, we will pack our bags.

The last point, of course, is where the ethical and social responsibility controversies erupt. Relatively small Western economies, such as Sweden, the Netherlands, and Canada, run the risk of losing a number of their leading firms once they "make it." Although the absolute number of jobs lost is not great, these are high-quality (and high-paying) jobs that every government would prefer to keep. More alarmingly, if a sufficient number of HQs move overseas, there is a serious ramification that other high-quality service providers, such as lawyers, bankers, and accountants, will follow them. In response, proposals are floating to offer tax incentives for these "footloose" MNEs to keep HQ at home. However, critics question why these wealthy MNEs (and executives) need to be subsidized (or bribed), whereas many other sectors and individuals are struggling.

Case Discussion Questions:

1. What are the drawbacks and benefits associated with moving business unit and corporate HQ to another country?
2. If you were a CEO or a business unit head, under what conditions would you consider moving HQ?
3. If you were a government official in the MNE's home country, what can you do to discourage such moves of multinational HQ out of the country?

Sources: Based on (1) J. Birkinshaw, P. Braunerhjelm, U. Holm, & S. Terjesen, 2006, Why do some multinational corporations relocate their headquarters overseas? *Strategic Management Journal*, 27: 681–700; (2) *BusinessWeek*, 2009, NYSE chief Duncan Niederauer on Obama and business, June 8: 15–16; (3) IBM, 2006, IBM Procurement headquarters moves to Shenzhen, China, May 22, www-03.ibm.com; (4) *Wall Street Journal*, 2009, HSBC re-emphasizes its "H," September 26, www.wsj.com.

NOTES

[Journal acronyms] **AME**—*Academy of Management Executive*; **AMJ**—*Academy of Management Journal*; **AMR**—*Academy of Management Review*; **APJM**—*Asia Pacific Journal of Management*; **ASQ**—*Administrative Science Quarterly*; **BW**—*BusinessWeek*; **HBR**—*Harvard Business Review*; **JIBS**—*Journal of International Business Studies*; **JIM**—*Journal of International Management*; **JMS**—*Journal of Management Studies*; **JWB**—*Journal of World Business*; **MIR**—*Management International Review*; **OSc**—*Organization Science*; **SMJ**—*Strategic Management Journal*

[1] C. K. Prahalad & Y. Doz, 1987, *The Multinational Mission*, New York: Free Press; J. Stopford & L. Wells, 1972, *Managing the Multinational Enterprise*, New York: Basic Books.

[2] T. Levitt, 1983, The globalization of markets, *HBR*, May–June: 92–102.

[3] A. Harzing, 2000, An empirical analysis and extension of the Bartlett and Ghoshal typology of MNCs, *JIBS*, 31: 101–120.

[4] T. Frost, J. Birkinshaw, & P. Ensign, 2002, Centers of excellence in MNCs (p. 997), *SMJ*, 23: 997–1018.

[5] J. Barbe & R. Richter, 2009, Causal analysis of the internationalization and performance relationship based on neural networks, *JIM*, 15: 413–431; C. Bartlett & S. Ghoshal, 1989, *Managing Across Borders*, Boston: Harvard Business School Press.

[6] B. Ambos & B. Schlegelmilch, 2007, Innovation and control in the multinational firm, *SMJ*, 28: 473–486; N. Anand, H. Gardner, & T. Orris, 2007, Knowledge-based innovation, *AMJ*, 50: 406–428; H. Berry, 2006, Leaders, laggards, and the pursuit of foreign knowledge, *SMJ*, 27: 151–168; W. Chen & K. Miller, 2007, Situational and institutional determinants of firm's R&D search intensity, *SMJ*, 28: 369–381.

[7] J. Cantwell & R. Mudambi, 2005, MNE competence-creating subsidiary mandates, *SMJ*, 26: 1109–1128; K. Ruckman, 2005, Technology sourcing through acquisitions, *JIBS*, 36: 89–103.

[8] *BW*, 2009, Kia Motors: Still cheap, now chic, June 1: 58.

[9] Y. Ling, S. Floyd, & D. Baldrige, 2005, Toward a model of issue-selling by subsidiary managers in MNCs, *JIBS*, 36: 637–654.

[10] R. Edwards, A. Ahmad, & S. Ross, 2002, Subsidiary autonomy, *JIBS*, 33: 183–191.

[11] T. Devinney, D. Midgley, & S. Venaik, 2000, The optimal performance of the global firm, *OSc*, 11: 674–695; J. Johnson, 1995, An empirical analysis of the integration-responsiveness framework, *JIBS*, 26: 621–635.

[12] R. Hodgetts, 1999, Dow Chemical CEO William Stavropoulos on structure (p. 30), *AME*, 13: 29–35.

[13] J. Galan & M. Sanchez-Bueno, 2009, The continuing validity of the strategy-structure nexus, *SMJ*, 1234–1243; W. C. Kim & R. Mauborgne, 2009, How strategy shapes structure, *HBR*, September: 73–80; J. Wolf & W. Egelhoff, 2002, A reexamination and extension of international strategy-structure theory, *SMJ*, 23: 181–189.

[14] G. Benito, B. Grogaard, & R. Narula, 2003, Environmental influences on MNE subsidiary roles, *JIBS*, 34: 443–456; S. Venaik, D. Midgley, & T. Devinney, 2005, Dual paths to performance,

JIBS, 36: 655–675; R. Whitley, G. Morgan, W. Kelley, & D. Sharpe, 2003, The changing Japanese multinational, *JMS*, 40: 643–672.

[15] X. Ma & A. Delios, 2010, Home country headquarters and an MNE's subsequent within-country diversification, *JIBS* (in press).

[16] *BW*, 2008, Cisco's brave new world, November 24: 56–66.

[17] T. Kostova & S. Zaheer, 1999, Organizational legitimacy under conditions of complexity, *AMR*, 24: 64–81; J. Laurila & M. Ropponen, 2003, Institutional conditioning of foreign expansion, *JMS*, 40: 725–751.

[18] W. Sine, H. Mitsuhashi, & D. Kirsch, 2006, Revisiting Burns and Stalker, *AMJ*, 49: 121–132.

[19] R. Belderbos & M. Heijltjes, 2005, The determinants of expatriate staffing by Japanese multinationals in Asia, *JIBS*, 36: 341–354.

[20] Y. Paik & J. Sohn, 2004, Expatriate managers and MNCs' ability to control international subsidiaries, *JWB*, 39: 61–71.

[21] C. K. Prahalad & K. Lieberthal, 1998, The end of corporate imperialism, *HBR*, 76 (4): 68–79.

[22] O. Richard, T. Barnett, S. Dwyer, & K. Chadwick, 2004, Cultural diversity in management, firm performance, and the moderating role of entrepreneurial orientation, *AMJ*, 47: 227–240.

[23] R. Durand, O. Bruiyaka, & V. Mangematin, 2008, Do science and money go together? *SMJ*, 29: 1281–1299; K. Ojah & L. Monplaisir, 2003, Investors' valuation of global product R&D, *JIBS*, 34: 457–472.

[24] F. Damanpour, R. Walker, & C. Avellaneda, 2009, Combinative effects of innovation types and organizational performance, *JMS*, 46: 650–674; G. Markman, P. Gianiodis, & P. Phan, 2009, Supply-side innovation and technology commercialization, *JMS*, 46: 625–648.

[25] Bartlett & Ghoshal, 1989, *Managing Across Borders* (p. 209).

[26] N. Foss & T. Pedersen, 2005, Organizing knowledge processes in the MNC, *JIBS*, 35: 340–349; A. Leiponen, 2008, Control of intellectual assets in client relationships, *SMJ*, 29: 1371–1394; G. Szulanski & R. Jensen, 2006, Presumptive adaptation and the effectiveness of knowledge transfer, *SMJ*, 27: 937–957.

[27] A. Gupta & V. Govindarajan, 2004, *Global Strategy and Organization* (p. 104), New York: Wiley.

[28] R. Coff, D. Coff, & R. Eastvold, 2006, The knowledge-leveraging paradox, *AMR*, 31: 452–465; T. Felin & W. Hesterly, 2007, The knowledge-based view, *AMR*, 32: 195–218; X. Martin & R. Salomon, 2003, Knowledge transfer capacity and its implications for the theory of the MNE, *JIBS*, 34: 356–373.

[29] K. Hewett, M. Roth, & K. Roth, 2003, Conditions influencing headquarters and foreign subsidiary roles in marketing activities and their effects on performance, *JIBS*, 34: 567–585; M. Kotabe, D. Dunlap-Hinkler, R. Parente, & H. Mishra, 2007, Determinants of cross-national knowledge transfer and its effect on firm innovation, *JIBS*, 38: 259–282; Y. Luo & H. Zhao, 2004, Corporate link and competitive strategy in MNEs, *JIM*, 10: 77–105.

[30] M. Porter, H. Takeuchi, & M. Sakakibara, 2000, *Can Japan Compete?* (p. 80), Cambridge, MA: Perseus.

[31] T. Frost & C. Zhou, 2005, R&D co-practice and "reverse" knowledge integration in MNCs, *JIBS*, 36: 676–687; Y. Luo & M. W. Peng, 1999, Learning to compete in a transition economy, *JIBS*, 30: 269–296.

[32] Y. Doz, J. Santos, & P. Williamson, 2001, *From Global to Metanational*, Boston: Harvard Business School Press.

[33] K. Asakawa & M. Lehrer, 2003, Managing local knowledge assets globally, *JWB*, 38: 31–42; R. Belderbos, 2003, Entry mode, organizational learning, and R&D in foreign affiliates, *SMJ*, 24: 235–255.

[34] M. W. Peng & D. Wang, 2000, Innovation capability and foreign direct investment, *MIR*, 40: 79–83; J. Penner-Hahn & J. M. Shaver, 2005, Does international R&D increase patent output? *SMJ*, 26: 121–140.

[35] G. Vegt, E. Vliert, & X. Huang, 2005, Location-level links between diversity and innovative climate depend on national power distance, *AMJ*, 48: 1171–1182; G. Verona, 1999, A resource-based view of product development, *AMR*, 24: 132–142.

[36] P. Bierly, F. Damanpour, & M. Santoro, 2009, The application of external knowledge, *JMS*, 46: 481–508; F. Sanna-Randaccio & R. Veugelers, 2007, Multinational knowledge spillovers with decentralized R&D, *JIBS*, 38: 47–63; J. Zhao & J. Anand, 2009, A multilevel perspective on knowledge transfer, *SMJ*, 30: 959–983.

[37] This section draws heavily from Gupta & Govindarajan, 2004, *Global Strategy and Organization*.

[38] H. Greve, 2003, A behavioral theory of R&D expenditures and innovations, *AMJ*, 46: 685–702.

[39] Y.-S. Su, E. Tsang, & M. W. Peng, 2009, How do internal capabilities and external partnerships affect innovativeness? *APJM*, 26: 309–331.

[40] K. Laursen & A. Salter, 2006. Open for innovation, *SMJ*, 27: 131–150; J. Spencer, 2003, Firms' knowledge-sharing strategies in the global innovation system, *SMJ*, 24: 217–233.

[41] Q. Yang & C. Jiang, 2007, Location advantages and subsidiaries' R&D activities, *APJM*, 24: 341–358.

[42] I. Bjorkman, W. Barner-Rasmussen, & L. Li, 2004, Managing knowledge transfer in MNCs, *JIBS*, 35: 443–455; R. Mudambi & P. Navarra, 2004, Is knowledge power? *JIBS*, 35: 385–406.

[43] G. Szulanski & R. Jensen, 2006, Presumptive adaptation and the effectiveness of knowledge transfer, *SMJ*, 27: 937–957.

[44] J. Salk & M. Brannen, 2000, National culture, networks, and individual performance in a multinational management team, *AMJ*, 43: 191–202; D. Schweiger, T. Atamer, & R. Calori, 2003, Transnational project teams and networks, *JWB*, 38: 127–140; M. Zellmer-Bruhn & C. Gibson, 2006, Multinational organization context, *AMJ*, 49: 501–518.

[45] W. Cohen & D. Levinthal, 1990, Absorptive capacity, *ASQ*, 35: 128–152; J. Hong, R. Snell, & M. Easterby-Smith, 2006, Cross-cultural influences on organizational learning in MNCs, *JIM*, 12: 408–429; J. Jansen, F. Bosch, & H. Volberda, 2005, Managing potential and realized absorptive capacity, *AMJ*, 48: 999–1015; P. Lane, B. Koka, & S. Pathak, 2006, The reification of absorptive capacity, *AMR*, 31: 833–863; D. Minbaeva, T. Pedersen, I. Bjorkman, C. Fey, & H. Park, 2003, MNC knowledge transfer, subsidiary absorptive capacity, and HRM, *JIBS*, 34: 586–599.

[46] T. Ambos & B. Ambos, 2009, The impact of distance on knowledge transfer effectiveness in MNCs, *JIM*, 15: 1–14; D. Gnyawali, M. Singal, & S. Mu, 2009, Knowledge ties among subsidiaries in MNC, *JIM*, 15: 387–400; S. O'Donnell, 2000, Managing foreign subsidiaries, *SMJ*, 21: 525–548; N. Noorderhaven & A. Harzing, 2009, Knowledge-sharing and social interaction within MNEs, *JIBS*, 40: 719–741.

[47] A. Bjorkman & R. Piekkari, 2009, Language and foreign subsidiary control, *JIM*, 15: 105–117; A. Dinur, R. Hamilton, & A. Inkpen, 2009, Critical context and international intrafirm best-practice transfers, *JIM*, 15: 432–446; A. Inkpen & E. Tsang, 2005, Social capital, networks, and knowledge transfer, *AMR*, 30: 146–165; R. Teigland & M. Wasko, 2009, Knowledge transfer in MNCs, *JIM*, 15: 15–31.

[48] M. W. Peng & Y. Luo, 2000, Managerial ties and firm performance in a transition economy, *AMJ*, 43: 486–501.

[49] R. Edwards, A. Ahmad, & S. Moss, 2002, Subsidiary autonomy, *JIBS*, 33: 183–192; T. Kostova & K. Roth, 2002, Adoption of an organizational practice by subsidiaries of multinational corporations, *AMJ*, 45: 215–233.

[50] B. Allred & K. S. Swan, 2004, Contextual influences on international subsidiaries' product technology strategy, *JIM*, 10: 259–286; C. Garcia-Pont, J. Canales, & F. Noboa, 2009, Subsidiary strategy, *JMS*, 46: 182–214; C. Williams, 2009, Subsidiary-level determinants of global initiatives in MNCs, *JIM*, 15: 92–104; Y. Wang & C. Suh, 2009, Towards a re-conceptualization of firm internationalization, *JIM*, 15: 447–459.

[51] J. Birkinshaw, 2000, *Entrepreneurship in the Global Firm* (p. 8), London: Sage.

[52] J. Birkinshaw & S. Terjesen, 2003, The customer-focused multinational, in J. Birkinshaw, S. Ghoshal, C. Markides, J. Stopford, & G. Yip (eds.), 2003, *The Future of the Multinational Company* (pp. 115–127), London: Wiley. See also S. Segal-Horn & A. Dean, 2009, Delivering "effortless" experience across borders, *JWB*, 44: 41–50.

pengatlas Part 3

MAP 3.1   EASE OF DOING BUSINESS: TOP TEN AND BOTTOM TEN

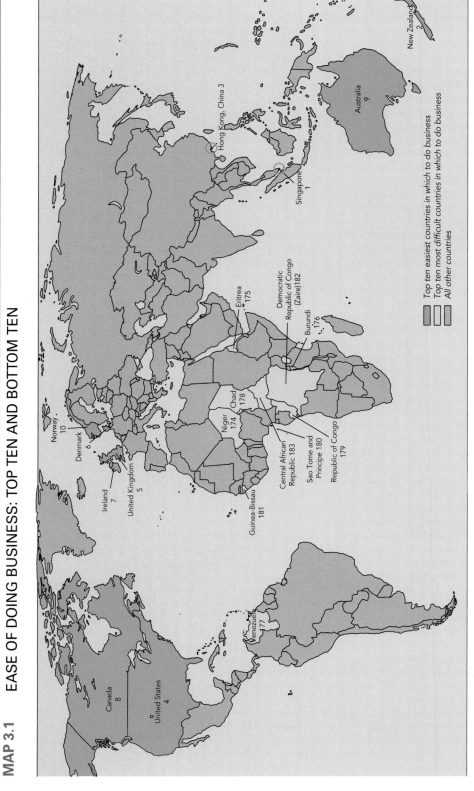

Norway 10

Denmark 6

Ireland 7

United Kingdom 5

Canada 8

United States 4

Hong Kong, China 3

Singapore 1

Australia 9

New Zealand

Eritrea 175

Democratic Republic of Congo (Zaire) 182

Burundi 176

Chad 178

Niger 174

Central African Republic 183

Sao Tome and Principe 180

Republic of Congo 179

Guinea-Bissau 181

Venezuela 177

Top ten easiest countries in which to do business
Top ten most difficult countries in which to do business
All other countries

Source: Data extracted from World Bank, 2010, *Doing Business 2010* (database at www.doingbusiness.org).

MAP 3.2   TOP REFORMERS IN 2008–2009

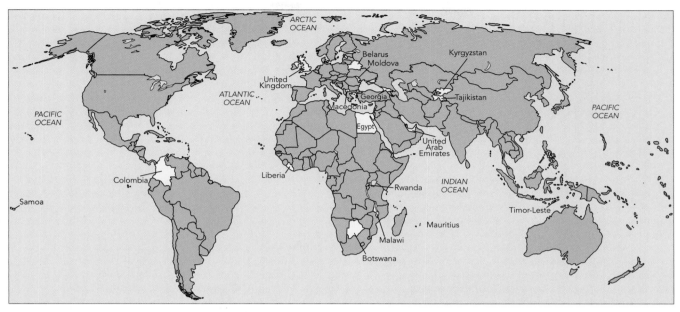

Source: World Bank, 2010, *Doing Business 2010* (database at www.worldbank.org).

MAP 3.3   ROTTERDAM—CENTRALLY LOCATED IN THE EU

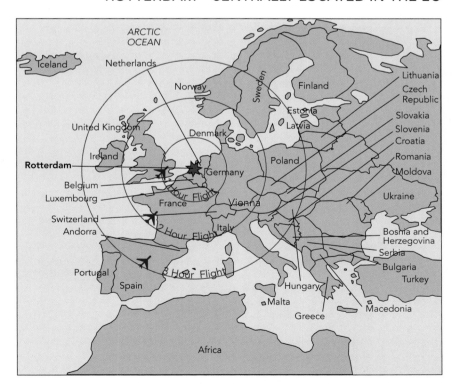

MAP 3.4   TOP TEN AND BOTTOM TEN COUNTRIES BY PER CAPITA INCOME

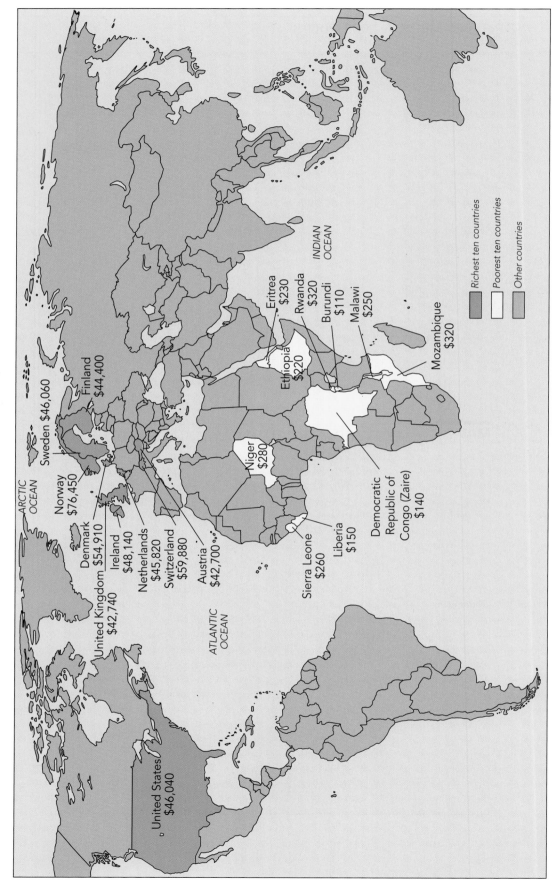

ARCTIC
OCEAN

Norway
$76,450

Sweden $46,060

Finland
$44,400

Denmark
$54,910

United Kingdom
$42,740

Ireland
$48,140

Netherlands
$45,820

Switzerland
$59,880

Austria
$42,700

Eritrea
$230

Rwanda
$320

Burundi
$110

Malawi
$250

Ethiopia
$220

Niger
$280

Sierra Leone
$260

Liberia
$150

Democratic
Republic of
Congo (Zaire)
$140

Mozambique
$320

INDIAN
OCEAN

United States
$46,040

ATLANTIC
OCEAN

Richest ten countries

Poorest ten countries

Other countries

Source: Adapted from The World Bank, 2009, *World Development Report 2009: Reshaping Economic Geography*, Washington: The World Bank. "Income" here refers to per capita gross national income (GNI), which is gross domestic product (GDP) plus net receipts of income from nonresident sources. GNI is also known as gross national product (GNP).

INTEGRATIVE CASE 3.1

PRIVATE MILITARY COMPANIES

Mike W. Peng, *University of Texas at Dallas*

Are entrepreneurial private military companies dogs of war or pussycats of peace?

This industry dates back to thousands of years ago, is visible in TV news almost everyday (at least since September 11, 2001), is global in nature, and has annual sales of $100 billion. Yet, participants do not even agree on how to label it, and most outsiders are clueless about its entrepreneurial nature and ethical dilemma. So, what industry is this? Many journalists and scholars call it the "private military industry." Others label it the "private security industry"—a leading British industry association, formed in 2006, calls itself the British Association of Private Security Companies (BAPSC). A leading American industry association, founded in 2001, names itself the International Peace Operations Association (IPOA) and has coined post-modern labels the "peace and stability industry" and the "peace operations industry." For compositional simplicity, in this case, we call this industry "private military industry" to emphasize its twin nature of private and military. Companies in this industry are thus called "private military companies" (PMCs).

From Rome to Iraq

The roots of this industry can be found in mercenaries. In fact, the very word "soldier" derives from *solidus*, the Roman gold coin. In other words, a soldier, by classical definition, is one who fought for money. During the American Revolution, mercenaries from Germany fought on the British side. The stereotype of mercenaries is the "dogs of war" who help win civil wars and topple governments (usually in resource-rich African countries).

A DynCorp employee guarding an Afghan official

© John Moore/Getty Images

However, modern PMCs hate to be associated with mercenaries. Today's PMCs are proud of their professionalism and value added. Led by entrepreneurs who are often retired military officers, PMCs compete globally. There are three main types. First, closest to the battlefield are "military provider firms" that supply hired guns (often known as "private contractors") who serve alongside national military forces. Blackwater is perhaps the best-known military provider firm. Second, "military consulting firms" offer assistance but do not engage in the battlefield. One example is Military Professional Resources, Inc. Third, "military support firms," such as Halliburton, provide non-lethal support, such as intelligence, logistics, technical support, and transportation. One of the rare publicly listed PMCs is DynCorp International, which went public in May 2006 (NYSE: DCP). It has more than 16,800 employees and generates over $2 billion revenue around the world.

Entrepreneurs thrive on chaos. To PMCs, the war in Iraq and Afghanistan has been a pot of gold. While US allies have been withdrawing their forces, PMCs rush in. By 2009, PMCs represented the *second largest* military contingent in Iraq (113,000 personnel),

This case was written by Mike W. Peng (University of Texas at Dallas). Its preparation was supported in part by a National Science Foundation CAREER grant (SES 0552089). This case is entirely based on published sources. The views expressed are those of the author and not those of the NSF. © Mike W. Peng. Reprinted with permission.

after the US (national) forces (130,000 personnel). In Afghanistan, in 2009, PMCs were the *largest* military force (130,000 personnel), outnumbering both the Afghan National Army (100,000 personnel) and the US (national) forces (64,000 personnel). Private soldiers drive convoy trucks, build camps, guard dignitaries, and gather intelligence. The most lucrative job is not "guns on trucks" but less glamorous but more steady work such as logistics. Well-muscled men with wrap-around sunglasses may steal headlines (especially after they allegedly shoot Iraqi civilians), but the real money is in other lines of work.

Long before Iraq, the use of PMCs alongside US troops had become an indispensable component of America's "Total Force." In an age of outsourcing, the Pentagon has followed suit, contracting dozens of PMCs to carry out essential military work that were once exclusively performed by uniformed soldiers. Not surprisingly, the driver behind such outsourcing is cost—both political and financial. Dead private soldiers mean fewer dead uniformed soldiers. Military casualties in Iraq are carefully recorded and provoke fierce antiwar protests. Neither the media nor the public seem to care about PMC casualties, although about 700 have died in Iraq. Overall, given the scale and scope of PMC involvement (representing 50% of the defense workforce deployed to the Balkans, Iraq, and Afghanistan shown in Exhibit 1), many experts now believe that the US (national) military is incapable of successfully carrying out large missions without PMCs.

Global Competition and Challenges

While well-connected American PMCs often win big contracts handed out by the US government, the competition is global. British PMCs, whose services represent Britain's biggest export to Iraq, grab more work from the private sector. Why are the British so competitive in this line of work? Three reasons. First, many British PMCs are first movers, tracing their roots to the days when they were real mercenaries active in Africa when the British Empire collapsed in the 1950s and

1960s. Second, British PMCs benefit from the clustering of many energy and mining companies in London, whose dangerous work often demands more security services. Third, British PMCs recruit from the British army, whose soldiers patrolled the mean streets of Northern Ireland without killing too many civilians. Such portable skills are highly sought after in Iraq and Afghanistan now.

There are two ethical challenges associated with PMCs. The first is the morality issue associated with their deployment. For regular soldiers, aid workers, and government officials, an instinctive reaction is: "Why should we respect these people who fight for money?" Nevertheless, privatization of government services is a global trend in general. In the military arena, the cost effectiveness of PMCs is compelling. Some argue that the UN Security Council should have contracted PMC services to limit the Rwanda genocide in the 1990s, as it was contemplating at the time but failed to do so. The new genocide in Sudan's Darfur region and UN member countries' hesitation to commit national troops as Blue Helmets have again led to calls for PMCs, which, in theory, can be deployed more rapidly and at a lower cost than Blue Helmets.

The second and probably larger challenge confronting PMCs is accountability—or the apparent lack of it. For example, private contractors were involved in the torture scandal at the Abu Ghraib prison in Baghdad, but only military personnel were court-martialed while private contractors were outside the scope of court-martial jurisdiction. Further, contracts are often impossible to monitor, particularly when private soldiers are deployed in dangerous situations. Where there is no accountability, "rogue" firms and individuals may enter, severely undermining the industry's reputation.

The presence of PMCs in conflict and post-conflict environments creates a significant institutional challenge as to what and whose rules of the game should govern PMCs. During a traditional war, national

---

EXHIBIT 1   PERSONNEL OF PRIVATE MILITARY COMPANIES AS PERCENTAGE OF DEFENSE WORKFORCE IN THREE RECENT US OPERATIONS

Balkans	Afghanistan	Iraq	Three operations combined
50%	62%	47%	50%

Source: Based on Figure 1 in M. Schwartz, 2009, *Department of Defense Contractors in Iraq and Afghanistan: Background and Analysis* (p. 2), Washington, DC: Congressional Research Service. "Defense workforce" is defined as the combination of contractor (PMC) and uniformed (national military) workforce deployed to these theaters of operations. Civilian employees working for the Department of Defense (DOD) are excluded from these calculations. If they were included, the percentage would not change much, because the DOD civilian employees represented less than 1% of the total force deployed there.

militaries are governed by the law of war or more specifically law of armed conflicts, whose most famous institution is the Geneva Convention. At all other times, the law of peace prevails and civilian casualties are not acceptable. However, the distinction between "war" and "peace" has broken down. Technically, US Congress has never issued a declaration of war against Iraq, but nobody can argue there is "peace" in Iraq since 2003. Given such ambiguity of "neither war nor peace," PMCs are essentially unregulated.

In 2004, Paul Bremer, head of the Coalition Provisional Authority (CPA) in charge of Iraq, signed CPA Order 17 stating that "[private military] contractors shall not be subject to Iraqi laws or regulations in matters relating to the terms and conditions of their contracts." In other words, PMCs working for the CPA, or the US government, were granted immunity from Iraqi law.

In October 2007, Blackwater found itself in hot water. The Iraqi government alleged that on September 16, 2007, Blackwater personnel opened fire indiscriminately at a Baghdad crossroads and killed 17 innocent civilians. Blackwater maintained that its men were under fire. Because, thanks to Order 17, Blackwater (and other PMCs) were formally immune from Iraqi law, the best that the Iraqi government could do was to demand that Blackwater leave the country. US Congress was in uproar concerning such an embarrassing incident and in October 2007 held a hearing on Blackwater—and in fact on the entire private military industry. Naturally, Blackwater's staunchest defenders were the US officials protected by its private soldiers. US officials preferred Blackwater and other PMCs because PMC personnel were regarded as more highly trained than (national) military guards. Blackwater's founder, Erik Prince, told the Congressional committee that "no individual protected by Blackwater has ever been killed or seriously injured," while 30 of its staff died on the job. While measures for increased legal and regulatory oversight were called for by the highest levels of the US government, whether these measures would be implemented on the messy and dangerous ground in Iraq (and elsewhere) remains to be seen.

Because Blackwater had immunity from Iraqi law at the time of the incident, the most severe punishment it received for its alleged misconduct was the US government's decision not to renew its contract for Iraq in January 2009. However, the Iraqi government leveraged this incident and forced the US government to repudiate *all* PMCs' immunity from Iraqi law in a Status of Force Agreement signed in December 2008.

In other words, PMCs no longer have the "get out of jail free card" in Iraq. In February 2009, Blackwater's notoriety forced it to rename itself Xe Services LLC (pronounced "zee").

In December 2009, President Obama announced the surge of 30,000 additional US troops to be sent to Afghanistan. What he did not announce was that according to a study by the Congressional Research Service (CRS), these 30,000 US (national) troops would be accompanied by *another* surge of 26,000–56,000 PMC personnel, bringing the total number of PMC personnel in Afghanistan to anywhere from 130,000 to 160,000. Prior to these two surges, the percentage of people working for Pentagon who were PMC personnel already reached over 60%, which, according to the same CRS study, "apparently represented the highest recorded percentage of contractors used by the Defense Department in any conflict in the history of the United States." Clearly, despite the notoriety of some PMCs such as Blackwater (now known as Xe), the private military industry has no problem *increasing* their "market share" in the business of war. In another development, pirates in the Somali waters have generated tremendous new business for PMCs that offer maritime security services.

Enlightened Self-Regulation?

As the industry aspires to become a "mature" one by diversifying into post-conflict reconstruction and risk management (after all, there are only so many shooting wars to fight), its current unregulated nature is not sustainable. In the absence of regulation, PMCs' seemingly secretive nature prevents them from being recognized as legitimate players. In response, the PMC community has recently set up the IPOA and BAPSC in order to advocate self-regulation. A very un-mercenary Code of Conduct governing all IPOA members went into effect in 2001. Its 11th revision, publicized in 2006, promised that member PMCs only work for legitimate governments and organizations and that all rules of engagement must "emphasize appropriate restraint and caution to minimize casualties and damage." In the long run, PMCs adhering to "aggressive self-regulation" hope to be perceived as reliable, professional, and high-quality service providers. Far from being the dogs of war, declared BAPSC's director-general, "we are actually the pussycats of peace." This thought-provoking statement is indicative of the ethical dilemma of PMCs: while they prefer to dispel any mercenary notion that they are dogs of war, they also thrive on the mean-and-tough warrior mystique. After all, wrote the *Economist*, "who would use a pussycat as a guard-dog?"

Case Discussion Questions:

1. From an institution-based view, explain what is behind the rise of this industry.

2. From a resource-based standpoint, explain (1) how PMCs can outperform national militaries and (2) how certain PMCs outperform others.

3. Why are industry associations such as the IPOA and BAPSC so interested in self-regulation?

4. As an investor, would you consider buying stock of a PMC such as DynCorp? (Imagine a scenario that all other listed firms suffered from the financial meltdown, but DynCorp's stock outperforms the market.) Why or why not? Do you have any ethical reservations?

5. As an oil company executive setting up operations in a politically unstable and dangerous country, would you consider hiring security personnel from Blackwater (which is now known as Xe)?

Sources: Based on (1) A. Bearpark & S. Schulz, 2006, The regulation of the private security industry and the future of the market, bapsc.org.uk; (2) *BusinessWeek*, 2006, Tainted past? No problem, July 17; (3) *The Economist*, 2006, Blood and treasure, November 4; (4) *The Economist*, 2006, Who dares profits? May 20; (5) *The Economist*, 2007, Blackwater in hot water, October 13; (6) *The Economist*, 2009, Splashing and clashing in murky waters, August 22; (7) International Peace Operations Association, 2006, Code of conduct, ipoaonline.org; (8) *Newsweek*, 2007, Blackwater is soaked, October 15; (9) C. Ortiz, 2007, Assessing the accountability of private security provision, *Journal of International Peace Operations*, January; (10) P. Singer, 2004, *Corporate Warriors*, Ithaca, NY: Cornell University Press; (11) M. Schwartz, 2009, *Department of Defense Contractors in Iraq and Afghanistan: Background and Analysis*, Washington, DC: Congressional Research Service.

INTEGRATIVE CASE 3.2

HUAWEI'S INTERNATIONALIZATION
Sunny Li Sun, *University of Texas at Dallas*

How does Huawei, a leading telecom network solutions and equipment manufacturer based in China, overcome challenges associated with its ambitious internationalization?

Established in 1988, China's Huawei Technologies has risen as one of the leading global telecommunications network solutions and equipment providers. In 2008, Huawei applied for the largest number of patents in the world under the World Intellectual Property Organization (WIPO) Patent Cooperation Treaty (PCT). In 2007, it applied for the fourth largest number of patents. In 2008, Huawei's revenues rose 36% to $17 billion, and in 2009 they rose 17% to $21.5 billion. Amid the global economic turmoil, this enviable performance suggests that Huawei outperformed most of its Western rivals, such as Alcatel-Lucent, Cisco, Ericsson, Motorola, and Nortel (Nortel filed for bankruptcy protection in 2009).[1] In January 2009, Huawei won the first global commercial contract to supply equipment for an advanced, fourth-generation (4G) LTE mobile network in Oslo, Norway.

China watchers often tout Huawei as one of the companies most likely to become China's first big global brand, although some of its foreign employees have trouble pronouncing the company's name (pronounced "hwa-way").[2] *BusinessWeek* listed Huawei as one of the "World's Ten Most Influential Companies" during 2008. With 75% of its sales from outside of China in 2008, Huawei is a significant example of an emerging economy-based multinational enterprise (EE MNE), which first nurtured its capabilities in the low-end domestic market, then treated global competition as an opportunity to grow, moved into more profitable segments, and adopted strategies that turn its latecomer status into a source of competitive advantage. How does it overcome challenges associated with its ambitious internationalization?

Overview of Huawei

Founded with a $9 million bank loan in 1988 and 30 employees, Huawei grew rapidly to revenues of $1.2 billion and 6,000 employees in 1998. Then, Huawei started to jump from being a local player to a global competitor with international revenues of $17 billion in 2008 (see Exhibit 1). In 2008, 75% sales of Huawei came from overseas markets. In the third quarter of

---

EXHIBIT 1   HUAWEI'S FAST INTERNATIONALIZATION (IN US$ BILLION)

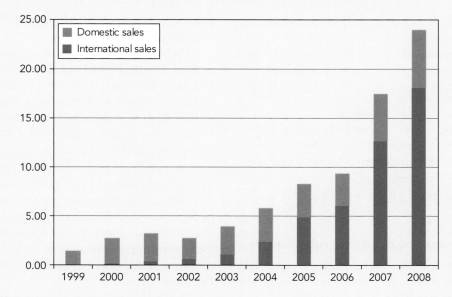

This case was written by Sunny Li Sun (University of Texas at Dallas) under the supervision of Professor Mike Peng. © Sunny Li Sun. Reprinted with permission.

2009, Huawei was number two (behind Ericsson) in the global mobile network equipment market, almost doubling its market share (20%) from a year ago (11%) and surpassing Nokia Siemens.[3]

Huawei is a leader in providing next generation telecommunications networks, and now serves 31 of the world's top 50 carriers, along with over one billion users worldwide. Since its start-up days, Huawei reinvests no less than 10% of its revenues in R&D and 10% of the R&D budget in cutting-edge and fundamental technologies. The company is committed to providing innovative and customized products, services, and solutions to create long-term value and growth potential for customers.

At present, Huawei has over 87,000 employees, of whom 48% are dedicated to R&D. Huawei's global R&D centers are located in Dallas, Texas, and the Silicon Valley, California (USA), Bangalore (India), Moscow (Russia), and Stockholm (Sweden), in addition to those in Beijing, Shanghai, Nanjing, Shenzhen, Hangzhou, and Chengdu in China.

With over 100 subsidiaries abroad, Huawei's global markets are divided into nine different zones:[4]

- China (headquartered in Shenzhen)
- Asia Pacific (headquartered in Kuala Lumpur, Malaysia)
- East Pacific (headquartered in Sydney, Australia, and includes Australia, Hong Kong, Japan, Korea, Macau, New Zealand, and Taiwan)
- Commonwealth of Independent States (headquartered in Moscow, Russia)
- Europe (headquartered in London, UK)
- Latin America (headquartered in Brasilia, Brazil)
- Middle East and North Africa (headquartered in Cairo, Egypt)
- North America (headquartered in Plano, Texas, in the Dallas area—this subsidiary is named Futurewei)
- Southern Africa (headquartered in Johannesburg, South Africa)

A vice president heads each of Huawei's eight regional headquarters outside China. The regional offices are organized by different product lines and have a technical support department and two departments in charge of client relations and business development.

From Domestic Dominance to Overseas Markets

Many Western reporters who highlight Huawei's military background are puzzled by its eccentric, earnest company culture. Other than CEO Ren Zhengfei's 14 years of military service, Huawei has no linkage with the Chinese military and only receives a very small contract from the military. However, in its early years, Huawei's culture was strongly influenced by its CEO's military background. Discipline, hard work, and purpose were the main drivers of Huawei's employees.

Compared with government-supported state-owned rivals, privately owned Huawei had no close linkages with its clients, all of which are state-owned telecommunications carriers. Huawei developed ferocious competitive skills, similar to those of wolves, firmly believing in the crucial *natural selection* in the marketplace. It was widely reported that Huawei incorporated three components of the wolf spirit as part of its indispensable corporate culture: (1) a sensitive nose, (2) aggressiveness, and (3) persistence on attack.

The first is a sensitive nose for opportunities. Wolves always activate their noses and keep their eyes fixed on their prey, closely observing the movements of sheep and even those of the shepherds. Once an opportunity emerges, they will immediately mount an attack. In Huawei, this inquisitiveness is vital in tracing the development of new technology, formulating strategies, studying price fluctuations, and surveying competitor moves. Starting as a telecom switch agent for PBX machines, Huawei heavily invested in R&D, and in 1993 became the second innovator on C&C08 digital switches, a segment dominated by foreign suppliers such as Siemens and Alcatel. Huawei's machines met a popular demand generated by the rapidly developing Chinese telecommunications industry in the 1990s. Based on excellent technology and low price, Huawei triumphed over foreign companies, and ranked fourth among local switch suppliers in 1998 (all three leading suppliers were state-owned).

The second aspect is aggressiveness. When wolves attack a flock of sheep, wolves will firmly bite into their prey and will not let go easily. Wolves are not satisfied with getting enough food from the killing of one sheep, but are determined to kill as many as possible in a short time. This aggressiveness describes precisely how Huawei grew by six-fold from 1996 to 1998, and how Huawei developed the leading GSM mobile switch system. In 1999 Huawei was selected as the principal supplier for China Mobile's nationwide CAMEL Phase II compliant IN network. This aggressiveness makes Huawei the number one local supplier in the mobile communications equity market, which was never dominated by Nokia and Ericsson before.

The third aspect is persistence. Huawei persistently attacks its target markets with its comparatively low cost of R&D—in other words, leveraging the cheaper intellectual resources from an EE. Data from Siemens indicates that European R&D workers, on average, work only 1,300 to 1,400 hours per year, while Huawei's Chinese R&D workers reach 2,750 hours a year—twice as many as Europeans working in the same field. The average annual R&D personnel cost at European MNEs is $120,000–$150,000. At Huawei, the cost is only $25,000. The input-to-output ratio of Huawei's R&D work is thus ten times larger than that of its European counterparts. This is where Huawei's advantages largely rest.

Gaining 85% sales growth in 2000, Ren sensed the incoming stagnation of the domestic market. If Huawei only focused on China, he believed that Huawei would experience a "long winter." He boldly sold Avansys Power Co., Huawei's fast growing subsidiary on telecom and data network power conversion products, to Emerson with 20 times of the price/earnings (P/E) ratio in October 2001, and raised US$750 million to initiate a large-scale attack on global markets. Ren gave a penetrating speech to managers who would lead troops into overseas markets on January 18, 2001.

> In this era, an entrepreneur is awesome if he has the vision of global strategy. A nation is thriving and prosperous if it can leverage the power of globalization. A company grows forever if it can build a global commercial ecosystem. An employee has a bright future career if he treats every strange place as his familiar home.

Huawei's Pain in the US and Happiness in EE and the EU

Huawei began to attack the North American market aggressively in 2001. Rather than targeting traditional telecommunications products, the company chose to explore the burgeoning market of digital communications. It adopted a very aggressive marketing strategy. Huawei's products directly challenged Cisco with prices 30% lower. Huawei also aired an extremely hostile advertisement: it featured Huawei products against the background of the Golden Gate Bridge in San Francisco, which happened to be Cisco's logo. The message line read, "The only difference between us and them is price."

Corporate buyers quickly recognized the high-quality performance of Huawei's routers. Cisco's first reaction was to discuss the possibility with Huawei that Cisco would give all its low-end products' OEM orders to Huawei if Huawei would give up its R&D in high-end products and not build its brand in the United States. Such requests were flatly rejected by Huawei.

In June 2002, Cisco's CEO, John Chambers, visited Huawei's booth as an unidentified visitor at Super-Comm, a trade show in Atlanta. Later, a counterattack plan against Huawei was formulated. In January 2003, Cisco sued Huawei for intellectual property rights (IPRs) infringement. A federal judge in East Texas was considering Cisco's motion for a preliminary injunction to prevent Huawei from selling its products in the United States.[5]

Huawei needed a partner: a friendly American partner. It decided to give up its brand to 3Com in overseas markets, when Huawei signed a sweeping joint venture (JV) agreement with this struggling networking company, just one week after it had been sued by Cisco. The JV was called "3Com-Huawei" in English but "Huawei-3Com" in Chinese.

3Com helped to increase Huawei's bargaining power in settling the lawsuit. Its American CEO Bruce Claflin said, "If Cisco were to sue the JV, it's 100% certain that we would countersue. It would be very different than just suing Huawei [which, unlike 3Com, had no US patents with which to negotiate a settlement]." Cisco and Huawei finally reached an agreement in July 2003. Cisco withdrew the lawsuit and both companies resolved all patent litigation, with each party paying for its own legal fees. Neither side revealed the terms, which were confidential. However, Huawei withdrew almost all of its products from the United States over the next several months, presumably due to the settlement agreement.

Huawei decided to focus on EEs and the European Union (EU). The deregulation wave around the world helped Huawei win a lot of orders from EEs. Many low-budget EE carriers were attracted by Huawei's low-cost, high-quality products and were apparently not troubled by allegations of its IPR problems. In 2003, Huawei's overseas sales soared to $1 billion, doubling what they were the year before. Most of its revenues came from the Asia Pacific, Southern Africa, and the Middle East and North Africa.

In addition to EE, Huawei also had a persistent attack on the EU. It won the first national network contract from France's second-largest fixed-line telecom carrier LDCom Networks. LDCom had used Cisco's Metro Ethernet switches and routers in its network already. However, Huawei swiftly finished a temporary project, and its low price and quick response to customers defeated Cisco. In 2001, Huawei also targeted BT, Britain's incumbent carrier. After three years of trials, Huawei joined the "short list" of BT's 21st Century Network planning in 2004.

Since Huawei took huge pressures of alleged IPR violation in Cisco's lawsuit, it scaled up the application patents in the US Patent and Trademarks Office (USPTO). Since 2004, its registered patents had rapid growth. For six consecutive years, Huawei was ranked first in the number of patent applications in China. At the end of 2007, Huawei had a total number of 26,880 patent applications. According to WIPO, Huawei became the world's largest patent applicant under the PCT, with 1,737 applications published in 2008.

Six years after resolving Cisco's IPRs charges, Huawei went back to North America, and opened a 4G wireless technology lab in Richardson, Texas, in July 2009. It won contracts from Cox Communications and Clearwire, the largest WiMAX operator in the United States.[6] Huawei's sales in the United States increased to $250 million in 2008, a 60% increase from 2007. Huawei currently has about 900 employees in North America. To expand its presence in the world's largest but toughest telecom equipment market, Huawei plans to add 600 employees in 2010.

Linkage, Leverage, and Learning

After various failed attacks, Huawei began to realize that it could not win the global game as a lone wolf; instead it needed to modify its wolf spirit to foster collaborative teamwork. Consequently, Huawei toned down its predatory attitude and began to emphasize cooperation with established telecom equipment suppliers, hoping to obtain access to global markets through them. Since 1999, Huawei has established joint R&D labs with Texas Instruments, Motorola, IBM, Intel, Agere Systems, Sun Microsystems, Altera, Qualcomm, Infineon, and Microsoft. Huawei now maintains in-depth cooperation with Motorola for wireless equipment, with Siemens for digital communications and TD-SCDMA, and with NEC for digital communications and mobile terminals. In other areas, they still remain rivals. This paints a very complex picture of competition and cooperation.

While few of these ventures are directed towards the North American market, Huawei used its Huawei-3Com JV as a new route to enter international markets, especially those in developed regions. Even after it sold its 49% stake in the JV to 3Com for $882 million in 2006, Huawei partnered with a private equity firm, Bain Capital, and made a plan to take over 3Com in 2007. Unfortunately, in 2008, this acquisition failed to pass the national security reviews by the Committee on Foreign Investment in the United States (CFIUS) and thus had to be abandoned.

Huawei also jointly developed with Vodafone and supply mobile phones to this largest mobile carrier in the EU since 2006. Huawei and Vodafone set up a closer strategic alliance in 2009, extending Huawei's service orders from Vodafone to Greece, Hungary, Romania, Spain, and Turkey. Huawei also built strategic alliances with Intel in WiMax technology in 2005 and with the Google-backed Open Handset Alliance to launch an Android phone in 2009.

Although Huawei has a low-cost advantage in R&D based on cheaper intellectual resources and engineers, as international business plays an ever bigger role, its costs have also increased. In global resources distribution, global services, materials and product parts purchasing, financing, and marketing, Huawei's advantages are starting to erode. For example, there is more urgent demand on the quality of products and services, academic qualifications of staff, and product delivery capacity. All these factors lead to increasing costs. In addition, Huawei's relatively lower R&D costs may actually lead to higher total costs of ownership, since products out of such "cheap and dirty" R&D may have defects that have to cost more money and manpower to fix in the long run.[7]

Since 1997, Huawei has realized this management challenge. IBM, Towers Perrin, Hay Group, PricewaterhouseCoopers, and Fraunhofer-Gesellschaft have been acting as its consultants, respectively, on process transformation, employee stock option plan, human resource management, financial management, and quality control. Huawei has learned management skills from these leading multinational consultancy firms in an effort to keep up with the best practices in the industry.

The benchmark learning has borne fruits. The employee productivity (per capita sales) of Huawei in 1996 were only $73,300 even when employees often worked overtime every day. This figure increased to $266,280 in 2008.[8]

This success was achieved despite a decreasing amount of overtime work. Overall, Huawei has built up its capabilities in world-class R&D management models, not only relying on personal cleverness and diligence, but also organizational integration in "speed, quality, and low cost."

Currently, Huawei has joined 83 international standard organizations, taken up nearly 100 roles in these organizations, and actively participated in international standard-setting. In 4G, LTE, SAE, NGN, IPTV, and other fields, Huawei has submitted over 3,000 proposals. Through these linkages, Huawei has built its global learning networks and brought dispersed knowledge together to fuel its innovations, while ensuring that it has a say at the table setting standards for tomorrow's technology.

Case Discussion Questions:

1. From a resource-based view, where do Huawei's competitive advantages come from?
2. From an institution-based view, what are the lessons Huawei can draw from its internationalization?

3. What constraints do Huawei face in its internationalization? How does it deal with them?
4. How do Huawei and other EE MNEs establish themselves successfully against the fierce resistance of MNEs from developed economies?

NOTES

[1] *Wall Street Journal*, 2008, Huawei posts sales growth, even as rivals slump, January 16.

[2] C. Simons, 2009, Production lines at Huawei are perfect, marketing isn't, *Newsweek*, July 27, http://www.newsweek.com/id/207381.

[3] Reuters, 2009, China's Huawei takes No. 2 spot in mobile gear, November 13.

[4] *Economist*, 2009, Up, up and Huawei, September 24.

[5] B. Einhorn, 2003, Cisco: In hot pursuit of a Chinese rival, *BusinessWeek*, May 19; B. Einhorn, 2003. Huawei vs. Cisco just got nastier, *BusinessWeek*, June 3.

[6] L. Luk, 2009, Huawei to beef up North America ops, adding staff, *Dow Jones Newswires*, November 23.

[7] Total cost of ownership (TCO) is a financial estimate designed to help consumers and enterprise managers assess direct and indirect costs related to the purchase of any capital investment.

[8] A comparative data point: Ericsson's employee productivity per capita: $396,563 in 2007. See Ericsson's annual report: http://www.ericsson.com/ericsson/investors/financial_reports/annual_reports/index.shtml.

INTEGRATIVE CASE 3.3

HONG KONG'S OCEAN PARK: LEARNING TO LIVE WITH DISNEYLAND
Michael N. Young and Yuan Yi Chen, *Hong Kong Baptist University*

Despite predictions of its demise, Ocean Park has not only survived the onslaught of Hong Kong Disneyland, but has also outperformed the multinational giant in attendance. What happened? How can Ocean Peak learn to coexist with Disneyland?

By 2010, Thomas Mehrmann, CEO of Hong Kong's Ocean Park, had not only overcome the challenges posed by a new Disneyland that had opened in 2005, but had even managed to turn a potential threat into an opportunity. When Hong Kong Disneyland opened, many people predicted that the demise of the then 28-year-old Ocean Park would only be a matter of time. Far from being the death knell as predicted by some analysts, Disneyland's arrival in Hong Kong had been a *boon* for Ocean Park. Disney's opening had spurred Ocean Park into action and it had achieved a dramatic turnaround. It had some of its best performance—partially as a direct *result* of Disney's arrival. In 2005, Ocean Park achieved the highest recorded attendance in its history; compared to the prior year, overall visitor attendance increased by 9% in 2004/2005 topping 4 million. Gross revenues grew 12% year-on-year and were HK$684 million[1] in 2005, giving the Park a surplus of HK$119.5 million.[2]

In fact, some commentators suggested that Ocean Park was a bigger benefactor from Disneyland than was Disney itself. In a survey conducted by Hong Kong Polytechnic University, 75% of respondents said the opening of Disneyland did not reduce their desire to visit Ocean Park. The opening of Hong Kong Disneyland had rejuvenated local interest in amusement parks and local people took notice of the competition between the parks that resulted in an attendance boost. Furthermore, Hong Kong Disneyland increased the number of tourists from China and Southeast Asia to Hong Kong—particularly families interested in amusement parks. In addition to seeing Disney, it was natural for them to want to see the other major amusement park: Ocean Park. As a result, by 2007/2008, Ocean Park enjoyed a surplus of HK$240 million, which was a 19% increase compared to the previous year.[3] Meanwhile,

Hong Kong Disneyland continued to struggle—with missing attendance goals and doubtful profitability.[4] In 2007, Ocean Park passed Hong Kong Disney in total attendance (see Exhibit 1). In 2008, Ocean Park climbed to become the fifteenth largest theme park in the world with 5 million visitors.

Mehrmann and his management team knew they could not rest on these past achievements. They had successfully ridden the Disney challenge to scale even greater heights. Now the strategy needed to shift from defense to offense. As suggested by some tourism professionals, these two theme parks could benefit from each other. Au King-chi, Commissioner for Tourism, pointed out: "The opening of Hong Kong Disneyland provided a driving force for Ocean Park to improve and the two theme parks could cooperate to attract more theme park tourists." Could Ocean Park benefit further from this relationship? Should Ocean Park try to grab some of Disneyland's market share? Was it in the best interest of Ocean Park to see Disneyland be successful? Were there further opportunities that the management team was overlooking?

Background on Ocean Park

Ocean Park opened in 1977 with thrill rides and an aquarium. Its construction was funded by the Hong Kong Jockey Club with profits earned from horse race gaming. The land for Ocean Park was provided by the British colonial government (Hong Kong returned to Chinese rule as a Special Administrative Region [SAR] in 1997). The Park was situated on the southern side

EXHIBIT 1   ATTENDANCE WARS

	Hong Kong Disneyland	Ocean Park
2006	5,200,000	4,380,000
2007	4,150,000	4,920,000
2008	4,500,000	5,030,000

This case was written by Michael N. Young and Yuan Yi Chen (Hong Kong Baptist University). The purpose of the case is to serve as a basis for classroom discussion rather than to illustrate either effective or ineffective handling of an administrative situation. We wish to acknowledge the help of Mr. Thomas Mehrmann, CEO of Ocean Park, for contributing his valuable time to give this case nuances that otherwise would have been be lacking. © Michael N. Young. Reprinted with permission.

of Hong Kong Island, not far from the central business district. By 2010, the Park was a major tourist attraction in Hong Kong and one of the world's leading amusement parks and oceanariums. Its vision was to be the world leader in providing excellent guest experiences in an amusement park environment connecting people with nature.[5] Since 1987, Ocean Park had been owned by the Hong Kong Government, supported by the Home Affairs Bureau and the Tourism Board and managed by the Ocean Park Corporation. The park's mascot, a sea lion with the name of *Wai Wai* (Whiskers in English), was introduced to the park in 2000. He became a household name in Hong Kong, particularly with children and families.

It had not always been smooth sailing for Ocean Park. The 1997 Asian financial crisis contributed to four consecutive years of losses from 1999 to 2002. In 2002, Ocean Park lost HK$80 million. During this extremely difficult period there was even some talk of closing the park. To make matters worse, the outbreak of Severe Acute Respiratory Syndrome (SARS) greatly affected tourism in Hong Kong. Ocean Park lost an additional HK$60 million during 2003 thanks to SARS. In addition to these external shocks, the Park had operated under monopoly conditions for years. This lack of competition had bred complacency; the park had failed to innovate and the characters, rides, and marine exhibits were beginning to look dated and shabby. Paul Pei, Ocean Park's Sales and Marketing Director, said of the Park before the reengineering that "customers did not understand and did not like what they were paying for." Nor did the Park establish a winning brand image or corporate logo. Human resource management (HRM) practices had also failed to keep up with the times. Most staff members at the Park were unskilled workers with long hours, low pay, and monotonous jobs that made turnover a problem. In Hong Kong, tourism workers were highly mobile. As sales continued to slide, management became increasingly aware of the need for a renovation of the Park's brand image, HRM, and operations.

Hong Kong's Ocean Park welcomes visitors

© Panorama Media (Beijing) Ltd./Alamy

In 2000, Ocean Park took on a program of reengineering, which consisted of brand repositioning and product updates. As Pei commented: "You could say that we had no brand image at all at that time." The Park brought in new attractions, such as the Abyss Turbo Drop thrill ride, which cost approximately HK$70 million. The Park also began having festival events and activities to vary the atmosphere throughout the year. There were five seasonal holiday themes—Chinese New Year, Easter Holiday, Summer Holiday, Halloween, and Christmas. For example, during the Easter Holiday of 2005, Ocean Park organized an anniversary party for the pandas. Translated from Chinese, the party was called "Lovely Giant Panda Party." This event also served as a fund raising event for the Hong Kong Society for Panda Conservation. By launching this party, Ocean Park hoped to further its image of social responsibility. During the hot Hong Kong summer holiday, the Park targeted teenagers by organizing several popular water-related activities, such as Water-war and Water-bomb. Around Halloween, the Park put on horror shows and opened haunted houses.

Ocean Park had also introduced a variety of interactive activities with animals, such as having meals with pandas and sea lions. In addition, "edutainment" programs gave visitors a chance to learn more about the animals and have fun at the same time. Examples included Honorary Giant Panda Keeper, Dolphin Encounter, Animal Meet and Greet, Animal Academy, and Panda Time Theatre. All of these carefully focused special events and seasonal promotions have encouraged customers to visit more often and stay longer with each visit, allowing the Park to sell additional souvenirs and refreshments.

By attempting to provide value for money, Ocean Park did not engage in glitzy, high-profile advertising and publicity stunts. Instead, the Park tended to rely more on word-of-mouth to generate additional business. As Pei stated, "If customers believe that going to Ocean Park is worth their money and their time, then they would visit again with friends and family." Management also tried to implement a culture of innovation. It was believed that continually adding new features and attractions would encourage visitors return to the Park. This was difficult because of the short life cycle of new fixed-asset attractions. For example, the new HK$70 million Abyss Turbo Drop thrill ride was initially a big success, but it was difficult to come up with an encore. As one visitor stated, "it is really exciting and attractive to try that new Abyss Turbo ride, however, not for the second time." Ocean Park

lacked the budget or space to provide a continuous supply of big-ticket thrill rides. Thus, management tried to find alternatives to attract repeat customers. It appeared that seasonal and special events were in a better position to provide novelty to get repeat visits.

Enter Hong Kong Disneyland

Hong Kong Disneyland was the third Disneyland to ever open outside of the United States. Disney's arrival seemed to shake Ocean Park out of its slumber and spurred it to action. Ocean Park now faced a competitor that not only had very deep pockets, but also was legendary for its world-renowned innovation, unparalleled service, and ruthless competitiveness. The dazzling commencement ceremony of Hong Kong Disneyland had taken place on September 12, 2005. Pundits had begun speculating as to what the "Disney effect" would be for Ocean Park. Several of Disney's characters, like Mickey Mouse, Donald Duck, and Winnie the Pooh, were household names all over the world, including in Hong Kong. With Disney's legendary "Imagineering," the company was cranking out amazing new animated characters that debuted in movies, making them well-known by the time visitors encountered them in the parks.

Hong Kong Disneyland was set up as a joint venture between the Walt Disney Company and the Hong Kong SAR Government. Located on Lantau Island, Disneyland could be reached in just 10 minutes from the new airport and in just 30 minutes from downtown Hong Kong. The Hong Kong Disneyland was based on other Disneyland parks and was divided into four parts, including Main Street USA, Fantasyland, Adventureland, and Tomorrowland. Guests visiting a Disneyland park could disengage from the real world and enter into a fairytale kingdom and the world of tomorrow in a flavor of adventure. In addition, two hotels were constructed to provide on-site lodging.

Hong Kong Disneyland's admission price was initially set at HK$295 during the week and HK$350 on weekends and peak days (In February 2009, the price on weekdays was adjusted to as the same as on special days). This was acclaimed to be the least expensive among the five Disney parks around the world.[6] Moreover, the construction of a second amusement park of Disneyland was scheduled to begin soon at the same resort.

As Ocean Park had been undergoing renovation programs that would increase over to 70 attractions from the current 44, the expansion of Disneyland would start soon. In July 2009, after two years of negotiation, Disneyland's two shareholders, the Hong Kong SAR Government and Walt Disney, have agreed to invest US$465 million to expand over the next five years. The Government hoped the plan, which would add another 30 attractions and three themed "lands," would answer critics' complaints of overcrowding and boring rides, and increase visitor numbers by 60% by 2014.

Ocean Park's Response

Local people had viewed Ocean Park's position as a classic David versus Goliath competition. Ocean Park had been a long-time favorite of several generations of Hong Kong parents and children and many people from mainland China had also heard of Ocean Park. So when Disney first announced it would come to Hong Kong, there was some community alarm over the fate of Ocean Park. Pundits predicted that Ocean Park could not survive. Immediately after its inception, Disneyland captivated Hong Kong. Compared with the fabulous glitz and glamour of Disney with its cosmopolitan appeal and reputation for creating magical experiences, Ocean Park was forced to devise a response. There was the real possibility that Ocean Park would come up short in face-to-face competition.

Yet, when comparing the two parks, one would be struck by their unique and different resources and competencies (see Exhibit 2). While Ocean Park did have thrill rides, its primary focus was on nature and wildlife with many animal-related activities. It had an Ocean Theater that staged dolphin and sea lion shows every day. Furthermore, the world-class Atoll Reef, Shark Aquarium, Bird Aviary, and Pacific Pier

gave visitors opportunities to view wild animals and beautiful scenery up close—a real rarity in urban Hong Kong. What's more, Ocean Park had distinct Chinese characteristics that reflected its roots in Hong Kong, a quintessentially Chinese city.

On the other hand, Disneyland's core competencies stemmed from its pioneering efforts in animation with the first widely appealing animated cartoon character (*Mickey Mouse®*) and the first full-length animated movie (*Snow White and the Seven Dwarfs®*). All of these gave Disney the ability to create fantasy and virtual situations, which center around the personalities of its numerous characters. Disney called this process "Imagineering" and attempted to leverage the benefits of animation into movies, TV shows, toys, and merchandise as well as amusement parks. Hong Kong Disneyland, like the other two Disney parks in Tokyo and Paris, allowed Disney to further leverage its core competencies to international markets. Almost all of the Hong Kong Disneyland attractions build off of Disney's library of animated characters and movies. Buzz Lightyear inhabits Tomorrowland, Winnie the Pooh, Mickey Mouse, and Snow White inhabit Fantasyland, and Tarzan and Lion King inhabit Adventureland. These features of Disneyland target the same demographic set and customer base in Hong Kong as Ocean Park.

In response to Disney's onslaught, Ocean Park proposed spending HK$5.55 billion, obtained from private and government loans, to revamp its well-worn product line. "We are receiving challenges from a formidable giant, and we need to survive," stated Allan Zeman, Ocean Park's Board Chairman. "The only way we can survive is to make our park world class," he

EXHIBIT 2   OCEAN PARK VERSUS HONG KONG DISNEYLAND

	Ocean Park	Hong Kong Disneyland
Date of opening	January 1977	September 2005
Selling points	Sea world, marine life, and real animals: 35 rides and attractions	Disney cartoon characters, fantasy, and famous American brands: 23 rides and attractions
Admission price	Adult: HK$250* Child: HK$125*	Adult: HK$350 Child: HK$250
Area	215 acres	310 acres
Daily maximum capacity	35,000 people	30,000 people
Number of jobs created	37,100	18,000
Economic contribution	HK$145 billion	HK$148 billion
Investment	HK$5.6 billion	HK$22.4 billion

* US$1 = HK$7.8.

added. Ocean Park's management was convinced that hesitation would be lethal in the increasingly competitive and globalized tourism market. However, Ocean Park made a clear decision early on that it would not try to beat Disneyland at its own game. Zeman stated: "We do not want to try to 'out-Disney' Disney." By this, he meant that Ocean Park would focus on its unique core competencies and not try to beat Disney at creating characters and fantasy. Vivian Lee, Ocean Park's Marketing Manager, stated: "A key decision was made that Ocean Park should go back to its roots and build on its strengths rather than trying to imitate its competitor. By positioning itself as the much-loved Hong Kong people's park that prides itself on connecting people with nature, Ocean Park could differentiate itself from Disneyland while complementing Disneyland to further promote Hong Kong as a must-visit tourist destination."

The result was an ambitious HK$5.55 billion master plan, including schemes for a new roller coaster that will be operating by 2012, a subzero "Ice Palace," and a 7.6-million liter aquarium with an underwater restaurant. An extra 33 animal species were to be brought in and the number of rides was doubled to 70. The redevelopment plan of Ocean Park also called for a two- or three-star hotel at the Mass Transit Railway (MTR) subway station: construction of the new MTR station will begin in 2011 and will be in operation by 2015. A five-star "boutique, spa-type" hotel will sit atop the hillside with a 360-degree view of the surrounding sea and mountains. This would be head-on confrontation with Disney, which traditionally offered accommodation within its amusement parks. These improvements were planned on the assumption that the government would build a new MTR station near Ocean Park. Zeman believed that an underground transport link to Ocean Park would help it compete with Disney, which had its own MTR station. According to the ambitious plan, Ocean Park was to have a new look to be divided into two major areas—Waterfront and Summit, which together would boast more than 70 distinctive attractions.

Just as its name designated, Ocean Park hoped to position itself as a world-class marine-based attraction with real animals in this ambitious overhaul. The Park would also continue in its efforts of wild life conservation and would continue to supply visitors with experiences that combined entertainment and education. Ocean Park's management hoped that the redevelopment of the Park would further strengthen its core competencies in "real" nature rather in contrast to Disney's strengths in cartoon characters, castles, virtual reality, and fantasy. It was hoped that Ocean Park

could differentiate itself more clearly from Disneyland. In this way, some of the tourists with families from China and Southeast Asia who came to Hong Kong would "spill over" into additional attendance for Ocean Park.

Accordingly, the plan called for more animal species to be introduced and the lower area would be renamed the Waterfront. Three themed zones would be: Aqua City aquarium, Birds of Paradise aviary, and Whiskers Harbor family area. Ocean Park would be transformed into a spectacular, marine-based theme park with 33 new species of animals, including whales, polar bears, and penguins. In addition to enhanced promotion activities in Hong Kong, the Park planned to open offices in major, affluent urban areas of Guangzhou, Shanghai, and Beijing to attract more mainland visitors, who, it was hoped, would make up an ever larger portion of the Park's clientele.

The pending overhaul plan would have a decisive influence on Ocean Park's future. Still, as with any major reorientation of strategy, the ultimate outcomes were uncertain. A major factor in success would depend upon implementation. While Ocean Park's location was quite convenient, the proposed MTR line extending to the southern region of Hong Kong Island would be of immense benefit.

In addition, the huge HK$5.55 billion investment would put a severe financial burden on Ocean Park as half of the investment would come from bank loans. Ocean Park's profit in 2005 was only HK$119.5 million. It would be difficult to service the loans from ticket receipts and consumption in the Park. Management was counting on the hotels to generate sufficient operating income for Ocean Park. The construction of the hotels required the approval of the Town Planning Board as well.

Although the proposed redevelopment plan would be expensive, Ocean Park still maintained its ticket prices upon the opening of Disneyland. "In particular, visitors from mainland China are very price sensitive but they represent a major source of Ocean Park's income," said Mehrmann. In the very beginning, management kept Ocean Park's admission fee at HK$185 for an adult compared to Disney's price of HK$295 on weekdays and HK$350 on special days. In the following years, to repay the principal and interest on its HK$5.5 billion redevelopment project, Ocean Park adjusted its admission price to HK$208 for an adult in October 2007, and then to HK$250 in October 2009. Disney only made one price adjustment to make the price on weekdays and special days the same in February 2009. However, the price of Ocean Park is still 40% lower than Disney's. As Mehrmann said: "It is premature to discuss whether the price will increase or drop in 2010. But it must be lower than Disneyland's."

Moreover, to boost the attendance frequency of local visitors, Ocean Park introduced a unique Smart-Fun Annual Pass program, which entitled annual pass holders to unlimited admission for an entire year. There would be three different types of SmartFun Annual Pass: gold pass, silver pass, and full-time student pass. It was hoped that this program would encourage annual pass holders to visit the park many more times. Hopefully, annual pass holders might also bring along other visitors. It was hoped that both the lower price and SmartFun Annual Pass program could draw larger crowds. The low-price policy, on the other had, was designed to immediately address the threat in the increasingly competitive tourism industry.

Besides price campaign, seasonal holiday theme was another field of battle between Ocean Park and Hong Kong Disneyland. This battle highlighted the different approaches taken by East and West. For instance, in the Halloween of 2009, a creative campaign was laid out. While Hong Kong Disneyland was fashioning a sinister, dark world, like the one we see in Hollywood blockbusters full of creepy zombies and aliens and patented Disney adventures, Ocean Park tapped into the local psyche. It presented a legion of incorporeal apparitions straight out of local lore, derived from old tales like the madness at the high street police station and the long-haired girl who was said to haunt a university laboratory. There was a great contrast between Ocean Park that played the Hong Kong card and Disneyland that deployed strong Western elements. Moreover, the former offered a 10% discount for advanced booking of Halloween Bash tickets, and the latter opened a week earlier than the former in order to beef up visitor numbers.

The MTR's Ngong Ping 360 cable car that opened in 2007 could have been another local competitor of Ocean Park and Disneyland. This was a 5.7 kilometer glass encased cable car ride near the new Hong Kong International Airport that took visitors up to the 26 meter high "Big Buddha" statue, the Po Lin Buddhist Monastery, and the Ngong Ping tourist village. What Ocean Park chose to do was to cooperate with the operator of the cable car. A discount was announced that visitors to either attraction would get a 10% discount when they visit the other. Disneyland may be at risk of even greater competition now that its rival, Ocean Park, is partnering with Ngong Ping 360.[7]

With a history of over 30 years, Ocean Park had developed better relations with travel agencies compared to Disneyland. Ocean Park was almost always included in inbound tour itineraries, but only 30% of visitors would go to Disneyland because of the extra time and money needed. Moreover, Ocean Park succeeded in touching Hong Kong people's hearts whereas Disneyland was seen as an American product.[8]

Challenges Ahead

Hong Kong tourism was becoming more challenging and dynamic. Zeman, Mehrmann, and other members of Ocean Park's management team were convinced that in order to remain competitive, Ocean Park could not be complacent. As a result, the campaign for the imaginations of the people between the two theme parks never stopped since Disney came to Hong Kong. Although Ocean Park seemed to be ahead for now in the amusement park battles, there was always the threat that Disney might pull ahead. In August 2008, Disneyland has been exclusively selected for a pilot scheme to bring in tourists from among Shenzhen's 12 million migrants.[9] As tourists from mainland China consisted of the majority of visitors for both parks, this represented a potential threat to Ocean Park—or was it? As Hong Kong tourism was in a state of flux, tourists from the mainland made up an ever increasing proportion of the visitors.

The global financial crisis that began in 2008 has battered the local tourism industry. Additionally, swine flu has been an uncertainty that made the attendance of Ocean Park in the summer of 2009 fall for the first time in three years since 2006. Facing these challenges, what should the management team of Ocean Park do? Is it possible to have a win-win situation between these two large-scale amusement parks in Hong Kong? Whatever strategies the management team developed, Ocean Park has to learn to live with Disneyland.

Case Discussion Questions:

1. Ocean Park made the decision not to compete head-to-head with Disneyland. Rather, Ocean Park took a strategy of co-existence. Will this strategy always work when local companies face giant multinational competitors? Explain.

2. How does the influx of mainland Chinese tourists resulting from Disneyland affect the tourism industry in Hong Kong?

3. How can Ocean Park further capitalize on Disneyland's presence? (Hint: Check out how other parks surrounding Disney, such as Sea World and Universal Studio, survive in Anaheim, California, and Orlando, Florida.)

4. Should Ocean Park intensify or reduce its head-to-head competition with Disneyland? Explain.

NOTES

[1] Since 1983, the Hong Kong dollar has been pegged to the US dollar at approximately US$1 = HK$7.8.

[2] *South China Morning Post*, 2006, Ocean Park puts on a great show, December 15.

[3] Information is partly from Ocean Park Annual Report 2004-2005.

[4] *Media*, 2009, Mickey must put his Hong Kong house in order, October 7.

[5] Information is partly from Ocean Park's website at http://www.oceanpark.com.hk/eng/main/index.html.

[6] D. Lee & K. Christensen, 2005, Translating Anaheim for Asia, *Los Angels Times*, September 6.

[7] *South China Morning Post*, 2007, Cable car and Ocean Park is discount deal, December 29.

[8] *The Standard*, 2007, Disneyland looks to local partners for visitor magic, December 22.

[9] *The Standard*, 2008, Ocean Park aims for 'fair' share of Disney CEPA deal, July 31.

INTEGRATIVE CASE 3.4

DHL BANGLADESH

Hemant Merchant, *Florida Atlantic University*

Masud Chand, *Simon Fraser University*

How should DHL Bangladesh proceed with a decision on a human resource information system, given the preferences of regional headquarters, the interests of sister subsidiaries, and the reservations of the Bangladesh subsidiary?

Late in October 2001, Nurul Rahman, Special Assistant to Vice President–Human Resources at DHL Bangladesh (DHLB), contemplated his options regarding the adoption of a human resource information system (HRIS) that the firm's regional headquarters (HQ) in Singapore had proposed. The HRIS would computerize various human resource management (HRM) routines and provide much needed infrastructure to DHLB's HR department which had difficulty coping with the organization's rapid growth. Yet, the proposed HRIS was an expensive initiative that DHLB seemed reluctant to adopt not only due to its uncertain payoffs but also because its implementation would solely be DHLB's responsibility. The charge of making an initial recommendation fell on Nurul who knew his counsel would be heeded by his boss, Mr. Jahar Saha, VP-HR and a DHLB veteran. Mr. Saha would almost certainly endorse Nurul's recommendation to the Board. Nurul was also aware of the likely political fallout of a "wrong" choice.

In reaching a decision, Nurul had to balance the claims of various stakeholders, particularly DHLB and its regional HQ (in Singapore) that had often expressed a strong preference for streamlining HR systems across its Asian subsidiaries. Was the HRIS recommended by Singapore appropriate for DHLB? If so, where could DHLB find resources for the initiative's adoption? If not, what modifications would be needed to augment HRIS' suitability for DHLB? Nurul had less than a week to make a recommendation.

DHL Bangladesh

A subsidiary of the privately held DHL Worldwide Express, DHLB was a pioneer and the acknowledged market leader in the "air express" industry in Bangladesh. DHLB's principal business consisted of delivering time-sensitive documents and parcels worldwide to and from Bangladesh. Created in 1979, DHLB had grown into a US$10 million business by 2002. During this period, DHLB's employee base had increased from 5 to almost 300. Most of them were based in Dhaka, Bangladesh's capital, where the bulk of DHLB's clientele had their offices.

The rapid economic growth in Bangladesh created opportunities as well as challenges for DHLB. On the one hand, it allowed DHLB to increase its revenues and profitability, and to achieve greater visibility within the DHL Worldwide network. On the other hand, this growth significantly increased the workload for DHLB employees, who were overworked and stressed.

Although DHLB's organizational structure enabled the firm to grow with Bangladesh's anticipated expansion, the company's various departments had not grown evenly. Nurul recalled:

In 2000, DHL Asia had implemented a region-wide cost management program. An important aspect of that program was to reduce back-line costs. Consequently, recruitment for back-line departments [such as HR] was frozen, and any new hiring for these departments had to be approved by the regional HQ. In fact, the cost-reduction initiative was so vital that DHL subsidiaries needed regional approval even if they wanted to fill vacancies created by retirements or turnover. There had been instances where such replacement hiring had not been approved by the regional HQ.

The lopsided growth in DHLB's organizational structure created a bottleneck. Nowhere was this bottleneck more evident than in the HR department which had been operating with just three employees since 1994, when DHLB had 150 employees. This situation

This is the condensed version of "DHL Bangladesh: Managing HQ-Subsidiary Relations," published in *Thunderbird International Business Review*, Volume 50, Issue 3, May–June 2008, pp. 201–214. The award-winning case was written by Dr. Hemant Merchant (Florida Atlantic University) with assistance from Masud Chand (Simon Fraser University) solely to provide material for class discussion. The authors do not intend to illustrate either effective or ineffective handling of a managerial situation, and may have disguised certain names and other identifying information to protect confidentiality. However, all essential facts and relationships remain unchanged. © Hemant Merchant. Reprinted with permission. Copyright of the longer version rests with Wiley/*TIBR*.

presented a major constraint because DHLB considered "people" to be its principal resource. This made it imperative that all DHLB employees were well trained and highly motivated. Thus—despite being widely viewed as a "support" function—HR, in fact, played a vital role in DHLB's growth.

HR Department in DHLB

Despite its small size, the HR department in DHLB performed multiple functions whose discharge strained the two executives who were involved in its day-to-day functioning. A key priority for DHLB was employee recruitment at various levels. The bulk of this hiring was at the entry level, where demands upon the HR department were the greatest.

Over the past three years, these HR responsibilities not only had increased greatly because of employee hiring in various departments, but also focused on development of generalist skills in the long term. There was also a sharp increase in the training and development of senior executives who were sent abroad for skills-enhancement workshops. Keeping track of these activities and ensuring a structure in which employees could perform multiple tasks increased the demands on the HR department significantly more than it had done at any other period in DHLB's history.

Perhaps the fastest growing HR function was the administration of compensation and benefits. Until 1998, employee benefits were decided on a company-wide basis while salary increments were based on recommendations of individual department managers. Over the last four years, this policy had changed drastically. Now, all non-salary benefits were being streamlined to DHL's standards for its Asia-Pacific region.

Likewise, salary increments were now being modelled on latest techniques and merit matrices were being implemented across all levels of DHLB. The "new" protocols for administering benefits and compensation created significant pressure on the two HR executives, who were already struggling with keeping up with their other HR obligations.

HRIS Requirements at DHLB

Currently, the core HR functions were managed with non-specialized software, usually Microsoft's Excel spreadsheet. This software solution had served DHLB well even though it limited ways in which HR data could be manipulated or viewed. With the recent growth in DHLB staff, the HR department found it increasingly difficult to rely upon a system that now seemed both "primitive and increasingly unwieldy" to manage. Sensing the imperative for better computerization within the HR department, DHLB management

had (in November 2000) approved the acquisition of a HRIS that met the growing company's needs.

After consulting with various DHLB stakeholders, the HR department had identified five criteria for selecting a HRIS: (1) ability to automate multiple HR functions, (2) ability to link various HR databases, (3) user-friendliness, (4) adaptability to current and anticipated needs, and (5) initial purchase price and operating costs. By December 2000, HR had begun evaluating systems that were being offered by local vendors. Although none of the vendors had an existing software application that exactly matched DHLB's needs, most vendors assured DHLB they would be able to develop a satisfactory solution within a reasonable period. All vendors offered DHLB free long-term technical support. Once DHLB decided on a vendor, it would take the vendor about 2–3 months to customize the solution to the subsidiary's requirements. If all went well, DHLB was expected to have an HRIS operating in approximately six months from the time DHLB placed its order. The system would adequately meet DHLB's needs for the foreseeable future.

Despite their merits, a major limitation of HRIS vendors was that their proposed software solutions would not be compatible with their counterparts in other DHL subsidiaries in the region. This did not seem to matter to some DHLB executives who simply viewed HRIS as an instrument to ease the increasing HR burden on their subsidiary. Such sentiments were not endemic to DHLB. Other DHL subsidiaries in the region, including those in Pakistan, Nepal, and Sri Lanka, were also considering solutions that suited their unique needs. On various occasions, these subsidiaries had informed regional HQ of their desire to develop customized systems. Indeed, in 2000, DHL's Pakistan subsidiary had already developed an HRIS that it had customized to its own needs. Eager to assist other DHL subsidiaries, and perhaps to share some of its developmental costs, Pakistan had been keen to recommend its own system to other DHL units.

Regional HQ and HRIS

The fungibility of Pakistan's HRIS appealed to the regional HQ that seriously considered it for the entire region. The regional HQ played multiple roles within the DHL Worldwide network. It was also responsible for the overall well-being of DHL's regional operations.

In the latter role, one of the main functions of regional HQ was to take data from its individual Asian subsidiaries and combine them into region-wide reports to facilitate subsidiary management and control. The HR function did not lend itself well to such region-wide analysis. Due to country-specific differences in HR practices, subsidiaries in each country where

DHL operated used different types of information and reporting systems. This diversity had strained the regional HQ's personnel in their efforts to consolidate and analyze HR data from DHL Asian subsidiaries. As such, regional HQ always had an interest in standardizing the HR reporting practices across countries. Pakistan's proposal seemed to be just the tool regional HQ was looking for to reduce differences in the functional and reporting styles of DHL subsidiaries across Asia. Nurul recalled:

> From the regional HQ's viewpoint, a single HRIS that worked across different countries made perfect sense. It would considerably reduce the work of regional HR staff as they would no longer need to spend time consolidating and analyzing data from different countries. Besides, standardizing processes across the region was one of regional HQ's main functions. However, differences in reporting styles across countries were not merely cosmetic; they were the products of inherently different HR systems which reflected distinct corporate and legal environments of each country.

In December 2000, the regional HQ asked DHLB to suspend evaluating local vendors and consider DHL Pakistan's offer. In response, the HR manager at DHLB asked for an opportunity to acquaint himself with the Pakistan HRIS system. As he would later learn, the HR managers in DHL Nepal and DHL Sri Lanka had also made similar requests, to which the regional HQ had replied favorably. The meeting to evaluate Pakistan HRIS was scheduled in late February 2001 in Karachi, Pakistan, where DHL Pakistan was headquartered. It was expected that the meeting would be attended by senior HR managers of DHL Bangladesh and DHL Sri Lanka, the country manager of DHL Nepal, and Bruce Newton, the regional VP-HR. DHL Pakistan's HR manager and a technical specialist from the subsidiary's IT department were expected as well. The responsibility of representing DHLB at the Karachi meeting had fallen on Nurul because of a scheduling conflict involving Mr. Saha, the VP-HR at DHLB, who would normally have represented his country.

HRIS Search at DHLB

Nurul had joined DHLB relatively recently, and was one of the newest and youngest members of the DHLB team. He had graduated from the country's premier business school which was affiliated with the University of Dhaka. Nurul's ability to deliver "quality" on special HR projects had earned him the respect of his colleagues and brought him to the attention of DHLB's senior management. Nurul had moved up through DHLB's ranks quickly and had earned the trust of Mr. Saha who had often assigned him to work on key HR projects under his personal supervision. One such project was the search for a suitable HRIS vendor—that is, until the regional HQ put a stop to that search with its own suggestion.

After an extensive analysis, Nurul had shortlisted two local vendors who could easily demonstrate their solutions within a week of being told to do so. Now Nurul had to consider a third option that regional HQ had proposed: the Pakistan HRIS. Doing so would not only significantly delay DHLB's decision about adopting a customized HRIS, but also require a very careful scrutiny of the broader context in which the HRIS acquisition decision was situated. Mr. Saha had been informed that regional HQ had now set a date for the HRIS project meeting during which DHL Pakistan would demonstrate its HRIS to the regional HQ and other subsidiary managers. DHL Pakistan hoped to persuade other subsidiaries that its own HRIS was the "right" software solution to their individual needs.

The Karachi Meeting

The Karachi meeting was as "interesting" as Nurul had expected. During the three-day meeting, DHL Pakistan managers briefed other DHL participants on the HRIS system currently used in Pakistan and acquainted them with the system. The hosts also gave the visitors short user-training related to different functionalities of the Pakistan HRIS. Nurul recalled:

> The Pakistan HRIS was a complicated software solution that required a lot of familiarization to become comfortable with. Although the HR employees at DHL Pakistan appeared to be comfortable with its use, it was clear that this software required a lot of first hand involvement to attain proficiency using it. Despite this, I was surprised that Pakistan had not yet developed any user- or technical-training manuals. While the Pakistan system brought all HR functions together under a comprehensive database, it would require a great deal of customization to be brought up to DHL Bangladesh's requirements. DHL Bangladesh and DHL Pakistan were very different in terms of their operations and size, and the two countries' HRIS requirements reflected that divergence.

DHL Pakistan was roughly twice the size of DHL Bangladesh, both in terms of revenue and personnel.

The Pakistan subsidiary's operations were also much more geographically widespread. Moreover, the roles of HR departments in the two countries were generally different. Indeed, the demonstrated HRIS was primarily designed to meet the Pakistan subsidiary's needs—many of them quite different from those of the Bangladesh subsidiary.

The differences in HR practices manifested itself in the expectations of the HRIS in each DHL subsidiary. For example, there were variances in the process of calculating gross salary for personnel. Although the calculation algorithm itself was easy to amend, the routine was hardwired into the system so that users could not change the settings from their side. To convert the system to do things in the DHLB style would require changes from the technical side, which is from the original designers of the system. The DHL Pakistan staff could make these changes before the system was operational in Bangladesh. However, if there were any further changes—even minor ones—based on DHL Bangladesh's methods, or if there were any changes in industrial laws brought about by the government of Bangladesh, the system would have to be reconfigured from the technical side by its designers.

Another major difference was that DHLB often recruited temporary employees who were not eligible for many company benefits, whereas Pakistan regulations required DHL there to treat all employees as regular employees. Such adjustments would further complicate the Pakistan HRIS.

Yet, another difference pertained to training records. DHLB maintained a database on training imparted to all employees. In contrast, DHL Pakistan maintained training records only for the last three years. Because these record-keeping protocols were hardwired into the Pakistan HRIS, they could be not be modified by the user. This meant the existing HRIS software would have to be rewritten by engineers before it could become useful to DHLB. All of these issues suggested DHLB not only would incur significant financial and non-financial costs if it adopted the Pakistani HRIS, it ran the additional risk of downtime and operational dependency on another subsidiary.

Such concerns were downplayed by DHL Pakistan managers. In fact, they assured the visiting executives that their technical team could make country-specific customizations relatively quickly, and at a reasonable price. Nurul believed if an application designed by Pakistan were adopted by DHL subsidiaries in the region, it would provide a major boost to DHL Pakistan's standing and influence. It would also raise the odds for Pakistan staff (especially from HR) to move upwards to the regional level. Bruce Newton, the regional VP-HR,

was highly impressed with the software and was confident of Pakistan HRIS' ability to be the platform for standardizing DHL's HR systems in the region. He let the executives know where he stood. Bruce said at the meeting:

> The Pakistan team has done a fine job of designing this software and I thank them for it. I can see they have put a great deal of thought and effort in designing it. Based on the demonstration we have viewed today, I am confident the Pakistan HRIS can be modified to meet the purposes of all DHL subsidiaries in the region. The only question I have is whether Pakistan can provide the level of technical support that might be needed by DHL's Asian subsidiaries.

The regional HQ's apparent liking for the Pakistani HRIS appeared to be driven by a variety of factors. First, the above HRIS not only was fully functional but also worked well in Pakistan. Second, given the above, the Pakistani HRIS was the quickest way for HQ to achieve its goal to standardize HR reporting systems across the Asian region. Third, the Pakistan team had assured Bruce that it could easily customize its HRIS to suit other DHL subsidiaries' requirements and that it also had the ability and willingness to provide technical assistance whenever needed. Given Pakistan's continued assurances of support, and perhaps because of Bruce's enthusiasm, the visiting DHL delegates also expressed confidence in the Pakistan HRIS.

Nurul, however, had reservations about the system he had just seen. Although he did not share his thoughts in Karachi, Nurul let his boss know about them when he returned to Dhaka. First, the financial burden of buying into Pakistan HRIS would be five times that of finding a local solution. A locally developed solution would cost DHLB less than $5,000, whereas the Pakistan system (inclusive of ancillary expenses) would cost approximately $100,000 which would be split four ways among the three countries and the regional HQ. While DHLB management would probably approve this $25,000 expense, the funds would represent the HR department's biggest outlay for the year. Indeed, the outlay would constitute the largest HRIS investment in Bangladesh's "air express" industry.

Nurul's second reservation pertained to the variety of customized modules needed to make the demonstrated HRIS suitable for DHLB's needs. Nurul was particularly concerned about the range of these changes for they would have to be developed around the Pakistan HRIS architecture. Doing so was expected to needlessly complicate DHLB's system:

> The problems with the Pakistan HRIS suitability for DHLB were both short and long run. In the short run, DHLB would inherit a system that was expensive (probably the single largest line item after salaries on our budget) and complicated. In the long run, DHLB would have a system that not only was extremely inflexible from the user front, but also dependent on another DHL subsidiary on the technical front.

Nurul was also concerned about DHLB's technical dependency on the Pakistan subsidiary. He had noticed that DHL Pakistan had an IT specialist whose sole responsibility was to maintain the subsidiary's HRIS. This reinforced Nurul's suspicion that the demonstrated HRIS needed regular technical upkeep. Although DHLB also had IT specialists on its staff, there were fewer of them. Given that all software changes would be designed in Pakistan—over whom Bangladesh had no authority—DHLB would be at the Pakistan subsidiary's mercy vis-à-vis any and all technical assistance. Seeking the regional HQ's intervention was not a sustainable solution and, moreover, would make DHLB staff "look bad" to the regional office. Additionally, software documentation on user as well as technical platforms was either inadequate or non-existent. DHL Pakistan would have to provide this documentation before its reconfigured HRIS system could be implemented in Bangladesh.

DHLB and Its Regional HQ

Mr. Saha relayed these concerns to regional HQ that had psychologically bought into what DHL Pakistan had to offer other DHL subsidiaries in the region. This was an important point that DLHB could not afford to ignore. DHLB reported directly to the Singapore-based regional HQ that played an important strategic role in the DHL system.

The responsibility for fulfilling this role fell on the regional management team that consisted of Asia region VPs and some other top-level executives. This group had line authority over country-level top management and was ultimately responsible for the overall success of DHL in Asia. The regional VPs were important members of the group and served as principal advisers to the functional area VPs in individual countries: it was very rare that their "advice" was not heeded by subsidiary VPs. Although regional VPs did not have direct control over subsidiary VPs, the

regional VPs had "very real power" and could significantly enhance or diminish the career prospects of subsidiary-level managers.

At the country level, all functional area VPs were in a quasi-matrix reporting structure (see Exhibit 1). A functional area VP reported directly to his country manager and also, indirectly, to the regional VP holding that particular functional portfolio. Thus, Mr. Saha also reported to Bruce Newton, the regional VP-HR. The regional VPs did not have line authority over their country-level counterparts, and could not issue direct orders to subsidiary VPs. Rather, the regional VPs' role was to coach, guide, provide expert knowledge, and lead cross-national projects. At least on paper, the regional HQ played a paternal role.

In reality, however, the regional VPs often wielded significant influence over country-level VPs as most major country-level decisions required regional approval. Subsidiary-initiated projects not supported by a regional VP were rarely approved at the country level. Thus, regional VPs were crucial individuals to get on board whenever any major country-level program was initiated. Their influence was further magnified by their role as functional advisors to the regional president who had direct authority over country management teams.

DHL also followed a 360-degree feedback model for evaluating the performance of its senior managers worldwide. This process involved seeking feedback from an individual's immediate supervisor, peers, subordinates, and customers as well as the regional management team. Thus, a regional VP's feedback played a crucial role in the career progression of an individual senior manager—especially if a country-level VP had any regional-level aspirations. The regional VP's strong endorsement was absolutely essential for any move to the regional office. An ambitious and upwardly mobile VP at the country level would think long and hard before turning down any advice from his regional VP. One written negative comment by a regional VP in a performance appraisal could easily be a career killer for the concerned country-level VP.

The HRIS Decision

Given the competing interests of various stakeholders, Nurul knew he had a tough recommendation to make. On the one hand, dropping the Pakistan HRIS customization idea was worth consideration. The modification might not live up to its potential in DHLB and there still were Bangladeshi vendors willing to do the job at a fraction of the cost. On the other hand, DHLB had already spent considerable time and money on this project, and could not afford further delays. The

EXHIBIT 1   **DHL BANGLADESH MATRIX STRUCTURE**

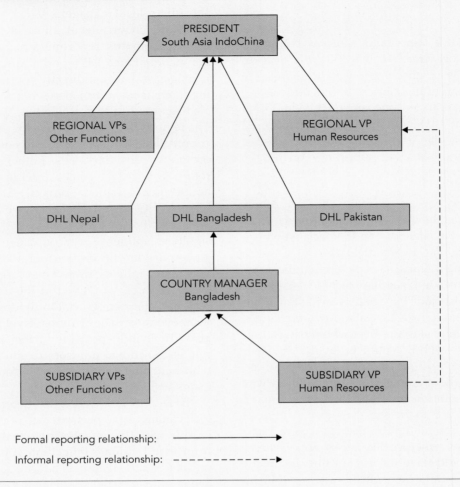

Formal reporting relationship: ⟶

Informal reporting relationship: ⇢

subsidiary's discussions with regional HQ and the Pakistan subsidiary managers had exhausted the HR department and, ironically, set it further behind in its day-to-day task completion. In any case, the regional HQ had constantly assured DHLB about Pakistan's commitment and technical support vis-à-vis the HRIS project. Would it not be better to continue with the Pakistan offer and solve potential problems when they arose? After all, the project had backing from the regional HQ.

Whatever Nurul recommended would have major ramifications at all levels. For DHLB, it was foremost a question about possessing the HRIS. Without it, there was no way the HR staff could stretch itself for much longer. It was also imperative to consider relations between the regional HQ and DHLB, and between DHLB and other DHL subsidiaries in Asia. How

might regional HQ view a deviation—even a "justified" one—from its position? Would it invite greater scrutiny in the future? Would it curtail the subsidiary's operational and strategic freedom? Would it be prudent for DHLB to accede to regional HQ's choice and save organizational energies for a "bigger battle" which might arise in the future? At an individual level, Nurul had to consider potential reprisals from a very powerful stakeholder. Indeed, how would his recommendation affect his own career at DHL? How might other HR staff be affected? What about Mr. Saha himself? How would Saha view his (Nurul's) integrity? These questions occupied Nurul's thoughts as he looked out of his office window into the winter sunshine: "What do I tell my boss three days from now? How—and how much—do I justify my recommendation?"

Case Discussion Questions:

1. What advantages and disadvantages associated with a matrix structure does this case reveal?
2. For Nurul, identify the advantages and disadvantages for the three options: (1) proceeding with DHL Pakistan's HRIS, (2) proceedings with a local Bangladesh vendor, and (3) negotiating with regional HQ.
3. Rank in order the advantages and disadvantages listed in the question above, in terms of their (1) potential for solving DHLB's problems and (2) political importance from the viewpoint of DHLB and regional HQ. For a more detailed analysis, include the following stakeholders: (1) Nurul Rahman, (2) DHLB's HR department, (3) Mr. Saha, and (4) DHL Pakistan.
4. If you were Nurul Rahman, what would you recommend?

Building Functional Excellence

© Ian Mckinnell

Chapter
14

© Sarah Peters

LEARNING OBJECTIVES

After studying this chapter, you should be able to:

1. articulate three of the four marketing Ps (product, price, and promotion) in a global context.

2. explain how the fourth marketing P (place) has changed into supply chain management.

3. outline the three As of supply chain management (agility, adaptability, and alignment).

4. discuss how institutions and resources affect marketing and supply chain management.

5. participate in two leading debates on marketing and supply chain management.

6. draw implications for action.

Competing on Marketing and Supply Chain Management

Zara: Rewriting Rules on Marketing and Supply Chain Management

Zara is one of the hottest fashion chains of the 21st century. Founded in 1975, Zara's parent, Inditex, has become one of the leading global apparel retailers. Since its initial public offering (IPO) in 2001, Inditex has tripled its sales and profits and doubled the number of stores. Of the company's eight brands, Zara contributes two-thirds of total sales. Zara succeeds by breaking and then rewriting rules on marketing and supply chain management.

Rule number one: The origin of a fashion house usually carries some cachet. However, Zara does not hail from Italy or France—it is from Spain. Even within Spain, Zara is not based in a cosmopolitan city like Barcelona or Madrid but in Arteixo, a town of only 25,000 people in a remote corner of Northwestern Spain. Yet, Zara is active not only throughout Europe, but also in Asia and North America. As of 2009, there are more than 4,200 Zara stores in 64 countries—in some of the priciest locations: Champs-Elysées in Paris, Ginza in Tokyo, Fifth Avenue in New York, and the Galleria in Dallas.

Rule number two: Avoid stock-outs (a store running out of items in demand). Actually, occasional shortages contribute to an urge to buy now. New items arrive at stores *twice* a week, so experienced Zara shoppers know that "If you see something and don't buy it, you can forget about coming back for it because it will be gone." The small batch of merchandise available for a short time motivates shoppers to visit Zara stores more frequently. In London, the average shopper will only visit a typical clothing store four times per year, but will go to Zara 17 times per year. Shoppers make so many trips because Zara makes about 20,000 different items a year, about triple what Gap does. As a result, "at Gap, everything is the same," according to a Zara fan, "and buying from Zara, you'll never end up looking like someone else."

Rule number three: Bombarding shoppers with ads is a must. Gap and H&M spend on average 3% to 4% of their sales on ads. Zara devotes just 0.3% of its sales to ads. High store traffic alleviates some need for media advertising, most of which only serves as a reminder to visit the stores.

Rule number four: Outsource. Gap and H&M do not own any production facilities. However, outsourcing production (mostly to Asia) requires a long lead time, usually several months ahead. Again, Zara has decisively deviated from the industry norm. By concentrating most of its production in-house and in Spain, Zara has developed a super-responsive supply chain. It designs, produces, and delivers a new garment to its stores worldwide in a mere 15 *days*, a pace that is unheard of in the industry. The best speed the rivals can achieve is two *months*. Outsourcing may not necessarily be "low cost," because errors in prediction can easily lead to unsold inventory, forcing retailers to offer steep discounts. The industry average is to offer 40% discounts across all merchandise. In contrast, Zara sells more at full price and, when it discounts, it averages only 15%.

Rule number five: Strive for efficiency through large batches. In contrast, Zara intentionally deals with small batches. Because of its flexibility, Zara does not worry about "missing the boat" for a season. When new trends emerge, Zara can react quickly. More interestingly, Zara runs its supply chain like clockwork, with a fast but predictable rhythm: Every store places orders on Tuesday/Wednesday and Friday/Saturday. Trucks and cargo flights run on established schedules—like a bus service. From Spain, shipments reach most European stores in 24 hours, US stores in 48 hours, and Asian stores in 72 hours. Not only does store staff know exactly when shipments will arrive, regular customers know too, thus motivating them to check out the new merchandise more frequently on those days, which are known as "Z days" in some cities.

Overall, marketing and supply chain management have become an integrated system that mutually reinforces each other and has propelled Zara's formidable rise around the globe. In the fiscal year ending January 31, 2009, Gap was still bigger ($14.5 billion sales) compared to Inditex ($14.1 billion)—but barely. What is more striking is that in the middle of the worst global economic crisis since the Great Depression, Inditex reported a 10% sales *gain*. In contrast, Gap suffered a 23% sales *decline* in the same year. Out of desperation, Gap and other rivals have resorted to deep discounting, a practice Zara has resisted thus far. In 2009, for the first time, *BusinessWeek* ranked Zara's fashionable but affordable brand as one of the top 50 best global brands (see Table 14.1). Although Gap also made the top 100, it was 78 and trailed behind Zara (50).

Sources: Based on (1) *BusinessWeek*, 2006, Fashion conquistador, September 4: 38–39; (2) *BusinessWeek*, 2009, 100 best global brands, September 28: 44–60; (3) K. Ferdows, M. Lewis, & J. Machuca, 2004, Rapid-fire fulfillment, *Harvard Business Review*, November: 104–110; (4) *Wall Street Journal*, 2009, Zara grows as retail rivals struggle, http://online.wsj.com/article/SB123801606310041287. html (accessed August 31, 2009); (5) www.zara.com.

Marketing
Efforts to create, develop, and defend markets that satisfy the needs and wants of individual and business customers.

Supply chain
Flow of products, services, finances, and information that passes through a set of entities from a source to the customer.

Supply chain management
Activities to plan, organize, lead, and control the supply chain.

Marketing mix
The four underlying components of marketing: (1) product, (2) price, (3) promotion, and (4) place.

How can firms such as Zara market themselves and attract customers? Having attracted customers, how can firms ensure a steady supply of products and services? This chapter deals with these and other important questions associated with marketing and supply chain management. **Marketing** refers to efforts to create, develop, and defend markets that satisfy the needs and wants of individual and business customers. **Supply chain** is the flow of products, services, finances, and information that passes through a set of entities from a source to the customer.[1] **Supply chain management** refers to activities to plan, organize, lead, and control the supply chain.[2] In this chapter, instead of viewing marketing and supply chain as two separate, stand-alone functions, we view them as one integrated function that may make or break a firm.

We first outline major marketing and supply chain activities in global business. Then we discuss how the institution-based and resource-based views enhance our understanding of the drivers behind marketing and supply chain management success. Finally, debates and implications follow.

Articulate three of the four marketing Ps (product, price, and promotion) in a global context.

THREE OF THE FOUR MARKETING Ps

Figure 14.1 shows the four Ps that collectively make up the **marketing mix**: (1) product, (2) price, (3) promotion, and (4) place.[3] We start with the first three Ps. The last P—place (where the product is sourced, produced, and distributed)—will be discussed in the next section.

FIGURE 14.1   THE FOUR Ps OF MARKETING MIX

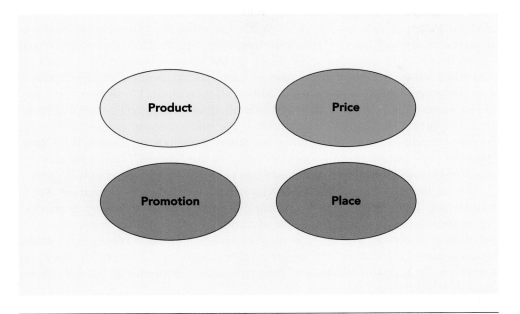

Product

Product refers to offerings that customers purchase. Although the word "product" originally referred to a physical product, its modern use may include services. To avoid confusion, however, we will use "products and services" in this chapter. This makes sense because in a broad sense when a customer purchases a product, this product also embodies service elements (such as maintenance and upgrades).

Even for a single category (such as women's dresses or sports cars), product attributes vary tremendously. For multinational enterprises (MNEs) doing business around the world, a leading concern is standardization versus localization.[4] Localization is natural. McDonald's, for example, sells wine in France, beer in Germany, mutton pot pies in Australia, and Maharaja Mac and McCurry Pan in India. What is interesting is the rise of standardization, which is often attributed to Theodore Levitt's 1983 article, "The Globalization of Markets"[5] (first discussed in Chapter 13). This article advocated globally standardized products and services, as evidenced by Hollywood movies and Coke Classic. However, numerous subsequent experiments such as Ford's "world car" and MTV's "global programming" have backfired. Marketers thus face a dilemma: Although one size does not fit all, most firms cannot afford to create products and services for just one group of customers. Thus, how much to standardize and how much to localize remains a challenge.[6]

As first noted in Chapter 13, local consumers and governments find localization appealing but firms find it expensive. A sensible solution is to have a product that *appears* to be locally adapted while deriving as much synergy (commonality) as possible in ways that customers cannot easily recognize. Consider the two weekly global business magazines, the US-based *BusinessWeek* and the UK-based *Economist*.

Why does McDonald's offer localized products in its restaurants based outside the United States?

Product
Offerings that customers purchase.

In addition to its US edition, *BusinessWeek* publishes two English-language editions for Asia and Europe and a Chinese edition for China. Although these four editions share certain content, they do not share a lot of local content, which is expensive to produce. In comparison, each issue of the *Economist* has the following regional sections (in alphabetical order): (1) the Americas (excluding the United States), (2) Asia, (3) Britain, (4) Europe (excluding Britain), (5) the Middle East and Africa, and (6) the United States. Although the content for each issue is identical, the regional sections are arranged differently. The US edition starts with the US section; the Asian edition starts with the Asia section; and so forth. By so doing, the *Economist* appears to be responsive to readers with different regional interests without incurring the costs of running multiple editions for different regions, as *BusinessWeek* does. Therefore, how many editions does one issue of the *Economist* have? We can say one—or six if we count the six different ways of stapling regional sections together.

One of the major concerns for MNEs is to decide whether to market global brands (see Table 14.1) or local brands in their portfolio.[7] The key is **market segmentation**—identifying segments of consumers who differ from others in purchasing behavior.[8] Markets can be segmented limitless ways, such as males versus females, urban dwellers versus rural residents, and Africans versus Latin Americans. In Focus 14.1 illustrates four new customer segments that have been identified in the recent recession.

For international marketers, the million dollar question is: How does one generalize from a wide variety of market segmentation in different countries in order to generate products that can cater to a few of these segments *around the world*? One globally useful way of segmentation is to divide consumers in four categories.

- Global citizens favor buying global brands that signal prestige and cachet.
- Global dreamers may not be able to afford to buy global brands but admire them nevertheless.
- Antiglobals are skeptical about whether global brands deliver higher-quality goods.
- Global agnostics are most likely to lead antiglobalization demonstrations.

Market segmentation
Identifying segments of consumers who differ from others in purchasing behavior.

Figure 14.2 shows that the distribution of these different groups within each country is uneven. Interestingly, Brazil, China, and Indonesia have higher percentages of global citizens compared to the United States and the UK, which correspondingly have higher percentages of global agnostics.[9]

TABLE 14.1   TOP 20 GLOBAL BRANDS

1	Coca-Cola (USA)	11	Hewlett-Packard (USA)
2	IBM (USA)	12	Mercedes-Benz (Germany)
3	Microsoft (USA)	13	Gillette (USA)
4	GE (USA)	14	Cisco (USA)
5	Nokia (Finland)	15	BMW (Germany)
6	McDonald's (USA)	16	Louis Vuitton (France)
7	Google (USA)	17	Marlboro (USA)
8	Toyota (Japan)	18	Honda (Japan)
9	Intel (USA)	19	Samsung (South Korea)
10	Disney (USA)	20	Apple (USA)

Source: Adapted from "100 Best Global Brands" in the September 28, 2009 issue of Bloomberg *BusinessWeek* by special permission. Copyright © 2009 by Bloomberg L.P.

Customer Segmentation in a Recession

In a recession, traditional segmentation based on demographic differences (such as males versus females, high school dropouts versus college educated, and teenagers versus retired) may need to be supplemented by a new scheme of segmentation based on psychological reactions to a recession. Four groups have emerged.

- *Slam-on-the-brakes*: Typically the hardest hit financially, these customers feel the most vulnerable and consequently curtail all spending.
- *Pained-but-patient*: Often representing the majority, these customers are not confident about maintaining their standard of living in the short term and economize in all areas, but less aggressively.
- *Comfortably-well-off*: Often in the top 5% income bracket, these customers continue to make high-end purchases, but do so less conspicuously.
- *Live-for-today*: Typically urban and young, these customers are unlikely to change their consumption behavior unless they become unemployed.

Consequently, marketers need to target different segments with different messages. For slam-on-the-brakes types, in addition to promoting lower prices and better value, marketers need to challenge "penny-wise, pound-foolish" behavior, such as postponing replacing worn out tires, which could not only result in a safety hazard but also a much higher expense. To the pained-but-patient, marketers can shrink product sizes and offer simpler models. To the comfortably-well-off, marketers can advertise their products' outstanding quality and emphasize the savings from buying now. Finally, to the live-for-today types, marketers can promote exciting "must have" products and make it more enticing to buy by offering convenient automatic credit card billing.

Sources: Based on (1) G. Johnson, 2009, Marketing through recession, Agryle CMO Leadership Forum, San Francisco, June 2, www.slideshare.net (accessed September 1, 2009); (2) J. Quelch & K. Jocz, 2009, How to market in a downturn, *Harvard Business Review*, April: 52–62; (3) D. Yankelovich & D. Meer, 2006, Rediscovering market segmentation, *Harvard Business Review*, February: 122–131.

The implications are clear. For the first two categories of global citizens and global dreamers (who make up approximately 78% of the consumers surveyed), firms are advised to leverage the global brands and their relatively more standardized products and services. "Global brands make us feel like citizens of the world," an Argentinean consumer observed. However, MNEs do not necessarily have to write off the antiglobals and global agnostics as lost customers because MNEs can market localized products and services under local brands. Nestlé, for example, owns 8,000 (!) brands around the world, most of which are local, country-specific (or region-specific) brands not marketed elsewhere.

Overall, Levitt may be *both* right and wrong. A large percentage of consumers around the world indeed have converging interests and preferences centered on global brands. However, a substantial percentage of them also resist globally standardized brands, products, and services. Armed with this knowledge, firms—both MNEs and locals—can better craft their products and services.

Price

Price refers to the expenditures that customers are willing to pay for a product. Most consumers are "price sensitive." The jargon is **price elasticity**—how demand changes when price changes. The basic economic theory of supply and demand suggests that when price drops, consumers will buy more and thus generate stronger demand.

Price
The expenditures that customers are willing to pay for a product.

Price elasticity
How demand changes when price changes.

FIGURE 14.2   SEGMENTATION OF CONSUMERS AS THEY RELATE TO GLOBAL BRANDS

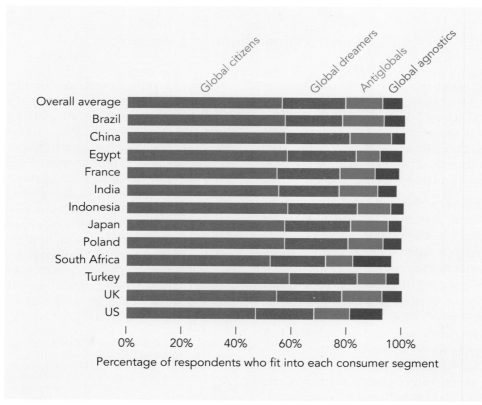

Source: D. Holt, J. Quelch, & E. Taylor, "How global brands compete", *Harvard Business Review*, September 2004, p. 73. Reprinted by permission of Harvard Business Publishing. Results are based on a survey of 1,500 urban consumers between 20 and 35 years old in 41 countries.

Firms in turn are motivated to expand production to meet the increased demand. This theory, of course, underpins the relentless drive around the world to cut costs and then prices. The question is: *How* "price sensitive" are consumers? Holding the product (such as shampoo) constant, in general the lower consumers' income, the more price sensitive they are. Although American, European, and Japanese consumers take it for granted that shampoo is sold by the bottle, in India shampoo is often sold in single-use sachets, each costing anywhere from 1 to 10 cents (in US dollars). Many Indian consumers find the cost for a bottle of shampoo to be prohibitive. Similarly, some African telecommunications operators charge customers by the *second* (not by the minute)—a big deal for those making pennies a day.[10]

In addition to the point of purchase price, another dimension of price is the **total cost of ownership**. An example in consumer products is the ubiquitous HP inkjet printer. Owners typically spend 2 to 3 times more on replacement ink cartridges than on the printer itself. Although individual consumers may not pay explicit attention to the total cost of ownership, businesses do. An important part of business-to-business marketing, total cost of ownership is often explicitly evaluated prior to purchase decisions. Companies such as Airbus and Boeing know that when they sell an aircraft, they can expect revenue for as long as 20 to 30 years in parts and service. More importantly, after-sales products and services are less price sensitive and thus have higher margin.[11] Consequently, many firms compete on winning the initial sale with a lower price, with the aim to capture more revenue through after-sales products and services.

Finally, in international marketing, it is important to note that aggressively low prices abroad may cause a firm to be accused of dumping, thus triggering

Total cost of ownership

Total cost needed to own a product, consisting of initial purchase cost and follow-up maintenance/service cost.

protectionist measures. Because Chapter 11 has already discussed the antidumping issue at length, we will not repeat it here other than stressing its importance.

Promotion

Promotion refers to all the communications that marketers insert into the marketplace. Promotion includes TV, radio, print, and online advertising, as well as coupons, direct mail, billboards, public relations, direct marketing (personal selling), and social media marketing. Marketers face a strategic choice of whether to standardize or localize promotional efforts. Standardized promotion not only projects a globally consistent message (crucial for global brands), but can also save a lot of money. One large campaign may be more cost effective than 100 smaller campaigns.

However, the effectiveness of standardized promotion may be limited. In the 1990s, Coca-Cola ran a worldwide campaign featuring a cute polar bear cartoon character. Research later showed that viewers in warmer weather countries had a hard time relating to this ice-bound animal with which they had no direct experience. In response, Coca-Cola switched to more costly but more effective country-specific advertisements. For instance, the Indian subsidiary launched a campaign that equated Coke with "thanda," the Hindi word for "cold." The German subsidiary developed commercials that showed a "hidden" kind of eroticism (!).[12] Although this is merely one example, it does suggest that even some of the most global brands (such as Coca-Cola) can benefit from localized promotion.

Many firms have promoted products and services overseas without doing the proper homework and ended up with campaigns that did not deliver the intended message. GM marketed its Chevrolet Nova in Latin America without realizing that "no va" means "no go" in Spanish. When Coors Beer translated "Turn it loose" from English into Spanish, its previously successful slogan became "Drink Coors, get diarrhea."[13] Table 14.2 outlines some blunders that are hilarious to readers but painful to marketers, some of whom were fired because of these huge mistakes.

In international marketing, the country-of-origin effect refers to the positive or negative perception of firms and products from a certain country.[14] Marketers have to decide whether to enhance or downplay such an effect, which can be very tricky. Disneyland Tokyo became popular in Japan because it played up its American image. Disneyland Paris, in contrast, received relentless negative press coverage in France because it insisted on marketing a "wholesome American look."[15] Singapore Airlines projects a "Singapore girl" image around the world, but Li Ning downplays its Chinese origin by using American NBA players in its commercials. What is the nationality of Häagen-Dazs ice cream? Many consumers think Häagen-Dazs is a German, Austrian, Belgian, or Swiss brand (and happily pay a premium price for "European" ice cream), but it is actually a US brand.

In addition to the domestic versus international challenge, a new challenge lies in the pursuit of online versus offline (traditional) advertising. As the first cohort to grow up Internet savvy, today's teens and twenty-somethings flock to social networks such as Facebook, Twitter, and MySpace. These young people "do not buy stuff because they see a magazine ad," according to one expert, "they buy stuff because other kids tell them to online."[16] What is challenging is how marketers can reach such youth. Firms such as Apple and P&G experiment with a variety of formats including sponsorships and blogs, with some hits, some misses, and lots of uncertainty. The basic threat to such social networks is the whim of their users, whose interest in certain topics or in the networks themselves may change or even evaporate overnight.

Promotion
Communications that marketers insert into the marketplace.

Country-of-origin effect
The positive or negative perception of firms and products from a certain country.

TABLE 14.2 SOME BLUNDERS IN INTERNATIONAL MARKETING

- One US toymaker received numerous complaints from American mothers, because a talking doll told their children, "Kill mommy!" Made in Hong Kong, the dolls were shipped around the world. They carried messages in the language of the country of destination. A packing error sent some Spanish-speaking dolls to the United States. The message in Spanish "Quiero mommy!" means "I love mommy!" (This is also a supply chain blunder.)

- AT&T submitted a proposal to sell phone equipment in Thailand. Despite its excellent technology, the proposal was rejected out of hand by telecom authorities, because Thailand required a 10-year warranty but AT&T only offered a 5-year warranty—thanks to standardization on warranty imposed by US headquarters.

- To better adapt its products to Egypt, one Chinese shoe manufacturer placed Arabic characters on the soles of the shoes. Unfortunately, the designers did not know Arabic and merely copied words from elsewhere. The words they chose meant "God." China's ambassador to Egypt had to apologize for this blunder.

- Japan's Olympia tried to market a photocopier to Latin America under the name "Roto." Sales were minimal. Why? "Roto" means "broken" in Spanish. (This happened after Chevrolet tried to sell its Nova car in the region—"no va" means "no go" in Spanish.)

- In their eagerness to export to the English-speaking world, Chinese firms have marketed the following products: White Elephant brand batteries, Sea Cucumber brand shirts, and Maxipuke brand poker cards. The two Chinese characters, *pu ke*, means poker, and it should have been translated as Maxi brand poker cards—but its package said "Maxipuke."

Sources: Based on text in (1) T. Dalgic & R. Heijblom, 1996, International marketing blunders revisited—some lessons for managers, *Journal of International Marketing*, 4 (1): 81–91; (2) D. Ricks, 1999, *Blunders in International Business*, 3rd ed., Oxford, UK: Blackwell.

Overall, marketers need to experiment with a variety of configurations of the three Ps (product, price, and promotion) around the world in order to optimize the marketing mix. What has not yet been discussed is the fourth P, place, to which we turn in the next section.

Explain how the fourth marketing P (place) has changed into supply chain management.

Place
The location where products and services are provided.

Distribution channel
The set of firms that facilitates the movement of goods from producers to consumers.

FROM DISTRIBUTION CHANNEL TO SUPPLY CHAIN MANAGEMENT

As the fourth P in the marketing mix, **place** refers to the location where products and services are provided (which now, of course, includes the online marketplace). Technically, "place" is also often referred to as the **distribution channel**—the set of firms that facilitates the movement of goods from producers to consumers. Until the 1980s, a majority of producers made most goods in-house, and one of the key concerns was distribution. Since then, production outsourcing has grown significantly (see Chapter 4). Many producers (such as Nike) do not physically produce their branded products at all; they rely on contract manufacturers to get the job done. Other producers that still produce in-house (such as Dell) rely on their suppliers to provide an increasingly higher percentage of the value added. Therefore, the new challenge is how to manage the longer distribution channel—more specifically, the distribution from suppliers (and contract manufacturers) all the way to consumers[17] (see Figure 14.3).

FIGURE 14.3   SUPPLY CHAIN MANAGEMENT

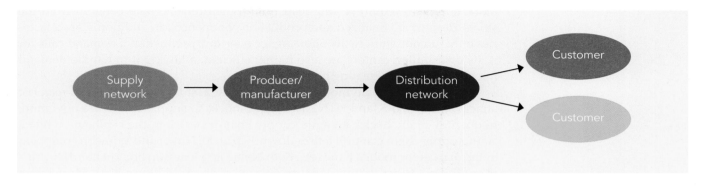

Consequently, the term "supply chain" has almost replaced the old-fashioned "distribution channel." To be sure, the focal firm has always dealt with suppliers. Strategy guru Michael Porter labels this function as "inbound logistics" (and the traditional distribution channel as "outbound logistics").[18] In a broad sense, the new term "supply chain" is almost synonymous with "value chain" encompassing both inbound and outbound logistics (see Chapter 4). In the military, logistics is widely acknowledged as a contributor to wartime success. But no army recruitment material would brag about a glamorous career in logistics in the military to attract new soldiers. Similarly, traditional business logistics tends to be tactical and lacks prestige. However, if supply chain is value chain, then supply chain management essentially handles the *entire* process of value creation, which is the core mission of the firm. Consequently, supply chain management has now taken on new strategic importance and gained tremendous prestige. As illustrated in the Closing Case, Hong Kong–based Li & Fung has become the largest sourcing company in the world by specializing and excelling in managing supply chains for leading retailers such as Victoria's Secret, Liz Claiborne, Timberland, Toys 'R' Us, and Sanrio.

One indication that supply chain management has gained traction is that instead of being obscure players, leading supply chain management firms, such as UPS and FedEx, have now become household names. On any given day, 2% of the world's GDP can be found in UPS trucks and planes. "FedEx" has become a verb, and even live *whales* have reportedly been "FedExed."[19] Modern supply chains aim to "get the right product to the right place at the right time—all the time."[20] (See PengAtlas Maps 4.1 and 4.2 for more information.) Next, we discuss the triple As underpinning supply chains: (1) agility, (2) adaptability, and (3) alignment.[21]

THREE As OF SUPPLY CHAIN MANAGEMENT

Agility

Agility refers to the ability to react quickly to unexpected shifts in supply and demand. To reduce inventory, many firms now use their suppliers and carriers' trucks, ships, and planes as their warehouse. In the quest for supply chain speed, cost, and efficiency, many firms fail to realize the costs they incur when they disregard agility. On the other hand, firms such as Zara thrive in large part because of the agility of their supply chain (see the Opening Case). Zara's agility permeates its

Outline the three As of supply chain management (agility, adaptability, and alignment).

Agility
The ability to react quickly to unexpected shifts in supply and demand.

entire operations. As soon as designers spot certain trends, they create sketches and can order fabrics without finalizing designs. This speeds things up because fabric suppliers require a long lead time. When reliable data come in from the stores, designs are finalized and production commences. In addition, Zara's factories only run one shift, easily allowing for overtime production if demand calls for it. Its distribution centers are also highly efficient, allowing it to handle demand fluctuation without creating bottlenecks.

Agility may become more important in the 21st century. Thanks to terrorist attacks, wars, SARS, and H1N1 swine flu, shocks to supply chains are now more frequent. Under shocks, an agile supply chain can rise to the challenge while a static supply chain can pull a firm down.[22] In 2000, Nokia and Ericsson competed in the market for mobile handsets. Both Nokia and Ericsson bought handset chips from Philips. When a thunderstorm started a fire at Philips's New Mexico factory, the two companies had different reactions. Reportedly, the factory damage was minor, and Philips expected to resume production within a week. However, Nokia took no chances and quickly carried out design changes so that two other suppliers, one in Japan and another in the United States, could manufacture similar chips for Nokia. (These were the only two suppliers in the world other than Philips that were capable of delivering similar chips.) Nokia then quickly placed orders from these two suppliers. In contrast, Ericsson's supply chain had no such agility: It was set up to function exclusively with the chips produced at the damaged Philips plant in New Mexico. In other words, Ericsson had no plan B. Unfortunately, Philips later found out that the damage was larger than first reported, and production was delayed for months. Turning to the other two suppliers, Ericsson found that Nokia had locked up all of their output for the next few months. The upshot? By 2001, Ericsson was out of the handset market as an independent player (although it later re-entered the market with a joint venture with Sony called Sony Ericsson).[23]

Adaptability

Although agility focuses on flexibility that can overcome short-term fluctuation in the supply chain, adaptability refers to the ability to change supply chain configurations in response to longer-term changes in the environment and technology. Adaptability is often enhanced through a series of make-or-buy decisions. This requires firms to *continuously* monitor major geopolitical, social, and technological trends in the world, make sense of them, and reconfigure the supply chain accordingly.[24] Failing to assess and respond to trends may not lead to immediate, visible damage, but over time could drive a firm out of the market.

Consider Lucent, the American telecommunications equipment giant. In the mid-1990s, its rivals Siemens and Alcatel benefited from low-cost, Asia-based production in switching systems. In response, Lucent successfully adapted its supply chain by phasing out production in high-cost developed economies and setting up plants in China and Taiwan. But Lucent stopped short and did not adapt continuously. Lucent concentrated its production in its own Asia-based plants, but its rivals outsourced their manufacturing to Asian suppliers, who in turn developed greater capabilities and could take on more complex work. In other words, Lucent used foreign direct investment (FDI) to "make" whereas rivals adopted outsourcing to "buy." Ultimately, Lucent was stuck with its own relatively higher cost (although Asia-based) plants and was overwhelmed by rivals. By 2002, Lucent was forced to shut down its Taiwan factory and to create an outsourced supply chain. But it was too late. By 2006, Lucent lost its independence and was acquired by its archrival Alcatel.

Adaptability
The ability to change supply chain configurations in response to longer-term changes in the environment and technology.

Make-or-buy decision
The decision on whether to produce in-house ("make") or to outsource ("buy").

Alignment

Alignment refers to the alignment of interests of various players involved in the supply chain. In a broad sense, each supply chain is a strategic alliance involving a variety of players, each of which is a profit-maximizing, stand-alone firm.[25] As a result, conflicts are natural (see Chapter 12). However, players associated with one supply chain must effectively coordinate to achieve desirable outcomes. Therefore, this is a crucial dilemma. Supply chains that can better solve this dilemma may be able to outperform other supply chains. Boeing's 787 Dreamliner, for example, has some 40% of the $8 billion development cost outsourced to suppliers: Mitsubishi makes the wings, Messier-Dowty provides the landing gear, and so forth.[26] Many suppliers are responsible for end-to-end design of whole subsections. Headed by a vice president MNE for global partnerships, Boeing treats its suppliers as partners, has "partner councils" with regular meetings, and fosters long-term collaboration.

Conceptually, two elements are key to achieving alignment: (1) power and (2) trust. Not all players in a supply chain are equal, and more powerful players such as Boeing naturally exercise greater bargaining power.[27] Having a recognized leader exercising power facilitates legitimacy and efficiency of the whole supply chain, such as the case with De Beers in diamonds. Otherwise, excessive bargaining will have to be conducted among supply chain members of more or less equal standing.

Trust stems from perceived fairness and justice from all supply chain members.[28] Supply chains have become ever more complex and extended. Modern practices, such as low (or zero) inventory, frequent just-in-time (JIT) deliveries, and more geographic dispersion of production, have made all parties more vulnerable if the *weakest* link breaks down. Therefore, it is in the best interest of all parties to invest in trust-building mechanisms in order to foster more collaboration (see Chapter 12). For instance, Seven-Eleven Japan exercised a great deal of power by dictating that vendors resupply its 9,000 stores at three *specific* times a day. If a truck is late by more than 30 minutes, the vendor has to pay a penalty equal to the gross margin of the products carried to the store. This may seem harsh, but it is necessary. Seven-Eleven Japan staff reconfigure store shelves three times a day to cater to different consumers at different *hours*, such as commuters in the morning and school kids in the afternoon. Time, literally, means money. However, Seven-Eleven Japan softens the blow by trusting its vendors. It does not verify the contents of deliveries, which allows vendors to save time and money. After deliveries, truck drivers do not have to wait for verification and can immediately move on to make other trips. The alignment of interest of such a supply chain is legendary. Hours after the Kobe earthquake in January 1995, relief trucks moved at two miles an hour (if they moved at all) on the damaged roads. In contrast, Seven-Eleven Japan's vendors deployed seven helicopters and 125 motorcycles to deliver 64,000 rice balls to the ravaged city.

Sometimes, introducing a neutral intermediary (middleman)—more specifically, third-party logistics (3PL) providers—may more effectively align the interests in the supply chain. In the case of outsourcing in Asia, buyers (importers) tend to be large Western MNEs, such as Gap, Nike, and Marks & Spencer, and suppliers (exporters) are often smaller Asian manufacturers. Despite the best of intentions, both sides may still distrust each other. MNE buyers are not sure of the quality and timeliness of delivery. MNE buyers are also unable to control labor practices in supplier factories, some of which may be dubious (such as running "sweatshops"). In the 1990s, Nike's reputation took a severe hit due to allegations of questionable labor practices at its supplier factories. But suppliers may also be suspicious. Since most contracts for shoes, clothing, toys, and electronics are written several months ahead of time, suppliers are not confident about MNE

Alignment
Alignment of interests of various players.

Third-party logistics (3PL)
A neutral, third-party intermediary in the supply chain that provides logistics and other support services.

buyers' ability to correctly forecast demand. Suppliers thus worry that in case of lower-than-anticipated demand, buyers may reject shipments to reduce excess inventory, using excuses such as labor practices or quality issues.[29] The involvement of 3PL intermediaries, such as the Hong Kong–based Li & Fung, provides one possible solution (see the Closing Case). Overall, 3PL firms may add value by aligning the interests of all parties.

From its humble roots as low-profile "logistics," supply chain management has come of age. A huge logistics industry has grown (see In Focus 14.2). Thomas

Focus 14.2

Ocean Shipping: The Perfect Storm

Compared with the high-profile FedEx and UPS jets, ships are slow. From Shanghai to Los Angeles it takes 12 to 13 days. Yet the slow-moving container ships do the heavy lifting in modern supply chains. Everyday, container ships carry 90% of the world's traded cargo by value, and such ocean shipping is known as the "box trade." Taking off since the 1970s, container shipping has facilitated the emergence of a global supply chain. This is because "box trade" has reduced the cost of ocean shipping so significantly that brand owners in the West can afford to search the world for the lowest-cost suppliers.

© Dan Barnes/iStock Photo

Thanks to the "box trade," China's location in the *Far East* does not seem to be too far away from major markets in North America and Europe.

However, container shipping is now in its first decline in history. In 2007, there were not enough ships to carry the rapidly growing global volume. On top of the 4,000 container ships, the industry ordered another 1,300 and the average ship size became more gigantic. But in 2009, thanks to the global recession and the shrinking trade volume, 15% of the industry capacity has become idle. Approximately 750 ships are sheltering in Asian waters, with no container boxes to carry. Another 280 are laid up in European ports. The price to move one container from China to Europe has dropped

from $1,400 in summer 2008 to $400 in summer 2009. A fight for a slice of the shrinking pie has been unleashed.

To make matters worse, pirates have increased the cost of shipping for those ships that do sail, particularly off the coast of East Africa. Kidnapping insurance usually covers legal fees and ransom (including the cost of the drop). Since 2009, a new type of insurance, simply known as pirate insurance, has emerged, costing between $30,000 and $50,000 for a one-way transit through dangerous waters.

Although numerous industries are hurting in the global economic crisis, few have to weather such a perfect storm: Rapid growth attracted significant new capacity, but was followed by demand shrinkage and pricing collapse on the one hand and pirate attacks and skyrocketing insurance cost on the other. Although proposals for an industry-wide scheme to scrap the surplus ships have been proposed, they are unlikely to be implemented. But clearly, the growth that occurred since the 1970s has come to an end.

Sources: Based on (1) *BusinessWeek*, 2009, Hedging bets on the high seas, April 27: 10; (2) *Economist*, 2007, Container ships, March 3: 71; (3) *Economist*, 2009, Sea of troubles, August 1: 55–56; (4) G. Stalk, 2006, The costly secret of China sourcing, *Harvard Business Review*, February: 64–66.

Friedman in *The World is Flat* offers an interesting "Dell theory" of world peace: No two countries that are both part of Dell's global supply chain will fight a war against each other.[30] First introduced in our Chapter 2, this theory is of course offered tongue in cheek—how can a "lowly" supply chain now become a guardian of world peace? The more serious point is that as various firms and countries are woven into a global supply chain that benefits all participants, which is symbolized by Dell, the cost of war may become too prohibitive.

HOW INSITITUTIONS AND RESOURCES AFFECT MARKETING AND SUPPLY CHAIN MANAGEMENT

Discuss how institutions and resources affect marketing and supply chain management.

Having outlined the basic features of marketing and supply chain management, let us now use the institution-based and resource-based views to shed additional light on these topics (Figure 14.4).

Institutions, Marketing, and Supply Chain Management

Formal rules of the game obviously have a significant impact. Most countries impose restrictions, ranging from taboos in advertising to constraints on the equity level held by foreign retailers and 3PL providers. Germany bans advertisement that portrays another product as inferior. Goodyear Tire ran a successful ad in the United States that showed that its tire cord could break a steel chain. But when Goodyear tried to run the same ad in Germany, it was banned because the German

FIGURE 14.4 INSTITUTIONS, RESOURCES, MARKETING, AND SUPPLY CHAIN MANAGEMENT

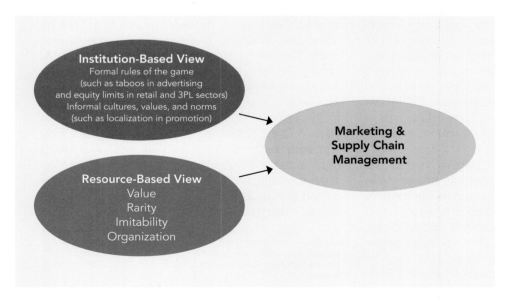

government said the ad was insulting to German steel chain manufacturers. Until 2009, FDI in India had not been allowed in the retail sector (see In Focus 14.3). Likewise, China forbids foreign retailers from operating wholly-owned stores and only approves joint-venture stores. In China, France's Carrefour is the most aggressive foreign retailer with sales ahead of Wal-Mart. In some cities, Carrefour struck sweetheart deals with officials and operated wholly-owned stores, which provoked Beijing's wrath. The upshot? Carrefour was forced to sell a portion of its equity to Chinese partners and convert its wholly-owned stores to joint-venture stores to be in compliance with regulations.

(IN) Focus 14.3

ETHICAL DILEMMA

India: Forthcoming Retail Revolution + Supply Chain Revolution?

India has the world's highest density of retail outlets of any country. It has more than 15 million retail outlets, compared with 900,000 in the United States, whose market (by revenue) is 13 times bigger. At present, 97% of retail sales in India are made in tiny mom-and-pop shops, mostly of less than 500 square feet (46 square meters). In Indian jargon, this is known, quite accurately, as the "unorganized" retail sector. The "organized" (more modern) retail sector commands only 3% of total sales, of which 96% is in the top ten cities. The retail industry is the largest provider of jobs after agriculture, accounting for 6% to 7% of jobs and 10% of GDP.

With a booming economy and a fast-growing middle class, it is not surprising that foreign retailers, such as America's Wal-Mart, France's Carrefour, Germany's Metro, and Britain's Tesco, are knocking at the door trying to expand the "organized" retail sector. However, here is one catch: The door is still closed to foreign direct investment (FDI) in the retail sector. Millions of shopkeepers, supported by leftist politicians and trade unionists, are worried about the onslaught of multinationals. Citing the controversial "Wal-Mart effect," one Indian union leader labeled Wal-Mart "one of the ten worst corporations in the world."

In response, the reformist government that brought India into the global spotlight beginning in 1991 has delicately tried to balance the interests of various stakeholders. FDI is still officially banned in *mass* retailing. However, a side door is now open. Foreign firms can take up to 51% equity in *single-brand* shops that sell their own products, such as Nike, Nokia, and Starbucks shops. Further, FDI in the supply chain is now permitted. Foreign firms can set up wholesale and sourcing subsidiaries that supply local mass retail partners. The first to do this was Australia's Woolworths, which in 2006 started to supply Croma stores owned by Tata Group, India's second-largest conglomerate. In June 2009, a 42-member Parliamentary committee in its report, *Foreign and Domestic Investment in Retail Sector*, recommended that no further licenses be granted to allow for partnerships between Indian and foreign retailers, because such partnerships are "merely a camouflage for foreigners doing retail trade through back door, which will result in unemployment of indigenous retail traders."

On average, Indians are still poor. Only one in 50 households has a credit card; only one in six has a refrigerator. However, as in China 15 years ago, such statistics do not deter foreign entrants; instead, they suggest tremendous potential. Despite objections, Wal-Mart is visibly leading the foreign lobby. One of its arguments is that efficient retail operations will enhance supply chain efficiency. At present, 35% to 40% of food products in India rot while in transit. Food processing adds just 7% to the value of agricultural output, compared with 40% in China, which embraced Wal-Mart. As local suppliers become more familiar with Wal-Mart's requirements, exports may naturally follow—Wal-Mart now accounts for 10% of China's exports to the United States. In sum, both a retail revolution and a supply chain revolution may be under way in India.

Sources: Based on (1) *Business Standard*, 2009, Panel opposes domestic corporate and foreign investment in retail, June 8, www.business-standard.com (accessed September 1, 2009); (2) *Economist*, 2006, Coming to market, April 15: 69–71; (3) *Economist*, 2006, Setting up shop, November 4: 73–74.

Informal rules also place significant constraints on marketing and supply chain management. In marketing, most of the blunders documented in Table 14.2 happened because firms failed to appreciate the deep underlying differences in cultures, languages, and norms—all part of the informal institutions. In supply chains, leading firms headquartered in developed economies may be able to spread leading edge practices around the world. In the 1990s, large numbers of European firms adopted the ISO 9000 series of quality management systems as a new norm. They then imposed the standard on their suppliers and partners throughout the world. Over time, these suppliers and partners spread ISO 9000 standards to other domestic firms. At present, over 560,000 sites in over 150 countries have been ISO 9000 certified. In other words, due to the normative influence, suppliers and partners that export goods and services to a particular country in a supply chain may be simultaneously *importing* that country's norms and practices.[31]

In supply chain management, the norm is to source from Asia. Even Zara does a fair amount of such outsourcing. This does not contradict the Opening Case, which states that Zara concentrates *most* of its production in-house and in Spain. While Zara's in-house work focuses on fast-turnaround, high-margin merchandise, it has outsourced basic T-shirts, for which demand is relatively stable and easy to predict, to low-cost suppliers in Asia. Overall, a new trend is that procurement executives are trickling toward Asia to be closer to where the action is. In 2006, IBM's chief procurement officer and the global procurement office moved to Shenzhen, China. This is IBM's first time to base a *corporate*-wide function outside the United States. Asia accounts for a lion's share of IBM's supply base, so it makes sense for key supply chain managers to be located in the region.

Resources, Marketing, and Supply Chain Management

As before, we can evaluate marketing and supply chain management activities based on the VRIO criteria (see Figure 14.4). First, managers need to ask: Do these activities add *value*?[32] Increasingly, as traditional media loses viewers and readers, and thus effectiveness, marketers do not have a good handle on how to add value with new forms of advertising, particularly online. The recession has added pressure as stores try hard to add value for their increasingly frugal customers. One interesting idea is to focus on the *disloyal*, not loyal, customers.[33] For example, Starbucks already has 90% of the coffee dollars of its most loyal customers, leaving little room for further growth in this group. However, it is the sizable group of "switchers"—those who go to both Starbucks and other coffee houses—that may represent the largest potential for growth. The challenge is: how to add value to these "switchers" who are loyal to neither Starbucks nor competitors.

Second, managers need to assess the *rarity* of marketing and supply chain activities. If all rival firms advertise in the *Economist* and use FedEx to manage logistics (all of which do add value), these activities, in themselves, are not rare. In supply chain management, first movers in radio frequency identification (RFID) tags may derive benefits because they are rare. Wal-Mart has been experimenting with RFID in 150 stores in the Dallas area and reaped some benefits (such as 16% reduction in out-of-stock items).[34] However, as RFID becomes more available, its rarity will drop.

Third, having identified valuable and rare capabilities, managers need to assess how likely it is for rivals and partners to *imitate* those capabilities. Although

© Aly Song/Reuters/Landov

In a VRIO analysis of a manufacturer's supply chain, how might this activity give the firm a competitive advantage?

there is no need to waste more ink on the necessity to watch out for rivals, firms need to be careful about partners in the supply chain. As more Western MNEs outsource production to suppliers (or, using a new jargon, contract manufacturers), it is always possible that some of the aggressive contract manufacturers may in turn directly imitate and compete with Western MNEs. This is not necessarily opportunism. It is natural for ambitious contract manufacturers to flex their muscle. Such muscle is often directly strengthened by the Western MNEs themselves that willingly transfer technology and share know-how, which is often known as supplier (or vendor) development.[35] China's Haier (household appliances), TCL (televisions), and Galanz (microwaves) have become global leaders in just that way. Although it is possible to imitate and acquire world-class manufacturing capabilities, marketing prowess and brand power are more intangible and thus harder to imitate. Western MNEs often cope by (1) being careful about what they outsource and (2) strengthening customer loyalty to their brands (such as Nike) to fend off contract manufacturers.[36]

Finally, managers need to ask: Is our firm *organizationally* ready to accomplish our objectives? Oddly, in many firms, Marketing and Sales functions do not get along well. When revenues are disappointing, the blame game begins: Marketing blames Sales for failing to execute a brilliant plan, and Sales blames Marketing for setting the price too high and burning too much of the budget in high-flying but useless promotion. Marketing staff tend to be better educated, more analytical, and disappointed when certain initiatives fail. In contrast, Sales people are often "street smart," persuasive, and accustomed to constant rejection. It is not surprising that Marketing and Sales have a hard time working together.[37] Yet, work together they must. Some leading firms have disbanded Marketing and Sales as separate functions and have created an integrated function—called Channel Enablement at IBM. Clearly, an organization with warring functions will be dysfunctional.

LEARNING OBJECTIVE

5

Participate in two leading debates on marketing and supply chain management.

DEBATES AND EXTENSIONS

There are some long-standing debates in this field, such as the standardization versus localization debate discussed earlier. Here, we focus on two important debates not previously discussed: (1) manufacturing versus services and (2) market orientation versus relationship orientation.

Manufacturing versus Services

This debate deals with the nature of certain economic activities. Consider contract manufacturing service. Is it manufacturing? Service? Both? Does it matter? Our vocabulary evolves with—and is also trapped by—the history of economic development. As the first sector for organized economic activities, agriculture was usually seen as *primary*. When manufacturing emerged during the Industrial Revolution of the 18th and 19th centuries, it was often the *secondary* sector (after agriculture). Consequently, the residual service activities were typically viewed as *tertiary* (third sector).

Throughout the first half of the 20th century, agriculture declined in importance, and "economic development" often meant industrialization centered on manufacturing. However, in the second half of the 20th century, services came to the forefront.[38] In 2007, services accounted for 83% of US employment whereas manufacturing accounted for only 10%.[39] The 2008–2009 recession has reduced the number of US manufacturing jobs even further.

Despite the recent prominence of the service sector, it historically lacks prestige. Service has a much longer history than manufacturing. The word "service" originated from the Latin word *servus*, which means slave or servant. Nothing could be lower than this. To add insult to injury, in *The Wealth of Nations* (1776) Adam Smith labeled service as "nonproductive activities." Believing "real men make stuff," the Soviet Union and China during the heyday of socialism had highly developed heavy manufacturing industries but a severely underdeveloped service sector. Thus, they were able to launch rockets to outer space but did not have enough skilled plumbers to fix toilets.

Towards the end of the 20th century, as Russia and China shifted and looked to developed economies for inspiration, they found a highly developed service sector. In fact, innovations in services drive much of current economic growth. Consider McDonald's. In the 1950s, McDonald's drew on the principle of the assembly line, a core manufacturing principle dating back to Henry Ford in the 1910s, to develop high-volume, fast, and standardized food services.

Historically marketing and supply chain management are regarded as services, but this classification may not matter that much. Half-jokingly, we can ask: Does McDonald's manufacture hamburgers? Seriously, how much difference is there between McDonald's and Airbus? Both market new products, both make-to-order (finalize a product based on an order), and both extensively rely on powerful supply chain management systems around the world. As alluded to earlier, if the difference between manufacturing and services was "black-and-white," then "contract manufacturing service" would be an oxymoron. Yet today, *integrating* manufacturing and services is both a reality and a necessity.

Market Orientation versus Relationship Orientation

Market orientation refers to a philosophy or way of thinking that places the highest priority on the creation of superior customer value in the marketplace.[40] A market-oriented firm genuinely listens to customer feedback and allocates resources accordingly in order to meet customer expectation. For example, Boeing used to be an engineering-driven firm and believed that its engineers were doing airlines a favor by sharing Boeing's technological wonders with them. Since the development of the 777 in the 1990s, Boeing has transformed itself by involving not only its customers (airlines) but also its suppliers in the conceptualization and design process. Thus, after a period of being outfoxed by Airbus, Boeing is once again dominant. The Boeing experience is not isolated. Many firms around the world have enjoyed better performance by being more market oriented. The debate centers on how firms benefit from market orientation *differently* around the world.

Market orientation
A philosophy or way of thinking that places the highest priority on the creation of superior customer value in the marketplace.

Another concept is **relationship orientation**, defined as a focus to establish, maintain, and enhance relationships with customers.[41] Like market orientation, relationship orientation has expanded to include many functions beyond marketing. Given the necessity for building trust and coordinating operations, supply chains certainly can benefit from a relationship orientation. Instead of selling airplane engines and then waiting for customers to order spare parts, Rolls-Royce now builds deeper relationships with airlines. It rents engines to airlines, provides 24/7 monitoring on every engine, carries out full maintenance, and gets paid for every hour the engine is in flight.[42] In short, Rolls-Royce can fix a problem before it creates damage, thus offering superior value for airlines.

Marketers have heavily debated whether a market orientation or a relationship orientation is more effective in global markets. Key to the debate is how firms benefit from market or relationship orientation *differently* around the world. Consider competition in China, where *guanxi* (relationship) reportedly is crucial.[43] Firms have to allocate resources between building market-oriented capabilities (such as quality, pricing, and delivery) and relationship-oriented assets (such as wining and dining). China thus offers a strong test for the debate between market and relationship orientation. Researchers find two interesting results. First, relationship-oriented assets do add value. Second, for truly outstanding performance, relationships are necessary but not sufficient. Market-oriented capabilities contribute *more* toward performance.[44] These results make sense, in light of China's increasingly market-driven competition that gradually reduces (but not eliminates) the importance of *guanxi*.

Viewed globally, market orientation has had the strongest effect on performance in US firms, which operate in arguably the most developed market economy.[45] In weak market economies such as Russia and Ukraine, the returns from being market oriented are limited.[46] In other words, firms there can get by with a minimal amount of market orientation. Viewed collectively, these findings support the *institution-based* view: By definition, market orientation functions more effectively in a market economy.[47]

Although it is always the *combination* of market and relationship orientation that differentiates winning firms from losers, the debate boils down to the relative distribution between the two. There is reason to believe that as China, Russia, and other emerging economies develop further and follow more global "rules of the game," market orientation may play an increasingly important role.

LEARNING OBJECTIVE 6

Draw implications for action.

Relationship orientation
A focus to establish, maintain, and enhance relationships with customers.

MANAGEMENT SAVVY

What determines the success and failure in marketing and supply chain management? The institution-based view points out the impact of formal and informal rules of the game. In a nonmarket economy (such as North Korea), marketing would be irrelevant. In a world with high barriers to trade and investment, globetrotting FedEx jets would be unimaginable. The resource-based view argues that holding institutions constant, firms such as Zara and Li & Fung that develop the best capabilities in marketing and supply chain management will emerge as winners (see the Opening and Closing Cases).

Consequently, three implications for action emerge (Table 14.3). First, marketers and supply chain managers need to know the rules of the game inside and out in order to craft savvy responses. For example, given the limited formal regulatory frameworks for prosecuting cross-border credit card crimes, some US e-commerce firms refuse to ship to overseas addresses. Thus legitimate overseas purchasers are denied business. As online shopping became a more widespread informal norm,

---

TABLE 14.3   IMPLICATIONS FOR ACTION

- Know the formal and informal rules of the game on marketing and supply chain management inside and out.

- In marketing, focus on product, price, promotion, and place (the four Ps) and do all it takes to avoid blunders.

- In supply chain management, focus on agility, adaptability, and alignment (the three As).

TABLE 14.4   DO'S AND DON'TS TO AVOID BLUNDERS IN INTERNATIONAL MARKETING

Do's	*Don'ts*
• Avoid ethnocentrism. Be sensitive to nationalistic feelings of local consumers, employees, and governments.	• Don't be overconfident about the potential of your products or services—firms will be better off by continuously testing the "water" and experimenting.
• Do your homework about the new market. Pay attention to details and nuances, especially those related to cultures, values, and norms.	• Don't cut corners and save back-translation cost—always back-translate. (After translating from English to Russian, get someone else to translate it from Russian to English to check accuracy.)
• Avoid the pushy salesman approach. The pace of business may seem too slow in some countries, but impatience does not bring sales.	• Don't use jokes in international advertising. Humor is usually impossible to translate. What is viewed funny by some may be offensive to others.
• Act like a diplomat—build relationships.	

Sources: Based on text in (1) T. Dalgic & R. Heijblom, 1996, International marketing blunders revisited—some lessons for managers, *Journal of International Marketing*, 4 (1): 81–91; (2) D. Ricks, 1999, *Blunders in International Business*, 3rd ed., Oxford, UK: Blackwell.

FedEx acquired Kinkos (which was turned into FedEx Office stores) and UPS took over Mail Boxes Etc (which was turned into UPS Stores). E-commerce firms can now have products shipped to FedEx Offices and UPS Stores in the United States, and FedEx and UPS then forward the products to the overseas purchasers. This is but one example of superb problem solving in the face of cumbersome formal rules and changing informal norms.

Second, marketing should focus on the four Ps. Every marketing textbook emphasizes this point, but in international marketing, managers need to do all it takes to avoid costly and embarrassing blunders (see Table 14.4). Remember: despite their magnitude, blunders are *avoidable* mistakes. In other words, international marketers should try very hard to avoid being written up for committing new blunders in a future edition of this book.

Finally, in supply chain management, focus on the triple As, which are a relatively new framework. Many firms are still unaware of the importance of the triple As and only deliver container-loads to minimize the number of deliveries and freight costs (see In Focus 14.2). When demand for a particular product suddenly rises, these firms cannot react quickly; they have to wait until the container (or sometimes even the entire container *ship*) is full. Such a so-called "best" practice typically delays shipment by a week or more, forcing stock-outs in stores and disappointing consumers. When firms eventually ship container-loads, they often result in excess inventory because most buyers do not need a full container-load. To get rid of such inventory, as much as a third of the merchandise carried by department stores ends up in sales. Such discounts not only destroy profits for every firm in the supply chain, but also undermine brand equity by upsetting consumers who recently bought the discounted items at full price. In contrast, the triple As urge savvy supply chain managers to focus on agility, adaptability, and alignment of interests of the entire chain.

CHAPTER SUMMARY

1. Articulate three of the four marketing Ps (product, price, and promotion) in a global context.
   - In international marketing, the number one product concern is standardization versus localization.
   - Marketers care about price elasticity—how responsive purchasing behavior is when prices change.
   - In promotion, marketers need to decide whether to enhance or downplay the country-of-origin effect.

2. Explain how the fourth marketing P (place) has changed into supply chain management.
   - Technically, "place" used to refer to distribution channel—the location where products are provided.
   - More recently, the term "distribution channel" has been replaced by "supply chain management," in response to more outsourcing to suppliers, contract manufacturers, and 3PL providers.

3. Outline the three As of supply chain management (agility, adaptability, and alignment).
   - Agility deals with the ability to react quickly to unexpected shifts in supply and demand.
   - Adaptability refers to the ability to reconfigure the supply chain in response to longer-term external changes.
   - Alignment focuses on the alignment of interests of various players in the supply chain.

4. Discuss how institutions and resources affect marketing and supply chain management.
   - Formal and informal rules of the game around the world significantly impact these two areas.
   - Managers need to assess marketing and supply chain management based on the VRIO criteria.

5. Participate in two leading debates on marketing and supply chain management.
   - (1) Manufacturing versus service and (2) market orientation versus relationship orientation

6. Draw implications for action.
   - Know the formal and informal rules of the game inside and out.
   - In marketing, focus on product, price, promotion, and place (the four Ps).
   - In supply chain management, focus on agility, adaptability, and alignment (the three As).

KEY TERMS

Adaptability 480
Agility 479
Alignment 481
Country-of-origin
   effect 477
Distribution channel 478
Make-or-buy decision 480
Market orientation 487
Market segmentation 474

Marketing 472
Marketing mix 472
Place 478
Price 475
Price elasticity 475
Product 473
Promotion 477
Relationship
   orientation 488

Supply chain 472
Supply chain
   management 472
Third-party logistics
   (3PL) 481
Total cost of
   ownership 476

REVIEW QUESTIONS

1. Describe the four components of the marketing mix.

2. In your home country, how much price elasticity do you think there is among consumers for cars? Cell (mobile) phones? Rice?

3. Is outsourcing the same thing as supply chain management? What is their relationship?

4. Why has supply chain management become an integral part of the place in the marketing mix?

5. Name and describe the three As in supply chain management.

6. How might a make-or-buy decision relate to an alliance or an acquisition?

7. List two examples of how formal and informal institutions affect marketing and/or supply chain management.

8. If a firm was using a VRIO framework to analyze its marketing mix, which of the four qualities do you think would be most significant? Why?

9. For firms that are both manufacturing and service oriented, which function do you think deserves more time and attention? Explain your answer.

10. Devise your own example of a common business situation, and explain how a market-oriented firm would handle it as opposed to a relationship-oriented firm.

11. If you were a manager of a firm that was planning to begin marketing its product internationally, what steps would you take to avoid marketing blunders?

12. How might a savvy manager use the three As to enhance a firm's supply chain?

13. As you look at PengAtlas Map 4.1 you may recall recent news stories about piracy along these routes, especially off Eastern Africa and Southeast Asia. Pirates have successfully taken over the ships of some of the wealthiest and most powerful nations on earth. How would you recommend dealing with this threat to world trade?

CRITICAL DISCUSSION QUESTIONS

1. The national animal of Canada is the beaver. In 2007, the Canadian prime minister suggested replacing it with the wolverine, and the suggestion stirred up a national debate. Does your country have a national animal? If you were hired as a marketing expert by the government of Canada (or another country), how would you best market the country using the animal?

2. *ON ETHICS:* You are a supply chain manager at a UK firm. In 2009, the H1N1 swine flu broke out in Mexico and the United States, potentially affecting your suppliers in the region. You are considering switching to a new supplier in Central Europe, but you feel bad about abandoning your Mexican and US suppliers, with whom you have built a pleasant personal and business relationship. However, your tightly coordinated production cannot afford to miss one supply shipment. How do you proceed?

3. *ON ETHICS:* Hollywood movies commonly have product placement (that is, products from sponsored companies, such as cars, appear in movies without telling viewers that these are effectively commercials). As a marketer, you are concerned about the ethical implications of product placement in Hollywood movies, but you also know traditional advertising is less and less effective. How do you proceed?

4. *ON ETHICS:* Look at PengAtlas Map 4.1 and the current trade routes. Although current routes do not go through the Arctic Ocean, global warming has made some shipping possible there for limited periods. Also, some farming is returning to Arctic areas such as Greenland. Given the area's natural resources, emerging agriculture, and potential new trade routes, make a case for how potential problems, such as flooding in port cities, may be at least partially offset with potential benefits from higher temperatures in the Arctic and Arctic Ocean.

globalEDGE
YOUR SOURCE FOR
global business
knowledge
http://globalEDGE.msu.edu

GLOBAL ACTION

1. Your company has developed a dominant global supply network that has contact with nearly every country in the world. However, recent internal initiatives have encouraged managers to reconfigure your company's supply network to increase efficiency. As a part of this process, you must use established logistics

performance metrics to identify the country that has the highest logistics competence on each continent (Africa, Asia, Europe, North America, and South America). Using resources from the globalEDGE website, prepare a report that indicates your recommendations and rationale for each continent. What could explain the results of your analysis?

2. You are conducting an international survey concerning possible acceptance of a new leisure activity: space tourism. One issue that can influence whether individuals in a country find this new concept interesting is culture. Based on a data source on globalEDGE that assesses culture around the world, identify the cultural trait that could measure general acceptance of space tourism by country. Then, determine which countries are ideal to target for commercialization. Be sure to support your position thoroughly in your report.

VIDEO CASES

Watch "Connecting Your Suppliers with Your Values" by Jean Sweeney of 3M.

1. Sweeney indicated that she expects her company's suppliers to be in compliance with her company's core values. Does it seem right to impose one's values on others? Can you think of any instances in which the failure to do so could hurt an organization?

2. When a supplier fails to comply with 3M's values, Ms. Sweeney indicates that 3M ceases to do business with a supplier. What might limit a firm's ability to do that?

3. Global corporations have complex supply chains with suppliers from around the world. How does that reality impact on how a firm can connect suppliers with its values?

4. Suppose Company A seeks to use only those suppliers that are in compliance with the highest standards regarding labor force and the environment. Suppose Company B, its competitor, seeks to gain market share through lower price by using less expensive suppliers that keep their costs down by applying very low standards. What can or should Company A do? Why?

5. How might the ability to connect suppliers with a firm's values depend on its industry and its size within that industry? Under what circumstances might a big firm have an advantage? When might the small firm have an advantage?

Closing Case

Li & Fung: From Trading Company to Supply Chain Manager

Founded in 1906 in Guangzhou (then known as Canton), China, the Li & Fung Group has been headquartered in Hong Kong since the 1930s. Originally a trading company, Li & Fung has emerged as the largest sourcing firm in the world. It manages the supply chain of high-volume, time-sensitive consumer goods (especially clothes and toys) produced throughout Asia for some of the major retail brands, such as Liz Claiborne, Talbots, Timberland, Toys 'R' Us, Limited Brands (which includes Victoria's Secret and Bath and Body Works), and Sanrio, the Japanese merchandiser of Hello Kitty.

Although Li & Fung has over 70 offices in more than 40 countries, it does not own any factories. As an intermediary, it adds value by linking smaller suppliers in Asia with larger retailers in the developed world. Li & Fung maintains a network of 8,300 suppliers and factories throughout Asia. By bargaining on behalf of the "small guys," Li & Fung enhances their bargaining power vis-à-vis multinational buyers. In exchange, Li & Fung enforces a code of conduct that prevents substandard quality and labor abuses. Suppliers found to violate this code are excluded from accessing Li & Fung's buyers. Li & Fung also keeps multinational buyers honest. If they refuse shipments due to their own problems (such as faulty forecast or demand collapse), Li & Fung denies them future access to its supplier network. Of course, Li & Fung's buyers and suppliers pay a fee for its services, but the fee is lower than the transaction costs associated with the haggling, uncertainties, and headaches when buyers and suppliers bargain directly.

Life as a trader and now a supply chain manager is not easy. In an effort for disintermediation, both

© Mike Clarke/AFP/Getty Images

buyers and suppliers relentlessly imitate Li & Fung's capabilities. Intermediaries such as Li & Fung thrive by working with small and medium-sized client firms on *both* sides. When buyers such as IBM grow and expand their purchasing volume, they often set up their own procurement channels in Asia directly. Therefore, Li & Fung is bypassed. When suppliers such as Taiwan's BenQ become more successful overseas, their export volume justifies the investment in their own distribution channels to the West, again bypassing Li & Fung. Thus, Li & Fung exists in a precarious world, constantly under the threat of being bypassed from both sides of its clients. The solution is to make some of its capabilities *untouchable*. For Li & Fung, this means constantly developing and leveraging its intimate knowledge of both sides as a hard-to-imitate strategic weapon. Li & Fung often scouts for smaller and lower-cost Asian manufacturers and for smaller Western buyers that would benefit from the wide selection and reliability that Li & Fung's network provides.

During the 2008–2009 recession, the value from Li & Fung's services has shined even brighter. For example, Liz Claiborne in early 2009 sold its sourcing operations to Li & Fung for $83 million. Liz Claiborne still designs and markets for brands such as Juicy Couture, Kate Spade, Liz Claiborne, and Lucky Brand, but Li & Fung handles the rest of the supply chain. As US retailers cope with tough times, more are following Liz Claiborne's lead by turning to Li & Fung. "As retailers slash costs," said Li & Fung managing director William Fung in an interview, "they are asking themselves, 'Is having our own buying office the way to go?'" The answer is increasingly no. For an order of 300,000 men's shorts, Li & Fung has unrivaled abilities to tap into the best-in-breed suppliers in buttons, zippers, yarn, fabric, and final production (sewing) scattered in various Asian countries and then to orchestrate the network to deliver high-quality products in a timely fashion. Although Li & Fung doubled its revenue to $12 billion between 2004 and 2007, its revenue in 2009 is likely to reach a record $16 billion. As of May 2009, its Hong Kong–listed stock was up 63%, compared with a mere 7% increase for the Hang Seng Index. This does not mean all is rosy for Li & Fung. The devastated US retail sector has exposed Li & Fung's crucial vulnerability: 62% of its revenues come from the United States, evidently too many eggs in one basket. It is trying to diversify away from the US retail market. Nevertheless, "we expect to emerge stronger after this crisis," said Fung.

Sources: Based on (1) *Business Week*, 2009, How not to sweat the retail details, May 25: 52–54; (2) A. Chintakananda, A. York, H. O'Neill, & M. W. Peng, 2009, Structuring dyadic relationships between export producers and intermediaries, *European Journal of International Management*, 3: 302–327; (3) V. Fung, W. Fung, & Y. Wind, 2008, *Competing in a Flat World*, Philadelphia: Wharton School Publishing; (4) V. Narayanan & A. Raman, 2004, Aligning incentives in supply chains, *Harvard Business Review*, November: 94–102; (5) M. W. Peng, 1998, *Behind the Success and Failure of US Export Intermediaries*, Westport, CT: Quorum; (6) M. W. Peng & A. York, 2001, Behind intermediary performance in export trade, *Journal of International Business Studies*, 32: 327–346.

Case Discussion Questions:

1. From a VRIO standpoint, what distinguishes Li & Fung from suppliers, buyers, and other intermediaries?
2. Intermediaries such as Li & Fung need to be paid. After paying Li & Fung a fee, why do buyers and suppliers still find it valuable to deal through an intermediary? In other words, why don't they trade directly?
3. Why was Li & Fung able to emerge stronger during the 2008–2009 global economic crisis?

NOTES

[Journal acronyms] AMJ—*Academy of Management Journal*; AMR—*Academy of Management Review*; BW—*BusinessWeek*; EJM—*European Journal of Marketing*; HBR—*Harvard Business Review*; IMR—*International Marketing Review*; JAMS—*Journal of the Academy of Marketing Science*; JIBS—*Journal of International Business Studies*; JIMktg—*Journal of International Marketing*; JMktg—*Journal of Marketing*; JMS—*Journal of Management Studies*; JOM—*Journal of Operations Management*; JWB—*Journal of World Business*; MIR—*Management International Review*; MSOM—*Manufacturing and Service Operations Management*; SMJ—*Strategic Management Journal*

[1] M. Lejeune & N. Yakova, 2005, On characterizing the 4 C's in supply chain management, *JOM*, 23: 81–100.

[2] T. Choi & D. Krause, 2006, The supply base and its complexity, *JOM*, 24: 637–652; G. T. Hult, D. Ketchen, & S. Slater, 2004, Information processing, knowledge management, and strategic supply chain performance, *AMJ*, 47: 241–253.

[3] P. Kotler & K. Keller, 2005, *Marketing Management*, 12th ed., Upper Saddle River, NJ: Prentice Hall.

[4] D. Dow, 2006, Adaptation and performance in foreign markets, *JIBS*, 37: 212–226; C. Katsikeas, S. Samiee, & M. Theodosiou, 2006, Strategy fit and performance consequences of international marketing standardization, *SMJ*, 27: 867–890; L. Lim, F. Acito, & A. Rusetski, 2006, Development of archetypes of international marketing strategy, *JIBS*, 37: 499–524.

[5] T. Levitt, 1983, The globalization of markets, *HBR*, May–June: 92–102.

[6] D. Rigby & V. Vishwanath, 2006, Localization, *HBR*, April: 82–92; A. Schuh, 2000, Global standardization as a success formula for marketing in Central Eastern Europe? *JWB*, 35: 133–148.

[7] J. Townsend, S. Yeniyurt, & M. Talay, 2009, Getting to global, *JIBS*, 40: 539–558.

[8] D. Yankelovich & D. Meer, 2006, Rediscovering market segmentation, *HBR*, February: 122–131.

[9] D. Holt, J. Quelch, & E. Taylor, 2004, How global brands compete, *HBR*, September: 68–75.

[10] *Economist*, 2008, Africa calling, June 7: 78.

[11] M. Cohen, N. Agrawal, & V. Agrawal, 2006, Winning in the aftermarket, *HBR*, May: 129–138.

[12] K. Macharzina, 2001, The end of pure global strategies? (p. 106), *MIR*, 41: 105–108.

[13] D. Ricks, 1999, Blunders in International Business, 3rd ed. (p. 88), Oxford: Blackwell

[14] L. Brouthers, E. O'Connell, & J. Hadjimarcou, 2005, Generic product strategies for emerging market exports into Triad nation markets, *JMS*, 42: 225–245; J. Knight, D. Holdsworth, & D. Mather, 2007, Country-of-origin and choice of food imports, *JIBS*, 38: 107–125; S. Samiee, T. Shimps, & S. Sharma, 2005, Brand

origin recognition accuracy, *JIBS*, 36: 379–397; P. Verlegh, 2007, Home country bias in product evaluation, *JIBS*, 38: 361–373.

[15] M. Brannen, 2004, When Mickey loses face, *AMR*, 29: 593–616.

[16] *BW*, 2005, The MySpace generation (p. 92), December 12: 86–96.

[17] E. Rabinovich, A. M. Knemeyer, & C. Mayer, 2007, Why do Internet commerce firms incorporate logistics service providers in their distribution channels? *JOM*, 25: 661–681.

[18] M. Porter, 1985, *Competitive Advantage*, New York: Free Press.

[19] *Economist*, 2006, The physical Internet, June 17: 3–4.

[20] R. Slone, 2004, Leading a supply chain turnaround (p. 116), *HBR*, October: 114–121.

[21] The following discussion draws heavily from H. Lee, 2004, The triple-A supply chain, *HBR*, October: 102–112.

[22] B. Avittathur & P. Swamidass, 2007, Matching plant flexibility and supplier flexibility, *JOM*, 25: 717–735.

[23] *Economist*, 2006, When the chain breaks, June 17: 18–19.

[24] R. Belderbos & L. Sleuwaegen, 2005, Competitive drivers and international plant configuration strategies, *SMJ*, 26: 577–593; F. Rothaermel, M. Hitt, & L. Jobe, 2006, Balancing vertical integration and strategic outsourcing, *SMJ*, 27: 1033–56.

[25] J. Murray, M. Kotabe, & J. Zhou, 2005, Strategic alliance-based sourcing and market performance, *JIBS*, 36: 187–208.

[26] C. Niezen & W. Weller, 2006, Procurement as strategy, *HBR*, September: 22–23.

[27] W. C. Benton & M. Maloni, 2005, The influence of power driven buyer/supplier relationships on supply chain satisfaction, *JOM*, 23: 1–22; T. R. Crook & J. Combs, 2007, Sources and consequences of bargaining power in supply chains, *JOM*, 25: 546–555.

[28] D. Krause, R. Handfield, & B. Tyler, 2007, The relationships between supplier development, commitment, social capital accumulation, and performance improvement, *JOM*, 25: 528–545.

[29] N. Morgan, A. Kaleka, & R. Gooner, 2007, Focal supplier opportunism in supermarket retailer category management, *JOM*, 25: 512–527.

[30] T. Friedman, 2005, *The World is Flat*, New York: Farrar, Straus, and Giroux.

[31] C. Corbett, 2006, Global diffusion of ISO 9000 certification through supply chains, *MSOM*, 8: 330–350.

[32] J. Anderson, J. Narus, & W. Rossum, 2006, Customer value propositions in business markets, *HBR*, March: 91–99; R. Priem, 2007, A consumer perspective on value creation, *AMR*, 32: 219–235.

[33] K. Favaro, T. Romberger, & D. Meer, 2009, Five rules for retailing in a recession, *HBR*, April: 64–72.

[34] *Economist*, 2006, Chain reactions, June 17: 14–18.

[35] S. Modi & V. Mabert, 2007, Supplier development, *JOM*, 25: 42–64; K. Rogers, L. Purdy, F. Safayeni, & P. R. Dimering, 2007, A supplier development program, *JOM*, 25: 556–572.

[36] S. Fournier & L. Lee, 2009, Getting brand communities right, *HBR*, April: 105–111.

[37] P. Kotler, N. Rackham, & S. Krishnaswamy, 2006, Ending the war between sales and marketing, *HBR*, July: 68–78.

[38] J. Heineke & M. Davis, 2007, The emergence of service operations management as an academic discipline, *JOM*, 25: 364–374.

[39] R. Chase & U. Apte, 2007, A history of research in service operations, *JOM*, 25: 375–386.

[40] A. Kohli & B. Jaworski, 1990, Market orientation, *JMktg*, 54: 1–18; N. Morgan, D. Vorhies, & C. Mason, 2009, Market orientation, marketing capabilities, and firm performance, *SMJ*, 30: 909–920; J. Narver & S. Slater, 1990, The effect of a market orientation on business profitability, *JMktg*, 54: 20–35; K. Zhou, J. Brown, C. Dev, & S. Agarwal, 2007, The effects of customer and competitor orientations on performance in global markets, *JIBS*, 38: 303–319; K. Zhou, C. Yim, & D. Tse, 2005, The effects of strategic orientations on technology- and market-based breakthrough innovations, *JMktg*, 69: 42–60.

[41] L. Berry, 1995, Relationship marketing of services, *JAMS*, 23: 236–245; G. Hoetker, 2005, How much do you know versus how well I know you, *SMJ*, 26: 75–96.

[42] *BW*, 2005, Rolls-Royce, at your service, November 14: 92–93.

[43] Y. Li, E. Xie, H. Teo, & M. W. Peng, 2010, Formal control and social control in domestic and international buyer-supplier relationships, *JOM* (in press).

[44] M. W. Peng & Y. Luo, 2000, Managerial ties and firm performance in a transition economy, *AMJ*, 43: 486–501.

[45] P. Ellis, 2006, Market orientation and performance, *JMS*, 43: 1089–1107.

[46] I. Akimova, 2000, Development of market orientation and competitiveness of Ukrainian firms, *EJM*, 34: 1128–1148; P. Golden, P. Doney, D. Johnson, & J. Smith, 1995, The dynamics of marketing orientation in transition economies, *JIMktg*, 3: 29–49.

[47] J. Fahy, G. Hooley, T. Cox, J. Beracs, K. Fonfoara, & B. Snoj, 2000. The development and impact of marketing capabilities in Central Europe, *JIBS*, 31: 63–81; K. Zhou, J. Brown, C. Dev, & S. Agarwal, 2007, The effects of customer and competitor orientations on performance in global markets, *JIBS*, 38: 303–319.

Chapter

15

© Don Klumpp

LEARNING OBJECTIVES

After studying this chapter, you should be able to:

1. explain staffing decisions with a focus on expatriates.

2. identify training and development needs for expatriates and host country nationals.

3. identify and discuss compensation and performance appraisal issues.

4. list factors that affect labor relations in both home and host countries.

5. discuss how the institution-based and resource-based views shed additional light on HRM.

6. participate in three leading debates on HRM.

7. draw implications for action.

Managing Human Resources Globally

ETHICAL DILEMMA

Managing Human Resources in Recession

During the 2008–2009 recession, the world economy faced the greatest increase in unemployment in decades. In China, 20 million people, mostly migrant workers, lost their jobs. In India, about 10 million became unemployed. The US unemployment level hit 9%, which broke a record, but Spain's 18% unemployment was double the US level and the highest in the EU. As the recession intensified its grip on the world, the role of human resource management (HRM) also intensified. HR managers were at the center stage in the recession's bad news. Armed with boxes of tissues, HR managers held layoff meetings, typically tearful events. Although they often played no role in making layoff decisions (which were usually made by line managers), HR managers had to answer angry calls about broken promises and do the dirty work of managing termination details. "If there was ever a time to underscore the importance of HR," *BusinessWeek* announced, "it has arrived."

Particularly as unemployment numbers around the world soar, how to manage layoffs and the survivors remains a major challenge for HRM. The consensus among experts is that firms need to treat laid-off employees with dignity, fairness, and respect. For plant closures and large-scale layoffs, key milestones and dates need to be communicated well in advance. The business case needs to be explained in detail. Affected employees should be given options for finding other jobs inside the company or the resources to hunt for jobs outside. HR managers are advised to show compassion and understanding. This can be done not only in words but also in concrete ways, such as offering to serve as a reference to prospective employers.

Unfortunately, too many firms do not do it right. Many line managers do not have the guts to face laid-off employees, and hide behind HR managers who have to deliver the bad news. Losing one's job is dehumanizing in any event, but many employees leave feeling alienated and unfairly treated. Worse yet is when a firm gives in to the temptation to shortchange employees on severance when downsizing. As a result, employee lawsuits for unlawful termination have skyrocketed. Around the world, different countries have different rules for severance arrangements. In France, employees are entitled to 30 days of severance pay for each year of service—an employee with 20 years of service can walk away with 20 months of pay. In Germany and India, severance pay is two weeks pay per year of service. In Britain, it is a minimum of $470 per year of service. In China and Russia, workers can be fired with only one month of wages. The United States does not have a legal requirement for severance pay in the Fair Labor Standards Act (FLSA) and the Worker Adjustment and Retraining Notification Act (WARN). Severance pay is strictly a matter of agreement between US employers and employees.

In addition to the stress of managing layoffs, managing surviving employees is no less challenging. Even when jobs are relatively safe, employees still ask: When are the layoffs coming? Survivors often see their salaries and work hours cut, budgets reduced, and perks eliminated. When dealing with international or multiethnic workforces, inappropriate or insensitive management can cause major trouble or even disaster. In June 2009, when a Hong Kong–owned toy factory in Guangdong, China, found demand reduced for its products, fights erupted between the majority Han Chinese employees and Uyghur employees (a minority group typically residing in Xinjiang province of China). A week later, a mob of mostly unemployed Uyghur killed several hundred Han Chinese in Urumqi, Xinjiang, apparently in retaliation, causing significant upheaval in the region. Typically, in most firms around the world, surviving employees are not unruly and violent, but many are taking preemptive measures and organizing unions or calling hotlines about suspected corporate wrongdoing. Under US law, once employees report any corporate wrongdoing (whether real or bogus), the employees become a protected class ("whistleblowers"). If whistleblowers are fired, then employers can be easily dragged into court on charges of retaliation. As a result, the loudmouths and the litigious often end up becoming an influential group among the surviving rank and file, undermining firms' ability to get the real job done.

Not all HR news is bad news in this tough time. One innovative practice emerging out of the recent recession is to tell laid-off employees: "You're fired—but please stay in touch." From Dow Chemical to JP Morgan Chase, many firms now label laid-off, former employees as "alumni," and cultivate online alumni networks as forums for opportunities in networking and for possible future rehiring. When the economy recovers, firms hope to recruit some of these "alumni" back. Such hire-back cases are now called "boomerangs" in the new HR jargon. By showing compassion and understanding to laid-off employees, such firms hope to preserve some goodwill in a tough time in order to create firm-specific advantage when the economy turns north. Advising CEOs, two experts wrote: "HR matters enormously in good times. It defines you in bad times."

Sources: Based on (1) *BusinessWeek*, 2009, The hidden perils of layoffs, March 2: 52–53; (2) *BusinessWeek*, 2009, You're fired—but stay in touch, May 4: 54–55; (3) *BusinessWeek*, 2009, Human resources: They're human, too, July 27: 19; (4) *Economist*, 2009, When jobs disappear, March 14: 71–73; (5) R. Sutton, 2009, How to be a good boss in a bad economy, *Harvard Business Review*, June: 42–50; (6) US Department of Labor, 2009, eLaws: FLSA advisor, www.dol.gov; (7) J. Welch & S. Welch, 2009, Layoffs: HR's moment of truth, *BusinessWeek*, March 23 & 30: 104.

How can firms select, retain, reward, and motivate the best employees that they can attract? How can they link the management of people with firm performance? During a recession, how can they manage both the laid-off workers and the surviving employees? These are some of the crucial questions we will address in this chapter. This chapter is devoted to **human resource management (HRM)**, which refers to activities that attract, select, and manage employees.[1] As a function, HRM used to be called "personnel" and before that "records management." Few of you are HRM experts, but everyone can appreciate HRM's rising importance just by looking at the evolution of the terminology. The term "HRM" clearly indicates that people are key resources of the firm to be actively managed and developed (see PengAtlas Maps 4.3 and 4.4). In the last two decades, HRM has become more important, and often sports the word "strategic" to make it "strategic HRM." From a lowly administrative support function, HRM has increasingly been recognized as a strategic function that, together with other crucial functions such as finance and marketing, helps accomplish organizational effectiveness and financial performance.[2]

This chapter first reviews the four main areas of HRM: (1) staffing, (2) training and development, (3) compensation and performance appraisal, and (4) labor relations. Then, we use the institution-based and resource-based views to shed light on these issues. We will also discuss three leading debates and conclude with a discussion on the five Cs associated with HRM.

Human resource management (HRM)

Activities that attract, select, and manage employees.

STAFFING

Staffing refers to HRM activities associated with hiring employees and filling positions.[3] In multinational enterprises (MNEs), there are two types of employees. **Host country nationals (HCNs)** are from the host country and are often known as "locals." Expatriates (expats for short) are individuals working in a foreign country. For example, the general manager at the Portman Ritz-Carlton Hotel in Shanghai, China, Mark DeCocinis, is an expatriate, and all the Chinese employees he hired are HCNs. Expatriates come in two types. **Parent country nationals (PCNs)** come from the parent country of the MNE and work at its local subsidiary. For the US-based Ritz-Carlton, PCNs would be Americans. **Third country nationals (TCNs)** come from neither the parent country nor the host country.

The majority of an MNE's employees (that is, those in the lower and mid ranks) would be HCNs. For example, of HSBC's 28,000 employees worldwide, only a small cadre of 400 executives are expatriates and another 1,600 employees are short-term assignees abroad. A leading concern is how to staff the *top* executive positions abroad, such as the subsidiary CEO, country manager, and key functional heads such as CFO and CIO. The three choices for top positions—PCNs, TCNs, and HCNs—all have their pros and cons (Table 15.1). The staffing choices are not random and are often a reflection of the strategic posture of the MNE, as discussed next.

Ethnocentric, Polycentric, and Geocentric Approaches in Staffing

There are three primary approaches for making staffing decisions for top positions at subsidiaries. An **ethnocentric approach** emphasizes the norms and practices of the parent company (and the parent country of the MNE) by relying on PCNs. Not only can PCNs ensure and facilitate control and coordination by headquarters, they may also be the best qualified people for the job because of special skills and

LEARNING OBJECTIVE 1

Explain staffing decisions with a focus on expatriates.

Staffing
HRM activities associated with hiring employees and filling positions.

Host country national (HCN)
An individual from the host country who works for an MNE.

Parent country national (PCN)
An individual who comes from the parent country of the MNE and works at its local subsidiary.

Third country national (TCN)
An individual who is from neither the parent country nor the host country of the MNE.

Ethnocentric approach
An emphasis on the norms and practices of the parent company (and the parent country of the MNE) by relying on PCNs.

TABLE 15.1   PARENT, THIRD, AND HOST COUNTRY NATIONALS

	Advantages	Disadvantages
Parent country nationals (PCNs)	• Control by headquarters is facilitated. • PCNs may be the most qualified people. • Managers are given international experience.	• Opportunities for HCNs are limited. • Adaptation may take a long time. • PCNs are usually very expensive.
Third country nationals (TCNs)	• TCNs may bridge the gap between headquarters and the subsidiary (and between PCNs and HCNs). • TCNs may be less expensive than PCNs.	• Host government and employees may resent TCNs. • Similar to disadvantages for PCNs.
Host country nationals (HCNs)	• Language and cultural barriers are eliminated. • Continuity of management improves, since HCNs stay longer in positions. • Usually cheaper.	• Control and coordination by headquarters may be impeded. • HCNs may have limited career opportunity. • Limits international experience opportunities for PCNs.

Source: Adapted from P. Dowling & D. Welch, 2005, *International Human Resource Management*, 4th ed. (p. 63), Cincinnati: South-Western Cengage Learning.

experience. A perceived lack of talent and skills among HCNs often necessitates an ethnocentric approach. In addition, a cadre of internationally mobile and experienced managers, who are often PCNs, can emerge to spearhead further expansion around the world.

A polycentric approach is the opposite of an ethnocentric approach. A **polycentric approach** focuses on the norms and practices of the host country. In short, "when in Rome, do as the Romans do." Who would make the best managers of operations in Rome? Naturally Roman (or Italian) managers—technically, HCNs. HCNs have no language or cultural barriers. Unlike PCNs who often pack their bags and move after several years, HCNs stay in their positions longer, thus providing more continuity of management. Further, placing HCNs in top subsidiary positions sends a morale-boosting signal to other HCNs who may feel that they can reach the top, too (at least in that subsidiary).

Disregarding nationality, a **geocentric approach** focuses on finding the most suitable managers, who can be PCNs, HCNs, or TCNs. In other words, a geocentric approach is "color-blind"—the color of a manager's passport does not matter. For a geographically dispersed MNE, a geocentric approach can help create a corporate-wide culture and identity. This can reduce the typical us-versus-them feeling in firms that use either ethnocentric or polycentric approaches. On the other hand, molding managers from a variety of nationalities is a lot more complex than integrating individuals from two (parent and host) countries.

Overall, there is a systematic link between the strategic posture of an MNE (see Chapter 13) and its staffing approaches (Table 15.2). MNEs pursuing a home replication strategy usually use an ethnocentric approach, staffing subsidiaries with PCNs. MNEs interested in a localization strategy are typically polycentric in nature, often hiring HCNs to head subsidiaries. Global standardization or transnational strategies often require a geocentric approach, resulting in a mix of HCNs, PCNs, and TCNs. In Focus 15.1 features some foreign-born bosses at MNEs aspiring to globalize their operations.

The Role of Expatriates

Polycentric approach
An emphasis on the norms and practices of the host country.

Geocentric approach
A focus on finding the most suitable managers, who can be PCNs, HCNs, or TCNs.

Expatriation
The process of selecting, managing, and motivating expatriates to work abroad.

Expatriation is leaving one's home country to work in another country. Shown in Figure 15.1, expatriates play four important roles:

- Expatriates are *strategists* representing the interests of the MNE's headquarters.[4] Expatriates, especially PCNs who have a long tenure with a particular MNE, may have internalized the parent firm's values and norms. They may not only enable headquarters to control subsidiaries, but also facilitate the socialization process to bring subsidiaries into an MNE's global "orbit."
- Expatriates act as *daily managers* to run operations and to build local capabilities. Generally, they are necessary when local management talent is lacking.

TABLE 15.2 MULTINATIONAL STRATEGIES AND STAFFING APPROACHES

MNE strategies	Typical staffing approaches	Typical top managers at local subsidiaries
Home replication	Ethnocentric	Parent country nationals
Localization	Polycentric	Host country nationals
Global standardization	Geocentric	A mix of parent, host, and third country nationals
Transnational	Geocentric	A mix of parent, host, and third country nationals

Foreign-Born Bosses

An increasingly large number of foreign-born bosses are now running the show at some of the world's largest and most visible MNEs. Since 1999, Nissan's CEO has been Carlos Ghosn, who more recently (since 2005) has also become CEO of Renault. Born in Brazil to Lebanese immigrants, Ghosn was educated in France and rose to the ranks in French MNEs Michelin and Renault. Soon after Ghosn took over Nissan, he was receiving hate mail from Japanese employees slated to lose their jobs. Now he is revered in Japan and considered a national hero for successfully turning around Nissan.

Because of Renault's acquisition of a chunk of Nissan's equity, Ghosn was appointed to Nissan as a PCN. However, at many other MNEs, foreign-born CEOs have been promoted from within. In 1993, the Scottish-born Alex Trotman took over as Ford's chairman and CEO, and then in 1999 he promoted the Lebanese-born Australian Jacques Nasser as his successor. In 2004, Coca-Cola named the Irish-born Neville Isdell its chairman and CEO. In 2005, Sony appointed the Welsh-born American Howard Stringer as its CEO. In 2006, Pepsi promoted the Indian-born Indra Nooyi to be its CEO.

Appointing foreign-born executives has become a trend for companies aspiring to globalize. After China's Lenovo acquired IBM's PC Division (PCD), Lenovo first appointed PCD's former head, an American, to be its CEO. Then Lenovo replaced him with another American CEO recruited from Dell. As Korea's LG generates four-fifths of its revenue from overseas, it has embarked on a drive to globalize its top echelon. Although its chairman and CEO are still Korean, five of its key units—namely, marketing, procurement, supply chain, HRM, and retailer relations—are now headed by Western executives recruited from HP, Novartis, Pfizer, and Unilever. The once-stodgy Korean company is counting on these expats to boost its global image and, ultimately, its profits. Whether these expats can make it happen remains to be seen. So stay tuned . . .

Sources: Based on (1) *BusinessWeek*, 2006, Smoothest handover, December 18: 62; (2) *BusinessWeek*, 2009, The foreigners at the top of LG, December 22: 56–57; (3) *Economist*, 2005, Outside in, January 1: 42.

- Expatriates are *ambassadors*.[5] Representing headquarters' interests, they build relationships with host-country stakeholders such as local managers, employees, suppliers, customers, and government officials. Importantly, expatriates also serve as ambassadors representing the interests of the *subsidiaries* when interacting with headquarters.
- Finally, expatriates are *trainers* for their replacements. Over time, some localization in staffing is inevitable, calling for expatriates to train local employees.

FIGURE 15.1   THE ROLES OF EXPATRIATES

What steps can expatriates take to prepare for an assignment and improve their chances of success?

Expatriate Failure and Selection

Few expatriates can play the challenging multidimensional roles effectively.[6] It is not surprising that expatriate failure rates are high. Expatriate failure can be defined several ways, including (1) premature (earlier-than-expected) return, (2) unmet business objectives, and (3) unfulfilled career development objectives. Using the easiest-to-observe measure of premature return, earlier studies reported that 76% of US MNEs have expatriate failure rates of more than 10% and that 41% and 24% of European and Japanese MNEs, respectively, have comparable failure rates.[7] More recent studies find that the failure rates have declined a little.[8] However, given the much larger number of expatriates now (at present, 1.3 million from the United States alone), expatriate failure rates are still high enough to justify attention. Since expatriates typically are the most expensive group of managers, the cost of each failure is tremendous—between a quarter of a million and one million dollars.

Expatriation can fail for a variety of reasons. Surveys of US and European MNEs find that the leading cause is the spouse and family's inability to adjust to life in a foreign country. In the case of Japanese MNEs, the leading cause is the inability to cope with the larger scope of responsibilities overseas. It usually is a *combination* of work-related and family-related problems that leads to expatriate failures.

Given the importance of expatriates and their reported high failure rates, how can firms enhance the odds for expatriate success? Figure 15.2 outlines a model for expatriate selection, with six underlying factors grouped along situation and individual dimensions. In terms of situation dimensions, the preferences of both headquarters and the subsidiary are important (Table 15.2). In some Asian countries where seniority is highly respected, younger expatriates may be ineffective.[9] The subsidiary may also have specific requests, such as "Send a strong IT person." It is preferable for expatriates to have some command—or better yet, mastery—of the local language.

In terms of individual dimensions, both technical ability and cross-cultural adaptability are a must. Desirable attributes include a positive attitude, emotional stability, and previous international experience.[10] Last (but certainly not least), spouse and family preferences must be considered.[11] The accompanying spouse may leave behind a career and a social network. The spouse has to find meaningful endeavors abroad, but many countries protect local jobs by not permitting the spouse to work. It is not surprising that many families find expatriation frustrating and that this frustration leads to expatriate failure.

Expatriates are expensive and failure rates are high in general, but middle-aged expatriates (forty-somethings) are the most expensive. This age group typically has children still in school so the employer often has to provide a heavy allowance for children's education. High-quality schools can be expensive. In places such as Manila, Mexico City, and Moscow, international or American schools cost $10,000 to $30,000 per year. Unfortunately, these expatriates also have the highest percentage of failure rates in part because of their family responsibilities. In response,

FIGURE 15.2   FACTORS IN EXPATRIATE SELECTION

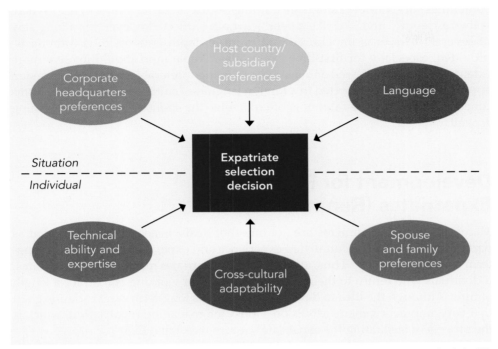

Source: Adapted from P. Dowling & D. Welch, 2005, *International Human Resource Management*, 4th ed. (p. 98), Cincinnati: South-Western Cengage Learning.

many MNEs either select expatriates in their fifties, who are less likely to have school-age children, and/or promote younger expatriates in their late twenties and early thirties who may not yet have children. The younger expatriates typically do not need a large home or education allowance. The second preference has strong implications for students studying this book now: Overseas opportunities may come sooner than you expect. Are *you* ready?

TRAINING AND DEVELOPMENT

Training is specific preparation to do a particular job. **Development** refers to longer term, broader preparation to improve managerial skills for a better career.[12] Training and development programs focus on two groups: expatriates and HCNs. Each is discussed in turn.

Training for Expatriates

The importance and cost of expatriates and their reported high failure rates make training necessary. Yet, about one third of MNEs do not provide any pre-departure training for expatriates, sending them off with little more than a wish for "good luck."[13] Even for firms that provide training, many offer short, one-day-type programs that are inadequate. Not surprisingly, many MNEs and expatriates get burned by such underinvestment in preparation for what are arguably some of the most challenging managerial assignments.

Identify training and development needs for expatriates and host country nationals.

Training
Specific preparation to do a particular job.

Development
Long-term, broader preparation to improve managerial skills for a better career.

Ideally, training length and rigor should correspond to the expatriate's expected length of stay. For a short stay, training can be short and less rigorous. Sometimes survival-level language training—such as learning how to say "Where is the restroom?" and "I'd like a beer"—would suffice. However, for a long stay of several years, it is imperative that more in-depth and rigorous training be provided, especially for first-time expatriates. Preparation should involve more extensive language as well as sensitivity training, preferably with an immersion approach (training conducted in a foreign language/culture environment). Firms concerned about failure rates now often involve the spouse in expatriate training as well.

Development for Returning Expatriates (Repatriates)

Many expatriate assignments are not one-shot deals; instead they are viewed as part of the manager's accumulated experience and expertise and enhance a long-term career in the firm.[14] Thus, at some point, expatriates may become **repatriates**, individuals who return to their home countries after working abroad for a length of time. Although the idea to develop a repatriate's long-term career sounds good in theory, in practice, many MNEs do a lousy job managing **repatriation**, which is the process of facilitating the expatriate's return (see Table 15.3).

Chief among the problems experienced by repatriates is career anxiety. A leading concern is "What kind of position will I have when I return?" Prior to departure, many expatriates are encouraged by their boss: "You should take (or volunteer for) this overseas assignment. It's a smart move for your career." Theoretically, this is known as a **psychological contract**, an informal understanding of expected delivery of benefits in the future for current services. A psychological contract is easy to violate. Bosses may change their minds. Or they may be replaced by new bosses. Violated psychological contracts naturally lead to disappointments.

Many returning expatriates find readjusting to the domestic workplace to be a painful experience. Ethnocentrism continues to characterize many MNEs. For example, many MNE employees at headquarters have a bias when it comes to knowledge transfer, which typically moves from headquarters to subsidiaries via expatriates. Consequently, they are not interested in learning from the returning expatriate's international experience, which would mean knowledge moving from subsidiaries to headquarters.[15] This attitude typically leads repatriates to feel that their international experience is not appreciated. After being a big fish in a small

Repatriate
Returning expatriate.

Repatriation
The process of facilitating the expatriate's return.

Psychological contract
An informal understanding of expected delivery of benefits in the future for current services.

TABLE 15.3 PROBLEMS ASSOCIATED WITH REPATRIATION

- Career anxiety—what kind of position will I have when I return (if I will have a position)?
- Work adjustment—from a big fish in a small pond (at the subsidiary) to a small fish in a big pond (at headquarters).
- Loss of status and pay—expatriate premiums are gone, chauffeured cars and maids are probably unavailable.
- Difficult for the spouse and children to adjust—"going home" is not that easy.

pond at the subsidiary, repatriates often feel like a small fish in a big pond at head-quarters. Instead of being promoted, many end up taking comparable (or lower-level) positions.

Repatriates may also experience a loss of status. Overseas, they are big shots, rubbing shoulders with local politicians and visiting dignitaries. They often command lavish expatriate premiums, with chauffeured cars and maids. But most of these perks disappear once they return home.

Lastly, the spouse and the children may also find it difficult to adjust back home. The feeling of being a part of a relatively high-class, close-knit expatriate community is gone. Instead, life at home may now seem lonely, dull, and unexciting. In the United States, some wives of Honda executives enjoy being Avon Ladies who are involved in direct selling. When the long-anticipated repatriation notice comes, they are excited about expanding their business back to Japan. However, prior to returning home, all husbands receive a letter from headquarters, demanding that their wives quit direct selling. This is because direct selling is viewed as a low-prestige occupation not worthy for the spouses of executives at a prestigious firm such as Honda—doesn't Honda pay executives enough? The letter ends with a warning that if their wives are found to continue to hawk Avon cosmetics in Japan, their husbands would be *fired*.[16] Likewise, children, being out of touch with current slang, sports, and fashion, may struggle to regain acceptance into peer groups back home. Having been brought up overseas, (re)adjusting back to the home country educational system may be especially problematic. Some of the returning Japanese teenagers committed suicide after failing to make the grade back home.

Overall, if not managed well, repatriation can be traumatic not only for expatriates and their families but also for the firm. Unhappy returning expatriates do not stay around long. Approximately one in four repatriates leave the firm within one year. Since a US MNE spends on average around one million dollars on each expatriate over the duration of a foreign assignment, losing that individual can wipe out any return on investment.[17] Worse yet, the returnee may end up working for a rival firm.

The best way to reduce expatriate turnover is a career development plan. A good plan also comes with a mentor (also known as a champion, sponsor, or god-father).[18] The mentor helps alleviate the "out-of-sight, out-of-mind" feeling by ensuring that the expatriate is not forgotten at headquarters and by helping secure a challenging position for the expatriate upon return.

Overall, despite the numerous horror stories, many expatriates do succeed. For example, Carlos Ghosn, after successfully turning around Nissan as a PCN, went on to become CEO of the parent company, Renault (see In Focus 15.1). To reach the top at most MNEs today, international experience is a must. Therefore, despite the drawbacks, aspiring managers should not be deterred from taking overseas assignments. Who said being a manager was easy?

Training and Development for Host Country Nationals

Although most international HRM practice and research focus on expatriates, it is important to note that the training and development needs of HCNs deserve significant attention as well. In the ongoing "war for talent" in Brazil, Russia, India, China (BRIC), and other emerging economies, a key factor in retaining or losing top talent is whether employers can provide better training and development opportunities. To slow turnover, many MNEs in China now have formal career development plans and processes for HCNs. Kodak, for example, strives for the "Four Greats:" (1) great hires, (2) great moves (fast promotion), (3) great assignments, and (4) great feedback.

LEARNING OBJECTIVE 3

Identify and discuss compensation and performance appraisal issues.

COMPENSATION AND PERFORMANCE APPRAISAL

As an HRM area, compensation refers to the determination of salary and benefits.[19] Performance appraisal is the evaluation of employee performance for the purpose of promotion, retention, or ending employment. Three related issues are discussed here: (1) compensation for expatriates, (2) compensation for HCNs, and (3) performance appraisal.

Compensation for Expatriates

A leading issue in international HRM is how to properly compensate, motivate, and retain expatriates. There are two primary approaches: going rate and balance sheet (Table 15.4).

The going rate approach pays expatriates the prevailing (going) rate for comparable positions in a host country. When Lenovo acquired IBM's PC division, it sent Chinese expatriates to New York and paid them the going rate for comparable positions for HCNs and other expatriates in New York. The going rate approach fosters equality among PCNs, TCNs, and HCNs within the same subsidiary. It also makes locations where pay is higher than the home country a more attractive place to work for PCNs and TCNs. Overall, this approach excels in its simplicity and fosters strong identification with the host country.

However, the going rate for the same position differs around the world, with the United States leading in managerial compensation. For example, the typical US CEO commands a total compensation package of over $2 million, whereas a British CEO fetches less than $1 million, a Japanese CEO $500,000, and a Chinese CEO $200,000. According to the going rate approach, returning Lenovo expatriates,

Compensation
The determination of salary and benefits.

Performance appraisal
The evaluation of employee performance for promotion, retention, or termination purposes.

Going rate approach
A compensation approach that pays expatriates the prevailing (going) rate for comparable positions in a host country.

TABLE 15.4   GOING RATE VERSUS BALANCE SHEET APPROACH IN EXPATRIATE COMPENSATION

	Advantages	Disadvantages
Going rate	• Equality among parent, third, and host country nationals in the same location • Simplicity • Identification with host country	• Variation between assignments in different locations for the same employee • Re-entry problem if the going rate of parent country is less than that of host country
Balance sheet	• Equity between assignments for the same employee • Facilitates expatriate re-entry	• Costly and complex to administer • Great disparities between expatriates and host country nationals

accustomed to New York–level salaries, will have a hard time accepting relatively lower Beijing-level salaries, thus triggering repatriation problems.

A second approach is the **balance sheet approach**, which balances the cost-of-living differences relative to parent country levels and adds a financial inducement to make the package attractive. This method is the most widely used in expatriate compensation. Historically this approach was justified on the grounds that a majority of expatriates were coming from higher-pay, developed economies and going to lower-pay locations. Under these conditions, the going rate approach would not work because an expatriate from New York probably would not accept the lower going rate in Beijing. The balance sheet approach essentially pays Beijing-bound expatriates "New York Plus." The "Plus" is nontrivial: additional financial inducement (premium), cost-of-living allowance (for housing and children's education), and a hardship allowance (fewer companies now pay a hardship allowance for Beijing, but many MNEs used to). Table 15.5 shows one hypothetical example. Adding housing and taxation that the MNE pays (not shown in the table), the total cost may reach $300,000.

The balance sheet approach has two advantages (see Table 15.4). First, there is equity between assignments for the same employee, whose compensation is always anchored to the going rate in the parent country. Second, it also facilitates repatriation, because there is relatively little fluctuation between overseas and parent country pay despite the cost-of-living differences around the world (Figure 15.3).

However, there are three disadvantages. The first is cost. Using the example in Table 15.5, the cost can add up to one million dollars for a three-year tour of duty. The second disadvantage is the great disparities in pay between expatriates (especially PCNs) and HCNs, causing resentment among HCNs.

Lastly, the balance sheet approach is organizationally complex to administer. For a US firm operating in South Africa, both the American PCNs and Australian TCNs are likely to be compensated more than the South African HCNs. The situation becomes more complicated when the US firm recruits South African MBAs before they finish business school training in the United States. Should they be paid as locally hired HCNs in South Africa or as expatriates from the United States? What about TCNs from Kenya, Morocco, and Nigeria who also finish US MBA training and are interested in going to work for the US MNE in South Africa? Ideally, firms pay for a position regardless of passport color. However, the market for expatriate compensation is not quite there yet.

Balance sheet approach

A compensation approach that balances the cost of living differences relative to parent country levels and adds a financial inducement to make the package attractive.

TABLE 15.5 A HYPOTHETICAL EXPATRIATE COMPENSATION PACKAGE USING THE BALANCE SHEET APPROACH

Items for a hypothetical US expatriate	Amount (US$)
Base salary	$150,000
Cost-of-living allowance (25%)	$37,500
Overseas premium (20%)	$30,000
Hardship allowance (20%)	$30,000
Housing deduction (–7%)	–$10,500
TOTAL (pretax)	$237,000

Note: The host country has a cost-of-living index of 150 relative to the United States. *Not* shown here are the full cost of housing and the cost to pay the difference between a higher income tax in a host country and a lower income tax in the parent country. Adding housing and taxation, the net cost on the MNE can reach $300,000 in this case.

FIGURE 15.3   DIFFERENCES IN COST OF LIVING FOR EXPATRIATES IN SELECTED CITIES (NEW YORK = 100)

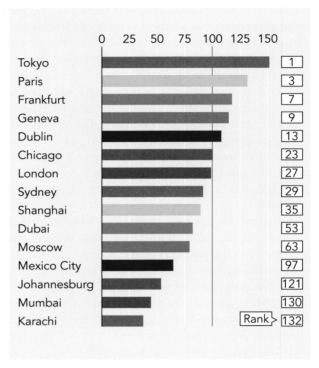

Source: Adapted from "The Cost of Living", *The Economist* March 14, 2009, p. 102. Copyright © 2009 The Economist Newspaper Limited. Reprinted with permission. All rights reserved. All data are for February 2009.

Compensation for Host Country Nationals

At the bottom end of the compensation scale, low-level HCNs, especially those in developing countries, have relatively little bargaining power. The very reason that they have jobs at the MNE subsidiaries is often because of their low labor cost—that is, they are willing to accept wage levels substantially lower than those in developed countries. The HCNs compare their pay to the farmhands sweating in the fields and making much less, or to the unemployed who make nothing and still have a family to feed. Despite accusations of exploitation by some social activists, MNEs in developing countries typically pay *higher* wages compared to similar positions in the local market.

On the other hand, HCNs in management and professional positions have increasing bargaining power. MNEs are rushing into emerging economies, where local supply of top talent is limited. This may be hard to believe, but the most populous country in the world has a shortage of people—executives. To fuel their growth, Chinese and foreign firms need 75,000 globally competitive executives in China. At present, approximately 3,000 to 5,000 Chinese executives fit the profile. Likewise, until the 2008–2009 recession, wage inflation in India's hot IT sector had been 16% a year, with a 40% turnover.[20] Although such increase has slowed down, the "war for talent" (specifically, the bidding war for top-notch HCNs) is real. It is not surprising that high-caliber HCNs, because of their scarcity, will fetch more pay. The question is: How much more? Most MNEs plan to eventually replace even top-level expatriates with HCNs, in part to save on costs. However, if HCNs occupying the same top-level positions are paid the same as expatriates, then there will be no cost savings. However, MNEs unwilling to pay top dollar for local talent may end up losing high-caliber HCNs to competitors that are willing to do so.[21] MNEs may eventually have to pay international rates for qualified individuals in top positions, regardless of nationality.

Performance Appraisal

Although initial compensation is determined upon entering a firm, follow-up compensation usually depends on performance appraisal. It focuses on decision making regarding pay and promotion, development, documentation, and subordinate expression. In our case, performance appraisal is based on how expatriates provide performance appraisal to HCNs and how expatriates are evaluated.

When expatriates evaluate HCNs, cultural differences may create problems. Western MNEs typically see performance appraisals as an opportunity for subordinates to express themselves. In high power-distance countries such as those in Asia and Latin America, however, such an expression could potentially undermine the power and status of supervisors. Employees themselves do not place a lot of importance on self-expression. So Western expatriates who push HCNs in these cultures to express themselves in performance appraisal meetings would be viewed as indecisive and lacking integrity.

Expatriates need to be evaluated by their own supervisors. In some cases, however, expatriates are the top manager in a subsidiary (such as country manager), and their supervisors are more senior executives based at headquarters. Some of these off-site managers have no experience as expatriates themselves. They often evaluate expatriates based on hard numbers (such as productivity and market growth), but sometimes these numbers are beyond the expatriate's control (such as effects from a currency crisis). This is one of the reasons why many expatriates think they are not evaluated fairly. The solution lies in fostering more visits and communication between on-site expatriates and off-site supervisors and in relying on former expatriates now based at headquarters to serve as off-site supervisors.

LABOR RELATIONS

Labor relations refer to a firm's relations with organized labor (unions) in both home and host countries. Each is discussed in turn.

LEARNING OBJECTIVE

4

List factors that affect labor relations in both home and host countries.

Managing Labor Relations at Home

In developed economies, a firm's key concern is to cut costs and enhance competitiveness to fight off low-cost rivals from emerging economies such as China and India. Labor unions, on the other hand, are organized with the purpose of helping workers earn higher wages and obtain more benefits through collective bargaining. In the United States, unionized employees earn 30% more than nonunionized employees. As a result, disagreements and conflicts between managers and unions are natural.

Labor relations

A firm's relations with organized labor (unions) in both home and host countries.

Labor unions' bargaining chip is their credible threat to strike, slow down, refuse to work overtime, or some other form of disruption. Managers' bargaining chip is the threat to shut down operations and move jobs overseas. It is clear which side is winning. In the United States, union membership dropped from 20% of the workforce in 1983 to 12% now.[22] In the private sector in the United States, only 7% of employees are union members at present.[23]

Unlike MNEs, which can move operations around the world, unions are organized on a country-by-country basis. Efforts to establish multinational labor organizations have not been effective. In the 1990s, US MNEs moved aggressively to shift operations to Mexico to take advantage of NAFTA. The leading US union, the AFL-CIO, contacted the Mexican government and requested permission to recruit members in Mexico. It was flatly rejected. In 2007, the US House of Representatives passed a new Employee Free Choice Act, which was designed to make it easier to organize unions in the United States. It has provoked fierce debates and been criticized by GE's former CEO Jack Welch as an "insidious" blow to American competitiveness (see In Focus 15.2).

The Unemployment Act

In 2007, a *BusinessWeek* reader wrote and asked columnists Jack Welch (former CEO of General Electric) and Suzy Welch (former editor of *Harvard Business Review*): *Are you at all concerned about American competitiveness in the future?* They wrote the following column titled "The Unemployment Act:"

Yes . . . We are as worried as can be that American competitiveness is about to be whacked by something no one seems to be talking about: the Employee Free Choice Act, which is currently [March 2007] weaving an insidious path through Congress toward becoming law. If it does, the long-thriving American economy will finally meet its match.

You didn't read wrong. We know it must sound strange to oppose legislation that promises "free choice." But the title of this bill is pure propaganda. It won't encourage liberty or self-determination in the workplace; more likely it will introduce intimidation and coercion by labor organizers, who after a long slide into near-oblivion, finally see a glorious new route to millions of dues-paying members. Their campaign could trigger a surge in unionization across US industry—

and in time, a reversion to the bloated economy that brought America to its knees in the late 1970s and early '80s and that today cripples much of European business. . .

Make no mistake. We don't unilaterally oppose unions. Indeed, if a company is habitually unfair or unreasonable, it deserves what it gets from organized labor. But the problem with unions is that they make a sport out of killing productivity even when companies are providing good wages, benefits, and working conditions. It is not uncommon in a union shop to shut down production rather than allow a nonunion worker to flip a switch. Only a union or millwright electrician can do that job! Come on. Companies today can't afford such petty bureaucracy or the other excesses unions so often lead to, such as two people for every job and a litigious approach to even the smallest matters. Yes, managers and employees will sometimes disagree. But in the global economy, they have to work through these differences not as adversaries but as partners.

The Employee Free Choice Act undermines that. Here's how. Currently, when labor organizers want to launch a unionization effort, they ask each worker to sign a card as a show of support. If 30% or more employees do so, a federally supervised election can be called and conducted within one of the most revered mechanisms in democracy, the secret ballot. Thus, employees can vote their conscience, without fear of retribution from either union leaders or management.

By contrast, under the Employee Free Choice Act, organizers could start a union if 50% of employees, plus one more worker, sign cards. That's right—no more secret ballot. Instead, employees would likely get a phone call with a pointed solicitation, or worse, a home visit from a small team of organizers. You can just imagine the scenario. The organizers sit around the kitchen table and make their case, likely with a lot of passion. Then they slide a card in front of the employee with a pen. Who would say no? Who could?

Now, union supporters will tell you that they won't intimidate employees for votes, and regardless, management intimidates all the time by threatening to fire employees who vote union. But the system as it exists has safeguards, including heavy fines against companies that misbehave.

Still, the advance of the Employee Free Choice Act continues unabated. And so pretty soon, if enough business leaders and legislators don't stand up, it may well be: Hello again, unions. So long, American competitiveness. The change won't happen instantly. Companies will fight unions as if they lives dependent on it, because they do. But given the logistics of the Employee Free Choice Act, any management campaign is hobbled. If you can't be at the kitchen table with the organizers and their hard stares, you probably can't win.

It's too bad. In fact, it's terrible. And ironic. First, because the ability to unionize already exists in America, thanks to the secret ballot. And second, because the Employee Free Choice Act ultimately only provides a free choice nobody would ever want: how to spend a government-issued unemployment check.

Jack Welch and Suzy Welch published their piece in *BusinessWeek* in 2007. Since then, debate on the Employee Free Choice Act (EFCA), commonly referred to as the "Card Check Bill," continues to rage. In April 2009, Dallas Regional Chamber of Commerce chairman Bob Best argued:

> The "Card Check Bill" will curtail the rights of both employees and employers to have a fair process regarding a decision to unionize companies, plants, and facilities of all sizes. If passed, this ill-considered proposal has the potential to hamper economic recovery and further curtail employment opportunities at just the wrong time.

Although President Obama supported EFCA when he was a presidential candidate, he modified his position on the eve of his inauguration. When questioned about a timetable for pushing EFCA, Obama was quoted in a media interview on January 16, 2009 (four days before his inauguration):

> If we are losing half a million jobs a month then there are no jobs to unionize. So my focus first is on the economic priority items (such as the stimulus package).

However, times change. Fears of a global recession unmatched since the Great Depression seemed to have passed. On September 7, 2009 (Labor Day), Obama told a crowd at a Labor Day rally that EFCA was his top legislative priority. In his own words:

> Why do I support the Employee Free Choice Act? To level the playing field so it's easier for employees who want a union to have a union. Because when labor is strong, America is strong. When we all stand together, we all rise together.

Sources: Excerpts from J. Welch & S. Welch, 2007, The unemployment act, *BusinessWeek*, March 12: 108. Additional sources are (1) *The Atlantic*, 2009, Obama on the Employee Free Choice Act, January 16 (marcambinder .theatlantic.com); (2) *BusinessWeek*, 2009, Labor's favorite bill hits a wall, March 23 & 30: 24; (3) Dallas Regional Chamber, 2009, Dallas Regional Chamber urges Congress to oppose Employee Free Choice Act (EFCA), April (www.dallaschamber.org); (4) Reuters, 2009, Obama, Biden reaffirm support for Employee Free Choice Act, September 7 (www. reuters.com).

Managing Labor Relations Abroad

If given a choice, MNEs prefer to deal with nonunionized workforces. When Japanese and German automakers came to the United States, they avoided the Midwest, a union stronghold. Instead, these MNEs went to the rural South and set up nonunion plants in small towns in Alabama (Mercedes and Hyundai), Kentucky (Toyota), and South Carolina (BMW). When MNEs have to deal with unions abroad, they often rely on experienced HCNs instead of locally inexperienced PCNs or TCNs.

Throughout many developing countries, governments welcome MNEs and simultaneously silence unions. In China, the right to strike was removed from the constitution in 1982. Only 10% of the half a million foreign-invested firms in China have unions. However, in a recent high-profile case, Wal-Mart decided to allow its 31,000-strong Chinese workforce to organize unions. The power of unions in developing countries certainly deserves some attention from MNE management.

Discuss how the institution-based and resource-based views shed additional light on HRM.

INSTITUTIONS, RESOURCES, AND HUMAN RESOURCE MANAGEMENT

Having outlined the four basic areas of HRM, let us now turn to the institution-based and resource-based views to see how they shed additional light (see Figure 15.4).

Institutions and Human Resource Management

Formal and informal rules of the game shape HRM significantly, both at home and abroad.[24] Let us start with *formal* institutions. Every country has rules, laws, and regulations governing the do's and don'ts of HRM. Foreign firms ignoring such rules do so at their own peril. For example, in Japan, firms routinely discriminate against women and minorities. However, when Japanese MNEs engage in such usual practices in the United States, they face legal charges. By the late 1980s, 60%

FIGURE 15.4   INSTITUTIONS, RESOURCES, AND HUMAN RESOURCE MANAGEMENT

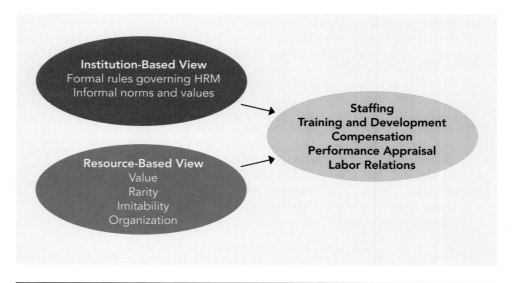

of Japanese MNEs doing business in the United States were charged with possible equal employment opportunity (EEO) violations.[25]

On the other hand, foreign firms well versed in local regulations may take advantage of them. For example, the legal hurdles for firing full-time workers in France are legendary. When HP announced a plan to lay off 1,200 employees in France, then-president Jacques Chirac called HP directly and complained.[26] However, it is this very difficulty in firing full-time workers that has made France a highly lucrative market for the US-based Manpower. French firms reluctant or unwilling to hire full-time employees value Manpower's expertise in providing part-time workers. France is now Manpower's *largest* market ahead of the United States.

Informal rules of the game, embodied in cultures, norms, and values, also assert powerful influence (see Table 15.6). MNEs from different countries have different norms in staffing. Most Japanese MNEs follow an informal rule: Heads of foreign subsidiaries, at least initially, need to be PCNs.[27] In comparison, European

TABLE 15.6   SOME BLUNDERS IN INTERNATIONAL HRM

- An American expatriate made a presentation to the prime minister of a small Caribbean country and his cabinet members, by starting with "Honorable Mr. Tollis and esteemed members of the cabinet." The prime minister immediately interrupted him and asked him to start over. This went back and forth several times. Eventually, someone advised the bewildered and then embarrassed expatriate that Mr. Tollis was the *former* prime minister, who had been deposed by the current prime minister (the man sitting in front of the expatriate).

- A Spanish company sent a team of expatriates to Saudi Arabia. Included in the team were a number of young, intelligent women dressed in current Western style. Upon arrival, the Saudi immigration official took a look at their miniskirts and immediately sent the entire team on the next flight back to Spain. The expatriate team and the company belatedly learned that despite the heat, women in Saudi Arabia never show their bare legs.

- In Malaysia, an American expatriate was introduced to an important potential client he thought was named "Roger." He proceeded to call this person "Rog." Unfortunately, this person was a "Rajah," which is an important title of nobility. In this case, the American tendency to liberally use another person's first name—and to proactively shorten it—appeared disrespectful and insensitive. The Rajah walked away from the deal.

- A Japanese subsidiary CEO in New York, at a staff meeting entirely consisting of Americans (except himself), informed everybody of the firm's grave financial losses and passed the request from headquarters in Japan that everybody redouble efforts. The staff immediately redoubled their efforts—by sending their resumes out to other employers.

- A female South Korean expatriate at a textile plant in Vietnam confronted a worker. She yelled in Korean "Move!" The Vietnamese worker did not move, because he did not understand Korean. The South Korean expatriate then kicked and slapped him—according to the media, in South Korea, it is common for employers to scold or even beat employees if they make a big mistake. But in this case, ten Vietnamese colleagues retaliated by beating up the expatriate, who was wounded, hospitalized, and then deported. The workers went on to strike for four days and obtained 10% to 15% pay raises.

Sources: Based on text in (1) P. Dowling & D. Welch, 2005, *International Human Resource Management*, 4th ed. (p. 59), Cincinnati: South-Western Cengage Learning; (2) D. Ricks, 1999, *Blunders in International Business*, 3rd ed. (pp. 95–105), Oxford, UK: Blackwell.

MNEs are more likely to appoint HCNs and TCNs to lead subsidiaries. There is a historical reason for such differences: Most European MNEs expanded globally before low-cost telephones, faxes, e-mails, and Skype were available. Thus, a localization strategy relying on HCNs and TCNs was necessary. Most Japanese MNEs went abroad in the 1980s, when modern communication technology enabled more centralized control from headquarters. In addition to technology, the Japanese cultural preference for low uncertainty also translated into a higher interest in headquarters' control. Thus, Japanese MNEs often implemented a home replication strategy that relied on PCNs who constantly communicated with headquarters.[28]

Although informal cultures, norms, and values are important, HR managers need to avoid stereotyping and instead consider changes. In the area of compensation, one study hypothesized that presumably collectivistic Chinese managers would prefer a more egalitarian compensation compared to what their individualistic US counterparts would prefer. The results turned out to be surprising: Chinese managers actually preferred *more* merit-based pay, whereas US managers behaved exactly the opposite. In other words, the Chinese seemed more "American" than Americans![29] Further digging revealed that these were not average Chinese; they were HCNs working for some of the most competitive Western MNEs in China. The upshot? Naïve adaptation to presumed local norms and values, often based on outdated stereotypes, may backfire. HR managers must do more homework to better understand their HCNs.

Consider expatriation, which has roots in colonialism. During the age of colonialism, hardship allowance was paid not only as an inducement but also as a path to riches. Before India's independence, British officers in the Indian Administrative Service, which ran the colonial government in India, were the *highest*-paid civil servants in the world. At that time, HCNs were unlikely to view themselves as equals of PCNs.[30] In the 21st century, many well-educated Indians, often with degrees from Western universities, are as qualified as some Western expatriates. Such HCNs naturally resent being treated as second-class citizens. Thus, the stereotypical expatriate, leading a life of luxury to compensate for hardship overseas, may become increasingly rare.

Even expatriates from the West, who tend to be younger, may not necessarily qualify for the most senior positions overseas. They may be sent abroad to gain experience—often with more down-to-earth titles such as "assignees" or "secondees." Also, more expatriates are now being sent on short-term, commuter-type assignments for which they do not need to uproot their families.[31] They may work weekdays in Budapest, and then fly home to Berlin for the weekend. Overall, the norms and images associated with the expatriate are changing rapidly.

Resources and Human Resource Management

As HRM becomes more strategic, the VRIO dimensions are increasingly at center stage. To start, managers need to ask: Does a particular HR activity add *value*?[32] Consider two examples. First, labor-intensive chores such as administering payroll, benefits, and basic training may not add value. They can often be outsourced. Second, training is expensive. Does it really add value? Results pooled from 397 studies find that on average, training adds value by improving individual performance by 20%.[33] Thus, training is often justified.

Next, are particular HR activities *rare*? The relentless drive to learn, share, and adopt best practices may reduce their rarity and thus usefulness. If every MNE in India provides training to high-caliber HCNs, such training, which is valuable, will be taken for granted but not viewed as rare.

Further, how *imitable* are certain HR activities? It is relatively easy to imitate a single practice, but it is much more difficult to imitate a complex HR *system* (or *architecture*) consisting of multiple, mutually reinforcing practices that work together.[34] Consider the Portman Ritz-Carlton hotel in Shanghai, which has been repeatedly voted the Best Employer in Asia. Its expatriate general manager personally interviews *every* new hire. It selects HCNs genuinely interested in helping guests. It cares deeply about employee satisfaction, which has led to superb guest satisfaction. Each single practice here may be imitable, and the Portman Ritz-Carlton has been studied meticulously by rivals (and numerous nonrivals) in China and around the world. Yet, none has been able to successfully imitate its system. On the surface, every firm says "We care about our people." But the reality at many firms is increasing underinvestment by employers and declining loyalty and commitment from employees.[35] Studies find that firm performance is the best with a mutual investment approach, as exemplified by the Portman Ritz-Carlton.[36] However, it is very difficult to imitate a mutual investment approach that comes together as a system (or architecture).

Finally, do HR practices support *organizational* capabilities to help the firm accomplish its performance goals? Consider teamwork and diversity, especially multinational teams that have members from different subsidiaries.[37] Although most firms promote some sort of teamwork and diversity, it is challenging to organizationally leverage such teamwork and diversity to enhance performance.[38] Too little or too much diversity may hurt performance.[39] In teamwork, certain disagreements may help promote learning. But obviously too many disagreements may lead to conflicts and destroy team effectiveness.[40] However, few managers (and few firms) know where to draw the line to keep team disagreements from getting out of control.

DEBATES AND EXTENSIONS

This chapter has already alluded to a number of HR debates, such as the value of expatriates. Here we focus on three debates previously untouched in this chapter: (1) best fit versus best practice, (2) expatriation versus inpatriation, and (3) across-the-board pay cut versus reduction in force.

Participate in three leading debates on HRM.

Best Fit versus Best Practice

The best fit school argues that a firm needs to search for HRM practices that are both the best external and internal fit. Externally, HRM is shaped by national and industry contexts. Internally, HRM is driven by firm strategy. On the product dimension, a firm pursuing a differentiation strategy needs to reinforce the passion for higher quality, better service, and more sustained learning. On the international dimension, a firm using a localization strategy needs to utilize more HCNs (Table 15.2). Moreover, the quest for the best fit is *continuous*. Even for the same MNE in the same country, a good fit now may not be good enough ten years later. In two words, the best fit school argues: it depends.[41]

Best practice proponents argue that firms should adopt best practices irrespective of context. Such best practices often include extensive training, high pay for high performance, and self-managed teams (emphasizing teamwork). Although the list of best practices may vary, the underlying spirit seems to be the same around the world.[42]

Critics of best practice make two points. First, they point out that "there is overwhelming evidence against a universal set of HR practices based on national variations."[43] Second, they argue that from a resource-based view, if all firms adopt universal best practices, such practices lose their value. To reconcile the debate, experts note that "it is not a question of either/or but a question of the appropriate balance."[44] They argue that during the next decade, most firms may still benefit from adopting some best practices because most firms are not yet at that frontier.

IN Focus 15.3

Dallas versus Delhi

© Sanjit Das/Bloomberg via Getty Images

Prashant Sarkar is director for corporate development for the New Delhi, India, subsidiary of the US-based Dallas Instruments. Sarkar has an engineering degree from the Indian Institute of Technology and an MBA from the University of Texas at Dallas. After obtaining his MBA in 1990, Sarkar worked at a Dallas Instruments facility in Richardson, Texas (a suburb of Dallas), and picked up a green card (US permanent residency) while maintaining his Indian passport. In 2000, when Dallas Instruments opened its first Indian subsidiary in New Delhi, Sarkar was tapped to be one of the first managers sent from the United States. India of the early 21st century is certainly different from the India of the mid-1980s that Sarkar had left behind. Reform is now in the air, MNEs are coming left and right, and an exhilarating self-confidence permeates the country.

As a manager, Sarkar has shined in his native New Delhi. His wife and two children (born in 1995 and 1998 in the United States) are also happy. After all, curry in New Delhi is a lot more authentic and fresher than that in Indian grocery stores in Dallas. Grandparents, relatives, and friends are all happy to see the family back. In Dallas, Prashant's wife, Neeli, a teacher by training, taught on a part-time basis, but couldn't secure a full-time teaching position because she did not have a US degree. Now she is principal of a great school. The two children are enrolled in the elite New Delhi American School, the cost of which is paid for by the company. New Delhi is not perfect, but the Sarkars feel good about coming back.

"Prashant, I have great news for you!" the American CEO of the subsidiary tells Sarkar at the end of 2011, "Headquarters wants you to move back to Dallas. You'll be in charge of strategy development for *global* expansion, working directly under the Group Vice President. Isn't that exciting? They want someone with proven success. You are my best candidate. I don't know what design they have for you after this assignment, but I suspect it'll be highly promising. Don't quote me, but I'd say you may have a shot to eventually replace me or the next American CEO here. Although I personally enjoy working here, my family sometimes still complains a bit about the curry smell. Or folks in Dallas may eventually want you to go somewhere else—frankly, I don't know but I'm just trying to help you speculate. I know it's a big decision. Talk to Neeli and the kids. But they lived in Dallas before, so they should be fine going back. Of course, I'll put you in touch with the folks in Dallas directly so that you can ask them all kinds of questions. Let me know what you think in a week."

Instead of calling his wife immediately, Sarkar has decided to wait till he gets home in the evening so that he can have a few hours to think about this. Going from Dallas to New Delhi, Sarkar, with his Indian passport, is an HCN. However, with his green card, he is also considered a US national and thus an expatriate. He wonders whether he would accept the new assignment and whether he would be an expatriate or inpatriate if he decides to go to Dallas from New Delhi.

Source: Based on the author's interviews. All individual and corporate names are fictitious.

Expatriation versus Inpatriation

One proposed solution to the expatriation problem is inpatriation—relocating employees of a foreign subsidiary to the MNE's headquarters for the purposes of filling skill shortages at headquarters and developing a global mind-set for such inpatriates. The term "inpatriation" is derived from "expatriation," and most inpatriates are expected to eventually return to their home country to replace expatriates (see In Focus 15.3). Examples would include IT inpatriates from India who work at IBM in the United States and telecom inpatriates from China who work at Alcatel in France. Technically, these inpatriates are expatriates from India and China, who will experience some of the same problems expatriates experience, as discussed earlier in this chapter.

Some inpatriates are paid according to the going rate in their home (typically developing) countries, which usually is lower than what colleagues in the same firm in developed economies doing equivalent work are paid. Indian IT professionals on average are paid 10% to 12% less than American workers. For this reason, some inpatriates refuse to go back to their home countries and instead find work in the host countries. Other inpatriates do return to their home countries but quit their sponsoring MNE. They go to work for rival MNEs that are willing to pay more.

Even for inpatriates who do return and assume leadership positions in subsidiaries in their home countries (as planned), many are ineffective. In China, inpatriated ethnic Chinese often struggle with an ambiguous identity: Western headquarters views them as "us," whereas HCNs also expect them to be "us." When headquarters and locals conflict over an issue (such as HCN pay), managers who favor headquarters are viewed as "traitors" of sorts by HCNs. These problems erupt in spite of inpatriates' Chinese roots—or perhaps, *because* of their Chinese roots (see In Focus 12.2, "Making M&As Fly in China"). Overall, one lesson is that inpatriates do not provide a panacea for international staffing. Inpatriates, just like expatriates, have their fair share of headaches.

Across-the-Board Pay Cut versus Reduction in Force

Both HR and line managers often have to make tough decisions. One of the most challenging decisions is how to cope with a downturn. Reduction in force (RIF), a euphemism for mass layoffs, is often used in the US and UK. However, outside the Anglo-American world, mass layoffs are often viewed as unethical. Some critics label mass layoffs as "corporate cannibalism." One alternative is for the entire firm to have an across-the-board pay cut while preserving all current jobs. Which approach is better?

During the SARS crisis in 2003, the Portman Ritz-Carlton hotel in Shanghai implemented an across-the-board pay cut, resulting in a 99.9% employee satisfaction rate. According to its general manager, "this was one of those negative things that turned out to be extremely positive."[45] However, when US firms experiment with an across-the-board pay cut, the results tend to be very *negative*. To avoid RIF in the post-2001 downturn, Applied Materials implemented an across-the-board pay cut in the United States: Executives took a 10% hit, managers and professionals 5%, and hourly production

Inpatriation
Relocating employees of a foreign subsidiary to the MNE's headquarters for the purposes of filling skill shortages at headquarters and developing a global mind-set for such inpatriates.

workers 3%. The pay cut lasted for 18 months. An HR executive at Applied Materials commented:

> This across-the-board pay cut has a longer lasting and far greater negative impact on morale than an RIF would have. RIFs are very hard on the impacted employees as well as the survivors. However, when managed correctly, impacted employees are able to separate from the company with dignity and in the case of Applied Materials, with a very generous financial package. . . . I don't know of any surviving employees that appreciated having their paycheck impacted every two weeks for 18 months. . . . Ultimately, pay levels were restored. However, employee memories are very long and this particular event was pointed to over and over again throughout multiple employee surveys as an indicator of poor leadership and a major cause of employee dissatisfaction.[46]

Applied Materials and other US firms that implemented across-the-board pay cuts have lost numerous star performers who leave to find "greener pastures" elsewhere. Although more US firms such as AMD, FedEx, HP, and *New York Times* have cut pay across the board in an effort to preserve jobs during the 2008–2009 recession, Applied Materials' experience raises serious concerns as to whether such large-scale sacrifice is worth it, at least in an individualistic culture (see the Closing Case).

LEARNING OBJECTIVE 7

Draw implications for action.

MANAGEMENT SAVVY

What determines the success and failure of HRM around the world? A simple answer is effectiveness of HR activities in areas such as staffing, training and development, compensation, and labor relations. A more interesting question is: How much does effective HRM impact firm performance?[47] Results from 3,200 firms find that change of one standard deviation in the HR system affects 10% to 20% of a firm's market value.[48] Findings from 92 studies suggest that an increase of one standard deviation in the use of an effective HR system is associated with a 4.6% increase in return on assets (ROA).[49] These recent findings validate a long-held belief among HRM practitioners and scholars: HRM is indeed *strategic*, as it has become a direct answer to the fundamental question of our field: What determines the success and failure of firms around the world?

Consequently, we identify five implications for actions (see Table 15.7). The first four Cs were developed by Susan Meisinger, president of the Society for Human Resource Management, for HR managers,[50] and the last C is for non-HR managers.

First, savvy HR managers need to be *curious*. They need to be well versed in the numerous formal and informal rules of the game governing HRM worldwide. They must be curious about emerging trends in the world and create people strategies to respond to these trends.

Second, HR managers must be *competent*. Far from its lowly roots as a lackluster administrative support function, HRM is now acknowledged as a more strategic function that directly contributes to the bottom line. As a result, HR managers need to develop organizational capabilities that drive business success. This starts with enhancing the basic business competencies of HR managers, who may have been trained more narrowly and with a more micro (nonstrategic)

TABLE 15.7 IMPLICATIONS FOR ACTION

For HR managers: The four Cs

- Be *curious*—know formal and informal rules of the game governing HRM in all regions of operations.

- Be *competent*—develop organizational capabilities that drive business success.

- Be *courageous* and *caring*—as guardians of talent, HR managers need to nurture and develop people.

For non-HR managers: The fifth C

- Be proactive in managing your international *career*.

---

focus. Now, HR managers must be able to not only contribute to the strategy conversation, but also to take things off the CEO's desk as full-fledged business partners.

Finally, HR managers must be *courageous* and *caring*. As guardians of talent, HR managers need to nurture and develop employees. This often means that as employee advocates, HR managers sometimes need to be courageous enough to disagree with the CEO and other line managers if necessary. This attribute is especially important in challenging times (such as in a recession) when the CEO and other line managers may be interested in reducing the head count, but HR managers want to preserve human talent (see the Opening Case). GE's recently retired head of HR, William Conaty, is just such an example. "If you just get closer to the CEO, you're dead," Conaty shared with a reporter, "I need to be independent. I need to be credible."[51] GE's CEO Jeff Immelt called Conaty "the first friend, the guy that could walk in my office and kick my butt when it needed to be"—exactly how a full-fledged "business partner" should behave.

In addition, there is a fifth "C" for non-HR managers: Proactively manage your *career* in order to develop a global mind-set.[52] Since international experience is a prerequisite for reaching the top at many firms, managers need to prepare by investing in their own technical expertise, cross-cultural adaptability, and language training. Some of these investments (such as language training) are long-term in nature. This point thus has strategic implications for students who are studying this book *now*: Have you learned a foreign language? Have you spent one semester or year abroad? Have you made any friends from abroad, perhaps fellow students who are taking *this* class with you now? Have you put this course on your resume? Imagine a scenario for expatriate selection five or ten years down the road: A non-Chinese colleague who was a former classmate with you and who speaks Chinese is tapped to go to China as a high-profile expat, but you are passed over because you have never studied Chinese. Your colleague took the time to learn Chinese, and you didn't. To make yourself "China ready" when such an opportunity comes, you have to start now. The point is not just about China. It is about how to arm yourself with the knowledge now, make proper investments, and maneuver yourself to be picked eventually. In the global economy, your career is in your hands.

CHAPTER SUMMARY

1. Explain staffing decisions with a focus on expatriates.
   - International staffing primarily relies on ethnocentric, polycentric, and geo-centric approaches.
   - Expatriates (primarily PCNs and to a lesser extent TCNs) play multiple challenging roles, and often have high failure rates. They need to be carefully selected, taking into account a variety of factors.

2. Identify training and development needs for expatriates and HCNs.
   - Expatriates need to be properly trained and cared for during expatriation and repatriation.
   - Training and development of HCNs are now an area of differentiation among many MNEs.

3. Discuss compensation and performance appraisal issues.
   - Expatriates are compensated using the going rate and balance sheet approaches.
   - Top talent HCNs now increasingly command higher compensation.
   - Performance appraisal needs to be carefully provided to achieve its intended purposes.

4. List factors that affect labor relations in both home and host countries.
   - Despite efforts to revive unions, the power of unions has been declining in developed countries.
   - The power of unions in most developing countries requires some attention but is mostly limited.

5. Discuss how the institution-based and resource-based views shed additional light on HRM.
   - HRM is significantly shaped by formal and informal rules of the game—both at home and abroad.
   - As HRM becomes more strategic, VRIO dimensions are now more important.

6. Participate in three leading debates on HRM.
   - They are (1) best fit versus best practice, and (2) expatriation versus inpatriation, and (3) across-the-board pay cut versus reduction in force.

7. Draw implications for action.
   - HR managers need to cultivate the four Cs: be curious, be competent, be courageous, and care about people.
   - Non-HR managers need to proactively develop their career by developing a global mind-set.

KEY TERMS

Balance sheet
    approach   509
Compensation   508
Development   505
Ethnocentric
    approach   501
Expatriation   502
Geocentric approach   502
Going rate approach   508

Host country national
    (HCN)   501
Human resource
    management (HRM)   500
Inpatriation   519
Labor relations   511
Parent country national
    (PCN)   501
Performance appraisal   508

Polycentric approach   502
Psychological contract   506
Repatriate   506
Repatriation   506
Staffing   501
Third country
    national (TCN)   501
Training   505

REVIEW QUESTIONS

1. Name and describe three staffing approaches.

2. What factors often lead to an expatriate experiencing difficulties or even failure on an overseas assignment?

3. Describe some of the problems experienced by repatriates and how training and development may alleviate those problems.

4. In the area of expatriate compensation, what is the difference between the going rate approach and the balance sheet approach?

5. What are some of the problems inherent in evaluating an expatriate's job performance?

6. Why has union power declined in developed countries?

7. Why have efforts to establish multinational labor organizations not been unsuccessful?

8. How can an understanding of informal institutions help HR managers avoid problematic stereotypes?

9. Look at India and China on PengAtlas Map 4.3. Compared to the United States, these two countries' economies are growing at a much faster pace and they have a much larger labor force. Even if the GDP of India and China equaled that of the United States, how would the per capita GDP compare? Do you think that the *size* of their labor force is an asset or a liability?

10. Compare PengAtlas Maps 4.3 and 4.4. Why wouldn't some of the countries with the largest labor force be among those with the largest number of unemployed?

11. What concept can be used to reconcile the best fit versus best practice debate, and how does it work?

12. What are the benefits of inpatriation?

13. What are the four Cs that can benefit HR managers?

14. What can you do to develop a global mind-set and help your career?

CRITICAL DISCUSSION QUESTIONS

1. You have been offered a reasonably lucrative three-year expatriate assignment and you will be meeting with your boss next week. What issues touching on this opportunity would you want to discuss with your boss?

2. *ON ETHICS:* If you were a HCN, do you think pay should be equal between HCNs and expatriates in equivalent positions? If you were president of a subsidiary in a host country, as a PCN your pay is five times higher than the pay for the highest-paid HCN (your vice president). What do you think?

3. *ON ETHICS:* As HR director for an oil company, you are responsible for selecting 15 expatriates to go to work in Iraq. However, you are personally concerned about the safety there. How do you proceed?

GLOBAL ACTION

1. You work at a large MNE that operates in every one of the top 100 metropolitan areas worldwide. One of the most pressing concerns in your firm at the moment is to control costs. Therefore, you have been asked to develop a forecast for the coming year that identifies the markets in which the firm can expect an increase in the cost of living and, as a result, general salary expenditures. After the report needed for your evaluation is secured, classify the cities that have experienced cost increases into their respective countries. Which countries have more than one city that meets the criteria for your forecast? What are the salary increase traits associated with each city identified?

2. Currently, your European company is evaluating its standing in the fast-growing emerging economies known as BRIC (Brazil, Russia, India, and China). Based on your evaluation of the cost of living in each country, the company may reconfigure some of its operations to increase profitability. Your company's manufacturing facilities are located in Shanghai, China; Mumbai, India; Sao Paulo, Brazil; and St. Petersburg, Russia. How much could be saved if the company consolidated into one BRIC location that has the lowest cost of living?

VIDEO CASES

Watch "Getting the Best Out of a Diverse Team" by Clive Mather of Shell Canada.

1. In describing his experience in dealing with a diverse group in Africa, Mather stated that not only did the group change but he also changed. What valuable lesson does that suggest for those who may assume a management position in a different country or culture?

2. Mather stressed that although various groups differ, group members should be treated as individuals who may not be exactly identical to the rest of the group. How does one do that in a collectivistic society that places more emphasis on the group than on the individual?

3. Mather pointed out that starting with projects and problems that people can be involved in may help build relationships that will ultimately produce greater teamwork. Shouldn't one first build the relationships before getting a diverse group together to work on something? What do you think?

4. Some countries have very little diversity. In contrast, people are continually coming to the United States from all around the world. If you were going to expand a US-based company into overseas markets, how could experience with US diversity be of value to you?

Closing Case

ETHICAL DILEMMA

Cut Salaries or Cut Jobs?

© Justin Pumfrey

As a Japanese expatriate in charge of US operations of Yamakawa Corporation, you are confronting a difficult decision: Facing a horrific economic downturn with major losses, should you cut salaries across the board or cut jobs? Headquarters in Osaka has advised that earnings at home are bad, and you cannot expect headquarters to bail out your operations. US government bailouts are only good for US-owned firms and are thus irrelevant for your unit, which is 100% owned by the Japanese parent company.

As a person brought up in a collectivistic culture, you instinctively feel compelled to suggest an across-the-board pay cut for all 1,000 employees in the United States. Personally, as the highest-paid US-based employee, you are willing to take the *highest* percentage of a pay cut (you are thinking of 30%). If implemented, this plan would call for other executives, who are mostly Americans, to take a 20% to 25% pay cut, mid-level managers and professionals a 15% to 20% pay cut, and all the rank-and-file employees a 10% to 15% pay cut. In a previous experience at Yamakawa in Japan, you did this

with positive results among all affected Japanese employees. In fact, at this time, most executive colleagues in Japan are doing the same. However, since you are now managing US operations, headquarters in Osaka, being more globally minded and sensitive, does not want to impose any uniform solutions around the world and asks you to make the call.

As a conscientious executive, you have studied all the HRM books—in both Japanese and English—that you can find on this tough decision. Most recently, you have meticulously studied Chapter 15 in Mike Peng's *Global Business*, and paid particular attention to the section on the debate regarding across-the-board pay cuts versus reduction in force (RIF). Although you understand that US executives routinely undertake RIF, which is a euphemism for mass layoffs, you have also noticed that in the recent recession, even "bona-fide" US firms such as AMD, FedEx, HP, and *New York Times* have instead trimmed the base pay for all employees. According to some US executives quoted in the media, if there is a time to change the norm and move towards more across-the-board pay cuts in an effort to preserve jobs and avoid RIF, this time may be it.

At the same time, you have also read that across-the-board pay cuts are *anathema* to a performance culture enshrined in the United States and taught in virtually all HRM textbooks. "The last thing you want is for your A players—or people in key strategic positions delivering the most value—to leave because you have mismanaged your compensation system," said Mark Huselid, a Rutgers University professor and a leading expert on HRM, in a media interview. You have also read in a recent (September 2009) *Harvard Business Review* survey that despite the worst recession, 20% of high-potential players in US firms have voluntarily left their jobs in search of better pay elsewhere. Naturally, you are worried that should you decide to implement the across-the-board pay cut you have

envisioned, you may end up losing a lot of American star performers and end up with a bunch of mediocre players who cannot go elsewhere—and you may be stuck with the mediocre folks even after the economy recovers.

After spending two days reading all the materials you have gathered, you still do not have a clear picture. Instead, you have a big headache. How do you proceed?

Case Discussion Questions:

1. What are the benefits of across-the-board pay cuts?
2. What are the benefits of reduction in force (mass layoffs)?
3. How would you advise this Japanese expatriate working in the United States?

Sources: This case is fictitious. It is based on (1) M. Y. Brannen, 2008, Global talent management and learning for the future: Pressing concerns for Japanese multinationals, *AIB Insights*, 8: 8–12; (2) *BusinessWeek*, 2009, Pay cuts made palatable, May 4: 67; (3) *BusinessWeek*, 2009, Cutting salaries instead of jobs, June 8: 46–48; (4) N. Carter & C. Silva, 2009, High potentials in the downturn: Sharing the pain? *Harvard Business Review*, September: 25.

NOTES

[Journal acronyms] AME—*Academy of Management Executive*; AMJ—*Academy of Management Journal*; AMR—*Academy of Management Review*; APJM—*Asia Pacific Journal of Management*; BW—*BusinessWeek*; CMR—*California Management Review*; HBR—*Harvard Business Review*; HRM—*Human Resource Management*; HRMR—*Human Resource Management Review*; IJHRM—*International Journal of Human Resource Management*; IJMR—*International Journal of Management Reviews*; JAP—*Journal of Applied Psychology*; JIBS—*Journal of International Business Studies*; JIM—*Journal of International Management*; JM—*Journal of Management*; JMS—*Journal of Management Studies*; JOB—*Journal of Organizational Behavior*; JWB—*Journal of World Business*; MIR—*Management International Review*; PP—*Personnel Psychology*; SMJ—*Strategic Management Journal*; TIBR—*Thunderbird International Business Review*

[1] P. Budhwar & Y. Debrah, 2009, Future research on HRM systems in Asia, *APJM*, 26: 197–218.

[2] W. Cascio, 2005, From business partner to driving business success, *HRM*, 44: 159–163; C. Fey, S. Morgulis-Yukushev, H. Park, & I. Bjorkman, 2009, Opening the black box of the relationship between HRM practices and firm performance, *JIBS*, 40: 690–712; E. Lawler, 2005, From HRM to organizational effectiveness, *HRM*, 44: 165–169; J. Paauwe, 2009, HRM and performance, *JMS*, 46: 129–142; L. Wei & C. Lau, 2008, The impact of market orientation and strategic HRM on firm performance, *JIBS*, 39: 980–995.

[3] R. Ployhart, 2006, Staffing in the 21st century, *JM*, 32: 868–897.

[4] C. Chung & P. Beamish, 2005, Investment mode strategy and expatriate strategy during times of economic crisis, *JIM*, 11: 331–355; A. Goerzen & P. Beamish, 2007, The Penrose effect, *MIR*, 47: 221–239; D. Tan & J. Mahoney, 2006, Why a multinational firm chooses expatriates, *JMS*, 43: 457–484.

[5] M. Janssens, T. Cappellen, & P. Zanoni, 2006, Successful female expatriates as agents, *JWB*, 41: 133–148; B. Reiche, A. Harzing, & M. Kraimer, 2009, The role of international assignees' social capital in creating inter-unit intellectual capital, *JIBS*, 40: 509–526; D. Vora & T. Kostova, 2007, A model of dual organizational identification in the context of the multinational enterprise, *JOB*, 28: 327–350.

[6] P. Bhaskar-Shrinivas, D. Harrison, M. Shaffer, & D. Luk, 2005, Input-based and time-based models of international adjustment, *AMJ*, 48: 257–281.

[7] R. L. Tung, 1982, Selection and training procedures for US, European, and Japanese multinationals, *CMR*, 25: 57–71. See also A. Harzing, 2002, Are our referencing errors undermining our scholarship and credibility? *JOB*, 23: 127–148.

[8] P. Dowling & D. Welch, 2005, *International Human Resource Management*, 4th ed. (p. 87), Cincinnati: Thomson.

[9] G. Graen, R. Dharwadkar, R. Grewal, & M. Wakabayashi, 2006, Japanese career progress, *JIBS*, 37: 148–161; E. Pellegrini &

T. Scandura, 2006. Leader-member exchange (LMX), paternalism, and delegation in the Turkish business culture, *JIBS*, 37: 264–279.

10 P. Caligiuri, 2006, Developing global leaders, *HRMR*, 16: 219–228; A. Molinsky, 2007, Cross-cultural code-switching, *AMR*, 32: 622–640; S. Shin, F. Morgeson, & M. Campion, 2007, What you do depends on where you are, *JIBS*, 38: 64–83; R. Takeuchi, P. Tesluk, S. Yun, & D. Lepak, 2005, An integrative view of international experience, *AMJ*, 48: 85–100.

11 M. Shaffer & D. Harrison, 2001, Forgotten partners of international assignments, *JAP*, 86: 238–254.

12 L. Dragoni, P. Tesluk, J. Russell, & I. Oh, 2009, Understanding managerial development, *AMJ*, 52: 731–743; E. Drost, C. Frayne, K. Lowe, & J. M. Geringer, 2002, Benchmarking training and development practices, *HRM*, 41: 67–86; C. Mabey, 2008, Management development and firm performance in Germany, Norway, Spain, and the UK, *JIBS*, 39: 1327–1342.

13 A major 2002 survey cited in Dowling & Welch, 2005, *International Human Resource Management* (p. 119).

14 M. Lazarova & J. Cerdin, 2007, Revisiting repatriation concerns, *JIBS*, 38: 404–429.

15 N. Furuya, M. Stevens, A. Bird, G. Oddou, & M. Mendenhall, 2009, Managing the learning and transfer of global management competence, *JIBS*, 40: 200–215; G. Oddou, J. Osland, & R. Blakeney, 2009, Repatriating knowledge, *JIBS*, 40: 181–199.

16 T. Amino, a retired US-based Honda executive and a friend of the author, personal communication, May 2002.

17 L. Bassi & D. McMurrer, 2007, Maximizing your return on people, *HBR*, March: 115–123.

18 S. Carraher, S. Sullivan, & M. Crocitto, 2009, Mentoring across global boundaries, *JIBS*, 39: 1310–1326; J. Mezias & T. Scandura, 2005, A needs-driven approach to expatriate adjustment and career development, *JIBS*, 36: 519–38.

19 J. DeVaro, 2006, Strategic promotion tournaments and worker performance, *SMJ*, 27: 721–740; K. Lowe, J. Milliman, H. De Cieri, & P. Dowling, 2002, International compensation practices, *HRM*, 41: 45–66; Y. Yanadori & J. Marler, 2006, Compensation strategy, *SMJ*, 27: 559–570.

20 *Economist*, 2006, The world is our oyster, October 7: 9.

21 T. Gardner, 2005, Interfirm competition for HR, *AMJ*, 48: 237–256.

22 AFL-CIO, 2007, Ten key facts for the Employee Free Choice Act, www.aflcio.org; Bureau of Labor Statistics, 2007, Union members in 2006, Washington: Department of Labor, www.bls.gov.

23 Bureau of Labor Statistics, 2007, Union member summary, Washington: Department of Labor, www.bls.gov.

24 I. Bjorkman, C. Fey, & H. Park, 2007, Institutional theory and MNC subsidiary HRM practices, *JIBS*, 38: 430–446.

25 R. Schuler, P. Budhwar, & G. Florkowski, 2002, International HRM (p. 56), *IJMR*, 4: 71–70.

26 *BW*, 2005, HP's French twist, October 10: 52–53.

27 N. Ando, D. Rhee, & N. Park, 2008, Parent country nationals or local nationals for executive positions in foreign affiliates, *APJM*, 25: 113–134; R. Belderbos & M. Heijltjes, 2005, The determinants of expatriate staffing by Japanese multinationals in Asia, *JIBS*, 36: 341–354; D. Brock, O. Shenkar, A. Shoham, &

I. Siscovick, 2008, National culture and expatriate deployment, *JIBS*, 39: 1293–1309.

28 Y. Paik & J. Sohn, 2004, Expatriate managers and MNCs' ability to control international subsidiaries, *JWB*, 39: 61–71.

29 C. Chen, 1995, New trends in allocation preferences, *AMJ*, 38: 408–428.

30 S. Toh & A. DeNisi, 2005, A local perspective to expatriate success, *AME*, 19: 132–146.

31 D. Collings, H. Scullion, & M. Morley, 2007, Changing patterns of global staffing in the MNE, *JWB*, 42: 198–213.

32 S. Kang, S. Morris, & S. Snell, 2007, Relational archetypes, organizational learning, and value creation, *AMR*, 32: 236–256; K. Law, D. Tse, & N. Zhou, 2003, Does HR matter in a transition economy? *JIBS*, 34: 255–265.

33 W. Arthur, W. Bennett, P. Edens, & S. Bell, 2003, Effectiveness of training in organizations, *JAP*, 88: 234–245.

34 J. Arthur & T. Boyles, 2007. Validating the HR system structure, *HRMR*, 12: 77–92; B. Colbert, 2004, The complex resource-based view, *AMR*, 28: 341–358; D. Lepak & S. Snell, 1999, The HR architecture, *AMR*, 24: 31–48.

35 A. Tsui & J. Wu, 2005, The new employment relationship versus the mutual investment approach, *HRM*, 44: 115–121.

36 J. Shaw, M. Dufy, J. Johnson, & D. Lockhart, 2005, Turnover, social capital losses, and performance, *AMJ*, 48: 594–606; D. Wang, A. Tsui, Y. Zhang, & L. Ma, 2003, Employment relationships and firm performance, *JOB*, 24: 511–535.

37 D. Zoogah, D. Vora, O. Richard, & M. W. Peng, 2010, Strategic alliance team diversity, coordination, and effectiveness, *IJHRM* (in press).

38 A. Joshi & H. Roh, 2009, The role of context in work team diversity research, *AMJ*, 52: 599–627; O. Richard, B. Murthi, & K. Ismail, 2007, The impact of racial diversity on intermediate and long-term performance, *SMJ*, 28: 1213–1233.

39 K. Dahlin, L. Weingart, & P. Hinds, 2005, Team diversity and information use, *AMJ*, 48: 1107–1123.

40 P. Balkundi & D. Harrison, 2006, Ties, leaders, and time in teams, *AMJ*, 49: 49–68; J. Brett, K. Behfar, & M. Kern, 2006, Managing multicultural teams, *HBR*, November: 84–91; M. Zellmer-Bruhn & C. Gibson, 2006, Multinational organization context, *AMJ*, 49: 501–518.

41 J. Delery & D. Doty, 1996, Modes of theorizing in strategic HRM, *AMJ*, 39: 802–835.

42 J. M. Geringer, C. Frayne, & J. Milliman, 2002, In search of "best practices" in international HRM, *HRM*, 41: 5–30; M. von Glinow, E. Drost, & M. Teagarden, 2002, Converging on IHRM best practices, *HRM*, 41: 123–140.

43 P. Boxall & J. Purcell, 2000. Strategic HRM (p. 190), *IJMR*, 2: 183–203. See A. Ferner, P. Almond, & T. Colling, 2005, Institutional theory and the cross-national transfer of employment policy, *JIBS*, 36: 304–321; J. Gamble, 2006, Introducing Western-style HRM practices to China, *JWB*, 41: 328–343; P. Huo, J. Huang, & N. Napier, 2002, Divergence or convergence, *HRM*, 41: 31–44; W. Newburry & N. Yakova, 2006, Standardization preferences, *JIBS*, 37: 44–60; O. Tregaski & C. Brewster, 2006. Converging or diverging? *JIBS*, 37: 111–126.

44 B. Becker & M. Huselid, 2006, Strategic HRM (p. 905), *JM*, 32: 898–925.

45 A. Yeung, 2006, Setting the people up for success, *HRM*, 45: 267–275.

46 S. Parker, EMBA student in the author's class, individual assignment 1, University of Texas at Dallas, January 2007.

47 S. Colakoglu, D. Lepak, & Y. Hong, 2006, Measuring HRM effectiveness, *HRMR*, 16: 209–218; D. Datta, J. Guthrie, & P. Wright, 2005, HRM and labor productivity, *AMJ*, 48: 135–145.

48 Becker & Huselid, 2006, Strategic HRM (p. 907).

49 J. Combs, D. Ketchen, A. Hall, & Y. Liu, 2006, Do high performance work practices matter? *PP*, 59: 501–528.

50 S. Meisinger, 2005, The four Cs of the HR profession, *HRM*, 44: 189–194.

51 *BW*, 2007, Secrets of an HR superstar (p. 66), April 19: 66–67.

52 W. Arruda, 2009, Personal brand communication, *TIBR*, 51: 409–416; T. Cappellen & M. Janssens, 2005, Career paths for global managers, *JWB*, 40: 348–360; M. Dickman & H. Harris, 2005, Developing career capital for global careers, *JWB*, 40: 399–408; O. Levy, S. Beechler, S. Taylor, & N. Boyacigiller, 2007, What we talk about when we talk about "global mindset," *JIBS*, 38: 231–258; D. Thomas, M. Lazarova, & K. Inkson, 2005, Global careers, *JWB*, 40: 340–347; C. Vance, 2005, The personal quest for building global competence, *JWB*, 40: 374–385.

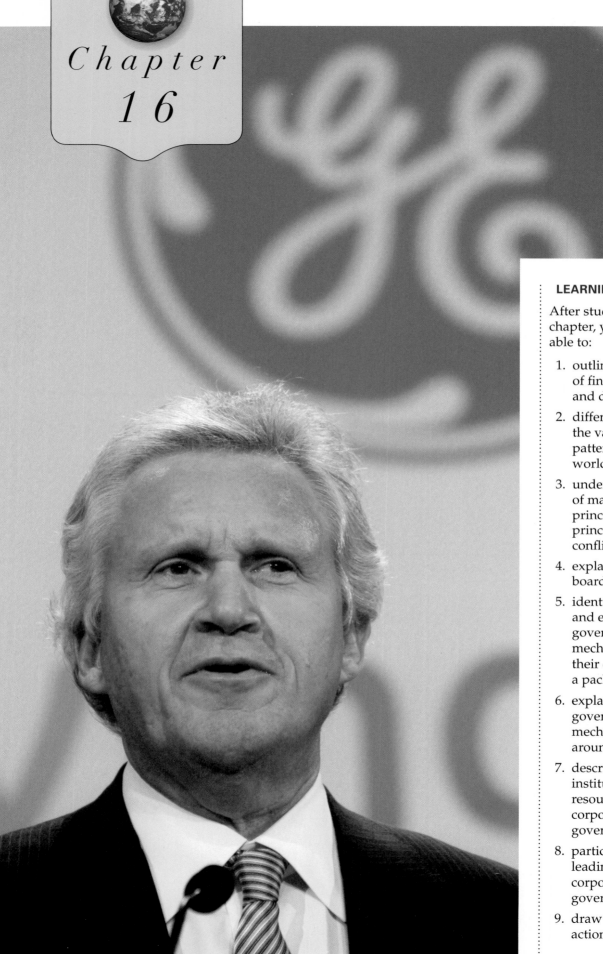

LEARNING OBJECTIVES

After studying this chapter, you should be able to:

1. outline the two means of financing: equity and debt.

2. differentiate among the various ownership patterns around the world.

3. understand the role of managers in both principal-agent and principal-principal conflicts.

4. explain the role of the board of directors.

5. identify voice-based and exit-based governance mechanisms and their combination as a package.

6. explain how governance mechanisms vary around the world.

7. describe how institutions and resources affect corporate finance and governance.

8. participate in two leading debates on corporate finance and governance.

9. draw implications for action.

© Mike Segar/Reuters/Landov

Financing and Governing the Corporation Globally

O P E N I N G   C A S E

GE Capital

Prior to the 2008–2009 recession, GE Capital had been the poster child among GE's many units that operate in numerous unrelated product industries ranging from aircraft engines to television broadcasting. GE Capital relates to all of these diverse businesses by financing their customers. Founded in 1932 as General Electric Contracts Corporation, GE Capital grew to be the largest and most important unit within GE, contributing 37% of GE's revenues but 55% of the profits in 2007. In addition to financing customer purchases of GE products, GE Capital undertook a series of activities that are purely financial in nature, such as property loans and credit cards. Geographically, GE Capital is active globally. If GE Capital were a bank, it would be the seventh-largest bank in the United States, after JP Morgan Chase, Citigroup, Bank of America, Wells Fargo, Goldman Sachs, and Morgan Stanley (in descending order of size).

GE Capital's funding model is systematically related to the risk of the wider financial markets. As a nonbank financial institution, it had little retail deposits. To fund its lending, GE Capital actively borrowed from credit markets, taking advantage of GE's prized AAA credit rating. When credit was plenty, these cheap funds propelled GE Capital to scale new heights. But

when financial markets took a nasty turn in 2008, the results were disastrous: Since the beginning of 2008, GE saw $269 billion wiped off its stock market value due to concerns about the quality of some of the loans made by GE Capital. In March 2009, both GE and GE Capital lost their AAA credit rating, being downgraded by Standard & Poor's (S&P) to AA+.

In response, GE tried to shore up confidence in GE Capital. It tapped cheap credit lines backed by the US government's Temporary Liquidity Guarantee Program (TLGP), reduced its exposure to the short-term commercial-paper market, and secured more long-term debt. In October 2008, GE raised $15 billion from a group of investors, including Warren Buffett's Berkshire Hathaway. In an effort to preserve cash to stem GE Capital's losses, GE slashed dividends by two-thirds in 2009. A bitter blow to GE's shareholders, this cut was the first time GE reduced its dividends since 1938.

There were rumors that after nursing GE Capital back to health, GE might sell it. GE CEO Jeff Immelt insisted that he was committed to GE Capital. But the goal would be to shrink its scale so that it would represent no more than 30% of GE's profit and to reduce its leverage. Given GE Capital's competitive advantage in GE's core product areas, such as aviation, media, and energy infrastructure, giving it up would be inadvisable. To some extent, the rescue efforts undertaken by GE to save GE Capital, in the worst of economic times, were similar to the bailout efforts undertaken by Washington to save Wall Street. As some financial services firms became "too big to fail," Washington felt compelled to bail them out at taxpayers' expenses. Likewise, as GE Capital became "too big to fail" within the GE family of many businesses, Immelt had to mobilize resources to bail out the financial services division at the expense of GE's other units and shareholders. In comparison with the mess in which other financial services firms was in, GE Capital's was not too bad. In 2009, GE Capital passed the Federal Reserve's stress test, requiring no further injections of capital. When compared to banks, GE Capital had less consumer exposure and no US mortgage or auto loan exposure, and GE Capital's holdings were more global. However, as a company that has long been regarded a model of management excellence, GE Capital tarnished GE's reputation, causing *The Economist* to use the following unflattering title to write about GE: "Losing Its Magic Touch."

Sources: Based on (1) *The Economist*, 2009, General Electric: Losing its magic touch, March 21: 73–75; (2) GE, 2009, GE Capital receives approval for PLGP exit plan, July 22, www.genewescenter.com; (3) GE, 2009, Live from New York, it's GE Capital, March 19, www.gereports.com.

How is GE Capital financed? How does it finance the purchase of GE products such as aircraft engines and power generators? How are firms such as GE governed? If GE Capital had had a different governance structure, would it have avoided the financial mess? How can GE Capital improve the effectiveness of its financing and governance in the future? These are some of the key questions addressed in this chapter, which focuses on how to finance and govern the corporation around the world. **Financing** refers to how a firm's money, banking, investments, and credit are managed. **Corporate governance** is "the relationship among various participants in determining the direction and performance of corporations."[1] The primary participants in corporate governance are (1) owners, (2) managers, and (3) boards of directors—collectively known as the "tripod" (see Figure 16.1).

We start by outlining the two means of financing decisions, issue equity or bonds. Then we discuss each of the three legs of the governance "tripod." Next, we introduce internal and external governance mechanisms from a global perspective. Then, institution-based and resource-based views on corporate finance and governance are outlined. As before, debates and extensions follow.

Financing

How a firm's money, banking, investments, and credit are managed.

Corporate governance

The relationship among various participants in determining the direction and performance of corporations.

FIGURE 16.1   THE TRIPOD OF CORPORATE GOVERNANCE

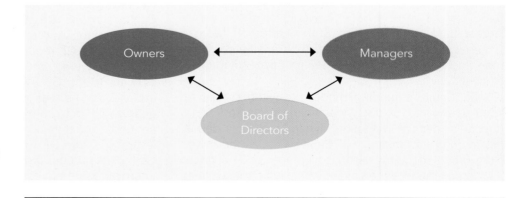

FINANCING DECISIONS

Providing the lifeblood of the firm, financing decisions are critical. Firms, of course, can finance their operations using their own money. But beyond a firm's own money, what are the *external* sources of financing? Broadly, external sources of financing can be classified as either equity or debt.[2] Deciding which one to use boils down to the cost of financing.

LEARNING OBJECTIVE

1

Outline the two means of financing: equity and debt.

Equity and Debt

Equity refers to the stock in a firm (usually expressed in shares), which represents equityholders' rights as firm owners. Firm owners are often known as **shareholders**. All firms, from entrepreneurial start-ups to multinational enterprises (MNEs), need to raise capital. Recall from Chapter 9 that when entrepreneurial firms are started, sources of financing include founders, family, friends, and "fools" (outside investors)—the "4F" sources of entrepreneurial financing. Technically, all the "4F" parties become shareholders.

Firms issue equity to attract investors to become shareholders so that firms can access a larger pool of capital and use it at management's discretion. One reason shareholders invest in a firm is because they share in the income generated by the firm's operations, which is paid out in the form of dividends. However, the amount of dividends is not fixed and is determined by management. As shown in the Opening Case, if a firm needs to preserve cash, management may decide to curtail or cancel dividends.[3]

Debt, in the context of financing, refers to a loan that the firm needs to pay back at a given time with an interest. The loan is called a **bond** and is issued by the firm and held by creditors known as **bondholders**. Management has little discretion over a bond. Unlike dividends, which can be curtailed or cancelled, the firm has to pay its bondholders back on time. If it does not, it is in **default**, which is failure to satisfy the terms of a loan obligation. For example, in December 2009, Dubai World defaulted on $26 billion of debt.[4] Short of a default, bondholders will get their money back with interest.[5] In other words, relative to shareholders, bondholders face a lower level of uncertainty.

Reducing the Cost of Capital

Financing decisions are primarily driven by the **cost of capital**, which is the rate of return that a firm needs to pay to capital providers.[6] For equity, the cost of capital is the dividend. For bonds, the cost of capital is the interest. Basic laws of supply and demand suggest that in general, the larger the pool of capital providers, the lower the cost of capital.[7] This is illustrated in Figure 16.2, using basic supply and demand curves. Hypothetically, if GE Capital (in the Opening Case) could only borrow from the United States, then to sell a $10 million bond, it would have to pay a 15% interest rate (point A). However, if GE Capital could tap into a global pool of capital providers, which by definition is larger than the domestic pool, then it could sell a $10 million bond at only a 10% interest rate (point B). Further, GE Capital may be able to raise $20 million at a 12% interest rate (point C).

This analysis has major ramifications both for firms' appetite to tap into global capital markets and for financial services providers' interest in serving this

Equity
The stock in a firm (usually expressed in shares), which represents the owners' rights.

Shareholder
Firm owner.

Debt
A loan that the firm needs to pay back at a given time with an interest.

Bond
Loan issued by the firm and held by creditors.

Bondholder
Buyer of bonds.

Default
A firm's failure to satisfy the terms of a loan obligation.

Cost of capital
The rate of return that a firm needs to pay to capital providers.

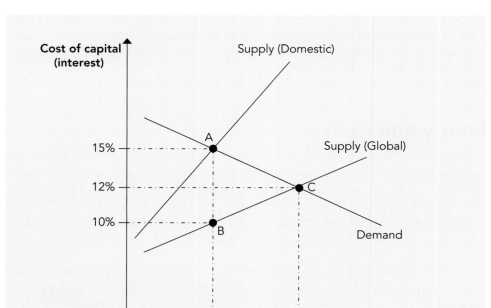

FIGURE 16.2   COST OF CAPITAL IS LOWER GLOBALLY THAN DOMESTICALLY

demand on a worldwide basis. Many firms have not only listed their stocks on their domestic stock exchanges but also on foreign stock exchanges as well. Listing shares on a foreign stock exchange is known as **cross-listing**. The New York Stock Exchange (NYSE) and NASDAQ have a lot of non-US firms listed. The London Stock Exchange (LSE) attracts numerous non-UK firms. The Hong Kong Stock Exchange has benefited from a gush of mainland Chinese listings. Cross-listing has numerous costs, however. In particular, the reporting and compliance requirements of foreign securities authorities can be expensive to comply. Nonetheless, numerous firms have cross-listed their shares overseas because the benefits, which are primarily derived from a lower cost of capital, outweigh the costs. Likewise, approximately 30% of current bonds are international bonds because they can be sold at a lower interest rate internationally as compared to domestically.

Obviously, financing decisions—whether to issue stocks or bonds—are crucial, because they can make or break a firm. Drawing from our Opening Case, we can say that GE became such a powerful MNE, in part, because until recently GE Capital made a series of smart financing decisions. We can also suggest that one of the primary reasons that GE is in trouble lately is because GE Capital messed up a number of financing decisions—first overborrowing from the bond markets when financing was cheap, and then overlending to many customers around the world who were not creditworthy. Overall, how firms safeguard and advance the interest of owners as providers of capital is at the heart of corporate governance, a topic that we turn to next.

Cross-listing

Listing shares on a foreign stock exchange.

OWNERS

Owners provide capital, bear risks, and own the firm. Three broad patterns exist: (1) concentrated versus diffused ownership, (2) family ownership, and (3) state ownership.

Differentiate among the various ownership patterns around the world.

Concentrated versus Diffused Ownership

Founders usually start up firms and completely own and control them. This is referred to as **concentrated ownership and control**. However, at some point, if the firm aspires to grow and needs more capital, the owners' desire to keep the firm in familiar hands will have to accommodate the arrival of other shareholders. Approximately 80% of listed US firms and 90% of listed UK firms are now characterized by **diffused ownership**, with numerous small shareholders but none with a dominant level of control.[8] Such firms have a **separation of ownership and control**, in that ownership is dispersed among many small shareholders and control is largely concentrated in the hands of salaried professional managers who own little (or no) equity.

Dispersed owners, each with a small stake, have neither incentives nor resources to keep a close eye on how the firm is run. Most small shareholders do not bother to show up at annual shareholder meetings. They prefer to free ride and hope that other shareholders will properly monitor and discipline managers. If small shareholders are not happy, they will simply sell the stock and invest elsewhere. However, if *all* shareholders behave in this manner, then *none* of them would care and managers would end up with significant *de facto* control and power.

The rise of institutional investors, such as professionally managed mutual funds and pension pools, has significantly changed this picture.[9] Institutional investors have both incentives and resources to closely monitor and control managerial activities. The increased size of institutional holdings limits the ability of institutional investors to dump the stock, because when one's stake is large enough, selling out depresses the share price and harms the seller.

Although the image of widely held corporations is a reasonably accurate description of most modern large US and UK firms, it is *not* the case in other parts of the world. Outside the Anglo-American world, most large firms are typically owned and controlled either by families or by the state with relatively little separation of ownership and control.[10] Each is discussed next.

Family Ownership

The vast majority of large firms throughout continental Europe, Asia, Latin America, and Africa feature concentrated family ownership and control (see In Focus 16.1).[11] On the positive side, family ownership and control may provide better incentives for the firm to focus on long-run performance. It may also minimize the conflicts between owners and professional managers typically encountered in firms owned by many small shareholders and managed by professional managers.[12] However, on the negative side, family ownership and control may lead to the selection of less qualified managers (who happen to be the sons, daughters, or other relatives of the founders), the destruction of value because of family conflicts, and the expropriation of minority shareholders (discussed below).[13] At present, there is no conclusive evidence on either the positive or negative role of family ownership and control on the performance of large firms.[14]

Concentrated ownership and control

Founders start up firms and completely own and control them on an individual or family basis.

Diffused ownership

Publicly traded corporations owned by numerous small shareholders but none with a dominant level of control.

Separation of ownership and control

The dispersal of ownership among many small shareholders, in which control is largely concentrated in the hands of salaried, professional managers who own little (or no) equity.

Family Ownership and Control

In mid-2005, few investors in Porsche would have guessed that only 18 months later their firm would be the dominant shareholder in Volkswagen. Then again, it is none of their business, because they have little say over the sports-car maker's managers or strategy. The Porsche and Piëch families have total voting control over Porsche, despite owning only half of its equity. The publicly traded shares, providing the other half of Porsche's capital, have no right to vote.

Porsche is an extreme example of how a family can wield great power by harnessing large amounts of other people's money. But it is not unusual. In America, 6% by number and 8% by capitalization of quoted companies had dual-class shares in 2002. Only two-thirds of large European companies rigorously apply the principle that one share should command one vote.

Some of the best-known North American companies use dual-class shares. The Ford family may no longer own the company—it has a slender 3.75% of the shares—but nobody can doubt who is in control. When the firm went public in 1956, the family's shares were converted into a special class that is guaranteed 40% of the voting power, no matter how many ordinary shares are in issue.

Dual-class shares are no hangover from the past. When Google went public in 2004, its founders, Larry Page and Sergey Brin, insisted on a dual-class share structure. Google sold the public new A shares with one vote per share; its existing shares, mostly held by Page and Brin, became B shares with ten times as many votes per share. With around one-fifth of Google's total equity, the founders still command about three-fifths of votes, and thus retain control.

Source: "Our Company Right or Wrong", *The Economist*, March 17, 2007, pp. 75–76. Copyright © 2007 The Economist Newspaper Limited. Reprinted with permission. All rights reserved.

State Ownership

Other than families, the state is another major owner of firms in many parts of the world. State-owned enterprises (SOEs) suffer from an incentive problem. Although in theory all citizens (including employees) are owners, in practice, they have neither rights to enjoy dividends generated from SOEs (as shareholders would), nor rights to transfer or sell "their" property. SOEs are *de facto* owned and controlled by government agencies and officials far removed from ordinary citizens and employees. Thus, there is little motivation for SOE managers and employees to improve performance because it could hardly benefit them personally. In a most cynical fashion, SOE employees in the former Soviet Union summed it up well: "They pretend to pay us and we pretend to work."

Since the 1980s, one country after another—ranging from Britain to Brazil to Belarus—realized that their SOEs often performed poorly, which resulted in a wave of privatization.[15] The SOE share declined around the world—until 2008.[16] Events since 2008 created a major reversal: Many governments in developed economies bailed out numerous failing private firms using public funds, effectively turning them into SOEs. Since SOEs have such a dreadful reputation (essentially a "dirty word"), the US government has refused to acknowledge it has SOEs. Instead, it acknowledges that the United States has "government-sponsored enterprises" (GSEs). GSEs include General Motors (now nicknamed "Government Motors") and Citigroup ("Citigovernment"). Like the swing of a pendulum (see Chapter 1), the upsurge of state ownership has wiped out a substantial chunk of the gains of privatization.

MANAGERS

Managers represent another crucial leg of the corporate governance "tripod." Of particular importance are executives on the **top management team (TMT)**, which is led by the **chief executive officer (CEO)**.

LEARNING OBJECTIVE **3**

Understand the role of managers in both principal-agent and principal-principal conflicts.

Principal-Agent Conflicts

The relationship between shareholders and professional managers is a relationship between principals and agents—in short, an **agency relationship**. Principals (owners) delegate authority, and **agents** (managers) are those to whom authority is delegated. **Agency theory** suggests a simple yet profound proposition: To the extent that the interests of principals and agents do not completely overlap, there will *inherently* be **principal-agent conflicts**. These conflicts result in **agency costs**, including (1) principals' costs of monitoring and controlling agents and (2) agents' costs of bonding (signaling that they are trustworthy).[17] In a corporate setting, although shareholders (principals) are interested in maximizing the long-term value of their stock, managers (agents) may be more interested in maximizing their own power, income, and perks.

Manifestations of agency problems include excessive executive compensation, on-the-job consumption (such as corporate jets), and empire-building (such as value-destroying acquisitions). Consider executive compensation. In 1980, the average US CEO earned approximately 40 times what the average blue-collar worker earned. Today, the ratio is 400 times. Despite some performance improvement, it seems difficult to argue that on average, CEOs improved performance 10 times faster than workers did since 1980, and thus deserved a pay package worth 400 worker salaries today.[18] In other words, one can "smell" some agency costs.

Directly measuring agency costs, however, is difficult. In one of the most innovative (and hair-raising) attempts to measure agency costs directly, one study finds that the sudden *deaths* (plane crashes or heart attacks) of some CEOs led to an increase in share prices of their firms.[19] In other words, to reduce agency costs that shareholders had shouldered, CEOs had to drop dead (!). Conversely, we could imagine how much value these CEOs destroyed when they were alive. In a sad (or, some may say, cruel) way, the capital market seemed to be pleased with such human tragedies.

The primary reason agency problems persist is because of **information asymmetries** between principals and agents—that

Do you think US CEOs and other top executives deserve high-end benefits, such as private transportation, substantial bonuses, and salaries as much as 400 times the average blue-collar worker?

© Comstock Images

Top management team (TMT)
The team consisting of the highest level of executives of a firm led by the CEO.

Chief executive officer (CEO)
The main executive manager in charge of the firm.

Agency relationship
The relationship between principals (such as shareholders) and agents (such as professional managers).

Principal
A person (such as owner) delegating authority.

Agent
A person (such as manager) to whom authority is delegated.

Agency theory
A theory that focuses on principal-agent relationships (or in short, agency relationships).

Principal-agent conflicts
Conflicts between principals and agents.

Agency costs
The costs associated with principal-agent relationships.

Information asymmetries
Asymmetric distribution and possession of information between two sides.

is, agents such as managers almost always know more about the property they manage than principals do. Although it is possible to reduce information asymmetries through governance mechanisms, it is not realistic to completely eliminate agency problems.

Principal-Principal Conflicts

Since concentrated ownership and control by families is the norm in many parts of the world, different kinds of conflicts are at play. One of the leading indicators of concentrated family ownership and control is the appointment of family members as board chairman, CEO, and other TMT members. In East Asia, approximately 57% of the corporations have board chairmen and CEOs from the controlling families.[20] In continental Europe, the number is 68%.[21] The families are able to do so because they are controlling (although not necessarily majority) shareholders. For example, in 2003, 30-year-old James Murdoch became CEO of British Sky Broadcasting (BSkyB), Europe's largest satellite broadcaster, despite strong resistance from minority shareholders. So why was he selected? James' father, Rupert Murdoch, controlled 35% of BSkyB and chaired the board.

The BSkyB case is a classic example of the conflicts in family-owned and family-controlled firms. Instead of between principals (shareholders) and agents (professional managers), the primary conflicts are between two classes of principals, controlling shareholders and minority shareholders—in other words, **principal-principal conflicts**[22] (see Figure 16.3 and Table 16.1). Family managers such as Rupert and James Murdoch, who represent (or are) controlling shareholders, may advance family interests at the expense of minority shareholders.

FIGURE 16.3 PRINCIPAL-AGENT CONFLICTS AND PRINCIPAL-PRINCIPAL CONFLICTS

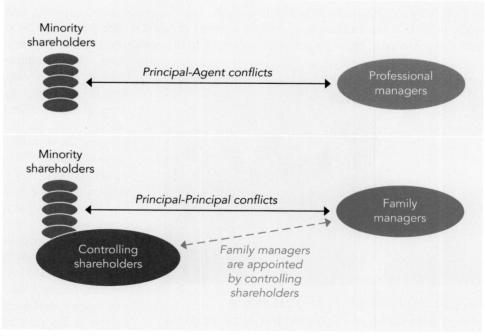

Principal-principal conflicts

Conflicts between two classes of principals: controlling shareholders and minority shareholders.

Source: M. Young, M. W. Peng, D. Ahlstrom, G. Bruton, & Y. Jiang, 2008, Corporate governance in emerging economies: A review of the principal-principal perspective (p. 200), *Journal of Management Studies*, 45: 196–220.

TABLE 16.1 PRINCIPAL-AGENT VERSUS PRINCIPAL-PRINCIPAL CONFLICTS

	Principal-Agent conflicts	Principal-Principal conflicts
Ownership pattern	Dispersed—shareholders holding 5% of equity are regarded as "blockholders"	Dominant—often greater than 50% of equity is controlled by the largest shareholders
Manifestations	Strategies that benefit entrenched managers at the expense of shareholders (such as shirking, excessive compensation, and empire building)	Strategies that benefit controlling shareholders at the expense of minority shareholders (such as minority shareholder expropriation and cronyism)
Protection of minority shareholders	Courts are more protective of minority shareholder rights; informal norms support this view	Formal institutional protection is often lacking; informal norms favor controlling shareholders
Market for corporate control	Active, at least in principle as the "governance mechanism of last resort"	Inactive even in principle; concentrated ownership thwarts notions of takeover

Source: Adapted from M. Young, M. W. Peng, D. Ahlstrom, G. Bruton, & Y. Jiang, 2008, Corporate governance in emerging economies: A review of the principal-principal perspective (p. 202), *Journal of Management Studies*, 45: 196–220.

Controlling shareholders' dominant position as *both* principals and agents (managers) may allow them to override traditional governance mechanisms designed to curtail principal-agent conflicts. For example, the board of directors will hardly be effective when the CEO being evaluated is the son of the board chairman.

The result of concentrated ownership by families is that family managers may engage in **expropriation** of minority shareholders, defined as activities that enrich controlling shareholders at the expense of minority shareholders. For example, managers from the controlling family may simply divert resources from the firm for personal or family use (see In Focus 16.2). This activity is vividly nicknamed **"tunneling"**—digging a tunnel to sneak out. Although such "tunneling" (also known as "corporate theft") is illegal, expropriation can be legally done through **related transactions**, whereby controlling owners sell firm assets to another firm they own at below-market prices or spin off the most profitable part of a public firm and merge it with another private firm they own (see the Closing Case).

Expropriation
Activities that enrich controlling shareholders at the expense of minority shareholders.

Tunneling
A form of corporate theft that diverts resources from the firm for personal or family use.

Related transactions
Controlling shareholders sell firm assets to another firm they own at below-market prices or spin off the most profitable part of a public firm and merge it with another private firm they own.

(IN) Focus 16.2

Satyam: A Corporate Governance Crisis in India

Satyam, which means "truth" in Sanskrit, an ancient Indian language, once belonged to the top tier of India's most celebrated industry: IT. But now it stands as India's largest corporate fraud. In January 2009, Satyam's founder and chairman, B. Ramalinga Raju, confessed to falsifying the company's books for years, inflating revenues and fabricating cash of about $1 billion that did not really exist. Raju also stole profits and saddled Satyam with debt-ridden companies owned by his sons, persuading his board to approve the deals. His auditors, PricewaterhouseCoopers,

endorsed Satyam's books even as hundreds of millions of dollars were unaccounted for. Critics point out that a majority of Indian companies are family-owned. Their founders, although eager to tap into global capital markets, are reluctant to give up control. So books are often cooked, complex cross-holdings among subsidiaries are linked, and disasters like Satyam's are bound to happen.

Sources: Based on (1) *BusinessWeek*, 2009, Corporate India's governance crisis, February 2: 78; (2) *The Economist*, 2009, Salvaging the truth, April 18: 68–69.

Explain the role of the board of directors.

BOARD OF DIRECTORS

As an intermediary between owners and managers, the board of directors oversees and ratifies strategic decisions and evaluates, rewards, and if necessary penalizes top managers.

Board Composition

Otherwise known as the insider/outsider mix, **board composition** has recently attracted significant attention. **Inside directors** are top executives of the firm. The trend around the world is to introduce more **outside directors,** defined as nonmanagement members of the board. Outside directors presumably are more independent and can better safeguard shareholder interests.[23]

Although conventional wisdom favors a board with a higher proportion of outside directors, academic research has *failed* to empirically establish a link between the outsider/insider ratio and firm performance.[24] Even "stellar" firms with a majority of outside directors on the board can still be plagued by governance problems. On average, 74% of the board members at Enron, Global Crossing, and Tyco were outside directors before each company's respective scandals.[25] It is possible that some of these outside directors are *affiliated* directors who may have family ties and/or professional relationships with the firm or firm management. In other words, such affiliated outside directors are not necessarily "independent." For example, outside directors on Japanese boards often come from banks, other member firms of the same *keiretsu* (a set of companies with interlocking business relationships and shareholdings), and their parent firms.[26]

Leadership Structure

Whether the board is led by a separate chairman or by the CEO who doubles as a chairman—a situation known as **CEO duality**—is also important. From an agency theory standpoint, if the board is to supervise the CEO, it seems imperative that the board be chaired by a separate individual. Otherwise, how can the CEO be evaluated by the body which he/she chairs? However, a corporation led by two top leaders (a board chairman and a CEO) may lack a unity of command and experience top-level conflicts. Not surprisingly, there is significant divergence across countries. Although a majority of the large UK firms separate the two top jobs, most large US firms combine them. A difficulty often cited by US boards is that it is very hard to recruit a capable CEO without the board chairman title.

Academic research is inconclusive on whether CEO duality (or nonduality) is more effective.[27] However, around the world firms are under increasing pressure to split the two jobs to at least show that they are serious about controlling the CEO.

The Role of Boards of Directors

In a nutshell, boards of directors are responsible for control, service, and resource acquisition functions. As discussed next, a board's effectiveness in serving the control function stems from its independence, deterrence, and norms.

- The ability to effectively control managers boils down to how independent directors are. Outside directors who are personally friendly and loyal to the CEO are unlikely to challenge managerial decisions. Exactly for this reason, CEOs often

Board composition

The insider/outsider mix on a board of directors.

Inside director

A member of the board who is a top executive of the firm.

Outside director

A nonmanagement member of the board.

CEO duality

The CEO doubles as a chairman of the board.

nominate family members, personal friends, and other independent but passive directors.[28]

- Directors are not at risk if they fail to protect shareholder interests. Courts usually will not second-guess board decisions in the absence of bad faith or insider dealing. Directors are often protected from the consequences of bad decisions.
- Directors who challenge management are outside the norm. When directors "stick their necks out" by confronting the CEO in meetings to raise a point, nobody picks it up.[29]

In addition to control, another important function of the board is service—primarily advising the CEO.[30] Finally, another crucial board function is resource acquisition for the focal firm.

What are some of the functions performed by corporate board members?

For example, in China, outside directors from buyers, suppliers, and alliance partners bring in more resources, resulting in higher sales growth.[31]

GOVERNANCE MECHANISMS AS A PACKAGE

LEARNING OBJECTIVE 5

Governance mechanisms can be classified as internal or external—otherwise known as voice-based and exit-based mechanisms, respectively. **Voice-based mechanisms** refer to shareholders' willingness to work with managers, usually through the board, by "voicing" their concerns. **Exit-based mechanisms** indicate that shareholders no longer have patience and are willing to "exit" by selling their shares. This section outlines these mechanisms.

Identify voice-based and exit-based governance mechanisms and their combination as a package.

Internal (Voice-Based) Governance Mechanisms

Boards typically employ two internal governance mechanisms: "carrots" and "sticks." The underlying idea behind "carrots" is pay for performance.[32] Increasing executive compensation is the most obvious. Stock options that help align the interests of managers and shareholders have become increasingly popular.[33] Although in principle this idea is sound, in practice it has a number of drawbacks. If accounting-based measures (such as return on sales) are used, managers are often able to manipulate numbers to make them look better. If market-based measures (such as stock prices) are adopted, stock prices obviously are subject to many forces beyond managers' control. Consequently, the pay-for-performance link in executive compensation is weak.[34]

In general, boards are likely to use "carrots" before considering "sticks." However, when facing continued performance failures, boards may have to dismiss the CEO.[35] Approximately 40% of all CEO changes in recent years are dismissals

Voice-based mechanisms

Corporate governance mechanisms that focus on shareholders' willingness to work with managers, usually through the board, by "voicing" their concerns.

Exit-based mechanisms

Corporate governance mechanisms that focus on exit, indicating that shareholders no longer have patience and are willing to "exit" by selling their shares.

for underachievement. In brief, recent boards seem to be quicker to dismiss CEOs. A new CEO faces substantial firm-specific employment risk because if fired, the CEO is extremely unlikely to run another publicly traded company. To offset the risk of being fired, new CEOs naturally demand generous compensation—a premium on the order of 30% or more—before taking on the job. This, in part, explains the rapidly rising levels of executive compensation.

External (Exit-Based) Governance Mechanisms

There are three external governance mechanisms: (1) the market for product competition, (2) the market for corporate control, and (3) the market for private equity. Product market competition is a powerful force compelling managers to maximize profits and, in turn, shareholder value. However, from a corporate governance perspective, product market competition *complements* the market for corporate control and the market for private equity, each of which is outlined next.

The Market for Corporate Control   This is the main external governance mechanism, otherwise known as the takeover market or the mergers and acquisitions (M&A) market (see Chapter 12). It is essentially an arena where different management teams compete for controlling rights of corporate assets. As an external governance mechanism, the market for corporate control serves as a disciplining mechanism of last resort when internal governance mechanisms fail. The underlying logic is spelled out by agency theory, which suggests that when managers engage in self-interested actions and internal governance mechanisms fail, a firm's stock will be undervalued by investors. Under these circumstances, other management teams, which recognize an opportunity to reorganize or redeploy the firm's assets and hence to create new value, bid for the rights to manage the firm. How effective is the market for corporate control? Three findings have emerged:[36]

- On average, shareholders of target firms earn sizable acquisition premiums.
- Shareholders of acquiring firms experience slight but insignificant losses.
- A substantially higher level of top management turnover follows M&As.

In summary, although internal mechanisms aim at "fine-tuning" management, the market for corporate control enables the "wholesale" removal of entrenched managers. As a radical approach, the market for corporate control has limitations. It is very costly to wage such financial battles. In addition, a large number of M&As seem to be driven by acquirers' sheer hubris or empire building, and the long-run profitability of post-merger firms is not particularly impressive (see Chapter 12).

Nevertheless, the net impact, at least in the short run, seems to be positive, because the threat of takeovers does help keep managers focused on shareholder wealth maximization. In Japan, an increasingly credible threat of takeovers has been rising. For example, Minolta was recently taken over by HOYA. Thus, Japanese managers now pay more attention to stock prices.

Private equity

Equity capital invested in private companies that, by definition, are not publicly traded.

Leveraged buyout (LBO)

A means by which investors, often in partnership with incumbent managers, issue bonds and use the cash raised to buy the firm's stock.

The Market for Private Equity   Instead of being taken over, a large number of publicly listed firms have gone private by tapping into private equity, primarily through leveraged buyouts (LBOs). In an LBO, private investors, often in partnership with incumbent managers, issue bonds and use the cash raised to buy the firm's stock—in essence replacing shareholders with bondholders and transforming the firm from a public to a private entity. As another external governance mechanism, private equity utilizes the bond market, as opposed to the stock market, to discipline managers. LBO-based private equity transactions are associated with three major changes in corporate governance:

- LBOs change the incentives of managers by providing them with substantial equity stakes.
- The high amount of debt imposes strong financial discipline.
- LBO sponsors closely monitor the firms in which they have invested.

Overall, evidence suggests that LBOs improve efficiency, at least in the short run.[37] However, the picture is less clear over the long run, because LBOs may have forced managers to reduce investments in long-run R&D. Around the world, private equity grew by leaps and bounds before 2008, from 0.25% of world GDP in 2000 to 1.5% in 2007, now representing approximately 20% of all M&A activities. Because of the recent recession, private equity activities declined a bit.

Internal Mechanisms + External Mechanisms = Governance Package

Taken together, the internal and external mechanisms can be considered a "package." Michael Jensen, a leading agency theorist, argues that failures of internal governance mechanisms in the United States in the 1970s activated the market for corporate control in the 1980s.[38] Managers initially resisted (see In Focus 16.3).

IN Focus 16.3

Michael Jensen as an Outside Director

Harvard professor Michael Jensen is a leading agency theorist, who served on the board of Armstrong World Industries between 1990 and 1996 as an outside director. He described this experience at a conference:

Let me say that there were very good people on that board. But what was true at Armstrong is that even the outside directors basically see themselves as employees of the CEO. That's just the way it is. And the outside directors in this case seemed even more deferential and beholden to the CEO than the managers who actually reported to him.

I was put on the compensation committee. And at the first meeting of that committee, there was a proposal to give the management a substantial bonus for the excellent performance they'd had that year. The problem, however, was that the equity value of the company had fallen by roughly 50% over that period. So I was listening to this discussion— and, by the way, the CEO was there running the meeting whose main focus was his own compensation. And when I pointed out that it was really hard to argue that management

had done a good job when the value of the company had fallen by 50%, my fellow members of the compensation committee acted as if they were shocked. The response I got was, "How did you calculate that?"

My own experience suggests that one person on a board can make a difference. It took a couple of years, but we did fire the CEO for poor performance. I would show up at every board meeting and say, "We've destroyed $50 million since the last meeting." And finally things moved.

After we eventually fired the CEO, I kept asking hard questions. And then the next CEO fired me from the board because, as he put it, I had a tendency to ask "trick questions." And that, apparently, was inappropriate behavior. A trick question, as I gathered from this experience, is one that the CEO either can't answer or finds it uncomfortable to do so.

Source: Excerpts from *Journal of Applied Corporate Finance*, 2008, US corporate governance accomplishments and failings: A discussion with Michael Jensen and Robert Monks (p. 34), 20(1): 28–46.

However, over time, many firms that are not takeover targets or that have successfully defended themselves against such attempts end up restructuring and downsizing—doing exactly what "raiders" would have done had these firms been taken over. In other words, the strengthened external mechanisms led to improved internal mechanisms.

Overall, since the 1980s, American managers have become much more focused on stock prices, resulting in a new term, "shareholder capitalism," which has been spreading around the world.[39] In Europe, executive stock options have become popular and M&As more frequent.[40] In Russia, after the 1998 collapse, there are now some traces of modern corporate governance.[41]

LEARNING OBJECTIVE

6

Explain how governance mechanisms vary around the world.

A GLOBAL PERSPECTIVE ON CORPORATE GOVERNANCE

Figure 16.4 illustrates how different corporate ownership and control patterns around the world lead to a different mix of internal and external mechanisms. The most familiar type is Cell 4, exemplified by most large US and UK firms. Although external governance mechanisms (M&As and private equity) are strong, internal mechanisms are relatively weak due to the separation of ownership and control that gives managers significant *de facto* control power.

The opposite mix can be found in Cell 1, which is typically seen in firms in continental Europe and Japan where the market for corporate control is relatively weak (although there is more activity recently). Consequently, the primary governance mechanisms remain concentrated ownership and control.

FIGURE 16.4   INTERNAL AND EXTERNAL GOVERNANCE MECHANISMS: A GLOBAL PERSPECTIVE

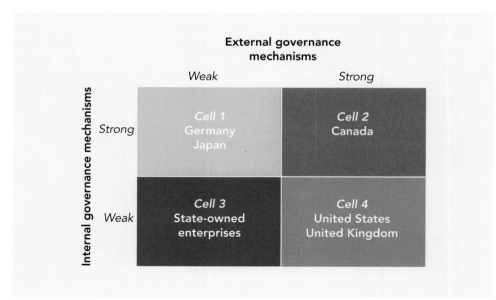

Shareholder capitalism

A view of capitalism that suggests that the most fundamental purpose for firms to exist is to serve the economic interests of shareholders (also known as capitalists).

Source: Cells 1, 2, and 4 are adapted from E. R. Gedajlovic & D. M. Shapiro, 1998, Management and ownership effects: Evidence from five countries (p. 539), *Strategic Management Journal*, 19: 533–553. The label of Cell 3 is suggested by the present author.

TABLE 16.2   TWO PRIMARY FAMILIES OF CORPORATE GOVERNANCE SYSTEMS

Corporations in the United States and United Kingdom	Corporations in Continental Europe and Japan
Anglo-American corporate governance models	German-Japanese corporate governance models
Market-oriented, high-tension systems	Bank-oriented, network-based systems
Rely mostly on exit-based, external mechanisms	Rely mostly on voice-based, internal mechanisms
Shareholder capitalism	Stakeholder capitalism

Overall, the Anglo-American and continental European-Japanese (otherwise known as German-Japanese) systems represent the two primary corporate governance families in the world, with a variety of labels (see Table 16.2). Given that both the United States and United Kingdom as a group and continental Europe and Japan as another group are highly developed, successful economies, it is difficult and probably not meaningful to argue whether the Anglo-American or German-Japanese system is better. Evidently, each has different strengths and weaknesses.

There are other systems that do not easily fit into such an either/or world. Placed in Cell 2, Canada has *both* a relatively active market for corporate control and a large number of firms with concentrated ownership and control—over 350 of the 400 largest Canadian firms are controlled by a single shareholder.[42] Canadian managers thus face powerful internal and external constraints.

Finally, SOEs (of all nationalities) are in an unfortunate position of both weak external and internal governance mechanisms (Cell 3). Pre-reform SOEs in the former Soviet bloc and China serve as a case in point. Externally, the market for corporate control simply did not exist. Internally, managers were supervised by officials who acted as *de facto* "owners" with ineffective control.

INSTITUTIONS, RESOURCES, AND CORPORATE FINANCE AND GOVERNANCE

Describe how institutions and resources affect corporate finance and governance.

The institution-based view posits that differences around the world are affected by (1) *formal* securities laws, corporate charters, and codes and (2) *informal* conventions, norms, and values—collectively known as institutions.[43] The resource-based view argues that among a number of firms financed in the same way and governed by the same set of rules, some excel more than others because of differences in firm-specific capabilities (Figure 16.5). This section examines these views.

Institutions and Corporate Finance and Governance

Formal Institutional Frameworks
Other than firms' founders and their families, external providers of capital—shareholders or bondholders—need to have some reasonable degree of assurance that their investment is protected and

FIGURE 16.5   INSTITUTIONS, RESOURCES, AND CORPORATE FINANCE AND GOVERNANCE

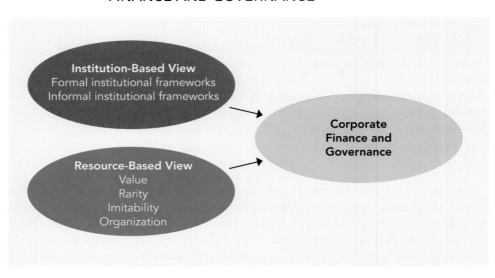

will not be abused. Such assurance is typically provided by formal institutional frameworks that protect investor rights.[44]

A fundamental difference in corporate finance and governance is between the separation of ownership and control in (most) Anglo-American firms and the concentration of ownership and control in the rest of the world. Among many explanations, an institutional explanation is a leading one. In brief, better formal legal protection of shareholder rights in the United States and United Kingdom, especially the rights of *minority* shareholders, encourages founding families to dilute their equity to attract minority shareholders and delegate day-to-day management to professional managers. Given reasonable investor protection, founding families themselves (such as the Rockefellers) may over time feel comfortable becoming minority shareholders of the firms they founded. On the other hand, when formal legal and regulatory institutions are dysfunctional, founding families *must* run their firms directly. In the absence of investor protection, bestowing management rights to outside, professional managers may invite abuse and theft.

Evidence suggests that the weaker the formal legal and regulatory institutions protecting shareholders, the more concentrated ownership and control rights become—in other words, there is some substitution between the two. Common-law countries (the US, UK, and former British colonies) generally have the strongest legal protection of investors and lowest concentration of corporate ownership.[45] In short, the absence of sufficient legal protection of shareholder rights leads to concentrated ownership and control as an answer to potentially rampant principal-agent conflicts.

However, what is good for controlling shareholders is not necessarily good for minority shareholders or for an economy. As noted earlier, minimizing principal-agent conflicts by concentrating ownership and control, unfortunately, introduces more principal-principal conflicts (see In Focus 16.1, 16.2, and the Closing Case). Consequently, many potential minority shareholders may refuse to invest. "How do you avoid being expropriated as a minority shareholder?" One popular saying in Asia suggests, "Don't be one!" If minority shareholders are informed enough to be aware of these possibilities and still decide to invest, they are likely to discount the shares floated by family owners, resulting in lower corporate valuations, fewer publicly traded firms, inactive and smaller capital markets, and, in turn, lower levels of economic development in general.

Given that almost every country desires vibrant capital markets and economic development, it seems puzzling that the Anglo-American-style investor protection is not universally embraced. It is important to note, however, that corporate governance at its core is ultimately a choice about *political* governance. For largely historical reasons, most countries have made hard-to-reverse political choices. For example, the German practice of "codetermination" (employees control 50% of the votes on supervisory boards) is an outcome of political decisions made by post-war German governments.[46] If German firms were to have US/UK-style dispersed ownership and still allowed employees to control 50% of the votes on supervisory boards, these firms would end up becoming *employee*-dominated firms. Thus, concentrated ownership and control becomes a natural response.

Changing corporate governance, although not impossible, will encounter significant resistance, especially from incumbents (such as German labor unions or Asian families) who benefit from the present system.[47] Some of the leading families not only have great connections with the government, sometimes they *are* the government. Two recent prime ministers of Italy and Thailand—Silvio Berlusconi and Thaksin Shinawatra, respectively—came from leading business families.

Only under extraordinary circumstances would some politicians muster sufficient political will to initiate major corporate governance reforms. The spectacular corporate scandals in the United States (such as Enron) are an example of such extraordinary events prompting more serious political reforms in the form of Sarbanes-Oxley (SOX) Act and other regulatory changes.

Informal Institutional Frameworks In the last two decades around the world, why and how have informal norms and values concerning corporate governance changed to such a great extent? In the United States and United Kingdom, the idea of shareholder capitalism has graduated from minority view to orthodoxy. This idea is spreading rapidly in the rest of the world as well. Why? At least three reasons for these changes can be identified: (1) the rise of capitalism, (2) the impact of globalization, and (3) the global diffusion of "best practices."

The recent changes in corporate governance around the world are part of the greater political, economic, and social movement embracing capitalism. The triumph of capitalism naturally boils down to the triumph of *capitalists* (otherwise known as shareholders). However, "free markets" are not necessarily free. Even some of the most developed countries have experienced significant governance failures, calling for a sharper focus on shareholder value.

At least three aspects of recent globalization have a bearing on corporate governance. First, thanks to more trade and investment, firms with different governance norms increasingly come into contact. Being aware of alternatives, shareholders are no longer easily persuaded that "our way" is the most natural and most efficient way of corporate governance.[48] Second, foreign portfolio investment (FPI)—foreigners purchasing stocks and bonds (see Chapter 6)—has scaled new heights. These investors naturally demand better shareholder protection before committing their funds. Finally, the global thirst for capital has prompted many firms to pay attention to corporate governance. Many foreign firms, for example, have cross-listed their stock in New York and London. In exchange for such privileges, they have to be in compliance with US and UK listing requirements.

In addition, the changing norms and values are also directly promoted by the global diffusion of codes of "best practices."[49] Led by Britain's Cadbury Report in

TABLE 16.3 SELECTED CORPORATE GOVERNANCE CODES AROUND THE WORLD SINCE THE 1990s

Developed economies	Emerging economies
Cadbury Report (United Kingdom, 1992)	King Report (South Africa, 1994)
Dey Report (Canada, 1994)	Confederation of Indian Industry Code of Corporate Governance (India, 1998)
Bosch Report (Australia, 1995)	Korean Stock Exchange Code of Best Practice (Korea, 1999)
Corporate Governance Forum of Japan Code (Japan, 1998)	Mexican Code of Corporate Governance (Mexico, 1999)
German Corporate Governance Code (Germany, 2000)	Code of Corporate Governance for Listed Companies (China, 2001)
Sarbanes-Oxley Act (United States, 2002)	Code of Corporate Conduct (Russia, 2002)

1992, the global proliferation of such codes is striking (Table 16.3). A lot of these codes are advisory and not legally binding. However, pressure is strong for firms to "voluntarily" adopt these codes. In Russia, although adopting the 2002 Code of Corporate Conduct is in theory voluntary, firms that opt not to adopt have to publicly explain why, essentially naming and shaming themselves.

The Organization for Economic Cooperation and Development (OECD) has spearheaded the efforts to globally diffuse "best practices." In 1999, it published the *OECD Principles of Corporate Governance*, suggesting that the overriding objective of the corporation should be to optimize shareholder returns over time. The *Principles* are nonbinding even for the 30 OECD member countries. Nevertheless, the global norms seem to be moving toward the *Principles*.[50]

The revival of state ownership and the reemergence of SOEs around the world, however, has reignited the debate on whether the firm exists to serve the interests of shareholders or to serve other "social" purposes (see Chapters 2 and 17). If governments are now providing major sources of financing for firms ranging from GM to the Royal Bank of Scotland, shouldn't governments, as owners (who theoretically act on behalf of all citizens and taxpayers), exercise their ownership rights by calling the shots?

Resources and Corporate Finance and Governance

From a corporate finance and governance standpoint, the ability to successfully list on a high-profile exchange such as NYSE and LSE is *valuable, rare,* and hard-to-*imitate* (the first three criteria in the VRIO framework). In 1997, the valuations of foreign firms listed on the NYSE were 17% higher than their domestic counterparts in the same country.[51] Despite hurdles such as SOX, the select few that are now able to list on the NYSE are rewarded even more handsomely: Their valuations are now 37% higher than comparable groups of domestic firms in the same country.[52] London-listed foreign firms do not enjoy such high valuations. This is classic resource-based logic at work: Precisely because it is much more challenging to list on the NYSE after SOX, the small number of foreign firms that are able to do so are truly exceptional. Thus, they deserve higher valuations.

Some of the most valuable, rare, and hard-to-imitate firm-specific resources are top managers and directors—often regarded as managerial human capital. Some of these resources, such as the social networks of these executives, are highly unique and likely to add value.[53] Also, top managerial talents are hard to imitate—unless they are hired away by competitor firms.

The last crucial component in the VRIO framework is *organizational*. It is within an organizational setting (in TMTs and boards) that managers and directors function.[54] Overall, the few people at the top of a firm can make a world of difference. Governance mechanisms need to properly motivate and discipline them to make sure that they make a positive impact.

DEBATES AND EXTENSIONS

Corporate finance and governance often generate significant debates. This section discusses two: (1) opportunistic agents versus managerial stewards and (2) global convergence versus divergence.

Participate in two leading debates on corporate finance and governance.

Opportunistic Agents versus Managerial Stewards

Agency theory assumes managers are agents who may engage in self-serving, opportunistic activities if left to their own devices. However, critics contend that most managers are likely to be honest and trustworthy. Managerial mistakes may be due to a lack of competence, information, or luck but not necessarily due to self-serving. Thus, it may not be fair to characterize all managers as opportunistic agents. Although influential, agency theory has been criticized as an "anti-management theory of management."[55] A new "pro-management" theory, stewardship theory, has emerged recently. It suggests that most managers can be viewed as owners' stewards.[56] Safeguarding shareholders' interests and advancing organizational goals, as opposed to serving one's own agenda, will maximize (most) managers' own utility functions.

Stewardship theorists agree that agency theory is useful when describing a certain portion of managers and under certain circumstances (such as being "under siege" during takeover battles). However, if all principals view all managers as self-serving agents who need control mechanisms to keep them on a "tight leash," then some managers, who initially view themselves as stewards, may become so frustrated that they end up engaging in the very self-serving behavior agency theory seeks to minimize. Therefore, as a self-fulfilling prophecy, agency theory may *induce* such behavior.[57]

Global Convergence versus Divergence

Another leading debate is whether corporate finance and governance is converging or diverging globally. Convergence advocates argue that globalization unleashes a "survival-of-the-fittest" process by which firms, in search of the lowest cost of capital, will be forced to adopt globally best (essentially Anglo-American) practices.[58] Global investors are willing to pay a premium for stock in firms with Anglo-American-style governance, prompting others to follow. Most of the recent

Managerial human capital
The skills and abilities acquired by top managers.

Stewardship theory
A "pro-management" theory that suggests that most managers can be viewed as owners' stewards interested in safeguarding shareholders' interests.

governance codes (Table 16.3) largely draw from Anglo-American concepts. Shareholder activism, an unheard-of phenomenon in many parts of the world, is now more visible (see the Closing Case on David Webb in Hong Kong).

One interesting phenomenon often cited by convergence advocates is cross-listing, which is primarily driven by the desire to tap into larger pools of capital. Foreign firms thus have to comply with US and UK securities laws and adopt Anglo-American governance norms if they want to be listed in New York or London.[59] There is evidence, for instance, that Japanese firms listed in New York and London, compared with those listed at home, are more concerned about shareholder value.[60]

Critics, on the other hand, contend that governance practices will continue to diverge throughout the world.[61] For example, promoting more concentrated ownership and control is often recommended as a solution to combat principal-agent conflicts in US and UK firms. However, making the same recommendation to reform firms in continental Europe, Asia, and Latin America may be counterproductive or even disastrous. The main problem in these regions is that controlling shareholders typically already have too much ownership and control.

In the case of cross-listed firms, divergence advocates make two points. First, compared to US firms, these foreign firms have significantly larger boards, more inside directors, lower institutional ownership, and more concentrated ownership.[62] In other words, cross-listed foreign firms do not necessarily adopt US governance practices before or after listing. Second, despite the popular belief that US and UK securities laws would apply to cross-listed foreign firms, in practice, these laws have rarely been enforced effectively against foreign firms' "tunneling."[63]

At present, complete divergence is probably unrealistic, especially for large firms in search of capital from global investors. Complete convergence also seems unlikely. What is more likely is "cross-vergence" balancing the expectations of global investors and those of local stakeholders.

LEARNING OBJECTIVE 9

Draw implications for action.

MANAGEMENT SAVVY

From the institution-based and resource-based views, two straightforward implications for action emerge (Table 16.4). First, savvy managers need to understand both the formal and informal rules, anticipate changes, and be aware of differences when dealing with financing and governance issues.[64] Consider executive compensation. In 2008, while many Wall Street firms had to be bailed out with billions of taxpayer dollars, Wall Street executives paid themselves $18 billion in bonuses. Although these practices did not break any formal laws, what the executives failed to read was the informal but very tangible normative pressures coming from an angry public fanned by the media and fueled by politicians who wanted to show they were "tough." As a result, formal efforts to limit executive compensation

TABLE 16.4 IMPLICATIONS FOR ACTION

- Understand the rules affecting corporate finance and governance, anticipate changes, and be aware of differences
- Develop firm-specific capabilities to differentiate a firm on corporate finance and governance dimensions

have been initiated in most countries. Although critics may argue that governments have no business in limiting executive compensation at private-sector firms, unfortunately, the rules have changed. As controlling shareholders of many formerly private-sector firms that have now become SOEs financed by public funds, governments do have legitimate ownership rights to intervene.

Second, managers need to develop firm-specific capabilities to differentiate their firms in terms of corporate finance and governance.[65] In India, whereas Satyam has emerged as a "bad apple" (In Focus 16.2), Infosys has served as a role model.[66] Infosys leads the competition by being the first Indian firm to follow US generally accepted accounting principles (GAAP) and one of the first to introduce outside directors. Since its listings in Bombay in 1993 and NASDAQ in 1999, it has gone far beyond disclosure requirements mandated by both Indian and US standards. On NASDAQ, Infosys *voluntarily* behaves like a US domestic issuer, rather than subjecting itself to the less stringent standards of a foreign issuer. The primary reason for such practices, according to Infosys executives, is to gain credibility with Western customers in the rough-and-tumble software market. In other words, excellent financing and governance practices make Infosys stand out in the product market.

CHAPTER SUMMARY

1. Outline the two means of financing: equity and debt.
   - Equity refers to the stock (usually expressed in shares) in a firm, and debt refers to the loan that the firm needs to pay back at a given time at a pre-specified interest rate.
   - Tapping into a larger pool of capital available globally allows firms to lower their cost of capital.

2. Differentiate among the various ownership patterns around the world.
   - In the United States and United Kingdom, firms with separation of ownership and control dominate.
   - Elsewhere, firms with concentrated ownership and control in the hands of families or governments dominate.

3. Understand the role of managers in both principal-agent and principal-principal conflicts.
   - In firms with separation of ownership and control, the primary conflicts are principal-agent conflicts.
   - In firms with concentrated ownership, principal-principal conflicts prevail.

4. Explain the role of the board of directors.
   - The board of directors performs (1) control, (2) service, and (3) resource acquisition functions.
   - Around the world, boards differ in composition and leadership structure.

5. Identify voice-based and exit-based governance mechanisms and their combination as a package.
   - Internal, voice-based mechanisms and external, exit-based mechanisms combine as a package to determine corporate governance effectiveness.
   - The market for corporate control and the market for private equity are two primary means of external mechanisms.

6. Explain how governance mechanisms vary around the world.
   • Different combinations of internal and external governance mechanisms lead to four main groups.

7. Describe how institutions and resources affect corporate finance and governance.
   • Institution-based and resource-based views shed light on corporate finance and governance issues.

8. Participate in two leading debates on corporate finance and governance.
   • (1) Opportunistic agents versus managerial stewards and (2) global convergence versus divergence.

9. Draw implications for action.
   • Understand the rules, anticipate changes, and be aware of differences.
   • Develop firm-specific capabilities to differentiate on corporate finance and governance dimensions.

KEY TERMS

Agency costs   537
Agency relationship   537
Agency theory   537
Agent   537
Board composition   540
Bond   533
Bondholders   533
CEO duality   540
Chief executive officer
  (CEO)   537
Concentrated ownership
  and control   535
Corporate governance   532
Cost of capital   533
Cross-listing   534
Debt   533

Default   533
Diffused ownership   535
Equity   533
Exit-based
  mechanisms   541
Expropriation   539
Financing   532
Information
  asymmetries   537
Inside director   540
Leveraged buyout
  (LBO)   542
Managerial human
  capital   549
Outside director   540
Principal   537

Principal-agent
  conflicts   537
Principal-principal
  conflicts   538
Private equity   542
Related transactions   539
Separation of ownership
  and control   535
Shareholder   533
Shareholder capitalism   544
Stewardship theory   549
Top management team
  (TMT)   537
Tunneling   539
Voice-based
  mechanisms   541

REVIEW QUESTIONS

1. What are the two primary means of financing? How do they differ?

2. Why can tapping into a global pool of capital providers result in a lower cost of capital?

3. How would you characterize a corporation with diffused ownership?

4. What are some of the pros and cons of family ownership?

5. Describe the differences between principal-agent conflicts and principal-principal conflicts.

6. Define the concept of expropriation of minority shareholders.

7. What do inside directors bring to a board of directors? What do outside directors have to offer?

8. What are the advantages and disadvantages of having two different individuals hold the positions of board chair and CEO rather than combining these two positions?

9. Name and describe the two internal governance mechanisms typically employed by boards.

10. Briefly summarize the three external governance mechanisms.

11. Why do most SOEs suffer from weak external and internal governance mechanisms?

12. What are some of the formal institutions that affect corporate finance and governance?

13. Explain how three aspects of recent globalization have influenced corporate finance and governance.

14. Where does managerial human capital fit into a VRIO framework?

15. Explain stewardship theory.

16. Given the arguments for converging versus diverging corporate governance around the world, which do you think is more likely to occur and why?

17. Compare Map 1.1 with Map 3.4. Countries that have low levels of development often benefit from outsourcing due to their low wages. Assume that a firm's board of directors is truly independent and makes decisions based only on economic considerations. Why would it not also outsource the top executive jobs? To the extent that such a thing might be possible, how might it be done?

CRITICAL DISCUSSION QUESTIONS

1. Some argue that the Anglo-American style separation of ownership and control is an inevitable outcome. Other contend that this is only one variant (among several) of how large firms can be effectively governed and that it is not necessarily the most efficient form. What do you think?

2. Recent corporate governance reforms in various countries urge (and often require) firms to add more outside directors to their boards and to separate the jobs of board chairman and CEO. Yet academic research has not been able to conclusively confirm the merits of both practices. Why?

3. *ON ETHICS*: As a chairman/CEO, you are choosing two candidates for one outside independent director position on your board. One of the candidates is another CEO and a long-time friend whose board you have served on

for many years. The other candidate is a known shareholder activist whose tag line is "No need to make fat cats fatter." Placing him on the board will earn you kudos among analysts and journalists for inviting a leading critic to scrutinize your work. But he may try to prove his theory that CEOs are overpaid—in other words, your compensation could be on the line. Who would you choose?

YOUR SOURCE FOR
global business knowledge

http://globalEDGE.msu.edu

GLOBAL ACTION

1. Your privately owned company consistently balances the interests of business freedom and labor freedom in its operations. As such, it has become an example for other firms worldwide to emulate. Since the tension between wages and prices at both the labor and business levels must be constantly reevaluated and improved, use globalEDGE to evaluate the leading countries that your firm can use as a model for continued commitment to the freedom of business as well as labor.

2. As CEO of a large multinational firm, the financial globalization level of a country can present different problems and solutions for success. Using a well-known index of financial globalization, evaluate and discuss specific countries in which the concerns of a high and low level of globalization must be addressed.

VIDEO CASES

Watch "Use Nonexecutive Directors Effectively" by Sir George Cox of the Institute of Directors.

1. Do you think that the primary value of nonexecutive (outside) directors is to serve as policemen or provide words of wisdom? Why or why not? Why did Cox think that this is not their primary value?

2. In comparing concentrated versus diffused ownership, make a case that nonexecutive directors can be of greatest value in firms with concentrated ownership. Now make a case that they could also be of greatest value in the case of diffused ownership.

3. In your opinion, in a global corporation with directors from various countries, are there any potential cultural issues that may affect the selection of nonexecutive directors?

4. As an example of how to make effective use of nonexecutive directors, Cox pointed to a situation in which he yielded to the recommendation of such directors. However, because the nonexecutive directors are not involved in the day-to-day operations, it would be easy to dismiss their disagreements on the grounds that they do not understand what is going on. What would you suggest that a CEO do to keep an open mind toward such directors?

Closing Case

David Webb: A Shareholder Activist in Hong Kong

Although Hong Kong may have a reputation as one of the world's most sophisticated financial markets, minority shareholders have a tradition of being abused by controlling shareholders. Although Hong Kong regulations were largely cut and pasted from British statutes, the nature of Hong Kong's listed firms means

that the laws leave gaping loopholes that are exploited by controlling shareholders. Since most listed British firms do not have controlling shareholders, the board is apt to fairly reflect the interests of all shareholders. However, in Hong Kong, 32 of the 33 "blue chips" in the Hang Seng Index, except HSBC, have controlling shareholders—a single person or group of persons, typically from a family, who control the board.

Crusading against such an establishment, David Webb, who was one of the 50 "Stars of Asia" featured by *BusinessWeek*, is a unique character in the emerging shareholder activism movement in Hong Kong. Webb, a native of England and an Oxford University graduate, moved to Hong Kong in 1991. He worked in investment banking and corporate finance until 1998 when he retired to become a full-time investor. His website (*www.webb-site.com*) now boasts 9,000 subscribers.

Webb is an outspoken critic at many shareholder meetings and an advocate for minority shareholders. He said that over 90% of listed companies in Hong Kong have a shareholder who owns more than 20% and has *de facto* control. He believed where either a family or a government controls listed companies, minority shareholders tend to be abused. As it stands now, the families that control most Hong Kong companies simply appoint directors and railroad their elections through at shareholder meetings. After buying 10 shares in each of the 33 companies that make up the Hang Seng Index, Webb has been regularly attending shareholder

meetings and demanding formal votes on *all* proposals. That does not win him friends among the tycoon set accustomed to doing cozy deals without outside scrutiny. Webb recognizes that the primary problems in corporate governance in Hong Kong—and also across Asia—arise from the concentrated ownership and control of companies.

Webb has been using his website to help increase the awareness of the benefits of minority shareholders. In the "Hall of Shame" on his website, he lists the companies under investigation by the Hong Kong authorities and frequently tackles what he sees as disenfranchisement of minority shareholders. In 2007, Webb lobbied against a proposed related transaction—Henderson Investment Ltd.'s planned buyout offer from the parent company Henderson Land Development Co. Following his advice, Henderson Investment Ltd.'s shareholders vetoed this related transaction.

In 2008, Webb quit as an independent director of the Hong Kong Stock Exchange (HKEX). Webb said Hong Kong Exchanges & Clearing Ltd., operator of HKEX, refused to provide information he needed to fulfill his role as an independent director. In resigning, Webb made serious allegations against the exchange, citing political interference and poor governance. One was that meetings were held with unnamed third parties on the express condition that the meetings not be reported to the board, raising the question of how the board can supervise management if it was denied the right to know of substantive meetings.

In 2009, HKEX announced the membership on the Listing Committee, which is responsible for approvals of initial public offerings as well as monitoring other listing and trading requirements. Webb noted that the majority of committee members have direct and indirect business relationships with the powerful tycoons in Hong Kong who have massive influence on the city's stock market. He said that was good news for the tycoons and their friends, but bad news for ordinary investors.

As for small local investors, those most hurt by poor corporate governance and high transaction costs, they never have much of a voice. Webb's surrogate role on their behalf will have to be conducted through his role on the Takeovers Panel of the Securities and Futures Commission (SFC), a position he has held since 2007. The panel resisted pressure from tycoons to relax a rule that requires stockholders with 30% ownership to issue a general offer for the entire company. Loosening the requirement would have made it easier for business owners to gain control of their companies without having to compensate minority shareholders. Webb opined: "I take the

position that it's better to lobby from the inside rather than the outside. . . . You can't rock the boat if you are swimming around outside it."

Case Discussion Questions:

1. What is the primary type of conflict in corporate governance in Hong Kong? Why do transplanted British laws and regulations seem ineffective?
2. What are Webb's motivations? Why aren't there many minority shareholders in Hong Kong who actively participate in corporate governance like Webb?
3. If you were Webb, what would be your recommendations to reform corporate governance in Hong Kong, Asia, and emerging economies in general?

Sources: This case was written by Professor **Yi Jiang** (California State University, East Bay). It is based on (1) P. Bowring, 2008, Hong Kong loses an independent watchdog, *Asia Sentinel*, May 16; (2) V. W. Kwok, 2009, Corporate governance, tycoon style, *Forbes*, June 2; (3) M. W. Peng & Y. Jiang, 2010, Institutions behind family ownership and control in large firms, *Journal of Management Studies*, 47: 253–273; (4) L. Santini, 209, David Webb continues Hong Kong quest, *Wall Street Journal*, April 27 (online); (5) M. Young, M. W. Peng, D. Ahlstrom, G. Bruton, & Y. Jiang, 2008, Corporate governance in emerging economies, *Journal of Management Studies*, 45: 196–220; (6) www.webb-site.com.

NOTES

[Journal acronyms] **AER**—*American Economic Review*; **AME**—*Academy of Management Executive*; **AMJ**—*Academy of Management Journal*; **AMP**—*Academy of Management Perspectives*; **AMR**—*Academy of Management Review*; **APJM**—*Asia Pacific Journal of Management*; **ASQ**—*Administrative Science Quarterly*; **BW**—*BusinessWeek*; **JAE**—*Journal of Accounting and Economics*; **JEL**—*Journal of Economic Literature*; **JEP**—*Journal of Economic Perspectives*; **JF**—*Journal of Finance*; **JFE**—*Journal of Financial Economics*; **JIBS**—*Journal of International Business Studies*; **JMS**—*Journal of Management Studies*; **JPE**—*Journal of Political Economy*; **JWB**—*Journal of World Business*; **MIR**—*Management International Review*; **OSc**—*Organization Science*; **OSt**—*Organization Studies*; **SMJ**—*Strategic Management Journal*

[1] R. Monks & N. Minow, 2001, *Corporate Governance* (p. 1), Oxford, UK: Blackwell. See also M. Benz & B. Frey, 2007, Corporate governance, *AMR*, 32: 92–104.

[2] E. Lim, S. Das, & A. Das, 2009, Diversification strategy, capital structure, and the Asian financial crisis, *SMJ*, 30: 577–594; M. Simlerly & M. Li, 2000, Environmental dynamism, capital structure, and performance, *SMJ*, 21: 31–49.

[3] X. Zhao, 2009, Determinants of flows into retail international equity finds, *JIBS*, 39: 1169–1177.

[4] *BW*, 2009, Why Dubai matters, December 14: 35–38.

[5] G. Dissanaike & I. Markar, 2009, Corporate financing in East Asia before the 1997 crash, *JIBS*, 40: 990–1004.

[6] F. Modigliani & M. Miller, 1958, The cost of capital, corporate finance and the theory of investment, *AER*, 48: 261–297.

[7] G. Bekaert & C. Harvey, 2000, Foreign speculators and emerging equity markets, *JF*, 55: 565–613.

[8] R. Stulz, 2005, The limits of financial globalization (p. 1618), *JF*, 60: 1595–1638.

[9] L. Tihanyi, R. Johnson, R. Hoskisson, & M. Hitt, 2003, Institutional ownership differences and international diversification, *AMJ*, 46: 195–211.

[10] R. La Porta, F. Lopez-de-Silanes, & A. Shleifer, 1999, Corporate ownership around the world, *JF*, 54: 471–517.

[11] M. Carney & E. Gedajlovic, 2002, The coupling of ownership and control and the allocation of financial resources, *JMS*, 39: 123–146; S. Thomsen & T. Pedersen, 2000, Ownership structure and economic performance in the largest European companies, *SMJ*, 21: 689–705.

[12] R. Anderson & D. Reeb, 2003, Founding-family ownership and firm performance, *JF*, 58: 1301–1328.

[13] S. Chang, 2003, Ownership structure, expropriation, and performance of group-affiliated companies in Korea, *AMJ*, 46: 238–254.

14 M. W. Peng & Y. Jiang, 2010, Institutions behind family ownership and control in large firms, *JMS*, 47: 253–273.

15 M. W. Peng, T. Buck, & I. Filatotchev, 2003, Do outside directors and new managers help improve firm performance? *JWB*, 38: 348–360.

16 W. Megginson & J. Netter, 2001, From state to market, *JEL*, 39: 321–389; R. Ramamurti, 2000, A multilevel model of privatization in emerging economies, *AMR*, 25: 525–551; P. Vaaler & B. Schrage, 2009, Residual state ownership, policy stability, and financial performance following strategic decisions by privatizing telecoms, *JIBS*, 40: 621–641.

17 M. Jensen & W. Meckling, 1976, Theory of the firm, *JFE*, 3: 305–360.

18 J. Combs & M. Skill, 2003, Managerialist and human capital explanations for key executive pay premiums, *AMJ*, 46: 63–77.

19 W. Johnson, R. Magee, N. Nagarajan, & H. Newman, 1985, An analysis of the stock price reaction to sudden executive deaths, *JAE*, 7: 151–174.

20 S. Claessens, S. Djankov, & L. Lang, 2000, The separation of ownership and control in East Asian corporations, *JFE*, 58: 81–112.

21 M. Faccio & L. Lang, 2002, The ultimate ownership of Western European corporations, *JFE*, 65: 365–395.

22 M. Young, M. W. Peng, D. Ahlstrom, G. Bruton, & Y. Jiang, 2008, Corporate governance in emerging economies, *JMS*, 45: 196–220.

23 A. Ellstrand, L. Tihanyi, & J. Johnson, 2002, Board structure and international political risk, *AMJ*, 45: 769–777.

24 D. Dalton, C. Daily, A. Ellstrand, & J. Johnson, 1998, Meta-analytic reviews of board composition, leadership structure, and financial performance, *SMJ*, 19: 269–290.

25 S. Finkelstein & A. Mooney, 2003, Not the usual suspects, *AME*, 17: 101–113.

26 T. Yoshikawa & J. McGuire, 2008, Change and continuity in Japanese corporate governance, *APJM*, 25: 5–24.

27 M. W. Peng, Y. Li, E. Xie, & Z. Su, 2010, CEO duality, organizational slack, and firm performance in China, *APJM* (in press).

28 J. Westphal & I. Stern, 2007, Flattery will get you everywhere, *AMJ*, 50: 267–288.

29 J. Westphal & P. Khanna, 2004, Keeping directors in line, *ASQ*, 48: 361–399.

30 Y. Kor & V. Misangyi, 2008, Outside directors' industry-specific experience and firms' liability of newness, *SMJ*, 29: 1345–1355; M. McDonald, J. Westphal, & M. Graebner, 2008, What do they know? *SMJ*, 29: 1155–1177.

31 M. W. Peng, 2004, Outside directors and firm performance during institutional transitions, *SMJ*, 25: 453–471.

32 A. Bruce, T. Buck, & B. Main, 2005, Top executive remuneration, *JMS*, 42: 1493–1506; C. Cadsby, F. Song, & F. Tapon, 2007, Sorting and incentive effects of pay for performance, *AMJ*, 50: 387–405; M. Makri, P. Lane, & L. Gomez-Mejia, 2006, CEO incentives, innovation, and performance in technology-intensive firms, *SMJ*, 27: 1057–1080; P. Wright, M. Kroll, J. Krug, & M. Pettus, 2007, Influences of top management team incentives on firm risk taking, *SMJ*, 28: 81–89.

33 C. Devers, R. Wiseman, & R. M. Holmes, 2007, The effects of endowment and loss aversion in managerial stock option valuation, *AMJ*, 50: 191–208; M. Goranova, T. Alessandri, P. Brandes, & R. Dharwadkar, 2007, Managerial ownership and corporate diversification, *SMJ*, 28: 211–225; J. O'Conner, R. Priem, J. Coombs, & K. M. Gilley, 2006, Do CEO stock options prevent or promote fraudulent financial reporting? *AMJ*, 49: 483–500.

34 L. Bebchuk & J. Fried, 2004, *Pay without Performance*, Cambridge, MA: Harvard University Press.

35 W. Shen & T. Cho, 2005, Exploring involuntary executive turnover through a managerial discretion framework, *AMR*, 30: 843–854; Y. Zhang & M. Wiersema, 2009, Stock market reaction to CEO certification, *SMJ*, 30: 693–710.

36 G. Andrade, M. Mitchell, & E. Stafford, 2001, New evidence and perspective on mergers, *JEP*, 15: 103–120; R. Masulis, C. Wang, & F. Xie, 2007, Corporate governance and acquirer returns, *JF*, 62: 1851–1889.

37 P. Phan & C. Hill, 1995, Organizational restructuring and economic performance in leveraged buyouts, *AMJ*, 38: 704–739.

38 M. Jensen, 1993, The modern industrial revolution, exit, and failure of internal control systems, *JF*, 48: 831–880.

39 P. Fiss & E. Zajac, 2004, The diffusion of ideas over contested terrain, *ASQ*, 49: 501–534; W. Schneper & M. Guillen, 2004, Stakeholder rights and corporate governance, *ASQ*, 49: 263–295.

40 A. Tuschke & W. G. Sanders, 2003, Antecedents and consequences of corporate governance reform, *SMJ*, 24: 631–649.

41 T. Buck, 2003, Modern Russian corporate governance, *JWB*, 38: 299–313; D. McCarthy & S. Puffer, 2003, Corporate governance in Russia, *JWB*, 38: 397–415.

42 E. Gedajlovic & D. Shapiro, 1998, Management and ownership effects (p. 536), *SMJ*, 19: 533–553.

43 C. Kwok & S. Tadesse, 2006, National culture and financial systems, *JIBS*, 37: 227–247; J. Siegel, 2009, Is there a better commitment mechanism than cross-listings for emerging-economy firms? *JIBS*, 40: 1171–1191.

44 L. Capron & M. Guillen, 2009, National corporate governance institutions and post-acquisition target reorganization, *SMJ*, 30: 803–833; L. Purda, 2008, Risk perception and the financial system, *JIBS*, 39: 1178–1196.

45 R. La Porta, F. Lopez-de-Silanes, A. Shleifer, & R. Vishny, 1998, Law and finance, *JPE*, 106: 1113–1155.

46 T. Buck & A. Shahrim, 2005, The translation of corporate governance changes across national cultures, *JIBS*, 36: 42–61.

47 R. Rajan & L. Zingales, 2003, The great reversals, *JFE*, 69: 5–50.

48 P. David, T. Yoshikawa, M. Chari, & A. Rasheed, 2006, Strategic investments in Japanese corporations, *SMJ*, 27: 591–600; L. Oxelheim & T. Randoy, 2005, The Anglo-American financial minfluence on CEO compensation in non-Anglo-American firms, *JIBS*, 36: 470–483.

49 R. Aguilera & A. Cuervo-Cazurra, 2004, Codes of good governance worldwide, *OSt*, 25: 415–443.

50 OECD, 2003, *Experiences from the Regional Corporate Governance Roundtables* (p. 23), Paris: OECD.

[51] C. Doidge, A. Karolyi, & R. Stulz, 2004, Why are foreign firms listed in the US worth more? *JFE*, 71: 205–238.

[52] *The Economist*, 2007, Down on the street (p. 70), November 25: 69–71.

[53] M. W. Peng & Y. Luo, 2000, Managerial ties and firm performance in a transition economy, *AMJ*, 43: 486-501. See also C. Collins & K. Clark, 2003, Strategic human resource practices, top management team social networks, and firm performance, *AMJ*, 46: 740–751; A. Mackey, 2008, The effects of CEOs on firm performance, *SMJ*, 29: 1357–1367.

[54] Z. Simsek, 2007, CEO tenure and organizational performance, *SMJ*, 28: 653–662.

[55] L. Donaldson, 1995, *American Anti-management Theories of Management*, Cambridge, UK: Cambridge University Press.

[56] J. Davis, F. D. Schoorman, & L. Donaldson, 1997, Toward a stewardship theory of management, *AMR*, 22: 20–47.

[57] S. Ghoshal & P. Moran, 1996, Bad for practice, *AMR*, 21: 31–47.

[58] P. Witt, 2004, The competition of international corporate governance systems, *MIR*, 44: 309–333.

[59] C. Doidge, G. A. Karolyi, K. Lins, D. Miller, & R. Stulz, 2009, Private benefits of control, ownership, and the cross-listing decision, *JF*, 69: 425–466.

[60] T. Yoshikawa & E. Gedajlovic, 2002, The impact of global capital market exposure and stable ownership on investor relations practices and performance of Japanese firms, *APJM*, 19: 525–540.

[61] R. Aguilera & G. Jackson, 2003, The cross-national diversity of corporate governance, *AMR*, 28: 447–465.

[62] G. Davis & C. Marquis, 2003, The globalization of stock markets and convergence in corporate governance, in R. Swedberg (eds.), *Economic Sociology of Capitalist Institutions*, Cambridge, UK: Cambridge University Press.

[63] J. Siegel, 2005, Can foreign firms bond themselves effectively by renting US securities laws? *JFE*, 75: 319–359.

[64] G. Davis, 2009, The rise and fall of finance and the end of the society of organizations, *AMP*, August: 27–44.

[65] T. Yoshikawa, L. Tsui-Auch, & J. McGuire, 2007, Corporate governance reform as institutional innovation, *OSc*, 18: 973–988.

[66] T. Khanna & K. Palepu, 2004, Globalization and convergence in corporate governance, *JIBS*, 35: 484–507.

Chapter 17

LEARNING OBJECTIVES

After studying this chapter, you should be able to:

1. articulate a stakeholder view of the firm.

2. apply the institution-based and resource-based views to analyze corporate social responsibility.

3. participate in three leading debates on corporate social responsibility.

4. draw implications for action.

© Mark Blinch/Reuters/Landov

Managing Corporate Social Responsibility Globally

O P E N I N G   C A S E

Which Side Is Toyota On?

Toyota has carefully crafted its "green" image, substantiated by its market-leading Prius hybrid model first unleashed in 1997. Unfortunately, Toyota has recently become a target for environmental groups, its usual allies. A new coalition of environmental groups simply named itself Truth About Toyota and dedicated itself to naming and shaming Toyota's alleged hypocrisy. Some of the unflattering pieces this group wrote included: (1) Stuck in some green mud, (2) Toyota: Moving backward, and (3) Toyota's betrayal.

So, what happened? In the eyes of some environmentalists, Toyota betrayed them by joining the "bad boys"—General Motors (GM), Ford, and Chrysler—to lobby against efforts in the US Congress to aggressively increase fuel economy standards, known as the corporate average fuel economy (CAFE) regulations. Supporters for tougher CAFE regulations wanted to pass legislation that would mandate an average of 35 miles per gallon for *both* cars and light trucks by 2020—up from 27.5 miles per gallon for cars and 22.2 for light trucks (including minivans and sports utility vehicles [SUVs]) in 2007. Toyota and its allies supported an alternative, less progressive proposal that would set the CAFE levels at 35 miles per gallon for cars and 32 for light trucks by 2022. Toyota's decision to support the less aggressive increase of fuel efficiency was most likely driven by its recent introduction of fuel-thirsty trucks, especially its giant Tundra pickup.

In response to Toyota's alleged "betrayal," outraged Prius owners in several US cities staged protests against Toyota. In a public letter to Toyota, nine US environmental leaders wrote on October 11, 2007:

> Toyota Motor Corporation's efforts to lobby Congress to weaken, delay, or eliminate the bipartisan Senate measure stands in marked contrast to its public statements and its marketing to consumers. Furthermore, it appears that Toyota is applying a double standard when the company simultaneously complied with strict Japanese fuel economy standards yet lobbies members of the US House and Senate against more modest improvements here in the United States. . . . As the world's leading automaker and a leader in advanced vehicle technology, Toyota should be setting the industry standard, not stooping to the lowest common denominator.

In Toyota's defense, a *Wall Street Journal* article opined: "The profitless Prius wouldn't exist if not for the nonhybrids that keep Toyota in business . . . [Toyota's position] would let automakers continue to make big vehicles that happen to be the ones Americans, with their dollars, show they actually want."

In the end, Toyota and its allies lost. On December 6, 2007, the Energy Independence and Security Act was passed, calling for a 35 miles per gallon CAFE level for *both* cars and light trucks by 2020. On January 13, 2008, Toyota's president Katsuaki Watanabe gave a speech at a Detroit auto show:

> Last month, the US Congress agreed on an energy bill calling for a 35-mpg CAFE by 2020. Toyota strongly supports this long, overdue legislation. However, as always, we will not wait until the deadline to comply. I have issued a challenge to our engineers to meet the new standard well in advance of 2020. I believe it can be done, it should be done, and Toyota is capable of doing it.

After Toyota and its allies lost the CAFE battle, it soon found itself engulfed in the debate on climate change and greenhouse gases (see the Closing Case). Toyota is a member of the US Chamber of Commerce, which lobbied against the "cap and trade" legislation because proposed offsets to pay for carbon emissions would allegedly be a massive tax hurting US firms. Toyota was consequently criticized by environmentalists. In response, Toyota issued the following statement:

> Toyota is a member of a wide array of groups, but none has our full proxy. Our association with any one of them [such as the US Chamber of Commerce] does not signify that we agree with all of their policies. It means that we are there to have a dialogue and engage in making good public policy. Toyota speaks for itself and has its own position on mitigating climate change, backed up by a strong track record of reducing greenhouse gas emissions. . . . As the record shows, Toyota has long supported global economy-wide reduction of greenhouse gases, and we are committed to working cooperatively with the US and other governments to achieve these reductions in every market where we operate.

Overall, such controversies did not stop Toyota from dethroning GM in 2008 to become the world's largest automaker by sales. By 2009, Prius's worldwide cumulative sales reached 1.5 million, more than half of which were sold in the United States. Among the 38 Toyota, Lexus, and Scion models available in the United States, Prius is now the third most popular model—only behind Camry and Corolla.

Sources: Based on (1) H. Jenkins, 2007, Cheap shot at Toyota, *Wall Street Journal*, October 24, online.wsj.com; (2) S. Nadel et al., 2007, Letter to Shigeru Hayakawa, Chairman and CEO, Toyota Motor North America, October 11, www.truthabouttoyota.com; (3) Toyota, 2008, Remarks by Katsuaki Watanbe at Toyota International Media Reception, 2008 NAIAS Detroit, January 13, pressroom.toyota.com; (4) Toyota, 2009, Toyota retail sales, December 1, pressroom.toyota.com; (5) Toyota, 2009, Toyota supports economy-wide reductions of greenhouse gases, October 22, pressroom.toyota.com.

Although Toyota is widely regarded as a leading "green" automaker, the Opening Case raises two crucial questions: Can a firm ever be socially responsible enough? When a firm pursues a social mission, is it setting itself up to be a target? Obviously these questions have no easy answers. This chapter helps answer these and other questions concerning **corporate social responsibility (CSR)**, which refers to "consideration of, and response to, issues beyond the narrow economic, technical, and legal requirements of the firm to accomplish social benefits along with the traditional economic gains which the firm seeks."[1] Historically CSR issues have been on the back burner for managers, but these issues are increasingly being brought to the forefront of corporate agendas.[2] Although this chapter is positioned as the last in this book, by no means do we suggest that CSR is the least important topic. Instead, we believe that this chapter is one of the best ways to *integrate* all previous chapters concerning international trade, investment, strategy, and human resources.[3] The comprehensive nature of CSR is evident in our Opening Case on Toyota.

At the heart of CSR is the concept of the **stakeholder**, which is "any group or individual who can affect or is affected by the achievement of the organization's objectives."[4] Shown in Figure 17.1, shareholders are important but are not the only group of stakeholders; others include managers, nonmanagerial employees

Corporate social responsibility (CSR)

Consideration of, and response to, issues beyond the narrow economic, technical, and legal requirements of the firm to accomplish social benefits along with the traditional economic gains which the firm seeks.

Stakeholder

Any group or individual who can affect or is affected by the achievement of the organization's objectives.

FIGURE 17.1   A STAKEHOLDER VIEW OF THE FIRM

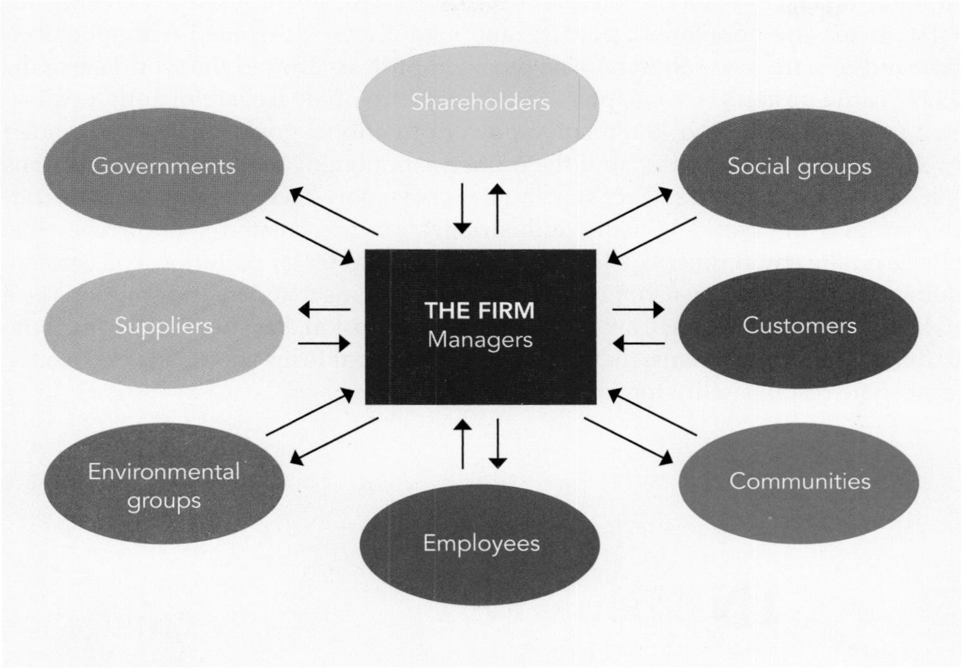

Source: Adapted from T. Donaldson & L. Preston, 1995, The stakeholder theory of the corporation: Concepts, evidence, and implications (p. 69), *Academy of Management Review*, 20: 65–91.

(hereafter "employees"), suppliers, customers, communities, governments, and social and environmental groups. Since Chapter 16 has dealt with shareholders at length, this chapter focuses on *nonshareholder stakeholders*, which we will call "stakeholders" here for simplicity. A leading debate on CSR is whether managers' efforts to promote the interests of these other stakeholders are at odds with their fiduciary duty to safeguard shareholder interests.[5] To the extent that firms are *not* social agencies and that their primary function is to serve as economic enterprises, it is certainly true that firms should not (and are not able to) take on all the social problems of the world. However, failing to heed certain CSR imperatives may be self-defeating in the long run. Therefore, the key is how to prioritize.

The remainder of this chapter first introduces a stakeholder view of the firm. Next we discuss how the institution-based and resource-based views inform the CSR discussion. We will then consider three debates on CSR in both domestic and overseas contexts. Finally, we will consider how savvy managers can best manage CSR issues.

A STAKEHOLDER VIEW OF THE FIRM

A Big Picture Perspective

A stakeholder view of the firm, with a quest for global sustainability, represents a "big picture." A key goal for CSR is **global sustainability**, which is defined as the ability "to meet the needs of the present without compromising the ability

Articulate a stakeholder view of the firm.

LEARNING OBJECTIVE

1

Global sustainability
The ability to meet the needs of the present without compromising the ability of future generations to meet their needs around the world.

of future generations to meet their needs."[6] It refers not only to a sustainable social and natural environment, but also sustainable capitalism.[7] Globally, the urgency of sustainability in the 21st century is driven by at least three concerns. First, increasing population, poverty, and inequity are associated with globalization and require new solutions. The repeated protests around the world since the 1999 Seattle protests (see Chapter 1) are but the tip of the iceberg of antiglobalization sentiments. Second, the relative power of national governments has eroded in the wake of globalization, but the influence of nongovernmental organizations (NGOs) and other civil society stakeholders have now become increasingly assertive around the world.[8] Finally, industrialization has created some irreversible effects on the environment.[9] Global warming, air and water pollution, soil erosion, deforestation, and over-fishing have become problems that demand solutions (see In Focus 17.1, the Closing Case, and PengAtlas Map 4.5). Because firms contribute to many of these problems, many citizens believe that firms should also take on at least some responsibility for solving them.

Salmon: Chicken of the Sea

There is an explosion of global supply of salmon recently. This rising supply is not due to any increase of wild salmon catch, which has been in steady decline for decades—thanks to dams, pollution, and over-fishing. As the wild Atlantic salmon disappear (wild Pacific salmon are still relatively safe), salmon farming (aquaculture) has been on the rise.

Starting in Norway as a cottage industry in the late 1960s, salmon farming quickly spread to Britain, Canada, Ireland, and Iceland in the 1970s, the United States in the 1980s, and Chile in the 1990s. Farm-raised salmon live in sea cages. They are fed pellets to speed their growth (twice as fast as in the wild), pigments to mimic the pink wild salmon flesh, and pesticides to kill the lice that go hand-in-hand with an industrial feedlot. Atlantic salmon farming (still dominated by Norwegian firms and followed by Chilean companies) has exploded into a $2 billion a year global business that produces approximately 700,000 tons of fish annually. In comparison, wild salmon catch in the Atlantic (only allowed by Britain and Ireland) is only 3,000 tons a year. In essence, it is Atlantic salmon farming companies that have brought you all the delicious and nutritious salmon, which has been transformed from a rare, expensive seasonal delicacy to a common chicken of the sea

to be enjoyed by everyone year-round. In addition, Atlantic salmon farming has brought undeniable benefits, such as taking commercial fishing pressure off wild salmon stocks and providing employment to depressed maritime regions. For example, in economically depressed western Scotland, salmon aquaculture employs approximately 6,000 workers.

But here is the catch: farm-raised salmon have (1) fouled the nearby sea, (2) spread diseases and sea lice, and (3) led to a large number of escaped fish. Each of these problems has become a growing controversy. First, heavy concentration of fish in a tiny area—up to 800,000 in one floating cage—leads to food and fecal waste that promotes toxic algae blooms, which, in turn, have led to closure of shellfishing in nearby waters. Second, sea lice outbreaks at fish farms in Ireland, Norway, and Scotland have had devastating effects on wild salmon and other fish. In Cobscook Bay, the aquaculture center of Maine, 2.1 million tainted fish had to be slaughtered recently. The third and probably most serious problem lies in escaped salmon. Many salmon have escaped whenever seals chewed through pens, storms demolished cages, or fish were spilled during handling. Research has found that escaped salmon interbreed with wild salmon. In Norwegian rivers that are salmon spawning grounds, 10% to 35% of the "wild" fish are found to be escaped salmon.

Wild salmon are an amazing species, genetically programmed to be able to find their spawning grounds in rivers after years of wandering in the sea. Although at present, only one egg out of every 4,000 is likely to complete such an epic journey, salmon has been a magic fish in the legends of Iceland, Ireland, Norway, and Scotland. These legends are threatened by the escaped farm-raised salmon and the hybrid they produce with wild salmon, because genetically homogenous salmon, descended from aquaculture fish, are ill suited to find these rivers and could also leave the species less able to cope with threats such as disease and climate change. In short, the biodiversity of the wild salmon stocks, already at dangerously low levels, is threatened by fish farming. Defenders of fish farming, however, argue that *all* farming alters, and sometimes damages, the environment. If modern agriculture featuring pesticides, fertilizers, and growth hormones were invented today, it probably would be banned. They argue that there is no reason that the emerging aquaculture industry needs to be held by higher standards. What do *you* think?

Sources: Based on (1) *BusinessWeek*, 2006, Fished out, September 4: 56–64; (2) *Economist*, 2003, A new way to feed the world, August 9: 9; (3) *Economist*, 2003, The promise of a blue revolution, August 9: 19–21; (4) F. Montaigne, 2003, Everybody loves Atlantic Salmon: Here's the catch, *National Geographic*, 204 (1): 100–123.

Drivers underpinning global sustainability are complex and multidimensional. For multinational enterprises (MNEs) with operations spanning the globe, their CSR areas, shown in Table 17.1, seem mind-boggling. This bewilderingly complex "big picture" forces managers to *prioritize*.[10] To be able to do that, primary and secondary stakeholders must be identified.[11]

Primary and Secondary Stakeholder Groups

Primary stakeholder groups are constituents on which the firm relies for its continuous survival and prosperity. Primary stakeholders typically refer to shareholders, managers, employees, suppliers, customers, and governments and communities whose laws and regulations must be obeyed and to whom taxes and other obligations may be due.

Secondary stakeholder groups are defined as "those who influence or affect, or are influenced or affected by, the corporation, but they are not engaged in transactions with the corporation and are not essential for its survival."[12] Examples include environmental groups (such as Greenpeace) and labor practice groups (such as the Fair Labor Association). Although firms do not depend on secondary stakeholder groups for survival, such groups may have the potential to cause significant embarrassment and damage. Think of Nike in the 1990s.

A key proposition of the stakeholder view is that firms should not simply pursue the economic bottom line (such as profits and shareholder returns). Instead, firms should pursue a more balanced set of criteria called the **triple bottom line**—*economic, social,* and *environmental* performance measures that simultaneously satisfy the demands of all stakeholder groups. To the extent that some competing demands obviously exist, it seems evident that the CSR proposition represents a dilemma. In fact, it has provoked a fundamental debate, which is introduced next.

The Fundamental Debate on CSR

The CSR debate centers on the nature of the firm in society. Why does the firm exist? Most people would intuitively answer: "To make money." Milton Friedman was a former University of Chicago economist and a Nobel laureate who passed

Primary stakeholder groups
Constituents on which the firm relies for its continuous survival and prosperity.

Secondary stakeholder groups
Those who influence or affect, or are influenced or affected by, the corporation but are not engaged in transactions with the firm and are not essential for its survival.

Triple bottom line
Economic, social, and environmental performance that simultaneously satisfies the demands of all stakeholder groups.

TABLE 17.1   CORPORATE SOCIAL RESPONSIBILITIES FOR MULTINATIONAL ENTERPRISES (MNEs) RECOMMENDED BY INTERNATIONAL ORGANIZATIONS

MNEs and Host Governments

- Should not interfere in the internal political affairs of the host country (OECD, UN)
- Should consult governmental authorities and national employers' and workers' organizations to ensure that their investments conform to the economic and social development policies of the host country (ICC, ILO, OECD, UN)
- Should reinvest some profits in the host country (ICC)

MNEs and Laws, Regulations, and Politics

- Should respect the right of every country to exercise control over its natural resources (UN)
- Should refrain from improper or illegal involvement in local politics (OECD)
- Should not pay bribes or render improper benefits to public servants (OECD, UN)

MNEs and Technology Transfer

- Should develop and adapt technologies to the needs of host countries (ICC, ILO, OECD)
- Should provide reasonable terms and conditions when granting licenses for industrial property rights (ICC, OECD)

MNEs and Environmental Protection

- Should respect the host country laws and regulations concerning environmental protection (OECD, UN)
- Should supply host governments with information concerning the environmental impact of MNE activities (ICC, UN)

MNEs and Consumer Protection

- Should preserve the safety and health of consumers by disclosing appropriate information, labeling correctly, and advertising accurately (UN)

MNEs and Employment Practices

- Should cooperate with host governments to create jobs in certain locations (ICC)
- Should give advance notice of plant closures and mitigate the adverse effects (ICC, OECD)
- Should respect the rights for employees to engage in collective bargaining (ILO, OECD)

MNEs and Human Rights

- Should respect human rights and fundamental freedoms in host countries (UN)

Sources: Based on (1) ICC: The International Chamber of Commerce Guidelines for International Investment (www.iccwbo.org); (2) ILO: The International Labor Office Tripartite Declarations of Principles Concerning Multinational Enterprises and Social Policy (www.ilo.org); (3) OECD: The Organizations for Economic Cooperation and Development Guidelines for Multinational Enterprises (www.oecd.org); (4) UN: The United Nations Code of Conduct on Transnational Corporations (www.un.org).

away in 2006. In an influential article published in 1970, he eloquently argued: "The business of business is business."[13] The idea that the firm is an economic enterprise seems to be uncontroversial. At issue is whether the firm is *only* an economic enterprise.

One side of the debate argues that "the social responsibility of business is to increase its profits." In fact, that is the title of Friedman's article quoted above. The free market school of thought goes back to Adam Smith's idea that pursuit of economic self-interest (within legal and ethical bounds) leads to efficient markets. Free market advocates such as Friedman believe that the firm's first and foremost stakeholder group are the shareholders, and managers have a fiduciary duty (required by law) to look after shareholders' interests. To the extent that the hallmark of our economic system remains capitalism, the providers of capital—namely, capitalists or shareholders—deserve a commanding height in managerial attention. In fact, since the 1980s, *shareholder capitalism* explicitly places shareholders as the single most important stakeholder group and has become increasingly influential (see Chapter 16) around the world.

Free market advocates argue that if firms attempt to attain social goals, such as providing employment and social welfare, managers will lose their focus on profit maximization (and its derivative, shareholder value maximization).[14] Consequently, firms may lose their character as capitalistic enterprises and become *socialist* organizations. The idea of a socialist organization is not a pure argumentative point but is derived from accurate characterization of numerous state-owned enterprises (SOEs) throughout the pre-reform Soviet Union, Central and Eastern Europe, and China as well as other developing countries in Africa, Asia, and Latin America. Privatization, in essence, is to remove the social function of these firms and restore their economic focus through private ownership. Overall, the free market school has also provided much of the intellectual underpinning for privatization around the world.

It is against such a formidable and influential school of thought that the CSR movement has emerged. A free market system is, in theory, constrained by rules, contracts, and property rights. But CSR advocates argue that a free market system that takes the pursuit of self-interest and profit as its guiding light may in practice fail to constrain itself, thus often breeding greed and excesses.[15] The financial meltdown in 2008–2009 is often fingered as a case in point. Although not denying that shareholders are important stakeholders, CSR advocates argue that all stakeholders have an *equal* right to bargain for a fair deal.[16] Given stakeholders' often conflicting demands, a very thorny issue in the debate is whether all stakeholders indeed have an equal right and how to manage their (sometimes inevitable) conflicts.

Starting in the 1970s as a peripheral voice in an ocean of free market believers, the CSR school of thought has slowly but surely become a more central part of management discussions. There are two driving forces. First, even as free markets spread around the world, the gap between the haves and have-nots has *widened*. Although many emerging economies have been growing, the per capita income gap between developed economies and much of Africa, Asia (except the Four Tigers), and Latin America has widened. Although only 2% of the world's children live in the United States, they enjoy 50% of the world's toys. In contrast, one-quarter of the children in Bangladesh and Nigeria are in these two countries' workforce.[17] Even within developed economies such as the United States, the income gap between the upper and lower echelons of society has widened. In 1980, the average American CEO was paid 40 times more than the average worker. The ratio is now above 400. Although American society accepts a greater income inequality than many others do, aggregate data of such widening inequality, which both inform and numb, often serve as a stimulus for reforming a leaner and meaner capitalism. Such sentiments have become especially strong in the 2008–2009 recession. However, the response from free market advocates is that, to the extent there is competition, there will always be *both* winners and losers. What CSR critics describe as "greed" is often translated as "incentive" in the vocabulary of free market advocates.

© Golin Harris

If you had the power to create employment laws, what would you do to protect child laborers?

IN Focus 17.2

Dow Chemical Company in China

Dow Chemical Company is a leading US-based MNE that has a presence in more than 175 countries. Dow has paid considerable attention to CSR. Since 1999, Dow has advocated the Guiding Principles of Responsible Care, a voluntary initiative within the global chemical industry to safely handle its products from inception to ultimate disposal.

China naturally has become an increasingly important market for Dow. However, beyond Dow's immediate market reach, the general deterioration of the environment in China, an unfortunate byproduct of the strong economic growth, is visible and getting worse. For example, on a "sunny" day, pedestrians in Beijing have a hard time to see through the smog to actually see the sun. As a result, China's leadership is putting increasing focus on environmental sustainability as a key national policy.

Aspiring to serve as a multinational role model fully aligned with Dow's own CSR commitment and with the government's concern to reduce pollution, Dow partnered with the State Environmental Protection Administration (SEPA) of China to launch a SEPA-Dow National Cleaner Production Pilot Project in 2005. Dow agreed to contribute $750,000 over the first three years. Cleaner Production is the continuous application of an integrated preventive environmental strategy to processes, products, and services to increase efficiency and reduce risks and possible damage to humans and the environment. The Pilot Project has focused on training local environmental protection agencies and officials as well as managers at small- and medium-sized enterprises (SMEs), a category of firms in China that, on average, tend to be less professional and more reckless in environmental management.

In the Pilot Project's first year, 19 SMEs in the chemical, dyeing, electronics, brewery, and food industries participated. The Project generated a combined reduction of waste water by 3.3 million cubic meters, of exhaust gas emissions by 554 tons, and of solid waste by 487 tons. This resulted in 538 cleaner production measures and an annual economic profit of approximately $130,000 for the 19 participating firms. Overall, these achievements, in Dow's own words, "confirm Dow's belief that Cleaner Production not only reduces waste in the production processes, it also increases the efficiency of energy resources and ultimately improves competitiveness of enterprises." Further, Dow intends to diffuse such "best practices" in China and beyond.

Sources: Based on (1) *China Business Review*, 2007, Dow partners with China's SEPA, May-June: 17; (2) Dow, 2006, SEPA-Dow Cleaner Production National Pilot Project achieves strong start and outstanding results, news.dow.com; (3) M. W. Peng, 2006, Dow Chemical in America and China, in M. W. Peng, *Global Strategy* (pp. 511–512), Cincinnati: South-Western Cengage Learning.

Second, disasters and scandals also drive the CSR movement. For example, in 1984, a toxic accident at a Union Carbide plant in Bhopal, India, killed 3,000 people and injured another 300,000. In 1989, the oil tanker *Exxon Valdez* spilled 11 million gallons of oil in the pristine waters off Alaska. In the 2000s, corporate scandals at Enron, Lehman Brothers, and Satyam rocked the world. In 2008–2009, excessive amounts of Wall Street bonuses distributed by financial services firms receiving government bailout funds were criticized for being socially insensitive and irresponsible. Not surprisingly, new disasters and scandals often propel CSR to the forefront of public policy and management discussions. For example, the rise of the CSR movement in China can be directly attributed to worsening environmental problems in the country (see In Focus 17.2).

Overall, managers as a stakeholder group are unique in that they are the only group that is positioned at the center of all these relationships. It is important to understand how they make decisions concerning CSR, as illustrated next.

INSTITUTIONS, RESOURCES, AND CORPORATE SOCIAL RESPONSIBILITY

LEARNING OBJECTIVE 2

Apply the institution-based and resource-based views to analyze corporate social responsibility.

Although some people do not consider CSR an integral part of global business, Figure 17.2 shows that the institution-based and resource-based views can inform the CSR discussion with relatively little adaptation. This section articulates why this is the case.

Institutions and CSR

The institution-based view sheds considerable light on the gradual diffusion of the CSR movement and the strategic responses of firms.[18] At the most fundamental level, regulatory pressures underpin *formal* institutions, whereas normative and cognitive pressures support *informal* institutions. The strategic response framework consists of (1) reactive, (2) defensive, (3) accommodative, and (4) proactive

---

FIGURE 17.2   INSTITUTIONS, RESOURCES, AND CORPORATE SOCIAL RESPONSIBILITY

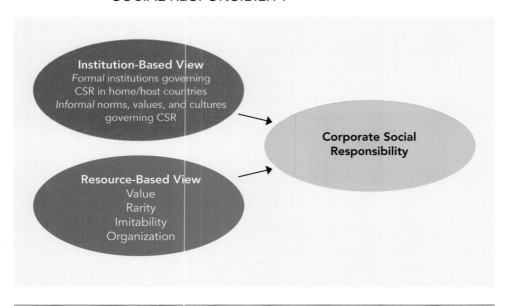

strategies, as first introduced in Chapter 3 (see Table 3.5). This framework can be extended to explore how firms make CSR decisions, as illustrated in Table 17.2.

A **reactive strategy** is indicated by relatively little or no support by top management of CSR causes. Firms do not feel compelled to act in the absence of disasters and outcries. Even when problems arise, denial is usually the first line of defense. Put another way, the need to accept some CSR is neither internalized through cognitive beliefs nor does it result in any norms in practice. That leaves only formal regulatory pressures to compel firms to comply. For example, in the United States, food and drug safety standards that we take for granted today were fought by food and drug companies in the early half of the 20th century. The basic idea that food and drugs should be tested before being sold to customers and patients was bitterly contested even as unsafe foods and drugs killed thousands of people. As a result, the Food and Drug Administration (FDA) was progressively granted more powers. This era is not necessarily over. Today, many dietary-supplement makers, whose products are beyond the FDA's regulatory reach, continue to sell untested supplements and deny responsibility.[19]

A **defensive strategy** focuses on regulatory compliance. Top management involvement is piecemeal at best, and the general attitude is that CSR is an added cost or nuisance. Firms admit responsibility but often fight it. After the establishment of the Environmental Protection Agency (EPA) in 1970, the US chemical industry resisted its intrusion (see Table 17.2). The regulatory requirements were at significant odds with the norms and cognitive beliefs held by the industry at that time.

How do various institutional pressures change firm behavior? In the absence of informal normative and cognitive beliefs, formal regulatory pressures are the only feasible way to push firms ahead. A key insight of the institution-based view is that individuals and organizations make *rational* choices given the right kind of incentives. For example, one efficient way to control pollution is to make polluters pay some "green" taxes. These can range from gasoline retail taxes to landfill charges on waste disposal. Yet controversy remains over how demanding these regulatory pressures should be. One side of the debate argues that tough environmental

Reactive strategy

A strategy that would only respond to CSR causes when required by disasters and outcries.

Defensive strategy

A strategy that focuses on regulatory compliance but with little actual commitment to CSR by top management.

TABLE 17.2   THE US CHEMICAL INDUSTRY RESPONDS TO ENVIRONMENTAL PRESSURES

Phase	Primary strategy	Representative statements from the industry's trade journal, *Chemical Week*
1. 1962–1970	Reactive	Denied the severity of environmental problems and argued that these problems could be solved independently through the industry's technological prowess.
2. 1971–1982	Defensive	"Congress seems determined to add one more regulation to the already 27 health and safety regulations we must answer to. This will make EPA [Environmental Protection Agency] a chemical czar. No agency in a democracy should have that authority" (1975).
3. 1983–1988	Accommodative	"EPA has been criticized for going too slow . . . Still, we think that it is doing a good job" (1982). "Critics expect overnight fix. EPA deserves credit for its pace and accomplishments" (1982).
4. 1989–present	Proactive	"Green line equals bottom line—The Clean Air Act (CAA) equals efficiency. Everything you hear about the 'costs' of complying with CAA is probably wrong . . . Wiser competitors will rush to exploit the Green Revolution" (1990).

Sources: Adapted from A. Hoffman, 1999, Institutional evolution and change: Environmentalism and the US chemical industry, *Academy of Management Journal*, 42: 351–371 for the phases and statements. Hoffman's last phase ended in 1993; its extension to the present is done by the present author.

regulations may lead to higher costs and reduced competitiveness, especially when competing with foreign rivals not subject to such demanding regulations. In short, there is no "free environmental lunch." This is the heart of the debate on climate change (see the Closing Case). However, CSR advocates, endorsed by former vice president Al Gore and strategy guru Michael Porter, argue that stringent environmental regulation may force firms to innovate, however reluctantly, thus benefiting the competitiveness of both the industry and country.[20]

The accommodative strategy is characterized by some support from top managers, who may increasingly view CSR as a worthwhile endeavor. Since formal regulations may be in place and informal social and environmental pressures may be increasing, a number of firms themselves may be concerned about CSR, leading to the emergence of some new industry norms. Further, new managers who are passionate about or sympathetic toward CSR causes may join the organization, or some traditional managers may change their outlook, leading to increasingly strong cognitive beliefs that CSR is the right thing to do. In other words, from both normative and cognitive standpoints, it becomes legitimate or a matter of social obligation to accept responsibility and do all that is required.[21] For example, in the US chemical industry, such a transformation probably took place in the early 1980s (see Table 17.2).

Adopting a code of conduct is a tangible indication of a firm's willingness to accept CSR. A code of conduct (sometimes called a code of ethics) is a set of written policies and standards outlining the proper practices for a firm or organization. The global diffusion of codes of conduct is subject to intense debate. First, some argue that firms may not necessarily be sincere. This *negative* view suggests that an apparent interest in CSR may simply be window dressing.[22] Some firms feel compelled to appear sensitive to CSR, following what others are doing, but have not truly and genuinely internalized CSR concerns. Second, an *instrumental* view suggests that CSR activities simply represent a useful instrument to make good profits.[23] Firms are not necessarily becoming more ethical. Finally, a *positive* view believes that (at least some) firms may be self-motivated to do it right regardless of social pressures. Codes of conduct tangibly express values that organizational members view as central and enduring.[24]

The institution-based view suggests that all three perspectives are probably valid. This is to be expected given how institutional pressures work to instill value. Regardless of actual motive, the fact that firms are practicing CSR is encouraging, indicative of the rising *legitimacy* of CSR on the management agenda. Even firms that adopt a code of conduct simply for window dressing purposes open doors for more scrutiny by concerned stakeholders, because these firms have publicized a set of CSR criteria against which they can be judged (see the Opening Case). Such pressures are likely to transform these firms into more self-motivated, better corporate citizens. For example, it probably is fair to say that Nike is a more responsible corporate citizen in 2010 than it was in 1990.

From a CSR perspective, the best firms take a proactive strategy when engaging in CSR, constantly anticipating responsibility and endeavoring to do more than is required. Top management at a proactive firm not only supports and champions CSR activities, but also views CSR as a source of differentiation.[25] In 2007, Marks & Spencer (M&S), a leading UK retailer, launched Plan A—an ambitious corporate-wide CSR plan with 100 concrete commitments that it aspired to achieve by 2012. The goals included becoming carbon neutral for all its UK and Irish stores and sending no waste to landfill. In Plan A's first year, M&S reduced energy-related CO_2 emissions from its stores and offices by 55,000 tons and reduced its use of plastic shopping bags by 11% (that is, a total of 37 million fewer bags given out). The reduction of plastic bags was accomplished by charging 5 pence (US$0.10) for

Accommodative strategy
A strategy characterized by some support from top managers, who may increasingly view CSR as a worthwhile endeavor.

Proactive strategy
A strategy that endeavors to do more than is required in CSR.

each plastic bag. M&S argued that plastic bags are not "free"—derived from petroleum products, plastic bags cost energy to produce and will be stuck in landfills forever because they are not biodegradable. Leading the global retail sector in the Dow Jones Sustainability Index, M&S has earned a number of kudos from CSR groups.

Proactive firms often engage in three areas of activity. First, like Toyota, they actively participate in regional, national, and international policy discussions (see the Opening Case and In Focus 17.3). To the extent that policy discussions today may become regulations in the future, it seems better to get involved early and (hopefully) steer the course toward a favorable direction. Otherwise, relatively passive firms are likely to see regulations to which they have little input being imposed on them.[26] In short, "if you're not at the table, you're on the menu."[27]

Second, proactive firms often build alliances with stakeholder groups.[28] For example, many firms collaborate with NGOs. Because of the historical tension and distrust, these "sleeping-with-the-enemy" alliances are not easy to handle. The key lies in identifying relatively short-term, manageable projects of mutual interest. For instance, UPS collaborated with the Alliance for Environmental Innovation to help packaging material suppliers reduce air pollution and energy use.

Third, proactive firms often engage in *voluntary* activities that go beyond what is required by regulations. Although examples of industry-specific self-regulation abound,[29] an area of intense global interest is the pursuit of the International Standards Organization (ISO) 14001 certification of environment management system (EMS). Headquartered in Switzerland, ISO is an influential NGO consisting of

IN Focus 17.3

Swiss Re's Climate-Smart Strategy

Founded in Zurich, Switzerland, in 1863, Swiss Re is the world's largest reinsurer operating in more than 20 countries. Reinsurance is a low-profile business, which insures the insurance companies. Although Swiss Re has been in the United States for over 100 years and was the lead insurer of the World Trade Center during 9/11 attacks, few people outside the industry knew it. In recent years, Swiss Re's quiet existence has been transformed by its strategic choice to be a vanguard in the climate change battle. This is because climate change poses significant climate-related risks in the form of floods, storms, and tsunamis. Although other industries avoid risk, Swiss Re embraces risk by offering financial services products that enable risk taking by other firms. As a result, Swiss Re has developed a special interest in understanding more about the risk associated with climate change, and played a leading role in disseminating this knowledge and enhancing public awareness. Since the 1990s, Swiss Re has placed climate change at the core of what it does, sponsoring a series of high-profile public forums, research projects, and TV documentaries. Swiss Re is obviously not totally altruistic. It has deployed its considerable expertise in climate risk modeling to develop innovative products such as weather derivatives and catastrophe bonds, in which it is the world market leader.

Sources: Based on (1) A. Hoffman, 2006, *Getting Ahead of the Curve: Corporate Strategies that Address Climate Change* (pp. 76–87), Arlington, VA: Pew Center on Global Climate Change; (2) www.swissre.com.

national standards bodies in 111 countries. Launched in 1996, the ISO 14001 EMS has become the gold standard for CSR-conscious firms.[30] Although not required by law, many MNEs, such as Ford, IBM, and Skanska, have adopted ISO 14001 standards in all their facilities worldwide. Firms such as Toyota, Siemens, and GM have demanded that their top-tier suppliers be ISO 14001 certified.

From an institutional perspective, these proactive activities are indicative of the normative and cognitive beliefs held by many managers on the importance of doing the right thing.[31] Although there is probably a certain element of window dressing and a quest for better profits, it is obvious that these efforts provide some tangible social and environmental benefits.

Resources and CSR

CSR-related resources can include *tangible* technologies and processes as well as *intangible* skills and attitudes.[32] The VRIO framework can shed considerable light on CSR.

Do CSR-related resources and capabilities add *value*? For many large firms, especially MNEs, financial, technological, and human resources can be applied toward a variety of CSR causes. For example, firms can choose to appease environmental groups by purchasing energy only from power plants utilizing green sources, such as wind-generated power. Or firms can respond to human rights groups by not doing business in or with countries accused of human rights violations. These activities can be categorized as social issue participation, which refers to a firm's participation in social causes not directly related to the management of its primary stakeholders. Research suggests that these activities may actually *reduce* shareholder value.[33] Overall, although social issue participation may create some remote social and environmental value, it does not add economic value.

In contrast, expertise, techniques, and processes associated with the direct management of primary stakeholder groups are likely to add value. For example, US companies excelling in diversity programs may gain a leg up when dealing with two primary stakeholder groups: employees and customers. By 2020, the number of Hispanics, African, Asian, and Native Americans will reportedly grow by 42 million, whereas Caucasians will rise by a mere 10 million.[34] Many companies compete on diversity via internships, scholarships, ad campaigns, and aggressive recruiting of minority candidates. Firms most sought after by minority employees and customers must have possessed some valuable resources and capabilities in the competition for the hearts and minds (and wallets) of the future.

CSR-related resources are not always *rare*. Remember that even a valuable resource is not likely to provide a significant advantage if competitors also possess it. For example, both Home Depot and Lowe's have NGOs such as the Forest Stewardship Council that certify their wood product suppliers in Brazil, Indonesia, and Malaysia use only material from renewable forests. These complex processes require strong management capabilities such as negotiating with local suppliers, undertaking internal verification, coordinating with NGOs for external verification, and disseminating such information to stakeholders. Such capabilities are valuable. But, since both competitors possess capabilities to manage these processes, they are common (but not rare) resources.

Although valuable and rare resources may provide some competitive advantage, the advantage will only be temporary if competitors can *imitate* it. Resources must be not only valuable and rare but also hard to imitate in order to give firms a sustainable (not merely temporary) competitive advantage. For example, pollution *prevention* technologies may provide firms with a significant advantage,

Social issue participation
Firms' participation in social causes not directly related to the management of primary stakeholders.

whereas pollution *reduction* technologies may offer no such advantage. This is because the relatively simple, "end-of-pipe" pollution reduction technologies can be more easily imitated. On the other hand, pollution prevention technologies are more complex, more integrated with the entire chain of production, and harder to imitate.

At some firms, CSR-related capabilities are deeply embedded in idiosyncratic managerial and employee skills and attitudes.[35] The socially complex way of channeling such energy and conviction toward CSR cannot be easily imitated. For example, the enthusiasm and energy that Starbucks devotes to CSR are very difficult to imitate. Although Starbucks may not please every NGO, it is difficult to argue that Starbucks is faking. Just consider all the expenses devoted to purchasing a large quantity of Fair Trade coffee, supporting 143 fair labor practice verifiers, and preparing its CSR annual report in six languages.

Does the firm have *organizational* capabilities to do a good job on CSR? Is the firm organized to exploit the full potential of CSR?[36] Numerous components within a firm may be relevant, such as formal management control systems and informal relationships between managers and employees. These components are often called *complementary assets* (see Chapter 4), because, by themselves, they typically do not generate advantage. However, complementary assets, when combined with valuable, rare, and hard-to-imitate capabilities, may enable a firm to fully utilize its CSR potential.

Complementary assets are not developed as part of new environmental strategies; rather, they are grown from more general business strategies (such as differentiation).[37] If such complementary assets are already in place, they can be leveraged in the new pursuit of CSR practices. Otherwise, single-minded imitation is not likely to be effective.

The resource-based view helps solve a major puzzle in the CSR debate: the CSR-economic performance puzzle. The puzzle—and a source of frustration to CSR advocates—is why there is no conclusive evidence on a direct, positive link between CSR and *economic* performance such as profits and shareholder returns.[38] Although some studies do indeed report a *positive* relationship,[39] others find a *negative* relationship[40] or *no* relationship.[41] Viewed together, "CSR does not hurt performance, but there is no concrete support to believe that it leads to supranormal returns."[42] Although there can be a number of explanations for this intriguing mess, a resource-based explanation suggests that because of capability constraints discussed above, many firms are not cut out for a CSR-intensive (differentiation) strategy. Since all studies have some sampling bias (no study is perfect), studies that over-sample firms not yet ready for a high level of CSR activities are likely to report a negative relationship between CSR and economic performance. Likewise, studies that over-sample firms ready for CSR may find a positive relationship. Also, studies with more balanced (more random) samples may fail to find any statistically significant relationship. In summary, since each firm is different (a basic assumption of the resource-based view), not every firm's economic performance is likely to benefit from CSR.

LEARNING OBJECTIVE 3

Participate in three leading debates on corporate social responsibility.

DEBATES AND EXTENSIONS

CSR has no shortage of debates. Here, we discuss three previously unexplored debates particularly relevant for international operations: (1) domestic versus overseas social responsibility, (2) race to the bottom versus race to the top, and (3) active versus inactive CSR engagement overseas.

Domestic versus Overseas Social Responsibility

Given that corporate resources are limited, resources devoted to overseas CSR often mean fewer resources devoted to domestic CSR. Consider two *primary* stakeholder groups: domestic employees and communities. Expanding overseas may not only increase corporate profits and shareholder returns, but also provide employment in host countries and develop many economies at the "base of the pyramid," all of which have noble CSR dimensions (see the Chapter 1 Closing Case and In Focus 17.2). However, this is often done at the expense of domestic employees and communities.

To the extent that few (or no) laid-off rank-and-file employees in developed economies are likely to move to emerging economies in search of work, many of the unemployed workers in developed economies could end up being social welfare recipients. Thus, one may argue that MNEs' actions shirk their CSR by increasing the social burdens of their home countries. However, from a corporate governance perspective, MNEs are doing nothing wrong by maximizing shareholder returns (see Chapter 16).

The heart of this debate boils down to a fundamental point that frustrates CSR advocates: In a capitalist society, it is shareholders (otherwise known as *capitalists*) who matter at the end of the day.[43] According to Jack Welch, GE's former chairman and CEO:

> Unions, politicians, activists—companies face a Babel of interests. But there's only one owner. A company is for its shareholders. They own it. They control it. That's the way it is, and the way it should be.[44]

When companies have enough resources, it would be nice to take care of domestic employees and communities. However, when confronted with relentless pressures for cost cutting and restructuring, managers have to prioritize.[45] Although people and countries at the base of the global pyramid welcome the migration of capital, technology, and jobs into their economies, domestic employees and communities as well as unions and politicians in developed economies frankly hate it. Given the lack of a clear solution, this debate is likely to heat up in the years to come.

Race to the Bottom ("Pollution Haven") versus Race to the Top

In global business, the "pollution haven" debate is controversial. One side argues that because of heavier environmental regulations in developed economies, MNEs may have an incentive to shift pollution-intensive production to developing countries, where environmental standards may be lower. To attract investment, developing countries may enter a "race to the bottom" by lowering (or at least not tightening) environmental standards and some may become "pollution havens."[46] The recent debate on climate change heightens this conflict, because firms in developed economies that are committed to reducing greenhouse gas emissions now may have stronger incentives to move pollution-intensive production to developing economies without such commitments (see the Closing Case).

Do you think a firm that locates its pollution-heavy manufacturing in a developing country is acting responsibly?

© Modern Landscapes/Alamy

The other side points out that many MNEs *voluntarily* adhere to environmental standards higher than those required by host countries (see In Focus 17.2).[47] In general, MNEs reportedly outperform local firms in environmental management.[48] The underlying motivations behind MNEs' voluntary "green practices" can be attributed to worldwide CSR pressures in general and CSR demands made by customers in developed economies. Although it is difficult to suggest that the "race to the bottom" does not exist, MNEs do not necessarily add to the environmental burden in host countries.

Active versus Inactive CSR Engagement Overseas

Increasingly MNEs are expected to actively engage in CSR.[49] MNEs that fail to do so are often criticized by NGOs. In the 1990s, Shell was harshly criticized for "not lifting a finger" when the Nigerian government brutally cracked down on rebels in the Ogoni region in which Shell operated. In 2009, Shell paid $15.5 million to the Ogoni people to end a long-running court battle brought by NGOs. Shell denied any wrongdoing, and pointed out the settlement was a "humanitarian gesture."[50]

However well-intentioned, calls for greater CSR engagement are in direct conflict with a long-standing principle governing the relationship between MNEs and host countries: nonintervention in local affairs (see the *first* bullet point in Table 17.1). The nonintervention principle originated from concerns that MNEs might engage in political activities against the host country. Chile in the 1970s serves as a case in point. After the democratically elected socialist President Salvador Allende had threatened to expropriate the assets of ITT (a US-based MNE) and other MNEs, ITT, in connection with the Central Intelligence Agency (CIA), allegedly promoted a coup that killed President Allende.[51] Consequently, the idea that MNEs should not interfere in the domestic political affairs of the host country has been enshrined in a number of codes of MNE conduct (see Table 17.1).

However, CSR advocates have been emboldened by some MNEs' actions during the apartheid era in South Africa, when local laws required racial segregation of the workforce. Although many MNEs withdrew, those that remained were encouraged by the Sullivan Principles to challenge, breach, and seek to dismantle the apartheid system, undermining the government's base of power. BP, for example, desegregated its employees. Emboldened by the successful removal of the apartheid regime in South Africa in 1994, CSR advocates have unleashed a new campaign that stresses the need for MNEs to engage in actions that often constitute political activity, particularly in the human rights area.

Trouble is, in almost every country, MNEs will find some local laws and norms objectionable. In Malaysia, ethnic Chinese are discriminated against by law. In Saudi Arabia, women are not allowed to drive cars. In the United States, groups ranging from Native Americans to homosexuals claim to be discriminated against. At the heart of this explosive debate is whether MNEs should spearhead efforts to remove some of these discriminatory practices or remain politically neutral by conforming to current host country laws and norms.

MANAGEMENT SAVVY

LEARNING OBJECTIVE

4

Draw implications for action.

Concerning CSR, the institution-based and resource-based views suggest three clear implications for action (see Table 17.3). First, savvy managers need to understand the formal and informal rules of the game, anticipate changes, and seek to shape such changes. Although the US government has refused to ratify the Kyoto

TABLE 17.3   IMPLICATIONS FOR ACTION

- Understand the rules of the game, anticipate changes, and seek to shape and influence such changes
- Pick your CSR battles carefully—don't blindly imitate other firms' CSR activities
- Integrate CSR as part of the core activities and processes of the firm—faking it does not last very long

Protocol and did not agree to any binding target in the Copenhagen Accord, many far-sighted US managers realize that competitors based in countries whose governments support serious efforts in greenhouse gas reduction may gain a strong "green" advantage.[52] Therefore, many US firms voluntarily participate in CSR activities not (yet) mandated by law, in anticipation of more stringent environmental requirements down the road (see the Closing Case).

Second, savvy managers need to pick CSR battles carefully. The resource-based view suggests an important lesson, which is captured by Sun Tzu's timeless teaching: "Know yourself, know your opponents." Although your opponents may engage in high-profile CSR activities that allow them to earn bragging rights while contributing to their triple bottom line, blindly imitating these practices without knowing enough about yourself as a manager and the firm/unit you lead may lead to some disappointment. Instead of always chasing the newest best practices, firms are advised to select CSR practices that fit with their *existing* resources and capabilities. In a recession, launching expensive new CSR initiatives may be inadvisable. Managers have to put profitability first and be more selective about CSR involvement. The point is simple: "You have to make money first to give it away."[53]

Third, given the increasingly inescapable responsibility to be good corporate citizens, managers may want to integrate CSR as part of the core activities and processes of the firm instead of faking it and making only cosmetic changes. For example, instead of treating NGOs as threats, Home Depot, Lowe's, and Unilever have their sourcing policies certified by NGOs. Dow Chemical has established community advisory panels in most of its locations worldwide. Many managers traditionally treated CSR as a nuisance, involving regulation, added costs, and liability. Such an attitude may underestimate potential business opportunities associated with CSR.

What determines the success and failure of firms around the world? No doubt, CSR will increasingly become an important part of the answer. The best performing firms are likely to be those that can integrate CSR activities into their core economic functions while addressing social and environmental concerns.[54] It is important to note that we live in a dangerous period of global capitalism devastated by financial meltdown, economic crisis, and climate change. In a post-Copenhagen world (see the Closing Case), managers, as a unique group of stakeholders, have an important and challenging responsibility to safeguard and advance capitalism. From a CSR standpoint, this means building more humane, more inclusive, and fairer firms that not only generate wealth and develop economies, but also respond to changing societal expectations concerning CSR around the world.[55]

CHAPTER SUMMARY

1. Articulate a stakeholder view of the firm.
   - A stakeholder view of the firm urges companies to pursue a more balanced triple bottom line, consisting of economic, social, and environmental performance.
   - Despite the fierce defense of the free market school, especially its shareholder capitalism variant, the CSR movement has now become a more central part of management discussions.

2. Apply the institution-based and resource-based views to analyze corporate social responsibility.
   - The institution-based view suggests that when confronting CSR pressures, firms may employ (1) reactive, (2) defensive, (3) accommodative, or (4) proactive strategies.
   - The resource-based view suggests that not all CSR satisfy the VRIO requirements.

3. Participate in three leading debates concerning corporate social responsibility.
   - (1) Domestic versus overseas social responsibility, (2) race to the bottom versus race to the top, and (3) active versus inactive CSR engagement overseas.

4. Draw implications for action.
   - Understand the rules of the game, anticipate changes, and seek to influence such changes.
   - Pick your CSR battles carefully—don't blindly imitate other firms' CSR activities.
   - Integrate CSR as part of the core activities and processes of the firm.

KEY TERMS

Accommodative strategy   571
Corporate social responsibility (CSR)   562
Defensive strategy   570
Global sustainability   564

Primary stakeholder groups   565
Proactive strategy   571
Reactive strategy   570
Secondary stakeholder groups   565

Social issue participation   573
Stakeholder   562
Triple bottom line   565

REVIEW QUESTIONS

1. How do you define global sustainability?

2. How do the concerns of a primary stakeholder differ from those of a secondary stakeholder?

3. What does it mean for a corporation to have a triple bottom line?

4. Using Table 17.2, summarize the four types of strategies that can be used to make CSR decisions.

5. Devise two examples: one in which a corporation's participation in a social issue adds value to the firm and one in which it decreases value in the eyes of the shareholders.

6. Using a resource-based view, explain why some firms improve their economic performance by adopting a CSR strategy, whereas others achieve either no results or damaging results.

7. Do you think "green practices" should be voluntary or mandatory for businesses?

8. In your opinion, do you think an MNE should remain politically neutral and adopt practices and laws of the host country?

9. As a manager, what are some of the considerations you would take into account before adopting any CSR-related policy?

10. Compare PengAtlas Map 4.5 with PengAtlas Map 1.1. Note which countries among the major sources of carbon emissions are developed and which are emerging economies. Developed economies have produced emissions for many years. Do you think they should now begin to curb their emissions while emerging economies remain relatively free of curbs until they can catch up with developed economies?

11. Compare PengAtlas Map. 4.5 with PengAtlas Map 1.1. Suppose your firm is located in a developed economy that is considering curbing carbon emissions, which could create problems for your firm. Would you recommend relocating operations to an emerging economy where the government is defiantly resisting any restrictions to curb such emissions? What are the pros and cons of relocation?

CRITICAL DISCUSSION QUESTIONS

1. In 1919, the landmark *Dodge v. Ford* case was brought before the Michigan State Supreme Court. The question before the court was whether Henry Ford could withhold dividends from the Dodge brothers and other shareholders of the Ford Motor Company to engage in what today would be called CSR activities. Returning a resounding "No," the court opined that "A business organization is organized and carried on primarily for the profits of the stockholders." If the court in your country were to decide on this case this year (or in 2019), what do you think would be the likely outcome?

2. *ON ETHICS:* Some argue that investing in emerging economies encourages global economic development. Others contend that moving jobs to low-cost countries not only abandons firms' domestic CSR in developed economies, but also exploits the poor in low-cost countries and destroys the environment. If you were (1) the CEO of an MNE headquartered in a developed economy moving production to a low-cost country, (2) the leader of a labor union in the home country of the MNE above, or (3) the leader of an environmental NGO in the low-cost country in which the MNE invests, how would you participate in this debate?

3. *ON ETHICS:* Hypothetically, your MNE is the largest foreign investor in Vietnam where dissidents and religious leaders are reportedly being persecuted.

As the country manager there, you understand that the MNE is being pressured by NGOs to help the oppressed groups in Vietnam. But you also understand that the host government would be upset if your firm is caught engaging in local political activities deemed inappropriate. These alleged government activities, which you personally find distasteful, are not directly related to your operations. How would you proceed?

YOUR SOURCE FOR
global business knowledge

http://globalEDGE.msu.edu

GLOBAL ACTION

1. China has been a recipient of considerable investment recently. However, little research has been conducted by the green technologies company for which you work concerning the exact nature of socially responsible technology investment. Since your firm's goal is to operate in China that promotes social responsibility, you must identify the sectors of green technology that receive the most investment. Using globalEDGE, develop a report that responds to this issue and adds to the development of your company's strategy in China. Based on your analysis, be sure to include possible new products that could be introduced in the Chinese market.

2. Microfinance is an emerging area of individualized financial investment in developing countries that is based on social responsibility principles (see In Focus 9.3). However, since it involves the investment of resources with the expectation that a profit will be made, microfinance investors tend to search for regions and portfolios that have the highest profitability. Analyze information in a global data set on globalEDGE to determine which areas of the world seem to have the most profitable microfinance activities. What conclusions can you draw from this information?

VIDEO CASES

Watch "The Importance of Follow-Through with CSR" by Andrew Kakabadse of Cranfield University, School of Management.

1. In Kakabadse's food company example, to what extent was lack of communication (from the organizations' top to bottom and bottom to top) causing a CSR problem?

2. In the food company example, to what extent was lack of penalties and incentives for CSR compliance causing a CSR problem? What would you recommend be done to deal with the problem?

3. In the food company example, to what extent was cost competition from competitors causing a CSR problem? If competitors are in different countries around the world and thus not subject to any given government regulation, what would you suggest be done for a given company to compete while demonstrating CSR for growers?

4. As Kakabadse pointed out, Africans were abusing Africans and poor families would be even poorer without child labor. Does that suggest that CSR is impossible in that situation? What about avoiding the CSR problem in Africa by shifting production to India?

Closing Case

ETHICAL DILEMMA

From Kyoto to Copenhagen: Cut Emissions or Cut Jobs?

© Doug Mills/The New York Times/Redux Pictures

Lately, the world has been hit by more droughts, more floods, more storms, and more heat waves. It seems clear that global warming and climate change caused by greenhouse gas (GHG) emissions require decisive actions to stem the trend. The scale of the problem and the uncertainty demand extraordinary ingenuity and cooperation among governments, firms, and consumers around the world. Unfortunately, since the United Nations Framework Convention on Climate Change (UNFCCC) was signed in 1992, global emissions of carbon dioxide (CO_2), the most potent GHG, have *risen* by a third.

Stimulated by UNFCCC, the Kyoto Protocol signed in 1997 was a hard-fought attempt to do something immensely difficult. Under Kyoto, developed countries pledged to cut emissions by 6% from 1990 levels by 2012. Each country is permitted to emit a certain quantity of CO_2. Governments issue emission permits to polluting firms within their borders, and such permits (essentially rights to pollute) can be bought and sold by firms worldwide. Through this carbon trading system, polluting firms in developed countries can pay someone else (at home or abroad) to cut emissions and claim credit.

Although the EU and Japan took Kyoto most seriously, the United States, which had been the world's number one emitter of GHG until recently, refused to ratify it. China (the current world champion in GHG emissions), India, and many developing countries essentially argued: "Sorry, we have to develop our economy first—and have to forget about Kyoto now." Not covering the world's top two emitting countries, Kyoto, despite noble intentions, did not seem to have any noticeable effect in achieving its goals. Since Kyoto's first commitment period would run out in 2012, the fifteenth UNFCCC conference in December 2009, popularly known as the Copenhagen Climate Conference, thus became extremely important in reaching a more effective, more inclusive, and more equitable global deal.

By the time of the Copenhagen conference, the scientific evidence about climate change became stronger. Thanks to the burning of fossil fuels, the average temperature on Earth has increased by 1°C since the Industrial Revolution. A decade after Kyoto, GHGs in the atmosphere are still increasing. Worse, they are increasing at an accelerating rate. Because GHGs stay in the atmosphere for decades (and often centuries), continuous and accelerated pumping of GHGs is likely to lead to global warming of 5°C by the end of this century, with disastrous ramifications. How dangerous is 5°C warming? To put things in perspective, this is the difference between today's climate and the last ice age's—when glaciers reached Central Europe and the northern United States. In addition to more droughts, storms, and heat waves, global warming and rising sea levels on this scale will cause the permanent flooding of a lot of low-lying coastal areas (including whole countries and major ports), famine, and possibly wars. Clearly, climate change is a global problem. No country is immune. The solution has to be global.

Although the global community convening in Copenhagen in principle agreed with the necessity to do something (the goal was to control the level of global warming to 2°C by century's end), countries strongly disagreed with what each of them needed to do. The timing was also unfortunate, because few governments would agree to major cuts on their CO_2 emissions when their countries had not recovered from the 2008–2009 crisis and the number of unemployed remained high.

Since there is no "free environmental lunch," the debate boils down to who is going to pay most of the cost to combat climate change. Although developed countries have been pumping more GHGs into the atmosphere on a per capita and cumulative basis, 1.6 billion people in the developing world still suffer from poverty and lack access to electricity, which will most likely be generated by old-tech, high-carbon technologies. The World Bank in the *World Development Report 2010*, released before the Copenhagen conference, urged developed countries to take aggressive action to reduce their own emissions, which "would free some 'pollution space' for developing countries, but more importantly, it would stimulate innovation and the demand for new technologies so they can be rapidly scaled up."

A crucial bone of contention is coal-fired power plants. Relative to oil, gas, nuclear, wind, solar, and biofuel sources, coal is not only the cheapest and the dirtiest, but also the most widely used energy source in Australia, China, Germany, India, and the United States. Displacing a third of power generation from coal in the United States by 2015 will put 1.2 million Americans out of work, and displacing two-thirds will result in 2.7 million lost jobs. Of course, the new wind, solar, and biofuel industries generate new jobs. However, these new sources of energy are so expensive that for now, they stand little chance in the absence of subsidies, and the jobs they create are far fewer than the jobs that will be lost if coal is drastically reduced. Not surprisingly, few politicians in the coal-dependent countries are politically suicidal enough to advocate the aggressive displacement of coal in power plants.

Proposals are numerous but solutions are few, because every new proposal generates new loopholes. In the same spirit of Kyoto, the "cap and trade" legislation discussed in the United States in 2009 called for polluters to pay for permits ("caps") and buy and sell them ("trade"). However, critics argued that this would be a stealth tax that would be a job killer, encouraging US firms to shift more production abroad. Then the next proposal called for import duties on goods from countries that have laxer rules on emissions. Not surprisingly, China and other developing countries vehemently opposed such "climate protectionism."

It is clear that with so much at stake, no solution will be perfect and trade-offs will be inevitable. The *Economist* suggests that climate change "is a prisoner's dilemma, a free-rider problem, and the tragedy of the commons all rolled into one." Until the last day of the Copenhagen conference, no deal had been in sight and countries were locked into bitter arguments because no one wanted to pay the "sucker's cost." Although the United States, despite its sky-

rocketing national debt, offered $100 billion in long-term financing to help developing countries adapt to climate change on the condition of verification of efforts, China disagreed with the notion of verification, claiming this to be an affront to national sovereignty. Of course, China's real concerns were economic slowdown and job losses given the need to continuously find jobs for the world's largest population. The choice boils down to: cut emissions or cut jobs?

However, inaction was not an option. The longer the world waited now, the more drastic future actions would have to be and the larger future sacrifices would have to be endured. It was in this spirit of urgency that leaders of Brazil, China, India, South Africa, and the United States reluctantly agreed, on the last day of the conference, December 18, 2009, to reach a very weak, nonbinding Copenhagen Accord. The Accord agreed to limit the level of global warming to no more than 2°C by century's end. Developed countries committed to reducing their GHG emissions by 80% by 2050. Developing countries committed to reducing GHG emissions but with no specific targets, and agreed in broad terms to some sort of reporting and verification—again with no specifics. In essence, countries agreed to keep talking. Although some politicians such as President Obama called the Copenhagen Accord "a meaningful first step," other politicians and numerous activists were deeply disappointed by the lack of a binding agreement.

Although the impact of proposed actions is uncertain, they can be regarded as investing in an insurance policy for the future health of our planet. The World Bank and the *Economist* estimate the cost to be 0.5% to 1% of global GDP, and argue that this amount should be socially acceptable. In comparison, the world spends 3% of GDP on (traditional) insurance, and governments recently burned 5% of GDP to bail out failed banks. Overall, deals such as Kyoto and Copenhagen are clearly flawed and do not make every country (let alone all countries) happy, but, given the downside risk, they seem better than nothing.

Case Discussion Questions:

1. From an institution-based view, how can firms play the game when the rules are uncertain?
2. From a resource-based view, identify potential first mover advantages in climate-smart strategies.

3. As CEO of a coal-fired utility in Australia, Germany, or the United States, how can your firm reduce greenhouse gas emissions? As CEO of a similar utility in China or India, what are your options?

Sources: Based on (1) *BusinessWeek*, 2009, Why Copenhagen will be good for business, December 14: 65; (2) *Economist*, 2009, Getting warmer, December 5: 22; (3) *Economist*, 2009, Stopping climate change, December 5: 11; (4) *Economist*, 2009, The grass is always greener, April 24: 81; (5) *New York Times*, 2009, Climate deal announced, but falls short of expectations, December 18, www.nytimes.com; (6) World Bank, 2010, *World Development Report 2010*, Washington: World Bank.

NOTES

[Journal acronyms] **AME**—*Academy of Management Executive*; **AMJ**—*Academy of Management Journal*; **AMP**—*Academy of Management Perspectives*; **AMR**—*Academy of Management Review*; **APJM**—*Asia Pacific Journal of Management*; **ASQ**—*Administrative Science Quarterly*; **BEQ**—*Business Ethics Quarterly*; **BSR**—*Business and Society Review*; **BW**—*BusinessWeek*; **CMR**—*California Management Review*; **HBR**—*Harvard Business Review*; **JBE**—*Journal of Business Ethics*; **JIBS**—*Journal of International Business Studies*; **JIM**—*Journal of International Management*; **JM**—*Journal of Management*; **JMS**—*Journal of Management Studies*; **JWB**—*Journal of World Business*; **NYTM**—*New York Times Magazine*; **OSc**—*Organization Science*; **SMJ**—*Strategic Management Journal*; **TC**—*Transnational Corporation*; **TIBR**—*Thunderbird International Business Review*

[1] K. Davis, 1973, The case for and against business assumption of social responsibilities (p. 312), *AMJ*, 16: 312–322. See also A. McWilliams, D. Siegel, & P. Wright, 2006, CSR, *JMS*, 43: 1–18.

[2] R. Aguilera, D. Rupp, C. Williams, & J. Ganapathi, 2007, Putting the S back in CSR, *AMR*, 32: 836–863; C. Egri & D. Ralston, 2008, Corporate responsibility, *JIM*, 14: 319–339; P. Godfrey, 2005, The relationship between corporate philanthropy and shareholder wealth, *AMR*, 30: 777–798; T. Hemphill, 2004, Corporate citizenship, *BSR*, 109: 339–361; T. Jones, W. Felps, & G. Bigley, 2007, Ethical theory and stakeholder-related decisions, *AMR*, 32: 137–155; T. London, 2009, Making better investments at the base of the pyramid, *HBR*, May: 106–113; A. Markus & A. Fremeth, 2009, Green management matters regardless, *AMP*, August: 17–26; S. Puffer & D. McCarthy, 2008, Ethical turnarounds and transformational leadership, *TIBR*, 50: 303–314.

[3] K. O'Shaughnessy, E. Gedajlovic, & P. Reinmoeller, 2007, The influence of firm, industry, and network on the corporate social performance of Japanese firms, *APJM*, 24: 283–304.

[4] E. Freeman, 1984, *Strategic Management: A Stakeholder Approach* (p. 46), Boston: Pitman.

[5] P. David, M. Bloom, & A. Hillman, 2007, Investor activism, managerial responsiveness, and corporate social performance, *SMJ*, 28: 91–100; P. David, J. O'Brien, T. Yoshikawa, & A. Delios, 2010, Do shareholders or stakeholders appropriate the rents from corporate diversification? *AMJ* (in press).

[6] World Commission on Environment and Development, 1987, *Our Common Future* (p. 8), Oxford: Oxford University Press. See also P. Bansal, 2005, Evolving sustainably, *SMJ*, 26: 187–218.

[7] S. Hart, 2005, *Capitalism at the Crossroads*, Philadelphia: Wharton School Publishing; R. Rajan & L. Zingales, 2003, *Saving Capitalism from the Capitalists*, New York: Crown.

[8] J. Doh & T. Guay, 2006, CSR, public policy, and NGO activism in Europe and the United States, *JMS*, 43: 47–73; B. Gifford & A. Kestler, 2008, Toward a theory of local legitimacy by MNEs in developing nations, *JIM*, 14: 340–352; G. Moore, 2004, The Fair Trade movement, *JBE*, 53: 73–86.

[9] P. Romilly, 2007, Business and climate change risk, *JIBS*, 38: 474–480.

[10] J. Coombs & K. M. Gilley, 2005, Stakeholder management as a predictor of CEO compensation, *SMJ*, 26: 827–840; B. Husted & D. Allen, 2006, CSR in the MNE, *JIBS*, 37: 838–849; A. Kacperczyk, 2009, With greater power comes greater responsibility? *SMJ*, 30: 261–285; G. Kassinis & N. Vafeas, 2006, Stakeholder pressures and environmental performance, *AMJ*, 49: 145–159; S. Sharma & I. Henriques, 2005, Stakeholder influences on sustainability practices in the Canadian forest products industry, *SMJ*, 26: 159–180.

[11] C. Eesley & M. Lenox, 2006, Firm responses to secondary stakeholder action, *SMJ*, 27: 765–781.

[12] M. Clarkson, 1995, A stakeholder framework for analyzing and evaluating corporate social performance (p. 107), *AMR*, 20: 92–117.

[13] M. Friedman, 1970, The social responsibility of business is to increase its profits, *NYTM*, September 13: 32–33.

[14] M. Jensen, 2002, Value maximization, stakeholder theory, and the corporate objective function, *BEQ*, 12: 235–256.

[15] C. Nielsen, 2005, Competition within the US national security regime, *JIM*, 11: 497–517.

[16] R. Buchholz, 2004, The natural environment, *AME*, 18: 130–133.

[17] J. Margolis & J. Walsh, 2003, Misery loves companies, *ASQ*, 48: 268–305.

[18] J. Murillo-Luna, C. Garces-Ayerbe, & P. Rivera-Torres, 2008, Why do patterns of environmental response differ? *SMJ*, 29: 1225–1240; D. Waldman et al., 2006, Cultural and leadership predictions of CSR values of top management, *JIBS*, 37: 823–837.

[19] P. Hilts, 2003, *Protecting America's Health*, New York: Knopf.

[20] A. Gore, 2006, *An Inconvenient Truth*, New York: Viking; M. Porter & M. Kramer, 2006, Strategy and society, *HBR*, December: 78–92.

[21] D. Matten & A. Crane, 2005, Corporate citizenship, *AMR*, 30: 166–179.

[22] P. Bansal & I. Clelland, 2004, Talking trash, *AMJ*, 47: 93–103.

[23] J. Lynes & M. Andrachuk, 2008, Motivations for corporate social and environmental responsibility, *JIM*, 14: 377–390; D. Siegel, 2009, Green management matters only if it yields more green, *AMP*, August: 5–16.

[24] C. Robertson & W. Crittenden, 2003, Mapping moral philosophies, *SMJ*, 24: 385–392; J. van Oosterhout, P. Heugens, & M. Kaptein, 2006, The internal morality of contracting, *AMR*, 31: 521–539.

[25] O. Branzei, T. Ursacki-Bryant, I. Vertinsky, & W. Zhang, 2004, The formation of green strategies in Chinese firms, *SMJ*, 25: 1075–1095.

[26] D. Schuler, K. Rehbein, & R. Cramer, 2002, Pursuing strategic advantage through political means, *AMJ*, 45: 659–672.

[27] *Economist*, 2007, Everybody's green now June 2: 6.

[28] P. Perez-Aleman & M. Sandilands, 2008, Building value at the top and the bottom of the global supply chain, *CMR*, Fall: 24–49; J. Selsky & B. Parker, 2005, Cross-sector partnerships to address social issues, *JM*, 31: 849–873.

[29] M. Barnett & A. King, 2008, Good fences make good neighbors, *AMJ*, 51: 1150–1170.

[30] R. Jiang & P. Bansal, 2003, Seeing the need for ISO 14001, *JMS*, 40: 1047–1067; A. King, M. Lenox, & A. Terlaak, 2005, The strategic use of decentralized institutions, *AMJ*, 48: 1091–1106.

[31] B. Arya & G. Zhang, 2009, Institutional reforms and investor reactions to CSR announcements, *JMS*, 46: 1089–1112; E. Reid & M. Toffel, 2009, Responding to public and private politics, *SMJ*, 30: 1157–1178.

[32] R. Chan, 2005, Does the natural-resource-based view of the firm apply in an emerging economy? *JMS*, 42: 625–675; A. Marcus & M. Anderson, 2006, A general dynamic capability, *JMS*, 43: 19–46.

[33] A. Hillman & G. Keim, 2001, Shareholder value, stakeholder management, and social issues, *SMJ*, 22: 125–139.

[34] *BW*, 2003, Diversity is about to get more elusive, not less, July 7: 30–31.

[35] M. Cordano & I. Frieze, 2000, Pollution reduction preferences of US environmental managers, *AMJ*, 43: 627–641; C. Egri & S. Herman, 2000, Leadership in the North American environmental sector, *AMJ*, 43: 571–604.

[36] N. Darnall & D. Edwards, 2006, Predicting the cost of environmental management system adoption, *SMJ*, 27: 301–320; M. Russo & N. Harrison, 2005, Organizational design and environmental performance, *AMJ*, 48: 582–593.

[37] P. Christmann, 2000, Effects of best practices of environmental management on cost advantage, *AMJ*, 43: 663–680; M. Delmas, M. Russo, & M. Montes-Sancho, 2007, Deregulation and environmental differentiation in the electric utility industry, *SMJ*, 28: 189–209.

[38] M. Barnett & R. Salomon, 2006, Beyond dichotomy, *SMJ*, 27: 1101–1122; A. Lockett, J. Moon, & W. Visser, 2006, CSR in management research, *JMS*, 43: 115–136; D. Schuler & M. Cording, 2006, A corporate social performance-corporate financial performance behavioral model for consumers, *AMR*, 31: 540–558; V. Strike, J. Gao, & P. Bansal, 2006, Being good while being bad, *JIBS*, 37: 850–862.

[39] J. Choi & H. Wang, 2009, Stakeholder relations and the persistence of corporate financial performance, *SMJ*, 30: 895–907; N. Darnall, I. Henriques, & P. Sadorsky, 2008, Do environmental management system improve business performance in an international setting? *JIM*, 14: 364–376; P. Godfrey, C. Merrill, & J. Hansen, 2009, The relationship between CSR and shareholder value, *SMJ*, 30: 425–445.

[40] S. Ambec & P. Lanoie, 2008, Does it pay to be green? *AMP*, November: 45–62; D. Vogel, 2005, The low value of virtue, *HBR*, June: 26.

[41] S. Brammer & A. Millington, 2008, Does it pay to be different? *SMJ*, 29: 1325–1343; A. McWilliams & D. Siegel, 2000, CSR and financial performance, *SMJ*, 21: 603–609.

[42] T. Devinney, 2009, Is the socially responsible corporation a myth? (p. 53), *AMP*, May: 44–56.

[43] R. E. Freeman, A. Wicks, & B. Parmar, 2004, Stakeholder theory and "The Corporate Objective Revisited," *OSc*, 15: 364–369.

[44] J. Welch & S. Welch, 2006, Whose company is it anyway? *BW*, October 9: 122.

[45] A. Sundaram & A. Inkpen, 2004, The corporate objective revisited, *OSc*, 15: 350–363.

[46] H. J. Leonard, 1988, *Pollution and the Struggle for a World Product*, Cambridge: Cambridge University Press.

[47] P. Christmann & G. Taylor, 2006, Firm self-regulation through international certifiable standards, *JIBS*, 37: 863–878.

[48] J. Child & T. Tsai, 2005, The dynamic between MNC strategy and institutional constraints in emerging economies, *JMS*, 42: 95–126.

[49] S. Brammer, S. Pavelin, & L. Porter, 2009, Corporate charitable giving, MNCs, and countries of concern, *JMS*, 46: 575–596; B. Scholtens, 2009, CSR in the international banking industry, *JBE*, 86: 159–175.

[50] *Economist*, 2009, Shell in Nigeria: Spilling over, June 13: 51.

[51] J. Kline, 2003, Political activities by transnational corporations, *TC*, 12: 1–26.

[52] J. Lash & F. Wellington, 2007, Competitive advantage on a warming planet, *HBR*, March: 95–102.

[53] A. McWilliams & D. Siegel, 2001, Corporate social responsibility, *AMR*, 26: 117–127.

[54] B. Husted & J. Salazar, 2006, Taking Friedman seriously, *JMS*, 43: 75–91.

[55] N. Gardberg & C. Fombrun, 2006, Corporate citizenship, *AMR*, 31: 329–346; A. Peredo & J. Chrisman, 2006, Toward a theory of community-based enterprise, *AMR*, 31: 309–328; P. Sethi, 1995, Societal expectations and corporate performance, *AMR*, 20: 18–21.

pengatlas Part 4

MAP 4.1
MAJOR SHIPPING AND TRANSPORTATION ROUTES

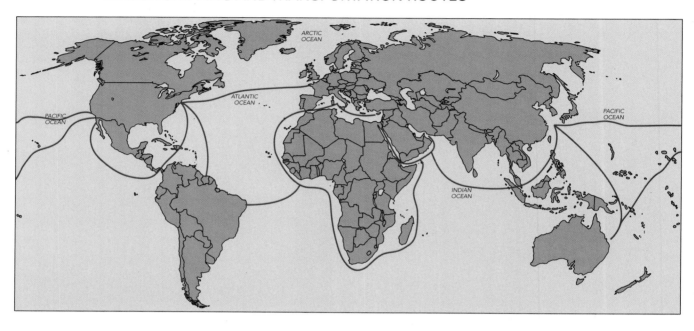

MAP 4.2
BUSIEST AIRPORTS

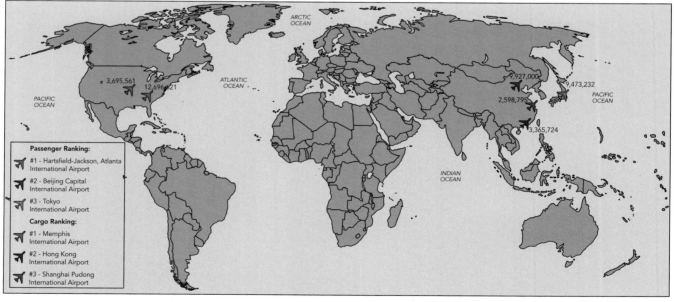

3,695,561
12,696,021
9,927,000
9,473,232
2,598,795
3,365,724

Passenger Ranking:
#1 - Hartsfield-Jackson, Atlanta International Airport
#2 - Beijing Capital International Airport
#3 - Tokyo International Airport

Cargo Ranking:
#1 - Memphis International Airport
#2 - Hong Kong International Airport
#3 - Shanghai Pudong International Airport

Source: http://encarta.msn.com/media_461532917/major_shipping_trade_routes.html.

MAP 4.3   COUNTRIES WITH THE LARGEST LABOR FORCES

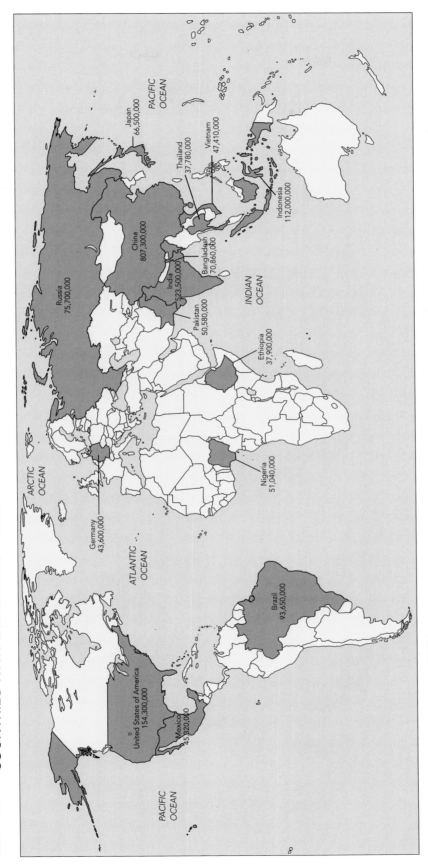

Russia
75,700,000

China
807,300,000

Japan
66,500,000

PACIFIC
OCEAN

Thailand
37,780,000

Vietnam
47,410,000

Indonesia
112,000,000

Bangladesh
70,860,000

India
523,500,000

Pakistan
50,580,000

INDIAN
OCEAN

Ethiopia
37,900,000

Nigeria
51,040,000

Germany
43,600,000

ARCTIC
OCEAN

ATLANTIC
OCEAN

Brazil
93,650,000

United States of America
154,300,000

Mexico
45,320,000

PACIFIC
OCEAN

Source: http://world.bymap.org/LaborForce.html, 2008.

MAP 4.4   COUNTRIES WITH THE HIGHEST UNEMPLOYMENT RATES

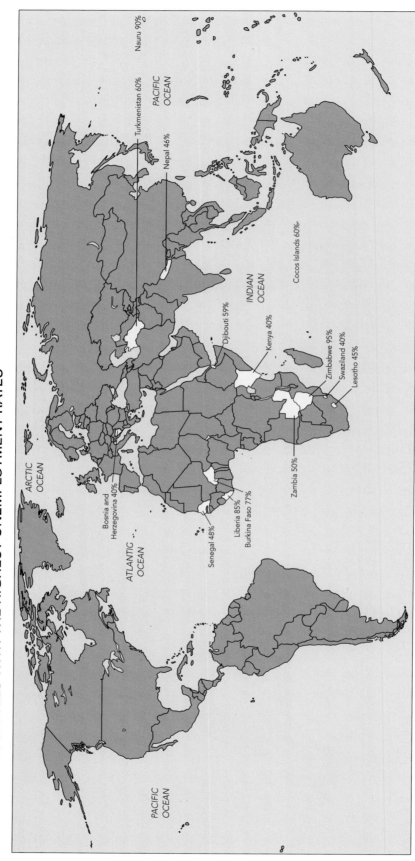

Source: CIA World Factbook, 2009.

MAP 4.5   TOP 20 COUNTRIES IN CO$_2$ EMISSIONS (IN MIO TONNES)

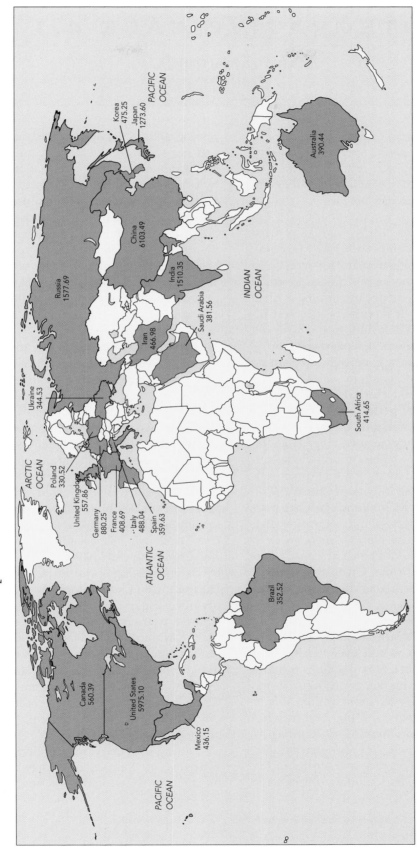

Source: http://unstats.un.org/unsd/environment/air_co2_emissions.htm, 2009.

INTEGRATIVE CASE 4.1

MARY KAY IN CHINA

Habte G. Woldu, *University of Texas at Dallas*

Two years after Mary Kay entered China, direct selling was banned by the Chinese government. Instead of collapsing, Mary Kay grew from its rocky start in China, adapted its marketing strategy, and made its China subsidiary the number one contributor to its global sales and profits.

Headquartered in Dallas, Texas, Mary Kay Cosmetics was founded in September 1963 by Mary Kay Ash, who constructed a sales domain for women at a time when women had few opportunities to work. Mary Kay grows and makes money by forming a direct selling distribution model. It recruits beauty consultants, who are independent distributors and who sell products directly to consumers. Its payment plan is principally commission based and multilevel, meaning that it pays commissions to agents for sales reported by them individually as well as for sales of the agents they recruit. Agents' goal for performance recognition is to get diamond bumble bee pins or pink Cadillac cars. Focusing on "improving women's lives" as the corporate goal, Mary Kay, the iconic, middle-American direct sales cosmetics firm, has shown that direct selling can work in America. Can it work in China?

In 1996, Mary Kay entered China and started to market its products through direct selling (see Appendix). China was attractive, because North American sales (not only in the United States, but also in Canada and Mexico) were down at that time. Given that China's population was four times higher than that of the United States, sales in China could boost corporate sales. It is interesting to underline that when Mary Kay Ash founded Mary Kay Cosmetics in 1963, she did not envisage that her products would ever reach China and become so popular. That China would eventually become the largest foreign market contributor to the company's profits would be even more unthinkable.

The pink-themed company is a big deal in what Americans used to call Red China. Mary Kay has its headquarters in China in Tower 2 of Shanghai's multiuse complex Plaza 66 and occupies four stories of the building. The huge, glossy, and spotless offices have photographs of the ornamented, heavily made-up Ash and her several proverbs and sayings in English and Mandarin, along with information about the company's background, beliefs, culture, and standards. The workforce of Mary Kay China includes about 250,000 beauty consultants, who are independent contractors doing direct selling to consumers, with a focus on the principle of women helping other women. It also has about 370 employees who work full-time, about 50 suppliers who are responsible for delivering the product and motivating consultants, and another 120 who work in the industrial unit manufacturing skin-care and other products.

Mary Kay's entry was not that easy, because in the mid-1990s, Chinese consumers did not readily accept the concept of direct selling. Different schemes like the pyramid and the Ponzi scheme thrived in the Wild West days of early Chinese capitalism. To make the matter worse, in 1998, two years after Mary Kay's entry, direct selling as a business model was *banned* by the Chinese government due to numerous reported cases of fraud.

Despite such a rocky start, Mary Kay showed a great deal of flexibility and resilience. Instead of collapsing, packing, and leaving the country, Mary Kay chose to change its marketing strategy for China. Mary Kay China showed loyalty to the Chinese government by demonstrating social responsibility to employees. During the ban, not a single Mary Kay employee was fired because of budget constraints or as a reaction to Chinese restrictions on its business practices. In fact, Mary Kay decided to go farther and be accommodative of the Chinese traditions. Mary Kay's corporate motto in the United States is "God first, family second, career third." However, a little adjustment was required for China because "God" is not a comfortable topic in this officially atheist state. As a result, "Principle" was substituted in place of "God."

During the ban on direct selling, the only way forward was to completely change the business model by offering showrooms and engaging in traditional

This case was written by Habte Woldu (University of Texas at Dallas). © Habte Woldu. Reprinted with permission.

retail operations—something that Mary Kay and other direct selling firms such as Amway and Avon claimed that they would never do. However, Amway and Avon seemed more relaxed than Mary Kay. Why? It was principally because of two reasons. The first was that "door-to-door" selling—to be precise, multilevel marketing by direct sellers—remained a subtle endeavor. The ban might not be totally complete. Second, the competitors found out workarounds for doing business in China without violating the boundaries of existing rules. Mary Kay, on the other hand, employed a different corporate strategy. Breaking from tradition, Mary Kay established various showrooms, appointed in-store agents, and paid them to represent its products. Implementing this strategy, Mary Kay managed to maintain corporate control of the product inventory.

In 2006, a new law was passed in China allowing direct selling. The revival of the direct sales market was made possible after the government decreed to open up its market to foreign players in an effort to adhere with rules pertaining to World Trade Organization (WTO) agreements. According to these new rules, foreign players were permitted to carry out single-level direct selling but were restricted from doing multilevel direct selling. This restriction implied that the foreign players might have sales representatives on a direct contract with the company. Hence, the sales representatives did not have the right to purchase and/or resell company products. They were also prohibited from receiving perks apart from product commissions earned by selling products directly. The new rules also restricted them to particular districts, while the companies engaged in direct selling were accountable for their conduct. The rules cost Mary Kay a lot of time, and left most people at its China subsidiary uncertain on whether they would be able to sustain the China market or they needed to quit. Subsequently, by offering discount programs to entry-level sales representatives, conducting training and referral benefit programs for mid-level reps, keeping official positions exposed to top-level reps, and encouraging proprietorship for independent individuals, Mary Kay eventually succeeded in finding ways to uphold the key elements of its direct selling approach in China while abiding the law.

In addition to Mary Kay, major players in China's multilevel marketing industry include Amway, Avon, and Nu Skin. At present, Mary Kay has 35 showrooms in China. It has customized its products based on the tastes of the locals. Although Chinese women do not apply too much makeup, the skin-care products of Mary Kay there include few anti-aging and whitening creams that are expensive as compared to other competing products. For example, it costs about $120 for a four-week supply of one cream. Although Mary Kay is not recognized as a super-premium luxury brand, it has managed to market itself quite well, positioning its showrooms in some of the busiest streets in major cities. If one peeps through the car window at Shanghai's traffic-clogged skyline, a huge sign flashing Mary Kay in English and Chinese is clearly visible in the distance, and people who drive by notice it.

From its rocky start in the mid-1990s, Mary Kay China has gained a substantial market share. While it has more than 30 subsidiaries throughout the world, today its China subsidiary is a juggernaut that is the largest contributor to its corporate profits. In 2008, Mary Kay China's sales soared by 50%. "This year, even with the economic situation, we have about 20% growth over last year," said Paul Mak, president of Mary Kay China. At present, the company books about 25% of its global sales from China. Emboldened by its China experience that found that the Asian market was favorable for its product line, Mary Kay recently opened a retail store in India.

Mary Kay's accomplishments have been widely recognized in China. In 2003 and 2004, the China Statistics Bureau rated Mary Kay as the most profitable Chinese cosmetics firm. In 2005, it was rated as the chemical firm with the highest return on investment in China by the China Chemical Industry Enterprise Management Association. In 2003 and 2005, *Fortune* (China) and Watson Wyatt acknowledged Mary Kay China as the Best Employer in China. As China encourages more international players for direct sales investment opportunities, the number of market players trying to enter into such a flourishing growth market increases. These new entrants have a formidable competitor waiting for them in China—Mary Kay.

Case Discussion Questions:

1. How do you characterize the nature of Mary Kay's business model?
2. Was it worth it for Mary Kay to change its marketing strategy for China?
3. What lessons can international corporations moving to China learn from the case?

Sources: (1) The Economist Intelligence Unit, 2005, *Business China*, June; (2) Mary Kay (China) Cosmetics Co., Ltd., case study, China Europe International Business School; (3) *Workforce Management*, 2005, Sales force at Mary Kay China embraces the American way, 84(4), April: 24; (4) http://hbr.org/product/mary-kay-inc-direct-selling-and-the-challenge-of-o/an/KEL034-PDF-ENG; (5) http://www.marykay.com/; (6) http://www.slate.com/id/2235897/.

Appendix: Key Development Milestones for Mary Kay China

1963 On Friday, September 13, Mary Kay Ash established Mary Kay Cosmetics—a "dream" company that she envisioned would offer women unprecedented opportunities for financial independence, advancement, and personal fulfillment. Mary Kay opened a 500-square-foot storefront in Dallas, Texas, with the help of her 20-year-old son Richard Rogers, her life savings of $5,000, and nine independent beauty consultants.

1995 Mary Kay established its first overseas manufacturing facility in Hangzhou, China.

1996 Mary Kay China was formally established and the first branch started to operate in Shanghai.

1997 The company awarded its first pink Volkswagen Santana car in China.

1998 Mary Kay China's change of direct selling model was approved by the government.

2001 Mary Kay China jointly established Mary Kay Women Entrepreneur Fund with National Women's Association and donated 300,000 yuan to support laid-off female workers and poor women in rural areas.

2002 Mary Kay China cooperated with many nongovernmental organizations (NGOs) on charity work.

2003 Mary Kay was recognized as one of the "10 Best Employers in China" by *Fortune* (China) magazine.

2004 Mary Kay built a new manufacturing facility in Hangzhou, China.

2005 Mary Kay awarded the first pink Cadillac car in China. Recognized again as one of the "10 Best Employers in China" by *Fortune* (China) magazine.

2006 New Hangzhou manufacturing plant began operating in March.

NOTE

[1] In 1995, Mary Kay established its first overseas manufacturing facility in Hangzhou, China. But direct selling had not started until 1996.

INTEGRATIVE CASE 4.2

BAOSTEEL EUROPE

Bernd Michael Linke, *Friedrich Schiller University of Jena, Germany*

Andreas Klossek, *Technical University of Freiberg, Germany*

Internationalization of a leading Chinese steelmaker and management of its European headquarters in Germany.

The Making of a Global Corporation

The name "Baosteel" combines Baoshan, a district in Shanghai, China, and the English word "steel." "Baosteel" stands for a Chinese company with global outreach. However, experts on Asia think that there is an additional twist at play, as is often the case with company names in this region. In Chinese "bao" also signifies "valuable" or "precious," and a literal translation of Baosteel may be "premium steel"—certainly something to which the company aspires.

Baosteel's home market is staggering. On the demand side, the market reflects the sheer and insatiable needs of the largest and most successful emerging economy in the world. However, on the supply side, it is fragmented unlike any other market in the world. Currently, the Chinese steel market is divided by 260 steelmakers of various sizes, and some sources say this number could be greater than 1,000. While some of these firms are profitable, most are not. Thus, it is not surprising that the Chinese government is urging them to turn themselves into large steelmaking corporations following the lead of Baosteel.

Baosteel Group was founded in Shanghai in December 1978 under the name of Baoshan Iron and Steel Complex. Skipping some of the historical details, it is sufficient to say that the current-day corporation is the result of a large merger between Shanghai Metallurgical Holding Group Corporation and Shanghai Meishan Group Co., Ltd. carried out in 1998 on the basis of a government decree. With continued growth, the most recent acquisition took place in April 2008, when Baosteel acquired the Bayi Steel Group in the province of Xinjiang.

Baosteel Group is a holding company consisting of five divisions: (1) financial, (2) steel trading, (3) equipment and spare parts engineering, (4) steel products, and (5) Shanghai headquarters office (administrative and service). The company produces and sells steel primarily to carmakers, shipbuilders, electronics and household appliances makers, oil drilling and pipeline companies, and construction companies. Baosteel has further diversified into areas such as financial services, trading, and logistics services. In sum, the company's operational philosophy is to continue to "diversify trading functions and operation products" while "gradually expanding non-Baosteel trading business."[1]

In comparison to international rivals, Baosteel displays a high degree of diversification. However, this is typical for many large Asian firms. Baosteel is a wholly owned state-owned enterprise (SOE). The largest business unit, Baoshan Iron and Steel Co., Ltd. (Baosteel Co., Ltd.), has been listed on the Shanghai Stock Exchange since 2000. Currently 78% of the shares are held by Baosteel Group, and thus ultimately by the Chinese government.

In recent years, the turnover of Baosteel has risen annually by 10%, from $19.5 billion in 2004 to $26.3 billion in 2007. During the same period, steel production has risen from 21.4 million to 28.6 million tons. Baosteel, which currently employs 122,780 workers, is China's largest producer of steel. It has worked on prestigious and complex building projects such as the principal venue of the 2008 Summer Olympic Games (the national stadium nicknamed "Bird's Nest" in Beijing), the headquarters of CCTV state television in Beijing, and the terminals of international airports in Beijing and Shanghai. In international terms the company is also one of the largest corporations of its kind. Since 2006, Baosteel has been in fifth place in the global steelmaker category. In 2004, Baosteel was the first Chinese manufacturing company to be included in the *Fortune* 500 list at 372—by 2008 it had climbed to 259. Baosteel aims to become one of the three largest

---

This case was written by Bernd Michael Linke (Friedrich Schiller University of Jena, Germany) and Andreas Klossek (Technical University of Freiberg, Germany). It was first published in the authors' study *Chinese Companies in Germany: Chances and Challenges*, which was sponsored by Bertelsmann Foundation and Deloitte (the full study can be accessed at http://www.bertelsmann-stiftung.de/cps/rde/xbcr/SID-12ED87F3-5090242B/bst_engl/xcms_bst_dms_27517_27534_2.pdf). The authors would like to thank both for granting the permission to reprint this case. © Bertelsmann Foundation. Reprinted with permission. Case discussion questions were added by Mike Peng.

steel producers in the world as soon as possible, and is well on its way to achieving this goal.

Strategic Positioning and Global Activities

Many experts believe that Baosteel's goal is attainable. Its accomplishments, which the Western media traditionally would not have thought possible in the case of a Chinese SOE, speak for themselves. Over the course of the most recent merger, the workforce was cut 43% from 176,000 to 122,780. Baosteel believes that its future success is no longer going to be based on cheap labor, but instead on automated production. The main plant in Shanghai is considered to be one of the most modern and most efficient manufacturing sites for steel products in the *world*. At Baosteel, the new management focus is visible in many areas. For example, the "Six Sigma" quality management system was successfully introduced in 2005. Further, Baosteel engages in strategic planning and has an integrated management system designed to regulate and assign responsibilities, executive order powers, and communication channels between business entities.

Corporate social responsibility (CSR) has also become increasingly important in recent years. Baosteel is ahead of this social trend, embracing CSR and bankrolling numerous social projects as early as 1990. For example, the establishment of Baosteel Education Fund is one of the most visible education awards nationwide. Its foundation has set up 38 Hope elementary schools[2] and provides support for sustainability and environmental projects. To further substantiate its dedication to CSR, Baosteel is the first Chinese company to publish annual sustainability reports, which have appeared since 2005. Moreover, in 2006 the management announced a new slogan and goal centered around CSR. The slogan, "Green Baosteel, our common home," is aligned with its goal of turning Baosteel into the cleanest and most sustainable steelmaker in the world.

The preconditions for turning the company into a global player are in place. First, Baosteel, since its founding, has never been a typical Chinese SOE. Second, it dates back only to December 1978, which coincides with the exact point at which the Chinese economic reforms got off the ground. Thus, unlike many SOEs, it was not burdened with the legacy of the Chinese communist past. Finally, it has been shaped by the cosmopolitan tradition of Shanghai, which is reflected in the long-lasting relationships and numerous joint ventures that the Baosteel Group holds with other global players.

Baosteel is prepared to confront the future and recognizes the enormous challenges it will bring. Special market segments in China have, for some time, seen higher growth rates and much higher demand levels than in other emerging markets such as India and Russia. To some extent, they have even caught up with those of industrialized countries such as the United States. The latest OECD research suggests that this trend is visible in every segment of the Chinese steel market and is projected to become more pronounced. At the same time, exports continue to grow despite the gigantic demand in China. In 2004, Chinese steel exports exceeded imports for the first time in history.

Endeavoring to meet the high demand at home, more than 90% of Baosteel's turnover is in China. Additionally, to enhance its negotiating position in the competition for scarcer natural resources, it is planning further mergers and acquisitions at home and abroad, both horizontally and vertically (upstream and downstream) across the value chain. The current consolidation of the Chinese steel market and open access to international markets are making this strategy of acquiring new plants and integrating important mining sites possible. For example, currently, Baosteel imports 80% of the iron ore it needs. However, as early as in 2001 the company took a 50% share in the Brazilian iron ore mine Água Limpa, and in 2003 it acquired shares in Hamersley Iron, an Australian subsidiary of Rio Tinto. These equity positions are examples of Baosteel's vertical movement on the value chain. Moreover, loose partnerships and numerous meetings with other steel giants in Asia, such as Nippon Steel in Japan and Posco in Korea, nurture rumors that a merger may emerge.

Of decisive importance for the Baosteel Group's strategic planning are not only the economic goals, but also the acquisition of international management experience. As such, internationalization efforts, such as those detailed in the remainder of the case with a focus on Baosteel Europe, are crucial.

Setting up a Subsidiary in Hamburg, Germany

Baosteel has been conducting business in Germany for a long time, though its activities have changed significantly over the years. In the beginning, it was impossible to think about selling steel products; rather its main task was to supply Chinese companies with vital replacement parts sourced in Germany for domestic production. This changed in 1993, when senior management decided to expand and founded Baosteel Europe GmbH with $6.64 million. Baosteel selected Germany for a very specific reason: the local courts provide European customers and suppliers with more legal protection than if business were to be conducted in Hong Kong or China. In other words, Baosteel considered the "rules of the game" regarding the legal infrastructure and enforcement across countries and made its location decision using the institution-based view.

After deciding to locate in Germany, Baosteel also evaluated a number of German cities. Its decision to locate the business in the Hamburg metropolis was based on both economical motives (such as direct access to shipping routes) and cultural aspects. For example, Ye Meng, the current President of Baosteel Europe, states, "Hamburg and China can look back on a long history of partnership. There really are quite a lot of Chinese companies and trading entities here. The parent of Baosteel Europe GmbH comes from Hamburg's sister city, Shanghai, which is also a port city. Both from a cultural perspective and for geographical reasons Hamburg in our opinion provides us with favorable conditions for the development of our company." Additionally, the workforce, technology, and infrastructure in Germany are known to be world class. Further, Meng believes that earning the trust of German clients and selling "Made in Germany" steel parts in China have benefited the company greatly.[3]

Indeed, Baosteel Europe's business has been booming. In the last three years, turnover increased to $732 million. This means that Baosteel Europe is among the largest Chinese companies in Germany. While making a profit, Baosteel Europe is certainly not resting on its laurels. Not only is Baosteel Europe strategizing to increase its share of the global market, it is also seeking to expand in Germany and Europe with new products and innovations. As such, the Hamburg subsidiary is due for expansion with new specialists recruited. Under Meng, the structure of Baosteel Europe GmbH has changed considerably in the last four years. For example, in 2004, there were 30 Baosteel employees in Germany, and today there are 55—with additional employees in other offices throughout Europe, the Middle East, and Shanghai. The finance department and the Shanghai office are responsible for the internal organization of what happens in Hamburg. Looking after customers and suppliers is the task of each business areas (i.e., steel trading, spare parts and equipment, and metal products). Recently, the new business department has been given the mandate of expanding into new business areas. In order to manage a variety of tasks, the company employs individuals from a number of countries. In Hamburg, Chinese expatriates work side by side with Germans. In other subsidiaries in Europe, employees from the various host countries are in the majority. Taken together, it is apparent that Baosteel is a transnational company with a global outlook.

Business Areas of the Baosteel Subsidiary in Germany

Procurement, which was of considerable importance at the start of Baosteel's activities in Germany, continues to play an important role today. The transactions involved are complicated and inter-culturally demanding, requiring good coordination. The procurement process is set in motion by a firm in a given location— for example a Chinese steelmaker in a province, which needs spare parts obtainable only from Europe. This requirement is relayed to the Baosteel head office in Shanghai, which subsequently transmits an inquiry to Baosteel Europe. The inquiry is received by a Chinese or German employee in Hamburg, who then places an order with a local (German) supplier. After the spare parts arrive, another Chinese or German Baosteel employee arranges for them to be sent to China. Inquiry, order processing, and transport are dealt with in Chinese, German, and English, meaning that employees of both nations transact on many tasks together and must engage in an ongoing dialogue. Thus, at the Hamburg location business success absolutely depends on Sino-German cooperation, which is based on years of experience and mutual understanding. A Chinese department head supervises four tandems, each consisting of a Chinese and a German employee, who know each other and work together in a coordinated manner.

Steel trading, however, has a fundamentally different procurement process, wherein ten Chinese co-workers—most of whom are engineers—work under the direction of the internationally experienced deputy managing director, Guo Zheng. The working language is Chinese and in keeping with international business practices, English is used when communicating with the "outside" world. In steel trading, the German market plays a subordinate role. Sales orders are sent via Hamburg, where the contracts are concluded, to the whole of Europe and the rest of the world. The majority of customers value Baosteel's quality, reliability, punctual delivery, and service. Although price is important in certain countries, Baosteel does not position itself in the lower price segment, preferring to have a price level akin to that of ThyssenKrupp and ArcelorMittal. In order to increase its market share in Europe, Baosteel is pinning its hopes on premium quality and customer orientation. The turnover volume, currently about 500,000 to 600,000 tons annually, is still a very small percentage of the total output.

The new business department is also managed by a Chinese expatriate with international experience. "New" refers both to new regions (such as the Middle East, Eastern Europe, and Africa) and to new activities (such as investments in sectors other than the steel industry). The current planning phase involves conducting feasibility studies (with the help of external expertise) and studying market entry methods.

Corporate Culture and Work Atmosphere

In recent years, Baosteel's senior management has come to realize the importance of a common corporate culture—for both Chinese and foreign employees. In 2004, Baosteel implemented a program that stresses "good faith" and "synergy" as basic values and emphasizes the significance of culture as the basis of all economic action. It has been said that "Baosteel's culture is the soul of management, while Baosteel's management is the vehicle of culture." The executives at Baosteel Europe emphasize words such as "integrity," "teamwork," and "loyalty," and are thus transferring to all employees the essence and level of their cooperation with the head office in Shanghai. To stress the high opinion and importance of the local workforce, all German employees of Baosteel Europe were invited to stay in Shanghai for a week. There they were shown the organization of the head office, met their counterparts with whom they often telephoned or exchanged emails, and experienced Chinese hospitality—along with gratitude for their achievement and loyalty to the company. The German employees have also been included in the Chinese bonus system in order to encourage their participation in the success of the company.

At the bi-annual meeting involving all Baosteel Europe employees, management reports at length about the success and goals of the parent company and the Hamburg subsidiary, hoping to foster a community spirit. The German employees were also pleasantly surprised that the Chinese executives clearly try to respect German habits and customs by not expecting German employees to stay in the office until late in the evening, as is often the case with Chinese expatriates. Baosteel has come to understand and acknowledge that despite different work habits, in the end, the efficiency is the same.

The German employees are also particularly appreciative of the respect with which Chinese superiors treat their subordinates. The experience of working together on a daily basis means that German employees at Baosteel certainly do not share the typically negative picture of China that is often painted by the media. Instead, most have developed a far more positive picture of China.

Apart from the good atmosphere in the workplace, employees have additional motivations. Specifically,

a large and expanding company is synonymous with safe jobs. This is especially true for Chinese companies, where protection against dismissal is based on the Chinese and Confucian belief that one has a duty to look after the well-being of others. The high one-off bonuses for special accomplishments confirm the appreciative attitude of the senior management. Therefore, employee turnover is quite small in comparison to other companies within this industry.

To advance within Baosteel, it is necessary to occupy a position of responsibility at the head office. As such, it is necessary for individuals to possess not only professional qualifications, but also have the ability to speak fluent Chinese. Thus, many German employees who do not speak Chinese find it extremely difficult to reach the senior management level at Baosteel Europe. Overall, while challenges remain, Baosteel has overcome many of the cultural differences by taking time to understand those differences and finding ways to embed both the German and Chinese cultures within its organizational culture.

Human Resource Management (HRM)

In China, Baosteel enjoys a good reputation for its excellent compensation and career opportunities. To maintain its reputation and recruit top talent, Baosteel implements a very thorough recruiting process. Candidates for its comprehensive examination procedure are selected from a large number of applicants—all of which are university graduates. Unlike most companies in East Asia, Baosteel rarely recruits candidates jumping ship from other employers or at job fairs. However, once candidates are selected, the successful applicants are introduced to and trained in Baosteel's corporate culture, which is a customary practice in Chinese firms. If the candidate does well over the course of the year, the company may cover the cost of further education—for example, a one-year higher education program at home or abroad. After this, the individual is likely to be promoted within the company and employed as a senior executive, alternating between China and other countries. Interestingly, until recently it had been considered a welcome opportunity for Chinese employees to be offered the opportunity to work abroad for a number of years, since it coincided with good pay and enhanced qualifications. However, because income and career opportunities have developed enormously within China in recent years, many consider this same "opportunity" or assignment to be a burden, especially since the quality of life in Shanghai is now higher than that in many Western cities.

In other words, Chinese expatriates now experience the same types of burdens as expatriates from developed countries, such as separation from their family or problems with their children's schools overseas. Although Baosteel takes into account these reservations and offers its Chinese expatriates numerous incentives such as increased compensation and job guarantees for spouses, the willingness to work in other countries is declining. However, for individuals trying to climb the career ladder, successful stints abroad considerably facilitate access to the senior management level and to executive posts in the subsidiaries and at the head office.

More recently, Baosteel has expanded the scope of its HRM, becoming more strategic in nature. In addition to regular assessments, the skills of its employees are continually being enhanced by means of systematic training. Further, preparatory country-specific or culture-specific instruction for foreign assignments is now available, as are returnees' programs. Finally, the mentoring system is well organized and highly valued. Talented young executives are watched over and given advice by mentors appointed to look after and guide them. As mentors rise in the company hierarchy, it will eventually lead to advancement for their "mentees," who may also receive recommendations for employment elsewhere. This network system not only leads to good professional work, but is indispensable if one wishes to advance to a decision-making position.

Baosteel Europe Paves the Way for Integration and Expansion

For Baosteel, numerous economic and cultural aspects were of decisive importance when it chose Hamburg as its European location. Endeavoring for a win-win outcome, Baosteel Europe has developed a great relationship with the Hamburg city government, especially with its departments involved in economic development. Baosteel continuously manages this relationship by staying in touch with the media and having company representatives participate in and sponsor public events. Interestingly, Baosteel has also incorporated its German-oriented practices of external representation back in China, demonstrating its dedication to learning from global best practices. Baosteel has also begun to develop ideas regarding networking strategies with other Chinese organizations in Germany geared toward the joint promotion of their interests, and maintained loose partnerships with two other large Chinese corporations also located in Hamburg—COSCO and Bank of China.

Baosteel Europe is said to exemplify the "large Chinese corporation abroad" and it occupies a front-runner role in two senses—being both a "test case" and a "model."[4] Many Chinese companies still find it difficult to be internationally competitive, and there is often a discrepancy between an impressive success story told at home and the hesitant progress overseas that may be marred by setbacks. This could change quickly if "pilot projects," such as the internationalization of Baosteel, are a success and the senior management of other companies draws the right conclusions. However, it is not only the views within an industry that are of importance. Chinese companies, especially those with international ambitions, must assume that they are being watched intently by the public both at home and abroad, and must behave in a responsible manner.

After a rough start, Baosteel has made significant progress in recent years. Admittedly, the situation has been rather auspicious for the steel industry. An essential basis for further expansion in the international sector is a systematic development of HR beginning with recruiting, and leading to career planning and further education. Baosteel aims to use the talents of both German and third-country specialists and to form international leadership teams that will be in a position to meet the challenges of international management. Further, in the case of international customer-supplier relationships, it is important to preempt cross-cultural conflicts by increasing the level of intercultural competence and strengthening an overarching corporate culture.

Baosteel is well on its way to mastering these challenges, having already united a variety of very different companies in Shanghai and developing a distinct corporate culture among its employees. When discussing Baosteel's "hard skills," the former chairwoman Qihua Xie once coined the slogan "quality, not quantity." The same can just as well be applied to Baosteel's "soft skills." Overall, the Baosteel Group is an exemplary company from which other Chinese companies can learn.

Case Discussion Questions:

1. What location-specific advantages did Hamburg, Germany, provide Baosteel? Evaluate other European locations that might offer similar advantages.
2. How did Baosteel manage its entry into Europe? What factors have enhanced its success?
3. What are the lessons on how to manage human resources in a subsidiary that we can draw based on Baosteel Europe's experience in Germany?
4. Why does Baosteel devote considerable resources to corporate social responsibility?
5. As the director of human resources for Baosteel, outline a strategic plan that will be implemented over the next three years that focuses on organizational culture and learning.

NOTES

[1] Baosteel, 2009, Address by the President, www.baosteel.eu, Accessed November 11, 2009.

[2] In Chinese jargon, Hope schools refer to schools set up in poor rural areas, where children would not have been educated had these schools not been set up. These schools are known to offer "hope."

[3] Hamburg provides Chinese company with link to Germany, Europe, and the World, http://www.gtai.com/homepage/info-service/publications/our-publications/germany-investment-magazine/vol-2008/vol-032008/foreign-direct-investment1, Accessed November 12, 2009.

[4] Handelsblatt no. 43, March 1, 2007.

INTEGRATIVE CASE 4.3

Socially Responsible to Whom? The Case of the US Ethanol Industry

Erin Pleggenkuhle-Miles, *University of Texas at Dallas*

Facing pressures from various stakeholder groups, managers in the US ethanol industry need to confront a leading challenge: To whom are they socially responsible?

In this day and age, most firms engage in some form of corporate social responsibility (CSR). Therefore, these firms must identify to whom they are socially responsible, which raises a number of questions as well as trade-offs. While this can be problematic for many firms, it is perhaps most discernible for firms in the US ethanol industry when we consider that *everyone* in the United States has a stake in national energy security and in climate change. Both of these are issues that the ethanol industry is facing head-on. To understand the multifaceted issues this industry confronts, it is necessary to understand its beginning and how it has influenced present conditions.

Background

The industry's emergence was marked and initiated by government sponsorship in response to the 1973 energy crisis. Despite initial governmental support, support for the industry waned as oil prices decreased in the early 1980s. It was brought to the forefront again in the 1990s riding on the coattails of global warming. Again, government-led initiatives in the form of legislature spurred growth and external support for the industry. It was during this period that the industry

really began to emerge with rapid growth in investment, capacity, and revenues (see Exhibit 1). However, this period of rapid growth has been relatively short-lived, as more recent industry growth has stagnated and many ventures have filed for bankruptcy. Yet the US government, as well as a number of other governments (e.g., China, the EU, India), has continued to incorporate biofuels into its energy plans and offer incentives to biofuel start-ups.

Current Conditions and Controversies

At present, due to the number of controversies surrounding this industry, US ethanol refineries find it necessary to pull together in order to speak to the diverse and numerous stakeholders. These stakeholders, notably farmers, foresters, policy makers, consumers, and environmentalists, have a wide range of motivations, and it is up to firms to understand how stakeholders view, evaluate, and make decisions in light of the operations of the ethanol firms. Only a few years ago ethanol was cited as the answer to both reduce oil dependence and combat global warming. However, it is now accused of triggering a global food crisis and critics contend that it does not combat climate change as was first thought.

In response, the industry has pulled together to address the swirling controversies, which are far more

EXHIBIT 1   US ETHANOL INDUSTRY OVERVIEW*

	1999	2000	2001	2002	2003	2004	2005	2006	2007	2008	2009
Total ethanol plants	50	54	56	61	68	72	81	95	110	139	170***
Production capacity (mgy)**	1,701	1,748	1,921	2,347	2,706	3,100	3,643	4,336	5,493	7,888	10,569****
Plants under construction/expanding	5	6	5	13	11	15	16	31	76	61	24
Capacity under construction/expanding (mgy)	77	91	64	390	483	598	754	1778	5635	5536	2066
States with ethanol plants	17	17	18	19	20	19	18	20	21	21	26

* All data refer to January of each year.
** mgy: million gallons per year.
*** Operating plants.
**** Including idled capacity, production capacity is 12,475 mgy.
Source: Renewable Fuels Association, www.ethanolrfa.org.

This case was written by Erin Pleggenkuhle-Miles (University of Texas at Dallas) under the supervision of Professor Mike Peng. © Erin Pleggenkuhle-Miles. Reprinted with permission.

complex than is often observed in the media. While one ethanol industry association—the Renewable Fuel Association (RFA)—has been in existence since 1980, another industry association has emerged—Growth Energy—as ethanol's reputation has declined. Both of these industry associations are working different angles to (1) correct myths regarding the production and use of ethanol and (2) restore ethanol's reputation. In doing so, they have launched public relations (PR) campaigns and are working closely with lobbyists and supporting state representatives in Washington, DC. The main focus of both groups is the food versus fuel debate and the climate change dispute.

First, in response to the food versus fuel debate, the industry argues that its member firms are consuming no more than was already available. However, this argument may simply shift the blame to many farmers who switched production to corn when prices were high in 2007, leaving a shortage of production in other crops. Such switches have global ramifications, which take time to correct. Since 2007, corn prices have decreased and farmers have gone back to more traditional methods of alternating crops yearly. Two additional factors must also be contemplated when considering this debate: (1) increased growing yield and efficiency and (2) increased food demand in developing countries. These are both important, yet often overlooked. Yield continues to increase. Today, more corn is produced per acre than ever before, meaning that it takes fewer acres to produce the same yield as in previous years. This makes analysis a bit trickier when weighing the different sides since analysts have to factor in the type of corn, its yield, how it is planted, whether it is irrigated, how it is fertilized, as well as various other variables. Because such up-to-date information is not readily available, analysts must rely heavily on assumptions and estimates in their analyses. Further, as diets are changing in developing countries from starchy foods to meat and poultry, there is increasing demand for grain, which is necessary to feed cattle, pigs, and poultry. This demand also places a higher value on corn. These different factors all fuel the food versus fuel debate and begins to demonstrate the number of stakeholders at play in the ethanol industry.

Second, the view of ethanol as a (partial) "solution" to climate change is also wrought with contradictory facts and opinions. For example, many studies base their estimates on older refineries, which are much less efficient than the refineries being built today—modern facilities are reportedly using 25% less energy than the industry average five years ago. Further, trying to calculate the amount of energy that goes into growing and harvesting is also challenging since there are

a variety of ways to farm. Some farming techniques that appear more energy-intensive in the short run are actually more energy-efficient in the long run; this is especially true when comparing intensive farming to organic farming. For example, organically raised chickens do not need high levels of antibiotics to protect them from the diseases that often spread like wildfire in broiler sheds. However, they take longer to reach slaughter weight, and thus consume more energy and produce more waste during their longer lives. In general, agriculture on the whole is an energy-intensive industry with its fuel, chemical, electricity, and natural gas costs, each of which must be accounted for and factored into analyses. Thus, it is not surprising that studies often produce contradictory results—depending on estimates used, personal opinions, and research sponsors.

For some, the analyses and arguments presented regarding ethanol and climate change dwell too much on past conditions and do not focus enough on current and future conditions. In other words, it is often forgotten that the primary goal of ethanol and other biofuels was, and is, to reduce oil dependence, and the climate change benefit was an added bonus. While current production is ripe with problems, it is not that different than many other infant industries during the same stage of their development. It is typical for first-generation products to be less efficient than second- and third-generation products—for example, consider how different computers are today versus ten years ago, or how the efficiency of washers and dryers has improved. Further, it is difficult to predict the shape and form of any industry ten years down the road based solely on old data. Instead, more focus needs to be given to the promise of next-generation feedstocks. Currently there are more than 200 companies in the United States using an array of technologies that are working on next-generation biofuels. Examples include Solazyme, which uses algae to produce ethanol, and Coskata, which uses biomass and municipal waste (garbage) to produce ethanol. Such enthusiasm for biofuel is not limited to the United States, but has grown globally (see Exhibit 2).

Global Stakeholders

Agriculture is a global issue. What is grown in Country A matters to Countries B, C, and D, because it impacts the global food chain. For example, when farmers in the United States begin growing more corn for biofuel production instead of soybeans, this creates a decrease in the supply of soybeans, thereby directly impacting global food availability. As countries around the world strive for energy and food security, the global

EXHIBIT 2   WORLD ANNUAL FUEL ETHANOL PRODUCTION, 1975–2009

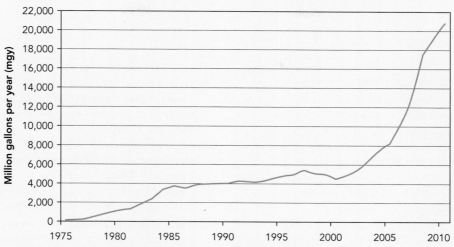

Source: F. O. Licht, 2009, *World Ethanol and Biofuels Report* (p. 365), 7 (18): May 26. 2009 and 2010 figures are based on estimates.

food chain has been shaken up, which has greatly impacted less developed countries. Currently, massive tracts of land in African countries such as Congo, Ethiopia, Madagascar, Malawi, Mali, and Sudan are being acquired by firms and individuals from other countries as sources for food and biofuel production. While additional investments in agriculture in developing countries are welcome in principle—injecting money into rural areas, creating more jobs, improving infrastructure, and aiding technology transfer—locals lose control over land on which they depend. Further, locals may not have formal titles for the land, because they often use custom tenure arrangements. They can thus be pushed off the land when richer investors, such as those coming from the US ethanol industry, come looking to buy. Taken together, it is easy to see the multitude of stakeholders that the ethanol industry need to be accounted for when making socially

responsible decisions. However, a "million dollar" question remains regarding to whom firms in the US ethanol industry should be responsible to first.

Case Discussion Questions:

1. As a US ethanol producer, who is your primary stakeholder?
2. From a US citizen perspective, how is the production of ethanol socially responsible (or irresponsible)?
3. From an international government perspective, how does the production of ethanol influence your policy?

Sources: Based on (1) J. Carey, 2008, Is ethanol getting a bum rap? *BusinessWeek*, May 1; (2) J. Carey, 2009, Controversies continue to swirl over corn ethanol, *BusinessWeek*, April 16; (3) L. Phillips, 2009, Europe's overseas push into biofuels, *BusinessWeek*, May 13; (4) Renewable Fuels Association, www.ethanolrfa.org; (5) US Department of Agriculture, 2008, Sustainability of Biofuels: Future research opportunities. Report from the October 2008 workshop: DOE/SC-0114; (6) *World Development Report 2008: Agriculture for Development*.

GLOSSARY

Absolute advantage. The economic advantage one nation enjoys that is absolutely superior to other nations.

Absorptive capacity. The ability to recognize the value of new information, assimilate it, and apply it.

Accommodative strategy. A strategy characterized by some support from top managers, who may increasingly view CSR as a worthwhile endeavor.

Acquisition. Transfer of the control of operations and management from one firm (target) to another (acquirer), the former becoming a unit of the latter.

Acquisition premium. The difference between the acquisition price and the market value of target firms.

Adaptability. The ability to change supply chain configurations in response to longer-term changes in the environment and technology.

Administrative policy. Bureaucratic rules that make it harder to import foreign goods.

Agency costs. The costs associated with principal-agent relationships.

Agency relationship. The relationship between principals (such as shareholders) and agents (such as professional managers).

Agency theory. A theory that focuses on principal-agent relationships (or in short, agency relationships).

Agent. A person (such as manager) to whom authority is delegated.

Agglomeration. Clustering of economic activities in certain locations.

Agility. The ability to react quickly to unexpected shifts in supply and demand.

Alignment. Alignment of interests of various players.

Andean Community. A customs union in South America that was launched in 1969.

Antidumping duty. Tariffs levied on imports that have been "dumped" (selling below costs to "unfairly" drive domestic firms out of business).

Antidumping laws. Laws that make it illegal for an exporter to sell goods below cost abroad with the intent to raise prices after eliminating local rivals.

Antitrust laws. Laws in various countries that outlaw cartels (trusts).

Antitrust policy. Government policy designed to combat monopolies and cartels.

Asia-Pacific Economic Cooperation (APEC). The official title for regional economic integration involving 21 member economies around the Pacific.

Association of Southeast Asian Nations (ASEAN). The organization underpinning regional economic integration in Southeast Asia.

Attack. An initial set of actions to gain competitive advantage.

Australia-New Zealand Closer Economic Relations Trade Agreement (ANZCERTA or CER). A free trade agreement between Australia and New Zealand that was launched in 1983.

Balance of payments. A country's international transaction statement, which includes merchandise trade, service trade, and capital movement.

Balance of trade. The aggregation of importing and exporting that leads to the country-level trade surplus or deficit.

Balance sheet approach. A compensation approach that balances the cost of living differences relative to parent country levels and adds a financial inducement to make the package attractive.

Bandwagon effect. The effect of investors moving in the same direction at the same time, like a herd.

Bargaining power. Ability to extract favorable outcome from negotiations due to one party's strengths.

Base of the pyramid. Economies where people make less than $2,000 per capita a year.

Benchmarking. An examination on whether a firm has resources and capabilities to perform a particular activity in a manner superior to competitors.

Bid rate. The price to buy a currency.

Blue ocean strategy. Strategy that focuses on developing new markets ("blue ocean") and avoids attacking core markets defended by rivals, which is likely to result in a bloody price war or a "red ocean."

Board composition. The insider/outsider mix on a board of directors.

Bond. Loan issued by the firm and held by creditors.

Bondholder. Buyer of bonds.

Born global. Start-up companies that attempt to do business abroad from inception.

Bretton Woods system. A system in which all currencies were pegged at a fixed rate to the US dollar.

BRIC. Brazil, Russia, India, and China.

Build-operate-transfer (BOT) agreement. A nonequity mode of entry used to build a longer-term presence by building and then operating a facility for a period of time before transferring operations to a domestic agency or firm.

Capability. The tangible and intangible assets a firm uses to choose and implement its strategies.

Capacity to punish. Sufficient resources possessed by a price leader to deter and combat defection.

Capital flight. A phenomenon in which a large number of individuals and companies exchange domestic currency for a foreign currency.

Captive sourcing. Setting up subsidiaries abroad so that the work done is in-house but the location is foreign. Also known as foreign direct investment (FDI).

Cartel (trust). An output- and price-fixing entity involving multiple competitors.

Causal ambiguity. The difficulty of identifying the causal determinants of successful firm performance.

Center of excellence. An MNE subsidiary explicitly recognized as a source of important capabilities, with the intention that these capabilities be leveraged by and/or disseminated to other subsidiaries.

CEO duality. The CEO doubles as a chairman of the board.

Chief executive officer (CEO). The main executive manager in charge of the firm.

Civil law. A legal tradition that uses comprehensive statutes and codes as a primary means to form legal judgments.

Civilization. The highest cultural grouping of people and the broadest level of cultural identity people have.

Classical trade theories. The major theories of international trade that were advanced before the 20th century, which consist of (1) mercantilism, (2) absolute advantage, and (3) comparative advantage.

Clean (or free) float. A pure market solution to determine exchange rates.

Cluster. Countries that share similar cultures.

Code of conduct (code of ethics). A set of guidelines for making ethical decision.

Cognitive pillar. The internalized (or taken-for-granted) values and beliefs that guide individual and firm behavior.

Collectivism. The idea that an individual's identity is fundamentally tied to the identity of his or her collective group.

Collusion. Collective attempts between competing firms to reduce competition.

Collusive price setting. Price setting by monopolists or collusion parties at a level higher than the competitive level.

Co-marketing. Efforts among a number of firms to jointly market their products and services.

Command economy. An economy that is characterized by government ownership and control of factors of production.

Commoditization. A process of market competition through which unique products that command high prices and high margins gradually lose their ability to do so, thus becoming commodities.

Common denominator. A currency or commodity to which the value of all currencies are pegged.

Common law. A legal tradition that is shaped by precedents and traditions from previous judicial decisions.

Common market. Combining everything a customs union has, a common market, in addition, permits the free movement of goods and people.

Comparative advantage. Relative (not absolute) advantage in one economic activity that one nation enjoys in comparison with other nations.

Compensation. The determination of salary and benefits.

Competition policy. Government policy governing the rules of the game in competition.

Competitive dynamics. Actions and responses undertaken by competing firms.

Competitor analysis. The process of anticipating rivals' actions in order to both revise a firm's plan and prepare to deal with rivals' response.

Complementary assets. The combination of numerous resources and assets that enable a firm to gain a competitive advantage.

Concentrated ownership and control. Founders start up firms and completely own and control them on an individual or family basis.

Concentration ratio. The percentage of total industry sales accounted for by the top four, eight, or twenty firms.

Contagion (imitation) effect. The reaction of local firms to rise to the challenge demonstrated by MNEs through learning and imitation.

Contender strategy. Strategy that centers on a firm engaging in rapid learning and then expand overseas.

Context. The underlying background upon which social interaction takes place.

Contractual (non-equity-based) alliances. Alliances between firms that are based on contracts and do not involve the sharing of ownership.

Copyright. Exclusive legal rights of authors and publishers to publish and disseminate their work.

Corporate governance. The relationship among various participants in determining the direction and performance of corporations.

Corporate social responsibility (CSR). Consideration of, and response to, issues beyond the narrow economic, technical, and legal requirements of the firm to accomplish social benefits along with the traditional economic gains which the firm seeks.

Corruption. The abuse of public power for private benefits, usually in the form of bribery.

Cost of capital. The rate of return that a firm needs to pay to capital providers.

Counterattack. A set of actions in response to attack.

Country-of-origin effect. The positive or negative perception of firms and products from a certain country.

Country (regional) manager. Manager of a geographic area, either a country or a region.

Cross-listing. Listing shares on a foreign stock exchange.

Cross-market retaliation. Retaliatory attacks on a competitor's other markets if this competitor attacks a firm's original market.

Cross-shareholding. Both firms invest in each other to become cross-shareholders.

Cultural distance. The difference between two cultures along identifiable dimensions such as individualism.

Cultural intelligence. An individual's ability to understand and adjust to new cultures.

Culture. The collective programming of the mind that distinguishes the members of one group or category of people from another.

Currency board. A monetary authority that issues notes and coins convertible into a key foreign currency at a fixed exchange rate.

Currency hedging. A transaction that protects traders and investors from exposure to the fluctuations of the spot rate.

Currency risk. The potential for loss associated with fluctuations in the foreign exchange market.

Currency swap. A foreign exchange transaction between two firms in which one currency is converted into another at Time 1, with an agreement to revert it back to the original currency at a specified Time 2 in the future.

Customs union. One step beyond a free trade area (FTA), a customs union imposes common external policies on nonparticipating countries.

Deadweight cost. Net losses that occur in an economy as a result of tariffs.

Debt. A loan that the firm needs to pay back at a given time with an interest.

Default. A firm's failure to satisfy the terms of a loan obligation.

Defender strategy. Strategy that centers on local assets in areas in which MNEs are weak.

Defensive strategy. A strategy that focuses on regulatory compliance but with little actual commitment to CSR by top management.

Democracy. A political system in which citizens elect representatives to govern the country on their behalf.

Demonstration effect. The reaction of local firms to rise to the challenge demonstrated by MNEs through learning and imitation.

Development. Long-term, broader preparation to improve managerial skills for a better career.

Diffused ownership. Publicly traded corporations owned by numerous small shareholders but none with a dominant level of control.

Direct exports. The sale of products made by firms in their home country to customers in other countries.

Dirty (or managed) float. Using selective government intervention to determine exchange rates.

Dissemination risk. The risk associated with unauthorized diffusion of firm-specific know-how.

Distribution channel. The set of firms that facilitates the movement of goods from producers to consumers.

Dodger strategy. Strategy that centers on cooperating through joint ventures with MNEs and sell-offs to MNEs.

Doha Round. A round of WTO negotiations to reduce agricultural subsidies, slash tariffs, and strengthen intellectual property protection that started in Doha, Qatar, in 2001. Officially known as the "Doha Development Agenda," it was suspended in 2006 due to disagreements.

Downstream vertical FDI. A type of vertical FDI in which a firm engages in a downstream stage of the value chain in a host country.

Dumping. An exporter selling goods at below cost.

Economic system. Rules of the game on how a country is governed economically.

Economic union. Having all the features of a common market, members also coordinate and harmonize economic policies (in areas such as monetary, fiscal, and taxation) to blend their economies into a single economic entity.

Emerging economies. A term that has gradually replaced the term "developing countries" since the 1990s.

Emerging markets. A term that is often used interchangeably with "emerging economies."

Entrepreneurs. Founders and/or owners of new businesses or managers of existing firms who identify and exploit new opportunities.

Entrepreneurship. The identification and exploitation of previously unexplored opportunities.

Equity. The stock in a firm (usually expressed in shares), which represents the owners' rights.

Equity-based alliances. Alliances based on ownership or financial interest between firms.

Equity mode. A mode of entry (JV and WOS) that indicates a relatively larger, harder-to-reverse commitment.

Ethical imperialism. A perspective that suggests that "there is one set of Ethics (with a capital E) and we have it."

Ethical relativism. A perspective that suggests that all ethical standards are relative.

Ethics. The principles, standards, and norms of conduct that govern individual and firm behavior.

Ethnocentric approach. An emphasis on the norms and practices of the parent company (and the parent country of the MNE) by relying on PCNs.

Ethnocentrism. A self-centered mentality by a group of people who perceive their own culture, ethics, and norms as natural, rational, and morally right.

Euro. The currency currently used in 16 EU countries.

Euro area. The 16 EU countries that currently use the euro as the official currency.

European Union (EU). The official title of European economic integration since 1993.

Exit-based mechanisms. Corporate governance mechanisms that focus on exit, indicating that shareholders no longer have patience and are willing to "exit" by selling their shares.

Expatriate manager (expat). A manager who works abroad.

Expatriation. The process of selecting, managing, and motivating expatriates to work abroad.

Explicit collusion. Firms directly negotiate output and pricing and divide markets.

Explicit knowledge. Knowledge that is codifiable (can be written down and transferred with little loss of richness).

Export intermediary. A firm that performs an important middleman function by linking domestic sellers and foreign buyers that otherwise would not have been connected.

Exporting. Selling abroad.

Expropriation. (1) Government's confiscation of foreign assets. (2) Activities that enrich controlling shareholders at the expense of minority shareholders.

Extender strategy. Strategy that centers on leveraging homegrown competencies abroad.

Factor endowment. The extent to which different countries possess various factors of production such as labor, land, and technology.

Factor endowment theory (Heckscher-Ohlin theory). A theory that suggests that nations will develop comparative advantages based on their locally abundant factors.

FDI flow. The amount of FDI moving in a given period (usually a year) in a certain direction.

FDI inflow. Inbound FDI moving into a country in a year.

FDI outflow. Outbound FDI moving out of a country in a year.

FDI stock. Total accumulation of inbound FDI in a country or outbound FDI from a country across a given period (usually several years).

Femininity. A relatively weak form of societal-level sex role differentiation whereby more women occupy positions that reward assertiveness and more men work in caring professions.

Financing. How a firm's money, banking, investments, and credit are managed.

First-mover advantages. Benefits that accrue to firms that enter the market first and that late entrants do not enjoy.

Fixed exchange rate policy. A government policy to set the exchange rate of a currency relative to other currencies.

Floating (or flexible) exchange rate policy. A government policy to let supply-and-demand conditions determine exchange rates.

Foreign Corrupt Practices Act (FCPA). A US law enacted in 1977 that bans bribery of foreign officials.

Foreign direct investment (FDI). Investment in, controlling, and managing value-added activities in other countries.

Foreign exchange market. The market where individuals, firms, governments, and banks buy and sell foreign currencies.

Foreign exchange rate. The price of one currency in terms of another.

Foreign portfolio investment (FPI). Investment in a portfolio of foreign securities such as stocks and bonds.

Formal institutions. Institutions represented by laws, regulations, and rules.

Forward discount. A condition under which the forward rate of one currency relative to another currency is higher than the spot rate.

Forward premium. A condition under which the forward rate of one currency relative to another currency is lower than the spot rate.

Forward transaction. A foreign exchange transaction in which participants buy and sell currencies now for future delivery.

Franchising. Firm A's agreement to give Firm B the rights to use A's proprietary assets for a royalty fee paid to A by B. This is typically done in service industries.

Free market view on FDI. A political view that suggests that FDI unrestricted by government intervention is the best.

Free trade. The idea that free market forces should determine how much to trade with little or no government intervention.

Free trade area (FTA). A group of countries that remove trade barriers among themselves.

Free Trade Area of the Americas (FTAA.) A proposed free trade area for the entire Western Hemisphere.

Game theory. A theory that studies the interactions between two parties that compete and/or cooperate with each other.

General Agreement on Tariffs and Trade (GATT). A multilateral agreement governing the international trade of goods (merchandise).

General Agreement on Trade in Services (GATS). A WTO agreement governing the international trade of services.

Geocentric approach. A focus on finding the most suitable managers, who can be PCNs, HCNs, or TCNs.

Geographic area structure. An organizational structure that organizes the MNE according to different geographic areas (countries and regions).

Global account structure. A customer-focused dimension that supplies customers (often other MNEs) in a coordinated and consistent way across various countries.

Global business. Business around the globe.

Global economic integration. Efforts to reduce trade and investment barriers around the globe.

Global matrix. An organizational structure often used to alleviate the disadvantages associated with both geographic area and global product division structures, especially for MNEs adopting a transnational strategy.

Global product division structure. An organizational structure that assigns global responsibilities to each product division.

Global standardization strategy. A strategy that focuses on development and distribution of standardized products worldwide in order to reap the maximum benefits from low-cost advantages.

Global sustainability. The ability to meet the needs of the present without compromising the ability of future generations to meet their needs around the world.

Global virtual team. A team whose members are physically dispersed in multiple locations in the world and often operate on a virtual basis.

Globalization. The close integration of countries and peoples of the world.

Going rate approach. A compensation approach that pays expatriates the prevailing (going) rate for comparable positions in a host country.

Gold standard. A system in which the value of most major currencies was maintained by fixing their prices in terms of gold.

Green-field operations. Building factories and offices from scratch (on a proverbial piece of "green field" formerly used for agricultural purposes).

Gross domestic product (GDP). The sum of value added by resident firms, households, and government operating in an economy.

Gross national income (GNI). Gross domestic product (GDP) plus income from income from nonresident sources abroad. GNI is the term used by the World Bank and other international organizations to supersede the term GNP.

Gross national product (GNP). Gross domestic product (GDP) plus income from nonresident sources abroad.

Group of 20 (G-20). The group of 19 major countries plus the European Union (EU) whose leaders meet on a biannual basis to solve global economic problems.

High-context culture. A culture in which communication relies a lot on the underlying unspoken context, which is as important as the words used.

Home replication strategy. A strategy that emphasizes the replication of home country-based competencies in foreign countries.

Horizontal FDI. A type of FDI in which a firm duplicates its home country-based activities at the same value chain stage in a host country.

Host country national (HCN). An individual from the host country who works for an MNE.

Hubris. Over-confidence in one's capabilities.

Human resource management (HRM). Activities that attract, select, and manage employees.

Import quota. Restriction on the quantity of imports.

Import tariff. A tax imposed on imports.

Importing. Buying from abroad.

Indirect exports. A way to reach overseas customers by exporting through domestic-based export intermediaries.

Individualism. The idea that an individual's identity is fundamentally his or her own.

Infant industry argument. The argument that if domestic firms are as young as "infants," in the absence of government intervention, they stand no chances of surviving and will be crushed by mature foreign rivals.

Informal institutions. Cultures, ethics, and norms.

Information asymmetries. Asymmetric distribution and possession of information between two sides.

In-group. Individuals and firms regarded as a part of us.

Initiator. The party who begins the process of ending the alliance.

Inpatriation. Relocating employees of a foreign subsidiary to the MNE's headquarters for the purposes of filling skill shortages at headquarters and developing a global mind-set for such inpatriates.

Inshoring. Outsourcing to a domestic firm.

Inside director. A member of the board who is a top executive of the firm.

Institution-based view. A leading perspective in global business that suggests that the success and failure of firms are enabled and constrained by institutions.

Institutional distance. The extent of similarity or dissimilarity between the regulatory, normative, and cognitive institutions of two countries.

Institutional framework. Formal and informal institutions that govern individual and firm behavior.

Institutional transitions. Fundamental and comprehensive changes introduced to the formal and informal rules of the game that affect firms as players.

Institutions. Formal and informal rules of the game.

Intangible resources and capabilities. Assets that are hard to observe and difficult (if not impossible) to quantify.

Integration-responsiveness framework. A framework of MNE management on how to simultaneously deal with two sets of pressures for global integration and local responsiveness.

Intellectual property. Intangible property that is the result of intellectual activity.

Intellectual property rights (IPR). Rights associated with the ownership of intellectual property.

Internalization. The replacement of cross-border markets (such as exporting and importing) with one firm (the MNE) locating and operating in two or more countries.

International business (IB). (1) A business (firm) that engages in international (cross-border) economic activities and/or (2) the action of doing business abroad.

International division. An organizational structure that is typically set up when firms initially expand abroad, often engaging in a home replication strategy.

International entrepreneurship. A combination of innovative, proactive, and risk-seeking behavior that crosses national borders and is intended to create wealth in organizations.

International Monetary Fund (IMF). An international organization that was established to promote international monetary cooperation, exchange stability, and orderly exchange arrangements.

International premium. A significant pay raise when working overseas.

Intrafirm trade. International transactions between two subsidiaries in two countries controlled by the same MNE.

Joint venture (JV). A new corporate entity created and jointly owned by two or more parent companies.

Knowledge management. The structures, processes, and systems that actively develop, leverage, and transfer knowledge.

Knowledge spillover. Knowledge diffused from one firm to others among closely located firms.

Labor relations. A firm's relations with organized labor (unions) in both home and host countries.

Late-mover advantages. Benefits that accrue to firms that enter the market later and that early entrants do not enjoy.

Learning race. A situation in which alliance partners aim to outrun each other by learning the "tricks" from the other side as fast as possible.

Legal system. The rules of the game on how a country's laws are enacted and enforced.

Letter of credit (L/C). A financial contract that states that the importer's bank will pay a specific sum of money to the exporter upon delivery of the merchandise.

Leveraged buyout (LBO). A means by which investors, often in partnership with incumbent managers, issue bonds and use the cash raised to buy the firm's stock.

Liability of foreignness. The *inherent* disadvantage that foreign firms experience in host countries because of their nonnative status.

Licensing. Firm A's agreement to give Firm B the rights to use A's proprietary technology (such as a patent) or trademark (such as a corporate logo) for a royalty fee paid to A by B. This is typically done in manufacturing industries.

Lingua franca. A global business language.

Local content requirement. A requirement stipulating that a certain proportion of the value of the goods made in one country must originate from that country.

Local responsiveness. The necessity to be responsive to different customer preferences around the world.

Localization (multidomestic) strategy. A strategy that focuses on a number of foreign countries/regions, each of which is regarded as a stand-alone local (domestic) market worthy of significant attention and adaptation.

Location. Advantages enjoyed by firms operating in a certain location.

Location-specific advantages. The benefits a firm reaps from the features specific to a place.

Long-term orientation. Dimension of how much emphasis is placed on perseverance and savings for future betterment.

Low-context culture. A culture in which communication is usually taken at face value without much reliance on unspoken context.

Make-or-buy decision. The decision on whether to produce in-house ("make") or to outsource ("buy").

Management control rights. The rights to appoint key managers and establish control mechanisms.

Managerial human capital. The skills and abilities acquired by top managers.

Managerial motives. Managers' desire for power, prestige, and money, which may lead to decisions that do not benefit the firm overall in the long run.

Market commonality. The overlap between two rivals' markets.

Market economy. An economy that is characterized by the "invisible hand" of market forces.

Market imperfection (market failure). The imperfect rules governing international transactions.

Market orientation. A philosophy or way of thinking that places the highest priority on the creation of superior customer value in the marketplace.

Market segmentation. Identifying segments of consumers who differ from others in purchasing behavior.

Marketing. Efforts to create, develop, and defend markets that satisfy the needs and wants of individual and business customers.

Marketing mix. The four underlying components of marketing: (1) product, (2) price, (3) promotion, and (4) place.

Masculinity. A relatively strong form of societal-level sex role differentiation whereby men tend to have occupations that reward assertiveness and women tend to work in caring professions.

Merchandise. Tangible products being traded.

Mercosur. A customs union in South America that was launched in 1991.

Merger. The combination of operations and management of two firms to establish a new legal entity.

Microfinance. A practice to provide micro loans ($50–$300) used to start small businesses with the intention of ultimately lifting the entrepreneurs out of poverty.

Micro-macro link. The micro, informal interpersonal relationships among managers of various units that may greatly facilitate macro, inter-subsidiary cooperation among these units.

Mixed economy. An economy that has elements of both a market economy and a command economy.

Mode of entry. Method used to enter a foreign market.

Modern trade theories. The major theories of international trade that were advanced in the 20th century, which consist of (1) product life cycle, (2) strategic trade, and (3) national competitive advantage of industries.

Monetary union. A group of countries that use a common currency.

Moral hazard. Recklessness when people and organizations (including firms and governments) do not have to face the full consequences of their actions.

Multilateral trading system. The global system that governs international trade among countries—otherwise known as the GATT/WTO system.

Multimarket competition. Firms engage the same rivals in multiple markets.

Multinational enterprise (MNE). A firm that engages in foreign direct investment (FDI).

Mutual forbearance. Multimarket firms respect their rivals' spheres of influence in certain markets, and their rivals reciprocate, leading to tacit collusion.

Nondiscrimination. A principle that a country cannot discriminate among its trading partners.

Nonequity mode. A mode of entry (exports and contractual agreements) that tends to reflect relatively smaller commitments to overseas markets.

Nongovernmental organizations (NGOs). Organizations that are not affiliated with governments.

Nontariff barrier (NTB). Trade barrier that relies on nontariff means to discourage imports.

Normative pillar. The mechanism through which norms influence individual and firm behavior.

Norms. Values, beliefs, and actions of relevant players that influence the focal individuals and firms.

North American Free Trade Agreement (NAFTA). A free trade agreement among Canada, Mexico, and the United States.

Obsolescing bargain. The deal struck by MNEs and host governments, which change their requirements after the initial FDI entry.

Offer rate. The price to sell a currency.

Offshoring. Outsourcing to an international or foreign firm.

OLI advantages. A firm's quest for ownership (O) advantages, location (L) advantages, and internalization (I) advantages via FDI.

Oligopoly. Industry dominated by a small number of players.

Opportunism. The act of seeking self-interest with guile.

Opportunity cost. Cost of pursuing one activity at the expense of another activity, given the alternatives (other opportunities).

Organizational culture. The collective programming of the mind that distinguishes the members of one organization from another.

Organizational fit. The similarity in cultures, systems, and structures between firms.

Original brand manufacturer (OBM). A firm that designs, manufactures, and markets branded products.

Original design manufacturer (ODM). A firm that both designs and manufactures products.

Original equipment manufacturer (OEM). A firm that executes design blueprints provided by other firms and manufactures such products.

Out-group. Members individuals and firms not regarded as a part of "us."

Outside director. A nonmanagement member of the board.

Outsourcing. Turning over an organizational activity to an outside supplier that will perform it on behalf of the focal firm.

Ownership. An MNE's possession and leveraging of certain valuable, rare, hard-to-imitate, and organizationally embedded (VRIO) assets overseas in the context of FDI.

Parent country national (PCN). An individual who comes from the parent country of the MNE and works at its local subsidiary.

Patent. Exclusive legal rights of inventors of new products or processes to derive income from such inventions.

Peg. A stabilizing policy of linking a developing contry's currency to a key currency.

Performance appraisal. The evaluation of employee performance for promotion, retention, or termination purposes.

Place. The location where products and services are provided.

Political risk. Risk associated with political changes that may negatively impact domestic and foreign firms.

Political system. The rules of the game on how a country is governed politically.

Political union. The integration of political and economic affairs of a region.

Polycentric approach. An emphasis on the norms and practices of the host country.

Post-Bretton Woods system. A system of flexible exchange rate regimes with no official common denominator.

Power distance. The extent to which less powerful members within a country expect and accept that power is distributed unequally.

Pragmatic nationalism on FDI. A political view that only approves FDI when its benefits outweigh its costs.

Predatory pricing. An attempt to monopolize a market by setting prices below cost and intending to raise prices to cover losses in the long run after eliminating rivals.

Price. The expenditures that customers are willing to pay for a product.

Price elasticity. How demand changes when price changes.

Price leader. A firm that has a dominant market share and sets "acceptable" prices and margins in the industry.

Primary stakeholder groups. Constituents on which the firm relies for its continuous survival and prosperity.

Principal. A person (such as owner) delegating authority.

Principal-agent conflicts. Conflicts between principals and agents.

Principal-principal conflicts. Conflicts between two classes of principals: controlling shareholders and minority shareholders.

Prisoners' dilemma. In game theory, a type of game in which the outcome depends on two parties deciding whether to cooperate or to defect.

Private equity. Equity capital invested in private companies that, by definition, are not publicly traded.

Proactive strategy. A strategy that endeavors to do more than is required in CSR.

Product. Offerings that customers purchase.

Product life cycle theory. A theory that accounts for changes in the patterns of trade over time by focusing on product life cycles.

Promotion. Communicatons that marketers insert into the marketplace.

Property rights. The legal rights to use an economic property (resource) and to derive income and benefits from it.

Protectionism. The idea that governments should actively protect domestic industries from imports and vigorously promote exports.

Psychological contract. An informal understanding of expected delivery of benefits in the future for current services.

Purchasing power parity (PPP). A conversion that determines the equivalent amount of goods and services different currencies can purchase.

Quota. The weight a member country carries within the IMF, which determines the amount of its financial contribution (technically known as its "subscription"), its capacity to borrow from the IMF, and its voting power.

R&D contract. Outsourcing agreement in R&D between firms.

Radical view on FDI. A political view that is hostile to FDI.

Reactive strategy. A strategy that would only respond to CSR causes when required by disasters and outcries.

Real option. An investment in real operations as opposed to financial capital.

Regional economic integration. Efforts to reduce trade and investment barriers within one region.

Regulatory pillar. The coercive power of governments.

Related transactions. Controlling shareholders sell firm assets to another firm they own at below-market prices or spin off the most profitable part of a public firm and merge it with another private firm they own.

Relational (or collaborative) capability. Capability to successfully manage interfirm relationships.

Relationship orientation. A focus to establish, maintain, and enhance relationships with customers.

Repatriate. Returning expatriate.

Repatriation. The process of facilitating the return of expatriates.

Resource. The tangible and intangible assets a firm uses to choose and implement its strategies.

Resource-based view. A leading perspective in global business that posits that firm performance is fundamentally driven by differences in firm-specific resources and capabilities.

Resource mobility. Assumption that a resource used in producing a product for one industry can be shifted and put to use in another industry.

Resource similarity. The extent to which a given competitor possesses strategic endowment comparable, in terms of both type and amount, to those of the focal firm.

Risk management. The identification and assessment of risks and the preparation to minimize the impact of high-risk, unfortunate events.

Scale of entry. The amount of resources committed to entering a foreign market.

Scenario planning. A technique to prepare and plan for multiple scenarios (either high or low risk).

Schengen. A passport-free travel zone within the EU.

Secondary stakeholder groups. Those who influence or affect, or are influenced or affected by, the corporation but are not engaged in transactions with the firm and are not essential for its survival.

Semiglobalization. A perspective that suggests that barriers to market integration at borders are high, but not high enough to completely insulate countries from each other.

Separation of ownership and control. The dispersal of ownership among many small shareholders, in which control is largely concentrated in the hands of salaried, professional managers who own little (or no) equity.

Services. Intangible services being traded.

Shareholder. Firm owner.

Shareholder capitalism. A view of capitalism that suggests that the most fundamental purpose for firms to exist is to serve the economic interests of shareholders (also known as capitalists).

Small- and medium-sized enterprises (SMEs). Firms with fewer than 500 employees in the United States and with fewer than 250 employees in the European Union.

Social capital. The informal benefits individuals and organizations derive from their social structures and networks.

Social complexity. The socially intricate and interdependent ways firms are typically organized.

Social issue participation. Firms' participation in social causes not directly related to the management of primary stakeholders.

Social mobility. The degree to which members from a lower social category can rise to a higher status.

Social stratification. The hierarchical arrangement of individuals into social categories (strata) such as classes, castes, or divisions within a society.

Solutions-based structure. A customer-focused solution in which a provider sells whatever combination of goods and services the customers prefer, including rivals' offerings.

Sovereign wealth fund (SWF). A state-owned investment fund composed of financial assets such as stocks, bonds, real estate, or other financial instruments funded by foreign exchange assets.

Spot transaction. The classic single-shot exchange of one currency for another.

Spread. The difference between the offer price and the bid price.

Staffing. HRM activities associated with hiring employees and filling positions.

Stage model. Model of internationalization that portrays the slow step-by-step (stage-by-stage) process an SME must go through to internationalize its business.

Stakeholder. Any group or individual who can affect or is affected by the achievement of the organization's objectives.

Stewardship theory. A "pro-management" theory that suggests that most managers can be viewed as owners' stewards interested in safeguarding shareholders' interests.

Strategic alliance. A voluntary agreement between firms involving exchange, sharing, or co-developing of products, technologies, or services.

Strategic fit. The effective matching of complementary strategic capabilities between firms.

Strategic hedging. Spreading out activities in a number of countries in different currency zones to offset any currency losses in one region through gains in other regions.

Strategic investment. One firm invests in another as a strategic investor.

Strategic trade policy. Government policy that provides companies a strategic advantage in international trade through subsidies and other supports.

Strategic trade theory. A theory that suggests that strategic intervention by governments in certain industries can enhance their odds for international success.

Subsidiary initiative. The proactive and deliberate pursuit of new opportunities by a subsidiary to expand its scope of responsibility.

Subsidy. Government payment to domestic firms.

Sunk cost. Cost that a firm has to endure even when its investment turns out to be unsatisfactory.

Supply chain. Flow of products, services, finances, and information that passes through a set of entities from a source to the customer.

Supply chain management. Activities to plan, organize, lead, and control the supply chain.

SWOT analysis. An analytical tool for determining a firm's strengths (S), weaknesses (W), opportunities (O), and threats (T).

Tacit collusion. Firms indirectly coordinate actions by signaling their intention to reduce output and maintain pricing above competitive levels.

Tacit knowledge. Knowledge that is non-codifiable, and its acquisition and transfer require hands-on practice.

Tangible resources and capabilities. Assets that are observable and easily quantified.

Target exchange rates (or crawling bands). Specified upper or lower bounds within which an exchange rate is allowed to fluctuate.

Tariff barrier. Trade barrier that relies on tariffs to discourage imports.

Technology spillover. Technology diffused from foreign firms to domestic firms.

Theocratic law. A legal system based on religious teachings.

Theory of absolute advantage. A theory that suggests that under free trade, a nation gains by specializing in economic activities in which it has an absolute advantage.

Theory of comparative advantage. A theory that focuses on the relative (not absolute) advantage in one economic activity that one nation enjoys in comparison with other nations.

Theory of mercantilism. A theory that suggests that the wealth of the world is fixed and that a nation that exports more and imports less will be richer.

Theory of national competitive advantage of industries (diamond theory). A theory that suggests that the competitive advantage of certain industries in different nations depends on four aspects that form a "diamond."

Third country national (TCN). An individual who is from neither the parent country nor the host country of the MNE.

Third-party logistics (3PL). A neutral, third-party intermediary in the supply chain that provides logistics and other support services.

Top management team (TMT). The team consisting of the highest level of executives of a firm led by the CEO.

Total cost of ownership. Total cost needed to own a product, consisting of initial purchase cost and follow-up maintenance/service cost.

Totalitarianism (dictatorship). A political system in which one person or party exercises absolute political control over the population.

Trade deficit. An economic condition in which a nation imports more than it exports.

Trade embargo. Politically motivated trade sanctions against foreign countries to signal displeasure.

Trade-Related Aspects of Intellectual Property Rights (TRIPS). A WTO agreement governing intellectual property rights.

Trade surplus. An economic condition in which a nation exports more than it imports.

Trademark. Exclusive legal rights of firms to use specific names, brands, and designs to differentiate their products from others.

Training. Specific preparation to do a particular job.

Transaction costs. The costs associated with economic transactions or, more broadly, the costs of doing business.

Transnational strategy. A strategy that endeavors to be cost efficient, locally responsive, and learning driven simultaneously around the world.

Triad. North America, Western Europe, and Japan.

Triple bottom line. Economic, social, and environmental performance that simultaneously satisfies the demands of all stakeholder groups.

Tunneling. A form of corporate theft that diverts resources from the firm for personal or family use.

Turnkey project. A project in which clients pay contractors to design and construct new facilities and train personnel.

Uncertainty avoidance. The extent to which members in a culture accept or avoid ambiguous situations and uncertainty.

Union of South American Nations (USAN/UNASUR). A regional integration mechanism integrating two existing customs unions (Andean Community and Mercosur) in South America.

United States-Dominican Republic-Central America Free Trade Agreement (CAFTA). A free trade agreement between the United States and five Central American countries and the Dominican Republic.

Upstream vertical FDI. A type of vertical FDI in which a firm engages in an upstream stage of the value chain in a host country.

Value chain. A chain of vertical activities used in the production of goods and services that add value.

Vertical FDI. A type of FDI in which a firm moves upstream or downstream at different value chain stages in a host country.

Voice-based mechanisms. Corporate governance mechanisms that focus on shareholders' willingness to work with managers, usually through the board, by "voicing" their concerns.

Voluntary export restraint (VER). An international agreement that shows that exporting countries voluntarily agree to restrict their exports.

VRIO framework. The resource-based framework that focuses on the value (V), rarity (R), imitability (I), and organizational (O) aspects of resources and capabilities.

Washington Consensus. A view centered on the unquestioned belief in the superiority of private ownership over state ownership in economic policy making, which is often spearheaded by two Washington-based international organizations: the International Monetary Fund and the World Bank.

Wholly owned subsidiary (WOS). A subsidiary located in a foreign country that is entirely owned by the parent multinational.

World Trade Organization (WTO). The official title of the multilateral trading system and the organization underpinning this system since 2005.

Worldwide (global) mandate. A charter to be responsible for one MNE function throughout the world.

NAME INDEX

A

Acedo, F., 117n3
Acemoglu, D., 58n34
Acito, F., 495n4
Acquaah, M., 410n48
Acs, Z., 321n4
Adams, G., 117n4
Adams, M., 350n31
Adegbesan, J. A., 117n3
Adner, R., 118n18, 323n49
Advertising and Marketing Review, 64
AFL-CIO, 527n22
Agarwal, S., 496n40, 496n47
Aggarwal, V., 322n36
Agmon, T., 208n28
Agrawal, N., 495n11
Agrawal, V., 495n11
Aguilera, R., 410n44, 557n49, 558n61, 583n2
Ahlstrom, D., 322n24, 538, 539, 556, 557n22
Ahmad, A., 439n10, 440n49
Ahuja, G., 409n16
Ainuddin, R. Z., 409n9
Akimova, I., 496n46
Albertson, P., 129
Alessandri, T., 557n33
Alexander, N., 410n64
Al-Issawi, T., 287n8
Allen, D., 583n10
Allende, S., 576
Allred, B., 118n15, 440n50
Almeida, J., 323n44
Almond, P., 527n43
Altomonte, C., 208n23
Ambec, S., 584n40
Ambos, B., 439n6, 440n46
Ambos, T., 440n46
Amino, T., 527n16
Anand, J., 378n19, 409n6, 410n50, 440n36
Anand, N., 439n6
Anderson, J., 118n18, 496n32
Anderson, M., 584n32
Anderson, R., 556n12
Ando, N., 527n27
Andrachuk, M., 584n23
Andrade, G., 409n26, 557n36
Ang, S., 85, 409n11
APEC Secretariat, 268n30
Apte, U., 496n39
Apud, S., 93n54
Ardichvili, A., 92n46
Arino, A., 410nn39,40
Armington, C., 321n4
Arnold, W., 294
Arregele, J., 350n47
Arruda, W., 528n52
Arthur, J., 527n34
Arthur, W., 527n33

Arya, B., 409n17, 584n31
Asaba, S., 118n25
Asakawa, K., 440n33
ASEAN Secretariat, 268n29
Ash, M. K., 590
Asmussen, C., 349n4, 350n47
Atamer, T., 440n44
The Atlantic, 513
Au, K., 321n5, 322n24, 454
Audretsch, D., 322n12
Augier, M., 349n6
Aulakh, P., 29nn8,32, 350nn38,48, 409n23
Autio, E., 307, 308, 322n41, 323n44
Avellaneda, C., 439n24
Avittathur, B., 496n22
Aycan, Z., 92n22

B

Bachrack, M., 370
Baggs, J., 177n2
Baghdasaryan, D., 349n14
Bailey, W., 92n28
Baldrige, D., 439n9
Balkundi, P., 527n40
Ballmer, S., 398
Bansal, P., 583n6, 584nn22,30,38
Bao, Y., 91n2
Barbe, J., 439n5
Barden, J., 410n43
Barner-Rasmussen, W., 440n42
Barnett, M., 92n40, 584nn29,38
Barnett, T., 439n22
Barnett, W., 322n22
Barney, J., 29n16, 97, 103, 117nn1,5, 118nn7,17,22,29, 321, 322n11, 377n6
Barr, P., 91n2
Barringer, B., 322n38
Barro, R., 58n34
Barroso, C., 117n3
Barry, D., 322n13
Barry, F., 208n25
Barry, K., 129
Barthelemy, J., 350n38
Bartikowski, B., 64
Bartlett, C., 92n21, 426, 439nn5,25
Basdeo, D., 378n18
Bassi, L., 527n17
Bastiat, F., 167, 177n19
Bastin, D., 59n37
Baum, J., 322n12, 378n15
Beal, B., 349n5
Beamish, P., 322n28, 350n47, 409nn2,9, 410nn41,65, 526n4
Bearpark, A., 448
Beaulieu, M., 58n20
Bebchuk, L., 557n34
Becerra, M., 377n2
Becker, B., 528nn44,48

Beechler, S., 528n52
Begley, T., 92n32
Behfar, K., 527n40
Beijing Review, 326
Bekaert, G., 556n7
Belderbos, R., 349n8, 409n15, 439n19, 440n33, 496n24, 527n27
Bell, D., 89
Bell, J., 322n34
Bell, S., 527n33
Benito, G., 439n14
Bennett, W., 527n33
Benton, W. C., 496n27
Benz, M., 556n1
Beracs, J., 496n47
Berg, D., 349n10
Bergh, R., 58n17
Berlusconi, S., 547
Bernardes, R., 133
Bernhofen, D., 177n10
Berns, S., 92n33
Bernstein, A., 22
Bernstein, P., 59n37
Berry, H., 349n7, 439n6
Berry, L., 496n41
Berry, R., 3
Best, B., 513
Bestor, T., 83
Beugelsdijk, S., 118n14
Bhagat, R., 29n6, 74, 92n43, 350n51
Bhagwati, J., 170–171, 177nn13,28,29, 260, 261, 268n31
Bhaskar-Shrinivas, P., 526n6
Bhattacharya, A., 29n7
Bhaumik, S., 29n14, 117n2, 349n1
Bialik, C., 129
Bierly, P., 440n36
Biggart, N., 58n10
Bigley, G., 29n17, 583n2
Bilkey, T., 286
Bird, A., 29n34, 92n22, 527n15
Birkinshaw, J., 350n30, 430, 438, 439n4, 440nn51,52
Björk, 66
Bjorkman, A., 440n47
Bjorkman, I., 92n19, 440nn42,45, 526n2, 527n24
Blakeney, R., 527n15
Blalock, G., 208n24
Bloom, M., 583n5
Bloomberg, 133
Boddewyn, J., 28n2
Bonardi, J., 58n17
Bond, M., 92n42
Bosch, F., 440n45
Bouquet, C., 350n30
Bourdreau, B., 409n13
Bowen, D., 410n59

Bowring, P., 556
Boxall, P., 527n43
Boyacigiller, N., 528n52
Boyd, J., 350n25
Boyd, N., 118n26
Boyles, T., 527n34
Brammer, S., 584n41, 584n49
Brander, J., 161, 177n2, 177n6
Brandes, P., 557n33
Brannen, M., 91n1, 410n56, 440n44, 496n15
Brannen, M. Y., 526
Branzei, O., 584n25
Braunerhjelm, P., 438
Bremer, J., 447
Bresser, R., 350n25
Brett, J., 527n40
Brewster, C., 527n43
Bridis, T., 287n4
Brin, S., 536
Brock, D., 349n6, 527n27
Brouthers, K., 350n30, 410n49
Brouthers, L., 350nn30,43, 495n14
Brown, J., 177n10, 496nn40,47
Browne, A., 62
Bruce, A., 557n32
Bruiyaka, O., 439n23
Bruton, G., 29n7, 208n12, 322nn14,24, 538, 539, 556, 557n22
Bucerius, M., 410n56
Buchan, N., 74
Buchholtz, A., 377n2
Buchholz, R., 583n16
Buck, T., 557nn15,32,41,46
Budhwar, P., 91n1, 92n47, 526n1, 527n25
Bunyaratavej, K., 118n14
Burbridge, J., 92n33
Burgess, S., 57, 179
Busenitz, L., 91n5, 322nn11,39
Bush, D., 356
Bush, G. W., 18, 61
BusinessWeek (BW), 4, 6, 28, 32, 36, 58nn12,13,14, 83, 91, 102, 111, 117, 118nn12,23, 162, 170, 177nn11,23,31, 179, 207, 208nn16,31, 212, 268nn15,20,22,24, 305, 309, 322n17, 349n3, 350n23, 365, 378n22, 408, 409n12, 410nn55,60, 432, 438, 439nn8,16, 448, 472, 482, 495, 496nn16,42, 500, 503, 513, 526, 527n26, 528n51, 539, 556n4, 565, 583, 584n34
Bygrave, W., 307, 308
Bynke, H., 238

ORGANIZATION INDEX

SUBJECT INDEX

How has the markets changed

- Economic

- Political

- Investment   ste we inest now or before

- Currency $ ↗↘

- Trade with U.S.

How Lybia $\overset{5\ ways}{}$ or Chng $\overset{5\ ways}{}$

10 ways they are changing Business
in the world.